THE
COLLECTIONS
of the
BRITISH
MUSEUM

THE
COLLECTIONS
of The
BRITISH
MUSEUM

EDITED BY

DAVID M. WILSON

THE BRITISH MUSEUM PRESS

FRONT COVER The Reading Room in the Great Court of the British Museum. Designed by Fosters & Partners, the Great Court opened in December 2000.
Photograph: Dudley Hubbard

BACK COVER Painted lid of the coffin of Pasenhor, 25th Dynasty, *c*. 700 BC, Egypt. Much of the decoration is drawn from the *Book of the Dead* and describes the judgement of the dead by a divine tribunal presided over by Osiris.

HALF-TITLE PAGE Earthenware tile painted in enamel colours on a white slip. Designed by William De Morgan (1839–1917) and made at Sands End Pottery, Fulham, 1897–1909. 15 × 15 cm.

TITLE PAGE The Portland Vase, a masterpiece of glass-blowing and cameo-cutting. The identification of the figures is much disputed. Roman, about 25 BC, H 24.8 cm.

THIS PAGE Silver-gilt drinking horn from Turkey, Achaemenid period (5th–4th century BC). See no. 318.

ISBN 0-7141-2759-0

© 1989, 2001, 2003 The Trustees of The British Museum

Third edition 2003

Published by The British Museum Press
A division of The British Museum Company Ltd
46 Bloomsbury Street, London WC1B 3QQ

Designed by Behram Kapadia

Typeset in Linotron Ehrhardt by
Rowland Phototypesetting, Ltd,
Bury St Edmunds, Suffolk,
and printed in Spain by Grafos S. A.

CONTENTS

INTRODUCTION

The British Museum can claim to be the earliest national museum of its kind in the world, its foundation marking the transition point between the privately owned cabinet of curiosities and the public museum. It was established on the death, in 1753, of the great collector Sir Hans Sloane, who left his collection to the British nation. This was at the height of the European Enlightenment, when knowledge was being scientifically categorised and great encyclopaedias were being compiled. In a sense, the founding collection of the British Museum, and the collecting activities which followed, created an encyclopaedia not of words, but of objects. Its purpose was to enable a better understanding of man and his environment.

Sloane did not set limits to his collecting activities: he acquired archaeological objects, historical antiquities, prints and drawings, books and manuscripts, and natural history specimens. It was within this framework of universality that the early Museum continued its founder's activities. Over the two and a half centuries since, the British Museum has had to refine its ambitions. The Natural History Museum was built in South Kensington and the collections moved there in the 1880s. The British Library was created in 1973 and the St Pancras building was opened in 1998. The British Museum also took account of other, independent institutions such as the National Gallery of 1824 and the Victoria and Albert Museum, founded on its current site as the South Kensington Museum in 1857: very few oil paintings and very little European costume and furniture are to be found in Bloomsbury.

The British Museum appointed its first director, Dr Gowin Knight, in 1756, and opened its doors to the public on 15 January 1759. The Board of Trustees of the Museum, under the chairmanship of the Archbishop of Canterbury, made it clear that the Museum was to be open to all, and that admission was to be free. The laudable tradition of there being no entrance charge continues to the present time. However, access to the Museum and its collections was not a simple matter in the early years. Tickets had to be obtained and visits were tightly controlled, a guide being provided who decided what should be shown and what the length of the visit was to be. The Museum was firmly shut at weekends and on the rare holidays when ordinary workers might have been able to attend. This situation eased bit by bit in the course of the nineteenth century, when the opening hours were extended and restrictions eliminated. An Easter Monday visit to the British Museum was a favoured activity of the London populace: in 1837, the building filled rapidly with 23,895 visitors, the most popular exhibits being the stuffed birds, minerals, Mexican and Peruvian antiquities and Magna Carta.

The initial task of the first Trustees was to find a suitable building for Sloane's collection. Their choice was between two large houses at what were then the boundaries of London: Buckingham House and Montagu House. The latter was cheaper (though in worse repair) and was the chosen option; the former was to become, as Buckingham Palace, the home of the monarch. Montagu House had been designed in 1675 by the polymath Robert Hooke, though after only a decade it had burnt down and had been reconstructed in a fashionable French style. The house provided reasonable accommodation, at least in the early years. On the ground floor were installed libraries, including the Old Royal Library, presented in 1757 by King George II. On the first floor were more books, manuscripts, medals, antiquities and natural history. Dr Knight managed to sneak in his magnetical laboratory (he designed compasses for the Royal Navy) and his residence was contained in one of the wings. Since then, there has been a tradition that the director always lives on-site. This initial state of equilibrium was not to last for long, for very soon collecting was being actively pursued. Natural history specimens poured in: 'vertebra and other bones of a monstrous size supposed to be a large sea animal' (1758); a 'monstrous pig from Chalfont St Giles' (1770). Captain Cook's three Pacific voyages (between 1767 and 1779) resulted in hitherto unknown ethnographic material and more natural history (including the remains of the first kangaroo seen in Europe). The British ambassador in Naples, Sir William Hamilton, amassed a huge collection of Greek vases which arrived at the Museum in 1772. By the end of the eighteenth century not only Montagu House, but also the sheds erected in its gardens, were full. In the early years of the following century, the government called in one of the outstanding architects of the day, Sir Robert Smirke, to consider the problem.

Smirke's first idea was to extend Montagu House, but it became apparent, with major new acquisitions, such

1 *The portico of the British Museum, perhaps the finest, and certainly the grandest Greek Revival Building in Britain.*

2 LEFT *Sir Hans Sloane (1660–1753), physician, naturalist and antiquary. His collections formed the core round which the collections of the British Museum, the British Library and the Natural History Museum were built. Bust by Michael Rysbrack.*

as the marbles from the Parthenon in 1816, that a more drastic solution was needed. In 1823 he presented the Trustees with his ideas for replacing the original museum house with a vast new building in Greek Revival style. The urgency to implement Smirke's plan became greater with the donation of King George III's library by his son in the same year; by 1827 this eastern part of the planned quadrangle was complete. The final section, the huge southern portico, was not finished until mid-century. Another accommodation crisis had become apparent by this time, the need for considerably more space for books (the British Museum Library was entitled to a copy of every book published in the British Isles) and for readers. The principal librarian (that is, the director) proposed a circular, domed structure in the middle of the courtyard formed by the quadrangle surrounding it, instead of the garden which was originally intended. Thus it was that the famous Round Reading Room was created, to the designs of Robert Smirke's younger brother, Sydney. The remainder of the courtyard space was filled with bookstacks and service buildings and the public soon forgot about one of the fundamental aspects of Robert Smirke's plan. Collecting had maintained its buoyant level of activity, and the many archaeological excavations supported by the Museum were returning large quantities of significant material. The British Museum, in interpreting relics of the ancient past, had become a world leader in scholarship. Smirke's building was itself clearly too small for the encyclopaedic ambitions of its founders, and debates raged over whether ethnography or natural history should be hived off to another site. The eloquent keeper of natural history, Richard Owen, argued for the latter, and by 1881 Alfred Waterhouse's impressive building had been constructed and opened on the site of the 1862 International Exhibition, alongside the South Kensington Museum. (The Natural History Museum did not, however, gain complete independence from its Bloomsbury parent until 1963.)

Although the collection of antiquities was enormous by the middle of the nineteenth century, there were concerns about its balance. A Royal Commission of 1849–50 expressed concern that antiquities from Britain, as opposed to those from Greece, Rome, Egypt and the Ancient Near East, were inadequately represented in the British Museum. In 1851 a young curator, Augustus Wollaston Franks, was appointed to deal with this lacuna. Over a career of nearly half a century, Franks transformed the collections, adding greatly to medieval,

3 *Moving the head of Ramesses II to the new Egyptian Sculpture Gallery in 1834.*

4 *This reconstruction of a* sarangbang *or scholar's study was made by Korean craftsmen according to traditional specifications and building techniques. The Korea Foundation Gallery was opened in 2000.*

Renaissance and later material from Europe, as well as revitalising the collecting of ethnography and stimulating Far Eastern acquisitions.

Further galleries to the south-east, forming the White Wing, were added by 1884, using a bequest which had been left to the Museum some sixty-two years earlier. Even this was not enough, and plans were drawn up in 1904 by the architect Sir John Burnet to envelop Smirke' building to the north, west and east, which would have entailed demolishing large numbers of eighteenth- and nineteenth-century houses around the site. In the event, only the north part was built, this being opened in 1914 as King Edward VII's Galleries. The greater part of the main floor of the building was used to display the medieval and later collections of ceramics and glass, along with oriental material, but all this not until 1920 when the British Museum could return to a semblance of normality after the First World War. In fact, the two World Wars had a major effect on the development of the twentieth-century Museum. The Duveen Gallery, constructed to house the Parthenon Marbles, was complete by 1939 but the sculptures were not installed but safely stored. The Gallery was dam-

aged by bombing a year later and it was not until 1962 that it was finally opened.

The constant pressure on space resulted in a radical solution being adopted for the Ethnographic collection in 1970. It moved, together with its staff, to the former Senate House of London University in Burlington Gardens (just behind the Royal Academy in Piccadilly). Here, though remaining part of the British Museum, the building was renamed the Museum of Mankind, and for the next thirty years a series of innovative exhibitions was to delight its visitors. The move was not intended to be a permanent one; just as soon as space became available at Bloomsbury, the collection would return.

The accommodation problem was in part solved by the extramural development of stores for objects not currently on display. But there were other pressures building up. When Smirke designed his Museum in 1823, he probably considered that 100,000 visits per year would be a high annual level of attendance. This figure rose through the century, and very significantly after the First World War: from the 1920s until 1939, there was an average of just over one million visits per year.

In 1969 the two million mark was attained for the first

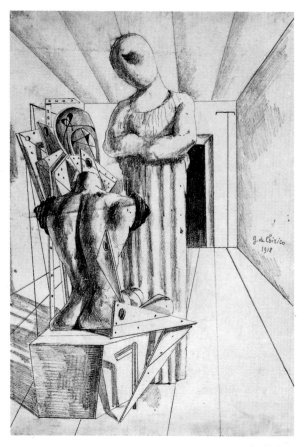

5 *The Museum does not concentrate exclusively on antiquities but has always collected contemporary material. Above pencil drawing,* Figure Metafisiche *by Giorgio de Chirico (1888–1978), executed in 1918 and acquired in 1982.*

time. This was to double by 1977. The British Museum was becoming an uncomfortably crowded place. The solution arose from the decision to separate the library departments from the antiquities, numismatic and fine art departments. Ideas had been proposed in the mid-1960s to construct a new building for the library to the south of Great Russell Street, but these had come to naught. Then the government decided that the library departments should not simply be geographically separated, but that they should form a new institution, the British Library. Legislation was enacted in 1972. Though the Library could not immediately move out of its existing location within the Museum, eventually a site for a new building was identified one mile to the north, at St Pancras. Construction started in April 1982 but progress was spasmodic because of uneven government funding. The last book did not leave the British Museum at Bloomsbury until 1998.

Though progress in the move of the British Library was frustratingly slow at times, the Museum started developing schemes in the late 1980s which would allow the expansion of space for its visitors, provide proper purpose-built public facilities which it had always lacked (such as lecture theatres, space for school parties, shops and a restaurant) and develop galleries for the Ethnographic collection to enable its return from Piccadilly. An architectural competition was held in 1993 and the winning firm, Norman Foster and Partners, was selected in July 1994. Construction work commenced in March 1998 and Her Majesty The Queen ceremonially opened the Great Court on 6 December 2000. The Great Court has transformed the visitor experience from the point of view of its users, providing a monumental space at the heart of the Museum, from which the public can easily find their way to the hundred or so galleries which surround it. The 1820s Greek Revival architecture of the quadrangle has been joined to the High Victorian Reading Room at its centre by an airy roof of glass and steel. To the back of the Reading Room, and under the pavement, Foster has provided many of the facilities which were so badly needed. The Reading Room itself has been turned into a reference library of books relating to the collections and the cultures which produced them, for any visitors who care to use it. One section has a display of books written by authors who are known to have used the Reading Room: Marx's complete works sit on the shelves close to those of Beatrix Potter. The Clore Education Centre provides, perhaps surprisingly for the first time, specially designed lecture theatres. Also for the first time, there is now a public route through the Museum at ground floor level which connects the Great Russell Street and Montague Place entrances. The Great Court has been called a new covered square for London, and it is true that a new urban space has been created, one which is open to the public for significantly longer hours than the Museum itself (though the opening hours of the latter have also been extended).

With all the building activities that occurred during the 1990s, it should not be thought that the traditional role of the Museum was neglected. Collections are at the core of the service which the British Museum provides, and access to them through display, publication and hands-on study is fundamental. Technological developments in recent years now allow electronic access to the collection around the world. The Museum's COMPASS programme, featuring some 4,000 objects, is available on the Museum's website (www.thebritishmuseum.ac.uk). COMPASS was launched in June 2000, and is also available locally in the Museum in the Reading Room and in the Clore Centre. Redevelopment of the Museum's galleries is constantly being considered. Between 1992 and 2000, twenty-eight galleries were renewed or created. One of the most recent, in 2000, was the Korea Foundation Gallery: the

6 *The Queen with the President of the People's Republic of China, Jiang Zemin, at the opening of the* Gilded Dragons: Buried Treasures from China's Golden Ages *exhibition in October 1999. (Right) The curator, Mrs Carol Michaelson.*

Museum has never dedicated a permanent gallery to this culture before. A scheme of gallery work and development of former British Library space has been devised, the next major milestone being the 250th anniversary of the Museum's foundation in 2003.

The curatorial departments of the Museum (there are also administrative ones) are ten in number. Two – Coins and Medals, and Prints and Drawings – specialise in the materials contained in their titles ('Drawings' includes paintings in watercolours on paper). Eight are named for the cultures that they study and display: Greek and Roman, Prehistory and Early Europe, Medieval and Modern Europe, Ancient Near East, Egyptian, Oriental, Japanese, and Ethnography. Two deal with objects in a different manner. Scientific Research works chiefly on the physical analysis of antiquities to determine their age, origin, method of manufacture, authenticity and composition. The Department of Conservation monitors the physical condition of the collections and the environmental conditions in the galleries and stores; it also stabilises damaged or deteriorating objects and cleans objects for display. The Education Department is active with the public at all levels. It makes arrangements for school visits (schools at last have their own space in the Ford Centre for Young Visitors) and arranges programmes of lectures, films, seminars and performances. It is deeply involved in the concept of lifelong learning and in the development of ways of responding to school curriculum requirements, and it has been involved in devising multi-media programmes for young people (these are also available on the web). Finally, Library Services have

been brought together under the wing of the David Eccles Librarian, a new post. Although the British Library has gone (and its holdings were on the Bloomsbury site for 245 years), significant and rich collections of books remain to enable the staff of the Museum and visitors to acquire understanding from printed sources and artefacts together.

The curatorial departments propose and develop plans for the exhibition programme. The British Museum has been very active in promoting exhibitions, and in recent years these have numbered between twenty and thirty each year. Not every one is large, but all are expected to throw light on an aspect of knowledge which can be illuminated by the collections of the Museum, or by borrowing objects from other museums to make particular points. Exhibitions are sometimes developed with other museum partners: *Greek Gold* was created by bringing together the Classical Greek jewellery collections from the British Museum, the Metropolitan Museum of Art in New York and the State Hermitage Museum of St Petersburg. *Ancient Faces*, an exhibition which considered portraits incorporated in mummies of the second and third centuries AD, travelled to several venues which had lent examples for the original British Museum showing. Some exhibitions attain an almost diplomatic role: in 1997, *The Enduring Image* was prepared to celebrate the fiftieth anniversary of Indian Independence and was shown to large audiences in Delhi and Mumbai after being opened by The Queen and the President of India. Another exhibition developed by the British Museum, *Gilded Dragons*, consisting of gold and silver objects from the Han and

Tang Dynasties of China, was lent by museums in Shaanxi Province to coincide with the state visit to the United Kingdom of the Chinese President, Jiang Zemin, in October 1999. An example of an innovatory exhibition can be found in *Human Image*, the first display arranged for the new Joseph Hotung Great Court Gallery in December 2000. Its intent was to stimulate thoughts about how different cultures, at different moments in their histories, portray the human body. This was achieved by bringing together items from all object-holding departments, thereby also providing the public with an unusual overview of the breadth of the collections. Nearly all exhibitions have publications associated with them: the exhibition itself may last only three or four months, but the ideas generated by the exercise live on in the catalogue. The British Museum has an enviable publication record in general, with its own publishing house, The British Museum Press, producing more than fifty books a year. They cover the widest range of approaches. Some publications are intended for young children, while others are produced for profound scholars; indeed, there are publications for all levels of background and understanding. Sometimes the curators wish to get research results circulated quickly to their peers. In such cases, the British Museum Occasional Paper series is available – between six and eight of these monographs are published every year.

7 The Warren Cup. This Roman silver cup with relief decoration of homoerotic scenes was purchased with the aid of the Heritage Lottery Fund, the National Art Collections Fund and a number of private donors. Said to have been found at Bittir (ancient Bethther, near Jerusalem), mid-1st century AD. H 11cm.

Naturally curators also publish their work in periodicals of learned societies; in a typical year, more than 200 papers will be issued in this form. Indeed, a number of curators edit, or sit on the editorial boards of such journals.

New galleries and exhibitions incorporate new ideas and new objects. Acquisition is a vitally important aspect in the life of the curator: it is a responsibility which must be approached with thought and care. It is always necessary to be able to produce a lucid and coherent argument about why an object should be added to the collections. This is the case even when something is donated to the Museum; if for no other reason, the addition of an object implies a continuing cost, in terms of storage, conservation and curation in general. Once an object is part of the collection, the Act of Parliament under which the Museum operates effectively prohibits its disposal. The public has traditionally been generous to the British Museum, and this generosity continues to the present day. Often the Museum is unable to find the cost of an object from its limited resources, but there are friends who are willing to help. For nearly a century, the National Art Collections Fund has made a real difference to the ability of the Museum to acquire significant objects. In recent years, a Chinese handscroll painting by Xie Chufang, dated 1321 and titled *Fascination of Nature*, was purchased: the Chairman of the National Art Collections Fund, Sir Nicholas Goodison, referred to it as 'one of the most marvellous objects that has ever come before us.' One of the most remarkable objects ever bought by the Museum must be the Warren Cup, a unique first-century AD Roman silver cup portraying homoerotic scenes. This provides evidence of practices not available from other sources: it could not have been incorporated in the collection of the Greek and Roman Department without the combined assistance of the Heritage Lottery Fund, the National Art Collections Fund and a number of private donors.

These two examples are of exceptional items. Few of the other 6,000 acquisitions made in 1999 would be regarded in the same way, but that does not mean that the smallest fragment of pottery added to the collection might not contain vitally important information. Many acquisitions come from excavations run by the Museum, but some are from excavations run by others with the participation of Museum staff. In 1999 the British Museum was associated with forty-one fieldwork or excavation projects in the United Kingdom or abroad. Often archaeological work takes part in countries which do not allow the export of antiquities, but important relationships are forged with foreign colleagues and new work sheds light on collections made long ago.

The Museum makes strenuous efforts not to acquire material which is not legally held by those who offer it, and evidence of provenance is always requested. Many

8 *Working on a Coptic textile. The care and meticulous conservation of the objects in the collection are major elements of the work of the Museum. Scientific research in this field is also carried out. See also 105.*

items on the market have been illegally excavated or exported. Clandestine excavation destroys vital evidence associated with such objects, evidence which can never be recovered. The British Museum is a history museum rather than an art museum, and it feels these sentiments very deeply. It offered evidence to the Select Committee for Culture, Media and Sport, which issued a report on cultural property and illicit trade in 2000, and the Director of the Museum sat on a panel established by the government to offer advice on how the illicit trade can be combated. A number of objects acquired by the Museum in the distant past are continually the subject of repatriation claims, notably the Parthenon Marbles and the Benin Bronzes. However, the Trustees, as owners of the collection, consider that they have legal title to all objects within the Museum. On the rarest of occasions, as in the recent case of the miniature Iron Age bronze shields from what is now known to have been an illegal excavation at Netherhampton in Wiltshire, objects have been returned to their rightful owners. The Museum assists the government in various ways in relation to cultural material. It is involved in the implementation of the Treasure Act, receiving objects with gold or silver content which have been buried in the past, identifying them and performing necessary conservation. In a number of cases, such material is acquired by the

Museum, but only when proper compensation is provided for the finder. Also associated with excavated material has been the Museum's help in the development of the Portable Antiquities scheme, a new, voluntary recording activity for excavated finds, providing important data which before were simply not available.

The British Museum is a complex institution which has continuously evolved over its long history. It is known the world over, receiving very large numbers of visitors from home and abroad, to make it one of the best-attended museums to be found anywhere. Even through the turmoil created by the building of the Great Court between 1998 and 2000, the Museum remained open as usual and visitor figures remained buoyant. The Rosetta Stone, the Assyrian Lion Hunt reliefs, the Parthenon Marbles, the Egyptian mummies, all of these and many others, attract millions to the British Museum year after year. It is the collection which is sought, a collection which belongs to the whole world and which is held in trust for generations of the present and of the future.

THE CLASSICAL
COLLECTIONS

◆

The collections in the Department of Greek and Roman Antiquities range in date from the beginning of the Bronze Age in Greek lands about 3200 BC to the establishment of Christianity as the official religion of the Roman Empire by the Edict of Milan in AD 313. The Greek material comes not only from the Greek mainland and the islands of the Aegean, but also from many lands around the Mediterranean, including Asia Minor and Egypt in the east and the Italian peninsula and Sicily in the west. Some non-Greek eastern cultures, in particular those of Cyprus, Lycia and Caria, are also represented. The collection of material from the native cultures of Italy, including the Etruscans, begins in the early Bronze Age. There is little material from the Roman Republic, but later the whole of the Roman Empire except for Britain falls within the scope of the Department.

9 *Terracotta relief. A four-horse racing chariot approaches the three columns of the turning-post. A jubilator (rider who encouraged the contestants) has already turned. First century* AD. H 30cm.

THE GREEK BRONZE AGE

The Greek Bronze Age, so called because bronze gradually replaced stone as the material most commonly used for tools and weapons, began in about 3200 BC. During the Early Bronze Age (*c.* 3200–2000 BC) the Cyclades, in the middle of the Aegean Sea, were the home of a flourishing and influential culture. Perhaps the most characteristic products of this culture are Cycladic figurines. Carved from local marble, these naked female figures with tranquilly folded arms exhibit a simplicity of form and purity of line which make them most attractive to the modern eye. Fine examples were brought to the Museum by J. T. Bent, who excavated in the Cyclades in the 1880s and whose finds, including pottery and stone vessels, form the core of the Museum's Cycladic collection.

Towards the beginning of the Middle Bronze Age (*c.* 2000 BC) the Cycladic islands came ever more under the growing influence of Minoan Crete. The palaces of Crete were established in about 1900 BC, and it was the largest and most important of these that Sir Arthur Evans discovered when he began his excavations at Knossos. He revealed an elaborate, multi-storeyed and richly decorated building that he called the 'Palace of Minos', naming it after the legendary King of Crete. The large Minoan 'pithos' (storage jar) in the British Museum came from an early excavation at the palace, before Evans began work there.

Minoan artistry and craftsmanship reached high levels of achievement, and the British Museum's collections include fine pottery and bronzes. Notable is a bronze group of an athlete leaping over the back of a bull. The miniature art of gem-engraving was particularly skilfully practised, and both Minoan and Mycenaean seals of high quality are preserved in the Museum. Minoan jewellery is represented particularly by the Aegina Treasure. Found on the island of Aegina, this jewellery is actually of Minoan craftsmanship, dating from about 1700–1500 BC. It includes four remarkably large and elaborate ear-rings, a pendant showing a nature god, and a variety of other ornaments.

The Late Bronze Age, beginning about 1550 BC, saw Crete in a position of considerable influence in the Aegean world. The Mycenaean civilisation of the Greek mainland, centred on the citadel of Mycenae, was beginning to come to prominence and felt this influence strongly. While indebted to Crete in artistic matters, however, the Mycenaeans were more warlike, and were destined to take over Crete's dominant position.

Amongst the most impressive remains of the Mycenaean civilisation are the tholos tombs. 'Tholos' is the Greek word for a circular building, and these large, stone-built, domed tombs were circular in plan. Probably the finest example is the so-called 'Treasury

10 *Marble Cycladic figurine with traces of black and red painted decoration. Such figurines, usually found in graves, perhaps represented their owners, or may have been representations of a goddess, possibly connected with fertility. About 2800–2300 BC. H 76.8cm.*

of Atreus' at Mycenae, which dates from about 1350–1250 BC. Special features of this tomb included the elaborately decorated façade, and the British Museum contains sections of two carved pillars which flanked the doorway, as well as fragments of green and red decorative marble slabs which originally faced the triangular space above the door lintel.

During the fourteenth and thirteenth centuries BC civilisation became remarkably uniform throughout the Aegean, as colonisation and trade extended Mycenaean culture over a large part of the Greek mainland, Crete

11 *A Minoan gold pendant from the Aegina Treasure. A nature god, the 'Master of Animals', is shown holding two geese. He stands amongst lotus flowers, an indication of Egyptian influence. About 1700–1500 BC. H 6cm.*

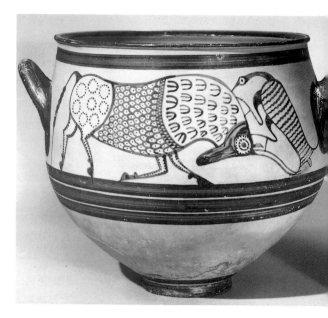

12 *A pottery bowl found at Enkomi in Cyprus, decorated with a bull and a bird, perhaps removing a tick from its hide. The vase is typical of Mycenaean pottery imported into Cyprus. About 1300–1200 BC. H 27.2cm.*

and the islands. Much of the Mycenaean material in the British Museum comes from tombs at Ialysos on Rhodes, which produced pottery, bronzes, jewellery, weapons and ivories. Further fine Mycenaean pottery came from excavations in Cyprus: a result of Mycenaean trade with that island, where pictorial vases, and particularly those showing chariot scenes, were popular.

In about 1100 BC, after a century of warfare and disruption, Mycenaean civilisation came to an end. The following Dark Age (c. 1100–900 BC) was a period of depopulation, poverty and isolation in many parts of Greece, and most of the arts and crafts of the Bronze Age were forgotten. Though some areas remained relatively prosperous, in general archaeological finds of the period are few. However, pottery continued to be made, and its continuous development can be traced in the British Museum's collections.

The Geometric period (c. 900–700 BC) saw Greece gradually emerging from the Dark Age, and by late Geometric times (c. 760–700 BC) this process was well advanced. The British Museum's late Geometric pottery includes vases with figured scenes. Particularly interesting is a large krater (mixing bowl) showing a man and a woman beside an oared ship. This may be an early representation of Greek myth, perhaps showing Theseus and Ariadne. Small votive bronzes of the Geometric period are well represented, while luxury objects can be seen in the Elgin jewellery. By the end of the Geometric period the Greek renaissance was complete, and the stage set for the achievements of the Archaic and Classical periods.

THE GREEKS: ORIENTALISING TO HELLENISTIC

In Greece the eighth and seventh centuries BC are often described as the Orientalising period, because the major advances in Greek culture at this time were the result of contact with great eastern civilisations, such as Syria, Phoenicia and Egypt. Making contact with the east through trade and colonisation, the Greeks learned new techniques of metalworking and ivory-carving, and new decorative motifs, including floral patterns, lions and fantastic animals like griffins, sphinxes and sirens. Many of these motifs appear on the gold and electrum plaques found in tombs at Camirus on the island of Rhodes; they were worn in rows, strung across the chest and fastened to the garment at the shoulders. Eastern models were modified and adapted by Greek artists, and gradually the linear formality of the old Geometric tradition was dissolved into a new and less restricted style of art. This process may be observed very clearly on the painted vases of the period, especially those of Corinth, where a delicate, miniaturist style ('Protocorinthian') was developed to decorate tiny perfume flasks and bottles, often no more than 5 or 6 cm high. At first the animal and human figures in these intricate scenes were shown in pure silhouette, or occasionally in outline, but as time went on details were incised through the silhouette with a sharp engraving tool, and so the 'black-figure' technique was born; this technique was to dominate the decoration of painted vases throughout Greece until about 530 BC. A perfect example of the developed Protocorinthian style is the Macmillan Aryballos, named after a Mr Malcolm Macmillan, who is said to have bought the vase on the platform of Corinth station, giving it to the Museum in 1889. Less than 7 cm high, this perfume pot, with its beautifully modelled lion-head mouth, bears three friezes of decoration: a battle scene with eighteen fully equipped warriors, a horse-race and a hare-hunt, all rendered in immaculate detail.

In the Archaic period of Greek art, the sixth century BC, the techniques learned in the Orientalising period were refined and developed. The sixth century saw the emergence of distinct regional styles in the minor arts,

alongside the rise of monumental sculpture and architecture.

During the sixth century the inspiration of the Corinthian vase-painters began to flag, and vase after vase carried the same friezes of animals prowling nose to tail through thickets of blob-like filling ornament; Athens now became the centre for the production of painted pottery. The Sophilos Dinos, made in Athens around 570 BC, is a bowl and stand designed to hold wine at a feast, and while the lower registers of the bowl, and the whole of the stand, are occupied by Corinthian-like animals, the upper frieze has a mythological, and appropriately festive subject, the arrival of guests at the wedding of Peleus and Thetis. Peleus stands at the door of his house, to receive the gods, goddesses, nymphs, Muses and others, who arrive either by chariot or on foot. Garments, chariots, harness, even horses' manes and tails, are shown in minute detail, and to aid identification and enhance the decorative effect of the whole, the names of all participants are written up beside them.

As the sixth century wore on the black-figure technique grew to perfection in Athens. In Rhodes and the coastal cities of Asia Minor a more relaxed and decorative animal style was favoured, but in Athens it was the human figure, in both mythological and everyday contexts, which absorbed the artists' attention. Two of the finest were Exekias and the Amasis Painter, both artists

13 *Detail from the Sophilos Dinos. Guests arrive for the wedding of Peleus and Thetis. The centaur Cheiron brings game; Hebe and Dionysos follow Leto and Chariklo, goddesses associated with marriage. About 570 BC. H (frieze) 8cm*

of enormous precision and imagination, sympathetic describers of the human form, past masters at the art of fitting their designs to the rounded surfaces of their pots.

Most of the British Museum's collection of Greek vases, bronzes and terracottas comes from Greek and Etruscan tombs, but some of it was found in sanctuaries. In the comparatively humble sanctuaries of Naucratis, a Greek trading port in the Nile Delta, were found vases, terracottas, bronzes and limestone statuettes which vividly illustrate the cosmopolitan life of a community in contact with Egypt, Cyprus and most parts of the Greek world; of very immediate appeal are the graffiti scratched on some of the pots, showing they were offerings made to the gods by named individuals. On a much more sumptuous scale was the sanctuary of Artemis at Ephesus, where, as we shall see, the first large-scale temple was built in the sixth century BC, with the financial support of King Croesus of Lydia. In

14 *Detail from an Athenian red-figured stamnos (jar). Odysseus passes the Sirens' island. Odysseus has plugged his crew's ears with wax, and is himself bound to the mast so that he can hear the Sirens' alluring song with impunity. 480–470 BC.*

the foundations of this temple was found the earliest known coin hoard, along with a votive deposit of small objects in gold, electrum, bronze and ivory – mostly articles of personal adornment offered as gifts to the goddess.

Wealthy visitors to sanctuaries dedicated statues in bronze or marble, usually, in the Archaic period, *kouroi* (naked youths, standing stiffly with one leg slightly forward and their hands by their sides) and *korai* (girls in similar pose, usually dressed in elaborately draped and patterned garments). At the oracular sanctuary of Apollo at Didyma, however, the preferred type of dedication was a seated figure, possibly a representation of the donor. Twelve of these seated figures, who formerly lined the route of the Sacred Way leading from the sea to the temple, are now in the British Museum. Even in their weathered state these statues still evoke the characteristics of Archaic east Greek sculpture, with its massive, smoothly rounded forms, punctuated and articulated by crisp, precisely cut fold-lines of drapery.

Around 530 BC the 'red-figure' technique of vase-painting was invented at Athens. On a red-figured vase the figures are left in the reddish colour of the clay, while the background is filled in with black glaze, and

14

15 ABOVE *Three white-ground lekythoi (oil flasks), showing the development of technique and style between about 460 and 400 BC; the white slip grows whiter and the range of colours expands to include blue, green, and violet.* H *(tallest, centre) 36.3cm.*

inner details are painted in in glaze. Black-figured vases continued to be made for many years, but most enterprising painters switched to the new technique. Some of the first, like Epiktetos, were equally fluent in both techniques, and would sometimes combine them on one vase. At much the same time the white-ground technique was pioneered. This involved applying a thin layer of white clay to the surface of a vase, on which figures could be drawn partly in outline and partly with washes of colour. Between about 500 and 480 BC the finest red-figure vases ever produced were made by such artists as the Berlin and Kleophrades Painters. As the century wore on, the red-figure style became looser and more florid, as seen in the elaborate creations of the Meidias Painter, working around 420–400 BC. Throughout the century on red-figured vases a wide variety of subjects drawn from both daily life and mythology appear. On white-ground vases the range

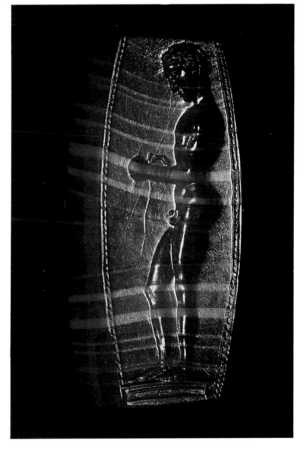

16 RIGHT *Agate sealstone showing a boxer binding thongs around his wrists. Many sealstones were originally set in rings. They were both worn as jewellery and used to mark and seal their owners' property. Greek, 450–400 BC.* H *2.2cm.*

17 ABOVE *The Chatsworth Head, perhaps a representation of the god Apollo. The finest Classical sculptures were of bronze, but very few survive intact, since most were melted down in antiquity. From Cyprus, about 470–460 BC. H 31.6cm.*

was more limited. The commonest white-ground shape was the lekythos, designed to hold perfumed oil offered as a gift to the dead, and this function is often reflected in its iconography, which may show two people parting, or a woman engaged in the domestic pursuits which no longer concern her after death.

Many other minor arts, including the manufacture of terracotta plaques and figurines, the casting of bronze statuettes, and the engraving of sealstones, flourished at Athens and elsewhere in Greece during the Archaic and Classical periods. But throughout antiquity the most highly regarded branch of art was sculpture. A rare surviving bronze example of the earlier Classical style is the Chatsworth Head, an over-life-size head, perhaps from a statue of Apollo, found in Cyprus in 1836 and preserved for many years at Chatsworth House in Derbyshire. The eyes were originally inlaid, probably in glass and marble, the curly locks of hair cast separately and attached.

The finest extant Classical sculpture in marble is that of the Parthenon, the great Doric temple of Athena on the Acropolis at Athens, built and decorated between

447 and 432 BC. The architect of the temple was Iktinos, and the artist whose name is associated with the sculptural decoration is Pheidias. Pheidias' exact role is uncertain: he very probably worked on the gold and ivory cult statue of the goddess, and he may also have had some say in the overall conception of the sculptural programme. This was basically in three parts. At the east and west ends the pediments were filled with groups carved in the round. Above the columns of the colonnade on all four sides was a Doric frieze of panels carved in high relief (metopes), alternating with vertically grooved blocks (triglyphs). Over the inner porches this arrangement was replaced by a continuous Ionic

18 RIGHT *A metope from the Parthenon. The wounded centaur tries to flee, but the Lapith restrains him with one hand, drawing back the other to deliver the final blow. Straining apart, the two figures are drawn back together by their struggle and by the Lapith's magnificent cloak. 447–432 BC. H 1.34m.*

19 BELOW *Three figures from the east pediment of the Parthenon, perhaps Hestia, goddess of the hearth, Aphrodite, goddess of love, and her mother, Dione. 447–432 BC. L (group) 3.15m.*

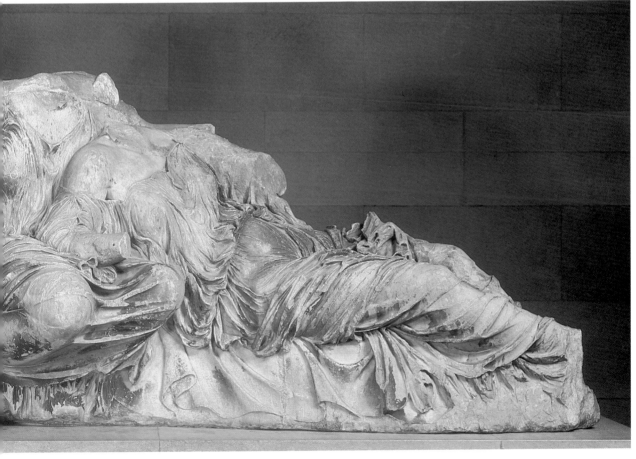

frieze carved in low relief. This extended down the sides of the inner building to form an uninterrupted band around it, below the ceiling of the colonnade.

The Parthenon was designed to glorify Athena, goddess of the city. It was a replacement for a temple which had been unfinished when the Acropolis was sacked by the Persians in 480 BC, before their decisive expulsion from Greece in 479. The subject matter of the Parthenon sculptures reflects both the idea of the triumphs of civilisation over the barbarian, and the self-conscious pride of Athens in the leading role she had played during the Persian wars and subsequently. The metopes were carved with such traditional heroic themes as the battle of gods and giants, the struggles between Greeks and Amazons, Greeks and centaurs, or the sack of Troy. While these subjects showed the triumphs of civilisation, the pedimental compositions were more specifically Athenian. At the west end Poseidon and Athena were represented competing for control of Attica, Poseidon striking the rock with his

20 RIGHT *Athenian grave stele of Xanthippos. Seated on an elegant chair, Xanthippos holds up a model of a foot, perhaps a last, suggesting he was a shoe-maker. His two daughters are shown as miniature adults. About 430 BC. H 83.3cm.*

21 BELOW *Detail of the frieze of the temple of Apollo at Bassae, showing the battle between Greeks and Amazons, a subject of perennial appeal for the Greeks, who may have felt it reflected their victories in the Persian Wars. About 410–400 BC. H 64.2cm.*

22 Marble head of Demeter from Cnidus. The mantle drawn up over her head like a veil recalls the myth of Demeter mourning the loss of her daughter Persephone, abducted by Hades, god of the Underworld. About 330 BC. w (face) 14.5cm.

trident to produce a spring of salt water, Athena winning the day with her olive tree. At the east end was shown the birth of Athena from the head of Zeus. Most Athenocentric of all, however, was the continuous Ionic frieze: interpretations of this vary in detail, but there is general agreement that it must evoke the Panathenaic procession, in which the people of Athens brought, every fourth year, a new robe for the statue of Athena.

The sculptures from the Parthenon now displayed in the British Museum were removed from the temple and brought back to England by the seventh Earl of Elgin between 1801 and 1804. Greece was at this time under Turkish rule, and it was from the Turkish government in Constantinople, where Lord Elgin was British Ambassador, that he obtained a permit entitling him not only to commission artists and other workmen to examine, draw and make casts of any sculpture on the Acropolis, but also to remove 'any pieces of stone with figures and inscriptions'. After protracted negotiations, the British Government bought the Elgin Marbles for the British Museum in 1816.

Amongst the antiquities from the Athenian Acropolis shipped back to England by Lord Elgin were frieze blocks from the temple of Athena Nike (Wingless Victory), depicting battle scenes, and architectural members and sculpture from the Erechtheion. This temple, which housed the cults of, amongst others, Poseidon and Erechtheus, besides the ancient olive-wood statue of Athena, was completed in 408 BC. By then Athens was losing the Peloponnesian War to Sparta and her allies, and the pride and confidence which had characterised the building of the Parthenon was giving way to a mood of retrospective nostalgia. Traces of this may be detected in the Caryatid from the Erechtheion's north porch: one of six, with her archaic stance, formally patterned drapery and flowing hair, she is slightly archaising in style, recalling the earlier statues of *korai*.

There are, however, no traces of nostalgia detectable in the sculptured frieze from the temple of Apollo at Bassae in Arcadia, built between about 430 and 400 BC. Like the Parthenon, the Doric temple at Bassae incorporated an Ionic sculptural frieze, running along the top of the wall of the inner building, but inside rather than outside as on the Parthenon. The subjects of the frieze are the battle of Lapiths and centaurs, and of the Greeks and Amazons. The frieze is carved in much higher relief than that of the Parthenon, and cruder in style, yet in its own way lively and characterful.

Around the time that the Parthenon was completed the tradition of sculptured gravestones, curbed by legislation around 500 BC, was revived in Athens, and a fine series of funeral monuments was produced down into the fourth century. Free-standing sculpture also flourished into the fourth century, at the hands of such masters as Praxiteles. The Aberdeen Head, named from a former owner, the fourth Earl of Aberdeen, exhibits many of the known characteristics of the Praxitelean style – soft, full contours, protuberant forehead, deep-set eyes and exuberantly carved hair. If not the work of Praxiteles himself, it should be attributed to one of his followers. Belonging to much the same date, around 330 BC, is a seated statue of Demeter, found in a sanctuary of Underworld deities at Cnidus in Asia Minor. The goddess is heavily draped, and sits on a cushioned throne. Her face and neck are made of a separate piece of marble, highly polished so as to contrast with her hair and drapery. Her expression, like her attitude, is calm and pensive.

A new period in Greek history was inaugurated by the conquests of Alexander the Great, which embraced Asia Minor, Egypt, Persia and Western Asia to the Indus. On Alexander's death in 323 BC this enormous empire was carved up by his generals into a series of independent kingdoms, and the Hellenistic period began. Hellenistic art was markedly different from that of the Classical period. It displays a greater interest in the

24 ABOVE *Terracotta figurine of a youth seated on a rock, from Tanagra. Most Tanagra figurines were found in tombs; others were dedicated in sanctuaries or served as decorative ornaments in private houses. About 330–300 BC. H 20cm.*

23 LEFT *Hellenistic gold jewellery: rich polychrome effects were created with the aid of enamelling and precious stones like garnets, imported from India in the wake of Alexander's conquests. New motifs were also introduced, such as the reef-knot, the 'knot of Herakles'. 300–100 BC. L (diadem, centre) 8.6cm.*

individual – in youth, old age, physical deformity, or racial differences. It is more cosmopolitan than before; it is often ostentatious, even theatrical; and its subject matter not infrequently displays an obsession with the ideas of chance and fortune. Most of these characteristics are more easily observable on the large-scale sculpture and architecture commissioned by Hellenistic rulers to embellish their states. Yet the interest in realism, at least, is readily observable in the terracotta figurines from Tanagra, produced in quantity in the third century BC: these are remarkably life-like in terms not only of poses and drapery, but also of their subject matter – ordinary people going about, dressed for shopping or travel, rather than the gods and goddesses of earlier years. An ivory statuette from the Townley Collection portrays a hunchback in such detail that it is possible to diagnose his condition as Pott's disease. Small objects also demonstrate the taste for show and luxury, from glass bowls decorated with gold leaf to intricately worked gold jewellery, lavishly inlaid with precious stones.

Macedonia became a Roman province in 148 BC; and with the defeat of Antony and Cleopatra at Actium in 31 BC the whole of Alexander's empire came under Roman rule. But this was by no means the end of Greek art, for Greek artists continued to work for Roman patrons, and much of the art of the Roman period is their work.

CYPRUS

The first settlers reached Cyprus some time before 7000 BC, probably from the nearby Syrian coast, but the Museum possesses little or no material belonging to the earliest prehistoric phases. The collections begin with the Early Bronze Age (2300–1900 BC), and include fine examples of red polished ware, the dominant pottery during this period. A series of weapons, wedge-shaped axeheads and dress-pins are all typical of early Cypriot metalwork, which, after a spectacular beginning, changed little until about 1600 BC. A new tradition of painted wares marks the beginning of the Middle Bronze Age around 1900 BC. Towards the end of that era Cyprus emerged from her isolation. Goods were imported and Cypriot products reached Egypt and the Near East.

The Late Bronze Age (1650–1050 BC) was a period of great prosperity and wide-ranging commercial connections. Life was particularly prosperous in the towns established mainly on the east and south coasts. Many had good harbours, including Enkomi, where excavations were carried out by the British Museum in 1896. Finds from here and other sites excavated by the Museum provide a fine picture of the civilisation of Late Bronze Age Cyprus. Cypriot workshops made pottery, bronzework, jewellery, sealstones and artefacts of glass, ivory and faience. Raw materials like gold, ivory and faience were imported, as were some finished articles, including a great quantity of pottery from Mycenaean Greece. Cyprus exported copper, her principal natural resource, and perhaps opium and perishable goods like textiles, grain and timber.

In the twelfth century some settlers may have arrived from the Greek world, but large-scale immigration probably occurred around 1100 BC. New Mycenaean Greek burial customs were practised in some eleventh-century BC cemeteries and the native Cypro-Minoan script died out to be replaced by Cypro-Syllabic and the Greek language.

The beginning of the Iron Age is dated about 1050

25 LEFT *Ivory gaming-box from Enkomi, decorated with hunting scenes and animals. The squares on the top are arranged for the Egyptian game of* tjau; *underneath is a drawer for the gaming-pieces. Probably carved in Cyprus in the twelfth century* BC *from imported ivory.* L 29.1cm.

BC; the bulk of the Museum's collection from that era again comes from excavations. The first two hundred years are usually described as a Dark Age, although contacts were maintained with both east and west. The arrival of the Phoenicians in the mid-ninth century prompted a Cypriot revival. Typical 'Phoenician' pottery was now made locally, and a fine series of metalwork produced by Phoenician residents is represented in the Museum's collection by decorated metal bowls and lampstands. The following centuries saw the island, now divided into autonomous city-kingdoms, ruled by a succession of foreign overlords, Assyria (*c.* 709–669 BC), Egypt (*c.* 570/60–526/5 BC) and Persia (*c.* 526/5–333 BC). Among the products of the seventh and sixth centuries are vases with pictorial decoration, including flowers, birds, human figures and mythological beasts. Around the middle of the seventh century, during a period of independence, large-scale sculpture in limestone and terracotta began. Many of the sculptures in the Museum's collection come from the excavations at the sanctuary of Apollo at Idalion. Some of the fine jewellery of the fifth and fourth centuries was imported from the Greek world, but bangles, hair spirals and ear-rings with animal-head terminals, were made in Cyprus.

The beginning of the true Hellenisation of Cypriot culture and the end of the city-kingdoms were marked by the voluntary submission of the Cypriot kings to Alexander the Great in 333 BC. In 294 BC Cyprus became part of the large state of Egypt ruled by Ptolemy I (one of Alexander's generals) and his Greek successors. She remained in Ptolemaic hands for nearly 250 years. Her closest relations were now with the Greek world.

Rome annexed Cyprus in 58 BC, but the island was briefly returned to Ptolemaic rule during the civil wars of the Roman Republic. In 30 BC Cyprus again became a Roman province. The language and culture remained basically Greek, in common with the rest of the eastern Roman Empire. In both the Hellenistic and Roman periods (323 BC–AD 395) Cypriot craftsmen followed cosmopolitan fashions, and although the limestone sculpture retains some of its native qualities, it is

26 *Painted terracotta head from a statue of a bearded worshipper in the earliest style of large-scale Cypriot sculpture which began in the middle of the seventh century* BC. *From the Sanctuary of Apollo at Phrangissa, Tamassos, 650–600* BC. H *36cm.*

27 *Bronze four-sided vessel-stand with openwork decoration showing on each side a man approaching a stylised tree. Here he carries an ingot shaped like an ox-hide, the form in which copper was transported at the time. Made in Cyprus in the twelfth century* BC. H *11cm.*

difficult to distinguish between locally produced artefacts and those made elsewhere. This is well illustrated by the Museum's collections. The events of the fourth century, with Constantinope replacing Rome as the capital of the Roman world in AD 330 and the allocation of Cyprus to the eastern Roman Empire in AD 395, mark the end of this era in the island's history.

THE GREEKS' EASTERN NEIGHBOURS

Since remote antiquity south-western Asia Minor has been isolated from the mainstream of Anatolian life. The history, language and art of the people of ancient Lycia reflects their dogged determination to maintain an independent identity. From 540 to 470 BC and again from 400 to 334 the Lycians were controlled, remotely through the agency of local nobles, by the Persian Great King. In the interim (470–400 BC) Lycia fell within the orbit of the Athenian Empire. Persepolis and Athens influenced Lycian funerary architecture, which was nonetheless dominated by a distinctive local style,

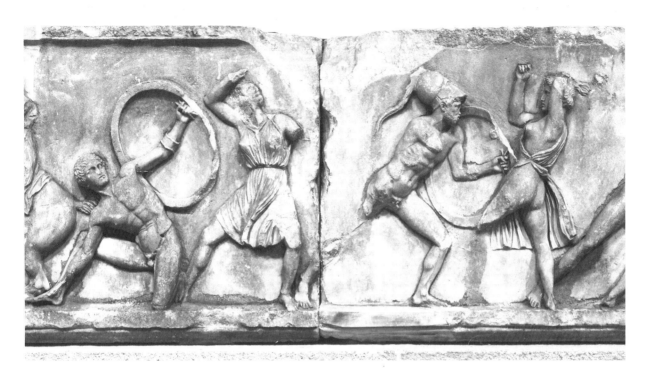

29 ABOVE *Part of a frieze from the Mausoleum at Halicarnassus showing Greeks fighting Amazons. The frieze originally ran around the monument just below the colonnade. These slabs were excavated by C. T. Newton in 1857. About 350 BC. H (slab) 90.2cm.*

28 LEFT *Reconstructed façade of the Nereid Monument from Xanthos. The elegant Nereids were set between the columns of this temple-like tomb, made for a dynast about 400 BC. On the podium are friezes with real and mythological battle-scenes. H 8.3m.*

featuring projecting rectangular frames and, on free-standing sarcophagi, steep ogival roofs. These surely reflect the direct translation into stone of the features of less durable timber-framed buildings.

The surviving monuments date to the two periods of Persian rule. The later tombs were expressly intended as an eternal record of the pursuit of advantage and privilege for the Lycian cities. Thus his inscribed sarcophagus represents Payava, a noble responsible for the administration of the lower Xanthos Valley, in audience with Autophradates, satrap of Sardis. Sadly more frequent are scenes of battle, gruesomely rendered on the otherwise decorative Nereid Monument from Xanthos, named for the lovely figures poised between its columns.

The Nereid Monument and earlier tombs also portray the traditional aristocratic pursuits of hunting, banqueting and cock-breeding. Though ferociously independent, no Lycian would wish to appear un-

cultured, and Greek influence is as apparent in the choice of decorative motifs as in the execution of the work. The earlier monuments such as the Harpy Tomb were evidently inspired by the art of Ionian Greece.

Persian authority was eventually undermined in western Lycia; the vacuum was filled by a powerful neighbour, Mausolus of Caria (d. 353 BC). Mausolus, too, preserved the memory of his splendid court in a tomb which has given us the word 'mausoleum'. One of the Seven Wonders of the Ancient World, the Mausoleum at Halicarnassus profoundly influenced Roman architectural design. The leading Greek architects Pytheos and Satyros and the sculptors Scopas, Bryaxis, Timotheos and Leochares designed and decorated the tomb. They contrived a three-dimensional tableau of courtly life animated by portraits of the ruling family and their courtiers. The figures were set on a stepped podium. Lions patrolled the base of the pyramidal roof, which was crowned with a chariot group. A conventionally Greek frieze depicting the battles against the Amazons decorated the top of the podium.

Another formidable neighbour of the Greeks, King Croesus of Lydia, contributed columns to the Temple of Artemis at Ephesus (550–500 BC). Fragments of exquisite sculptural decoration survive from this temple, destroyed in 356 BC by the arsonist Herostratus. A second temple was promptly commissioned. With striking figured decoration on its columns, this too became a Wonder of the Ancient World.

THE GREEKS IN THE WEST

The contacts re-established with the peoples of the eastern Mediterranean after the fall of the Mycenaean world were closely followed by exploration in the west. Traders from the island of Euboea led the way, as they had in the east. By 750 BC they had established a thriving trading post on the beautiful island of Ischia (ancient Pithekoussai), off the coast of central Italy, near Naples. Several Greek cities, from the mainland, the islands and the coast of Asia Minor, soon followed this lead and established colonies along the coasts of southern Italy and Sicily: some had superb harbours, like Syracuse in Sicily, others had access to rich agricultural plains, such as Metaponto, whose badge on coins was to be an ear of corn. The heyday of this great colonial adventure was the late eighth and seventh centuries BC.

The Greeks brought with them their language, their religion and their customs, but they also brought their arts and crafts. In the sixth and early fifth centuries the Greek artists in southern Italy produced many fine bronzes, decorated vases of fired clay and terracottas. The British Museum has a rich collection of bronze statuettes, one of the finest of which came from Armentum in Apulia. It was probably made at Taras (modern Taranto) in about 550 BC, and shows a warrior on horseback. It is remarkable for both its size and its quality, and is particularly evocative of the military power of the Greeks in southern Italy. On mainland Greece heavily armed cavalry was rare, but in southern Italy the wide plains allowed the rearing of fine horses and their deployment in battle.

Each of the Greek city-states followed its own independent course and almost all flourished, although there were inevitably clashes with neighbours, both native and Greek. Syracuse was to emerge in the fifth century as perhaps the greatest Greek city in the west, ruled by a succession of vigorous tyrants: an Etruscan

30 Bronze cavalryman from Armentum, made in southern Italy about 550 BC. It was cast solid in two main pieces – horse and rider – with smaller pieces (reins, spear and shield, all now missing) added separately. H 25.3cm.

32 RIGHT Gold choker-necklace made in Taras (modern Taranto) about 350 BC. The individual elements were produced by hammering thin sheets to shape and adding details in wire in the delicate technique of filigree. L 30.6cm.

31 BELOW Detail from a bell-shaped krater (mixing-bowl) painted by Python at Paestum about 330 BC. Alkmene is on a pyre which is being lit by her husband Amphitryon; Zeus orders the Clouds to put out the fire. H (picture) 26m.

bronze helmet from Olympia is a dedication by one of them after their victory over the Etruscans at the battle of Cumae in 473 BC.

The colony founded by Athens in 443 BC at Thurii seems to have encouraged some Athenian potters to emigrate to the neighbourhood of Metaponto, for from this date begins a series of vases decorated in the red-figure technique. A number of local schools of vase-painting soon developed, not only in Lucania and nearby Apulia, but also to the north in Campania and to the south in Sicily. The finest school, which is well represented in the British Museum, was the Apulian, based at Taras. It produced a host of monumental funerary vases covered with elaborate decoration. At Paestum, however, a rich city on the borders of Lucania and Campania, a potter called Python also produced some particularly fine vases decorated with scenes from plays both tragic and comic, for the Greeks brought with them their love of the theatre.

By the early fourth century Syracuse had gained control of most of Sicily and much of southern Italy, with the exception of Taras, which became particularly powerful in the fourth century and a flourishing artistic centre. Indeed, at Taras, in addition to talented potters and makers of terracottas, there was a school of jewellers, active from the middle of the century, that produced a series of exceptional pieces. From a single tomb, perhaps that of a priestess of Hera, comes a wonderful sceptre, a splendid ring and a spectacular necklace with pendant female heads, two of which have horns, identifying the figure as Io, the priestess of Hera who was turned by her into a heifer.

In the later fourth century, however, the power of Rome began to be felt and by 272 BC all of Greek Italy was in Roman hands. Sicily held out longer, but by the end of the third century it too had been absorbed into the centralised culture and economy of the Roman world, a fate that spelled the inevitable decline of all the fiercely independent Greek communities in Italy. Greek artists, however, continued to work for their new patrons and much in Roman art owes both its origins and its creators to the Greek artistic traditions of southern Italy.

THE NATIVE ITALIC CULTURES AND THE ETRUSCANS

The impact of Greek settlement in southern Italy was all the more powerful because the native population was culturally and technologically less advanced. Nonetheless research into Early Iron Age Italy (9th–8th centuries BC) now presents a complex picture of a multitude of peoples, each with its own customs, religion, occasionally also its own language, and types of artefact. Distinctive local products of the Italic peoples as represented in the British Museum include a

33 *Gypsum figure of a lady. This is a rare surviving example of a carved statue from the Etruscan Archaic period, found in the so-called Isis Tomb in the Polledrara Cemetery near Vulci. About 570–560 BC. H (figure) 85cm.*

34 *Bronze statuette of a young man wearing pointed boots and a tebenna (Etruscan form of toga). This figure is one of the finest Etruscan Archaic bronzes in existence. From Pizzirimonte, near Prato, about 500–480 BC. H 17.1cm.*

35 *Etruscan bronze mirror with a bone handle. The engraved back shows Perseus (Pherse), who has just decapitated Medusa, Athena (Menerfa), holding aloft the head, and, on the right, Hermes (Turms). From Perugia, about 350–325 BC. H 24cm.*

comprehensive collection of native Apulian pottery, Samnite bronze armour, including breastplates and broad belts, impasto pottery from Latium and the Faliscan territory, and bronze jewellery from Picenum. From a much earlier period, the Italian Bronze Age (*c.* 2000–900 BC), there is an impressive array of bronze weapons, brooches and implements, and a selection of Nuraghic bronzes, including statuettes, from Sardinia (12th–9th centuries BC or later).

The boundaries of the territories inhabited by the Italic tribes are blurred; each was influenced by its neighbours and, especially in the south, in Sicily and in Sardinia, not only by the Greeks but also by the Phoenicians who settled there. The most dramatic effects of foreign contact, however, are demonstrated by the

inhabitants of Etruria, who by the eighth century BC were already the most sophisticated and developed people in Italy. They lived in part of the western central region, broadly speaking between the valleys of the Arno and Tiber, where they benefited from rich agricultural resources and plentiful metal ores which enabled their craftsmen to excel in the production of metalwork throughout Etruscan history. The Etruscan civilisation had developed out of the so-called Villanovan culture of the ninth and eight centuries BC, but it has become customary to use the term Etruscan for the period following 700 BC only, when the Etruscans began to write, using a version of the Greek alphabet, and we know that Etruscan was spoken.

In the seventh century BC increasing trade and many

imports from the eastern Mediterranean brought new wealth to Etruria; this is known as the Orientalising period. Beautifully carved ivory, sea-shells and other luxury goods appear, and much Greek pottery, and perhaps also Greek craftsmen, arrived in Etruria. The most characteristic native Etruscan pottery was bucchero, a distinctive black, lustrous ware whose production lasted down to the early fifth century BC; painted Etruscan pottery through the centuries generally followed Greek styles and shapes. Ostentatious gold jewellery, famed for its decoration with filigree and granulation (minute gold spheres formed into patterns) was produced by Etruscan craftsmen, and many examples have been found in the fine family tombs built by the nobility of the seventh and sixth centuries. Cemeteries of all periods have yielded the greatest quantity of Etruscan artefacts.

Among the most impressive objects of the Etruscan Archaic period (600–475 BC) in the British Museum are the contents of the so-called Isis Tomb, excavated by Lucien Bonaparte, Prince of Canino, from the Polledrara cemetery on his estate near Vulci. The tomb-goods, mainly dating from 600 to 550 BC, include many sumptuous objects, some imported and others made locally. From the Archaic period also are two limestone cinerary urns in the form of male figures, examples of the monumental sculpture which, along with the practice of tomb-painting, had begun to appear in Etruria at the end of the previous century. In addition, there are numerous examples of the exquisite bronze sculpture, including many votive statuettes dedicated at shrines, and decorated utensils, especially mirrors with scenes engraved on the backs. These continued to be produced by the Etruscans down to the second and first centuries BC. This fine metalwork and engraved sealstones attracted discerning nineteenth-century collectors such as Richard Payne Knight, who bequeathed his collection of classical antiquities to the British Museum in 1824. In the sixth century BC Etruscan power and prosperity were at their zenith; Etruscan kings ruled Rome, and Etruscan colonies flourished in Campania and the lower Po Valley. By the end of the century, however, defeats by the Greeks at sea and on land severely reduced Etruscan domination; according to tradition the last Etruscan king was expelled from Rome in 509 BC, when the Roman Republic was established.

The Etruscan Classical period (475–300 BC) saw a continuing decline of Etruscan fortunes at the hands of the Greeks, Romans and Gauls who were now settled

36 *Painted terracotta sarcophagus of Seianti Thanunia Tlesnasa. She is shown reclining on the lid, wearing rich jewellery and holding a mirror while she adjusts her mantle. From a tomb at Poggio Cantarello, near Chiusi (ancient Clusium), about 150–130 BC. H 1.22m.*

in the Po Valley. Lacking outside stimulus, Etruscan art retained the Archaic style much longer than Greek art, and it occasionally became rather provincial-looking. Nonetheless, tomb-painting and engraved bronzework reached new heights, and painted terracotta roof decorations from Etruscan temples of the sixth to third centuries BC give a lively impression of the colour and showiness of the religious architecture of the period.

During the Hellenistic period Etruria shared an artistic style in common with most areas around the Mediterranean, but some traditional Etruscan elements persisted, particularly in the production of painted terracotta and carved stone cinerary urns and sarcophagi. It was during this period that Rome conquered the Mediterranean world, and by 280 BC the Etruscan city-states were subject allies of Rome. The Etruscans were given Roman citizenship after the Social War in 89 BC and were finally assimilated into the Roman world: the latest art of Etruria, especially the bronze figures depicting Herakles, priests and priestesses, heralds the beginnings of Roman Imperial art.

ROME AND THE EMPIRE

Some elements of Etruscan and Italic religions and civic ritual survived at Rome, but most Roman patricians (men of noble family) were educated by Greeks. Their taste for Greek culture was strengthened by the removal to Rome of classical works of art stripped from Greek cities and sanctuaries following Roman domination of the eastern Mediterranean in the second century BC. The generals of the later Roman Republic were rightly perceived in the Greek world as the successors to the Hellenistic kings. At home, amidst criticism from men of more traditional views, some generals acquired personal collections of Greek art. As the fashion spread, marble copies of Greek bronze originals were commissioned to adorn the houses and gardens of the wealthy. Greek artists were much in demand.

In Republican Rome the right to portraiture was restricted to the families of magistrates and the nobility. Portrait busts, of wax, terracotta and, later, stone, were arranged in cupboards at home to form a three-dimensional family tree. At funerals the busts were paraded and ancestral masks were worn to encourage the younger members of noble families to live up to the reputations of their ancestors. The unflattering portraits expressed respect for the traditional Roman virtues of authority and austerity.

By the reign of the emperor Augustus (27 BC–AD 14) the court favoured a Greek style of portrait, and the old patrician style was taken up by freed slaves of alien origin who now enjoyed prospects of citizenship. The growth of enfranchisement and opportunities to hold

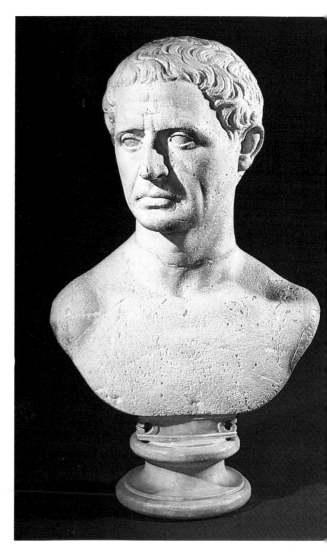

37 *Marble portrait bust of a Roman. The shape of the bust suggests that it was made about AD 100, but the subject's severe expression deliberately recalls the style of Republican portraits of the first century BC. H (with base) 54.8cm.*

public office encouraged the spread of the traditional Roman portrait to the provinces. The style was to re-emerge at Rome at the courts of emperors of relatively humble origin, such as Vespasian (AD 69–79) and many of the third-century emperors.

Such complex currents of artistic influence, generated by the relatively open nature of Roman society, and by the mobility of the army and wealthy provincials, give Roman art an eclectic and uncertain identity. But many Roman works have a striking historical immediacy. A bronze head of Augustus, cut from a statue in a Roman fort in Egypt by raiders from the kingdom of Meroë (Sudan), brilliantly portrays the first Roman emperor as

38 *Sardonyx cameo portrait of the first emperor, Augustus (27 BC–AD 14), wearing the protective aegis of Zeus with the heads of Phobos (Fear) and Medusa. The jewelled diadem was added later, and may have replaced a laurel wreath. H 12.8cm.*

39 *Gold mouthplate of a scabbard. As head of state Augustus receives a statuette of Victory from his stepson and field commander Tiberius. The emperor's victory is confirmed by Victoria. From Mainz (Germany), about 15 BC. W 8.6cm.*

successor to the Hellenistic kings. A softer regal image is offered by the Blacas Cameo. On the mouthplate of a scabbard of a ceremonial sword from Mainz (Germany), Augustus appears in the pose of the god Jupiter. Cameos and ceremonial weapons were made for loyal individuals; in sculptures and on coins seen by many Augustus was more modestly presented. 38 39

Made of glass cut in layers like a cameo, the Portland Vase is the finest example in the collections of the Augustan taste for Greek culture. That the interpretation of its scenes is still disputed is perhaps a reflection of the profound Hellenisation of the Augustan court. title page

The Roman imperial army, increasingly recruited from provincials, was instrumental in spreading Roman citizenship and culture to the frontier provinces. A diploma from Pannonia (Hungary) offers a precise record of the enfranchisement by the emperor Hadrian on 17 July AD 122 of the auxiliary cavalryman Gemellus after twenty-five years of military service. Also of historical interest is the set of inscribed silvered bronze horse-trappings from Xanten (Germany), most likely awarded to an officer serving under the prefect of cavalry Gaius Plinius Secundus, better known to us as the writer Pliny the Elder. Pliny's German command overlapped the reigns of the emperors Claudius (AD 41–54) and Nero (AD 54–68).

Nero's passion for the theatre, considered unseemly in an emperor, reflected the apparently insatiable Roman appetite for entertainment. Even more popular with the populace than mime were gladiatorial fights and chariot-races. A terracotta plaque of first-century date, possibly from a tomb, illustrates a race in progress. An ivory bust of a charioteer closely resembling the emperor Caracalla (AD 203–17) is said to come from the Roman amphitheatre at Arles (southern France). 40 9 42

As in their pleasures and cultural life, so in religious belief the Romans were open to external influence. A highly superstitious people, the Romans worshipped many deities beyond the Latin version of the classical Greek pantheon. The surviving traces of civic and personal commitment are legion.

The growth of material prosperity under the *Pax Romana* encouraged the building of houses of refined comfort and decoration for the wealthy. The large Roman townhouse was designed for the formal reception of clients and friends of the owner. An impression of cultured ease was evidently desirable. Rare intact survivals suggest the careful coordination of decorative schemes on painted walls and mosaic floors (and presumably painted or stuccoed ceilings).

The frequent reuse and recutting in late antiquity of marble statues and architectural decoration reflects the dependence of Roman sculptors and architects upon a fluctuating trade in white marbles. Mosaics, popular throughout the Empire, were not subject to such constraints; a mosaic floor could be assembled from off-

cuts of stone, glass and tile, and the many surviving late Roman examples are of striking appearance and lively design. The portrayal of the rich at their favourite sports of hunting and fishing was especially popular in North Africa. The wild beasts destined for the universally popular games were another favourite subject, possibly illustrating a lucrative source of income for the owners of North African estates.

Large quantities of surviving Roman tablewares offer further evidence of sustained material prosperity. The perfection of the technique of glass-blowing in the later first century BC led for the first time in classical antiquity to the manufacture of large glass vessels for common use at table. Production of decorative glasses spread from Syria, which remained a key centre of glass-making, to north-east Italy and the Rhineland. Plain wares were made in numerous local centres. The more luxurious glass vessels were elaborately decorated with coloured glass blobs or trails, or with applied figures. Glass was also wheel-cut; late Roman glasscutters were very proficient at figured scenes.

The earliest imperial ceramics rivalled fine glassware. Unsurprisingly, Roman potters imitated the fine

40 ABOVE Three terracotta figures of actors performing a mime. First century AD. H 16.9cm.

41 RIGHT Roman gold jewellery. The necklace with butterfly pendant is from Rome, and was made in the first century AD. On a second-century necklace, probably from Italy, gold links alternate with emeralds. A third-century hair ornament from Tunis is decorated with emeralds, pearls and sapphires. H (hair ornament) 10.7cm.

ceramic and metal wares of Hellenistic Greece and Asia Minor. The most elaborate vessels were thrown into moulds decorated with as many as thirty stamped impressions; the potter's name, or that of the owner of the workshop, was often stamped on the pot. Most Roman fine wares were given a distinctive red gloss, inspired by the finish of Hellenistic fine wares from Pergamon. Many Roman decorative motifs, like those of contemporary sculpture and painting, were drawn from the Classical Greek repertoire, and served the same purpose of endowing the owner with an air of cultured refinement.

By the mid-first century AD the production of fine ceramic tableware had moved from Arezzo (Italy) first to Lyons and La Graufesenque, then to Lezoux (central France). The owners of the kilns could thus more easily supply their main clients, the armies in Gaul and the Rhineland. The design and decoration of the vessels became less refined. New centures of production emerged to the north and east, but by the third century AD the Gaulish producers had been supplanted in the Mediterranean basin by workshops based in northern Africa and western Asia Minor. African Red Slip ware was often undecorated, or adorned with figured appliqués closely related in form to contemporary silverwork. In the northern provinces red wares were supplanted by local products.

A red slip was also applied to pottery lamps made in Italy. The workshops are approximately contemporary with those producing Arretine tableware, but the lamp workshops lasted into the second century AD. They produced innovative designs, mostly with figured decoration on the disc. Italian lamps were exported and copied throughout the Empire.

The third century AD was to see centralised imperial authority drastically weakened. Hoards of precious

42 ABOVE *Ivory bust of a charioteer closely resembling the emperor Caracalla (AD 198–217), who rebuilt the Circus at Rome. Said to be from the amphitheatre at Arles (France), early third century AD. H 5.3cm.*

43 ABOVE *Silver statuette of Tyche, the good fortune of a city. The wings of the goddess support a crescent with seven busts representing the gods of the days of the week. From Mâcon (France), second–third century AD. H 14cm.*

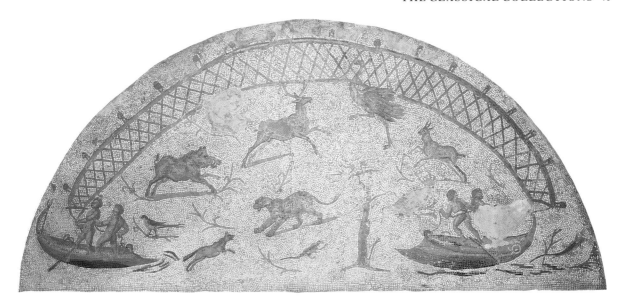

metals have been found in various provinces, where communities were threatened by political instability and barbarian invasion. Among the most spectacular of surviving hoards is that from Mâcon (central France), buried about AD 261 and sadly dispersed since its discovery in 1764. The hoard originally comprised silver vessels and statuettes, jewellery and some 30,000 gold and silver coins. The statuettes may have been dedicated in a private shrine.

The restoration of central authority after fifty years of chaos under a college of emperors led by the Illyrian Diocletian (AD 284–305), was to change for ever the nature of Roman society, and to accentuate the distinctions, long masked by Romanisation, between the Greek east and Latin west. A new eastern capital was founded by Constantine (AD 307–37) at Byzantium (modern Istanbul), and the city was renamed Constantinople (city of Constantine). As Rome centuries earlier had been furnished as an imperial capital with looted Greek statues, so under Constantine and later emperors works of art and symbols of culture still surviving in the Greek cities and sanctuaries were stripped for the adornment of Constantinople. Even today the serpent column from Delphi may be admired in that most Roman of settings, the hippodrome.

45 Mosaic pavement. Men in boats hunt animals in marshland with a long net. From Utica (Tunisia), early third century AD. W 3.39m.

The drastically changed presentation of the emperor to his subjects encapsulates for the modern viewer the distinction between the early imperial principate, or rule by 'the first citizen', and the later Roman dominate, or absolute rule. The anonymous image of the college of four emperors was thus replaced by that of a distant figure, his eyes no longer gazing reassuringly at his subjects but raised as if in search of divine approval of his authority. The portrayal of various levels of Roman society in sharply divided horizontal bands, in Augustan art discreetly employed in objects of restricted circulation, became a commonplace on monumental relief sculpture seen by the masses.

Bastions of pagan culture survived the adoption of Christianity as the official religion of empire. To these we owe the transmission of classical culture into the medieval and modern worlds. Some indication of the prosperity of the late Roman university town of Athens is offered by the chance survival of a gold ring set with precious stones, as by the traces of extensive city walls designed to protect the residences of the rich. It is fitting that Athens, since the days of Pericles a model of cultural supremacy, played a major role in the preservation of pagan culture in late antiquity.

44 LEFT Roman pottery and glass: a) Arretine krater from Capua, made about 20 BC–AD 20; b) red-slipped jug with applied decoration celebrating the victory of a team of gladiators, made in Tunisia in the third century AD; c) lamp with boxers, made in Italy about AD 1–50; d) glass flask with snake-thread decoration, made in Cologne in the third century AD. H 14cm.

COINS AND MEDALS

◆

*T*he Department of Coins and Medals contains the national collection of coins, medals, tokens and paper money. It embraces all cultures and periods, and is thus uniquely equipped to cover the history of coinage and money in East and West. As in other areas of the British Museum's collections, the Department has expanded its holdings by purchase and by the generosity of innumerable donors, but it is also able to buy gold or silver objects which have been declared Treasure Trove, and the vast majority of these are coins. In this way important hoards of coins, buried during the many periods of crisis and instability throughout Britain's history, have entered the collections of the British Museum. This has proved a useful source for filling gaps in the collection of common coins, as well as allowing the acquisition of some spectacular pieces.

46 *Treasure Trove of thirty-seven Roman gold aurei from Bredgar, Kent. They probably belonged to an officer with the Roman invasion of* AD *43, who may have fallen in the battle to cross the River Medway.*

All coins in this chapter are reproduced 1¹/₃ actual size.

GREEK COINS

The history of coinage has its origins in the Greek world of the early seventh century BC: the first metal coin was struck in the kingdom of Lydia in western Turkey around 625 BC and was long erroneously associated with King Croesus. The Department's collections chart the development of coinage in Greek lands from its earliest beginnings to the last of the Greek city coinages in Asia Minor about AD 276. Nearly 1,500 states and cities are represented, both large and small; many of the rulers and some of the cities themselves are known only from their surviving coins. Geographically the collection includes not only the heartland of the Greek world, but also the areas on its fringes whose peoples adopted the form of Greek coins for their own issues: from Spain to India, and from South Russia to North Africa. It embraces, therefore, a broad range of cultures with inscriptions not only in Greek, but also in Aramaic and other western scripts, such as Kharosthi, and even in demotic Egyptian.

The coins provide a closely dated sequence of designs that trace the history of art in different areas over this period; at the same time, because of their official nature, they provide a considerable amount of information, not available from other sources, about the social, religious and political history of the areas. The early

48 Portrait of Cleopatra I on a gold octadrachm of Ptolemy V of Egypt, issued under her regency (180–176 BC). The obverse bears a portrait of Ptolemy, and this is the only coin to portray Cleopatra I with her son.

coins in silver and gold carried a design on one side only, but were to be recognised by the distinguishing badge of the issuing authority – such as the tortoise of Aegina, the griffin of Abdera, or the Pegasus of Corinth. By the fifth century BC coinage was attracting engravers of the highest calibre, and dies cut deeply and in exquisite detail were being made. Those of south

47 Silver coins of Greek cities: a) tetradrachm of Athens with a Gorgon's head (c. 515 BC); b) stater of Poseidonia (Paestum, Italy), with Poseidon, patron deity of the colony (c. 520 BC); c) half-stater of Sardis, Turkey, with the fore-parts of a lion and a bull.

49 BELOW *a) silver tetradrachm (c. 315 BC) of the Carthaginians struck while campaigning against the Greeks in Sicily; b) silver five-shekel piece depicting Alexander the Great victorious against an Indian potentate (c. 325 BC); c) bronze coin of Commodus (AD 80–92), Abydos, Turkey.*

50 ABOVE *Silver tetradrachms of the Greek kings of Bactria, illustrating the distinctive and striking portraiture found in this series (from the top, left to right): a) Demetrius I (c. 200–185 BC); b) Antimachus (c. 185–170 BC); Eucratides (c. 170–145 BC).*

7b Italy (Magna Graecia) and Sicily, in which the collection is particularly strong, are especially beautiful, and occasionally bear the name of the artist. A great variety of different designs is found.

9b The Persian Empire had already absorbed the tradition of coinage in its western realms, but it was the spread of direct Greek influence under Alexander the Great (336–323 BC) that suddenly resulted in purely Greek coins being struck as far east as India.

48 Portraiture, although rarely used before the fourth century BC, provides a gallery of the rulers of the Hellenistic kingdoms unparalleled in any other

50 medium. The series issued by the Greek kings of Bactria and north-west India is noteworthy. The coming of the Romans had a dramatic effect on the coinage of the Greeks and political decline was matched by artistic decline. A particularly fine collection of the

9a coinage of Rome's enemy, Carthage, illuminates the course of the struggle for power. Under the Empire coinage in gold was not permitted to the cities of the Roman provinces, and coinage in silver was much restricted, eventually becoming purely imperial in char-

9c acter. The bronze coins of the Greek cities under the Roman Empire, however, many of them of large medallion size, provide a fascinating array of designs, usually associated on the obverse of the coin with the portrait of the emperor or of members of his immediate family. Reverses illustrate local temples and statues, refer to periodic games, and generally provide copious evidence of the preoccupations of the cities in the first three centuries of our era. Economic and political changes in the Empire led to their cessation, though a few quasi-civic coins inscribed in Latin were issued in the early fourth century.

ROMAN COINS

The British Museum has one of the finest collections of Roman coins in the world, spanning the period from the beginning of Roman coinage around 300 BC to the death of the last emperor in the west in AD 480. The

51 earliest Roman coins in the collection are a small group of relatively rare silver and bronze coins of the third century BC, struck in imitation of the coinage of the Greek colonies of southern Italy. At the same time the Romans were continuing to cast large bronze 'bricks' and discs; this was a practice they had copied and adapted from their central Italic or Etruscan neighbours, who used heavy cast-bronze ingots as currency.

This dual system survived until the crippling cost of the war against Hannibal (218–201 BC) forced the Romans to debase their silver and reduce the weight of the bronze coinage. The Museum has a particularly good collection of the cast bronzes and of the struck silver, notably of the latest issue known as 'quadrigati', because of the design of a four-horse chariot.

51 *Silver didrachm of the Roman Republic (c. 265 BC). On one side Hercules is depicted; on the other Romulus and Remus with the she-wolf.*

In about 210 BC the new 'denarius system' was inaugurated. This coinage was named after its principal denomination, and it lasted for some four and a half centuries. Although the early bronze 'asses' are not very well represented in the Museum, it has an excellent collection of silver denarii from the latter part of the Roman Republic (c. 150 BC–c. 31 BC).

During the civil wars following the death in 44 BC of Julius Caesar, the first living man to be portrayed on a Roman coin, the leaders of the various factions tried to buy the loyalty of their armies, and minted large quantities of money; some of them continued the Hellenistic Greek practice of adding their portrait. This had two permanent consequences for Roman coinage. First, it added a gold coin to the range of denominations regularly produced – the aureus, worth 25 denarii. Thereafter gold remained important until the end of the second century AD. The Museum has one of the world's best collections of aurei, deriving principally from the British royal and other eighteenth- and nineteenth-century private collections; in addition, hoards of Roman gold coins found in Britain have been acquired, notably those from Bredgar, dating from AD 46 43, the very year of the Roman invasion, and Corbridge, deposited just after the middle of the second century. The second change, portraiture, was continued by the emperors and became a normal feature of imperial coins. The series of fine portraits of the early Empire were eagerly acquired by early collectors to illustrate the events described by Roman historians, and so have come to represent one of the main strengths of the Museum's Roman collection, notable for its remarkable state of preservation as well as its comprehensiveness.

From the end of the second century AD the stability of the Roman monetary system was strained by a shortage of precious metals and an expensive succession of frontier wars against the Germans and Persians. The consequence was a reduction in the quantity of gold issued and in the weight and purity of the silver coinage, and an increase in the number of mints and their output. At the same time bronze coins ceased to be

53 *Gold solidus of the Byzantine emperor Justinian* II *(AD 685–95). On the obverse Christ is shown as ruler of the world, with the emperor as his humble servant on the reverse.*

52 *The obverse of a gold coin of the Roman emperor Maxentius (AD 306–12). The depiction of Maxentius is characteristic of the powerful portraiture of emperors of this period. The value of the coin was four aurei.*

struck. Although poorly made and unattractive, these coins are an important source for the history of an otherwise poorly documented period and recent acquisitions, particularly from British coin hoards, have increased the Museum's holdings in this area. The most notable of these was the find of almost 55,000 at Mildenhall (Wiltshire) in 1978, and generally known by its ancient name of Cunetio, in order to avoid confusion with its Suffolk namesake.

The main elements of the coinage system of the late Roman Empire as established by Diocletian (AD 284–305) were the gold solidus and a plentiful base metal coinage, produced at a dozen or more mints, including London for a time; it consisted of coins of various weight-standards during the first half of the fourth century, most issues containing a small quantity of silver. This fourth-century coinage is well represented in the Museum collections, partly as a result of the acquisition of gold hoards from Water Newton, Corbridge and Rockbourne, important finds respectively of the 380s and 390s. Late fourth-century silver coinage is particularly characteristic of British finds, and the Museum has an especially rich series. Base metal coinage has also been systematically collected, with the issues of the London mint and of the so-called 'British Empire' of Carausius and Allectus (AD 286–96) receiving notable attention.

The fifth century AD saw the break up of the Roman Empire and the cessation of its coinage in Western Europe. Britain had already been abandoned in about 410, after which time no coinage circulated for two centuries. This and a lack of antiquarian interest in the fifth century has deprived the Museum of one of its main traditional sources of acquisition, British hoards. However, private collections, particularly drawing upon finds from the Balkans, North Africa and Egypt, have ensured as good and representative a collection of base metal coins as can be found in any museum, and many important pieces in gold and silver are here.

Successor kingdoms to the western Roman Empire, the Vandals, Visigoths, Ostrogoths, Franks and others, began coinages of their own based on the Roman model in the course of the fifth century. Together with issues of later migrants such as the Lombards, these ultimately gave rise to the national coinages of Western Europe and good representative collections may be found in the Museum, thanks mainly to Count de Salis. Roman coinage continued in the eastern Mediterranean basin, where it eventually adopted characteristic inscriptions and types that we call Byzantine. This coinage, together with numerous derivatives in eastern Europe as far west as Italy, lasted almost down to the fall of Constantinople to the Turks in 1453. Though not large, the Museum's Byzantine collection is fully representative and contains a high proportion of unusual pieces.

EUROPE AND GREAT BRITAIN

Outside the immediate political influence of the Greeks and Romans, gold and silver coinage came to be produced by the Celts and other inhabitants of Central Europe during the last three centuries before Christ. At first these were mostly barbarous copies of issues of the kings of Macedon, and even in faraway Britain gold coins showed evidence of this origin. The Museum has only a representative collection of Continental material, but has an excellent series of ancient British pieces, built up in recent years by acquisitions from such hoards as Waltham St Lawrence (Berkshire) and Wanborough (Surrey). Something of the political structure

54 *The Celts in Britain: gold 'staters' of the Catuvellauni (left to right): a) King Tasciovanus (late 1st century BC), an important ruler in southern Britain; b) his son and successor Cunobelinus (Cymbeline), who died shortly before the Roman invasion.*

56 *Coins of Offa, King of Mercia, England (AD 757–96): a) gold copy of an 'Abbasid dinar, said to have been found at Rome; b) silver penny: following Frankish coinage, Offa made the regal penny the normal coinage in England.*

of this period is revealed by the find spot distribution and designs of the coins of such rulers as the 'Great King' Tasciovanus And his son Cunobelinus, Shakespeare's Cymbeline.

All non-Roman coinage in Europe ceased during the heyday of the Roman Empire. It began to revive tentatively during the fifth century AD, imitating first Roman

55 *Barbarian successors to the Roman Empire (from top to bottom): a) gold solidus of Theoderic (AD 489–523), founder of the Ostrogothic kingdom, struck at Rome; b) gold tremissis, struck at Saragossa, Spain, by the Visigothic ruler Reccared I (AD 586–601); c) Merovingian gold tremissis, struck at Limoges, France, by the moneyer Saturnus.*

and later Byzantine prototypes. By the seventh century national characteristics were well developed in Spain and France, whose easily recognisable gold tremisses reintroduced the notion of coinage to England. The burial at Sutton Hoo (c. AD 625), included a purse and thirty-seven such coins, and within two decades similar pieces, now of rather debased gold, were being struck in England.

For the next six centuries little gold was struck in Europe away from the shores of the Mediterranean. Such few as there are, such as Charlemagne's coin minted at Dorestadt or that of Offa struck in imitation of a Muslim 'Abbasid dinar, must have been made for offerings rather than commerce.

Continental silver of this period tended to name its place of mintage as well as the ruler. That struck in England more usually bore the name of a moneyer, and only gradually came to include a mint name. Many Continental series, too, remained almost unchanged over long periods – their types were 'immobilised' – whereas from the reign of Edgar (959–75) to that of Stephen (1135–54) designs on English pennies were periodically changed, testimony to the much closer control that was maintained over the coinage in England.

Gold coinage began to revive in Europe during the thirteenth century, the 'florin' of Florence being particularly influential. English gold coinage hardly began before the mid-fourteenth century, but then the profits from the wool trade and from success in the Hundred Years' War against France led to a huge output, whose stability over a long period is well attested by the Fishpool (Nottinghamshire) hoard, which also shows how Continental gold entered the country to redress a favourable trade balance. The celebrated design of the noble, showing the warlike figure of the king in a ship, was a potent symbol of a strong island power. For

57 ABOVE *(top) Silver denier of the Frankish king Charles the Bald (AD 843–77); (below) a group of English silver pennies: Alfred (AD 871–99), Edgar (AD 959–75), Stephen (AD 1135–54) and Edward I (AD 1272–1307).*

58 BELOW *a) Gold lion of Philip the Good (AD 1419–67), Duke of Burgundy, struck in Flanders; b) gold salut of Henry VI (AD 1422–61): this type of salut is an allegory of the hoped-for union between France and England under the infant king.*

almost three centuries the kings of England had extensive lands in what is now France, and this coinage, too, is well represented in the collection. Remarkable is the design of the 'salute', in which the Angel Gabriel's salutation of the Virgin is made a symbol of the hoped-for union of England and France by the marriage of Henry V with Katherine of France. 58b

A dramatic change – though it took almost a century to accomplish – came about in European coinage after about 1470 under a triple stimulus. First was the impact of immense new supplies of precious metal, particularly of silver, from new mines in Europe and the New World. Secondly came technical developments leading to the increasing mechanisation of coin production. Third was the artistic change brought about by the influence of the Renaissance, starting in Italy and expressed in the revival of realistic portraiture and the use of Roman letters for inscriptions. These features did not of course necessarily come in together; in England, for example, a realistic portrait was normal after 1504, whereas Roman letters did not become invariable until fifty years later. 60

The financial systems of Central and Western Europe all originally stemmed from the eighth-century Carolingian pounds, shillings and pence. By the sixteenth century the same system was applied to widely differing coins in different countries; in Scotland, the pound of 1600 was worth only a twelfth of its English counterpart, the Scots shilling being the equivalent of an English penny. As the value of the unit of currency was eroded by inflation, so the use of money became

59 ABOVE *Medieval gold coins: a) florin, Florence: first issued in 1252, these coins were the basis of Western European commerce in the early fourteenth century; b) noble of Edward III (AD 1327–77): this coin was first struck in 1344 as England became rich from the wool trade and the profits of war.*

60 BELOW *Renaissance gold coinage: a) double-ducat of Louis XII of France, minted in the Duchy of Milan: a classic example of Italian Renaissance coinage; b) 30-shilling sovereign of Elizabeth I of England (AD 1558–1603), which retains many medieval characteristics.*

61 *Gold coins of the nineteenth and twentieth century:*
a) 20-shilling sovereign of George IV (1820–30), Great
Britain: Pistrucci's vision of St George and the dragon has
continued in use to the present; b) napoléon of Napoleon I
(AD 1804–14), France; c) Britannia, Elizabeth II (1952–),
Great Britain: a typical modern coin-like ingot, its value
expressed as a weight of fine gold rather than as a
denomination.

increasingly common until it spread to virtually all transactions. Base metal coins of very low value existed, for example, in Portugal and Sicily from the thirteenth century, but modest inflation in England meant that no copper coins existed until the seventeenth century. Until the last quarter of the century lead and copper farthings were often produced by municipalities and tradesmen. These are an important source of personal and economic information, and a very large collection, arranged by county and town or village, is kept in the Museum.

The great days of silver coinage lasted until the eighteenth century when new discoveries of gold, first in Brazil and later in North America, Australia and South Africa, made coins of that metal the dominant high value currency in the nineteenth century. However, the supremacy of gold was short-lived, as paper money was already encroaching on the traditional role of precious metal coinage. In the twentieth century the pressures of two world wars have eliminated all precious metal coinage from currency; it survives only as bullion and in commemorative pieces, like 'Britannia'. Modern coinage is wholly token and is confined to use in minor transactions, yet vast quantities are needed for this purpose and the mechanisation process has advanced from the seventeenth-century screw press through steam power to modern electrically powered coining machines. Now every country sees it as a matter of national pride to have its own issues and thus the variety of coins produced in the world remains as great as ever. The Museum endeavours to collect as much of this as possible, for the time will come when it will be of historical interest.

ORIENTAL COINS

The history of coinage in Asia is well documented in the Museum's holdings. If Lydia, in Western Asia, was the birth-place of the Western coinage tradition, Asia saw the origin and development of three other distinct

62 *Coins of the Chinese series: a) Bronze 'hoe' coin of the Zhou*
kings, China (c. 450 BC); b) bronze '5-grain' coin, Han
dynasty, China (c. 75 BC); c) bronze Guangxu 10-cash coin,
Qing dynasty, China (AD 1875–1908); d) brass cash, Bantam,
Java (16th century AD); e) silver 2¹/₂-bat of Rama III
(AD 1824–51), Thailand; f) gold 1-bu, Japan (AD 1601).

61a,b

coinage traditions: Chinese, Indian and Islamic, and two lesser independent coinage systems in Japan and Thailand.

China's coinage is the oldest in the world after the Lydian. It originated independently in North China by the sixth century BC and spread during the following centuries to Central Asia, Korea, Japan, Vietnam, Indonesia, Malaysia and Thailand. During the medieval period Chinese coins even circulated as far afield as South India, Iran and East Africa.

China's first coins were cast-bronze copies of hoes, knives and cowrie shells. These objects had all previously been used by the Chinese to make payments, and the first coins standardised their use as money. By the end of the third century BC these curiously shaped coins had all been replaced by flat round coins, each with a square central hole. Coins of this shape remained in use in China until the present century. Throughout their long history Chinese coins retained three other distinctive features: the coins were cast in moulds; they

were made from base metals – bronze, brass, iron or lead; and they were decorated only with inscriptions. Chinese-style coinage was adopted by other nations in the Far East, but these distinctive features were always retained.

The Museum's Far Eastern coins cover the full range of the Chinese coinage tradition, including rare examples of the earliest phases of coinage in China, Japan and Central Asia. The collection is a valuable record of the Far East's economic and political history, and also provides an important visual account of the development of the Chinese writing system.

Together with the coins, the Department also holds an outstanding collection of the gold and silver ingots and paper money which circulated alongside the base metal coins in China and Japan. Included in the Far Eastern coin collection is an extensive series of religious charms made in the shape of Chinese coins. These represent a shared tradition from China, Japan, Korea, Vietnam and Indonesia of using coins as religious charms. The charms carry inscriptions and images relating to a broad range of Far Eastern religions.

India's coinage is almost as old as that of China, but it was not an independent invention and began as an offshoot of Greek coinage. It quickly developed characteristics of its own and spread its influence south and east to Sri Lanka, Burma, Thailand, Cambodia, Malaysia and Indonesia, and northwards in Central Asia.

63 Coins of the Indian series: a) silver punch-marked coin of Mauryan kings of India (c. 300 BC); b) gold double stater of Kushan king Wima Kadphises (c. AD 75), N.W. India; c) gold dinara of Gupta king Samudragupta (AD c. 335–80), N. India; d) silver tangka from the kingdom of Srikshetra, Burma (c. AD 800); e) gold 5-muhar of the Mughal emperor Akbar (AD 1556–1605), India; f) gold muhar dated 1770 of the British East India Company, Bombay Presidency, India.

India seems to have derived the idea of coinage from the Greek world via Iran. During the fifth century BC Greek-style coins circulating as money in Iran entered the north-west corner of the South Asian sub-continent. By the end of the fourth century BC silver coins with Indian designs were in circulation throughout northern India. The Greek idea of using stamped pieces of metal as money was modified by the Indians; India's first coins were not stamped in the Greek manner on both sides, but only on one side, and the designs were applied by several punches. The early coins were rarely round like Greek coins, but were often square. The designs mostly consisted of small symbols, stylised images of the sun, moon, animals, trees and so on. The occasional use of square coins has persisted throughout the Indian coinage. Although India has always maintained a distinct coinage tradition, it is possible to trace the impact of successive cultural intrusions by Greek, Iranian, Scythian, Hunnish, Turkic, Mongol and European invaders.

The British Museum's collection of South Asian coins is probably the finest in the world. The full range of Indian coins is represented, with particularly spec-tacular holdings of Indo-Greek, Kushan, Gupta, Sultanate, Mughal and British Indian coins. Much of the chronology of Indian history has been established through a study of its coins. They also give a significant insight into the development of Indian religious thought, providing in many cases the earliest datable and identifiable representations of deities.

The third main Asian coinage tradition, Islamic, began its development in the seventh century BC. It grew directly out of the Western coinage tradition but, in response to the restraints of Islam, it soon established an identity of its own which was carried along with the Islamic faith out of the Middle East, north into Central

64 *Coins from the Islamic series: a) bronze imitation of Byzantine follis, issued in the name of Allah, from Syria, Arabs in Hims (Emesa), c. AD 680; b) gold dinar dated AH 77 (AD 696) of Umayyad caliph Abd al-Malik, Syria; c) bronze coin of Ayyubid ruler Salah al-Din (Saladin, AD 1169–93), Syria; d) gold dinar of Umayyad ruler Hisham II (AD 976–1010), Spain; e) gold kupang of Sultan Muhammad al-Sa'id, Sulawesi, Indonesia; f) silver coin of Timur (Tamerlane, AD 1390–1402), Afghanistan.*

Asia, east to India and Indonesia, and out of Asia, south to East Africa and west into North Africa and Europe.

The first coins struck in the name of Allah, the God of Islam, and his prophet Muhammad were simply copies of Byzantine gold and copper and Sassanian silver coins with short added religious inscriptions, proclaiming the Islamic faith. From AD 696 these imitations were replaced by coins with purely Islamic designs. The Islamic faith was hostile to the use of pictorial representations, so the new designs were inscriptional. The new inscriptions proclaimed Islam, and referred to the denomination, date and place of issue of the coin.

Inscriptional coin designs were used wherever the followers of Muhammad carried his faith. Later additional information relating to local rulers, governors and religious leaders was included in the inscriptions. Departures from the rule against pictures were unusual and, where they occurred, tended to be on bronze coins. In India the regular Islamic coin design was retained, but modified to fit the Indian tradition, often being used on square coins and with symbols to identify the issuing mint or ruler. Remarkable examples are the zodiacal and portrait issues of the Mughals Akbar and Jahangir. Islamic coins, imported from Central Asia by Viking trade through the Baltic and Russia, played an important part in the monetary history of Northern Europe during the ninth and tenth centuries, and they even occur in British hoards.

In addition to these main Asian coinages, the Museum collection also covers two other independent minor traditions which developed in Japan and Thailand. Both these traditions were adaptations of an earlier use of precious metal ingots as money. In Thailand the ingots were bracelet-shaped and the fully developed coinage consisted of stamped bars of silver bent into a tight sphere. Japan's ingots were both gold and silver, slab- or bar-shaped; the coins were the same shape, but stamped with several punches.

62e
62f

In both Central and South-East Asia, where Chinese, Indian and Islamic cultures coexisted, the three main coinage traditions of Asia met and mingled, giving rise to interesting hybrid coinages, such as coins of Chinese shape with Islamic inscriptions, or Indian shape with Chinese inscriptions.

From the late fifteenth century onwards European commercial, imperial and colonial expansion into Asia had a marked effect upon the traditional coinage systems. Apart from a few residual features, Asia's coinages have lost their distinctive identities and become part of the Western coinage tradition. This process of change is particularly well documented by the Museum's collection.

MEDALS

The art of medal-making has its origin in the Italian Renaissance, and flourished throughout Western Europe in the succeeding centuries. The British Museum's collections are drawn from every European and many non-European countries from the fifteenth century to the present day. The oldest medal in the collection, in fact the first modern medal, was struck to celebrate the capture of Padua by Francesco II da Carrara in AD 1390.

Many early medallists, such as Pisanello, produced

65 LEFT *Gold and silver medals of the seventeenth and eighteenth centuries: a) James I: Peace with Spain (1604), perhaps by Nicholas Hilliard; b) Elizabeth I: Dangers Averted (c. 1588), perhaps by Hilliard, executed shortly after the defeat of the Armada; c) Mary I: The Happy State of England (1555), by Jacopo da Trezzo; d) John Thurloe (c. 1653), by Abraham and Thomas Simon; e) Oliver Cromwell (1653), by Thomas Simon; f) Second Treaty of Vienna (1731), by John Croker.*

66 ABOVE *Medals of the twentieth century: a) Prague (1909), by Stanislas Sucharda; b) Pax (1919), by Erzsebet von Esseö; c) Toulouse-Lautrec (1964), by André Galtié; d) bison (1975), by Elizabeth Frink: presented to eminent British zoologists. All bronze except a), which is silver.*

67 *Bronze medal of John* VIII *Palaeologus, Byzantine emperor 1423–48, made by Pisanello in 1438.*

cast pieces far more closely related to paintings and sculpture than to coins, and have left us superb likenesses of the appearance of notable contemporaries, such as John Palaeologus, the Byzantine emperor (AD 1421–48), of whom the numismatic record is disappointing.

Between about 1500 and the end of the last century there was a tendency to assimilate the style and technique of coins and medals, but since that time the genres have once more separated, with medals losing much of their official character. Casting is again a normal technique, and there have been remarkable instances of experimentation in style and form, emphasising anew the medal as an art form rather than as a vehicle for commemoration.

The Department contains a comprehensive collection of British medals of all periods, including two versions of Nicholas Hilliard's famous 'Dangers Averted' medal of the time of the Armada, a fine series of portraits by Thomas and Abraham Simon, and a complete set of the beautiful medals engraved by John Roettiers after the Restoration. Italian Renaissance and sixteenth-century medals are well represented, as are French and Dutch, Swiss and Scandinavian seventeenth- and eighteenth-century medals. The German medals of this period, accumulated by the Hanoverians, are particularly worthy of note, as are the outstanding collection of German First World War material, the wide-ranging, if not yet entirely representative, collec-

tions of late nineteenth- and early twentieth-century European and American medals and the growing number of late twentieth-century pieces. Dies and models for medals, political and satirical badges and tokens, military medals and decorations also contribute to the unusually comprehensive nature of the Museum's medallic collection.

PAPER MONEY

Circulating paper money was first used in China in the late tenth century AD, but did not appear in Europe and the West until the seventeenth century, with issues in Scandinavia, Britain and America. Growth of trade and industry encouraged the rise of banking and the convenience of paper in the eighteenth and nineteenth centuries. Many ventures were heavily based on credit, showing more optimism than business sense, and legislation to place banks and note issue on a firmer financial footing resulted in the rationalisation and centralisation of banking services. Today the right to issue notes is almost exclusively the privilege of central banks and state treasuries.

The British Museum's collection of banknotes and related items illustrates the historical development and geographical spread of paper currency. Altogether almost two hundred countries are represented, with material dating from such early examples as notes issued by the Chinese Board of Revenue during the Ming dynasty (AD 1368–1644) and seventeenth-century issues from Sweden and Norway, to modern state issues from developing Third World countries. The collection includes not only state and privately issued banknotes, but also emergency and political issues, cheques, postal orders, printers' specimens, and artwork for note designs. Even credit cards have a place. All British paper money is well represented, with particularly good collections of notes from Scotland, the Isle of Man, and the English country banks of the nineteenth century.

The Museum's paper money is acquired by donations, loans and purchases. Several important series of notes have come from major private collections and many countries around the world help to keep the collection up to date by sending examples of their current note issues. We house on permanent loan the Chartered Institute of Bankers' collection of paper money, comprising some 10,000 British notes and 20,000 notes from the rest of the world. Combining this excellent collection with our own holdings has ensured that the British Museum contains one of the foremost collections of paper money in the world.

68 BELOW *Unissued five-pound note of the Hull Banking Co.,*
Kingston-upon-Hull, England, 1840–49.

69 ABOVE *Réunion, 1,000-franc note (equivalent to 20 new*
francs), 1958–73.

EGYPTIAN ANTIQUITIES

The British Museum houses one of the world's great collections from ancient Egypt. Every aspect of this civilisation over six thousand years is illustrated, from the Predynastic cultures to early Christian times. The collections of the Department of Egyptian Antiquities include all types of object in many different materials – from paintings, inscribed and written documents, metalwork, stone-carving and woodwork, to pottery, glass, jewellery and textiles. The early Christian, or Coptic collections, including inscribed gravestones, textiles and domestic objects, bring the collections up to the ninth century AD, while Islamic material from Egypt, dating from the seventh century onwards, is kept in the Department of Oriental Antiquities.

The oldest objects in the British Museum's Egyptian collections date from the fifth millennium BC. The Predynastic inhabitants of the Nile Valley were hunters who gradually settled in permanent villages and learned the skills of agriculture. Their tools are carefully worked from flint; the finest example, the Pitt-Rivers knife, has an ivory handle carved with scenes of animals and hunting. A distinctive range of fine handmade ceramics and stone vessels was produced at this early period. Some objects remain enigmatic, such as a series of slate palettes, shaped as animals, birds and fish. These may embody divine representations. Many show the stains of eye-paint and were undoubtedly used for grinding pigments – their primary purpose; others are larger and more elaborate, and carry carved scenes which may reflect events of historical importance. The Battlefield Palette, for example, which shows a lion attacking men, is probably an allegorical scene of a king slaying his enemies. A similar symbolic reference to a national struggle may be contained in the marvellous scenes on the Hunters' Palette, where men hunt lions and other wild animals.

By far the most striking element of the Museum's Egyptian collection is its large and impressive array of sculpture. Statues were produced almost entirely for religious purposes, to promote the worship of deities, to glorify the power of specific kings, to obtain benefits for private persons, or to act in a more specific funerary role, representing the person of the deceased. Some sculpture was monumental in the strictest sense of the term being part of the architectural embellishment of temples, but most pieces were conceived in private roles, to be consigned to the darkness of the tomb or to the unfrequented courts of temples.

Among the very earliest datable sculptures is an ivory figurine of a woman of the Badarian culture, from the early fourth millennium BC. This piece is crudely executed and has no recognisably Egyptian features. An exceptionally fine early sculpture is a small ivory of an unidentified king of the First or Second Dynasty (c.

72 *Ivory figure of a king wearing the White Crown of Upper Egypt and the cloak of the* Sed-*festival. From Abydos, Early Dynastic Period, about 2900 BC.* H *8.8cm.*

71 *Carved slate palette, known as the Hunters' Palette from the scenes of hunting wild animals with which it is decorated. Late Predynastic Period, about 3100 BC.* L *66.5cm.*

70 LEFT *Part of a tomb-painting on plaster, showing the nobleman Nebamun hunting birds in the marshes. From Thebes, Eighteenth Dynasty, about 1400 BC.* H *81cm.*

73 *Standing tomb-statue of Nenkheftka, carved in limestone and painted. From Deshasha, Fifth Dynasty, about 2400 BC.* H *1.34cm.*

2800 BC), which is delicately carved. Perhaps the most outstanding piece of Old Kingdom sculpture in the collections is a figure dating to the Fifth Dynasty (*c.* 2494–2345 BC) and representing a nobleman, Nenkheftka, in the classic pose of the Egyptian standing figure: left foot forward, arms held straight by the sides. Breaking away from this conventional pose is a wooden figure of the Sixth Dynasty (*c.* 2200 BC) of the youthful Meryrehashtef. One of the most striking and expressive of Old Kingdom sculptures, this is one of a series of figures from Meryrehashtef's tomb showing him at different stages of his life.

Statues such as these were intended to act as a residence for the soul of the deceased in his tomb, and offerings made to them could be enjoyed by the spirit of the dead. Colouring as well as pose was conventional: the flesh tones of male figures were rendered by red paint (as, for example, on the figure of Nenkheftka), female yellow. This contrast is particularly well illustrated by a tomb group of the Fourth Dynasty (*c.* 2600 BC), a painted limestone sculpture showing the seated figures of Katep and his wife Hetepheres.

During the Middle Kingdom (*c.* 2050–1786 BC) the range and style of sculpture changed quite dramatically. Royal statues show a new realism in depicting the care-worn features of the ruler, revealing him as a man rather than as a detached god-king. Three almost identical black granite statues of Sesostris III (*c.* 1878–1843 BC) from Deir el-Bahri are fine examples of the genre. The realism of Middle Kingdom royal portraiture is reflected to a lesser extent in private sculpture of the period. For the first time statues of private individuals began to appear in temples as well as in tombs, enabling the owner to partake of any offerings made to the god of the temple. Changes in usage were accompanied by changes in form, the so-called 'blockstatue' making its first appearance. The British Museum possesses one of the earliest known examples of this type, the statue of Sihathor; the figure, in its original niche, squats on the ground, his limbs covered by an all-enveloping cloak. As a form it was to become increasingly popular, since it removed the need to carve the body in detail and provided large, relatively flat surfaces which could be used for inscriptions. This was important, since it was the inscription rather than the features which gave precise identity to the statue.

The most important series of sculptures belongs to the New Kingdom, outstanding among which is a royal head in green schist, possibly depicting Queen Hatshepsut (*c.* 1503–1482 BC) or her co-regent and successor Tuthmosis III (*c.* 1504–1450 BC). There are several representations of Amenophis III, including the head and an arm from a colossal statue in red granite; its torso still lies in the precincts of the temple of Mut at Karnak. A number of statues may be attributed by their youthful features to Tutankhamun, but the inscriptions

74 *Three black granite statues of King Sesostris III. From Deir el-Bahri, Twelfth Dynasty, about 1850 BC. H (average) 1.40m.*

75 *Limestone funerary stele of Sihathor, with a recess for a statue of the same material. The squatting figure of Sihathor is one of the earliest known examples of a block-statue. Twelfth Dynasty, about 1850 BC. H 1.12m.*

are of Horemheb, who usurped many of Tutankhamun's portraits.

A remarkable sculpture of the Nineteenth Dynasty, the so-called Younger Memnon, was removed from the Ramesseum at Thebes by Giovanni Battista Belzoni. This is the upper part of a colossus of King Ramesses II (*c.* 1304–1237 BC), striking for its use of two-tone granite. A standing sculpture of Ramesses II's son Khaemwese is carved from breccia, another unusual material. This very hard conglomerate stone presented enormous technical difficulties which the sculptor of this fine piece was only partially able to surmount. A fragmentary black granite sculpture of a young prince wearing the sidelock of youth may represent Ramesses II's eventual successor, Merneptah, or the future Sethos II.

The British Museum's collections are particularly rich in private sculpture of the New Kingdom on both large and small scale. Two interesting statues of the influential official Senenmut date to the reign of Queen Hatshepsut. One is a block-statue in quartz; the other, in black granite, is more unusual, and shows Senenmut with the princess Neferure on his lap. The recent acquisition of a fragmentary scribe-statue of the general Djehuty has a particular historical interest: Djehuty's capture of the city of Joppa in Palestine is recounted in a papyrus in this collection. One of the most skilful and charming pieces from this period, a little less than life size and evidently originating from the Memphite necropolis, shows an unnamed official and his wife seated hand in hand. Carved in limestone, the piece is uninscribed and is probably unfinished.

76 *Head of green schist, representing either Queen Hatshepsut or her successor, Tuthmosis* III. *Eighteenth Dynasty, about 1480* BC. H *45.7cm.*

77 *Upper part of a colossal granite statue of Ramesses* II, *known as the Younger Memnon. From Ramesses' mortuary temple at Thebes. Nineteenth Dynasty, about 1250* BC. H *2.67m.*

Sculpture of animals became increasingly common during the New Kingdom, and the British Museum possesses many fine examples. On a monumental scale are two red granite lions, dating from the reign of Amenophis III (*c.* 1417–1379 BC). Both were set up as guardian figures before Amenophis' temple at Soleb in Nubia, but in the third century BC were moved south to Gebel Barkal. From early times animals were connected with the worship of deities, and many gods were represented either wholly or partially as animals. Thirty lion-headed figures of the goddess Sakhmet also date from the reign of Amenophis III: over six hundred were set up by the king in his mortuary temple and in the temple of Mut at Thebes, some of which are still in situ. The British Museum possesses the largest collection of these outside Egypt. Of the many other animal sculptures in the collections mention may be made of a life-size figure of a baboon, sacred to the god Thoth, and a fine head of a cow carved in alabaster from a cult statue of the goddess Hathor at Deir el-Bahri.

Royal sculpture of the Late Dynastic Period is particularly well represented by two fine pieces of Nubian origin: a sphinx and a large ram incorporating an image of the king Taharqa of the Twenty-Fifth Dynasty (*c.* 690–664 BC). Much private sculpture of the period harks back to forms of the Old Kingdom. For example, a limestone statue of Tjayasetimu is based on a standing mortuary figure like that of Nenkheftka, while a head from a statue of a high official (the so-called Benson Head) from Karnak wears a wig commonly encountered in the Old Kingdom.

From the seventh century BC it became a common practice to deposit bronze figures of gods in their sanctuaries: the donor hoped thereby to partake of the beneficence of the particular deity. Most of the Department's bronze sculpture consists of votive figures of gods or sacred animals, although some depict kings and

79

78 *Statue of an unnamed nobleman and his wife carved in limestone. Eighteenth Dynasty, about 1325* BC. H *1.3m.*

80 BELOW *Schist head of a young man. The sculpture features Greek as well as Egyptian characteristics and is finished with excellent detail. From Alexandria, Roman Period, after 30 BC. H 24.5cm.*

79 ABOVE *Statue in red granite of a recumbent lion, one of a pair originally set up at the temple of Soleb in Nubia. It has inscriptions of Tutankhamun and the much later Meroitic ruler Amanislo. Eighteenth Dynasty, about 1380 BC. H 1.17m.*

private individuals. Examples of most of the Egyptian pantheon are represented. Perhaps the finest bronze is the Gayer-Anderson Cat, incarnation of the goddess Bastet, cast hollow with ear-rings of gold and an inlaid pectoral of sheet silver. Another splendid piece, cast in silver and embellished with gold foil, depicts the god Amen-Re.

During the Graeco-Roman period a degree of realism unknown since the Middle Kingdom began to reappear in Egyptian sculpture. Though not yet able to be classed as true portraiture, the treatment of heads was less stereotyped, and statues of this period can be said to attempt a likeness of their subject. The most striking example of this type of work is a schist head of a young man from Alexandria. The face has the high finish characteristic of Egyptian sculpture of the Late Period, although the treatment of the features and the unpolished, random curls on the head betray Greek influence.

Closely related to sculpture in the round is the technique of relief carving, which was used extensively to decorate not only the walls of temples and tombs, but also funerary and dedicatory stelae, of which the De-

81 *Evidence of the Late Period animal cults. The bronze Gayer Anderson Cat (left) represents the goddess Bastet. A silvered pectoral bears the sacred eye of Horus. The intricately wrapped mummy of a cat (right) is from Abydos. Roman Period, after 30 BC. H (Gayer Anderson Cat) 38cm.*

partment has a large and wide-ranging collection. Two principal techniques were in use: in raised relief the background was cut away leaving the figures standing out from the surface, while in sunk relief the figures were cut into the background. Both techniques allow the figures to be modelled. On the whole the quality of sunk relief tends to be less good, although it is more effective in bright sunlight, where the sharp shadows make the decoration stand out. Some of the best-quality raised reliefs belong to the Old Kingdom, and fine examples can be seen in the stele of Rahotpe, the

false door of Kaihap, and the reliefs of Iry and Int. From the Late Period a relief of Osorkon II from the Twenty-Second Dynasty (*c.* 874–850 BC), and a slab of Nectanebo I of the Thirtieth Dynasty (380–362 BC) are good illustrations of sunk relief.

Both raised and sunk reliefs were painted, although much of the paint has now vanished. Where carved relief was not possible, the decoration could be provided in the form of wall-paintings. Although this may have been considered second best by the Egyptians themselves, the wall-paintings are perhaps the liveliest and most appealing products of Egyptian decorative art to have come down to us. The principal colours used were white, black, red, green and yellow, produced from naturally occurring minerals. While a brush was employed for larger areas, for fine detail the colour was applied with a reed chewed at one end. A wide range of Egyptian artists' equipment is to be found in the British Museum, from brushes, palettes, grinders and pig-

82 *Limestone stele of Rahotpe from his tomb at Maidum. It is decorated in low relief with a figure of the owner before a table of offerings. Fourth Dynasty, about 2600 BC. H 79cm.*

ment, to the lengths of paint-daubed string used for marking out a grid in preparation for the transfer of the artist's preliminary sketches onto the prepared surface of the wall. The method is well illustrated by a wooden 83 drawing board on which, within a grid, is sketched a seated figure of Tuthmosis III.

The earliest paintings in the British Museum belong to the Fourth Dynasty and come from the tomb of Nefermaat and Itet at Maidum. Although only fragments, they display a high level of skill. On the first is part of a bird-trapping scene in which one figure holds a well-observed decoy duck, while a second man pulls on the rope of a clap net. The second painting shows a man leading an antelope. The majority of tomb-paintings in the collection date from the New Kingdom and originate from the tombs of the vast Theban necropolis. A group of six paintings from the tomb of an official of Tuthmosis IV called Sobkhotpe includes a striking series of scenes representing the presentation of tribute

by foreigners (Nubians and Asiatics); another fragment from the tomb shows jewellery- and metal-workers making beads and vessels of precious metal.

An outstanding group of eleven paintings comes from a tomb which has never been identified to the complete satisfaction of Egyptologists. It belonged to an official with the titles 'scribe and counter of grain', whose name may be restored as Nebamun. The artistic quality of these paintings is of the very highest standard. Probably the best-known scene, full of life and interest, shows Nebamun and his family fowling in the marshes; 7 the detail and precision with which the animals are portrayed are striking. Three paintings originally formed part of a banqueting scene. One fragment shows two graceful dancers accompanied by four female musicians; two of the figures are depicted full-face, contrary to normal convention. Other fragments illustrate life on the estate of Nebamun: his garden and pool; the counting of cattle and geese; the estimation of the harvest yield for taxation purposes. These scenes, too, display remarkable skill in the depiction of the animals and in their composition.

Some of the paintings in the collection are from the tombs of the necropolis workforce at Deir el-Medina; 8 their relative stiffness demonstrates how far Theban

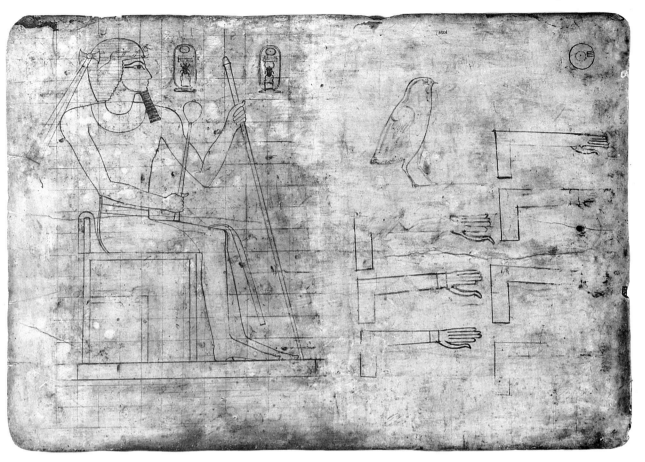

83 *Drawing board covered with a thin layer of plaster, marked out in red with a grid within which is drawn a seated figure of Tuthmosis III. Eighteenth Dynasty, about 1450 BC. H 36.4cm.*

painting had declined since the great days of the Eighteenth Dynasty. Another series of fragments comes from the city of the heretic king Akhenaten at El-Amarna: among the most free in design, these paintings originate not in tombs but in the palaces and houses of the new capital. Scenes of animals and plants are the most popular, life in the marshes being a particularly favoured motif.

One of the strengths of the British Museum's Egyptian collection lies in its wide range of written and inscribed material. Most ancient Egyptian sculpture was inscribed with texts which play an important part in establishing the statues' function and significance. The other main sources are relief fragments, stelae, papyri and ostraca. The best-known of the British Museum's inscribed monuments is the Rosetta Stone. It was among the antiquities gathered by the *savants* of Napoleon's military expedition to Egypt and ceded to British forces in 1801. The stone is part of a monument containing a decree dated to year 9 of Ptolemy V (196 BC), inscribed in Egyptian (in both hieroglyphic and demotic scripts) and in Greek. From the first it promised to provide the means by which the secrets of ancient Egypt might be revealed, and it provoked great interest among scholars and public alike. It was with the help of the Greek version that scholars were finally able to decipher the Egyptian scripts. The subsequent study of the Egyptian language and scripts made it possible for the many inscribed objects and written texts which have survived to be read and understood.

Another valuable historical document is the King List, recovered from the temple of Ramesses II at Abydos. Compiled under Ramesses II, it records all previous kings he thought worthy of commemoration. It is one of several such lists, the best preserved of which still exists in the temple of Sethos I at Abydos. Although damaged and incomplete – they have several important omissions, notably the kings associated with the period of 'heretical' rule introduced by Akhenaten – the King Lists have provided an invaluable source for establishing a chronological framework of ancient Egyptian history.

Other reliefs in the collections contain important religious texts. One such is found on the Shabaka

84 *Painting of King Amenophis I from the Ramesside tomb of Kynebu at Deir el-Medina. The king is shown in his regalia, holding a lotus flower and a sceptre. Twentieth Dynasty, about 1140 BC. H 44cm.*

85 *Part of the rural decoration in the 'Green Room' of the Northern Palace at El-Amarna. A kingfisher swoops down through the papyrus thicket to fish in the waters below. Eighteenth Dynasty, about 1350 BC.*

Stone, a carefully carved inscription of the eighth century BC which was partially destroyed in late antiquity or medieval times when the slab carrying the text was used as a millstone. This is a treatise on the Memphite theological system in which the god of Memphis, Ptah, takes a prominent role. Another interesting religious inscription dates from an earlier period: the stele of the brothers Suty and Hor, architects in the reign of Amenophis III (c. 1417–1379 BC). This impressive monument includes prayers to different forms of the sun-god; one in particular is addressed to Aten, the solar disc, which later became the sole object of official worship under Akhenaten (c. 1379–1362 BC).

Funerary stelae such as that of Suty and Hor are a rich source of information about the ancient Egyptians. The earliest stelae were simple memorials, bearing the name and titles of the deceased, as, for example, that of the Second Dynasty king Peribsen. By the end of the First Dynasty truly funerary stelae were being pro-

86 ABOVE *The Rosetta Stone. A slab of black basalt incised with the same priestly decree concerning Ptolemy V in three scripts (hieroglyphs, demotic and Greek) but only two languages (Egyptian and Greek). From Rosetta, 196 BC. H 1.14m.*

87 RIGHT *Part of a list of the kings of Egypt from the temple of Ramesses II at Abydos. Several lists of this kind have survived, the most complete example being in the temple of Ramesses' father, Seti I, also at Abydos. Nineteenth Dynasty, about 1250 BC. H 1.38m.*

duced; these were carved with scenes and texts directly connected with securing posthumous benefits for the deceased. From the start these scenes took a standard form: the deceased seated at an offering table upon which are loaves of bread, with simple texts enumerating the various food and drink offerings and the name and titles of the deceased.

During the Old Kingdom the predominant type is the large, false door stele, so called because it takes the form of a blind door. The false door of Kaihap is a fine

example from the Fifth Dynasty; its carvings in low relief are of the highest quality. The false door was gradually superseded by a new, smaller type of funerary stele on which it was not uncommon to include an account of the career of the deceased. The niche-stele of Sihathor, for example, records that he directed the making of sixteen statues of the king to be set up near the royal pyramid; on the stele of Inyotef the owner describes his own virtues and qualities, additionally explaining his methods of dealing with superiors,

88

75

equals and inferiors in the course of his daily work. Many of the Middle Kingdom stelae, including that of Sihathor, come from Abydos, traditionally the principal burial place of the dismembered Osiris, and consequently a favoured location for cenotaphs of persons actually buried elsewhere.

Stelae of the New Kingdom frequently show the deceased worshipping gods of the Underworld, such as Osiris and Anubis; examples include the stelae of Sobkhotpe, scribe of the wine cellar, and of Bakenamun, chief cook in the household of Queen Tiy. Each of these stelae retains its original paint. The official religion of ancient Egypt was designed to stress and enhance the relationship between the king and the gods, and its material remains offer a poor reflection of the beliefs of the average Egyptian. Personal piety is well illustrated, however, by an interesting series of stelae from the workmen's village at Deir el-Medina.

89 ABOVE *Weighing of the heart of the deceased, from an illustration in the papyrus of the royal scribe Hunefer. The weighing of the heart against the feather of Truth was a major part of the Egyptian Judgement of the Dead. Nineteenth Dynasty, about 1250 BC. H 39cm.*

88 LEFT *Limestone false-door stele of Kaihap, decorated with figures of the owner in low relief: The hieroglyphs are finely executed in both raised and sunk relief. From Saqqara, Fifth Dynasty, about 2400 BC. H 2.07m.*

Several small shrines within the settlement were available at which individuals might offer prayers, often by means of a votive stele showing the donor worshipping his chosen deity. Occasionally the design incorporates a number of ears, which were intended to ensure that the prayer be heard. The texts on these stelae, which date to the Ramesside period, sometimes take the form of a plea for mercy; afflictions of the body, such as blindness, are frequently attributed to the god as a punishment for some transgression against him – as on a stele offered to Ptah by the workman Neferabu. The custom of making funerary stelae continued through to the Graeco-Roman period. Hellenistic funerary stelae bear Greek inscriptions and often represent the deceased in Greek costume with the jackal-headed god Anubis.

By far the most extensive and important class of documentary material held by the Museum comprises the papyri written in the hieroglyphic, hieratic and demotic scripts. The best known of these are the funerary documents described as *Book of the Dead* papyri, collections of religious and magical texts which were intended to ensure a satisfactory afterlife and to enable the deceased to leave his tomb when necessary. Descended from the earlier *Pyramid Texts* and *Coffin Texts*, the earliest *Book of the Dead* papyri date from the Eighteenth Dynasty (c. 1567–1320 BC) and the finest copies are beautifully illustrated with coloured vignettes, such as those prepared for Ani, Hunefer and Anhai. In the Late New Kingdom and the Saite period the vignettes are sometimes rendered as brush and ink drawings, good examples of which include those of Nesitanebtashru (the Greenfield Papyrus) and Ankhwahibre.

Apart from magical and religious texts, the papyri in the collection cover a wide range of subject matter. Wisdom literature includes didactic works composed of maxims and precepts; *The Instruction of Ammenemes I* is a typical example, consisting of advice from the king to his son. The collections also contain one of the earliest copies of the *Maxims of Ptahhotep*, an Old Kingdom high official (c. 2380 AD) and the *Instructions of Onkhsheshonqy*, written in demotic. Another class of literature is pessimistic in character; many other papyri contain poetry, lyrics and hymns. A number of stories have also been preserved, such as *The Tale of Two*

89

Brothers, The Blinding of Truth by Falsehood, The Prince who knew his Fate, and *The Capture of Joppa.* Scientific writings include texts on mathematics (such as the Rhind Mathematical Papyri), astronomy and medicine (for example, the London Medical Papyrus and the Chester Beatty Papyrus). A fascinating glimpse into Egyptian life is offered by private letters, and business and legal documents, written at first in hieratic script and later in demotic. Particularly fascinating are the documents that chronicle the investigations into Theban tomb-robberies in the Twentieth Dynasty; these include records of the evidence given by the accused, and lists of objects found in the possession of the guilty parties.

Other forms of document include inscribed tablets of wood, frequently overlaid with gesso, and ostraca (flakes of white limestone or potsherds). The latter tend to contain texts of an ephemeral nature, such as school exercises, drafts of contracts, deeds and letters, records of attendance at work, inventories, magical texts and oracles; the British Museum has thousands of documents of this sort.

Since much of our evidence for the life of the Egyptians comes from their tombs, material relating to their funerary beliefs and customs is abundant in the collections. During the Predynastic Period (before 3100 BC) graves consisted of shallow pits in the ground; a reconstruction of such a burial in the British Museum shows the body surrounded by a typical selection of grave-goods. The body owes its preservation to the desiccating effect of the sand in which it was buried. Small coffins of basketwork or wood are from a slightly later date. The use of coffins removed the body from contact with the sand and encouraged rapid decomposition. Since the Egyptians believed it necessary for the body to be preserved for the next life, the first tentative steps towards artificial preservation were made. Evisceration of the body was practised from at least the Fourth Dynasty (*c.* 2600 BC), and the British Museum's collections chart the development of mummification and ancient Egyptian burial practice to Roman times.

Simple rectangular wooden coffins were used throughout the Old and Middle Kingdoms. The tendency towards increasingly elaborate decoration can be illustrated by comparing the simplicity of the Sixth Dynasty coffin of Nebhotep, decorated merely with bands of text, with that of Gua, a high official of the Twelfth Dynasty. Gua had two coffins, which fitted inside each other, both painted inside and out. On the

90 BELOW *Limestone ostracon inscribed with a hieratic text forming part of the record of an enquiry into the ownership of a tomb. Nineteenth Dynasty, about 1300 BC. H 16.3cm.*

91 RIGHT *Reconstructed shallow grave containing a naturally preserved body lying in a contracted position, with examples of grave-goods of similar age. From Gebelein, Predynastic Period, about 3250 BC. L (body) 1.63m.*

interior of the coffins are extracts from magical texts written in black ink (the so-called *Coffin Texts*) intended to safeguard the passage of the deceased through the Underworld and to ensure his eternal survival. The painted scenes show objects which were included in the funerary equipment, such as weapons and stone vessels intended for the use of the tomb-owner.

In the Twelfth Dynasty (c. 1991–1786 BC) masks of plaster-reinforced linen were sometimes placed over the faces of mummies, a custom which led ultimately to the appearance of coffins in human form. A particularly interesting coffin of this type is that of King Nub-kheperre Inyotef, which consists of gilded wood with surface decoration in the form of feathers: this design was characteristic of the period, and was thought to represent the wings of the goddess Isis protecting the body of Osiris.

Coffins of the New Kingdom were normally made of wood or cartonnage (moulded linen and plaster). These human-form coffins are in most cases covered with religious texts and scenes inside and out. Rich burials were frequently supplied with a 'nest' of several such coffins. One of the finest examples in the British Museum belonged to Henutmehit, a priestess of Amun who probably lived during the Nineteenth Dynasty (c.

1290 BC). Each of her two splendid coffins was gilded and fitted with inlaid eyes. In addition, her mummy was overlaid by a cartonnage cover which fitted within the inner coffin. The painted decoration normally encountered at this period is mythological, with scenes showing the deceased praising the gods; typical examples are found on the Twenty-First Dynasty wooden coffin of Djedhoriufankh. On the floor of the coffin is painted a large figure of Amenophis I, an Eighteenth Dynasty king who by now was revered as patron of the Theban necropolis. The inner surfaces of the sides are covered with offering scenes, while the interior of the canopy bears a painting of a vulture goddess hovering protectively over the deceased.

The art of mummification reached its peak in the Twenty-First Dynasty. A finely bandaged mummy of an unnamed Theban priestess, still in her original painted wood coffin, may date from this period. Other mummies from the Twenty-Second Dynasty are preserved in their cartonnage inner coffins, which are covered wth painted scenes and funerary inscriptions. The standard of mummification declined from this point on, but in the Roman Period bandaging became more elaborate. A particularly good example from the first century AD is the mummy of a boy wrapped in

bandages which are arranged in intricate geometric patterns. The face of the mummy is covered with a portrait of the deceased in coloured wax on a wooden panel. The Museum possesses many fine portraits of this type, executed in a naturalistic if idealised style, as well as a number of three-dimensional portraits of the deceased in painted plaster.

Inner and outer coffins continued to be used until Roman times, and even in the third century AD they were still decorated with traditional Egyptian scenes, although by this date the style was increasingly debased. In the early fourth century AD the rise of Christianity led to the abandonment of mummification.

Besides human mummies, the Museum possesses many mummified animals, birds, fish and reptiles, extraordinary relics of the Late Period cults which revived the worship of ancient deities in their animal forms. The carefully wrapped bodies deposited in the great cemeteries of Saqqara, Bubastis, Abydos and elsewhere are probably to be seen as a formal acknowledgement of these deities' powers, which were invoked by visitors to their shrines.

X-ray photography of the mummies has revealed much information about the body itself, and the presence of any objects still in position beneath the wrappings. In one case, that of an unnamed man, X-ray photography has shown the presence of artificial eyes. The mummy of a Theban priestess of the Late Period, Tjentmutengebtyu, was shown to have a winged scarab amulet over her feet. Amulets of various kinds were wrapped with the mummy, the most important of which was the heart scarab, inscribed with a text from Chapter 30B of the *Book of the Dead* intended to prevent the heart from revealing any of the deceased's earthly sins. The most interesting, and one of the earliest examples in the British Museum is carved from green jasper and mounted in gold. This belonged to the Seventeenth Dynasty king Sobkemsaf and was stolen by tomb-robbers more than five hundred years later. Ordinary small scarabs are also encountered on mummies of the New Kingdom and later, engraved with divine symbols and short amuletic texts. The eye of Horus, the *djed*-pillar, the girdle of Isis, and the *wadj*-sceptre are other common funerary amulets.

A number of objects connected with the mortuary ritual have already been mentioned: tomb-paintings, stelae, funerary papyri. But the range of equipment included in the grave was wide indeed. From the earliest times the tombs of the Egyptians were provided with objects designed to satisfy the needs of the de-

92 LEFT *Gilded and painted mummy mask showing the deceased richly adorned with a wide selection of jewellery, including a number of real finger-rings. Nineteenth Dynasty, about 1250 BC.* H *58cm.*

93 *Painted and modelled wooden mummy board of an unnamed Theban priestess. Late Twenty-First Dynasty, about 950 BC.* H *1.62m.*

94 *Mummy of a youth wrapped in the intricate bandaging characteristic of the Roman Period. Over the face is a portrait of the deceased, executed in coloured wax. From Hawara, first century* AD. H *1.32m.*

ceased in the afterlife, including food and drink, tools, utensils, furniture, clothing and jewellery. Many of the objects in the Department which come from tombs would have originally been made for use in daily life. Other types of object were made specifically as funerary equipment and were more closely connected to the fate of the deceased in the Underworld. The internal organs removed from the body before mummification were placed in special vessels known as Canopic jars. From the Middle Kingdom sets of four jars were regularly placed in tombs, stored in wooden chests.

From this time too tomb equipment commonly included figures known as *shabtis*. They were intended to act as deputies of the deceased in the agricultural work which would be required from him in the next world as in earthly life. The earliest Middle Kingdom *shabtis* are quite simple wood, stone or wax figures, inscribed with little more than the name of the deceased owner and in the form of a mummy. In the New Kingdom glazed composition became the most common material for *shabtis*, though several fine wooden or stone examples survive, such as the *shabti* of Amenophis II, carved from serpentine. From this date most *shabtis* have tools in their hands – mattocks, hoes and one or more baskets slung over the shoulder. From the end of the New Kingdom it became customary to bury quite large

numbers of *shabtis*, and sets of as many as 401 were frequent: 1 'worker' *shabti* for each day of the year, with 36 'overseer' figures. Such large sets of *shabtis* were accommodated in special chests, such as the fine painted box of the priestess Henutmehit.

Another type of figure commonly found in burials of the Late Period is that of Ptah-Seker-Osiris, a deity embodying the characteristics of Ptah (god of creation), Seker or Sokar (god of the necropolis) and Osiris (god of the Underworld). Some of these figures were hollow and held a copy of the *Book of the Dead* inscribed for the owner. The British Museum's papyrus of Anhai, a Theban high priestess in the Twentieth Dynasty, and that of Hunefer, both sumptuously illustrated with coloured vignettes, were recovered from such statues.

Tombs of the later Old to Middle Kingdoms were frequently supplied with wooden models representing various sorts of domestic and agricultural activities and crafts. The Museum's collections include scenes of butchery, brewing, baking, ploughing and brick-making as well as miniature granaries, boats and funerary barges. In the Middle Kingdom burials of the less affluent frequently contained pottery model houses, in the forecourts of which were represented offerings. These soul-houses, as they are known, were intended to provide sustenance and a home for the *Ka* (spirit) of the deceased.

Along with the wall-paintings and papyrus illustrations, these models supplement the evidence from objects of daily use to give an extraordinarily vivid impression of everyday life in ancient Egypt. The

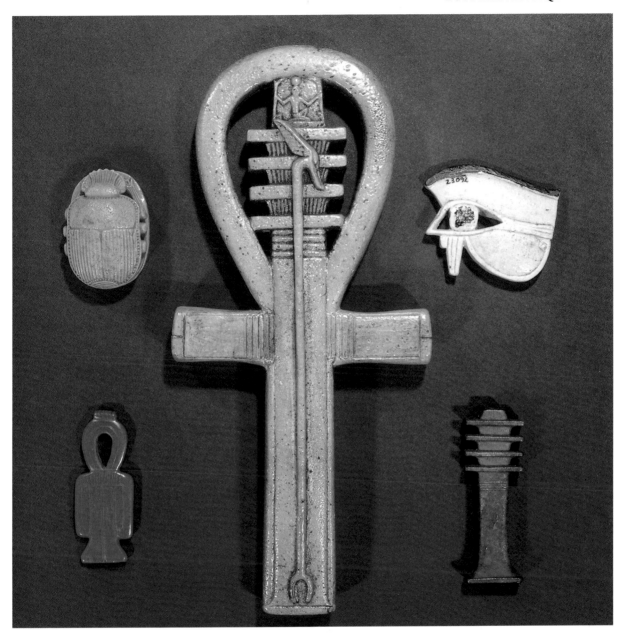

95 *A collection of popular amulets. At the top are the scarab beetle, associated with the Sun-god, and the eye of Horus, a protective device. Below are the* tyet-*symbol and the* djed-*pillar, linked to Isis and Osiris respectively. The central amulet combines the signs* ankh, djed *and* was, *meaning 'life, stability and power'.* H *(tyet-symbol) 6.5cm.*

annual innundation of the Nile, which fertilised the valley, provided a firm and continuing basis for agricultural prosperity. The principal crops were emmer and barley, cereals used almost exclusively for making bread and beer. The Museum possesses many tools used on the land: hoes, baskets and even a plough. Diet could be supplemented by hunting and fishing: the Nile teemed with fish, and the marshy areas of the Delta and the Faiyum abounded with wild birds. Throw-sticks or boomerangs were used for fowling, while bows and arrows were needed for hunting larger animals, such as the antelope, oryx and wild bull. The bow was not just a hunting weapon, but was also important in warfare, used mainly by Nubian auxiliaries. Other weapons are also represented in the collections: the axe and shield of the native infantryman, supplemented by the dagger and spear. More advanced military equipment (including coats of mail made of small bronze plates riveted to

96 LEFT *Painted wooden shabtis of the Theban priestess Henutmehit, with her wooden painted shabti box on which she is depicted adoring three of the Four Sons of Horus. Nineteenth Dynasty, about 1290 BC. H 33.5cm.*

97 TOP RIGHT *Painted wooden tomb model showing a peasant ploughing with a pair of oxen. Middle Kingdom, about 1900 BC. L 43cm.*

98 BOTTOM RIGHT *Furniture including a three-legged table with splayed legs, an ornate stool and a low, wide chair inlaid with ebony and ivory. The decorated wine jar is from El-Amarna. Eighteenth Dynasty, 1400–1350 BC. H (table) 50.8cm.*

leather jerkins) and a curved scimitar-like sword with its blade and handle cast in one piece date from the warlike period of the New Kingdom, when Egypt established an empire in Syria and Palestine.

Egypt's almost total self-sufficiency in basic natural resources was a vital factor in the growth of Egyptian civilisation. The British Museum's wide-ranging collection illustrates particularly well the variety of techniques and industries developed to exploit these resources. The woven-fibre industries, such as rope- and mat-making, basketry and textile weaving, were known from earliest times. The principal materials were palm leaves, reeds, rushes, papyrus, flax and various kinds of grass. Baskets, after clay pots, were the most common form of household container, used to store fruit, seeds, linen-cloth and bronze tools. Surviving fragments of

basketwork in the collection date from as early as the Predynastic Period. Closely allied to basketry, though more advanced, is the technique of textile weaving. The woven cloth of Egypt was invariably of linen thread, the source of which was flax. The cultivation and processing of this crop are often illustrated in painted vignettes on funerary papyri, such as that of Nakht. Tools employed in the processing of flax include sharp-toothed 'hackling' combs, which were used for separating the fibres from the woody tissue, and wooden spindles in the form of slender sticks weighted towards the top with a whorl. A few fragments of woven textile remain from before 3100 BC. The vast majority of woven fabric from the Dynastic period consists of mummy wrappings and bandages, or lengths of cloth which were placed in the tomb for the use of the

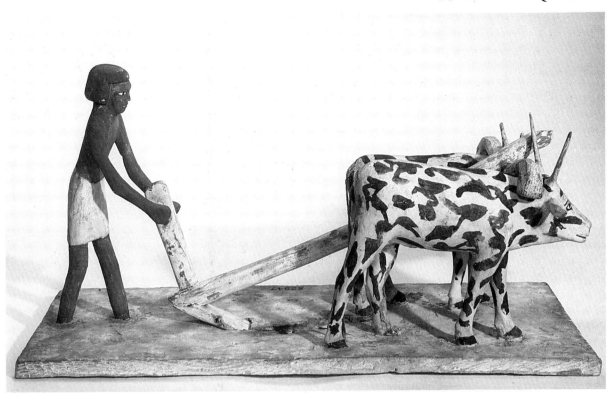

99 *A linen cloth painted with a scene in which six named ladies adore and present offerings to the goddess Hathor, portrayed as a cow emerging from the Western Desert hills. From Deir el-Bahri, Eighteenth Dynasty, about 1400 BC. L 46cm.*

deceased in the next life. Actual garments are less common and those that do survive are mostly extremely fragmentary. A fine exception is a large linen tunic or shirt which may have been worn as an undergarment.

The increasing availability of copper for tools from about the First Dynasty is thought to have greatly influenced the development of the earliest stone architecture around this time. However, the skill of the Egyptian stone-carver is evident from even earlier periods in the large quantity of beautifully worked stone vessels from Predynastic times. It was during this period that the widest range of shapes was produced in the greatest vareity of materials, including basalt, breccia, alabaster, granite, limestone, diorite, schist and serpentine. Alabaster continued to be popular into the Old Kingdom and later.

100 *Stone vessels dating from the Predynastic Period to the Eighteenth Dynasty. These examples show something of the wide range of shapes of the vessels, and of the materials used. H (tall marble vase) 34.2cm.*

101 *Group of objects mostly of New Kingdom date made from glazed composition, including bowls and a chalice, a tile for inlaying, an amuletic pectoral and a* shabti *figure.* D *(larger) bowl) 25 cm.*

The early period is also well represented in pottery; indeed, some of the most attractive Egyptian pottery is of Predynastic date. Of special interest are pots from the Naqada period in buff-coloured ware decorated in purple with boats, human figures and deities. The majority of Dynastic pottery consists of utilitarian cooking and storage vessels, and painted wares only reappear in the Eighteenth Dynasty. The most striking examples come from Malqata and El-Amarna. The jars are painted with mostly floral designs in light blue on a buff-coloured background, with details picked out in red and black. Among the finest examples in the British Museum are two wine jars inscribed for the lady Nodjmet, with hieratic dockets identifying the Delta origin of the contents.

Superior types of ware were made of Egyptian faience, more properly referred to as glazed composition. The material consisted of a core of quartz sand crushed into a fine powder. This, when heated with a colorant, fused into a glass-like material, enabling small objects to be mass-produced in moulds, usually of blue, green or greenish-blue colour, although other colours are known. Glazed composition was used for making all manner of objects, well represented in the Museum's collection: delicate vessels, jewellery, amulets, *shabtis*, figures of gods, tiles and inlays. Glass was in common

use from the Eighteenth Dynasty onwards. Glass vessels are frequently decorated with patterns formed by fusing together rods of different colours; blue, yellow and white were the most frequent. The British Museum possesses one of the finest collections of Egyptian glass vessels, including an outstanding glass cosmetic vessel in the form of a fish from El-Amarna.

A large number of cosmetic vessels and toilet implements are preserved in the collection, reflecting the concern of the ancient Egyptians with their personal appearance. Glass was only one of a variety of materials used to make these small objects, which offered the craftsman opportunities to display his artistic skills in a way denied the artist working in the strictly circumscribed field of Egyptian funerary art. During the New Kingdom this freedom resulted in a wealth of imaginative and delicate forms and designs, executed in a variety of techniques. Among the most striking are a bronze toilet implement in the form of a rider on horseback, and a wooden figure of a swimming girl pushing before her an ointment box in the form of a duck.

One area in which Egyptian craftsmen excelled was metalworking. Copper and bronze were used in the manufacture of tools and weapons, and cast to produce sculpture, as well as utensils and all manner of ritual objects, such as censers, a sceptre, libation vessels and other containers for sacred liquids.

The precious metals of gold and silver were used in conjunction with richly coloured semi-precious stones such as cornelian, lapis lazuli, turquoise and amethyst to produce jewellery of outstanding quality. Glazed composition and glass were both used as substitutes for hardstones. The imaginative ways in which the jewellery-maker combined these disparate materials to produce such pleasing results are particularly well exemplified by the elaborate collars and necklaces of the New Kingdom. Pieces of particular interest include an openwork gold pectoral showing Ammenemes IV making offerings to the god Atum; the gold bracelet terminals of King Inyotef embellished with figures of reclining cats, and the gold inlaid bracelets of prince Nemareth, son of Sheshonq I.

Egyptian jewellery often incorporated scarabs, which are found in large quantities in all collections. The designs and inscriptions engraved on them are often commonplace and of little interest; others represent some of the finest achievements of the ancient carver in miniature. The large scarabs issued by Amenophis III to commemorate important events and royal achievements are of particular interest. The Museum possesses the only complete series of these scarabs, with subjects including a lion-hunt, a wild bull hunt, his marriage to Queen Tiy, the digging of a lake and the arrival of a foreign princess with her retinue.

103 RIGHT *Royal jewellery of gold and electrum, including an openwork plaque of Ammenemes* IV, *a pair of bracelet terminals of Inyotef* VII, *and the heart scarab of Sobkemsaf (bottom). Middle Kingdom and Second Intermediate Period, about 1885–1650* BC. W *(winged scarab) 3.5cm.*

102 BELOW *Cosmetic vessel in the form of a fish, made in polychrome glass. From El-Amarna, Eighteenth Dynasty, about 1350* BC. L *14.5cm.*

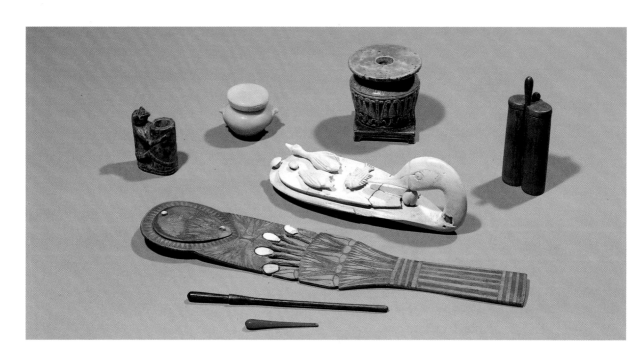

The use of scarabs as amulets in a funerary context has already been mentioned, but amuletic and magical objects were also widely employed in everyday life. Large numbers of small figures of protective deities exist, such as the hippopotamus goddess Thoeris, revered as a protectoress of women in childbirth; or Bes, a dwarf with the features of a lion who was thought to bring happiness to the home and to protect it against harmful creatures, such as snakes. Magical spells written on papyrus to protect the carrier, incantations against disease, dream books to interpret omens, oracles, and calendars of lucky and unlucky days are among the many texts in the Museum's rich collections.

Incorporation into the Roman Empire marked a vital turning point in Egypt's history, bringing this ancient civilisation into the wider sphere of eastern Mediterranean culture. A more decisive break with the Dynastic past is signalled with the abandonment of mummification in the early fourth century AD. The Egyptian collections, however, include material from early Christian and Coptic Egypt. Both pagan and Christian antiquities occur in Egypt during the third to sixth centuries AD, and it is not always easy to assign one object to one culture or the other. Gravestones of Christian origin show the typical form of the funerary inscriptions, and some have crosses in the form of the ancient Egyptian *ankh*, the hieroglyph for 'life'. Other examples of stonework from this period, fragmentary architectural pieces and reliefs, are decorated with traditional Hellenistic motifs, figures of classical divinities and foliate designs.

Hellenistic influence is also apparent in the decorated textiles which occur in the fourth century AD, of which the Museum possesses a good collection, including tapestries in wool with mythological motifs and floral designs. Subjects of a purely Christian nature do not become common until the eighth century, and they continue until the twelfth, when the textiles themselves disappear – and with them the last vestiges of pharaonic civilisation.

104 TOP LEFT *A group of cosmetic objects of New Kingdom date. At the back are containers for eye-paint applicators. The duck-shaped box and floral spoon probably contained cosmetic creams. L (floral spoon) 31cm.*

105 BOTTOM LEFT *Tapestry with two large divine figures between vertical bands of decoration, formed of coloured wool on a linen base. Fourth–fifth centuries AD. H 1.8m.*

106 *Memorial stone inscribed for Pleinos, bearing a form of cross derived from the hieroglyphic* ankh, *the sign for 'life'. Seventh–eighth centuries AD. H 61cm.*

THE ETHNOGRAPHIC COLLECTIONS

*T*he Department of Ethnography, formerly better known as the Museum of Mankind,
houses the anthropological collections of the British Museum, the finest of their kind in the
world. They derive mainly from recent and contemporary cultures, but also include
important archaeological collections from Africa, the Americas and the Pacific. The
emphasis is generally on small-scale indigenous societies, but some larger, more complex states
in Africa, Asia and elsewhere are also represented. Today the Department's collecting policy
is focused on fieldwork, undertaken by Museum staff or outside colleagues, through which
properly documented materials are acquired to enhance existing collections and to reflect new
perspectives on how cultures operate and change.

THE AMERICAS

The American collections contain artefacts from most of the major historical and cultural traditions in the New World. Those from North America derive from both the agriculturalists of eastern and south-western parts of the continent, and from the highly diversified hunters, fishermen and gatherers in the rest of the United Stated and Canada. The American collections are strongest in those areas either visited by early explorers, or affected by colonisation from the seventeenth century onwards. Most of the objects were made by often highly mobile hunters; as one would expect, they consist of clothing, always highly utilitarian but often also superbly decorated with painted and embroidered designs, and deceptively simple hunting equipment, lightweight, but often of great technical perfection. The materials from the farmers of the eastern United States are slight, although they include perhaps the earliest examples of a Cherokee basket and Cherokee gourd rattle. From the Puebloan peoples of Arizona and New Mexico come an extensive series of matt painted pottery, including water jars, bowls and canteens, particularly from Zuni. The neighbouring Navajo, who became sheep farmers in the centuries after Spanish contact, are best known for their wool, wearing-blankets and rugs, of which there is a good representative collection in the Museum.

The peoples of the Northwest Coast were, and are still, fishermen occupying ancient villages in the rain-forest coast fringing the Rocky Mountains between Southeast Alaska and Northern California. Hierarchical societies developed here. Hereditary chiefs express their status by giving potlatches or feasts, at which masked dances are performed celebrating the status of the feast-giver. The Museum has important masks, feast bowls and ceremonial weaponry and clothing from the period of early contact at the end of the eighteenth century. Vast poles and doorways carved with animal crests are from a later date.

The Arctic collections from Eskimoan peoples such as the Canadian Inuit, like those from the Northwest

107 LEFT *Cast-brass plaque from Benin, Nigeria. The central figure on horseback is the Oba (king), probably engaged in a ritual marking his supremacy over the birds, whose cry is used in divination. Such plaques were used to cover the wooden beams supporting the palace roof. It probably dates from the mid-sixteenth to seventeenth century.* H 41.5cm.

108 ABOVE *Ceramic vessel in the form of a reclining woman, from Casas Grandes, Chihuahua, Mexico. The geometric patterns incorporate a lightning motif which may suggest that the woman represents a fertility deity. The distinctive style originated after Casas Grandes had been settled by Central Mexican peoples who represented their deities using the local style.* AD 1060–1340. H 12.7cm.

109 *Chilkat dancing blanket of twined wool and vegetable fibre from the Northwest Coast of America. It would probably have been used by a man of high rank at a feast. The design represents an animal crest belonging to the owner. W 2.2m.*

Coast, were made largely during the voyages in search of the Northwest Passage between 1818 and 1880. From northern Greenland came a now unique sled from the Polar Inuit, collected by Sir John Ross in 1818 on the first recorded occasion of contact between these people and anyone, European or Inuit, from the outside world. It is constructed entirely of whale and walrus bone and ivory, strapped together with sealskin. These people possessed little wood, and used meteoric iron for their cutting tools. Further to the west the searches for Sir John Franklin, the explorer lost in the 1840s, brought contact with Copper Inuit and the earliest collection of Inuit tools furnished with native copper blades. From Northwest Alaska large quantities of tools used in sealing, bird spearing and the hunting of bowhead whales were collected from the Inupiat Eskimo from the 1820s onwards. Many of the finest of these are of ancient mammoth ivory, a tougher substance than walrus ivory.

To the south of the Eskimoan peoples live groups of Subarctic Indians who hunt moose and caribou, fish and sell furs to southern markets. The Department possesses fifteen examples of superb caribou summer clothing from this area. The Dene clothing from the west is decorated with porcupine quillwork, while in the east the coats made by the Naskapi are delicately covered with multi-coloured stamped designs in pigments mixed with fish oil.

On the great North American Plains the aboriginal peoples were also big-game hunters. The Museum's collections from this area as elsewhere consist mostly of highly decorated skin clothing, as well as riding equipment, hunting gear, and a long series of excellent calumets, or smoking pipes; these were used in ceremonies expressing group solidarity, for instance at the time of making peace or undertaking trade. From the far west there are highly important collections from California. At the time of European contact in the eighteenth century California was an abundant wilderness teeming with big game – deer, antelope and bear. The aboriginal peoples, who all but disappeared after the gold rush of the mid-nineteenth century, were hunters and fishermen. But above all they collected acorns, from which they prepared acorn mush, a limitless source of carbohydrates. A fine group of coiled baskets dating from the eighteenth century was used in food preparation. From the Chumash of the Santa Barbara region in southern California come more baskets, as well as a unique basketry hat made in the style

110 A Plains Indian shirt and leggings of European cloth decorated with glass beads, hair and fur trim. This costume was presented in 1881 by its owner Osoop, a Saulteaux head man, to the Governor-General of Canada, the Marquis of Lorne, who later gave it to the Museum. L (coat) 88cm.

used by Spanish priests, shell ornaments, and a series of harpoons thought to have been used in the hunting of tuna and sea-lion.

Most of the material from North American collections was collected before 1910, but since the late 1970s the Museum has extended its range, with, for example, contemporary twined basketry from the Yurok of northern California, and the coastal peoples of British Columbia. More general series of artefacts have been acquired in the Arctic and Subarctic to illustrate the maintenance of traditional skin clothing, embroidery styles and hunting technology. Other contemporary collections have been made from peoples as diverse as the Seminole of southern Florida and the agricultural peoples of the Southwest. Contemporary prints from the Northwest Coast, Arctic and Subarctic are housed in the library.

The major cultures of ancient Middle, Central and South America are, with few exceptions, well represented in the collections. Typical of the earliest artefacts from Mexico and the other countries of Mesoamerica are the small pottery votive figurines of the pre-Classic periods (*c.* 2000–1000 BC). These usually depict nude females, sometimes with elaborate hair-styles and head-dresses.

The first major civilisation of this region was that of the Olmec (*c.* 1000–400 BC), which developed in the swampy Gulf Coast area of Mexico. As well as creating architecture and sculpture on a monumental scale, the Olmec produced some of the finest small carvings in jade and other greenstones known from the New World. Outstanding examples of this work are a cer-

111 *A Yupik Eskimo painted wood shaman's mask, representing a half-animal, half-human creature of great strength; in this form the spirit is half-fox, half-man. From Nunivak Island, Alaska, twentieth century AD. H 50cm.*

112 *Olmec jade pectoral from Mexico (c. 1000 BC). It is probably meant to depict an Olmec ruler or noble. Some early hieroglyph forms are incised on the panel. H 10.5cm.*

emonial adze in the form of an anthropomorphised jaguar deity and a fine portrait pendant.

In the central valleys of Mexico the most important civilisation of the Classic period (c. AD 200–800) was centred at Teotihuacan. The builders of the massive temple-pyramids at this site were also skilled muralists, potters and stone-workers. Typical examples of their work are stone masks and an offering vessel in the form of a stylised jaguar or ocelot.

Maya civilisation developed in southern Mexico, Guatemala and parts of the adjacent countries, attaining in its Classic phase (c. AD 300–900) an organisational complexity and cultural sophistication unsurpassed in Mesoamerica. The great temple-pyramids characteristic of Maya sites were decorated with superb sculptures in stone and stucco-work representing rulers and deities. Massive stone stelae, usually representing rulers and with carved hieroglyphic texts, and altars were erected within the temple precincts to commemorate important events. Stone lintels from the site of Yaxchilan in Chiapas, Mexico, and the figure of a Maize God from Copan in Honduras, attest to the excellence of Maya sculptors.

As with the Olmec, jade and greenstone were highly valued by the Maya, and worked to form very elaborate beads and pendants. Their superb polychrome pottery provides much information concerning religious cer-

emony and mythology. Maya civilisation was waning by about AD 900, and there is evidence that the rise of the post-Classic civilisations which dominated central Mexico at this time contributed to this decline. New elements of style and content enter the archaeological record, with greater emphasis upon militarism and increasing interest in human sacrificial cults.

The post-Classic civilisations of Mesoamerica (c. AD 1000–1519) are represented by good examples of the major ceramic traditions and stone sculptures. The most notable sculptures are those of the Huastec people of Veracruz on the Gulf Coast and the Aztecs of the central valleys of Mexico. An exceptional Aztec sculpture is a highly polished representation of a coiled rattlesnake. The underside is also carved and has the original red painted decoration representing the snake's markings. Another striking sculpture is a carving of a mythological creature, the *xiucoatl* or fire-serpent.

113 *Carved stone lintel from Yaxchilan, Mexico. One of the finest examples of Maya sculpture, it depicts Lady Xoc, a wife of Shield Jaguar, the ruler of the city, participating in a ritual blood-letting ceremony. The hieroglypic inscription dates the ceremony to 23 October AD 681. 130.1 × 86.3cm.*

114 *Ornament of wood in the form of a serpent, with turquoise and shell mosaic decoration. Mixtec/Aztec, AD 1400–1520. L 43.5cm.*

114   Probably the most outstanding examples of the art of this period are the nine turquoise mosaic decorated objects of the Aztec period. The masks, sacrificial knife, helmet, small animal carvings and serpent ornament which comprise this group were probably among the earliest objects from the New World to be seen in Europe.

From the ancient cultures of the Central American countries – Nicaragua, Costa Rica and Panama – the collection contains a wealth of pottery vessels and examples of typical elaborately carved stone metates (grinding stones). There are also examples of the fine lost-wax cast-gold ornaments of these regions, and the highly polished jade celts, often decorated with zoomorphic figures.

The pre-Columbian inhabitants of the Caribbean were linguistically related to some of the lowland tribes of South America, though some aspects of the cultures of the Greater Antilles show ties with Mesoamerica. The most impressive items from this area are a small group of Taino wood-carvings. These include *duhos* (ceremonial stools) and three figures, a standing male, a bird-headed figure, possibly a deity, and a female

figure of great beauty with a canopy above the head which probably served as a tray for the inhalation of hallucinogenic snuff used in religious rites.

A few pottery vessels only represent the first of the great civilisations of ancient South America, that of Chavin de Huantar in the northern highlands of Peru (*c.* 1000–400 BC). For the subsequent Andean cultures of Peru, Colombia and Ecuador there is a wealth of pottery, textiles, stone-carvings and metalwork. There are fine examples of the characteristic red and cream painted pottery of the Moche people of Peru (*c.* AD 300–800). Representations of human and animal figures provide information concerning many aspects of Moche culture, particularly its religious and ceremonial practices. The fine polychrome pottery of the Nasca civilisation from the south coast of Peru (*c.* 200 BC–AD 600), is decorated with highly stylised depictions of deities and mythological creatures from their complex pantheon. There is also a rare example of Nazca feather-mosaic work among the textiles of this period. Among the finest textiles are those in the style of Tiahuanaco, the great kingdom which flourished in the region of Lake Titicaca (*c.* 500 BC–AD 1000).

From Colombia there are many superb examples of gold ornaments from the succession of regional chiefdoms which arose in its northern provinces from the early centuries AD to the sixteenth century. Especially notable are the gold and *tumbaga* (gold/copper alloy)

ornaments and limeflasks of the Quimbaya (*c.* AD 1000), and a dramatic anthropomorphic pendant in the style of Popayan in the Upper Cauca region. 115

The ethnographic collections from Middle, Central and South America began to enter the British Museum in the nineteenth century. The most notable of these early collections were from the tropical forest regions of South America, especially Guyana, although there are also important groups of material from Tierra del Fuego, Paraguay and Panama. In recent years there have been considerable efforts to enlarge this area of the collections with a programme of Latin American field research which has resulted in the acquisition of a wide range of well-documented materials from Mexico, Guatemala, Panama, Colombia, Peru, and Bolivia. This work is still in progress. 116

115 LEFT *Limeflask of* tumbaga *(a gold–copper alloy), probably from the Cauca Valley area, Colombia, Quimbaya style.* AD 400–900. H 14.5cm.

116 BELOW *Mortar surmounting a double-headed animal carved from a dark wood. The rim has a carved geometric border, while the animal's body is decorated by scrollwork. From Lowland South America.* L 20.3cm.

AFRICA

The collections from West and North Africa reflect the great ecological and cultural diversity of these areas. The influence of Islam in the north is shown by the lack of representational images and a wider concern with the decoration of household objects. Rich ornamentation characterises both the textiles and the metalwork of the urban Arab cultures and the mountain-dwelling Berber peoples. The African collections also contain examples of the highly distinctive decorated pottery of the Kabyle people of Algeria.

The collections from south of the Sahara come from both centralised states, especially those in the tropical rainforest zone, such as Benin (Nigeria), Asante (Ghana) and the Yoruba kingdoms of Nigeria, and the smaller, chiefless people of the Savanah and Sahel zones to the north. Many of these collections come from the areas formerly under British colonial control, but recent policy has been to complement these with major works, especially of wood sculpture, from other areas.

When Europeans first began to voyage along the African coast in the fifteenth century they found many well-established kingdoms. Early white visitors commissioned works from African craftsmen and these are important evidence for the artistic skills and sophistication of coastal societies. An Afro-Portuguese salt cellar is one of a group of similar works, including spoons, forks and horns made by African craftsmen for visitors to Benin (Nigeria) and Sherbro (Sierra Leone) at the end of the fifteenth or early sixteenth century. A number of virtually identical pieces are known – suggesting the establishment of permanent workshops, which would also have catered for a local demand. In these pieces we see African carvers struggling to interpret forms that were unfamiliar in their own tradition. For example, wood joinery seems to have been uncommon in traditional Africa, most wooden products being carved from a single piece of wood. When called upon to represent the planking of a Western ship, the carver interprets them as being fixed in the same way as the tiles on the King of Benin's palace roof – as demonstrated in later brass castings of the court made for the king.

It seems to have been as a response to the local needs of kingship that many of the ancient bronze and brass castings of West Africa were produced – indeed, copper alloys were largely a royal prerogative. The earliest documented casting tradition in the region is that of

117

117 *Ivory salt cellar from Benin, Nigeria. Such works were carved for European visitors in the late fifteenth to early sixteenth centuries and show a mixture of Western and African forms.* H *24cm.*

Igbo-Ukwu (Nigeria). A number of sites, including the grave of a notable, have yielded evidence of a tradition of high technological and artistic ability that flourished between the ninth and eleventh centuries. Examples of these superb leaded bronze castings are in the collection.

Later casting traditions, such as those of the Yoruba kingdoms and that of Benin, are clearly related, but the precise relationship between these remains unclear. The Benin collection provides a comprehensive example of the sacral regalia of a powerful empire. The brass head is from the royal altars in the palace and dates from the sixteenth century. It would have been used to support an elephant tusk and is in the form of an Oba (king) in beaded ceremonial dress. Heads of this sort could only be made for a king and were produced under rigorous control by the guild of brass-workers.

The arts from some other parts of West Africa clearly show the effects of interaction with the West. The Kalabari screen is a commemorative image made for a trading house of the Nigerian city-state of New Calabar. Social changes brought about by the rapid generation of wealth through involvement in Atlantic trade and the absorption of large number of slave members led to shifts of power in the leadership. New images of power were produced, based upon European two-dimensional illustrations that were becoming familiar to the Kalabari in the late eighteenth to early nineteenth centuries. The Museum has eight of these carved wood screens, which were about to be destroyed early this century during a Christian movement. They were, instead, presented to a colonial administrator from whom they eventually came to the Museum.

The Yoruba people of Nigeria are among the most prolific wood-carvers of Black Africa and the collections contain many of their elaborately carved and coloured masks, as well as images used in the worship of particular deities. The special status of twins in many areas of Africa (where twin births are often far more frequent than in Europe) is shown by Yoruba *ibejis*, small carvings made after the death of a twin and subsequently carried by its mother. Other Yoruba items are associated with its kings – the elaborate crowns decorated by coloured glass beads, other items of regalia and the carved doors and roof pillars from palaces.

The great kingdom of Asante in Ghana was based, in a large part, on mining its vast gold deposits and exporting slaves. The first item to come from this area was a drum which was in Sir Hans Sloane's collection on his death in 1753. In 1817 T. E. Bowdich visited the Asante capital and collected gold castings, pottery, leatherwork and a wooden stool for the Museum. The Asante's skill in casting gold by the lost-wax method, and the use of elaborately worked gold to adorn the king and his servants is represented by many superb pieces

which came to the Museum after British military intervention in Asante in 1874, 1896 and 1900.

West Africa is particularly renowned for its wood sculpture, both in the form of the human figure and in masks or other images worn on or over the head, usually in performances which also include music and dance, concerned with representing, in some way, spiritual powers. There is considerable stylistic variation between groups that produce carvings and the collections contain examples from many areas. Especially noteworthy are the masks of the Dogon of Mali and the figure sculpture of the nearby Bamana people, the helmet masks worn at female initiation among the Mende of Sierra Leone, and the carvings from the Igbo, Ibibio, Jukan and Tiv Nigerian peoples which show clearly the varying ways of representing the human form. Few wood-carvings last more than a generation or two in the climatic conditions of tropical Africa, but a hundred or so stone-carvings from the coastal areas of Sierra Leone and Western Liberia show earlier artistic forms. Some of these probably date from the fifteenth century, and some are clearly related to the ivories carved for the Portuguese around 1500.

118 Wood carving of five birds, covered in sheet gold, from Asante, central Ghana. It would have been used as the top of a ceremonial umbrella, which shaded a senior chief when he appeared in public. H 26.5cm.

The Department also possesses many everyday arte-facts, and especially tools and utensils. The usual tool for cultivation in Africa is the hoe. One of these, from McCarthy Island in the Gambia, shows the high value of iron in this particular place: the blade is made of wood and only edged with metal.

In recent years the Museum has striven to obtain comprehensive collections from West African societies, most of which are undergoing change at an unpre-cedented rate. Wherever possible one artefact of each type, with full documentation, is obtained. A collection made among the Baka of Cameroon, a forest-dwelling pygmy group contained virtually all their artefacts, including a shelter made from leaves and branches. Change is also shown by the use of recycled Western manufactured items: shoes made of old lorry tyres, lamps made from burnt-out light-bulbs and musical instruments made of tin cans.

The area of West Africa that includes the modern states of Zaire and Angola is well represented in the Museum's holdings, as to a lesser extent are Gabon and the Republic of Congo. The main collection here was formed in the opening decades of this century, and ranges from masks and figure sculpture to magical devices, textiles, pottery and other domestic objects. Most of the objects came from the southern parts of the Equatorial forests amongst such peoples as the Mbala, 120 Pende, Wongo, Lele, Songye and Tetela. The most important section documents the culture of the Kuba Kingdom in Kasai region of Zaire, an elaborate and impressive traditional state.

Three commemorative carvings represent Kuba 119 kings. One of these depicts the founder of the ruling Kuba dynasty, Shyaam aMbul aNgoong, who ruled in the first quarter of the seventeenth century. However, although all these king figures are frequently referred to as 'portraits', it is unlikely that any were carved much before the mid-eighteenth century. Even so they rank amongst the oldest extant examples of wood sculpture from Africa. What makes them 'portraits' is not any physical resemblance between the figures and the kings with whom they are associated, but small emblems carved on the front of the plinths on which they sit. In the case of Shyaam this is a game-board, with whose introduction amongst the Kuba he is credited. In ad-dition to objects with such royal associations the collec-tion also includes many examples of the distinctive Kuba tradition of decorating surfaces with intricate geometric patterning. This practice can be seen on items of wood and horn, and on mats, textiles and

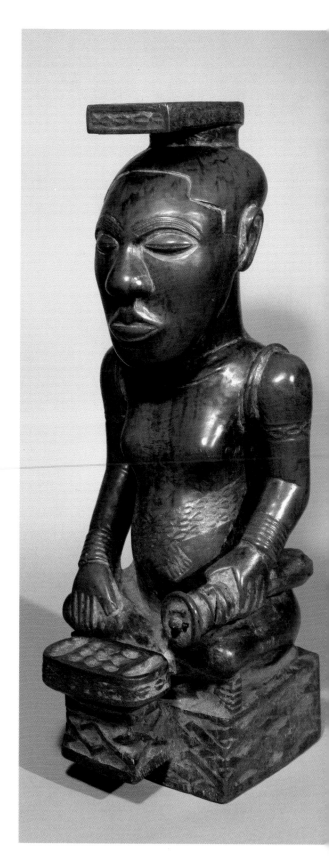

119 *Dynastic statue commemorating Shyaam aMbul aNgoong, the founder of the Kuba Kingdom, Zaire.* H 54cm.

beadwork. Not only is this the hallmark of the arts of the Kuba, it is also an apt reflection of the systematic and orderly operation of the state itself.

Another early collection made in the north of Zaire is also comprehensive, though within the narrower category of weaponry. Here more than anywhere else on the continent knives, both to be held in the hand and thrown, assume the greatest variety of forms. Equally, they had both practical and ceremonial functions, as most notably in the Mangbetu and the Azande kingdoms.

The way of life of the peoples of the Equatorial forests and of those in the woodlands immediately to their south is essentially that of agriculturalists. Moving to the east and south-east, however, traditional economies are much more mixed, and the keeping of cattle assumes a more significant role. Recent field collections from the Sudan and older material from elsewhere in Eastern Africa serve to document the transhumant life that is associated with purer forms of cattle pastoralism. Here more portable and robust objects are noticeable. Furniture is largely limited to light stools and head-rests that can comfortably be carried, whilst such fragile objects as pottery are relatively rare. Items made of readily available cattle-hide range from shields and sheaths to items of clothing.

120 *Polychrome mask incorporating fur horns and a raffia costume. Tetela, Zaire.* L *48.3cm.*

121 *Decorated calabash, or gourd, used for preparing medicines. From the Kamba people, Kenya.* H *24.9cm.*

Traditions of sculpture are usually presented as being largely absent from Eastern and Southern Africa. The mask and figure sculpture of the Makonde of Mozambique and Tanzania is the major exception and is illustrated by a small but important collection of traditional examples in the Museum's holdings. Among other sculpture from Eastern and Southern Africa is a reconstructed pottery head excavated at Luzira Hill in Uganda. It remains a unique and thus far undated find. Wood sculpture from Tanzania, Kenya, Zambia and Malawi also testifies to carving traditions in these regions. Frequently the function of such figurative works is unrecorded though some appear to have been presentation and prestige objects. One large figure, for instance, seems to have been given to the Kabaka (king) of the Ganda of Uganda, but was in fact carved by a Nyamwezi sculptor in Tanzania.

However, it is the decorative arts that are most obvious from these parts of Africa and particularly in such materials as beadwork. The most prominent are the abundant examples from such peoples as the Zulu, Xhosa, and Ndebele of South Africa. Together with

122 ABOVE *Water pot with graphite glaze made in the form of a calabash ladle. Probably from the Ganda people of Uganda.* H *22cm.*

123 BELOW *Narrow-strip woven silk textile (*kente*) from the Asante people of central Ghana. Such textiles are worn by senior men on especially important occasions.*

124 *Bead necklace, South-East Africa. The patterned beadwork of the peoples of southern and eastern Africa can convey messages by the use of certain colours and motifs. Young girls work beaded panels to present to their admirers.* L *(central panel)* 7.5 cm.

weaponry, pottery, wood vessels, ivory ornaments and snuff-spoons, these are the basis of the collections from the south of the continent. Illustrative collections have also been formed amongst the Khoisan (Bushman and Hottentot) peoples of Southern Africa and the various Pygmy groups of Equatorial Africa.

The collection of textiles from Africa illustrates well the wide variety of materials used by African weavers, the extensive distribution of weaving technology across the continent, and the range of patterns and motifs that are characteristic of textiles from Islamic peoples to the north of the Sahara and throughout Black Africa. Cotton is perhaps the most widely exploited of

materials, being found everywhere but in the Congo Basin (the modern country of Zaire), where raffia is exclusively used. Silk textiles are found in West Africa and on the island of Madagascar, whilst wool is the primary material for weaving in North Africa.

Pattern is applied to cloth both in the process of weaving itself and subsequently – principally by methods of dyeing and appliqué. The collections from West Africa give perhaps the fullest impression of the colourful results achieved. A collection of weaving equipment, including working examples of looms, supports this important textile collection.

Two other, and exceptional, collections deserve mention within the African context. One is material of Ethiopic Christian origin, mostly collected in the nineteenth century. Included are processional crosses, censers, sistrums, and other liturgical items. Secondly, the island of Madagascar, off the south-east coast of the continent, is well represented in the Museum.

Older collections, mostly from mission sources, concentrate on the Merina and Betsileo areas of central Madagascar and include textiles (many of them burial shrouds), charms and jewellery. Recently formed field collections from the east and south of the island have sought to build on these historical materials. All, however, ultimately demonstrate the mixed Asian and African ancestry of the people of this large island in the Indian Ocean.

THE MIDDLE EAST

Despite the long association of the British with the Middle East as colonialists, traders and travellers, there were few objects from the area in the Department's collections before the 1960s, and it is only in the last two decades that the main collections in the Middle Eastern section have been acquired. The Department specialises particularly in material from rural cultures. The

first important Middle Eastern collection was a group of fine, mainly nineteenth-century Palestinian Arab costumes. These had once been worn by the village farmers of Palestine, as distinct from the townspeople, who wore simpler costumes modelled on the fashions which prevailed among the ruling Ottoman Turks or later the British. These costumes have been complemented by subsequent acquisitions, including costume and other artefacts (such as looms) collected for the Museum during research visits to the Palestine area (Israel and Jordan) in the late 1960s and 1970s.

Until the mid-twentieth century the dresses, head-veils and head-dresses of the village women of Palestine were lavishly embroidered in predominantly red silk thread in a variety of beautiful geometric designs, and were decorated with satin and taffeta patchwork in brilliant colours. These garments have an intrinsic artistic value which can easily be appreciated by members of other cultures, and are also filled with social significance and symbolic meanings, which only research among the women who created and wore them has been able to reveal. Village costumes indicated village and regional origins within Palestine, demonstrated marital and economic status, and constituted a women's language and aesthetic which only they fully understood.

Another important group of material which has entered the Museum's collections in recent years is village pottery from South Arabia. A great variety of pots are represented, including huge water-storage vessels, cooking pots, coffee pots and delicately moulded incense-burners from the home of the ancient coffee and incense trades. These pots were made in many different centres in the former British Aden Protectorate (now the Peoples' Democratic Republic of Yemen), and were traded over a wide area of the southern Arabian peninsula.

Another collection from the sedentary peoples of South Arabia comes from a small community of farmers and traders in the Yemen Arab Republic. During the 1970s increasing financial prosperity brought about social changes in the community, and many, though not all, traditional artefacts were replaced by articles imported from the industrial world. The collection of pottery, baskets, jewellery, costume and farming implements preserves many of the objects which were rapidly going out of use and being discarded. Of particular interest is the ornate silver jewellery which was presented to the bride by the groom at marriage, the colourful baskets for displaying bread at meals and for

126 Incense-burner from South Arabia. Incense is often burned when welcoming guests to the house throughout Arabia. From antiquity to recent times South Arabia was the important centre for the production and trade in incense. Mid-twentieth century H 16.5 cm.

storing clothes and incense, and cooking bowls carved from locally quarried stone.

Other important Middle Eastern collections come from various tent-dwelling nomadic peoples, who traditionally depended on livestock for their livelihood. Today most formerly nomadic peoples are integrated into national and urban economies, and pursue a variety of occupations. The collections include 'mobile homes' and their furnishings from the Türkmen of Iran and the Bedouin of Jordan. The Türkmen material includes a magnificent domed tent (*yurt*) with a wooden frame and felt covers, as well as examples of bold heavy jewellery, with beautiful designs in different metals, set with various stones. Among the Bedouin collection are a goat-hair tent and a ground loom of the type on which Bedouin weave their tent cloth, woven animal-trappings, and a wooden camel saddle. Also included is a set of utensils for making and serving coffee: an iron

125 Dress from Beit Dajan, near Jaffa, Palestine. Richly embroidered in silk cross-stitch with taffeta and satin patchwork. Dresses such as this were embroidered by girls to be worn at their wedding ceremonies. 1920s. H 1.4m.

127 ABOVE *Silver necklace from Razih, North-West Yemen Arab Republic. Such jewellery is part of a woman's dowry. Mid-twentieth century* AD. L *39cm.*

128 BELOW *Silver ceremonial buckle from the Turnovo district, north-east Bulgaria. It is ornamented in repoussé with birds, a popular motif on such buckles. Late nineteenth century* AD. L *19.5cm.*

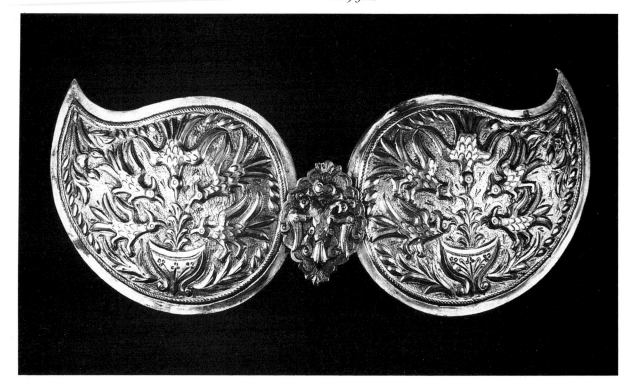

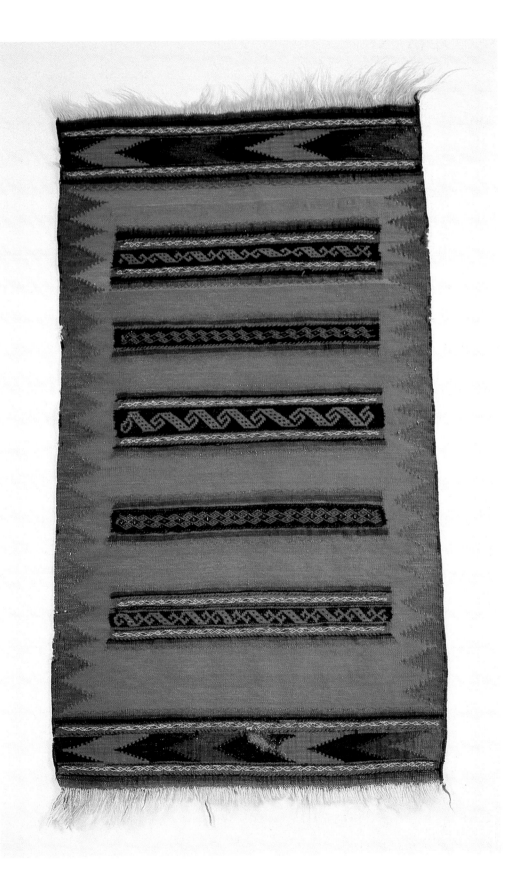

129 *Woven wool meal cloth from Baluchistan. Such cloths were used for laying out meals to serve to guests. This piece may derive from the Rakhshani or Reki tribe (Chakhansur, Afghanistan) or the Janbegi tribe (Iran).*
114 × 63cm.

ladle for roasting the beans, a carved wooden mortar and pestle for grinding them, and a set of brass coffee pots. Offering bitter coffee flavoured with cardamon is an important expression of hospitality among the Bedouin. There are also several looms among a collection of beautiful flat-woven rugs and saddle-bags from the nomads of Baluchistan in Pakistan. These are in natural wools and dyed mainly shades of red, with geometric designs. The bags are ornamented with finely worked tassels and shells.

The Department contains little material from Europe, but worthy of note are a collection of Bulgarian costumes donated by the Bulgarian government and shadow puppets from Turkey and Greece. The costumes show the different styles of dress worn by the village people in various parts of Bulgaria, and include finely woven and embroidered dresses, jackets and blouses. The puppets were used in a popular form of street threatre which showed the farcical exploits of a comic hero.

Asia

The Department's Asian collections reflect a great variety of natural and cultural environments. From India and China the collections are relatively sparse and uneven, although one group of material that deserves attention gives an interesting if superficial glance at mainstream rural culture. The most typical specimens are realistic models of houses, boats, mechanical devices and native figures in different occupations or social positions. These indicate not only the influence of a relatively advanced technology and division of labour (and, of course, the practical difficulty of collecting full-sized examples), but also the readiness of traditional artisans to cater to European tastes. This happened not only in India and China, for instance, but also in Java and Japan.

In contrast, the Department has more material from the tribal cultures of Asia. South Asian hunters and gatherers are represented by collections from the

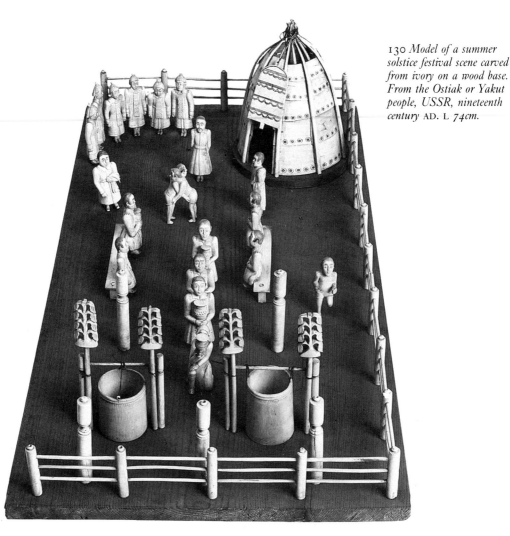

130 *Model of a summer solstice festival scene carved from ivory on a wood base. From the Ostiak or Yakut people, USSR, nineteenth century* AD. L *74cm.*

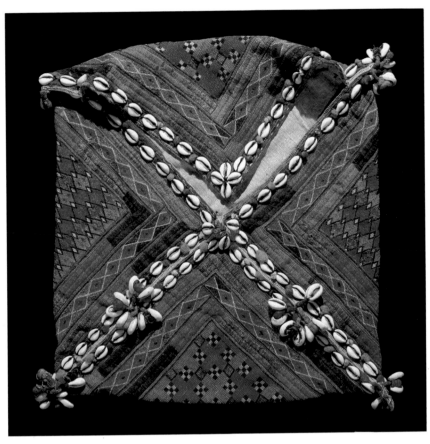

131 *Dowry bag of embroidered cotton with cowrie shells. From the Banjara people of the Deccan, India, late twentieth century* AD. H 43cm.

Andaman and Nicobar Islands acquired around the turn of this century and in the 1920s. Between the world wars colonial officers stationed among the Nagas of north-east India compiled rich collections for the British Museum and Oxford and Cambridge Universities. Prominent among these are ivory armlets, amber necklaces, basketry hats adorned with feathers, and brass or wood heads that are related to a head-hunting tradition, and human figures which reflect the importance of ancestors.

People with a similar mode of economy and relatively egalitarian social structure, the Chhindwara Gonds of Madhya Pradesh in central India, are represented in the remarkably comprehensive collection made around 1914 by Hira Lal – a rare and particularly interesting example from the colonial period of an ethnographic collection compiled by a non-European. Even at that time the Gonds' natural environment gave them much less protection from outside influence than the Nagas enjoyed in their own hillier country further from the

main concentrations of Hindu or European culture in the sub-continent.

Material from Sri Lanka documents many aspects of non-tribal Sinhalese (and, to a limited extent, Tamil) culture, and is especially rich in ritual objects, including many masks used for ritual healing. One mask represents Dala Kumara in the unique form of a human 133 face superimposed on a woman's bosom, and is from the *Kolam* masked theatre, which is probably related to Indian traditions and is today maintained only in the south-western part of the island.

From further east on the Asiatic mainland come well-documented textiles and other tribal material from south-west China and northern Thailand, some of them received in recent years, as well as earlier collections from nomadic hunter-gatherers of the forests of the Malayan peninsula. The tribal cultures of upland Burma are also well represented, particularly by traditional costumes acquired during the colonial period.

The Department's holdings of textiles and costumes from Tibet and neighbouring territories complement other material from the same region in the Department of Oriental Antiquities, which together comprise an outstanding resource. More miscellaneous are the collections from Central Asia, although there is some notable jewellery and examples of fine, vivid

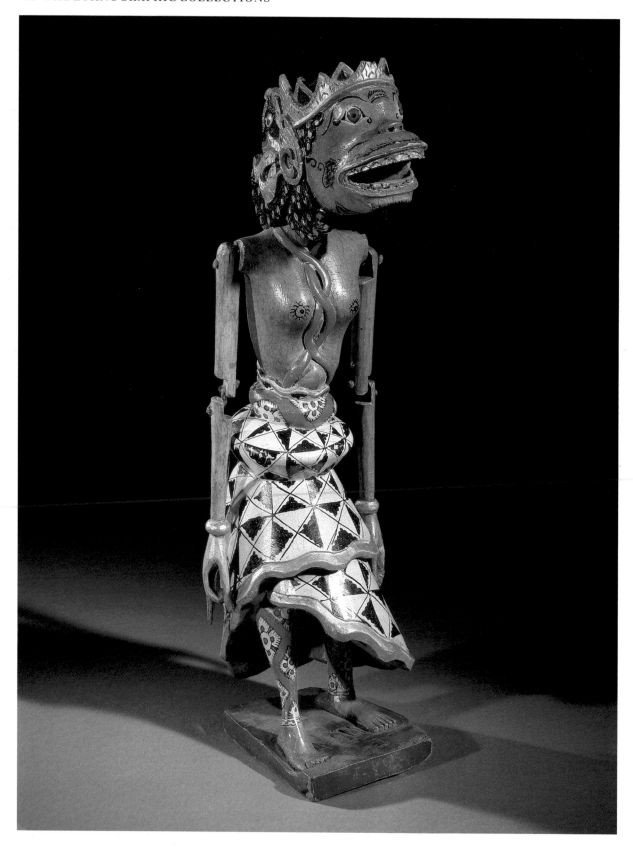

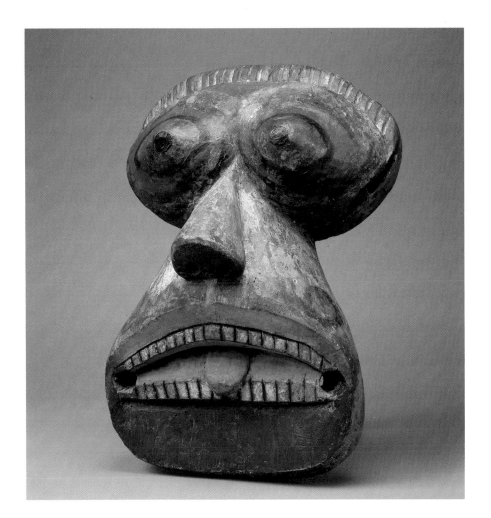

132 LEFT *Javanese painted and gilded wood puppet*, wayang klitik, *representing a mythological king. Late eighteenth century or early nineteenth century* AD. H *32cm.*

133 RIGHT *Sinhalese* Kolam *mask of painted wood depicting Dala Kumara, Lord of benevolent demons. From Sri Lanka, nineteenth century* AD. H *40cm.*

ikat-dyed textiles. The Department also holds artefacts from tribal peoples of Siberia that compare with native North American work in the resourceful use of local materials, such as birch-bark containers, fish-skin garments and delicate carvings in bone and ivory. Among these collections is a shaman's drum with a painted drum-head that was part of Sir Hans Sloane's bequest on which the British Museum was founded in 1753.

Collections from eastern Asia include important material from the tribal people of Taiwan, such as carved wooden objects and blankets of red-dyed dog-hair, and from the Ainu of Hokkaidō, the northern island of Japan. The Ainu are culturally related to certain Siberian peoples. Among the Department's finest Ainu items are outstanding barkcloth coats with bold curvilinear designs in cotton appliqué and embroidery. These people also observed a bear-cult, represented in the collection by a striking skin-covered bear's skull mounted on a post.

The collections from the South-East Asian archipelago, between Sumatra in the west, the Philippines in the north, and the tiny Kei Islands in the east, show dramatic cultural variation. This is partly due to a long history of outside influence, through immigration, trade and conquest, but it is also the result of environmental contrasts between the interior uplands, valleys and plains of the larger islands and the more restricted habitats of the smaller islands and atolls.

Steep and densely forested hills in central Borneo, for example, encouraged cultural variation as communities developed their own patterns in relative isolation from each other; elsewhere strong currents, sea-raiders, or historical differences also acted to reduce contact between separate islands. Immediate neighbours Java and Bali both practise rice cultivation and fishing, and there are similarities in their culture. Java is Islamic and Bali Hindu, but despite corresponding social and religious differences both developed aristocratic court traditions characterised by elaborate products, like superbly decorated textiles, the semi-sacred *keris*, and theatrical and musical repertoires of great finesse. The great collection acquired by Sir Stamford Raffles when he was Lieutenant Governor of Java from 1811 to 1816 probably contains the earliest datable and certainly some of the finest examples of puppets, including shadow-puppets, masks and musical instruments from Java, and also pieces from Bali and other parts of Indonesia.

134 LEFT *Wood figure,* kenyalang, *of a hornbill, a type used in head-hunting ceremonies among the Kenyah people of the Upper Baram River, Sarawak, Borneo. This example was employed by a colonial officer to promote peace.* L 1.1m.

135 RIGHT *Hawaiian cloak. Such full-sized cloaks, with scarce red and yellow feathers, were restricted to high chiefs. The brown cocks' feathers of this cloak are unusual. Its straight neckline suggests an eighteenth-century origin.* W 2.43m.

Tribal material from insular South-East Asia includes ancestral figures from the Nias Islands off south-west Sumatra, and a wide range of traditional objects from various people of the Philippine Islands, such as figures, shields, weapons, and examples of the entire range of artefacts of a nomadic group of negrito hunter-gatherers. Of special importance is a well-documented and detailed collection from Seram of recent, everyday equipment and samples of raw materials. Many of the pieces are particularly perishable and ephemeral, and are therefore rarely found in musuem collections.

Finally, the Department has an outstanding collection of tribal material from Borneo, largely from Sarawak in the north-west of the island. Most of it derives from Charles Hose, an officer in Rajah Sir Charles Brooke's administration between 1884 and 1907. Among the most striking objects in the Hose collection are some magnificent wood sculptures – free-standing anthropomorphic figures of very varied form and expression, as well as canoe-prows and house-boards depicting stylised animals, and elaborately carved hornbill effigies to enlist the support of a deity in head-hunting raids. Hose not only collected artefacts, but could turn them to advantage in his work. A photograph in one of his books shows that before it was sent to London, he reversed the traditional function of one of the hornbill images now in the Department, to suggest supernatural approval of a peace-making ceremony he organised in 1899 between hostile communities.

OCEANIA

The British Museum's Oceanic collections come from that vast area stretching from New Guinea's western tip to Easter Island, and from the Hawaiian Islands in the north, to New Zealand's South Island. The great size of this area is reflected in the diversity of the societies found there. Nevertheless, three broad generalisations can be made about these societies' traditional material culture, and hence about the collections. Metalworking was not indigenous to Oceania except in the extreme west of New Guinea, where it was introduced from Indonesia. Instead, stone, shell, bone and bamboo provided the tools for felling and cutting, carving and killing. Nor is weaving a traditional Oceanic craft, save in Micronesia, on some outliers of the Solomon Islands, and locally in the Bismarck Archipelago. Other fabrics, in particular barkcloth, generally served the functions of woven fabrics elsewhere. Finally, pottery was not known in Australia, and only in prehistoric times in Polynesia.

Oceania is conventionally subdivided into Polynesia, Micronesia, Melanesia and Australia; Fiji, sometimes assimilated to Polynesia, is here treated as part of Melanesia.

Polynesia

Well-founded knowledge of Polynesia began in the West with Captain Cook's three voyages of exploration (1768–79), which were also the origin, both directly and indirectly, of many of the most important pieces in the Museum's collections. Today this great scatter of islands, of which New Zealand is much the largest, is known to have been settled by a single people, ultimately of South-East Asian origin. These proto-Polynesians

134

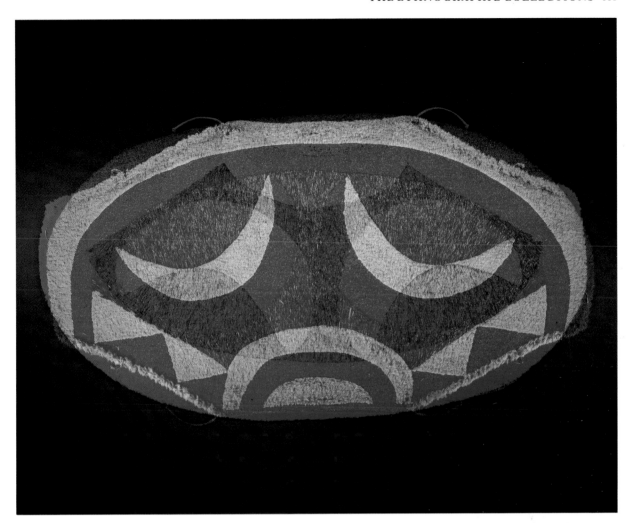

may well have brought with them the notions of rank and hierarchy, based upon genealogical proximity to chiefly lines, which Cook and other early visitors found to be expressed more or less strongly throughout the islands. These ranking systems, which were comparatively muted on the more sparsely populated Polynesian atolls, reached their fullest development on the populous volcanic islands, such as the Tahitian and Hawaiian Islands. This is reflected in their material culture. For example, in the Hawaiian Islands, from which the Museum has excellent collections, men of the chiefly class were distinguished by their feather-work regalia – capes, cloaks, helmets, which were worn on ceremonial occasions and in battle. Feathers were similarly important in Tahiti: in fact, Cook used red feathers that he had earlier obtained in Tonga to trade for food in Tahiti. However, undoubtedly the most spectacular item in the collections from Tahiti is the mourning dress presented to Cook on his second voyage. Such dresses were donned on the death of a high-ranking individual by one of his close relatives or by a priest who, in the company of other mourners, toured the neighbourhood, terrorising the inhabitants. Further important early material from both the Hawaiian and Tahitian Islands was collected by G. C. Hewitt, the surgeon's mate on Captain Vancouver's voyage in the area at the end of the eighteenth century.

The European impact upon Polynesia was swift, marked and often catastrophic. In some island groups, such as the Australs, the combination of introduced diseases and missionary fervour devastated the indigenous culture before the full significance of such items as the representation of the god A'a from Rurutu Island could be appreciated. At the same time the introduction of metal tools often appears to have given a short-lived stimulus to local wood-carving traditions, allowing the production of artefacts that were larger (as in the case of some Hawaiian images in the collection) and more intricate (as with Mangaian adzes and Ra'iva-vaean drum bases) than before. The finer designs on Hawaiian barkcloth also seem to have been related to the acquisition of iron tools, enabling Hawaiians to

136 *Tahitian mourning dress presented to Captain Cook. The dress is of barkcloth and the face-mask of pearl shell. Whole pearl shells decorate the wooden breast ornament, while the chest piece is made from pearl shell slivers.* H 2.2m.

produce more intricate barkcloth-beaters and stamps.

The European intrusion into Polynesia was not the sole source of destructive change. By 1774 many of the massive stone statues for which Easter Island is so well known had been toppled by the islanders themselves, perhaps as the consequence of warfare associated with the indigenous degradation of the environment. The collections include two such statues, brought back to Britain by HMS *Topaze* after a visit to the island in 1868. However, the social significance of these statues and of the Museum's extensive collection of wood-carvings – including examples of the undeciphered *rongorongo* script – remains unclear. The combination of raids by Peruvian slavers in the early 1860s and smallpox so reduced the island's population that this cultural knowledge was lost.

Like Easter Island, New Zealand is one of the very few Polynesian islands outside the tropics. On New Zealand's South Island, in particular, the crops which are important food sources elsewhere in Polynesia did not grow, and the eighteenth-century inhabitants lived largely by hunting, gathering and fishing. Throughout New Zealand the climate also restricted cultivation of the paper mulberry, from which barkcloth is otherwise made. Instead, native flax was fashioned (using a plaiting technique known as finger-weaving) into cloaks, belts and kilts. The collections are particularly rich in cloaks and, more generally, in a host of Maori wooden artefacts carved in characteristic curvilinear style. Amongst the most elaborate carving was that done on war canoes. In New Zealand, more than elsewhere in Polynesia, the European impact – expressed in part through the sale of guns – aggravated local patterns of warfare, and was one of the factors leading to the eclipse of Maori culture in the nineteenth century.

138

137 ABOVE *This unique figure of the god A'a from Rurutu Island in Polynesia is one of the most famous pieces in the Museum's collections. A large cavity in the figure's back once contained a number of smaller images. Probably eighteenth century* AD. H *1.17m.*

138 RIGHT *Prow of a Maori war canoe, with several* manaia, *a motif ubiquitous in Maori carving, combining elements of man, bird and lizard. Only one other prow in the northern style, such as this one, is known. Probably eighteenth or early nineteenth century* AD. H *(max.) 89cm.*

139 *Wood container with shell inlay from the Palau Islands (Republic of Belau). Such decorated containers were used traditionally for storing sweetmeats. This one is unusual in showing warriors carrying heads. Probably eighteenth century AD.* H *22cm.*

Micronesia

As in Polynesia, the four island groups of Micronesia – the Mariana, Caroline, and Marshall Islands, and Kiribati – are a combination of resource-rich volcanic islands and poorer atolls. They, too, were originally settled by immigrants (probably from the Philippines and Indonesia, and later Fiji and the New Hebrides), and their inhabitants depended both upon marine resources and horticulture. In most parts of Micronesia (the Marianas are an exception) the impact of the West was not extensively felt until the mid-nineteenth century. Thereafter introduced diseases had a similar depleting effect as in Polynesia, and the islands passed variously and successively under Spanish, German, Japanese, British and American control.

The collections include examples of characteristic Micronesian arts and crafts: wooden bowls, shell ornaments and plaited mats and baskets. Weaponry is well represented, particularly from Kiribati which, as the Gilbert Islands, was the only Micronesian island group under British control. Here the shark-tooth weapons and coconut-fibre armour are particularly notable.

139

The collections also include what may be the earliest documented holdings from any part of Micronesia. In August 1783 the East India Company packet *Antelope* was wrecked in the Palau Islands (now Republic of Belau). The captain and the crew forged such amicable relations with the Palauans that when they left they carried not only an impressive collection of artefacts, some of which found their way to the Museum, but also the High Chief's son who, sadly, died before he could be returned to the islands.

Melanesia

Almost all areas of Melanesia (which comprises the large island of New Guinea, the Bismarck Archipelago, Solomon Islands, New Hebrides, New Caledonia and Fiji) are substantially represented in the Museum's collections. The bias, however, is towards those parts, such as Papua and the Solomon Islands, which had closer historical links with Britain. Traditional Melane-

140 *Canoe-prow ornament, from the Solomon Islands. Such carvings, attached to the prow just above the waterline, are believed to protect the canoe and its occupants from dangers ahead.* H *22.5cm.*

141 ABOVE Malangan *sculpture in the form of a horizontal frieze from New Ireland, Papua New Guinea.* L *1.33m.*

sian political systems are typically decentralised and fairly small-scale. Their material culture does not generally reflect the hierarchical values, or the power of chiefs, apparent in Polynesia.

Social life in many parts of Melanesia revolves around the ceremonial exchange of goods between individuals and communities. The best known of such exchange systems was that studied during the First World War by Malinowski, one of the founding fathers of contemporary anthropology. Known as the *kula*, this exchange system links many of the island communities in the Massim area, off New Guinea's south-eastern tip. The Museum has excellent Massim collections (among them, Malinowski's), and includes fine examples both of the exchange items themselves, and of the intricately carved end-boards of the canoes in which those on *kula* expeditions travelled. Inter-island *kula* trips are still made today, sometimes by canoe, sometimes in modern vessels. Nineteenth-century European impact in the neighbouring Solomon Islands was far more disruptive of local societies. The large plank-built Solomon Island canoes, inlaid with pearl-shell and with striking prow carvings, are no longer made.

142 RIGHT *Wood rack for trophy skulls, from the Papuan Gulf, Papua New Guinea. Skull racks, together with ceremonial boards, also made of wood and similarly decorated, were kept in men's houses. Nineteenth or very early twentieth century* AD. H *1.17m.*

On the New Guinea mainland the Sepik region was particularly noted for its art forms. In its diversity and expressiveness, this is perhaps the richest art-producing area in the world. The Sepik area fell into what was, until 1914, German New Guinea, and German institutions possess the finest early Sepik material. Recently, however, the Museum has added to its existing Sepik holdings, making in particular an extensive collection from the Abelam people, whose bold figurative sculpture is produced in connection with initiation ceremonies. In 1964 a comprehensive range of material from the Tifalmin people of the upper Sepik was acquired as a result of an expedition by members of the Department's staff. Field collecting by members of staff has since become a regular way of adding well-documented items to the collections.

Few artefacts survive very long in a tropical environment, but some categories of artwork are notably ephemeral. The magnificent filigree *malangan* constructions of New Ireland may be discarded and left to rot, or sold to Europeans, after having been briefly displayed in the commemorative rites for the dead for which they are made. Here the collections include in particular some fifty very early *malangan*, purchased from a single site in exchange for 'a gigantic pig', and presented to the Museum in 1884. In the Papuan Gulf, on New Guinea's southern coast, the polychrome bark-cloth masks made for a now discontinued ritual cycle were ceremonially burned at the end of festivities. Not all Papuan Gulf material culture was so transient: the skull racks and ceremonial boards in the collection would have been more enduring items.

The dense populations of the Highland areas of New Guinea were the last major Melanesian societies to be contacted by outsiders, in the 1920s and 1930s. Theirs is generally a sparser material culture, but with a particular emphasis on elaborate personal adornment worn for festivals and exchanges.

Australia

The Aboriginal peoples of Australia lived by hunting gathering and, in some areas, fishing; for the most part by moving in small bands across vast territories, living off the land as they went. To survive they developed a subtle and deep understanding of their natural environment. Although their artefacts are generally simple, sometimes multi-functional (a shield could serve as a container and also be used in making fire), they were well adapted to a life of frequent movement. Besides the wooden shield collected at Botany Bay on one of Cook's voyages, the Museum possesses many other examples of Aboriginal tools and weapons, including various forms of boomerang, as well as baskets, fishing equipment and a double raft from the Worora people. The most substantial collections come from Western Australia, the Northern Territories and Queensland. The research expedition of the Cambridge anthropologist A. C. Haddon in 1888–9 added many items from the Torres Straits area, and two other pioneering anthropologists, Baldwin Spencer and F. J. Gillen, collected among the Aranda tribe of central Australia, whose ceremonial life they studied and recorded. The complex religious beliefs of the Aborigines are represented by several examples of sacred engraved stones, *churinga*, which record the journeys of the ancestral beings who are believed to have created important features of the landscape as they travelled.

European impact had a devastating effect on Aboriginal societies, dispossessing and destroying many, and radically affecting most of the remainder. However, recent decades have seen a revival of Aboriginal culture. Many groups in central Australia and in the Northern Territory have re-established a presence on traditional lands, a move they have partly financed from the sale of works of art. The Museum has acquired a number of collections of such contemporary Aboriginal art which, though it often employs modern materials, also refers back through the motifs it uses to the long-standing Aboriginal concern with the land.

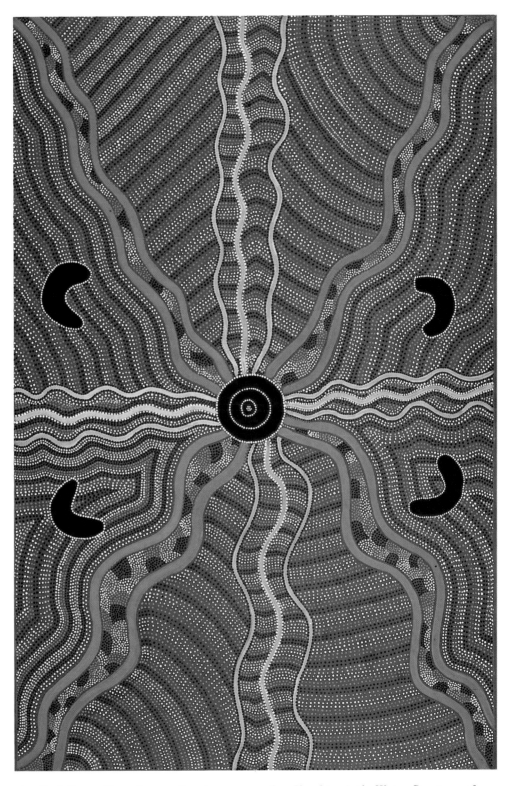

143 Bush Potato Dreaming: *acrylic paint on canvas, from Yuendumu in the Western Desert area of Australia's Northern Territory. 1986. 145 × 94cm.*

THE MEDIEVAL
AND
MODERN COLLECTIONS

◆

The Department of Medieval and Modern Europe, formerly Medieval and Later Antiquities, contains a vast and heterogeneous collection of the post-classical art and archaeology of Europe. Other Christian and Jewish cultures of this period outside Europe are included, for instance Byzantium. The Museum does not, however, attempt to make comprehensive collections in every medium: furniture, textiles, European folk life, arms and armour, manuscripts, paintings, printed books and pamphlets and modern technology are collected by other national institutions.

144 *Shoulder-clasps of gold, garnet and* millefiore *glass from the Sutton Hoo ship burial (c. AD 625–30). The clasps would have been fixed to two halves of a leather overgarment. Each is fastened on a hinge by a gold animal-headed pin. L 12.7cm.*

THE LATE ANTIQUE COLLECTIONS

The Department is responsible for those late Roman collections which date from after the Edict of Milan (AD 313) but do not come from Roman Britain. With the Edict of Milan Christians throughout the Roman Empire gained the freedom to practise their religion, and it is the emergence of a Christian art from its secular, Jewish and pagan background which gives the Department's superb late Roman collections their particular interest and importance.

Two sizeable silver treasures demonstrate the gradual development of the religion. The first, from the fourth century AD, found on the Esquiline Hill in Rome, includes two large caskets, plates and furniture fittings; a slightly later hoard unearthed at Carthage is composed predominantly of bowls and spoons with Christian symbols. The emergence of an unambiguous Christian iconography is reflected in some remarkable

145 The Projecta Casket from the Esquiline Treasure. The partly gilt silver casket is embossed with mythological and secular scenes but engraved with the inscription: 'Secundus and Projecta, may you live in Christ'. Second half of the fourth century AD. L 56cm.

ivories, among them four sides of a box carved with scenes of Christ's Passion. A substantial collection of jewellery, much of it bearing Christian symbols, includes a large number of precious and semi-precious stones engraved in intaglio with various devices; also noteworthy is a small group of gold objects executed in *opus interrasile* ('pierced work'). The collection contains some 750 magical gems, cut to magicians' 'prescriptions', mostly to cure or protect against such illnesses and misfortunes as colic, backache and shipwreck.

The collection of glass includes the unique dichromic Lycurgus Cup, carved with a mythological scene, but especially notable is the gold-glass: vessels decorated with gold foil cut to shape and sandwiched between layers of glass. Examples include pagan, Jewish and Christian designs. The Department also holds a large group of bronze and glass weights, tokens and amuletic pendants, pottery, and a wide range of everyday objects. Stone is represented by a more or less complete sarcophagus, carved with the story of Jonah, a number of architectural and sarcophagus fragments, and a few grave stelae. Few textiles survive from this early period, and then only from Egyptian soil; the Department's small collection complements textiles cared for by the Department of Egyptian Antiquities.

145

146

146 *Gold–glass fragments of drinking vessels, with gold foil between layers of glass. These fragments, found in the Roman catacombs, show bridal couples blessed by Cupid (top) and Christ (bottom). Fourth century AD. D (top) 7cm.*

BARBARIAN EUROPE

During the fourth and fifth centuries AD the power of the Roman Empire in the west crumbled, and land-hungry Germanic tribes expanded to occupy much of Western Europe. Before they were firmly converted to Christianity Germanic tribes buried objects with their dead. Thus, until the seventh century in large areas of

Western Europe, and the eleventh century in Scandinavia, significant objects from daily life are preserved in many graves. The collections are particularly rich in jewellery of the fifth to seventh centuries associated with tribes such as the Goths, Ostrogoths, Franks and Lombards, whose wealth in gold and silver, use of red garnet inlays and love of rich colour contrasts owe much to late antique traditions. Stylised animal ornament, a characteristically Germanic development, was particularly long lived in Scandinavia, where the changing styles are seen in a range of objects from Gotland of the fifth to eleventh centuries. Double-edged swords, sometimes richly decorated and skilfully smithed by Rhenish craftsmen, were marks of the powerful throughout the period; freemen carried a spear and shield, or heavy knife.

From the eighth to ninth centuries onwards new urban trading sites developed in strategic locations throughout Europe and parts of Scandinavia. From these comes extensive evidence of local industries and trading which is reflected in material, for example, from Dorestad in the Netherlands.

From the late eighth to early eleventh centuries Europe was again convulsed as Scandinavian Vikings raided widely in the west and occupied some areas for permanent settlement. A range of treasures and heavily decorated jewellery from Gotland shows the Vikings' technical skill and artistry. Objects of iron, bronze and whalebone found in Norwegian graves show more everyday aspects of their life. Roman and Byzantine gold coins of the fourth to sixth centuries, and Islamic and Anglo-Saxon silver of the ninth to eleventh centuries found in Scandinavia are evidence of the wealth derived from periods of military service, trade and piracy.

In Eastern and Central Europe from the sixth to eighth centuries the Slavs expanded to occupy lands as far as the Baltic coast, the River Elbe and the Adriatic Sea. In the east they penetrated deep into modern Russia and the Ukraine. The collections illustrate little of the complex political and economic developments in this important area of Europe. A western Slav hoard of the eleventh century contains sheet-silver beads and ear-rings with delicate use of filigree and granulation. Modest rings, worn in a woman's hair or as head-dress pendants, display regional variations, especially among the eastern Slavs. The most spectacular (called 'kolts') are of eleventh- to thirteenth-century date and are of silver, sometimes nielloed, or of gold with enamelled decoration. Kiev, the centre of the most powerful eastern Slav principality, is represented by a silver hoard of the thirteenth century, buried just before its sack by the Tartars from the east.

The Balts and Finno-Ugrians, two distinct ethnic and linguistic groups, inhabited lands bordering those of the Slavs, very broadly in the present Baltic States

147 ABOVE *Germanic polychrome jewellery. Sixth-century female brooches and a belt buckle, from different parts of Europe. The predominant red of the cloisonné garnet inlay is highlighted by the sparing use of a second inlay and the glitter of gold or gilt.* L *(buckle) 9.8cm.*

and northern Russia respectively. Their traditional bronze jewellery during the ninth to twelfth centuries reflects very distinctive local fashions. That of the Balts is characterised by its weight of bronze and delicate decoration, while the Finno-Ugrians display a fondness for naturalistic representations of animals and birds.

Throughout the first millennium periodic invasions of peoples from the Eurasian Steppes brought upheaval to Central Europe and sometimes further west: the Huns in the late fourth and fifth centuries, the Avars in the sixth century, the Bulgars in the late seventh century, the Magyars in the later ninth and tenth centuries. Characteristic of these semi-nomadic groups are richly worked objects in organic materials, which unfortunately seldom survive. The importance of these peoples is only hinted at through the minor objects contained in the collections. Avar ear-rings, for example, and other gold ornaments, are made of melted-down coins extorted in massive amounts as tribute from the Byzantine

148 *Finno-Ugrian copper alloy pendant. The upper part is in the form of the head and fore-leg of two horses in profile. The chains support pendants resembling webbed feet, which would have jingled as the wearer moved.* W *5.1cm.*

Empire. The vine-scroll decoration on their elaborately cast fittings from composite belts shows further Byzantine influence. Saddle-mounts and richly decorated iron horse-fittings survive, along with the rider's characteristic weapons such as the sabre.

THE ANGLO-SAXONS

In the fifth century southern and eastern areas of Britain saw the settlement of Anglo-Saxons, a blanket term for folk from a variety of tribes with homelands on the North German Plain and in southern Scandinavia. The early phases of the Anglo-Saxon settlement are represented by a range of metalwork and pottery that reveals the Continental backgrounds of the Germanic immigrants. The grave-goods of these pagan Anglo-Saxons, dating from the fifth to the seventh centuries, are exceptionally well represented in the collections, supplemented by a growing body of material from modern settlement excavations. They illustrate considerable diversity of wealth and culture, from the cremation urns and cruciform brooches of the Angles, to Saxon saucer brooches, and the lavish garnet-inlaid metalwork, prestige weapons and Continental imports characteristic of Kent, richest of the early kingdoms.

The collections also contain an unrivalled group of material from royal and princely graves. The most famous of these is the Sutton Hoo (Suffolk) ship burial,

the grave of an East Anglian king. The burial is renowned for its wealth of gold and garnet jewellery, its Byzantine silver and its weapons and armour. Lesser princely graves in the collection – notably those from Taplow (Buckinghamshire) and Broomfield (Essex) – were also lavishly equipped with gold jewellery, sets of fine drinking and storage vessels and weapons.

After the conversion of the English to Christianity the practice of burying personal possessions with the dead gradually ceased. In the collections individual finds, hoards and assemblages from rural and urban

149 The Fuller Brooch. A large silver Anglo-Saxon disc brooch, decorated in niello with scenes representing the five senses. One of the most lavish forms of late Saxon jewellery, disc brooches were worn by both men and women. D 11.4cm.

settlements replace the grave-goods of the earlier cemeteries. Although from the mid-seventh century onwards fewer objects have survived, these include a high proportion of personal possessions, such as jewellery and weapons. The role of the Church in society is reflected in memorial stones and standing crosses, liturgical metalwork, and a fine series of tenth- and eleventh-century ivory-carvings, such as the pen-case from London. Craft and technology as well as the domestic side of Anglo-Saxon life in the eighth to eleventh centuries are well represented by a range of objects including pottery and other kitchen utensils, iron knives and weaving implements. Carpenters' tools from the Hurbuck (Durham) hoard and iron fish-hooks and spade shoes, as well as metalworking equipment, give glimpses of rural life and industry otherwise known from manuscript sources.

Contemporary with the late Anglo-Saxon material is a small but rich collection of Viking objects from England, Ireland and Scotland. Through gold and silver jewellery, predominantly male, it reflects Viking wealth from loot and trade, while the significance of warfare is revealed through axes, spears, swords and their fittings. The collections include some impressive hoards of hack-silver, most famous among them that from Cuerdale (Lancashire), the largest Viking hoard outside Russia, which contained over a thousand pieces of cut-up silver bullion, as well as many thousands of coins.

The gradual development of literacy is reflected in a varied group of objects inscribed with runic inscriptions, some clearly magical. Of outstanding interest are the unique rune-inscribed box of whale's bone known

150 Anglo-Saxon pen-case made of walrus ivory with glass inlays. It has a sliding lid and is carved in high relief with plant and animal scenes. Its shape suggests that it was used to hold quill pens. Mid-eleventh century AD. L 23.2cm.

as the Franks Casket and two gold ninth-century rings associated by their inscriptions with the royal house of Wessex. The lighter side of Anglo-Saxon life can be seen in bone chessmen and gaming-pieces, and in a number of lyre fittings, which testify to the importance of music and poetry. Finally, the abiding pleasure that the Anglo-Saxons took in intricate decoration and fine craftsmanship is demonstrated in metalwork and sculpture covering five hundred years in which the development of the animal-based ornament brought by the earliest Germanic settlers can be traced.

The Celts in Britain and Ireland

The Museum has the most extensive collection outside Ireland of material from the early medieval phase of the western Celtic peoples. In Britain this is the period of the Anglo-Saxon settlement of lowland Britain, when the Celtic kingdoms held the highland areas of the north, modern Wales and the south-west. Fine metalwork from the kingdoms of Celtic Britain is represented primarily by the remains of more than thirty hanging-bowls, many handsomely decorated with applied enamels in characteristic scroll and spiral designs. Almost all, such as the three bowls from Sutton Hoo, have been recovered from Anglo-Saxon pagan burials.

The greater part of the Celtic collection comes from Ireland. It is rich in metalwork, particularly relating to dress. The characteristic Celtic dress fastening was the open-ring or 'penannular' brooch, well represented here, with examples from the fifth century onwards. A few come from Wales and some from the kingdom of the Picts, a major power in the early Middle Ages in northern Britain. Dress pins are also common; like them, the brooches demonstrate the variety of form and styles in the early Christian period, in particular the absorption of Anglo-Saxon and Mediterranean motifs in the eighth century, a period of brilliant craftsmanship. In the tenth and eleventh centuries Vikings in Ireland adopted new styles of brooch and pin reflecting Scandinavian taste, the most flamboyant of which are the great silver penannular brooches with thistle-shaped terminals; examples have been found in Cumbria, at Clonkeen in Co. Longford (Ireland), and elsewhere.

151 BELOW *Silver bossed penannular brooch from Co. Galway, Ireland. This is one of a small group of elaborate Irish–Viking brooches of the late ninth to early tenth centuries* AD. *It is decorated on the front with panels of animal interlace between the high-relief bosses.* L *39cm.*

152 ABOVE *Pictish symbol stone carved with the figure of a bull, one of numerous bull carvings from the vitrified fort at Burghead, Moray Firth. The powerful bull symbol occurs only at Burghead and may indicate tribal or dynastic identity.* H *5.25cm.*

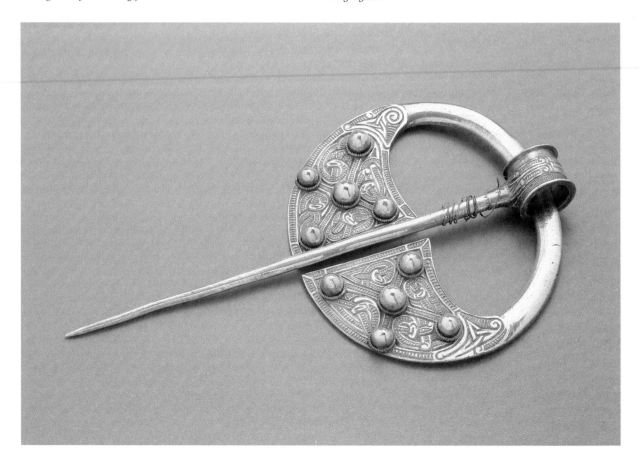

The collection also contains an important group of ecclesiastical metalwork dating from the eighth century onwards. This was a period of travel and exchange amongst the monks and clergy, when the Church was the major patron of the arts. The find-places of a few fine Irish-style pieces reflect this interchange: the gilt-bronze boss from Steeple Bumpstead (Essex), material from the Anglo-Saxon abbey at Whitby (North Yorkshire), and a Carolingian brooch from Ballycottin (Co. Cork, Ireland). The flowering of Christian culture in Ireland is also seen in an important group of early bells, some associated with holy men and enclosed later in lavish containers. The 'Kells' crozier is justly famous and the collection contains parts of other croziers, ornamental figures and plaques from other shrines.

A variety of tools, utensils and other objects illustrate domestic and rural life. Although pottery was not in common use in the Celtic kingdoms, the collections include some early imported Mediterranean sherds and later domestic ware. There are also examples of less readily portable material: among a small group of sculptured stones are a memorial stone with both Ogham and Latin script from Llywel (Powys, Wales) and a finely incised Pictish bull on a slab from Burghead (Grampian, Scotland).

BYZANTIUM

In AD 330 Constantinople (present-day Istanbul) had become the capital of the Roman Empire; the fall of Rome and the western part of the Empire to Germanic peoples during the fifth century marked the beginning of the early Byzantine period. The Roman legacy is reflected in the Department's Byzantine collections by items which preserve the classical tradition through a continuing interest in pagan motifs and yet represent a development into a fully fledged Christian art. Two silver treasures, from the sixth and seventh centuries, found near Constantinople and on the island of Cyprus, are characteristic of the period. Among the Department's collection of ivory carvings is one of the masterpieces of early Byzantine art, an ivory panel decorated with the figure of an archangel; notable also are six boxes carved with classical and Christian scenes. More extensive is the collection of jewellery, which includes medallions, buckles, crosses, rings and ear-rings, as well as an impressive gold body-chain, one of the largest pieces of Byzantine jewellery to have survived. Liturgical vessels and objects of devotion in precious

153 *Leaf of an ivory diptych, carved with the figure of an archangel: one of the great masterpieces of Byzantine art. The inscription 'Receive these, and having learnt the cause . . .' would have continued on the other, lost leaf. From Constantinople, sixth century* AD. H 41 cm.

155 Gold cloisonné pendant reliquary with representations of St George (seen here) and St Demetrios, inscribed '[The bearer] prays that you will be his fiery defence in battle' and, round the edge, 'Anointed with your blood and myrrh'. From Salonica, thirteenth century AD. D 3.25cm.

metal, bronze, glass and pottery are numerous. These include a fine collection of pilgrims' tokens and *ampullae* (pilgrims' flasks) in pottery, and hinged bronze reliquary-crosses.

The collections from Byzantine Egypt are shared between this Department and the Department of Egyptian Antiquities, the numerous finds from the Wadi Sarga excavations (apart from the *ostraca*) being housed here.

From the middle of the seventh century onwards the Byzantine Empire contracted considerably: wealthy eastern provinces such as Syria and Egypt were lost to the Arabs, and the northern borders of the Empire were continually assailed by nomadic tribes. Because of the destruction and abandonment of many of the great cities of the eastern Mediterranean, fewer everyday objects have survived from this time onwards.

Between AD 726 and 843, with one interruption, images were officially banned in the Byzantine Empire, and their restoration marked the so-called middle

154 Icon of St John the Baptist, painted in egg-tempera on gold-leaf on a linen-faced panel. The icon was probably painted for the personal devotions of someone of high rank. From Constantinople, about AD 1300. 25 × 20cm.

Byzantine period. This 'renaissance' is mainly represented by some particularly fine ivory-carvings and a few important items of jewellery, on which the technique of cloisonné enamel, new to Byzantine craftsmen, is used to remarkable effect. Other metalwork includes bronze reliquary-crosses, belt-buckles, and seals. 155

Between 1204 and 1261 Constantinople was ruled from the west, and the resulting influences are particularly noticeable in such items as an extensive collection of glass pilgrim-tokens, steatite (soapstone) carvings and a rare 'Crusader' icon of St George, painted by a western artist in the Byzantine manner. The Department also has a small collection of pottery vessels known as sgraffito ware.

The last centuries of the Byzantine Empire, from 1261 until the fall of Constantinople to Mehmet the Conqueror in 1453, are principally represented by four superb icons; three (of St Peter, St John the Baptist, and a scene representing the end of Iconoclasm) were painted in Constantinople, and the fourth (a 'festival' icon with four New Testament scenes) either in Constantinople or Thessaloniki. These icons form the nucleus of the national icon collection, which also comprises Russian icons painted between the fourteenth and nineteenth centuries. 154

THE MIDDLE AGES

Ever since a new interest in the Middle Ages was rekindled among British antiquaries in the late seventeenth century the precious objects made for the Church and laity between about AD 800 and 1500 have been collected for their historical interest as well as their aesthetic appeal. Few of the Museum's benefactors have regarded their objects merely as works of art, rather as counterparts to the archaeology and historical documents of the period, and it is as such that they still retain a special resonance in the Museum, the 'high profile' luxury side of life, as opposed to the more day-to-day artefacts, which form the nucleus of the collections.

The Museum boasts a rich collection of precious objects of the Carolingian period, associated with the Emperor Charlemagne (crowned in AD 800) and his successors, whose literate circle in church and court sought to recreate the splendours of late antique art. These include elephant-ivory carvings and engraved rock-crystals, such as the Lothar Crystal. In the German lands during the Ottonian and Salian period small-scale carving of precious materials, particularly ivory, continued to flourish. Ottonian art reached its apogee around AD 1000 in the Rhineland and Trier, where the Townley Brooch, a rare gold cloisonné enamel, was probably made. From the Saxon heartland comes a small square ivory plaque from Otto the Great's Magdeburg Cathedral of the 960s.

156 ABOVE *A King and Queen from a hoard of walrus-ivory chessmen from the Isle of Lewis in the Outer Hebrides. The greatest surviving series of medieval chessmen, they date from the middle of the twelfth century AD. H (King) 10.6cm.*

The British Museum has never systematically collected the sculpture and wall-paintings from churches, monasteries and castles, although it does possess a few important twelfth-century English capitals. On a smaller scale, too, there is a remarkable series of ivories, mostly walrus ivory. Twelfth-century gaming pieces are more richly represented here than perhaps in any museum in the world. The most famous are, of course, the eighty pieces from the hoard of chessmen found on the Isle of Lewis in the Outer Hebrides in 1831, perhaps the work of a Scandinavian artist, but the collections also contain numerous bone and ivory counters, carved with all manner of biblical and mythological scenes and exotic beasts. Other Romanesque ivories, either English or European, were commissioned by the Church, for book-covers, croziers, reliquaries, and so on. So too were many of the metalwork objects in the collections: crucifix figures, censers and reliquaries. The cult of relics inevitably led to the creation of reliquaries echoing the original form of the relic they contained: a relic of the skull of St Eustace originally owned by the Cathedral of Basle was enclosed within a carved wooden 'portrait-head' of St Eustace, itself encased in silver-gilt sheeting of about 1200.

The revival of champlevé enamel during the twelfth century finds remarkable expression in the Museum's collections. The Limoges enamels of south-west France and northern Spain are numerically by far the largest group and include some famous pieces, among them an early secular casket of about 1180 with elegantly drawn lovers, musicians, hunters and warriors. In the Meuse Valley and Middle Rhine great masterpieces of enamel were also made in the twelfth century. The collections reflect their variety: an altar cross, decorated with scenes from the Old Testament, and two plaques made for Henry of Blois, Bishop of

157 *Silver-gilt head-reliquary from the Cathedral at Basle, Switzerland. Inside a cavity in the wooden core relics were kept, including a relic of the skull of St Eustace, the hunter. About AD 1200. H 34cm.*

158 LEFT *Altar-cross of gilt copper and champlevé enamel, a masterpiece of Romanesque enamel. Made in the Mosan region or Middle Rhineland in the third quarter of the twelfth century AD. The five scenes on the cross were chosen as Old Testament prefigurations of the Crucifixion. H 37cm.*

159 ABOVE *The Royal Gold Cup, probably made in Paris about AD 1370–80 for Charles V of France, and later in the royal English collections in the fifteenth and sixteenth centuries. The cup is of solid gold decorated in* basse-taille *enamel with the story of St Agnes. H 23.5cm.*

Winchester (1129–71) by one of the greatest of the Mosan enamellers are but three examples.

From the thirteenth and fourteenth centuries comes a rich series of ecclesiastical metalwork: chalices and patens, altar crosses and other altar furniture and liturgical items. In the late thirteenth century brasses appear on monuments. The Department's English and Continental brasses include a fine fourteenth-century head of a bishop and a small group of the type known as palimpsest brasses, in which the plain reverse has been engraved with a new figure or inscription. Brass rubbings are not kept here, but in the Department of Manuscripts of the British Library.

The collections also contain a large number of Gothic ivory-carvings. Many of them were originally made in major urban centres such as Paris, where by the fourteenth century not only devotional objects but also secular caskets, mirror-cases, cosmetic boxes, and so on, were being produced. A unique group of devotional ivories is carved with the arms of John Grandisson, Bishop of Exeter (1327–69). Among the famous enamels of the fourteenth century are a chalice signed by the two Sienese Tondino di Guerrino and Andrea Riguardi, and a small crystal-set 'bean-shaped' gold reliquary which opens like a book into enamelled leaves. A set of elaborate enamelled silver altar plate from the Hospital de Vera Cruz at Medina de Pomar

160 *Copper alloy aquamanile, used to contain water for washing hands before meals. It was filled through the helmet and emptied through the spout on the horse's forehead. Found in the River Tyne, near Hexham, Northumberland, it dates from* AD *1250–1300.* H *33.7cm.*

near Burgos (Spain) is of mid-fifteenth century date.

Among the most precious possessions of the Museum are the few melancholy but beautiful fragmentary wall-paintings from the royal chapel of St Stephen's within the Palace of Westminster, executed for Edward III in the 1350s. The fragments were painted in oil medium on the plastered wall, with minutely refined details and delicate brushwork.

Secular material from great households in the later Middle Ages ranges from Gothic ivories and metalwork to tooled leather items and table vessels. One of the most important surviving medieval musical instruments is an early fourteenth-century English gittern (an early form of guitar). A silver cup (on loan from Lacock, Wiltshire) was made to stand on the table of some lord or rich city merchant in the early fifteenth century, and an ivory hunting-horn, associated with the tenure of Savernake Forest (Wiltshire), has rich fourteenth-century enamel mounts. Little survives of the household jewels and plate of the fourteenth and fifteenth centuries, but an exceptional piece is the Royal Gold Cup. Of solid gold and richly decorated in red, blue, brown and green translucent enamels with scenes from the Passion of St Agnes, this was probably made for Charles V of France about 1380.

Medieval warfare is illustrated by a collection of armour and weapons, many of them now on loan to the Royal Armouries at the Tower of London. A ceremonial object, never intended for use in battle, is the tournament shield, painted in the Netherlands in the late fifteenth century, which shows a young knight kneeling before his lady, while Death in the form of a skeleton reaches out for him from behind.

In stark contrast to the brilliance of the jewels, ivories and enamels of the medieval church and nobility is the large group of material, much of it from archaeological excavations, that reflects medieval daily life in all its many facets. As well as small metal objects, the collections include a wide range of pottery vessels from storage jars to cooking pots and jugs that represent types used all over England for storing food, cooking and drinking. Some, such as those from Toynton All Saints (Lincolnshire) or Ashton (Cheshire), were discovered at the actual kiln site. The discovery and excavation of such manufacturing sites has led to the establishment of the national reference collection of medieval pottery in the British Museum; this provides a comprehensive visual collection for students of medieval pottery.

Bronze vessels, jugs, cauldrons and aquamaniles were also used both for cooking and drinking. A striking example is a ewer bearing the arms and devices of Richard II (1377–99), which was discovered in the West African kingdom of Asante in 1896. Bronze was also used for cauldrons, skillets and chafing dishes. Occasionally wooden vessels survive: mazers, shallow

161 *Gold fifteenth-century brooches found in the River Meuse, decorated with stones and enamelling. The largest, with a lady holding a sapphire, shows the elaborate modelling and decoration of late medieval North European jewellery.* H *(largest) 3.9cm.*

wooden bowls used as drinking cups, are often decorated with silver mounts. The finest example in the Museum's small collection is the bowl of Robert Pecham given to the refectory of Rochester in 1532–3.

The Department's collection of medieval jewellery consists of some important single finds, such as the white-enamelled Dunstable Swan Jewel of about 1400, but it also contains rings and brooches found with coin hoards which have come to the Museum through the operation of Treasure Trove. Such material is included in the hoards from Lark Hill (Worcestershire), Coventry, and the fifteenth-century hoard from Fishpool (Nottinghamshire). A large collection of medieval rings ranges over all the known types from signet rings, decorative rings and inscribed rings to ecclesiastical rings. Although the collection is mainly English, it also includes rings from France and Germany and an important series from Italy.

A prominent feature of medieval life was the pilgrimage. Pilgrim signs of lead or pewter were distributed at famous shrines to pilgrims to wear as proof of their journey. Examples come from important English shrines, as well as from Continental shrines, such as the scallop shell, the sign of St James, indicative of the pilgrimage to Santiago de Compostella. Among the subjects in the collection are the figures of St Thomas (Canterbury) and the Virgin and Child (Walsingham),

162 *Wall-tile decorated in sgraffito with apocryphal stories of the childhood of Christ: Jesus being hit by a schoolmaster and Jesus blessing two schoolmasters after healing two cripples. From Tring church, Hertfordshire, early fourteenth century* AD. *32.5 × 16.3cm.*

the head of St John the Baptist (Amiens), the horn of St Hubert, the Axe of St Olave, and the comb of St Blaise. The collections also contain stone moulds for casting pilgrim signs.

An unrivalled collection of some 14,000 medieval decorated tiles comes from the flooring of monastic and parish churches, royal palaces and manor houses. The collection was greatly enhanced by the collection formed by the Duke of Rutland, containing tiles from a wide variety of monastic sites and the late fifteenth-century pavement from the house of William Canynges at Bristol. One of the most important groups is of the thirteenth century and was found at the Benedictine Abbey of Chertsey (Surrey) in the 1850s. This series includes roundels with scenes of the romance of Tristram and Iseult, as well as a series of combat scenes including Richard and Saladin. The pavement and kiln from Clarendon Palace (Wiltshire) are evidence of royal use of tiles in the thirteenth century. Apart from the impressive quality of the finer tiles, the collection is important for understanding the geographical spread of this form of medieval craftsmanship.

The Department also houses the important national collection of medieval seal matrices.

FROM THE RENAISSANCE TO THE TWENTIETH CENTURY

The explosion of creative energy that we call the Renaissance is illustrated in the British Museum mainly in the 'applied arts'. The great strength of the collections from the Renaissance up to more recent times lies in ceramics, glass, precious metalwork, jewellery and small-scale sculpture. These collections were essentially accumulated in the second half of the nineteenth century and reflect the Victorian fascination with the application of art to industry. The historical and archaeological traditions of the Museum are reflected in the collection's richness in pieces of documentary or historic association.

The Department has little Renaissance sculpture, although examples include small works by Michelangelo and Giambologna and, from north of the Alps, fine wood-carvings by Tilman Riemenschneider and Conrad Meit. The great collection of Renaissance medals in the Department of Coins and Medals is complemented by an important series of single-sided metal reliefs called plaquettes, which ornamented larger objects and helped diffuse the designs of great original artists down to the other arts. The Museum holds collections among the richest in the world illustrating aspects of virtuoso Renaissance craftsmanship, particularly the painted tin-glazed Italian pottery known as 'maiolica', the elaborate drinking glasses made in sixteenth-century Venice and the painted enamels of Limoges in southern France.

Spectacular examples of goldsmiths' work, jewellery and precious *objets d'art* are to be found particularly in the Waddesdon Bequest. This collection, from Waddesdon Manor in Buckinghamshire, was bequeathed by Baron Ferdinand Rothschild in 1898 and forms the nearest equivalent to be found in Britain of the varied *Schatzkammer* (treasure chamber) of a Renaissance prince. Among the treasures of the Bequest are the enamelled gold Holy Thorn reliquary, made in France about 1405–10 for the great art patron Jean duc de Berry to contain a thorn from the Crown of Thorns; a parade shield of damascened iron by Giorgio Ghisi of Mantua (1554); and the Lyte Jewel, an English gold locket with a miniature by Hilliard of James I (1610).

England was slow to absorb the cultural revolution emanating from Renaissance Italy and the importance of immigrant craftsmen in bringing England into the mainstream of European art is illustrated by pieces like an astrolabe made for Henry VIII by the French maker Sebastian Le Seney; or the glass tankard made around 1575 in the London glass-house of a Venetian immigrant, Jacopo Verzelini, which has mounts bearing the arms of Lord Burghley, chief minister to Queen Elizabeth I. A distinguished group of pieces of English Renaissance silver plate includes the silver-gilt Wyndham Ewer (1554–5), the earliest surviving piece of English plate in the Continental Mannerist style.

The Department's splendid series of luxury objects from Tudor England and later is complemented by wide-ranging collections of more modest items illustrating social history up to the nineteenth century. The kitchen- and tableware provide dating evidence for developments in design and consumer demand. The development in cutlery design is a major indication of increased domestic sophistication, and an extraordinary range of materials and techniques were used in furnishing the handles of knives and forks. The influence of magic on the Renaissance mind is illustrated by the 'crystal ball' and astrological equipment of Dr John Dee, the astrologer favoured by Queen Elizabeth I.

163 *Exotic natural history curiosities in silver-gilt mounts from the Waddesdon Bequest. Left is a nut from the Seychelles in mid-sixteenth-century German mounts; centre, a nautilus shell in Antwerp mounts of 1555–6; right, an ostrich egg in Prague mounts of the late sixteenth century.* H *(ostrich egg and mount) 38.7cm.*

164 *One of a pair of silver-gilt vases with ivory sleeves carved by a Continental artist; the cups have the London hallmark and the maker's mark of David Willaume, a talented French Protestant craftsman who settled in London. 1711. From the Peter Wilding Bequest.* H 42.4cm.

The impact of the tobacco trade is visible in the wide range of smoking accessories, such as clay pipes and pipe-stoppers. Typical reminders of the fashion for smoking in the seventeenth and eighteenth centuries are the brass and copper tobacco boxes from Germany and Holland, many of which were imported into Britain and which were often decorated with mythological and biblical scenes. Such objects also reflect contemporary history in their decoration, and the battles and personalities of the Seven Years War (1756–63) and the career of Frederick the Great of Prussia provided popular decorative themes.

Silversmiths' work in England was heavily influenced in the late seventeenth century by the arrival of Huguenot refugees from France. The Museum possesses the superb Wilding Bequest of Huguenot silver by the leading first- and second-generation immigrant craftsmen in London between 1699 and 1723. Huguenot work was cast in solid silver, in contrast to most English ware, which was raised in hollow silver with thin walls. The French immigrants soon attracted commissions from the British aristocracy, such as the silver-gilt ewer and basin by Pierre Harache with the arms of the Duke of Devonshire (1697). London goldsmiths were forced to improve the quality of their work and adopted the French designs and techniques.

One of the most impressive items of late seventeenth-century plate is the pair of ice-pails made for the Duke of Marlborough, which were cast in pure gold. A later, even more spectacular example of work in gold is the Portland Font, commissioned by the third Duke of Portland on the birth of his grandson in 1796; designed by landscape gardener Humphrey Repton, it was executed in the London workshop of Paul Storr, and is one of the greatest monuments of English goldsmiths' work in the neo-classical style.

A more modest category of gold and silver work is found in boxes and containers of different sorts. These include Tudor and Stuart counter boxes, curiosities such as the delicately pierced cases for Goa stones (c. 1700), and snuff-boxes ranging from plain silver examples to the superb-quality gold and enamel boxes made by Parisian goldsmiths in the late eighteenth century. Also represented is the technique of *piqué* work, that is the inlaying of gold and silver into malleable materials, such as tortoiseshell or ivory, practised throughout Europe from the seventeenth to the nineteenth centuries.

A speciality of the Department is its collection of material illustrating the history of heraldry and seals. The department holds the main national collection of seal dies (or 'matrices') from the late Saxon period to the early twentieth century, and considerable collections of French, German and Italian seal matrices. The collection of wax seal impressions as applied to documents is in the Department of Manuscripts in the

165 ABOVE *The Portland Font. The 22-carat gold font with figures of Faith, Hope and Charity, was designed in the neo-classical style by Humphrey Repton and made in the London workshop of Paul Storr, 1797–8.* W *(pedestal) 34.9cm.*

British Library. From the medieval period the seal matrices include seals connected with trade and administration, such as customs seals, seals for the delivery of wool and hides, wool staple seals, and seals of officials. A wide variety of seals for medieval ecclesiastical officials and institutions are joined by those of guilds and fraternities. The great seal matrices of the medieval kings do not survive, and from Tudor times

166 *The seal matrix of Richard, Duke of Gloucester (later King Richard* III*) as Admiral of England for Dorset and Somerset. The matrix is engraved with a single masted ship, the mainsail bearing the Duke's arms.* AD 1462. D 7.55cm.

the seals of state were often melted down and made into presentation plate, such as the sixteenth-century 'Bacon cups', one of which is in the Museum. The earliest surviving great seal of an English king here is that of William IV, dated 1831. The collection includes an extensive series of colonial seals and many personal seals, some with coats of arms. A signet ring of the sixteenth century once belonged to Mary Queen of Scots. Other highlights of the heraldic series are Tudor stall plates of the Order of the Garter made for St George's Chapel, Windsor, and a lavish set of Garter insignia made of enamelled gold and jewels, commissioned by the Earl of Northampton in 1628.

The most comprehensive area of the Department's holdings is its collection of ceramics, illustrating the history of firing, glazing and decorative techniques in Western Europe up to recent times. From medieval times earthenwares coated with lead glaze were made throughout Europe, largely for domestic use. Pieces decorated with slip (liquid clay) include posset-pots, loving cups and mugs, principally made in the London area, Wrotham (Kent), Staffordshire and Sussex. During the eighteenth century the making of pottery in Staffordshire became progressively more industrialised. This phase of production is represented by eighteenth-century green- and yellow-glazed earthenwares made by Thomas Whieldon in partnership with Josiah Wedgwood, cream-coloured earthenwares, one of Wedgwood's greatest successes, and pearlwares.

The lead-glazed wares from Continental Europe are often ornamental in character. A group of pieces with bizarre, naturalistically modelled ornament, including shells and sea creatures, decorated with coloured glazes, demonstrates the skill of France's most revered potter, Bernard Palissy. Lead glazes coloured with metal oxides were also used in sixteenth-century Germany in the manufacture of stove tiles moulded in high relief with figure scenes. The technique of scratching through a coloured slip to reveal the colour of the body beneath was frequently used by German potters in the Rhineland and elsewhere.

Coating earthenware with an opaque white glaze containing tin provided a good surface for painting. Tin-glazed earthenwares made in Spain, above all in the Valencia region (eastern Spain), in the fifteenth century inherited an Islamic tradition, and the lustred pottery of Valencia was exported all over Europe. The Museum's collection of Valencian lustreware is one of the world's richest.

168 *Slipware dish by Thomas Toft, Staffordshire, of about 1670. The red clay dish, probably intended to stand on a dresser, is covered with white slip. The design of the Pelican in her Piety is trailed in red-brown and dark-brown slip.* D 44cm.

The pictorial potential of tin-glazed pottery was developed above all in Italy, and the brilliantly coloured maiolica dishes of centres like Faenza and Urbino were painted like pictures with overall narrative scenes, using a wealth of classical, biblical and contemporary subjects. The Museum's collection is virtually unrivalled in its series of pieces with dates and artists' signatures, key documents in the history of this art. The techniques of Italian maiolica were taken abroad in the sixteenth century by emigrant craftsmen, who helped establish native traditions of tin-glazed pottery in France, the Low Countries, England and elsewhere. Tin-glazed pottery was produced in England from the sixteenth century, and by the seventeenth century it was in common use for drug and ointment pots, bottles, dishes and mugs, many decorated in blue in the Chinese style. The tradition continued, and a large bowl inscribed *Clay got over the Primate's Coals Dublin 1753* shows that tin-glazed ware was made in Ireland too. Tin-glazed jugs and dishes from German pottery centres include skilfully painted examples by the late seventeenth-century Nuremberg artists Wolf Rössler and Johann Schaper. The collection also includes seventeenth- to nineteenth-century French, Spanish, Portuguese and East European tin-glazed wares, as well as Dutch Delftwares. The tin-glazed tradition in England and on the Continent was virtually destroyed by the new industrial wares of eighteenth-century Staffordshire.

By the fifteenth century a new type of high-fired

167 *Lustred pottery vase, made in Valencia, Spain, about 1465–75. It bears the arms of the Medici family and was probably made for Piero 'the Gouty' or his son Lorenzo the Magnificent, successive rulers of Florence.* H 57cm.

pottery, stoneware, had been developed in the Rhineland, and fragments of fifteenth-century stoneware excavated at Savignies show that the technology also existed in France. The Department's comprehensive collection of German salt-glazed stoneware comprises more than two hundred pieces from all over Germany. Stonewares were produced in England and the Low Countries from the seventeenth century. In the 1670s John Dwight, from his Fulham pottery, was producing fine greyish or whitish stonewares, some of which were as translucent as porcelains. Amongst the examples of Dwight's superlative sculptural work are a monumental bust of Prince Rupert (1619–82) and small-scale figures of mythological subjects, such as Mars, Meleager and Flora.

In the late eighteenth century the Staffordshire potter Josiah Wedgwood produced new varieties of unglazed stoneware which enjoyed notable success, in particular his jasper ware, a fine white stoneware,

169 Jasper ware vase and cover known as the Pegasus Vase from the figure of the flying horse on the cover. Made at Josiah Wedgwood's factory, Etruria, Staffordshire, and presented by him in 1786. H 46cm.

frequently tinted blue. Among the Museum's examples of jasper ware is the Pegasus Vase, presented by Wedgwood himself in 1786 and considered by him to be his finest vase, and blue and black jasper copies of the Roman cameo glass Portland Vase.

Porcelain, a hard translucent ceramic material first manufactured by the Chinese, was greatly admired by European potters, who attempted to imitate it. The earliest known examples of the so-called 'artificial' type (soft-paste) were made in Florence around 1575–87, with underglaze blue decoration directly copying Chinese porcelain. The British Museum has four examples of this very rare ware. France was next to produce porcelain, which was certainly made at St Cloud near Paris in the early eighteenth century. True porcelain containing china clay and china stone was first made at Dresden around 1710, when Friedrich Böttger discovered the secret of its manufacture. The Department has a fine series of Continental porcelain, including Meissen baroque figures and Sèvres rococo porcelains.

The collections of eighteenth-century porcelain show the development of the new material in England. From the earliest established concern at Bow, London, comes the famous mongrammed bowl, housed in a wooden box with a manuscript note, dated 1790, on the history of the factory by the china-painter Thomas Craft. A white figure of a sleeping child inscribed JUNE YE 26 1746 is the earliest known dated figure from the Chelsea factory. A group of over one hundred Chelsea 'toys' – scent-bottles, buckles and seals – includes many rarities. A magnificent pair of blue-ground porcelain vases made at the Chelsea factory during the 1760s are painted with scenes connected with the death of Cleopatra and exotic birds.

A group of late eighteenth-century unglazed Derby figures includes some, such as the 'Russian shepherd' group, which are otherwise unknown. The collection also contains several hundred pieces, both painted and transfer-printed, from the Worcester factory, as well as porcelain from almost every other eighteenth-century concern. The small group of nineteenth- and twentieth-century English porcelain is now being supplemented by acquisitions on a systematic basis.

The Museum's collection of Western European glass ranks among the best in the world. Pride of place goes to the Venetian glass of the fifteenth to eighteenth centuries, with hundreds of examples illustrating the whole range of decorative techniques. Glass from Ger-

170 RIGHT Soft-paste porcelain vase painted with Roman soldiers attacking Cleopatra. Made at the Chelsea porcelain factory, London, about 1762. With its pair, this is the earliest piece of 'modern' ceramics to enter the Museum. Both were presented in 1763 only ten years after its foundation. H 50cm.

171 LEFT *Enamelled silver-gilt bowl, the central medallion painted with two swans, the sides with flowers, birds and portraits on a white ground. Made in Solvychegodsk, Northern Russia, late seventeenth century.* D 20.5 cm.

many, where there were important advances in wheel-engraving and colouring of the glass itself, as well as from Spain, France, Bohemia and Holland, includes numbers of signed or dated items from the most re-nowned glass-houses. Two jugs in the Venetian style have London-made silver mounts and may have been made by Venetian craftsmen in London in the 1540s. A serving bottle bearing the seal used by George Ravens-croft (*c.* 1680) is a remarkable example of the earliest lead glass made in England.

Over two hundred hand-painted enamels of mytho-logical and biblical subjects made in Limoges, France, in the sixteenth century represent the art of working coloured glassy substances on copper. Examples of this technique in eighteenth-century England, notably from Staffordshire and London, demonstrate its popularity. A number of enamels with printed subjects of a ma-sonic or historical character complete the collection, famous for its signed and dated pieces.

Among the Department's huge and varied collec-tions are smaller areas of more special interest. One such speciality is the collection of objects belonging to famous people. In addition to those already discussed are a casket made in 1769 for the actor David Garrick of wood from the mulberry tree in Shakespeare's garden, and a punch-bowl of Inverary marble made for the Scottish poet Robert Burns in 1788. Alongside such curiosities are a gold watch owned by the composer Handel, two gold rings of the poets Elizabeth Barrett Browning and Robert Browning, and a gold box bequeathed by Napoleon to Lady Holland in 1821.

The core of the Department's collection of eight-eenth-century portrait sculpture is an unparalleled group of plaster and terracotta models from Roubiliac's studio purchased soon after the sculptor's death in 1759. A series of portrait busts from the eighteenth to the twentieth century represents people connected with the British Museum, such as the terracotta bust by Rysbrack of the Museum's founder, Sir Hans Sloane.

The British Museum houses the national collection of engraved gems, and the Department has over a thousand intaglios and cameos from about AD 400 to about 1900. Among the cameo carvings of the Renaiss-ance is a remarkable Italian onyx cameo of 1520-30,

173 *Glass goblet, enamelled with the portraits of a man and a woman and the motto* AMOR. VOL. FEE *(love requires faith). Perhaps a betrothal gift. Venetian, about 1480-1500.* H 22.3 cm.

carved with Hercules on one side and Omphale on the other. Engraved gems of the sixteenth and seventeenth centuries are often anonymous, unlike those of the eighteenth and nineteenth centuries, when the taste for cameos and intaglios reflected the influence of the classical world and engravers tended to sign their names after the antique. The collection is rich in works of the great European neo-classical masters – Mar-chant, Burch, the Pichler family, Morelli, Berini, Pistrucci, Girometti, Hecker, Lebas and the Saulini

172 *Pair of hard-paste porcelain busts of children modelled by Franz Anton Bustelli about 1760-1 and made at the Nymphenburg factory, Bavaria. Bustelli is considered one of the greatest porcelain modellers in the rococo style.* H 24.8 cm.

174 *Life-size marble statue of William Shakespeare by Louis-François Roubiliac; made in 1758 for the actor David Garrick (1717–79), who placed it in a Temple of Shakespeare in his garden, and left it to the Museum in his will.*

Cameos and intaglios were often set into boxes and other precious objects or mounted in jewellery.

The Hull Grundy Gift of over 1,200 pieces of jewellery, engraved gems and goldsmiths' work has extended the Department's already rich collection of post-medieval jewellery into the twentieth century, and illustrates European and American taste in jewellery, from opulent eighteenth-century diamond ornaments to Victorian naturalistic 'message jewellery' in the form of flowers and plants, each with sentimental significance. The collection is especially noted for its nineteenth-century revivalist jewellery, such as the gold and gem-set medieval-style cross designed about 1860 by the architect William Burges, or the minutely detailed gold granulation work carried out by the Castellani workshop in Rome and Naples in imitation of Etruscan jewellery. Alongside these artistic jewels are examples of mass-produced industrial jewellery made in Birmingham at the end of the nineteenth century. The curvilinear Art Nouveau style fashionable at the turn of the century is represented by pieces from the major Parisian firms designed by notable European sculptors and medallists, and some astonishingly delicate pieces by Réné Lalique with *plique-à-jour* or open-back enamelling.

The Department's collections have recently been extended into the twentieth century, to illustrate the development of the international modern movement. Nineteenth-century eclecticism can be seen in the work of two Gothic Revival architects, A. W. N. Pugin and William Burges, while the applied arts designed by Christopher Dresser look not only to the past, but to other contemporary cultures, such as Japan. The collections also encompass the many avant-garde applied arts movements of the turn of the century in Europe and America, from the Art Nouveau style of the Belgian architect Henri van de Velde to the rectilinear geometric style of the American architect Frank Lloyd Wright, whose copper vase designed for his own studio in Chicago is a rare example of his small-scale metalwork. In addition, the British Museum holds the most comprehensive collection outside Germany of German applied arts of the period 1890 to 1930, culminating in the achievements of the Bauhaus school, where Marianne Brandt's constructivist tea-pot of 1924 was made. The 1920s and 1930s elsewhere in Europe are

family. Intaglio gems, often used as sealstones, are usually carved from a stone of one colour, the subject engraved in reverse below the surface. Cameos are carved in relief, with the subject silhouetted against a ground of a different colour. The skill of the cameo engraver lies in exploiting the different layers; a spectacular example of unparalleled virtuosity is the cameo carved in 1830 by Domenico Calabresi of Rome in an agate of seven layers showing Vulcan casting his net over Mars and Venus, in which the upper layer forming the net has been undercut to reveal the scene below.

175 *Nineteenth-century gold and enamel jewellery set with hardstones or mosaics: a) Italian plasma cameo of Medusa; b) miniature glass mosaic with Greek inscription 'Bravo', made by the Castellani firm, Rome; c) agate cameo engraved in England by Benedetto Pistucci; d) onyx cameo engraved in Milan by Antonio Berini; e) hardstone mosaic or* pietra dura, *Florence. From the Hull Grundy Gift, except a (top). w (b) 5.4cm.*

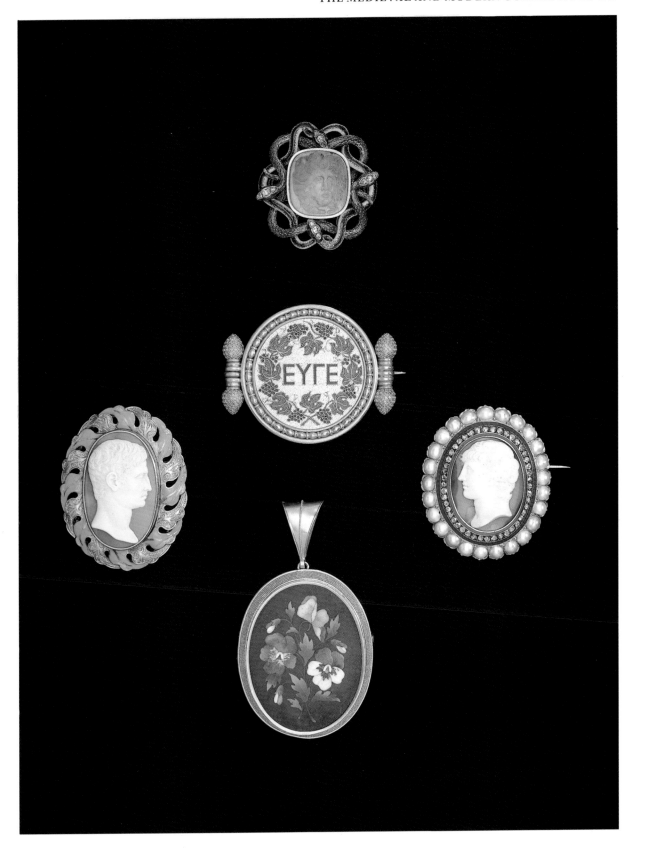

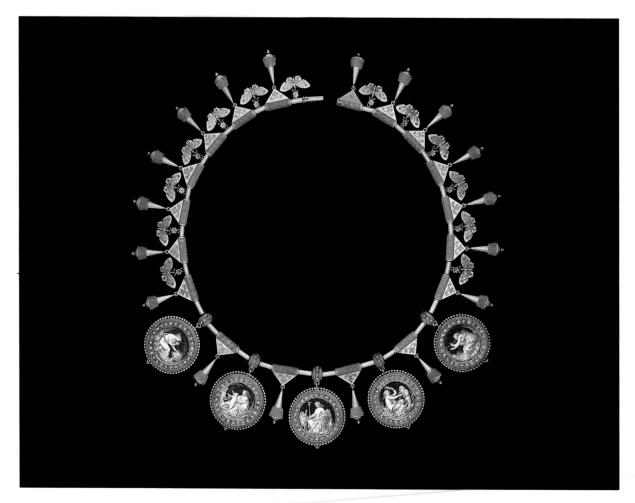

176 ABOVE *Gold and diamond necklace, made up of elements derived from jewellery of the classical world. The medallions were inspired by the Roman wall-paintings at Pompeii and painted by Eugène Richet. Made by the firm of Eugène Fontenay, Paris, about 1870. From the Hull Grundy Gift.* D *(central pendant) 2.95cm.*

177 BELOW *Silver tea-infuser with an ebony handle and knop. Designed in 1924 by Marianne Brandt and handmade at the Bauhaus school of design in Germany between 1924 and 1932.* H *7cm.*

also represented, while notable recent acquisitions include examples of Soviet porcelain decorated in the early years of the Revolution in the style of the Suprematist movement.

CLOCKS, WATCHES AND SCIENTIFIC INSTRUMENTS

The Museum houses what is probably the most comprehensive horological collection in the world. The earliest clocks in the Museum date from the sixteenth century. Thereafter both weight-driven and spring-driven clocks from the main European centres of clock-making are represented. While the Museum does not possess an early turret clock, the Cassiobury Park clock made about 1620 displays many of the features found in those of the fourteenth century. Particularly fine

178 *Year-going table-clock with quarter repeat by Thomas Tompion, London (c. 1690). Commissioned for William III and Queen Mary in 1689, the year of the coronation, this is the earliest known spring-driven pendulum clock to go for one year at a winding.* H *71 cm.*

examples from the late sixteenth century are the fascinating 'nef' table clock/automaton of about 1580 made by Hans Schlottheim, and the magnificent carillon clock by Isaac Habrecht made in 1589. Standing over 1.5m in height, this domestic version of Habrecht's great astronomical clock in Strasbourg Cathedral is an impressive combination of Renaissance decoration and mechanical virtuosity. There were few clockmakers in England in the sixteenth century but Nicholas Vallin's carillon clock of 1598, which plays musical quarter chimes on 13 bells, is a fine example of their high-quality work.

Probably the most fundamental and important advance towards accurate time-keeping was the application of the pendulum to clockwork by Christiaan Huygens in 1657. Clockmakers were quick to adopt this innovation and in England the wooden cased table clock with pendulum soon became common. Of the Museum's many examples perhaps the most outstanding is the 'Mostyn' year-going table clock by Thomas Tompion. Made for William III in about 1689, this clock is a prime example of Tompion's mechanical genius and also displays some of the finest silver and ormolu decoration of the period.

With the introduction of the pendulum in England came the beginning of a new design in clocks – the long-case clock. This basic design, introduced in the 1660s by Fromanteel and other leading London makers, was to last for almost two centuries. The Museum collections contain long-case clocks from the earliest period to the nineteenth century, including examples by Fromanteel and Knibb, the famous 'mulberry' clock by Tompion and a magnificent year-going equation clock by Daniel Quare. The Museum also possesses one of a

179 *Silver watches with* piqué *outer cases: (left) made shortly before 1675 by Charles Gretton, London: seconds dial on the back of the movement; (right) by Thomas Tompion, London (c. 1688): dial with subsidiary seconds.* D *(left) 5.2cm.*

178

180 *Astronomical compendium by Johann Anton Londen, Heilbronn (1596), made for Christoph Leibfried of Würzburg. The compendium contains a range of instruments for astronomical, astrological and calendrical purposes.* H 12.6cm.

series of vast astronomical long-case clocks by Edward Cockey of Warminster of about 1760.

The age of precision had its origins in the late seventeenth century when the Royal Observatory, Greenwich, was built. In the Great Room of the Observatory were three regulators by Thomas Tompion, one of which, made for Sir Jonas Moore in 1676, survives in the collections. Precision 'regulators' with maintaining power and temperature compensation became an essential tool for scientists and astronomers in the eighteenth century and the Museum has a fine example by George Graham with dead-beat escapement and mercurial compensation pendulum.

The successful sea trials of John Harrison's marine time-keeper in 1761 proved that a sea-going chronometer could be used to establish longtitude at sea. Harrison's pioneering work was later improved upon by Thomas Mudge, John Arnold and Thomas Earnshaw and examples of their work as well as that of the leading

Continental makers can be found amongst the Museum's forty or so marine chronometers.

The Department's collection of over 2,500 watches comprehensively covers every aspect of the history and development of the watch as a portable time-keeper. It is probably the finest collection in the world, extending from examples of the German stackfreed watches of the mid-sixteenth century to the advent of quartz technology in the modern age. All the leading watchmakers are represented and, while the collection is perhaps oriented towards the mechanical aspects of watchmaking, it is also rich in fine examples of the casemaker's and jeweller's art.

The collection of European scientific instruments, although small, covers a wide variety of areas. It includes instruments for measuring time, such as sundials, quadrants and nocturnals from the medieval period to the twentieth century, instruments for mathematics, astronomy, surveying, and so on. Many of the well-known makers are represented in the collection, including a number of instruments by Humphrey Cole, astrolabes by Vulparia, Hartman and Volkmer and sundials by Charles Whitewell, Erasmus Habermel and Hans Tucher.

THE ORIENTAL
COLLECTIONS

The Oriental collections of the British Museum are divided between the Departments of Ethnography, Japanese Antiquities and Oriental Antiquities. The Oriental Department deals with the cultures of Asia from the Neolithic period to the twentieth century, with the exception of Japan, and Iran and the Near East before the Arab conquests. Its vast geographical span thus stretches from North Africa to Korea, and includes the islands of South-East Asia. Unlike the Department of Ethnography, many of whose collections cover the same geographical area, it has tended to concentrate on urban, rather than traditional rural societies. The collections in the Department of Japanese Antiquities range in date from the third millennium BC to the present day.

181 *Brass pen-box decorated with astrological figures in roundels on a ground of animal interlace, and inlaid with silver and gold. The signature of the craftsman Mahmud ibn Sunqur and the date* AH 680 (AD 1281) *appear beneath the clasp.* L 19.7cm.

CHINA

The earliest Chinese artefacts in the British Museum date from the Neolithic period. Finds from Banpo, an important western site near Xi'an dating to about 4500 BC, belong to the Yangshao culture and illustrate the beginnings of the fine painted pottery that characterises many of the western Neolithic cultures. Early pottery from south-eastern China, whose lobed and articulated shapes influenced later bronze vessels, is not represented in the collection. However, there are fine examples of stone and jade tools, discs, and tall tubes known as *cong*, made by the peoples of the later Liang-zhu culture (*c.* 2500 BC), which display the skill of early Chinese jade-carving. Face designs on the *cong* were the starting point for zoomorphic motifs which form such a fundamental element of bronze ornament.

Cast-bronze vessels appear in China with little metallurgical precedent. The simplest are found at Erlitou, a site after which the first major phase of

182 *Bronze* zun, *a container, presumably for wine. The two rams are naturalistic and thus quite different from animals on metropolitan bronzes, which are more two-dimensional and usually imaginary. It probably comes from south China. Shang dynasty (*c. 1700–1050* BC). H *43.2cm.*

casting is named. The second phase is known as Erligang, the name of a site at Zhengzhou in Henan. This has been identified as one of the capitals of the Shang (*c.* 1700–*c.* 1050 BC), the first ruling house or dynasty for whose existence there is incontrovertible evidence. Unlike most other ancient bronze-workers, the Chinese used cast bronze rather than wrought metal to make vessels which were used to offer food and wine to ancestors. Ornament on these bronzes comprised monsters, animals and geometric motifs organised within units determined by casting techniques.

The last of the Shang kings was overthrown in the eleventh century BC by the Zhou peoples of northwestern China. Before their conquest of the Shang, the Zhou (*c.* 1050–221 BC) had already adopted Shang ritual practices and their ritual vessels, and so there is no very clear distinction between late Shang and early Zhou bronzes. By the last quarter of the eleventh century, however, a Zhou style of bronze vessels had emerged, which is well illustrated by a bronze vessel in the British Museum's collection called the Kang Hou *gui*. The *gui* bears a highly important inscription recording the enfeoffment of the Marquis of Kang as a reward for his part played in quelling Shang insurrection. Major changes in ritual practice seem to have taken place rather more than a century later, with numbers of vessel types being much reduced at that time. Decoration also changed, with sweeping wave designs dominating large vessels, as may be seen on the Museum's Shi Wang *hu*. The designs of the early Zhou period contracted into a dense geometric interlace during the Eastern Zhou. From the eighth century BC China was divided into many small states, of which the major seven were constantly engaged in warfare. One of

these states was the southern state of Chu, whose working of lacquer, silk and wood contributed new motifs and styles to bronze art. Beliefs in protective spirits is illustrated in the art of Chu by an antlered wood sculpture in the British Museum.

Qin Shihuangdi, the first Emperor of China, united the former Zhou states under one rule in 221 BC. His awesome power is reflected in his burial mound and the nearby pits containing the magnificent army of thousands of life-size terracotta warriors, which were discovered in 1974. Qin Shihuangdi's unpopularity led, however, to the overthrow of his dynasty. It was followed by the Han dynasty (206 BC–AD 220), a time of the restoration of Confucian values, military expansionism and the beginning of the system of recruiting officials by examination. The philosophy of Daoism was formulated at this time, with its emphasis on everlasting life and its portrayal of immortals in paradise. The Queen Mother of the West, who ruled over the Daoist paradise, is often portrayed in art of the Han, as are Dong Fang Gong (the Lord of the East), the animals of the four directions and the sun and moon.

Chamber tombs replaced earlier simple shafts and were decorated with wall-paintings, stone friezes or moulded bricks, as if to create a dwelling-place for the person's afterlife. Burial objects changed too, with

183 The Admonitions of the Instructress to Court Ladies. *Eighth-century copy in ink and colours on silk of a handscroll attributed to Gu Kaizhi (*c. AD 344–405*), with illustrations to a text by Zhang Hua (AD 232–309) on correct behaviour of imperial concubines.* H 25cm.

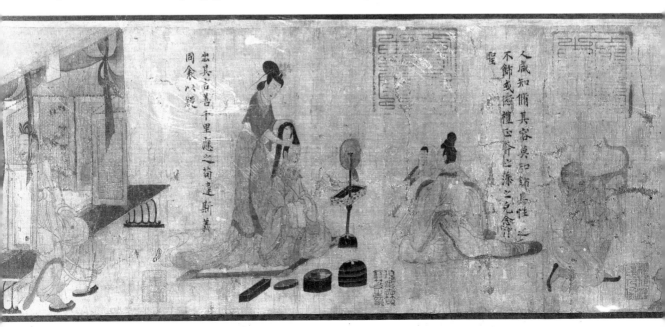

ceramics, lacquer and silk replacing bronzes. Burial suits were made of jade, thought erroneously to preserve the body. The Museum's set of glass plaques would have had the same function.

There was also a lively portrayal of the mundane activities of everyday life in the tomb figures of the Han dynasty, which were made in low-fired lead-glazed earthenware, as opposed to the high-fired ceramics with a greenish lime-based ash glaze, which had been used for high-quality vessels from the Shang period. During the Six Dynasties period (AD 220–589) the manufacture of fine high-fired, green-glazed stoneware flourished in south-east China. Known today as Yue wares, these ceramics were made in the shapes of toads and lions, imitating small bronzes, and were also used for teabowls and tall funerary vases with small figures and houses modelled on the top.

The British Museum's most important painting is a Tang dynasty copy of a handscroll by the early figure-painter Gu Kaizhi (b. AD 345). It is called *Admonitions of the Instructress to Court Ladies* and illustrates advice on correct behaviour given to ladies in the Imperial harem by the court preceptress. The painting is in ink and colour, mainly vermilion, on silk. The fine-line drawing and the floating draperies show courtly figure painting of the time.

The division of the country into many small kingdoms, some ruled by foreigners, allowed Buddhism to be assimilated into Chinese culture. In the north large complexes of caves containing enormous Buddhist sculptures were created, particularly under the Northern Wei (AD 386–535) and Northern Qi (AD 550–77) dynasties. A number of stone sculptures and small gilt bronzes date from these periods. The massive figure of the white marble Amitābha Buddha is dated AD 585. It was produced under the Sui dynasty (AD 581–618), who unified the former small kingdoms under one ruling house.

The capital of China under the Tang dynasty (AD 618–906) was Chang'an, meaning 'long peace' (present-day Xi'an). Chang'an was the most civilised and cosmopolitan city in the world and stood at the eastern end of the Silk Route. It was a centre for trade in exotic goods from Central Asia and the Near East. The influence of Central Asia and of Sassanian Iran can be seen on Tang silver, jewellery and ceramics, many examples of which have survived in tomb deposits. 'Three-colour' ceramic lead-glazed tomb figures of camels and horses, foreigners and dancing girls, with their vivid splashed colours, served the deceased after death. Fierce guardian figures reflected Buddhist influence, which fluctuated during the Tang according to the religious inclinations of different emperors. The earliest true porcelain dates from the Tang, although it was solid and heavy, unlike European preconceptions of porcelain, derived from much later wares.

A large collection of paintings and other antiquities from sites in Chinese Central Asia was acquired for the British Museum by Aurel Stein. Stein led three expeditions to Central Asia between 1900 and 1915. The antiquities he collected mostly date from the Tang and Five Dynasties period (AD 618–960).

The paintings were found in cave 17 at Dunhuang and range from large works on silk and paper to sutra illustrations in handscrolls and books. They are valuable sources for the history of Chinese figure painting and architecture, and contain some fine examples of early landscape painting in the scenes of the life of the Buddha. Terracottas and architectural fragments show an interesting mixture of cultures, with influences from Greece, Gandhara, the Near East and China.

After the Tang dynasty the Central Asian domains came under the control of Tibet, while in northern China the Khitan tribes seized control and took the title of Liao dynasty (AD 907–1125). Under the Liao fine porcelains, similar to famous Ding wares of the Northern Song, and green-glazed low-fired wares in the style of the Tang dynasty were produced. The nomadic origins of the Khitan are reflected in the shapes of their pots, some of which were based on the leather bags which would have been slung on horse's saddles. A figure in green, brown and buff glazed ceramic from this period showing a seated Buddhist holy man is one of the British Museum's most compelling Chinese sculptures.

The classic ceramic wares of the Song dynasty are famous for their subtle glazes and elegant shapes. In the Northern Song (AD 960–1127), when the capital was at Kaifeng, stonewares and porcelains, such as Northern Celadons, Ding, Jun and Ru were produced. Many of these were offered at court as tribute for the first time. Both white Ding wares and the olive green Northern Celadons were decorated with incised and carved motifs of flowers, waves and children at play. As ceramics came to be produced in greater quantities, moulded decoration was introduced. Apart from the refined porcelains and stonewares of court taste, there was also a tradition of boldly decorated coarser stonewares for popular use, called Cizhou wares. A fine example of these wares is a pillow decorated with a dancing bear in the Museum's collection.

The Song period was a time of great achievement in painting, and court patronage played an important role in establishing the taste that dominated later generations. The Museum possesses only copies of the classic landscape painting of the Song, but it does have an important handscroll attributed to the Southern Song figure painter, Ma Hezhi (fl. c. AD 1130–70), entitled the *Odes of Chen*. Several fine wooden sculptures illustrate the graceful style that the Song had inherited from the Tang.

The development of appreciation of Chinese art has

185 ABOVE *Seated Lohan of lead-glazed earthenware. From a set of sixteen or eighteen Lohans in the Yizhou caves in Hebei province, which are so individually modelled that they have been considered as portraits of individual monks. The influence of Tang 'three-colour' ware can be seen in the brilliant glazes. H 1.03m.*

184 LEFT *Avalokiteśvara. Painting in ink and colours on silk. From Dunhuang. Five Dynasties, but dated tenth year of Tianfu (the penultimate reign of Tang AD 910). 77 × 48.9cm.*

much to do with the history of collecting in China. From as early as the Han dynasty ancient bronzes were discovered by chance and accorded respect, often being interpreted as omens. Possession of such bronzes was indeed regarded as evidence of the legitimacy of a dynasty. Emperors were just as eager to obtain calligraphy of renowned masters, whose famous works were treated almost as talismans. From such origins emerged the great art collections of the Song period, whose principal components were bronzes, calligraphy and painting. The famous collector Emperor Song Huizong had a catalogue of his treasures made that can still be consulted today. Calligraphy was particularly treasured, and the southern tradition with its flowing lines and elegant brush-strokes, as practised by the master calligrapher Wang Xizhi (AD 306–65), was

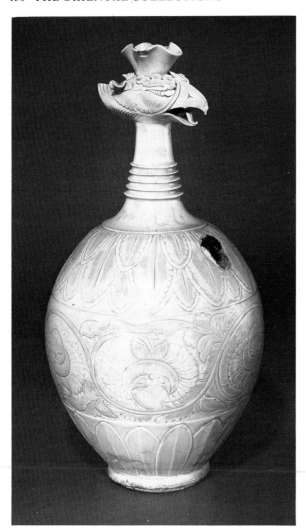

186 ABOVE *Phoenix-head ewer of white porcelain. The influence of metalwork can be seen in the rings around the neck, the punched decoration and the phoenix's head. The greenish tinge in the glaze suggests a southern origin. Eleventh century AD. H 39.8cm.*

In 1280 the Mongols under Khubilai Khan conquered both the Jurchen (who had succeeded the Liao) in the north and the Southern Song, setting up the capital of the Yuan dynasty (AD 1260–1368) in Peking. There was much mercantile contact with Central Asia and the Near East, which led to the development of new styles and techniques. The many Arab communities in the ports of the south-east coast stimulated the use of cobalt 'Persian blue', which was used on underglaze painted porcelain at Jingdezhen, the important ceramic centre in central south-east China. The dense and decorative style, with fish, dragons, figures and landscapes, was influenced by metalwork, textiles and

187 BELOW *Large porcelain flask with peony scrolls in underglaze cobalt blue. Peony and lotus scrolls are a favourite design on Chinese ceramics and on applied art originating in Western architectural ornament. Jingdezhn ware, Ming dynasty, Xuande period (AD 1426–35). H 51.2cm.*

adopted as the classic style, as opposed to the more regular and angular northern style, which derived from stone inscriptions.

Ceramics of the Southern Song (AD 1137–1279), such as Longquan celadons with a milky-green glaze and Guan wares with their finely controlled crackle glazes, were made in the shapes of ancient bronzes, which would have been known from the catalogues of bronze shapes which scholars started to compile during this period. The tradition of archaism continued for centuries. Black teabowls of Jizhou and Jian made in the Southern Song were particularly prized in Japan and were taken home by visiting Zen monks.

woodblock prints, elaborating the patterns used by the Song and the Jin. Cizhou stonewares continued to be made, as did Longquan celadons. Both the celadons and the underglaze blue porcelain were very popular in the Near East and South-East Asia, where they are found in great quantities.

The native Chinese Ming dynasty overthrew the Mongols in 1368. Decoration on underglaze blue porcelain reached its high point in the fifteenth century, particularly under the Xuande (AD 1426–35) and Chenghua (AD 1465–87) emperors. The elegant designs can be directly related to the academy-style bird and flower painting of the time. Some of the Museum's best Yuan and early Ming pieces come from the John Addis Bequest. Interesting copies of Islamic metalwork shapes were also made at this time. Painting in overglaze enamels was introduced in the late fifteenth century, at first in combination with underglaze blue. The reign of the Wanli emperor (AD 1573–1619) was a period of particularly vigorous designs. Many of the

later Ming wares were exported to South-East Asia, the Near East, Africa and Japan, even reaching the West. They can often be seen in Dutch still-life paintings of the period.

The Ming dynasty was also a time of development and refinement in the manufacture of lacquer and cloisonné enamels. In earlier periods lacquer had been embellished with painting or used for inlay in mother-of-pearl and gold and silver foil and wire. The Yuan had introduced the technique of carving through the many different layers of lacquer. This art was perfected in the Ming, with carved decoration of landscapes, flowers of the four seasons, dragons and lions, which was shared with that on metalwork and on porcelains of

188 *Large cloisonné foliate dish with dragon design, dating from the Wanli period (AD 1573–1619). This shows the vigorous and lively nature of Wanli design, which can also be seen on ceramics of the same period.* D 50cm.

the period. In the sixteenth century polychrome carved lacquer became popular, as did inlaid lacquer and the practice of incising a design and then gilding. These methods were introduced to the Ryūkyū Islands, where they were highly developed. The art of cloisonné enamelling, used for decorating copper vessels, was introduced from the West and also reached a high point in the fifteenth century. In this technique the enamels are contained within small cells, or 'cloisons' and so prevented from running into each other. Related to these enamels are the *fahua* ceramics, which have designs painted in glazes, also separated by 'cloisons' of applied clay. Their brilliant colours on a dark-blue or turquoise ground are particularly distinctive. Buddhist sculpture of the period was influenced by Tibetan taste and several striking bronzes in this style are in the collection.

Under the foreign Mongol dynasty scholars had withdrawn into exile away from court, devoting themselves to calligraphy and painting. Zhao Mengfu alone of the great artists had continued to serve this court. By the Ming dynasty a tradition of literati painting had become established by educated men, who based their painting on the style of landscape masters from the Five Dynasties, Song and Yuan dynasties.

The Museum's collection of Ming paintings includes works by the literati painters of the *Wu* school, Wen Zhengming (AD 1470–1559) and Dong Qichang (AD 1555–1636). In parallel a group of painters from the Zhe school revitalised the style of Southern Song Academy. The Museum has fine examples of these works from the fifteenth and sixteenth centuries.

When the Manchus defeated the Ming in 1644 to set up the Qing dynasty (AD 1644–1911), certain Ming loyalists such as Kuncan (2nd half of the 17th century) developed their own style, which was based on the Ming scholar-amateur tradition. The Museum has two superb album leaves by Kuncan, which are dated 1666 and depict autumn and winter. He was one of a group of highly eccentric painters who became Buddhist monks. Zhu Da (AD 1625–c. 1705) and Daoji (AD 1641–c. 1717) were other such painters, who worked more directly from nature than many of their predecessors. Their brush-strokes were unorthodox, and Daoji stressed the importance of the 'single brush-stroke'. The more orthodox landscape style, seen in the paintings of the 'Four Wangs', was based on the writings of Dong Qichang and the celebrated Four Masters of the Yuan dynasty. The Yangzhou individualists are also represented in the Museum collections by a set of fan paintings by Gao Fenghan (AD 1683–1749) and a scroll by Luo Ping (AD 1733–99).

The reigns of the Kangxi (AD 1662–1722), Yongzheng (AD 1723–35) and Qianlong (AD 1736–95) emperors were times of particularly strong government, and the court could command high standards of workmanship. Overglaze enamels in the *famille verte* palette are characteristic of the Kangxi period, while the pink derived from colloidal gold was introduced by Jesuits at

189 Autumn. *Album leaf mounted in handscroll form, painted in ink and colours on paper by Kuncan (fl. c. AD 1650–75). Kuncan was a native of Hunan province who entered a Chan Buddhist order. He was an individualist painter, remarkable for the dryness of his brushwork. 31.4 × 64.1cm.*

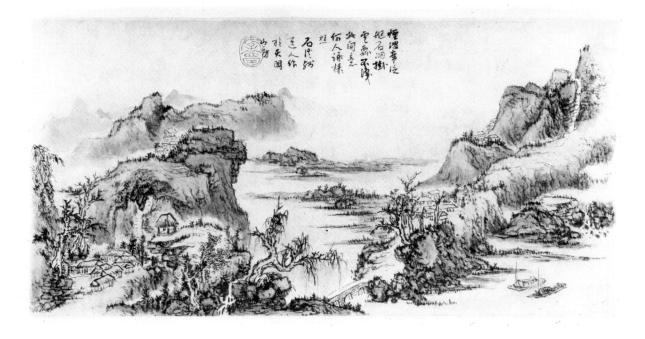

190 *Porcelain bowl decorated in* famille rose *enamels with narcissi, bamboo and fungus among rocks. The delicate overglaze painting is in Chinese taste whereas the heavier crowded decoration on some* famille rose *wares was for the Western market. Qing dynasty, Yongzheng period (AD 1723–35).* H 6.5cm.

court to produce the *famille rose* palette under Yongzheng. The ceramic complex at Jingdezhen was managed at this time by able directors and enjoyed court patronage. Innovations in monochrome glazes such as the *sang de boeuf* red, 'teadust' green, 'robin's egg' blue and many others were products of this great period of high technical quality.

While in the West the porcelains of the Ming and Qing have been prized since the fifteenth century, in China bamboo-carving, jade and other materials employed by scholars, such as ink-stones and brushes, water droppers and table screens, have been much more highly esteemed. Jade, ivory, bamboo and rhinoceros horn were all carved with exquisite precision during the Qing. The arts of lacquer and enamels continued to flourish, as did that of glass-making and miniature arts, such as snuff-bottles. There was a continuing tradition of archaism, with bronzes, ceramics and jades all being made in ancient shapes. Copies of Song dynasty celadons were of particularly high quality. The Qianlong emperor, in particular, accumulated a large collection of the finest works of art and literature from the past. Sculpture, however, was never regarded as an art in China. Figures of popular gods, Daoist immortals and literary figures in porcelain,

ivory and wood would have adorned homes and temples for worship not for appreciation.

Much of the previously high standards of workmanship and design declined during the nineteenth century. Painting continued in the styles established in earlier centuries. The painting of the four artists known as the 'Four Rens' was a development of the work of the eighteenth-century individualists. The Museum has a set of paintings of the Four Seasons by Ren Xun (dated 1835), whose bold style and elongated compositions are found in the Shanghai school of the early twentieth century epitomised by the work of Qi Baishi (1863–1957). His work is also represented in the Museum's collection, along with a growing collection of other modern painters and printmakers and representative examples of modern ceramics.

KOREA

Korea, a peninsula off north-east China, has been greatly influenced and often dominated by China, to whom she owed Buddhism and many elements of her culture. The Koreans, however, are one of the most creative peoples of Asia and an effortless grace and vitality are apparent in their earliest work.

During the Three Kingdoms period (57 BC–AD 668) the art of the northern state of Koguryŏ showed strong influence from Han dynasty China, particularly in wall-paintings in tombs. Buddhism was introduced first to Koguryŏ and later to Paekche, the kingdom in the south-west which is well known for its high-fired pottery of great technical elegance. The third kingdom, ·

191 *Sutra box with clasped lid, made of lacquer and inlaid with chrysanthemum scroll decoration in mother-of-pearl and bronze wire. From Korea, Koryŏ dynasty, thirteenth century* AD. L *47.2cm.*

Silla, in south-east Korea, produced gold-working of an astonishingly high standard, using thinly rolled gold foil and wire.

After the unification of Korea in the Great Silla period (AD 668–918) Buddhism provided the basis for a cultured society centred on the capital Kyŏngju. The Museum has four small gilt-bronze figures of the Buddha Amitābha dating from this period.

The ceramics of the Koryŏ dynasty (AD 918–1392) are perhaps the finest expression of Korean art. While stonewares with a celadon glaze show influence from Song dynasty China, a certain Korean innovation is the use of white and black slip inlaid into engraved designs under the glaze. Indeed, inlay dominated the taste of the later Koryŏ and can be seen in silver inlaid on bronze and in mother-of-pearl and silver inlaid on lacquer. The British Museum has a fine inlaid lacquer sutra box of the thirteenth century and a good collection of Koryŏ metalwork and celadons, as well as some of the *punch'ŏng* wares of the early Yi (or Chosŏn) dynasty (AD 1398–1910), which continued the tradition of inlaid ceramics, often having stamped designs filled

with slip. After the Japanese invasions in 1592–8 many of the potters moved to Japan and *punch'ŏng* wares declined, giving way to the white porcelain with its careless decoration in blue or iron-brown under the glaze, favoured by the upper classes.

One of the most important items in the Museum's Korean collection is a fine Koryŏ period manuscript of the Amitābha Sūtra, illustrated in gold and silver paint. The Museum also has a small collection of Korean paintings, including a sixteenth-century painting on silk of the white-robed Avalokiteśvara and two very large eighteenth- to nineteenth-century paintings on hemp, from a temple at Taegu, of the Buddhist guardians of the East and West.

A nineteenth-century album of scenes from everyday life after Kim Hong-do (1745–after 1814) and a set of export drawings of Korean games and pastimes by the late nineteenth-century artist Kisan give a picture of life in late Yi dynasty Korea.

THE INDIAN SUBCONTINENT

The British Museum's Indian collections are particularly strong in the rich sculptural traditions of the subcontinent, especially in the sculptures from Amaravati, the Gandhara area and medieval eastern India; the sculptures were used in the construction and decoration of temples. But the collections also include

191

arms and armour, ritual objects, textiles, jewellery, and a large collection of Tibetan banner paintings, as well as paintings from all the major Indian schools.

The oldest objects in the collections – sherds, terracottas, stone tools, and so on – date from the Neolithic, which began in the seventh millennium BC in the subcontinent. A small group of archaeological material represents the great city culture which flourished in the Indus Valley between about 2500 and 2000 BC. The three major cities of the period were Harappa, after which this civilisation is named, Mohenjo-daro and Kalibangan. Objects from this period, mostly from Mohenjo-daro, include painted pottery, terracotta figures, copper and stone tools, as well as finely carved steatite seals. From the Ganges basin to the east of the

192 *Objects from prehistoric cemeteries in the Nilgiri Hills, South India: bronze bowl, iron short sword, an earthenware funerary urn and urn lids with animal or human ornaments. About first century* BC *to* AD *500.* H *(urn with lid) 43.8cm.*

Indus Valley comes a group of copper implements and weapons of unusual forms. These distinctive objects are from the so-called 'Copper Hoard Culture' of the first millennium BC. A selection of iron implements is evidence of the introduction, around 1000 BC, of that metal to North India.

From about 1500 BC North India began to be populated by people entering the subcontinent from the north-west. They were speakers of an Indo-European

193 *The Bimaran Reliquary. Made of gold and set with garnets, this object was found inside an inscribed stone box in a stupa in Afghanistan. It depicts the Buddha, the gods Indra and Brahma and a worshipper. About first–second century* AD. H *6.7cm.*

language, the parent of Sanskrit and the modern dialects of North India. These people brought with them their religious beliefs, laid down in sacred texts known as the Vedas. In the sixth century BC two great teachers, the Buddha and Mahavira, preached the path of non-attachment to this world and the negation of all desire. The religions they founded, Buddhism and Jainism, continue to this day. The gods of the Vedas survived the growth of these religions, but were slowly superseded by the two great deities Shiva and Vishnu, and by a supreme Mother Goddess. This new complex of beliefs, Hinduism, eventually grew to become the dominant Indian religion.

In the third century North India was unified for a brief period under Ashoka (c. 269–232 BC), one of the greatest of all Indian rulers. He proclaimed his own conversion to Buddhism through inscriptions on rocks and polished pillars set up throughout his empire. These texts are the earliest examples of continuous writing in India. The collection contains a fragment of one of these pillars, which are usually associated with monasteries or stupas (solid domes set on a plinth and containing relics of the Buddha or some great saint). A stone bracket depicting a nature spirit embracing a tree comes from Sanchi, the important early group of stupas

in North India (1st century BC–1st century AD).

After the death of Ashoka North India was invaded by the Bactrian Greeks, descendants of Alexander's colonists who in the early second century BC occupied the north-western part of the subcontinent. They are best known for their magnificent portrait coins. In about 50 BC they were followed by nomadic Scythian tribes, known as Sakas, who penetrated as far as Mathura, whence comes the famous Mathura Lion capitol inscribed with the names of the Saka kings.

Under the Kushan dynasty (1st–3rd centuries AD) two principal artistic centres flourished, one in what was then called Gandhara (the north-west of Pakistan, and Afghanistan), the other at Mathura. All aspects of the Buddhist art of Gandhara are represented in the British Museum's collection, which is one of the finest in the world. Stone friezes depict vivid scenes of the main incidents of the Buddha's life and previous existences; large and small cult images in stone and stucco portray the Buddha and the other benevolent deities (Bodhisattvas); and there are two rare, standing Buddhas in bronze. The celebrated cylindrical reliquary from a stupa at Bimaran, in eastern Afghanistan is of gold, set with garnets, and is decorated with arcaded figures of the Buddha and divine attendants. The powerful influence of the Western classical world is clear in Gandharan art.

Mathuran art, serving the Buddhist, Jain and Hindu religions, is less well represented. A group of Jain heads in characteristic mottled red sandstone (2nd–3rd centuries AD) are among the most important pieces.

From the fourth to sixth centuries AD, for the second and last time in its history, the whole of North India was controlled by a native dynasty, the Guptas, who ruled from Pataliputra, the old capital of Ashoka. There were two main schools of Gupta art, one centred on Sarnath (near Banaras), the other on Mathura. Sarnath created a refined type of Buddha image of dignified spirituality which was to become the model for future Buddhist art. Two monumental Buddha figures in the British Museum, one seated and one standing, splendidly represent this style. The Mathura style, stronger and more tense, is illustrated by an exquisite bronze figure, the 'Danesar Khera' Buddha.

The break-up of the Gupta Empire in the sixth century AD led to the rise of numerous provincial dynasties. Although the Gupta heritage was common to all, it developed in the seventh to thirteenth centuries into four parallel but distinctive regional styles: western Indian (the modern states of Gujarat and Rajasthan), central Indian (the state of Madhya Pradesh), Kashmiri and eastern Indian (the states of Bihar and Bengal, together with Bangladesh).

The Museum's earliest western Indian sculpture is a beautiful Mother and Child of the seventh century AD, one of the Mother Goddesses of Hinduism. The eighth

194 *Sandstone figure of the Buddha, with hand raised in the sign signifying reassurance. He wears the close-fitting monastic garments typical of the Eastern Indian school of sculpture. Probably from Sarnath, fifth century* AD. H 1.45m.

century is represented by a powerful seated image of the elephant-headed god Ganesha. A large pillar base carved with female figures dating from the eleventh century shows the ambitious scale of the temples of this period. Many were built of white marble, also used for a large panel of a rearing lion-headed monster.

The central Indian style retained the weight and power of the Mathura school. The most notable early sculptures here, in the sandstone characteristic of the region, are a standing Shiva and a magnificent large image of the Boar incarnation of Vishnu, both of the eighth century. An important group of Jain sculptures of the Gurjara-Pratihara style are dated to about 900. As the style developed the cutting became sharper and the detail more abundant. The Chandella dynasty, associated with the well-known group of temples at Khajuraho, controlled most of central India from the tenth century. The sculptural style is lush and detailed, as seen in a headless female torso, once the property of Sir Jacob Epstein. From Dhar in Malwa comes a famous marble Sarasvati. A magnificent three-faced figure of Brahma, also from Malwa, is dated to about AD 1000.

In the art of Kashmir and the surrounding region the Gupta style was modified by influences absorbed from the earlier Gandhara school. The collection is exceptionally rich in this field. Among the many important pieces is a group of eighth-century terracotta heads from Akhnur and Ushkur. An ivory-carving of a Bodhisattva and attendants is part of a very fine miniature shrine set in a wooden frame. Other pieces include a number of excellent Hindu and Buddhist bronzes and a rich collection of stone images. The unique Kashmir Smats wood-carvings (9th–10th century AD) and two white marble sculptures of Hindu deities represent the art of the Hindu Shahi period in the region.

The chief source of the eastern Indian style was the Gupta school of Sarnath, which continued as an artistic centre after the fall of the Empire. The main patrons were the Buddhist Pala dynasty (*c.* AD 770–1050) and the Hindu Sena dynasty (*c.* AD 1050–1220). This collection is the finest outside India and Bangladesh, and contains a wide range of Hindu and Buddhist images in basalt and an outstanding selection of bronzes. Notable in the latter group is an early image of Manasa, the snake-goddess, and a superbly inlaid and decorated Balarama of the twelfth century.

The art of the Deccan is thinly represented outside India and the British Museum's collection of Buddhist stone sculpture from this area is unique in the West. The Buddhist stupa at Amaravati on the Krishna River was the most famous monument of the Satavahana dynasty, which ruled the Deccan for the first two centuries AD. The stupa, founded in the third century BC, was extensively excavated in the nineteenth century. Most of the surviving sculptures, carved in a luxuriant

naturalistic style, are now divided between the Madras Museum and the British Museum; the latter possesses over a hundred large fragments.

Other fine examples of the art of the Deccan include a fine male head from Elephanta Island in Bombay Harbour (6th–8th century AD), and a group of Buddhist bronzes from Buddhapad (7th–11th century AD). A single stone figure of Vishnu comes from the greatest rock-cut temple in India, the Kailasanatha at Ellora, built under the Rashtrakuta dynasty (AD 753–973).

195 ABOVE Krishna and the Maidens. *A fine example of the Basohli Style of painting from the Punjab Hills, from the large and comprehensive collection of Indian paintings housed at the British Museum. About* AD *1710. 19.2 × 18cm.*

196 RIGHT *Mahakala, a powerful protector and an aspect of Shiva absorbed by Buddhism. Seen here as the 'Protector of Science' in a Tibetan banner painting or* thangka. *At his waist is a row of severed heads; all around are various deities and Buddhist notables. Nineteenth century* AD. *155 × 91.5cm.*

197 *Solid cast-bronze statue of Shiva as Lord of the Dance (Nataraja) performing an act of simultaneous destruction and creation in a ring of cosmic fire as he tramples the dwarf of ignorance. South India, Chola Dynasty, about AD 1100. H 89.5cm.*

The southern Deccan contributes much to the collections: three famous bronzes of Sarasvati, Shiva and a seated Jain figure from the Western Ganga dynasty of Mysore (8th–10th century); a small group of stone sculpture of the Nolamba dynasty; three female dancers which once adorned the pillar capitals of temples and a splendid figure of Shiva as Bhairava which date from the Hoysala dynasty (12th–13th century).

Orissa, on the east coast of India, is stylistically an integral part of the Deccan. Its three great artistic centres were the temple cities of Bhuvaneshvar and Puri, and the now-ruined coastal site of Konarak. The Museum's fine collection contains a vigorous eighth-century figure of Durga killing the buffalo demon and a later, smoother Jain Mother Goddess and child. A magnificent series of black schist sculptures of the thirteenth century illustrates the artistic splendours of the Ganga dynasty, and includes a set of Hindu planets.

In South India the first great artistic flowering took place under the Pallava dynasty (c. AD 600–900), famous for their rock-cut temples and sculpture in granite. The collection contains a magnificent Garuda

(the vehicle of Vishnu) of about AD 750: a taut and imperious figure, half bird, half man.

From the late ninth to the thirteenth century the Chola dynasty ruled from Tanjavur. Their empire extended at its height to include much of Sri Lanka. The collection is rich in Chola sculpture, including (in stone) Shiva bursting from the Lingam, and Shiva seated as teacher. In bronze, a grand Nataraja (Shiva as Lord of the Dance) is an early example of this popular type of image (c. AD 1100), while the finest bronze in the collection is a seated Shiva Vishapaharana (c. 950).

Indian painting

The Museum's collection of Indian two-dimensional art is extensive and comprehensive, the vast majority dating from the last three or four centuries. Chief among the non-Mughal paintings in the collections are those from the Deccan, the Punjab Hills and Rajasthan. From Bijapur, in the Deccan, the often published portrait of Sultan Ibrahim Adil Shah II (AD 1579–1627) and that of a contemporary standing courtier are most notable. Among the earliest and finest examples from the Punjab Hills is that of *Krishna and the Maidens*, in Basohli style (c. 1710). From Guler comes a sense of *Krishna on a Swing* (c. 1750).

Some of the finest of all Indian paintings came from the royal courts of Rajasthan, and the riches of that region are justly represented in the Museum's collection. It includes the famous Manley Ragamala (c. 1610), a bound set of miniatures depicting musical modes, possibly from Amber, and the magnificent *Krishna Supporting Mount Govardhana* by Shahadin (Bikaner school, c. 1690).

The Company school is represented by many paintings of architectural, occupational or iconographical subjects, some on mica. Nineteenth-century Calcutta is represented in a number of Kalighat paintings of Hindu deities.

NEPAL AND TIBET

Indian art had a profound influence on that of Nepal and Tibet. While the Pala style of eastern India was strongest in Nepal and southern Tibet, western Tibet followed the direction of her neighbour, Kashmir. Both countries soon expressed these influences in their own idiom, producing a fresh interpretation of the Indian model. The most creative period of Nepalese art, serving both the Buddhist and Hindu religions, lasted from the ninth to the sixteenth centuries AD. Chief among a group of early bronzes is a dignified seated Maitreya (the Buddha to come) of the tenth century. Outstanding stone sculptures include an eighth-century standing Buddha, a teaching Buddha of the ninth to tenth centuries, and a twelfth-century sculpture of Shiva and his consort.

A group of bronzes of the eleventh to thirteenth centuries show that the art of southern Tibet had already acquired a character of its own, with a marked preference for inlays of gold and silver. The collection is rich in Tibetan metal images, ritual equipment and banner paintings, or *thangkas*. An early painting, probably of the thirteenth century, perfectly preserved on a large wooden book-cover, is probably the finest Tibetan work in the collection. In the fourteenth century Tibet felt the impact of her powerful eastern neighbour, China, and Indian and Chinese influences begin to appear side by side.

By the seventeenth century the arts in Nepal and Tibet were content to repeat the old formulas. Craftsmanship, however, remained of a high order, especially in the elaborate inlaying of semi-precious stones, as seen in jewellery and musical instruments.

SRI LANKA

Both the Buddhist religion and the Sinhalese language find their origins in North India. However, the most dominant influences on the art of Sri Lanka came from

198 *The Bodhisattva Tara. Solid cast in gilded bronze, this image from Sri Lanka of the shakti or female essence of the Bodhisattva Avalokiteśvara is possibly the finest of all South Asian bronzes. It combines a ravishing naturalism with great spiritual dignity. Tenth century* AD. H *1.43m.*

199 *The Buddha in the earth-touching posture, symbolising his enlightenment. This gesture of the right hand is the commonest in Burmese Buddha images. This is one of the finest of the bronzes of Burma's Pagan period. Twelfth–thirteenth century* AD. H *33cm.*

the eastern Deccan (Amaravati) and South India. A small group of Buddhist bronzes belongs to the Anuradhapura period, which came to an end in the early eleventh century with the Chola invasion. The greatest of all Sri Lankan works of art, an almost life-size gilt-bronze figure of the Bodhisattva Tara, dates from the flowering of Sri Lankan art in the Polonnaruwa period between the tenth and thirteenth centuries AD. The collection contains a good selection of small bronzes and ivory-carvings, including a magnificent carved casket of AD 1600.

SOUTH-EAST ASIA

During the first millennium AD Indian forms of society, religion and art were carried all over South-East Asia by sea-going traders and colonists. The collections from South-East Asia include objects from Burma, Thailand, Cambodia, Malaysia, Indonesia, Vietnam, Laos and the Philippines.

Burma

A golden age of Burmese art began with the Pagan kingdom (AD 1044–1287) on the Irrawaddy River, drawing heavily on the Buddhist art of neighbouring eastern India. The finest Pagan bronze outside Burma, a seated Buddha, graces the British Museum's collection. In later Pagan style is a dignified standing wooden Buddha of about the fifteenth century. Later Burmese art is often characterised by the addition of gilt lacquer and coloured mirror glass. From the nineteenth century a figure of a kneeling monk shows genuine sensitivity in what is a very repetitive later style of art.

Thailand

The earliest kingdom in Thailand was that of the Mons (7th–11th centuries AD). The best-known early style of art is named after the capital of the Mon kingdom, Dvaravati. Influenced to a degree by the Sarnath school of Gupta India, this distinctive style is represented by a powerful stone Buddha head, and another in stucco. The legacy of Khmer domination of southern Thailand can be seen in stone sculpture from Lopburi and bronze Buddha heads from U'Tong (13th–14th centuries).

The first Thai dynasties were founded in the thirteenth century at Chiengmai and, later, Ayuthia (14th–18th centuries AD). A Thai art style, inspired by Burmese and Sri Lankan forms, developed quickly. The walking Buddha is a highly original Thai contribution to the history of the Buddha image. In the fourteenth and fifteenth centuries Thailand became famous for its ceramic production, including the celebrated Sawankhalok and Sukhothai wares, along with celadons.

Cambodia

The greatest of the Indianised kingdoms of ancient mainland South-East Asia was that of the Khmers of Cambodia. Its highly original art is sparsely represented here, but from the early period comes an exquisite eighth-century female head. The greatest complex of temple architecture of the region is at Angkor, the Khmer capital founded in the ninth century. In the Museum's collection are a tenth-century Angkor male torso, a later three-headed stone Bodhisattva of the twelfth or thirteenth century and a small collection of bronzes (11th–12th centuries).

Indonesia

A great Indianised kingdom was established in Java by the eighth century. Under the Shailendra dynasty in central Java, between AD 750 and 950, art and architecture were influenced by South India. From that period dates the greatest of all Buddhist monuments, the vast stupa at Borabudur, and the collection contains Buddha heads from that site, as well as a magnificent male torso. A rich body of Buddhist bronzes illustrates an artistic debt to eastern India. Also of this period is the famous Sambas hoard of gold and silver images from Borneo.

The Eastern Javanese period (c. 950–late 14th century), a period of excellent craftsmanship and powerful sculpture, is scarcely represented here.

Vietnam

The two principal ancient divisions of this country were the Chinese-influenced north (Annam) and Champa, the Indianised coastal south. Annam is represented mainly by a collection of porcelain, remarkable amongst which are two dated altar vases (1582) and an inscribed, pillared censer (dated 1575), both of which are decorated with raised dragons in unmistakable Annamese style. From Champa come three sculpture fragments including a lively eleventh-century rampant lion with a curly mane.

THE LANDS OF ISLAM

The Islamic religion was founded by the Prophet Muhammad, who was born at Mecca in western Arabia about AD 570. His flight to Medina in AD 622 marks the beginning of the Islamic era. Those countries in which the Islamic religion came to prevail constituted the *Dar al-Islam*, 'the World of Islam'. Its peoples were governed by Muslim rulers, and however much they differed in race and language Islam gave them a common purpose and way of life, though in the course of centuries distinctive Islamic cultures were created. The lands represented in the British Museum's Islamic collections are, in modern political terms, Egypt, Syria, Lebanon, Israel, Turkey, Iraq, Iran, Afghanistan, the Soviet Central Asian Republics, Pakistan and India.

From the earliest days Muslim patrons demanded superb craftsmanship and design in everyday objects, and it is in the forms and decoration of pottery, glass and inlaid metalwork that Islam excelled. A decisive Arab contribution to Islamic art was the script: Kufic, an early angular style, and Naskhi, a later, more rounded hand whose remarkable dignity and flexibility were exploited in all Islamic art. Among important specimens of Arabic script in the Museum's collections are a gravestone of AD 858, a stone cenotaph of AD 991, and a building dedication of AD 1084, all inscribed in the Kufic script, reserved in the early centuries of Islam for the Quran and for monumental inscriptions. The Islamic proscription against human representation was not enforced in the case of the minor arts; only when it was intended for religious architecture (tile revetments and stucco panels) or for Koranic illumination did the decoration revolve entirely around geometric forms of the arabesque – a continuous stem with split palmette leaves, convoluted in an infinite variety of forms.

During the seventh and eighth centuries AD the Arabs conquered Egypt, Syria, North Africa, Spain, Mesopotamia, Persia, Transoxania and Sind. The caliphs of the Umayyad dynasty (AD 661–749) ruled their empire from Damascus in Syria. Early Islamic art, in its architecture as well as in the decorative arts, is heavily dependent on the cultures of the conquered peoples, the Sassanian tradition in Persia and the Graeco-Roman tradition in Syria. Thus a turquoise-glazed vase of the Umayyad period from Mesopotamia follows the style and technique of the green-glazed amphorae of the late Parthian period (2nd–3rd centuries AD).

The Umayyads were succeeded by the ᶜAbbasid caliphs (AD 749–1258), whose capital was Baghdad in

201 *Glass bottle with the silhouette of a running hare which has been carved from an overlay of green glass. The lively but abstract appearance of the hare is typical of Persian art in the tenth century* AD. H *15 cm.*

200 *Shallow bowl, painted in black slip with a fine Kufic inscription. The inscription reads: He who speaks his speech is silver, but silence is a ruby: With good health and prosperity. From Nishapur, Iran, later eleventh century* AD. D *34.6 cm.*

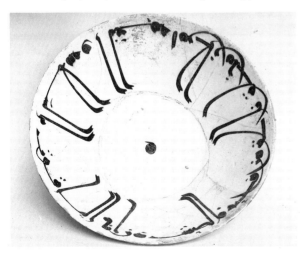

Mesopotamia. ᶜAbbasid power and the ᶜAbbasid court were greatest in the ninth century AD. Highly regarded at the ᶜAbbasid court were Tang stonewares imported from China; these greatly inspired the Arab potters. A ninth- to tenth-century Tang white ware dish with foliate rim, found at Nishapur (Iran), has an exact ᶜAbbasid parallel. Unable to manufacture stoneware, the potters achieved a cosmetic likeness by applying an opaque white tin-glaze to the surface of their earthenware vessels. Sometimes they added elegant foliate and geometric designs in blue and green. The ᶜAbbasid potters' greatest technical achievement was lustre, a technique first used in Egypt in the eighth and ninth centuries to decorate glass; metallic pigments were painted onto the tin-glazed surface of a vessel to create a lustrous sheen that may have been intended to imitate precious metal. Early examples combine two or more colours, as on fragments of tiles from the short-lived capital of the ᶜAbbasids at Samarra. These brilliant shades, however, were abandoned in favour of a single yellow lustre, which seems to coincide with a change from organic to figural decoration.

Precious metalwork of the Umayyad and ᶜAbbasid periods is often in the Sassanian tradition; vessels are worked in repoussé and often parcel gilt with characteristic scenes of rulers engaged in courtly pastimes. Silver and gold continued to be worked until the twelfth century: an important hoard found at Nihavand in western Iran includes a complete belt of silver, parcel gilt and nielloed. Simple bronze objects were also produced in Iran and the western Islamic lands up to 1200. Early examples, particularly ewers, follow the Roman or Sassanian tradition; later objects from Iran – mortars, lamps, dishes and boxes – have fine engraved decoration. Particularly popular in the twelfth century were mirrors, often decorated on their backs with harpies and bands of Kufic calligraphy. Painting of this period is represented by illustrations from an Arabic translation of the ancient Greek pharmacopeia *Materia Medica* by Dioscorides, copied in 1224 and painted in Baghdad. A fifteenth-century page from the *Ajaᶜib al-Makhluqat* (Wonders of Creation) depicts the emblems of the four evangelists; this very popular text was much illustrated in Iraq in the fourteenth and fifteenth centuries, perpetuating the great school of painting in Baghdad under the last ᶜAbbasid caliphs.

In the ninth and tenth centuries Persian dynasties were established independently of the Umayyad caliphs of Baghdad. The Samanids in eastern Iran and Transoxania (AD 874–999), for example, ruled from their capital at Nishapur, where excavations have re-
200 vealed quantities of earthenware pottery. Painted in thickly applied slips to prevent the colours from running beneath a transparent lead glaze, the finest are boldly painted with Kufic inscriptions. Also from Nishapur are buff ware bowls, whose figural decoration continues the subject matter of Sassanian relief-worked silver.

In Persia, Mesopotamia and Egypt the Muslims
201 inherited an ancient tradition of glass-making. The most prized glasses were carved in relief; the so-called Hedwig Glass is a magnificent example. Mould-blown glass was also produced, and the ancient technique of making mosaic glass was revived by the glass-makers of Mesopotamia in the ninth century AD. Rock-crystal is singled out for praise by early chroniclers who saw the famous and opulent Cairo treasury of the Fatimid caliphs, rulers of Egypt between AD 969 and 1171. These rock-crystals range in date from the ninth to the eleventh centuries and are often carved with animals or Kufic inscriptions. Many found their way to Europe, where they were mounted in precious metal and used as

202 *The Vaso Vescovali. Bronze vessel, inlaid with silver with depictions of the planets and signs of the Zodiac, mounted warriors and a frieze of musicians. Probably from Eastern Iran or Afghanistan, about AD 1200. H 22cm.*

reliquaries. Recent research suggests that rock-crystal may also have been carved in Basra in Iraq, and a fine goblet in the collection may perhaps come from this source.

Jewellery, too, is known from the Fatimid period; several examples show the continuity of the traditions and techniques of classical and Byzantine jewellery in the use of intricate filigree-work and enamelling. But best known of the arts of the Fatimids of Egypt is their lustreware, which follows on, both technically and stylistically, from the lustrewares of Iraq. Excavations of the potters' quarters at Fustat, south of Cairo, have yielded quantities of locally produced and imported lustrewares.

In the eleventh century Persia was invaded by the Seljuk Turks, nomads from Central Asia, who established their rule over the greater part of Persia, Mesopotamia, Syria and ultimately Asia Minor. Under their patronage a style of architecture was developed, which was continued by their successors: the Atabegs in

Persia, Mesopotamia and Syria, and the Seljuk Sulans of Konya in Turkey. A major influence on pottery at this time was Chinese porcelain of the Song dynasty (AD 960–1279), which was exported into the Islamic heartlands. Islamic potters, attempting to recreate this ware, produced a new, more versatile ceramic fabric, composed of frit made from a high percentage of ground quartz and pure white clay and used in conjunction with new alkaline glazes. Iran, with its ceramic centre at Kashan, produced a whole range of ceramics in this new medium. Designs on their overglaze enamelled wares (*minai*) and lustre vessels are strongly linked to miniature-painting in manuscripts. The underglaze painted wares of Kashan were to have a tremendous impact on the Chinese for, along with Persian cobalt imported into China at this period, they created the vogue for blue and white porcelain under the Yuan and Ming dynasties.

Metalwork, too, at this time saw a revolution in form and technique. Perhaps because of a shortage of silver in the Near East from about AD 1100, craftsmen turned to brass or bronze, which they inlaid with silver and copper. The collection has fine examples of fluted brass ewers, pen-boxes and ink-wells, many of them produced in the eastern Iranian province of Khurasan. These were often decorated with the signs of the zodiac, combined with dense scrollwork and animated inscriptions. A remarkable footed bowl and lid in this style is the Vaso Vescovali, a bronze vessel inlaid with silver, dating from about 1200.

In the first quarter of the thirteenth century Persia was devastated by the Mongol invasions. A number of metalworkers may have found asylum at the court of the Atabeg Badr al-Din Lulu at Mosul in northern Iraq (AD 1218–59), where the metalworking industry reached new heights of refinement. The Museum has a number of pieces inscribed with his name and titles, and many objects are signed by craftsmen with a Mosul connection. Among the most important is a brass ewer signed by Shujaᶜ ibn Manᶜa and made in Mosul; it is inlaid with silver and copper, with intricately worked roundels containing genre scenes of life and entertainment at the Mosul court.

In Egypt the Fatimids were succeeded by the Ayyubids (AD 1171–1250), who added Syria to their domains. Syria had produced glass since antiquity, but now a new technique was developed – gilding. A fragmentary flask with gilded decoration is inscribed with the name of ᶜImad al-Din Zangi (AD 1127–46), who ruled at Mosul and Aleppo in Syria prior to the Ayyubids. In the thirteenth and fourteenth centuries enamelling was combined with gilding. A fine example is a pilgrim's flask painted with horsemen and musicians. In northern Syria at towns like Raqqa and Balis/Meskene on the Euphrates underglaze pottery, contemporary with that of Kashan in Iran, was being produced. Using the newly discovered ceramic fabric (frit), Syrian potters perfected the art of underglaze painting with geometric, arabesque or animal motifs under a brilliant turquoise glaze.

The Ayyubid period also saw the beginning of inlaid metalwork in Syria and Egypt. A superb brass astrolabe with silver and copper inlays was made in Cairo by a Cairene specialist ᶜAbd al-Karim in 1235–6. This instrument is the earliest known piece of inlaid metalwork produced in Egypt. Arab painting from Egypt is represented by rare thirteenth-century examples from Fustat. A number of objects from this period bear Christian scenes, demonstrating a wider patronage than simply the ruling Muslim élite. A handwarmer, or pomander, made in Syria for the emir Badr al-Din Baysari, bears a double-headed eagle, the blazon of the last reigning Ayyubid Sultan at Salih Ayyub.

In 1250 the Mamluks, an army of Turkish slaves built up by the Sultan Ayyub, seized power from their erstwhile masters. They made their capital at Cairo, and ruled until 1517, when they were overthrown by the Ottomans. Art flourished under Mamluk rule. Enamelled glass continued to be produced: characteristic are the mosque lamps, commissioned by sultans and emirs, of which the Museum has many fine examples. In the early fourteenth century a third wave of Chinese imports – textiles, blue and white porcelain and celadons of the Yuan period – had a dramatic effect on the decorative arts. *Chinoiserie* lotuses, peonies, phoenixes, and the blue and white colour scheme appeared on tiles and vessels. Metalwork, too, shows their influence: large basins and trays have *chinoiserie* lotuses or peonies incorporated into designs which also bear inscriptions in the large cursive script known as *thulth* often in the names of the Mamluk sultans or emirs. The Mamluks granted devices of rank to high officers of state and these are frequently depicted: a fine fourteenth-century steel mirror bears a pen-box, the emblem of a secretary of state.

In the middle of the thirteenth century Persia and Mesopotamia had been joined with Central Asia and China under the rule of the Mongol Great Khan. Political union brought close commercial relations between east and west Asia, and the exchange enriched the arts of Persia. Under the Mongol dynasty of the Ilkhans (AD 1245–c.1336) there was renewed activity in pottery and metalwork. The influx of Chinese motifs had the same effect on Persian art as it had on that of the Mamluks. Flowers and leaves were rendered more naturalistically and the lotus and phoenix now appear on ceramic wares of the 'Sultanabad' type, which are generally coarser that their Kashan predecessors.

In the fourteenth century Persia was invaded by Timur, known in the West as Tamerlane. This was only a temporary setback to Persian civilisation, however, thanks to his successors, who were enlightened patrons

204

of the arts. The British Museum has three vessels of dark-green jade which may have been made at Samarqand, the seat of Timur's grandson Ulugh Beg (AD 1409–47), an enthusiastic collector of jade-carvings. One of these, a vase, subsequently passed to Jahangir, Mughal Emperor of India (AD 1605–28), who recorded his ownership in an engraved inscription.

With the collapse of the Timurid Empire and that of its Turcoman successors at the close of the fifteenth century Persia came under the rule of the Safavids (1502–1736). Safavid art continued in the Timurid tradition: the brass jugs of the early sixteenth century are close in form and style to those of the Timurid period. The armourers and swordsmiths of the Safavid period, however, were famous. A superb helmet and arm-piece of steel, carved and inlaid with gold, bear dedicatory inscriptions to the greatest ruler of the Safavid dynasty, Shah ᶜAbbas I (AD 1588–1629). Two sabres, one signed by a swordsmith of Isfahan, are notable examples of the pattern-welded steel blade. The great astrolabe made in AD 1712 for the last of the Safavid rulers, Shah Sultan Husayn (AD 1694–1722), is a superb example of the high quality achieved by the Safavid instrument-makers.

Persian pottery of the seventeenth century compares in quality with that of the earlier periods. A large bowl decorated in underglaze blue and black with phoenixes and flying cranes was inspired by Chinese originals, as was a superb dish with a qilin. The turbanned head of a youth painted on a large dish is a typical invention of contemporary Safavid painting and belongs to a group associated with Kubachi in the Caucasus, where many of this type were found. A vase decorated in white slip on a soft-grey ground, and a hookah-base for a tobacco pipe painted in polychrome are examples of wares influenced by Chinese export wares from Swatow.

The political turmoil after the fall of the Safavids was ended by the Qajar dynasty (AD 1795–1924), which brought about a regeneration of Persia in the nineteenth century. Painted lacquer was popular at both the Safavid and Qajar courts, and a remarkable instrument box with the court of Solomon depicted on the lid probably belonged to an apothecary or a jeweller. A portrait of two Persian youths painted in oils on canvas employs a technique and style borrowed from Europe.

In Turkey the Byzantine Empire had succumbed to the Ottoman Turks with the fall of Constantinople to Sultan Mehmet I in 1453. By the sixteenth century Turkey was the centre of a powerful empire. The

203 *Miniature from a manuscript of the* Shah-nama, *or Persian Book of Kings, probably painted in Tabriz about AD 1500. It shows Rustam sleeping in a woody landscape while his horse Rakhsh saves him from an attacking lion. 31.5 × 21cm.*

204 *Brass astrolabe inlaid with silver and copper made by 'Abd al-Karim al-Misri in Egypt and dated AH 633 (AD 1235–6). Certain of the pointers are pictorial representations of fixed stars, such as Pisces, Pegasus and Cygnus.* H 39.4cm.

pointed steel helmet and breastplate are reminders of Turkey's military prowess at this time. A finely patterned steel sabre bears the name of Sultan Suleyman the Magnificent (1520–66).

The Museum has an unrivalled collection of Turkish pottery produced at Iznik from the end of the fifteenth century. Chinese taste after the capture of Chinese porcelain as booty at Tabriz in 1514 influenced the decoration of the earliest blue and white wares. Small-scale spiralling tendrils characterise the so-called Golden Horn wares, while the 'Damascus' group produced between the 1550s and the 1560s exhibit a range of colours hitherto unknown in the history of Islamic pottery. An important documentary piece is a mosque lamp dated 1549 from the Dome of the Rock in Jerusalem. The turning point for the Iznik potteries came with building of the Süleymaniye complex (inaugurated 1557) for which tiles from Iznik were ordered. This established a fashion for an underglaze bole-red used extensively on both tiles and vessels.

205 *Footed basin decorated with swirling leaves and fantastic flowers, with a border of tulips around the base. The colour range and fine draughtsmanship demonstrate the skill of the Iznik potters in sixteenth-century Ottoman Turkey.* H 27.3cm.

The collections also include some fine examples of Turkish miniature-painting. Of special interest are paintings of foppish European gentlemen by Levni (d. 1736). Other noteworthy items include an album of costumes and paper cuts acquired in Istanbul in 1618, a two-volume eighteenth-century album of costumes, and pages from biographies of the Shi'i martyrs, probably executed in Baghdad in about 1600.

In India Babur (AD 1526–30), a descendant of Timur, founded the Mughal Empire; by the seventeenth century it included North India and the greater part of the Deccan. Unlike other Islamic countries, the majority of its people were not Muslim, and Mughal society shows a distinctive fusion of Muslim and Hindu cultures. Mughal craftsmen were particularly skilled in the art of carving hardstones; the emperor Jahangir (AD 1605–28) is known to have patronised jade-carvers. To his reign probably belongs a magnificent terrapin carved from a great block of jade. A beautiful jade vessel carved in the form of a split gourd bears a dedication to Jahangir's son, the emperor Shah Jahan (AD 1628–58).

A pair of huqqa bases encrusted with gold and semi-precious stones have gold ormolu mounts made specially for them in the late eighteenth century. Other hardstones were also carved: a finely sculpted tiger's head of banded agate is probably from the arm of a throne. Mughal weapons of the sixteenth to eighteenth centuries include fine daggers with blades of pattern-welded steel and handles of jade, walrus ivory, or jewel-encrusted rock-crystal. Also popular were gilded coloured glass vessels, and jewellery set with emeralds, diamonds and rubies.

The gem-set jewellery of the Mughal period, worn by the ruling élite, was frequently depicted in contemporary miniatures. The most important of the Museum's collections of miniature-paintings belong to the Mughal period, particularly those associated with the reigns of Akbar (AD 1556–1605) and Jahangir. There are portraits of courtiers; calligraphy by famous Mughal practioners; illustrations to Hindu and Persian classics; books of fables; and illustrations from a brief life of Christ composed by the Jesuits for the emperor

206 *The Prophet Khidr saving the young prince Nur al-Dhahr from drowning in the Ganges. From the* Hamza-nama, *the legendary exploits of the Amir Hamza, made for the Mughal emperor Akbar about* AD 1567–82. 67 × 50cm.

207 *Terrapin carved from one piece of jade. Found in a tank at Allahabad in Northern India. Mughal, probably commissioned by the emperor Jahangir (AD 1605–27). L 50.2cm.*

Akbar. In addition there are illustrations to the major chronicles of the reigns: *Babur-nama, Akbar-nama* and the *Tuzuk-i Jahangiri.* Among the prizes of the collection is the fragmentary *Princes of the House of Timur*, possibly painted in Kabul about 1545–50; portraits of Akbar, Jahangir and Shah Jahan were added later. Equally fine are the pages from the late sixteenth-century *Hamza-nama*, the work of Akbar's studio.

JAPAN

The geographical area from which the British Museum's collection comes coincides with Japan's modern political boundaries. They include the large northern island of Hokkaidō, and the Southern Prefecture of Okinawa, formerly known as the Ryūkyū Islands, both of which lay historically outside the mainstreams of Japanese culture. The Japanese collection aims to cover all aspects of material culture from the Jōmon period (beginning *c.* 10,000 BC) until the present day. It is particularly recognised as the national collection of Japanese fine arts in traditional styles or formats, but excludes international-style easel-paintings of the last 130 years, which for reasons of conservation fall within the remit of the Tate Gallery. Items of anthropological interest, especially relating to the Ainu culture of Hokkaidō, are held in the Department of Ethnography, while a group of Japanese clocks is cared for by the Department of Medieval and Later Antiquities.

Japanese culture has since the fourth century BC been characterised by its relationship with countries of East Asia; and, from the sixteenth century AD onwards, with Western nations also. In all of that period cultural change has tended to come about by following foreign example. Because of Japan's distance from the nearest Asian country (Korea) overseas influences have typically arrived in comparatively short, powerful bursts, followed by periods of greater isolation in which they have been absorbed and slowly changed into more native forms. These patterns have been broken since 1945 by the interdependence of modern international society and the speed of communications. It is too early to predict if this is a permanent change in emphasis.

The earliest culture represented in the collections is known as Jōmon after the typical cord-impressed decoration on the inventively shaped low-fired pottery. The earliest Jōmon pottery is also so far the earliest datable pottery in the world (*c.* 10,000 BC). The British Museum's collection includes only a few undocumented pieces of pottery and sherds from the later part of the period (*c.* 3,000 BC onwards), together with some stone arrowheads and other stone implements.

The first major revolution in the life-style of the Japanese people occurred in the third century BC with the change to settled rice-cultivation and the use of metals. Known as the Yayoi period (*c.* 300 BC–AD 300), this ended a period of some ten thousand years of the hunting, gathering and fishing culture of Jōmon. The development of settled agriculture is assumed to have been due to close contacts with East Asia or immigration, though there is no conclusive evidence as yet to settle the question. Other continental introductions were wheel-thrown pottery and wood vessels, the cast-

The Kofun period (*c.* AD 300–710) saw the building of impressive tombs for the great, especially for the ruling family of the Yamato region (modern Nara Prefecture), which gradually established its dominance over much of Japan. The stone chambered tombs were protected under huge mounds of earth, the largest reaching over 800m in length. Low-fired red pottery figures in the form of people, animals, birds and houses were placed round the outer slopes as guardians. The British Museum has one such complete figure.

The contents of the tombs are close to objects from the contemporary kingdoms of Korea, which clearly exerted a strong influence on Japanese culture. This included improved furnace technology, which produced a hard grey pottery known as Sue, fired at a high temperature. The collection is rich in Sue ware; a particularly fine example is a tall jar with moulded 208 animals around the shoulder. Some Sue ware has a natural ash glaze resulting from the volatilisation of the kiln wall material, an affect which was contrived in later centuries as a major style in Japanese ceramic art. The British Museum owes much of its collection of material of the period to the activities of a metallurgist, Professor William Gowland, who lived in Japan during the years 1872–88. An amateur archaeologist, he was able to visit Kyūshū and, together with his Japanese helpers, to excavate dolmen graves. The collection includes pottery, bronze mirrors, iron swords, gilt horse-trappings, and groups of beads and jewellery.

Buddhism was introduced in the mid-sixth century, in the period (*c.* AD 550–710) sometimes called Asuka after the central district of administration of the imperial family. Asuka was also the site of Japan's earliest Buddhist temple. It was the Buddhist architecture transmitted from China through Korea which was to provide the initial setting for many of the newly imported higher arts of the continent, including lacquer, wood and metal sculpture, fine bronzes, and hand- 209 scrolls containing the Buddhist scriptures, written in characters in their Chinese translations. All of these arts, and many others, were to become the major forms also used in traditional secular culture, as Buddhism quickly spread and became in the eighth century the state religion.

The continuity of Buddhist material culture over the entire period until its eclipse after 1867 was nevertheless marked by changes of emphasis as different sects were introduced from the continent. The earliest, including the 'Six Sects of Nara', were monastic and contemplative in outlook; they dominated until the end of the Nara period (AD 710–794). Founders were especially revered, like the monk Jion Taishi (AD 632–682), of whom there is a fine fourteenth-century portrait on silk; or Prince Shōtoku (AD 574–622), the chief establisher of Japanese Buddhism. His life was often compared with that of the historical Buddha, as in a

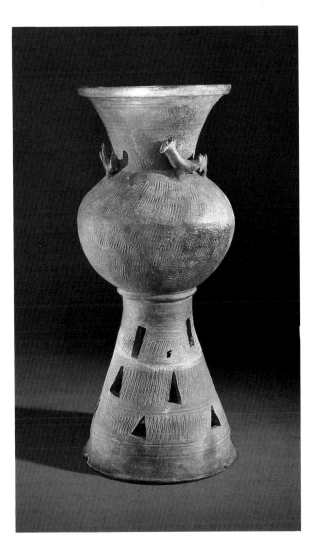

208 *Sue ware vase with applied stag, boar and bird figures. Such vases, found in the tumuli of the later Kofun period (sixth–seventh centuries* AD*), exist in a variety of forms. They probably contained offerings of different foods and liquids.* H *52.2cm.*

ing of bronze and iron, techniques of weaving, and the polishing of stone tools and jewellery. Settled and stratified society gradually spread east and north. The origins of the institutionalised Shinto religion also lie in this period, with its distinctive shrine architecture. The collection includes two splendid bronzes, cast from moulds, from the middle Yayoi period, thought to have been used in agricultural rituals. One, a *dōtaku* (bell-shaped bronze), is decorated with abstract patterns related to imported Chinese mirrors of the period; the other is a halberd. There is also one fine example of a large, wheel-thrown pottery jar, probably used for the storage of grain.

209 *Painted and lacquered wood figure of a mature man, with his head shaven in priest's style. The subject is probably the retired head of a merchant family who has taken Buddhist vows. Seventeenth century AD. H 40.5 cm.*

group of early sixteenth-century painted scenes from his life, the earliest narrative paintings in the collection. The earliest Buddhist objects, however, are eighth-century clay plaques crisply moulded with images very close to those of contemporary China; and a group of the turned-wood reliquaries called the *hyakumantō* (1,000,000 stupas) made in the years 764–770 on the orders of the Empress Kōken to hold printed *mantras*, and then distributed to major temples.

From the rare semi-secular arts of the Nara period comes a carved wooden *Gigaku* mask used in a court ritual dance-drama derived from Korea. Such masks are among the first surviving examples of the Japanese genius for sculpture. *Nō* drama masks, made from the fifteenth century onwards, are also well represented, the greater number coming from the Edo period (AD 1600–1867).

From the Heian period (AD 794–1185) the by now well-established court aristocracy patronised newly imported forms of Buddhism with a stronger ritual element, especially the Tendai and Shingon sects. The tantric Shingon beliefs recognised virtue in the production of images of the mystical deities, and the copying of formal *mandara* (mandalas). The fourteenth-century image of the Bodhisattva Kokuzō is the earliest of many in the collection. The complex allusiveness and ritual of Heian Buddhism found its counterpart in the subtle complexities of courtly society. The life of the nobility was dominated by etiquette and dress, sexual love and the arts, especially poetry, music and painting. In this period lie the origins of the Yamatoe ('Japanese pictures') style, based on simple colour, clear outline and a high point-of-view, with a very strong preference for human subjects, especially those associated with love,

nostalgia, sadness, and with a constant reference to the passing seasons. This broad style was carried on by many schools, including the Tosa (from the fifteenth century) and the Sumiyoshi (based in Edo from the seventeenth century) and Revival Yamatoe artists of around 1800 onwards. The collection includes many hundreds of paintings of these schools in all the usual formats – hanging scrolls, handscrolls, albums, screens,

210 *Lacquer writing-box, which originally contained writing brushes, a block of ink, an ink-stone and a water dropper. The design of Futamigaura Bay is made with* makie, *lacquer sprinkled with gold dust and carved and polished into shape. Sixteenth century* AD. *24.5 × 22.2 × 5cm.*

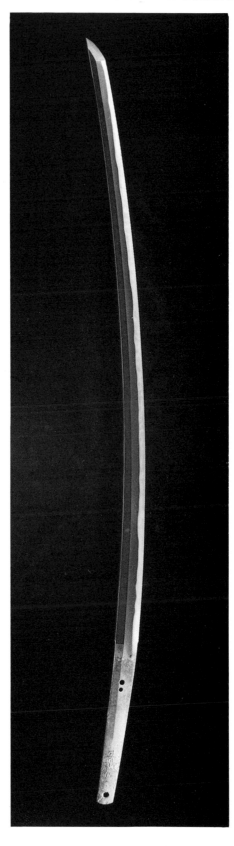

212 ABOVE *Ivory netsuke in the form of a tiger. The netsuke, or ornamental toggle, was used to fix to the sash of the kimono small pouches and containers such as* inrō *(seal or medicine boxes), which were carried suspended by cords. Nineteenth century* AD. H *4.4cm.*

211 LEFT *Portrait of Minamoto Yoritomo (*AD *1147–99), who established the Bakufu samurai government at Kamakura. This hanging scroll, in colours on silk, is a late Kamakura period copy (fourteenth century* AD*) of a portrait thought to have been painted in 1173 by Fujiwara Takenobu. 145 × 88.5cm.*

213 RIGHT *Tachi-type steel sword blade, signed Kageyasu. Although the sword has had several centimetres cut from its original length, it retains the characteristic elegant shape of work of the early Kamakura period. From Bizen province, early thirteenth century* AD. L *(blade) 68.5cm.*

fans. The earliest is from the early sixteenth century, and the holdings for the Edo period (1600–1867) are particularly rich.

Another product of early Heian courtly culture was the preference for lacquered pieces for tableware, storage boxes, and personal accoutrements, which soon came generally to be decorated with sprinkled gold and silver dust and gold and silver leaf in the process known as *makie*. Mother-of-pearl was also inlaid into lacquer. The Japanese became known throughout East Asia for the fineness of these wares, which have continued to be made to the present day. The collection includes many hundreds of examples, the earliest a document-box from the thirteenth century, and the finest perhaps the

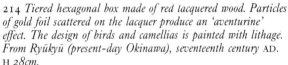

214 *Tiered hexagonal box made of red lacquered wood. Particles of gold foil scattered on the lacquer produce an 'aventurine' effect. The design of birds and camellias is painted with lithage. From Ryūkyū (present-day Okinawa), seventeenth century AD. H 28cm.*

215 *Hexagonal porcelain lidded jar with enamelled floral decoration. The finest quality coloured enamelling is known by the name of the family of the originator, Kakiemon. This jar was made in Arita (Hizen province) for export to Europe in the second half of the seventeenth century AD. H 27.1cm.*

sixteenth-century ink-stone box decorated with a view of Futamigaura Bay. From the later sixteenth century some lacquered pieces were made especially for export to Europe. A remarkable example is a large chest in *makie* and mother-of-pearl in export style, dating from the later seventeenth century. The most characteristic lacquer pieces of the seventeenth to nineteenth centuries are the *inrō* (seal cases), usually consisting of a series of interlocking compartments and elaborately decorated. These became items of personal adornment. In more recent times they became collectors' items in the West, and the British Museum's splendid holdings (approximately three hundred items) have been mainly

given or bequeathed by major collectors such as Oscar Raphael, Collingwood Ingram and Anne Hull Grundy. Netsuke and sword furniture were acquired in the same way.

The Heian period saw the steady rise of the samurai class of warriors. From the beginning of the Kamakura period (AD 1185–1333) until 1867 the Japanese government was always controlled by the military class, and samurai virtues, skills, tastes and equipment remained major themes in Japanese culture. Of the equipment, the incomparable steel sword-blade was the most prestigious, combining sharpness, durability, elegance of shape and complex patterned surfaces into

216 Tsukiji, *woodblock print from the series 'Tokyo after the Earthquake Fire', 1923. This poignant series was the earliest masterpiece by Hiratsuka Unichi (b. 1895), one of the founders of the Sōsaku Hanga (Creative Print) movement.* 26.3 × 34.5 cm.

a weapon which was also a work of art and of Shintō veneration. The British Museum's collection of over two hundred blades ranges from the thirteenth to the twentieth centuries. The decorated metal fittings were always kept separately from the blade themselves, and in the Edo period, when actual fighting almost ceased, they became the vehicle for displays of the inlayer's finest skills. The collection of *tsuba* (sword guards) of this period is particularly extensive.

During the Muromachi period (AD 1393–1573) the austerity of samurai taste encouraged the arts associated with meditative (Zen) Buddhism, including the Tea Ceremony. The hanging scroll (*kakemono*) became the prestige format for paintings, and the British Museum is very richly endowed with such paintings in ink or very restrained colour, especially those of the Kano and Nanga schools in the seventeenth, eighteenth

and nineteenth centuries. The Tea Ceremony itself led to the great development of more or less severe pottery styles, used for teabowls, tea-caddies, water jars and incense-containers, and also to hanging or standing vases for the flower arrangements which were another important element. A fine group of many hundreds of these utensils dates mainly from the seventeenth to nineteenth centuries.

While the samurai in the Kamakura period patronised Zen, the more popular Buddhist sects from China appealed to ordinary farmers and artisans, of which the most important was the Pure Land (Jōdo) doctrine which promised salvation to those who called on the name of the merciful Buddha Amida. Much surviving Buddhist art was produced for the Jōdo sects. It typically included gilded paintings illustrating Amida, and the collection is rich in such works of all periods from the fourteenth to nineteenth centuries. The fourteenth-century wooden figure of Amida is the earliest of a large group of Pure Land sculptures, many of them in more miniature forms for private devotion.

The brilliant Momoyama period (AD 1568–1603) saw the end of a century of intermittent civil war, the growth of a large urban class, and the decline of institutional Buddhism. Art became secular, gaudier, more middle-class. Style became bolder, notably in textiles, lacquer and the painted screens and sliding doors which had developed to suit the new castle architecture of the warlords. The expansive screen-painting style, often liberally adorned with gold leaf or gold powder, continues into the present century, and is well represented in the British Museum – perhaps the most striking example is a set of four sliding doors of geese, water, flowers and trees done by a pupil of Hasegawa Tōhaku in the early seventeenth century.

Despite Japanese isolation in the Edo period Dutch traders confined to Nagasaki carried to Europe the products of the young Japanese porcelain industry of the Arita district, prized above all for their harmoniously enamelled decoration. The Museum's large collection of seventeenth- eighteenth- and early nineteenth-century wares has been extended by recent purchases to include the fine white, celadon and underglaze painted wares made for export in the later nineteenth century. One of the great glories of the period is the growth of the Ukiyoe school of art, depicting the pleasures and entertainments of the increasingly rich city-dwellers. Beginning in the early seventeenth century with *genre* painting, Ukiyoe soon began to specialise in the subjects of the Kabuki theatre and portraits of the grand courtesans dressed in the latest fashions. From the mid-seventeenth century woodblock-printed illustrated books added to the Ukiyoe repertoire, followed by sheet prints, which by the 1750s were produced in a palette of dazzling colours. The British Museum's Ukiyoe collection is one of the greatest outside Japan, in all of its various forms, and amounts to some eight thousand items. The prints of the 'Golden Age' (*c.* 1780–1800) are of outstanding condition and quality.

The steady rise of aesthetic standards among a broad public in the Edo period resulted in many new schools of painting apart from Ukiyoe itself. The collections are most comprehensively represented in the Maruyama-Shijō school of the late eighteenth to late nineteenth centuries; with its emphasis on free brushwork and its unforced response to the natural world, it appeals strongly to Westerners, and continues to be vigorously collected.

The end of the isolation in the mid-nineteenth century brought Japan into strong contact with the Imperialistic, industrial nations. Japan rapidly modernised and industrialised, and her culture was for a while in danger of becoming swamped in wholesale Westernisation (Meiji period, 1867–1912). After a generation many traditional arts were reasserted, alongside international ones. The collection is naturally rich in the many adaptations of traditional crafts to produce exportable goods. One example was the change made by netsuke-carvers towards larger carv-

214
215
217

ings, usually of ivory, of 'typical' Japanese subjects for Western side-tables and mantelpieces (mostly in the period 1870–1900).

Japanese art and craft production has tended in the twentieth century to become more and more confined to self-conscious studio practitioners. The British Museum cannot keep up with all areas of activity but has successfully brought its collection of prints up to date. Indeed, its collection of graphic art in all mediums from Meiji until the present day is probably the most comprehensive in the world.

216

217 Asukayama at Cherry Blossom Time. *Woodblock print, signed Kiyonaga, about 1785. This is typical of the works of Tori Kiyonaga (AD 1752–1815), known for his plein-air compositions containing graceful figures which greatly vitalised Ukiyoe art at the end of the eighteenth century. Each sheet 37 × 25.5 cm.*

PREHISTORY
AND
ROMAN BRITAIN

*T*he collections in the Department of Prehistory and Early Europe, formerly Prehistoric and Romano-British Antiquities, represent virtually the whole span of human history from man's earliest appearance more than two million years ago up to the Christian era. Geographically the collections cover the Old World for the earlier periods (Palaeolithic and Mesolithic), Europe in the later prehistoric periods (Neolithic, Bronze and Iron Ages) and Roman Britain. Prehistory is concerned with the preliterate period of man's past, which must be reconstructed by archaeologists without the help of written records. The collections also illustrate the work of the archaeologist, for all the information we have about early man is inferred entirely from material remains, whether casually collected or scientifically excavated.

THE PALAEOLITHIC PERIOD

The oldest objects in the British Museum are those in the Quaternary Section of the Department of Pre-history and Early Europe. These collections consist of stone tools, bone and antler artefacts, personal ornaments and miniature art, excavated or collected in Britain, Western Europe, the Middle East, Africa, India, Australia and North America. They date from the time of the appearance of the first known tool-making humans just over two million years ago and end with the transition to agriculture about ten thousand years ago in the Old World, more recently elsewhere.

Amongst the oldest cultural remains in the world are those from the unparalleled sequence of sites excavated by Louis and Mary Leakey in Olduvai Gorge, Tanzania. The British Museum is fortunate in having a small but representative series of artefacts from these sites spanning about 1.5 million years of early human development. The choppers, spheroids and flake tools forming the 'Oldowan' tool-kits reveal that the deci-sion-making ability and manual skills, which have been the key to human success, were already a characteristic of the early human population evolving in Africa some two million years ago. These populations lived by hunting or scavenging meat from the carcasses of animals which had died through natural causes, and by collecting plant foods – a means of subsistence which was to persist throughout the Palaeolithic period.

The collection also contains a selection of Acheulian handaxes, which first appear at Olduvai about 1.4 million years ago. There are also small collections of Oldowan and Acheulian tools from a number of other African sites, including Kalambo Falls in Zambia, Stellenbosch in South Africa and Olorgesailie in Kenya, reflecting the spread of tool-making humans throughout the African continent.

In Africa handaxes seem to have died out around 120,000 years ago as flake production became more controlled and regular. The uniformity achieved can be seen in the typical retouched points and scrapers of the Middle Stone Age from sites like Kalambo Falls in Zambia, Elmenteita in Kenya and Cape Flats in South Africa. These flake tools may have been fixed into hafts made of wood, bone or antler to form a variety of tools and weapons, such as knives or spears, but there is no evidence to prove that this technology existed south of the Sahara.

Outside Africa no artefacts can undoubtedly be dated before one million years ago. Europe is not

219 *Handaxe of flint discovered in 1690 in Gray's Inn Lane, London.* L 16.5cm.

known to have been occupied before 700,000 years ago, and the largest part of the Quaternary Section's hold-ings comprise stone artefacts from Western Europe, principally Britain and France, dating from between 500,000 and 10,000 years ago. Among the older or 'Lower' Palaeolithic objects are handaxes from St Acheul and Abbeville in France. These specimens, found in ancient channels of the River Somme, are of historic interest as they formed part of the evidence which convinced late nineteenth-century scientists that human activity in Europe began far beyond 4004 BC, the estimated date of the Biblical Creation. Another early find came from Hoxne (Suffolk), and the Museum has recently acquired handaxes and flake tools excavated from the same site in the 1970s. These excavations showed that the tool-makers had estab-lished a camp in a woodland clearing by the side of a lake which had once existed there about 350,000 years ago.

The technological tradition displayed in the tool-kit from Hoxne is quite different from that derived from Clacton-on-Sea (Essex), and from the Museum's own excavations at High Lodge (Suffolk). At both of these 220 sites the tool-makers used flint, not to make handaxes but to produce thick flakes which could then be modi-fied to form a variety of tools. At High Lodge many flakes were found lying in clusters or 'scatters' and these have remained undisturbed since the time they were formed. By fitting the flakes back together well over 100,000 years later it is possible to see every step in the flake production.

Handaxes and flake tools from sites such as Oldbury (Kent), La Cotte de St Brelade on Jersey, and La Ferrassie, La Quina and Le Moustier in France show that very few changes occurred in tools or tool-making techniques during the Middle Palaeolithic.

Implements of the European Upper Palaeolithic dating from 35,000 to 10,000 years ago are more varied

218 *The Snettisham Torc. The finest surviving Celtic torc, made of eight strands of gold twisted together, each of which is in turn made of eight wires. From Snettisham, Norfolk, first century* BC. D 19.9cm.

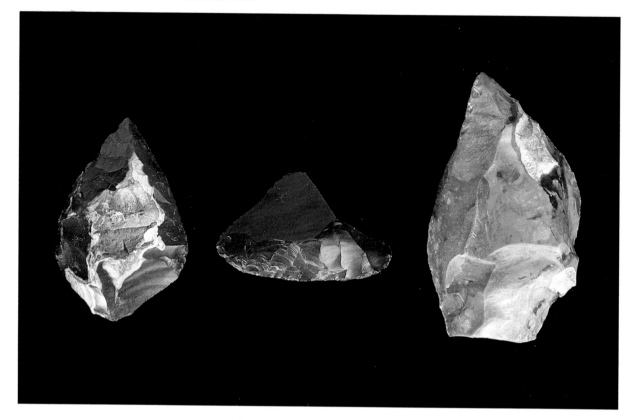

220 *Scrapers made on flint flakes from High Lodge, Suffolk, about 450,000 years ago. These tools form part of a tool-kit used by the earliest inhabitants yet known in Britain.* H (largest) 11cm.

than those from the earlier periods. There is a wider range of stone tools, many of which are made on long, narrow 'blades' rather than flakes, along with a great deal of bone and antler equipment, personal ornaments such as beads and pendants, and art objects. The technological innovations and variations in tool-kit composition suggest that successive, far-reaching cultural changes were taking place within relatively short periods of just a few thousand years.

The basic sequence of these changes was established in the late nineteenth century by pioneering archaeologists such as Edouard Lartet and Henry Christy, who sought cultural evidence of progress and development to substantiate the new theories of human evolution by excavating in the caves and rock-shelters of south-west France. From these sites came a fascinating series of artefacts and works of art which were donated to the British Museum. Additional important material from other parts of western Europe came by way of the Sturge Bequest, so that the Museum now holds Upper Palaeolithic collections without rival outside France.

The earlier Perigordian, Aurignacian and Gravettian phases of the Upper Palaeolithic are represented in collections from the type-sites of Perigord, Aurignac and La Gravette (France). These include examples of the blunted or 'backed' blades, particular types of scrapers and engraving tools known as burins which typify these periods. Amongst the Aurignacian material are also examples of bone points used as spear or lance tips. The collections of Solutrean material from Solutré and Laugerie Haute show that bone- and antler-working and blade production were less significant during the period following the Aurignacian from 20,000 to 16,000 years ago. They were replaced by finely worked points shaped like laurel and willow leaves, of which the specimen from Volgu is the supreme example. Indeed, this piece is so skilfully made that it can be regarded more as a brilliant expression of craftsmanship than as a purely functional item.

A variety of bone and antler objects reappears in the final Magdalenian phase of the Upper Palaeolithic from sites such as La Madeleine, Les Eyzies, Montastruc and Corbet (France). These include barbed points made as spear or harpoon tips, spear-throwers, perforated batons of unknown function and smaller items such as needles. Many of these are decorated with abstract or geometric designs, but art was not restricted to functional items. Thin discs of bone, pieces of ivory, antler rods and plaques of stone were engraved and

221 *Tip of a mammoth tusk carved into the shape of two reindeer swimming one behind another. From Montastruc, France, about 14,000 years old. L 20.7cm.*

sculpted, often with complex and possibly symbolic designs. The stone plaques from Montastruc, for example, are decorated with recognisable but rather stylised animals shown in twisted profile, some superimposed on others, displaying in miniature some of the features characteristic of the paintings and engravings found on cave walls. Among the decorated specimens from La Madeleine are antler batons engraved with beautifully drawn outlines of reindeer and horses which march nose to tail along the shafts, whilst the art objects from Courbet include carved heads of horses and musk ox, which originally formed parts of spear-throwers. The numerous pieces of miniature art from Montastruc include a second spear-thrower ingeniously carved as a mammoth, as well as one of the great masterpieces of the period, an ivory rod carved to the shape of two reindeer, a male following a female. The carving is detailed and naturalistic, showing the animals with their chins up and their antlers back, as if swimming. It is a work of genius in both its conception and technique, and its quality and beauty transcend the 14,000 years that have elapsed since its creation.

222 *Carving from reindeer antler of a mammoth, originally part of a spear-thrower with a wooden handle. The animal's tail provided the hook, which held the base of the spear. From Montastruc, France, about 14,000 years old. W 12.4cm.*

223 Antler frontlet and mattock head from the 10,000-year-old site of Star Carr, Yorkshire. The mattock head is made of elk antler. The frontlet is part of a red deer skull with antlers and the holes drilled through it suggest that it might have been worn as a head-dress or hung as a trophy. L (mattock) 20cm.

THE MESOLITHIC PERIOD

Implements dating from about 10,000 years ago exhibit considerable changes from those of the preceding Upper Palaeolithic. Some of these changes are to be seen in material from Wawcott (Berkshire) and Oakhanger (Hampshire). The tool-kits from these sites contain new, standardised tool forms made from small blades or bladelets. The most distinctive artefacts are the small neatly shaped bladelet segments known as *microliths*. These were fixed into wooden hafts to form tools and weapons, such as arrowheads and knives. Parallel-sided axes sharpened at one end by the removal of a single flake are also common and were presumably used for felling trees or wood-working. The collection from Star Carr (Yorkshire) reveals that a wide range of artefacts were also made of organic material. These include long, thin antler points with barbs along one side and perforated mattocks made from elk and red deer antlers. Most curious is part of a red deer skull which has two holes drilled through it. This skull might have been worn as a head-dress during ceremonies or as a disguise to enable hunters to get close to their prey.

223

THE NEOLITHIC PERIOD

The first domestic animals and cultivated crops appeared in the Near East some 10,000 years ago. By 5000 BC sizeable farming populations had occupied parts of Central and Western Europe and the Mediterranean area. Within the next two thousand years the knowledge of farming spread throughout Europe, save where the northern climate prevented crop growth. The production of food was to transform society: permanent settlements were established, and more stratified societies developed.

The artefacts of food production were limited but functional, and they are well represented in the collections. Axes with polished flint or stone blades were used to clear forests and were employed in increasingly sophisticated carpentry to construct timber houses. Flint-edged sickles were used for harvesting, and querns and rubbers reduced grain to flour. A range of flint tools helped to turn plants and animals into food, and their by-products into clothing, containers and bindings to satisfy the needs of everyday existence. A revolutionary new skill was the making of pottery, chiefly used for storing food, for cooking and tableware. The earliest wares were plain, but experimentation led to more complex shapes and decoration by painting and impression. The typical impressed and incised geometric decoration of, for example, Peterborough and Grooved ware in Britain during the third millennium BC strike a contrast with the simpler wares of the earlier period. In eastern Europe more ornate and varied painted styles occurred, as shown by trichrome painted pottery from the Ukraine.

Increasing economic surplus and social complexity were the impetus for developments beyond the strictly functional. The polishing of axeheads for a more efficient and durable cutting edge was widely practised, but this labour-intensive task was frequently extended to the whole surface, an action that could have no other purpose than for display. An axe of polished jadeite found near Canterbury in Kent is in pristine state and was clearly not intended for normal use. The stone from which it was made probably came from the Alpine region, and indeed jadeite deposits in northern Italy were quarried from an early date and large mirror-polished axes of this semi-precious stone were traded and exchanged far afield. A growing selectivity in raw materials becomes evident, and much effort went into quarrying and deep-mining for better-quality stone and flint, as at the Neolithic flint-mining complex at Grime's Graves (Norfolk), explored by the British Museum between 1972 and 1976.

Wood-working also became increasingly important. Little organic material has survived from this early date, although some examples have been preserved from waterlogged sites, such as the Alpine lakeside settle-

224 ABOVE *Peterborough ware bowl from Hedsor, Buckinghamshire, decorated with twisted cord impressions. Pottery decorated in this style was widely used in England and Wales in the second half of the third millennium BC. D 17.5 cm.*

ments; here the total range of domestic objects in use in the Neolithic was revealed in a remarkable series of excavations in the nineteenth century. In England the wetlands of the Somerset Levels and the East Anglian Fens have yielded up wooden implements, such as an axe-haft of ash from Etton (Cambridgeshire). A section of the Sweet Track, now in the British Museum, is a fine example of Neolithic carpentry, dating to the early fourth millennium BC; the two-kilometre track provided a dry path across the marshy Somerset Levels. Such finds offer a new perspective to a material culture otherwise known only from its less perishable components.

With these have also come objects which cast light on areas of belief otherwise unsuspected, like the remarkable god-dolly, a small wooden figure recovered from the Bell Track (Somerset). Very little naturalistic art survives from prehistoric Britain; the god-dolly, and a crude figure in chalk – the 'goddess' – from the Grime's Grave flint mines, are among the few examples. In contrast is a red-fired pottery figure from Vinča (Yugoslavia); this seated figure, with its hands on its

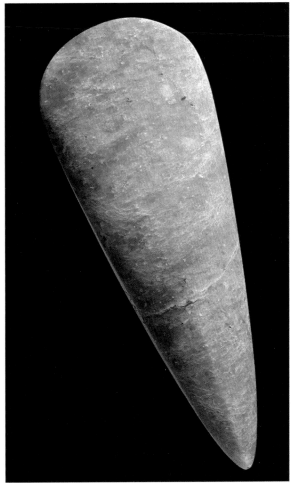

225 *Ground and highly polished ceremonial axehead made from jadeite from northern Italy, one of the earliest imports into Britain. From Canterbury, Kent, about 4000 BC. L 21.9 cm.*

226 *Decorated fired clay cult figurine, seated on a tripod stool, from Vinča, Yugoslavia. About 4500* BC. H *17cm.*

hips, has pierced shoulders, elbows and ears and a stylised head. The aesthetic and perhaps spiritual aspirations of Neolithic society are reflected in such figurines.

THE BRONZE AGE

By the end of the third millennium BC a pattern had been established of prosperous well-adapted agricultural communities with increasing technological sophistication. Meanwhile in eastern Europe a new era had already dawned with the discovery of metallurgy. The earliest metal tools were of unalloyed copper and, although it produced a less effective cutting edge than stone or flint, the new material held certain advantages. A damaged or broken tool could simply be melted down and recast, while the relative scarcity of copper and the mysteries of its production could confer prestige upon its owner. As copper – and tin, the other chief component of bronze – are found only in certain parts of Europe trade became a marked feature of the Bronze Age, bringing prosperity to those who controlled the sources and the routes by which the materials were dispersed. With trade came the exchange of other materials, in particular exotica such as gold and amber used for personal adornment.

The British Museum's collection traces the development of metalworking technology during the Bronze Age. Experimentation brought improvements in the quality of the metal itself and in casting techniques. The use of alloys improved the hardness and durability of the implement. Arsenical copper had such properties and its use became widespread. Around 3000 BC came the realisation that bronze – a copper-tin alloy – was superior in all respects, and this new, more durable alloy gradually replaced copper.

The development of casting technology is shown by the increasing sophistication of moulds. The early moulds are simple: shallow matrices cut into the surface of a suitable stone. A considerable improvement is represented by two-piece moulds, the separate halves being bound together and filled from one end. This form allowed the production of more complex shapes, and innovations such as sockets for hafting. In time moulds of clay and metal were added to the repertoire, providing even greater diversity in casting and an economy of labour in the production of formers. A founder's hoard from Brough-on-Humber included a two-part bronze mould complete with a socketed axe casting. The development of axe forms over this period reflects this technological improvement, from the flat axes of the Copper Age to the sophisticated socketed axes of the Late Bronze Age. Finds from Central Europe, eastern France and northern Italy particularly show technical artistry in the casting of daggers with well-crafted hilts and decorated blades.

In Western Europe the introduction of metallurgy can be linked to groups using a distinctive form of pottery, most familiar as a fine decorated drinking cup, or Beaker. The style is known from Spain to Denmark, and from Hungary to Ireland. The new Beaker pottery is very different from what went before. It is well made, thin walled and fired under controlled conditions often to give a handsome rich reddish-brown surface. The earliest carry the imprint of a fine twisted cord wound round the vessel from top to bottom or narrow horizontal zones of impressed lines made with a rectangular toothed comb stamp. On the finest vessels geometric patterns are set with great precision in evenly spaced bands around the pot.

227 ABOVE *Bronze spearhead, pin and dagger, and stone battleaxe from an Early Bronze Age burial at Snowshill, Gloucestershire. The spearhead, with tang and cast socket for attachment, illustrates the improvement in casting technology during this period. About 1500 BC. L (dagger) 22.1cm.*

228 BELOW *A range of Beaker pottery (from the left) from Hemp Knoll (Wiltshire), Rudston (Humberside), Goodmanham (Humberside), Lambourn (Berkshire) and Hitchin (Hertfordshire).* H *(tallest) 26.7cm.*

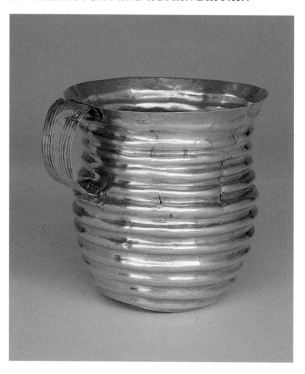

The Beaker groups were also responsible for another innovation: for the first time personal goods accompanied the deceased in the grave. In most graves the body was accompanied only by a Beaker, although some were equipped with additional objects: weaponry (a dagger, stone battle-axe, archer's equipment) and ornaments of bronze, gold, jet and amber. The Beaker itself may have contained nourishment for the deceased: analysis of the residues in a beaker from Scotland indicated a honey-sweetened drink or mead. In some areas exceptionally rich and exotic materials occasionally accompanied the dead. Among the most notable are grave finds in Wessex, southern England. Dating from the later part of the Beaker period, these graves featured prestige items such as weapons, a range of spectacular personal ornaments and beaker-shaped cups made from a variety of exotic materials, such as gold, shale and amber. Such an item is the gold cup from the Rillaton Barrow in Cornwall. This splendid piece is one of only three such found in temperate Europe, and is made of sheet gold, ribbed for reinforcement and decoration, with a remarkable ribbon-like handle.

229 ABOVE *Gold cup found in an Early Bronze Age burial at Rillaton, Cornwall. The body of the cup was beaten out from a single piece of gold; the handle, made separately, is attached by rivets. About 1700–1400 BC. H 8.3cm.*

230 BELOW *Solid chalk cylinders, ornately carved in a woodworking style, found with the skeleton of a child in a grave beneath a round barrow at Folkton, North Yorkshire. Early Bronze Age, about 2200–2000 BC. D (largest) 14.2cm.*

Also from the Beaker period are three of the most extraordinary objects to have survived from prehistoric Britain: the Folkton Drums. These chalk cylinders vary in diameter from 10.4 to 14.6 cm, and are carefully carved around the tops and sides. Some of the carving is reminiscent of earlier decoration on pottery, but two cylinders are carved with eyebrow and eye motifs. Although these items are unique, and their purpose is entirely unknown, they must have been highly valued, yet they were placed with the body of a child in one of a number of simple graves beneath an unremarkable mound.

One of the richest and most important discoveries from Bronze Age Britain was the group of burials in a barrow at Barnack in Cambridgeshire, excavated between 1974 and 1976. The barrow had been used for a number of burials over several centuries. The initial burial at the base of the great central grave is now reconstructed in the British Museum. At the foot of the body of an adult male stood an exceptionally large and fine Beaker, a copper or bronze dagger, an ivory pendant and a polished greenstone wristguard.

Evidence for ritual is sparce. Votive deposits, often consigned to river or bog, became increasingly common. Hoards of metalwork were frequently buried during the Bronze Age and many of these seem to have been for ritual or ceremonial purposes. In Britain, for example, a group of four bronze axes were buried at Willerby Wold (North Yorkshire), in association with a contemporary burial mound – clearly a sacred site. These axes are in pristine condition, three of them with punched ornament. Although sites such as the monumental stone circles and henges yield little in the way of precise information about the nature of the

231 *Bronze shield found in a bog at Moel Siabod, near Capel Curig, Wales. The raised decoration was beaten out from the back. The type is British, differing considerably from Continental forms. Late Bronze Age, about 800 BC. D 64.4cm.*

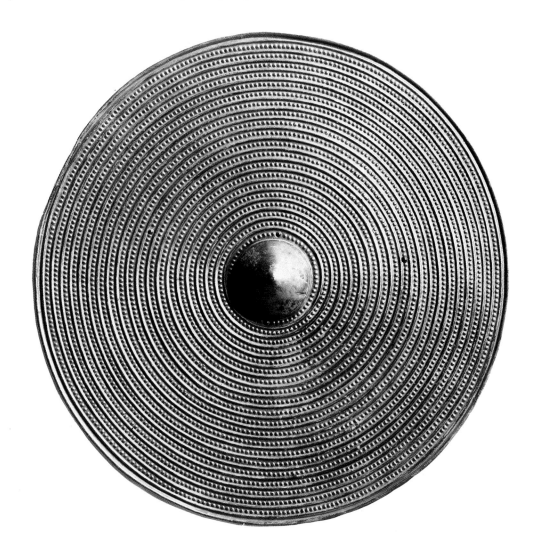

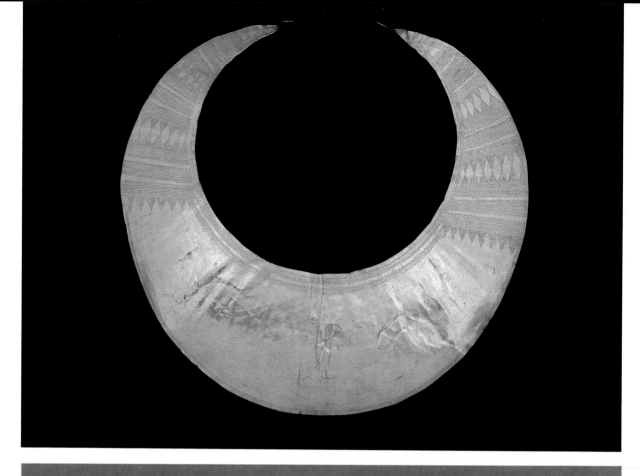

232 LEFT *Gold lunula from Ireland of 'classical' type, one of a group distinguished by their thinness, by their width and by the precision of their ornamentation. Early Bronze Age, about 2000–1500 BC. W 23.7cm.*

rituals enacted, they emphasise the preoccupation with power and prestige constantly in evidence. Hoards of the later Bronze Age make the same point: they reveal a considerable expenditure of effort on the elaboration of weaponry, especially swords and spears, together with the appearance of spectacular shields and bronze body-armour.

Western European craftsmen showed an early interest in the decorative possibilities of sheet gold. In Ireland Beaker ceramic motifs were transferred to crescent-shaped neck ornaments or *lunulae*. The zoned geometric designs often achieved a fine degree of intricate detail. Elsewhere this crescent form was re-produced in bead necklaces, the desired shape being maintained by complex bored spacer plates in amber and jet. The jet necklace from Melfort (Strathclyde), is a typical example and a characteristic find from Scot-land at this period. The acme of sheet goldwork in the West European Bronze Age tradition, dating to about 1200 BC, is the great gold cape found in a grave at Mold (Clwyd, Wales). Made from a continuous piece of metal, beaten out over a rock to obtain the shape, its surface is decorated with bosses and ribs in a pattern that may imitate the folds of cloth. The cape was presumably for ceremonial use, since the wearer could not have moved his arms once the cape was in place.

If the techniques of sheet-gold working reached their peak with the Mold gold cape, casting and the manipulation of wire offered new possibilities. The improvement in casting technology, involving the use of increasingly complex moulds, encouraged the elabora-tion of shape. Wire became prominent in such items as the fibula, or safety-pin brooch, a long-lived form invented at this period. Irish goldsmiths in particular produced fine goldwork, culminating in the develop-ment of the twisted bar torc: torcs continued to be manufactured for at least a millennium.

Most of the surviving evidence for the Bronze Age comes from either graves or hoards of metalwork. These enable us to study the widening range of tools and weapons in use and to gain some insight into the technological achievements of the age. A founder's hoard from Minster in Kent, for example, contained a quantity of raw metal and casting waste and bronze

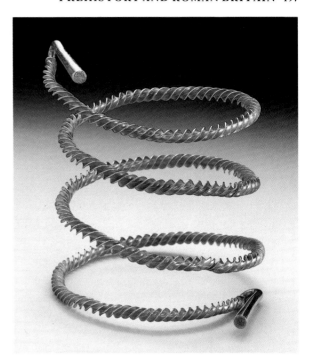

234 *A gold torc from Wales made from a twisted bar and wound into 3½ coils. It is an example of a type found in Britain, Ireland and northern France. Middle Bronze Age, about 1200–900 BC. L 11.6cm.*

implements, some of which were scrap, ready for re-casting. Hoards from southern Britain also reveal par-ticular local fashions; a hoard of bronzes from Brighton contained three coiled finger-rings, a torc and a pal-stave, as well as four 'Sussex loops', a type of coiled arm-ring known only from hoards in Sussex.

Recent archaeological work has concentrated on ex-cavating settlement sites. The rich yield of informa-tion from well-preserved sites such as Runnymede Bridge (Berkshire), now being explored by a team from the British Museum, is set to transform our under-standing of prehistoric Britain and so allow us to place the hoards and graves within the social systems which once existed. Here enormous quantities of finds as varied as pottery, metalwork, bone objects and flints have been recovered. Such sites can also yield valuable information on the trading patterns which provided the real motive-force of Bronze Age society and economy. Whereas hoards and grave groups are by definition selective, the loss or discarding of material which char-acterises all settlement sites provides a more accurate reflection of what was available and in current use. Trade was clearly highly organised, as shown by the retrieval of lost cargoes of bronzes from the estuary of the Huelva and off the modern port of Dover, the latter preserved in the British Museum.

233 *Ceremonial gold cape from Mold, Wales, found in a burial around the bones of a skeleton. The cape is made from a single sheet of gold and covered in repoussé ornament. Middle Bronze Age, about 1200 BC. H 23.5cm.*

235 *One of a pair of bronze flagons, decorated with inlays of coral and red enamel. This is one of the outstanding examples of early Celtic art of the La Tène period. From Basse-Yutz, France, about 400 BC. H 39.6cm*

Developments towards the end of the Bronze Age prefigured those of the succeeding Iron Age, when new technologies began to alter the long-standing social systems. The central position held by metal resources and their control is emphasised by a determination to maintain the pre-eminence of bronze. Iron implements have been found in later Bronze Age contexts, sufficient to show that the technology was available and understood, but the introduction of ironworking beyond south-east Europe was long delayed and, it must be assumed, long resisted.

THE IRON AGE

The European Iron Age is divided into two phases, Hallstatt (*c.* 700–450 BC) and La Tène (*c.* 450 BC to the Roman Conquest), named after type-sites where large collections of artefacts were excavated in the nine-

teenth century. At Hallstatt, in Upper Austria, almost 1,000 burials were excavated by J. G. Ramsauer between 1845 and 1863, and later in the 1860s more were unearthed by two British archaeologists, Sir John Evans and Sir John Lubbock. La Tène, on the edge of Lake Neuchâtel in Switzerland, seems to have been the site of a water-cult, where artefacts were deposited as votive offerings. Engineering works and subsequent archaeological excavations during 1880–85 and 1907–17 produced more than three thousand swords and scabbards, spearheads, brooches, tools, coins and wooden objects. Hallstatt and La Tène are representative of the kinds of site from which the British Museum collections draw their strength. There is a little from La Tène itself, rather more from Hallstatt (including most of the finds from the Evans/Lubbock excavations), but from other burial sites and votive deposits come many of the finest objects known from the period.

Many of the Iron Age peoples of Europe (mainly

Celts) buried their dead with great ceremony, accompanied by objects worn or used during life. Nowhere provides a better example of these rituals than Champagne, where the most spectacular finds are from a series of chariot-burials. The corpse was buried with a complete chariot surrounded by harness and other grave-goods. The majority of graves are less elaborate, but it was customary to bury women with their jewellery – a torc round the neck and often a couple of bracelets and one or two brooches – whilst warriors had an array of weapons. Both men and women were accompanied by pottery, and animal bones suggest that food was included to sustain the dead. In the second half of the nineteenth century many thousands of La Tène graves were excavated in Champagne, and one of the largest collections amassed by Léon Morel, of Rheims, was acquired by the British Museum in 1901. It includes one of the most spectacular chariot-burials, from Somme-Bionne (Marne), whose grave-goods included a Greek pottery cup and an Etruscan bronze flagon.

In Britain Iron Age burials are well represented in only two areas; eastern Yorkshire, where inhumation was practised from the fourth century BC; and south-eastern England, where cremation was the rule, but only in the century immediately before the Roman Conquest. The Yorkshire burials are less impressive than their Continental counterparts; most skeletons are without grave-goods, but some have the occasional brooch, bracelet, pot or sword. Finds from excavations by nineteenth-century antiquaries have now been supplemented by material from a modern excacation at Burton Fleming. Two chariot-burials have recently been excavated by the British Museum at Garton-on-the-Wolds and Kirkburn. In both the vehicle had been dismantled, the T-shaped chariot frame, a crouched skeleton and pieces of harness being distributed on the floor. Chain-mail had been placed over one of the bodies, the earliest occurrence so far found in Britain.

The cremation burials of south-eastern England belong to the 'Aylesford Culture', which takes its name from a cemetery in Kent excavated at the end of the last century. Again, the Department's old acquisitions (including material from Aylesford itself) have been supplemented by recent finds, noticeably from a huge cemetery of 471 burials found just outside the walls of Verulamium in 1966. Many of those burials comprised only a collection of cremated bone in an urn, but others were more elaborate, with up to ten pots in a grave and several were accompanied by brooches. None of the Verulamium burials was as rich as that found at Welwyn Garden City in 1965. Here the cremated bones were in a heap on the floor of the grave and included bear-claws from the fur-wrapping round the corpse. No fewer than thirty pots were ranged on the floor of the grave, and the five Roman amphorae leaning against the wall would have held about 100 litres of imported wine.

237 ABOVE *Reconstruction of a bucket with bronze fittings found in a burial at Aylesford, Kent. The repoussé decoration on the upper band includes pairs of stylised horses. First century BC. H (excluding handle mounts) 30cm.*

236 BELOW. *Four glass game-pieces from a complete set of twenty-four from a burial at Welwyn Garden City, Hertfordshire. First century BC. H 2–2.2cm.*

236 The most spectacular item in the Welwyn Garden City grave, however, was a unique set of glass game-pieces; divided by colour into four sets of six pieces, which seem to have been used for a race-game perhaps like ludo. Discoveries such as Welwyn Garden City show how Britons living in south-east England were 238 open to influences from Roman Gaul. They appear to have relished Italian wine, and imported the tableware to go with it, including silver cups. In return, according to Strabo, the Britons exported corn, cattle, gold, silver, hides, slaves and hunting dogs. Such trade gradually paved the way for the Roman Conquest.

Food and drink for the dead, and vehicles for transport to another world, suggest that the Celts anticipated an afterlife, but beyond such vague generalisations little can be said of the beliefs of people who left no written documents. The importance of some kind of water-cult is obvious, for some of the finest surviving artefacts come from lakes, rivers and bogs. In England the River Thames has pride of place, for this has produced some of the very finest decorated metalwork. The great shield 239 from Battersea, two shield-bosses from Wandsworth, and a magnificent horned helmet from near Waterloo Bridge are only the most outstanding of the finds

recovered from dredging in the nineteenth century, while even today the supply of treasures continues. In 1985 a unique bronze shield was discovered in a former water-course at Chertsey (Surrey). Smaller collections have come from the River Witham, near Lincoln (including the magnificent Witham Shield), the River Nene (swords and scabbards found between 1980 and 1984) and the River Bann, in Northern Ireland (a superb decorated scabbard-plate).

A further example of this water-ritual is the now-famous Lindow Man – the upper half of a human body whose skin has been perfectly preserved by the acids of the peat-bog. Found in 1984 by a peat-cutting machine (which destroyed his lower half) at Lindow Moss (Cheshire), Lindow Man had met his death perhaps two thousand years ago. First stunned by a couple of blows on the top of the head, he was then garrotted with a fine length of animal sinew, which strangled him and broke his neck. The killers then cut his throat before dropping their victim face-down in the bog. A ritual killing is suggested by this elaborate sequence of death, concluding with the flowing of blood and deposition in water, and it is known from classical sources that the Celts did not shrink from human sacrifice.

Impressive collections of metalwork, especially harness and vehicle fittings, were deposited at Stanwick (North Yorkshire), Polden Hills (Somerset) and Westhall (Suffolk) in the years shortly before and after the Roman Conquest. They convey a good idea of the range and decoration of such equipment, but leave no

238 Group of fine pottery of the early first century AD imported into southern England from north-eastern Gaul before the Roman invasion of AD 43. Found at St Albans, Hertfordshire, and Colchester, Essex. H (tallest) 19cm.

240 ABOVE *The iron handle of a sword, decorated with red enamel. From Kirkburn, North Humberside, second century* BC. L *(handle) 13.7cm.*

239 *The Battersea Shield: the bronze facing from a wooden shield, the flowing palmette and scroll ornament enhanced with red enamel. Found in the River Thames at Battersea, London, first century* BC. H *77cm.*

241 *Bronze mirror from Desborough, Northamptonshire. One of the finest surviving Celtic mirrors, it is decorated on the back with an elaborate symmetrical design. First century* BC. L *35cm.*

clue as to why these deposits were buried. Again, there seems every likelihood that they served some ritual purpose, but there is no way in which the ceremonies and beliefs associated with their deposition can be reconstructed. With another type of hoard, the gold torcs found especially in East Anglia, it seems reasonable to suppose that wealth was being buried for safe keeping in time of danger. At Snettisham, Norfolk, five separate hoards were uncovered in one field in 1948 and 1950. One included the magnificent Snettisham Torc, but in all fragments of at least 61 torcs were found in the hoards, together with 158 coins. It may well be that the entire collection was deposited on one occasion some time during the second half of the first century BC, buried in separate locations for greater security. In 1968 five complete gold torcs were found on a building site at Ipswich; another was later discovered nearby.

The bulk of the artefacts mentioned convey something of death and ritual in the Iron Age and throw light on such matters as fashion in jewellery and aspects of warfare. Much, too, can be learnt about the technology needed to manufacture these objects, but what of life itself in the Iron Age? The most impressive settlements are the hillforts, whose often massive earthwork defences remain spectacular even today. Some were in permanent occupation, whilst others seem to have served as refuges. Far more common than hillforts would have been the lowland settlements, especially farmsteads, many hundreds of which are now known from air photography. Most of the population would have lived in these, occupying circular wooden huts with thatched roofs, and earning their living on the land, growing grain to be stored in pits or in the wooden

242 TOP RIGHT *Roman weapons of the first century* AD. *The javelin-heads and the dagger and sheath are from Hod Hill, Dorset, while the sword and its highly decorated scabbard were found in the Thames at Fulham, London.* L *(sword blade) 57cm.*

243 BOTTOM RIGHT *The body of a man preserved in a peat-bog at Lindow Moss, Cheshire. First century* AD.

218

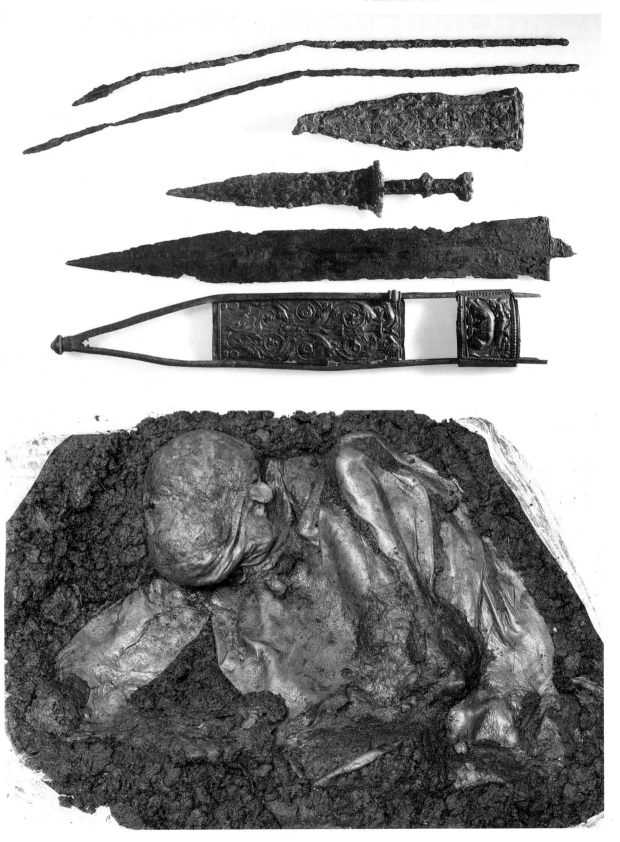

granaries whose ground-plan of four post-holes is such a distinctive feature of Iron Age settlements. Such communities were largely self-sufficient, rearing also cattle, sheep and pigs. The most common finds to come from these settlements, apart from animal bones, are sherds of pottery, whilst metal and bone artefacts are relatively rare. Occasionally we are offered a glimpse of other things. A pit on the settlement at Gussage All Saints (Dorset), had been used to dump the debris from a bronze-smith's workshop. This yielded more than 7,000 fragments of clay moulds, used for casting bronze by the lost-wax process, as well as some bone tools used in modelling the wax. The collection includes a type series of finds from a number of sites as well as the entire collection from excavations at Staple Howe, a small palisaded farmstead in Yorkshire, and the Hod Hill hillfort in Dorset.

Hod Hill, excavated by a team from the Museum between 1951 and 1958, was one of the hillforts attacked by the Roman Second Legion under the command of the future emperor Vespasian. The Britons there had no time to complete their defences, and were no match for the organisation of the Roman army. They had to suffer an attack that accurately concentrated its fire of ballista-bolts on the chieftain's hut, and in defeat saw their defences slighted. But Hod Hill marks the arrival of Rome in a still more obvious way. The conquerors expelled the defenders and built their own distinctive military fort within a corner of the Iron Age defences.

Roman Britain

When Britain became a province of the Roman Empire in AD 43 profound changes were to take place, not only in social organisation, but in administration, law, language and religion. The very appearance of the country was transformed by forts, roads, towns and buildings of brick and stone, while the lives of the inhabitants were enriched by a vastly increased choice of material goods. Celtic culture continued, certainly, but was now to become inextricably woven with the traditions of the classical world.

With the Conquest Britain also makes its appearance on the stage of written history, and though the greater part of our knowledge of the period is derived from archaeological rather than historical sources there are rare instances where the two combine. One such is the tombstone of Julius Classicianus, the procurator (senior fiscal administrator) of the province immediately after the unsuccessful rebellion led by the British Queen Boudica in AD 60–1. The Roman historian Tacitus relates how wisely Classicianus dealt with the aftermath of the revolt, overruling the desire for retaliation and revenge evinced by the Roman military leadership.

244 *Restored tombstone of Julius Classicianus, erected by his widow, Julia Pacata. The fragments were found in London, so although the date of his death is unknown, we may infer that Classicianus died in office.* L 2.3m.

Evidence for the presence of the army is abundant, and the collections contain a wide range of armour and weaponry. They range from fragments of armour and an array of iron spears and javelin-heads from Hod Hill (Dorset), to exceptional objects, like the highly decorated cavalry parade-helmet found at Ribchester (Lancashire), in the late eighteenth century. One of the most remarkable finds of recent years is the collection of wooden writing-tablets from Vindolanda (Chesterholm), near Hadrian's Wall. These tablets are a striking illustration of the fact that the most interesting and important objects are not necessarily beautiful or intrinsically valuable, being simply paper-thin slivers of wood, with faint traces of writing in ink, hardly seeming to merit a second glance. Yet these are the earliest written documents from Britain, and afford a unique glimpse into the everyday affairs of a garrison in a remote frontier post of the Empire.

The dividends paid by careful study of often unspectacular material have long been known in the case of pottery. Detailed research on the huge quantity of ceramics from Roman sites has enabled scholars to build up a framework for dating, and to gain insights into the organisation of manufacturing industries and trading activities. Pottery was used for the majority of cooking utensils and tableware, and was manufactured throughout the country. Many existing pre-Roman industries simply developed and expanded under the new regime. Pottery was also imported from other provinces: the mass-produced red tableware known as *samian* was manufactured in Gaul and traded all over the western Empire in the first and second centuries AD. It can be very closely dated, sometimes to within

245 *A Roman cavalry helmet in bronze and iron, from Witcham Gravel, Ely, Cambridgeshire.* H *30cm.*

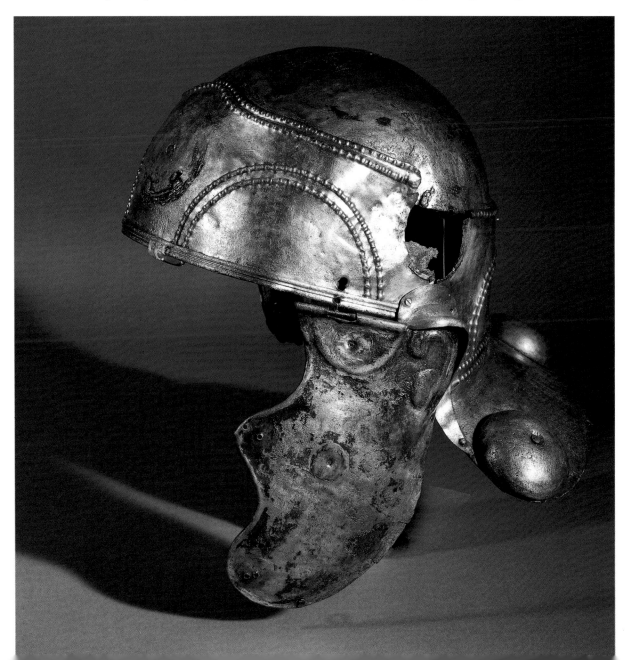

246 ABOVE *One of several hundred documents found at the Roman fort of Vindolanda. They were written on thin tablets of wood, and include official and personal correspondence.* L *17cm.*

247 BELOW *Group of pottery from Stonea, Cambridgeshire.* D *(central bowl) 31.6cm.*

twenty years or so, and the styles of individual potters and workshops, whose name-stamps appear on many of the vessels, can be recognised.

Stonea (Cambridgeshire) was excavated by the British Museum between 1980 and 1984 as part of a planned programme of research into a specific area of the Roman landscape. It was evidently an administrative centre, perhaps overseeing the development of agriculture and stock-raising in the Fenland during the earlier part of the Roman occupation. Finds from sites like Stonea and from the small rural settlements in the same area help to build up a picture of the life-style of

the inhabitants and the way in which Roman policy decisions impinged upon them.

Glass vessels, which first appear in Britain just before the Roman Conquest, must be classed as luxury goods. Because glass is fragile and reusable, settlement sites seldom yield complete vessels, but undamaged examples are sometimes found in graves. The collection includes some of the finest pieces known from Roman Britain, such as the perfect mould-blown beaker with a chariot-racing scene from Colchester, the elegant cut-glass cup from Barnwell (Cambridgeshire) and a superb flagon from Bayford (Kent). Window-

247

248 ABOVE *Mould-blown glass beaker of the first century* AD *from Colchester, Essex. It is decorated with a scene of chariot-racing and the names of charioteers.* H *8.3cm.*

249 RIGHT *Bronze head of the emperor Hadrian from the Thames at London Bridge. It is from a statue of well over life size.* H *43cm.*

glass is known, too, from many buildings, and a complete pane has survived from a villa at Garden Hill (Sussex).

Large-scale sculpture in bronze and stone was also new to Britain, and statues of the emperor, life size or even larger, would have featured in towns and public buildings. The fine bronze head of Hadrian (ruled AD 117–138) is from such a statue, which might well have adorned a square or government building in London. One of the most important pieces of Romano-British sculpture was found as recently as 1979, during the excavation of a temple to the god Mercury at Uley (Gloucestershire). It is the head from the cult-statue of the god, larger than life size, and carved from Cotswold limestone. Though surely the work of an outstanding local sculptor who was familiar with the distinctive properties of the stone, the graceful proportions and serene expression of the head place it in a tradition which has its origins in the work of the great artists of classical Greece.

The Uley temple site produced many other finds, including the bones of sacrificed animals and a large series of lead tablets with curses scratched upon them. Unlike the Vindolanda letters, these tend to be written to a formula, but even so, those which have been translated give a vivid picture of rural Gloucestershire at the time, with complainants seeking divine help from Mercury against thieves who had deprived them of such indispensible valuables as lengths of cloth and draught oxen. Gifts to the deity at this and other pagan temple sites comprise money, statuettes and other valuables, especially jewellery.

Certain types of personal adornment, whether made of precious metal or copper alloys, had been established well before the Roman period. The functional fibula, or safety-pin brooch, is the prime example. Brooches were made in a variety of imaginative and decorative forms, and were often embellished with enamel, a Celtic speciality which reached its fullest development under Roman rule. Other types of jewellery were purely

classical, and appear for the first time in Britain after the Conquest, though in due course they too came to be manufactured here. Examples include finger-rings set with engraved gems, and bracelets and rings in the form of snakes. A small pot full of coins and silver jewellery found at Snettisham (Norfolk) in 1985 is part of the stock of a local second-century jeweller and gem-cutter, and includes amongst other things over 40 snake-rings and 110 engraved cornelians ready for setting into the standard type of early Roman ring. Gold, silver, copper and other metals had long been skilfully worked in Britain: the Roman development of these crafts was built on an ancient and sound foundation.

Silver and bronze were also used for the most luxurious tableware. As already noted, Roman silver drinking cups were among items already imported by wealthy wine-drinking Celtic rulers before the Conquest. A group of silver wine cups from Hockwold (Norfolk) belong to the early Roman period, but it is from the fourth century that a truly impressive quantity of silver has come down to us, most of it found in hoards buried for safe-keeping.

The most spectacular of these treasures was ploughed up in 1942 at Mildenhall (Suffolk). The

250 ABOVE *A 'dragonesque' brooch in enamelled bronze, a typically Romano-British ornament. The pin is missing.* L *6.2cm.*

251 BELOW *A selection of items from the hoard of Christian silver found at Water Newton, Cambridgeshire. The Sacred Monogram, the Greek letters* chi *and* rho, *can be seen on the three triangular plaques.* H *(central vase) 20.3cm.*

252 *The Great Dish from the Mildenhall Treasure, one of the finest examples of silverware surviving from antiquity.* D *60.5cm.*

technical and aesthetic quality of some of the objects in this group remains unrivalled anywhere in the late Roman Empire. The largest piece is a shallow dish over 60 cm in diameter and weighing over 8 kilogrammes, entirely covered with figured decoration in low relief. In the centre is the head of a sea-god, surrounded by a circular frieze of sea creatures and nymphs; the main zone of decoration depicts the wine-god Bacchus and his unruly entourage, drinking, dancing and making music. The traditional pagan decoration of this magnificent work of art is reflected in most of the other decorated vessels in the treasure, but three spoons are engraved with unequivocally Christian symbols: the *chi-rho* monogram and the Greek letters alpha and omega. This combination of pagan and Christian icon-

253 *The central portrait roundel of the mosaic floor from the late Roman villa at Hinton St Mary, Dorset. The* chi-rho *monogram appears behind the head, which probably represents Christ.* D *(inner circle) 87.5cm.*

ography is characteristic of the unsettled fourth century, when the struggle between the old pagan values and the newly approved cult of Christianity became acute. The collections are particularly rich in objects which illustrate this religious crisis.

Foremost is another silver treasure, found at Water Newton (Cambridgeshire) in 1975. The objects in it comprise the earliest set of Christian liturgical silver yet discovered. Inscriptions on the vessels establish beyond doubt that they were in use in a Christian church, and record the names of one man and three women who must have belonged to the congregation: Publianus, Innocentia, Viventia and Amcilla. In addition to the

bowls, jugs and a chalice-like cup, are numerous triangular plaques made of thin sheet silver, intended as votive offerings to be displayed in the place of worship. Such plaques are well known from pagan temples, bearing dedications to deities such as Mars, Minerva and Jupiter, but the plaques from Water Newton are the first to demonstrate the practice within a Christian congregation.

Buildings, whether public or domestic, were fundamentally transformed by the influence of classical standards, and by the later Roman period decoratively painted walls and mosaic floors were commonplace in all but very humble dwellings. The subjects chosen for these forms of interior decoration were generally taken from the wide repertoire of Graeco-Roman religion and mythology, but they also provided a medium for expressing the spread of Christianity in the fourth century. At the Lullingstone Roman villa in Kent the painted walls in one room reveal it as a Christian chapel;

the decoration includes large *chi-rho* monograms and a frieze of figures standing with hands upraised in the ancient attitude of prayer. Equally evocative of Romano-British Christianity is the largest mosaic floor in the collections, excavated at Hinton St Mary (Dorset) in 1964. The design of the pavement is conventional, with hunting scenes and corner figures surrounding a circular panel containing a portrait head. A central portrait of this kind is usually the image of a pagan god or goddess. Here it depicts a young, beardless man, flanked by pomegranates (symbols of immortality), with the Christian monogram behind his head: almost certainly a picture of Christ. The Hinton pavement therefore stands at the beginning of the tradition of Byzantine Christian mosaics which are one of the glories of early medieval art.

The collections contain many other major relics of Christianity, but two small objects perhaps deserve special mention, gold finger-rings from Suffolk and Brentwood (Essex), bearing the Christian monogram engraved on their bezels. Finger-rings traditionally carried some religious device, such as the figure of a god or goddess, or an attribute of a deity. Here again can be seen early Christians adopting pagan customs to their own beliefs.

Even in the late fourth century AD, when Britain's days as a province of Rome were numbered, paganism continued to fight for existence against the increasing power of the new faith. An astounding illustration of this was found in late 1979 at Thetford (Norfolk). The Thetford Treasure consists of an assemblage of flamboyantly beautiful gold jewellery, including no fewer than twenty-two finger-rings, a set of thirty-three silver spoons and three strainers. Spoons with Christian inscriptions became increasingly common throughout the fourth century, and undoubtedly had a religious use. The Thetford spoons also have religious inscriptions engraved on them, but they are all to a pagan god, to the obscure Italian nature-deity Faunus, who by this time was probably perceived as part of the cult of Bacchus. Even more remarkable, the name of Faunus is combined in true Roman provincial fashion with by-names of unmistakably Celtic form, so there is no question of these spoons being some inexplicable import from the Mediterranean.

The wealthy Romano-British pagans who dedicated these precious things to the use of Faunus in fourth-century East Anglia must have seen themselves as the heirs and upholders of a precious tradition, a truly combined classical and Celtic tradition in the inexorably changing world of late antiquity. The treasure was probably concealed for safety in response to the Imperial decrees forbidding pagan practices in the early 390s. There is a poignancy in the ostentatious richness of the Thetford Treasure, for within a generation of its burial all that it represents, the ancient civilisation of one of the world's great empires, had already begun to vanish from Britain.

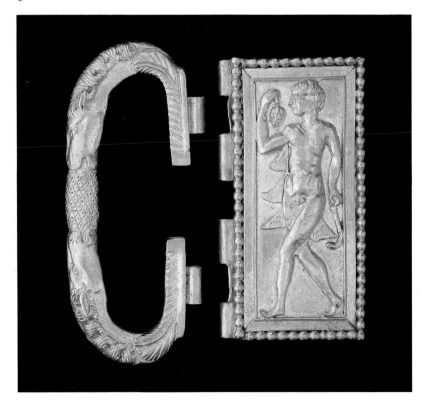

254 *The gold buckle from the Thetford Treasure, decorated with a dancing satyr.* H *5.9cm.*

PRINTS
AND DRAWINGS

◆

The Department of Prints and Drawings houses the national collection of Western graphic art. It possesses one of the great collections of prints, documenting the history of printmaking from its beginnings in the fifteenth century down to modern times. The collection of drawings, though relatively small by comparison with some of the great Continental accumulations, such as those in Paris and Florence, is one of the best balanced and most representative in the world, for in it most of the greatest masters of the major schools are represented.

255 CHARLES RENNIE MACKINTOSH (1868–1928). Port Vendres (c. 1926–7)
Watercolour over pencil. One of a series of large Mediterranean watercolours he painted between 1923 and 1927. The views of Port Vendres were executed out of doors and would often take two or three weeks to complete. 28 × 37.8cm.

DRAWINGS OF THE ITALIAN SCHOOL

The Early and High Renaissance in Italy are particularly well represented. Among outstanding drawings of the fifteenth century in Florence is *The Prisoner before a Judge* by Antonio Pollaiuolo, exemplifying the Florentine tradition that conceived the fundamental language of artistic expression in terms of the nude figure in action. This tradition was continued in the vigorous black-chalk nude studies by Pollaiuolo's younger contemporary and pupil Luca Signorelli, and was carried to its fullest pitch of expression by Michelangelo. The complementary aspect of Florentine art is the linear graceful style of Sandro Botticelli, whose drawing of *Abundance* or *Autumn* is one of the most beautiful Renaissance drawings to have come down to us. A drawing by Andrea Verrocchio depicts the magnificent head of a woman. The emphasis on the complexity of the *coiffure* anticipates the work of his pupil Leonardo da Vinci, twenty-one of whose drawings are in the collection.

In north Italy during the *quattrocento* the chief artistic centres were Venice, Padua and Verona. Nine drawings are kept under the name of Giovanni Bellini, the greatest Venetian artist of the period, but some of these are possibly by his brother-in-law, the Paduan Andrea Mantegna. Drawings by Mantegna are very rare, and the Museum's group, which numbers at least six and possibly as many as nine, is unrivalled both in quantity and quality. It includes the carefully finished and coloured *Mars, Venus and Diana* – a drawing as beautiful in its own way as the Botticelli *Abundance*. By Giovanni Bellini's elder brother Gentile, who visited Constantinople in about 1470, we have the drawings of a *Turkish Lady* and a *Janissary*; and by their father, Jacopo Bellini, the so-called 'sketchbook' of some hundred leaves, with black-chalk drawings of a great variety of subjects, religious, allegorical, mythological, architectural.

Fine drawings by Andrea del Sarto and Fra Bartolommeo illustrate the High Renaissance style in Florence; but in the early sixteenth century the artistic initiative had begun to shift from Florence to Rome,

256 RAFFAELLO SANTI, CALLED RAPHAEL (1483–1520). Head of a bearded man (*c.* 1519–20)
Black chalk over pounced-through underdrawing. An auxiliary cartoon for a foreground figure, usually identified as St Andrew, in Raphael's altarpiece The Transfiguration *in the Vatican Gallery. 39.9 × 35cm.*

257 ABOVE MICHELANGELO BUONARROTI (1475–1564).
Study for the *Bathers* (*c.* 1504–5)
*Pen and brown and greyish-brown ink and wash, heightened
with white. The* Bathers *formed part of the design for the*
Battle of Cascina, *a painting intended for the Palazzo Vecchio
in Florence but never completed. 42.1 × 28.7cm.*

258 RIGHT SANDRO BOTTICELLI (1444/5–1510).
Abundance
*Pen and brown ink and brown wash over black chalk
heightened with white bodycolour, on pink prepared paper. One
of the most beautiful drawings of the Italian* quattrocento, *this
may have been executed a few years after Botticelli's* Primavera
in the Uffizi of about 1478. 31.7 × 25.5cm.

259 GIOVANNI BATTISTA PIRANESI (1720–78). View of the Capitol, Rome
Pen and brown ink with red and black chalk. A study for the etching in Piranesi's famous series of prints, the 'Vedute di Roma', on which he worked from the late 1740s to his death. 40.3 × 70.1 cm.

where the Florentine-trained Michelangelo executed many of his greatest works, and the Umbrian Raphael all of his. Both artists are magnificently represented in the Museum. Raphael's thirty-nine drawings include an early self-portrait, done at the age of sixteen or seventeen, and studies for some of his greatest works – the *Parnassus* and the *Disputa* in the Vatican, the *Sibyls* in Sta Maria della Pace, Rome, and the Vatican *Transfiguration*. The group of over eighty Michelangelo drawings, the largest outside Italy, illustrates almost every phase of his long career: especially noteworthy are the study for a figure in the early cartoon of the *Bathers*, the sketch of the first, discarded scheme for the decoration of the Sistine Ceiling, the series of designs for the tombs in the Medici Chapel in S. Lorenzo in Florence, the group of very late *Crucifixion* drawings and his only surviving complete cartoon, the large-scale *Epifania*.

Michelangelo, essentially a solitary genius, had no pupils, but there are five drawings by his most important follower, Sebastiano del Piombo. Raphael, in contrast, headed a flourishing school, and the Museum possesses a very good representative collection of drawings by his pupils and/or associates: Giulio Romano, Perino del Vaga, Baldassare Peruzzi and Polidoro da Caravaggio. Towards the end of his life Raphael was developing in the direction of the graceful, decorative style which is usually called Mannerism, and after his premature death in 1520 the tendency was carried forward by his younger associates. The same development away from the ideals of the High Renaissance was formulated independently in Florence by Rosso and Pontormo. It was continued there by Bronzino, Francesco Salviati and Vasari, and in Rome by Daniele da Volterra, Taddeo and Federico Zuccaro, Pellegrino Tibaldi and Raffaellino da Reggio.

Although Rome was the most important theatre for the evolution of the High Renaissance style, Parma and Venice contributed their own local variants. Seventeen drawings are by the Parmese Correggio, and nearly one hundred by his more prolific compatriot and follower, Parmigianino. Only one drawing is certainly by the greatest Venetian painter of the sixteenth century, Titian, a small study in black chalk for an Apostle in the altarpiece of the *Assumption* in Sta Maria dei Frari, Venice; but his younger contemporaries Jacopo Tintoretto and Paolo Veronese are well represented, and there is an important group of about ninety composition-sketches in oil on paper by the younger Tintoretto, Domenico.

The beginning of the seventeenth century in Italy is marked by a naturalistic reaction. No drawings by

260 GIANDOMENICO TIEPOLO (1727–1804).
The Arrest of Christ
Pen and brown ink with brown wash over black chalk. From a series of eighty-two biblical subjects, this drawing reveals the artist's powerful imagination in his interpretation of religious themes.
47.5 × 37cm.

Michelangelo da Caravaggio, the exponent of a highly realistic style, are known; but Annibale Carracci, whose idealised naturalism was of seminal influence upon the development of both the classical and the Baroque style of the 1620s, returned to the High Renaissance example of Raphael and Michelangelo in making numerous preparatory studies for his paintings. The large group of some twenty-four drawings by him include, besides several landscape drawings in pen and ink, the cartoon of a helmsman for the fresco *Ulysses and the Sirens* in the *camerino* of the Palazzo Farnese in Rome.

As the influence of the followers of Caravaggio and Annibale Carracci waned, the true Baroque style developed in Rome. This is typified in the grandiose decorative works of Pietro da Cortona. Bernini, who was primarily a sculptor and architect, was another brilliant protagonist of the Baroque, and the Museum possesses several examples of his work as a draughtsman. Towards the end of the seventeenth century Roman painting came to be dominated by Maratta's High Baroque classicism. The essentially academic basis of his art is shown by the fact that most of the Museum's seventeen drawings by him are studies from the model.

In the eighteenth century it was above all in Venice that the great tradition of Italian painting continued. The lively rococo figure style of Giovanni Battista Tiepolo and his son Giandomenico parallels contemporary developments in France. The two great view-painters, Francesco Guardi and Antonio Canaletto, specialised in townscapes, particularly of Venice, but the collection also includes a number of Canaletto's views in England. Another mainly topographical draughtsman well represented in the collection is Giovanni Battista Piranesi; though a Venetian by birth he spent his working life largely in Rome, the city which is the subject of most of his etchings and drawings.

DRAWINGS OF THE GERMAN, DUTCH AND FLEMISH SCHOOLS

In Germany the Renaissance flowered briefly but intensely, and it is fortunate that the Department's holdings of this school are mainly concentrated in that period. Its collection of drawings by the greatest of all German artists, Albrecht Dürer, is the largest in the world, and is particularly strong in watercolour landscapes and portrait drawings. By the other great German artist of the early sixteenth century, Hans Holbein the Younger, who is best known as a portrait draughts-

260

259

261

261 ALBRECHT DÜRER (1471–1528). View of the castle at Trent
Pen and black ink with watercolour. The castle at Trent was reconstructed in 1468 and remains comparatively little altered. Dürer probably made the drawing in 1495 en route *from Italy to Nuremberg. 19.6 × 25cm.*

man, is a large group of designs for jewellery and metalwork, but only two drawings, both of ladies, one traditionally identified as Sir Thomas More's daughter, Margaret Roper, the other as Queen Anne Boleyn.

A small but choice group covers the rest of the German school (with which may be linked the Swiss) from the fifteenth century to the end of the seventeenth. Outstanding among drawings by the followers of Dürer in Nuremberg are those of Hans von Kulmbach and Hans Schäufelein, while those by Hans Holbein the Elder and Hans Burgkmair at Augsburg illustrate the rise of the Renaissance in southern Germany. Among the seventeenth-century drawings may be particularly

noted the group of technically accomplished landscapes in bodycolour that are traditionally attributed to Adam Elsheimer.

The late nineteenth and twentieth centuries are represented by a growing number of works by some of the most important figures: Paula Modersohn-Becker, Kirchner, Heckel, Grosz, Beckmann and, most recently of all, Anselm Kiefer and Gerhard Richter.

The Netherlandish school is subdivided into 'Dutch' and 'Flemish' because of the break-up, in the later sixteenth century, of the Low Countries into the Protestant north and the Catholic south. The collection starts at the beginning of the fifteenth century, with a group of portraits in silverpoint by or attributed to Jan van Eyck and Rogier van der Weyden. Subsequent developments can be studied in detail here, and include fine examples from all the important artistic centres, Bruges, Ghent and Antwerp, as well as the only known brush drawing by Hieronymus Bosch, *The Entombment.*

The two most important treasures of the sixteenth century are the unrivalled group of twelve drawings by the precocious genius, Lucas van Leyden, and the

262 HANS HOLBEIN THE YOUNGER (1497/8–1543).
Portrait of an English woman
Black and red chalk and brush and black ink, heightened with white bodycolour, on pink prepared paper. This was drawn during Holbein's second stay in England from 1532 to 1543. 27.6 × 19.1 cm.

group of landscape drawings by Pieter Bruegel the Elder, together with his only known drawing of an allegorical subject, *The Calumny of Apelles*. The leading draughtsmen of the next generation, Hendrick Goltzius and Jacob de Gheyn II, are well represented, together with many of their lesser contemporaries.

From the beginning of the seventeenth century in the Catholic south (Flanders) the artistic world was dominated by Peter Paul Rubens. All periods of his career and most aspects of his interests are illustrated. There are five studies after the model – perhaps the most impressive, both in the skill displayed and in the feeling expressed, is that of *Christ on the Cross* – and preparatory studies for compositions, for instance, a *Lioness* for 266 *Daniel in the Lion's Den*. Rubens closely studied the work of his predecessors, and the collection is rich in copies after Michelangelo, Raphael and others. His antiquarian and collecting interests are reflected in sketches after the antique as well as the numerous drawings by earlier masters that he improved by re-touching. A small but important group of landscapes

includes his *Sunset*, while among the portraits is one of the most outstanding, that of his first wife, *Isabella Brant*. His designs for title-pages and preparatory drawings for engravings after his paintings are also included.

The British Museum's collection of drawings by Rubens' brilliant assistant, Anthonie van Dyck, is without rival. There are several early pen studies, which are sometimes difficult to distinguish from those of Rubens. The 'Italian Sketchbook' contains drawings made during his travels in Italy between 1621 and 1627. After his return from Italy he was principally interested in portraiture. Four preparatory drawings for engravings in his *Iconography* are executed in black chalk on white paper with the occasional use of brown wash, and admirably illustrate his portrait style before he settled in England in 1632. Studies for portraits he painted in England are in black chalk on blue paper, perhaps inspired by the sixteenth-century Venetian school. The Museum's collection of drawings of this type is without parallel, including many studies for famous paintings.

263 ABOVE ERNST LUDWIG KIRCHNER (1880–1938). A nude woman standing in her bath (1914)
Pastel. Kirchner produced some of his most striking compositions in pastel between 1913 and 1914 while he was living in Berlin. 67.3 × 51.2cm.

264 TOP RIGHT HIERONYMUS BOSCH (c. 1450–1516). The Entombment
Brush drawing in grey over traces of an underdrawing in black chalk. The drawing was first discovered and identified as by Bosch in 1952. The high quality of the brush work and unusual iconography seem characteristic, and no convincing alternative attribution has been proposed. 25.3 × 30.4cm.

265 BOTTOM RIGHT ANTHONIE VAN DYCK (1599–1641). Study of trees
Pen and brown ink and watercolours. The drawing was almost certainly made in England in the 1630s, and was used by van Dyck in the background of the Equestrian Portrait of Charles I *in the National Gallery, London. 19.5 × 23.6cm.*

266 LEFT
PETER PAUL RUBENS
(1577–1640).
A lioness
*Black and yellow chalk,
with grey wash,
heightened with white
bodycolour. A
preliminary sketch for a
painting of* Daniel in
the Lions' Den *now
in the National Gallery
of Art, Washington.
The drawing was
probably made in or
before 1618, when
Rubens offered the
painting to the British
ambassador to The
Hague. 39.6 × 23.5cm.*

267 RIGHT
REMBRANDT VAN RIJN
(1606–69).
A sleeping girl
*Brush drawing in
brown wash. Drawn in
the mid-1650s. The
model was probably
Hendrickje Stoffels, who
had entered
Rembrandt's household
as a servant ten years
before. 24.5 × 20.3cm.*

5 An impressive group of his charming landscape drawings seem to date from his final years in England.

The only other Flemish artist of that period of any real importance is Jacob Jordaens. He was essentially a decorative artist, and this aspect is given full scope in his tapestry designs.

The collection of drawings by Rembrandt, though relatively small, is one of the most representative. Rembrandt was an extraordinarily versatile draughtsman, and his use of a kind of pen-and-ink shorthand to capture the mood of the moment makes the study of his drawings one of enormous fascination. In his maturity his disregard for conventional technique led to the

7 brilliant economy of brushwork in the *Sleeping girl*, for example, and the virtuosity with the reed pen in *A girl seated* (both possibly studies of Hendrickje Stoffels).

In addition to those undeniably by Rembrandt, a large group of drawings are by his pupils, some of whom aped his style so well that it is often difficult to distinguish their drawings from the master's; but his most important followers or associates, such as Jan Lievens and Gerard Dou, have quite distinctive styles.

The particular strengths of the rest of the seventeenth-century Dutch school are also represented: landscape by fine examples of Jan van Goyen, Jacob van Ruisdael, Anthonie Waterloo and Aelbert Cuyp; marine painting by Renier Zeeman and Ludolf van Backhuizen; and *genre* by Adriaen van Ostade.

Towards the end of the seventeenth century in both the Dutch and Flemish Schools we find an increasing use of watercolour and a growing dependence on French culture. These tendencies became even more evident in the eighteenth century. Dutch art of this period is well represented, but after the glories of the previous century its effect is inevitably one of anticlimax. Subsequent developments are sparsely illustrated, but there is a magnificent pen-and-ink landscape, *Le Crau from Montmajour*, by Vincent van Gogh, a sketchbook page by Piet Mondrian (*c.* 1911) and a gouache of 1958 by the COBRA artist, Karel Appel.

DRAWINGS OF THE FRENCH SCHOOL

In France a high level of excellence was achieved in portrait drawing in the early sixteenth century at the court of François I in the work of Jean and François Clouet; the Museum's large group of drawings by the Clouets and their successors provides a primary source for the study of this school. In the tradition of manuscript illumination are the fifty watercolours by the sixteenth-century Huguenot artist, Jacques Le Moyne de Morgues. His surviving work consists almost entirely of plant drawings and miniatures of great refinement and surprising naturalism. The 122 vellum sheets of French chateaux by Jacques Androuet Ducerceau are perhaps the most notable of such sixteenth-century French drawings extant.

The development in Lorraine in the early seventeenth century of a native Mannerist school produced two remarkable draughtsmen and etchers, Jacques Callot and Jacques Bellange. By the former there is a quite large group of drawings of landscape, small figure compositions and studies of horses, some of them

268 JACQUES LE MOYNE DE MORGUES (c. 1533–88).
Primrose and fly
Watercolour and bodycolour. Le Moyne was born in Dieppe, but little is known of his early life. In 1564 he accompanied an expedition to Florida to make a graphic record of the native Indians and the flora. A Huguenot, he eventually settled in London about 1580. This is from a series of more than eighty studies of flowers and fruit painted around 1585. 20.7 × 14.1 cm.

268

269 CLAUDE LORRAIN (1600–82). Landscape with the abandoned Psyche at the palace of Cupid
Pen and brown ink and brown wash, heightened with white bodycolour, over black chalk on blue paper. From the celebrated Liber Veritatis, *the drawing corresponds to a painting known as* The Enchanted Castle. *19.6 × 26.3 cm.*

connected with etchings. Bellange is represented by five drawings, including a remarkable study of a girl in pen and blue wash.

There are only a few authentic drawings by Nicolas Poussin, the greatest and most influential of the French 'classical' masters of the seventeenth century, or by the other artists working in the same tradition: Simon Vouet, Eustache Le Sueur, Laurent de la Hyre and Charles le Brun. On the other hand, the collection of some 500 drawings by Claude Lorrain, who, like Poussin, spent his working life in Rome and who as a landscape painter and draughtsman overshadows all his contemporaries, is the largest in existence. Most of them are sketches of an astonishing freedom and poetry made directly from nature in the Roman Campagna;

distinct from these, and in their own way no less beautiful, are the 205 drawings in the *Liber Veritatis*. 269 These were made by the artist, whose works were extensively forged and imitated even in his own lifetime, as a record of his work and a protection against forgery.

The classicism of Poussin and his followers survived into the eighteenth century, but the emphasis was shifting to the men and manners of the new age. Antoine Watteau was largely instrumental in bringing about this change. The Museum's sixty or so drawings by him cover every phase of his brief career from the elongated forms and timid handling of his maturity. By use of the technique *à trois crayons* – a combination of 270 black, red and white chalk – he achieved an unequalled effect of mingled richness and precision. One of the outstanding drawings by him is a design for a fan-leaf, the only one of its kind known.

The other leading masters of the eighteenth century, François Boucher and Jean-Honoré Fragonard, the two most characteristic personalities of the *rococo* period, and Hubert Robert and Gabriel de Saint-Aubin are represented, though less well, while there is a small

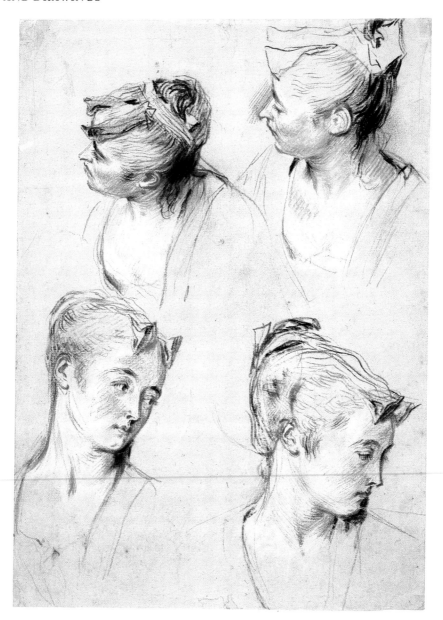

270 JEAN-ANTOINE WATTEAU (1684–1721). Four studies of the head of a young woman
Two shades of red chalk, and black and white chalk. Although Watteau made few formal portraits, there are a number of highly expressive and convincing drawings of heads of his friends. This is a particularly fine example. 33.1 × 23.8cm.

but interesting group of drawings of the neo-classical movement of the end of the century.

The collection contains relatively little from the nineteenth century, although there are some drawings in pencil, pen, watercolour and pastel by Eugène Delacroix; *Studies of a seated Arab* is a masterpiece of delicate and perceptive portraiture. His pupil Théodore Géricault has some effective drawings to his name, most of them from his English period, notably *The Coal Waggon*. Jean-August-Dominique Ingres, the upholder of a rigid classicism and the outstanding draughtsman of his age, can be studied in a group of preparatory and finished drawings including two remarkable portraits, *Sir John Hay and his Sister* and *M. Charles Hayard and his*

Daughter, as well as studies for the *Golden Age* and *Apotheosis of Homer*. From the Barbizon school of landscape are drawings by Théodore Rousseau, Jean-François Millet and Charles-François Daubigny. By Jean-Baptist-Camille Corot there is little in the way of landscape, but there are two excellent portraits in pencil. The few examples of the work of the Impressionists and the artists associated with them include a nude study by August Renoir; a group of drawings by Edgar Degas; several characteristic examples of the work of Camille Pissaro; two watercolours by Berthe Morisot; and five portraits and figure studies by Toulouse-Lautrec. Cézanne is represented by two works in pencil and a watercolour of 1878–80, *The*

271 PIERRE BONNARD (1867–1949). La salle à manger, Villa le Bosquet, le Cannet
Watercolour, bodycolour and pencil. Bonnard made numerous depictions of the little house just above Cannes which he acquired in 1926. In 1942 on one of the occasions when he was painting the dining room he commented: 'I'm trying to do what I have never done: give the impression one has on entering a room: one sees everything and at the same time nothing'. 46.5 × 48.7cm.

272 HENRI MATISSE (1869–1954). A seated woman wearing a taffeta dress (1938)
Charcoal. 66.3 × 50.5cm.

Apotheosis of Delacroix. Georges Seurat, the exponent of neo-Impressionism, can be studied in six drawings, including two studies for *La Grand Jatte.*

Of the major figures and movements of the twentieth century, from the Cubists onwards, there is only a small body of work, including a fine watercolour by Bonnard, dated about 1930, and a substantial drawing of 1938 by Matisse.

271
272

DRAWINGS OF THE SPANISH SCHOOL

The main strength of the small collection of the Spanish school lies in its drawings by some of the major seventeenth-century masters. There are seven drawings by Jusepe Ribera, who though a leading member of the Neapolitan school always insisted on his Spanish nationality; at least twenty by Bartolomé Esteban Murillo, and a few by other leading masters, including the only drawing generally accepted as being by Fran-

273 FRANCISCO GOYA Y LUCIENTES (1746–1828). Por linage de ebreos (For being of Jewish ancestry) *Brush and grey and brown wash. One of a series of drawings made between about 1814 and 1823 during the period of repression under Ferdinand VII. The subjects are victims of the Inquisition. 20.3 × 14.2cm.*

Pr linage de Cristos

cisco Zurbaran, a powerful study in black chalk of the head of a monk.

The greatest master of the Madrid school, Diego Velasquez, is virtually an unknown quantity as a draughtsman; but the black-chalk study of a man on a horse, attributed to him when in the collection of Mariette, the great French connoisseur of the eighteenth century, has been accepted by some authorities. Other examples of the Madrid school are by Vicente Carducho, Antonio Pereda, Juan Carreno and Claudio Coello.

The coverage of eighteenth-century works by Spanish masters is by comparison thin and of lower quality: designs for church decoration by Mosen Domingo Saura and Teodoro Ardemans are still in the seventeenth-century Baroque tradition, and there are two interesting and accomplished portraits, one by Luis Paret of Maria Luisa de Borbon, the other of Elizabeth Farnese by Miguel Jacinto Menendez.

273 By Francisco Goya, one of the greatest Spanish painters and unquestionably the greatest Spanish draughtsman, there are seven drawings. The earliest, *The Garotted Man*, dates from the 1780s and derives in technique, though not in subject matter or mood, from G. B. Tiepolo. The others include the red-chalk sketch of the Duke of Wellington, done from life in 1812 after the Battle of Salamanca, which served as basis for all Goya's painted portraits of him, and a brush drawing of a group of victims of the Inquisition, *For being of Jewish ancestry*, which can be dated after 1814. Goya's influence is all-pervading in the small group of drawings by his follower, Eugenio Lucas. Another nineteenth-century artist whose influence was felt within and outside Spain was Mariano Fortuny; the Department possesses eighteen characteristic drawings by him, mostly in watercolour.

DRAWINGS OF THE BRITISH SCHOOL

The Department's collection of drawings by British artists, or by artists from abroad who made their careers in England, is inevitably larger than that of any other school. It ranges from the mid-sixteenth century until the present day and includes, as well as drawings in chalk, black lead, ink, and pencil, a comprehensive selection from the English watercolour school from its origins in the seventeenth-century 'stained drawing'.

English drawings of the sixteenth century have survived in very small numbers, but the Department possesses one rare design in pen and ink by the miniaturist Nicholas Hilliard for the Irish Great Seal of Queen Elizabeth, and the earliest and finest set of ethnographical watercolours in John White's drawings of the Algonquin Indians and the flora and fauna of Sir Walter Raleigh's original colony of Virginia. Of English seventeenth-century draughtsmen, the most important are Inigo Jones, a number of whose architectural drawings in the collection include some for Whitehall Palace, and Francis Barlow, whose work as an illustrator is well represented, especially by the designs for the *Aesop's Fables with his Life*, 1666. There are also series of drawings by the York topographer, Francis Place, and by several of the Continental artists who worked in England at the period; in particular Wenceslas Hollar, Willem van de Velde the Elder, and Sir Peter Lely, by whom the Department possesses sixteen studies of figures in the Garter Procession at Windsor. There are

2

274 WENCESLAUS HOLLAR (1607–77). View of Westminster and the Thames from Lambeth House
Pen and brown ink over black lead. Born in Prague, Hollar settled in London in the late 1630s. His detailed views of the city are an unparalleled source of topographical information on its appearance before the Great Fire of 1666. Here we are looking north and down river, the Tower visible in the distance. 15.1 × 40.1cm.

examples of the portrait studies of Lely's German successor, Sir Godfrey Kneller, and of the Swedish portrait painter, Michael Dahl. The tradition of pastel portraiture in England is illustrated by the drawings of Edward Lutterell, Edmund Ashfield, John Greenhill and others, as well as a group of plumbago (lead pencil) miniatures by Thomas Forster, David Loggan and Robert White.

In the eighteenth century English artists became self-consciously concerned with founding a national school to vie with those of the Continent. Sir James Thornhill painted grandiose decorative schemes on the model of those by the Italians Verrio and Ricci and the Frenchman Laguerre, and the Department's book of sketches by him for schemes of this sort is one of the most important surviving documents of the English Baroque period. His son-in-law, William Hogarth, was even more influential in achieving a new status for the artist in England. An extensive group of his drawings include all the surviving designs for the series *Industry and Idleness*, and examples of his skill as a portrait draughtsman. An underrated contemporary of Hogarth's was Francis Hayman, also well represented by a series of illustrations to Smollett's translation of *Don Quixote* (1755).

275 THOMAS GAINSBOROUGH (1727–88). Study of a woman
Black chalk and stump, heightened with white bodycolour on buff paper. Dating from the mid-1780s, this study is one of a series Gainsborough probably made in connection with a projected painting, The Richmond Water Walk.
49.5 × 31.4cm.

276
J. M. W. Turner
(1775–1851).
The Vale of
Ashburnham
*Watercolour; signed:
J. M. W. Turner
RA 1816. One of a
series of views in
Sussex commissioned
from Turner by John
Fuller in 1815;
Beachy Head is visible
in the centre distance.
It is closely based on a
pencil drawing of the
view in the artist's*
Vale of Heathfield
*sketchbook. Together
with others in the
series, this was
engraved in 1817.
37.9 × 56.3cm.*

Sir Joshua Reynolds, the great portrait painter, did not practise drawing to any great extent, but the collection includes a large proportion of his studies, in addition to a self-portrait dated 1750 and two of the notebooks that he used in Italy in 1752. Reynolds's great rival, Gainsborough, can be seen both as portrait draughtsman and landscape artist, with several full-length figure studies and over eighty sketches of trees and plants and imaginary landscape compositions. Downman, Hoppner and Lawrence also figure, and Romney's romantic figure subjects are well represented by several dramatic wash studies. These, together with Fuseli's Roman sketchbook of the 1770s (one of the principal documents of the early Romantic and neo-classical movements) and the excellent group of drawings by Stothard and Flaxman, form a background to the Blake collection, which, apart from the illuminated books, includes the complete series of watercolours for Young's *Night Thoughts* and a number of the subjects from the late illustrations to Dante.

The humorous figure draughtsmen of this period are also present, with many good examples of Thomas Rowlandson's lively watercolours, preparatory studies by James Gillray for his savage political cartoons of the French Revolutionary and Napoleonic periods, and drawings of comic social observation by John Nixon, Henry Bunbury and Nathaniel Dance. These provide a general view of the social background of the period, as do the charming watercolours of Paul and Thomas Sandby and the minute rural scenes by Thomas Bewick, which he himself engraved on wood as vignettes in his classic *History of British Birds*. There is also a very large collection of sketches by George Cruikshank, who continued the tradition of comic and satirical draughtsmanship down to the middle of the nineteenth century.

The Romantic movement manifested itself as much by an interest in nature as by concern for the more passionate aspects of human behaviour. It was above all in landscape that colour came to be seen as an integral expressive part of a finished drawing, and the landscape watercolour is the most important British contribution to European art since the Middle Ages. The mood of Romanticism, already foreshadowed in the first half of the eighteenth century in the drawings of William Taverner and Jonathan Skelton, appears even more obviously in the views which William Pars made in Greece and Switzerland in the 1760s and 1770s, imbued as these are with the enthusiasm for ruins and mountain scenery that was to become widespread in the next generation. All Pars's finest drawings of these subjects are in the British Museum, along with numerous examples by his associates in the 1780s, Francis Towne and John 'Warwick' Smith. Two other artists of an earlier generation who were also inspired by Italy, but who did not work in watercolour, were Richard

275

277 RICHARD DADD (1817–86). The Halt in the Desert *Watercolour and bodycolour. This rare and important example of Dadd's early work was thought to have been lost since 1857 until its recent discovery. It was developed from sketches made in 1842 while on tour with his patron Sir Thomas Phillips. Here the travellers are bivouacked by the Dead Sea; Dadd himself is at the far right of the camp fire. 37 × 70.7 cm.*

278 HENRY MOORE (1898–1986). Crowd looking at a
tied-up object (1942)
Watercolour over coloured chalks. This is one of Henry Moore's
most famous compositions, probably influenced by a reproduction
he knew of Nupe tribesmen in Nigeria standing around two
immense, draped cult figures. 40 × 55cm.

Wilson and Alexander Cozens. The Department possesses a large number of studies of landscape and
details of landscape by Wilson in his characteristic
medium of black and white chalk on grey paper, and
several of Cozens's ideal 'blot' landscapes in brown
wash together with a group of pen-and-ink sketches
made in Rome when he was a young man. John Robert
Cozens, his son and arguably the finest English water-
colourist before the generation of Turner and Girtin, is
also represented. Both Wilson and John Robert Cozens
exercised a fundamental influence on the early development of J. M. W. Turner. The Henderson, Salt-
ing and Lloyd Bequests of finished watercolours give a
superb picture of this, the greatest, most versatile and
prolific of British painters. An unrivalled collection of
watercolours and drawings by Turner's contemporary

Thomas Girtin includes five well-preserved sections of
the preliminary design in watercolour for the *Panorama*
of London, which together constitute the artist's masterpiece.

The collection of drawings by John Constable,
though smaller than that in the Victoria & Albert
Museum, is well balanced, and includes a sketchbook
of 1819, and a fuller representation of the artist's figure
drawings than exists elsewhere. Watercolours by members of the Norwich school include a very large number
by John Sell Cotman, among them several of the
well-known 'Greta' subjects of 1805 and the famous
Dismasted Brig. A large view of Lincoln is the most
impressive of a small group of watercolours by Peter de
Wint; David Cox, on the other hand, is represented by a
comprehensive collection of works from all periods of
his life. The drawings by Richard Parkes Bonington are
mostly pencil studies, many of them made in the
Louvre, but there are a few watercolours, including the
lively *Château de Berri* and a striking self-portrait.

Two of Samuel Palmer's sketchbooks are in the
department, and one of the finest watercolours from his
Shoreham period, of *A Cornfield by Moonlight with the*
Evening Star (c. 1830). Another highly individual figure,

Richard Dadd, who was committed to Bethlem Hospital for the murder of his father in 1843, is represented by one of his most important watercolours, *The Halt in the Desert* (c. 1845)

277

From the second half of the nineteenth century there are good holdings of such artists as Edward Lear, William Müller and John Frederick Lewis, and a small but representative group of Pre-Raphaelite drawings, including fine examples by Rossetti and Millais, and a substantial quantity by Burne-Jones. The latter include two important sketchbooks, one a volume of pencil studies dating from the 1870s, including designs for the *Days of Creation*, the other containing a series of circular designs in watercolour suggested by the names of flowers and known as the 'Flower book'. There are also examples of the draughtsmanship of Lord Leighton, Alma-Tadema and Charles Ricketts; Ricketts's notebook of jewellery designs is a particularly telling record

279 PERCY WYNDHAM LEWIS (1882–1957). Woman with a sash (1920)
Pen and ink, crayon and watercolour. The sitter is Iris Barry (1895–1969), the writer and film critic who lived with Wyndham Lewis from 1918 to 1921; she was the subject of Praxitella (1920–1), one of his most striking portraits in oil, now in the Leeds City Art Gallery. 38.1 × 39.1 cm.

280 DAVID SMITH (1906–65). Untitled (1951)
Oil and gouache. David Smith's artistic reputation has rested largely upon his sculpture, yet painting and drawing also played a vital role throughout his career. The drawings were conceived more as a parallel means of exploring certain ideas rather than being direct preparatory studies for sculpture. 66.5 × 50.4cm.

of his delicacy of invention and technical refinement. Many of the great book illustrators of the period also feature in the collection: Beardsley, du Maurier, Charles Keene, Kate Greenaway, Edmund Dulac and Beatrix Potter among them – the last represented by the complete set of watercolours illustrating *The Tale of the Flopsy Bunnies*.

All the major figures in British art from the 1880s onwards are represented, with particularly strong concentrations of the work of W. R. Sickert, one of the main links between Continental Post-Impressionism and England, Muirhead Bone, Charles Rennie Mackintosh, Wyndham Lewis, David Bomberg, Ceri Richards, Graham Sutherland, Henry Moore and the St Ives artists among many others. A number of interesting sketchbooks and albums include Henry Moore's *Shelter* sketchbook 1940–1. The collection also embraces work by contemporary British artists such as Frank Auerbach, Lucian Freud and Howard Hodgkin.

A small group of drawings by American artists are mainly of the late-nineteenth and twentieth centuries. The most notable examples are an *Amsterdam Nocturne* (1883–4) by J. A. M. Whistler, a fine selection of J. S. Sargent watercolours and more recent works of the post-Second World War period by David Smith, Hans Hofmann, Franz Kline, Jim Dine and Sol LeWitt.

280

PRINTS

The multiplication of visual images began in Europe, in south Germany and Italy, in the first half of the fifteenth century, rather before the earliest dissemination of the written word by movable type. Prints have been used for many purposes: not only as original works of art and as reproductions of works of art, but also for book illustration, for religious or political propaganda, for the recording of historical events and the appearance of famous people and as patterns for decoration – to name only a few of their innumerable uses. Until the invention of photography in the mid-nineteenth century images could only be multiplied by means of the traditional hand-crafted techniques of the printmaker. The new photographically based technologies produced a further category of photomechanical print; prints of this type have in general not been acquired by the Museum. But before this point the most important distinction is between the 'original' print, in which the artist exploits the resources of the medium in order to produce a work of art, and the reproductive print, in which he reproduces a design by another. The Department possesses one of the finest and most complete collections of original prints in the world. Over and above these there is a vast mass of prints that are of interest primarily for the information of one kind or another that they convey.

Prints can also be categorised by technique. With intaglio prints (engravings, etchings, drypoints) the design is incised in a metal plate which, after being inked, is wiped clean and printed under pressure so that the ink remaining in the incised lines is forced out on to the paper. In the relief-printing process (woodcuts, wood-engravings and metal-cuts) the white areas are cut away on the block, leaving the lines that print standing in relief. In surface prints (lithographs and screenprints) the printing surface is neither raised nor lowered. In addition, there are the 'tone processes': stipple and aquatint (varieties of etching and almost always used in conjunction with the etched line) and mezzotint. In the latter the plate is first roughened so that if inked it would print dead black, and the lighter areas are then burnished down.

The earliest techniques were woodcut and engraving on metal. Relief printing from woodblocks was first used for the decoration of textiles and in the manufacture of playing-cards, and for the crudely executed representations of religious or devotional subjects made as souvenirs for pilgrims. The wider use of the process coincided with the invention of printing, for since text and block can be printed together it was ideally suited to book illustration. The history of woodcut in the fifteenth and sixteenth centuries is thus closely involved with that of the printed book, and the Department possesses, in addition to cuts either issued separately or extracted from books, a considerable

281 ANONYMOUS GERMAN. Christ before Herod (early 15th century AD)
Woodcut. One of the finest woodcuts surviving from the earliest period of the use of the medium in Europe. It is known in only two impressions, both found pasted inside the cover of a single book. 39.5 × 28.5cm.

collection of books with woodcut illustrations, chiefly German. The culmination comes at the beginning of the sixteenth century with Dürer, to whom about 150 woodcuts are attributed (some of the original woodblocks are in the collection), and with the woodcuts produced in Venice in the circle of Titian, many after his designs. An earlier Venetian masterpiece is the great bird's-eye view of Venice, dated 1500, by Jacopo de' Barbari.

Though the process was used throughout the sixteenth century, it gradually gave way to metal engraving; but a significant new development was the introduction of the 'chiaroscuro' woodcut, printed in colours from two or more blocks in imitation of a wash drawing. Of these the Department has a good collection, from Ugo da Carpi in the early sixteenth century to the English amateur John Skippe at the end of the eighteenth. Woodcut later came to be used mainly as a cheap method of illustrating chapbooks and broad-

290

281

282 ATTRIBUTED TO ESAIAS VAN DE VELDE
(*c.* 1590/1–1630). Arcadian landscape (*c.* 1615)
Woodcut with two tone blocks in shades of green. Only recently
attributed to van de Velde, this remarkable landscape shows the
method of 'chiaroscuro' colour woodcut printing invented in
Germany and Italy in the early sixteenth century.
18 × 24.8cm.

sides, but towards the end of the eighteenth century there was a revival of the process when it was discovered that a block of very hard wood, such as box, cut across the grain, could be worked with engravers' tools. The wood-engraving thus differs fundamentally from the woodcut, which is made with a knife on a block of softish wood cut along the grain, and its effect depends largely on the use of white line on black. Wood-engravings are usually small in scale, but some of the most beautiful work ever done on wood was produced in the early nineteenth century by Thomas Bewick, William Blake (in the illustrations to Thornton's *Virgil*) and, under Blake's inspiration, Edward Calvert. (The blocks of Blake's *Virgil* and of Calvert's five wood-engravings are in the Department). In the middle years of the nineteenth century wood-engraving was much

used as a reproductive process for book illustration, and its practitioners displayed astonishing skill in translating the pen-and-ink drawings made by the artist on the block. The Department owns a large collection of proofs from the workshop of the most famous of these engravers, the Dalziel brothers.

Towards the end of the nineteenth century the revival of fine printing, associated above all with William Morris and Charles Ricketts, brought with it a revival of woodcut illustration that was at first consciously inspired by fifteenth-century northern and Italian examples. The revival continued until well into the following century, mainly on traditional lines; but of particularly original work in this medium should be mentioned the woodcuts of William Nicholson and Paul Nash, and the semi-abstract experiments of Edward Wadsworth. In Germany the revival of the woodcut took a quite different direction, and it became the favoured technique of the Expressionists, mostly notably the members of the artists' group *Die Brücke* (The Bridge) founded in Dresden in 1905 (Ernst Ludwig Kirchner, Erich Heckel and Karl Schmidt-Rottluff).

A process which involved the use of metal plates but

283

283 KARL SCHMIDT-ROTTLUFF (1884–1976).
House behind trees (1911)
Woodcut. Schmidt-Rottluff was one of the four founding members of the Dresden group Die Brücke *(The Bridge), which played a pioneering role in the development of German Expressionism. 20.4 × 26.2cm.*

which is essentially analogous to woodcut rather than to metal engraving was the method of 'relief etching' invented by William Blake for the production of his illustrated books. The design was drawn with the 're-sist' so that the areas to be left white were bitten away, and the plate was printed in same way as a woodblock. The Department has a very good collection of Blake's illustrated books.

Printing from engraved metal plates originated, like woodcut, in south Germany and Italy in the early fifteenth century, and developed from the goldsmiths' practice of taking impressions from ornamental engraving on their works. This origin is reflected in the timid technique of the earliest German engravings and in those Florentine ones classified as the 'Fine Manner'. (Closely related in style to these is the volume of drawings in the Department known as the 'Florentine Picture Chronicle'.) Another group of Florentine engravings is classified as the 'Broad Manner', and to that tradition belongs not only the one indisputable master-piece of the Florentine school, Antonio Pollaiuolo's *Battle of Naked Men*, but also the engravings of the Mantuan master, Andrea Mantegna. The seven plates now accepted as being from Mantegna's hand repro-duce the effect of his vigorous style of drawing in pen

and ink. As an original creative process, line-engraving reached its height in the late fifteenth and early six-teenth centuries with Mantegna, Dürer and the Ger-man 'Little Masters' (Beham, Pencz, Aldegrever and others, so-called because of the small scale of their plates), Marcantonio Raimondi in Italy, and Lucas van Leyden in Holland. Dürer and Lucas van Leyden were wholly original engravers, responsible for the design and the execution of their plates. Marcantonio's early original plates are of little interest, but those after Raphael, with whom he worked in close collaboration, are among the greatest and most influential reproduc-tive engravings. The last major exponent of original engraving, at the beginning of the seventeenth century, was the Dutch Mannerist Hendrick Goltzius; tech-nically brilliant though he was, with him virtuosity seems to have become an end in itself. From the early seventeenth century onwards line-engraving was more and more confined to reproduction; and though an ever-increasing degree of technical skill was developed, engraving as a medium of original creative expression gave way to the altogether freer and more rapid process of etching.

In an engraving the line has to be laboriously incised into the metal, whereas in etching the plate is coated

284 WILLIAM BLAKE (1757–1827). God creating the Universe (1794)
Relief etching. This plate was originally made as the frontispiece to Europe, a Prophecy, *written and illustrated by Blake in 1794, using a method of relief etching of copper plates that he had invented himself. 23.3 × 16.8cm.*

In his hand, he took, the Golden Compasses, prepared
In Gods eternal store, to circumscribe
This Universe, and all created things.
One foot he center'd, and the other turn'd,
Round through the vast profundity obscure,
And said, thus far extend, thus far thy bounds
This be thy just circumference, O world!

Milton

with an acid-resisting substance, either wax or resin (the 'resist'), through which the design is scratched with an etching needle and then bitten by immersion in acid. The potentialities of the medium for free and direct expression were not all at once recognised. Dürer, for example, experimented with it but the results do not differ fundamentally in treatment from his engravings, and it is broadly true to say that in the sixteenth century the process was mainly used either in combination with line-engraving or as a short cut to achieving the same effect. There are a few exceptions, notably Parmigianino, who has the distinction of being the first 'painter-etcher', and from whose hand seventeen etchings are known, characterised by the same graceful elegance as his drawings, and Federico Barocci. But it was not until the first half of the seventeenth century, in Holland, that the process was first properly exploited, by Hercules Segers and, even more, by Rembrandt.

Segers's landscape etchings, often printed in coloured ink on tinted paper or even cloth, display an extraordinary degree of freedom and fantasy. They are extremely rare, but the Department possesses twenty-four – a number exceeded only by the considerably larger group in the Amsterdam Printroom. Rembrandt's output was far greater and his range far wider. The three hundred or so etchings that are generally accepted as his represent landscapes, portraits, biblical subjects and *genre* scenes. Many, particularly the later ones, use much drypoint (direct incision into the plate with a sharp point) in addition to etching, and most plates are known in several 'states' (a term denoting any alteration to a plate). In the vast majority of prints differences of state, when they exist, are of trivial importance; but Rembrandt's show him developing his ideas as he went along, and by preserving his successive changes of mind they provide a unique insight into the creative process.

288 Francisco Goya (1746–1828). A caza de dientes (Hunting for teeth)
Etching and aquatint. Plate 12 of Los Caprichos *(1799). This set of eighty plates satirises the vices and follies of his time. The teeth of a hanged man were regarded as aphrodisiacs. 21.5 × 15cm.*

289 PABLO PICASSO (1881–1973). Minotaur and sleeping girl (1933)
Drypoint. One of the so-called Vollard Suite, *a collection of a hundred of Picasso's finest plates of the 1930s published together by Ambrose Vollard. 30 × 37cm.*

Original etching was widely practised in Holland in the seventeenth century by many besides Rembrandt and his followers. The work of all these artists is very fully represented in the Department. But in his range of subject matter and profundity of treatment, as well as in his technical mastery of the medium, Rembrandt stands alone in his own period and overshadows all but one or two of his successors. There were others working in the early seventeenth century for whom etching was the primary means of expression: Jacques Callot, a native of Nancy who worked in Florence, and Stefano della Bella, a Florentine by birth, both of whom etched more than 1,000 plates; and Wenceslas Hollar, a native of Bohemia who worked in England, and who produced as many as 2,700. The etchings of all three are of very varied subject matter and tend to be small in scale. In the eighteenth century the most outstanding original etcher was Giovanni Battista Piranesi, who worked on a large scale and specialised in architectural fantasies and in views, equally touched with fantasy, of ancient and modern Rome.

Two technical innovations were introduced in the course of the eighteenth century: soft-ground etching, which reproduces the effect of a chalk drawing, and aquatint, in which an area of tone is achieved by biting the plate through a partly porous granular resist. These were mainly used in reproductive engraving, though Gainsborough etched a number of soft-ground landscapes and in many of Goya's etchings aquatint is used to great effect in combination with the etched line. Francisco Goya is the only etcher unquestionably in the same rank as Rembrandt. The series that he produced, *Los Caprichos* (a series of satirical prints on the vices of his times), *The Disasters of Wars* (on the atrocities of the Napoleonic invasion of Spain and the reaction after the

288

290 WILLIAM DOUGHTY (1757–82) Dr Samuel Johnson
(1779)
After Sir Joshua Reynolds (1723–92)
*Mezzotint. Doughty was apprenticed as a painter to Reynolds
and married one of his servants. This is one of six prints after
Reynolds' paintings that Doughty made in 1779–80 before
leaving England to seek his fortune in Bengal. 45.4 × 32.9cm.*

restoration of the royal family) and the mysterious
Disparates (Follies), are unique in their powerful and
unforgettable combination of satirical bitterness, fantastic imagination, brutality and compassion. The other
late eighteenth- and early nineteenth-century etchers,
in Germany, France and Britain, were mainly inspired
by Dutch seventeenth-century masters. What has been
called the 'etching revival' began in the middle of the
nineteenth century in France, with the painters of the
Barbizon school – Rousseau, Daubigny, Millet and the
rest – Charles Meryon (who was exclusively an etcher),
and James McNeill Whistler, equally well known as a
painter. Many of Whistler's best etchings (e.g. the
'Thames Set') were produced in England, and his
technique owes much to his years in France and to the
example of Meryon. In his artistic aims he differs so
completely from Rembrandt and Goya that comparison
is hardly possible, but he certainly approaches them in
technical mastery. Other nineteenth-century etchers
include Seymour Haden, whose landscape etchings are
strongly influenced by Whistler, his brother-in-law,
and the more isolated figure of Samuel Palmer, best
remembered for his early visionary landscape drawings

of the 1820s, who etched a few plates that are among
the best work of his later years. Of succeeding generations, the Department has excellent collections of
the work of almost all the leading figures in Britain,
from the Scotsmen Cameron, Bone and McBey to the
Englishmen Augustus John and Sickert. The greatest
etcher of the twentieth century is Picasso, and by him
the Department has a small but reasonably representative collection of prints.

Mezzotint, invented in the middle of the seventeenth
century by Ludwig von Siegen, is a tone process,
differing essentially from all others in that the artist
works from dark to light. Although its earliest masters
such as Prince Rupert and Vaillant worked on the
Continent, the process soon came to be associated with
England, where in the eighteenth century mezzotint
engravers attained an extraordinary degree of technical
skill in the reproduction of portraits by Reynolds,
Gainsborough and their followers. In the early
nineteenth century mezzotint on steel was used to great
effect by John Martin and J. M. W. Turner, impressions of whose very rare *Little Liber Studiorum* are
in the Department. Stipple was another process that
came to be an English speciality, and its most famous
practitioner, Francesco Bartolozzi, made over a
thousand plates while resident in London.

Lithography was invented at the very end of the
eighteenth century by the German Alois Senefelder. It
involves the use of a particular kind of limestone and the
chemical fact that grease repels water. The design is
drawn in a greasy ink-absorbent chalk or ink either
directly on the stone or on lithographic transfer-paper
from which it is transferred to the stone, which is then
wetted, inked, and printed. The essence of printmaking
as a creative art lies in the skill with which the artist
adapts his conception to the technical limitations of the
process. This element of conflict hardly exists in
lithography, which provides an exact facsimile of a
free-hand drawing, and the process was in fact mainly
used as a cheap and convenient means of reproduction.
There were, however, a number of 'artist lithographers'
who produced original work in this medium; the most
successful were the chalk lithographs which took
advantage of the grained surface of the stone and the
possibilities of scratching down the surface to create
highlights to produce uniquely beautiful effects: Goya
(the first major artist to experiment with the process); in
France, Géricault, Delacroix, Daumier, Manet,
Toulouse-Lautrec, and the symbolist Odilon Redon; in
England above all Whistler and C. R. W. Nevinson.

Since the Second World War lithography has become perhaps the most popular medium of printmaking, partly because it can easily be adapted for colour
printing. In France the major figures were Picasso and
Dubuffet; in America a number of specialist workshops
devoted to lithography opened around 1960, and pro-

291 EDOUARD VUILLARD (1868–1940). Interior with red wallpaper (1899)
Colour lithograph. From a series of twelve colour lithographs Paysages et Intérieurs *(Landscapes and Interiors) commissioned by the publisher Ambrose Vollard.34 × 27cm.*

292 VASILY KANDINSKY (1866–1944). *The Mirror* (1907)
Linocut printed in five colours from two blocks. An example of Kandinsky's early style, made in Munich in the years shortly before his development of abstract art. Later in the 1920s Kandinsky taught at the Bauhaus in Weimar and Dessau. 32 × 15.8cm.

293 RIGHT ROBERT GWATHMEY (b. 1903). Hitch-hiker (1943)
Screenprint in colours. Screenprinting, a variety of stencil printing, was originally developed for commercial purposes in advertising and packaging. It was first adopted by artists for printmaking in the United States during the Depression of the 1930s. 42.7 × 33.2cm.

Screenprinting (or silkscreen or serigraphy as it is often called) is the youngest of the printmaking processes to be applied to fine art. It is in essence a stencil process by which parts of a silk or nylon mesh are stopped out with a paper stencil or with a brushed-on liquid, and ink forced through with a squeegee to the paper on the other side. Screenprinting was originally developed for commercial purposes in the early years of this century, and first used to make artists' prints in America in the 1930s. Its use spread to Europe in the 1950s, and a number of specialist firms established (the most famous in England is Kelpra, in Germany Domberger). It has been particularly liked by 'Pop' artists, who relished the intense colours that can be produced by thick layers of pigment, and the Super-realists who could build up their images with layer after layer of colour using no line at all. Examples of the main figures and types of screenprint may be seen in the Department.

The collection is not confined to original prints. Notable features of the reference collection are: reproductive engravings, classified by designers; reproductions of drawings, including the Gernsheim *Corpus Photographicum* of more than 120,000 photographs (still in progress); portrait engravings, classified by sitter; prints illustrating British and foreign history, classified by date; topographical prints and drawings, especially of London (these include the Crace collection of nearly six thousand London drawings and prints, the twenty-two volumes of the Potter collection of material relating to North London and seventeen portfolios of watercolour views of London made in the 1840s and 1850s by J. W. Archer); satirical prints, both political and personal, especially British from the seventeenth to the early nineteenth century; the three thousand photographs of the National Photographic Record made by Sir Benjamin Stone about 1900; the Banks and Heal collections of trade cards; Lady Charlotte Schreiber's collections of playing-cards, fans and fan-leaves; and the Franks, Rosenheim and Viner collections of bookplates.

vided facilities for Jasper Johns, Robert Rauschenberg and their numerous successors. The Department has a few representative works by all those artists, but, in keeping with the historical nature of the collection, makes no attempt to buy contemporary works as they are published, leaving this to the Tate Gallery and Victoria & Albert Museum.

WESTERN ASIATIC
ANTIQUITIES

*T*he collections of the Department of the Ancient Near East, formerly Western Asiatic
Antiquities, include objects from many different areas and civilisations. Their geographical
range covers virtually all those lands east of Egypt, south of the USSR, and west of
Afghanistan and Pakistan. Greek and Roman remains from Western Asia itself are
excluded, but the range extends westwards to include Phoenician colonies throughout the
Mediterranean. The earliest items in the collections date from about 6000 BC, the latest are
from the time of the first Muslim conquests in the seventh century AD.

294 *Gold jewellery from Tell el-'Ajjul, southern Palestine. This was a prosperous city in the Middle and Late Bronze
Ages. The jewellery, from the sixteenth century* BC, *well displays the artistry and skill of the Canaanite craftsmen.*
W *(bottom pendant) 4.57cm.*

The prehistoric periods

The earliest peoples represented in the collections had a way of life comparable with that of the unwesternised cultures which still exist here and there across the world. Material in the Department of Ethnography indicates the extraordinary richness and variety of surviving pre-industrial cultures, not only in material goods but also in social conventions and imaginative thought. The articles in daily use among them, however, are often made of perishable materials, such as wood, textiles, or skin. The same was evidently true of the primitive cultures of ancient Western Asia, and the things which are preserved in the earth for the archaeologist to discover give an unavoidably distorted picture of what life was then like.

The prehistoric collections of the Department consist largely of pottery, which has been found in large quantities on settlement sites, as well as a variety of stone and bone tools, terracottas and stone figures, beads and amulets. Such finds allow us to reconstruct something of the economic basis of prehistoric communities, and see that similar evolutionary pressures led time and again to similar solutions in widely separated areas.

The people relied basically on their own local resources, mainly as settled farmers or as migrant herdsmen or hunters. The smallest groups may have contained only a few families, but circumstances sometimes favoured the growth and survival of larger groups, where several thousand people were associated in interdependent units, or in single towns and tribes. Some groups lived in areas with local resources that were more than adequate for their own needs: resources like obsidian, a volcanic glass with a fine cutting edge; volcanic lava, which makes excellent grinding stones for grain; natural bitumen, for glueing and water-proofing; metals and metal ores; decorative coloured stones such as lapis lazuli; cowrie shells, and so on. Some items were exchanged over hundreds or even thousands of miles, perhaps accompanied by travelling merchants or craftsmen. At the same time there had to be occasional contact and competition between previously unrelated groups of people. Factors such as these ensured that widely separated areas shared, in some respects, a common culture.

Evidence of crafts is offered by bone and stone awls and needles from Mesopotamia of the Halaf period (*c.* 4500–4000 BC); these were used in leather-working. Spindle-whorls of clay indicate spinning. Other finds show that by about 3500 BC metalworking was estab-

295 *Handmade pottery jar and bowl, each with a design of geometric ornament shown in black paint. From Tell al-'Ubaid, fifth millennium* BC. H *(jar)* 5cm.

lished over a wide area of Western Asia. If excavation of sites yields information about the living conditions, a tiny steatite amulet in the shape of a hut from Arpachiyeh gives a more immediate picture, with its pitched roof. A terracotta model of a hut dated about 3300 BC from Azor in Palestine also has a pitched roof and overhanging eaves. This was a receptacle for the bones of the dead, and other similar ossuaries show further architectural details, such as windows, thatched roofs and pillars.

The pottery found at prehistoric sites provides an invaluable aid to the archaeologist in distinguishing one period from another. In Mesopotamia, for instance, incised wares of the Hassuna period (6th millennium BC) could never be confused with the fine painted wares of the Halaf period. There are many more such distinctions, seldom so conspicuous, which can even enable us to date an ancient site by an examination of the pottery fragments found on its surface. Studies of pottery also help to trace cultural influences across wide areas. For example, design motifs in the painted decoration of Halaf period pottery are found as far afield as north Syria and southern Anatolia.

Most of the prehistoric pottery was made on a slow wheel rotated by hand. Before being fired the smaller vessels were often painted with patterns which are 295 sometimes reminiscent of basketwork. Pictures of

296 RIGHT *Pottery figurine showing a woman with prominent breasts, perhaps a goddess of fertility. From Chagar Bazar, Syria. Halaf period, about 5000 BC. H 8cm.*

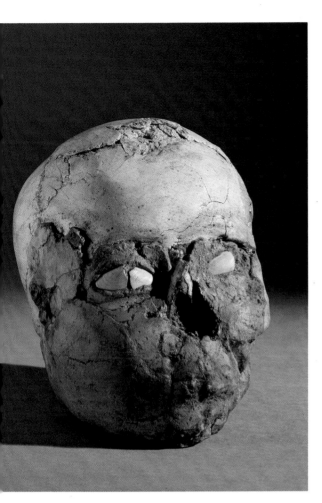

several found in an early level (6000 BC or earlier) at Jericho in Palestine. There is evidence that the head represented a dead relative and had been preserved in a family shrine.

Fortifications and religious buildings on a monumental scale were already being built in the prehistoric period. A reconstruction in the Museum using original materials shows part of a half-columned façade from a temple at Uruk in southern Mesopotamia dated about 2900 BC: geometric patterns were created by pressing coloured cones into wet plaster.

The same kind of mosaic decoration was used as far away as Brak in Syria. Fragments of the embellishment of the Eye Temple at Tell Brak, also dated about 2900 BC, include part of a frieze from the altar made from gold, limestone and shale; a rosette of marble, shale and pink limestone was one of several decorating the façade of the temple. Excavations at the Brak temple produced thousands of small amulets and 'eye-idols', probably offerings made to win the god's favour. An elegantly stylised human head also comes from this temple. The architecture of the temple and the artefacts found there have no identifiable local characteristics, and are further evidence of the strong cultural influence exerted by Mesopotamia.

THE INVENTION OF WRITING

The invention of writing and the keeping of permanent records allow us a much fuller glimpse of ancient society. The collections of the Department well illustrate the history of writing in the ancient Near East. A preliminary step towards the invention of writing was taken with the manufacture of stone seal stamps. The oldest date from before 6000 BC, but some of the finest in the collection are from the late prehistoric period, about 3500–2800 BC. They were used in much the same way as seals and signatures are today. To prove, for instance, that he was responsible for a delivery of oil, a particular person applied his personal seal to wet clay covering the stopper of the oil-jar; no-one could then open it without breaking the seal.

The first written records seem to have been receipts, sealed lumps of clay on which rows of circular impressions, representing numbers, were written; such receipts have been found from Syria to central Iran and may date back to 3500 BC. The British Museum's collection begins slightly later, when the impressed numbers were accompanied by simple pictures (pictograms). The head of an ox, for example, was used to indicate that the number of dots referred to the number of oxen. As it was not easy to incise curved lines on clay, the scribes simplified the characters to forms made up of straight lines. These were made by pressing one end of a wooden or reed stylus into clay; as the end of the stylus struck the clay first, it made a wider mark than the

297 LEFT *Group of stone amulets from the Tell Brak temple, Syria. The amulets, representing a pig, a ram and a fox, have the form of stamp-seals, with patterns on the base, but were apparently left in the temple as offerings. Jamdat Nasr period, about 3000 BC. L (ram) 4.5cm.*

298 ABOVE *Plastered skull from Jericho. Several such skulls, dating to the seventh millennium BC, were found at Jericho, and are thought to have been connected with some form of ancestor cult. L 20.3cm.*

people and animals are relatively scarce, and they are drawn, when they do appear, in a schematic form which exaggerates some physical characteristics and omits others. The attitude to living subjects can also be seen in prehistoric figures. Some of these, notably two from Chagar Bazar in Syria which seem to show women offering the breast, emphasise the importance of fertility beliefs in many early farming communities. The nature of the subject is tolerably obvious, but there is no attempt at realism. Another aspect of prehistoric religion is represented by a plastered human skull, one of

299 ABOVE *Clay tablet of the Jamdat Nasr period, about 3000 BC, with an administrative text. Although the pictographic origin of the script is still clear, individual signs are beginning to evolve into a truly cuneiform script. 7.8 × 7.8cm.*

301 BELOW *Akkadian cylinder-seal of lapis lazuli with gold mounts. The seal is carved with scenes of combat between heroes and animals, and there are traces of the owner's name. From Ur, Iraq, about 2100 BC. H 4.3cm.*

300 LEFT *Clay tablet from Nineveh with the Babylonian account of the Flood, from the Epic of Gilgamesh. At the instruction of the god Ea the hero Utnapishtim successfully builds a boat. Seventh century BC. 13.5 × 15,3cm.*

shaft, so that the impression formed was characteristically wedge-shaped. The pictograms were increasingly stylised until in time the characters were no longer recognisable as pictures of objects. The signs or characters included word signs (logograms) and phonetic signs (phonograms) representing syllables which could be used to spell out words.

This script is now known as cuneiform ('wedge shape'), and was eventually used to write records of many kinds in several different languages. The material on which it was written remained, most commonly, damp clay; this was available everywhere, retained its shape when dry, and could always be baked if a permanent record was required. The British Museum possesses a vast collection of cuneiform tablets, representing a wide range of literature, from economic and administrative records, legal documents and letters, magical, astrological and mathematical texts, to historical records, and myths and legends.

Cuneiform tablets, like prehistoric receipts, were often authenticated by means of seals in stamp form in the early period, about 3000 BC. These were generally cylindrical in shape, and were rolled over the surface of the clay. The carvings on these seals, though miniature in size, are among the finest products of ancient Mesopotamian art.

There are many different styles, but the best of all are perhaps those produced in the Akkad period (c. 2370–2100 BC). One has to look at them very closely to appreciate the quality of the workmanship and the concentrated vitality of the figures. The subject matter ranges from offering scenes to contests between men and animals and depictions of deities.

The development of cuneiform for use in complex documents was a gradual process, but it had been completed by about 2500 BC, when it was in use in the Sumerian cities of southern Mesopotamia.

THE HISTORICAL PERIODS

The Sumerians appear to have been the heirs of the prehistoric culture of Mesopotamia, whose influence was widely felt throughout the Near East: certainly their civilisation was strongly influenced by what had gone before. A gypsum trough, which shows sheep returning to the fold where their lambs are waiting, is the Museum's finest example of Mesopotamian art about 3000 BC. This may have come from Uruk, where a magnificent temple complex continued to flourish in the Early Dynastic Period (c. 2800–2370 BC).

The inlaid decoration from the façade of a temple at al-'Ubaid (c. 2600 BC) included another series of pastoral scenes. Still more imposing, and of great technical interest for the history of metallurgy, are the copper heads and plaques representing lions, cattle, and deer. The columns of this same temple façade were found fallen in a heap, together with the rest of the decoration, but have been restored on reliable evidence. They were originally made of palm-tree trunks coated with bitumen, and their surface was then covered with shaped pieces of pink limestone and mother-of-pearl.

The temples of Sumer owed their great wealth to the theocratic system of government which existed in many Sumerian sites. The priests and controllers of the temple bureaucracies established themselves in power, and spent the surplus wealth of the community not only on the temples but also on themselves. The results of this policy are seen most dramatically in the Royal Tombs of Ur.

The city of Ur lay close to the Euphrates. Archaeologists were first attracted by its 'ziggurat', a massive brick tower which once had a temple on top, but excavations in the 1920s also uncovered a cemetery which had remained in use for centuries. The excavator, Sir Leonard Woolley, was working on behalf of the British Museum and the University Museum, Philadelphia, and these two institutions were each awarded a quarter of what the expedition found; the other half remained in Baghdad. Even the British Museum's share, however, amply demonstrates the lavish way in which the tombs were furnished, and the extraordinary skill which Woolley brought to the task of excavating them. The finest articles in the collection are

302 Sumerian stone trough showing lambs emerging from a reed hut to meet a flock of sheep. This trough, from Uruk, Iraq, probably comes from a temple of Inanna, goddess of fertility. About 3500–3000 BC. L 96.5cm.

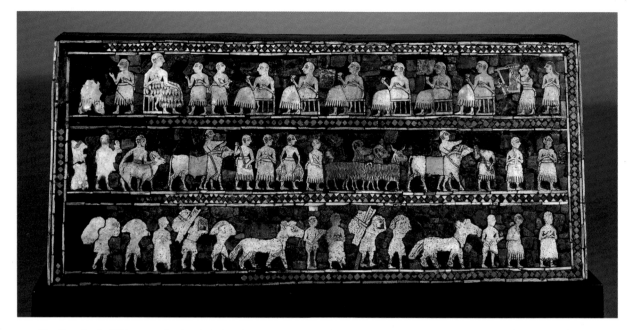

303 *The Standard of Ur: a wooden box inlaid with stones and shells. This side shows the king celebrating at a banquet (top row), while servants bring animals and other goods below. From the Royal Cemetery at Ur, about 2500 BC. L 49.5cm.*

thought to have belonged to the ruling family at a time, about 2500 BC, when Ur was the most powerful city in Mesopotamia. Sometimes the dead man or woman had been accompanied to the grave by as many as sixty attendants, who brought with them everything necessary to ensure that their master continued to live, after death, in the style to which he had been accustomed. Woolley's discovery of these 'death-pits' aroused extensive controversy among scholars at the time, as Mesopotamian literature is singularly devoid of reference to any such macabre ceremonies.

We can still see the skulls of a helmeted soldier and of a female attendant wearing a jewelled headband, as they were found crushed in the ground. Some of the finest objects, however, have been restored to their original shapes. The goat with his forelegs resting on a tree – often called the Ram in the Thicket because of a fancied connection with the story of Abraham and Isaac – is one of a pair. The two probably supported a small table on which delicate vessels of gold and silver, or the Sumerian equivalent of a chess-set may once have stood. This highly ornamental goat was made on a simple wooden core; the surface consists of carved stones, shell and sheet metal, with bitumen as glue. Musical instruments were constructed in the same way: the British Museum has one silver lyre, and another pair of inlaid instruments, a harp and a lyre, which have been restored in wood. The sounding-boxes of the lyres represent bulls, and a text tells us that the music was imagined as coming out of the animals' mouths.

A lyre of the same kind is shown in a scene on the so-called Standard of Ur, a lectern-shaped box with mosaic panels all round. One of the two main sides shows people bringing gifts and tribute; the lyre-player is entertaining the king and his high officials at a banquet in the top row. The other side shows a different aspect of Sumerian civilisation, with chariots charging, and warriors bringing captives into the royal presence. The chariots are pulled not by horses but by a kind of ass native to Mesopotamia; one of these animals is represented on an electrum rein-ring which was part of the harness attached to a queen's ox-drawn sledge. The collections also include a large quantity of jewellery, such as the queen's attendants wore. It is worth noting that all the metals used, together with the cornelian and lapis lazuli, must have been imported.

Life-size Sumerian sculpture is represented by the statue of a slightly later ruler, about 2100 BC, almost certainly Gudea of the state of Lagash. This statue would have been set up in a temple, to encourage the god to look after the ruler's interests. Most Mesopotamian statues are far smaller than this, as the blocks of stone had to be brought from outside the Tigris-Euphrates plain, and the problems of moving them must have been considerable.

In the early part of the second millennium BC Baby-

304 *Ram feeding at a bush. This figure is decorated with gold, copper, shell, lapis lazuli and other stones. It comes from one of the Royal Tombs at Ur, Iraq, and may once have been part of a stand. About 2500 BC. H 46cm.*

305 *Assyrian and Babylonian stone weights in the shape of ducks. Mesopotamian rulers took great trouble to ensure that traders used correct weights. Their* mina *weighed about half a kilogram. From Iraq, about 2000–500 BC.* L (largest) 14cm.

Ionia achieved supremacy in Mesopotamia under its most famous king, Hammurapi (1792–1750 BC), whose capital was at Babylon. The Old Babylonian levels at the site have scarcely been excavated, but the collections contain much material of the same date from other sites in Mesopotamia. Particularly interesting are the series of terracotta plaques showing scenes of daily life, female fertility figures and erotic pleasures. The collections also contain vast numbers of cuneiform tablets from the site of Sippar, including economic and legal texts. Perhaps the most interesting item is an inscribed model of a sheep's liver, used by diviners to interpret omens.

Syrian civilisation shared the same prehistoric background as Mesopotamia on the one hand and Palestine on the other. During the third millennium BC, however, a distinctive culture flourished in the central and northern parts of the country which was distinctively Syrian. Characterised by wonderfully fine, almost metallically hard pottery, this culture became known as 'calciform', on account of the ubiquitous cup- or goblet-shaped vessels present in the repertoire. Excavations at major sites such as Hama, Qatna and Ebla have revealed a level of cultural sophistication and architectural refinement to rival that of Mesopotamia. Terracotta figurines

were produced in great quantity, and the collections contain many examples of the distinctive types found in the Euphrates area, which have pillar bases in place of legs, exaggerated facial features and elaborate hairstyles.

During the second millennium BC the city-states of Syria exerted considerable political influence. One of the most important was Alalakh, and the collections contain many of the finds recovered during excavations between 1937 and 1949. Perhaps the most impressive of these is the statue of one of the city's rulers, King Idrimi (c. 1550 BC), carved in a somewhat austere and simplistic style, quite unlike contemporary sculptures in Mesopotamia.

Palestine, during the third millennium, was an active commercial centre. An economy based on productive agriculture and trade led to the development of sophisticated urban centres, with well-planned houses, palaces, temples and, in many cases, substantial fortifications. Tombs of the period were often large, and contained multiple successive burials. The Museum has objects from such tombs excavated at Lachish in the 1930s. The elegant pottery vessels, many covered with a bright red slip and highly burnished, testify to the skill and artistry of the Early Bronze Age potters. The collections also contain many of the impressive copper weapons (daggers and javelins) and bead necklaces recovered from these tombs.

Towards the end of the third millennium Palestine's main trading partner, Egypt, failed, with the collapse of the Old Kingdom. Objects from this period reflect the

306 *Statue of Idrimi, King of Alalakh, Syria, in the sixteenth century* BC. *The statue would almost certainly have been painted, and the eyes and eyebrows were inlaid with black stone.* H *1.1m.*

recession that followed in Palestine: tools and weapons become heavier, pottery becomes simpler and more functional. Examples of the pottery and metalwork of this interesting period are illustrated by the finds from Tiwal esh-Sharqi in Jordan. Dating to about 2300 BC, the objects placed in the deep shaft-tombs as funerary offerings include fine handmade pottery jars, copper daggers and javelins, necklaces of cornelian beads and distinctive four-spouted pottery lamps.

In the second millennium BC the re-establishment of trade routes led to a return to city life in Palestine. The population, which is now referred to as 'Canaanite', generally chose to re-occupy sites which had been abandoned during the period of recession, creating high mounds (or *tells*), which they then fortified with smooth plastered slopes and massive ramparts. The

Canaanites soon established a firm reputation as skilled artists and craftsmen. Examples of rarely preserved carpentry can be seen in the furniture excavated from tombs at Jericho near the Dead Sea. The Museum has reconstructed one of these tombs, which in addition to 307 the furniture, includes pottery vessels, wooden boxes and platters, and baskets. Jewellery of this period shows highly developed techniques of granulation and re- 294 poussée. The fine collection from Tell el-'Ajjul well illustrates these features, and also includes pendants bearing highly stylised representations of the goddess Astarte.

Canaanite Palestine, open to sea-faring traders of the eastern Mediterranean became a cosmopolitan centre. Cypriot and Myceanaean objects were imported, and these were skilfully imitated by local craftsment. One of the most characteristic imported Cyptiot juglets was modelled in the form of a poppy-head. Known as 'bil-bils', these vessels are thought to have been used to transport opium. The 'bil-bil' was copied by the Canaanite potters and became a popular and elegant tableware.

During the second half of the second millennium Palestine (and part of Syria) formed part of Egypt's New Kingdom empire, and the diplomatic correspondence between the pharoahs and their subject Canaanite princes has been preserved in the fascinating documents known as the Amarna letters. Found at Amarna in Egypt, they include appeals for help from attacks of the 'Hapiru', identified by some as the biblical 'Hebrews'.

The Amarna letters were written in Akkadian cuneiform, as indeed was most of the formal diplomatic correspondence at this time. It was the Canaanites who, during the second millennium BC, developed a new and much simpler writing system, which was to have a major and lasting impact upon later civilisations. In its earliest stages, as illustrated by the Sinai Inscriptions, this system used pictograms to represent the initial consonantal value of the word depicted. By selecting and standardising a set of these pictograms every sound in the language could be represented by a single symbol. This was the basis of the alphabet, and because it relied upon single consonants (plus signs to stand for the vowels) rather than syllables, only twenty-five or so signs were needed, unlike the cumbersome Akkadian system which required over six hundred.

The alphabet system spread among the Phoenicians 308 and other Semitic-speaking peoples of the eastern coast of the Mediterranean. The inhabitants of Ugarit, modern Ras Shamra near Lattakia, and subsequently the Achaemenid kings, used alphabets written in types of cuneiform. Both were eventually replaced by alphabets drived from the Phoenician, which could be written at greater speed on materials like paper.

The Semitic alphabet developed in several direc-

307 ABOVE *Reconstructed tomb from Jericho. In the Middle Bronze Age (c. 1750–1650 BC) first one, then subsequently six other individuals were interred in this tomb. It contained pottery, as well as wooden furniture, rarely preserved elsewhere in Palestine.*

tions. Hebrew, as written on the tomb of Shebnaiah at Jerusalem, eventually became the square Hebrew script still used today. The Aramaic script, used through much of Western Asia for centuries, had several descendants, including Armenian. The Arabic script is again derived from the early Semitic alphabet. The Greeks borrowed their own alphabet from the Phoenicians, and the Russians took theirs from the Greek. Most Western European languages now use the Latin alphabet, which derived from the same source.

The end of the second millennium was, in the Levant, one of the most confused and turbulent phases of its history, with the historically documented incursions of new peoples such as the Sea Peoples (including the Philistines), the Aramaeans and the Israelites. Amidst the confusion the Egyptians struggled to maintain control of their dwindling empire, establishing garrisons at key strategic sites, such as Beth Shan in the

308 *Carved limestone stele with a Punic inscription in the alphabetic Phoenician script of the western Mediterranean, which records its dedication to the goddess Tinnit and the god Ba'al Hammon. Third to second century BC. H 26.7cm.*

north and Gaza in the south. Excavations at Tell
es-Sa'idiyeh in Jordan have brilliantly illuminated this
final phase of Egyptian control. The site, which is
identified as biblical Zarathan, was a major Egyptian
outpost on the eastern side of the River Jordan, and
excavations have revealed a part of the governor's
residency. A rich and extensive cemetery has also been
excavated, and the finds, many of which are now in the
Museum's collections, reflect not only the prosperity of
the city, but also the unusual and mixed nature of its
population. For many of the objects show influences
from Egypt, Anatolia, Cyprus and the Aegean,
suggesting perhaps that the Egyptians had in their
employ, in addition to local Canaanites, many other
peoples of foreign origin. One of the most interesting
objects is a beautiful ivory cosmetic box in the form of a
fish. This piece, which is almost certainly of Egyptian
manufacture, was found inside a bronze bowl which
covered the genitals of the deceased.

In prehistoric times some of the earliest towns had
developed on the Anatolian plateau, in what is now
Turkey, but urban civilisation did not expand there as
rapidly as in Mesopotamia. In the third millennium BC
Anatolia was probably an important source of copper,
and fine examples of metalwork have been found in
tombs at Alaça Hüyük, about 2300 BC. A silver bull with
high horns probably derives from this group. In the
Yortan area, to the south of Troy, an undistinguished
type of black burnished pottery was used, but those who
could afford it possessed metal vessels, such as an
elegant two-handled silver cup.

In the second millennium Hittites, who spoke an
Indo-European language, built an empire in Anatolia,
which extended into Syria and shared a border with
the Egyptians. A cuneiform tablet in the Hittite and
Luvian languages is one of thousands of tablets found
in the royal archives at the Hittite capital of Hattusa
(Bogazköy). The Museum's most remarkable example
of Hittite workmanship is a series of miniature figures
made of gold, lapis lazuli and stealite which represent Hittite gods and dignitaries. These were found in a
grave at Carchemish on the Euphrates, a town which
retained some aspects of Hittite culture long after the
empire had collapsed around 1200 BC. Also from
Carchemish is a series of sculptural slabs with texts in
the language of Carchemish, which was related to
Hittite but written in a heiroglyphic script. The style of
the sculptures themselves is clearly reminiscent of
Assyrian art; most of were in fact made in the ninth and
eighth centuries BC, when Carchemish was an important trading centre under Assyrian protection. Other
articles from Carchemish indicate the cosmopolitan
character of what is sometimes called 'Syro-Hittite' art.

Despite the upheavals at the close of the second
millennium BC, the Canaanite legacy of artistry and
craftsmanship was preserved in a small area of the

309 *Silver bull, probably the decorative terminal of a pole or
staff, with gold inlay and standing on a base of copper. It is
thought to have come from one of the rich graves at Alaça
Hüyük, and dates to about 2300 BC. H 24cm.*

Levantine coast, which became known as Phoenicia.
The Phoenicians, during the first millennium BC, refined and developed the already sophisticated eclectic
style of the Canaanites, and their products, and at times
the craftsmen themselves, were in great demand
throughout the Near East.

The biggest contributor to their distinctive style was
undoubtedly Egypt, and this influence can be clearly
seen in the sphinxes and decorative motifs on a series of
bronze bowls found in the Assyrian capital city of
Nimrud; these must have been made between 900 and
700 BC. In addition to fine metalwork, the Phoenicians
were renowned for their manufacture of jewellery, glass
and, of course, the famous purple dye. However, it is
perhaps in the field of ivory-carving that their artistic
excellence can best be illustrated and judged.

The Museum possesses a fine collection of Phoenician ivories. Most were excavated in Assyrian palaces,

310 *Gold Hittite figure, probably representing a king. The collections contain a series of such miniature figures in gold, lapis lazuli and steatite. Fourteenth century* BC. H *3.94cm.*

311 *Ivory figurine from Nimrud, depicting a kilted male figure carrying a gazelle on his shoulders and leading a bull or calf. The ivory has been discoloured by burning. About eighth century* BC. H *11cm.*

where they had been taken as booty. Many are panels which would have been used as furniture decoration; some have alphabetic marks on the back, which indicated to the carpenter where to fix them. Some pieces came from toilet boxes, and others were fan- or whisk-handles. Occasionally a larger object, such as a chair, might be made entirely of ivory members: one piece in the collection is apparently a furniture-leg.

Some of the items are blackened by fire, but others retain the brilliant whiteness of fresh ivory. This can be misleading, as ivories were sometimes stained in different colours, and the richer pieces were covered with gold-leaf. Colour was also provided by red and blue inlays; these were normally made of glass, but we occasionally encounter cornelian and lapis lazuli too,

for instance on a plaque which shows a lioness holding an African by the neck. The delicate carving of this small panel is among the finest examples of Phoenician workmanship. It must be dated between 900 and 700 BC, a period during which large quantities of ivory furniture were transported to Assyria as war booty or as tribute.

The Phoenician ivories were often inspired by Egyptian models, so much so that some of them at first sight might seem to be Egyptian work. Towns in inland Syria, including probably Damascus and Hama, had their own schools of ivory craftsmen; ivories were also carved in Urartu, Babylonia, and in Assyria itself. Notable motifs on the Syrian and Phoenician ivories include the sphinx, the griffin, the grazing deer, the cow

312 ABOVE *Ivory panel from Nimrud, originally part of a piece of furniture. The female head wearing an Egyptian-style wig and looking out of a window is thought to be an acolyte of the goddess Ashtarte. About eighth century* BC. H *10.7cm.*

313 RIGHT *Gold amulet-case, probably from Tharros, Sardinia. The lion's head surmounted by a disc and uraeus indicates the Egyptian goddess Sakhmet. The hollow lower section once held an amulet. Sixth to fifth century* BC. L *4.5cm.*

turning to lick her suckling calf, and the 'woman at the window', believed to be a picture of one of the Phoenician goddesses of reproduction and fertility. Although the ivories were mass-produced, each one seems to have some individual felicity of carving. We can see that the Phoenician reputation for ingenuity, mentioned by the early Greeks, was thoroughly well deserved.

With almost no effective hinterland to support an agricultural economy, Phoenicia turned to the sea in order to secure its prosperity. During the first millennium colonies were established throughout the Mediterranean, and expeditions were undertaken to places beyond. Cyprus was among the islands colonised from Phoenicia; an elaborate silver bowl, showing both Egyptian and Assyrian influence, comes from a grave at Amathus. A Phoenician cemetery has also been discovered as far west as Tharros in Sardinia. A large collection of material from the Tharros cemeteries is preserved in the Museum and includes fine pottery and much jewellery of high quality. The most famous of all Phoenician settlements, however, was the city of Carthage in what is now Tunisia; the Carthaginian

empire was at one time a serious rival of Rome. There are a number of stelae inscribed in the Phoenician (Punic) script; some were erected over the graves of children who had probably been sacrificed to the local god, a practice noted by several Greek and Roman authors.

Politically, the first millennium BC was dominated by the military campaigns of the Assyrians. Based in the valley of the River Tigris, Assyrian culture was distinctive, with its own dialect, and its own arts and institutions. The military expeditions of the neo-Assyrian kings, between the ninth and seventh centuries BC, extended their power from Egypt to the Persian Gulf, and deep into what are now Iran and Turkey. Their exploits were commemorated on carved stone slabs which lined the palace walls in the successive capital cities of Nimrud (ancient Kalhu), Khorsabad (Dur-Sharrukin), and Nineveh. The subject matter of these narrative carvings include military expeditions – sieges and battles, victories, and processions of tribute-bearers – as well of scenes of hunting and banqueting. These carvings offer an extraordinarily detailed picture

314 *Dying lioness: gypsum carving from the palace of Ashurbanipal at Nineveh. Hunting lions was a favourite sport of Assyrian kings. Such wild animals symbolised the forces of evil against which the king, as the champion of civilisation, was obliged to struggle. About 645* BC.

of the Assyrian world as seen through contemporary eyes. The palaces which contained them were eventually destroyed in 612 BC by a combined army of Iranians and Babylonians.

The slabs in the British Museum were excavated between 1845 and 1855 principally by two men, Layard and Rassam. At that time Great Britain was a valued ally of the Ottoman Empire, and the excavators were allowed to remove the lion's share of what they found. Their discoveries, together with some already made by a Frenchman, Botta, first opened European eyes to the high achievements of Mesopotamian civilisation. The collection of sculptures brought back by them to England is still much the finest in the world. The British Museum is the only place where one can see so many sequences of magnificently preserved slabs, re-erected in their original order.

In addition to the sculptured slabs, the collections contain a number of free-standing sculptures, such as the imposing statue of Ashurbanipal II (883–859 BC). There is no pretence of naturalism: the king's features are no portrait, but simply an ideal of static dignity.

Assyrian obelisks, like Egyptian ones, were probably set up outside temple doors. Only two have ever been found complete and both are now in the British Museum. The better preserved, the Black Obelisk, made for Shalmaneser III (858–824 BC), shows people from the extreme ends of the Assyrian Empire bringing tribute before the king. He himself appears twice, once as a conqueror with bow and arrow, and a second time carrying a cup. The tributaries, and the nature of the tribute, are described in captions above the rows of carving. We see among them elephants, monkeys and other exotic animals. One group of tribute is provided by Jehu, King of Israel.

Perhaps the most impressive monuments of Assyrian art are the two magnificent winged bulls, each weighing some 16 tons. Colossal animals such as these frequently flanked magnificent doorways: these are from the palace of Sargon II at Khorsabad. From Balawat near Nimrud, came two massive pairs of gates. Made of wood, the gates were decorated with strips of worked bronze illustrating the full range of Assyrian narrative art: battles, sieges and tribute-bearers. The larger pair of gates, dating from the reign of Shalmaneser III

(858–824 BC) illustrate the king's expeditions to Turkey.

As well as these large items, the collections include many small articles made in Assyria or under Assyrian influence. Arms and armour are well represented: the Assyrians generally used iron weapons, but their protective armour was sometimes bronze. An iron saw-blade was probably used for cutting slabs of stone, such as those on which the sculptures were carved. 305

A silver cup with gold foil round its rim, which was buried before the sack of Nimrud and crushed by the weight of earth above it, is one of the few Assyrian articles in precious metal to have survived. Weights were often made of bronze: one complete set, in the shape of lions, was found in a palace at Nimrud. A much larger bronze object is the hip-bath from Ur. This had been used as a coffin when it was found, but the delicate incisions on its sides are typically Assyrian in style.

Most of the earlier excavations concentrated on the major royal sites, and consequently the Museum's collections reflect the opulent taste of the Assyrian court. A more balanced perspective has recently been added by a series of excavations of late Assyrian and post-Assyrian sites in the Eski Mosul region of northern Iraq. The results and finds shed interesting light on the material culture of smaller settlements.

One of the most interesting sequences of sculptural slabs from the final royal capital, Nineveh, vividly portrays the Assyrian king Sennacherib's siege and capture of the city of Lachish in southern Palestine in 701 BC. It was not, however, the Assyrians who finally destroyed this great city, but the inheritors of the Empire, the Babylonians. In 587 BC, shortly before the fall of Jerusalem brought an end to the southern kingdom of Judah, Nebuchadnezzar attacked Lachish. The last few days before the fall of the city are poignantly documented by a group of ostraca, letters written on potsherds in black ink, which were found amidst the burned debris of the gateway at Lachish. Written in ancient Hebrew, they represent the correspondence sent to the military commander of the city from an outlying watch-post where the Babylonian advance was being monitored. 316

To the north-east the kingdom of Urartu (c. 850–600 BC) included the eastern provinces of modern Turkey, Russian Armenia, and part of Iran. It, too, was strongly influenced by Assyrian civilisation, as can be seen in the fine collection of Urartian bronzes from Toprak Kale near Van. The collection contains several

315 The Black Obelisk. This black stone monument from Nimrud, Iraq, displays the achievements of Shalmaneser III, King of Assyria 858–824 BC. The carved panels show people bringing tribute, and the inscription describes his many campaigns. About 825 BC. H 1.98m.

316 *The capture of Lachish: gypsum panel from the palace of Sennacherib, King of Assyria, at Nineveh, Iraq. A siege-engine attacks from the left, and prisoners stream out of the gate below. Lachish was a town in the biblical kingdom of Judah, captured by Sennacherib in 701 BC. About 700 BC.*

318   fragments of bronze furniture, which may have belonged to a throne of the national god Haldi. A winged figure with a female head probably derives from the rim of a cauldron; this shape was widely imitated in Greek and Etruscan art. Other bronzes include an Utartian model castle, and arms and armour; one round bronze shield is elaborately decorated with processions of animals. Some examples of Urartian texts are written in a version of the cuneiform script.

During this period the cultures of Iran were also highly developed, showing rich and varied artistic traditions, especially in the fields of metalworking and pottery manufacture. Mesopotamian influence can still be recognised in many silver and bronze objects from Iran during the second millennium, but the bronze horse harness and dress pins from Luristan are distinctive in style. It is unfortunate, if not tragic, that the majority of the quite exceptional objects that have

317 *Glazed tile, probably showing the Assyrian king Ashurnasirpal II (883–859 BC). He stands under a canopy with bodyguards behind him, and takes a cup of wine from a servant. From Nimrud, Iraq, ninth century BC. H 30cm.*

318 ABOVE *Urartian bronze furniture-fitting, in the form of a bar surmounted by a snarling lion. This piece was twisted out of shape in antiquity. From Toprak Kale, eighth to seventh century* BC. H *30cm.*

The rich cross-fertilisation of techniques and motifs between the cultures of ancient Western Asia is nowhere more apparent than in the Oxus Treasure. This impressive hoard of gold and silver objects probably belonged to a temple where offerings had accumulated for several centuries. It was buried, perhaps about 200 BC, and rediscovered in 1877 by a group of merchants who carried it to India. There it was sold to a British officer and most of it eventually came to the British Museum as part of the Franks Bequest.

The Oxus Treasure provides ample confirmation of the wealth and sophistication of the Achaemenid court. The style of the ornament is typical of the Achaemenian Persians; as in much Iranian art great use is made of animal forms, both real and mythical, sometimes naturalistically rendered, but more often subordinated to the total design. While the main treasure is Achaemenian, it contains some earlier, perhaps Median pieces, and since it had a chequered history after its discovery

319 BELOW *Silver sword hilt from Luristan. The handle and split pommel are elaborately decorated with embossed lions. Eighth to seventh century* BC. H *16.8cm.*

survived come from looted tombs and lack, therefore, any archaeological context.

The most famous site in Iran is undoubtedly Persepolis, capital of the Achaemenid Persian Empire. The Empire was established through the capture of Babylon by Cyrus in 539 BC. A cylinder seal in the British Museum records the event, asserting that the Persian conquest liberated the people from their oppressors. The Museum is singularly fortunate in its collection of Achaemenid work. The Susa archer is a large-scale example in glazed brick. Among smaller works of art one of the finest is a silver and partly gilded rhyton with a griffin's head. This was a drinking vessel, the liquid being poured into the mouth through a hole in the griffin's chest.

Fragments of wall-carvings, which once adorned the walls of palaces and public buildings in Persepolis, are also in the collections. These slabs are carved in a distinctive, highly finished style, characteristic of the art of the Persian Empire which, extending from Egypt to Turkestan, borrowed freely from all the ancient cultures it superseded.

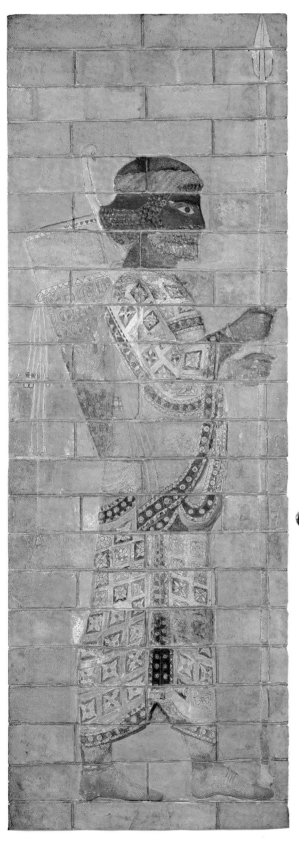

321 ABOVE *Silver-gilt drinking horn: the base is in the form of a griffin, a fabulous bird-headed creature with horns and wings. From Erzincan, Turkey, Achaemenid period, fifth–fourth century* BC. H *25cm.*

320 *Relief of polychrome glazed bricks from the palace of Darius the Great (521–486* BC*) at Susa. This panel is part of a frieze showing a parade of the king's bodyguard, special troops known as the 'Immortals'. On loan from the Louvre.* H *1.47m.*

some later pieces have become associated with it which do not strictly belong.

One item of particular interest is the model chariot drawn by four small ponies. Others worth noting include the pair of armlets decorated with griffins' heads and once inlaid with glass or semi-precious stones, and the large gold fish, really a bottle, with an aperture at its mouth. A simpler form of art is represented on a series of gold plaques for sewing on clothes, while an elaborate scabbard, with scenes of lion-hunts, recalls some of the Assyrian sculptures. The 1500 or so gold and silver coins which were sold with the Treasure may not have been part of the hoard. These are now housed in the Department of Coins and Medals.

The conquests of Alexander the Great destroyed the Persian Empire, but from about 250 BC his Greek successors were gradually replaced by a local dynasty, the Parthians, who had their early capital at Hecatompylos in north-eastern Iran. Work produced in the

323 ABOVE *Gold model of a chariot pulled by four horses, from the Oxus Treasure. The charioteer stands holding the reins while his passenger, represented at a larger size and probably a person of high rank, is seated. Achaemenid, fifth to fourth century* BC. L *18.8cm.*

322 LEFT *Gold armlet from the Oxus Treasure, its terminals in the form of fabulous bird-headed creatures with horns and wings. The armlet was originally inlaid with precious stones. One of a pair, the other belonging to the Victoria and Albert Museum. Achaemenid, fifth to fourth century* BC. H *12.3cm.*

324 RIGHT *Gold face-mask from a tomb of the Parthain period at Nineveh. Gold masks were sometimes used to cover the faces of corpses, thereby concealing the decay of organs such as the eyes, nose and mouth that would be needed in the afterlife. First century* AD. H *16.5cm.*

Parthian period (*c.* 150 BC–AD 224) is often based on Greek models, but older Iranian themes tend to intrude. The gold masks from Nineveh were originally 324 placed in graves, over the faces of the dead. The blue-glazed coffin from Uruk is decorated with figures of armed men, made by pressing a mould into the damp clay.

The period of the Parthian Empire witnessed in the west the rapid expansion of the Roman Empire, which reached eastwards to incorporate Anatolia, Mesopo-

tamia, Palestine, Syria and Arabia. Syria was a frontier province, and the desert city of Palmyra, or Tadmor, retained a considerable degree of freedom. It was situated on an oasis dominating the most direct trade-route between the Syrian coast and the important Mesopotamian territories of the Parthian and, later Sassanian empires. Its control of the transit trade greatly enriched the city, especially in the second and third centuries AD, and the principal families built themselves imposing tombs in the suburbs. Each grave was provided with a stone portrait of the deceased, and their style is a strange amalgam of eastern and western influences. They are worth comparing with some of the painted portraits from Roman Egypt in the Department of Egyptian Antiquities.

Other late objects from Syria, including stone statuary from the Hauran, are variable in style, but the glassware shows great originality; indeed, the blowing of glass was probably invented in Syria. Some pottery bowls, with Aramaic incantations written across them, were originally buried for magical purposes.

Although later a Roman province, Palestine in the first century BC was independent, under Roman protection, and the centre of the expanding Jewish religion. It seems to have been prosperous, and it possessed its own characteristic culture. The British Museum has two elegantly carved ossuaries or stone chests which were designed to contain the bones of the dead; one belonged to the family of a man who had presented a new set of gates to the temple at Jerusalem. These chests date from about the time of Christ, and this is also approximately the period of the Dead Sea scrolls.

A frequently overlooked, but very important area of the ancient Near East represented in the Department is South Arabia. Most South Arabian antiquities have come from what are now the territories of Yemen and South Yemen, the home of the legendary Queen of Sheba. The ancient history of this area is virtually unknown, but it was famous for the production of aromatic spices and incense; its reputed wealth attracted invaders from Roma, Iran and Ethiopia. One of the more delicate objects is, appropriately, a bronze incense-burner; its handle represents an oryx, or antelope with highly exaggerated horns.

The South Arabians had their own alphabetic script, which appears on several monuments, and a distinctive style of primitive sculpture, sometimes reminiscent of modern work. A great bronze altar with projecting bulls' heads and massive rows of sphinxes, recalls the art of Western Asia before the Greeks. Two fine heads, however, in bronze and translucent stone, are obviously influenced by Graeco-Roman standards of portraiture.

In Iran the Parthian Empire was overthrown in AD 224 by Ardashir I, founder of the Sassanian dynasty. The Sassanians regarded themselves as the heirs of the Achaemenids, and retained a religious centre at Istakhr, a city in the neighbourhood of Persepolis.

325 LEFT *Bust of a woman from Palmyra. During the Greek and Roman periods Palmyra was a major commercial centre in the Syrian desert. The wealthy citizens buried their dead in tomb towers or hypogea, with plaques bearing portrait busts. The inscription records that this lady was a certain 'Herta, daughter of Ogilu'.* H 53 cm.

326 BELOW *Limestone ossuary, originally decorated with red paint, with a Greek inscription indicating that it contained the bones of Nicanor, a wealthy Jew of Alexandria. First century* AD. H 38 cm.

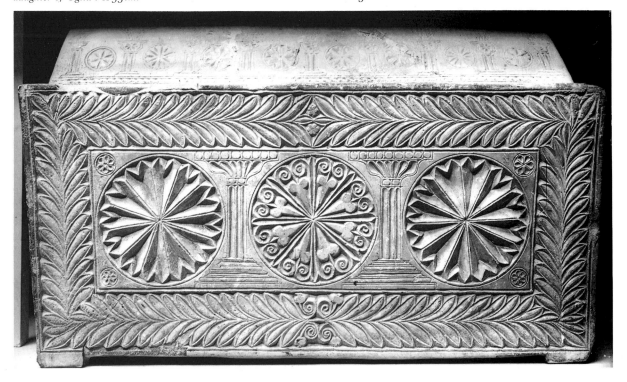

327 ABOVE *Silver-gilt dish, showing a Sassanian king, probably Shapur II (AD 309–79) hunting stags. The king sits astride one stag while another (perhaps the same animal) lies fatally wounded beneath. D 18cm.*

328 BELOW *Sassanian iron swords, with gold and silver hilts and scabbards. The gold scabbard is decorated with an embossed scallop pattern, and the silver with applied wire spirals. Sixth to seventh century AD. L (max.) 108cm.*

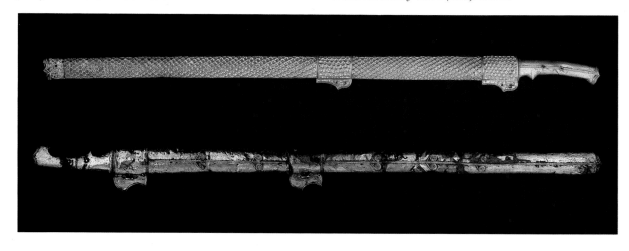

329 *Silver-gilt Sassanian vase. The decoration, which includes birds and foxes between vines, is based on the Roman cult of Bacchus. This scene shows two naked boys picking grapes. From Mazanderan, Iran, sixth to seventh century AD. H 18.5 cm.*

Their goldsmiths and silversmiths showed great skill in the use of embossing, chasing, engraving and gilding, and other craftsmen continued ancient Near Eastern traditions of fine workmanship. One silver dish shows Shapur II hunting stags; on another Bahram V is shown hunting lions, and a partially gilded silver vase is decorated with vineyard scenes framed in stylised grape vines. Contacts with the classical world are shown by seals depicting Leda and the swan, and Romulus and Remus suckled by a wolf.

At the height of their power the Sassanians ruled an area extending from the Euphrates in the west to the Indus in the east, and in the north to Armenia and Soviet Central Asia. They were, therefore, the heirs to all the great civilisations of ancient Western Asia. However, in the early seventh century AD Arab invaders swept through the Near East and carried all before them. The defeat in AD 642 of the Sassanian forces marks the end of the Persian empires and the coming of Islam.

330 *Calcite statue of a woman from South Arabia. She may well have held an offering in her outstretched hands. About first century BC to first century AD. H 74.5 cm.*

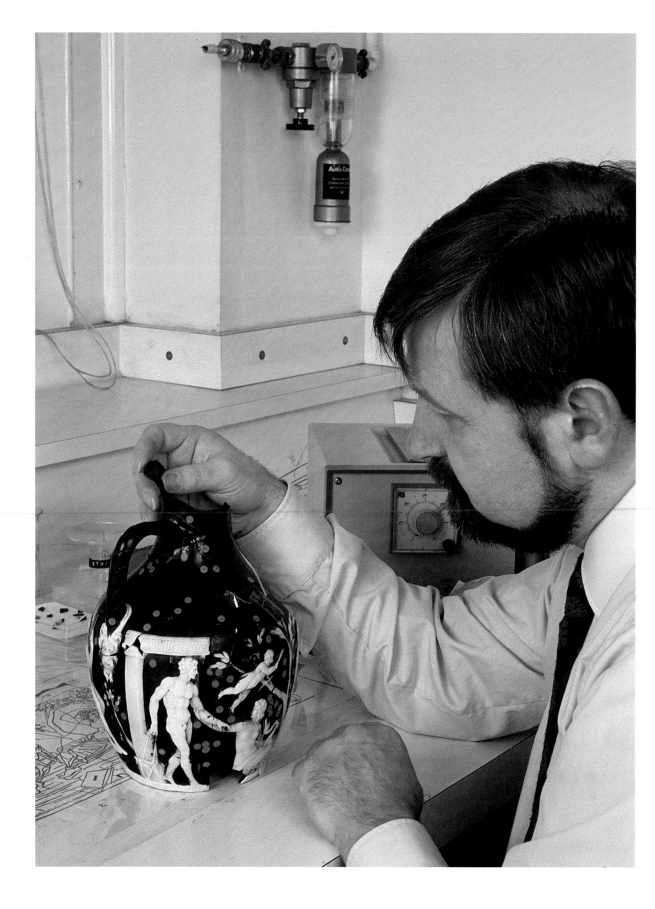

CONSERVATION AND SCIENTIFIC RESEARCH

—◆—

CONSERVATION

Conservation in the British Museum has its origins in the work of craftsmen who were employed to clean and restore objects from the earliest days of the Museum. Since 1924, however, the Museum has had its own permanent conservation research facility staffed by fully trained scientists, and these scientists have worked alongside a growing number of conservators to improve the methods and materials of conservation. The Department of Conservation now employs nearly sixty conservators working in six specialised sections: ceramics and glass; metals; organic materials (wood, leaves, fur, feather, leather, bone and ivory) and textiles; stone, wall-paintings and mosaics; Eastern pictorial art; and Western pictorial art. In addition there are the Conservation Research Section manned by scientists, and a small team of craftsmen who make replicas of museum objects for other institutions.

The work of a conservator today is highly specialised, demanding both manual dexterity and some knowledge of science, particularly chemistry. Within any of the categories listed above the work can be very varied, so that a ceramic conservator may be working on Greek vases one month, eighteenth-century porcelain the next, and crude prehistoric pottery a few weeks later. The overriding principle is to preserve whatever remains of an object for the future. Usually conservation begins with cleaning and stabilisation (that is the counteracting of any active decay mechanisms), followed by any necessary restoration. Finally, the object may be mounted to safeguard it in storage or on display.

Needless to say, these four processes vary enormously from object to object and from one type of object to another. For instance, cleaning porcelain may involve

331 *The Portland Vase undergoing conservation in 1988/9. Because the adhesive used in the previous restoration, during late 1940s, was deteriorating, the vase was dismantled into its two hundred or so separate pieces and reassembled using the most modern adhesives. See title page.*

simple washing to remove dust and finger grease, or it may involve the use of chemicals to remove more stubborn stains. In many cases conservation will involve the undoing of previous restoration, using water or organic solvents to dissolve adhesives, and physical or chemical treatments to soften and remove restored areas. The cleaning of excavated metal objects presents special problems, as they are often covered in layers of corrosion which may obscure decoration. The conservator must decide how much of these to remove and radiography is a useful aid for revealing what lies below 332 the surface. In modern conservation a combination of manual treatments and the local application of small quantities of chemicals enables the process to be totally controlled.

Organic objects, textiles and works of art on paper are often very fragile, but in many cases either washing in water or 'dry cleaning' can be used, although only if any pigments or dyes which may be present are not fugitive. Cleaning, however, must never remove evidence of the use to which an object was put. Hence evidence of libations, food remains on the inside of a vessel, or smoke marks on the outside must be left in place.

Stabilisation is important where, as a result of burial or storage in a hostile environment, an object is undergoing spontaneous decay. Atmospheric pollutants, for 335 example, may attack limestone and many plant and animal products (including paper); the movements of soluble salts (absorbed during burial) caused by daily or seasonal changes in the humidity of the surrounding air may have a deleterious effect on porous objects. The presence of chemicals absorbed from the soil may also promote corrosion on bronze or iron objects. Sometimes stabilisation will seek to remove the agent of decay – for example, washing pottery can remove soluble chloride – but in other cases this may be impossible, and the conservator must control the humidity and pollution in the atmosphere to prevent further deterioration.

Once an object is clean and stable the conservator can proceed to carry out any necessary restoration. Here he or she is guided by a very strict ethic – the

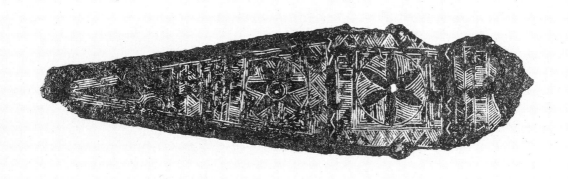

extent of the restoration should be fully recorded and (usually) visible to the naked eye on close inspection. This means, again taking pottery as an example, that any gap-filling should be clearly visible on close inspection, although it may go unnoticed by the casual museum visitor who strolls past the display. The same is true of scupture, although here the tendency is not to restore missing parts, as we can never know exactly how they looked. Indeed, in recent years conservators have been removing restorations from sculpture carried out by earlier generations. For works of art on paper, however, surface blemishes may be camouflaged and areas where pigment has been lost discreetly restored.

Finally, the mounting of an object ensures its safe handling, storage and exhibition in the future. Sculpture and other heavy objects are often fixed permanently to a base in such a way as to ensure that no undue strain is put on the object. Works of art on paper are usually mounted between sheets of acid-free cardboard, with an aperture cut in the front to the size of the picture. Small three-dimensional objects are usually only mounted for display purposes, unless they are very fragile, in which case a mount will be specially designed to double as a splint. A good example is the collection of early medieval swords, which are stored on specially made plastic mounts moulded to the contours of the corroded blades. These give excellent support when the swords are handled.

332 LEFT *Roman dagger sheath plate made of iron, from Hod Hill in Dorset: (top) before cleaning; (centre) an x-radiograph revealed extensive decoration hidden below the layers of corrosion; (bottom) cleaning by hand revealed the decoration formed of silver wires inlaid into the iron.*

333 BELOW *The conservation of an Egyptian papyrus document dating from about 1100 BC. The use of a frosted glass table top with a light below facilitates the examination of the papyrus fibre structure and assists in the repositioning of the fragments.*

334 *Sarcophagus lid from Clazomenae, near Izmir, Turkey, which was damaged by a bomb on the night of 10 May 1941. It dates from about 500 BC and weighs 900kg. The view below shows it on display (Room 3) after cleaning and repair.*

335 *Nineteenth-century Chinese painting from Canton which has been adversely affected by damp and mould growth (above). Conservation included the removal of the disintegrating backing paper and relining with modern high quality Japanese paper.*

Much of the conservation done in the British Museum is common to many museums with similar collections throughout the world, but there are also three specialist studios, each devoted to one type of object: mosaics, cuneiform tablets and scroll-paintings from the Far East. In the latter case the studio has been designed and built to a traditional Japanese format, and the tools and techniques in use are those which have been developed in Japan by traditional craftsmen over several centuries. For the mosaic pavements and cuneiform tablets, however, the workshops are of the most modern design and the techniques of conservation in use have been developed by scientists within the British Museum.

In order that conservation in the British Museum stays at the forefront of the subject, the conservators are backed up by a team of scientists who research into the mechanisms by which objects decay. Once the decay mechanism is understood, ways of arresting the decay can be developed. The corrosion of metals, the flaking of stone, discoloration of paper, the fading of dyes and pigments are just a few of the topics being investigated. In addition, there is a continuous programme of testing

adhesives and chemicals which may be of use for conservation, and of the materials used to make or line show-cases and storage cupboards (wood, glues, textiles, plastics and so on) to ensure that these materials are not slowly giving off chemicals which may react with the antiquities. For instance, it has long been known that vapours emitted by certain types of wood will corrode lead; recently it has been discovered that many textiles will cause silver to tarnish. In fact, it is only relatively recently that the scale of the problem of air pollution has been recognised, and methods are now being researched for eliminating the harmful gases from inside show-cases.

Conservators are intimately involved in the planning and setting up of exhibitions, so new scientific developments will ensure that the objects on display will not be harmed by excessive light, the degree of humidity, air pollution or rapid changes in temperature. Such advice is also given when loans are made to other institutions and the objects are carefully inspected for any signs of physical weakness, so that essential conservation can be carried out and the correct environment specified.

Practical conservation work is not confined to the

336 *The Eastern Pictorial Art conservation studio, where the Japanese tradition is followed of conservators working in a kneeling position at low work-benches on a floor covered in tatami matting. Traditional tools and drying boards are visible on the walls.*

Museum's premises; conservators frequently work on site at excavations, both in Britain and abroad. This is a natural extension of the process of conservation to the moment when the object is discovered. The Department of Conservation also plays a significant role in the training of future generations of conservators by taking students into the workshops and studios as interns, and by providing lectures and demonstrations for various conservation courses in Britain.

The work of the Department of Conservation has an enormous and visible impact on the display of the Museum's collections, although this may not be evident to the majority of visitors. Reflection for a moment, however, on problems of deterioration at home – yellowing of newspapers left in the sun, breaking of pots, corrosion of car bodies, tearing of clothes – will give some idea of the damage from the past that conservators have to deal with every day.

THE RESEARCH LABORATORY

The Research Laboratory is responsible for the scientific examination of the collections of the British Museum. It essentially provides important information on when, how and where objects were made and what materials they were made of. It commands a wide range of scientific equipment to assist in its investigations, as well as computer systems for handling scientific data, for statistical analysis, and for the documentation of the Museum's collections.

For determining when an object was made two main methods are available to the scientist. Radiocarbon dates can be provided for organic materials, such as charcoal, wood, bone and antler. The radioactive isotope carbon-14 is present as a fixed proportion of the total carbon in all living substances but decays at a known rate when a substance ceases to live. By measuring the amount of carbon-14 in a given sample, the date at which an artefact was made can be calculated. Samples up to a few thousand years old can be dated typically to within about fifty years, but the inaccuracy increases with the age of the sample: the upper limit is about 40,000 years. Another problem with radiocarbon dating is that the quantity of material required using the conventional equipment available in the Research

Laboratory is about 10g of charcoal or 150g of bone. This equipment cannot, therefore, normally be used to date museum objects, since the extent of damage in obtaining a sample would be unacceptable. However, recent developments in other laboratories involving the use of a particle accelerator have reduced the sample size required to a few milligrams, making it possible to obtain radiocarbon dates for museum objects.

The other scientific dating technique – thermoluminescence – is used on materials such as pottery, burnt flint, calcite and sediments from archaeological excavations. The method involves measuring the light emitted when samples from such materials are heated. This light is the result of radioactive impurities present within the samples themselves and in their burial environment. For pottery or burnt flint the amount of light emitted is proportional to the length of time elapsed since its last heating; for calcite, since its formation; and for sediments, since their last exposure to sunlight. A particularly important application of this method has been the provision of dates for Palaeolithic sites which

were occupied at times beyond the range of radiocarbon dating. In addition to dating archaeological sites, the method is now routinely used to establish whether ceramics on offer to the Museum for purchase are genuine or forgeries. It has also been applied to objects which were acquired before the advent of thermoluminescence and which curatorial staff now regard as suspect on stylistic grounds.

The Research Laboratory is also concerned with the study of ancient technology, researching into the raw materials and production methods used in antiquity, as well as investigating the more fundamental question of why particular materials and methods were used. A

337 *The synthesis rig in the Research Laboratory: it is used to convert pretreated samples to benzene for radiocarbon dating. Using a method known as liquid scintillation counting, the decay of the radiocarbon atoms can be detected and the age of the sample evaluated.*

338 ABOVE *X-ray fluorescence spectrometer, used to analyse a Chinese Ming dynasty brass figure. When x-rays from a high-voltage tube strike the area to be analysed fluorescent x-rays are emitted which are characteristic of the elements present.*

wide range of analytical techniques are employed, including atomic absorption spectrometry, x-ray fluorescence spectrometry, and x-ray diffraction, together with x-ray radiography and both optical and electron microscopy.

The study of the microstructure of ancient ceramics with an electron microscope can reveal particle size and shape, degree of interconnection and porosity. This allows scientists to trace the development from low-fired, coarse undecorated pottery, through the Greek and Roman fine wares with their characteristic high-gloss surface finish, to high-fired glazed stonewares and porcelains, which were first made in China and ultimately imitated in Europe. In such investigations the aim is to determine what type of clay and what firing temperature were employed to make the bodies and what methods were used to produce the different types of surface decoration. Similarly, in the case of glass, a major interest is the identification of the colorants and opacifiers used.

The development of metalworking has also been the subject of close scientific scrutiny. The method of manufacturing iron sword blades, for example, is of particular interest. Modern analytical techniques have allowed scientists to examine their very structure. From their first use iron sword blades were made up of several strips of iron welded together. We can see that Roman

339 *Attic Greek vase of the fifth century* BC, *with the characteristic high-gloss finish of its black surface. Great skill was required to retain the black reduced surface coat while firing the body to a red-oxidised colour. This was achieved by preparing a very fine-grained clay for the surface coat, as shown by the photomicrograph (below), so that it was highly impermeable as compared to the porous body. Scale of micrograph: bar = 10μm*

340 *Sword blade from the Sutton Hoo ship burial. An X-radiograph (slightly enlarged) of this totally corroded blade reveals the complex structure of the iron still preserved in the corrosion. Rods of iron have been repeatedly welded, twisted and beaten out to form the intricate pattern shown (pattern welding).*

technology achieved considerable improvements in quality, and in the Dark Ages the blades were made from large numbers of rods welded together to produce a very complex structure referred to as pattern welding, which both strengthens the sword and produces a decorative pattern on the blade. The development in techniques such as gilding, silvering and tinning used to decorate metals has also been investigated. For example, it has been shown that prior to the Hellenistic period (c. 325–27 BC) metals were gilded by the application of gold-leaf to their surfaces, but subsequently mercury or fire-gilding became common. This technique involves applying a gold-mercury amalgam to the surface of an object; when heated the mercury evaporates, leaving a layer of gold on the surface.

The historical development of the composition of metal alloys, from copper, through arsenical copper to

341 *A bronze arm from a life-size Roman statue found in Gaul, providing an example of leaf-gilding. Squares of gold-leaf were burnished in place; in this case the outline of the leaf can still be seen.*

342 *Excavation of furnaces at Zawar, Rajasthan, India, used in the fifteenth century* AD *to produce metallic zinc by distillation. The retorts, filled with ore and charcoal, were placed in the furnace with the necks protruding through the perforations in the floor into the cool-chamber below, where the zinc was collected.*

tin-bronze and ultimately brass (a copper-zinc alloy) has also been examined. Coinage offers some useful data, as coins provide comparatively well-dated series from which the chronology for the introduction of a specific metal alloy can be inferred. Thus the analysis of a large number of Hellenistic coins from the eastern Mediterranean has revealed that the use of brass occurred as early as the beginning of the first century BC.

The analysis of metals is also of special importance to numismatic studies, since it provides crucial data on the debasement of coinage. For example, during the seventh century AD the gold content in Merovingian gold coinage fell from more than 95 per cent to as low as 20 per cent, probably as a result of the breakdown of supplies of the precious metal from the Byzantine Empire. It has been possible, using these data and by analysing the compositions of the coins found in the

Anglo-Saxon ship burial at Sutton Hoo, Suffolk, to suggest a date of about AD 625 for the burial.

For a fuller understanding of how metal objects were made, it is important, as well as examining the finished artefacts, also to investigate the complete production process, from mining the ore through to the extraction and purification of the metal. The Research Laboratory has, therefore, collaborated in the excavation of ancient metal-production sites and has acquired for the Museum representative groups of smelting debris, such as furnace fragments, crucibles and, of course, slags from these sites. At Zawar in India the earliest known furnaces used to produce metallic zinc (15th century AD) have been excavated. The major obstacle to the production of metallic zinc in antiquity was that it volatilises at about 900°C and would have been lost in any normal smelting process. At Zawar a distillation process analogous to that used in the production of alcohol was evolved in which zinc vapour was condensed under reducing conditions.

Another important area of the Laboratory's work is its contribution to provenance studies: ascertaining where an object was made. Here the aim is to determine whether artefacts found on an archaeological site were manufactured locally or whether they were imported, and if so from where. Provenance studies involve

343 *Fragments of Hispano-Moresque lustreware. Neutron activation analysis has been used to identify the production centres. The dish fragment (left), found in Bristol, was made in Valencia, and the vase fragment (right) from London, was made in the Malaga region.*

finding some fingerprint for distinguishing different sources of raw materials and thus identifying production centres. One approach is the analysis, using for example neutron activation, of minor and trace element impurities, since their patterns of concentration can characterise a particular raw material source. Where the raw material has been chemically altered by man during manufacture, as in the case of metals, great difficulties have been encountered. However, with stone and pottery which has undergone only slight or no chemical change it has proved successful. For example, comparison of the minor and trace element concentrations in flint artefacts and in the possible sources has enabled the identification of the areas in southern Britain which provided the material for Neolithic polished flint axes. Similarly, it has been possible to establish whether fragments of Hispano-Moresque lustre pottery dating from the thirteenth to fifteenth centuries AD, found on urban excavations in southern Britain, were produced at the Malaga or Valencia pottery production centres in Spain.

In the case of pottery and stone artefacts a complementary technique involves the careful preparation of thin cross-sections of the material. These sections – which may be only a few hundredths of a millimetre thick – are translucent, and under the microscope the type of geological deposit from which the clay and stone were obtained may be recognised. In some cases the restricted occurrence or juxtaposition of specific rock types even allows a geographical origin to be identified.

With marble a different approach is necessary. Marble is a form of calcium carbonate, and here the ratios of the stable isotopes of carbon and oxygen provide the key. These ratios are affected by the conditions under which the marble is formed, so that different quarry areas have different isotope signatures which can be measured by mass spectrometry. In principle, therefore, the quarry exploited for marble for specific statues or carvings can be determined. This technique has been used to analyse various elements from the Mausoleum at Halicarnassus (4th century BC). It has shown that marble was imported from widely distributed sources, such as the Greek mainland for the statues (Pentelic marble) and nearby Asia Minor for the architectural components.

Scientific examination is invaluable in the authentication of an object. Artefacts from the Museum's own collections, or on offer for purchase, are routinely sent to the Research Laboratory for investigation. Usually the questions are not simply whether the object is fake or genuine, but how much it has been restored, whether new parts have been added or whether it has been assembled from otherwise genuine but unrelated components.

The research of the Laboratory into ancient technology provides the basic control data for establishing whether the materials and techniques used to make any object are appropriate to the age and place of origin ascribed to it. Further, if the object is ceramic, or of cast metal with a clay core present, then thermoluminescence can establish whether it is ancient or modern. The patination of a metal is also a useful guide it is antiquity. Patina which has been forming on the metal in the ground over thousands of years will be firmly attached.

If, however, it has been only recently applied in the form of a pigment, then normally it can be easily removed mechanically or by using an appropriate solvent.

The work of the Research Laboratory remains largely unseen by the Museum's visitors, but it is of immense importance. It provides the curators with basic information which is vital to the understanding both of individual objects and of the Museum's collections as a whole. A long-term project of documentation and inventory is now under way to compile computerised records containing such information as object type, material, provenance, period and donor for all of the Museum's collections. Not only will this assist the curators, but in due course it will be possible to provide academic and public enquirers with on-line or printed listings of, for example, all the objects of a particular type and provenance held by the Museum, offering a degree of access to the Museum's vast collections possible only in the computer age.

344 *Thermoluminescence can be used to test the authenticity of ceramic objects. The Museum's collection of seventy-three ceramics attributed to the Zapotec culture which flourished in the Mexican state of Oaxaca from AD 200 to 800, was tested by this process. Twenty items, including the one illustrated here, were shown to be forgeries.*

FURTHER READING

The following list is a selection of books on the Museum's collections from British Museum Press. A full and up-to-date list of all British Museum publications, including scholarly catalogues on specific aspects of the collections, can be obtained by writing to the Marketing Manager at:

British Museum Press
46 Bloomsbury Street
London WC1B 3QQ

GENERAL

The British Museum, 1997: also available in French, German, Italian, Spanish, Chinese, Japanese and Korean translations
BURNETT, A. AND REEVE, J. *Behind the Scenes at the British Museum,* 2001
CAYGILL, M. *The British Museum A–Z Companion,* 1999
CAYGILL, M. *The Story of the British Museum,* 2nd edn 2002
CAYGILL, M. *Treasures of the British Museum,* 1992
CAYGILL, M. AND Date, C. *Building the British Museum,* 1999
TAIT, H. *Seven Thousand Years of Jewellery,* 1989
TAIT, H. *Five Thousand Years of Glass,* 2nd edn 1995
Wilson, D. *The British Museum, A history,* 2002

CLASSICAL COLLECTIONS

BURN, L. *The British Museum Book of Greek and Roman Art,* 1991
COOK, B.F. *The Elgin Marbles,* 1984
COOK, B.F. *The Townley Marbles,* 1985
FRITTON, L. *Cycladic Art,* 1989
JENKINS, I. *Greek and Roman Life,* 1986
JENKINS, I. *The Parthenon Frieze,* 2nd edn 2002
MACNAMARA, E. *The Etruscans,* 1990
SWADDLING, J. *The Ancient Olympic Games,* 1980
TATTON-BROWN, V. *Ancient Cyprus,* 1988
WALKER, S. *Roman Art,* 1991
WALKER, S. *Memorials to the Roman Dead,* 1985
WILLIAMS, D. *Greek Vases,* 1985
WILLIAMS, N. *The Breaking and Remaking of the Portland Vase,* 1989

COINS AND MEDALS

BLAND, R. *The Chalfont Hoard,* 1992
BURNETT, A. *Interpreting the Past: Coins,* 1991
JONES, M. *Contemporary British Medals,* 1986
JONES, M. *Medals of the French Revolution,* 1977
PRICE, M. *Sylloge Nummorum Graecorum, vol ix, I The Black Sea,* 1993

EGYPTIAN ANTIQUITIES

ANDREWS, C. *Egyptian Mummies,* 1984
ANDREWS, C. *The Rosetta Stone,* 1981
JAMES, T.G.H. *Egyptian Painting,* 1985
JAMES, T.G.H. AND DAVIES, W.V. *Egyptian Sculpture,* 1983
MALEK, J. *The Cat in Ancient Egypt,* 1993
QUIRKE, S. AND ANDREWS, C. (introduction and trans.) *The Rosetta Stone: Facsimile Drawing,* 1988
QUIRKE, S. AND SPENCER, J. *The British Museum Book of Ancient Egypt,* 1992
STEAD, M. *Egyptian Life,* 1986
TAYLOR, J. *Egypt and Nubia,* 1991

ETHNOGRAPHIC COLLECTIONS

* BAQUEDANO, E. *Aztec Sculpture,* 1984
CARMICHAEL, E. AND SAYER, C. *The Skeleton at the Feast: the Day of the Dead in Mexico,* 1991
HOUSTON, S.D. *Maya Glyphs,* 1989
KING, J.C.H. *Arctic Hunters, Indians and Inuit of Northern Canada,* 1987
MACK, J. *Madagascar: Island of the Ancestors,* 1986
MACK, J. *Emil Torday and the Art of the Congo,* 1990
MACK, J. (ED.) *Ethnic Jewellery,* 3rd edn 2002
RICHARDSON, J. *From Aztecs to Zulus: Inside the Museum of Mankind,* 1986
WEIR, S. *Palestinian Costume,* 1989

MEDIEVAL AND MODERN COLLECTIONS

CHERRY, J. *Medieval Decorative Art,* 1991
EVANS, A.C. *The Sutton Hoo Ship Burial,* 4th edn 2000
LOVERANCE, R. *Byzantium,* 1988
RUDOE, J. *Decorative Arts, 1850–1950,* 1991
TAIT, H. *Clocks and Watches,* 1983
* TAIT, H. *The Waddesdon Bequest,* 1981
TAYLOR, M. *The Lewis Chessman,* 1978

ORIENTAL COLLECTIONS

CANBY, S. *Persian Paintings*, 1993
HARRIS, V. *Netsuke: The Hull Grundy Collection*, 1987
HARRISON-HALL, J. *Ming Ceramics in the British Museum*, 2001
KNOX, R. Amaravati: *Buddhist Sculpture from the Great Stupa*, 1992
RAWSON, J. *The British Museum Book of Chinese Art*, 1992
RAWSON, J. *Chinese Ornament, The Lotus and the Dragon*, 1984
ROGERS, M. *Mughal Miniatures*, 1993
SMITH, L. *Contemporary Japanese Prints, Images of a Society in Transition*, 1985
SMITH, L., HARRIS, V. AND CLARK, T. *Japanese Art*, 1990
VAINKER, S.J. *Chinese Pottery and Porcelain from Prehistory to the Present*, 1991
WARD, R. *Islamic Metalwork*, 1993
WHITFIELD, R. AND FARRER, A. *Caves of the Thousand Buddhas: Chinese Art from the Silk Route*, 1990

PREHISTORY AND ROMAN BRITAIN

BOWMAN, A.K. *Roman Writing Tablets from Vindolanda*, 1983
BROTHWELL, E. *The Bog Man*, 1986
LONGWORTH, I.H. *Prehistoric Britain*, 1985
POTTER, T.W. AND JOHNS, C. *Exploring the Roman World: Roman Britain*, 2nd edn 2002
STEAD, I.M. *The Battersea Shield*, 1985
STEAD, I.M. *Celtic Art*, 1985
STEAD, I.M., Bourke., J.B. AND BROTHWELL, D. *Lindow Man*, 1986

PRINTS AND DRAWINGS

CAREY, F. AND GRIFFITHS, A., *Avant-Garde British Printmaking 1914-60*, 1990
CAREY, F. AND GRIFFITHS, A., *The Print in Germany*, 1993
CHRISTIAN, J. *Letters to Katie from Edward Burne-Jones*, 1988
GERE, J.A. AND TURNER, N. *Drawings by Raphael*, 1983
GOLDMAN, P. *Looking at Prints, Drawings and Watercolours*, 1988
GRIFFITHS, A. *Prints and Printmaking*, 1980
GRIFFITHS, A. AND WILLIAMS, R. *The Department of Prints and Drawings in the British Museum – User's Guide*, 1987
HAYDEN, R. *Mrs Delany and her Flower Collages*, 1992
*HULTON, P. *America 1585: The Complete Drawings of John White*, 1984
ROWLANDS, J. AND BARTRUM, G. *Drawings by German Artists*, 1993
ROYALTON-KISCH, M. *Adriaen van de Venne's Album*, 1988
STAINTON, L. *Turner's Venice*, 1985

WESTERN ASIATIC ANTIQUITIES

COLLON, D. *First Impressions: Cylinder Seals in the Ancient Near East*, 1987
CURTIS, J. *Ancient Persia*, 1989
MITCHELL, T.C. *The Bible in the British Museum*, 1988
READE, J. *Assyrian Sculpture*, 1983
READE, J. *Mesopotamia*, 1991
TUBB, J. *Archaeology and the Bible*, 1991
WALKER, C.B.F. *Cuneiform*, 1987

CONSERVATION AND RESEARCH

BOWMAN, S. (ED.) *Science and the Past*, 1991
ODDY, A. (ED.) *The Art of the Conservator*, 1992
WILLIAMS, N. *The Breaking and Remaking of the Portland Vase*, 1989
WILLIAMS, N.R. *Porcelain Repair and Restoration*, 2002

* Books available only from British Museum Bookshops

THE GALLERIES OF THE BRITISH MUSEUM

While every effort has been made to ensure that the information given below is correct, the Museum's continual programme of renewal means that galleries may be rearranged from time to time. The most up-to-date information and a gallery plan is available from the Information Desk in the Front Hall.

ANCIENT NEAR EAST

ROOM 16
Khorsabad Entrance Sculptures from the palace of Sargon at Khorsabad

ROOM 17
Assyrian Saloon Sculptures and reliefs from the palaces of Sennacherib (seige of Lachish) and Ashurbanipal (lion-hunts) at Nineveh

ROOM 19
Nimrud Gallery Sculptures from the palace of Ashurnasirpal at Nimrud

ROOM 20
Nimrud Central Saloon Sculptures from the palace of Tiglath-pileser at Nimrud

ROOM 21
Nineveh Gallery Sculptures from the palace of Sennacherib at Nineveh

ROOM 26
Assyrian Transept Assyrian gateway figures; stelae; Balawat Gates; Black Obelisk

ROOM 51
Palmyra and Ancient South Arabia

ROOM 52
Ancient Iran Oxus Treasure Luristan bronzes, Persepolis reliefs

ROOMS 53–54
The Raymond and Beverly Sackler Gallery of Ancient Anatolia Antiquities from Ancient Turkey from 6000–536 BC, with emphasis on Hittite and Urartian kingdoms

ROOM 55
The Raymond and Beverly Sackler Gallery of Later Mesopotamia Babylonian and Assyrian antiquities from 1600–539 BC, including cuneiform tablets from the Royal Library at Nineveh

ROOM 56
The Raymond and Beverly Sackler Gallery of Early Mesopotamia Sumerian and Babylonian antiquities down to 1600 BC, including material from The Royal Cemetery at Ur

ROOMS 57-59
The Raymond and Beverly Sackler Gallery of Ancient Levant Antiquities from Syria and Palestine from 6000 BC to 539 BC. Statues from 'Ain Ghazal; Jericho tomb; Phoenician art

ROOM 88
Special Ancient Near East exhibitions

ROOMS 88a–89
Assyrian Art Sculptures of Sennacherib and Ashurbanipal; daily life

COINS AND MEDALS

ROOM 68
HSBC Money Gallery The history of money from ancient Babylonia to the present day; coins, banknotes and related monetery objects

ROOM 69a
Temporary displays of coins, medals, paper money, tokens and badges from the Department's collections

Coins and Medals are also displayed in other galleries in the contexts of the cultures in which they have been used (a fuller listing is available from the department):

Ancient Anatolia: Room 54
Ancient Iran: Room 52
Celtic Europe: Room 50
Greek and Roman: Rooms 3, 14, 40, 52, 65, 69, 70, 71, 72, 73
Roman Britain: Room 49
Medieval Europe: Rooms 41, 42
Renaissance and later Europe: Rooms 46, 47, 48
Islam: Room 34
South Asia: Room 33
Far East: Room 33

EGYPTIAN ANTIQUITIES

ROOM 4
Egyptian Sculpture Gallery Sculpture; architecture from temples and tombs; inscriptions

ROOM 60
First Egyptian Room Closed

ROOM 61

Second Egyptian Room
Understanding Ancient Egyptian
Culture. Interim exhibition examining
hieroglyphs, written sources and life in
ancient Egypt. New research and
excavation material is included

ROOMS 62-63

**The Roxie Walker Galleries of
Egyptian Funerary Archaeology**
A new display of Egyptian funerary
material

ROOM 64

**The Raymond and Beverly Sackler
Gallery of Early Egypt**
The collections from prehistory to the
beginning of the Old Kingdom

ROOM 65

**The Raymond and Beverly Sackler
Gallery of Egypt and Africa**
The Nubian and Sudanese collections

ROOM 66

Coptic Corridor Carved stonework
textiles, jewellery and ritual objects
from the second to the ninth
century AD

ETHNOGRAPHY

ROOM 24

The Wellcome Trust Gallery
A gallery exploring themes of
wellbeing and health with reference to
a diversity of cultures

ROOM 26

The Mexican Gallery
A gallery offering a representative
range of material from Mexico's
pre-Columbian cultures

ROOM 27

**The JPMorgan Chase Gallery of
North America**
A gallery devoted to the arts and
cultures of Native North America

ROOM 25

Sainsbury African Galleries
Three linked galleries providing
insight into the cultural life of Africa,
past and present

From 1970 to 1997 the Department of
Ethnography occupied the Museum of
Mankind in Piccadilly. During this
period the Department created a path-
breaking programme of temporary
exhibitions supported by educational
activities and daily film screenings.
At the end of 1997, the Museum of
Mankind closed to the public so
collections could be packed for the
Department's long-planned return to
Bloomsbury.

The Anthropology Library and the
Study Room will reopen in late 2003 as
a new Centre for Anthropology near
the Museum's North entrance. Some
study collections will be stored nearby
but most will remain at the Museum's
premises at Orsman Road. Some
20,000 textiles will join Maya casts
and other Museum collections at
Blythe House in West Kensington
early in 2003. Departmental offices
and staff will relocate to the East
Residence in the first part of 2004 and
access to the off-site study collections
will be resumed as soon as possible
thereafter. The Museum is also
planning a major new Ethnography
gallery which will feature the
outstanding Australian and Pacific
collections, the earliest of which derive
from Captain Cook's voyages.

GREEK AND ROMAN
ANTIQUITIES

ROOM 11

Cycladic Room Bronze Age artefacts
from the Cycladic Islands

ROOM 12

**The Arthur I. Fleischman Gallery
of the Greek Bronze Age** Pottery,
statuettes, jewellery, stonework,
weapons of the Bronze Age and Early
Iron Age

ROOM 13

Archaic Greek Room Geometric,
Orientalising and black-figured
pottery; statuettes; stone sculpture;
jewellery; coins

ROOM 13a

First Vase Room Early Greek vases
(temporarily closed)

ROOM 14

Andokides Room 'New Techniques
in Vase-painting': red-figure and
other pottery techniques

ROOM 15

Room of the Harpy Tomb The
Harpy Tomb; red-figured vases;
bronze and terracotta statuettes;
sculpture

ROOM 16

Bassae Room Marble sculpture
from the Temple of Apollo at Bassae

ROOM 17

Nereid Room The Nereid
Monument from Xanthos

ROOM 18

Duveen Gallery Sculptures from
the Parthenon; computer graphics
video, installation for the visually
impaired, audio guide

ROOM 19

Caryatid Room Sculptures from the
Acropolis at Athens; Greek pottery,
terracottas, bronzes, 430–400 BC

ROOM 20

Payava Room The tomb of Payava
from Xanthos; Greek pottery,
sculpture, terracottas and bronzes,
400–330 BC

ROOM 20a

Second Vase Room Athenian and South Italian red-figure, white-ground and black-glazed vases

ROOM 21

Mausoleum Room Statues and relief sculpture from the Mausoleum at Halicarnassus

ROOM 22

Hellenistic World: Art and Culture Sculptures from Ephesos, Knidos and Priene; pottery, jewellery, coins, glass, and small-scale sculpture

ROOM 23

Greek and Roman Sculpture Room Sculpture

ROOM 69

Greek and Roman Life Room Objects used in daily life

ROOM 70

Rome: City and Empire Portraits and other sculptures; Portland Vase and Warren Cup; pottery; glass; jewellery; mosaics; inscriptions; coins

ROOM 71

'Italy before the Roman Empire' Etruscan and other cultures of Italy: sculpture; painting; pottery; metalwork, including arms and armour; jewellery and mirrors; coins

ROOM 72

A.G. Leventis Gallery of Cypriot Antiquities Bronze, copper and limestone artefacts from ancient Cyprus; Cypriot sculpture, jewellery and weaponry

ROOM 73

'The Greeks in Southern Italy' Pottery; terracottas; coins; bronzes; jewellery

ROOM 77

Architecture Gallery Greek and Roman architecture

ROOMS 78–85 The Wolfson Galleries

ROOM 78

Room of Latin and Greek Inscriptions

ROOM 79

Lycian Room Sculpture from Lycia (temporarily closed)

ROOM 80

Archaic and Classical sculpture from Greece and Asia Minor; Athenian grave reliefs (temporarily closed)

ROOM 81

Later Greek Sculpture: monuments from Greek Asia Minor, including the Mausoleum, the temple of Artemis at Ephesus, and the temple of Athena at Priene; later funerary monuments (temporarily closed)

ROOM 82

Ephesus Gallery Sculpture from Ephesus and Greek sites; small sculptures from the Townley Collection; Roman funerary reliefs

ROOM 83

Roman Room Large sculptures from sanctuaries and public buildings; sarcophagi

ROOM 84

Townley Room Charles Townley's collection of sculpture

ROOM 85

Portrait Room Roman portraits and heads of deities and heroes

JAPANESE ANTIQUITIES

The new Japanese galleries which opened in Spring 1990 consist of Rooms 92 (Urasenke Gallery), 93 (Main Japanese Gallery), 94 (Konika Gallery).

The lobby outside the Urasenke Gallery houses a permanent display of netsuke, *inrō* and sword furniture.

The Urasenke Gallery houses on permanent display a tea-house and classic teawares.

The other two galleries house both general and thematic exhibitions from the Museum's wide collections and also loans from Japanese collections.

MEDIEVAL AND MODERN EUROPE

ROOM 41

Early Medieval Room Antiquities from the British Isles, Europe and the Mediterranean, fourth–eleventh centuries AD; the Sutton Hoo Ship Burial, Lycurgus Cup

ROOM 42

Medieval Room Religious and secular antiquities from Western Europe and Byzantium, ninth–fifteenth centuries AD; the Lewis Chessmen, Royal Gold Cup

ROOM 43

Medieval Tile and Pottery Room English pottery and manufacturing processes, seventh–fifteen centuries AD. the production and design of tiles thirteenth–sixteenth centuries AD; the Canynges pavement

ROOM 44

Clocks and Watches Technical development of mechanical horology in Europe, sixteenth–twentieth centuries; the Strasbourg Clock

ROOM 45

Waddesdon Room The Waddesdon Bequest of medieval and Renaissance treasures

ROOM 46

Europe: Fifteenth to Eighteenth Centuries Continental and British applied arts and archaeology from the Renaissance to the end of the eighteenth century. The Armada Service. The Wilding Bequest

ROOM 47

Europe: Nineteenth Century Continental and British applied arts. The Hull Grundy Gift of Jewellery

ROOM 48

Modern Gallery Twentieth-century European American applied arts; changing displays

ORIENTAL ANTIQUITIES

ROOM 33

The Joseph E. Hotung Gallery Sculpture from South and South-East Asia; bronzes, sculpture, decorative arts and ceramics from China. In the North Entrance is a display of Vietnamese blue and white ceramics

ROOM 33a

The Asahi Shimbun Gallery of Amaravati Sculpture Buddhist sculpture from the Great Stupa at Amaravati in southeast India

ROOM 33b

The Selwyn and Ellie Alleyne Gallery Chinese jades from the collection of Sir Joseph Hotung

ROOM 34

The John Addis Gallery Antiquities from the Islamic collections, especially ceramics, metalwork and painting

ROOM 67

The Korean Foundation Gallery Korean art and archaeology including a reconstructed scholars' studio

ROOM 91

Changing exhibitions of Asian material in all media

PREHISTORY AND EARLY EUROPE

ROOMS 36–37

Prehistory: Objects of Power An exhibition exploring two million years of human development from the Old Stone Age to the Bronze Age. The stone, bone, bronze, pottery and gold objects show the practical, artistic and symbolic aspects of life in prehistoric communities

ROOM 49

The Weston Gallery of Roman Britain The Roman army; medicine; burials; written records (Vindolanda tablets, inscriptions); coins, pottery; glassware and silver plate; treasure hoards, ironwork; building materials; mosaics; religion; sculpture

ROOM 50

Celtic Europe Celtic arts; crafts; pottery; weapons; jewellery and goldwork; chariotry; coins; Lindow Man

The Later Bronze Age in Europe Ornaments; weapons; horses; farming; pottery; food and feasting

PRINTS AND DRAWINGS

The collections of this Department are not on permanent display because of their fragility and susceptibility to damage from exposure to light. Selections from the collection are shown as temporary exhibitions in Room 90.

KEY TO THE ILLUSTRATIONS

With the following exceptions, all of the photographs in this book were provided by the Photographic Service of the British Museum:

Lee Boltin 2, 102, 114, 221

The references given in the list below are to the British Museum accession numbers. The abbreviations used below for the Museum Departments are:

CM   Coins and Medals
EA   Egyptian Antiquities
ETH   Ethnography
GR   Greek and Roman
JA   Japanese Antiquities
MLA   Medieval and Later
       Antiquities
OA   Oriental Antiquities
PD   Prints and Drawings
PRB   Prehistoric and
       Romano-British Antiquities
WA   Western Asiatic Antiquities

Half-title page MLA 1980,3–7,118
Title page GR 1945.9–27.1
Back cover MLA 1980.5–19,1
2. MLA 1756,6–19,1 (photo Lee Boltin)
5. PD 1982.3–27.4 (© DACS 2001)
9. GR 1805.7–3.337
10. GR 1971.5–21.1
11. GR 1982.5–20.8
12. GR 1897.4–1.1150
13. GR 1971.11–1.1
14. GR 1843.11–3.31
15. GR 1863.7–28.312; 1874.11–10.1; 1873.8–20.303
16. GR 1892.7–21.1
17. GR 1958.4–18.1
18. GR 1816.6–10.11
19. GR 1816.6–10.97
20. GR 1805.7–3.183
21. GR 1815.10–20.18
22. GR 1859.11–26.26

23. GR 1872.6–4.815; 1867.5–8.537; 1914.10–16.1
24. GR 1874.3–5.69
25. GR 1897.4–1.996
26. GR 1910.6–20.1
27. GR 1920.12–20.1
28. GR 1848.10–20.34, etc.
29. GR 1847.4–24.270 & 269
30. GR 1904.7–3.1
31. GR 1890.2–10.1
32. GR 1872.6–4.667
33. GR 1850.2–27.1
34. GR 1824.4–97.1
35. GR 1888.11–10.1
36. GR 1887.4–2.1
37. GR 1875.3–13.30
38. GR 1867.5–7.484
39. GR 1866.8–6.1
40. GR 1907.5–18.8–10
41. GR 1872.6–4.670; 1814.7–4.1203; 1903.7–17.3
42. GR 1851.8–13.175
43. GR 1824.4–24.1
44. GR 1869.2–5.4; 1972.9–27.1; 1867.5–8.686; 1868.5–1.257
45. GR 1859.4–2.102
46. CM 1957.10–10.1–34; 1965.12–2.1–3
47. CM 1873.7–2.9; 1846.6–30.11; 1982.7–35.3
48. CM 1978.10–21.1
49. CM 1987.6–49.303; 1887.6–9.1; 1969.6–8.1
50. CM BMC 1; BMC 1; BMC 9
51. CM 1867.1–1.31
52. CM 1959.7–4.1
53. CM 1964.12–3.235
54. CM 1919.2–13.318; 1919.2–13.338
55. CM BMC 65; De Salis Coll.; 1924.6–3.15
56. CM 1913.12–13.1; Bank Collection M1
57. CM 1857.9–1.8; 1838.7–10.285; 1935.11–17.476; BMC 19; E2203
58. CM 1909.10–6.48; 1915.5–7.599

59. CM 1885.4–5.36; 1915.5–7.469
60. CM 1956.4–8.1; 1935.4–1.2021
61. CM 1855.3–21.15; S. S. Banks, pp. 132–60; 1988.1–30.1
62. CM 1983. 8–17.2; 1897.12–7.4; 1976.9–16.40; 1979.3–2.12; 1921.10–18.3; CH 0150
63. CM 1894.5–7.4; BMC 1; BMC 52; 1918.6–3.2; BMC 23; 1844.4–25.49
64. CM BMC 27; 1874.7–6.1; 1974.9–16.341; 1865.8–4.40; 1875.5–1.20; CH 0420; BMC 36
65. CM 1844.4–25.24; M6903; George III, English Medals 67; M7357; M7364; George III, English Medals 15
66. CM 1979.5–17.71; 1920.2–33.71; 1982.5–3.2; 1976.4–5.1
67. CM George III, Naples 9
68. CM 1981.11–22.258
69. CM 1984.6–5.1711
70. EA 37977
71. EA 20790
72. EA 37996
73. EA 1239
74. EA 684–6
75. EA 569, 570
76. EA 986
77. EA 19
78. EA 36
79. EA 2
80. EA 55253
81. EA 64391, 37348
82. EA 1242
83. EA 5601
84. EA 37993
85. EA From a copy by Nina de Garis Davies
86. EA 24
87. EA 117
88. EA 1848
89. EA 9901/3
90. EA 5624
91. EA 32751
92. EA 6665

93. EA 22542
94. EA 13595
95. EA 64659 (top left); 23092 (top right); 54412 (centre); 20639 (bottom left); 12235 (bottom right)
96. EA 41548
97. EA 52947
98. EA 2469 (table); 2472 (stool); 2480 (chair); 26227 (cup); 41578 (sandals); 59775 (jar)
99. EA 42515
100. EA (back row) 32531, 29923, 35297, 36347; (centre) 4716 (bowl), 43034 (jug), 36358, 26242, 26971, 35074, 22823; (front) 4735 (vase), 56843, 35306, 24416
101. EA (back row) 57385, 4790, 26226; (front row) 12968, 65802, 7865
102. EA 55193 (photo Lee Boltin)
103. EA 54460; 59194; 57699–700; 57698; 7876
104. EA (back row, left to right) 21895, 12753, 37234, 2598; (centre to foreground) 5946, 5965, 2662, 37187
105. EA 43049
106. EA 679
107. ETH 98.1–15.44
108. ETH 1979.Am8.7
109. ETH 1976.Am3.28
110. ETH Q72.Am17
111. ETH 1976.Am3.79
112. ETH 1929.7–12.1
113. ETH
114. ETH 1894–634 (photo Lee Boltin)
115. ETH 1940.Am11.2
116. ETH 7204
117. ETH 78.11–1.48a,b,c
118. ETH Q74.Af2925
119. ETH 1909.12–10.1
120. ETH 1979.Af1.2397
121. ETH 1925.11–23.35
122. ETH 1901.11–13.51
123. ETH 1934.3–7.198
124. ETH 1937.2–20.3
125. ETH 1968.As4.31
126. ETH 1965.As7.10
127. ETH 1981.As2.4
128. ETH 1971.Eu1.260
129. ETH 1973.As7.3
130. ETH 5068
131. ETH 1986.As9.29
132. ETH 1859.12–28.448

133. ETH 98.7–3.134
134. ETH 1905–818
135. ETH HAW 133
136. ETH TAH 78
137. ETH IMS 19
138. ETH 1900.7–21.1
139. ETH Q72.Oc.95
140. ETH 1927–113
141. ETH 1954.Oc6.158
142. ETH 1906.10–13.5
143. ETH 1987.Oc4.7
144. MLA 1939,10–10,4–5
145. MLA 66,12–29,1
146. MLA 63,7–27,11; 98,7–19,1
147. MLA 1921,11–1,221; 91,10–19,24; 1978,5–3,1; 65,3–18,1
148. MLA 1922, 6–1, 244
149. MLA 1952,4–4,1
150. MLA 1870,8–11,1
151. MLA 69,3–1,1
152. MLA 61,10–24,1
153. MLA OA4312
154. MLA 1986,7–8,1
155. MLA 1926,4–9,1
156. MLA 78–159 (complete set)
157. MLA 50,11–27,1
158. MLA 56,7–18,1
159. MLA 92,5–1,1
160. MLA 53,3–15,1
161. MLA Af 2768–70
162. MLA 1922,12–2,4
163. MLA Waddesdon cat. 125, 115, 111
164. MLA 1969,7–5,11
165. MLA 1986,4–3,1
166. MLA 80,3–10,1
167. MLA G619
168. MLA Pottery cat. D49
169. MLA Pottery cat. I 712
170. MLA Porcelain cat. II 28
171. MLA 78,12–30,660
172. MLA 1948,12–3,69 & 70
173. MLA Slade cat. 361
174. MLA 1823,1–1,1
175. MLA Dalton no. 181; HG 898 (left); HG 877 (right); HG 952 (centre); HG 940 (bottom)
176. MLA HG 983
177. MLA 1979,11–2,1
178. MLA 1982,7–2,1
179. MLA CA1–2316; CA1–2381
180. MLA 57,11–16,1
181. OA 91.6–23.5
182. OA 1936.11–18.1
183. OA 1903.4–8.1

184. OA 1919.1–1.014
185. OA 1913.11–12.1
186. OA 1936.10–12.206
187. OA 1975.10–28.19
188. OA 1885.12–28.79
189. OA 1963.5–20.03
190. OA 1983.12–12.1
191. OA 1966.12–21.1
192. OA 1880–482; 1880–615; 1879.12–1.9, 31; 1882.10–9.9; 1880–459
193. OA 1900.2–9.1
194. OA 1880.6
195. OA 1955.10–8.069
196. OA 1949.11–12.01
197. OA 1987.3–14.1
198. OA 1830.6–12.4
199. OA 1971.7–27.1
200. OA 1958.12–18.1
201. OA 1967.12–11.1
202. OA 1950.7–25.1
203. OA 1948.12–11.023
204. OA 1855.7–9.1
205. OA 1983.66
206. OA 1925.9–29.01
207. OA 1830.6–12.1
208. JA F2228
209. JA 1885.12–27.98
210. JA 1974.5–13.13
211. JA HG 700
212. JA 1920.7–13.1
213. JA 1984.7–23.1
214. JA 1974.2–26.81
215. JA F498A
216. JA 1987.10–14.04
217. JA 1906.12–20.220
218. PRB 1951.4–2.2
219. PRB SL24
220. PRB P1964.12–6.1059
221. PRB Peccadeau 550 (photo Lee Boltin)
222. PRB Peccadeau 551
223. PRB 1953.2–8.1; P1976.12–1 & 2
224. PRB 1921.3–15.1
225. PRB 1901.2–6.1
226. PRB 1939.7–4.1
227. PRB WG 2126–9
228. PRB P1981.3–1.1; 1879.12–9.700; 1879.12–9.1201; 1862.7–7.5; 1915.12–8.206
229. PRB On loan from His Majesty King Edward VIII
230. PRB 1893.12–28.15–17
231. PRB 1873.2–10.1
232. PRB 45.1–22.1

233. PRB 1836.9−2.1
234. PRB 1838.1−28.1
235. PRB 1929.5−11.1
236. PRB 1967.2−2.42−65
237. PRB 1886.11−12.3−5
238. PRB 1953.4−2,1; P1976.5−1
239. PRB 1857.7−15.1
240. PRB P1987.4−4
241. PRB 1924.1−9.1
242. PRB 1892.9−1 (Hod Hill);
    1883.4−7.1 (Fulham)
243. PRB P1984.10−2.1
244. PRB 1852.8−6.2; 1935.7−12.1
245. PRB 1891.11−17.1
246. PRB P1980.3−3.28
247. PRB P1983.11−3
248. PRB 1870.2−24.3
249. PRB 1848.11−3.1
250. PRB POA 201
251. PRB P1975.10−2
252. PRB 1946.10−7.1
253. PRB 1965.4−9.1
254. PRB P1981.2−1.1
255. PD 1981.12−12.17
256. PD PG 37
257. PD 1887.5−2.116
258. PD 1895.9−15.447
259. PD 1908.6−16.45
260. PD 1986.7−26.32
261. PD 1895.9−15.975
262. PD 1910.2−12.105
263. PD 1982.3−27.5
264. PD 1952.4−5.9
265. PD 1824, Oo.9−50
266. PD 1973.U.1344
267. PD 1895.9−15.1279
268. PD 1962.7−14.1(4)
269. PD 1957.12−14.168
270. PD 1895.9−15.941
271. PD 1981.2−21.1 (© ADAGP,
    Paris and DACS, London 2003)
272. PD 1979.12−15.17 (©
    Succession H. Matisse/DACS
    2003)
273. PD 1862.7−12.187
274. PD 1882.8−12.224
275. PD 1910.2−12.250
276. PD 1910.2−12.272
277. PD 1987.4−11.4
278. PD 1988.3−5.7
279. PD 1983.4−16.4
280. PD 1988.10−1.44 (© Estate of
    David Smith/DACS, London/
    VAGA, NY 2003)
281. PD 1972.U.1047
282. PD 1868.6−12.1
283. PD 1984.6−9.7 (© DACS 2003)

284. PD 1936.11−16.31
285. PD 1860.7−14.41
286. PD 1854.6−28.73
287. PD V8−182
288. PD 1848.7−21.41
289. PD 1979.7−21.67 (© Succession
    Picasso/DACS 2003)
290. PD 1868.8−22.2113
291. PD 1949.4−16.3600 (© ADAGP,
    Paris and DACS, London 2003)
292. PD 1983.7−23.24 (© ADAGP,
    Paris and DACS, London 2003)
293. PD 1981.7−25.14 (© Estate of
    Robert Gwathmey/DACS,
    London/VAGA, NY 2003)
294. WA 130762−4; 130767
295. WA 117007; 117119
296. WA 125381
297. WA 126251; 126445; 126448
298. WA 127414
299. WA 116730
300. WA K3375
301. WA 122216
302. WA 120000
303. WA 121201
304. WA 122200
305. WA 91435; 91440; 91442;
    118572; 128487; 128493
306. WA 139738−9
307. WA Jericho tomb P19
308. WA 125091
309. WA 135851
310. WA 126389
311. WA 132915
312. WA 118158
313. WA 135781
314. WA 124864
315. WA 118885
316. WA 124906
317. WA 90859
318. WA 91253
319. WA 129378
320. WA 132525
321. WA 124081
322. WA 124017
323. WA 123908
324. WA 123894
325. WA 125019
326. WA 126395
327. WA 124091
328. WA 135738; 135158
329. WA 124094
330. WA 134693
332. PRB 1960.4−5.906
334. GR 1869.6−15.1
335. OA + 0323
339. GR 1939.10−10.95

340. MLA 1868.6−6.7
341. GR 1904.2−4.1249
343. MLA 1901,4−27,3; 1896−2−1, 79
344. ETH 1946. Am16.7

INDEX

The numbers in italic type refer to illustrations

THE GOVT SOLUTION

Every 4LTR Press solution includes:

Heading Numbers Connect Print & eBook

Visually Engaging Textbook

Online Study Tools

Tear-out Review Cards

Interactive eBook

STUDENT RESOURCES:

- Interactive eBook
- Auto-Graded Quizzes
- Flashcards
- Videos
- Crossword Puzzles
- Review Cards
- Animated Learning Modules

INSTRUCTOR RESOURCES:

- All Student Resources
- Engagement Tracker
- First Day of Class Instructions
- LMS Integration
- Instructor's Resource Manual
- Test Bank
- PowerPoint® Slides
- Instructor Prep Cards

Students sign in at **www.cengagebrain.com**

Instructors sign in at **www.cengage.com/login**

"Like a good recipe, you simply can't alter things that are already great. Love this layout and the study tools provided online are fantastic!"

– Amanda Brenek, Student, *University of Texas at San Antonio*

GOVT6

Sixth Edition

Edward Sidlow • Beth Henschen

Product Director: Suzanne Jeans

Product Team Manager: Carolyn Merrill

Associate Product Manager: Scott Greenan

Content Developer: Rebecca Green

Content Coordinator: Jessica Wang

Product Assistant: Abigail Hess

Marketing Manager: Valerie Hartman

Senior Media Developer: Laura Hildebrand

4LTR Press Project Manager: Riccardo Nuzzo

Senior Content Project Manager: Ann Borman

Print Buyer: Fola Orekoya

Copy Editor: Jeanne Yost

Proofreader: Pat Lewis

Indexer: Terry Casey

Art Director: Linda May

Interior Designer: RHDG

Cover Design: Lisa Kuhn

Cover Images: Lou Jones/Lonely Planet Images/ Getty Images; and © pashabo/ShutterStock.com

Compositor: Parkwood Composition Service

For product information and technology assistance, contact us at
Cengage Learning Customer & Sales Support
1-800-354-9706

For permission to use material from this text or product, submit all requests online at
www.cengage.com/permissions.

Further permissions questions can be e-mailed to
permissionrequest@cengage.com.

Library of Congress Control Number: 2013954642

ISBN-13: 978-1-285-43742-2

Cengage Learning
20 Channel Center
Boston, MA 02210
USA

Cengage Learning is a leading provider of customized learning solutions with office locations around the globe, including Singapore, the United Kingdom, Australia, Mexico, Brazil, and Japan. Locate your local office at: **www.cengage.com/global.**

Cengage Learning products are represented in Canada by Nelson Education, Ltd.

To learn more about Cengage Learning, visit **www.cengage.com.**

Purchase any of our products at your local college store or at our preferred online store **www.cengagebrain.com.**

Printed in the United States of America
2 3 4 5 6 7 17 16 15 14

GOVT BRIEF CONTENTS

GOVT CONTENTS

© BONNIE FINK/ SHUTTERSTOCK.COM

CHAPTER 3
Federalism 45

PART II Our Liberties and Rights 72

MLADEN ANTONOV/AFP/ GETTY IMAGES

CHAPTER 4
Civil Liberties 68

MARIO TAMA/GETTY IMAGES

CHAPTER 5
Civil Rights 92

TOM WILLIAMS/GETTY IMAGES/
CQ ROLL CALL

CHAPTER 7
Political Parties 141

JOHN GRESS/GETTY IMAGES

CHAPTER 6
Interest Groups 118

DAVID BECKER/GETTY IMAGES

CHAPTER 8
Public Opinion and Voting 163

TOM WILLIAMS/CQ ROLL CALL

CHAPTER 9
Campaigns and Elections 187

ALEX WONG/GETTY IMAGES FOR MEET THE PRESS

CHAPTER 10
Politics and the Media 212

PART IV Institutions 233

TOM WILLIAMS/CQ ROLL CALL

CHAPTER 11
The Congress 233

CHAPTER 12
The Presidency 257

CHAPTER 13
The Bureaucracy 283

CHAPTER 14
The Judiciary 306

PART V   Public Policy 330

CHIP SOMODEVILLA/GETTY IMAGES

CHAPTER 15
Domestic Policy 330

WIN MCNAMEE/GETTY IMAGES

CHAPTER 16
Foreign Policy 352

APPENDICES

SKILL PREP
A Study Skills Module

Want to make the most of your study time & ace the test?
Having trouble getting started on the paper that's due soon?

Use the study skills guide on the next few pages to
get the grade you want
in your American Government course. You'll find:

- **Study Prep:** Pointers for reading to learn and retain the key concepts and for taking great notes
- **Test Prep:** Tips and tricks for passing your exams
- **Write Prep:** Steps for writing A+ papers and essays

STUDY PREP

What does it take to be a successful student? Like many people, you may think that success depends on how naturally smart you are, that some people are just better at school than others. But in reality, successful students aren't born, they're made. What this means is that even if you don't consider yourself naturally "book smart," you can do well in this course by developing study skills that will help you understand, remember, and apply key concepts.

READING FOR LEARNING

Your textbook is the foundation for information in a course. It contains key concepts and terms that are important to your understanding of the subject. For this reason, it is essential that you develop good reading skills. As you read your textbook with the goal of learning as much of the information as possible, work on establishing the following habits:

FOCUS

Make an effort to focus on the book and tune out other distractions so that you can understand and remember the information it presents.

TAKE TIME

To learn the key concepts presented in each chapter, you need to read slowly, carefully, and with great attention.

REPEAT

To read for learning, you have to read your textbook a number of times. Follow a preview-read-review process:

1. **Preview**: The first time you read a section of the book, you should preview it. Look over the chapter title, section headings, and highlighted or bold words. This will give you a good preview of important ideas in the chapter. (Notice that each major section heading in this textbook has a corresponding Learning Outcome. By turning headings or subheadings in all of your textbooks into questions or learning objectives—and then answering them—you will increase your understanding of the material.) Note graphs, pictures, and other visual illustrations of important concepts. Pay special attention to the first and last sentence of each paragraph. First sentences usually introduce the main point of the paragraph, while last sentences usually sum up what was presented in each paragraph. For each section, try to answer the question "What is the main idea?" The point is to develop some general ideas about what the section is about so that when you do read it in full, you can have a guide for what to look for.

2. **Read**: After the preview, read through each passage in detail. During this phase, it is important to read with a few of questions in mind: What is the main point of this paragraph? What does the author want me to learn from this? How does this relate to what I read before? Keeping these questions in mind will help you to be an attentive reader who is actively focusing on the main ideas of the passage.

   It is helpful to take notes while reading in detail. You can mark your text or write an outline, as explained below. Taking notes will help you read actively, identify important concepts, and remember them. Then when it comes time to review for the exam, the notes you've made will make your studying more efficient. After you have completed a detailed read of the chapter and taken a break, try writing a brief summary or paraphrase of what you read, identifying the most important ideas.

3. **Review**: After you've finished a detailed reading of the chapter, you should take the time to review the chapter at least once (but maybe even two or more times) before your exam. Review each paragraph and the notes you made, asking this question: "What was this paragraph about?" You'll want to answer the question

in some detail, readily identifying the important points.

A reading group is a great way to review the chapter. After completing the reading individually, group members should meet and take turns sharing what they learned. Explaining the material to others will reinforce and clarify what you already know. It also provides an opportunity to learn from others. Getting a different perspective on a passage will increase your knowledge, since different people will find different things important during a reading.

ASK QUESTIONS

If you are really engaged in your American government course, you will ask a question or two whenever you do not understand something. You can also ask a question to get your instructor to share her or his opinion on a subject. However you do it, true engagement requires you to be a participant in your class. The more you participate, the more you will learn (and the more your instructor will know who you are!).

TAKE NOTES

Being *engaged* means listening to discover (and remember) something. Not only do you have to hear what the professor is saying in class, you have to pay attention to it. And as you listen with attention, you will hear what your instructor believes is important. One way to make sure that you are listening attentively is to take notes. Doing so will help you focus on the professor's words and will help you identify the most important parts of the lecture.

The physical act of writing makes you a more efficient learner. In addition, your notes provide a guide to what your instructor thinks is important. That means you will have a better idea of what to study before the next exam if you have a set of notes that you took during class.

MAKE AN OUTLINE

As you read through each chapter of your textbook, you might want to make an outline—a simple method for organizing information. You can create an outline as part of your reading or at the end of your reading. Or you can make an outline when you reread a section before moving on to the next. The act of physically writing an outline for a chapter will help you retain the material in this text and master it, thereby obtaining a higher grade in class.

To make an effective outline, you have to be selective. Your objectives in outlining are, first, to identify the main concepts and, then, to add the details that support those main concepts.

Your outline should consist of several levels written in a standard format. The most important concepts are assigned Roman numerals; the second most important, capital letters; the third most important, numbers; and the fourth most important, lowercase letters. Here is a quick example:

I. Why Is Government Necessary?
   A. The Need for Security
      1. Order: a state of peace and security
      2. The example of Afghanistan
   B. Protecting Citizens' Freedoms
      1. To protect the liberties of the people: the greatest freedom of the individual that is equal to the freedom of other individuals in the society
   C. Authority and Legitimacy
      1. Authority: The right and power of a government to enforce its decisions and compel obedience
      2. Legitimacy: Popular acceptance of the right and power of government authority
         a. North Korea as an example of authority without legitimacy

MARK YOUR TEXT

If you own your own textbook for this course, you can greatly improve your learning by (marking) your text. By doing so, you will identify the most important concepts of each chapter, and at the same time, you'll be making a handy study guide for reviewing material at a later time. It allows you to become an active participant in the mastery of the material. Researchers have shown that the physical act of marking, just like the physical acts of note-taking during class and outlining, increases concentration and helps you better retain the material.

WAYS OF MARKING The most common form of marking is to underline important points. The second most commonly used method is to use a felt-tipped highlighter, or marker, in yellow or some other transparent color. Put a check mark next to material that you do not understand. Work on better comprehension of the checkmarked material after you've finished the chapter. Marking also includes circling, numbering, using arrows, jotting brief notes, or any other method that allows you to remember things when you go back to skim the pages in your textbook prior to an exam.

IMPORTANT

TWO POINTS TO REMEMBER WHEN MARKING

★ Read one section at a time before you do any extensive marking. You can't mark a section until you know what is important, and you can't know what is important until you read the whole section.

★ Don't overmark. Don't fool yourself into thinking that you have done a good job just because each page is filled up with arrows, circles, and underlines. The key to marking is *selective* activity. Mark each page in a way that allows you to see the most impor-

tant points at a glance. You can follow up your marking by writing out more in your subject outline.

TRY THESE TIPS

With these skills in hand, you will be well on your way to becoming a great student. Here are a few more hints that will help you develop effective study skills.

- As a rule, do schoolwork as soon as possible when you get home after class. The longer you wait, the more likely you will be distracted by television, video games, phone calls from friends, or social networking.

- We study best when we are free from distractions. Set aside time and a quiet, comfortable space where you can focus on reading. Your school library is often the best place to work. Set aside several hours a week of "library time" to study in peace and quiet. A neat, organized study space is also important. The only work items that should be on your desk are those that you are working on that day.

- Reward yourself for studying! Rest your eyes and your mind by taking a short break every twenty to thirty minutes. From time to time, allow yourself a break for surfing the Internet, going for a jog, taking a nap, or doing something else that you enjoy. These interludes will refresh your mind, give you more energy required for concentration, and enable you to study longer and more efficiently.

- Often, studying involves pure memorization. To help with this task, create flash (or note) cards. On one side of the card, write the question or term. On the other side, write the answer or definition. Then, use the cards to test yourself on the material.

- Mnemonic (pronounced ne-mon-ik) devices are tricks that increase our ability to memorize. A well-known mnemonic device

winterling/iStockphoto.com

is the phrase ROY G BIV, which helps people remember the colors of the rainbow—Red, Orange, Yellow, Green, Blue, Indigo, Violet. You can create your own for whatever you need to memorize. The more fun you have coming up with mnemonics for yourself, the more useful they will be.

- Take notes twice. First, take notes in class. Then, when you get back home, rewrite your notes. The rewrite will act as a study session by forcing you to think about the material. It will also, invariably, lead to questions that are crucial to the study process.

TEST PREP

You have worked hard throughout the term, reading the book, paying close attention in class, and taking good notes. Now it's test time, when all that hard work pays off. To do well on an exam, of course, it is important that you learn the concepts in each chapter as thoroughly as possible, but there are additional strategies for taking exams. You should know which reading materials and lectures will be covered. You should also know in advance what type of exam you are going to take—essay or objective or both. Finally, you should know how much time will be allowed for the exam. By taking these steps, you will reduce any anxiety you feel as you begin the exam, and you'll be better prepared to work through the entire exam.

FOLLOW DIRECTIONS

Jesus Jauregui/iStockphoto.com

Students are often in a hurry to start an exam, so they take little time to read the instructions. The instructions can be critical, however. In a multiple-choice exam, for example, if there is no indication that there is a penalty for guessing, then you should never leave a question unanswered. Even if only a few minutes are left at the end of an exam, you should guess on the questions that you remain uncertain about.

Additionally, you need to know the weight given to each section of an exam. In a typical multiple-choice exam, all questions have equal weight. In other types of exams, particularly those with essay questions, different parts of the exam carry different weights. You should use these weights to apportion your time accordingly. If the essay portion of an exam accounts for 20 percent of the total points on the exam, you should not spend 60 percent of your time on the essay.

Finally, you need to make sure you are marking the answers correctly. Some exams require a No. 2 pencil to fill in the dots on a machine-graded answer sheet. Other exams require underlining or circling. In short, you have to read and follow the instructions carefully.

OBJECTIVE EXAMS

An objective exam consists of multiple-choice, true/false, fill-in-the-blank, or matching questions that have only one correct answer. Students usually commit one of two errors when they read objective exam questions: (1) they read things into the questions that do not exist, or (2) they skip over words or phrases. Most test questions include key words such as:

- all
- never
- always
- only

If you miss any of these key words, you may answer the question wrong even if you know the information.

Whenever the answer to an objective question is not obvious, start with the process of elimination. Throw out the answers that are clearly incorrect. Typically, the easiest way to eliminate incorrect answers is to look for those that are meaningless, illogical, or inconsistent. Often, test authors put in choices that make perfect sense and are indeed true, but they are not the answer to the question under study.

If you follow the above tips, you will be well on your way to becoming an efficient, results-oriented student. Here are a few more that will help you get there.

- Instructors usually lecture on subjects they think are important, so those same subjects are also likely to be on the exam. Therefore, be sure to take extensive notes in class. Then, review your notes thoroughly as part of your exam preparation.
- At times, you will find yourself studying for several exams at once. When this happens, make a list of each study topic and the amount of time needed to prepare for that topic. Then, create a study schedule to reduce stress and give yourself the best chance for success.
- When preparing for an exam, you might want to get together a small group for a study session. Discussing a topic out loud can improve your understanding of that topic and will help you remember the key points that often come up on exams.
- If the test requires you to read a passage and then answer questions about that passage, read the questions first. This way, you will know what to look for as you read.
- When you first receive your exam, look it over quickly to make sure that you have all the pages. If you are uncertain, ask your professor or exam proctor. This initial scan may uncover other problems as well, such as illegible print or unclear instructions.
- Grades aren't a matter of life and death, and worrying too much about a single exam can have a negative effect on your performance. Keep exams in perspective. If you do poorly on one test, it's not the end of the world. Rather, it should motivate you to do better on the next one.
- Review your lecture notes immediately after each class, when the material is still fresh in your mind. Then, review each subject once a week, giving yourself an hour to go back over what you have learned. Reviews make tests easier because you will feel comfortable with the material.
- Some professors make old exams available, either by posting them online or by putting them on file in the library. Old tests can give you an

Get together with a small group for a

study session.

Discussing a topic out loud can improve your understanding.

idea of the kinds of questions the professor likes to ask. You can also use them to take practice exams.

- With essay questions, look for key words such as "compare," "contrast," and "explain." These will guide your answer. If you have time, make a quick outline. Most important, get to the point without wasting your time (or your professor's) with statements such as "There are many possible reasons for . . . ."
- Cramming just before the exam is a dangerous proposition. Cramming tires the brain unnecessarily and adds to stress, which can severely hamper your testing performance. If you've studied wisely, have confidence that the information will be available to you when you need it.
- When you finish a test early, it is always a good idea to review your answers. You may find a mistake or an area where some extra writing will improve your grade.
- Be prepared. Make a list of everything you will need for the exam, such as a pen or pencil, watch, and calculator. Arrive at the exam early to avoid having to rush, which will only add to your stress. Good preparation helps you focus on the task at hand.
- Be sure to eat before taking a test so you will have the energy you need to concentrate. Don't go overboard, however. Too much food or heavy foods will make you sleepy.

Mlenny/iStockphoto

WRITE PREP

kyoshino/iStockphoto.com

A key part of succeeding as a student is learning how to write well. Whether writing papers, presentations, essays, or even e-mails to your instructor, you have to be able to put your thoughts into words and do so with force, clarity, and precision. In this section, we outline a three-phase process that you can use to write almost anything.

PHASE 1: GETTING READY TO WRITE

First, make a list. Divide the ultimate goal—a finished paper—into smaller steps that you can tackle right away. Estimate how long it will take to complete each step. Start with the date your paper is due and work backward to the present: For example, if the due date is December 1, and you have about three months to write the paper, give yourself a cushion and schedule November 20 as your targeted completion date. Plan what you want to get done by November 1, and then list what you want to get done by October 1.

PICK a TOPIC To generate ideas for a topic, any of the following approaches work well:

- **Brainstorm with a group.** There is no need to create in isolation. You can harness the energy and the natural creative power of a group to assist you.
- **Speak it.** To get ideas flowing, start talking. Admit your confusion or lack of clear ideas. Then just speak. By putting your thoughts into words, you'll start thinking more clearly.
- **Use free writing.** Free writing, a technique championed by writing teacher Peter Elbow, is also very effective when trying to come up with a topic. There's only one rule in free writing: Write without stopping. Set a time limit—say, ten minutes—and keep your fingers dancing across the keyboard the whole time. Ignore the urge to stop and rewrite. There is no need to worry about spelling, punctuation, or grammar during this process.

REFINE YOUR IDEA After you've come up with some initial ideas, it's time to refine them:

- **Select a topic and working title.** Using your instructor's guidelines for the paper or speech, write down a list of topics that interest you. Write down all of the ideas you think of in two minutes. Then choose one topic. The most common pitfall is selecting a topic that is too broad. "Political Campaigns" is probably not a useful topic for your paper. Instead, consider "The Financing of Political Campaigns."
- **Write a thesis statement.** Clarify what you want to say by summarizing it in one concise sentence. This sentence, called a *thesis statement*, refines your working title. A thesis is the main point of the paper—it is a declaration of some sort. You might write a thesis statement such as "Recent decisions by the Supreme Court have dramatically changed the way that political campaigns are funded."

SET GOALS Effective writing flows from a purpose. Think about how you'd like your reader or listener to respond after considering your ideas.

- If you want someone to think differently, make your writing clear and logical. Support your assertions with evidence.
- If your purpose is to move the reader into action, explain exactly what steps to take and offer solid benefits for doing so.

To clarify your purpose, state it in one sentence—for example, "The purpose of this paper is to discuss and analyze the various explanations for the increasing partisanship in Congress."

BEGIN RESEARCH At the initial stage, the objective of your research is not to uncover specific facts about your topic. That comes later. First, you want to gain an overview of the subject. Say that you want to persuade the reader to vote against a voter ID requirement in your state. You must first learn enough about voter ID laws to summarize for your reader the problems such laws may cause for some voters and whether the laws actually deter voting fraud.

MAKE AN OUTLINE An outline is a kind of map. When you follow a map, you avoid getting lost. Likewise, an outline keeps you from wandering off topic. To create your outline, follow these steps:

1. Review your thesis statement and identify the three to five main points you need to address in your paper to support or prove your thesis.

2. Next, look closely at those three to five major points or categories and think about what minor points or subcategories you want to cover in your paper. Your major points are your big ideas. Your minor points are the details you need to fill in under each of those ideas.

3. Ask for feedback. Have your instructor or a classmate review your outline and offer suggestions for improvement. Did you choose the right categories and subcategories? Do you need more detail anywhere? Does the flow from idea to idea make sense?

DO IN-DEPTH RESEARCH Three-by-five-inch index cards are an invaluable tool for in-depth research. Simply write down one idea or piece of information per card. This makes it easy to organize—and reorganize—your ideas and information. Organizing research cards as you create them saves time. Use rubber bands to keep *source cards* (cards that include the bibliographical information for a source) separate from *information cards* (cards that include nuggets of information from a source) and to maintain general categories.

When creating your cards, be sure to:

- Copy all of the information correctly.
- Always include the source and page number on information cards.
- Be neat and organized. Write legibly, using the same format for all of your cards.

In addition to source cards and information cards, generate *idea cards*. If you have a thought while you are researching, write it down on a card. Label these cards clearly as containing your own ideas.

PHASE 2: WRITING A FIRST DRAFT

To create your draft, gather your index cards and confirm that they are arranged to follow your outline. Then write about the ideas in your notes. It's that simple. Look at your cards and start writing. Write in paragraphs, with one idea per paragraph. As you complete this task, keep the following suggestions in mind:

- **Remember that the first draft is not for keeps.** You can worry about quality later. Your goal at this point is simply to generate words and ideas.

- **Write freely.** Many writers prefer to get their first draft down quickly and would advise you to keep writing, much as in free writing. You may pause to glance at your cards and outline, but avoid stopping to edit your work.

- **Be yourself.** Let go of the urge to sound "scholarly" and avoid using unnecessary big words or phrases. Instead, write in a natural voice. Address your thoughts to an intelligent student. Visualize this person, and choose the three or four most important things you'd say to her or him about the topic.

- **Make writing a habit.** Don't wait for inspiration to strike. Make a habit of writing at a certain time each day.

- **Get physical.** While working on the first draft, take breaks. Go for a walk. From time to time, practice relaxation techniques and breathe deeply.

- **Hide your draft in your drawer for a while.** Schedule time for rewrites, and schedule at least one day between revisions so that you can let the material sit. The brain needs that much time to disengage itself from the project.

PHASE 3: REVISING YOUR DRAFT

During this phase, keep in mind the saying "Write in haste; revise at leisure." When you are working on your first draft, the goal is to produce ideas and write them down. During the revision phase, however, you need to slow down and take a close look at your work. One guideline is to allow 50 percent of writing time for planning, researching, and writing the first draft. Then use the remaining 50 percent for revising.

There are a number of good ways to revise your paper:

Izabela Habur/iStockphoto.com

1. **Read it out loud.**

   The combination of voice and ears forces us to pay attention to the details. Is the thesis statement clear and supported by enough evidence? Does the introduction tell your reader what's coming? Do you end with a strong conclusion that expands on what's in your introduction rather than just restating it?

2. **Have a friend look over your paper.**

   This is never a substitute for your own review, but a friend can often see mistakes you miss. With a little practice, you will learn to welcome feedback because it is one of the fastest ways to approach the revision process.

3. **Cut.**

   Look for excess baggage. Avoid at all costs and at all times the really, really terrible mistake of using way too many unnecessary words, a mistake that some student writers often make when they sit down to write papers for the various courses in which they participate at the fine institutions of higher learning that they are fortunate enough to attend. (Example: The previous sentence could be edited to "Avoid unnecessary words.") Also, look for places where two (or more sentences) could be rewritten as one. Resist the temptation to think that by cutting text you are losing something. You are actually gaining a clearer, more polished product. For maximum efficiency, make the larger cuts first—sections, chapters, pages. Then go for the smaller cuts—paragraphs, sentences, phrases, words.

4. **Paste.**

   In deleting both larger and smaller passages in your first draft, you've probably removed some of the original transitions and connecting ideas. The next task is to rearrange what's left of your paper or speech so that it flows logically. Look for consistency within paragraphs and for transitions from paragraph to paragraph and section to section.

5. **Fix.**

   Now it's time to look at individual words and phrases. Define any terms that the reader might not know. In general, focus on nouns and verbs. Using too many adjectives and adverbs weakens your message and adds unnecessary bulk to your writing. Write about the details, and be specific. Also, check your writing to ensure that you are:

   - Using the active voice. Write "*The research team began the project*" rather than (passively) "*A project was initiated.*"

   - Writing concisely. Instead of "*After making a timely arrival and perspicaciously observing the unfolding events, I emerged totally and gloriously victorious,*" be concise with "*I came, I saw, I conquered.*"

   - Communicating clearly. Instead of "*The speaker made effective use of the television medium, asking in no uncertain terms that we change our belief systems,*" you can write specifically, "*The senatorial candidate stared straight into the television camera and said, 'Take a good look at what my opponent is doing! Do you really want six more years of this?'*"

6. **Prepare.**

   Format your paper following accepted standards for margin widths, endnotes, title pages, and other details. Ask your instructor for specific instructions on how to cite the sources used in writing your paper. You can find useful guidelines in the *MLA Handbook for Writers of Research Papers*, Use quality paper for the final version of your paper. For an even more professional appearance, bind your paper with a plastic or paper cover.

7. Proof.

As you ease down the home stretch, read your revised paper one more time. This time, go for the big picture and look for the following:

Proofreading checklist

- A clear thesis statement.
- Sentences that introduce your topic, guide the reader through the major sections of your paper, and summarize your conclusions.
- Details—such as quotations, examples, and statistics—that support your conclusions.
- Lean sentences that have been purged of needless words.
- Plenty of action verbs and concrete, specific nouns.
- Finally, look over your paper with an eye for spelling and grammar mistakes. Use contractions sparingly if at all. Use your word processor's spell-check by all means, but do not rely on it completely as it will not catch everything.

ACADEMIC INTEGRITY: AVOIDING PLAGIARISM

Using another person's words, images, or other original creations without giving proper credit is called *plagiarism*. Plagiarism amounts to taking someone else's work and presenting it as your own—the equivalent of cheating on a test. The consequences of plagiarism can range from a failing grade to expulsion from school.

To avoid plagiarism, ask an instructor where you can find your school's written policy on this issue. Don't assume that you can resubmit a paper you wrote for another class for a current class. Many schools will regard this as plagiarism even though you wrote the paper. The basic guidelines for preventing plagiarism are to cite a source for each phrase, sequence of ideas, or visual image created by another person. While ideas cannot be copyrighted, the specific way that an idea is *expressed* can be. You also need to list a source for any idea that is closely identified with a particular person. The goal is to clearly distinguish your own work from the work of others. There are several ways to ensure that you do this consistently:

- **Identify direct quotes.** If you use a direct quote from another source, put those words in quotation marks. If you do research online, you might copy text from a Web page and paste it directly into your notes. This is the same as taking direct quotes from your source. Always identify such passages in an obvious way.

- **Paraphrase carefully.** Paraphrasing means restating the original passage in your own words, usually making it shorter and simpler. Students who copy a passage word for word and then just rearrange or delete a few phrases are running a serious risk of plagiarism. Remember to cite a source for paraphrases, just as you do for direct quotes. When you use the same sequence of ideas as one of your sources—even if you have not paraphrased or directly quoted—cite that source.

- **Note details about each source.** For books, details about each source include the author, title, publisher, publication date, location of publisher, and page number. For articles from print sources, record the article title and the name of the magazine or journal as well. If you found the article in an academic or technical journal, also record the volume and number of the publication. A librarian can help identify these details. If your source is a Web page, record as many identifying details as you can find—author, title, sponsoring organization, URL, publication date, and revision date. In addition, list the date that you accessed the page. Be careful when using Web resources, as not all Web sites are considered legitimate sources. Wikipedia, for instance, is not regarded as a legitimate source.

- **Cite your sources as endnotes or footnotes to your paper.** Ask your instructor for examples of the format to use. You do not need to credit wording that is wholly your own. Nor do you need to credit general ideas, such as the suggestion that people use a to-do list to plan their time. When you use your own words to describe such an idea, there's no need to credit a source. But if you borrow someone else's words or images to explain the idea, do give credit.

TAKE ACTION:
A GUIDE TO POLITICAL PARTICIPATION

It's easy to think of politics as a spectator sport— something that politicians do, pundits analyze, and citizens watch. But there are many ways to get engaged with politics, to interact with the political world and participate in it, and even to effect change.

GET INFORMED. GET CONNECTED. GET INVOLVED.

GET INFORMED.

FIND OUT WHERE YOU FIT AND WHAT YOU KNOW

- You already have some opinions about a variety of political issues. Do you have a sense of where your views place you on the political map? Get a feel for your ideological leanings by taking *The World's Smallest Political Quiz*: **www.theadvocates.org/quiz/**.

- Which Founder Are You? The National Constitutional Center can help you with that. Go to **constitutioncenter.org/foundersquiz/** to discover which Founding Father's personality most resembles your own.

- The U.S. Constitution is an important part of the context in which American politics takes place. Do you know what the Constitution says? Take the *Constitution I.Q. Quiz*: **www.constitutionfacts.com/**. Was your score higher than the national average?

LIGHTPOET/SHUTTERSTOCK.COM

- At the National Constitution Center, you can explore the interactive Constitution and learn more about the provisions in that document: **constitutioncenter.org/**.

- Find out what those who want to become U.S. citizens have to do—and what they have to know.

PAUL MATTHEW PHOTOGRAPHY/SHUTTERSTOCK.COM

Go to the U.S. Citizenship and Immigration Services Web site at **www.uscis.gov/**. What is involved in applying for citizenship? Take the *Naturalization Self-Test*. How did you do?

THINK ABOUT HOW YOUR POLITICAL VIEWS HAVE BEEN SHAPED

- Giving some thought to how agents of political socialization—your family, your schools, your peers, for example—have contributed to your political beliefs and attitudes may help you understand why others might *not* share your views on politics. Have some conversations with people in your classes or in your residence hall about the people, institutions, and experiences that influenced the way they view the political world.

- Now explore how your views on political issues compare with those of a majority of Americans. There are a number of good polling sites that report public opinion on a range of topics.

  - The Pew Research Center for the People & the Press conducts monthly polls on politics and policy issues: **www.people-press.org/**.

  - Public Agenda reports poll data and material on major issues: **publicagenda.org/**.

  - The results of recent polls and an archive of past polls can be found at Gallup: **www.gallup.com/**.

  - The Roper Center for Public Opinion Research is a leading archive of data from surveys of public opinion: **www.ropercenter.uconn.edu/**.

  - PollingReport organizes public opinion data from various sources by keyword: **pollingreport.com/**.

GET CONNECTED.

NEWS

Keep up with news—print and broadcast. Remember that different news organizations (or media brands) will report the same information in different ways. Don't avoid certain news sources because you think you might not agree with the way they report the news. It's just as important to know how people are talking about issues as it is to know about the issues themselves.

- One of the best ways to get to the source of the news is to get your information from the same place that journalists do. Often they take their cues or are alerted to news events by news agencies like the nonprofit cooperative, Associated Press: **ap.org/**.

- Installing a few key apps on your phone or tablet can make all the difference in being informed. Try downloading the Associated Press (AP) app for short updates from news around the world, as they happen. There are tons of other great political apps—some that are fairly polarized, others that are neutral, and still others that are just plain silly.

BLOGS

The blogosphere affords views of politics that may be presented differently than the way the mainstream media do it.

- **Shortformblog.com** provides snippets of news and information from the White House and around the world in small, digestible amounts.

- **Technorati.com/politics** is a great place to explore hundreds of blogs about politics (or anything else you want), rated by political authority.

SOCIAL MEDIA

Staying connected can be as simple as following local, national, or international politics on social media. U.S. House Majority Whip Kevin McCarthy, President Barack Obama, Senator Elizabeth Warren, House Speaker John Boehner, and even the White House have Instagram accounts worth following. Numerous politicians and political outlets are also on Twitter and Facebook.

CHECK THE DATA

- It's not always easy to figure out if what newsmakers are saying is accurate. Politifact, a project of the *Tampa Bay Times*, is a good place to go to get the facts: **www.politifact.com/**. Check out the Truth-O-Meter, and get it on your smartphone or tablet.

- A project of the Annenberg Public Policy Center, **www.factcheck.org/** is a nonpartisan, nonprofit "consumer advocate" for voters that monitors the factual accuracy of what political players are saying in TV ads, speeches, and interviews.

KEEP UP DURING ELECTION SEASON

- Project Vote Smart offers information on elections and candidates: **votesmart.org/**.

- Nate Silver's FiveThirtyEight features election analysis, in addition to covering sports and economics: **www.fivethirtyeight.com/**.

- Stay connected to the horse-race aspect of electoral politics by tracking election polls. There are many good sources:

- For a comprehensive collection of election polls, go to the RealClearPolitics Web site: **realclearpolitics.com/polls/**.

RINECA/SHUTTERSTOCK.COM

RealClearPolitics is a good source for other political news and opinions as well.

- Polls for U.S. federal elections, including state-by-state polls, can be found at **electoral -vote.com/**.

- HuffPost Pollster publishes pre-election poll results combined into interactive charts: **elections.huffingtonpost.com/pollster/**. During presidential elections, additional maps and electoral vote counts can be found at HuffPost Politics Election Dashboard.

- Interactive electoral vote maps are available at 270 to Win: **www.270towin.com/**.

- If you have the opportunity, attend a speech by a candidate you're interested in.

MONITOR MONEY AND INFLUENCE IN POLITICS

The Center for Responsive Politics Web site is an excellent source for information about who's contributing what amounts to which candidates: **www.open secrets.org/**. You can also use the lobbying database to identify the top lobbying firms, the agencies most frequently lobbied, and the industries that spend the most on lobbying activities. Explore the site's information on the revolving door, which identifies the lobbying firms, agencies, and industries that have the highest numbers of people who have moved between government and interest group positions.

CONNECT WITH CONGRESS

You can, of course, learn a lot about what's going on in Congress from the Web sites of the House of Representatives and the Senate: **www.house.gov/** and **www.senate.gov/**. Look up the names and contact information for the senators and the representative from your area. If you want to let your voice be heard, you can do so simply by phoning

or e-mailing your senators or your representative. Your chances of influencing your members of Congress will be greater if you can convince others, including your friends and family members, to do likewise. Members of Congress do listen to their constituents and often do act in response to their constituents' wishes. Indeed, next to voting, contacting those who represent you in Congress is probably the most effective way to influence government decision making.

Check GovTrack to find out where your representative and senators fall on the leadership and ideology charts, as well as their most recently sponsored bills and votes on legislation: **www.govtrack.us/**.

GET INVOLVED.

TAKE AN INTEREST IN YOUR COMMUNITY—HOWEVER YOU DEFINE IT. OFFER TO HELP.

Every community—large or small—can use energetic people willing to help where there is a need. Local nonprofit agencies serving the homeless, or battered women, or troubled teens often welcome volunteers who are willing to pitch in. You can learn a lot about the public policies that focus on social services while doing some good for others.

The Internet also has abundant resources about nonprofits and charities and how you can get involved:

- **Idealist.org** is a great place to find organizations and events that are looking for employees, interns, and volunteers. Filter by type and area of focus (women, disaster relief, animals, etc.) to find a cause that fits you.

- **Tinyspark.org** is a watchdog for nonprofits and charity organizations. It highlights individuals and groups that are doing good things in communities and around the globe and checks on those who may not be doing as much good as you'd think. Tinyspark also has a podcast.

- **Charitynavigator.org** is another tool for checking on charities. It reports on charities in terms of how much of their donations go to the cause, which charities are in the red, which are worth promoting, and the like—it's kind of like *opensecrets.org* for charities.

DESIGN YOUR OWN WAYS TO TAKE ACTION

- Are there people on your campus who, because of disability or recent injury, need someone to help carry belongings, open doors, or push wheelchairs? Start a network to match those who need assistance and those who want to help.

- Do you want to raise awareness about an issue? Is there a cause that you think needs attention? Talk with friends. Find out if they share your concerns. Turn your discussions into a blog. Create videos of events you think are newsworthy and share them online. Sign or start a petition.

The citizens of the United States are responsible for the **greatest trust** *ever confided to a political society."*

— JAMES MADISON

JOIN A GROUP ON CAMPUS

You see flyers promoting groups and recruiting members posted all over campus—in the student center, in the residence halls, in classroom buildings. Chances are, there's a group organized around something you're interested in or care about.

Maybe it's an organization that works to bring clean water to remote parts of the world. Perhaps it's an organization that works to foster tolerance on campus. The American Civil Liberties Union may have a chapter on your campus. The American Red Cross may be there, too. You'll find College Republicans, College Democrats, groups organized around race or culture, groups that go on alternative spring break trips to give direct service to communities in need, service organizations of all kinds, groups that serve to create community among culturally underrepresented students, and groups that care about the environment. The list goes on and on.

If you have an interest that isn't represented by the groups on your campus, start your own. Your college or university has an office of campus life (or

something similar) that can help you navigate the process for establishing a student organization.

Remember, too, that there are hundreds of political interest groups with national reach. Check out their Web sites to see if you want to join.

VOTE (BUT FIRST YOU HAVE TO REGISTER)

- Voting is one of the most widely shared acts of participation in American democracy. You can learn about the laws governing voting in your state—and all of the others—by going to the Web site of the National Conference of State Legislatures and its link to Voter Identification Requirements: **www.ncsl.org/research/elections-and-campaigns/voter-id/**.

- **Register:** Enter "register to vote in [your state]" in a search engine. The office in your state that administers voting and elections (in some states it's the office of the secretary of state, in others it might be the State Board of Elections) will have a Web site that outlines the steps you will need to follow. If you need to vote absentee, you'll find out how to do that here, too.

- If you want to view a sample ballot to familiarize yourself with what you'll be looking at when you go to the polls, you will probably be able to view one online. Just enter "sample ballot" in a search

engine. Your local election board, the League of Women Voters, or your district library often post a sample ballot online.

- **Vote:** Familiarize yourself with the candidates and issues before you go to the polls. If you'd like to influence the way things are done in your community, state, or Washington, D.C., you can do so by helping to elect state and local officials, a president, and members of Congress whose views you endorse and who you think would do a good job of running the government. Make sure you know the location and hours for your polling place.

SUPPORT A POLITICAL PARTY

Getting involved in political parties is as simple as going to the polls and casting your vote for the candidate of one of the major parties—or of a third party. You can also consider becoming a delegate to a party convention. Depending on the state, parties may hold conventions by U.S. House district, by county, or by state legislative district. In many states, the lowest-level conventions are open to anyone who shows up. Voting rights at a convention, however, may be restricted to those who are elected as precinct delegates in a party primary.

In much of the country, precinct delegate slots go unfilled. If this is true in your area, you can become a precinct delegate with a simple write-in campaign, writing in your own name and persuading a handful of friends or neighbors to write you in as well. Whether you attend a convention as a voting delegate or as a guest, you'll have a firsthand look at how politics operates. You'll hear debates on resolutions. You might participate in electing delegates to higher-level conventions—perhaps even the national convention if it is a presidential election year.

WORK FOR A CAMPAIGN

Candidates welcome energetic volunteers. So do groups that are supporting (or opposing) ballot measures. While sometimes tiring and frustrating, working in campaign politics can also be exhilarating and very rewarding.

Find the contact information for a campaign you're interested in on its Web site and inquire about volunteer opportunities. Volunteers can assemble mailings, answer the telephone, or make calls to encourage voters to support their candidate or cause. Even if you have little free time or are not comfortable talking to strangers, most campaigns can find a way for you to participate.

BE PART OF CAMPUS MEDIA

Do you have a nose for news and do you write well? Try reporting for the university newspaper. Work your way up to an editor's position. If broadcast media are your thing, get involved with your college radio station or go on air on campus TV.

ENGAGE WITH POLITICAL INSTITUTIONS, GOVERNMENT AGENCIES, AND PUBLIC POLICYMAKERS—AT HOME AND ABROAD

- Consider that an individual or a small group can have much more influence on local and state politics than on the national level. Visit the government Web sites for your state and community and learn about your representatives. Contact them with your thoughts on the matters that are important to you. Attend a city council meeting. You can find date, location, and agenda information on the Web site for your city. And if you're passionate about a local issue, you can even sign up to speak.

- Remember that your U.S. representative has district offices—one may be in the town in which you live. Your U.S. senators also have offices in various locations around the state. Check to see if internships are available or if there are opportunities for volunteering. If you plan to be in

M. DYKSTRA/SHUTTERSTOCK.COM

Try your hand at Governing

Get involved with student government.Serve on committees. Run for office.

Washington, D.C., and want to visit Capitol Hill, you can book a tour in advance through your senators' or representative's offices. That's where you get gallery passes, too.

- Spend some time in Washington. Many colleges and universities have established internship programs with government agencies and institutions. Some have semester-long programs that will bring you into contact with policymakers in Congress and in the bureaucracy, with journalists, and with a variety of other prominent newsmakers. Politics and government come alive, and the contacts you make while participating in such programs can often lead to jobs after graduation.

- If you're interested in the Supreme Court and you're planning a trip to Washington, try to watch oral argument. Go to the Court's Web site to access the link for oral arguments: **www.supremecourt.gov/**. You'll find the argument calendar and a visitor's guide. (The secret is to get in line early.)

- If you can't make it to Washington, D.C., for a semester-long program or even a few days, become a virtual tourist. Take the U.S. Capitol Virtual Tour: **www.senate.gov/vtour/**.

- You can take a virtual tour of the Supreme Court at the Web site of the Oyez Project at IIT Chicago-Kent College of Law:

www.oyez.org/. And you can listen to Supreme Court oral arguments wherever you are. Go to the Oyez site and check out ISCOTUSnow.

- Studying abroad, of course, is a great way to expand your horizons and to get a feel for different cultures and the global nature of politics and the economy. There are programs that will take you almost anywhere in the world. Check with the Study Abroad Office at your college or university to find out more.

- You can gain some insight into dealing with global issues even if you stay stateside. Participate in the Model UN Club on your campus (or start a Model UN Club if there isn't one). By participating in Model UN, you will become aware of international issues and conflicts and recognize the role that the United Nations can play in forging collective responses to global concerns. Model UN conferences are simulations of a session of the United Nations; your work as part of a country's UN delegation will give you hands-on experience in diplomacy.

GET INFORMED. GET CONNECTED. GET INVOLVED.

America in the Twenty-First Century

ROBERT ROSAMILIO/NY DAILY NEWS ARCHIVE VIA GETTY IMAGES

The **Learning Outcomes** labeled 1 through 4 are designed to help improve your understanding of the chapter. After reading this chapter, you should be able to:

1–1 Explain what is meant by the terms *politics* and *government*.

1–2 Identify the various types of government systems.

1–3 Summarize some of the basic principles of American democracy and basic American political values.

1–4 Define common American ideological positions, such as "conservatism" and "liberalism."

Remember to visit page 20 for additional Study Tools

LearningOutcomes

AMERICA AT
ODDS
Has Our Government Grown Too Large?

JUSTIN SULLIVAN/GETTY IMAGES

For much of America's history, there was little discussion about whether our government had grown too large. The government, after all, wasn't that big. Since the Great Depression of the 1930s, however, the government has grown by leaps and bounds.

Americans are at odds over the proper size of government. Indeed, the size of government lies at the very heart of the differences between Republicans and Democrats. Republicans have called for trillions of dollars in federal budget cuts over the next decade. Democrats, however, believe that cuts of this size may endanger important programs such as Medicare and Medicaid. Following the 2012 elections, the presidency and the U.S. Senate were once again in the hands of the Democrats, while the Republicans continued to control the U.S. House. Under such circumstances, arguments over the size of the government should continue for the foreseeable future.

Big Government Must Shrink

Many of those who believe that big government must shrink admit that government programs can help many people in need of, for example, medical care or better education. The problem is that once government programs are in place, they expand. The result is an "assisted society." Opponents of big government believe that too many people spend too much time seeking government assistance rather than taking care of their problems by themselves or with the help of family and friends.

Conservatives argue that government spending must be cut to avoid higher taxes. So far, though, increases in federal government spending have meant larger budget deficits rather than increased taxes. The government has simply borrowed what it needs. Conservative economists believe that this new government borrowing means there are fewer funds available for private individuals and businesses to borrow. Moreover, they say, the higher taxes that will eventually be needed to pay back the sums the government has borrowed will reduce people's incentives to work and to invest, now and in the future. Ultimately, that means less economic growth.

We Need What the Government Does

Liberal economists dismiss the conservative worry that government spending will "crowd out" private spending. Liberals admit that could happen during a boom, but they also contend that when millions of people are unemployed, government spending puts people back to work.

More generally, liberals argue that we need the programs that a big government can provide. Medicare, Medicaid, Social Security, and national defense together make up well over half of all federal spending. The first three programs assist people who cannot get by just with the help of family or friends. Most of the smaller programs, such as education and veterans' benefits, serve equally important purposes.

Liberals agree that we should do whatever we can to limit wasteful spending and get more "bang" for the taxpayer's buck. But when we must choose between higher taxes and eliminating crucial services, then we will simply have to pay for the benefits we need. We can do this. Until December 2012, when some taxes increased, taxes were lower as a share of our economy than in any year since the 1950s.

Where do you stand?

1. Is big government necessary in times of crisis, such as after the terrorist attacks of 9/11 and during the Great Recession that began in December 2007? Explain your answer.
2. Would you favor a law that reduced the budget of every federal, state, and local agency by, say, 15 percent? What would be the consequences?

Explore this issue online

- The issue of big government divides liberals and conservatives. You can find examples of conservative views by typing that term into a search engine such as Google. Entering "liberal," however, brings up more sites hostile to liberalism than ones that actually represent the philosophy. Instead, try using terms such as "progressive blogs" or "progressive politics."

Introduction

Regardless of how Americans feel about government, one thing is certain: they can't live without it. James Madison (1751–1836) once said, "If men were angels, no government would be necessary." Today, his statement still holds true. People are not perfect. People need an organized form of government and a set of rules by which to live.

Government performs a wide range of extremely important functions. From the time we are born until the day we die, we constantly interact with various levels of government. Most (although not all) students attend government-run schools. All of us travel on government-owned streets and highways. Many of us serve in the military—a completely government-controlled environment. A few of us get into trouble and meet up with the government's law enforcement system.

Every citizen after reaching the age of sixty-five can expect the government to help with medical and living expenses. When the new health-care reform legislation—Obamacare—finally takes full effect, the government will ensure that the medical needs of most citizens are met, regardless of age or income. To fund all these functions, the government collects taxes.

In a representative democracy such as ours, it is politics that controls what the government decides to do. As discussed in this chapter's opening *America at Odds* feature, the primary question is: How big should the government be? This leads to other questions, including the following: What combination of taxes and government services is best? Should industries such as agriculture and alternative energy be subsidized? When should our leaders use military force against foreign nations or rebellions in foreign countries? How the nation answers these and many other questions will have a major impact on your life—and participation in politics is the only way you can influence what happens.

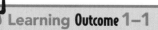

Learning Outcome 1–1

Explain what is meant by the terms *politics* and *government*.

1–1 What Are Politics and Government?

Even if—contrary to Madison's observation—people were perfect, they would still need to establish rules to guide their behavior. They would somehow have to agree on how to divide up a society's resources, such as its land, among themselves and how to balance individual needs and wants against those of society generally.

These perfect people would also have to decide *how* to make these decisions. They would need to create a process for making rules and a form of government to enforce those rules. It is thus not difficult to understand why government is one of humanity's oldest and most universal **institutions.**

As you will read in this chapter, a number of different systems of government exist in the world today. In the United States, we have a democracy in which decisions about pressing issues ultimately are made politically, by the people's representatives in government.

Because people rarely have identical thoughts and feelings about issues, it is not surprising that in any democracy citizens are often at odds over many political and social problems. Throughout this book, you will read about contemporary controversies that have brought various groups of Americans into conflict with one another.

Differences in political opinion are part and parcel of a democratic government. Ultimately, these differences are resolved, one way or another, through the American political process and our government institutions.

1–1a Defining Politics and Government

Politics means many things to many people. There are also many different notions about the meaning of government. How should we define these two central concepts?

Politics and Conflict To some, politics is an expensive and extravagant game played in Washington, D.C., in state capitols, and in city halls, particularly during election time. To others, politics involves all of the tactics and maneuvers carried out by the president and Congress. Most formal definitions of politics, however, begin with the assumption that **social conflict**—disagreements among people in a

> **institution** An ongoing organization that performs certain functions for society.
>
> **social conflict** Disagreements among people in a society over what the society's priorities should be.

> ## "THE ULTIMATE RULERS
> of our democracy are . . .
> the voters of this country."
>
> ~ FRANKLIN D. ROOSEVELT ~
> THIRTY-SECOND PRESIDENT
> OF THE UNITED STATES
> 1933–1945

society over what the society's priorities should be—is inevitable. Conflicts will naturally arise over how the society should use its scarce resources and who should receive various benefits, such as status, health care, and higher education. Resolving such conflicts is the essence of **politics.** Political scientist Harold Lasswell perhaps said it best when he defined politics as the process of determining "who gets what, when, and how" in a society.[1]

Government and Authority From the perspective of political science, **government** can best be defined as the individuals and institutions that make society's rules and also possess the *power* and *authority* to enforce those rules. Although this definition of government sounds remote and abstract, what the government does is very real indeed. As one scholar put it, "Make no mistake. What Congress does directly and powerfully affects our daily lives."[2] The same can be said for decisions made by state legislators and local government officials, as well as for decisions rendered by the courts—the judicial branch of government.

Of course, a key question remains: How do specific individuals obtain the power and authority to govern? As you will read shortly, the answer to this question varies from one type of political system to another.

> ## "The thing about democracy,
> beloveds, is that it is not neat, orderly or quiet. It requires a certain relish for confusion."
>
> ~ MOLLY IVINS ~
> AMERICAN JOURNALIST
> 1944–2007

To understand what government is, you need to understand what it actually does for people and society. Generally, in any country government serves at least three essential purposes: (1) it resolves conflicts, (2) it provides public services, and (3) it defends the nation and its culture against attacks by other nations.

1–1b Resolving Conflicts

Even though people have lived together in groups since the beginning of time, none of these groups has been free of social conflict. Disputes over how to distribute a society's resources inevitably arise because valued resources, such as property, are limited, while people's wants are unlimited. To resolve such disputes, people need ways to determine who wins and who loses, and how to get the losers to accept those decisions. Who has the legitimate power—the authority—to make such decisions? This is where governments step in.

Governments decide how conflicts will be resolved so that public order can be maintained. Governments have **power**—the ability to influence the behavior of others. Power is getting someone to do something that he or she would not otherwise do. Power may involve the use of force (often called coercion), persuasion, or rewards. Governments typically also have

politics The process of resolving conflicts over how society should use its scarce resources and who should receive various benefits, such as public health care and public higher education.

government The individuals and institutions that make society's rules and possess the power and authority to enforce those rules.

power The ability to influence the behavior of others, usually through the use of force, persuasion, or rewards.

CAROL GUZY/WASHINGTON POST/GETTY IMAGES

First-year dental hygiene students at Northern Virginia Community College show techniques to the school's president. In what ways are college faculty members different from other government employees?

authority, which they can exercise only if their power is legitimate. As used here, the term *authority* means the ability to use power that is collectively recognized and accepted by society as legally and morally correct. Power and authority are central to a government's ability to resolve conflicts by making and enforcing laws, placing limits on what people can do, and developing court systems to make final decisions.

For example, the judicial branch of government—specifically, the United States Supreme Court—resolved the highly controversial question of whether the Second Amendment to the Constitution grants individuals the right to bear arms. In 2008 and 2010, the Court affirmed that such a right does exist. Because of the Court's stature and authority as a government body, there was little resistance to its decision, even from gun control advocates.

1–1c Providing Public Services

Another important purpose of government is to provide **public services**—essential services that many individuals cannot provide for themselves. Governments undertake projects that individuals usually would not or could not carry out on their own, such as building and maintaining roads, establishing welfare programs, operating public schools, and preserving national parks. Governments also provide such services as law enforcement, fire protection, and public health and safety programs. As Abraham Lincoln once stated:

> The legitimate object of government is to do for a community of people, whatever they need to have done, but cannot do, *at all*, or cannot, *so well* do, for themselves—in their separate, individual capacities. In all that the people can individually do as well for themselves, government ought not to interfere.[3]

Services for All and Services for Some

Some public services are provided equally to all citizens of the United States. For example, government services such as national defense and domestic law enforcement allow all citizens, at least in theory, to feel that their lives and property are safe. Laws governing clean air and safe drinking water benefit all Americans.

Other services are provided only to citizens who are in need at a particular time, even though they are paid for by all citizens through taxes. Examples of such services include health and welfare benefits, as well as public housing. Laws such as the Americans with Disabilities Act explicitly protect the rights of people with disabilities, although all Americans pay for such protections whether they have disabilities or not.

Managing the Economy One of the most crucial public services that the government is expected to provide is protection from hardship caused by economic recessions or depressions. From 2008 on, this governmental objective became more important than almost any other, due to the severity of the recession that began in December 2007. One of the most damaging consequences of the recession has been high rates of unemployment, which have continued into the present, even though the recession officially ended in June 2009 when economic growth resumed. We examine the unemployment problem in the *Perception versus Reality* feature on the following page.

1–1d Defending the Nation and Its Culture

Historically, matters of national security and defense have been given high priority by governments and have demanded considerable time, effort, and expense. The U.S. government provides for the common defense and national security with its Army, Navy, Marines, Air Force, and Coast Guard. The departments of State, Defense, and Homeland Security, plus the Central Intelligence Agency, National Security Agency, and other agencies, also contribute to this defense network.

As part of an ongoing policy of national security, many departments and agencies in the federal government are constantly dealing with other nations. The Constitution gives our national government exclusive power over relations with foreign nations. No individual state can negotiate a treaty with a foreign nation.

Of course, in defending the nation against attacks by other nations, a government helps to preserve the nation's culture, as well as its integrity as an independent unit. Failure to defend successfully against foreign attacks may have significant consequences for a nation's culture. For example, consider what happened in Tibet in the 1950s. When that country was taken over by the People's Republic of China, the conquering Chinese set out on a systematic program, the effective result of which was large-scale cultural destruction.

Since the terrorist attacks on the World Trade Center and the Pentagon in 2001, defending the homeland against future terrorist attacks has become a priority of our government.

authority The ability to legitimately exercise power, such as the power to make and enforce laws.

public services Essential services that individuals cannot provide for themselves, such as building and maintaining roads, establishing welfare programs, operating public schools, and preserving national parks.

Perception versus Reality
Do We Still Need to Worry about Unemployment?

In 2009, the nation's unemployment rate—about 5 percent in 2007—shot up to 10 percent. In 2012, five years after the Great Recession first struck, the rate was still above 8 percent. By mid-2013, it had declined slightly to 7.5 percent. The United States has not seen so much long-term unemployment since the Great Depression of the 1930s.

THE PERCEPTION

In 2009, President Obama advertised many of his initiatives—including the February 2009 stimulus package, the 2009 federal budget, and the bailout of automakers GM and Chrysler—as ways to combat unemployment. In the 2010 elections, however, Republicans argued that the federal budget deficit was the nation's number-one economic problem. That election year proved to be very good for Republicans. After the elections, Obama "pivoted" to address the deficit. Since then, arguments over the economy in Washington, D.C., have largely centered on the deficit. It would appear that unemployment is yesterday's issue, and we need to worry about other matters instead.

THE REALITY

Regardless of what Washington insiders say, Americans continue to tell public opinion pollsters that unemployment is the nation's most important issue. Also, while the unemployment rate may be coming down, many economists look beyond the unemployment rate to another, underlying statistic. This figure is the percentage of adults who have jobs, regardless of whether they are looking for work or any other factor. From 2000 to 2007, that figure averaged about 62 to 63 percent. Since 2010, however, it has been stuck at about 58 to 59 percent. The jobs that have been created in recent years are just enough to compensate for population growth.

Young people who are entering the workforce have been especially hard hit by our stagnating economy. About half of the population aged sixteen to twenty-four is in the labor force. (Many of the rest are in school or the military and not yet seeking employment.) In mid-2013, these young people had an unemployment rate of 16 percent. African American teenagers faced even bleaker circumstances. For black youth aged sixteen to twenty-four, the unemployment rate was 30 percent. Studies have shown that youthful unemployment can cripple a person's income prospects for the rest of his or her life.

BLOG ON For basic statistics on unemployment, enter "unemployment quandL" into an Internet search engine such as Google. For a liberal perspective, search on "unemployment demos cha." For conservative proposals on how to increase employment, check out "justin quinn job growth."

FOR CRITICAL THINKING

Young Americans have the lowest voter-turnout rate of any group in the country. Some believe that if voting were made easier, young Americans would turn out in greater numbers. Others believe that America's youth stay away from the polls because they are not interested in politics. *What is your position on this issue?*

1-2 Different Systems of Government

Through the centuries, the functions of government just discussed have been performed by many different types of structures. A government's structure is influenced by a number of factors, such as a country's history, customs, values, geography, resources, and human experiences and needs. No two nations have exactly the same form of government. Over time, however, political analysts have developed ways to classify

different systems of government. One of the most meaningful ways is according to *who* governs. Who has the power to make the rules and laws that all must obey?

1–2a Undemocratic Systems

Before the development of democratic systems, the power of the government was typically in the hands of an authoritarian individual or group. When such power is exercised by an individual, the system is called **autocracy.** Autocrats can gain power by traditional or nontraditional means.

Monarchy   One form of autocracy, known as a **monarchy,** is government by a king, queen, emperor, empress, tsar, or tsarina. In a monarchy, the monarch, who usually acquires power through inheritance, is the highest authority in the government.

Historically, many monarchies were *absolute monarchies,* in which the ruler held complete and unlimited power. Until the eighteenth century, the theory of "divine right" was widely accepted in Europe. This **divine right theory,** variations of which had existed since ancient times, held that God gave those of royal birth the unlimited right to govern other men and women. In other words, those of royal birth had a "divine right" to rule, and only God could judge them. Thus, all citizens were bound to obey their monarchs, no matter how unfair or unjust they seemed to be. Challenging this power was regarded not only as treason against the government but also as a sin against God.

Most modern monarchies, however, are *constitutional monarchies,* in which the monarch shares governmental power with elected lawmakers. Over time, the monarch's power has come to be limited, or checked, by other government leaders and perhaps by a constitution or a bill of rights. Most constitutional monarchs today serve merely as ceremonial leaders of their nations, as in Spain, Sweden, and the United Kingdom (Britain).

Dictatorship   Undemocratic systems that are not supported by tradition are called **dictatorships.** Often, a dictator is a single individual, although dictatorial power can be exercised by a group, such as the Communist Party of China. Dictators are not accountable to anyone else.

A dictatorship can also be *totalitarian,* which means that a leader or group of leaders seeks to control almost all aspects of social and economic life. The needs of the nation come before the needs of individuals, and all citizens must work for the common goals established by the government.

Examples of the totalitarian form of government include Adolf Hitler's Nazi regime in Germany from 1933 to 1945 and Joseph Stalin's dictatorship in the Soviet Union (Russia) from 1929 to 1953. A more contemporary example of a totalitarian dictator is the latest leader of North Korea, Kim Jong Un.

1–2b Democratic Systems

The most familiar form of government to Americans is **democracy,** in which the supreme political authority rests with the people. The word *democracy* comes from the Greek *demos,* meaning "the people," and *kratia,* meaning "rule." The main idea of democracy is that government exists only by the consent of the people and reflects the will of the majority. Figure 1–1 on the following page shows the extent of democracy in the world today—with "democratic" defined as "free."

The Athenian Model of Direct Democracy

Democracy as a form of government began long ago. In its earliest form, democracy was simpler than the system we know today. What we now call **direct democracy** exists when the people participate directly in government decision making.

autocracy A form of government in which the power and authority of the government are in the hands of a single person.

monarchy A form of autocracy in which a king, queen, emperor, empress, tsar, or tsarina is the highest authority in the government. Monarchs usually obtain their power through inheritance.

divine right theory The theory that a monarch's right to rule was derived directly from God rather than from the consent of the people.

dictatorship A form of government in which absolute power is exercised by an individual or group whose power is not supported by tradition.

democracy A system of government in which the people have ultimate political authority. The word is derived from the Greek *demos* ("the people") and *kratia* ("rule").

direct democracy A system of government in which political decisions are made by the people themselves rather than by elected representatives. This form of government was practiced in some parts of ancient Greece.

FIGURE 1–1

Free and Unfree Nations
of the World, 2013

In this classification of nations by Freedom House, green means free, yellow means partly free, and purple means unfree. Bear in mind that these are the assessments of a single organization. Judgments may differ on how any particular nation should be classified.

Sources: Arch Puddington, *Freedom in the World 2013: Democratic Breakthroughs in the Balance* (Washington, D.C.: Freedom House, 2013). Outline map adapted from Wikimedia.

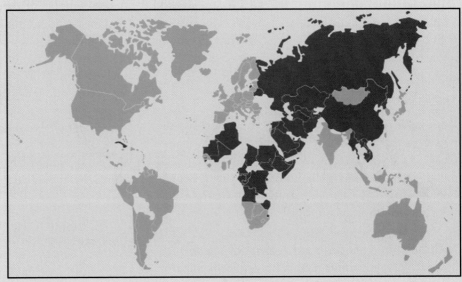

In its purest form, direct democracy was practiced in Athens and several other ancient Greek city-states about 2,500 years ago. Every Athenian citizen participated in the governing assembly and voted on all major issues. Although some consider the Athenian form of direct democracy ideal because it demanded a high degree of citizen participation, others point out that most residents in the Athenian city-state (women, foreigners, and slaves) were not considered citizens and thus were not allowed to participate in government.

Clearly, direct democracy is possible only in small communities in which citizens can meet in a chosen place and decide key issues and policies. Nowhere in the world does pure direct democracy exist today. Some New England towns, though, and a few of the smaller political subunits, or cantons, of Switzerland still use a modified form of direct democracy.

Representative Democracy Although the founders of the United States were aware of the Athenian model and agreed that government should be based on the consent of the governed, they believed that direct democracy would deteriorate into mob rule. They thought that large groups of people meeting together would ignore the rights and opinions of people in the minority and would make decisions without careful thought. They believed that representative assemblies were superior because they would enable public decisions to be made in a calmer and more deliberate manner.

In a **representative democracy,** the will of the majority is expressed through smaller groups of individuals elected by the people to act as their representatives. These representatives are responsible to the people for their conduct and can be voted out of office. Our founders preferred to use the term **republic,** which means essentially a representative democracy—with one qualification.

representative democracy A form of democracy in which the will of the majority is expressed through groups of individuals elected by the people to act as their representatives.

republic Essentially, a representative democracy in which there is no king or queen and the people are sovereign.

"People often say that, in a democracy, decisions are made by a majority of the people. Of course, that is not true. **DECISIONS ARE MADE BY A MAJORITY OF . . . THE PEOPLE WHO VOTE—** a very different thing."

~ WALTER H. JUDD ~
U.S. REPRESENTATIVE FROM MINNESOTA
1943–1963

These voters are listening to a debate at a town hall meeting in Plainfield, Vermont. Some New England towns use such meetings to engage in a form of direct democracy. Why doesn't the United States as a nation have direct democracy?

AP IMAGES/TOBY TALBOT

A republic, by definition, has no king or queen. Rather, the people are sovereign. In contrast, a representative democracy may be headed by a monarch. For example, as Britain evolved into a representative democracy, it retained its monarch as the head of state (but with no real power).

Types of Representative Democracy In the modern world, there are basically two forms of representative democracy: presidential and parliamentary. In a *presidential democracy,* the lawmaking and law-enforcing branches of government are separate but equal. For example, in the United States, Congress is charged with the power to make laws, and the president is charged with the power to carry them out.

In a *parliamentary democracy,* the lawmaking and law-enforcing branches of government are united. In Britain, for example, the prime minister and the cabinet are members of the legislature, called Parliament, and are responsible to that body. Parliament thus both enacts the laws and carries them out.

1–2c Other Forms of Government

Monarchy, dictatorship, and *democracy* are three of the most common terms for describing systems of government, but there are others. For example, the term *aristocracy,* which in Greek means "rule by the best," describes a government run by members of old, noble families. Aristocracies have rarely had complete power, but have usually shared power with other forces, such as a monarch. *Plutocracy,* a somewhat similar form, means "government by the wealthy." The term typically refers to systems in which the rich have a disproportionate influence.

A difficult form of government for Americans to understand is *theocracy*—a term derived from the Greek words meaning "rule by the deity" or "rule by God." In a theocracy, there is no separation of church and state. Rather, the government rules according to religious precepts. In Iran, the Council of Guardians, an unelected group of religious leaders, ensures that laws and lawmakers conform to their interpretation of the teachings of Islam.

FOR CRITICAL THINKING Chinese Communist leader Mao Zedong (1893–1976) once said, "Political power grows out of the barrel of a gun." *Are there governments in today's world that tend to confirm Mao's point? Are there forms of government that disprove his statement?*

1–3 American Democracy

This country, with all its institutions, belongs to the people who inhabit it. Whenever they shall grow weary of the existing government, they can exercise their constitutional right to amend it, or their revolutionary right to dismember or overthrow it.[4]

With these words, Abraham Lincoln underscored the most fundamental concept of American government: that the people, not the government, are ultimately in control.

1–3a The British Legacy

In writing the U.S. Constitution, the framers incorporated two basic principles of government that had evolved in England: *limited government* and *representative government.* In a sense, then, the beginnings of our form of government are linked to events that occurred centuries

Learning Outcome 1–3

Summarize some of the basic principles of American democracy and basic American political values.

writings, the founders of our nation derived ideas to justify their rebellion against Britain and their establishment of a "government by the people."

Limited Government

At one time, the English monarch claimed to have almost unrestricted powers. This changed in 1215, when King John was forced by his nobles to accept the Magna Carta, or the Great Charter. This monumental document provided for a trial by a jury of one's peers (equals). It prohibited the taking of a free man's life, liberty, or property except through due process of law. The Magna Carta also forced the king to obtain the nobles' approval of any taxes he imposed on them. Government thus became a contract between the king and his subjects.

The importance of the Magna Carta to England cannot be overemphasized, because it clearly established the principle of **limited government**—a government on which strict limits are placed, usually by a constitution. This form of government is characterized by institutional checks to ensure that it serves public rather than private interests. Hence, the Magna Carta signaled the end of the monarch's absolute power. Although many of the rights provided under the original Magna Carta applied only to the nobility, the document formed the basis of the future constitutional government for England and eventually the United States.

limited government A form of government based on the principle that the powers of government should be clearly limited either through a written document or through wide public understanding. It is characterized by institutional checks to ensure that government serves public rather than private interests.

parliament The name of the national legislative body in countries governed by a parliamentary system, such as Britain and Canada.

social contract A voluntary agreement among individuals to create a government and to give that government adequate power to secure the mutual protection and welfare of all individuals.

natural rights Rights that are not bestowed by governments but are inherent within every man, woman, and child by virtue of the fact that he or she is a human being.

earlier in England. They are also linked to the writings of European philosophers, particularly the English political philosopher John Locke. From these

The English Bill of Rights

In 1689, the English Parliament passed the English Bill of Rights, which further extended the concept of limited government. This document included several important ideas:

- The king or queen could not interfere with parliamentary elections.

- The king or queen had to have Parliament's approval to levy (collect) taxes or to maintain an army.

- The king or queen had to rule with the consent of the people's representatives in Parliament.

The English colonists in North America were also English citizens, and nearly all of the major concepts in the English Bill of Rights became part of the American system of government.

Representative Government

In a representative government, the people, by whatever means, elect individuals to make governmental decisions for all of the citizens. Usually, these representatives of the people are elected to their offices for specific periods of time. In England, as mentioned earlier, this group of representatives is called a **parliament.** The English form of government provided a model for Americans to follow. Each of the American colonies established its own legislature.

Political Philosophy: Social Contracts and Natural Rights

Our democracy resulted from what can be viewed as a type of **social contract** among early Americans to create and abide by a set of governing rules. Social-contract theory was developed in the seventeenth and eighteenth centuries by philosophers such as John Locke (1632–1704). According to this theory, individuals voluntarily agree with one another, in a "social contract," to give up some of their freedoms to obtain the benefits of orderly government. The government is given adequate power to secure the mutual protection and welfare of all individuals.

Locke also argued that people are born with **natural rights** to life, liberty, and property. He theorized that the purpose of government was to protect those rights. If it did not, it would lose its legitimacy and need not

CORBIS YELLOW/RF

be obeyed. As you will read in Chapter 2, when the American colonists rebelled against British rule, such concepts as natural rights and a government based on a social contract became important theoretical tools in justifying the rebellion.

1–3b Principles of American Democracy

We can say that American democracy is based on five fundamental principles:

- *Equality in voting.* Citizens need equal opportunities to express their preferences about policies and leaders.

- *Individual freedom.* All individuals must have the greatest amount of freedom possible without interfering with the rights of others.

- *Equal protection of the law.* The law must entitle all persons to equal protection.

- *Majority rule and minority rights.* The majority should rule, while guaranteeing the rights of minorities.

- *Voluntary consent to be governed.* The people who make up a democracy must collectively agree to be governed by the rules laid down by their representatives.

These principles frame many of the political issues that you will read about in this book. They also frequently lie at the heart of America's political conflicts. Does the principle of minority rights mean that minorities should receive preferential treatment in hiring and firing decisions to make up for past mistreatment? Does the principle of individual freedom mean that individuals can express whatever they want on the Internet, including hateful, racist comments? Such conflicts over individual rights and freedoms and over society's priorities are natural and inevitable. Resolving these conflicts is what politics is all about. The key point is that Americans are frequently able to reach acceptable compromises because of their common political heritage.

1–3c American Political Values

Historically, as the nations of the world emerged, the boundaries of each nation normally coincided with the boundaries of a population that shared a common ethnic heritage, language, and culture.

From its beginnings as a nation, however, America has been defined less by the culture shared by its diverse population than by a set of ideas, or its political culture. A **political culture** can be defined as a patterned set of ideas, values, and ways of thinking about government and politics.

Our political culture is passed from one generation to another through families, schools, and the media. This culture is powerful enough to win over most new immigrants. Indeed, some immigrants come to America precisely because they are attracted by American values.

The ideals and standards that constitute American political culture are embodied in the Declaration of Independence, one of the founding documents of this nation, which will be discussed further in Chapter 2 and presented in its entirety in Appendix A. The political values outlined in the Declaration of Independence include natural rights (to life, liberty, and the pursuit of happiness), equality under the law, government by the consent of the governed, and limited government powers. In some ways, the Declaration of Independence defines Americans' sense of right and wrong. It presents a challenge to anyone who might wish to overthrow our democratic processes or deny our citizens their natural rights.

The rights to liberty, equality, and property are fundamental political values shared by most Americans. These values provide a basic framework for American political discourse and debate because they are shared, yet Americans often interpret their meanings quite differently. The result of these differences can be sharp conflict in the political arena.

Liberty The term *liberty* refers to a state of being free from external controls or restrictions. In the United States, the Constitution sets forth our *civil liberties* (see Chapter 4), including the freedom to practice whatever religion we choose and to be free from any state-imposed religion. Our liberties also include the freedom to speak freely on any topic and issue. Because people cannot govern themselves unless they are free to voice their opinions, freedom of speech is a basic requirement in a true democracy.

Clearly, though, if we are to live together with others, there have to be some restrictions on individual liberties. If people were allowed to do whatever they wished, without regard for the rights or liberties of others, pandemonium would result. Hence, a more accurate definition of **liberty**

political culture The set of ideas, values, and attitudes about government and the political process held by a community or a nation.

liberty The freedom of individuals to believe, act, and express themselves as they choose so long as doing so does not infringe on the rights of other individuals in the society.

would be as follows: *liberty is the freedom of individuals to believe, act, and express themselves as they choose so long as doing so does not infringe on the rights of other individuals in the society.*

While almost all Americans believe strongly in liberty, differing ideas of what, in practice, liberty should mean have led to some of our most heated political disputes. Should women be free to obtain abortions? Should employers be free to set the wages and working conditions of their employees? Should individuals be free to smoke marijuana? Over the years, Americans have been at odds over these and many other issues that concern liberty.

What function does "flag waving" have?

Equality

The goal of **equality** has always been a central part of American political culture. The Declaration of Independence confirmed the importance of equality to early Americans by stating, "We hold these Truths to be self-evident, that all Men are created equal." Because of the goal of equality, the Constitution prohibited the government from granting titles of nobility. Article I, Section 9, of the Constitution states, "No Title of Nobility shall be granted by the United States." (The Constitution did not prohibit slavery, however—see Chapter 2.)

But what, exactly, does equality mean? Does it mean simply political equality—the right to vote and run for political office? Does it mean that individuals should have equal opportunities to develop their talents and skills? What about those who are poor, suffer from disabilities, or are otherwise at a competitive disadvantage? Should it be the government's responsibility to ensure that such individuals also have equal opportunities?

Although most Americans believe that all per-

equality A concept that holds, at a minimum, that all people are entitled to equal protection under the law.

capitalism An economic system based on the private ownership of wealth-producing property, free markets, and freedom of contract. The privately owned corporation is the preeminent capitalist institution.

sons should have the opportunity to fulfill their potential, few contend that it is the government's responsibility to totally eliminate the economic and social differences that lead to unequal opportunities. Indeed, some contend that efforts to achieve equality, in the sense of equal treatment for all, are fundamentally incompatible with the value of liberty.

Property

As noted earlier, the English philosopher John Locke asserted that people are born with natural rights and that among these rights are life, liberty, and *property*. The Declaration of Independence makes a similar assertion: people are born with certain "unalienable" rights, including the right to life, liberty, and the pursuit of happiness. For Americans, property and the *pursuit of happiness* are closely related. Americans place a great value on land ownership, on material possessions, and on their businesses. Property gives its owners political power and the liberty to do what they want—within limits.

PROPERTY AND CAPITALISM. Private property in America is not limited to personal possessions such as automobiles and houses. Property also consists of assets that can be used to create and sell goods and services, such as factories, farms, and shops. Private ownership of wealth-producing property is at the heart of our capitalist economic system. **Capitalism** enjoys such widespread support in the United States that we can reasonably call it one of the nation's fundamental political values. In addition to the private ownership of productive property, capitalism is based on *free markets*—markets in which people can freely buy and sell goods, services, and financial investments without undue constraint by the government. Freedom to make binding contracts is another element of the capitalist system. The preeminent capitalist institution is the privately owned corporation.

CAPITALISM AND GOVERNMENT. Although capitalism is supported by almost all Americans, there is no equivalent agreement on the relationship between capitalism and the government. Is it best for the government to leave businesses alone in almost all circumstances—or would this lead to excessive inequality and unethical business practices that injure consumers? As with the values of liberty and equality, Americans are divided over what the right to property should mean.

1–3d Political Values and a Divided Electorate

Differences among Americans in interpreting our collectively held values underlie the division between the Republican and Democratic parties. Recent election results suggest that the voters are split right down the middle. Elections have often been close. In 2000, for example, Republican George W. Bush narrowly won the presidency in a contested election. Since then, support for the parties has swung back and forth without giving either one a long-term advantage.

The Democrats in Power Public rejection of the war in Iraq was enough to give the Democrats control of Congress in the 2006 elections. The economic crisis of 2008 then handed Democrat Barack Obama the presidency and gave the Democrats large margins in the U.S. House and Senate. Within a year, many voters had turned away from the Democrats, believing that they had failed to heal the economy and were letting the government grow too fast. In 2010, Republicans took control of the House, gained six senators and six governors, and won control of many state legislatures.

Republican Ambitions Some argue that the Democrats overreached in 2009 and 2010, but the Republicans may have done the same in the following years. For example, House Republicans, many of them aligned with the Tea Party movement, proposed changes to the government's Medicare and Medicaid programs that would have made them less generous. (Medicare is a federal health-insurance program for the elderly, and Medicaid provides health-care funding for the poor, including the elderly poor.) By 2012, many moderate voters were apparently concerned that Republican threats to popular social programs outweighed worries about Democratic fondness for "big government."

The 2012 Elections In the 2012 elections, President Barack Obama was reelected over Republican Mitt Romney by a 3.9 percent margin. Many observers had predicted that the Democrats would lose control of the U.S. Senate, but they gained two seats. In

the U.S. House, however, the Democrats won 201 seats to the Republicans' 234, leaving the Republicans again in control. The election results meant that Republican plans for a more limited government were frustrated. The health-care reforms known as Obamacare would survive. Finally, in the December 2012 negotiations to resolve the so-called fiscal cliff crisis, Republicans were forced to accept tax rate increases on high-income taxpayers.

1–3e Political Values in a Changing Society

From the earliest English and European settlers to the many cultural groups that today call America their home, American society has always been multicultural. Until recently, most Americans accepted that American society included numerous ethnic and cultural groups, but they expected that the members of these groups would abandon their cultural distinctions and assimilate the language and customs of earlier Americans. One of the outgrowths of the civil rights movement of the 1960s, however, was an emphasis on *multiculturalism,* the belief that the many cultures that make up American society should remain distinct and be protected—and even encouraged—by our laws.

Despite the growth in multiculturalism, Americans of all backgrounds remain committed to the values described in the last few sections of this text. Inevitably, however, different groups will interpret these values in varying ways, thus adding to our political divisions. African Americans, for example, given their collective history, will often have a different sense of what equality means than do Americans whose ancestors came from Europe.

Race and Ethicity The racial and ethnic makeup of the United States has changed dramatically in the last two decades and will continue to change (see Figure 1–2 on the following page). Already, non-Hispanic whites are a minority in California. For the nation as a whole, non-Hispanic whites will be in the minority before 2050. Some Americans fear that rising numbers of immigrants will threaten traditional American political values and culture. Others are confident that newcomers will adopt American values. We take a closer look at the immigration issue in this chapter's *Join the Debate* feature on page 15.

An Older Society In 2010, Americans aged 65 or above made up 13 percent of the total population. By 2040, however, that figure is expected to reach 20 percent. The aging of America means that in future years there will be more retired people collecting Social Security, Medicare, and private pensions, compared with the number of working adults. Inevitably, the question of how to share the national income among the generations will become an ever-greater problem. In many foreign countries, however, the aging population poses a much greater threat than in the United States. Our population is expected to grow throughout the coming century. Nations such as Germany, Japan, Russia, and even China can expect to see their populations shrink, which will make it much harder for them to support their older citizens.

FOR CRITICAL THINKING

Describe some ways in which the values of equality and property can come into conflict with each other. *Many people see liberty and property as highly compatible values, but can you think of ways in which these values, too, might come into conflict?*

1–4 American Political Ideology

In a general sense, **ideology** refers to a system of political ideas. These ideas typically are rooted in religious or philosophical beliefs about human nature, society, and government.

When it comes to ideology, Americans are often placed in two broad political camps: conservatives and liberals. The term *conservative* originally referred to persons who wished to conserve—keep—traditional social and political habits and institutions. The term *liberal* referred to those who wanted to be free from tradition and to establish new policies and practices. In today's American political arena, however, these simple definitions of *liberalism* and *conservatism* are incomplete. Both terms mean much more.

ideology Generally, a system of political ideas that are rooted in religious or philosophical beliefs concerning human nature, society, and government.

conservatism A set of political beliefs that include a limited role for the national government in helping individuals and in the economic affairs of the nation, as well as support for traditional values and lifestyles.

1–4a Conservatism

Modern American **conservatism** does indeed value traditions—specifically, American ones. For

---

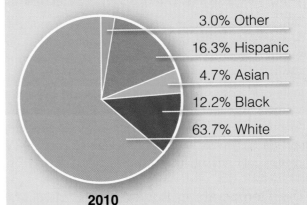

FIGURE 1–2

Distribution of the U.S. Population by Race and Hispanic Origin, 2010 to 2050

By 2050, minorities will constitute a majority of the U.S. population.

2010
- 3.0% Other
- 16.3% Hispanic
- 4.7% Asian
- 12.2% Black
- 63.7% White

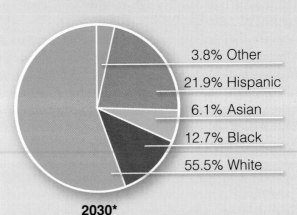

2030*
- 3.8% Other
- 21.9% Hispanic
- 6.1% Asian
- 12.7% Black
- 55.5% White

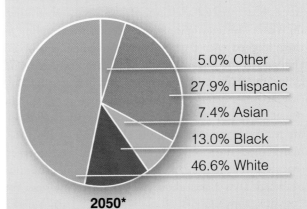

2050*
- 5.0% Other
- 27.9% Hispanic
- 7.4% Asian
- 13.0% Black
- 46.6% White

*Data for 2030 and 2050 are projections.

Figures do not necessarily sum to 100%, because of rounding. Hispanics may be of any race. The chart categories "White," "Black," "Asian," and "Other" are limited to non-Hispanics.
"Other" consists of the following non-Hispanic groups: "American Indian," "Alaska Native," "Native Hawaiian," "Other Pacific Islander," and "Two or More Races."
Sources: U.S. Bureau of the Census and authors' calculations.

Should We Encourage Immigration?

Most discussions about immigration focus on what we should do about illegal immigration, a topic we will address later in this text. For now, we consider immigration in general. America was founded by immigrants, and few restrictions on immigration existed until the twentieth century. Should the federal government change our immigration laws to allow more foreigners to immigrate legally and eventually become citizens of the United States? Or should we reduce immigration because we already have so many immigrants that they threaten to dilute our national character?

What Was Good Once Is Not Good Now

Those who oppose additional immigration admit that we are a nation founded by immigrants. Immigration opponents say, however, that new immigrants resist assimilation into American society and do not acquire core American values such as individualism and self-reliance. These opponents believe that the loyalty of new immigrants—even well-educated ones—to the United States and its core culture is fragile.

Increased legal immigration will bring in more low-skilled, poorly educated residents. That is not going to help our economy. Some second- and third-generation Latinos, for example, have fallen into the underclass culture. If current immigration patterns hold, in the future we will see a decline in U.S. literacy and numeracy. If we want to continue to compete in the global economy, we must have an advanced labor force. If we allow some immigration, we should limit it, as much as possible, to professionals and highly skilled tradespeople.

A Nation Founded by Immigrants Needs More of Them

Immigration supporters believe that we benefit when people flow across borders. Indeed, if we made it easier for talented foreigners to move to this country, America would become even richer than it is now. Immigrants fill jobs, but they also create jobs. A quarter of the engineering and technology companies started in the United States from 1995 to 2005 had at least one founder who was foreign-born. Some of the world's brightest brains and most cutting-edge innovators come to the United States to study—and often to stay. Foreign students earn 44 percent of U.S. science and engineering doctorates. Yet many of these students are forced to leave the country after graduation because there are not enough visas available for professionals.

Immigration supporters are aware that many immigrants are unskilled. The United States, however, has jobs available at the bottom as well as the top. Even with unemployment at 10 percent in 2009 and 2010, farmers on the West Coast still could not find U.S. citizens willing to pick fruits and vegetables. And as far as assimilation is concerned, studies have shown that the new immigrants assimilate just as quickly as did newly arrived immigrants in past decades.

FOR CRITICAL ANALYSIS What are some of the reasons that people from around the world want to come to America and become U.S. citizens?

much of U.S. history, business enterprise was largely free from government control or regulation. That freedom began to break down during the administration of Franklin D. Roosevelt (1933–1945). Roosevelt's New Deal programs, launched in an attempt to counter the effects of the Great Depression, involved the government in the American economy to an extent previously unknown. Roosevelt gave conservatives a common cause: opposition to the New Deal and to big government. The tradition that conservatives sought to maintain was a version of capitalism that was free of government regulation or control.

The Conservative Movement The emergence of the **conservative movement** in the 1950s and 1960s was essential to the development of modern conservatism. Previously, economic

conservative movement An ideological movement that arose in the 1950s and 1960s and continues to shape conservative beliefs.

#SenateMustAct

U.S. House Speaker John Boehner speaking on the eve of the "government shutdown" crisis of October 2013. After the 2012 elections, Boehner was the highest-ranking Republican in National office. What is his ideology?

ally optimum. Conservatives believe that individuals and families should take responsibility for their own economic circumstances, and if that means that some people have less, so be it. Conservatives also place a high value on the principle of order, on family values, and on patriotism. Conservatism has always included those who want society and the government to reflect traditional religious values, and Christian conservatives remain an important part of the conservative coalition today.

1–4b Liberalism

While modern American **liberalism** can trace its roots to the New Deal programs of Franklin D. Roosevelt, the ideology did not take its fully modern form until the 1960s, during the Johnson administration. Johnson went well beyond the programs of Roosevelt with new economic initiatives, such as Medicare and Medicaid. These programs—and more recent health-care reforms—reflect the strong liberal belief that the social and economic outcomes that exist in the absence of government action are frequently unfair. Conservatives commonly accuse liberals of valuing "big government" for its own sake. Liberals reject that characterization and argue that big government is simply a necessary tool for promoting the common welfare.

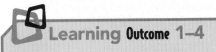

Learning Outcome 1–4

Define common American ideological positions, such as "conservatism" and "liberalism."

conservatives were often seen as individuals who feared that government activity might personally cost them wealth or power. The conservative movement, in contrast, was clearly ideological. It provided a complete way of viewing the world, and it attracted millions of followers who were not necessarily motivated by narrow economic self-interest. The conservative movement emerged as a major force in 1964, when Arizona senator Barry Goldwater won the Republican presidential nomination on a relatively radical platform. Goldwater was soundly defeated by Democrat Lyndon B. Johnson (1963–1969). In 1980, however, Republican Ronald Reagan became the first "movement conservative" to win the White House.

The Civil Rights Revolution In the 1960s, liberals in the Democratic Party were able to commit their party firmly to the cause of African American equality, permanently overriding those Democratic conservatives who still supported legal segregation of the races. In a matching development, conservatives in the Republican Party began to appeal to traditionalist whites who were upset by the African American civil rights movement. As the party

liberalism A set of political beliefs that include the advocacy of active government, including government intervention to improve the welfare of individuals and to protect civil rights.

Conservatism Today

A key element in conservative thinking is the belief that the distribution of social and economic benefits that would exist if the government took little or no action is usu-

SOCIAL MEDIA
In Politics

You can follow top conservative and liberal opinion pieces on Facebook and Twitter. In either system, search on "national review" for conservative commentary. For a liberal take on the issues, try "think progress" on either Facebook or Twitter.

Hillary Clinton has been the First Lady, a senator from New York, a presidential candidate, and during President Obama's first term, the U.S. secretary of state. If she chooses to run for president in 2016, she will have very strong support within the Democratic Party. Is Clinton a liberal?

Other Liberal Values The Vietnam War (1965–1975) also influenced liberal thinking. Although American participation in the conflict was initiated by President Johnson, liberals swung against the war more strongly than other Americans. Liberalism therefore came to include a relatively negative view of American military initiatives abroad. (That distrust has declined in recent years, however.)

Liberals strongly favor the separation of church and state. They generally think that the government should avoid laws that endorse or impose traditional religious values. These beliefs sharply contrast with those of religious conservatives. In this area, at least, liberals do not stand for big government, but rather the reverse.

Liberals and Progressives Not all political labels are equally popular, and the term *liberal* has taken a particular beating in the political wars of the last several decades. One result is that most politicians who might have called themselves liberals in the past have labeled their philosophy **progressivism** instead. The term *progressive* dates back to the first years of the twentieth century, when it referred to a reform movement that was active in both major political parties. Later, the progressive label fell into disuse, until it was resurrected in recent years.

1–4c The Traditional Political Spectrum

Traditionally, liberalism and conservatism have been regarded as falling within a political spectrum that ranges from the left to the right. As Figure 1–3 below illustrates, modern

> **progressivism** An alternative, more popular term for the set of political beliefs also known as liberalism.

of Lincoln, the Republicans had once been the natural political home of African Americans. This was no longer true. Support for minority rights of all kinds became an integral part of liberal ideology, while conservatism came to include skepticism toward minority claims.

FIGURE 1-3 The Traditional Political Spectrum

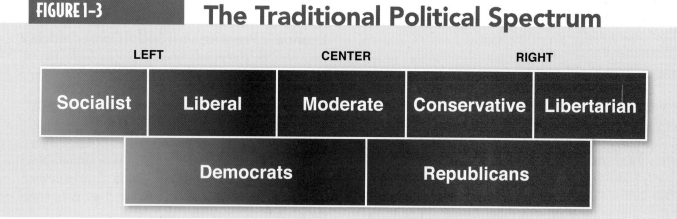

LEFT		CENTER		RIGHT
Socialist	Liberal	Moderate	Conservative	Libertarian

Democrats	Republicans

conservatives typically identify themselves politically as Republicans. Similarly, liberals—or progressives—identify with the Democratic Party. The identification of the parties with specific ideologies is clear today but was not always so noticeable in the past. Conservative Democrats and liberal Republicans were once common, but they are now rare.

People whose views fall in the middle of the traditional political spectrum are generally called **moderates.** By definition, moderates do not classify themselves as either liberal or conservative. Moderates may vote for either Republicans or Democrats, although in public opinion polls Democrats are about twice as likely as Republicans to identify themselves as moderates. Still, a large number of moderates do not support either major political party and often describe themselves as *independent* (see Chapter 7).

1–4d Beyond Conservatism and Liberalism

Many Americans do not adhere firmly to a particular political ideology. Some are not interested in political issues. Others may have opinions that do not neatly fit under the liberal or conservative label. For example, conservatives typically support restrictions on the availability of abortion. They also may favor banning the procedure altogether. Liberals usually favor the right to have an abortion. Many liberals believe that the government ought to guarantee that everyone can find a job. Conservatives generally reject this idea. Millions of Americans, however, support restrictions on abortion while supporting government jobs programs. Many other citizens would oppose both of these positions. Conservatism and liberalism, in other words, are not the only ideological possibilities.

moderates Persons whose views fall in the middle of the political spectrum.

socialism A political ideology that lies to the left of liberalism on the traditional political spectrum. Socialists are scarce in the United States but common in many other countries.

libertarianism The belief that government should do as little as possible, not only in the economic sphere, but also in regulating morality and personal behavior.

Tea Party movement A grassroots conservative movement that arose in 2009 after Barack Obama became president. The movement opposes big government and current levels of taxation, and also rejects political compromise.

Socialism To the left of liberalism on the traditional ideological spectrum lies **socialism.** This ideology has few adherents in the United States, although a small handful of Democrats and independents accept the label. In much of the world, however, the main left-of-center party describes itself as socialist. Socialists have a stronger commitment to egalitarianism than do U.S. liberals and a greater tolerance for strong government. Indeed, in the first half of the twentieth century, most socialists advocated government ownership of major businesses. Few European or American socialists endorse such proposals today, however.

Western socialists strongly support democracy, but early in the twentieth century an ultra-left breakaway from the socialist movement—the *Communists*—established a series of brutal dictatorships, initially in Russia (the Soviet Union). Communists remain in power in China and a few other nations. Despite Communist rule, in recent years capitalist businesses have thrived in China.

Libertarianism Even as socialism is weak in America compared with the rest of the world, the right-of-center ideology of **libertarianism** is unusually strong. Libertarians oppose almost all government regulation of the economy and government redistribution of income.

Many ardent conservatives, such as the members of the **Tea Party movement,** share these beliefs. What distinguishes true libertarians from Tea Party supporters, however, is that libertarians also oppose government involvement in issues of private morality. In this belief, they often have more in common with liberals than they do with conservatives. For most people, however, economic issues remain the more important ones, and a majority of libertarians ally with conservatives politically and support the Republicans.

Economic Progressives, Social Conservatives

Many other voters are liberal on economic issues even as they favor conservative positions on social matters. These people favor government intervention to promote both economic "fairness" *and* moral values. Low-income people frequently are economic progressives and social conservatives. A large number of African Americans and Hispanics fall into this camp. While it is widespread within the electorate, this "anti-libertarian" point of view has no agreed-upon name.

In sum, millions of Americans do not fit neatly into the traditional liberal-conservative spectrum. We illustrate an alternative, two-dimensional political classification in Figure 1–4.

FOR CRITICAL THINKING

Suppose you are a representative in Congress and ran for office on a platform that clearly articulated your strong beliefs. *Should you be willing to compromise with others in the hopes of obtaining at least some of what you favor—or is it better to stand on principle, even if you lose?*

FIGURE 1–4

A Two-Dimensional
Political Classification

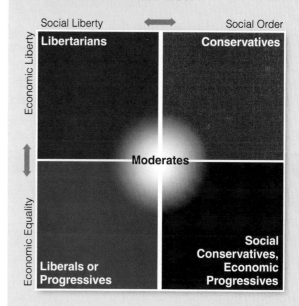

AMERICA AT
ODDS Key Conflicts in America in the Twenty-First Century

As you learned in this chapter, Americans are united by a common political culture. At the same time, however, Americans are at odds over how much weight should be given to various fundamental principles. We can summarize these most basic disputes as follows:

- How large should our government be? Should it offer a wide range of services, along with the resulting taxes—or should it provide relatively few services and collect less in taxes?

- Should businesses be strictly regulated to ensure the common good—or should regulation be minimized to promote economic freedom and growth?

- More generally, should we place a greater value on economic liberty and property rights—or on economic egalitarianism and improving the condition of those who are less well-off?

- How active should the government be in promoting moral behavior? Should the government support traditional values—or place a high value on social liberty?

- Are progressive or liberal policies best for the nation—or does conservatism provide better answers? Alternatively, is libertarianism the solution—or social conservatism combined with progressive economic policies?

STUDY TOOLS

Ready to study?

- **Review** what you've read with the quiz below.
- Check your answers on the **Chapter in Review** card at the back of the book.
- For any questions you miss, read the corresponding **Learning Outcome** section again to prepare for class and your exam.
- Rip out and study the **Chapter in Review** card (at the back of the book).

Fill-In

Learning Outcome 1–1

1. _____ can best be defined as the individuals and institutions that make society's rules and also possess the power and authority to enforce those rules.

2. In any country, government generally serves at least three essential purposes: _____.

Learning Outcome 1–2

3. In an _____, the power and authority of the government are in the hands of a single person.

4. In a _____, the will of the majority is expressed through groups of individuals elected by the people to act as their representatives.

Learning Outcome 1–3

5. The philosopher John Locke argued that people are born with natural rights to _____.

6. American democracy is based on five fundamental principles: _____.

Learning Outcome 1–4

7. When it comes to ideology, Americans are often placed in two broad political camps: _____.

8. People whose views fall in the middle of the traditional political spectrum are generally called _____.

9. _____ oppose almost all government regulation of the economy and government redistribution of income, while also opposing government involvement in issues of private morality.

Multiple Choice

Learning Outcome 1–1

10. Political scientist Harold Lasswell defined _____ as the process of determining "who gets what, when, and how" in a society.
    a. government   b. power   c. politics

Learning Outcome 1–2

11. The system of government in the United States is best described as a _____ democracy.
    a. parliamentary   b. presidential   c. direct

12. In _____, there is no separation of church and state. Rather, the government rules according to religious precepts.
    a. a plutocracy   b. an aristocracy   c. a theocracy

Learning Outcome 1–3

13. Which of the following best describes a social contract?
    a. The set of ideas, values, and attitudes about government and the political process held by a community or a nation.

    b. A voluntary agreement among individuals to create a government and to give that government adequate power to secure the mutual protection and welfare of all individuals.

    c. An economic system based on the private ownership of wealth-producing property, free markets, and freedom of contract.

14. Because of the political value of _____, Article I, Section 9, of the U.S. Constitution prohibits the government from granting titles of nobility.
    a. equality   b. liberty   c. multiculturalism

Learning Outcome 1–4

15. American liberalism took its fully modern form in the
    a. 1960s, during the administration of Lyndon Johnson.
    b. 1990s, during the administration of Bill Clinton.
    c. 2000s, during the administration of Barack Obama.

The Constitution

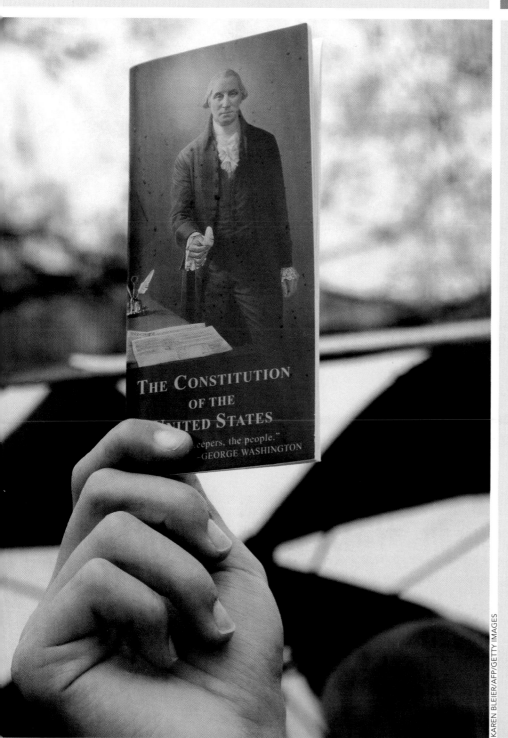

THE CONSTITUTION
OF THE
NITED STATES
...eepers, the people."
—GEORGE WASHINGTON

LearningOutcomes

The **Learning Outcomes** labeled 1 through 5 are designed to help improve your understanding of the chapter. After reading this chapter, you should be able to:

2–1 Point out some of the influences on the American political tradition in the colonial years.

2–2 Explain why the American colonies rebelled against Britain.

2–3 Describe the structure of government established by the Articles of Confederation and some of the strengths and weaknesses of the Articles.

2–4 List some of the major compromises made by the delegates at the Constitutional Convention, and discuss the Federalist and Anti-Federalist positions on ratifying the Constitution.

2–5 Summarize the Constitution's major principles of government, and describe how the Constitution can be amended.

Remember to visit page 44 for additional Study Tools

ODDS
Was the United States Meant to Be a Christian Nation?

© LORI HOWARD/SHUTTERSTOCK.COM

The Pilgrims sought to establish a religious colony when they landed in New England. In early Virginia, failure to attend Church of England services was a serious crime. By the time the Constitution was written, several states still had established (state-supported) churches. Christian beliefs were strong among the general population in that era. Most Americans considered themselves to be part of a Christian—indeed, a Protestant—people. Anti-Catholicism was widespread.

Yet the Declaration of Independence never refers to Christ. The Constitution does not contain the word *God*. It refers to religion twice. Article VI states: "no religious Test shall ever be required as a Qualification to any Office or public Trust under the United States." The world-famous First Amendment begins: "Congress shall make no law respecting an establishment of religion, or prohibiting the free exercise thereof."

Considering these facts, was the United States meant to be a Christian nation—or not? The answer to that question depends in part on what we mean by "Christian nation."

Yes, America Is a Christian Nation

By *nation*, do we mean a country's government or its people? If we say "people," it is hard to deny that the United States has been a Christian nation. Today, 78.5 percent of all Americans consider themselves to be Christians. Some conservatives, however, have argued that "Christian nation" should mean more than that. Most of the founders, even those whose private commitment to Christianity was questionable, agreed that religion was essential to a just and harmonious society. The founders would have been astonished to learn that public school teachers today may not lead their students in prayer. According to Christian conservatives, students should also learn that America has a divine mission in the world. In this view, constitutional principles are inseparable from Christianity, and the First Amendment means only that the government must not pick and choose among Christian denominations. Limits on "anti-Western" religions—such as bans on Islamic mosques—are appropriate.

The "Christian Nation" Idea Would Violate Our Rights

It is hard to imagine how the founders could have sought to establish a Christian nation when many of them were not Christians at all, in any modern sense. Consider our first five presidents. George Washington never took communion or referred to Christ in his speeches and correspondence. John Adams was a Unitarian—that is, he did not believe that Jesus was divine. Thomas Jefferson thought likewise. It is impossible to say what James Madison and James Monroe believed, because they avoided issues of doctrine even in their private correspondence. Not until Andrew Jackson (1829–1837) did we have a president who openly endorsed Christianity in the way we now expect of political candidates.

Opponents of the Christian nation concept argue that the First Amendment should be interpreted strictly. Whatever the beliefs of the majority, it is essential to tolerate the adherents of all religions—including Muslims and, for that matter, atheists. This is an issue about which the founders were quite explicit.

Where do you stand?

1. Christian conservatives argue that discrimination against Christians is widespread in modern America. Is anti-Christian discrimination a problem? Why or why not?
2. Should religiously affiliated colleges or hospitals have a right to reject health-insurance programs that pay for contraception? Should profit-making businesses have such a right?

Explore this issue online

- For a wealth of information about the religious beliefs and practices of Americans, visit the Web site of the Pew Forum on Religion and Public Life. Search on "pew religion."
- The First Amendment Center is a resource for information on First Amendment issues, including issues of religious freedom. Find its site by searching on its name.

Introduction

The Constitution, which was written more than two hundred years ago, continues to be the supreme law of the land. Time and again, its provisions have been adapted to the changing needs and conditions of society. The challenge before today's citizens and political leaders is to find a way to apply those provisions to a society and an economy that could not possibly have been anticipated by the founders. Will the Constitution survive this challenge? Most Americans assume that it will—and with good reason: no other written constitution in the world today is as old as the U.S. Constitution.

To understand the principles of government set forth in the Constitution, you have to go back to the beginnings of our nation's history.

2–1 The Beginnings of American Government

When the framers of the Constitution met in Philadelphia in 1787, they brought with them some valuable political assets. One asset was their English political heritage (see Chapter 1). Another was the hands-on political experience they had acquired during the colonial era. Their political knowledge and experience enabled them to establish a constitution that could meet not only the needs of their own time but also the needs of generations to come.

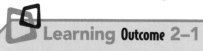

Learning Outcome 2–1

Point out some of the influences on the American political tradition in the colonial years.

The American colonies had been settled by individuals from many nations, including France, Germany, Ireland, the Netherlands, Spain, and Sweden. The majority of the colonists, though, came from England and Scotland. The British colonies in North America were established by private individuals and private trading companies and were under the rule of the British Crown. The colonies, which were located along the Atlantic seaboard of today's United States, eventually numbered thirteen.

Although American politics owes much to the English political tradition, the colonists actually derived most of their understanding of social compacts, the rights of the people, limited government, and representative government from their own experiences. Years before Parliament adopted the English Bill of Rights or John Locke wrote his *Two Treatises on Government* (1690),

the American colonists were putting the ideas expressed in those documents into practice.

2–1a The First English Settlements

The first permanent English settlement in North America was Jamestown, in what is now Virginia.[1] Jamestown was established in 1607 as a trading post of the Virginia Company of London.[2]

The first New England colony was founded by the Plymouth Company in 1620 at Plymouth, Massachusetts. Most of the settlers at Plymouth were Pilgrims, a group of English Protestants who came to the New World on the ship *Mayflower*. (We discussed religion and the Constitution in the chapter-opening *America at Odds* feature.) Even before the Pilgrims went ashore, they drew up the **Mayflower Compact,** in which they set up a government and promised to obey its laws.

The reason for the compact was that the group was outside the territory assigned to the Virginia Company, which had arranged for them to settle in what is now New York, not Massachusetts. Fearing that some of the passengers might decide that they were no longer subject to any rules of civil order, the leaders on board the *Mayflower* agreed that some form of governmental authority was necessary.

The Mayflower Compact was essentially a social contract. It has historical significance because it was the first of a series of similar contracts among the colonists to establish fundamental rules of government.[3]

The Massachusetts Bay Colony was established as another trading outpost in New England in 1630. In 1639, some of the Pilgrims at Plymouth, who felt that they were being persecuted by the Massachusetts Bay Colony, left Plymouth and settled in what is now Connecticut. They developed America's first written constitution, which was called the Fundamental Orders of Connecticut. This document called for the laws to be made by an assembly of elected representatives from each town. The document also provided for the popular election of a governor and judges.

Other colonies, in turn, established fundamental governing rules. The Massachusetts Body of Liberties protected individual rights. The Pennsylvania Frame of Government, passed in 1682, and the Pennsylvania Charter of Privileges of 1701 established principles that were later expressed in

Mayflower Compact
A document drawn up by Pilgrim leaders in 1620 on the ship *Mayflower*. The document stated that laws were to be made for the general good of the people.

the U.S. Constitution and **Bill of Rights** (the first ten amendments to the Constitution). By 1732, all thirteen colonies had been established, each with its own political documents and constitution (see Figure 2–1).

2–1b Colonial Legislatures

As mentioned, the British colonies in America were under the rule of the British monarchy. Britain, however, was thousands of miles away—it took two months to sail across the Atlantic. Thus, to a significant extent, colonial legislatures carried on the "nuts and bolts" of colonial government. These legislatures, or *representative assemblies,* consisted of representatives elected by the colonists. The earliest colonial legislature was the Virginia House of Burgesses, established in 1619. By the time of the American Revolution, all of the colonies had representative assemblies. Many had been in existence for more than a hundred years.

Through their participation in colonial governments, the colonists gained crucial political experience. Colonial leaders became familiar with the practical problems of governing. They learned how to build coalitions among groups with diverse interests and how to make compromises. Indeed, by the time of the American Revolution in 1776, Americans had formed a complex, sophisticated political system.

The colonists benefited from their political experiences. They were quickly able to establish their own constitutions and state systems of government after they declared their independence from Britain in 1776. Eventually, they were able to set up a national government as well.

FOR CRITICAL THINKING

When first founded, each of the colonies had very few people. *How might that have made it easier to draw up founding documents?*

Bill of Rights The first ten amendments to the U.S. Constitution. They list the freedoms—such as the freedoms of speech, press, and religion—that a citizen enjoys and that cannot be infringed on by the government.

FIGURE 2–1

The Thirteen Colonies
before the American Revolution

The western boundary of the colonies was set by the Proclamation Line of 1763, which banned European settlement in western territories that were reserved for Native Americans. Note that Vermont was claimed by both New York and New Hampshire.

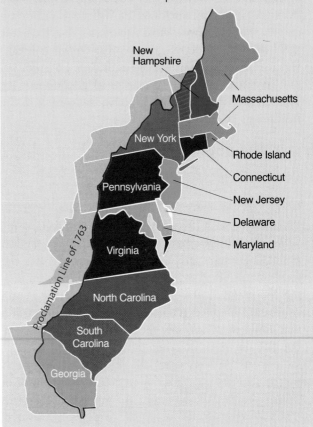

2–2 The Rebellion of the Colonists

Scholars of the American Revolution point out that by and large, the American colonists did not want to become independent of Britain. For the majority of the colonists, Britain was the homeland, and ties of loyalty were strong. Why, then, did the colonists revolt against Britain and declare their independence? What happened to sever the political, economic, and emotional bonds that tied the colonists to Britain? The answers to these questions lie in a series of events in the mid-1700s that culminated in a change in British policy toward the colonies. Table 2–1 on the following page shows some major political events in early U.S. history.

One of these events was the Seven Years' War (1756–1763) between Britain and France, which Americans often refer to as the French and Indian War. The British victory in the Seven Years' War permanently altered the relationship between Britain and its American colonies. After successfully ousting

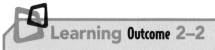

Explain why the American colonies rebelled against Britain.

the French from North America, the British expanded their authority over the colonies. To pay its war debts and to finance the defense of its expanded North American empire, Britain needed revenues. The British government decided to obtain some of these revenues by imposing taxes on the American colonists and exercising more direct control over colonial trade.

At the same time, Americans were beginning to distrust the expanding British presence in the colonies. Having fought alongside British forces, Americans thought that they deserved more credit for the victory. The British, however, attributed the victory solely to their own effort.

TABLE 2-1

Significant Events in Early U.S. Political History

1607	Jamestown established; Virginia Company lands settlers.
1620	Mayflower Compact signed.
1630	Massachusetts Bay Colony set up.
1639	Fundamental Orders of Connecticut adopted.
1641	Massachusetts Body of Liberties adopted.
1682	Pennsylvania Frame of Government passed.
1701	Pennsylvania Charter of Privileges written.
1732	Last of thirteen colonies established (Georgia).
1756	French and Indian War declared.
1765	Stamp Act; Stamp Act Congress meets.
1773	Boston Tea Party.
1774	First Continental Congress meets.
1775	Second Continental Congress; Revolutionary War begins.
1776	Declaration of Independence signed.
1777	Articles of Confederation drafted.
1781	Last state signs Articles of Confederation.
1783	"Critical period" in U.S. history begins; weak national government until 1789.
1786	Shays' Rebellion.
1787	Constitutional Convention held.
1788	Constitution ratified.
1791	Bill of Rights ratified.

Furthermore, the colonists began to develop a sense of identity separate from the British. Americans were shocked at the behavior of some of the British soldiers and the cruel punishments meted out to enforce discipline among the British troops. The British, in turn, had little good to say about the colonists alongside whom they had fought. They considered them brutish, uncivilized, and undisciplined. It was during this time that the colonists began to use the word *American* to describe themselves.

2-2a "Taxation without Representation"

In 1764, the British Parliament passed the Sugar Act, which imposed a tax on all sugar imported into the American colonies. Some colonists, particularly in Massachusetts, vigorously opposed this tax and proposed a boycott of certain British imports. This boycott developed into a "nonimportation" movement that soon spread to other colonies.

The Stamp Act of 1765 The following year, in 1765, Parliament passed the Stamp Act, which imposed the first direct tax on the colonists. Under the act, all legal documents and newspapers, as well as certain other items, including playing cards and dice, had to use specially embossed (stamped) paper that was purchased from the government.

The Stamp Act generated even stronger resentment among the colonists than the Sugar Act. James Otis, Jr., a Massachusetts attorney, declared that there could be "no taxation without representation." The American colonists were not represented in the British Parliament. They viewed Parliament's attempts to tax them as contrary to the principle of representative government. The British saw the matter differently. From the British perspective, it was only fair that the colonists pay taxes to help support the costs incurred by the British government in defending its American territories and maintaining the troops that were permanently stationed in the colonies following the Seven Years' War.

In October 1765, nine of the thirteen colonies sent delegates to the Stamp Act Congress in New York City. The delegates prepared a declaration of rights and grievances, which they sent to King George III. This action marked the first time that a majority of the colonies had joined together to oppose British rule. The British Parliament repealed the Stamp Act.

Further Taxes and the Coercive Acts Soon, however, Parliament passed new laws designed to bind the colonies more tightly to the central government

During the Boston Tea Party in 1773, the colonists dumped chests of British tea into Boston Harbor as a gesture of tax protest.

that all colonies select delegates to send to Philadelphia for the congress.

The First Continental Congress

The **First Continental Congress** met on September 5, 1774, at Carpenter's Hall in Philadelphia. Of the thirteen colonies, only Georgia did not participate. The congress decided that the colonies should send a petition to King George III to explain their grievances, which they did. The congress also called for a continued boycott of British goods and required each colony to establish an army.

To enforce the boycott and other acts of resistance against Britain, the delegates to the First Continental Congress urged that "a committee be chosen in every county, city and town . . . whose business it shall be attentively to observe the conduct of all persons." The committees of "safety" or "observation," as they were called, organized militias, held special courts, and suppressed the opinions of those who remained loyal to the British Crown. Committee members spied on neighbors' activities and reported to the press the names of those who violated the boycott against Britain. The names were then printed in the local papers, and the transgressors were harassed and ridiculed in their communities.

The Second Continental Congress

Almost immediately after receiving the petition from the First Continental Congress, the British government condemned the actions of the congress as open acts of rebellion. Britain responded with even stricter and more repressive measures. On April 19, 1775, British soldiers (Redcoats) fought against colonial citizen soldiers (Minutemen) in the towns of Lexington and Concord in Massachusetts—the first battles of the American Revolution.

Less than a month later, delegates from all thirteen colonies gathered in Pennsylvania for the **Second Continental Congress,** which immediately assumed the powers of a central government. The Second Continental Congress declared that the militiamen who had gathered around Boston were now a full army. It also named George Washington, a delegate to the congress who had some military experience, as its commander in chief.

The delegates to the Second Continental Congress still intended to reach a peaceful settlement with the British Parliament. One declaration stated specifically that "we [the congress] have not raised armies with ambitious designs of separating from Britain, and establishing independent States." The continued

in London. Laws that imposed taxes on glass, paint, lead, and many other items were passed in 1767. The colonists protested by boycotting all British goods. In 1773, anger over taxation reached a powerful climax at the Boston Tea Party, in which colonists dressed as Mohawk Indians dumped almost 350 chests of British tea into Boston Harbor as a gesture of tax protest.[4]

The British Parliament was quick to respond to the Tea Party. In 1774, Parliament passed the Coercive Acts (sometimes called the "Intolerable Acts"), which closed Boston Harbor and placed the government of Massachusetts under direct British control.

First Continental Congress A gathering of delegates from twelve of the thirteen colonies, held in 1774 to protest the Coercive Acts.

Second Continental Congress The congress of the colonies that met in 1775 to assume the powers of a central government and to establish an army.

2–2b The Continental Congresses

In response to the "Intolerable Acts," New York, Pennsylvania, and Rhode Island proposed a colonial congress. The Massachusetts House of Representatives requested attempts to effect a reconciliation with Britain, even after the outbreak of fighting, underscore the colonists' reluctance to sever their relationship with the home country.

2-2c Breaking the Ties: Independence

Public debate about the problems with Britain continued to rage, but the stage had been set for declaring independence. One of the most rousing arguments in favor of independence was presented by Thomas Paine, a former English schoolmaster and corset maker, who wrote a pamphlet called *Common Sense.*

Paine's *Common Sense* Paine's pamphlet was published in Philadelphia in January 1776. In it, Paine addressed the crisis using "simple fact, plain argument, and common sense." He mocked King George III and attacked every argument that favored loyalty to the king. He called the king a "royal brute" and a "hardened, sullen-tempered Pharaoh [Egyptian king in ancient times]."[5]

Paine's writing went beyond a personal attack on the king. He contended that America could survive economically on its own and no longer needed its British connection. He wanted the developing colonies to become a model republic in a world in which other nations were oppressed by strong central governments.

None of Paine's arguments was new. In fact, most of them were commonly heard in tavern debates throughout the land. Instead, it was the wit and eloquence of Paine's words that made *Common Sense* so effective:

> A government of our own is our natural right: and when a man seriously reflects on the precariousness of human affairs, he will become convinced, that it is infinitely wiser and safer, to form a constitution of our own in a cool and deliberate manner, while we have it in our power, than to trust such an interesting event to time and chance.[6]

Revolution and the Popular Mind Many historians regard Paine's *Common Sense* as the single most important publication of the American

Revolution. The pamphlet became a best seller. More than one hundred thousand copies were sold within a few months after its publication.[7] It put independence squarely on the agenda. Above all, *Common Sense* helped sever the remaining ties of loyalty to the British monarch, thus removing the final psychological barrier to independence. Indeed, later John Adams would ask,

> What do we mean by the Revolution? The War? That was no part of the Revolution. It was only an effect and consequence of it. The Revolution was in the minds of the people, and this was effected, from 1760 to 1775, in the course of fifteen years before a drop of blood was drawn at Lexington.[8]

Independence from Britain—The First Step

By June 1776, the Second Continental Congress had voted for free trade at all American ports with all countries except Britain. The congress had also suggested that all colonies establish state governments separate from Britain. The colonists realized that a formal separation from Britain was necessary if the new nation was to obtain supplies for its armies and commitments of military aid from foreign governments. On June 7, 1776, the first formal step toward independence was taken when Richard Henry Lee of Virginia placed the following resolution before the congress:

"The Constitution . . . is an instrument for the people to restrain the government— lest it come to dominate our lives and interests."

~ PATRICK HENRY ~
AMERICAN STATESMAN AND
OPPONENT OF THE CONSTITUTION
1736–1799

> RESOLVED, That these United Colonies are, and of right ought to be, free and independent States, that they are absolved from allegiance to the British Crown, and that all political connection between them and the state of Great Britain is, and ought to be, totally dissolved.

The congress postponed consideration of Lee's resolution until a formal statement of independence could be drafted. On June 11, a "Committee of Five" was appointed to draft a declaration that would present to the world the colonies' case for independence.

The Significance of the Declaration of Independence Adopted on July 4, 1776, the Declaration of Independence is one of the world's most famous documents. Like Paine, Thomas Jefferson,

The committee chosen to draft a declaration of independence is shown at work in this nineteenth-century engraving. They are, from the left, Benjamin Franklin, Thomas Jefferson, John Adams, Philip Livingston, and Roger Sherman.

LIBRARY OF CONGRESS

who wrote most of the document, elevated the dispute between Britain and the American colonies to a universal level. Jefferson opened the second paragraph of the declaration with the following words, which have since been memorized by countless American schoolchildren and admired the world over:

> We hold these Truths to be self-evident, that all Men are created equal, that they are endowed by their Creator with certain unalienable Rights, that among these are Life, Liberty, and the Pursuit of Happiness— That to secure these Rights, Governments are instituted among Men, deriving their just Powers from the Consent of the Governed, that whenever any Form of Government becomes destructive of these Ends, it is the Right of the People to alter or to abolish it, and to institute new Government.

The concepts expressed in the Declaration of Independence clearly reflect Jefferson's familiarity with European political philosophy, particularly the works of John Locke.[9] Locke's philosophy provided philosophical underpinnings by which the revolution could be justified.

unicameral legislature A legislature with only one chamber.

From Colonies to States

Even before the Declaration of Independence, some of the colonies had transformed themselves into sovereign states with their own permanent governments. In May 1776, the Second Continental Congress had directed each of the colonies to form "such government as shall . . . best be conducive to the happiness and safety of their constituents [those represented by the government]."

Before long, all thirteen colonies had created constitutions. Eleven of the colonies had completely new constitutions. The other two, Rhode Island and Connecticut, made minor modifications to old royal charters. Seven of the new constitutions contained bills of rights that defined the personal liberties of all state citizens. All constitutions called for limited governments.

Republicanism

Many citizens were fearful of a strong central government because of their recent experiences under the British Crown. They opposed any form of government that resembled monarchy in any way. This antiroyalist—or *republican*—sentiment pervaded the colonies.

THE IMPACT OF REPUBLICANISM. Wherever antiroyalist sentiment was strong, the legislature—composed of elected representatives—became all-powerful. In Pennsylvania and Georgia, for example, **unicameral** (one-chamber) **legislatures** were unchecked by any executive authority. Indeed, the executive branch was extremely weak in all thirteen states.

The republican spirit was strong enough to seriously interfere with the ability of the new nation to win the Revolutionary War. (For example, republican sentiments made it difficult for the national government to raise the funding needed to adequately supply General Washington's army.) Republicans of the Revolutionary Era (not to be confused with supporters of the later Republican Party) were suspicious not only of executive authority in their own states but also of national authority as represented by the Continental Congress. This anti-authoritarian, localist impulse contrasted with the *nationalist* sentiments of many of the nation's founders, especially such leaders as George Washington and Alexander Hamilton. Nationalists favored an effective central authority. Of course, many founders, such as Thomas Jefferson, harbored both republican and nationalist impulses.

WHO WERE THE REPUBLICANS? Like all political movements of the time, the republicans were led by men of "property and standing." Leaders who were strongly republican, however, tended to be less prominent than their nationalist or moderate counterparts. Small farmers may have been the one group that was disproportionately republican. Significantly, small farmers made up a majority of the voters in every state.

FOR CRITICAL THINKING

The American colonists did not have the right to elect members of the British Parliament. *How might American history have been different if the British had permitted such representation?*

2-3 The Confederation of States

Republican sentiments influenced the thinking of the delegates to the Second Continental Congress, who formed a committee to draft a plan of confederation. A **confederation** is a voluntary association of *independent* states (see Chapter 3). The member states agree to let the central government undertake a limited number of activities, such as forming an army, but do not allow the central government to place many restrictions on the states' own actions. The member states typically can still govern most state affairs as they see fit.

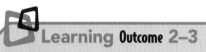

Learning Outcome 2-3

Describe the structure of government established by the Articles of Confederation and some of the strengths and weaknesses of the Articles.

On November 15, 1777, the Second Continental Congress agreed on a draft of the plan, which was finally signed by all thirteen colonies on March 1, 1781. The **Articles of Confederation,** the result of this plan, served as this nation's first national constitution and represented an important step in the creation of our governmental system.[10]

2-3a The Articles of Confederation

The Articles of Confederation established the Congress of the Confederation as the central governing body. This congress was a unicameral assembly of representatives—or ambassadors, as they were called—from the various states. Although each state could send from two to seven representatives to the congress, each state, no matter what its size, had only one vote.

The issue of sovereignty was an important part of the Articles of Confederation:

> Each State retains its sovereignty, freedom, and independence, and every power, jurisdiction, and right, which is not by this Confederation expressly delegated to the United States in Congress assembled.

The structure of government under the Articles of Confederation is shown in Figure 2–2 on the following page.

Powers under the Articles Congress had several powers under the Articles of Confederation, and these enabled the new nation to achieve a number of objectives (see Figure 2–3 on page 31). The Northwest Ordinance settled states' claims to many of the western lands and established a basic pattern for the government of new territories. Also, the 1783 peace treaty negotiated with Britain granted to the United States all of the territory from the Atlantic Ocean to the Mississippi River and from the Great Lakes and Canada to what is now northern Florida.

Weaknesses under the Articles In spite of these accomplishments, the central government created by the Articles of Confederation was quite weak. The Congress of the Confederation had no power to raise revenues for the militia or to force the states to meet military quotas. Essentially, this meant that the new government did not have the power to enforce its laws. Even passing laws was difficult because the Articles of Confederation provided that nine states had to approve any law before it was enacted. Figure 2–4 on page 32 lists these and other powers that the central government lacked under the Articles of Confederation.

The Articles and the Constitution Nonetheless, the Articles of Confederation proved to be a good "first draft" for the Constitution, and at least half of the text of the Articles would later appear in the Constitution. The Articles were an unplanned experiment that tested some of the principles of government that had been set forth

confederation A league of independent states that are united only for the purpose of achieving common goals.

Articles of Confederation The nation's first national constitution, which established a national form of government following the American Revolution. The Articles provided for a confederal form of government in which the central government had few powers.

FIGURE 2-2

American Government
under the Articles of Confederation

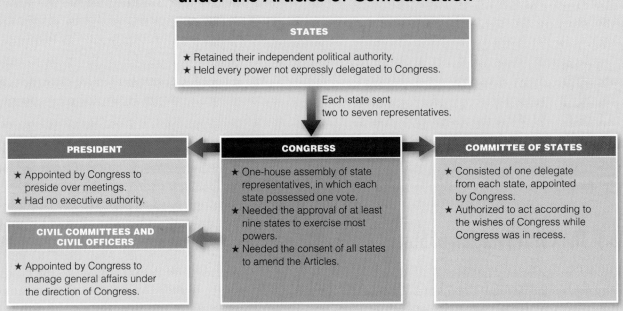

STATES

★ Retained their independent political authority.
★ Held every power not expressly delegated to Congress.

Each state sent two to seven representatives.

PRESIDENT

★ Appointed by Congress to preside over meetings.
★ Had no executive authority.

CIVIL COMMITTEES AND CIVIL OFFICERS

★ Appointed by Congress to manage general affairs under the direction of Congress.

CONGRESS

★ One-house assembly of state representatives, in which each state possessed one vote.
★ Needed the approval of at least nine states to exercise most powers.
★ Needed the consent of all states to amend the Articles.

COMMITTEE OF STATES

★ Consisted of one delegate from each state, appointed by Congress.
★ Authorized to act according to the wishes of Congress while Congress was in recess.

---

earlier in the Declaration of Independence. Some argue that without the experience of government under the Articles of Confederation, it would have been difficult, if not impossible, to arrive at the compromises that were necessary to create the Constitution several years later.

2-3b A Time of Crisis—The 1780s

The Revolutionary War ended on October 18, 1781. The Treaty of Paris, which confirmed the colonies' independence from Britain, was signed in 1783. Peace with the British may have been won, but peace within the new nation was hard to find. The states bickered among themselves and refused to support the new central government in almost any way. As George Washington stated, "We are one nation today and thirteen tomorrow. Who will treat [with] us on such terms?"

Indeed, the national government, such as it was, did not have the ability to prevent the various states from entering into agreements with foreign powers, despite the danger that such agreements could completely disrupt the confederation, pitting state against state. When Congress proved reluctant to admit Vermont into the Union, Britain began negotiations with influential Vermonters with the aim of annexing the district to Canada. Likewise, the Spanish governor of Louisiana energetically sought to detach Tennessee and the lands south of it from the United States. Several prominent individuals—including Daniel Boone—accepted Spanish gold.

The states also increasingly taxed each other's imports and at times even prevented trade altogether. By 1784, the new nation was suffering from a serious economic depression. States started printing their own money at dizzying rates, which led to inflation. Banks were calling in old loans and refusing to issue new ones. Individuals who could not pay their debts were often thrown into prison.

Shays' Rebellion The tempers of indebted farmers in western Massachusetts reached the boiling point in August 1786. Former Revolutionary War captain Daniel Shays, along with approximately two thousand armed farmers, seized county courthouses and disrupted the debtors' trials. Shays and his men then launched an attack on the national government's arsenal in Springfield. **Shays' Rebellion** continued to grow in intensity and lasted into the winter, when it was finally stopped by the Massachusetts volunteer army, which was paid by Boston merchants.[11]

Similar disruptions occurred throughout most of the New England states and in some other areas as well. The upheavals were an important catalyst

Shays' Rebellion A rebellion of angry farmers in western Massachusetts in 1786, led by former Revolutionary War captain Daniel Shays.

FIGURE 2-3

Although the Articles of Confederation were later scrapped, they did allow the early government of the United States to achieve several important goals, including winning the Revolutionary War.

Powers of the Central Government
under the Articles of Confederation

WHAT THE CONGRESS COULD DO	ACCOMPLISHMENT
Congress could establish and control the armed forces, declare war, and make peace.	The United States won the Revolutionary War.
Congress could enter into treaties and alliances.	Congress negotiated a peace treaty with Britain.
Congress could settle disputes among the states under certain circumstances.	Congress passed the Northwest Ordinance, which settled certain states' land claims.
Congress could regulate coinage (but not paper money) and set standards for weights and measures.	Congress carried out these functions, but the inability to regulate paper money proved a major weakness.
Congress could borrow money from the people.	Congress did borrow money, but without the power to tax, it had trouble repaying the loans or obtaining new ones.
Congress could create a postal system, courts to address issues related to ships at sea, and government departments.	Congress created a postal system and departments of foreign affairs, finance, and war.

for change. The revolts frightened American political and business leaders and caused more and more Americans to realize that a *true* national government had to be created.

The Annapolis Meeting The Virginia legislature called for a meeting of representatives from all of the states at Annapolis, Maryland, on September 11, 1786, to consider extending national authority to issues of commerce. Five of the thirteen states sent delegates, two of whom were Alexander Hamilton of New York and James Madison of Virginia. Both of these men favored a strong central government.[12] They persuaded the other delegates to issue a report calling on the states to hold a convention in Philadelphia in May of the following year.

The Congress of the Confederation at first was reluctant to give its approval to the Philadelphia convention. By mid-February 1787, however, seven of the states had named delegates to the Philadelphia meeting. Finally, on February 21, the Congress called on the states to send delegates to Philadelphia "for the sole and express purpose of revising the Articles of Confederation." That Philadelphia meeting became the **Constitutional Convention.**

FOR CRITICAL THINKING

Given that all Americans would have benefited from an army capable of keeping the peace and defending the country, why would the states have been so reluctant to fund the national government?

2-4 Drafting and Ratifying the Constitution

Although the convention was supposed to start on May 14, 1787, few of the delegates had actually arrived in Philadelphia on that date. The convention formally opened in the East Room of the

Constitutional Convention The convention of delegates from the states that was held in Philadelphia in 1787 for the purpose of amending the Articles of Confederation. In fact, the delegates wrote a new constitution (the U.S. Constitution) that established a federal form of government.

FIGURE 2-4

Lack of Central Government Powers
under the Articles of Confederation

The government's lack of certain powers under the Articles of Confederation taught the framers of the Constitution several important lessons, which helped them create a more effective government under that new document.

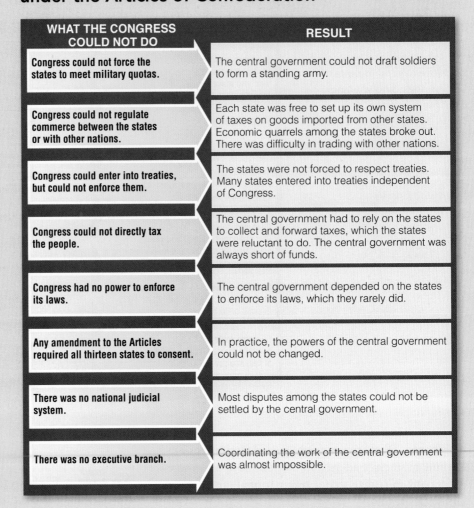

WHAT THE CONGRESS COULD NOT DO	RESULT
Congress could not force the states to meet military quotas.	The central government could not draft soldiers to form a standing army.
Congress could not regulate commerce between the states or with other nations.	Each state was free to set up its own system of taxes on goods imported from other states. Economic quarrels among the states broke out. There was difficulty in trading with other nations.
Congress could enter into treaties, but could not enforce them.	The states were not forced to respect treaties. Many states entered into treaties independent of Congress.
Congress could not directly tax the people.	The central government had to rely on the states to collect and forward taxes, which the states were reluctant to do. The central government was always short of funds.
Congress had no power to enforce its laws.	The central government depended on the states to enforce its laws, which they rarely did.
Any amendment to the Articles required all thirteen states to consent.	In practice, the powers of the central government could not be changed.
There was no national judicial system.	Most disputes among the states could not be settled by the central government.
There was no executive branch.	Coordinating the work of the central government was almost impossible.

Pennsylvania State House on May 25, after fifty-five of the seventy-four delegates had arrived.[13] Only Rhode Island, where feelings were strong against creating a more powerful central government, did not send any delegates.

2-4a Who Were the Delegates?

Among the delegates to the Constitutional Convention were some of the nation's best-known leaders. George Washington was present, as were Alexander Hamilton, James Madison, George Mason, Robert Morris, and Benjamin Franklin (who, at eighty-one years old, had to be carried to the convention on a portable chair).

Some notable leaders were absent, including Thomas Jefferson and John Adams, who were serving as ambassadors in Europe, and Patrick Henry, who did not attend because he "smelt a rat." (Henry was one of Virginia's most strongly republican leaders.)

For the most part, the delegates were from the best-educated and wealthiest classes. Thirty-three delegates were lawyers, nearly half of the delegates were college graduates, three were physicians, seven were former chief executives of their respective states, six owned large plantations, at least nineteen owned slaves, eight were important business owners, and twenty-one had fought in the Revolutionary War.

In other words, the delegates to the convention consti-

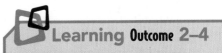

Learning Outcome 2-4

List some of the major compromises made by the delegates at the Constitutional Convention, and discuss the Federalist and Anti-Federalist positions on ratifying the Constitution.

Alexander Hamilton was among the key delegates at the Constitutional Convention that convened on May 25, 1787.

tuted an elite assembly. No ordinary farmers or merchants were present. Indeed, in his classic work on the Constitution, Charles Beard maintained that the Constitution was produced primarily by wealthy bondholders who had made loans to the government under the Articles and wanted a strong central government that could prevent state governments from repudiating debts.[14] Later historians, however, rejected Beard's thesis, concluding that bondholders played no special role in writing the Constitution.

2-4b The Virginia Plan

James Madison had spent months reviewing European political theory before he went to the Philadelphia convention. His Virginia delegation arrived before anybody else, and he immediately put its members to work. On the first day of the convention, Governor Edmund Randolph of Virginia was able to present fifteen resolutions outlining what was to become known as the *Virginia Plan*. This was a masterful political stroke on the part of the Virginia delegation. Its proposals immediately set the agenda for the remainder of the convention.

The fifteen resolutions contained in the Virginia Plan proposed an entirely new national government under a constitution. The plan, which favored large states such as Virginia, called for the following:

- A **bicameral** (two-chamber) **legislature.** The lower chamber was to be chosen by the people. The smaller,

upper chamber was to be chosen by the elected members of the lower chamber. The number of representatives would be in proportion to each state's population (the larger states would have more representatives). The legislature could void any state laws.

- A national executive branch, elected by the legislature.
- A national court system, created by the legislature.

The smaller states immediately complained because they would have fewer representatives in the legislature. After two weeks of debate, they offered their own plan—the *New Jersey Plan.*

2-4c The New Jersey Plan

William Paterson of New Jersey presented an alternative plan favorable to the smaller states. He argued that because each state had an equal vote under the Articles of Confederation, the convention had no power to change this arrangement. The New Jersey Plan proposed the following:

- Congress would be able to regulate trade and impose taxes.
- Each state would have only one vote.
- Acts of Congress would be the supreme law of the land.
- An executive office of more than one person would be elected by Congress.
- The executive office would appoint a national supreme court.

2-4d The Compromises

Most delegates were unwilling to consider the New Jersey Plan. When the Virginia Plan was brought up again, however, delegates from the smaller states threatened to leave, and the convention was in danger of dissolving. On July 16, Roger Sherman of Connecticut broke the deadlock by proposing a compromise plan. Compromises on other disputed issues followed.

The Great Compromise Roger Sherman's plan, which has become known as the **Great Compromise** (or the Connecticut Compromise), called for a legislature with two chambers:

bicameral legislature
A legislature made up of two chambers, or parts.

Great Compromise A plan for a bicameral legislature in which one chamber would be based on population and the other chamber would represent each state equally. The plan was also known as the Connecticut Compromise.

- A lower chamber (the House of Representatives), in which the number of representatives from each state would be determined by the number of people in that state.

- An upper chamber (the Senate), which would have two members from each state. The members would be elected by the state legislatures.

The Great Compromise gave something to both sides: the large states would have more representatives in the House of Representatives than the small states, yet each state would be granted equality in the Senate—because each state, regardless of size, would have two senators. The Great Compromise thus resolved the small-state/large-state controversy.

The Three-Fifths Compromise

A second compromise had to do with how many representatives each state would have in the House of Representatives. Although slavery was legal in parts of the North, most slaves and slave owners lived in the South. Indeed, in the southern states, slaves constituted about 40 percent of the population. Counting the slaves as part of the population would thus greatly increase the number of southern representatives in the House. The delegates from the southern states wanted the slaves to be counted as persons, but the delegates from the northern states disagreed.

Eventually, the **three-fifths compromise** settled this deadlock: each slave would count as three-fifths of a person in determining representation in Congress. (The three-fifths compromise was eventually overturned in 1868 by the Fourteenth Amendment.)

three-fifths compromise A compromise reached during the Constitutional Convention by which three-fifths of all slaves were to be counted for purposes of representation in the House of Representatives.

interstate commerce Trade that involves more than one state.

Slave Importation

The three-fifths compromise did not satisfy everyone at the Constitutional Convention. Many delegates wanted slavery to be banned completely in the United States. The delegates compromised on this question by agreeing that Congress could prohibit the importation of slaves into the country beginning in 1808. The issue of slavery itself, however, was never really addressed by the delegates to the Constitutional Convention. As a result, the South won twenty years of unrestricted slave trade and a requirement that escaped slaves who had fled to the northern states be returned to their owners. Domestic slave trading was untouched.

Banning Export Taxes

The South's economic health depended in large part on its exports of agricultural products. The South feared that the northern majority in Congress might pass taxes on these exports. This fear led to yet another compromise: the South agreed to let Congress have the power to regulate **interstate commerce** as well as commerce with other nations. In exchange, the Constitution guaranteed that no export taxes would be imposed on products exported by the states. Today, the United States is one of the few countries that does not tax its exports.

2–4e Defining the Executive and the Judiciary

The Great Compromise was reached by mid-July. Still to be determined was the makeup of the executive branch and the judiciary. One of the weaknesses of the Confederation had been the lack of an independent executive authority. The Constitution remedied this problem by creating an independent executive—the president—and by making the president the commander in chief of the army and navy and of the state militias when called into national service. The president was also given extensive appointment powers, although Senate approval was required for major appointments.

Another problem under the Confederation was the lack of a judiciary that was independent of the state courts. The Constitution established the United States Supreme Court and authorized Congress to establish other "inferior" federal courts.

To protect against possible wrongdoing, the Constitution also provided a way to remove federal officials from office—through the impeachment process. The Constitution provides that a federal official who commits "Treason, Bribery, or other high Crimes and Misdemeanors" may be *impeached* (accused of, or charged with, wrongdoing) by the

George Washington convenes one of the sessions of the Constitutional Convention in 1787. What advantages may have followed from naming Washington to preside over the convention?

House of Representatives and tried by the Senate. If found guilty of the charges by a two-thirds vote in the Senate, the official can be removed from office and prevented from ever assuming another federal government post.

2–4f The Final Draft Is Approved

A five-man Committee of Detail handled the executive and judicial issues, plus other remaining work. In August, it presented a rough draft to the convention. In September, a committee was named to "revise the stile [style] of, and arrange the Articles which had been agreed to" by the convention. The Committee of Style was headed by Gouverneur Morris of Pennsylvania.[15] On September 17, 1787, the final draft of the Constitution was approved by thirty-nine of the remaining forty-two delegates (some delegates had left early).

As we look back on the drafting of the Constitution, an obvious question emerges: Why didn't the founders ban slavery outright? Certainly, as already mentioned, many of the delegates thought that slavery was morally wrong and that the Constitution should ban it entirely. Many Americans have since regarded the framers' failure to deal with the slavery issue as

a betrayal of the Declaration of Independence, which proclaimed that "all Men are created equal."

A common argument supporting the framers' action (or lack of it) with respect to slavery is that they had no alternative but to ignore the issue. If they had taken a stand on slavery, the Constitution certainly would not have been ratified. Indeed, if the antislavery delegates had insisted on banning slavery, the delegates from the southern states might have walked out of the convention—and there would have been no Constitution to ratify. For another look at this issue, however, see this chapter's *Perception versus Reality* feature on the following page.

2–4g The Debate over Ratification

The ratification of the Constitution set off a national debate of unprecedented proportions. The battle was fought chiefly by two opposing groups— the **Federalists** (those who favored a strong central government and the new

> **Federalists** A political group, led by Alexander Hamilton and John Adams, that supported the adoption of the Constitution and the creation of a federal form of government.

Perception versus Reality

The Slavery Issue

In the Declaration of Independence, Thomas Jefferson, a Virginia slave owner, pronounced that "all Men are created equal." Jefferson considered slavery a "hideous blot" on America. George Washington, also a slave owner, regarded the institution of slavery as "repugnant." Patrick Henry, another southerner, also publicly deplored slavery. Given such views among the leading figures of the era, why didn't the founders stay true to the Declaration of Independence and free the slaves?

THE PERCEPTION

Most Americans assume that southern economic interests and racism alone led the founders to abandon the principles of equality expressed in the Declaration of Independence. African slaves were the backbone of American agriculture, particularly for tobacco, the most profitable export. Without their slaves, southern plantation owners would not have been able to earn such high profits. Presumably, southerners would not have ratified the Constitution unless it protected the institution of slavery.

THE REALITY

The third chief justice of the United States Supreme Court, Oliver Ellsworth, declared that "as population increases, poor laborers will be so plenty as to render slaves useless. Slavery in time will not be a speck in our country."[16] He was wrong, of course. But according to historian Gordon S. Wood, Ellsworth's sentiments mirrored those of most prominent leaders in the United States in the years leading up to the creation of our Constitution. Indeed, great thinkers of the time firmly believed that the liberal principles of the Revolution would destroy the institution of slavery.

At the time of the Constitutional Convention, slavery was disappearing in the northern states (it would be eliminated there by 1804). Many founders thought the same thing would happen in the southern states. After all, there were more antislavery societies in the South than in the North. The founders also thought that the ending of the international slave trade in 1808 would eventually end slavery in the United States. Consequently, the issue of slavery was taken off the table when the Constitution was created simply because the founders had a mistaken belief about the longevity of the institution. They could not have predicted that, within a relatively short time, rapid growth of cotton production in the southern states would give slavery a new lease on life.[17]

BLOG ON Slavery and the Constitution is just one of many subjects that you can read about in the Legal History Blog, which you can find by entering "legal history blog" into a search engine. If you enter "slavery" into the box at the top left of the screen, you will see the postings on this topic.

Constitution) and the **Anti-Federalists** (those who opposed a strong central government and the new Constitution).

In the debate over ratification, the Federalists had several advantages. They assumed a positive name, leaving their opposition with a negative label. (Instead, the Anti-Federalists could well have called themselves republicans and their opponents nationalists.) The Federalists also had attended the Constitutional Convention and thus were familiar with the arguments both in favor of and against various constitutional provisions. The Anti-Federalists, in contrast, had no actual knowledge of those discussions because they had not attended the convention.

The Federalists also had time, funding, and prestige on their side. Their impressive list of political thinkers and writers included Alexander Hamilton, John Jay, and James Madison. The Federalists could communicate with one another more readily because many of them were bankers, lawyers, and merchants who lived in urban areas, where communication was

Anti-Federalists A political group that opposed the adoption of the Constitution.

easier. Accordingly, the Federalists organized a quick and effective ratification campaign to elect themselves as delegates to each state's ratifying convention.

The Federalists Argue for Ratification

Alexander Hamilton, a leading Federalist, enlisted John Jay and James Madison to help him write newspaper columns in support of the new Constitution. In a period of less than a year, these three men wrote a series of eighty-five essays in defense of the Constitution. These essays, which were printed in newspapers throughout the states, are known collectively as the *Federalist Papers.*

Generally, the papers attempted to allay the fears expressed by the Constitution's critics. One fear was that the rights of those in the minority would not be protected. Many critics also feared that a republican form of government would not work in a nation the size of the United States. Various groups, or **factions**, would struggle for power, and chaos would result. Madison responded to the latter argument in *Federalist Paper* No. 10 (see Appendix F), which is considered a classic in political theory. Among other things, Madison argued that the nation's size was actually an advantage in controlling factions: in a large nation, there would be so many diverse interests and factions that no one faction would be able to gain control of the government.[18]

The Anti-Federalists' Response Perhaps the greatest advantage of the Anti-Federalists was that they stood for the status quo. Usually, it is more difficult to institute changes than it is to keep what is already known and understood. Among the Anti-Federalists were such patriots as Patrick Henry and Samuel Adams. Patrick Henry said of the proposed Constitution, "I look upon that paper as the most fatal plan that could possibly be conceived to enslave a free people."

In response to the *Federalist Papers,* the Anti-Federalists published their own essays. They also wrote brilliantly, attacking nearly every clause of the new document. Many Anti-Federalists contended that the Constitution had been written by aristocrats and would lead the nation to aristocratic **tyranny** (the exercise of absolute, unlimited power). Other Anti-Federalists feared that the Constitution would lead to an overly powerful central government that would limit personal freedom.[19]

The Anti-Federalists argued vigorously that the Constitution needed a bill of rights. They warned that without a bill of rights, a strong national government might take away the political rights won during the American Revolution. They demanded that the new Constitution clearly guarantee personal freedoms. The Federalists generally did not think that a bill of rights was all that important. Nevertheless, to gain the necessary support, the Federalists finally promised to add a bill of rights to the Constitution as the first order of business under the new government. This promise turned the tide in favor of the Constitution.

2–4h Ratification

The contest for ratification was close in several states, but the Federalists finally won in all of the state conventions. In 1787, Delaware, Pennsylvania, and New Jersey voted to ratify the Constitution, followed by Georgia and Connecticut early in the following year. Even though the Anti-Federalists were perhaps the majority in Massachusetts, a successful political campaign by the Federalists led to ratification by that state on February 6, 1788.

Following Maryland and South Carolina, New Hampshire became the ninth state to ratify the Constitution on June 21, 1788, thus formally putting the Constitution into effect. New York and Virginia had not yet ratified, however, and without them the Constitution would have no true power. That worry was dispelled in the summer of 1788, when both Virginia and New York ratified the new Constitution. North Carolina waited until November 21 of the following year to ratify the Constitution, and Rhode Island did not ratify until May 29, 1790.

2–4i Did a Majority of Americans Support the Constitution?

Some historians have called the Constitution an aristocratic document that lacked majority support. We cannot conclusively say what most Americans thought of the Constitution, however, because the great majority of adults did not have the right to vote.

Slaves, women, and Indians, of course, could not vote. Furthermore, free men could not vote unless they held sufficient property. A typical voting requirement, used by several states, was possession of land or other property worth forty British pounds. At the time, this sum would buy about a hundred acres of average U.S. farmland. Many of the men who could not vote, it has been argued, were strong republicans.

faction A group of persons forming a cohesive minority.

tyranny The arbitrary or unrestrained exercise of power by an oppressive individual or government.

Still, support for the Constitution seems to have been widespread in all social classes. Both rich and poor Americans were troubled by the weakness of the national government under the Articles of Confederation.

FOR CRITICAL THINKING

Suppose that Rhode Island had refused to ratify the Constitution and join the Union. *Would American history have been seriously altered by such an event?*

2–5 The Constitution's Major Principles of Government

The framers of the Constitution were fearful of the powerful British monarchy, against which they had so recently rebelled. At the same time, they wanted a central government strong enough to prevent the kinds of crises that had occurred under the weak central authority of the Articles of Confederation. The principles of government expressed in the Constitution reflect both of these concerns.

2–5a Limited Government, Popular Sovereignty, and the Rule of Law

The Constitution incorporated the principle of limited government, which means that government can do only what the people allow it to do through the exercise of a duly developed system of laws. This principle can be found in many parts of the Constitution. For example, while Articles I, II, and III indicate exactly what the national government *can* do, the first nine amendments to the Constitution list the ways in which the government *cannot* limit certain individual freedoms.

rule of law A basic principle of government that requires those who govern to act in accordance with established law.

federal system A form of government that provides for a division of powers between a central government and several regional governments.

commerce clause The clause in Article I, Section 8, of the Constitution that gives Congress the power to regulate interstate commerce (commerce involving more than one state).

Popular Sovereignty

Implicitly, the principle of limited government rests on the concept of popular sovereignty. Remember the phrases that frame the Preamble to the Constitution: "We the People of the United States . . . do ordain and establish this Constitution for the United States of America." In other words, it is the people who form the government and decide on the powers that the government can exercise. If the government exercises powers beyond those granted to it by the Constitution, it is acting illegally.

The Rule of Law The idea that no one, including government officers, is above the law is often called the **rule of law.** Ultimately, the viability of a democracy rests on the willingness of the people and their leaders to adhere to the rule of law. A nation's written constitution may guarantee numerous rights and liberties for its citizens. Yet, unless the government of that nation enforces those rights and liberties, the law does not rule the nation. Rather, the government decides what the rules will be.

2–5b The Principle of Federalism

The Constitution also incorporated the principle of *federalism*, or a **federal system** of government, in which the central (national) government shares sov-

Learning Outcome 2–5

Summarize the Constitution's major principles of government, and describe how the Constitution can be amended.

ereign powers with the various state governments. Federalism was the solution to the debate over whether the national government or the states should have ultimate sovereignty.

National Powers The Constitution gave the national government significant powers—powers that it had not had under the Articles of Confederation. For example, the Constitution expressly states that the president is the nation's chief executive as well as the commander in chief of the armed forces. The Constitution also declares that the Constitution and the laws created by the national government are supreme—that is, they take precedence over conflicting state laws. Other powers given to the national government include the power to coin money, to levy and collect taxes, and to regulate interstate commerce, a power granted by the **commerce clause.** Finally, the national government was authorized to undertake all laws that are "necessary and proper" for carrying out its expressly delegated powers.

State Powers Because the states feared too much centralized control, the Constitution also allowed for many states' rights. These rights include the power to regulate commerce within state borders and generally the authority to exercise any powers that are not delegated by the Constitution to the central government.

> "The truth is that all men having power **ought to be mistrusted."**
>
> ~ JAMES MADISON ~
> FOURTH PRESIDENT
> OF THE UNITED STATES
> 1809–1817

2–5c Separation of Powers

As James Madison once said, after you have given the government the ability to control its citizens, you have to "oblige it to control itself." To force the government to "control itself" and to prevent the rise of tyranny, Madison devised a scheme, the **Madisonian Model,** in which the powers of the national government were separated into different branches: legislative, executive, and judicial.[20] The legislative branch (Congress) passes laws, the executive branch (the president) administers and enforces the laws, and the judicial branch (the courts) interprets the laws. By separating the powers of government, the framers ensured that no one branch would have enough power to dominate the others. This principle of **separation of powers** is laid out in Articles I, II, and III of the Constitution.

2–5d Checks and Balances

A system of **checks and balances** was also devised to ensure that no one group or branch of government can exercise exclusive control. Even though each branch of government is independent of the others, it can also check the actions of the others.

Look at Figure 2–5 on the following page, and you can see how this is done. As the figure shows, the president checks Congress by holding a **veto power,** which is the ability to return bills to Congress for reconsideration. Congress, in turn, controls taxes and spending, and the Senate must approve presidential appointments. The judicial branch can check the other branches of government through *judicial review*— the power to rule congressional or presidential actions unconstitutional.[21] In turn, the president and the Senate exercise some control over the judiciary through the president's power to appoint federal judges and the Senate's role in confirming presidential appointments.

Among the other checks and balances built into the American system are staggered terms of

James Madison (1751–1836). Madison's contributions at the Constitutional Convention in 1787 earned him the title "Master Builder of the Constitution." Madison was also responsible for drafting the Bill of Rights. He became our fourth president in 1809.

Madisonian Model
The model of government devised by James Madison, in which the powers of the government are separated into three branches: legislative, executive, and judicial.

separation of powers
The principle of dividing governmental powers among the legislative, the executive, and the judicial branches of government.

checks and balances A major principle of American government in which each of the three branches is given the means to check (to restrain or balance) the actions of the others.

veto power A constitutional power that enables the chief executive (president or governor) to reject legislation and return it to the legislature with reasons for the rejection. This either prevents or delays the bill from becoming law.

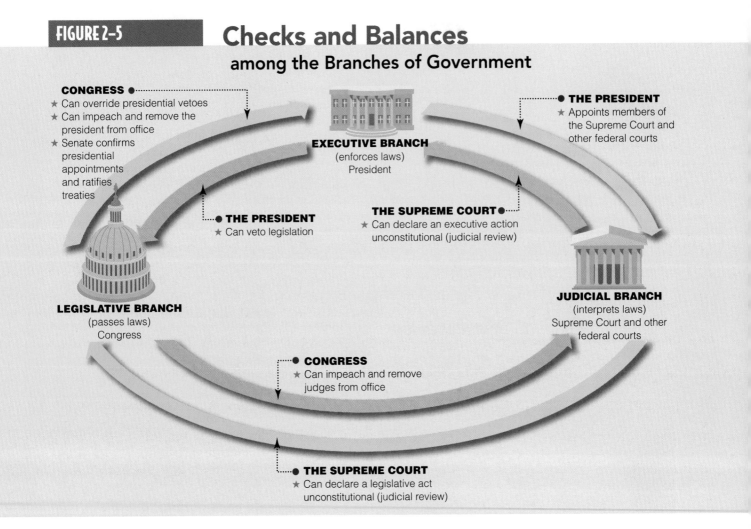

FIGURE 2-5   Checks and Balances
among the Branches of Government

CONGRESS
★ Can override presidential vetoes
★ Can impeach and remove the president from office
★ Senate confirms presidential appointments and ratifies treaties

EXECUTIVE BRANCH
(enforces laws)
President

THE PRESIDENT
★ Appoints members of the Supreme Court and other federal courts

THE PRESIDENT
★ Can veto legislation

THE SUPREME COURT
★ Can declare an executive action unconstitutional (judicial review)

LEGISLATIVE BRANCH
(passes laws)
Congress

JUDICIAL BRANCH
(interprets laws)
Supreme Court and other federal courts

CONGRESS
★ Can impeach and remove judges from office

THE SUPREME COURT
★ Can declare a legislative act unconstitutional (judicial review)

---

office. Members of the House of Representatives serve for two years, members of the Senate for six, and the president for four. Federal court judges are appointed for life but may be impeached and removed from office by Congress for misconduct. Staggered terms and changing government personnel make it difficult for individuals within the government to form controlling factions. The American system of government also includes many other checks and balances, which you will read about in later chapters of this book.

2–5e Limited versus Effective Government

Such American constitutional principles as the separation of powers and a system of checks and balances are not universal among representative democracies. Compared with the United States, many countries place less emphasis on limited government and a higher value on "effective government." The *parliamentary system* is a constitutional form that reflects such values. We describe it in this chapter's *The Rest of the World* feature on the following page.

2–5f The Bill of Rights

To secure the ratification of the Constitution in several important states, the Federalists had to provide assurances that amendments would be passed to protect individual liberties against violations by the national government. At the state ratifying conventions, delegates set forth specific rights that should be protected. James Madison considered these recommendations as he labored to draft what became the Bill of Rights.

After sorting through more than two hundred state recommendations, Madison came up with sixteen amendments. Congress tightened the language somewhat and eliminated four of the amendments. Of the remaining twelve, two—one dealing with the apportionment of representatives and the other with the compensation of the members of Congress—were not ratified by the states during the ratification process.[22] By 1791, all of the states had ratified the ten amendments that now constitute our Bill of Rights. We discuss the Bill of Rights in depth in Chapter 4.

The Parliamentary Alternative

An alternative to our form of government is the *parliamentary system*. Britain—the United Kingdom—has a typical parliamentary system. In contrast to the American system, the British one is based on the *fusion* of powers rather than the *separation* of powers.

First, a Few Basics

Members of Parliament (MPs) are elected just as we elect members of Congress. Here the similarity ends. British voters do not directly choose a chief executive, as we do when we vote for president. Rather, the chief executive is chosen by the lower house of Parliament—the House of Commons, analogous to our House of Representatives. (There is an upper house, the House of Lords, but it has little power.)

Each political party selects a leader well before the general elections. The leader then chooses other MPs who, if the party wins, will take cabinet posts, such as minister of defense or minister of justice. If one party wins a majority of the seats in the House of Commons, it can name its leader as the *prime minister*—the chief executive of the nation.

The Fusion of Powers

MPs who join the cabinet keep their seats in Parliament. The prime minister is both the chief executive of the nation and the leader of his or her party in the legislature. The legislature and the executive are fused, not separated. In contrast, the U.S. Constitution explicitly requires members of Congress who join the president's administration to resign from Congress.

Americans often view the parliamentary system as undemocratic because voters cannot choose the chief executive. Citizens of parliamentary countries do not see the system in quite that way, however. Voters know who the party leaders are in advance of the elections. When they vote, they are choosing a party and its leader. The identity of their own local MP usually has little impact on how they cast their ballot.

What the parliamentary system really does is prevent voters from choosing a chief executive from one party and a legislative representative from another. In America after the 2010 and 2012 elections, for example, Democratic president Barack Obama faced a House of Representatives controlled by the Republicans. That kind of divided government is impossible under the parliamentary system.

Coalition Governments

The parliamentary system does foster a different kind of divided government. It encourages the formation of multiple major parties, thus providing voters with more options than is common in America. But what if no party wins a majority in the lower house of Parliament? Two options are possible. The largest party can form a *minority government* with the acquiescence of other parties. Alternatively, two, three, or more parties can agree to form a *coalition government*.

Many countries that use the parliamentary system are normally governed by coalitions, but until 2010 Britain had not had one for decades. Following the elections in that year, the Conservative Party formed a coalition with the Liberal Democratic Party. The Labour Party then became "Her Majesty's Loyal Opposition."

FOR CRITICAL ANALYSIS Why is it so hard to form effective third parties in the United States?

2–5g Amending the Constitution

Since the Constitution was written, more than eleven thousand amendments have been introduced in Congress. Nonetheless, in the years since the ratification of the Bill of Rights, the first ten amendments to the Constitution, only seventeen proposed amendments have actually survived the amendment process and become a part of our Constitution. It is often contended that members of Congress use the amendment process simply as a political ploy. By introducing an amendment, a member of Congress can show her or his position on an issue, knowing that the odds *against* the amendment's being adopted are high.

One of the reasons there are so few amendments is that the framers, in Article V, made the formal amendment process difficult (although it was easier than it had been under the Articles of Confederation). There are two ways to propose an amendment and two ways to ratify one. As a result, there are four possible ways for an amendment to be added to the Constitution.

Methods of Proposing an Amendment The two methods of proposing an amendment are as follows:

1. A two-thirds vote in the Senate and in the House of Representatives is required. All of the twenty-seven existing amendments have been proposed in this way.

2. If two-thirds of the state legislatures request that Congress call a national amendment convention, then Congress must call one. The convention may propose amendments to the states for ratification. No such convention has ever been convened.

The notion of a national amendment convention is exciting to many people. Many leaders, however, are uneasy about the prospect of convening a body that conceivably could do what the Constitutional Convention did—create a new form of government.

Methods of Ratifying an Amendment There are two methods of ratifying a proposed amendment:

1. Three-fourths of the state legislatures can vote in favor of the proposed amendment. This method is considered the "traditional" ratification method and has been used twenty-six times.

2. The states can call special conventions to ratify the proposed amendment. If three-fourths of the states approve, the amendment is ratified. This method has been used only once—to ratify the Twenty-first Amendment.[23]

You can see the four methods for proposing and ratifying amendments in Figure 2–6 below. As you can imagine, to meet the requirements for proposal and ratification, any amendment must have wide popular support throughout the country.

FOR CRITICAL THINKING

Is amending the Constitution too difficult? Why or why not?

FIGURE 2–6

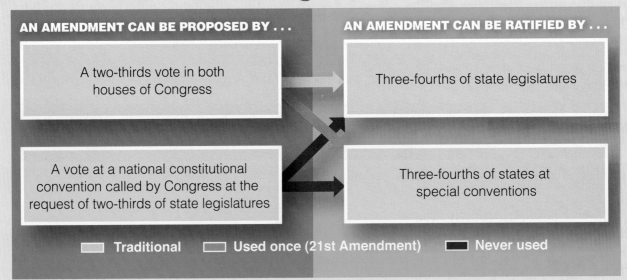

The Process of Amending the Constitution

AN AMENDMENT CAN BE PROPOSED BY . . .

A two-thirds vote in both houses of Congress

A vote at a national constitutional convention called by Congress at the request of two-thirds of state legislatures

AN AMENDMENT CAN BE RATIFIED BY . . .

Three-fourths of state legislatures

Three-fourths of states at special conventions

☐ Traditional ☐ Used once (21st Amendment) ■ Never used

AMERICA AT
ODDS The Constitution

Americans engaged in intense disputes about the ratification of the Constitution, as you have learned in this chapter. The most important of these disputes was over the relative power of the states and the national government. This dispute is central to the topic of federalism, which we will take up in Chapter 3. Proposed constitutional amendments have also been the source of many controversies throughout U.S. history. These controversies include the following:

- The Equal Rights Amendment of 1972 stated, "Equality of rights under the law shall not be denied or abridged by the United States or by any state on account of sex." The amendment failed to win approval from enough states. Should it be revived—or are equal rights for women unacceptable because women could not then be exempted from a military draft?

- Members of the Tea Party movement have advocated the repeal of the Seventeenth Amendment, which transferred the election of U.S. senators from state legislatures to the people of the respective states. The argument is that giving the choice of senators back to state legislatures would strengthen the relative power of the states. Is this a good argument—or is popular election of senators the superior system?

- Conservatives have campaigned for a constitutional amendment to ban same-sex marriage. Would such a measure be desirable—or repugnant as the first attempt to write a limit on freedoms into the Constitution?

- What about an amendment to ban the destruction of the American flag as an act of protest? Is such a ban important to the dignity of our fallen soldiers—or would it be an unacceptable limit on free speech?

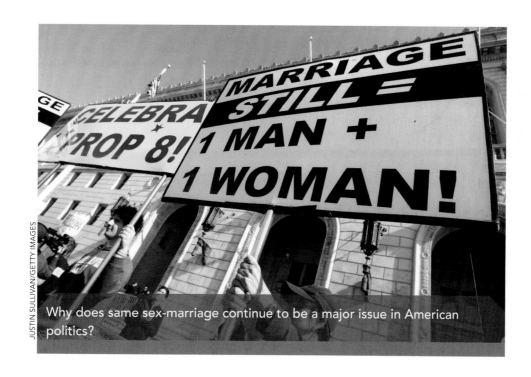

Why does same sex-marriage continue to be a major issue in American politics?

JUSTIN SULLIVAN/GETTY IMAGES

STUDY TOOLS

Ready to study?

- **Review** what you've read with the quiz below.
- Check your answers on the **Chapter in Review** card at the back of the book.
- For any questions you miss, read the corresponding **Learning Outcome** section again to prepare for class and your exam.
- Rip out and study the **Chapter in Review** card (at the back of the book).

Fill-In

Learning Outcome 2–1

1. Even before the Pilgrims went ashore, they drew up the _____, in which they set up a government and promised to obey its laws.

Learning Outcome 2–2

2. After the Seven Years' War, the British government decided to obtain revenues to pay its war debts and to finance the defense of its North American empire by _____.

3. The British Parliament imposed several taxes on the colonists, including the _____.

Learning Outcome 2–3

4. The Articles of Confederation established the _____ as the central governing body.

5. _____, a rebellion of angry farmers in western Massachusetts in 1786, along with similar uprisings throughout most of the New England states, emphasized the need for a true national government.

Learning Outcome 2–4

6. At the Constitutional Convention in 1787, the delegates forged the Great Compromise, which established a bicameral legislature composed of the _____.

7. The Constitution provides that a federal official who commits "_____" may be impeached by the House of Representatives and tried by the Senate.

8. During the debate over ratification, the Anti-Federalists argued that the Constitution needed a _____ because a strong national government might take away the political rights won during the American Revolution.

Learning Outcome 2–5

9. The principle of dividing governmental powers among the legislative, the executive, and the judicial branches of government is known as the _____.

10. Among the checks and balances built into the American system of government are the _____.

Multiple Choice

Learning Outcome 2–1

11. The majority of American colonists came from
    a. Germany and Spain.
    b. France and Ireland.
    c. England and Scotland.

Learning Outcome 2–2

12. Before the mid-1700s, the majority of American colonists were
    a. secretly planning to declare their independence from Britain.
    b. loyal to the British monarch and viewed Britain as their homeland.
    c. loyal to France.

Learning Outcome 2–3

13. Under the Articles of Confederation, the new nation
    a. could not declare war.
    b. could enter into treaties and alliances.
    c. regulated interstate commerce.

Learning Outcome 2–4

14. The three-fifths compromise reached at the Constitutional Convention had to do with
    a. how slaves would be counted in determining representation in Congress.
    b. the imposition of export taxes.
    c. the regulation of commerce.

Learning Outcome 2–5

15. All of the existing amendments to the Constitution have been proposed
    a. by a two-thirds vote in the Senate and in the House of Representatives.
    b. by a vote in three-fourths of the state legislatures.
    c. at national constitutional conventions.

Federalism

© BONNIE FINK/SHUTTERSTOCK.COM

The **Learning Outcomes** labeled 1 through 5 are designed to help improve your understanding of the chapter. After reading this chapter, you should be able to:

3–1 Explain what federalism means, how federalism differs from other systems of government, and why it exists in the United States.

3–2 Indicate how the Constitution divides governing powers in our federal system.

3–3 Summarize the evolution of federal–state relationships in the United States over time.

3–4 Describe developments in federalism in recent years.

3–5 Explain what is meant by the term *fiscal federalism*.

Remember to visit page 67 for additional Study Tools

AMERICA AT
ODDS
Should the States Lower the Drinking Age?

Our political system is a federal one in which power is shared between the states and the national government. The Tenth Amendment to the U.S. Constitution reserves all powers not delegated to the national government to the states and to the people. Nonetheless, the national—federal—government has been able to exercise power over matters that traditionally have been under the control of state governments, such as the minimum age for drinking alcoholic beverages. The federal government has been able to do so by its ability to give or withhold federal grants. In the 1980s, for example, the national government wanted the states to raise the minimum drinking age to twenty-one years. States that refused to do so were threatened with the loss of federal highway construction funds. The threat worked—it was not long before all of the states had changed their minimum drinking age laws. The federal government has used grants to control the actions of the states on many occasions. There may be limits to this power, though. In the Supreme Court ruling that upheld the health-care law known as Obamacare, Chief Justice John Roberts also held that the national government cannot pressure the states to expand Medicaid by threatening to take away all of their Medicaid funds. Roberts argued that cutting the states off completely would do too much damage to their budgets.

It's Time to End This Charade— College Students Still Drink

Underage drinking did not disappear when the minimum drinking age requirement was raised to twenty-one years. Indeed, the problem got worse. Millions of young people today are, in effect, criminals, because they are breaking the law by drinking. The minimum drinking age of twenty-one years has not reduced drunk driving among teenagers, because it is largely unenforceable. Additionally, it has bred contempt for the law in general among teenagers. That is why a group of 135 U.S. college presidents and chancellors endorsed the Amethyst Initiative, a movement calling for the reconsideration of U.S. drinking age laws. Prohibition did not work in the 1920s, and prohibiting those under twenty-one from drinking will not work in the twenty-first century. Almost no other country has such a high minimum drinking age. It is time to lower the drinking age everywhere in the United States. Responsible drinking can be taught through role modeling by parents and through educational programs.

Keep the Age-Twenty-One Requirement Because It's Working

Mothers Against Drunk Driving (MADD) leads the opposition to lowering the drinking age. That group contends that the current drinking age laws have saved more than twenty thousand lives. The National Transportation Safety Board, the American Medical Association, and the Insurance Institute for Highway Safety all agree. After all, young persons' brains are not fully developed, so they are more susceptible to alcohol. The drinking age limit of twenty-one helps to protect young people from being pressured to drink. Teenagers who drink are a danger not only to themselves but also to others—particularly when driving. Young people away at college must deal with enough new responsibilities. They don't need drinking as yet another problem. Fatalities involving eighteen- to twenty-year-old drivers have decreased since the laws establishing the minimum drinking age of twenty-one were enacted. These laws are working as planned, so we should keep them.

Where do you stand?

1. Is there any chance that the Supreme Court might extend its Obamacare reasoning to overturn the law that forces states to adopt a twenty-one-year-old drinking age? Why or why not?
2. Why might it be that almost every economically advanced nation other than the United States lets nineteen-year-olds drink alcohol?

Explore this issue online

- Professor David J. Hanson, of the State University of New York at Potsdam, maintains a Web site that explores alcohol-related issues, including the minimum drinking age controversy. You can find it by searching on his name—"david j hanson."
- You can find the Mothers Against Drunk Driving site by entering "madd" into your search engine. For a related organization, Students Against Destructive Decisions, enter "sadd."

Introduction

The controversy over the drinking age is just one example of how different levels of government in our federal system can be at odds with one another. Let's face it—those who work for the national government based in Washington, D.C., would like the states to cooperate fully with the national government in the implementation of national policies. At the same time, those who work in state government don't like to be told what to do by the national government, especially when the implementation of a national policy is costly for the states. Finally, those who work in local governments would like to run their affairs with the least amount of interference from both their state governments and the national government.

Such conflicts arise because our government is based on the principle of **federalism,** which means that government powers are shared by the national government and the states. When the founders of this nation opted for federalism, they created a practical and flexible form of government capable of enduring for centuries. At the same time, however, they planted the seeds for future conflict between the states and the national government over how government powers should be shared. As you will read in this chapter—and throughout this book—many of today's most pressing issues have to do with which level of government should exercise certain powers.

3–1 Federalism and Its Alternatives

There are various ways of ordering relations between central governments and local units. Federalism is one of these ways. Learning about federalism and how it differs from other forms of government is important to understanding the American political system.

3–1a What Is Federalism?

Nowhere in the Constitution does the word *federalism* appear. This is understandable, given that the concept of federalism was an invention of the founders. Since the Federalists and the Anti-Federalists argued more than two hundred years ago about what form of government we should have, hundreds of definitions of federalism have been offered. Basically, as mentioned in Chapter 2, government powers in a *federal system* are divided between a central government and regional, or subdivisional, governments.

Defining *Federalism* Although the definition given here seems straightforward, its application certainly is not. After all, almost all nations—even the most repressive totalitarian regimes—have some kind of subnational governmental units. Thus, the existence of national and subnational governmental units by itself does not make a system federal. *For a system to be truly federal, the powers of both the national units and the subnational units must be specified and limited.*

Under true federalism, individuals are governed by two separate governmental authorities (national and state authorities) whose expressly designated powers cannot be altered without changing the fundamental nature of the system—for example, by amending a written constitution. Table 3–1 on the following page lists some of the countries that the Central Intelligence Agency has classified as having a federal system of government.[1]

U.S. Federalism in Practice Federalism in theory is one thing—federalism in practice is another. As you will read shortly, the Constitution sets forth specific powers that can be exercised by the national government and provides that the national government has the implied power to undertake actions necessary to carry out its expressly designated powers. All other powers are "reserved" to the states. The broad language of the Constitution, though, has left much room for debate over the specific nature and scope of certain powers, such as the national government's implied powers and the powers reserved to the states. Thus, the actual workings of our federal form of government have depended, to a great extent, on the historical application of the broad principles outlined in the Constitution.

To further complicate matters, the term *federal government,* as it is used today, refers to the national, or central, government. When individuals talk of the federal government, they mean the

federalism A system of shared sovereignty between two levels of government—one national and one subnational—occupying the same geographic region.

TABLE 3-1

Countries That Have a Federal System Today

Country	Population (in Millions)
Argentina	42.6
Australia	23.0
Austria	8.5
Brazil	201.0
Canada	35.1
Ethiopia	86.6
Germany	80.3
India	1,220.8
Malaysia	29.7
Mexico	116.2
Nigeria	170.9
Pakistan	183.3
Switzerland	8.0
United States	316.0

Source: Official estimates by governments of the listed nations or by the Central Intelligence Agency.

national government based in Washington, D.C. They are *not* referring to the federal *system* of government, which is made up of both the national government and the state governments.

3–1b Alternatives to Federalism

Perhaps an easier way to define federalism is to discuss what it is *not*. Most of the nations in the world today have a **unitary system** of government. In such a system, the constitution vests all powers in the national government. If the national government so chooses, it can delegate certain activities to subnational units. The reverse is also true: the national government can take away, at will, powers delegated to subnational governmental units. In a unitary system, any subnational government is a "creature of the national government." The governments of Britain, France, Israel, Japan, and the Philippines are examples of unitary systems.

unitary system A centralized governmental system in which local or subdivisional governments exercise only those powers given to them by the central government.

confederal system A league of independent sovereign states, joined together by a central government that has only limited powers over them.

In the United States, because the Constitution does not mention local governments (cities and counties), we say that city and county governmental units are "creatures of state government." That means that state governments can—and do—both give powers to and take powers from local governments.

The Articles of Confederation, discussed in Chapter 2, created a confederal system. In a **confederal system**, the national government exists and operates only at the direction of the subnational governments. Few true confederal systems are in existence today, although some people contend that the European Union—a group of twenty-eight European nations that has established many common institutions—qualifies as such a system.

3–1c Federalism—An Optimal Choice for the United States?

The Articles of Confederation failed because they did not allow for a sufficiently strong central government. The framers of the Constitution, however, were fearful of tyranny and a too-powerful central government. The outcome had to be a compromise—a federal system.

The appeal of federalism was that it retained state powers and local traditions while establishing a strong national government capable of handling common problems, such as national defense. A federal form of government also furthered the goal of creating a division of powers (to be discussed shortly). There are other reasons why the founders opted for a federal system, and a federal structure of government continues to offer many advantages (as well as some disadvantages) for U.S. citizens.

Advantages of Federalism: Size One of the reasons a federal form of government is well suited to the United States is our country's large size. Even in the days when the United States consisted of only thirteen states, its geographic area was larger than that of England or France. In those days, travel was slow and communication was difficult, so people in outlying areas were isolated. The news of any particular political decision could take several weeks to reach everyone. Therefore, even if the framers of the Constitution had wanted a more centralized system (which most of them did not), such a system would have been unworkable.

Look at Figure 3–1 on the following page. As you can see, to a great extent the practical business of governing this country takes place in state and local governmental units. Federalism, by providing a multitude of

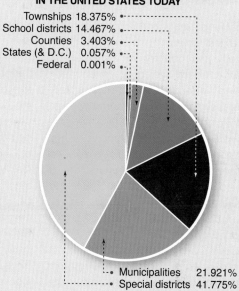

FIGURE 3–1

Governmental Units in the United States Today

The most common type of governmental unit in the United States is the special district, which is generally concerned with a specific issue such as solid waste disposal, mass transportation, or fire protection.

Often, the jurisdiction of special districts crosses the boundaries of other governmental units, such as cities or counties. Special districts also tend to have fewer restrictions than other local governments as to how much debt they can incur and so are created to finance large building projects.

THE NUMBER OF GOVERNMENTS IN THE UNITED STATES TODAY

Government	Number
Federal government	1
State governments and District of Columbia	51
Local governments	
Counties	3,031
Municipalities (mainly cities or towns)	19,522
Townships (less extensive powers)	16,364
Special districts (water, sewer, and so on)	37,203
School districts	12,884
Subtotal local governments	89,004
Total	**89,056**

Source: U.S. Census Bureau, 2012

PERCENTAGE OF ALL GOVERNMENTS IN THE UNITED STATES TODAY

Townships 18.375%
School districts 14.467%
Counties 3.403%
States (& D.C.) 0.057%
Federal 0.001%

Municipalities 21.921%
Special districts 41.775%

---

arenas for decision making, keeps government closer to the people and helps make democracy possible.

Advantages of Federalism: Experimentation

The existence of numerous government subunits in the United States also makes it possible to experiment with innovative policies and programs at the state or local level. Many observers, including Supreme Court justice Louis Brandeis (1856–1941), have emphasized that in a federal system, state governments can act as "laboratories" for public-policy experimentation. For example, many states have adopted minimum-wage laws that establish a higher minimum wage than the one set by national legislation. State governments also have a wide variety of policies on how or whether state employees can form labor unions.

Depending on the outcome of a specific experiment, other states may (or may not) implement similar programs. State innovations can also serve as models for federal programs. For instance, California was a pioneer in air-pollution control. Many of that state's regulations were later adapted by other states and eventually by the federal government.

Advantages of Federalism: Subcultures We

have always been a nation of different political subcultures. The Pilgrims who founded New England were different from the settlers who established the agricultural society of the South. Both of these groups were different from those who populated the Middle Atlantic states. The groups that founded New England had a religious focus, while those who populated the Middle Atlantic states were more business oriented. Those who settled in the South were more individualistic than the other groups. That is, they were less inclined to act as a collective and more inclined to act independently of each other. A federal system of government allows the political and cultural interests of regional groups to be reflected in the laws governing those groups.

As we noted earlier, nations other than the United States have benefited from the principle of federalism. One of them is Canada. Because federalism permits the expression of varying regional cultures, Canadian federalism naturally differs from the American version, as you will discover in this chapter's *The Rest of the World* feature on the following page.

Some Drawbacks to Federalism Federalism

offers many advantages, but it also has some drawbacks. Consider that although federalism in many ways promotes greater self-rule, or democracy, some scholars point out that local self-rule may not always be in society's best interests. These observers argue that the smaller the political unit, the higher the probability that

Canadian versus American Federalism

By land area, Canada is the second-largest country in the world. Physically, the country seems designed for a federal system of government. And indeed, Canada has a federal system similar in some ways to that of the United States—but also with some big differences. When the 1867 Constitution Act created modern Canada, the United States had just concluded the Civil War. Canada's founders blamed that war on the weakness of the U.S. central government. Therefore, the Canadian Constitution gave far more power to the central government than did the U.S. Constitution.

The Powers of Lower-Level Governments

Our lower levels of government are called states, whereas in Canada they are called provinces. Right there, the powers of the central government are emphasized. The word *state* implies sovereignty. A *province*, however, is never sovereign and is typically set up for the convenience of the central government.

In the United States, the powers of the national government are limited to those listed in the Constitution. In the Canadian Constitution, it is the powers of the provinces that are limited by a list. The Tenth Amendment to the U.S. Constitution reserves residual powers to the states or to the people. In Canada, residual powers rest with the national government. Under the 1867 Canadian Constitution, the central government could veto any provincial legislation. No such clause appears in the U.S. Constitution.

Changes over Time

Over time, the powers of the U.S. federal government grew at the expense of the states. The opposite happened in Canada. By the end of the nineteenth century, the Canadian government in practice had abandoned the power to veto provincial legislation. The Great Depression of the 1930s strengthened the national government in the United States. In Canada, it strengthened the provinces.

Two Languages

Another striking difference between Canada and the United States is that Canada has two national languages. A majority of Canadians speak English, but most of the population of Québec speak French. The Parti Québécois (PQ), which wants Québec to be a separate country, gained power in that province in 1976 and 1994. Both times, it held referenda on whether Québec should demand "sovereignty-association," a euphemism for independence. In 1995, the PQ almost obtained a majority vote for its position. The PQ returned to power in 2012 but without enough votes to hold another referendum. Nevertheless, the possibility exists that Canada could actually break apart.

FOR CRITICAL ANALYSIS The Canadian Constitution is based on the principles of "peace, order, and good government." Contrast that phrase with the words in the Declaration of Independence—"life, liberty, and the pursuit of happiness." How do the statements differ?

---

it will be dominated by a single political group, which may or may not be concerned with the welfare of many of the local unit's citizens. For example, entrenched segregationist politicians in southern states denied African Americans their civil rights and voting rights for decades, as we discuss further in Chapter 5.

Powerful state and local interests can block progress and impede national plans. State and local interests often diverge from those of the national government. For example, several of the states have recently been at odds with the national government over how to address possible climate change. Finding acceptable solutions to such conflicts has not always been easy. Indeed, as will be discussed shortly, in the 1860s, war—not politics—decided the outcome of a struggle over states' rights.

Federalism has other drawbacks as well. One of them is the lack of uniformity of state laws, which can complicate business transactions that cross state borders. Another problem is the difficulty of coordinating government policies at the national, state, and local levels. Additionally, the simultaneous regulation of business by all levels of government creates red tape that imposes substantial costs on the business community.

In a federal system, there is always the danger that national power will be expanded at the expense of the states. President Ronald Reagan (1981–1989) once said, "The Founding Fathers saw the federalist system as constructed something like a masonry wall. The States are the bricks, the national government is the mortar. . . . Unfortunately, over the years, many people have increasingly come to believe that Washington is the whole wall."[2]

FOR CRITICAL THINKING

The national government imposed a uniform highway speed limit on the entire country from 1974 until its repeal in 1995. *Why should we leave speed limits to the states—or why should they be a federal responsibility?*

3–2 The Constitutional Division of Powers

Learning Outcome 3–2

Indicate how the Constitution divides governing powers in our federal system.

The founders created a federal form of government by dividing sovereign powers into powers that could be exercised by the national government and powers that were reserved to the states. Although there is no systematic explanation of this **division of powers** between the national and state governments, the original Constitution, along with its amendments, provides statements on what the national and state governments can (and cannot) do.

3–2a The Powers of the National Government

The Constitution delegates certain powers to the national government. It also prohibits the national government from exercising certain powers.

Powers Delegated to the National Government
The national government possesses three types of powers: expressed powers, implied powers, and inherent powers.

EXPRESSED POWERS. Article I, Section 8, of the Constitution expressly enumerates twenty-seven powers that Congress may exercise. Two of these **expressed powers,** or *enumerated powers,* are the power to coin money and the power to regulate interstate commerce. Constitutional amendments have provided for other expressed powers. For example, the Sixteenth Amendment, added in 1913, gives Congress the power to impose a federal income tax.

One power expressly granted to the national government is the right to regulate commerce not only among the states, but also "with the Indian Tribes." As a result, relations between Native American tribal governments and the rest of the country have always been a national responsibility. A further consequence is that state governments face significant limits on their authority over Indian reservations within their borders.

IMPLIED POWERS. The constitutional basis for the **implied powers** of the national government is found in Article I, Section 8, Clause 18, often called the **necessary and proper clause.** This clause states that Congress has the power to make "all Laws which shall be necessary and proper for carrying into Execution the foregoing [expressed] Powers, and all other Powers vested by this Constitution in the Government of the United States, or in any Department or Officer thereof." The necessary and proper clause is often referred to as the *elastic clause,* because it gives elasticity to our constitutional system.

INHERENT POWERS. The national government also enjoys certain **inherent powers**—powers that governments must have simply to ensure the nation's integrity and survival as a political unit. For example, any national government must have the inherent ability to make treaties, regulate immigration, acquire territory, wage war, and make peace. While some inherent powers are also enumerated in the Constitution, such as the powers to wage war and make treaties, others are not. For example, the Constitution does not speak of regulating immigration

division of powers
A basic principle of federalism established by the U.S. Constitution, by which powers are divided between the national and state governments.

expressed powers
Constitutional or statutory powers that are expressly provided for by the U.S. Constitution; also called *enumerated powers.*

implied powers The powers of the federal government that are implied by the expressed powers in the Constitution, particularly in Article I, Section 8.

necessary and proper clause Article I, Section 8, Clause 18, of the Constitution, which gives Congress the power to make all laws "necessary and proper" for the federal government to carry out its responsibilities; also called the *elastic clause.*

inherent powers The powers of the national government that, although not always expressly granted by the Constitution, are necessary to ensure the nation's integrity and survival as a political unit.

or acquiring new territory. Although the national government's inherent powers are few, they are important.

FEDERAL LANDS. One inherent power is older than the Constitution itself—the power to own land. The United States collectively owned various western lands under the Articles of Confederation. The Northwest Territory, which included the modern states of Illinois, Indiana, Michigan, Ohio, Wisconsin, and part of Minnesota, joined United States' lands together with lands given up by New York and Virginia. The Northwest Territory was organized during the ratification of the Constitution. Indeed, establishing the territory as the collective property of the entire Union was necessary to secure support for ratification in several states, including Maryland.

The United States then sold land to new settlers—land sales were a major source of national government income throughout much of the 1800s. To this day, the national government owns most of the acres in many far western states, a fact that annoys many Westerners.

Powers Prohibited to the National Government

The Constitution expressly prohibits the national government from undertaking certain actions, such as imposing taxes on exports, and from passing laws restraining certain liberties, such as the freedom of speech or religion. Most of these prohibited powers are listed in Article I, Section 9, and in the first eight amendments to the Constitution. Additionally, the national government is implicitly prohibited from exercising certain powers. For example, most authorities believe that the federal government does not have the power to create a national public school system, because such power is not included among those that are expressed and implied.

police powers The powers of a government body that enable it to create laws for the protection of the health, safety, welfare, and morals of the people. In the United States, most police powers are reserved to the states.

3–2b The Powers of the States

The Tenth Amendment to the Constitution states that powers that are not delegated to the national government by the Constitution nor prohibited to the states "are reserved to the States respectively, or to the people." The Tenth Amendment thus gives numerous powers to the states, including the power to regulate commerce within their borders and the power to maintain a state militia.

Police Powers In principle, each state has the ability to regulate its internal affairs and to enact whatever laws are necessary to protect the health, safety, welfare, and morals of its people. These powers of the states are called **police powers**. The establishment of public schools and the regulation of marriage and divorce have traditionally been considered to be entirely within the purview of state and local governments.

Because the Tenth Amendment does not specify what powers are reserved to the states, these powers have been defined differently at different times in our history. In periods of widespread support for increased regulation by the national government, the Tenth Amendment tends to recede into the background. When the tide of support turns, the Tenth Amendment is resurrected to justify arguments supporting increased states' rights (see, for example, the discussion of the new federalism later in this chapter). Because the United States Supreme Court is the ultimate arbiter of the Constitution, the outcome of disputes over the extent of state powers often rests with the Court.

Powers Prohibited to the States Article I, Section 10, denies certain powers to state governments, such as the power to tax goods that are transported across state lines. States are also prohibited from entering into treaties with other countries. In addition, the Thirteenth, Fourteenth, Fifteenth, Nineteenth, Twenty-fourth, and Twenty-sixth Amendments prohibit certain state actions. (The complete text of these amendments is included in Appendix B.)

3–2c Interstate Relations

The Constitution also contains provisions relating to interstate relations. The states have constant commercial and social interactions among themselves, and these interactions often do not directly involve the national government. The relationships among the states in our federal system of government are sometimes referred to as *horizontal federalism*.

The Full Faith and Credit Clause The Constitution's full faith and credit clause requires each state to honor every other state's public acts, records, and judicial proceedings. The issue of gay marriage, however, has made this constitutional mandate difficult to follow. If a gay couple legally married in Massachusetts moves to a state that bans same-sex marriage, which state's law takes priority? The federal government attempted to answer that question through the 1996 Defense of Marriage Act (DOMA), which provided that no state is *required* to treat a relationship between persons of the same sex as a marriage, even if the relationship is considered a marriage in another state.

A second part of the law barred the national government from recognizing same-sex marriages in states that legalize them. From 2010 through 2012, however, U.S. district and appellate courts ruled in five different cases that this part of DOMA was unconstitutional. The federal government, in other words, was required to provide marriage-based benefits to couples who have been married in states where such unions are legal. In 2013, the United States Supreme Court backed the lower courts on this issue. Was it correct to do so? We examine that issue in the *Join the Debate* feature on the following page.

Interstate Compacts Horizontal federalism also includes agreements, known as *interstate compacts,* among two or more states to regulate the use or protection of certain resources, such as water or oil and gas. California and Nevada, for example, have formed an interstate compact to regulate the use and protection of Lake Tahoe, which lies on the border between those states.

3–2d Concurrent Powers

Concurrent powers can be exercised by both the state governments and the federal government. Generally, a state's concurrent powers apply only within the geographic area of the state and do not include functions that the Constitution delegates exclusively to the national government, such as the coinage of money and the negotiation of treaties.

An example of a concurrent power is the power to tax. Both the states and the national government have the power to impose income taxes—and a variety of other taxes. States, however, are prohibited from imposing tariffs (taxes on imported goods), and, as noted, the federal government may not tax articles exported by any state.

concurrent powers
Powers held by both the federal and the state governments in a federal system.

supremacy clause
Article VI, Clause 2, of the Constitution, which makes the Constitution and federal laws superior to all conflicting state and local laws.

Figure 3–2, on page 55, summarizes the powers granted and denied by the Constitution and lists other concurrent powers.

3–2e The Supremacy Clause

The Constitution makes it clear that the federal government holds ultimate power. Article VI, Clause 2, known as the **supremacy clause,** states that the U.S. Constitution and the laws of the federal government "shall be the supreme Law of

Few issues today are as controversial as state-legalized gay marriages. A federal judge in California ruled that Proposition 8, which nullified such marriages, was unconstitutional, and the United States Supreme Court refused to overturn that ruling.

DAVID BUTOW/REDUX

Can the Federal Government Decide Who Is Married?

Traditionally, the states have decided when individuals may legally marry. Until recently, state marriage laws have rarely been politically controversial. In the 1990s, however, state-recognized same-sex marriages became an issue. In response, the U.S. Congress passed the Defense of Marriage Act (DOMA) in 1996. That law allowed state governments to ignore same-sex marriages performed in other states and barred the national government from recognizing such marriages. DOMA raised this question: Under our federal system, does the national government have any business defining who is or is not married? The United States Supreme Court ruled on this issue in June 2013. The Court found that the national government was, in fact, required to accept state-authorized same-sex marriages. But was this the right decision?

Congress Should Stay Out of This Issue

America has a powerful interest in allowing same-sex couples to enjoy the institution of marriage. The institution promotes stability and a commitment to society. DOMA denied more than one thousand federal benefits to same-sex couples, and according to Supreme Court justice Ruth Bader Ginsburg, this denial effectively turned their relationships into "skim-milk marriages."

When the Defense of Marriage Act was passed, a House report indicated that Congress passed it to express "moral disapproval of homosexuality." But Congress has no business creating classes of people it doesn't like. In fact, the very act of establishing a class of people with inferior rights is a violation of the Fourteenth Amendment to the Constitution, which guarantees equal protection under the law. Congress cannot treat same-sex marriages differently than traditional marriages.

In any event, Congress has no expressed or implied authority to define marriage. That power has always been reserved to the states. An attempt by Congress to intervene in the states' business by claiming the right to decide who is married is an unacceptable power grab.

It Is the Courts That Are Overreaching

The recent Supreme Court ruling essentially says that the national government cannot determine who is or is not married—even for the purposes of allocating federal benefits. Under DOMA, though, the national government was not telling the states what to do. Rather, the national government was deciding what to do *with its own money.*

Many liberal- and moderate-minded young people have applauded the Court's action. They ought to consider, however, the possible consequences. When the Court places new limits on the powers of the national government, progressive causes are more likely to suffer than conservative ones. Consider Obamacare. In its ruling on this issue, the Court employed a novel legal theory to allow states to opt out of expanding Medicaid to cover more of their low-income citizens. The results are that in 2014, millions of low-income persons must do without health-care insurance.

Same-sex marriage is clearly on a roll. It shouldn't be too many years before Congress itself replaces DOMA with something more progressive. Let's rely on popularly elected leaders to make our decisions—not on unelected federal judges.

FOR CRITICAL ANALYSIS Why wasn't the topic of same-sex marriage important one hundred years ago?

the Land." In other words, states cannot use their reserved or concurrent powers to counter national policies. Whenever state or local officers, such as judges or sheriffs, take office, they become bound by an oath to support the U.S. Constitution. National government power always takes precedence over any conflicting state action.[3]

FOR CRITICAL THINKING

The national government also exercises police powers, such as environmental regulation. *Name some other federal activities that might fall into this category.*

FIGURE 3-2

The Constitutional Division of Powers

The Constitution grants certain powers to the national government and certain powers to the state governments, while denying them other powers. Some powers, called *concurrent powers*, can be exercised at either the national or the state level, but generally the states can exercise these powers only within their own borders.

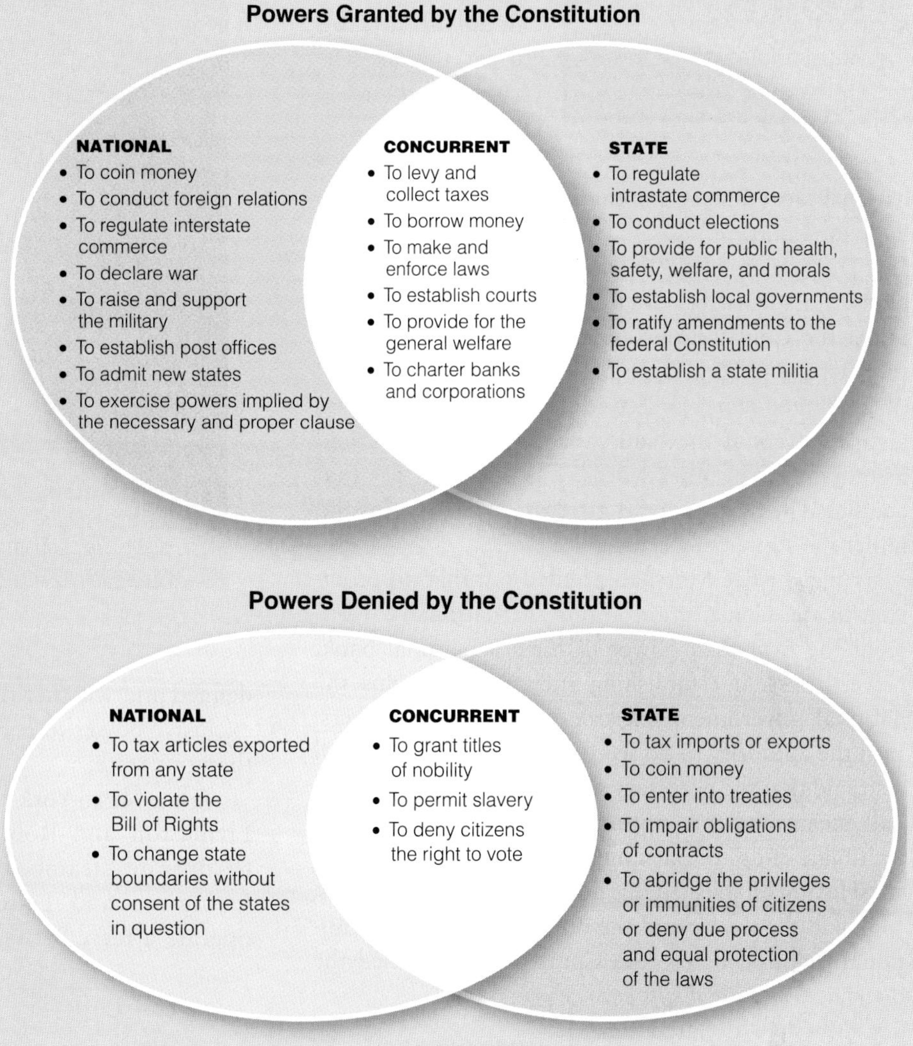

Powers Granted by the Constitution

NATIONAL
- To coin money
- To conduct foreign relations
- To regulate interstate commerce
- To declare war
- To raise and support the military
- To establish post offices
- To admit new states
- To exercise powers implied by the necessary and proper clause

CONCURRENT
- To levy and collect taxes
- To borrow money
- To make and enforce laws
- To establish courts
- To provide for the general welfare
- To charter banks and corporations

STATE
- To regulate intrastate commerce
- To conduct elections
- To provide for public health, safety, welfare, and morals
- To establish local governments
- To ratify amendments to the federal Constitution
- To establish a state militia

Powers Denied by the Constitution

NATIONAL
- To tax articles exported from any state
- To violate the Bill of Rights
- To change state boundaries without consent of the states in question

CONCURRENT
- To grant titles of nobility
- To permit slavery
- To deny citizens the right to vote

STATE
- To tax imports or exports
- To coin money
- To enter into treaties
- To impair obligations of contracts
- To abridge the privileges or immunities of citizens or deny due process and equal protection of the laws

3-3 The Struggle for Supremacy

Much of the political and legal history of the United States has involved conflicts between the supremacy of the national government and the desire of the states to preserve their sovereignty. The most extreme example of this conflict was the Civil War in the 1860s. Through the years, because of the Civil War and several important Supreme Court decisions, the national government has increased its power.

3-3a Early United States Supreme Court Decisions

Two Supreme Court cases, both of which were decided in the early 1800s, played a key role in establishing the constitutional foundations for the supremacy of the national government. Both decisions were issued while John Marshall was chief justice of the Supreme Court. In his thirty-four years as chief justice (1801–1835), Marshall did much to establish the prestige and the independence of the Court. In *Marbury v. Madison*,[4] he clearly enunciated the principle of *judicial review,* which has since become an important part of the checks and balances in the American system of government. Under his leadership, the Supreme Court also established, through the following cases, the superiority of federal authority under the Constitution.

***McCulloch v. Maryland* (1819)** The issue in *McCulloch v. Maryland*,[5] a case decided in 1819, involved both the necessary and proper clause and the supremacy clause. When the state of Maryland imposed a tax on the Baltimore branch of the Second Bank of the United

Learning Outcome 3-3

Summarize the evolution of federal–state relationships in the United States over time.

States, the branch's chief cashier, James McCulloch, declined to pay the tax. The state court ruled that McCulloch had to pay it, and the national government appealed to the United States Supreme Court.

The case involved much more than a question of taxes. At issue was whether Congress had the authority under the Constitution's necessary and proper clause to charter and contribute capital to the Second Bank of the United States. A second constitutional issue was also involved: If the bank was constitutional, could a state tax it? In other words, was a state action that conflicted with a national government action invalid under the supremacy clause?

Chief Justice Marshall pointed out that no provision in the Constitution grants the national government the *expressed* power to form a national bank. Nevertheless, if establishing such a bank helps the national government exercise its expressed powers, then the authority to do so could be implied. Marshall also said that the necessary and proper clause included "all means that are appropriate" to carry out "the legitimate ends" of the Constitution.

Having established this doctrine of implied powers, Marshall then answered the other important constitutional question before the Court and established the doctrine of *national supremacy*. Marshall declared that no state could use its taxing power to tax an arm of the national government. If it could, the Constitution's declaration that the Constitution "shall be the supreme Law of the Land" would be empty rhetoric without meaning. From that day on, Marshall's decision became the basis for strengthening the national government's power.

John Marshall, chief justice of the United States Supreme Court (1801–1835).

STOCK MONTAGE/ARCHIVE PHOTOS/GETTY IMAGES

defined and whether the national government had the exclusive power to regulate commerce involving more than one state.

The New York legislature had given Robert Livingston and Robert Fulton the exclusive right to operate steamboats in New York waters, and Livingston and Fulton licensed Aaron Ogden to operate a ferry between New York and New Jersey.

Thomas Gibbons, who had a license from the U.S. government to operate boats in interstate waters, decided to compete with Ogden, but he did so without New York's permission. Ogden sued Gibbons in the New York state courts and won. Gibbons appealed.

Chief Justice Marshall defined *commerce* as including all business dealings, including steamboat travel. Marshall also stated that the power to regulate interstate commerce was an *exclusive* national power and had no limitations other than those specifically found in the Constitution. Since this 1824 decision, the national government has used the commerce clause repeatedly to justify its regulation of almost all areas of economic activity.

"We here highly resolve that . . .

This Nation . . . shall have a new birth of freedom; and that government of the people, by the people, for the people, shall not perish from the earth."

~ ABRAHAM LINCOLN ~
GETTYSBURG ADDRESS
1863

Gibbons v. Ogden (1824)

As Chapter 2 explained, Article I, Section 8, gives Congress the power to regulate commerce "among the several States." But the framers of the Constitution did not define the word *commerce*. At issue in *Gibbons v. Ogden*[6] was how the *commerce clause* should be

3–3b The Civil War—The Ultimate Supremacy Battle

The great issue that provoked the Civil War (1861–1865) was the future of slavery. Because people in different sections of the country had radically different beliefs about slavery, the slavery issue took the form of a dispute over states' rights versus national supremacy. The war brought to a bloody climax the ideological debate that had been outlined by the Federalist and Anti-Federalist factions even before the Constitution was ratified.

Nullification and Secession As just discussed, the Supreme Court headed by John Marshall interpreted the commerce clause in such a way as to increase the power of the national government at the expense of state powers. By the late 1820s, however, a shift back to states' rights had begun, and the question of the regulation of commerce became one of the major issues in federal–state relations. When the national government, in 1828 and 1832, passed laws imposing tariffs (taxes) on goods imported into the United States, southern states objected, believing that such taxes were against their interests.

One southern state, South Carolina, attempted to *nullify* the tariffs, or to make them void. South Carolina claimed that in conflicts between state governments and the national government, the states should have the ultimate authority to determine the welfare of their citizens. President Andrew Jackson was prepared to use force to uphold national law, but Congress reduced the tariffs. The crisis passed.

Additionally, some Southerners believed that democratic decisions could be made only when all the segments of society affected by those decisions were in agreement. Without such agreement, a decision should not be binding on those whose interests it violates. This view was used to justify the **secession**—withdrawal—of the southern states from the Union in 1860 and 1861.

States' Rights and Slavery The defense of slavery and the promotion of states' rights were both important elements in the South's decision to secede, and the two concepts were commingled in the minds of Southerners of that era. Which of these two was the more important remains a matter of controversy even today. Modern defenders of states' rights and those who distrust governmental authority often present southern secession as entirely a matter of states' rights. Liberals and those who champion the rights of African Americans see slavery as the sole cause of the crisis. Indeed, the declarations of secession issued by the southern states left little doubt as to the importance of slavery.

When the South was defeated in the war, the idea that a state has a right to secede from the Union was defeated also. Although the Civil War occurred because of the South's desire for increased states' rights, the result was just the opposite—an increase in the political power of the national government.

3–3c Dual Federalism—From the Civil War to the 1930s

Scholars have devised various models to describe the relationship between the states and the national government at different times in our history. These models are useful in describing the evolution of federalism after the Civil War.

The model of **dual federalism** assumes that the states and the national government are more or less equals, with each level of government having separate and distinct functions and responsibilities. The states exercise sovereign powers over certain matters, and the national government exercises sovereign powers over others.

For much of our nation's history, this model of federalism prevailed. After the expansion of national authority during the Civil War, the courts again tended to support the states' rights to exercise police powers and tended to strictly limit the powers of the federal government under the commerce clause. In 1918, for example, the Supreme Court ruled unconstitutional a 1916 federal law excluding from interstate commerce the products created through the use of child labor. The law was held unconstitutional because it attempted to regulate a local problem.[7] The era of dual federalism came to an end in the

secession The act of formally withdrawing from membership in an alliance; the withdrawal of a state from the federal Union.

dual federalism A system of government in which the federal and the state governments maintain diverse but sovereign powers.

SOCIAL MEDIA In Politics

Searching on "civil war" in Facebook brings up the Civil War page of the *New York Times*. This page has a wealth of historical information plus popular discussions about these crucial events.

President Franklin D. Roosevelt supported many new federal programs during the Great Depression.

Depression, President Franklin D. Roosevelt (1933–1945) launched his **New Deal,** which involved many government-spending and public-assistance programs. Roosevelt's New Deal legislation not only ushered in an era of cooperative federalism, which has more or less continued until the present day, but also marked the real beginning of an era of national supremacy.

Before the period of cooperative federalism could be truly established, it was necessary to obtain the concurrence of the United States Supreme Court. As mentioned, in the early part of the twentieth century, the Court held a very restrictive view of what the federal government could do under the commerce clause. In the 1930s, the Court ruled again and again that various economic measures were unconstitutional.

In 1937, Roosevelt threatened to "pack" the Court with up to six new members who presumably would be more favorable to federal action. This move was widely considered to be an assault on the Constitution, and Congress refused to support it. Later that year, however, Roosevelt had the opportunity—for the first time since taking office—to appoint a new member of the Supreme Court. Hugo Black, the new justice, tipped the balance on the Court. After 1937, the Court ceased its attempts to limit the scope of the commerce clause.

1930s, when the United States was in the depths of the greatest economic depression it had ever experienced.

3–3d Cooperative Federalism and the Growth of the National Government

The model of **cooperative federalism,** as the term implies, involves cooperation by all branches of government. This model views the national and state governments as complementary parts of a single governmental mechanism, the purpose of which is to solve the problems facing the entire United States. For example, federal law enforcement agencies, such as the Federal Bureau of Investigation, lend technical expertise to solve local crimes, and local officials cooperate with federal agencies.

cooperative federalism A model of federalism in which the states and the federal government cooperate in solving problems.

New Deal The policies ushered in by the Roosevelt administration in 1933 in an attempt to bring the United States out of the Great Depression.

Roosevelt's New Deal

Cooperative federalism grew out of the desire to solve the pressing national problems caused by the Great Depression, which began in 1929. In an attempt to bring the United States out of the

Cooperative Federalism and the "Great Society" The 1960s and 1970s saw an even greater expansion of the national government's role in domestic policy. The Great Society legislation of President Lyndon B. Johnson (1963–1969) created Medicaid, Medicare, the Job Corps, Operation Head Start, and other programs. The Civil Rights Act of 1964 prohibited discrimination in public accommodations, employment, and other areas on the basis of race, color, national origin, religion, or gender. In the 1970s, national laws protecting consumers, employees, and the environment imposed further regulations on the economy. Today, few activities are beyond the reach of the regulatory arm of the national government.

Nonetheless, the massive social programs undertaken in the 1960s and 1970s also resulted in greater involvement by state and local governments. The national government simply could not implement those programs alone. For example, Head Start, a program that provides preschool services to children of low-income families, is administered by local nonprofit organizations and school systems, although it is funded by federal grants.

Head Start is a program initiated by the federal government but administered by local nonprofit organizations. Why doesn't the federal government operate this program directly?

JOHN MOORE/GETTY IMAGES

time since the 1930s, occasionally curbed Congress's regulatory powers under the commerce clause. You will read more about this development shortly.

Federal Preemption and Cooperative Federalism John Marshall's validation of the supremacy clause of the Constitution has also had significant consequences for federalism. One important effect of the supremacy clause today is that the clause allows for federal **preemption** of certain areas in which the national government and the states have concurrent powers. When Congress chooses to act exclusively in an area in which the states and the national government have concurrent powers, Congress is said to have *preempted* the area. In such cases, the courts have held that a valid federal law or regulation takes precedence over a conflicting state or local law or regulation covering the same general activity.

The model in which every level of government is involved in implementing a policy is sometimes referred to as **picket-fence federalism.** In this model, the policy area is the vertical picket on the fence, while the levels of government are the horizontal support boards.

The Commerce Clause and Cooperative Federalism

The two United States Supreme Court decisions discussed earlier, *McCulloch v. Maryland* and *Gibbons v. Ogden*, became the constitutional cornerstone of the regulatory powers that the national government enjoys today. From 1937 on, the Supreme Court consistently upheld Congress's power to regulate domestic policy under the commerce clause. Even activities that occur entirely within a state were rarely considered to be outside the regulatory power of the national government. For example, in 1942 the Supreme Court held that wheat production by an individual farmer intended wholly for consumption on his own farm was subject to federal regulation because the home consumption of wheat reduced the demand for wheat and thus could have an effect on interstate commerce.[8]

In 1980, the Supreme Court acknowledged that the commerce clause had "long been interpreted to extend beyond activities actually in interstate commerce to reach other activities that, while wholly local in nature, nevertheless substantially affect interstate commerce."[9] Today, Congress can regulate almost any kind of economic activity, no matter where it occurs. In recent years, though, the Supreme Court has, for the first

FOR CRITICAL THINKING

Although marijuana is illegal under national law, Colorado and Washington are trying to legalize and tax it. Should the federal government take a hands-off approach or crack down on these states? Why or why not?

3–4 Federalism Today

By the 1970s, some Americans had begun to question whether the national government had acquired too many powers. Had the national government gotten too big? Had it become, in fact, a threat to the power of the states and the liberties of the people? Should steps be taken to reduce the regulatory power and scope of the national government? Since that time, the model

picket-fence federalism
A model of federalism in which specific policies and programs are administered by all levels of government —national, state, and local.

preemption A doctrine rooted in the supremacy clause of the Constitution that provides that national laws or regulations governing a certain area take precedence over conflicting state laws or regulations governing that same area.

of federalism has evolved in ways that reflect these and other concerns.

3–4a The New Federalism— More Power to the States

Starting in the 1970s, several administrations attempted to revitalize the doctrine of dual federalism, which they renamed the "new federalism." The **new federalism** involved a shift from *nation-centered* federalism to *state-centered* federalism. One of the major goals of the new federalism was to return to the states certain powers that had been exercised by the national government since the 1930s. The term **devolution**—the transfer of powers to political subunits—is often used to describe this process.

Although a product of conservative thought and initiated by Republicans, the devolutionary goals of the new federalism were also espoused by the Clinton administration (1993–2001). An example of the new federalism is the welfare reform legislation passed by Congress in 1996, which gave the states more authority over welfare programs.

3–4b The Supreme Court and the New Federalism

new federalism A plan to limit the federal government's role in regulating state governments and to give the states increased power in deciding how they should spend government revenues.

devolution The surrender or transfer of powers to local authorities by a central government.

federal mandate A requirement in federal legislation that forces states and municipalities to comply with certain rules.

During and since the 1990s, the Supreme Court has played a significant role in furthering the cause of states' rights. All of the following decisions, for example, either limited the power of the federal government or enhanced the power of the states.

- In a landmark 1995 decision, *United States v. Lopez,*[10] the Supreme Court held, for the first time in sixty years, that Congress had exceeded its constitutional authority under the commerce clause. The Court concluded that the Gun-Free School Zones Act of 1990, which banned the possession of guns within one thousand feet of any school, was unconstitutional because it attempted to regulate an area that had "nothing to do with commerce."

- In a 1997 decision, the Court struck down portions of the Brady Handgun Violence Prevention Act of 1993, which obligated state and local law enforcement officers to do background checks on prospective handgun buyers until a national instant-check system could be implemented. The Court stated that Congress lacked the power to "dragoon" state employees into federal service through an unfunded **federal mandate** of this kind.[11]

- In 2000, the Court invalidated a key provision of the federal Violence Against Women Act of 1994, which allowed women to sue in federal court when they were victims of gender-motivated violence, such as rape. The Court upheld a federal appellate court's ruling that the commerce clause did not justify national regulation of noneconomic, criminal conduct.[12]

- In *Massachusetts v. Environmental Protection Agency,*[13] Massachusetts and several other states sued the Environmental Protection Agency (EPA) for failing to regulate greenhouse-gas emissions. The states asserted that the agency was required to do so by the Clean Air Act of 1990. The EPA argued that it lacked the authority under the Clean Air Act to regulate greenhouse-gas emissions alleged to promote climate change. In a 2007 decision, the Court ruled for the states, holding that the EPA did have the authority to regulate such emissions and should take steps to do so.

3–4c The Shifting Boundary between Federal and State Authority

Clearly, the boundary between federal and state authority has been shifting. Notably, issues relating to the federal structure of our government, which at one time were not at the forefront of the political arena, have in recent years been the subject of heated debate among Americans and their leaders. The federal government and the states seem to be in a constant tug-of-war over federal regulations, federal programs, and federal demands on the states.

The Politics of Federalism The Republican Party is often viewed as the champion of states' rights.

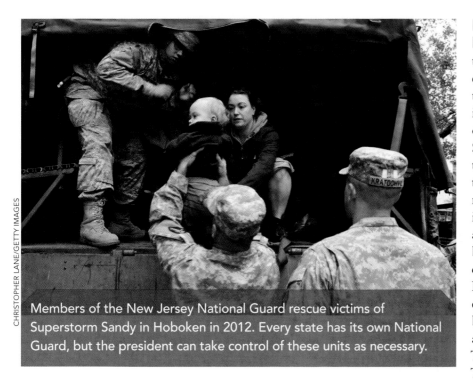

Members of the New Jersey National Guard rescue victims of Superstorm Sandy in Hoboken in 2012. Every state has its own National Guard, but the president can take control of these units as necessary.

Federalism and the Economic Crisis Unlike the federal government, state governments are supposed to balance their budgets. This requirement is written into the constitution of every state except Vermont. Such requirements do not prevent the states from borrowing, but typically when a state borrows, it must follow strict rules laid down in its constitution. Frequently, a vote of the people is required before a state or local government can go into debt by issuing bonds. In contrast, when the federal government runs a budget deficit, the borrowing that results takes place almost automatically—the U.S. Treasury continually issues new Treasury securities.

Certainly, the party has claimed such a role. For example, when the Republicans took control of both chambers of Congress in 1995, they promised devolution—which, as already noted, refers to a shifting of power from the national level to the individual states. Smaller central government and a state-centered federalism have long been regarded as the twin pillars of Republican ideology. In contrast, Democrats usually have sought greater centralization of power in Washington, D.C.

Since the Clinton administration, however, there have been times when the party tables seem to have turned. As mentioned earlier, it was under Clinton that welfare reform legislation giving more responsibility to the states—a goal that had been endorsed by the Republicans for some time—became a reality. Conversely, the No Child Left Behind Act of 2001, passed at the request of Republican president George W. Bush, gave the federal government a much greater role in education and educational funding than ever before.

Many Republicans also supported a constitutional amendment that would ban same-sex marriages nationwide. Liberals, recognizing that it was possible to win support for same-sex marriages only in a limited number of states, took a states' rights position on this issue. Finally, the Bush administration made repeated attempts to block California's medical-marijuana initiative and Oregon's physician-assisted suicide law.

STATE SPENDING IN A RECESSION. A practical result is that when a major recession occurs, the states are faced with severe budget problems. Because state citizens are earning and spending less, state income and sales taxes fall. At the same time, people who have lost their jobs require more state services. The costs of welfare, unemployment compensation, and Medicaid (health care for low-income persons) all rise. During a recession, state governments may be forced either to reduce spending and lay off staff—or to raise taxes. Either choice helps make the recession worse. State-spending patterns tend to make economic booms more energetic and busts more painful—in a word, they are *procyclical.*

FEDERAL SPENDING IN A RECESSION. The federal government has no difficulty in spending more on welfare, unemployment compensation, and Medicaid during a recession. Even though revenue raised through the federal income tax may fall, the federal government often cuts tax rates in a recession to spur the economy. It makes up the difference by going further into debt, an option not always available to the states. The federal government even has the power to reduce its debt by issuing new money. In a recession, the actions of the federal government are normally *anticyclical.*

One method of dealing with the procyclical nature of state spending is to increase federal grants to the

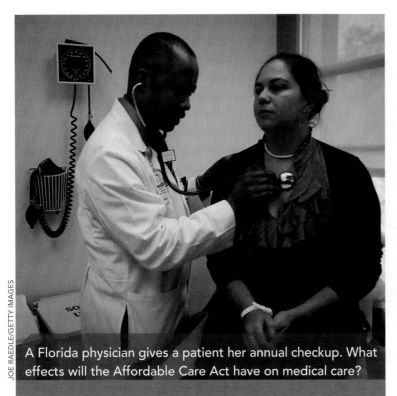

JOE RAEDLE/GETTY IMAGES

A Florida physician gives a patient her annual checkup. What effects will the Affordable Care Act have on medical care?

did allow Arizona to check the immigration status of individuals arrested for reasons other than immigration status. But it reserved the right to rule against Arizona on that issue, too, if the state was shown to practice racial discrimination in its arrests.[14]

HEALTH-CARE REFORM. The second of the Court's major rulings on federalism in 2012 concerned the constitutionality of the Affordable Care Act, popularly known as Obamacare. In this case, *National Federation of Independent Business v. Sebelius,* the Court upheld most of the law. Two of Chief Justice John Roberts's arguments, however, seemed to set new limits on the powers of the national government.

Roberts contended that the federal government could not, under the commerce clause of the Constitution, *require* individuals to purchase something—in this case, health-care insurance. Roberts did allow the government to encourage such behavior through the tax code, however. Roberts also ruled that the national government cannot force the states to expand Medicaid by threatening to take away all of their Medicaid funds if they do not. Roberts argued that cutting the states off completely would do too much damage to their budgets.[15]

Both of these arguments—on purchasing insurance and on forcing the states to expand Medicaid—were novel, at least in the opinion of most constitutional scholars. Many observers also doubt, however, that these two arguments will have much impact in the future. It is not likely that Congress would want to require individuals to purchase a service in contexts other than health-care insurance. Also, the ruling against the government on Medicaid was based on the enormous size of the penalty. If Congress in the future wanted to pressure the states to expand Medicaid, it presumably could do so by threatening to withhold, say, 10 percent of a state's Medicaid funds instead of all of them.

Although the decision did not substantially change Obamacare, the case did demonstrate that the Court was more willing to challenge the national government on its use of the commerce clause than at any time since 1937. Indeed, four of the nine justices advocated positions on the commerce clause that, in terms of recent legal understanding, were almost revolutionary.

states during a recession. Such grants were included in the February 2009 stimulus legislation championed by President Obama. By the middle of 2010, however, the grants had largely dried up. From 2010 through 2012, the states laid off a substantial number of employees.

The Supreme Court Weighs In Again
In June 2012, the United States Supreme Court issued two rulings that addressed the relative power of the national government and the states. One decision dealt with immigration and the other with health-care reform legislation.

IMMIGRATION. In *Arizona v. United States,* the Supreme Court confirmed national authority over immigration by striking down three provisions of a tough Arizona immigration law.

The rejected provisions would have (1) subjected illegal immigrants to criminal penalties for activities such as seeking work, (2) made it a state crime for immigrants to fail to register with the federal government, and (3) allowed police to arrest people without warrants if they had reason to believe that the individuals were deportable.

The Court stated that "Arizona may have understandable frustrations with the problems caused by illegal immigration . . . but the State may not pursue policies that undermine federal law." The Court

FOR CRITICAL THINKING

Do you think that the relative power of the state and national governments will be more of an issue in future years, or do you think the dispute will become less important? Explain your reasoning.

3-5 The Fiscal Side of Federalism

Learning Outcome 3-5

Explain what is meant by the term *fiscal federalism.*

Since the advent of cooperative federalism in the 1930s, the national government and the states have worked hand in hand to implement programs mandated by the national government. Whenever Congress passes a law that preempts a certain area, the states are, of course, obligated to comply with the requirements of that law. As already noted, a requirement that a state provide a service or undertake some activity to meet standards specified by a federal law is called a *federal mandate.* Many federal mandates concern civil rights or environmental protection. Recent federal mandates require the states to provide persons with disabilities with access to public buildings, sidewalks, and other areas; to establish minimum water-purity and air-purity standards; and to extend Medicaid coverage to all poor children.

To help the states pay for some of the costs associated with implementing national policies, the national government gives back some of the tax dollars it collects to the states in the form of grants. As you will see, the states have come to depend on grants as an important source of revenue. When taxes are collected by one level of government (typically the national government) and spent by another level (typically state or local governments), we call the process **fiscal federalism.**

3-5a Federal Grants

Even before the Constitution was adopted, the national government granted lands to the states to finance education. Using the proceeds from the sale of these lands, the states were able to establish elementary schools and, later, *land-grant colleges.* Cash grants started in 1808, when Congress gave funds to the states to pay for the state militias. Federal grants were also made available for other purposes, such as building roads and railroads.

Only in the twentieth century, though, did federal grants become an important source of funds to the states. The major growth began in the 1960s, when the dollar amount of grants quadrupled to help pay for the Great Society programs of the Johnson administration. Grants became available for education, pollution control, conservation, recreation, highway construction and maintenance, and other purposes. There are two basic types of federal grants: categorical grants and block grants.

Categorical Grants A **categorical grant** is targeted for a specific purpose as defined by federal law—the federal government defines hundreds of categories of state and local spending. Categorical grants give the national government control over how states use the funds by imposing certain conditions. For example, a categorical grant may require that the funds must be used for the purpose of repairing interstate highways and that the projects cannot pay below the local prevailing wage. Depending on the project, the government might require that an environmental impact statement be prepared.

Block Grants A **block grant** is given for a broad area, such as criminal justice or mental-health programs. The term *block grant* was coined in 1966 to describe a series of programs initiated by President Johnson, although a number of federal grants issued earlier in our history shared some of the characteristics of modern block grants. Block grants now constitute a growing percentage of all federal aid programs.

A block grant gives the states more discretion over how the funds will be spent. Nonetheless, the federal government can exercise control over state decision making through these grants by using *cross-cutting requirements,* or requirements that apply to all federal grants. Title

fiscal federalism The allocation of taxes collected by one level of government (typically the national government) to another level (typically state or local governments).

categorical grant A federal grant targeted for a specific purpose as defined by federal law.

block grant A federal grant given to a state for a broad area, such as criminal justice or mental-health programs.

VI of the 1964 Civil Rights Act, for example, bars racial discrimination in the use of all federal funds, regardless of their source.

3–5b Federal Grants and State Budgets

Currently, about one-fifth of state and local revenue comes from the national government. In fiscal year 2013, the federal government transferred about $635 billion to state and local governments—more than half a trillion dollars. By far, the largest transfer was for Medicaid, the health-care program for the poor. It totaled $334 billion. The federal government provided the states with about $104 billion for education. Highway grants ran more than $45 billion.

When the media discuss state and local budgets, they typically refer just to the general fund budgets, which are largely supported by state and local taxes. But, in fact, state and local taxes support just under half of state and local spending. Federal funds aren't listed in general fund budgets. Further, more than one-third of state and local spending goes to fee-for-service operations, in which governments charge for the services they provide. This spending applies to functions such as water supply, sewers, and other public utilities; fees charged by government-owned hospitals and airports; college tuition; and much else. Typically, these operations are also excluded from general fund budgets.

3–5c Using Federal Grants to Control the States

Grants of funds to the states from the national government are one way that the Tenth Amendment to the U.S. Constitution can be bridged. Remember that the Tenth Amendment reserves all powers not delegated to the national government to the states and to the people. You might well wonder, then, how the federal government has been able to exercise control over matters that traditionally have been under the authority of state governments, such as the minimum drinking age. The answer involves the giving or withholding of federal grant dollars.

For example, as noted in the *America at Odds* feature at the beginning of this chapter, the national government forced the states to raise the minimum

> **"Taxes,** after all, are the dues that we pay for the privilege of membership in an **organized society."**
>
> ~ FRANKLIN D. ROOSEVELT ~
> THIRTY-SECOND PRESIDENT
> OF THE UNITED STATES
> 1933–1945

drinking age to twenty-one by threatening to withhold federal highway funds from states that did not comply. Obamacare also raised questions about forcing the states to expand Medicaid, as discussed earlier in this chapter. The education reforms embodied in the No Child Left Behind Act rely on federal funding for their implementation as well. The states receive block grants for educational purposes and, in return, must meet federally imposed standards for testing and accountability.

3–5d The Cost of Federal Mandates

As mentioned earlier, when the national government passes a law preempting an area in which the states and the national government have concurrent powers, the states must comply with that law in accordance with the supremacy clause of the Constitution. Thus, when such laws require the states to implement certain programs, the states must comply—but compliance with federal mandates can be costly. The cost of compliance has been estimated by some at $29 billion annually, and some believe the true figure to be much higher. Although Congress passed legislation in 1995 to curb the use of unfunded federal mandates, that legislation was more rhetoric than reality.

Even when funding is provided, it may be insufficient, resulting in an *underfunded* federal mandate. As mentioned earlier, for example, states receive block grants for educational purposes in return for meeting standards imposed by the federal No Child Left Behind Act. Critics argue that the national government does not supply the states with enough funds to implement the act.

3–5e Competitive Federalism

The debate over federalism is sometimes reduced to a debate over taxes. Which level of government will raise taxes to pay for government programs, and which will cut services to avoid raising taxes?

The Right to Move How states answer that question gives citizens an option: they can move to a state with fewer services and lower taxes, or to a state with more services but higher taxes. Political

The City of Detroit filed for bankruptcy in 2013, and these Detroit firefighters are worried about their jobs and pensions. A major cause of the bankruptcy was a fall in the city's population from 1.8 million in 1950 to 700,000 today. If cities compete to attract residents, Detroit has clearly been losing. This loss helped make it impossible for the city to pay its debts, including its pension obligations.

scientist Thomas R. Dye calls this model of federalism **competitive federalism**. State and local governments compete for businesses and citizens. If the state of Ohio offers tax advantages for locating a factory there, for example, a business may be more likely to build its factory in Ohio, thereby providing more jobs for Ohio residents.

If Ohio has very strict environmental regulations, however, that same business may choose not to build there, no matter how beneficial the tax advantages, because complying with the regulations would be costly. Although Ohio citizens lose the opportunity for more jobs, they may enjoy better air and water quality than citizens of the state where the new factory is ultimately built.

Advantages and Disadvantages of Competition

Some observers consider such competition an advantage: Americans have several variables to consider when they choose a state in which to live. Others consider it a disadvantage: a state that offers more social services or lower taxes may experience an increase in population as people "vote with their feet" to take advantage of that state's laws. The resulting population increases can overwhelm the state's resources and force it to cut social services or raise taxes. Regulations that make it easier to build new

housing may also draw in new residents. Recent studies suggest that much of the difference in population growth rates among states in recent decades may be due to differences in the cost of housing.

It appears likely, then, that the debate over how our federal system functions, as well as the battle for control between the states and the federal government, will continue. The Supreme Court, which has played umpire in this battle, will also likely continue to issue rulings that influence the balance of power.

competitive federalism A model of federalism in which state and local governments compete for businesses and citizens, who in effect "vote with their feet" by moving to jurisdictions that offer a competitive advantage.

FOR CRITICAL THINKING

What kinds of factors might cause you to consider moving to a different state? Are any of these factors under the control of state governments?

AMERICA AT
ODDS Federalism

The topic of federalism raises one of the most enduring disputes in American history—the relative power of the national government versus that of the governments of the states. As you read in the last two chapters, Americans have been at odds over the strength of the central government since well before the American Revolution. The issue of centralization versus decentralization has taken a number of specific forms:

- Is it right for the national government to use its financial strength to pressure states into taking actions such as raising the drinking age by threatening to withhold subsidies—or are such pressures an abuse of the federal system?

- Should the national government intervene in the issue of legalizing or banning same-sex marriages—or leave such matters strictly to the states?

- Should the commerce clause be interpreted broadly, granting the federal government much power to regulate the economy—or should it be interpreted as narrowly as possible to keep the government from interfering with the rights of business owners?

- Should the federal government have a role in setting national policies for public education—or should that be left entirely to the states?

- Should the federal government establish a national system for funding health care—or should that, too, be left to the states or to the private sector?

STUDY TOOLS

Ready to study?

- **Review** what you've read with the quiz below.
- Check your answers on the **Chapter in Review** card at the back of the book.
- For any questions you miss, read the corresponding **Learning Outcome** section again to prepare for class and your exam.
- Rip out and study the **Chapter in Review** card (at the back of the book).

Fill-In

Learning Outcome 3–1

1. The advantages of a federal system of government in the United States include _____.

Learning Outcome 3–2

2. The constitutional basis for the implied powers of the national government is the _____ clause.

3. The Constitution's _____ clause requires each state to honor every other state's public acts, records, and judicial proceedings.

Learning Outcome 3–3

4. In *McCulloch v. Maryland*, a case decided in 1819, the United States Supreme Court established the doctrines of _____.

5. Cooperative federalism grew out of the need to solve the pressing problems caused by _____.

Learning Outcome 3–4

6. The relationship of national, state, and local levels of government in implementing massive social programs in the 1960s and 1970s is often referred to as _____ federalism.

7. A _____ is a requirement in federal legislation that forces states and municipalities to comply with certain rules.

Learning Outcome 3–5

8. The national government forced the states to raise the minimum drinking age to twenty-one by _____.

Multiple Choice

Learning Outcome 3–1

9. In a unitary system,
   a. subdivisional governments exercise only those powers given to them by the central government.
   b. sovereign states are joined together by a central government that has only limited powers over them.
   c. there are no local or subdivisional governments.

10. There are ___ governmental units in the United States today.
   a. 51   b. nearly 3,000   c. almost 90,000

Learning Outcome 3–2

11. Article I, Section 8, of the U.S. Constitution enumerates twenty-seven powers that Congress may exercise. Two of these _____ powers are the power to coin money and the power to regulate interstate commerce.
   a. concurrent   b. expressed   c. inherent

12. The relationships among the states in our federal system of government are sometimes referred to as _____ federalism.
   a. picket-fence   b. cooperative   c. horizontal

Learning Outcome 3–3

13. The era of _____ federalism came to an end in the 1930s.
   a. dual   b. new   c. competitive

Learning Outcome 3–4

14. The welfare reform legislation passed by Congress in 1996 is an example of _____ federalism.
   a. dual   b. cooperative   c. new

Learning Outcome 3–5

15. Block grants
   a. are targeted for specific purposes as defined by federal law.
   b. are federal grants given to a state for broad areas, such as criminal justice or mental-health programs.
   c. give the states less discretion than categorical grants over how funds will be spent.

Civil Liberties

MLADEN ANTONOV/AFP/GETTY IMAGES

The **Learning Outcomes** labeled 1 through 4 are designed to help improve your understanding of the chapter. After reading this chapter, you should be able to:

4–1 Define the term *civil liberties*, explain how civil liberties differ from civil rights, and state the constitutional basis for our civil liberties.

4–2 List and describe the freedoms guaranteed by the First Amendment and explain how the courts have interpreted and applied these freedoms.

4–3 Discuss why Americans are increasingly concerned about privacy rights.

4–4 Summarize how the Constitution and the Bill of Rights protect the rights of accused persons.

Remember to visit page 91 for additional Study Tools

AMERICA AT ODDS

Do U.S. Citizens Really Need Military-Style Rifles?

MELANIE STETSON FREEMAN/ THE CHRISTIAN SCIENCE MONITOR VIA GETTY IMAGES

The Second Amendment to the U.S. Constitution states that the people have the right "to keep and bear arms." The Supreme Court has ruled that this right is enjoyed by individuals, not just state militias. In these rulings, however, the Court has also said that the national and state governments may limit the types of weapons that individuals may hold. Should ordinary citizens have a right to own rifles based on military weapons?

This issue came to the fore after a shooter killed twenty-six children and teachers in December 2012 at the Sandy Hook Elementary School in Connecticut. The shooter used a semiautomatic rifle based on the military's M4 carbine. Earlier that year, a shooter used a similar rifle with a hundred-round magazine in a movie theater in Colorado. He killed twelve people and wounded fifty-eight. Proposed gun control legislation to ban such weapons and magazines failed to pass Congress in 2013. Nevertheless, Americans remain at odds about whether military-style rifles and high-round magazines should be legal.

The Second Amendment Means What It Says

Those who do not believe that Congress should ban military-style rifles maintain that such weapons are fully covered by the constitutional right to bear arms. The most popular military-style rifle is the AR-15, based on the military's M16. Other rifles are based on the similar but lighter M4. These civilian rifles are semiautomatic, which means that the trigger must be pulled once for each shot. That makes these weapons different from fully automatic military weapons that can spray bullets like water from a hose. Plenty of civilian weapons other than the AR-15 are semiautomatic, including many handguns and deer rifles. Yet they were exempt from the recent proposed legislation.

From 1994 to 2004, the Federal Assault Weapons Ban outlawed military-style semiautomatic rifles. This law did not reduce the national murder rate. Although the murder rate fell throughout this period, the decline would have occurred even if these weapons had not been banned. After all, only 2.6 percent of all murders are committed using any type of rifle.

Citizens Don't Need Military-Style Rifles

Although the National Rifle Association claims that semiautomatic military-style rifles are useful for hunting, target practice, and home defense, they are not. The AR-15's .223 caliber ammunition is too light for deer hunting and useless for waterfowl. The low-power .22 rimfire cartridge—not the high-power .223—is the international standard for target competition. An ordinary 12-gauge shotgun is vastly superior for home protection, and a handgun is best for self-defense in other circumstances.

The AR-15/M16 was designed in 1957 for the U.S. Army. This rifle, and its more recent M4 version, is optimized for one purpose only—killing the largest number of enemy possible on the battlefield. How can such a weapon be legitimate in a civilian context? Let's face it: military-style rifles are popular because they appeal to owners' dangerous fantasies of domestic chaos or insurrection. *World War Z* is not an acceptable basis for national policy.

Where do you stand?

1. Should the Second Amendment be interpreted to mean that anyone can own any weapon anywhere at anytime? Why or why not?
2. Could a citizens' militia possibly be effective against an attempt to install a dictator?

Explore this issue online

- For a defense of the right to bear the AR-15, search on "lott wsj assault weapons" for an article by John Lott.
- Justin Peters criticizes the usefulness of the AR-15—enter "slate peters hunting."
- Finally, Matt Steinglass attacks the fantasies of AR-15 owners at "economist treason."

Introduction

The debate over military-style rifles, discussed in the chapter-opening *America at Odds* feature, is but one of many controversies concerning our civil liberties. **Civil liberties** are legal and constitutional rights that protect citizens from government actions.

Perhaps the best way to understand what civil liberties are and why they are important to Americans is to look at what might happen if we did not have them. If you were a student in China, for example, you would have to exercise some care in what you said and did. That country prohibits a variety of kinds of speech, notably any criticism of the leading role of the Communist Party. If you criticized the government in e-mail messages to your friends or on your Web site, you could end up in court on charges that you had violated the law—and perhaps even go to prison.

Note that some Americans confuse *civil liberties* (discussed in this chapter) with *civil rights* (discussed in the next chapter) and use the terms interchangeably. Scholars, however, make a distinction between the two. They point out that whereas civil liberties are limitations on government action, setting forth what the government *cannot* do, civil rights specify what the government *must* do—for example, ensure equal protection under the law for all Americans.

4-1 The Constitutional Basis for Our Civil Liberties

The founders believed that the constitutions of the individual states contained ample provisions to protect citizens from government actions. Therefore, the founders did not include many references to individual civil liberties in the original version of the Constitution. Many of our liberties were added by the Bill of Rights, ratified in 1791. Nonetheless, the original Constitution did include some safeguards to protect citizens against an overly powerful government.

4-1a Safeguards in the Original Constitution

Article I, Section 9, of the Constitution provides that the writ of *habeas corpus* (a Latin phrase that roughly means "produce the body") will be available to all citizens except in times of rebellion or national invasion. A **writ of habeas corpus** is an order requiring that an official bring a specified prisoner into court and explain to the judge why the prisoner is being held in jail. If the court finds that the imprisonment is unlawful, it orders the prisoner to be released. If our country did not have such a constitutional provision, political leaders could jail their opponents without giving them the opportunity to plead their cases before a judge. Without this opportunity, many opponents might conveniently be left to rot away in prison.

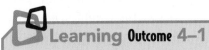

Learning Outcome 4-1

Define the term *civil liberties*, explain how civil liberties differ from civil rights, and state the constitutional basis for our civil liberties.

The Constitution also prohibits Congress and the state legislatures from passing bills of attainder. A **bill of attainder** is a legislative act that directly punishes a specifically named individual (or a group or class of individuals) without a trial. For example, no legislature can pass a law that punishes a named Hollywood celebrity for unpatriotic statements.

Finally, the Constitution also prohibits Congress from passing *ex post facto laws*. The Latin term *ex post facto* roughly means "after the fact." An ***ex post facto* law** punishes individuals for committing an act that was legal when it was committed.

4-1b The Bill of Rights

As you read in Chapter 2, one of the contentious issues in the debate over ratification of the Constitution was the lack of protections for citizens from government actions. Although many state constitutions provided such protections, the Anti-Federalists wanted more. The promise of the addition of a bill of rights to the Constitution ensured its ratification.

The Bill of Rights was ratified by the states and became part of the Constitution on December 15, 1791. Look at the text of the Bill of Rights in Table 4–1 on the following page. As you can see, the first eight

TABLE 4-1

The Bill of Rights

Amendment I.
Religion, Speech, Press, Assembly, and Petition

Congress shall make no law respecting an establishment of religion, or prohibiting the free exercise thereof; or abridging the freedom of speech, or of the press; or the right of the people peaceably to assemble, and to petition the Government for a redress of grievances.

Congress may not create an official church or enact laws limiting the freedom of religion, speech, the press, assembly, and petition. These guarantees, like the others in the Bill of Rights (the first ten amendments), are not absolute—each right may be exercised only with regard to the rights of other persons.

Amendment II.
Militia and the Right to Bear Arms

A well regulated Militia, being necessary to the security of a free State, the right of the people to keep and bear Arms, shall not be infringed.

Each state has the right to maintain a volunteer armed force. Although individuals have the right to bear arms, states and the federal government may regulate the possession and use of firearms by individuals.

Amendment III.
The Quartering of Soldiers

No Soldier shall, in time of peace be quartered in any house, without the consent of the Owner, nor in time of war, but in a manner to be prescribed by law.

Before the Revolutionary War, it had been common British practice to quarter soldiers in colonists' homes. Military troops do not have the power to take over private houses during peacetime.

Amendment IV.
Searches and Seizures

The right of the people to be secure in their persons, houses, papers, and effects, against unreasonable searches and seizures, shall not be violated, and no Warrants shall issue, but upon probable cause, supported by Oath or affirmation, and particularly describing the place to be searched, and the persons or things to be seized.

Here, the word warrant refers to a document issued by a magistrate or judge indicating the name, address, and possible offense committed. Anyone asking for a warrant, such as a police officer, must be able to convince the magistrate or judge that an offense probably has been committed.

Amendment V.
Grand Juries, Self-Incrimination, Double Jeopardy, Due Process, and Eminent Domain

No person shall be held to answer for a capital, or otherwise infamous crime, unless on a presentment or indictment of a Grand Jury, except in cases arising in the land or naval forces, or in the Militia, when in actual service in time of War or public danger; nor shall any person be subject for the same offense to be twice put in jeopardy of life or limb; nor shall be compelled in any criminal case to be a witness against himself, nor be deprived of life, liberty, or property, without due process of law; nor shall private property be taken for public use, without just compensation.

There are two types of juries. A grand jury considers physical evidence and the testimony of witnesses and decides whether there is sufficient reason to bring a case to trial. A petit jury hears the case at trial and decides it. "For the same offense to be twice put in jeopardy of life or limb" means to be tried twice for the same crime. A person

may not be tried for the same crime twice or forced to give evidence against herself or himself. No person's right to life, liberty, or property may be taken away except by lawful means, called the due process of law. Private property taken for public purposes must be paid for by the government.

Amendment VI.
Criminal Court Procedures

In all criminal prosecutions, the accused shall enjoy the right to a speedy and public trial, by an impartial jury of the State and district wherein the crime shall have been committed, which district shall have been previously ascertained by law, and to be informed of the nature and cause of the accusation; to be confronted with the witnesses against him; to have compulsory process for obtaining witnesses in his favor, and to have the Assistance of Counsel for his defence.

Any person accused of a crime has the right to a fair and public trial by a jury in the state in which the crime took place. The charges against that person must be made clear. Any accused person has the right to a lawyer to defend him or her and to question those who testify against him or her, as well as the right to call people to speak in his or her favor at trial.

Amendment VII.
Trial by Jury in Civil Cases

In Suits at common law, where the value in controversy shall exceed twenty dollars, the right of trial by jury shall be preserved, and no fact tried by a jury, shall be otherwise reexamined in any Court of the United States, than according to the rules of the common law.

A jury trial may be requested by either party in a dispute in any case involving more than $20. If both parties agree to a trial by a judge without a jury, the right to a jury trial may be put aside.

Amendment VIII.
Bail, Cruel and Unusual Punishment

Excessive bail shall not be required, nor excessive fines imposed, nor cruel and unusual punishments inflicted.

Bail is that amount of money that a person accused of a crime may be required to deposit with the court as a guarantee that she or he will appear in court when requested. The amount of bail required or the fine imposed as punishment for a crime must be reasonable compared with the seriousness of the crime involved. Any punishment judged to be too harsh or too severe for a crime shall be prohibited.

Amendment IX.
The Rights Retained by the People

The enumeration in the Constitution, of certain rights, shall not be construed to deny or disparage others retained by the people.

Many civil rights that are not explicitly enumerated in the Constitution are still held by the people.

Amendment X.
Reserved Powers of the States

The powers not delegated to the United States by the Constitution, nor prohibited by it to the States, are reserved to the States respectively, or to the people.

Those powers not delegated by the Constitution to the federal government or expressly denied to the states belong to the states and to the people. This clause in essence allows the states to pass laws under their "police powers."

amendments grant the people specific rights and liberties. The remaining two amendments reserve certain rights and powers to the people and to the states.

Basically, in a democracy, government policy tends to reflect the view of the majority. A key function of the Bill of Rights, therefore, is to protect the rights of those in the minority against the will of the majority. When there is disagreement over how to interpret the Bill of Rights, the courts step in.

The United States Supreme Court, as our nation's highest court, has the final say as to how the Constitution, including the Bill of Rights, should be interpreted. The civil liberties that you will read about in this chapter have all been shaped over time by Supreme Court decisions. For example, it is the Supreme Court that determines where freedom of speech ends and the right of society to be protected from certain forms of speech begins.

THE FIRST AMENDMENT to the Constitution mandates separation of church and state. Nonetheless, references to God are common in public life, as the phrase "In God We Trust" on this coin demonstrates.

v. Baltimore (1833), that the Bill of Rights did not apply to state laws.[1]

Eventually, however, the Supreme Court began to take a different view. Because the Fourteenth Amendment played a key role in this development, we look next at the provisions of that amendment.

The Right to Due Process In 1868, three years after the end of the Civil War, the Fourteenth Amendment was added to the Constitution. The **due process clause** of this amendment requires that state governments protect their citizens' rights. (A similar requirement, binding on the federal government, was provided by the Fifth Amendment.) The due process clause reads, in part, as follows:

> No State shall . . . deprive any person of life, liberty, or property, without due process of law.

The right to **due process of law** is simply the right to be treated fairly under the legal system. That system and its officers must follow "rules of fair play" in making decisions, in determining guilt or innocence, and in punishing those who have been found guilty. Due process has two aspects—procedural and substantive.

PROCEDURAL DUE PROCESS. *Procedural* due process requires that any governmental decision to take life, liberty, or property be made equitably. For example, the government must use "fair procedures" in determining whether a person will be subjected to punishment or have some burden imposed on him or her. Fair procedure has been interpreted as requiring that the person have at least an opportunity to object to a proposed action before an impartial, neutral decision maker (who need not be a judge).

SUBSTANTIVE DUE PROCESS. *Substantive* due process focuses on the content, or substance, of legislation. If a law or other governmental action limits a *fundamental right*, it will be held to violate substantive due process, unless it promotes a *compelling* or *overriding state interest*. All First Amendment rights plus the rights to interstate travel, privacy, and voting

4–1c The Incorporation Issue

For many years, the courts assumed that the Bill of Rights limited only the actions of the national government, not the actions of state or local governments. In other words, if a state or local law was contrary to a basic freedom, such as the freedom of speech or the right to due process of law, the federal Bill of Rights did not come into play. The founders believed that the states, being closer to the people, would be less likely to violate their own citizens' liberties. Moreover, state constitutions, most of which contain bills of rights, protect citizens against state government actions. The United States Supreme Court upheld this view when it decided, in *Barron*

due process clause The constitutional guarantee, set out in the Fifth and Fourteenth Amendments, that the government will not illegally or arbitrarily deprive a person of life, liberty, or property.

due process of law The requirement that the government use fair, reasonable, and standard procedures whenever it takes any legal action against an individual; required by the Fifth and Fourteenth Amendments.

are considered fundamental. Compelling state interests could include, for example, the public's safety.

Other Liberties Incorporated   The Fourteenth Amendment also states that no state "shall make or enforce any law which shall abridge the privileges or immunities of citizens of the United States." For some time, the Supreme Court considered the "privileges and immunities" referred to in the amendment to be those conferred by state laws or constitutions, not the federal Bill of Rights.

Starting in 1925, however, the Supreme Court gradually began using the due process clause to say that states could not abridge a civil liberty that the national government could not abridge. In other words, the Court *incorporated* the protections guaranteed by the national Bill of Rights into the liberties protected under the Fourteenth Amendment. As you can see in Table 4–2 below, the Supreme Court was particularly active during the 1960s in broadening its interpretation of the due process clause to ensure that states and localities could not infringe on civil liberties protected by the Bill of Rights.

Today, the liberties still not incorporated include the right to refuse to quarter soldiers and the right to a grand jury hearing. The right to bear arms described in the Second Amendment was incorporated only in 2010.

FOR CRITICAL THINKING   Congress often passes laws that are so narrowly defined that only one individual or corporation is covered by the legislation. *Should such laws be considered bills of attainder and thus unconstitutional? Why or why not?*

4–2 Protections under the First Amendment

The First Amendment sets forth some of our most important civil liberties. Specifically, the First Amendment guarantees the freedoms of religion, speech, the

TABLE 4–2

Incorporating the Bill of Rights into the Fourteenth Amendment

Year	Issue	Amendment Involved	Court Case
1925	Freedom of speech	I	*Gitlow v. New York*, 268 U.S. 652.
1931	Freedom of the press	I	*Near v. Minnesota*, 283 U.S. 697.
1932	Right to a lawyer in capital punishment cases	VI	*Powell v. Alabama*, 287 U.S. 45.
1937	Freedom of assembly and right to petition	I	*De Jonge v. Oregon*, 299 U.S. 353.
1940	Freedom of religion	I	*Cantwell v. Connecticut*, 310 U.S. 296.
1947	Separation of church and state	I	*Everson v. Board of Education*, 330 U.S. 1.
1948	Right to a public trial	VI	*In re Oliver*, 333 U.S. 257.
1949	No unreasonable searches and seizures	IV	*Wolf v. Colorado*, 338 U.S. 25.
1961	Exclusionary rule (See page 88.)	IV	*Mapp v. Ohio*, 367 U.S. 643.
1962	No cruel and unusual punishments	VIII	*Robinson v. California*, 370 U.S. 660.
1963	Right to a lawyer in all criminal felony cases	VI	*Gideon v. Wainwright*, 372 U.S. 335.
1964	No compulsory self-incrimination	V	*Malloy v. Hogan*, 378 U.S. 1.
1965	Right to privacy	Various	*Griswold v. Connecticut*, 381 U.S. 479.
1966	Right to an impartial jury	VI	*Parker v. Gladden*, 385 U.S. 363.
1967	Right to a speedy trial	VI	*Klopfer v. North Carolina*, 386 U.S. 213.
1969	No double jeopardy	V	*Benton v. Maryland*, 395 U.S. 784.
2010	Right to bear arms	II	*McDonald v. Chicago*, 561 U.S. 3025.

Learning **Outcome 4-2**

List and describe the freedoms guaranteed by the First Amendment and explain how the courts have interpreted and applied these freedoms.

press, and assembly, as well as the right to petition the government. In the pages that follow, we look closely at the first three of these freedoms and discuss how, over time, Supreme Court decisions have defined their meaning and determined their limits.

4-2a Freedom of Religion

The First Amendment prohibits Congress from passing laws "respecting an establishment of religion, or prohibiting the free exercise thereof." The first part of this amendment is known as the **establishment clause**. The second part is called the **free exercise clause**.

Laws on Religion in the Colonies

That freedom of religion was the first freedom mentioned in the Bill of Rights is not surprising. After all, many colonists came to America to escape religious persecution. Nonetheless, these same colonists showed little tolerance for religious freedom within the communities they established. For example, in 1610 the Jamestown colony enacted a law requiring attendance at religious services on Sunday "both in the morning and the afternoon." Repeat offenders were subjected to

particularly harsh punishments. For those who twice violated the law, for example, the punishment was a public whipping. For third-time offenders, the punishment was death. (We provided additional details on religion in the colonies in the *America at Odds* feature at the beginning of Chapter 2.)

These examples of religious laws provide a context that is helpful in understanding why, in 1802, President Thomas Jefferson—a great proponent of religious freedom and tolerance—wanted the establishment clause to be "a wall of separation between church and state." The context also helps to explain why even state leaders who supported state religions might have favored the establishment clause—to keep the national government from interfering in such state matters. After all, the First Amendment says only that *Congress* can make no law respecting an establishment of religion. It says nothing about whether the *states* can make such laws.

The Establishment Clause

The establishment clause forbids the government from establishing an official religion or church. This makes the United States different from countries that are ruled by religious governments, such as the Islamic government of Iran. It also makes us different from nations that have in the past strongly discouraged the practice of any religion at all, such as the People's Republic of China.

What does this separation of church and state mean in practice? For one thing, religion and government, though constitutionally separated in the United

Middle school students form a prayer circle. To what extent does the Constitution allow prayers in school?

STEVE LISS/TIME LIFE PICTURES/GETTY IMAGES

States, have never been enemies or strangers. The establishment clause does not prohibit government from supporting religion in *general*. Religion remains a part of public life.

Most government officials take an oath of office in the name of God, and our coins and paper currency carry the motto "In God We Trust." Clergy of different religions serve in each branch of the armed forces. Public meetings and even sessions of Congress open with prayers. Indeed, the establishment clause often masks the fact that Americans are, by and large, religious and prefer that their political leaders be people of faith.

THE WALL OF SEPARATION. The "wall of separation" that Thomas Jefferson referred to, however, does exist and has been upheld by the Supreme Court on many occasions. An important ruling by the Supreme Court on the establishment clause came in 1947 in *Everson v. Board of Education*.[2] The case involved a New Jersey law that allowed the state to pay for bus transportation of students who attended parochial schools (schools run by churches or other religious groups).

The Court stated: "No tax in any amount, large or small, can be levied to support any religious activities or institutions." Nevertheless, the Court upheld the New Jersey law because it did not aid the church *directly* but provided for the safety and benefit of the students. The ruling both affirmed the importance of separating church and state and set the precedent that not *all* forms of state and federal aid to church-related schools are forbidden under the Constitution.

A full discussion of the various church–state issues that have arisen in American politics would fill volumes. Here, we examine three of these issues: prayer in the schools, the teaching of evolution versus creationism or intelligent design, and government aid to parochial schools.

PRAYER IN THE SCHOOLS. On occasion, some public schools have promoted a general sense of religion without proclaiming allegiance to any particular church or sect. Whether the states have a right to allow this was the main question presented in 1962 in *Engel v. Vitale*,[3] also known as the "Regents' Prayer case." The State Board of Regents in New York had composed a nondenominational prayer (a prayer not associated with any particular church) and urged school districts to use it in classrooms at the start of each day. The prayer read as follows:

Almighty God, we acknowledge our dependence upon Thee, and we beg Thy blessings upon us, our parents, our teachers, and our Country.

Some parents objected to the prayer, contending that it violated the establishment clause. The Supreme Court agreed and ruled that the Regents' Prayer was unconstitutional. Speaking for the majority, Justice Hugo Black wrote that the First Amendment must at least mean "that in this country it is no part of the business of government to compose official prayers for any group of the American people to recite as a part of a religious program carried on by government."

PRAYER IN THE SCHOOLS—THE DEBATE CONTINUES. Since the *Engel v. Vitale* ruling, the Supreme Court has continued to shore up the wall of separation between church and state in a number of decisions. Generally, the Court has walked a fine line between the wishes of those who believe that religion should have a more prominent place in our public institutions and those who do not. For example, in a 1980 case, *Stone v. Graham*,[4] the Supreme Court ruled that a Kentucky law requiring that the Ten Commandments be posted in all public schools violated the establishment clause. Many groups around the country opposed this ruling.

MOMENTS OF SILENCE. Another controversial issue is whether "moments of silence" in the schools are constitutional. In 1985, the Supreme Court ruled that an Alabama law authorizing a daily one-minute period of silence for meditation and voluntary prayer was unconstitutional. Because the law specifically endorsed prayer, it appeared to support religion.[5]

Since then, the lower courts have generally held that a school may require a moment of silence, but only if it serves a clearly secular purpose (such as to meditate on the day's activities).[6] Yet another issue concerns prayers said before public school sporting events, such as football games. In 2000, the Supreme Court held that student-led pregame prayer using the school's public-address system was unconstitutional.[7]

In sum, the Supreme Court has ruled that public schools, which are agencies of government, cannot sponsor religious activities. It has *not*, however, held that individuals cannot pray, when and as they choose, in schools or in any other place. Nor has it held that the schools are barred from teaching *about* religion, as opposed to engaging in religious practices.

EVOLUTION VERSUS CREATIONISM. Certain religious groups have long opposed the teaching of evolution in public schools. These groups contend that evolutionary theory, a theory with overwhelming scientific support, directly counters their religious belief that human beings did not evolve but were created fully formed, as described in the biblical story of the creation. In fact, surveys have shown that up to one-third of Americans believe that humans were directly created by God rather than having evolved from other species. The Supreme Court, however, has held that state laws forbidding the teaching of evolution in the schools are unconstitutional.

For example, in *Epperson v. Arkansas*,[8] a case decided in 1968, the Supreme Court held that an Arkansas law prohibiting the teaching of evolution violated the establishment clause because it imposed religious beliefs on students. In 1987, the Supreme Court also held unconstitutional a Louisiana law requiring that the biblical story of the creation be taught along with evolution. The Court deemed the law unconstitutional in part because it had as its primary purpose the promotion of a particular religious belief.[9]

TEACHING THE CONTROVERSY. Nevertheless, some state and local groups continue their efforts against the teaching of evolution. In 2008, Louisiana adopted the Louisiana Science Education Act, which states, "The teaching of some scientific subjects can cause controversy." It encourages Louisiana teachers to "help students understand, analyze, critique, and review in an objective manner the scientific strengths and scientific weaknesses of existing scientific theories." Debate in the state legislature made it clear that the theories in question included evolution and global warming. Critic John Derbyshire commented, "The act will encourage Louisiana local school boards to unconstitutional behavior. That's what it's *meant* to do." The legislation has not yet been challenged in court, however.

EVOLUTION VERSUS INTELLIGENT DESIGN. Some activists have advocated the concept of "intelligent design" as an alternative to the teaching of evolution. This concept posits that an intelligent cause, rather than an undirected process such as natural selection, lies behind the creation and development of the universe and living things. Proponents of intelligent design claim that it is a scientific theory and thus that its teaching does not violate the establishment clause in any way. Opponents contend that the "intelligent cause" is simply another term for God.

These arguments were tested in 2004 in Dover, Pennsylvania, when the local school board required ninth-grade biology classes to use a textbook that endorsed intelligent design. In November 2005, the board members who supported the requirement were voted out of office. In December, a federal district court judge ruled that intelligent design was not science, that it was inherently religious, and that the school board's actions were unconstitutional.[10]

AID TO PAROCHIAL SCHOOLS. Americans have long been at odds over whether public tax dollars should be used to fund activities in parochial schools. Over the years, the courts have often had to decide whether specific types of aid do or do not violate the establishment clause. Aid to church-related schools in the form of transportation, equipment, or special educational services for disadvantaged students has been held permissible. Other forms of aid, such as funding teachers' salaries and paying for field trips, have been held unconstitutional.

MATTHEW CAVANAUGH/GETTY IMAGES

When an Oklahoma school attempted to bar a young Muslim girl from wearing a head scarf to school, the federal government intervened. Why would the U.S. government protect the right to wear religious symbols in public schools? What civil liberties ensured by the U.S. Constitution might protect the right to wear religious dress in public schools?

THE *LEMON* TEST. Since 1971, the Supreme Court has held that, to be constitutional, a state's school aid must meet three requirements: (1) the purpose of the financial aid must be clearly secular (not religious), (2) its primary effect must neither advance nor inhibit religion, and (3) it must avoid an "excessive government entanglement with religion." The Court first used this three-part test in *Lemon v. Kurtzman*,[11] and hence it is often referred to as the *Lemon* test.

In the 1971 *Lemon* case, the Court denied public aid to private and parochial schools for the salaries even of teachers of secular courses and for textbooks and instructional materials in certain secular subjects. The Court held that the establishment clause is designed to prevent three main evils: "sponsorship, financial support, and active involvement of the sovereign [the government] in religious activity."

SCHOOL VOUCHER PROGRAMS. Another contentious issue has to do with the use of **school vouchers**—educational certificates, provided by state governments, that students can use at any school, public or private. In an effort to improve their educational systems, several school districts have been experimenting with voucher systems. Twelve states now have limited voucher programs, under which some schoolchildren may attend private elementary or high schools using vouchers paid for by taxpayers' dollars. In eight of these states, vouchers are limited to special-needs children.

In 2002, the United States Supreme Court ruled that a voucher program in Cleveland, Ohio, was constitutional. Under the program, the state provided up to $2,250 to low-income families, who could use the funds to send their children to either public or private schools. The Court concluded that the taxpayer-paid voucher program did not unconstitutionally entangle church and state because the funds went to parents, not to schools. The parents theoretically could use the vouchers to send their children to nonreligious private academies or charter schools, even though 95 percent used the vouchers at religious schools.[12]

SCHOOL VOUCHERS AND STATE CONSTITUTIONS. Despite the 2002 Supreme Court ruling, several constitutional questions surrounding school vouchers remain unresolved. For example, some state constitutions are more explicit than the federal Constitution in denying the use of public funds for religious education. Even after the Supreme Court ruling in the Ohio case, a Florida court ruled in 2002 that a voucher program in that state violated Florida's constitution.[13]

The Free Exercise Clause

As mentioned, the second part of the First Amendment's statement on religion consists of the free exercise clause, which forbids the passage of laws "prohibiting the free exercise of religion." This clause protects a person's right to worship or to believe as he or she wishes without government interference. No law or act of government may violate this constitutional right.

BELIEF AND PRACTICE ARE DISTINCT. The free exercise clause does not necessarily mean that individuals can act in any way they want on the basis of their religious beliefs. There is an important distinction between belief and practice. The Supreme Court has ruled consistently that the right to hold any *belief* is absolute. The right to *practice* one's beliefs, however, may have some limits. As the Court itself once asked,

UPI PHOTO/LANDOV

Some of the members of fundamentalist Mormon sects engage in polygamy, which is against the law. What can the government do in such situations?

"Suppose one believed that human sacrifice were a necessary part of religious worship?"

The Supreme Court first dealt with the issue of belief versus practice in 1878 in *Reynolds v. United States*.[14] Reynolds was a member of the Latter-Day Saints (Mormons) who had two wives. Polygamy, or the practice of having more than one spouse simultaneously, was encouraged by the customs and teachings of his church at that time. Polygamy was also prohibited by federal law. Reynolds was convicted and appealed the case, arguing that the law violated his constitutional right to freely exercise his religious beliefs. The Court did not agree. It said that to allow Reynolds to practice polygamy would make religious doctrines superior to the law.

RELIGIOUS PRACTICES AND THE WORKPLACE. The free exercise of religion in the workplace was bolstered by Title VII of the Civil Rights Act of 1964, which requires employers to accommodate their employees' religious practices unless such accommodation causes an employer to suffer an "undue hardship." Thus, if an employee claims that religious beliefs prevent him or her from working on a particular day of the week, such as Saturday or Sunday, the employer must try to accommodate the employee's needs if possible.

Several cases have come before lower federal courts concerning employer dress codes that contradict the religious customs of employees. For example, in 1999 the Third Circuit Court of Appeals ruled in favor of two Muslim police officers in Newark, New Jersey, who claimed that they were required by their faith to wear beards and would not shave them to comply with the police department's grooming policy.[15] Muslims, Rastafarians, and others have refused to change the grooming habits required by their religions and have been successful in court.

INSURANCE FOR BIRTH CONTROL. A recent free exercise controversy involved the question of whether businesses could be required to supply health-insurance coverage for birth control measures. Such coverage was required in health-insurance plans that met the standards of the 2010 Affordable Care Act. Churches and other religious organizations that objected to contraception on principle were exempt from the requirement. In 2012, however, the government ruled that universities, hospitals, and similar organizations had to provide coverage for contraception even if they were affiliated with churches that opposed birth control.

The result was a storm of opposition from organizations such as the Roman Catholic Church, which rejects contraception. These groups argued that they were being forced to support activities to which they were morally opposed. Such a requirement was, in their opinion, a violation of their free exercise rights. This position gained broad support among Republicans in Congress. An alternative view was that the churches were attempting to impose their religious values on employees not directly involved in religious activities. Many employees of Catholic-affiliated universities and hospitals are in fact not Catholic.

President Barack Obama proposed a compromise under which church-affiliated hospitals and schools would not have to pay for the insurance coverage, but employees would still receive the benefit. This plan satisfied many schools and hospitals. It was not acceptable to the Catholic bishops, however, who filed a lawsuit aimed at overturning the requirement.

4–2b Freedom of Expression

No one in this country seems to have a problem protecting the free speech of those with whom they agree. The real challenge is protecting unpopular ideas. The protection needed is, in Justice Oliver Wendell Holmes's words, "not free thought for those who agree with us but freedom for the thought that we hate." The First Amendment is designed to protect the freedom to express *all* ideas, including those that may be unpopular. Many foreign nations do not protect unpopular ideas in the way that the United States does. Even in the United States, private organizations—such as Facebook—are not subject to the constraints of the First Amendment. We examine these issues in The *Rest of the World* feature on the following page.

The First Amendment has been interpreted to protect more than merely spoken words. It also protects **symbolic speech**—speech involving actions and other nonverbal expressions. Some common examples include picketing in a labor dispute or wearing a black armband in protest of a government policy. Even burning the American flag as a gesture of protest has been held to be protected by the First Amendment.

The Right to Free Speech Is Not Absolute

Although Americans have the right to free speech, not *all* speech is protected under the First Amendment. Our constitutional rights and liberties are not abso-

symbolic speech The expression of beliefs, opinions, or ideas through forms other than verbal speech or print; speech involving actions and other nonverbal expressions.

Social Media and Limits on Free Speech

There are over a billion Facebook users worldwide and hundreds of millions of Twitter users. Social media are everywhere. While free speech in social media is largely taken for granted in the United States, such is not the case in India, the Middle East, and elsewhere. (Of course, free speech of *all* types is seriously restricted in China, North Korea, and many other nations.)

Should Hate Speech Be Banned?

Many social media companies ban hate speech in their Terms of Service. Facebook, for example, consistently takes down pages that support alleged terrorist organizations such as Hezbollah. Facebook's policies specifically prohibit content that threatens or organizes violence or praises violent organizations. (Facebook also bans all forms of nudity, a policy that has caused problems for advocates of breastfeeding.)

Some free speech advocates believe that all expression, no matter how offensive, should be allowed on social media. Nonetheless, Facebook is adamant about its censorship rules. As a private corporation, it is not bound by the First Amendment. Facebook, along with Google and Twitter, is also a worldwide service that must deal with societies whose rules are very different from those in the United States.

Twitter versus India

Some call Twitter the world's largest public megaphone. Recently, the Indian government tried to pull Twitter's plug. Ethnic extremists in rival communities used Twitter to spread rumors that each group was attacking the other. In response, the Indian government asked Twitter to block the accounts of users who were encouraging violence. The government also banned text messages directed to more than five recipients. Twitter, for its part, agreed to remove a number of hate-content sources. It refused a request to block users who were ridiculing India's prime minister, however. The battle for free speech in social media continues in that country.

Social Media and Religion

Perhaps nowhere is there more tension concerning free speech than in areas involving religion. In the name of protecting religious sensitivities, many nations, chiefly those in the Middle East, restrict social media communications. In particular, criticisms of Islam are often dealt with quite harshly. In a way, this is not surprising—under the law in eight Middle Eastern countries, atheists can be put to death.

Even in Britain, there have been official reactions against anti-Islamic messages. A British soldier was gruesomely murdered by two Islamic extremists in London in 2013. The police subsequently cracked down on radical Islamists online—but they also charged a dozen anti-Islamic social media users with violating laws against inciting hatred and giving offense.

FOR CRITICAL ANALYSIS Should U.S. corporations such as Facebook and Twitter attempt to uphold American principles of free speech everywhere? Why or why not?

---

lute. Rather, they are what the Supreme Court—the ultimate interpreter of the Constitution—says they are. Although the Court has zealously safeguarded the right to free speech, at times it has imposed limits on speech in the interests of protecting other rights of Americans. These rights include security against harm to one's person or reputation, the need for public order, and the need to preserve the government.

Indeed, throughout our history, the Supreme Court has attempted to balance our rights to free speech against other needs of society. As Justice Holmes once said, even "the most stringent protection of free speech would not protect a man in falsely shouting fire in a theatre and causing a panic."[16] We look next at some of the ways that the Court has limited the right to free speech.

Restrictions on Expression At times in our nation's history, various individuals have opposed our form of government. The government, in responding to these individuals, has drawn a fine line between legitimate criticism and the expression of ideas that may seriously harm society. Clearly, the government may pass laws against violent acts. But what about **seditious speech**, which

> **seditious speech**
> Speech that urges resistance to lawful authority or that advocates the overthrow of a government.

urges resistance to lawful authority or advocates overthrowing the government?

As early as 1798, Congress took steps to curb seditious speech when it passed the Alien and Sedition Acts. The Sedition Act made it a crime to utter "any false, scandalous, and malicious" criticism of the government. The acts were considered unconstitutional by many but were never tested in the courts. Several dozen individuals were prosecuted under the Sedition Act, and some were actually convicted. In 1801, President Thomas Jefferson pardoned those sentenced under the act, and it was not renewed after it expired in 1801.

CLEAR AND PRESENT DANGER. During World War I, Congress passed the Espionage Act of 1917 and the Sedition Act of 1918. The 1917 act prohibited attempts to interfere with the operations of the military forces, the war effort, or the process of recruitment. The 1918 act made it a crime to "willfully utter, print, write, or publish any disloyal, profane, scurrilous [insulting], or abusive language" about the government. More than two thousand persons were tried and convicted under this act, which was repealed at the end of World War I. The Supreme Court upheld the constitutionality of the Espionage Act in 1919 when it issued the *clear and present danger test*. Under that test, expression may be restricted if it would cause a dangerous condition, actual or imminent, that Congress has the power to prevent.[17]

"FREE SPEECH
is the whole thing,
the whole ball game.
Free speech is life itself."

~ SALMAN RUSHDIE ~
INDIAN-BORN BRITISH WRITER
B. 1947

THE BAD TENDENCY RULE. In 1925, the Court adopted an even more restrictive doctrine, the *bad tendency rule*. Under this rule, speech could be restricted if it might lead to some "evil."[18]

In 1940, Congress passed the Smith Act, which forbade people from advocating the violent overthrow of the U.S. government. In 1951, the Supreme Court upheld the constitutionality of the Smith Act in *Dennis v. United States*,[19] which involved eleven top leaders of the Communist Party who had been convicted of violating the act. The Court found that their activities went beyond the permissible peaceful advocacy of change.

THE IMMINENT LAWLESS ACTION TEST. The current standard for evaluating the legality of advocacy speech was established by the Supreme Court in 1969. Under the **imminent lawless action test**, speech can be forbidden only when it is "directed to inciting . . . imminent lawless action."[20] This is a hard standard for prosecutors to meet. As a result, "subversive" speech receives far more protection today than it did in the past.

Limited Protection for Commercial Speech

Advertising, or **commercial speech,** is also protected by the First Amendment, but not as fully as regular speech. Generally, the Supreme Court has considered a restriction on commercial speech to be valid as long as the restriction "(1) seeks to implement a substantial government interest, (2) directly advances that interest, and (3) goes no further than necessary to accomplish its objective." Problems arise, though, when restrictions on commercial advertising achieve one substantial government interest yet are contrary to the interest in protecting free speech and the right of consumers to be informed. In such cases, the courts have to decide which interest takes priority.

Liquor advertising is a good illustration of this kind of conflict. In one case, Rhode Island argued that its law banning the advertising of liquor prices served the state's goal of discouraging liquor consumption (because the ban discouraged bargain hunting and thus kept liquor prices high). The Supreme Court, however, held that the ban was an unconstitutional restraint on commercial speech. The Court stated that the First Amendment "directs us to be especially skeptical of regulations that seek to keep people in the dark for what the government perceives to be their own good."[21]

Unprotected Speech
Certain types of speech receive no protection under the First Amendment. Speech has never been protected when the speech itself is part of a crime. An act of fraud, for exam-

imminent lawless action test The current Supreme Court doctrine for assessing the constitutionality of subversive speech. To be illegal, speech must be "directed to inciting . . . imminent lawless action."

commercial speech Advertising statements that describe products. Commercial speech receives less protection under the First Amendment than ordinary speech.

Protesters in Hong Kong support Edward Snowden, the national defense contractor who exposed U.S. surveillance programs in 2013. Does the First Amendment have any relevance to the Snowden case?

Miller.[22] To be ruled obscene, a work must: (1) excite "unwholesome sexual desire" under present-day community standards, (2) offensively depict prohibited sexual conduct, and (3) lack serious literary, artistic, political, or scientific value. Under "community standards," the definition of obscenity could vary from one part of the country to another.

The *Miller* test was handed down at a time when American attitudes toward sexual expression were undergoing a revolution. A few years earlier, major literary works such as *Ulysses* by James Joyce and *Lady Chatterley's Lover* by D. H. Lawrence were illegal. By the early 1980s, however, it was possible in almost all parts of the country to rent pornographic videotapes that left nothing to the imagination.

The Internet was the final blow to the concept of obscenity. By the end of the twentieth century, U.S. officials no longer tried to impose obscenity restrictions on printed or visual material. Attempts by Congress in 1996 and 1998 to ban Internet obscenity that might be seen by minors were ruled unconstitutional by the Supreme Court.[23]

ple, often may be carried out entirely through spoken words. Accused fraudsters who attempted to defend their actions by standing on their First Amendment rights would get nowhere. Other types of unprotected speech include defamation (libel and slander) and obscenity.

LIBEL AND SLANDER. No person has the right to libel or slander another. **Libel** is a published report of a falsehood that tends to injure a person's reputation or character. **Slander** is the public utterance (speaking) of a statement that holds a person up for contempt, ridicule, or hatred. To prove libel or slander, certain criteria must be met. The statements made must be untrue, must stem from an intent to do harm, and must result in actual harm.

The Supreme Court has ruled that public figures (public officials and others in the public limelight) cannot collect damages for remarks made against them unless they can prove the remarks were made with "reckless" disregard for accuracy. Generally, it is believed that because public figures have greater access to the media than ordinary persons do, they are in a better position to defend themselves against libelous or slanderous statements.

THE END OF OBSCENITY. Traditionally, obscenity was a form of expression not protected under the First Amendment. The courts, however, have found the term **obscenity** hard to define. In 1973, the Supreme Court finally came up with a three-part test in *California v.*

REMAINING RESTRICTIONS ON PORNOGRAPHY. Several types of restrictions survive. The First Amendment applies only to governments, so private, voluntary restrictions are possible. Most mainstream movie theaters, for example, will not show a film that has received a "No One 17 or Under Admitted" (NC-17) rating from the Motion Picture Association of America. In addition, the government retains the right to impose restrictions on activities that it subsidizes or media that it controls, such as the broadcast spectrum. Thus, restrictions on radio and broadcast television remain in effect.

Finally, the courts have upheld laws aimed at protecting children. Making or possessing pornographic videos or photographs of underage persons remains a serious crime, based on the argument that such depictions are acts of child abuse. Ironically, this argument demonstrates the collapse of obscenity as a legal concept—child pornography is *not* banned because it is obscene. Writings or drawings, including animation, that depict underage

libel A published report of a falsehood that tends to injure a person's reputation or character.

slander The public utterance (speaking) of a statement that holds a person up for contempt, ridicule, or hatred.

obscenity Indecency or offensiveness in speech, expression, behavior, or appearance.

sexuality are tolerated because no actual children are involved.

Free Speech for Students?

America's schools and college campuses experience an ongoing tension between the guarantee of free speech and the desire to restrain speech that is offensive to others. Typically, cases involving free speech in the schools raise the following question: Where should the line between unacceptable speech and merely offensive speech be drawn? Schools at all levels—elementary schools, high schools, and colleges and universities—have grappled with this issue.

ELEMENTARY AND HIGH SCHOOLS. Generally, the courts allow elementary schools wide latitude to define what students may and may not say to other students. At the high school level, the Supreme Court has allowed some restraints to be placed on the freedom of expression. For example, as you will read shortly in the discussion of freedom of the press, the Court allows school officials to exercise some censorship over high school publications. And, in a controversial 2007 case, the Court upheld a school principal's decision to suspend a high school student who unfurled a banner reading "Bong Hits 4 Jesus" at an event off the school premises. School officials maintained that the banner appeared to advocate illegal drug use in violation of school policy. Many legal commentators and scholars strongly criticized this decision.[24]

UNIVERSITY SPEECH CODES. A difficult question that many universities face today is whether the right to free speech includes the right to make hateful remarks about others based on their race, gender, or sexual orientation. Some claim that allowing people with extremist views to voice their opinions can lead to violence. In response to this question, several universities have gone so far as to institute speech codes to minimize the disturbances that hate speech might cause. Speech codes at public colleges have been ruled unconstitutional on the ground that they restrict freedom of speech.[25] Such codes continue to exist on many college campuses, however.

For example, the policy on acceptable e-mail usage at Claremont McKenna College (a private institution) provides that "the College's system must not be used to create or transmit material that is derogatory, defamatory, obscene or offensive. Such material includes, but is not limited to, slurs, epithets or anything that might be construed as harassment or disparagement based on race, color, national origin, sex, sexual orientation, age, disability, or religious or political beliefs." Presumably, under a policy such as this, it would be a violation to say "Democrats are idiots" or "Republicans are insane."

CYBERBULLYING. The courts have regularly upheld the right of schools to ban bullying even when bullying consists entirely of spoken or written words. Such bans are justified as a protection of a school's basic educational mission. Bullying can disrupt the educational process by making it difficult or impossible for the victim to carry on in school. Matters are less clear at the college level or when a perpetrator is an adult who is not even under the authority of the school system.

SOCIAL MEDIA
In Politics

As you might suspect, cyberbullying is a major topic in social media. Check out "stopcyberbullying" on Facebook.

AP IMAGES/DAVID GOLDMAN

Cyberbullying has become a serious problem for some young people. This girl, shown with her parents, was the victim of a phony Facebook page set up in her name that contained defamatory material. The family filed a libel lawsuit.

Recently, several cyberbullies have been charged with crimes. One example is the Rutgers student who secretly taped his roomate having a sexual encounter with another man and then posted the video online. When the roommate committed suicide, the student was convicted of multiple computer-related crimes but is appealing his convictions.

Another example is a woman who pretended online to be a boy so as to harass one of her daughter's classmates. After the young victim was told that "the world would be a better place without you," she committed suicide. The woman's conviction for computer crime was overturned on appeal. Both of these cases raise troubling questions about the extent to which verbal harassment is protected by the First Amendment.

4–2c Freedom of the Press

The framers of the Constitution believed that the press should be free to publish a wide range of opinions and information, and generally the free speech rights just discussed also apply to the press. The courts have placed certain restrictions on freedom of the press, however. Over the years, the Supreme Court has developed various guidelines and doctrines to use in deciding whether freedom of speech and the press can be restrained.

The Preferred-Position Doctrine One major guideline, called the *preferred-position doctrine,* states that certain freedoms are so essential to a democracy that they hold a preferred position. According to this doctrine, any law that limits these freedoms should be presumed unconstitutional unless the government can show that the law is absolutely necessary. The idea behind this doctrine is that freedom of speech and the press should rarely, if ever, be diminished, because spoken and printed words are the prime tools of the democratic process.

Prior Restraint Stopping an activity before it actually happens is known as *prior restraint.* With respect to freedom of the press, prior restraint involves *censorship,* which occurs when an official removes objectionable materials from an item before it is published or broadcast. An example of censorship and prior restraint would be a court's ruling that two paragraphs in an upcoming article in the local news-

"The only security of all is in a **FREE PRESS.**...
It is necessary, to keep the waters pure."

~ THOMAS JEFFERSON ~
THIRD PRESIDENT OF THE UNITED STATES
1801–1809

paper had to be removed before the article could be published. The Supreme Court has generally ruled against prior restraint, arguing that the government cannot curb ideas before they are expressed.

In certain circumstances, however, the Court has allowed prior restraint. For example, in a 1988 case, *Hazelwood School District v. Kuhlmeier,*[26] a high school principal deleted two pages from the school newspaper just before it was printed. The pages contained stories on students' experiences with pregnancy and discussed the impact of divorce on students at the school. The Supreme Court, noting that students in school do not have exactly the same rights as adults in other settings, ruled that high school administrators can censor school publications. The Court said that school newspapers are part of the school curriculum, not a public forum. Therefore, administrators have the right to censor speech that promotes conduct inconsistent with the "shared values of a civilized social order."

FOR CRITICAL THINKING The establishment of religious chaplains in the armed forces has been justified on the basis that otherwise, service members on active duty would have no access to religious services and counseling. *Do you agree with this argument? Why or why not?*

4–3 The Right to Privacy

In a dissenting opinion written in 1928, Supreme Court justice Louis Brandeis stated that the right to privacy is "the most comprehensive of rights and the right most valued by civilized men."[27] The majority of the justices on the Supreme Court at that time did not agree. In the 1960s, however, Court opinion began to change.

4–3a Court and Congressional Actions

In 1965, in the landmark case of *Griswold v. Connecticut,*[28] the Supreme Court held that a right to privacy is implied by other constitutional rights guaranteed in the First, Third, Fourth, Fifth, and Ninth Amendments. For

Learning Outcome 4–3

Discuss why Americans are increasingly concerned about privacy rights.

example, consider the words of the Ninth Amendment: "The enumeration in the Constitution, of certain rights, shall not be construed to deny or disparage others retained by the people." In other words, just because the Constitution, including its amendments, does not specifically mention the right to privacy does not mean that this right is denied to the people.

During recent decades, Congress has also passed laws ensuring the privacy rights of individuals. For example, in 1966 Congress passed the Freedom of Information Act, which, among other things, allows any person to request copies of any information about her or him contained in government files. In 1974, Congress passed the Privacy Act, which restricts government disclosure of data to third parties.

In 1994, Congress passed the Driver's Privacy Protection Act, which prevents states from disclosing or selling a driver's personal information without the driver's consent.[29] In late 2000, the federal Department of Health and Human Services issued a regulation ensuring the privacy of medical information. Healthcare providers and insurance companies are restricted from sharing confidential information about their patients. In 2011, however, the Supreme Court struck down a Vermont law that prevented pharmacies from selling the prescription records of physicians to drug companies.[30]

Although Congress and the courts have acknowledged a constitutional right to privacy, the nature and scope of this right are not always clear. For example, Americans continue to debate whether the right to privacy includes the right to have an abortion or the right of terminally ill persons to commit physician-assisted suicide. Since the terrorist attacks of September 11, 2001, another pressing privacy issue has been how to monitor potential terrorists to prevent another attack without violating the privacy rights of all Americans.

4–3b The Abortion Controversy

One of the most divisive and emotionally charged issues debated today is whether the right to privacy means that women can choose to have abortions.

Abortion and Privacy In 1973, in the landmark case of *Roe v. Wade,*[31] the Supreme Court, using the *Griswold* case as a precedent, held that the "right of

privacy . . . is broad enough to encompass a woman's decision whether or not to terminate her pregnancy." The right is not absolute throughout pregnancy, however. The Court also said that any state could impose certain regulations to safeguard the health of the mother after the first three months of pregnancy and, in the final stages of pregnancy, could act to protect potential life.

Since the *Roe v. Wade* decision, the Supreme Court has adopted a more conservative approach and has upheld restrictive state laws requiring counseling, waiting periods, notification of parents, and other actions prior to abortions.[32] Yet the Court has never overturned the *Roe* decision. In fact, in 1997 and again in 2000, the Supreme Court upheld laws requiring "buffer zones" around abortion clinics to protect those entering the clinics from unwanted counseling or harassment by antiabortion groups.[33]

Supporters of abortion rights in Texas rally at the state capitol in July 2013. They are supporting state senator Wendy Davis, who temporarily blocked an antiabortion law with a filibuster (a method of halting legislative action by continuous speech).

Partial-Birth Abortions   In 2000, the Supreme Court invalidated a Nebraska statute banning "partial-birth" abortions, a procedure used during the second trimester of pregnancy.[34] Undeterred by the fate of the Nebraska law, President George W. Bush signed the Partial Birth Abortion Ban Act in 2003. In a close (five-to-four) and controversial 2007 decision, the Supreme Court upheld the constitutionality of the 2003 act.[35]

Many were surprised at the Court's decision on partial-birth abortion, given that the federal act banning this practice was quite similar to the Nebraska law that had been struck down by the Court in 2000, just seven years earlier. The Court became more conservative in 2006, however, when President George W. Bush appointed Justice Samuel Alito to replace Sandra Day O'Connor. Dissenting from the majority opinion in the case, Justice Ruth Bader Ginsburg said that the ruling was an "alarming" departure from three decades of Supreme Court decisions on abortion.

In reality, how easy is it for women to access abortion services today? We examine that question in the *Perception versus Reality* feature below.

Perception versus Reality
The Availability of Abortion

Before 1973, abortion was illegal in much of the United States. In that year, the United States Supreme Court issued its decision in *Roe v. Wade*. The outcome of this landmark case seemed to settle the abortion issue once and for all. Women had the right to terminate their pregnancies.

THE PERCEPTION

The highest court in the land made it clear—women can have an abortion if they so decide, and no state laws may prevent this, at least during the first trimester of pregnancy. During the second trimester, only state laws that limit the procedure to protect the health of pregnant women are constitutional. It follows that abortion should be freely available throughout the land.

THE REALITY

The pro-life and pro-choice sides of the abortion debate seem to agree on one thing. In practice, *Roe v. Wade* is no longer the law of the land. In 2011, legislators in twenty-four states passed a record ninety-two laws restricting abortions. By 2012, hundreds of additional bills had been introduced around the country to limit abortions, and many had passed.

Several states now prohibit abortion beyond twenty weeks into a pregnancy. In 2013, Arkansas moved to ban abortion after twelve weeks. Virginia requires women seeking an abortion to have an abdominal ultrasound. Other states are considering this measure as well. In Mississippi, where in 2010 voters had rejected an antiabortion ballot proposal, the legislature in 2012 hit upon a new way to shut down the state's only abortion clinic. Physicians at the clinic would be required to have admission privileges at a local hospital. Legislators could rely on the hospitals to refuse such privileges. (A federal judge blocked implementation of the law.)

Most of these new laws violate *Roe v. Wade* and subsequent Supreme Court rulings. Supporters of abortion rights, however, have been reluctant to challenge the laws because they are afraid that the Supreme Court might narrow abortion rights further. After all, in 2007 the Supreme Court ruled that a federal ban on so-called partial-birth abortions was constitutional, reversing an earlier precedent. A few of the laws banning abortion after twenty weeks have been blocked by federal appeals courts. Still, state attempts to make abortion difficult or impossible are on the rise. Already, for all practical purposes, women cannot get an abortion in several small-population Great Plains and Rocky Mountain states.

BLOG ON   On the Slate Web site, pro-choice writer Dahlia Lithwick has written a call to alarm on the state of *Roe v. Wade*. If you enter "lithwick roe wade" into a search engine, you'll find both that article and a host of commentary, much of it written by pro-life advocates.

4-3c Do We Have the "Right to Die"?

Whether it is called euthanasia (mercy killing), assisted suicide, or a dignified way to leave this world, it all comes down to one basic question: Do terminally ill persons have, as part of their civil liberties, a right to die and to be assisted in the process by physicians or others? Phrased another way, are state laws banning physician-assisted suicide in such circumstances unconstitutional?

In 1997, the issue came before the Supreme Court, which characterized the question as follows: Does the liberty protected by the Constitution include a right to commit suicide, which itself includes a right to assistance in doing so? The Court's clear and categorical answer to this question was no. To hold otherwise, said the Court, would be "to reverse centuries of legal doctrine and practice, and strike down the considered policy choice of almost every state."[36]

Although the Court upheld the states' rights to ban such a practice, the Court did not hold that state laws *permitting* assisted suicide were unconstitutional. In 1997, Oregon became the first state to implement such a law. In 2008, Washington and Montana became the second and third states, respectively, to allow the practice. Oregon's law was upheld by the Supreme Court in 2006.[37]

4-3d Personal Privacy and National Security

Since the terrorist attacks of September 11, 2001, the news media and Congress have debated how the United States can strengthen national security while still protecting civil liberties, particularly the right to privacy.

The USA Patriot Act Several laws and programs that infringe on Americans' privacy rights were created in the wake of 9/11 in an attempt to protect the nation's security. For example, the USA Patriot Act of 2001 gave the government broad latitude to investigate people who are only vaguely associated with terrorists. Under this law, the government can access personal information on American citizens to an extent never before allowed.

The Federal Bureau of Investigation was also authorized to use "National Security Letters" to demand personal information about individuals from private companies (such as banks and phone companies). The companies supplying the information are not allowed to inform their customers about the requests. In one of the most controversial programs, the National Security Agency (NSA) was authorized to monitor certain domestic phone calls without first obtaining a warrant. When Americans learned of the NSA's actions in 2005, the ensuing public furor forced the Bush administration to obtain warrants for such activities.

National Security under President Obama

During his 2008 campaign, Obama promised to make a clean break with the policies of the Bush administration on national security. It did not take long, however, for observers to realize that the differences between the Obama and Bush administrations were more a matter of presentation than substance. For example, Obama restated the Bush policy that suspected terrorists could be held indefinitely without trial.

In June 2013, materials released to the press by an employee of a national security contractor revealed that government surveillance is more universal than most people had previously assumed. Under one program, the NSA has been collecting information about every phone call made in the entire country—not the content of the call, but the time, number called, and number calling.[38] Although this program was undertaken pursuant to a secret court-ordered search warrant, its scope seems hard to square with the text of the Fourth Amendment, which states that "no Warrants shall issue, but upon probable cause . . . and particularly describing the place to be searched, and the persons or things to be seized."

MARK WILSON/GETTY IMAGES

FBI director James Comey, Jr., faced congressional questioning on national security during his confirmation hearings.

A second program, known as PRISM, was designed to accumulate vast quantities of data from the servers of corporations such as AOL, Apple, Facebook, Google, and Skype. The information includes e-mails, chats, photos, and more. PRISM data collection is worldwide, a fact that has generated considerable consternation abroad, especially in Europe.

The Civil Liberties Debate   Some Americans wonder why the public outcry about the erosion of privacy rights has not been more vehement. They point out that trading off even a few civil liberties, including our privacy rights, for national security is senseless. After all, these liberties are at the heart of what this country stands for. When we abandon any of our civil liberties, we weaken our country rather than defend it. Essentially, say some members of this group, the federal government has achieved what the terrorists were unable to accomplish—the destruction of our freedoms.

Other Americans believe that we have little to worry about. Those who have nothing to hide should not be concerned about government surveillance and other privacy intrusions undertaken with the intention of making our nation more secure against terrorist attacks.

FOR CRITICAL THINKING

Could the government's current policies on screening airline passengers be considered a violation of privacy rights? Why or why not?

4-4 The Rights of the Accused

The United States has one of the highest murder rates in the industrialized world. It is therefore not surprising that many Americans have extremely strong opinions about the rights of persons accused of criminal offenses. Indeed, some Americans complain that criminal defendants have too many rights.

Why do criminal suspects have rights? The answer is that all persons are entitled to the protections afforded by the Bill of Rights. If criminal suspects were deprived of their basic constitutional liberties, all people would suffer the consequences, because there is nothing to stop the government from accusing anyone of being a criminal. In a criminal case, a state official (such as the district attorney, or D.A.) prosecutes the defendant,

and the state has immense resources that it can bring to bear against the accused person. By protecting the rights of accused persons, the Constitution helps to prevent the arbitrary use of power by the government.

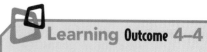

4-4a The Rights of Criminal Defendants

The basic rights, or constitutional safeguards, provided for criminal defendants are set forth in the Bill of Rights. These safeguards include the following:

- The Fourth Amendment protection from unreasonable searches and seizures.

- The Fourth Amendment requirement that no warrant for a search or an arrest be issued without **probable cause**—cause for believing that there is a substantial likelihood that a person has committed or is about to commit a crime.

- The Fifth Amendment requirement that no one be deprived of "life, liberty, or property, without due process of law." As discussed earlier in this chapter, this requirement is also included in the Fourteenth Amendment, which protects persons against actions by state governments.

- The Fifth Amendment prohibition against **double jeopardy**—being tried twice for the same criminal offense.

- The Fifth Amendment provision that no person can be required to be a witness against (incriminate) himself or herself. This is often referred to as the constitutional protection against **self-incrimination.** It is the basis for a criminal suspect's "right to remain silent" in criminal proceedings.

- The Sixth Amendment guarantees of a speedy trial, a trial by jury, a public trial, and the right to confront witnesses.

- The Sixth Amendment guarantee of the right to counsel at various

probable cause Cause for believing that there is a substantial likelihood that a person has committed or is about to commit a crime.

double jeopardy The prosecution of a person twice for the same criminal offense; prohibited by the Fifth Amendment in all but a few circumstances.

self-incrimination Providing damaging information or testimony against oneself in court.

stages in some criminal proceedings. The right to counsel was strengthened in 1963 in *Gideon v. Wainwright*.[39] The Supreme Court held that if a person is accused of a felony and cannot afford an attorney, an attorney must be made available to the accused person at the government's expense.

- The Eighth Amendment prohibitions against excessive bail and fines and against cruel and unusual punishments. Should the death penalty be considered a cruel and unusual punishment? We discuss that question in this chapter's *Join the Debate* feature on the following page.

BOSTON GLOBE/GETTY IMAGES

In June 2013, New England Patriots tight end Aaron Hernandez was arrested and charged with murder. Does he automatically have the right to counsel?

4–4b The Exclusionary Rule

Any evidence obtained in violation of the constitutional rights spelled out in the Fourth Amendment normally is not admissible at trial. This rule, which has been applied in the federal courts since at least 1914, is known as the **exclusionary rule**. The rule was extended to state court proceedings in 1961.[40]

The reasoning behind the exclusionary rule is that it forces law enforcement personnel to gather evidence properly. If they do not, they will be unable to introduce the evidence at trial to convince the jury that the defendant is guilty.

4–4c The *Miranda* Warnings

In the 1950s and 1960s, one of the questions facing the courts was not whether suspects had constitutional rights—that was not in doubt—but how and when those rights could be exercised. For example, could the right to remain silent (under the Fifth Amendment's prohibition against self-incrimination) be exercised during pretrial interrogation proceedings or only during the trial? Were confessions obtained from suspects admissible in court if the suspects had not been advised of their right to remain silent and other constitutional rights?

To clarify these issues, in 1966 the Supreme Court issued a landmark decision in *Miranda v. Arizona*.[41] In that case, the Court enunciated the *Miranda* **warnings** that are now familiar to almost all Americans:

> Prior to any questioning, the person must be warned that he has a right to remain silent, that any statement he does make may be used against him, and that he has a right to the presence of an attorney, either retained or appointed.

4–4d The Erosion of *Miranda*

As part of a continuing attempt to balance the rights of accused persons against the rights of society, the Supreme Court has made a number of exceptions to the *Miranda* ruling. In 1986, for example, the Court held that a confession need not be excluded even though the police failed to inform a suspect in custody that his attorney had tried to reach him by telephone.[42] In an important 1991 decision, the Court stated that a suspect's conviction will not be automatically overturned if the suspect was coerced into making a confession. If the other evidence admitted at trial was strong enough to justify the conviction without the confession, then the fact that the confession was obtained illegally can be, in effect, ignored.[43]

exclusionary rule
A criminal procedural rule stating that illegally obtained evidence is not admissible in court.

***Miranda* warnings**
A series of statements informing criminal suspects, on their arrest, of their constitutional rights, such as the right to remain silent and the right to counsel; required by the Supreme Court's 1966 decision in *Miranda v. Arizona*.

Is the Death Penalty a Cruel and Unusual Punishment?

The Eighth Amendment to the U.S. Constitution explicitly states that the government cannot inflict "cruel and unusual punishments." But what exactly is considered "cruel and unusual"? What about the death penalty, also called capital punishment?

Criminals have been executed in America since the earliest days of the republic. In addition to murder, a variety of crimes have been punished by death. In the 1700s, for example, citizens were executed for robbery, forgery, and illegally cutting down trees.

No state executes people for such crimes today. Furthermore, although a majority of Americans continue to support the death penalty for crimes such as murder, fewer states are executing people at all. Eighteen states (and the District of Columbia) have abolished the death penalty, and several governors have announced that they will not authorize executions even though their states permit them. Does this trend suggest that in our modern world the death penalty itself is cruel and unusual, and therefore a violation of the Eighth Amendment?

An Eye for an Eye Makes the Whole World Blind

Some argue that the death penalty is inappropriate even for someone who has committed murder. Violence and death may always be with us, but the law should not encourage violent sentiments. Already in 1764, the Italian jurist Cesare Beccaria asserted that "the death penalty cannot be useful, because of the example of barbarity it gives men."

Face it—capital punishment is barbaric whether it is carried out by a firing squad, an electric chair, a gas chamber, lethal injection, or hanging. Nations other than the United States that frequently employ capital punishment are not ones that we would seek to emulate: they include China, Iran, North Korea, and Saudi Arabia. Almost all of our allies have abolished the practice.

There Is Nothing Cruel and Unusual about Executing a Murderer

Strangely enough, some who are against capital punishment have argued that life in prison without parole is crueler than death. Prisoners are confined in an environment of violence where they are treated like animals, and the suffering goes on for decades. If you think about it, this is an argument that the death sentence can be merciful.

In any event, capital punishment is not cruel and unusual as meant by the Eighth Amendment. Indeed, the current method of execution used in most states—lethal injection—appears quite civilized compared with methods of execution used in England back in the 1700s, which included drawing and quartering and burning at the stake. Practices such as these are what the founders sought to ban.

FOR CRITICAL ANALYSIS Can there be a humane method of extinguishing someone's life? Why or why not?

Requesting One's Rights In yet another case related to *Miranda*, in 1994 the Supreme Court ruled that a suspect must unequivocally and assertively state his right to counsel in order to stop police questioning. Saying "Maybe I should talk to a lawyer" during an interrogation after being taken into custody is not enough. The Court held that police officers are not required to decipher the suspect's intentions in such situations.[44]

In a parallel ruling in 2010, the Court found that suspects must explicitly invoke the right to remain silent if they wish to avail themselves of that right.[45] In 2011, however, the Court ruled that because children are more susceptible to pressure than adults, police officers must take extra care in ensuring the *Miranda* rights of child suspects.[46]

Recording Confessions *Miranda* may eventually become obsolete regardless of any decisions made in the courts. A relatively new trend in law enforcement has been for agencies to digitally record interrogations and confessions. Thomas P. Sullivan, a former U.S. attorney in Chicago, and his staff interviewed personnel in more than 230 law enforcement agencies in thirty-eight states that record interviews of suspects who are in custody. Sullivan found that nearly all police officers said the procedure saved time and money, created valuable evidence to use in court, and made it more difficult for defense attorneys to claim that their clients had been illegally coerced.[47] Some scholars have suggested that recording all custodial interrogations would satisfy the Fifth Amendment's prohibition against coercion and in the process render the *Miranda* warnings unnecessary.

FOR CRITICAL THINKING

Regardless of whether executions can be carried out humanely, should the death penalty be abolished, or not? Explain your reasoning.

AMERICA AT
ODDS Civil Liberties

Civil liberties represent a contentious topic, and Americans are at odds over many of its issues. Almost all Americans claim to believe in individual rights, but how should this freedom be defined? Often, one right appears to interfere with another. Some of the resulting disputes include the following:

- Should the First Amendment's establishment clause be interpreted strictly, so that no one's rights are infringed on by government sponsorship of religion—or should it be interpreted loosely, to recognize that the United States is a very religious country?

- What kinds of religious practices should be allowed under the free exercise clause? In particular, should religious groups that limit or ban participation by gay men and lesbians receive the same government benefits as any other group—or may they be penalized for discrimination?

- Should advertising receive the same free speech rights as any other kind of speech—or should advertisers be held accountable for making false claims?

- Has the government gone too far in restricting liberties in an attempt to combat terrorism—or are the restrictions trivial compared with the benefits?

- Consider the most intense controversy of all: Should women have a privacy right to terminate a pregnancy for any reason—or should abortion be a crime?

STUDY TOOLS

Ready to study?

- **Review** what you've read with the quiz below.
- Check your answers on the **Chapter in Review** card at the back of the book.
- For any questions you miss, read the corresponding **Learning Outcome** section again to prepare for class and your exam.
- Rip out and study the **Chapter in Review** card (at the back of the book).

Fill-In

Learning Outcome 4–1

1. The _____ clause of the Fourteenth Amendment to the U.S. Constitution guarantees that state governments will not arbitrarily deprive any person of life, liberty, or property.

Learning Outcome 4–2

2. The *Lemon* test, enunciated by the Supreme Court in 1971 to determine whether government aid to parochial schools is constitutional, states that the aid must _____.

3. The current Supreme Court standard for assessing the constitutionality of _____ is the imminent lawless action test.

4. _____ is a published report of a falsehood that tends to injure a person's reputation or character.

5. The Supreme Court's _____ doctrine states that certain freedoms are so essential to a democracy that any law that limits these freedoms should be presumed to be unconstitutional unless the government can show that the law is absolutely necessary.

Learning Outcome 4–3

6. Under the USA Patriot Act of 2001, the FBI is authorized to use _____ to demand personal information about individuals from private companies, such as banks and phone companies.

7. In _____, the Supreme Court held that the "right of privacy . . . is broad enough to encompass a woman's decision whether or not to terminate her pregnancy."

Learning Outcome 4–4

8. The _____ Amendment includes protection from unreasonable searches and seizures.

9. The Eighth Amendment prohibits _____.

Multiple Choice

Learning Outcome 4–1

10. A(n) _____ is an order requiring that an official bring a specified prisoner into court and explain to the judge why the prisoner is being held.
    a. *ex post facto* law
    b. writ of *habeas corpus*
    c. bill of attainder

Learning Outcome 4–2

11. Thomas Jefferson wanted the establishment clause of the First Amendment to be a
    a. "bridge connecting government and religion."
    b. "barrier between government and the freedom of speech."
    c. "wall of separation between church and state."

12. The Supreme Court has ruled that public schools
    a. cannot sponsor religious activities.
    b. are allowed to determine for themselves the number of religious exercises they will sponsor.
    c. are barred from teaching about religion.

Learning Outcome 4–3

13. The Supreme Court, in *Griswold v. Connecticut* (1965), held that a right to privacy is implied by other constitutional rights guaranteed in the
    a. Magna Carta.
    b. First, Third, Fourth, Fifth, and Ninth Amendments.
    c. Declaration of Independence.

Learning Outcome 4–4

14 The Fifth Amendment
    a. includes a protection against self-incrimination.
    b. guarantees a speedy trial and a trial by jury.
    c. guarantees the right to counsel at various stages in some criminal proceedings.

15. _____ states that illegally obtained evidence is not admissible in court.
    a. Double jeopardy
    b. The exclusionary rule
    c. Probable cause

5

Civil Rights

The **Learning Outcomes** labeled 1 through 5 are designed to help improve your understanding of the chapter. After reading this chapter, you should be able to:

5–1 Explain the constitutional basis for our civil rights and for laws prohibiting discrimination.

5–2 Discuss the reasons for the civil rights movement and the changes it caused in American politics and government.

5–3 Describe the political and economic achievements of women in this country over time and identify some obstacles to equality that women continue to face.

5–4 Summarize the struggles for equality that other groups in America have experienced.

5–5 Explain what affirmative action is and why it has been so controversial.

Remember to visit page 117 for additional Study Tools

MARIO TAMA/GETTY IMAGES

AMERICA AT
ODDS
Should Unauthorized Immigrants Become Citizens?

Apart from Native Americans, all of us are either immigrants or the descendants of immigrants. Yet immigration remains one of the most divisive issues facing Americans today.

Congress has reacted in various ways to the issue of illegal immigration. Back in 1986, it established an amnesty program to allow unauthorized immigrants who had been working in the United States for five years to obtain legal residency. In the following years, however, many more people came to this country without authorization, and Congress has had little appetite for regularizing the status of these new arrivals. Following the 2012 elections, some Republicans argued in favor of immigration reform, as a way to make their party more attractive to Latino voters. Together with Democrats, these Republicans were able to get new legislation through the U.S. Senate, but not the House of Representatives.

In 2012, the Obama administration initiated, through an executive order, a program to freeze the deportation of young people brought into the country illegally before they were sixteen years old. Now such individuals can stay in the country and obtain work permits, if they meet certain conditions.

Today, there are about 11 million illegal immigrants living and working in this country. Should they be given a path to citizenship?

A Path to Citizenship Sends the Wrong Signal

Illegal immigrants have broken the law. If we give them a path to citizenship or even to legal status, we are sending the wrong signal to the rest of the world. As a result, we will end up with even more illegal immigrants, all of them hoping to find a path to citizenship one day. This is what happened after the 1986 legislation.

Most unauthorized immigrants have few job skills. Immigrants without high school diplomas now head about a third of immigrant households. Certainly, this country can use more high-skilled immigrants—those with scientific degrees and Ph.D.'s. Low-skilled immigrants, in contrast, simply take jobs away from Americans. To send the right signal to the world, we should also crack down on employers who hire illegal immigrants. These employers are adding to the problem.

How Can Americans Be Against Immigration?

Some find the "close the door after me" mentality to be very un-American. Immigrants pay more in taxes than they receive in government services. Unauthorized immigrants are not eligible to receive welfare benefits of any kind. The vast majority of illegal immigrants are working—they come here to work, not to receive government handouts.

Unauthorized immigrants don't compete with U.S. citizens for employment, because U.S. citizens are better qualified for jobs that require English-language skills. By increasing the size of the overall economy, immigration actually creates more jobs for citizens. It's true that unauthorized immigrants are not playing by the rules. But that is because the rules are too difficult to follow. We should make it easier for current unauthorized immigrants to gain legal status.

Where do you stand?

1. How might we rationalize the inconsistency between our being a country of immigrants and our wanting to keep out new ones?
2. From a Republican point of view, is it more helpful to build bridges to the Latino community—or to block citizenship rights for unauthorized immigrants who will probably vote for Democrats?

Explore this issue online

- The Catholic Church has long supported rights for unauthorized immigrants. Recently, many evangelical Protestants have joined the call for reform. Search on "immigration evangelicals" for news on this development.
- Tea Party groups remain opposed to anything that could be called amnesty for illegal immigrants. Check out their views at "immigration tea party."

Introduction

As noted in Chapter 4, people sometimes confuse civil rights with civil liberties. Generally, though, the term **civil rights** refers to the rights of all Americans to equal treatment under the law, as provided by the Fourteenth Amendment.

Although the democratic ideal is for all people to have equal rights and equal treatment under the law, and although the Constitution guarantees those rights today, this ideal has often remained just that—an ideal. As you will read in this chapter, the struggle of various groups in American society to obtain equal treatment has been a long one, and it continues. Latinos make up one such group, and we discussed an issue that concerns them in this chapter's opening *America at Odds* feature.

In a sense, the history of civil rights in the United States is a history of discrimination against various groups. Discrimination against women, African Americans, and Native Americans dates back to the early years of this nation. Later, as people from around the globe immigrated to this country, each immigrant group faced discrimination in one form or another. More recently, other groups, including persons with disabilities and gay men and lesbians, have struggled for equal treatment under the law. This chapter discusses each of these groups. Inevitably, though, a single short chapter must omit discussion of some groups that have experienced discrimination. Two such groups are American Muslims and older Americans.

Central to any discussion of civil rights is the

> All Americans are entitled to **EQUAL TREATMENT UNDER THE LAW,** as provided by the Fourteenth Amendment.

interpretation of the equal protection clause of the Fourteenth Amendment to the Constitution. For that reason, we look first at that clause.

5–1 The Equal Protection Clause

You read about the due process clause of the Fourteenth Amendment in Chapter 4. Equal in importance to the due process clause is the **equal protection clause** in Section 1 of that amendment, which reads as follows: "No State shall . . . deny to any person within its jurisdiction the equal protection of the laws." Section 5 of the amendment provides a legal basis for federal civil rights legislation: "The Congress shall have power to enforce, by appropriate legislation, the provisions of this article."

The equal protection clause has been interpreted by the courts, and especially the Supreme Court, to mean that states must treat all persons equally and may not discriminate *unreasonably* against a particular group or class of individuals. The task of distinguishing between reasonable and unreasonable discrimination is difficult. Generally, in deciding this question, the Supreme Court balances the constitutional rights of individuals to equal protection against government interests in protecting the safety and welfare of citizens.

Over time, the Court has developed various tests, or standards, for determining whether the equal protection clause has been violated. These standards are strict scrutiny, intermediate scrutiny, and ordinary scrutiny (the rational basis test).

Learning Outcome 5–1

Explain the constitutional basis for our civil rights and for laws prohibiting discrimination.

5–1a Strict Scrutiny

If a law or action prevents some group of persons from exercising a **fundamental right** (such as one of our First Amendment rights), the law or action will be subject to the **strict scrutiny standard.** Under this standard, the law or action must be necessary to promote a *compelling state interest* and must be narrowly tailored to meet that interest. A law based on

---

civil rights The rights of all Americans to equal treatment under the law, as provided by the Fourteenth Amendment to the Constitution.

equal protection clause Section 1 of the Fourteenth Amendment, which states that no state shall "deny to any person within its jurisdiction the equal protection of the laws."

fundamental right A basic right of all Americans, such as First Amendment rights. Any law or action that prevents some group of persons from exercising a fundamental right is subject to the *strict scrutiny standard*.

strict scrutiny standard A standard under which a law or action must be necessary to promote a compelling state interest and must be narrowly tailored to meet that interest.

a **suspect classification**, such as race, is also subject to strict scrutiny by the courts, meaning that the law must be justified by a compelling state interest.

5–1b Intermediate Scrutiny

Because the Supreme Court had difficulty deciding how to judge cases in which men and women were treated differently, another test was developed—the *intermediate scrutiny standard.* Under this standard, also known as *exacting scrutiny,* laws based on gender classifications are permissible if they are "substantially related to the achievement of an important governmental objective."

For example, a law punishing males but not females for statutory rape has been ruled valid by the courts. The reasoning is that there is an important governmental interest in preventing teenage pregnancy in those circumstances and almost all of the harmful and identifiable consequences of teenage pregnancies fall on young females.[1] A law prohibiting the sale of beer to males under twenty-one years of age and to females under eighteen years would not be valid, however.[2]

Declaring Gender-based Laws Unconstitutional

Generally, since the 1970s, the Supreme Court has scrutinized gender classifications closely and has declared many gender-based laws unconstitutional. In 1979, the Court held that a state law allowing wives to obtain alimony judgments against husbands but preventing husbands from receiving alimony from wives violated the equal protection clause.[3] In 1982, the Court declared that Mississippi's policy of excluding males from the School of Nursing at Mississippi University for Women was unconstitutional.[4]

The Virginia Military Institute Case

In a controversial 1996 case, *United States v. Virginia,*[5] the Court held that Virginia Military Institute, a state-financed institution, violated the equal protection clause by refusing to accept female applicants. The Court said that the state of Virginia had failed to provide sufficient justification for its gender-based classification.

5–1c The Rational Basis Test (Ordinary Scrutiny)

A third test used to decide whether a discriminatory law violates the equal protection clause is the **rational**

AP PHOTO/ANDY ALONSO

Women broke the state government–supported gender barrier at Virginia Military Institute in 1996.

basis test. This test is employed only when there is no classification—such as race or gender—that would require a higher level of scrutiny. When applying this test to a law that classifies or treats people or groups differently, the courts ask whether the discrimination is rational. In other words, is it a reasonable way to achieve a legitimate government objective? Few laws tested under the rational basis test—or the *ordinary scrutiny standard,* as it is also called—are found invalid, because few laws are truly unreasonable.

A municipal ordinance that prohibits certain vendors from selling their wares in a particular area of

suspect classification
A classification, such as race, that provides the basis for a discriminatory law. Any law based on a suspect classification is subject to strict scrutiny by the courts, meaning that the law must be justified by a compelling state interest.

rational basis test A test (also known as the *ordinary scrutiny standard*) used by the Supreme Court to decide whether a discriminatory law violates the equal protection clause of the Constitution. It is used only when there is no classification—such as race or gender—that would require a higher level of scrutiny.

the city, for example, will be upheld if the city can meet this rational basis test. The rational basis for the ordinance might be the city's legitimate government interest in reducing traffic congestion in that particular area.

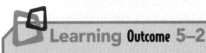

FOR CRITICAL THINKING When evaluating cases of discrimination against gay men or lesbians, some judges have employed the rational basis test, while others have applied intermediate scrutiny. *Which standard do you consider appropriate, and why?*

5–2 African Americans

Learning Outcome 5–2

Discuss the reasons for the civil rights movement and the changes it caused in American politics and government.

The equal protection clause was originally intended to protect the newly freed slaves after the Civil War (1861–1865). In the early years after the war, the U.S. government made an effort to protect the rights of blacks living in the states of the former Confederacy. The Thirteenth Amendment (which granted freedom to the slaves), the Fourteenth Amendment (which guaranteed equal protection under the law), and the Fifteenth Amendment (which stated that voting rights could not be abridged on account of race) were part of that effort.

By the late 1880s, however, southern legislatures had begun to pass a series of segregation laws—laws that separated the white community from the black community. Such laws were commonly called "Jim Crow" laws (from a song that was popular in minstrel shows that caricatured African Americans). Some of the most common Jim Crow laws called for racial segregation in the use of public facilities, such as schools, railroads, and, later, buses. These laws were also applied to housing, restaurants, hotels, and many other facilities.

separate-but-equal doctrine A Supreme Court doctrine holding that the equal protection clause of the Fourteenth Amendment did not forbid racial segregation as long as the facilities for blacks were equal to those for whites.

5–2a Separate but Equal

In 1892, a group of Louisiana citizens decided to challenge a state law that required railroads to provide separate railway cars for African Americans. A man named Homer Plessy, who was seven-eighths European and one-eighth African, boarded a train in New Orleans and sat in the railway car reserved for whites. When Plessy refused to move at the request of the conductor, he was arrested for breaking the law.

Four years later, in 1896, the Supreme Court provided a constitutional basis for segregation laws. In *Plessy v. Ferguson*,[6] the Court held that the law did not violate the equal protection clause if *separate* facilities for blacks were *equal* to those for whites.

The lone dissenter, Justice John Marshall Harlan, disagreed: "Our Constitution is colorblind, and neither knows nor tolerates classes among citizens." The majority opinion, however, established the **separate-but-equal doctrine**, which was used to justify segregation in many areas of American life for nearly sixty years. Separate facilities for African Americans, when they were provided at all, were in practice almost never truly equal.

A member of the Klu Klux Klan in Miami, Florida, in 1939. He was part of a campaign to intimidate potential black voters.

IMAGNO/GETTY IMAGES

5–2b Violence and Vote Suppression

Segregation was far from the only problem faced by African Americans in the years following the abolition of slavery. Perhaps the most important was denial of the right to vote.

Loss of the Franchise The Fifteenth Amendment explicitly extended the franchise (the right to vote) to African Americans, and for several decades following the Civil War, blacks were in fact able to vote throughout much of the former Confederacy. In the 1880s and 1890s, however, Southern leaders launched major efforts to disenfranchise black voters. They used a number of techniques to accomplish this goal, including the following:

- *Literacy tests*, which African Americans were guaranteed to fail.
- The *poll tax*, a tax on voting, which disenfranchised poor whites as well as blacks.
- The *grandfather clause*, which effectively limited voting to those whose ancestors could vote before the Civil War.
- The *white primary*, which prevented African Americans from voting in Democratic primary elections.

Social Control through Violence These restrictive laws were backed up by the threat of violence directed at African Americans who were brave enough to try to vote. The *Klu Klux Klan* was famous for its use of force to keep black citizens "in their place," but white violence was not limited to Klan members. The threat of *lynching*—execution and even torture at the hands of a mob—was employed not only to keep African Americans from voting but also to impose an elaborate code of social deference upon them.

5–2c The *Brown* Decisions and School Integration

In the late 1930s and the 1940s, the United States Supreme Court gradually moved away from the separate-but-equal doctrine discussed earlier. The major breakthrough, however, did not come until 1954, in a case involving an African American girl who lived in Topeka, Kansas.

In the 1950s, Topeka's schools, like those in many cities, were segregated. Mr. and Mrs. Oliver Brown wanted their daughter, Linda Carol Brown, to attend a white school a few blocks from their home instead of an all-black school that was twenty-one blocks away. With the help of lawyers from the National Association for the Advancement of Colored People (NAACP), Linda's parents sued the board of education to allow their daughter to attend the nearby school. (NAACP is always pronounced as "N-double-A-C-P.")

In 1954, in *Brown v. Board of Education of Topeka*,[7] the Supreme Court reversed *Plessy v. Ferguson*. The Court unanimously held that segregation by race in public education is unconstitutional. Chief Justice Earl Warren wrote as follows:

> Does segregation of children in public schools solely on the basis of race, even though the physical facilities and other "tangible" factors may be equal, deprive the children of the minority group of equal educational opportunities? We believe that it does. . . . [Segregation generates in children] a feeling of inferiority as to their status in the community that may affect their hearts and minds in a way unlikely ever to be undone. . . . We conclude that in the field of public education the doctrine of "separate but equal" has no place. Separate educational facilities are inherently unequal.

In 1955, in *Brown v. Board of Education*[8] (sometimes called *Brown II)*, the Supreme Court ordered desegregation to begin "with all deliberate speed," an ambiguous phrase that could be (and was) interpreted in a variety of ways.

Reactions to School Integration The Supreme Court ruling did not go unchallenged. Bureaucratic loopholes were used to delay desegregation. Another reaction was "white flight." As white parents sent their children to newly established private schools, some formerly white-only public schools became 100 percent black. In Arkansas, Governor Orval Faubus used the state's National Guard to block the integration of Central High School in Little Rock in 1957. A federal court demanded that the troops be withdrawn. Only after President Dwight D. Eisenhower federalized the Arkansas National Guard and sent in additional troops did Central High finally become integrated.

By 1970, *de jure segregation*—segregation that is established by law—had been abolished by school systems. But that meant only that no public school could

> **de jure segregation**
> Racial segregation that occurs because of laws or decisions by government agencies.

legally identify itself as being reserved for all whites or all blacks. It did not mean the end of *de facto segregation*—segregation that is not imposed by law but is produced by circumstances, such as the existence of neighborhoods or communities populated primarily by African Americans. Attempts to overcome *de facto* segregation have included redrawing school district lines, reassigning pupils, and establishing busing.

Busing In respect to civil rights, **busing** is the transporting of students by bus to schools physically outside their neighborhoods in an effort to achieve racially desegregated schools. The Supreme Court first endorsed busing in 1971 in a case involving the school system in Charlotte, North Carolina.[9] Following this decision, the Court upheld busing in several northern cities.[10] Proponents believed that busing improved the educational and career opportunities of minority children and also enhanced the ability of children from different ethnic groups to get along with one another.

Nevertheless, busing was unpopular with many groups from its inception. By the mid-1970s, the courts had begun to retreat from their former support for busing. In 1974, the Supreme Court rejected the idea of busing children across school district lines.[11] In 1986, the Court refused to review a lower court decision that ended a desegregation plan in Norfolk, Virginia.[12] Today, busing orders to end *de facto* segregation are not upheld by the courts. Indeed, *de facto* segregation in America's schools is still widespread.

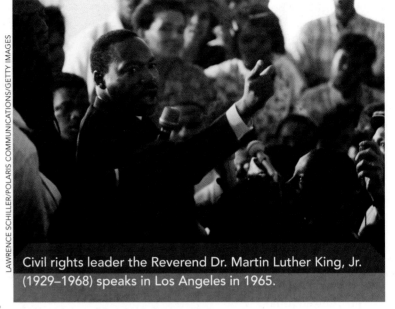

LAWRENCE SCHILLER/POLARIS COMMUNICATIONS/GETTY IMAGES

Civil rights leader the Reverend Dr. Martin Luther King, Jr. (1929–1968) speaks in Los Angeles in 1965.

5–2d The Civil Rights Movement

In 1955, one year after the first *Brown* decision, an African American woman named Rosa Parks, a longtime activist in the NAACP, boarded a public bus in Montgomery, Alabama. When it became crowded, she refused to move to the "colored section" at the rear of the bus. She was arrested and fined for violating local segregation laws. Her arrest spurred the local African American community to organize a year-long boycott of the entire Montgomery bus system.

The protest was led by a twenty-seven-year-old Baptist minister, the Reverend Dr. Martin Luther King, Jr. During the protest period, he was jailed and his house was bombed. Yet, despite white hostility and what appeared to be overwhelming odds against them, the protesters were triumphant in the end.

In 1956, a federal court prohibited the segregation of buses in Montgomery, and the era of the **civil rights movement**—the movement by minorities and concerned whites to end racial segregation—had begun. The movement was led by a number of groups and individuals, including Martin Luther King and his Southern Christian Leadership Conference (SCLC). Other groups, such as the Congress of Racial Equality (CORE), the NAACP, and the Student Nonviolent Coordinating Committee (SNCC), also sought to secure equal rights for African Americans.

Nonviolence as a Tactic Civil rights protesters in the 1960s began to apply the tactic of nonviolent **civil disobedience**—the deliberate and public refusal to obey laws considered unjust—in civil rights actions throughout the South. Activists were trained in the tools of nonviolence—how to use nonthreatening body language, how to go limp when dragged or

de facto segregation Racial segregation that occurs not as a result of deliberate intentions but because of social and economic conditions and residential patterns.

busing The transportation of public school students by bus to schools physically outside their neighborhoods to eliminate school segregation based on residential patterns.

civil rights movement The movement in the 1950s and 1960s, by minorities and concerned whites, to end racial segregation.

civil disobedience The deliberate and public act of refusing to obey laws thought to be unjust.

assaulted, and how to protect themselves from clubs and police dogs.

AN EXAMPLE. In 1960, for example, four African American students in Greensboro, North Carolina, sat at the "whites only" lunch counter at Woolworth's and ordered food. The waitress refused to serve them, and the store closed early, but more students returned the next day to sit at the counter, with supporters picketing outside. **Sit-ins** spread to other lunch counters across the South.

In some instances, students participating in sit-ins were heckled or even dragged from Woolworth's by angry whites. But the protesters never reacted with violence. They simply returned to their seats at the counter, day after day. Within months of the first sit-in, lunch counter managers began to reverse their policies of segregation.

THE NATIONAL REACTION. As the civil rights movement gained momentum, the media images of nonviolent protesters being assaulted by police, sprayed with fire hoses, and attacked by dogs shocked and angered Americans across the country. This public backlash led to nationwide demands for reform. The March on Washington for Jobs and Freedom, led by Martin Luther King in 1963, aimed in part to demonstrate the widespread public support for legislation to ban discrimination in all aspects of public life.

Civil Rights Legislation in the 1960s

As the civil rights movement demonstrated its strength, Congress began to pass civil rights laws. While the Fourteenth Amendment prevented the *government* from discriminating against individuals or groups, the private sector—businesses, restaurants, and the like—could still freely refuse to employ and serve nonwhites. Therefore, Congress sought to address this issue.

THE CIVIL RIGHTS ACT OF 1964. The Civil Rights Act of 1964 was the first and most comprehensive civil rights law. It forbade discrimination on the basis of race, color, religion, gender, and national origin. The major provisions of the act were as follows:

- It outlawed discrimination in public places of accommodation, such as hotels, restaurants, movie theaters, and public transportation.

- It provided that federal funds could be withheld from any federal or state government project or facility that practiced any form of discrimination.

- It banned discrimination in employment.

- It outlawed arbitrary discrimination in voter registration.

- It authorized the federal government to sue to desegregate public schools and facilities.

> **"INJUSTICE**
> anywhere is a threat to justice everywhere."
> ~ MARTIN LUTHER KING, JR. ~
> U.S. CIVIL RIGHTS LEADER
> 1929–1968

VOTING AND HOUSING RIGHTS. Other significant laws were passed by Congress during the 1960s as well. The Voting Rights Act of 1965 made it illegal to interfere with anyone's right to vote in any election held in this country. (Earlier in this chapter, we mentioned the historical restrictions on voting that African Americans faced, and we discuss them further in Chapter 8.) The Civil Rights Act of 1968 prohibited discrimination in housing.

The Black Power Movement

Not all African Americans embraced nonviolence. Several outspoken leaders in the mid-1960s were outraged at the slow pace of change in the social and economic status of blacks.

Malcolm X, a speaker and organizer for the Nation of Islam (also called the Black Muslims), rejected the goals of integration and racial equality espoused by the civil rights movement. He called instead for black separatism and "black pride." Although he later moderated some of his views, his rhetorical style and powerful message influenced many African American young people.

By the late 1960s, with the assassinations of Malcolm X in 1965 and Martin Luther King in 1968, the era of mass acts of civil disobedience in the name of civil rights had come to an end.

5–2e African Americans in Politics Today

As mentioned earlier, in many jurisdictions African Americans were prevented from voting for years

sit-in A tactic of nonviolent civil disobedience. Demonstrators enter a business, college building, or other public place and remain seated until they are forcibly removed or until their demands are met.

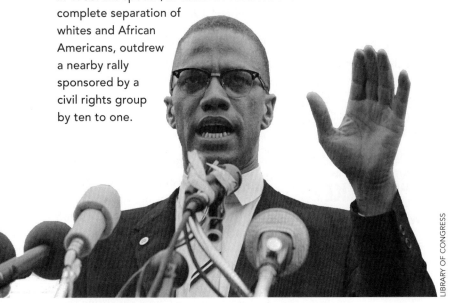

Black Muslim leader Malcolm X speaks to an audience at a Harlem rally in 1963. His speech, in which he restated the Black Muslim theme of complete separation of whites and African Americans, outdrew a nearby rally sponsored by a civil rights group by ten to one.

LIBRARY OF CONGRESS

after the Civil War, despite the Fifteenth Amendment (1870). These discriminatory practices persisted in the twentieth century. In the early 1960s, only 22 percent of African Americans of voting age in the South were registered to vote, compared with 63 percent of voting-age whites. In Mississippi, the most extreme example, only 6 percent of voting-age African Americans were registered to vote. Such disparities led to the enactment of the Voting Rights Act of 1965, which ended discriminatory voter-registration tests and gave federal voter registrars the power to prevent racial discrimination in voting.

Today, the percentages of eligible blacks and whites registered to vote are nearly equal. As a result of this dramatic change, political participation by African Americans has increased, as has the number of African American elected officials.

Representation in Office

More than nine thousand African Americans now serve in elective office in the United States. At least one congressional seat in each southern state is held by an African American, as are more than 15 percent of the state legislative seats in the South. A number of African Americans have achieved high government office, including Colin Powell, who served as President George W. Bush's first secretary of state, and Condoleezza Rice, his second secretary of state.

Of course, in 2008 Barack Obama, a U.S. senator from Illinois, became the first African American president of the United States. Obama's election reflects a

significant change in public opinion. Fifty years ago, only 38 percent of Americans said that they would be willing to vote for an African American as president. Today, this number has risen to more than 90 percent. Nonetheless, only two African Americans have been elected to a state governorship, and only a handful of African Americans have been elected to the U.S. Senate since 1900.

The Supreme Court Weakens the Voting Rights Act

In June 2013, the Voting Rights Act received a significant setback at the hands of the United States Supreme Court. In *Shelby County v. Holder,* the Court ruled that Section 4 of the Voting Rights Act was unconstitutional.[13] This section defined which state and local governments were subject to special federal oversight.

These governments could not change voting procedures or district boundaries without *preclearance,* or approval, from the federal government. The governments identified by Section 4 had a history of voting rights violations in the 1960s, but the Court argued that basing current law on events that far in the past was unacceptable. In principle, Congress could adopt a new Section 4, but the chances of such a measure passing a highly polarized Congress any time soon were remote.

The Impact of Voting Restrictions

Progressives feared that the Court's decision would result in new state laws that would make it difficult for many low-income persons to vote. Indeed, even before the 2012 elections, a substantial number of new laws threatened to reduce turnout among poor—and minority—voters. These laws included limits on early voting and requirements that voters produce photographic IDs.

As it turned out, there was no drop-off in the minority vote relative to the white vote in 2012. Some analysts concluded that anger over the restrictive laws drove up minority turnout, fully compensating for any fall in the number of voters due to the restrictions.

5–2f Continuing Challenges

Although African Americans no longer face *de jure* segregation, they continue to struggle for income and educational parity with whites. Recent census data show that average incomes in black households are only 59 percent of those in non-Hispanic white households. The poverty rate for blacks is roughly three times that for whites. The loss of jobs caused by the Great Recession tended to make matters worse for African Americans and other minority group members.

A related problem is crime. Criminal activity is commonplace in the impoverished neighborhoods where many African Americans live, and African Americans are disproportionately arrested for crimes of all types. Prejudice among law enforcement officials may account for some arrests of African Americans, but statistics suggest that blacks probably do commit a disproportionate share of violent crime. When it comes to illegal drug charges, the picture is more troubling. We examine that issue in the *Perception versus Reality* feature on the following page.

Problems with Education The education gap between blacks and whites also persists despite continuing efforts by educators—and by government, through programs such as the federal No Child Left Behind Act—to reduce it. Recent studies show that, on average, African American students in high school read and do math at the level of whites in junior high school. Also, while black adults have narrowed the gap with white adults in earning high school diplomas, the disparity has widened for college degrees.

These problems tend to feed on one another. Schools in poorer neighborhoods generally have fewer educational resources available, resulting in lower achievement levels for their students. Thus, some educational experts suggest that it all comes down to money. In fact, many parents of minority students in struggling school districts are less concerned about integration than they are about funds for their children's schools. A number of these parents have initiated lawsuits against their state governments, demanding that the states give poor districts more resources.

Class versus Race in Educational Outcomes
Researchers have known for decades that when students enrolled at a particular school come almost entirely from impoverished families, regardless of race, the performance of the students at that school is seriously depressed. When low-income students attend schools where the majority of the students are middle class, again regardless of race, their performance improves dramatically—without dragging down the performance of the middle-class students. Because of this research and recent United States Supreme Court rulings that have struck down some racial integration plans, several school systems have adopted policies that integrate students on the basis of socioeconomic class, not race.[14]

FOR CRITICAL THINKING

Why might low-income students do better in their studies, on average, when most of their classmates are middle class instead of poor?

5–3 Women

In 1848, Lucretia Mott and Elizabeth Cady Stanton organized the first "woman's rights" convention in Seneca Falls, New York. The three hundred people who attended approved a Declaration of Sentiments: "We hold these truths to be self-evident: that all men *and women* are created equal." In the following years, other women's groups held conventions in various cities in the Midwest and the East. With the outbreak of the Civil War, though, women's rights advocates devoted their energies to the war effort.

Learning Outcome 5–3

Describe the political and economic achievements of women in this country over time and identify some obstacles to equality that women continue to face.

5–3a The Struggle for Voting Rights

The movement for political rights gained momentum again in 1869, when Susan B. Anthony and Elizabeth Cady Stanton formed the National Woman Suffrage Association. **Suffrage**—the right to vote—became their goal. Members of this association saw suffrage as only one step on the road toward greater social and political rights for women. In contrast, Lucy Stone and other women, who founded the American Woman Suffrage Association, thought that the right to vote should be the only goal.

The Suffrage Campaign By 1890, the two organizations had joined forces, and the resulting National American Woman Suffrage Association had indeed

suffrage The right to vote; the franchise.

Perception versus Reality

Racial Disparities in Incarceration for Drug Violations

More than 2.3 million Americans are in jail or prison. Indeed, the United States, with only 5 percent of the world population, has 25 percent of the world's prisoners. If you consider as well those under parole or on probation, about one in thirty adults is subject to some form of correctional control. African Americans constitute nearly 1 million of the 2.3 million incarcerated. Add Hispanics, and those two groups make up almost 60 percent of all prisoners, even though they represent about 25 percent of the U.S. population.

THE PERCEPTION

The numbers tell it all—American law enforcement is at heart racist. Take marijuana arrests. African Americans are nearly four times as likely to be arrested for possession of marijuana as whites, even though studies show that the two groups use that particular drug at similar rates. African Americans represent 12 percent of the total population of drug users but almost 40 percent of those arrested for drug offenses and almost 60 percent of those in state prisons for drug offenses.

THE REALITY

Some law enforcement officials may have racist tendencies, but that is not a full explanation of why African Americans and Hispanics are routinely arrested more frequently for drug offenses than are whites. Rather, we can explain the disparities more accurately by looking at the incentives facing police personnel.

Imagine that you work for the police and want to get promoted. You are out on patrol, and you know your boss wants to see results. You suspect that there is illegal drug use in the homes of middle-class whites (or even in the offices of Wall Street stockbrokers) and also on the streets in a low-income part of town. Where are you going to do your investigations?

If you arrest a middle-class white stockbroker, that person has the resources to hire a good lawyer to fight the charge. The stockbroker is likely to get off. In contrast, if you arrest someone in a low-income, minority neighborhood, that person will not have the resources to fight back. You will get your "collar" and may see a successful prosecution. Do that often enough, and your boss will see how effective you are and promote you.

In other words, it is not so much race that leads the police to arrest more African Americans and Hispanics than middle-class whites for drug offenses. Rather, it is a matter of socioeconomic class. Consider George Zimmerman, who shot Trayvon Martin, a black youth, and who was found not guilty in 2013. If Zimmerman had been represented in court by a public defender instead of a legal team worth hundreds of thousands of dollars, what are the odds that he would have escaped conviction?

BLOG ON

- A Web search on "race arrests pot" will yield a variety of articles on racial disparities in marijuana arrests.
- One step that would dramatically reduce marijuana arrests is to legalize the drug. The Web site The Reality-Based Community contains many posts discussing the pros and cons of legalization.

only one goal—enfranchisement (being given the right to vote). When little progress was made, small, radical splinter groups took to the streets. Parades, hunger strikes, arrests, and jailings soon followed.

World War I (1914–1918) marked a turning point in the battle for women's rights. The war offered many opportunities for women. Several thousand women served in the U.S. Navy, and about a million women joined the workforce, holding jobs vacated by men who had entered military service.

The Nineteenth Amendment After the war, President Woodrow Wilson wrote to Carrie Chapman Catt, one of the leaders of the women's movement: "It is high time that [that] part of our debt should be acknowledged." Two years later, in 1920, seventy-two years after

5–3b The Feminist Movement

For many years after winning the right to vote, women engaged in little independent political activity. In the 1960s, however, a new women's movement arose—the feminist movement. Women who faced discrimination in employment and other circumstances were inspired in part by the civil rights movement and the campaign against the war in Vietnam.

The National Organization for Women (NOW), founded in 1966, was the most important new women's organization. But the feminist movement also consisted of thousands of small, independent "women's liberation" and "consciousness-raising" groups established on campuses and in neighborhoods throughout the nation. **Feminism,** the goal of the movement, meant full political, economic, and social equality for women.

Combating Gender Discrimination

During the 1970s, NOW and other organizations sought to win passage of the Equal Rights Amendment (ERA) to the Constitution, which would have written equality into the heart of the nation's laws. The amendment did not win support from enough state legislatures, however, and it failed. Campaigns to change state and national laws affecting women were much more successful. Congress and the various state legislatures enacted a range of measures to provide equal rights for women. The women's movement also enjoyed considerable success in legal action. Courts at all levels accepted the argument that *gender discrimination* violated the Fourteenth Amendment's equal protection clause.

Abortion and Other Issues

In addition to fighting against gender discrimination, the feminist movement took up a number of other issues impor-

the Seneca Falls convention, the Nineteenth Amendment to the Constitution was ratified: "The right of citizens of the United States to vote shall not be denied or abridged by the United States or by any State on account of sex."

> "The right of citizens of the United States to vote **shall not be denied or abridged . . . on account of sex."**
>
> ~ THE NINETEENTH AMENDMENT TO THE UNITED STATES CONSTITUTION ~
> 1920

tant to women. Some campaigns, such as the one to curb domestic violence, have been widely supported. Others have resulted in heated debate. Perhaps the most controversial issue of all has been the right to have an abortion, which we discussed in Chapter 4.

5–3c Women in American Politics Today

More than ten thousand members have served in the U.S. House of Representatives. Only 1 percent of them have been women, and women continue to face a "men's club" atmosphere in Congress. In 2002, however, a woman, Nancy Pelosi (D., Calif.), was elected minority leader of the House of Representatives. She was the first woman to hold this post. Pelosi again made history when, after the Democratic victories in the 2006 elections, she was elected Speaker of the House of Representatives, the first woman ever to lead the House. After the Republicans took control of the House in 2011, Pelosi again became minority leader.

Federal Offices Women have been underrepresented in receiving presidential appointments to federal offices. Franklin D. Roosevelt (1933–1945) appointed the first woman to a cabinet post—Frances Perkins, who was secretary of labor from 1933 to 1945. Several women have held cabinet posts in more recent administrations. All of the last three presidents have appointed women to the most senior cabinet post—secretary of state. Bill Clinton (1993–2001) appointed Madeleine Albright to this position, George W. Bush (2001–2009) picked Condoleezza Rice for the post in his second term, and most recently, Barack Obama chose New York senator Hillary Clinton to be secretary of state during his first term.

In addition, Ronald Reagan (1981–1989) appointed the first woman to sit on the Supreme Court, Sandra Day O'Connor. Bill Clinton appointed Ruth Bader Ginsburg to the Supreme Court. Barack Obama selected Sonia Sotomayor for the Court in 2009 and Elena Kagan in 2010.

State Politics Women have made greater progress at the state level, and

feminism A doctrine advocating full political, economic, and social equality for women.

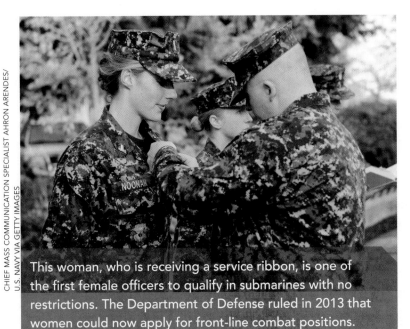

This woman, who is receiving a service ribbon, is one of the first female officers to qualify in submarines with no restrictions. The Department of Defense ruled in 2013 that women could now apply for front-line combat positions.

females who perform essentially the same job. The following year, Congress passed the Civil Rights Act of 1964, Title VII of which prohibits employment discrimination on the basis of race, color, national origin, gender, and religion. Women, however, continue to face wage discrimination.

It is estimated that for every dollar earned by men, women earn about 80 cents. Although the wage gap has narrowed significantly since 1963, when the Equal Pay Act was enacted (at that time, women earned 58 cents for every dollar earned by men), it still remains. This is particularly true for women in management positions and older women. Female managers now earn, on average, only 70 percent of what male managers earn. And women between the ages of forty-five and fifty-four make, on average, only 73 percent of what men in that age group earn. Notably, when the workers in a particular occupation include a disproportionately high number of women, the wages that are paid in that occupation tend to be relatively low.

the percentage of women in state legislatures has been rising steadily. Women now constitute nearly one-fourth of state legislators. In 1998, women won races for each of the top five offices in Arizona, the first such occurrence in U.S. history. Generally, women have been more successful politically in the western states than elsewhere. In Washington, more than one-third of the state's legislative seats are now held by women. At the other end of the spectrum are states such as Alabama. In that state, fewer than 10 percent of the lawmakers are women.

5–3d Women in the Workplace

An ongoing challenge for American women is to obtain equal pay and equal opportunity in the workplace. In spite of federal legislation and programs to promote equal treatment of women in the workplace, women continue to face various forms of discrimination.

Wage Discrimination

In 1963, Congress passed the Equal Pay Act. The act requires employers to pay an equal wage for substantially equal work—males cannot be paid more than

glass ceiling An invisible but real discriminatory barrier that prevents women and minorities from rising to top positions of power or responsibility.

sexual harassment Unwanted physical contact, verbal conduct, or abuse of a sexual nature that interferes with a recipient's job performance, creates a hostile environment, or carries with it an implicit or explicit threat of adverse employment consequences.

The Glass Ceiling Even though an increasing number of women now hold business and professional jobs once held only by men, relatively few of these women are able to rise to the top of the career ladder in their firms due to the lingering bias against women in the workplace. This bias has been described as the **glass ceiling**—an invisible but real discriminatory barrier that prevents women and minorities from rising to top positions of power or responsibility. Today, less than one-sixth of the top executive positions in the largest American corporations are held by women.

Sexual Harassment Title VII's prohibition of gender discrimination has also been extended to prohibit sexual harassment. **Sexual harassment** occurs when job opportunities, promotions, salary increases, or even the ability to retain a job depend on whether an employee complies with demands for sexual favors. A special form of sexual harassment, called *hostile environment harassment*, occurs when an employee is subjected to sexual conduct or comments in the workplace that interfere with the employee's job performance or that create an intimidating, hostile, or offensive environment.

The Supreme Court has upheld the right of persons to be free from sexual harassment on the job on a number of occasions. In 1998, the Court made it clear that sexual harassment includes harassment by members of the same sex.[15] In the same year, the Court held that employers are liable for the harassment of employees by supervisors unless the employers can show that (1) they exercised reasonable care in preventing such problems (by implementing anti-harassment policies and procedures, for example), and (2) the employees failed to take advantage of any corrective opportunities provided by the employers.[16]

The Civil Rights Act of 1991 greatly expanded the remedies available for victims of sexual harassment. Under the act, victims can seek damages as well as back pay, job reinstatement, and other compensation.

FOR CRITICAL THINKING

In recent years, the percentage of young women who have received college diplomas has exceeded the percentage for young men. *In the future, how might this development change the social and economic roles of women and men?*

5–4 Securing Rights for Other Groups

Learning Outcome 5–4

Summarize the struggles for equality that other groups in America have experienced.

In addition to African Americans and women, a number of other groups in U.S. society have faced discriminatory treatment. One lingering result of past discrimination can be that a group suffers from below-average incomes and relatively high rates of poverty. Figure 5–1 on the right shows the percentage of persons with incomes below the poverty line for five major racial or ethnic groups. The chart provides statistics for children as well as the overall population. Note that in all groups, children are much more likely than adults to live in poverty. This reality makes poverty that much more damaging.

Next, we look at three groups that have had to struggle for equal treatment—Latinos, Asian Americans, and Native Americans (or American Indians). Then we examine the struggles of several other groups of Americans—persons with disabilities and gay men and lesbians.

5–4a Latinos

Latinos, or Hispanics, constitute the largest ethnic minority in the United States. Whereas African Americans represent 13.1 percent of the U.S. population, Latinos now constitute 16.9 percent. Each year, the Hispanic population grows by nearly 1 million people, one-third of whom are newly arrived legal immigrants. By 2050, Latinos are expected to constitute almost 30 percent of the U.S. population.

Who Are the Hispanics? According to the U.S. Census Bureau definition, Hispanics can be of any race. Note that while *Hispanic* is official U.S. government terminology, some members of this group prefer the term *Latino*—or *Latina* in the feminine case. In fact, though, most Latinos prefer to identify with their

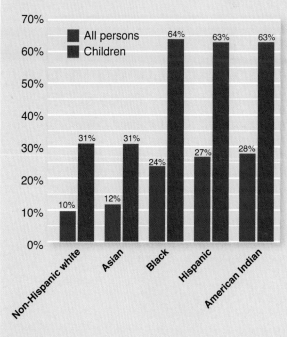

FIGURE 5–1

Persons in Poverty in the
United States by Race and Hispanic Origin, 2010

Blacks, Hispanics, and American Indians are more likely than whites or Asians to have incomes below the poverty line. Children are substantially more likely than adults to live in families with incomes below the poverty line.

Source: The 2010 Census.

country of origin rather than be categorized as either Hispanics or Latinos.

COUNTRIES OF ORIGIN.   As you can see in Figure 5–2 below, the largest Hispanic group consists of Mexican Americans, who constitute 64.6 percent of the Latino population living in the United States. Some 9.5 percent of Latinos are Puerto Ricans, and 3.6 percent are Cuban Americans. Most of the remaining Hispanics are from Central and South American countries.

LOW INCOMES.   Economically, Latino households are often members of this country's working poor. As Figure 5–1 shows, many have incomes below the government's official poverty line. Latino leaders tend to attribute the low income levels to language problems, lack of job training, and continuing immigration. Immigration disguises statistical progress because language problems and lack of job training are usually more notable among new immigrants than among those who have lived in the United States for many years.

Party Identification   In their party identification, Latinos tend to follow some fairly well-established patterns. Traditionally, Mexican Americans and Puerto Ricans identify with the Democratic Party, which has favored more government assistance and support programs for disadvantaged groups.

THE CUBAN EXCEPTION.   Cubans, in contrast, tend to identify with the Republican Party. This is largely because of a different history. Cuban émigrés fled from Cuba during and after the Communist revolution led by Fidel Castro. The strong anti-Communist sentiments of the Cubans propelled them toward the more conservative party—the Republicans. Today, relations with Communist Cuba continue to be a key political issue for Cuban Americans. Cubans of the younger generation, however, are much more open to voting for Democrats than their parents were.

THE IMMIGRATION ISSUE.   Immigration reform has been an important issue for many Latinos. Even legal immigrants often have friends or relatives who are in the country illegally. In recent years, the Republican Party has taken a stand against any reform that would let unauthorized immigrants regularize their status. This stand has pushed many Latinos toward the Democrats.

Since the 2012 elections, however, a number of Republicans have taken a stand in favor of immigration reform. We discussed that development in the *America at Odds* feature at the beginning of this chapter.

Latinos in American Politics Today   Generally, Latinos in the United States have had a comparatively low level of political participation. This is understandable, given that more than one-third of Hispanics are below voting age and also that more than one-fourth are not citizens and thus cannot vote. Although voter turnout among Latinos is generally low compared with the population at large, the Latino voting rate is rising as more immigrants become citizens and as more Hispanics reach voting age. Indeed, when comparing citizens of equal incomes and educational backgrounds, Latino citizens' participation rate is higher than average. In the 2012 elections, Latinos made up 10 percent of the electorate, up from 9 percent in 2008 and 8 percent in 2004.

Latinos increasingly hold political office, particularly in states with large Hispanic populations. Today, more than 5 percent of the state legislators in Arizona, California, Colorado, Florida, New Mexico, and Texas are of Hispanic ancestry. Cuban Americans have been notably successful in gaining local political power, particularly in Dade County, Florida. Latinos are also increasing their presence in Congress, albeit slowly. As of 2013, thirty-one Latinos serve in either the U.S. House of Representatives or the Senate.

FIGURE 5–2

Hispanics Living in the
United States by Place of Origin

As you can see in this chart, most Latinos (just under two-thirds) are from Mexico.

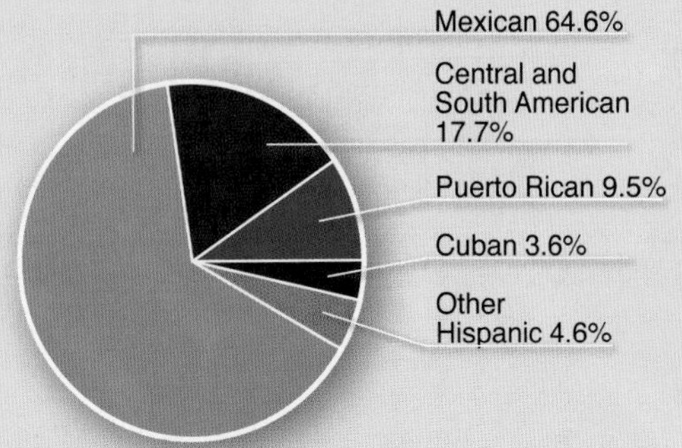

Mexican 64.6%

Central and South American 17.7%

Puerto Rican 9.5%

Cuban 3.6%

Other Hispanic 4.6%

Source: Pew Research Center.

5–4b Asian Americans

Asian Americans have also suffered, at times severely, from discriminatory treatment. The Chinese Exclusion Act of 1882 prevented people from China and Japan from coming to the United States to prospect for gold or to work on the railroads or in factories in the West. After 1900, immigration continued to be restricted—only limited numbers of Chinese or Japanese individuals were allowed to enter the United States. Those who were allowed into the country faced racial prejudice from Americans who had little respect for their customs and culture. In 1906, after the San Francisco earthquake, Japanese American students were segregated into special schools so that white children could use their buildings.

Internment of Japanese Americans The Japanese bombing of Pearl Harbor in 1941, which launched the entry of the United States into World War II (1939–1945), intensified Americans' fear of the Japanese. Actions taken under an executive order issued by President Franklin D. Roosevelt in 1942 subjected many Japanese Americans to curfews, excluded them from certain "military areas," and evacuated most of the West Coast Japanese American population to internment camps (also called "relocation centers").[17] In 1988, Congress provided funds to compensate former camp inhabitants—$1.25 billion for approximately 60,000 people.

Some Asians argue that they face discrimination in college admissions.

A "Model Minority"? Today, Asian Americans lead other minority groups in median income and median education. Indeed, Asians who have immigrated to the United States since 1965 (including immigrants from India) represent the most highly skilled immigrant groups in American history. Nearly 40 percent of Asian Americans over the age of twenty-five have college degrees.

The image of Asian Americans as a "model minority" has created certain problems for its members, however. Some argue that leading private colleges and universities have discriminated against Asian Americans in admissions because so many of them apply. We discuss that issue in this chapter's *Join the Debate* feature on the following page.

More than a million Indochinese war refugees, most from Vietnam, have immigrated to the United States since the 1970s. Many came with relatives and were sponsored by American families or organizations. Thus, they had support systems to help them get started. Some immigrants from other parts of Indochina, however, have experienced difficulties because they come from cultures that have had very little contact with the practices of developed industrial societies.

5–4c Native Americans

When we consider population figures since 1492, we see that the Native Americans experienced one catastrophe after another. We cannot know exactly how many people lived in America when Columbus arrived. Current research estimates the population of what is now the continental United States to have been anywhere from 3 million to 8 million. The Europeans brought with them diseases to which these Native Americans had no immunity. As a result, after a series of terrifying epidemics, the population of the continental United States was reduced to perhaps eight hundred thousand people by 1600. Death rates elsewhere in the New World were comparable. When the Pilgrims arrived at Plymouth, the Massachusetts coast was lined with abandoned village sites due to a recent epidemic.[18]

In subsequent centuries, the Native American population continued to decline, bottoming out at

JOIN THE DEBATE

Are Admissions at Top Schools Unfair to Asian Americans?

There are more than 18 million Asian Americans. They are a diverse group. Outside the United States, people from China, India, Japan, and Korea have little in common. Only in America are they lumped together—and in this country, people from East Asia and South Asia do have a few things in common. Their average family income is higher than that of whites. They are also well educated. By one estimate, Asian Americans make up as many as 30 percent of the top college candidates as determined by SAT scores. In the Ivy League, however, Asian admissions have consistently run below 20 percent. In other words, many excellent Asian American students are being turned away.

College Admission Isn't Just about Grades and Test Scores

While it may appear to high-scoring Asian Americans who don't get into their college of choice that they have suffered from discrimination, it is not necessarily true. Universities routinely manage admissions to obtain the freshman classes they wish to have. They try to include the right number of football and basketball players, for example, as well as minorities.

Only if you believe that high test scores should be the sole basis for admission can you argue that university admission preferences constitute discrimination.

The goal of a diverse freshman class is to expose all students to a mix of races, ethnicities, and viewpoints. A freshman class that is, say, 40 percent Asian American does not look like America.

Discrimination Is Discrimination—Period

Lately, Ivy League–level private universities have established techniques to limit the number of Asian American students admitted to their institutions. These same techniques were used before World War II (and sometimes even after) to limit the number of Jewish students. The basic scheme, then and now, is to award lots of extra points for being "well-rounded" and then to define *well-rounded* as everything that young Asian Americans aren't (or that the young Jews weren't).

There is no need to set Asian Americans in competition with other minorities in admissions. More than 20 percent of the spaces at top private universities are currently set aside for legacy students, children of the rich and famous, and athletes. (Legacy students are the children of alumni or alumnae.) If the number of these unjustified preferences were merely cut in half, there would be enough room for qualified Asian youths.

FOR CRITICAL ANALYSIS Why do some universities reserve spots for the children of their graduates?

---

about half a million in 1925. These were centuries in which the European American and African American populations experienced explosive growth. By 2010, the Native American population had recovered to almost 3 million, or more than 5 million if we count individuals who are only part Indian.

In 1789, Congress designated the Native American tribes as foreign nations so that the government could sign land and boundary treaties with them. As members of foreign nations, Native Americans had no civil rights under U.S. laws. This situation continued until 1924, when the citizenship rights spelled out in the Fourteenth Amendment to the Constitution were finally extended to American Indians.

Early Policies toward Native Americans

The Northwest Ordinance, passed by Congress under the Articles of Confederation in 1787, stated that "the utmost good faith shall always be observed towards the Indians; their lands and property shall never be taken from them without their consent." Over the next hundred years, these principles were violated more often than they were observed.

In 1830, Congress instructed the Bureau of Indian Affairs (BIA), which Congress had established in 1824 as part of the War Department, to remove all tribes to reservations west of the Mississippi River in order to free land east of the Mississippi for white settlement. The resettlement was a catastrophe for Indians in the eastern states.

In the late 1880s, the U.S. government changed its policy. The goal became the "assimilation" of Native Americans into American society. Each family was given a parcel of land within the reservation to farm. The remaining acreage was sold to whites, thus reducing the number of acres in reservation status from 140 million to about 47 million. Tribes that would not cooperate with this plan lost their reservations altogether.

The BIA also set up Native American boarding schools for children to remove them from their parents' influence. In these schools, American Indian children were taught to speak English, to practice Christianity, and to dress like white Americans.

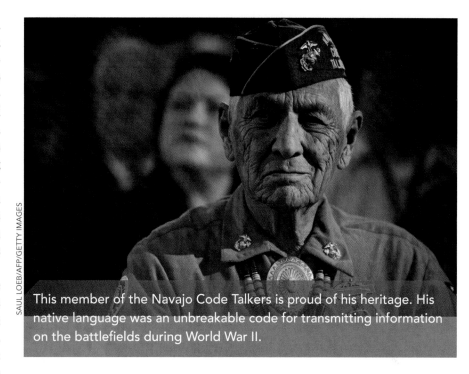

This member of the Navajo Code Talkers is proud of his heritage. His native language was an unbreakable code for transmitting information on the battlefields during World War II.

Native American Activism Native Americans have always found it difficult to obtain political power. In part, this is because the tribes are small and scattered, making organized political movements difficult. Today, American Indians remain fragmented politically because large numbers of their population live off the reservations.

Nonetheless, beginning in the 1960s, some Native Americans formed organizations to strike back at the U.S. government and to reclaim their heritage, including their lands. For example, in 1973, supporters of the American Indian Movement took over Wounded Knee, South Dakota, where about 150 Sioux Indians had been killed by the U.S. Army in 1890.[19] The occupation was undertaken to protest the government's policy toward Native Americans.

Compensation for Injustices of the Past
As more Americans became aware of the sufferings of Native Americans, Congress began to compensate them for past injustices. In 1990, Congress passed the Native American Languages Act, which declared that Native American languages are unique and serve an important role in maintaining Indian culture and continuity. Courts, too, have shown a greater willingness to recognize Native American treaty rights. For example, in 1985, the Supreme Court ruled that three tribes of

Oneida Indians could claim damages for the use of tribal land that had been unlawfully transferred in 1795.[20]

The Indian Gaming Regulatory Act of 1988 allows Native Americans to have gambling operations on their reservations. Although the profits from casinos have helped to improve the economic and social status of many Native Americans, poverty and unemployment remain widespread on the reservations.

5–4d Obtaining Rights for Persons with Disabilities

Discrimination based on disability crosses the boundaries of race, ethnicity, gender, and religion. Persons with disabilities, especially those with physical deformities or severe mental impairments, face social bias. Although attitudes toward persons with disabilities have changed considerably in the last several decades, such persons continue to suffer from discrimination.

Persons with disabilities first became a political force in the 1970s, and in 1973 Congress passed the initial legislation protecting this group—the Rehabilitation Act. This act prohibited discrimination against persons with disabilities in programs receiving federal aid. The Individuals with Disabilities Education Act (formerly called the Education for All Handicapped Children Act of 1975) requires public schools to provide children with disabilities with free, appropriate, and individualized education in the least restrictive environment appropriate to their needs.

The Americans with Disabilities Act (ADA) of 1990, however, is by far the most significant legislation protecting the rights of this group of Americans.

The Americans with Disabilities Act

The ADA requires that all public buildings and public services be accessible to persons with disabilities. The act also mandates that employers "reasonably accommodate" the needs of workers or job applicants with disabilities who are otherwise qualified for particular jobs unless to do so would cause the employer to suffer an "undue hardship."

The ADA defines persons with disabilities as persons who have physical or mental impairments that "substantially limit" their everyday activities. Health conditions that have been considered disabilities under federal law include blindness, a history of alcoholism, heart disease, cancer, muscular dystrophy, cerebral palsy, paraplegia, diabetes, and acquired immune deficiency syndrome (AIDS). The ADA, however, does not require employers to hire or retain workers who, because of their disabilities, pose a "direct threat to the health or safety" of their co-workers.

Limiting the Scope of the ADA

From 1999 to 2002, the Supreme Court handed down a series of rulings that substantially limited the scope of the ADA. The Court found that any limitation that could be remedied by medication or by corrective devices such as eyeglasses did not qualify as a protected disability. According to the Court, even carpal tunnel syndrome was not a disability.[21] In 2008, however, the ADA Amendments Act overturned most of these limits. Carpal tunnel syndrome and other ailments may again qualify as disabilities. (The need for eyeglasses was not, however, covered by the new law.)

In 2001, the Supreme Court reviewed a case raising the question of whether suits under the ADA could be brought against state employers. The Court concluded that states are immune from lawsuits brought to enforce rights under this federal law.[22]

5–4e Gay Men and Lesbians

Today, many Americans—including seven members of Congress—are openly gay, lesbian, or bisexual. Until the late 1960s and early 1970s, though, gay men and lesbians tended to keep quiet about their sexual orientation because exposure usually meant facing harsh consequences. This attitude began to change after a 1969 incident in the Greenwich Village neigh-

PETE MAROVICH/BLOOMBERG VIA GETTY IMAGES

U.S. Representative Tammy Duckworth, Democrat of Illinois. Duckworth lost both legs after her helicopter was shot down in Iraq in 2004.

borhood of New York City. When the police raided the Stonewall Inn—a bar popular with gay men and lesbians—on June 27 of that year, the bar's patrons responded by throwing beer cans and bottles at the police. The riot continued for two days. The Stonewall Inn uprising launched the "gay power" movement. By the end of the year, gay men and lesbians had formed fifty organizations, including the Gay Activist Alliance and the Gay Liberation Front.

A Changing Legal Landscape

The number of gay and lesbian organizations has grown from fifty in 1969 to several thousand today. These groups have exerted significant political pressure on legislatures, the media, schools, and churches. In the decades following Stonewall, more than half of the forty-nine states that had sodomy laws—laws prohibiting homosexual conduct and certain other forms of sexual activity—repealed them. In seven other states, the courts invalidated such laws. Then, in 2003, the United States

Supreme Court issued a ruling that effectively invalidated all remaining sodomy laws in the country.

GAINING LEGAL STATUS. In *Lawrence v. Texas,*[23] the Court ruled that sodomy laws violated the Fourteenth Amendment's due process clause. According to the Court, "The liberty protected by the Constitution allows homosexual persons the right to choose to enter upon relationships in the confines of their homes and their own private lives and still retain their dignity as free persons."

ANTIDISCRIMINATION LAWS. Today, twenty-one states and more than 170 cities and counties in the United States have laws prohibiting discrimination against homosexuals in at least some contexts. The laws may prohibit discrimination in housing, education, banking, employment, or public accommodations. In a landmark case in 1996, *Romer v. Evans,*[24] the Supreme Court held that a Colorado constitutional amendment that would have invalidated all state and local laws protecting homosexuals from discrimination violated the equal protection clause of the U.S. Constitution. The Court stated that the amendment would have denied to homosexuals in Colorado—but to no other Colorado residents—"the right to seek specific protection from the law."

Changing Attitudes

Laws and court decisions protecting the rights of gay men and lesbians reflect social attitudes that are much changed from the 1960s. Liberal political leaders have been supporting gay rights for at least two decades. Even some conservative politicians have softened their stance on the issue. For example, Republican U.S. senators from Alaska, Illinois, and Ohio now support same-sex marriage.

According to a Gallup poll taken in 2013, public support for gay and lesbian rights has continued to rise. The survey showed that 65 percent of respondents believed that gay or lesbian relations between consenting adults should be legal, up from 43 percent in 1978. In a separate poll, an even larger share of those interviewed—70 percent—believed that openly gay or lesbian persons should be allowed to serve in the military.

Support for same-sex marriage, which was endorsed by only 27 percent of Americans in 1996, has risen ever since. In a striking development, several polling organizations reported in mid-2011 that for the first time ever, an absolute majority of those questioned supported same-sex marriage. Support in current polls ranges from 49 to 57 percent.

Same-Sex Marriage

Today, same-sex marriage is legal in thirteen states—California, Connecticut, Delaware, Iowa, Maine, Maryland, Massachusetts, Minnesota, New Hampshire, New York, Rhode Island, Vermont, and Washington—and in the District of Columbia. Three states endorsed same-sex marriage in the 2012 elections—Maine, Maryland, and Washington. These votes marked the first time that voters had endorsed such marriages. Previously, state legislatures or the courts had legalized them.

SAME-SEX MARRIAGE IN THE COURTS. State supreme courts took the lead in legalizing same-sex marriage, beginning with the Massachusetts Supreme Judicial Court in 2003.[25] In May 2008, California became the second state to legalize gay marriage as

JUSTIN SULLIVAN/GETTY IMAGES

This California same-sex couple gained the right to marry in 2013.

a result of a ruling by the state's supreme court. In November of that year, however, California voters approved Proposition 8, which restricted marriage to "one man and one woman." California continued to recognize same-sex marriages conducted between May and Election Day in 2008.

In 2010, a U.S. district court declared that Proposition 8 violated the due process and equal protection clauses of the Fourteenth Amendment to the U.S. Constitution. The Ninth Circuit Court of Appeals upheld this decision in 2012. The inevitable result was to send the matter to the United States Supreme Court. In June 2013, the Court declined to decide the case on the merits, arguing that the private parties who had filed the appeal had no legal grounds for doing so. (The California state government had refused to appeal the case.) As a result, the district court ruling remained valid, and California immediately resumed conducting same-sex marriages.[26]

A second Supreme Court decision in 2013 had more sweeping consequences. As we mentioned in the *Join the Debate* feature in Chapter 3, Congress passed the Defense of Marriage Act (DOMA) in 1996. Section 3 of DOMA barred the national government from recognizing same-sex marriages performed under state law. In *United States v. Windsor,* the Court found Section 3 to be unconstitutional under the Fifth Amendment.[27] The result was to make same-sex couples eligible for thousands of federal benefits.

CIVIL UNIONS AND DOMESTIC PARTNERSHIPS. A number of states have civil union or domestic partnership laws that grant most of the benefits of marriage to registered same-sex couples. These include Illinois, Hawaii, Nevada, New Jersey, and Oregon. More limited benefits are provided in Colorado and Wisconsin.

In most states whose laws allow for neither same-sex marriage nor domestic partnership, same-sex marriage is explicitly banned, either through a constitutional amendment or through legislation. In fact, same-sex marriage is illegal in some of the states that do provide for domestic partnership.

affirmative action

A policy that gives special consideration, in jobs and college admissions, to members of groups that have been discriminated against in the past.

Gays and Lesbians in the Military Gay men and lesbians who wish to join the military have faced a number of obstacles. Until recently, one was the "don't ask, don't tell" policy. This policy, which banned openly gay men and lesbians from the military, was implemented in 1993 by President Bill Clinton when it became clear that more liberal alternatives would not be accepted. During his presidential campaign, Barack Obama pledged to abolish the policy. Later, gay and lesbian rights activists accused him of "putting the issue on a back burner."

The courts forced the issue, however. In September 2010, a U.S. district court ruled that "don't ask, don't tell" was unconstitutional.[28] A U.S. appeals court stayed (suspended) the ruling, but the possibility that "don't ask, don't tell" might be thrown out by the courts forced Congress to take action. In the "lame duck" session between the November 2010 elections and the swearing-in of new members in January 2011, Congress repealed the policy. Full repeal was implemented later in 2011. As a result, gay men and lesbians may now serve openly in the nation's armed forces.

FOR CRITICAL THINKING

The number of Latinos in the United States continues to grow. *What impact do you think this will have on American culture and politics?*

5–5 Beyond Equal Protection—Affirmative Action

One provision of the Civil Rights Act of 1964 called for prohibiting discrimination in employment. Soon after the act was passed, the federal government began to legislate programs promoting *equal employment opportunity.*

Such programs require that employers' hiring and promotion practices guarantee the same opportunities to all individuals. Experience soon showed that minorities often had fewer opportunities to obtain education and relevant work experience than did whites. Because of this, minorities were still excluded from many jobs. Even though discriminatory practices were made illegal, the change in the law did not make up for the results of years of discrimination. Consequently, under President Lyndon B. Johnson (1963–1969), a new policy was developed.

Called **affirmative action,** this policy required employers to take positive steps to remedy *past* discrimination. Affirmative action programs involved giving special consideration, in jobs and college admis-

LearningOutcome 5–5

Explain what affirmative action is and why it has been so controversial.

sions, to members of groups that were discriminated against in the past.

Until recently, all public and private employers who received federal funds were required to adopt and implement these programs. Thus, the policy of affirmative action was applied to all agencies of the federal, state, and local governments and to all private employers who sell goods to or perform services for any agency of the federal government. In short, it covered nearly all of the nation's major employers and many of its smaller ones.

5–5a Affirmative Action Tested

The Supreme Court first addressed the issue of affirmative action in 1978 in *Regents of the University of California v. Bakke*.[29] Allan Bakke, a white male, had been denied admission to the University of California's medical school at Davis. The school had set aside sixteen of the one hundred seats in each year's entering class for applicants who wished to be considered as members of designated minority groups. Many of the students admitted through this special program had lower test scores than Bakke.

Bakke sued the university, claiming that he was a victim of **reverse discrimination**—discrimination against whites. Bakke argued that the use of a **quota system**, in which a specific number of seats were reserved for minority applicants only, violated the equal protection clause. A majority on the Supreme Court concluded that although both the Constitution and the Civil Rights Act of 1964 allow race to be used as a factor in making admissions decisions, race cannot be the *sole* factor. Because the university's quota system was based solely on race, it was unconstitutional.

5–5b Strict Scrutiny Applied

In 1995, the Supreme Court issued a landmark decision in *Adarand Constructors, Inc. v. Peña*.[30] The Court held that any federal, state, or local affirmative action program that uses racial classifications as the basis for making decisions is subject to "strict scrutiny" by the courts. As discussed earlier in this chapter, this means that, to be constitutional, a discriminatory law or action must be narrowly tailored to meet a *compelling* government interest.

In effect, the *Adarand* decision narrowed the application of affirmative action programs. An affirmative action program can no longer make use of quotas or preferences and cannot be maintained simply to remedy past discrimination by society in general. It must be narrowly tailored to remedy actual discrimination that has occurred, and once the program has succeeded, it must be changed or dropped.

5–5c The Diversity Issue

Following the *Adarand* decision, several lower courts faced cases raising the question of whether affirmative action programs designed to achieve diversity on college campuses were constitutional. In a 1996 case, *Hopwood*

reverse discrimination Discrimination against those who have no minority status.

quota system A policy under which a specific number of jobs, promotions, or other types of placements, such as university admissions, are given to members of selected groups.

JUSTIN SULLIVAN/GETTY IMAGES

In 1996, California voters passed Proposition 209. This initiative prohibited affirmative action in all state government institutions, including universities.

v. State of Texas, a federal appellate court challenged the *Bakke* decision by stating that *any* use of race in college admissions, even when diversity was a goal, violated the Fourteenth Amendment.[31]

The University of Michigan Cases
In 2003, the United States Supreme Court reviewed two cases involving issues similar to that in the *Hopwood* case. Both cases involved admissions programs at the University of Michigan.

UNDERGRADUATE ADMISSIONS. In *Gratz v. Bollinger,*[32] two white applicants who were denied undergraduate admission to the university alleged reverse discrimination. The university's policy gave each applicant a score based on grade point average, standardized test scores, and personal achievements. The system *automatically* awarded every "underrepresented" minority (African American, Hispanic, and Native American) applicant one-fifth of the points needed to guarantee admission. The Court held that this policy violated the equal protection clause.

LAW SCHOOL ADMISSIONS. In contrast, in *Grutter v. Bollinger,*[33] the Court held that the University of Michigan Law School's admissions policy was constitutional. The significant difference between the two admissions policies, in the Court's view, was that the law school's approach did not apply a mechanical formula giving "diversity bonuses" based on race or ethnicity. In short, the Court concluded that diversity on college campuses was a legitimate goal and that limited affirmative action programs could be used to attain this goal.

5–5d The Supreme Court Revisits the Issue

By 2007, when another case involving affirmative action came before the Court, Justice Samuel Alito, Jr., had replaced Sandra Day O'Connor, who had often been the "swing" vote on the Court, sometimes voting with the more liberal justices and sometimes joining the conservative bloc. Alito was a more conservative jurist than O'Connor, and his appointment moved the Court to the right.

The Seattle and Louisville School Cases
Parents Involved in Community Schools v. Seattle School District No. 1 was decided in 2007.[34] The case concerned the policies of two school districts—one in Louisville, Kentucky, and one in Seattle, Washington.

Both schools were trying to achieve a more diversified student body by giving preference to minority students if space in the schools was limited and a choice among applicants had to be made.

Parents of white children who were turned away from schools because of these policies sued the school districts, claiming that the policies violated the equal protection clause. Ultimately, the Supreme Court held in favor of the parents. The Court's decision did not overrule the 2003 case involving the University of Michigan Law School, however, for the Court did not deny that race could be used as a factor in university admissions policies. Nonetheless, some claimed that the decision represented a significant change on the Court with respect to affirmative action policies.

Fisher v. University of Texas
Many observers thought that the Court might use a 2013 case, *Fisher v. University of Texas,* to finally overturn affirmative action in public college admissions altogether. In the end, however, the Court ruled narrowly. It sent the case back to the federal appeals court with instructions that race could be considered in University of Texas admissions if there was no other way to obtain the diversity sought by the university.[35]

5–5e State Actions

Beginning in the mid-1990s, some states have taken actions to ban affirmative action programs or replace them with alternative policies.

Bans on Affirmative Action
In 1996, by a ballot initiative, California amended its state constitution to prohibit any "preferential treatment to any individual or group on the basis of race, sex, color, ethnicity, or national origin in the operation of public employment, public education, or public contracting." Two years later, voters in the state of Washington approved a ballot measure ending all state-sponsored affirmative action. Florida has also ended affirmative action.

In 2006, a ballot initiative in Michigan banned affirmative action in that state just three years after the Supreme Court decisions discussed above. In the 2008 elections, Nebraska also banned affirmative action, but voters in Colorado rejected such a measure. Arizona banned affirmative action in 2010, and New Hampshire and Oklahoma did so in 2012.

Also in 2012, however, a federal appeals court overturned the affirmative action ban, as applied to higher education, approved by Michigan voters in 2006.[36] The Supreme Court was to take up this case in its 2013–2014 session.

"Race-Blind" Admissions In the meantime, many public universities are trying to find "race-blind" ways to attract more minority students to their campuses. For example, Texas has established a program under which the top students at every high school in the state are guaranteed admission to the University of Texas, Austin. Originally, the guarantee applied to students who were in the top 10 percent of their graduating class. Today, the percentage varies from year to year. For 2014, the guarantee was limited to students in the top 7 percent of their class. Beginning in 2005, the university reinstated an affirmative action plan, but it was limited to students who were not admitted as part of the top-student guarantee.

The guarantee ensures that the top students at minority-dominated inner-city schools can attend the state's leading public university. It also assures admission to the best white students from rural, often poor, communities. Previously, many of these students could not have hoped to attend the University of Texas. The losers are students from upscale metropolitan neighborhoods or suburbs who have high test scores but are not the top students at their schools. One result is that more students with high test scores enroll in less famous schools, such as Texas Tech University and the University of Texas, Dallas—to the benefit of these schools' reputations.

FOR CRITICAL THINKING

Is the Texas plan to admit the top students from each high school to the University of Texas fair? Why or why not?

MARK WILSON/GETTY IMAGES

These demonstrators wanted the Supreme Court to uphold affirmative action in the 2013 *Fisher v. University of Texas* case. Were their wishes fulfilled?

AMERICA AT

ODDS Civil Rights

During the first part of the twentieth century, discrimination against African Americans and members of other minority groups was a social norm in the United States. Indeed, much of the nation's white population believed that the ability to discriminate was a constitutionally protected right. Today, the "right to discriminate" has very few defenders. America's laws—and its culture—now hold that discrimination on the basis of race, gender, religion, national origin, and many other characteristics is flatly unacceptable.

Even if civil rights are now broadly supported and protected by law, however, questions remain as to how far these protections should extend. Americans are at odds over a number of civil rights issues, including the following:

- If unauthorized immigrants have certain rights as *persons* under the Fourteenth Amendment to the Constitution, should these rights be construed broadly—or as narrowly as possible?

- Should same-sex marriages by lesbians and gay men be recognized—or prohibited?

- Should we allow lesbians and gay men to serve openly in the nation's armed forces—or was it a mistake to abandon the "don't ask, don't tell" policy?

- Is affirmative action still a necessary policy—or should it be abandoned?

- When colleges and universities consider admissions, is it legitimate to promote racial, ethnic, gender, or socioeconomic diversity—or are such considerations just new forms of discrimination?

STUDY TOOLS

Ready to study?

- **Review** what you've read with the quiz below.
- Check your answers on the **Chapter in Review** card at the back of the book.
- For any questions you miss, read the corresponding **Learning Outcome** section again to prepare for class and your exam.
- Rip out and study the **Chapter in Review** card (at the back of the book).

Fill-In

Learning Outcome 5–1

1. A law based on a _____, such as race, is subject to strict scrutiny by the courts.

Learning Outcome 5–2

2. In *Plessy v. Ferguson* (1896), the Supreme Court established the _____ doctrine, which was used to justify racial segregation in many areas of life for nearly sixty years.

3. The Civil Rights Act of 1964 forbade discrimination on the basis of _____.

Learning Outcome 5–3

4. The feminist movement that began in the 1960s sought _____ for women.

5. It is estimated that for every dollar earned by men, women earn about _____.

Learning Outcome 5–4

6. _____ constitute the largest ethnic minority in the United States.

7. Actions taken under an executive order issued by President Franklin D. Roosevelt in 1942 subjected many _____ Americans to curfews and evacuated many of those on the West Coast to "relocation centers."

Learning Outcome 5–5

8. Affirmative action is best defined as a policy _____.

9. In *Adarand Constructors, Inc. v. Peña* (1995), the Supreme Court held that any federal, state, or local affirmative action program that uses racial classifications as the basis for making decisions is subject to _____ scrutiny by the courts.

Multiple Choice

Learning Outcome 5–1

10. The equal protection clause of the ____ Amendment reads: "No State shall . . . deny to any person within its jurisdiction the equal protection of the laws."
    a. Fifth   b. Fourteenth   c. Nineteenth

Learning Outcome 5–2

11. "Jim Crow" laws
    a. separated the white community from the black community.
    b. were justified by the Supreme Court's decision in *Brown v. Board of Education of Topeka* (1954).
    c. required an end to segregation.

12. In *Brown II* (1955), the Supreme Court ordered desegregation to begin
    a. "immediately."
    b. "with caution and care."
    c. "with all deliberate speed."

Learning Outcome 5–3

13. _____ appointed the first woman to serve as a justice of the United States Supreme Court.

    a. Ronald Reagan   c. Barack Obama
    b. George W. Bush

Learning Outcome 5–4

14. In 1789, Congress designated the Native American tribes as _____ so that the government could sign land and boundary treaties with them.
    a. enemies
    b. sovereign states composed of American citizens
    c. foreign nations

Learning Outcome 5–5

15. In *Gratz v. Bollinger* (2003), the Supreme Court held that the undergraduate admissions policy at the University of Michigan violated the equal protection clause because it
    a. automatically awarded every "underrepresented" minority applicant one-fifth of the points needed to guarantee admission.
    b. failed to take into account an applicant's race or ethnicity.
    c. failed to take into account an applicant's gender.

6

Interest Groups

JOHN GRESS/GETTY IMAGES

Remember to visit page 140 for additional Study Tools

AMERICA AT
ODDS
Are Farmers Getting a Deal That's Too Good?

JOHN MOORE/GETTY IMAGES

Many people, including those who live in large cities, have a romantic view of farming and farmers. This view is one of many reasons why interest groups representing farmers are so successful in winning support from the federal government. Over the last five years, about 2 million farmers received subsidies. These funds now include $1 billion per year in disaster assistance, $3 billion for conservation programs, $8 billion in subsidies for crop insurance, and $7 billion in commodity subsidies. These last payments are among the most controversial. Some are paid out when crop prices are low. But growers of corn, cotton, rice, soybeans, and wheat get a special, additional deal: they receive about $5 billion per year in *direct payments*, based solely on a history of planting particular crops.

The farm program is authorized by five-year farm bills, and the next one became due in 2012. In both 2012 and 2013, however, Congress was unable to agree on a new farm bill. Such gridlock is unprecedented—in earlier years, bipartisan farm legislation always passed easily. In part, this was possible because support for farmers was placed in the same bill as the Supplemental Nutrition Assistance Program (food stamps). That ensured that urban liberals would join with rural legislators to support the bill. Now, farm subsidies are up for debate. Should they be cut? Are farmers getting too good a deal?

Agriculture Works—Don't Mess with Success

Farming is one of the riskiest businesses around. Farmers are ten times as likely to be killed on the job as the average worker. The weather is a constant worry. Every year, thousands of farmers lose their crops to floods or drought—as in 2012. Further, unlike many businesses, farmers can't set their own prices for what they sell. If you manufacture dishwashers, you expect that you can set a price for them that will cover your costs. Not so in agriculture. Prices are set by world commodity markets, where prices can swing wildly from month to month.

Despite the dangers, agriculture is a success story. Farm exports are booming as poor countries become richer and their people demand better diets—and the United Nations predicts that farmers will need to produce 70 percent more food by 2050 to keep up with population increases. Farm programs are an important safety net that helps keep our farmers in business. At less than half a percent of the federal budget, these programs are also a bargain.

Wealthy Farmers Don't Need These Subsidies

Everybody loves small farmers, but most of the subsidies don't go to these farmers. Large commercial farms amass 62 percent of all federal payments. The average family income for these farmers exceeds $200,000 per year. Their subsidies average about $30,000 per year, as opposed to $7,000 for farms that are small (but still provide a full-time occupation for their owners). Why are we giving so much federal aid to people who are that well off?

There's no doubt that farming is risky. That's why the great majority of farmers carry crop insurance, which—as noted above—is subsidized. Insuring 50 percent of your crop is free. You can insure the rest at reduced rates. How can you lose? Some may claim that we still need disaster assistance and conservation programs. Insurance subsidies have a certain appeal, although they can encourage farmers to plant on marginal acres. But at the very least we can get rid of the direct payments. American food consumers and taxpayers have paid too much for too long.

Where do you stand?

1. What effect might farm programs have on rural residents who are not farmers?
2. Soybeans are the nation's second-largest crop, after corn. Half of all U.S. soybeans are exported, many of them to feed Chinese pigs. What benefits might we gain from this trade?

Explore this issue online

- You can find the site of the Environmental Working Group (EWG), a critic of farm subsidies, by entering "ewg database" into a search engine. The EWG database contains a complete record of farm program recipients and what they were paid.
- To find arguments in support of the farm programs, search on "farm policy facts."

Introduction

The groups supporting and opposing farm programs provide but one example of how Americans form groups to pursue or protect their interests. All of us have interests that we would like to have represented in government: labor unionists would like it to be easier to organize unions, young people want good educational opportunities, and environmentalists want cleaner air and water, for example.

The old saying that there is strength in numbers is certainly true in American politics. Special interests significantly influence American government and politics. Indeed, some Americans think that this influence is so great that it jeopardizes representative democracy. Others maintain that interest groups are a natural consequence of democracy. After all, throughout our nation's history, people have organized into groups to protect special interests. Because of the important role played by interest groups in the American system of government, we examine such groups in this chapter. We look at what they are, why they are formed, and how they influence policymaking.

> "Politics is about **people,** not politicians."
> ~ SCOTT SIMMS ~
> CANADIAN POLITICIAN
> B. 1969

Learning Outcome 6–1

Explain what an interest group is, why interest groups form, and how interest groups function in American politics.

6–1 Interest Groups and American Government

An **interest group** is an organized group of people sharing common objectives who actively attempt to influence government policymakers through direct and indirect methods. Whatever their goals—more or fewer social services, higher or lower prices—interest groups pursue these goals on every level and in every branch of government.

On any given day in Washington, D.C., you can see national interest groups in action. If you eat breakfast in the Senate dining room, you might see congressional committee staffers reviewing testimony with representatives from women's groups. Later that morning, you might

interest group An organized group of individuals sharing common objectives who actively attempt to influence policymakers.

visit the Supreme Court and watch a civil rights lawyer arguing on behalf of a client in a discrimination suit. Lunch in a popular Washington restaurant might find you listening in on a conversation between an agricultural lobbyist and a congressional representative.

That afternoon you might visit an executive department, such as the Department of Labor, and watch bureaucrats working out rules and regulations with representatives from a business interest group. Then you might stroll past the headquarters of the National Rifle Association (NRA), AARP (formerly the American Association of Retired Persons), or the National Wildlife Federation.

6–1a The Constitutional Right to Petition the Government

The right to form interest groups and to lobby the government is protected by the Bill of Rights. The First Amendment guarantees the right of the people "to petition the Government for a redress of grievances." This important right sometimes gets lost among the other, more well-known First Amendment guarantees, such as the freedoms of religion, speech, and the press. Nonetheless, the right to petition the government is as important and fundamental to our democracy as the other First Amendment rights.

The right to petition the government allows citizens and groups of citizens to lobby members of Congress and other government officials, to sue the government, and to submit petitions to the government. Whenever someone e-mails to her or his congressional representative for help with a problem, such as not receiving a Social Security payment, that person is petitioning the government.

6–1b Why Interest Groups Form

The United States is a vast country of many regions, scores of ethnic groups, and a huge variety of businesses and occupations. The number of potential interests that can be represented is therefore very large. Beyond the sheer size of the country, however, there are a number of specific reasons why the United States has as many interest groups as it does.

Becoming an Interest Group It is worth remembering that not all groups are interest groups. A group becomes an interest group when it seeks to affect the policies or practices of the government. Many groups do not meet this standard. A social group, for example, may be formed to entertain or educate its members, with no broader purpose. Churches, organized to facilitate worship and community, frequently have no political aims. (Indeed, certain political activities, such as campaigning for or against candidates for office, could cost a church its tax-exempt status.)

A group founded with little or no desire to influence the government can become an interest group, however, if its members decide that the government's policies are important to them. Alternatively, lobbying the government may initially be only one of several activities pursued by a group and then grow to become the group's primary purpose.

The National Rifle Association (NRA) provides an example of this process. From its establishment in 1871 until the 1930s, the group took little part in politics. As late as the 1970s, a large share of the NRA's members joined for reasons that had nothing to do with politics. Many joined solely to participate in firearms training programs or to win marksman certifications. The NRA continues to provide such services today, but it is now so heavily politicized that anyone likely to take out a membership is certain to broadly agree with the NRA's political positions.

More Government, More Interest Groups

Interest groups may form—and existing groups may become more politically active—when the government expands its scope of activities. More government, in other words, means more interest groups. Prior to the 1970s, for example, the various levels of government were not nearly as active in attempting to regulate the use of firearms as they were thereafter. This change provides one explanation of why the NRA is much more politically active today than it was years ago.

Consider another example—AARP, formerly the American Association of Retired Persons. AARP is a major lobbying force that seeks to preserve or enhance Social Security and Medicare benefits for citizens sixty-five years of age and older. Before the creation of Social Security in the 1930s, however, the federal government did not provide income support to the elderly, and there would have been little reason for an organization such as AARP to exist.

Defending the Group's Interests

Interest groups also may come into existence in response to a perceived threat to a group's interests. In the example of the NRA, the threat was an increase in the frequency of attempts to regulate or even ban firearms. This increase threatened the interests of gun owners. As another example, the National Right to Life Committee formed in response to *Roe v. Wade*, the United States Supreme Court's decision that legalized abortion. Interest groups can also form in reaction to the creation of other interest groups, thus pitting two groups against each other. Political scientist David B. Truman coined the term *disturbance theory* for his description of this kind of defensive formation of interest groups.[1]

The Importance of Leaders

Political scientist Robert H. Salisbury provided another analysis of the organization of interest groups that he dubbed *entrepreneurial theory*. This line of thought focuses on the importance of the leaders who establish the organization. The desire of such individuals to guarantee a viable organization is important to the group's survival.[2] AARP is an example of a group with a committed founder—Dr. Ethel Percy Andrus, a retired high school principal. Andrus organized the group in 1958 to let older Americans purchase health-care insurance collectively. Like the NRA, AARP did not develop into a lobbying powerhouse until years after it was founded.

Incentives to Join a Group

The French political observer and traveler Alexis de Tocqueville wrote in 1835 that Americans have a tendency to form "associations" and have perfected "the art of pursuing in common the object of their common desires. . . . In no other country of the world, has the principle of association been more successfully used or applied to a greater multitude of objectives than in America."[3] Of course, Tocqueville could not foresee the thousands of associations that now exist in this country. Surveys show that more than 85 percent of Americans belong to at least one group. Table 6–1 below shows

TABLE 6–1

Percentage of Americans Belonging to Various Groups

Social clubs	17%
Neighborhood groups	18
Hobby, garden, and computer clubs	19
PTA and school groups	21
Professional and trade associations	27
Health, sport, and country clubs	30
Religious groups	61

Source: AARP.

the percentage of Americans who belong to various types of groups today.

Political scientists have identified various reasons why people join interest groups. Often, people have one or more incentives to join such organizations.

- If a group stands for something that you believe is very important, you can gain considerable satisfaction in taking action from within that group. Such satisfaction is referred to as a **purposive incentive.**
- Some people enjoy the camaraderie and sense of belonging that come from associating with other people who share their interests and goals. That enjoyment can be called a **solidary incentive.**
- Some groups offer their members material incentives for joining, such as discounts on products, subscriptions, or group insurance programs. Each of these could be characterized as a **material incentive.**

Sometimes, though, none of these incentives is enough to persuade people to join a group.

The Free Rider Problem

The world in which we live is one of scarce resources that can be used to create *private goods* and *public goods.* Most of the goods and services that you use are private goods. If you consume them, no one else can consume them at the same time. If you eat a sandwich, no one else can have it.

With public goods, however, your use of a good does not diminish its use by someone else. National defense is a good example. If this country is protected through its national defense system, your protection from enemy invasion does not reduce any other person's protection.

People cannot be excluded from enjoying a public good, such as national defense, just because they did not pay for it. As a result, public goods are often provided by the government, which can force people to pay for the public good through taxation.

The existence of persons who benefit but do not contribute is called the **free rider problem.** Much of what we know about the free rider problem comes from Mancur Olson's classic work of political science, *The Logic of Collective Action.*[4]

INTEREST GROUPS AND PUBLIC GOODS. Lobbying, collective bargaining by labor unions, and other forms of representation can also be public goods. If an interest group is successful in lobbying for laws that will improve air quality, for example, everyone who breathes that air will benefit, whether they paid for the lobbying effort or not.

ADDRESSING THE PROBLEM. In some instances, the free rider problem can be overcome. For example, social pressure may persuade some people to join or donate to a group for fear of being ostracized. This motivation is more likely to be effective for small, localized groups than for large, widely dispersed groups like AARP, however.

The government can also step in to ensure that the burden of lobbying for the public good is shared by all. When the government classifies interest groups

Alexis de Tocqueville (1805–1859) was a well-known French political historian who took a keen interest in the new democracy in America. He toured the United States as a young man and collected his observations in *Democracy in America,* published in 1835.

PHOTO BY TIME LIFE PICTURES/MANSELL/TIME LIFE PICTURES/GETTY IMAGES

purposive incentive
A reason to join an interest group—satisfaction resulting from working for a cause in which one believes.

solidary incentive
A reason to join an interest group—pleasure in associating with like-minded individuals.

material incentive
A reason to join an interest group—practical benefits such as discounts, subscriptions, or group insurance.

free rider problem
The difficulty that exists when individuals can enjoy the outcome of an interest group's efforts without having to contribute, such as by becoming members of the group.

as nonprofit organizations, it confers on them tax-exempt status. The groups' operating costs are reduced because they do not have to pay taxes, and the impact of the government's lost revenue is absorbed by all taxpayers.

6–1c How Interest Groups Function in American Politics

Despite the bad press that interest groups tend to get in the United States, they do serve several purposes in American politics:

- Interest groups help bridge the gap between citizens and government and enable citizens to explain their views on policies to public officials.

- Interest groups help raise public awareness and inspire action on various issues.

- Interest groups often provide public officials with specialized and detailed information that might be difficult to obtain otherwise. This information may be useful in making policy choices.

- Interest groups serve as another check on public officials to make sure that they are carrying out their duties responsibly.

Access to Government In a sense, the American system of government invites the participation of interest groups by offering many points of access for groups wishing to influence policy. Consider the possibilities at just the federal level.

An interest group can lobby members of Congress to act in the interests of the group. If the Senate passes a bill opposed by the group, the group's lobbying efforts can shift to the House of Representatives. If the House passes the bill, the group can try to influence the new law's application by lobbying the executive agency that is responsible for implementing the law. The group might even challenge the law in court, directly (by filing a lawsuit) or indirectly (by filing a brief as an *amicus curiae*,[5] or "friend of the court").

Interest groups can seek a variety of different benefits when lobbying the government. A frequent goal is favorable treatment under federal or state regulations. Groups may also seek outright subsidies that benefit their members. An increasingly popular objective is special treatment in the tax code. Tax breaks for a special interest can be easier to obtain than subsidies because the breaks don't look like government spending. We take a closer look at that issue

in this chapter's *Join the Debate* feature on the following page.

Pluralist Theory The **pluralist theory** of American democracy focuses on the participation of groups in a decentralized government structure that offers many points of access to policymakers. According to the pluralist theory, politics is a contest among various interest groups. These groups vie with one another—at all levels of government—to gain benefits for their members. Pluralists maintain that the influence of interest groups on government is not undemocratic because individual interests are indirectly represented in the policymaking process through these groups.

Although not every American belongs to an interest group, inevitably some group will represent at least some of the interests of each individual. Thus, each interest is satisfied to some extent through the compromises made in settling conflicts among competing interest groups.

Pluralists also contend that because of the extensive number of interest groups vying for political benefits, no one group can dominate the political process. Additionally, because most people have more than one interest, conflicts among groups do not divide the nation into hostile camps. Not all scholars agree that this is how interest groups function, however.

6–1d How Do Interest Groups Differ from Political Parties?

Although interest groups and political parties are both groups of people joined together for political purposes, they differ in several important ways. As you will read in Chapter 7, a political party is a group of individuals who organize to win elections, operate the government, and determine policy. Interest groups, in contrast, do not seek to win elections or operate the government, although they do seek to influence policy. Interest groups differ from political parties in the following ways:

- Interest groups are often policy *specialists*, whereas political parties are policy *generalists*. Political parties are broad-based organizations that must attract the support of many opposing groups and consider a large number of issues. Interest groups, in contrast,

> **pluralist theory** A theory that views politics as a contest among various interest groups—at all levels of government—to gain benefits for their members.

Should We Close Tax Loopholes?

When you hear the words "tax loophole," you might think of tax breaks for the rich—perhaps the people who fly in corporate jets. (In fact, there is a tax loophole for corporate jets.) A tax loophole is a legal method to reduce taxes owed. Tax loopholes are also called *tax expenditures* in federal government bookkeeping circles. If your parents obtain a tax credit for your tuition, that is a tax loophole—a tax expenditure. People who own houses can usually reduce their federal income taxes by a percentage of whatever they paid in local property taxes. That's also a tax loophole.

The two examples above, though, are peanuts. The first one adds up to only $12 billion a year and the second to about $25 billion. The total amount of tax expenditures is closer to $1 trillion per year. The three largest are tax exclusions for employer contributions to health insurance, exclusions for pension contributions, and the deduction for mortgage interest.

Eliminate—or at Least Reduce—All Tax Loopholes

In 2012, a substantial number of politicians campaigned on a platform of closing tax loopholes. They pointed out that the federal government had been running up debts to the tune of over $1 trillion a year for the past four years. That's a sum roughly equivalent to the size of all tax expenditures. Some sacred cows would have to be slaughtered, such as the tax deduction homeowners are allowed for mortgage interest. As with all tax loopholes, this deduction is worth much more to the rich. Moreover, it may encourage less well-off families to buy homes that they can't really afford.

There is a basic fairness issue for all tax loopholes: Is it right to choose a particular expenditure, such as interest on a home mortgage, and declare that it is so vital to society that it must be subsidized? Why privilege such personal spending over everything else?

Not So Fast— Those Tax Loopholes Can Be Useful

Some tax experts say "not so fast" when it comes to abolishing tax expenditures. Blogger Matt Yglesias, for example, points out that we have tax loopholes because the government wants to attain real policy objectives. The employer-provided health-insurance tax break, for example, supports the health-insurance plans of most adults in the United States. The break makes it possible for large employers to turn their workforces into risk-sharing pools.

The tax break for charitable deductions is essential to funding higher education and research, including medical research. The tax breaks for certain private pension plans serve an important goal—they allow people to provide for themselves individually in old age, rather than relying completely on Social Security. Providing tax loopholes might not be the most efficient way to attain policy goals. But we need to think up other ways to accomplish these goals before we stop funding them through tax breaks.

FOR CRITICAL ANALYSIS How much should we worry about people who are negatively affected when a tax loophole is eliminated?

may have only a handful of key policies to push. An environmental group, obviously, will not be as concerned about the economic status of Hispanics as it is about polluters. A manufacturing group is more involved with pushing for fewer regulations than it is with inner-city poverty.

- Interest groups are usually more tightly organized than political parties. They are often financed through contributions or dues-paying memberships. Organizers of interest groups communicate with members and potential members through conferences, mailings, newsletters, and electronic formats such as e-mail, Facebook, and Twitter.

- A political party's main sphere of influence is the electoral system. Parties run candidates for political office. Interest groups may try to influence the outcome of elections, but unlike parties, they do not compete for public office. Although a candidate for office may be sympathetic to—or even be a member of—a certain group, he or she does not run for election as a candidate of that group.

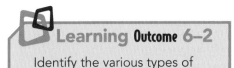

FOR CRITICAL THINKING

Identify some public goods other than national defense. *Are any of these public goods associated with a significant free rider problem? Why or why not?*

6–2 Different Types of Interest Groups

Learning Outcome 6–2

Identify the various types of interest groups.

American democracy embraces almost every conceivable type of interest group, and the number is increasing rapidly. No one has ever compiled a *Who's Who* of interest groups, but you can get an idea of the number and variety by looking through the annually published *Encyclopedia of Associations.*

Some interest groups have large memberships. AARP, for example, has about 40 million members. Others, such as the Colorado Auctioneers Association, have barely a hundred members. Some, such as the U.S. Chamber of Commerce, are household names and have been in existence for many years, while others crop up overnight. Some are highly structured and are run by full-time professionals, while others are loosely structured and informal.

6–2a Private- and Public-Interest Groups

The most common interest groups are those that promote private interests. These groups seek public policies that benefit the economic interests of their members and work against policies that threaten those interests. Other groups, sometimes called **public-interest groups,** are formed with the broader goal of working for the "public good." The American Civil Liberties Union and Common Cause are examples.

Let there be no mistake, though, about the name *public interest.* There is no such thing as a clear public interest in a nation of more than 315 million diverse people. The two so-called public-interest groups just mentioned do not represent all American people but only a relatively small part of the American population. In reality, all lobbying groups, organizations, and other political entities represent special interests.

> **public-interest group**
> An interest group formed for the purpose of working for the "public good." Examples are the American Civil Liberties Union and Common Cause.

6–2b Business Interest Groups

Business has long been well organized for effective action. Hundreds of business groups are now operating in Washington, D.C., in the fifty state capitals, and at the local level across the country. Table 6–2 on the following page lists some top business interests and their campaign contributions through the end of 2012. Two umbrella organizations that include small and large corporations and businesses are the U.S. Chamber of Commerce and the National Association of Manufacturers (NAM). In addition to representing about 3 million individual businesses, the Chamber has more than three thousand local, state, and regional affiliates. It has become a major voice for millions of small businesses.

AP/PRNEWSFOTO/NATIONAL BEER WHOLESALERS ASSOCIATION

Members of the National Beer Wholesalers Association. What kinds of laws might these people lobby for?

TABLE 6-2

Top Business Campaign Donors, 1989–2012

Firm or Group	Total, 1989–2012
1. AT&T, Inc.	$56,607,795
2. National Association of Realtors	$50,702,597
3. Goldman Sachs (bank)	$44,084,500
4. Citigroup, Inc. (bank)	$31,916,868
5. United Parcel Service	$31,745,440
6. National Auto Dealers Assn.	$31,537,599
7. American Bankers Assn.	$30,631,342
8. JPMorgan Chase & Co. (bank)	$29,365,372
9. Altria Group (cigarettes)	$28,794,623
10. Microsoft	$28,629,309

Trade Organizations The hundreds of **trade organizations** are far less visible than the Chamber of Commerce and the NAM, but they are also important in seeking policies that assist their members. Trade organizations usually support policies that benefit specific industries. For example, people in the oil industry work for policies that favor the development of oil as an energy resource. Other business groups work for policies that favor the development of coal, solar power, and nuclear power. Trucking companies work for policies that would lower their taxes. Railroad companies would, of course, not want other forms of transportation to receive special tax breaks, because that would hurt their business.

How Business Interest Groups Support Both Parties Traditionally, business interest groups have been viewed as staunch supporters of the Republican Party. This is because Republicans are more likely to promote a "hands-off" government policy toward business. Since 2000, however, donations from corporations to the Democratic National Committee have more than doubled. Why would business groups make contributions to the Democratic National Committee? One reason is that in some fields, business leaders are more likely to be Democrats than in the past. Financial industry leaders were once almost entirely Republican, but today many of them support the Democrats. Information technology, a relatively new industry, contains both Republicans and Democrats.

An additional reason why many business interests support both parties is to ensure that they will benefit regardless of who wins the elections. Fred McChesney, a professor of law and business, offers still another reason why business interests might want to contribute to both parties: campaign contributions are often made not to gain political favors but rather to avoid political disfavor. He argues that just as government officials can take away wealth from citizens (in the form of taxes, for example), politicians can implicitly extort payments from private enterprises in return for *not* damaging their business.[6]

6–2c Labor Interest Groups

Interest groups representing labor have been some of the most influential groups in our country's history. They date back to at least 1886, when the American Federation of Labor (AFL) was formed. The largest and most powerful labor interest group today is the AFL-CIO (the American Federation of Labor–Congress of Industrial Organizations), a confederation of fifty-seven unions representing 9 million organized workers and 3.2 million community affiliates.

Unions not affiliated with the AFL-CIO also represent millions of members. The Change to Win federation consists of four unions and 4.3 million workers. Dozens of other unions are independent. Examples include the National Education Association, the United Electrical Workers (UE), and the Major League Baseball Players Association. We list some top labor and professional groups in Table 6–3 on the following page.

Union Goals Like labor unions everywhere, American unions press for policies to improve working conditions and ensure better pay for their members. Unions may compete for new members. In many states, for example, the National Education

trade organization
An association formed by members of a particular industry, such as the oil industry or the trucking industry, to develop common standards and goals for the industry. Trade organizations, as interest groups, lobby government for legislation or regulations that specifically benefit their members.

TABLE 6-3

Top Labor and Professional Campaign Donors, 1989–2012

Union or Group	Total, 1989–2012
1. American Fed. of State, County & Municipal Employees	$57,614,514
2. National Education Assn.	$52,581,915
3. Int'l. Brotherhood of Electrical Workers	$43,786,207
4. American Assn. for Justice (trial lawyers)	$41,922,951
5. United Auto Workers	$41,807,589
6. Service Employees Int'l. Union	$37,344,202
7. American Federation of Teachers	$36,839,727
8. Laborers Union	$36,834,416
9. Carpenters & Joiners Union	$36,784,209
10. Communications Workers of America	$35,798,423

Association and the AFL-CIO's American Federation of Teachers compete fiercely for members.

The Decline of Unions   Although unions were highly influential in the 1930s, 1940s, and 1950s, their strength and political power have waned in the last several decades, as you can see in Figure 6–1 on the right. Today, members of organized labor make up only 11.3 percent of the **labor force**—defined as all of the people over the age of sixteen who are working or actively looking for jobs.

REASONS FOR LABOR'S DECLINE.   There are several reasons why the power of organized labor has declined in the United States. One is the continuing fall in the proportion of the nation's workforce employed in such blue-collar activities as manufacturing and transportation. These sectors have always been among the most heavily unionized.

Another important factor in labor's decline, however, is the general political environment. Forming and maintaining unions is more difficult in the United States than in most other industrial nations. Among the world's wealthy democracies, the United States is one of the most politically conservative, at least on economic issues. Economic conservatives are traditionally hostile to labor unions. Further, many business owners in the United States do not accept unions as legitimate institu-

tions and will make enormous efforts to ensure that their own businesses remain ununionized.

DIFFERING STATE LAWS. The impact of the political environment on labor's organizing ability can be easily seen by comparing rates of unionization in various states. These rates are especially low in conservative southern states. Georgia and North Carolina are both major manufacturing states, but unions represent only 4.6 percent of the workforce in Georgia and only 5 percent in North Carolina.

Compare these figures with rates in more liberal states, such as California and New York: unions represent 19.5 percent of the workforce in California and 26.6 percent in New York. One factor that depresses unionization rates in many states is the existence of so-called **right-to-work laws.**

labor force All of the people over the age of sixteen who are working or actively looking for jobs.

right-to-work laws Laws that ban unions from collecting dues or other fees from workers whom they represent but who have not actually joined the union.

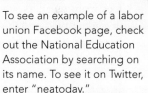

SOCIAL MEDIA
In Politics

To see an example of a labor union Facebook page, check out the National Education Association by searching on its name. To see it on Twitter, enter "neatoday."

FIGURE 6-1

Union Membership,
1952 to Present

This figure shows the percentage of wage and salary workers who have been union members from 1952 to the present. Unions represent many workers who are not members, so the percentage of workers represented by a union would be larger. As you can see, union membership has declined significantly since its highpoint in 1954.

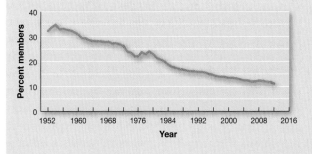

CHRIS MADDALONI/GETTY IMAGES/CQ ROLL CALL

Organic farmers rally in front of the White House to oppose GMO seeds produced by the Monsanto Company. (GMO stands for genetically modified organism.)

These laws ban unions from collecting dues or other fees from workers whom they represent but who have not actually joined the union. Such laws create a significant free rider problem for unions. Twenty-four states have right-to-work laws.

Public-Sector Unions While organized labor has suffered from declining numbers and a resulting loss in lobbying power, labor has held the line in one industry—government. In the 1960s and 1970s, public-sector unions enjoyed rapid growth. The percentage of government workers who are union members then leveled off, but it remains high. More than one-third of all public-sector workers are union members today.

In contrast to unions in the private sector, public-sector unions do not have the right to strike over wages and working conditions. Still, they are influential. Unlike workers in private industry, public-sector employees—as citizens—have the right to vote for their own bosses. As a result, elected officials are often reluctant to antagonize public-sector unions. One consequence of the influence of these unions is that government workers typically enjoy pension benefits that are substantially more generous than those received by equivalent employees in the private sector.

Following the 2010 elections, several Republican governors attempted to curtail the bargaining rights of state and local employee unions. These governors argued that pension benefits and other perks won by the unions threatened the financial stability of state and local governments. The role and status of state and local unions, therefore, have become important political issues.

6–2d Professional Interest Groups

Most professions that require advanced education or specialized training have organizations to protect and promote their interests. These groups are concerned mainly with the standards of their professions, but they also work to influence government policy. Major professional groups include the American Medical Association (AMA), representing physicians; the American Bar Association, representing lawyers; and the American Association for Justice, representing trial lawyers. In addition, there are dozens of less well-known and less politically active professional groups, such as the National Association of Social Workers and the American Political Science Association.

Competing interests sometimes divide professional interest groups from one another. For example, medical groups contend that it is too easy for lawyers to sue physicians, insurance companies, and other businesses, and that generous settlements drive up the cost of health care and other goods. The AMA generally favors restrictions on such lawsuits. The American Association for Justice, naturally, opposes such changes.

6–2e Agricultural Interest Groups

Many groups work for general agricultural interests at all levels of government. Three broad-based agricultural groups represent millions of American farmers, from peanut farmers to dairy producers to tobacco growers. They are the American Farm Bureau Federation (Farm Bureau), the National Grange, and the National Farmers Union.

The Farm Bureau, representing more than 5.5 million families (a majority of whom are not actually farm families), is the largest and generally the most effective of the three. Founded in 1919, the Farm Bureau achieved one of its greatest early successes when it helped to obtain government guarantees of "fair" prices during the Great Depression of the 1930s.[7] Producers of various specific farm commodities, such as dairy products, soybeans, grain, fruit, corn, cotton, beef, and sugar beets, have formed their own organizations.

Interest groups representing farmers have been spectacularly successful in winning subsidies from the federal government, as we explained in the chapter-opening *America at Odds* feature. Subsidies are not the only way in which the federal government can benefit growers of a particular crop. The government can also restrict imports of a specific commodity, such as sugar. The restrictions raise the price of sugar, which benefits sugar beet growers at the expense of consumers.

6–2f Consumer Interest Groups

Groups organized for the protection of consumer rights were very active in the 1960s and 1970s. Some are still active today. One well-known group is Consumers Union, a nonprofit organization started in 1936. In addition to publishing *Consumer Reports* magazine, Consumers Union has been influential in pushing for the removal of phosphates from detergents, lead from gasoline, and pesticides from food. Consumers Union strongly criticizes government agencies when they appear to act against consumer interests. Other major groups include Consumer Action, the Consumer Federation of America, and Public Citizen.

Consumer groups have been organized in every city as well. They deal with such problems as substandard housing, discrimination against minorities and women, discrimination in the granting of credit, and business inaction on consumer complaints.

6–2g Identity Interest Groups

Americans who share the same race, ethnicity, gender, or other characteristic often have important common interests. African Americans, for example, have a powerful interest in combating the racism and racial discrimination that have marked American history from the beginning. Slaves, of course, were not able to form interest groups. For many years after the abolition of slavery, organizing African American interest groups remained impossibly dangerous. Such groups did not come into existence until the twentieth century.

The National Association for the Advancement of Colored People was founded in 1909, and the National Urban League was created in 1910. During the civil rights movement of the 1950s and 1960s, African Americans organized a number of new groups, some of which lasted (the Southern Christian Leadership Conference, founded in 1957) and some of which did not (the Student Nonviolent Coordinating Committee, organized in 1960).

The campaigns for dignity and equality of Native Americans, Latinos, women, lesbians and gay men, Americans with disabilities, and many other groups have all resulted in important interest groups. You learned about many of these organizations in Chapter 5. One identity-based group not discussed in that chapter is older Americans. Senior citizens are numerous, are politically active, and have a great deal at stake in debates over certain programs, such as Social Security and Medicare. As a result, groups representing them, such as AARP, can be a potent political force.

6–2h Ideological Interest Groups

Some interest groups are organized to promote not an economic interest or a collective identity but a shared political perspective or ideology. Examples include MoveOn, an Internet-oriented liberal group, and the Club for Growth, a conservative antitax organization.

NICHOLAS KAMM/AFP/GETTY IMAGES

Members of the NAACP (National Association for the Advancement of Colored People) in front of the United States Supreme Court. They oppose the Court's decision to strike down part of the Voting Rights Act of 1965.

The Tea Party Movement The highly decentralized Tea Party movement, which sprang into life in 2009, has been described as an ideological interest group. The activities of the Tea Party movement, however, raise the question of whether it really is an interest group at all. The point is that interest groups, while they are often very concerned about who wins an election and may endorse candidates, do not themselves attempt to gain control of the machinery of government.

Most Tea Party leaders claim that the movement is nonpartisan and that it contains not only Republicans but independents, libertarians, and even a few Democrats. Still, some Tea Party groups have attempted to gain control of local Republican Party organizations. It may be only a matter of terminology, but political scientists refer to groups that compete for control of a political party as *factions*, not interest groups.

Environmental Groups

Environmental groups have supported pollution controls, wilderness protection, and clean-air legislation. They have opposed strip mining, nuclear power plants, logging activities, chemical waste dumps, and many other potential environmental hazards. Environmental interest groups range from traditional organizations, such as the National Wildlife Federation with 4 million members, to more radical groups, such as Greenpeace USA with a membership of 250,000.

In the past, environmental groups have been characterized as single-interest groups, not ideological organizations. Issues such as climate change, however, have led many modern environmental groups to advocate sweeping changes to the entire economy. Groups with such broad agendas could be considered a type of ideological interest group.

Religious Groups

Religious organizations are another type of group that could be included in the ideological category. Many religious groups work on behalf of conservative social causes. Others take a strong interest in the well-being of those suffering from poverty. How much representation do the poor receive in the political system? We look at that question in the *Perception versus Reality* feature on the following page. We also list some top ideological and miscellaneous interest groups in Table 6–4 above.

6–2i Single-Issue Interest Groups

Numerous interest groups focus on a single issue. For example, Mothers Against Drunk Driving (MADD)

TABLE 6–4

Top Ideological and Miscellaneous Campaign Donors, 1989–2012

Group	Total, 1989–2012
1. ActBlue (Democratic)	$88,679,138
2. EMILY's List (Democratic)	$28,099,958
3. National Rifle Assn.	$20,242,684
4. Club for Growth (conservative)	$17,057,095
5. Human Rights Campaign (gay and lesbian)	$11,982,496

lobbies for stiffer penalties for drunk driving. Formed in 1980, MADD now boasts more than 3 million members and supporters. The abortion debate has created various single-issue groups, such as the Right to Life organization (which opposes abortion) and NARAL Pro-Choice America (founded as the National Association for the Repeal of Abortion Laws in 1969, when abortion was widely illegal). Other examples of single-issue groups are the NRA and the American Israel Public Affairs Committee (a pro-Israel group).

6–2j Government Interest Groups

Efforts by state and local governments to lobby the federal government have escalated in recent years. When states experience budget shortfalls, these governments often lobby in Washington, D.C., for additional federal funds. The federal government has sometimes lobbied in individual states, too. Until 2009, for example, the U.S. Attorney General's office lobbied against medical marijuana use in states that were considering ballot measures on the issue.

FOR CRITICAL THINKING

Are you a member of any interest groups? If so, why? If not, which existing groups might best serve your interests? Again, why?

Perception versus Reality
The Unrepresented Poor

America has not eliminated poverty. Indeed, every year we read stories about poor Americans and about Americans who have fallen into poverty. Given that the poor are in no position to lobby for themselves, it seems obvious that rich individuals and major corporations, because they do lots of lobbying, must get all the benefits from government.

THE PERCEPTION

Because the poor have no access to the halls of government, they are underrepresented. Low-income persons simply do not have the time, funds, or spare energy to compete with moneyed interests, at either the state or the national level.

THE REALITY

While it may be true that lobbyists are often successful in getting "special deals" for the rich and for big corporations, the tax burden on wealthy individuals remains heavy. The richest 10 percent of Americans pay about half of all federal income and payroll taxes. (Payroll taxes are Social Security and Medicare taxes.) The top 1 percent of Americans pay about one-quarter of these taxes. Low-income taxpayers are largely exempt from the income tax. They pay only payroll taxes, and in many cases, they can get rebates on these. Even without being able to lobby for themselves, low-income families and individuals receive beneficial tax treatment.

Now consider spending. Ron Haskins of the Brookings Institution estimates that all federal low-income programs together cost more than $800 billion a year. One of the most important of these programs is food stamps (now called Supplemental Nutrition Assistance Program, or SNAP). Just since 2007, when the Great Recession struck, the number of food stamp recipients has risen from 26 million to 45 million. The average monthly value of the benefit is close to $300. Other programs for the poor include Medicaid and the refundable portions of the Earned-Income Tax Credit and the Additional Child Tax Credit.

The reality is that for decades, many liberal groups have lobbied on behalf of those suffering from poverty. Mainstream religious groups have done the same—including Catholic organizations, Lutherans, the National Council of Churches, the Friends (Quakers), and many others. Liberal and religious interests have done for the poor what the poor cannot do for themselves. The result: If there were no federal tax and spending programs aimed at low-income persons, as many as 25 percent of U.S. families would have incomes below the official poverty line. If you take into account all benefits that low-income families obtain, that number drops to about 10 percent.

BLOG ON

- For a vast collection of data on social services provided by the federal government, see the *Green Book* of the Ways and Means Committee of the U.S. House of Representatives. Enter "green book ways and means" into an Internet search engine.
- For another source of information, see the Web site of the University of Kentucky Center for Poverty Research. Search on "kentucky poverty."

6-3 How Interest Groups Shape Policy

Interest groups operate at all levels of government and use a variety of strategies to steer policies in ways beneficial to their interests. Sometimes, they attempt to influence policymakers directly, but at other times they try to exert indirect influence on policymakers by shaping public opinion. The extent and nature of the groups' activities depend on their goals and their resources.

6-3a Direct Techniques

Lobbying and providing election

Learning Outcome 6-3

Discuss how the activities of interest groups help to shape government policymaking.

Mega-lobbyist Heather Podesta (center) greets a government official at a Washington, D.C. reception.

LINDA DAVIDSON/THE WASHINGTON POST VIA GETTY

support are two important **direct techniques** used by interest groups to influence government policy.

Lobbying Today, **lobbying** refers to all of the attempts by organizations or by individuals to influence the passage, defeat, or contents of legislation or to influence the administrative decisions of government. (The term *lobbying* arose because, traditionally, individuals and groups interested in influencing government policy would gather in the foyer, or lobby, of the legislature to corner legislators and express their concerns.) A **lobbyist** is an individual who handles a particular interest group's lobbying efforts. Most of the larger interest groups have lobbyists in Washington, D.C. These lobbyists often include former members of Congress or former employees of executive bureaucracies who are experienced in the methods of political

influence and who "know people." Table 6–5 on the following page summarizes some of the basic methods by which lobbyists directly influence legislators and government officials.

Lobbying can be directed at the legislative branch of government, at administrative agencies, and even at the courts. Many lobbyists also work at state and local levels. In fact, lobbying at the state level has increased in recent years as states have begun to play a more significant role in policymaking.

Providing Election Support

Interest groups often become directly involved in the election process. Many group members join and work with political parties to influence party platforms and the nomination of candidates. Interest groups provide campaign support for legislators who favor their policies and sometimes encourage their own members to try to win posts in party organizations.

Most important, interest groups urge their members to vote for candidates who support the views of the group. They can also threaten legislators with the withdrawal of votes. No candidate can expect to have support from all interest groups, but if the candidate is to win, she or he must have support from many of the strongest ones.

POLITICAL ACTION COMMITTEES (PACs). Since the 1970s, federal laws governing campaign financing have allowed corporations, labor unions, and special interest groups to raise funds and make campaign contributions through **political action committees (PACs).** Both the number of PACs and the amount of money PACs spend on elections have grown astronomically in recent years. There were about 1,000 PACs in 1976. Today, there are more than 4,500 PACs. In 1973, total spending by PACs amounted to $19 million. In the 2011–2012 election cycle, contributions to federal candidates by PACs totaled about $440 million.

Even with their impressive growth, PACs provided a smaller share of campaign spending in the years after 1988, principally because of the development of other funding sources, such as "soft money" and issue ads. (We discuss these sources shortly.)

SUPER PACs. In 2010, the United States Supreme Court upended the world of campaign finance in

direct technique Any method used by an interest group to interact with government officials directly to further the group's goals.

lobbying All of the attempts by organizations or by individuals to influence the passage, defeat, or contents of legislation or to influence the administrative decisions of government.

lobbyist An individual who handles a particular interest group's lobbying efforts.

political action committee (PAC) A committee that is established by a corporation, labor union, or special interest group to raise funds and make campaign contributions on the establishing organization's behalf.

TABLE 6-5

Direct Lobbying Techniques

Technique	Description
Making Personal Contacts with Key Legislators	A lobbyist's personal contacts with key legislators or other government officials—in their offices, in the halls of Congress, or on social occasions such as dinners, boating expeditions, and the like—comprise one of the most effective direct lobbying techniques.
Providing Expertise and Research Results for Legislators	Lobbyists often have knowledge and expertise that are useful in drafting legislation, and this expertise can be a major strength for an interest group. Harried members of Congress cannot possibly be experts on everything they vote on and therefore eagerly seek information to help them make up their minds.
Offering "Expert" Testimony before Congressional Committees	Lobbyists often provide "expert" testimony before congressional committees for or against proposed legislation. Each expert offers as much evidence as possible to support her or his position.
Providing Legal Advice to Legislators	Many lobbyists assist legislators in drafting legislation or prospective regulations. Lobbyists are a source of ideas and sometimes offer legal advice on specific details.
Following Up on Legislation	Because executive agencies responsible for carrying out legislation can often change the scope of the new law, lobbyists may also try to influence the bureaucrats who implement the policy.

Citizens United v. Federal Election Commission.[8] The Court ruled that PACs could accept unlimited contributions from individuals, unions, and corporations for the purpose of making **independent expenditures.** These are expenditures that are not coordinated with a candidate's campaign or a political party. This ruling led, in short order, to the creation of super PACs, which channeled close to $1 billion into election spending in the 2012 election cycle. Many super PACs were funded by wealthy individuals, and many of them concentrated on negative ads.

Note that although campaign contributions do not guarantee that officials will vote the way the groups wish, contributions usually do ensure that the groups will have the ear of the public officials they have helped to elect. (We will discuss election finances in greater detail in Chapter 9.)

6–3b Indirect Techniques

Interest groups also try to influence public policy indirectly through third parties or the general public. The effects of such **indirect techniques** may appear to be spontaneous, but indirect techniques are generally as well planned as the direct lobbying techniques just discussed. Indirect techniques can be particularly effective because public officials are often more impressed by contacts from voters than from lobbyists.

Shaping Public Opinion Public opinion weighs significantly in the policymaking process, so interest groups cultivate their public images carefully. If public opinion favors a certain group's interests, then public officials will be more ready to listen and more willing to pass legislation favoring that group. An interest group's efforts to cultivate public opinion, may include online campaigns, television publicity, newspaper and magazine advertisements, mass mailings, and the use of public relations techniques to improve the group's image.

For example, environmental groups often run television ads to dramatize threats to the environment. Oil companies may respond to criticism about increased gasoline prices with advertising that shows how hard they are working to develop new sources of energy. The goal of all these activities is to influence public opinion.

independent expenditure An expenditure for activities that are independent from (not coordinated with) those of a political candidate or a political party.

indirect technique Any method used by interest groups to influence government officials through third parties, such as voters.

Pulitzer Prize–winning journalist José Antonio Vargas—himself an unauthorized immigrant—often speaks out on immigration reform.

Rating Systems

Some interest groups also try to influence legislators through **rating systems.** A group selects legislative issues that it believes are important to its goals and rates legislators according to the percentage of times they vote favorably on that legislation. For example, a score of 90 percent on the Americans for Democratic Action (ADA) rating scale means that the legislator supported that liberal group's position to a high degree.

Other groups use telling labels to tag members of Congress who support (or fail to support) their interests to a significant extent. For instance, the Communications Workers of America refers to policymakers who take a position consistent with its views as "Heroes" and those who take the opposite position as "Zeroes." Needless to say, such tactics can be an effective form of indirect lobbying, particularly with legislators who do not want to earn a low ADA score or be placed on the "Zeroes" list.

Issue Ads

One of the most powerful indirect techniques used by interest groups is the "issue ad"—a television or radio ad taking a position on a particular issue. The Supreme Court has made it clear that the First Amendment's guarantee of free speech protects interest groups' rights to set forth their positions on issues when they fund

rating system A system by which a particular interest group evaluates (rates) the performance of legislators based on how often the legislators have voted with the group's position on particular issues.

such activities through independent expenditures that are not coordinated with a candidate's campaign or a political party. Nevertheless, issue advocacy is controversial because the funds spent to air issue ads have had a clear effect on the outcome of elections. Both parties have benefited from such interest group spending.

527s and 501(c)4s

As you will read in Chapter 9, the Bipartisan Campaign Reform Act of 2002 banned unlimited donations to campaigns and political parties, called *soft money*. In subsequent years, interest groups that had previously given soft money to parties set up new groups called "527s" (after the provision of the tax code that covers them). The 527s engaged in such practices as voter registration, but they also began making large expenditures on issue ads—which were legal so long as the 527s did not coordinate their activities with candidates' campaigns.

In the run-up to the 2008 presidential elections, clever campaign finance lawyers hit upon a new type of group, the 501(c)4 organization, also named after a section of the tax code. Groups such as the Sierra Club and Citizens Against Government Waste have set up special 501(c)4 organizations.

Lawyers argued that a 501(c)4 group could spend some of its funds on direct campaign contributions as long as most of the group's spending was on issue advocacy. Further, a 501(c)4 group could conceal the identity of its contributors. Federal agencies and the courts have not yet determined the legality of these claims. We will discuss this issue in greater depth in Chapter 9.

Mobilizing Constituents

Interest groups sometimes urge members and other constituents to contact government officials—by letter, e-mail, Facebook, Twitter, or telephone—to show their support for or opposition to a certain policy. Such efforts are known as *grassroots organizing*.

Large interest groups can generate hundreds of thousands of letters, e-mail messages, tweets, and phone calls. Interest groups often provide form letters or postcards for constituents to fill out and mail. The NRA has successfully used this tactic to fight strict federal gun control legislation by delivering half a million letters to Congress within a few weeks. Policymakers recognize that such communications are initiated by interest groups, however, and are impressed only when the volume of letters or e-mail communications is very large.

Campaigns that masquerade as grassroots mobilizations, but are not, have been given the apt label *Astroturf lobbying*. An Astroturf lobbyist might, for example, make anonymous postings online that appear to be from concerned citizens but that actually come from the sponsoring organization.

Going to Court The legal system offers another avenue for interest groups to influence the political process. In the 1950s and 1960s, civil rights groups paved the way for interest group litigation with major victories in cases concerning equal housing, school desegregation, and employment discrimination. Environmental groups, such as the Sierra Club, have also successfully used litigation to press their concerns. For example, an environmental group might challenge in court an activity that threatens to pollute the environment or that will destroy the natural habitat of an endangered species. The legal challenge forces those engaging in the activity to defend their actions and may delay the project. In fact, much of the success of environmental groups has been linked to their use of lawsuits.

Interest groups can also influence the outcome of litigation without being a party to a lawsuit. Frequently, an interest group files an *amicus curiae* brief. The brief states the group's legal argument in support of its desired outcome in a case.

For example, the case *Arizona v. United States*, heard by the Supreme Court in 2012, turned on whether a state government could enact immigration laws tougher than those adopted by the federal government. The Court ruled that part, but not all, of the Arizona legislation was unconstitutional.[9] Dozens of organizations filed *amicus* briefs on one side or the other of the issue. Conservative and anti-immigration groups supported the state. Naturally, so did Arizona elected officials, including the state legislature. Those backing the federal government, which had challenged the Arizona law, included the Catholic bishops, labor unions, the American Bar Association, a variety of civil rights and civil liberties groups, and the government of Mexico.

Often, in such briefs, interest groups cite statistics and research that support their position on a certain issue. This research can have considerable influence on the judges deciding the case.

Demonstrations Some interest groups stage protests to make a statement in a dramatic way. The Boston Tea Party of 1773, in which American colonists dressed as Native Americans and threw tea into Boston Harbor to protest British taxes, is testimony to how long this tactic has been around. Over the years, many groups have organized protest marches and rallies to support or oppose legalized abortion, gay and lesbian rights, the treatment of Native Americans, restrictions on the use of federally owned lands in the West, and the activities of global organizations such as the World Trade Organization.

> "Never doubt that a small group of thoughtful, committed citizens can **CHANGE THE WORLD;** indeed, it's the only thing that ever has."
>
> ~ MARGARET MEAD ~
> AMERICAN ANTHROPOLOGIST
> 1902–1978

THE OCCUPY TOGETHER MOVEMENT. In 2011 and 2012, a major series of demonstrations swept across the United States. The first of these, Occupy Wall Street, began when activists set up a tent encampment to "occupy" Wall Street. Major demands were that the government should take steps to reduce economic inequality and to increase employment, especially for young people. The principal slogan was "We are the 99 percent," as opposed to the richest 1 percent. Several hundred encampments subsequently sprang up across the nation and around the world. The movement is credited with placing the issue of inequality squarely on the political agenda. By 2012, however, the protests were dying down.

VIOLENT DEMONSTRATIONS. Not all demonstration techniques are peaceful. Some environmental groups, for example, have used such dangerous tactics as spiking trees and setting traps on logging roads to puncture truck tires. Pro-life groups have bombed abortion clinics, and members of the Animal Liberation Front have broken into laboratories and freed animals being used for experimentation. Some evidence exists that violent demonstrations can be counterproductive—that is, that they can hurt the demonstrators' cause by angering the public. Historians continue to debate whether violent demonstrations against the Vietnam War (1964–1975) helped or hurt the antiwar cause.

Why might some lawmakers pay more attention to contacts by ordinary people than contacts by lobbyists?

6-4 Today's Lobbying Establishment

Learning Outcome 6-4

Describe how interest groups are regulated by government.

Without a doubt, interest groups and their lobbyists have become a permanent feature in the landscape of American government. All the major interest groups have headquarters in Washington, D.C., close to the center of government. Professional lobbyists and staff members of various interest groups move freely between their groups' headquarters and congressional offices and committee rooms. Interest group representatives are routinely consulted when Congress drafts new legislation. As already mentioned, interest group representatives are frequently asked to testify before congressional committees or subcommittees on the effect or potential effect of particular legislation or regulations. In sum, interest groups have become an integral part of the American government system.

As interest groups have become a permanent feature of American government, lobbying has developed into a profession. A professional lobbyist—one who has mastered the techniques of lobbying discussed earlier in this chapter—is a valuable ally to any interest group seeking to influence government. Professional lobbyists can and often do represent a number of different interest groups over the course of their careers.

In recent years, it has become increasingly common for those who leave positions with the federal government to become lobbyists or consultants for the private-interest groups they helped to regulate. In spite of legislation and regulations designed to reduce this "revolving door" syndrome, it is still functioning quite well.

6-4a Why Do Interest Groups Get Bad Press?

Despite their importance to democratic government, interest groups, like political parties, are often criticized by both the public and the press. Our image of interest groups and their special interests is not very favorable. You may have run across political cartoons depicting lobbyists standing in the hallways of Congress with briefcases stuffed with money. These cartoons are not entirely factual, but they are not entirely fictitious either.

Examples of Questionable Activities Consider a few examples. In 2004, the chief executive officer of a coal company donated $3 million to the election campaign of a candidate for the West Virginia Supreme Court. That sum amounted to most of what was spent in the race. At that time, the coal company had a $50 million case pending before the court, which eventually found in the coal company's favor. (In 2009, the United States Supreme Court ruled that the recipient of the largesse should not have participated in the court proceedings.)[10]

In 2007, Texas governor Rick Perry issued an executive order adding a new vaccine to the list required for public school students. The Gardasil vaccine protects against a sexually transmitted virus that can cause cervical cancer in women. As it turns out, Merck, the company that makes the vaccine, had given $5,000 to the governor's reelection campaign immediately before the executive order was issued. One of Merck's lobbyists was Perry's former chief of staff.

Concentrated Benefits, Dispersed Costs A major complaint by critics of interest groups is that the benefits these groups obtain are not in the general public interest. One reason for this situation is the so-called enthusiasm gap between supporters and opponents of any given subsidy. Sugar producers, for example, benefit greatly from restrictions on sugar imports. They work hard to ensure that these restrictions continue. Yet for sugar consumers—all the rest of us—the price of sugar is a trivial matter. End users of sugar have no incentive to organize. This enthusiasm gap, referred to as "concentrated benefits, dispersed costs," is especially important in issues of international trade, as we explain in *The Rest of the World* feature on the following page.

6-4b The Regulation of Interest Groups

In an attempt to control lobbying, Congress passed the Federal Regulation of Lobbying Act in 1946. The major provisions of the act are as follows:

Tailoring Trade Deals for Special Interests

Special interests are unusually powerful when it comes to the rules on international trade. Indeed, people who think that trade is boring are likely to miss some of the biggest rip-offs coming out of Congress. Furthermore, America's worldwide trade in goods and services is huge. We import about $2.8 trillion of goods and services from other countries each year, and we export about $2.2 trillion. That's 17 percent of our overall economy for imports and 13 percent for exports.

The Basics of International Trade

A belief in the benefits of foreign trade unites almost all economists, liberal and conservative. Economists argue that free trade results in more goods and services for every participating country. Unfortunately, not everyone benefits from free trade. When we import cars from Japan or Korea, there are fewer jobs available for American auto workers. Imports compete with many U.S.-made goods and services, so many people oppose free trade and support restrictions on imports, such as quotas or *tariffs* (taxes on imports).

Still, over the past several decades, the United States has negotiated a variety of trade deals aimed at lowering trade barriers. These include the North American Free Trade Agreement and the Central America–Dominican Republic–United States Free Trade Agreement. Currently, the federal government is sponsoring two large-scale trade talks—one with nations of East Asia and the Pacific, and another with the countries of Europe.

Special Interests Keep On Pushing

You might think that trade deals could be simple. If the only goal were to reduce tariffs and quotas, a straightforward formula might specify the rates at which these restrictions would be cut. To get a trade deal through Congress, however, an agreement must reward industry after industry so that those interests will support the deal. The pharmaceutical industry wants intellectual property protection that drives up the price of drugs in foreign countries. Banks want to force other countries to cut back on banking regulations—even though many

people believe that too little bank regulation helped cause the Great Recession. And, of course, each country works to make sure that favored industries are not negatively affected by the deal. Japan wants to maintain its quotas on rice imports. The U.S. government wants to keep cotton subsidies for U.S. producers that ruin African cotton farmers.

Concentrated Benefits, Dispersed Costs

Economists have identified a problem with legislation in a democracy that they call *concentrated benefits, dispersed costs*. If a special law, such a tax break, helps relatively few people, those who receive the benefit will fight like the devil to keep or enlarge it. The great majority, which winds up paying for the benefit, has little motivation to oppose it. After all, for members of the majority the cost may be a matter of pennies. Those who benefit from trade restrictions—called *protectionists*—are concentrated in specific industries that face foreign competition. As a result, they often win.

FOR CRITICAL ANALYSIS American humorist Mark Twain allegedly said, "The free traders win all the arguments and the protectionists win all the votes." Why would he have said that?

- Any person or organization that receives money to influence legislation must register with the clerk of the House and the secretary of the Senate.

- Any groups or persons registering must identify their employer, salary, amount and purpose of expenses, and duration of employment.

- Every registered lobbyist must make quarterly reports on his or her activities.

- Anyone violating this act can be fined up to $10,000 and be imprisoned for up to five years.

The act did not succeed in regulating lobbying to any great degree for several reasons. First, the

© 2009 HARLEY SCHWADRON

"MY GREATEST ASSET IS I'M SO RICH, I CAN'T BE BOUGHT BY ANY INTEREST GROUP."

Supreme Court restricted the application of the law to only those lobbyists who sought to influence federal legislation directly.[11] Any lobbyist seeking to influence legislation indirectly through public opinion did not fall within the scope of the law.

Second, only persons or organizations whose principal purpose was to influence legislation were required to register. Many groups avoided registration by claiming that their principal function was something else. Third, the act did not cover those whose lobbying was directed at agencies in the executive branch or lobbyists who testified before congressional committees. Fourth, the public was almost totally unaware of the information in the quarterly reports filed by lobbyists. Not until 1995 did Congress finally address those loopholes by enacting new legislation.

6-4c The Lobbying Disclosure Act of 1995

In 1995, Congress passed new expanded lobbying legislation—the Lobbying Disclosure Act—that reformed the 1946 act in the following ways:

- Strict definitions now apply to determine who must register with the clerk of the House and the secretary of the Senate as a lobbyist. A lobbyist is anyone who either spends at least 20 percent of his or her time lobbying members of Congress, their staffs, or executive-branch officials, or is

paid more than $5,000 in a six-month period for such work. Any organization that spends more than $20,000 in a six-month period conducting such lobbying activity must also register. These amounts have since been altered to $2,500 and $10,000 per quarter, respectively.

- Lobbyists must report their clients, the issues on which they lobbied, and the agency or chamber of Congress they contacted, although they do not need to disclose the names of those they contacted.

Tax-exempt organizations, such as religious groups, were exempted from these provisions, as were organizations that engage in grassroots lobbying, such as a media campaign that asks people to write or call their congressional representative. Nonetheless, the number of registered lobbyists nearly doubled in the first few years after the new legislation.

> ## "An honest politician
> is one who, when he is bought, will stay bought."
> ~ SIMON CAMERON ~
> U.S. FINANCIER AND POLITICIAN
> 1799–1889

6-4d Recent Reform Efforts

In 2005, a number of lobbying scandals in Washington, D.C., came to light. As a result, following the midterm elections of 2006, the new Democratic majority in the Senate and House of Representatives undertook a lobbying reform effort. This involved changes to the rules that the two chambers impose on their own members.

Bundled campaign contributions, in which a lobbyist arranges for contributions from a variety of sources, would have to be reported. Expenditures on the sometimes lavish parties to benefit candidates would have to be reported as well. (Of course, partygoers were expected to pay for their food and drink with a check written out to the candidate.) The new rules covered PACs as well as registered lobbyists, which led one lobbyist to observe sourly that this wasn't lobbying reform but campaign-finance reform.

President George W. Bush signed the Honest Leadership and Open Government Act in 2007. The new law increased lobbying disclosure requirements and placed further restrictions on the receipt of gifts and travel by members of Congress paid for by lobbyists and the organizations they represent. The act also included provisions requiring the disclosure of lawmakers' requests for earmarks in legislation. (We discuss earmarks in more depth in Chapter 11.)

FOR CRITICAL THINKING

As noted at the beginning of this chapter, the right to lobby is protected by the Constitution. *If that weren't so, would it be a good idea to ban lobbying? Why or why not?*

AMERICA AT
ODDS Interest Groups

Interest groups are one of the most controversial features of our democratic system. The right to lobby may be protected by the First Amendment, but many people consider lobbying by interest groups to be a source of corruption within the political system. Of course, people can readily see the problems with lobbying when it is done for a cause that they oppose. In contrast, it is easy to support political action for something you believe in, regardless of what others might think of it. Some of the controversies surrounding interest group lobbying include the following:

- Should labor unions be allowed to organize workplaces by obtaining signed cards—or are secret-ballot elections an essential safeguard?

- Are farm subsidies a valid protection for an important industry—or just another giveaway to the politically powerful?

- Does lobbying always harm legislation—or can lobbying improve it?

- Free riders benefit from a particular activity without paying their share of its costs. Is free riding inherently unfair—or is it only a problem when it is so pervasive that it makes the activity in question (for example, lobbying by consumer groups) unaffordable?

- Are there too many lobbyists—or is the real problem that there aren't enough lobbyists for ordinary people?

STUDY TOOLS

Ready to study?

- **Review** what you've read with the quiz below.
- Check your answers on the **Chapter in Review** card at the back of the book.
- For any questions you miss, read the corresponding **Learning Outcome** section again to prepare for class and your exam.
- Rip out and study the **Chapter in Review** card (at the back of the book).

Fill-In

Learning Outcome 6–1

1. The right to form interest groups and to lobby the government is protected by the _____ Amendment to the U.S. Constitution.

2. _____ theory describes the defensive formation of interest groups.

Learning Outcome 6–2

3. Today, members of organized labor make up only _____ percent of the labor force.

4. _____ laws ban unions from collecting dues or other fees from workers whom they represent but who have not actually joined the union.

Learning Outcome 6–3

5. Lobbying refers to _____.

6. Interest groups can influence the outcome of litigation without being a party to a lawsuit by filing _____.

Learning Outcome 6–4

7. It has become increasingly common for those who leave positions with the federal government to become lobbyists or consultants for the private-interest groups they helped to regulate. This is called the _____ syndrome.

Multiple Choice

Learning Outcome 6–1

8. There are various reasons why people join interest groups. Some people find that they gain considerable satisfaction from taking action from within that group. Such satisfaction is referred to as a _____ incentive.
   a. free rider   b. purposive   c. material

9. Interest groups
   a. are often policy generalists.
   b. compete for public office.
   c. help bridge the gap between citizens and government.

Learning Outcome 6–2

10. The American Association for Justice represents the interests of
    a. trial lawyers.   b. children.   c. senior citizens.

11. MoveOn and the Club for Growth are _____ interest groups.
    a. business   b. consumer   c. ideological

Learning Outcome 6–3

12. _____ is a direct technique used by interest groups to influence public policy.
    a. The use of rating systems
    b. Providing election support

c. Staging demonstrations

13. The Supreme Court has made it clear that the First Amendment's guarantee of free speech
    a. protects interest groups' rights to set forth their positions on issues when they fund such activities through independent expenditures that are not coordinated with a candidate's campaign or a political party.
    b. protects issue advocacy as long as that advocacy is coordinated with a candidate's campaign or a political party.
    c. does not include protection for interest groups to set forth their positions on issues.

Learning Outcome 6–4

14. Lobbying campaigns that masquerade as grass-roots mobilizations (but are not) have been labeled _____ lobbying.
    a. *Bluegrass*   b. *Turfgrass*   c. *Astroturf*

15. When a benefit is provided to a limited number of people, the enthusiasm gap between recipients of the benefit and everyone else is called:
    a. concentrated costs and dispersed benefits.
    b. the free rider problem.
    c. concentrated benefits and dispersed costs.

Political Parties

Learning Outcomes

The **Learning Outcomes** labeled 1 through 5 are designed to help improve your understanding of the chapter. After reading this chapter, you should be able to:

7–1 Summarize the origins and development of the two-party system in the United States.

7–2 Describe the current status of the two major parties.

7–3 Explain how political parties function in our democratic system.

7–4 Discuss the structure of American political parties.

7–5 Describe the different types of third parties and how they function in the American political system.

Remember to visit page 162 for additional Study Tools

AMERICA AT
ODDS

Does the Republican Party Need a New Strategy?

CHARLES OMMANNEY/GETTY IMAGES

In the 2010 midterm elections, conservative Republicans turned out in great numbers and took control of the U.S. House of Representatives away from the Democrats. Democrats continued to hold the Senate and the presidency. Still, conservatives interpreted these results to mean that they, not the Democrats, had a mandate from the voters. In 2012, voters reelected Democratic president Barack Obama, and the Democrats gained seats in the House and Senate. As a result, a few Republicans argued that the party should change its policies to attract moderate, independent voters, especially Hispanics. Other Republicans, however, often supported by Tea Party activists, claimed that Republican politicians were not conservative enough. Who has the more convincing argument?

Uncompromising Conservatism Is the Only Way Forward

Uncompromising conservatives believe that the Republicans must steer to the political right. Even though only 25 percent of voters call themselves Republicans, 40 percent say that they are conservatives. Support is rising for such conservative positions as the right to bear arms and opposition to abortion.

Conservative activists argue that their values are not only popular but also "correct" in a very deep sense. In their view, values such as religious belief, strong families, and individual self-reliance are the foundation of our civilization. Liberalism erodes these values and paves the road to cultural collapse.

According to some conservative commentators, the Republicans lost the 2012 presidential elections only because white working-class voters in states such as Ohio stayed home—they were turned off by the Republican candidate Mitt Romney, a wealthy financier. If Republicans support causes such as immigration reform, they will just alienate these voters further.

Americans are starting to rebel against big government and a culture of immorality. If the Republicans don't stand firm for true conservatism, these Americans won't have anyone to vote for.

Radical Conservatism Spells Disaster in the Long Run

A minority of Republicans point out that their party has won fewer votes than the Democrats in five of the last six presidential elections. The face of America is changing. Support for gay rights has risen dramatically. The number of Hispanic voters rises year by year, and by 2050, non-Hispanic whites will be a minority of the U.S. population. Despite these changes, some conservatives seem intent on ensuring that the Republicans are seen as the "nasty party"—the party that hates people.

Republicans require young voters, but tirades against gays are poison to that constituency. If the vast majority of Latinos come to reject the Republicans because of the party's anti-immigrant rhetoric, eventually the Republicans will even fail to carry Texas. If voters conclude that Republicans see large numbers of their fellow Americans as "the enemy," the party will lose future elections, no matter how well it did in 2010 or how well it does in 2014.

Finally, a complete refusal to compromise is not a winning formula. Many Americans, especially the independents who decide elections, strongly favor cooperation between the parties. If either party refuses to compromise, in time the voters are likely to take notice.

Where do you stand?

1. Pastor Rick Warren, author of *The Purpose Driven Life*, accepts that homosexuality is a sin, but he also emphasizes his belief in God's love for all people. Why might some members of the religious right reject Warren's formula?
2. American-style cultural conservatism is not popular in much of Europe. Many of these nations are also facing declines in their populations. Some conservatives would argue that these facts are connected. Is this argument reasonable? Why or why not?

Explore this issue online

- For full-throttle conservatism, try Rush Limbaugh's site by typing "limbaugh" into your favorite search engine.
- Blogger Josh Barro takes a combative approach to the need to "reform the conservatives." Reformer Reihan Salam is more sympathetic to the current state of the Republicans than Barro is. You can find the work of these writers by searching on their names.

Introduction

Political ideology can spark heated debates among Americans, as you read in the chapter-opening *America at Odds* feature. A **political party** can be defined as a group of individuals who organize to win elections, operate the government, and determine policy.

Political parties were an unforeseen development in American political history. The founders defined many other important institutions, such as the presidency and Congress, and described their functions in the Constitution. Political parties, however, are not even mentioned in the Constitution. In fact, the founders decried factions and parties. Thomas Jefferson probably best expressed the founders' antiparty sentiments when he declared, "If I could not go to heaven but with a party, I would not go there at all."[1]

If the founders did not want political parties, though, who was supposed to organize political campaigns and mobilize supporters of political can-

> "Both of our political parties . . . agree conscientiously in the same object:
> **the public good;** but they differ essentially in what they deem the means of promoting that good."
>
> ~ THOMAS JEFFERSON ~
> IN A LETTER TO ABIGAIL ADAMS, 1804

didates? Clearly, there was a practical need for some kind of organizing group to form a link between citizens and their government. Even our early national leaders, for all their antiparty feelings, soon realized this. Several of them were active in establishing or organizing the first political parties.

7–1 A Short History of American Political Parties

Throughout the course of our history, several parties have formed, and some have disappeared. Even today, although we have only two major political parties, a few others always exist at any one time, as will be discussed later in this chapter.

7–1a The First Political Parties

The founders rejected the idea of political parties because they believed, as George Washington said in his Farewell Address, that the "spirit of party . . . agitates the community with ill-founded jealousies and false alarms, kindles the animosity of one part against another, foments occasionally riot and insurrection."[2] At some point in the future, the founders feared, a party leader might even seize power as a dictator.

Learning Outcome 7–1

Summarize the origins and development of the two-party system in the United States.

Federalists and Anti-Federalists In spite of the founders' fears, two major political factions—the Federalists and the Anti-Federalists—were formed even before the Constitution was ratified. Remember from Chapter 2 that the Federalists pushed for the ratification of the Constitution because they wanted a stronger national government than the one that had existed under the Articles of Confederation. The Anti-Federalists argued against ratification. They supported states' rights and feared a too-powerful central government.

> **political party** A group of individuals who organize to win elections, operate the government, and determine policy.

John Adams (1735–1826) was the Federalists' candidate to succeed George Washington. Adams defeated Thomas Jefferson in 1796, but lost to him in 1800.

realignment A process in which the popular support for and relative strength of the parties shift and the parties are reestablished with different coalitions of supporters.

Federalists and Republicans

The Federalist and Anti-Federalist factions continued, in somewhat altered form, after the Constitution was ratified. Alexander Hamilton, the first secretary of the Treasury, became the leader of the Federalist Party, which Vice President John Adams also joined. The Federalists supported a strong central government that would encourage the development of commerce and manufacturing. The Federalists generally thought that a republic should be ruled by its wealthiest and best-educated citizens.

Opponents of the Federalists and Hamilton's policies referred to themselves as Republicans. Today, they are often referred to as Jeffersonian Republicans, or Democratic Republicans (a name never used at the time), to distinguish this group from the later-established Republican Party. The Jeffersonian Republicans favored a more limited role for government. They believed that the nation's welfare would be best served if the states had more power than the central government. In their view, Congress should dominate the government, and government policies should serve farming interests rather than promote commerce and manufacturing.

7-1b From 1796 to 1860

The nation's first two parties clashed openly in the elections of 1796, in which John Adams, the Federalists' candidate to succeed George Washington as president, defeated Thomas Jefferson. Over the next four years, Jefferson and James Madison worked to extend the influence of the Jeffersonian Republican Party. In the presidential elections of 1800 and 1804, Jefferson won the presidency, and his party also won control of Congress.

Triumph of the Jeffersonians The transition of political power from the Federalists to the Jeffersonian Republicans is the first example in American history of what political scientists have called a **realignment.** In a realignment, a substantial number of voters change their political allegiance, which usually also changes the balance of power between the two major parties. In fact, the Federalists never returned to power and thus became the first (but not the last) American party to go out of existence. (See the time line of American political parties in Figure 7–1 on the following page.)

The Jeffersonian Republicans dominated American politics for the next twenty years. Jefferson was succeeded in the White House by two other members of the party—James Madison and James Monroe. In the mid-1820s, however, the Jeffersonian Republicans split into two groups. This was the second realignment in American history. Supporters of Andrew Jackson,

Thomas Jefferson (1743–1826) became our third president and served two terms. The Jeffersonian Republicans (not to be confused with the later Republican Party of Abraham Lincoln) dominated American politics for more than two decades.

Andrew Jackson (1767–1845) led the newly formed Democratic Party. Jackson won the presidential election in 1828, defeating the candidate of the National Republicans.

LIBRARY OF CONGRESS

LIBRARY OF CONGRESS

FIGURE 7-1

A Time Line of U.S. Political Parties

Many of these parties—including the Constitutional Union Party, Henry Wallace's Progressive Party, and the States' Rights Democrats—were important during only one presidential election.

Evolution of the Major American Political Parties and Splinter Groups

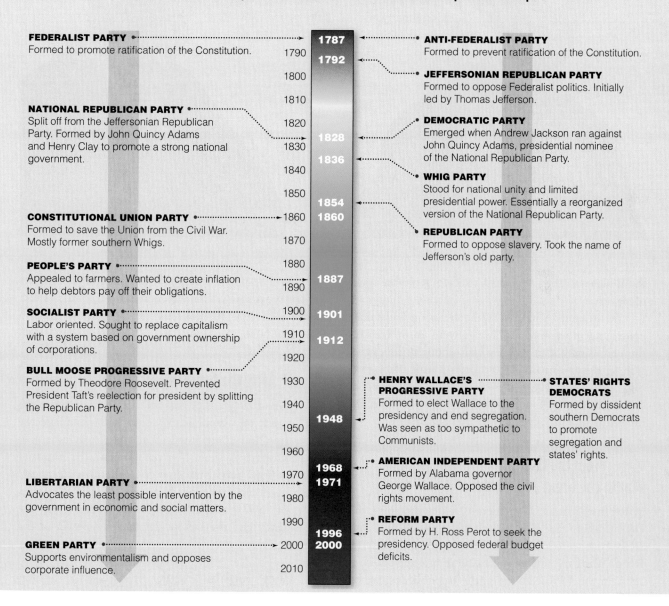

FEDERALIST PARTY
Formed to promote ratification of the Constitution.

NATIONAL REPUBLICAN PARTY
Split off from the Jeffersonian Republican Party. Formed by John Quincy Adams and Henry Clay to promote a strong national government.

CONSTITUTIONAL UNION PARTY
Formed to save the Union from the Civil War. Mostly former southern Whigs.

PEOPLE'S PARTY
Appealed to farmers. Wanted to create inflation to help debtors pay off their obligations.

SOCIALIST PARTY
Labor oriented. Sought to replace capitalism with a system based on government ownership of corporations.

BULL MOOSE PROGRESSIVE PARTY
Formed by Theodore Roosevelt. Prevented President Taft's reelection for president by splitting the Republican Party.

LIBERTARIAN PARTY
Advocates the least possible intervention by the government in economic and social matters.

GREEN PARTY
Supports environmentalism and opposes corporate influence.

1787 1792 1828 1836 1854 1860 1887 1901 1912 1948 1968 1971 1996 2000

1790 1800 1810 1820 1830 1840 1850 1860 1870 1880 1890 1900 1910 1920 1930 1940 1950 1960 1970 1980 1990 2000 2010

ANTI-FEDERALIST PARTY
Formed to prevent ratification of the Constitution.

JEFFERSONIAN REPUBLICAN PARTY
Formed to oppose Federalist politics. Initially led by Thomas Jefferson.

DEMOCRATIC PARTY
Emerged when Andrew Jackson ran against John Quincy Adams, presidential nominee of the National Republican Party.

WHIG PARTY
Stood for national unity and limited presidential power. Essentially a reorganized version of the National Republican Party.

REPUBLICAN PARTY
Formed to oppose slavery. Took the name of Jefferson's old party.

HENRY WALLACE'S PROGRESSIVE PARTY
Formed to elect Wallace to the presidency and end segregation. Was seen as too sympathetic to Communists.

STATES' RIGHTS DEMOCRATS
Formed by dissident southern Democrats to promote segregation and states' rights.

AMERICAN INDEPENDENT PARTY
Formed by Alabama governor George Wallace. Opposed the civil rights movement.

REFORM PARTY
Formed by H. Ross Perot to seek the presidency. Opposed federal budget deficits.

who was elected president in 1828, called themselves Democrats. The Democrats appealed to small farmers and the growing class of urbanized workers. The other group, the National Republicans (later the Whig Party), was led by John Quincy Adams, Henry Clay, and the great orator Daniel Webster. It had the support of bankers, business owners, and many southern planters.

The Impending Crisis As the Whigs and Democrats competed for the White House throughout the 1840s and 1850s, the two-party system as we know it today emerged. Both parties were large, with well-known leaders and supporters across the nation. Both had grassroots organizations of party workers committed to winning as many political offices (at all levels of government) for the party as possible. Both

From the election of Abraham Lincoln in 1860 until the election of Franklin Delano Roosevelt in 1932, the Republican Party was the more successful party in presidential politics.

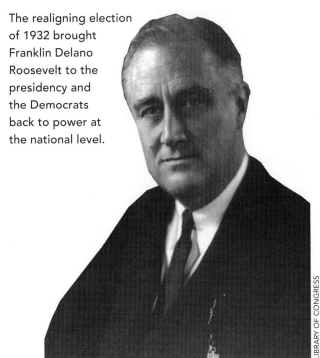

The realigning election of 1932 brought Franklin Delano Roosevelt to the presidency and the Democrats back to power at the national level.

the Whigs and the Democrats tried to avoid the issue of slavery.

By the mid-1850s, the Whig coalition had fallen apart, and most northern Whigs were absorbed into the new Republican Party, which opposed the extension of slavery into new territories. Campaigning on this platform in 1860, the Republicans succeeded in electing Abraham Lincoln—the first president elected under the banner of the new Republican Party.

7-1c From the Civil War to the Great Depression

When the former Confederate states rejoined the Union after the Civil War, the Republicans and Democrats were roughly even in strength, although the Republicans were more successful in presidential contests. In the 1890s, however, the Republicans gained a decisive advantage. In that decade, the Democrats allied themselves with the Populist movement, which consisted largely of indebted farmers in the West and South. The Populists—the People's Party—advocated inflation as a way of lessening their debts. Urban workers in the Midwest and East strongly opposed this program, which would erode the value of their paychecks. After the realigning election of 1896, the Republicans established themselves in the minds of many Americans as the party that knew how to manage the nation's economy.

As a result of a Republican split, the Democrats under Woodrow Wilson won power from 1912 to 1920. Otherwise, the Republicans remained dominant in national politics until the onset of the Great Depression.

7-1d After the Great Depression

The Great Depression of the 1930s destroyed the belief that the Republicans could better manage the economy and contributed to another realignment in the two-party system. In a realignment, the minority (opposition) party may emerge as the majority party, and this is certainly what happened in 1932. The election of 1932 brought Franklin D. Roosevelt to the presidency and the Democrats back to power at the national level.

A Civil Rights Plank Roosevelt's programs to fight the Depression were called the *New Deal*. Those who joined the Democrats during Roosevelt's New Deal included a substantial share of African Americans—Roosevelt's relief programs were open to people of all races. (Until the 1930s, African Americans had been overwhelmingly Republican.) In 1948, for the first time ever, the Democrats adopted a civil rights plank as part of the party platform at their national convention. A number of southern Democrats revolted and ran a separate States' Rights ticket for president.

In 1964, the Democrats, under incumbent president Lyndon Johnson, won a landslide victory, and liberals held a majority in Congress. In the political environment that produced this election result, a coalition of northern Democrats and Republicans crafted the major civil rights legislation that you read about in Chapter 5. The subsequent years were turbulent, with riots and marches in several major cities and student protests against the Vietnam War (1965–1975).

A "Rolling Realignment" Conservative Democrats did not like the direction in which their party seemed to be taking them. Under President Richard Nixon, the Republican Party was receptive to these conservative Democrats, and over a period of years, most of them became Republican voters. This was a major alteration in the political landscape, although it was not exclusively associated with a single election. Republican president Ronald Reagan helped cement the new Republican coalition.

TURNOVER IN CONGRESS. The Democrats continued to hold majorities in the House and Senate until 1994, but partisan labels were somewhat misleading. During the 1970s and 1980s, a large bloc of Democrats in Congress, mostly from the South, sided with the Republicans on almost all issues. In time, these conservative Democrats were replaced by conservative Republicans.

A CLOSELY DIVIDED NATION. The result of this "rolling realignment" was that the two major parties were fairly evenly matched. The elections of 2000 were a striking demonstration of how closely the electorate was now divided. Republican George W. Bush won the presidency in that year by carrying Florida with a margin of 537 votes. Democrat Al Gore actually received about half a million more popular votes than Bush. Following the elections, the Senate was made up of 50 Republicans and 50 Democrats. The Republicans controlled the House by a razor-thin margin of seven seats.

FOR CRITICAL THINKING

If you could create a new party, what would be its most important principles?

7–2 America's Political Parties Today

Historically, political parties drew together like-minded individuals. Today, too, individuals with similar characteristics tend to align themselves more often with one or the other major party. Such factors as race, age, income, education, marital status, and geography all influence party identification. For example, upper-income voters traditionally have been more likely to support the Republican Party. But is this still true today? We examine that question in this chapter's *Perception versus Reality* feature on page 150.

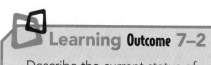

Learning **Outcome 7–2**

Describe the current status of the two major parties.

7–2a Red States versus Blue States

Geography is one of the many factors that can determine party identification. Examine the national electoral map shown in Figure 7–2 on the following page. In 2012, Republican Mitt Romney did well in the South, in the Great Plains, and in parts of the Midwest and Mountain West. Democrat Barack Obama did well in the Northeast, in parts of the Midwest, and on the West Coast. Beginning with the presidential elections of 2000, the press has made much of the supposed cultural differences between the "blue" states that vote for the Democratic candidate and the "red" states that vote for the Republican.[3] In reality, though, many states could better be described as "purple"—that is, a mixture of red and blue. These states could give their electoral votes to either party.

For another way to consider the influence of geography, see the map of Ohio in Figure 7–3 on page 149. Most of Ohio is red, and a quick glance might lead you to believe that Romney carried the state. In fact, Obama carried Ohio by a margin of 3 percentage points. Ohio looks red because Romney carried almost all of the rural parts of the state. The Obama counties had larger populations. This pattern was seen all over the country: the more urban the county, the more likely it was to vote Democratic.

7–2b Shifting Political Fortunes

As noted earlier, by 2000 the two major parties were very closely matched in terms of support. Public

FIGURE 7-2

The 2012 Presidential
Election Results

This map shows the 2012 presidential election results by state. While Barack Obama won the election, Mitt Romney picked up two states that Obama carried in 2008.

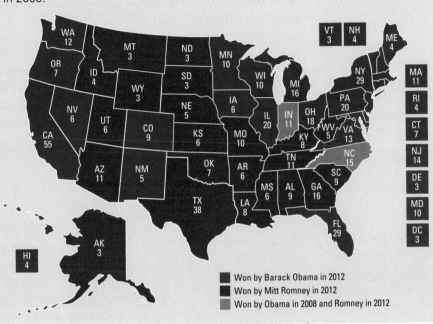

Won by Barack Obama in 2012
Won by Mitt Romney in 2012
Won by Obama in 2008 and Romney in 2012

sixty-three seats in the U.S. House to the Republicans, granting that party control of the chamber. (The Democrats still controlled the Senate.)

The 2012 Elections By 2011 and 2012, some were beginning to wonder whether the strong conservatism of the newly elected Republicans might be alienating independent voters. In fact, in the 2012 elections, Democratic presidential candidate Barack Obama prevailed by almost 4 percentage points. Democrats picked up a net two seats in the Senate and eight in the House. While these results were better for the Democrats than for the Republicans, they did nothing to change the partisan balance in the nation's capital.

opinion polls reported that voters continued to view the parties with roughly equal favor. But that situation soon began to shift.

Trouble for the Republicans During 2005, the seemingly endless war in Iraq began to cut into support for the Republicans. Even before the start of the Great Recession in December 2007, therefore, the Republicans were in trouble. In 2006, the Democrats regained control of the House and Senate. In 2008, in the shadow of a global financial crisis, Americans elected Democrat Barack Obama as president.

Trouble for the Democrats Within one year of Obama's inauguration, the Democratic advantage had vanished. Continued high rates of unemployment were one major reason. Also, a sharp increase in government activity during Obama's first two years in office appeared to bother many voters. A large economic stimulus package was followed by the bailout of Chrysler and General Motors. In 2010, Congress passed a major health-care reform package. Then, in November 2010, the voters handed an additional

The Triumph of Partisanship A key characteristic of recent politics has been the extreme partisanship of party activists and members of Congress. As noted earlier, in the 1960s, party coalitions included a variety of factions with differing politics. The rolling realignment after the elections of 1968 resulted in parties that were much more homogeneous. Political scientists have concluded that by 2009, the most conservative Democrat in the House was to the left of the most moderate Republican.

MAKING THE OTHER PARTY LOOK WEAK. Ideological uniformity has made it easier for the parties to maintain discipline in Congress. Personal friendships across party lines, once common in Congress, have become rare. The belief has grown that compromise with the other party is a form of betrayal. According to this view, the minority party should not attempt to improve legislation proposed by the majority. Instead, it should oppose majority-party measures in an effort to make the majority appear ineffective. The Republican Party has employed such tactics throughout Obama's term of office.

FIGURE 7-3

The 2012 Presidential
Election Results in Ohio

This map displays the Ohio counties carried by Barack Obama (blue) and Mitt Romney (red) in the 2012 presidential elections. The cities shown on the map are the ten most populous municipalities in Ohio. Obama did well in urban and suburban counties, but poorly in nonmetropolitan regions. (Note that one nonmetropolitan county that Obama carried contains a major university.)

THE IMPACT OF THE TEA PARTY MOVEMENT. Political polarization grew even more severe after the 2010 elections. Many of the new Republican members of Congress were pledged to the Tea Party philosophy of no-compromise conservatism. These members were fully prepared to revolt if the Republican leadership presented them with legislation that Democrats could support. Given that the Democrats still controlled the Senate and the presidency, political deadlock seemed inevitable.

THE DEBT-CEILING CRISIS. A key example of deadlock was the debt-ceiling crisis. Congress regularly must vote to lift the *debt ceiling*, the maximum sum that the federal government can borrow. Failure to lift the ceiling could force the federal government to default on its obligations. In the summer of 2011, House Republicans demanded massive federal spending cuts in exchange for raising the ceiling. The House leadership and President Obama reached a compromise at the very last moment. In a second confrontation in October 2013, House Republicans were forced to back down and suffered a serious loss in popularity.

7-2c Realignment, Dealignment, and Tipping

Despite the narrowness of the Republican margin after 2000, Republican strategists dreamed of a new realignment that would force the Democrats into the minority. These hopes were not fulfilled. After 2006, many Democrats anticipated a realignment that would benefit the Democrats. These dreams were shattered as well. For a major realignment to take place, a large number of voters must conclude that their party is no longer capable of representing their interests and ideals, and that another party can do better. It is hard to identify large groups of voters who could be swayed to support a different party today.

Dealignment One political development that may rule out realignment is the growth in the number of independent voters. By 2014, fully 42 percent of the electorate claimed to be independent. True, many of these voters admitted to leaning toward the Republicans or the Democrats. Still, anyone claiming to be an independent has a weakened attachment to the parties.

Some political scientists argue that with so many independent voters, the concept of realignment becomes irrelevant. Realignment has been replaced by **dealignment.** In such an environment, politics would be unusually volatile, because the large body of unattached independents could easily swing from one party to another. The dramatic changes in fortune experienced by the two major parties in recent years provide some evidence to support the dealignment theory. By 2013, as deadlock gripped the political system, the parties experienced record-high unfavorable scores in public opinion polls.

Tipping Realignment is not the only process that can alter the political landscape. What if the various types of voters maintain their political identifications—but one type of

> **dealignment** Among voters, a growing detachment from both major political parties.

Perception versus Reality

Wealthy People Are Republicans

Many people in the United States, as in most other countries, see the wealthy as conservative (on the political right). Likewise, the poor are seen as liberal (on the political left). In America, that means the wealthiest citizens should be Republicans and the poor should be Democrats.

THE PERCEPTION

The political left—Democrats and others—is united in favor of policies that help the poor. Democrats also dislike the rich and want to increase taxes on the wealthiest taxpayers. Consequently, the wealthy vote against Democrats because Democrats will raise their taxes. The rich therefore speak with one voice—a Republican voice.

THE REALITY

Consider the results of exit polling after the 2012 elections, in which Democrat Barack Obama won the presidency. As you move up the income ladder, you indeed see fewer votes for Obama. Families making from $100,000 to $200,000 per year were more Republican than those making $50,000 to $100,000. Moving up to the $200,000 to $250,000 category, however, support for Obama jumped from 44 percent to 47 percent. (It fell again above $250,000—but this last group consists precisely of those people whose taxes Obama proposed to raise.) We all know that many rich and famous Hollywood stars lean toward the left. In addition, many executives in high-tech companies are Democrats. Some are quite liberal indeed.

The fact is, there are conservatives *and* liberals among the rich—particularly, among the very rich. Class warfare is not on the American agenda. The cosmopolitan cultural attitudes of the wealthy cause many of them to favor liberal politics. Even when Democrats, including President Obama, talk about raising tax rates for the rich, many of these people believe that such policies are "fair." For example, at a Facebook forum with President Obama, Facebook founder Mark Zuckerberg said that he was "cool" with paying more in taxes.

Note, too, that many of the super-rich are not particularly affected by higher income tax rates. People like Zuckerberg receive most of their income as capital gains—notably as increases in the value of their stocks. Capital gains are taxed at a relatively low 15 percent rate. In contrast, tax rates on earned income can reach almost 40 percent. (Beginning in 2013, however, families with incomes over $250,000 pay 18.8 percent on capital gains, and those with incomes above $450,000 pay 23.8 percent.) In any event, it is certainly easier for the super-rich to support Democrats who want to raise income tax rates if they know that for the most part they are not going to pay those additional taxes.

BLOG ON You can check out recent exit polls for yourself. You'll see how income, education, race, religion, ideology, and many other variables affect people's votes. For the 2012 polls, try "exit polls 2012."

voter becomes substantially more numerous? This can happen due to migration between states or between nations, or even due to changes in education levels and occupations. The result could tip a state from one party to another. Many Democratic strategists believe that such *tipping* will benefit their party greatly in the future.

FOR CRITICAL THINKING

Demographers expect that minority group members will be a majority of the U.S. population by 2050. *How might this affect the two major parties?*

7–3 What Do Political Parties Do?

As noted earlier, the Constitution does not mention political parties. Historically, though, political parties have played a vital role in our democratic system. Their main function has been to link the people's policy preferences to actual government policies. Political parties also perform many other functions.

7–3a Selecting Candidates

One of the most important functions of the two political parties is to recruit and nominate candidates for political office. This function simplifies voting choices for the electorate. Political parties take the large number of people who want to run for office and narrow the field. They accomplish this by the use of the **primary,** which is a preliminary election to choose a party's final candidate. This candidate then runs against the opposing party's candidate in the general election.

Voter turnout for primaries is lower than it is for general elections. The voters who do go to the polls are often strong supporters of their party. Indeed, in many states, independents cannot participate in primary elections, even if they lean toward one or the other of the two major parties. As a result, the Republican primary electorate is very conservative, and Democratic primary voters are quite liberal. Candidates often find that they must run to the political right or left during the primaries. Traditionally, candidates then often moved to the center during the general election campaign. Chapter 9 provides much more detail on primary and general elections.

7–3b Informing the Public

Political parties help educate the public about important political issues. In recent years, these issues have included environmental policies, health-care reform, our tax system, immigration, and ways to stimulate the economy. Each party presents its views on these issues through television announcements, newspaper articles or ads, Web site materials, campaign speeches, and debates. These activities help citizens learn about the issues, form opinions, and consider proposed solutions.

7–3c Coordinating Policymaking

In our complex government, parties are essential for coordinating policy among the various branches of the government. The political party is usually the major institution through which the executive and legislative branches cooperate with each other. Each president, cabinet head, and member of Congress is normally a member of the Democratic Party or the Republican Party. The president works through party leaders in Congress to promote the administration's legislative program.

Ideally, the parties work together to fashion compromises—legislation that is acceptable to both parties and that serves the national interest. Yet in recent years, as we noted earlier, there has been little bipartisanship in Congress. (For a more detailed discussion of the role played by political parties in Congress, see Chapter 11.)

primary A preliminary election held for the purpose of choosing a party's final candidate.

SCOTT EELLS/BLOOMBERG VIA GETTY IMAGES

Delegates from Texas at the Republican National Convention Tampa, Florida, in August 2012. What kinds of people might Texas send to a Republican convention?

Parties also act as the glue of our federal structure by connecting the various levels of government—state and national—with a common bond.

7-3d Checking the Power of the Governing Party

The party with fewer members in the legislature is the **minority party.** The party with more members is the **majority party.** The party that does not control Congress or a state legislature, or the presidency or a state governorship, also plays a vital function in American politics. The "out" party does what it can to influence the "in" party and its policies, and to check the actions of the party in power.

For example, depending on how evenly Congress is divided, the out party, or minority party, may be able to attract to its side some of the members of the majority party to pass or defeat certain legislation. The minority party will also work to inform voters of the shortcomings of the majority party's agenda and to plan strategies for winning the next election.

7-3e Balancing Competing Interests

Political parties are often described as vast umbrellas under which Americans with diverse interests can gather. Political parties are essentially **coalitions**— alliances of individuals and groups with a variety of interests and opinions who join together to support the party's platform, or parts of it.

The Democratic Party, for example, includes a number of groups with different views on such issues as health care, immi-

minority party The political party that has fewer members in the legislature than the opposing party.

majority party The political party that has more members in the legislature than the opposing party.

coalition An alliance of individuals or groups with a variety of interests and opinions who join together to support all or part of a political party's platform.

electorate All of the citizens eligible to vote in a given election.

gration, and climate change. The role of party leaders in this situation is to adopt a view broad enough on these issues that no group will be alienated. In this way, different groups can hold their individual views and still come together under the umbrella of the Democratic Party.

Leaders of both the Democratic Party and the Republican Party modify contending views and arrange compromises among different groups. In so doing, the parties help to unify, rather than divide, their members.

7-3f Running Campaigns

Through their national, state, and local organizations, parties coordinate campaigns. Political parties take care of a large number of small and routine tasks that are essential to the smooth functioning of the electoral process. For example, they work at getting party members registered and at conducting drives to recruit new voters. Sometimes, party volunteers staff the polling places.

FOR CRITICAL THINKING

Presidents often have political goals that are different from those of senators and representatives from the president's own party. *What might such goals be?*

7-4 How American Political Parties Are Structured

Each of the two major American political parties consists of three components: the party in the electorate, the party organization, and the party in government.

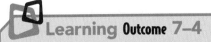

Learning Outcome 7-4

Discuss the structure of American political parties.

1. The party in the **electorate** is the largest component, consisting of all of those people who describe themselves as Democrats or Republicans. In most states, a voter can register as a Democrat or a Republican, but registration can be changed at will.

2. Each major party has a nationwide organization with national, state, and local offices. As will be

discussed later in this section, the party organizations include several levels of people who maintain the party's strength between elections, make its rules, raise money, organize conventions, help with elections, and recruit candidates.

3. The party in government consists of all of the party's candidates who have won elections and now hold public office. Even though candidates above the local level almost always run for office as either Democrats or Republicans, members of a given party do not always agree with one another on government policy. The party in government helps to organize the government's agenda by coaxing and convincing its own party members in office to vote for its policies. If the party is to translate its promises into public policies, the job must be done by the party in government.

7–4a The Party in the Electorate

Let's look more closely at the largest component of each party—the party in the electorate. What does it mean to belong to a political party? In many European countries, being a party member means that you actually join a political party. You get a membership card to carry in your wallet, you pay dues, and you vote to select your local and national party leaders. In the United States, becoming a member of a political party is far less involved.

In most states, voters may declare a party preference when they register to vote. This declaration allows them to participate in party primaries. Some states do not register party preferences, however. In short, to be a member of a political party, an American citizen has only to think of herself or himself as a Democrat or a Republican (or a member of a third party, such as the Green Party or the Libertarian Party). Members of parties do not have to work for the party or attend party meetings. Nor must they support the party platform.

Identifiers and Activists Generally, the party in the electorate consists of **party identifiers** (those who identify themselves as being members of the party) and **party activists**—party members who choose to work for the party and even become candidates for office. Political parties need year-round support from the latter group to survive. During election campaigns in particular, candidates depend on active party members and volunteers to answer phones, conduct door-to-door canvasses, participate in Web campaigns, organize speeches and appearances, and, of course, donate money.

Between elections, parties also need active members to plan the upcoming elections, organize fundraisers, and stay in touch with party leaders in other communities to keep the party strong. The major functions of American political parties are carried out by the party activists.

Why People Join Political Parties In a few countries, such as the People's Republic of China, people belong to a political party because they are required to do so to get ahead in life, regardless of whether they agree with the party's ideas and candidates. In the United States, though, people generally belong to a political party because they agree with many of its main ideas and support some of its candidates. Just as with interest groups, people's reasons for choosing one party over another may include solidarity, material, and purposive incentives.

SOLIDARITY INCENTIVES. Some people join a particular party to express their **solidarity,** or mutual agreement, with the views of friends, loved ones, and other like-minded people. People also join parties because they enjoy the excitement of engaging in politics with like-minded others.

MATERIAL INCENTIVES. Many believe that by joining a party, they will benefit materially through better employment or personal career advancement. The traditional institution of **patronage**—rewarding the party faithful with government jobs or contracts—lives on, even though it has been limited to prevent abuses.[4] Back in the nineteenth century, when almost all government employees got their jobs through patronage, people spoke of it as the "spoils system," as in "the spoils of war."

PURPOSIVE INCENTIVES. Finally, some join political parties because they wish to actively promote a set of ideals and principles that they feel are important to American politics and society. As a rule, people join

party identifier
A person who identifies himself or herself as being a supporter of a particular political party.

party activist A party member who helps to organize and oversee party functions and planning during and between campaigns, and may even become a candidate for office.

solidarity Mutual agreement among the members of a particular group.

patronage A system of rewarding the party faithful and workers with government jobs or contracts.

political parties because of their overall agreement with what a particular party stands for.

Thus, when asked why they support the Democratic Party, people may make such remarks as the following: "It seems that the economy is better when the Democrats are in control." "The Democrats are for the working people." People might say about the Republican Party: "The Republicans favor a smaller government than the Democrats do." "The Republicans deal better with national defense issues."

Texas delegates to the 2012 Democratic National Convention in Charlotte, North Carolina. What kinds of Texans are likely to attend a Democratic convention?

DANIEL ACKER/BLOOMBERG VIA GETTY IMAGES

7–4b The Party Organization

In theory, each of the major American political parties has a standard, pyramid-shaped organization. This theoretical structure is much like that of a large company, in which the bosses are at the top and the employees are at various lower levels.

Actually, neither major party is a closely knit or highly organized structure. Both parties are fragmented and *decentralized,* which means there is no central power with a direct chain of command. If there were, the national chairperson of the party, along with the national committee, could simply dictate how the organization would be run, just as if it were Apple or Google. In reality, state party organizations are all very different and are only loosely tied to the party's national structure. Local party organizations are often quite independent from the state organization.

In short, no single individual or group directs all party members. Instead, a number of personalities, frequently at odds with one another, form loosely identifiable leadership groups.

ward A local unit of a political party's organization, consisting of a division or district within a city.

precinct A political district within a city, such as a block or a neighborhood, or a rural portion of a county; the smallest voting district at the local level.

State Organizations

The powers and duties of state party organizations differ from state to state. In general, the state party organization is built around a central committee and a chairperson. The committee works to raise funds, recruit new party members, maintain a strong party organization, and help members running for state offices.

The state chairperson is usually a powerful party member chosen by the committee. In some instances, however, the chairperson is selected by the governor or a senator from that state.

Local Organizations

Local party organizations differ greatly, but generally there is a party unit for each district in which elective offices are to be filled. These districts include congressional and legislative districts, counties, cities and towns, wards, and precincts.

A **ward** is a political division or district within a city. A **precinct** can be either a political district within a

"Under democracy one party always devotes its chief energies to trying to prove that the other party is **unfit to rule**—and both commonly succeed."

~ H. L. MENCKEN ~
AMERICAN JOURNALIST
1880–1956

Representative Debbie Wasserman Schultz (D., Fla.) is chair of the Democratic National Committee, and Reince Priebus is chair of the Republican National Committee.

city, such as a block or a neighborhood, or a rural portion of a county. Polling places are located within the precincts. The local, grassroots foundations of politics are formed within voting precincts.

The National Party Organization

On the national level, the party's presidential candidate is considered to be the leader of the party. Well-known members of Congress may also be viewed as national party leaders. In addition to the party leaders, the structure of each party includes four major elements: the national convention, the national committee, the national chairperson, and the congressional campaign committees.

THE NATIONAL CONVENTION. Much of the public attention that the party receives comes at the **national convention,** which is held every four years during the summer before the presidential elections. The news media always cover these conventions, and as a result, they have become quite extravagant. Lobbyists, big business, and interest groups provide millions of dollars to put on these events. Such organizations have an interest in government subsidies, tax breaks, and regulatory favors.

The conventions inspire and mobilize party members throughout the nation. They provide the voters with an opportunity to see and hear the can-

didates directly, rather than through a media filter or characterizations provided by supporters and opponents. Candidates' speeches at conventions draw huge audiences. For example, in 2012 more than 30 million people watched the acceptance speeches of Barack Obama and Mitt Romney.

The national conventions are attended by delegates chosen by the states in various ways, which we describe in Chapter 9. The delegates' most important job is to nominate the party's presidential and vice-presidential candidates, who together make up the **party ticket.** Key delegates also write the **party platform,** which sets forth the party's positions on national issues. Essentially, through its platform, the party promises to initiate certain policies if it wins the presidency. Despite the widespread perception that candidates can and do ignore these promises once they are in office, in fact, many of the promises become law.

national convention The meeting held by each major party every four years to nominate presidential and vice-presidential candidates, write a party platform, and conduct other party business.

party ticket A list of a political party's candidates for various offices. In national elections, the party ticket consists of the presidential and vice-presidential candidates.

party platform The document drawn up by each party at its national convention that outlines the policies and positions of the party.

THE NATIONAL COMMITTEE. Each state elects a number of delegates to the **national party committee.** The Republican National Committee and the Democratic National Committee direct the business of their respective parties during the four years between national conventions. The committees' most important duties, however, are to organize the next national convention and to plan how to obtain a party victory in the next presidential election.

THE NATIONAL CHAIRPERSON. Each party's national committee elects a **national party chairperson** to serve as administrative head of the national party. The main duty of the national chairperson is to direct the work of the national committee from party headquarters in Washington, D.C. The chairperson is involved in raising funds, providing for publicity, promoting party unity, encouraging the development of state and local organizations, recruiting new voters, and other activities. In presidential election years, the chairperson's attention is focused on the national convention and the presidential campaign.

THE CONGRESSIONAL CAMPAIGN COMMITTEES. Each party has a campaign committee in each chamber of Congress. In each chamber, members are chosen by their colleagues and serve for two-year terms. The committees work to help elect party members to Congress.

7-4c The Party in Government: Developing Issues

When a political party wins the presidency or control of one or more chambers of Congress, it has the opportunity to carry out the party platform it developed at its national convention. The platform represents the official party position on various issues, although neither all party members nor all candidates running on the party's ticket are likely to share these positions exactly.

FOR CRITICAL THINKING

The parties often hope they can win additional votes in a state by holding their national convention in that state. *Do you think this strategy is likely to be effective? Why or why not?*

7-5 The Dominance of Our Two-Party System

In the United States, we have a **two-party system.** This means that the two major parties—the Democrats and the Republicans—dominate national politics. Why has the two-party system become so firmly entrenched in the United States? According to some scholars, the first major political division between the Federalists and the Anti-Federalists established a precedent that continued over time and ultimately resulted in the domination of the two-party system.

Learning Outcome 7-5

Describe the different types of third parties and how they function in the American political system.

7-5a The Self-Perpetuation of the Two-Party System

One of the major reasons for the perpetuation of the two-party system is simply that there is no alternative. Minor parties, called **third parties,**[5] have found it extremely difficult to compete with the major parties for votes. There are many reasons for this, some of which are described in the following subsections.

Political Socialization

When young people or new immigrants learn about U.S. politics, they tend to absorb the political views of those who are providing them with information. Parents find it easy to pass their political beliefs on to their children, often without even trying. Those beliefs frequently involve support for one of the two major parties. To be sure, up to two-fifths of voters today regard themselves as independents (although they may lean toward one party or another). These voters apparently believe that neither major party fully represents their views. Such attitudes, however, do not mean that independents are looking for a third party. Typically, true independents are content to swing between the Democrats and the Republicans.

Election Laws Favoring Two Parties

American election laws tend to favor the major parties. In many states, for example, the established major parties need relatively few signatures to place their candidates on the ballot, whereas a third party must get many more signatures. The number of signatures required is often based on the total party vote in the last election, which penalizes a new party that is competing for the first time. The rules governing campaign financing also favor the major parties.

Institutional Barriers to a Multiparty System

The structure of many of our institutions prevents third parties from enjoying electoral success. The nature of the election process works against third-party candidates, as does the nature of single-member districts.

THE ELECTION PROCESS. One of the major institutional barriers is the election, by the people, of governors and (through the electoral college) the president. Voting for governors and members of the electoral college takes place on a statewide, winner-take-all basis. (Maine and Nebraska are exceptions—they can, under certain circumstances, split their electoral votes.) Third-party candidates find it hard to win when they must campaign statewide instead of appealing to voters in a smaller district that might be more receptive to their political positions.

> "I am not a member of any organized political party.
> **I AM A DEMOCRAT."**
> ~ WILL ROGERS ~
> AMERICAN HUMORIST
> 1879–1935

BETTMANN/CORBIS

BETTMANN/CORBIS

Most colleges and universities have mascots that represent their athletic teams. So, too, do the two major political parties. On the left, you see the donkey that became the Democratic Party mascot. On the right, you see the elephant that became the Republican Party mascot.[6]

The popular election of executive officers contrasts with the parliamentary system described in *The Rest of the World* feature in Chapter 2. In that system, parliament—not the voters—chooses the nation's executive officers. Third-party voters therefore have a greater chance of affecting the outcome by electing a few members of parliament.

SINGLE-MEMBER DISTRICTS VERSUS PROPORTIONAL SYSTEMS. Another institutional barrier to a multiparty system is the single-member district. Today, all federal and most state legislative districts are single-member districts—that is, voters elect one member from their district to the House of Representatives and to their state legislature.[7] In some countries, by contrast, districts are drawn as multimember districts and are represented by multiple elected officials from different parties, according to the proportion of the vote each party received.

In many democracies that use single-member districts to choose members of parliament, additional members are chosen from statewide or nationwide party lists. The number of additional members elected from the party lists is calculated to guarantee that the election results are *proportional*. Under a proportional election system, one party might receive 40 percent of the national vote, another party 35 percent, and a third party 25 percent. Each party can expect to obtain a share of seats in the national parliament that closely reflects its percentage of the vote.

NONPARTISAN ELECTIONS. While third parties are rarely successful in the United States, the two major parties do not compete in all elections. Some state offices and many local offices are filled by *nonpartisan elections,* in which party identification never appears on the ballot. Are there benefits to the nonpartisan system? We examine that question in this chapter's *Join the Debate* feature on the following page.

7-5b Third Parties in American Politics

Despite difficulties, throughout American history third parties have competed for influence in the nation's two-party system. Indeed, as mentioned earlier, third parties

have been represented in most of our national elections. These parties are as varied as the causes they represent, but all have one thing in common: their members and leaders want to challenge the major parties because they believe that certain needs and values are not being properly addressed.

Some third parties have tried to appeal to the entire nation. Others have focused on particular regions, states, or local areas. Most third parties have been short lived. A few, however, such as the Socialist Party (founded in 1901 and disbanded in 1972), lasted for a long time. The number and variety of third parties make them difficult to classify, but most fall into one of the general categories discussed in the following subsections.

Issue-Oriented Parties An issue-oriented third party is formed to promote a particular cause or timely issue. For example, the Free Soil Party was organized in 1848 to oppose the expansion of slavery into the western territories. The Prohibition Party was formed in 1869 to advocate banning the manufacture and use of alcoholic beverages.

Most issue-oriented parties fade into history as the issue that brought them into existence fades from public attention, is taken up by a major party, or is resolved. Some issue-oriented parties endure, however, when they expand their focus beyond a single area of concern. For example, the Green Party was founded in 1972 to raise awareness of environmental issues, but it is no longer a single-issue party. Today, the Green Party campaigns against alleged corporate greed and the major parties' ostensible indifference to a number of issues, including poverty, the excesses of globalism, and the failure of the war on drugs.

Ideological Parties As discussed in Chapter 1, a *political ideology* is a system of political ideas rooted in beliefs about human nature, society, and government. An ideological party supports a particular political doctrine or a set of beliefs.

For example, the (still-existing) Socialist Labor Party believes that our free enterprise system should be replaced by one in which workers control all of the factories in the economy. The party's members believe that competition should be replaced by cooperation

"Let us not seek the Republican answer or the Democratic answer, but the **right answer.**"

~ JOHN FITZGERALD KENNEDY ~
THIRTY-FIFTH PRESIDENT
OF THE UNITED STATES
1961–1963

JOIN THE DEBATE

Are Nonpartisan Elections a Good Idea?

It's hard to miss the partisan battles in Washington, D.C. To a lesser extent, nasty fights also occur in state legislatures and even city councils. As you've learned, the framers of the U.S. Constitution never mentioned political parties. They thought that the nation would be better off without them. Dream on. We will never eliminate partisan elections at the federal level. But what about the state and, particularly, the local levels? Would the states be better off with nonpartisan elections?

Take the Nastiness Out of Elections—Go Nonpartisan

Advocates of nonpartisan elections believe that the two major political parties are the reason that many states are "ungovernable." Political deadlock would be eliminated if state senators and representatives were voted into office without a party label.

Currently, ideological activists—Republicans and Democrats—largely determine the identity of state legislative candidates. Where does that leave independents and moderates? The answer is: underrepresented.

More than two-thirds of American cities have embraced nonpartisan voting. After all, local issues are very different from national ones, and knowing that a candidate is a Republican or a Democrat tells you little about that candidate's policy positions on local issues. It's time to extend nonpartisan elections to state legislatures as well. Nebraska, for one, has such a legislature already.

Nonpartisan Elections Lead to Less-Informed Voters

While enticing in theory, nonpartisan elections do not result in better government. In some nonpartisan systems, candidates are still affiliated with political parties. Even so, without party labels on the ballot, citizens find it more difficult to cast an informed vote. Ordinary citizens cannot take the time to analyze in any detail the political positions of legislative candidates. Take the example of nonpartisan state elections in Minnesota before 1973. There, prominent local figures were able to win elections even when their politics were unrepresentative of their districts. After partisan labels were introduced in 1973, the state legislature was transformed.

According to law professor David Schleicher, nonpartisan balloting at the city level also leaves voters poorly informed and reduces turnout in elections. True, party labels provide less information in municipal contests than in national elections. They provide at least *some* information, however, and without them, citizens often know nothing at all. As a result, Schleicher says, voters tend to rely on racial or ethnic clues in candidates' names.

FOR CRITICAL ANALYSIS If you were independently wealthy and could finance an expensive campaign, would you prefer partisan or nonpartisan elections? Why?

---

and social responsibility so as to achieve an equitable distribution of income. In contrast, the Libertarian Party opposes almost all forms of government interference with personal liberties and private enterprise.

Splinter or Personality Parties A splinter party develops out of a split within a major party. This split may be part of an attempt to elect a specific person. For example, when Theodore Roosevelt did not receive the Republican Party's nomination for president in 1912, he created the Bull Moose Party (also called the Progressive Party) to promote his candi-

dacy. From the Democrats have come Henry Wallace's Progressive Party and the States' Rights (Dixiecrat) Party, both formed in 1948. In 1968, the American Independent Party was formed to support George Wallace's campaign for president.

Most splinter parties have been formed around a leader with a strong personality, which is why they are sometimes called *personality parties*. When that person steps aside, the party usually collapses. An example of a personality party is the Reform Party, which was formed in 1996 mainly to provide a campaign vehicle for H. Ross Perot.

Green Party presidential candidate Jill Stein and Libertarian Party candidate Gary Johnson at a debate hosted by the Free and Equal Elections Foundation in 2012.

BOTH PHOTOS BY SCOTT OLSON/GETTY IMAGES

Presidential Candidate
JILL STEIN
Green Party

Presidential Candidate
GARY JOHNSON
Libertarian Party

7–5c The Effects of Third Parties

Although most Americans do not support third parties or vote for their candidates, third parties have influenced American politics in several ways.

Third Parties Bring Issues to the Public's Attention

Third parties have brought many political issues to the public's attention. They have exposed and focused on unpopular or highly debated issues that major parties have preferred to ignore. Third parties are in a position to take bold stands on issues that major parties avoid because third parties are not trying to be all things to all people.

Some people have argued that third parties are often the unsung heroes of American politics, bringing new issues to the forefront of public debate. Progressive social reforms such as the minimum wage, women's right to vote, railroad and banking legislation, and old-age pensions were first proposed by third parties. The Free Soilers of the 1850s were the first true antislavery party, and the Populists and Progressives put many social reforms on the political agenda. Although some of the ideas proposed by third parties were never accepted, others were taken up by the major parties as those ideas became increasingly popular.

Third Parties Can Affect the Vote

Third parties can also influence election outcomes. On occasion, they have taken victory from one major party and given it to another, thus playing the "spoiler" role.

For example, in 1912, when the Progressive Party split from the Republican Party, the result was three major contenders for the presidency: Woodrow Wilson, the Democratic candidate; William Howard Taft, the regular Republican candidate; and Theodore Roosevelt, the Progressive candidate. The presence of the Progressive Party "spoiled" the Republicans' chances for victory and gave the election to Wilson, the Democrat. Without Roosevelt's third party, Taft might have won. Similarly, some commentators contended that Green Party candidate Ralph Nader "spoiled" the chances of Democratic candidate Al Gore in the 2000 elections, because many of those who voted for Nader would have voted Democratic had Nader not been on the ballot.

Third Parties Provide a Voice for Dissatisfied Americans

Third parties also provide a voice for voters who are frustrated with and alienated from the Republican and Democratic parties. Americans who are unhappy with the two major political parties can still participate in American politics through third parties that reflect their opinions on political issues. For example, many new Minnesota voters turned out during the 1998 elections to vote for Jesse Ventura, a Reform Party candidate for governor in that state. Ventura won.

Ultimately, third parties in national elections find it difficult to break through in an electoral system that perpetuates their failure. Because third parties normally do not win elections, Americans tend not to vote for them or to contribute to their campaigns, so they continue not to win. As long as Americans hold on to the perception that third parties can never win big in an election, the current two-party system is likely to persist.

FOR CRITICAL THINKING

Some have argued that, given the polarization of the two major parties, Americans should organize a new party based on moderate politics. *Why might such an initiative fail—or succeed?*

AMERICA AT ODDS Political Parties

By their very nature, arguments about the parties are some of the most divisive conflicts in politics. We can list only a sampling of the disputes:

- Is the Republican Party, through excessive conservatism, driving off voters that it needs—or can it win by upholding basic conservative values? For that matter, are the Democrats too liberal—or not liberal enough?

- Is it better when the two chambers of Congress and the presidency are held by the same party, thus guaranteeing effective government—or is it better when Congress and the presidency are held by different parties, so that the two parties can check each other?

- Is the increasing importance of political independents a positive development—or is it a sign that citizens are becoming dangerously detached from our political system?

- Are political parties desirable and inevitable—or should elections be nonpartisan whenever possible?

- Is it better to support a third party when you are in greater agreement with its positions than with those of either major party—or should you avoid wasting your vote and always support the major party that is closer to your politics?

- Finally, looking forward, do the Republicans or the Democrats offer the best solutions for our problems?

STUDY TOOLS

Ready to study?

- **Review** what you've read with the quiz below.
- Check your answers on the **Chapter in Review** card at the back of the book.
- For any questions you miss, read the corresponding **Learning Outcome** section again to prepare for class and your exam.
- Rip out and study the **Chapter in Review** card (at the back of the book).

Fill-In

Learning Outcome 7–1

1. The nation's first two political parties, the _____, clashed openly in the elections of 1796.

2. In 1860, Abraham Lincoln became the first president elected under the banner of the new _____ Party.

Learning Outcome 7–2

3. Dealignment among voters refers to _____.

Learning Outcome 7–3

4. Political parties link the people's policy preferences to actual government policies. Parties also perform many other functions, including _____.

5. A _____ is a preliminary election held for the purpose of choosing a party's final candidate.

Learning Outcome 7–4

6. The Republican and Democratic candidates for president and vice president are nominated at each party's _____.

7. A party platform is _____.

Learning Outcome 7–5

8. Third parties have influenced American politics in several ways, including _____.

Multiple Choice

Learning Outcome 7–1

9. _____ refers to a process in which a substantial number of voters change their political allegiance, which usually also changes the balance of power between the two major parties.
   a. Realignment   b. Dealignment   c. Tipping

10. After the election of 1896, the _____ established themselves in the minds of many Americans as the party that knew how to manage the nation's economy, and they remained dominant in national politics until the onset of the Great Depression.
    a. Democrats   b. Republicans   c. Whigs

Learning Outcome 7–2

11. After the 2010 elections, many of the new Republican members of Congress were pledged to the Tea Party philosophy of
    a. moving the Republican Party toward more liberal positions.
    b. breaking political deadlock in Washington to solve national problems.
    c. no-compromise conservatism.

Learning Outcome 7–3

12. Which of the following statements best describes the way in which political parties perform the function of balancing competing interests?
    a. The political party is usually the major institution through which the executive and legislative branches cooperate with each other.
    b. Political parties are essentially coalitions—alliances of individuals and groups with a variety of concerns and opinions who join together to support the party's platform or parts of it.
    c. Political parties take the large number of people who want to run for office and narrow the field.

Learning Outcome 7–4

13. To be a member of a political party in the United States, a citizen
    a. must join the party and pay membership dues.
    b. must support the party platform.
    c. has only to think of himself or herself as a Democrat or a Republican (or a member of a third party).

Learning Outcome 7–5

14. An issue-oriented third party
    a. supports a particular political doctrine or a set of beliefs.
    b. is formed to promote a particular cause.
    c. is also referred to as a splinter party.

GOVT

8

Public Opinion and Voting

The **Learning Outcomes** labeled 1 through 4 are designed to help improve your understanding of the chapter. After reading this chapter, you should be able to:

8–1 Explain how public opinion polls are conducted, problems with polls, and how they are used in the political process.

8–2 Describe the political socialization process.

8–3 Discuss the different factors that affect voter choices.

8–4 Indicate some of the factors that affect voter turnout, and discuss what has been done to improve voter turnout and voting procedures.

Remember to visit page 186 for additional Study Tools

Learning Outcomes

DAVID BECKER/GETTY IMAGES

163

AMERICA AT
ODDS
Do New State Laws Interfere with Voting Rights?

WILLIAM THOMAS CAIN/MCT VIA GETTY IMAGES

In 1965, Congress passed the Voting Rights Act. The goal was to stop efforts by state and local governments, particularly in the South, to keep African Americans from voting. One provision of the act was that state and local governments with a history of violating voters' rights must obtain "preclearance" for changes to voting rules and district boundaries from the federal government.

In 2013, however, the United States Supreme Court threw out the formula in the act that determined which states and localities must obtain preclearance. The Court argued that the formula was unacceptable because it was based on forty-year-old data. State governments in the South and elsewhere quickly implemented new voting laws. The most common change was to require voters to show photo identification at the polls, but other new laws were adopted as well.

The goal of the new state laws, according to state officials, was to reduce voter fraud. While no one is in favor of voter fraud, many argue that the new laws did more harm than good because they restricted voting rights. The Obama administration mounted challenges to many of these new laws under clauses of the Voting Rights Act that remained in effect. Attorney General Eric Holder said that the administration planned to "use every tool" at its disposal to maintain federal oversight of voting, despite the Supreme Court's decision. Did the attorney general overreact? Do new state laws truly interfere with voting rights?

Fewer Eligible Voters Will Vote

According to columnist Harold Meyerson of the *Los Angeles Times*, "Voter fraud is a myth—not an urban or a real myth, as such, but a Republican one." He argues that Republicans have raised the specter of voter fraud to pass laws that make it harder for disadvantaged persons (mostly Democrats) to vote.

For example, at least eight states have introduced legislation requiring proof of citizenship, such as a birth certificate or a passport, to register to vote. Many poorer citizens—especially minority group members—do not have these documents. Other states have eliminated same-day registration on Election Day. In some states, young citizens lost the right to "preregister" to vote before they turned eighteen. Some states decided to reduce early voting—a practice that minorities have used more than others. North Carolina, for example, eliminated Sunday early voting. In that state, African American church congregations had adopted the practice of marching as a group to polling places at the conclusion of Sunday services.

Much Ado About Nothing

Those who support the new state voting laws argue that photo ID requirements do not restrict anyone's rights. After all, Americans have to show their IDs when they cash a check or board an airplane. Violations of voting laws continue to occur. Felons, for example—who are not allowed to vote in many states—may end up voting anyway. Support for ID requirements exists even within some minority communities. Polls show that Hispanic Texans support the requirement. In Texas, anyone can get the necessary ID free of charge, so poverty cannot be an excuse not to obtain it.

Also, many states have recently passed laws to make voting more convenient. Colorado now allows Election Day registration, as well as preregistration of eligible young people. Maryland has expanded its early voting system. Today, Virginia and West Virginia provide online registration. True, some states have tightened the rules, but overall, it is as easy to vote now as it ever was.

Where do you stand?

1. Given that a photo ID is required to board an airplane, do you think one should be required to vote? If so, why? If not, why not?
2. Some people claim that minority groups can counteract any negative effect of restrictive voting rules by increased turnout at the polls. How easy would it be to do that? Explain.

Explore this issue online

- For a spirited defense of Texas voting laws by the state's attorney general, type "abbot washington times" into a search engine.
- The liberal Daily Kos blog opposes legislation that restricts voting—search on "kos voting."
- For a roundup of recent changes to state voting laws, visit the Brennan Center by entering "brennan voting."

Introduction

For a democracy to be effective, members of the public must form opinions and openly express them to their elected officials. Only when the opinions of Americans are communicated effectively to elected representatives can those opinions form the basis of government action.

Citizens use many methods to communicate with elected officials, including letters, e-mail, texting, telephone calls, and attendance at rallies or "town hall" meetings with representatives. The most accurate way of gauging overall public opinion between elections, however, is through public opinion polls, which we describe in this chapter.

The ultimate way that citizens communicate their views, of course, is by casting ballots for their preferred candidates. Many factors affect the political beliefs that motivate voters, and we discuss these factors in this chapter. We also look at the mechanics of voting, which can have a definite impact on election results.

8–1 Measuring Public Opinion

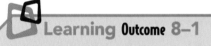

Learning Outcome 8–1

Explain how public opinion polls are conducted, problems with polls, and how they are used in the political process.

What exactly is **public opinion?** We define it as the sum total of a complex collection of opinions held by many people on issues in the public arena, such as taxes, health care, Social Security, clean-air legislation, and unemployment. When you hear a news report or read a magazine article stating that "a significant number of Americans" feel a certain way about an issue, you are probably hearing that a particular opinion is held by a large enough number of people to make government officials listen.

8–1a Public Opinion Polls

A **public opinion poll** is a survey of the public's opinion on a particular topic at a particular moment. The results of opinion polls are most often cast in terms of percentages: 62 percent feel this way, 31 percent do not, and 7 percent have no opinion.

Of course, a poll cannot survey the entire U.S. population. Therefore, public opinion pollsters have devised scientific polling techniques for measuring public opinion through the use of **samples**—groups of people who are typical of the general population.

8–1b Early Polling Efforts

Since the 1800s, magazines and newspapers have often spiced up their articles by conducting **straw polls** of readers' opinions. Straw polls simply ask a large number of people the same question. The problem with straw polls is that the opinions expressed usually represent an atypical subgroup of the population, or a **biased sample.** A survey of those who read *People* will most likely produce different results than a survey of those who read *Sports Illustrated*, for example.

The most famous of all straw-polling errors was committed by the *Literary Digest* in 1936 when it tried to predict the outcome of that year's presidential elections. The *Digest* forecast that Republican Alfred Landon would easily defeat Democratic incumbent Franklin D. Roosevelt. Instead, Roosevelt won by a landslide. The editors of the *Digest* had sent mail-in cards to names in telephone directories, to its own subscribers, and to automobile owners—a staggering 2,376,000 people. In the Depression year of 1936, however, people who owned a car or a telephone or who subscribed to the *Digest* were not representative of most Americans. The vast majority of Americans could not afford such luxuries. The sample turned out to be unrepresentative and consequently inaccurate.

Several newcomers to the public opinion poll industry, however, did

> "A government can be no better than the
> **PUBLIC OPINION**
> that sustains it."
>
> ~ FRANKLIN DELANO ROOSEVELT ~
> THIRTY-SECOND PRESIDENT
> OF THE UNITED STATES
> 1933–1945

public opinion The views of the citizenry about politics, public issues, and public policies; a complex collection of opinions held by many people on issues in the public arena.

public opinion poll A survey of the public's opinion on a particular topic at a particular moment.

sample In the context of opinion polling, a group of people selected to represent the population being studied.

straw poll A nonscientific poll in which there is no way to ensure that the opinions expressed are representative of the larger population.

biased sample A poll sample that does not accurately represent the population.

Nate Silver at a Chicago hotel. Silver, an unabashed numbers geek, correctly predicted the 2012 presidential winner in all fifty states and almost all the winners in the Senate races.

AP PHOTO/NAM Y. HUH

essential in the mid-twentieth century, when a surprisingly large number of homes did not have telephones.

In time, however, the number of homes without phones dwindled, and polling organizations determined that they could obtain satisfactory samples of voters through telephone interviews alone. In recent years, poll takers have even replaced human interviewers with prerecorded messages that solicit responses. Such methods allow companies to conduct very large numbers of polls at little cost. Questions have arisen as to whether automated polling is as accurate as polling that uses live interviewers, however.

Further complications for telephone poll takers include the increase in the use of cell phones—which not all pollsters bother to call. Today, many cell phone users no longer have a landline number. An additional problem is the public's growing use of Skype and other Internet-based telephone systems. Poll takers have not yet determined a way to integrate such users into their polls. Finally, a growing number of people simply refuse to participate in telephone surveys.

Technological advances have opened up a new possibility—the Internet survey. The Harris Poll now specializes in this type of research. As when telephone interviews were introduced, serious questions exist as to whether the samples obtained by Harris and other Internet polling firms can be representative. Internet usage has become extremely widespread, but it is still not universal.

SOCIAL MEDIA
In Politics

For a storm of tweets on public opinion polling—and sports—join statistical expert Nate Silver on Twitter by following "fivethirtyeight."

predict Roosevelt's victory. Two of these organizations are still at the forefront of the polling industry today: the Gallup Organization, started by George Gallup, and Roper Associates, founded by Elmo Roper and now known as the Roper Center.

8–1c Polling Today

Today, polling is used extensively by political candidates and policymakers. Politicians and the news media generally place a great deal of faith in the accuracy of poll results. Polls can be quite accurate when they are conducted properly. In the twenty presidential elections in which Gallup has participated, its polls conducted in late October correctly predicted the winner in sixteen of the races.[1] Even polls taken several months in advance have been able to predict the eventual winner.

random sample In the context of opinion polling, a sample in which each person within the entire population being polled has an equal chance of being chosen.

Types of Polls
In the earliest days of scientific polling, interviewers typically went door to door locating respondents. Such in-person surveys were

Sampling Today, the most reputable polls sample between 1,500 and 2,000 people. How can interviewing such a small group possibly indicate what millions of voters think? To be successful, a sample must consist of people who are typical of the population. If the sample is not properly chosen, then the results of the poll may not reflect the beliefs of the general population.

The most important principle in sampling is randomness. A **random sample** means that each person within the entire population being polled has an equal chance of being chosen. For example, if a poll is trying to measure how women feel about an issue, the sample should include respondents from all groups within the female population in proportion to their percentage in the entire population. A properly drawn random sample would include appropriate numbers of women in terms of age, race and ethnicity, geography, income, and religious affiliation.

What Polls Really Tell Us As noted earlier, poll results are almost always publicized using exact numbers. A typical result would be that 80 percent of those polled are partly or completely dissatisfied with the actions of the U.S. Congress, 12 percent are partly or completely satisfied, and 8 percent have no opinion. Figures such as these, though, can provide a misleading picture of what the poll is actually saying. Public opinion polls are fundamentally *statistical*. The true result of a poll is not a single figure, but a range of probabilities. In the example just given, the figure 80 percent is merely the midpoint of all the possible results.

A professional polling firm might state of a given poll that it has "95 percent confidence that the maximum margin of sampling error is plus or minus 4 percentage points." (**Sampling error** is the difference between what the poll shows and what the results would have been if *everyone* in the relevant population had been interviewed.) To claim "95 percent confidence" means that there is one chance in twenty that this poll is off by four points or more. The 95 percent figure is an industry standard. That means that out of the thousands of polls released every year, 5 percent are expected to yield results that are outside their own margin of error.

It follows that there is not much point in paying attention to small, short-lived changes in polling results. Consider a polling firm's report that President Barack Obama's popularity rating was, in five consecutive weeks, 45 percent, 43 percent, 44 percent, 47 percent, and 45 percent. Do these figures mean that Obama was less popular in week two and more popular in week four? Almost certainly not. The fluctuation in the figures is most likely due to random error—it is statistical "noise."

Statistical Modeling and House Effects

Sampling error is not the only source of inaccuracy in public opinion polling. Another source of error follows from the fact that it is almost impossible to obtain a body of respondents that truly reflects the population at large. Many people refuse to be interviewed. Some kinds of people—including poor people and students—are hard to reach. In addition, it happens that women answer the telephone more frequently than do men.

WEIGHTING. Polling firms respond to these difficulties by *weighting* the responses of various groups. If the survey did not locate enough evangelical Christians, for example, the responses of the evangelicals who were contacted will be weighted more heavily. Thus, a pollster might double the numerical value of the answers provided by the evangelicals before adding the results back into the total sample. A pollster would do this if, in the initial sample, the number of evangelicals interviewed was half what it should have been. If the model that the pollster uses to weight the responses is flawed, however, the poll results will be off as well.

Weighting for purely demographic variables is a small part of the modeling problem. Errors are much more common when pollsters attempt to adjust for the number of Republicans, Democrats, and independents in their samples. Perhaps the greatest difficulty is determining who is likely to turn out and vote. In the months leading up to the 2012 elections, each major polling firm had its own model for weighting groups of respondents and determining who was a likely voter. Most of these models were trade secrets. One result of the differing models was a substantial variation in predicted results.

HOUSE EFFECTS. Based on their differing models, some polling firms consistently published results more favorable to one or the other of the two major parties than the results released by other pollsters. When a pollster's results appear to consistently favor one of the parties, polling experts refer to the phenomenon as a *house*

> "A popular government without popular information, or the means of acquiring it, is but
> ## A PROLOGUE TO A FARCE OR A TRAGEDY,
> or perhaps both."
>
> ~ JAMES MADISON ~
> FOURTH PRESIDENT OF THE UNITED STATES
> 1809–1817

sampling error In the context of opinion polling, the difference between what the sample results show and what the true results would have been had everybody in the relevant population been interviewed.

effect. Not surprisingly, firms that exhibited house effects in 2012 frequently had ties to the political party favored by their results.

The connection was not exact, however. Some partisan firms did not exhibit a house effect, and some pollsters who were well known for nonpartisanship did have one. Also, a firm with a house effect is not always wrong. It may be noticing something that most of its competitors have missed.

Bias in Framing Questions

To obtain accurate results, poll takers also want to ensure that there is no bias in their polling questions. How a question is phrased can significantly affect how people answer it.

AN EXAMPLE: THE BIRTH CONTROL CONTROVERSY.

Consider a dispute that arose in 2012. The Affordable Care Act—Obamacare—included a provision stating that qualifying employer-provided health-insurance plans should cover contraception, or birth control services. Churches opposed to contraception were exempt. The Obama administration, however, ruled that hospitals and colleges with religious affiliations were not exempt. The Catholic Church and several other bodies objected vehemently to this ruling. Republicans in Congress backed the churches.

What did the public think about the issue? Public opinion depended overwhelmingly on how the question was phrased. One poll asked whether the insurance plans of religiously affiliated institutions should be required to cover contraception. Respondents supported coverage 61 percent to 31 percent. A later poll by the same organization included the language "opt out based on religious and moral objections." This time, those interviewed agreed 57 percent to 36 percent that the institutions ought to be able to opt out.

Polls, in other words, came up with differing results based on whether respondents were encouraged to think about women's health or to consider religious liberties. (In the end, the administration announced a compromise that was acceptable to most church-affiliated schools and hospitals—but not the Catholic bishops, who filed a lawsuit.)

YES AND NO QUESTIONS.

Polling questions also sometimes reduce complex issues to questions that simply call for "yes" or "no" answers. For example, a survey question might ask respondents whether they favor giving aid to foreign countries. A respondent's opinion on the issue might vary depending on the recipient country or the purpose of the aid. The poll would nonetheless force the respondent to give a "yes" or "no" answer that does not fully reflect his or her opinion.

INADEQUATE INFORMATION.

Respondents sometimes answer "I don't know" or "I don't have enough information to answer," even when the poll does not offer such options. Interestingly, a study of how polling is conducted on the complex issue of school vouchers (school vouchers were discussed in Chapter 4) found that about 4 percent volunteered the answer "I don't know" when asked if they favored or opposed vouchers. When respondents were offered the option of answering "I haven't heard or read enough to answer," however, the proportion choosing that answer jumped to about 30 percent.[2]

OTHER PROBLEMS.

In addition to potential bias in framing questions, poll takers must also be concerned about other issues that affect the reliability of their polls. For example, respondents interviewed may be influenced by the interviewer's personality or tone of voice. They may give the answer that they think will please the interviewer.

Timing of Polls

Opinion polls of voter preferences cannot reflect rapid shifts in public opinion unless they are taken frequently. One example of this problem was the polls taken during the presidential elections of 1980. The candidates in that year were incumbent Democratic president Jimmy Carter and Republican Ronald Reagan. Almost to the end of the campaign, polls showed Carter in the lead. Only the most capable analysts took note of the very large number of undecided voters. In the last week before the elections, these voters broke sharply for Reagan. Few polls were conducted late enough to detect this development.

Exit Polls

The reliability of polls was also called into question by the use of exit polls in the 2000 presidential elections. The Voter News Service (VNS)—a consortium that no longer exists—conducted polls of people exiting polling places on Election Day. These exit polls were used by the news networks to predict the winner of the Florida race—and they were wrong, not just once, but twice. First, they claimed that the Florida vote had gone to Al Gore. Then, a few hours later, they said it had gone to George W. Bush. Finally, they said the Florida race was too close to call.

The Accuracy of the Polls in 2012

As a whole, public opinion polls did a good job of predicting the 2012 election results, despite a bias toward the Republicans shown by a handful of pollsters. These pollsters, however, included some of the biggest names in the field. Gallup, for example, initially overestimated turnout among Republican voters and underestimated turnout among Democrats. In its last poll, Gallup corrected its results by 5 points, but it still had Romney as the winner. Rasmussen, a top Republican poll taker, made the mistake of weighting Republican responses more heavily than independent ones.

Many conservative bloggers refused to accept polls that showed Obama ahead. Some even accused pollsters of deliberately skewing the results. Nate Silver, a polling expert formerly with the *New York Times* and now with ESPN, was the target of many of these attacks. In the end, however, the results proved that Silver and other polling experts were correct. Figure 8–1 alongside shows the predictions of leading poll takers.

Misuse of Polls Today, a frequently heard complaint is that, instead of measuring public opinion, polls can end up creating it. For example, to gain popularity, a candidate might claim that all the polls show that he or she is ahead in the race. People who want to support the winner may back this candidate despite their true feelings. This is often called the "bandwagon" effect. Presidential approval ratings lend themselves to the bandwagon effect.

The media also sometimes misuse polls. Many journalists take the easy route during campaigns and base their political coverage almost exclusively on poll findings. Media companies often report only the polls conducted by their affiliated pollsters, announcing the results as the absolute truth regardless of whether the results are typical or are at serious variance with polls taken by other organizations.

Indeed, given the diversity of results among different polling organizations, savvy political analysts look at as many different polls as they can. Experts often average the results of polls that ask a particular question. Some of them even weight these polls based on how reliable they believe each firm to be. For additional information that is useful in evaluating polls, see this chapter's *Perception versus Reality* feature on the following page.

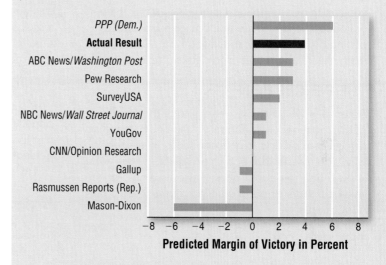

FIGURE 8–1

Final Poll Results for the
2012 Presidential Elections

The figure shows the predicted margin of victory for Democrat Barack Obama over Republican Mitt Romney, listed by polling firm. Note that one pollster reported a tie and three predicted that Romney would win. Two polling firms had ties to a major political party.

Predicted Margin of Victory in Percent

Source: Real Clear Politics and FiveThirtyEight blogs.

The Problem of Push Polls One tactic in political campaigns is to use **push polls,** which ask "fake" polling questions that are actually designed to "push" voters toward one candidate or another. The National Council on Public Polls describes push polls as outright political manipulation—the spreading of rumors and lies by one candidate about another. Push pollsters usually do not give their name or identify the poll's sponsor. The interviews last less than a minute, whereas legitimate pollsters typically interview a respondent for five to thirty minutes.

AN EXAMPLE: JOHN McCAIN. Republican presidential candidate John McCain was the target of a famous push poll in the 2000 Republican presidential primary in South Carolina. White voters were asked, "Would you be more likely or less likely to vote for John McCain for president if you knew

push poll A campaign tactic used to feed false or misleading information to potential voters, under the guise of taking an opinion poll, with the intent to "push" voters away from one candidate and toward another.

Perception versus Reality

Reliable Polls, Unreliable Polls, and Polls by Outright Crooks

Today, more than ever before, Americans are bombarded with the results of public opinion polls. If you can think of a political candidate, topic, issue, or concept, chances are that one or more public polling organizations can tell you what "Americans really think" about that candidate or topic.

THE PERCEPTION

Americans who hear or read about the results of public opinion polls naturally assume that polling organizations undertook those polls in a scientific way and presented accurate results. Those who know a little bit about polling also assume that the small numbers of people polled represented a random sample.

THE REALITY

Many "polls" are not based on a random sample, contrary to popular belief. Consider a "poll" recently published in an investment blog. The blogger asked his readers to estimate the rate of inflation and volunteer their answers. (*Inflation* is a sustained increase in average prices.) Readers reported an average rate of 8 percent, and the blogger claimed that this was the true inflation rate, not the lower rate published by those liars in the federal government.

Because answers were volunteered, though, this "poll" couldn't accurately reflect the opinion of the blog's own readers. Those who thought that inflation was high—and a problem—would be more likely to respond than readers who thought inflation was a non-issue. Many of the blog's readers doubtless shared the blogger's unconventional economic theories, and so the blog's readers themselves were a biased sample of the public.

Finally, determining the rate of inflation through a poll, even a scientific one, is like taking a poll to find out the number of people living in Alaska. The population of Alaska is what it is, regardless of public opinion. As of 2013, the inflation rate was about 2 percent, not 8.

On occasion, pollsters have been accused of issuing fraudulent reports. In 2009, polling experts accused a Georgia-based company of making up results without conducting any actual surveys. Immediately after the accusation was made, the firm ceased issuing polls and vanished from sight. In 2010, a polling firm was sued by its largest customer—the Daily Kos, a leading progressive blog. Kos accused the company of manufacturing its results. The case was settled out of court in 2011, with the firm paying a substantial penalty to Kos.

Polling expert Nate Silver has released calculations of pollster-introduced error (PIE) based on general election polls dating back to 1998. PIE is the average amount of error that a pollster introduces above and beyond ordinary sampling error. The worst results exceeded 4 percentage points.

BLOG ON For additional assessments of poll takers, including their performance in the 2012 elections, search on "rating polling firms nate silver."

he had fathered an illegitimate black child?" In fact, McCain and his wife had adopted a girl with a cleft palate from an orphanage in Bangladesh.

PUSH POLLS AND LEGITIMATE POLLS. Some researchers argue that identifying a push poll is not always straightforward. Political analyst Charlie Cook points out that "there are legitimate polls that can ask push questions, which test potential arguments against a rival to ascertain how effective those arguments might be in future advertising. . . . These are not only legitimate tools of survey research, but any political pollster who did not use them would be doing her or his clients a real disservice."[3]

Distinguishing between push polls and push questions, then, can be challenging—which is usually the intent of the push pollsters. A candidate does not want to be accused of conducting push polls, because the public considers them a "dirty trick" and may turn against the candidate who uses them.

children, "Let us explain to you the virtues of becoming a Republican," their children nevertheless come to know the parents' feelings, beliefs, and attitudes. The strong early influence of the family later gives way to the multiple influences of school, church, peers, television, co-workers, and other groups. People and institutions that influence the political views of others are called **agents of political socialization.**

8–2 How Do People Form Political Opinions?

Learning Outcome 8–2

Describe the political socialization process.

When asked, most Americans are willing to express an opinion on political issues. Not one of us, however, was born with such opinions. Most people acquire their political attitudes, opinions, beliefs, and knowledge through a complex learning process called **political socialization.** This process begins in childhood and continues throughout life.

Most political socialization is informal, and it usually begins during early childhood, when the dominant influence on a child is the family. Although parents normally do not sit down and say to their

8–2a The Importance of Family

As just suggested, most parents or caregivers do not deliberately set out to form their children's political ideas and beliefs. They are usually more concerned with the moral, religious, and ethical values of their offspring. Yet a child first sees the political world through the eyes of his or her family, which is perhaps the most important force in political socialization. Children do not "learn" political attitudes the same way they learn to master in-line skating. Rather, they learn by hearing their parents' everyday conversations and stories about politicians and issues and by observing their parents' actions and reactions.

The family's influence is strongest when children can clearly perceive their parents' attitudes, and most can. In one study, more high school students could identify their parents' political party affiliation than their parents' other attitudes or beliefs. The political party of the parents often becomes the political party of the children, particularly if both parents support the same party.

8–2b Schools and Churches

Education also strongly influences an individual's political attitudes.

Family support for going to college often matters.

HILL STREET STUDIOS/BLEND IMAGES/CORBIS

political socialization
The learning process through which most people acquire their political attitudes, opinions, beliefs, and knowledge.

agents of political socialization People and institutions that influence the political views of others.

From their earliest days in school, children learn about the American political system. They say the Pledge of Allegiance and sing patriotic songs. They celebrate national holidays, such as Presidents' Day and Veterans' Day, and learn about the history and symbols associated with them. In the upper grades, young people acquire more knowledge about government and democratic procedures through civics classes and participation in student government and various clubs. They also learn citizenship skills through school rules and regulations. Generally, those with more education have more knowledge about politics and policy than those with less education. The level of education also influences a person's political values, as will be discussed later in this chapter.

A majority of Americans hold strong religious beliefs, and these attitudes can also contribute significantly to political socialization. For example, if a family's church emphasizes that society has a collective obligation to care for the poor, the children in that family may be influenced in a liberal direction. If the church instead depicts the government as irreligious and morally threatening, children will receive a conservative message.

8–2c The Media

The **media**—newspapers, magazines, television, radio, and the Internet—also have an impact on political socialization. The most influential of these media is television, which continues to be a leading source of political information for older voters. As explained later in this chapter, older citizens turn out to vote significantly more often than younger ones.

Some contend that the media's role in shaping public opinion has increased to the point that the media are as influential as the family, particularly among high school students. For example, in her analysis of the media's role in American politics, media scholar Doris A. Graber points out that high school students, when asked where they obtain the information on which they base their attitudes, mention the Internet and social media far more than they mention their families, friends, and teachers.[4]

Other studies have shown that the media's influence on people's opinions may not be as great as some have thought.

media Newspapers, magazines, television, radio, the Internet, and any other printed or electronic means of communication.

Generally, people go online, watch television, or read articles with preconceived ideas about the issues. These preconceived ideas act as a kind of perceptual screen that blocks out information that is not consistent with the ideas. Generally, the media tend to wield the most influence over the views of persons who have not yet formed opinions about various issues or candidates. (See Chapter 10 for a more detailed discussion of the media's role in American politics.)

8–2d Opinion Leaders

Every state or community has well-known citizens who are able to influence the opinions of their fellow citizens. These people may be public officials, religious leaders, teachers, or celebrities. They are the people to whom others listen and from whom others draw ideas and convictions about various issues of public concern. These opinion leaders play a significant role in the formation of public opinion.

Opinion leaders often include politicians or former politicians. For example, President Barack Obama asked former U.S. presidents George W. Bush (2001–2009) and Bill Clinton (1993–2001) to lead a nationwide fund-raising drive following the January 2010 earthquake in Haiti, which destroyed much of that country.

Sometimes, however, opinion leaders can fall from grace when they express views radically different from what most Americans believe. One example is former president Jimmy Carter (1977–1981), who lost much popularity after he published a book that harshly criticized Israel's actions toward the Palestinians.[5] (Most Americans of both parties are strongly pro-Israel.)

8–2e Major Life Events

Often, the political attitudes of an entire generation of Americans are influenced by a major event. For example, the Great Depression (1929–1939), the most severe economic depression in modern U.S. history, persuaded many Americans who lived through it that the federal government should step in when the economy is in decline. A substantial number of voters came to believe that the New Deal programs and policies of President Franklin Roosevelt showed that the Democratic Party was concerned about the fate of ordinary people, and so they became supporters of that party.

The generation that lived through World War II (1939–1945) tends to believe that American intervention in foreign affairs is good. In contrast, the generation that came of age during the Vietnam War (1965–1975) is more skeptical of American interventionism. A national tragedy, such as the terrorist attacks of September 11, 2001, is also likely to influence the political attitudes of a generation, though in what way is still difficult to predict. The recent Great Recession and the financial crisis that struck in September 2008 will surely affect popular attitudes in years to come.

8–2f Peer Groups

Once children enter school, the views of friends begin to influence their attitudes and beliefs. From junior high school on, the **peer group**—friends, classmates, co-workers, club members, or religious group members—becomes a significant factor in the political socialization process.

Most of this socialization occurs when the peer group is involved with political activities or other causes. For example, your political beliefs might be influenced by a peer group with which you are working on a common cause, such as cleaning up a local river bank or campaigning for a favorite candidate. Your political beliefs probably are not as strongly influenced by peers with whom you, say, snowboard regularly or attend concerts.

8–2g Economic Status and Occupation

A person's economic status may influence her or his political views. For example, poorer people are more likely to favor government assistance programs. On an issue such as abortion, lower-income people are more likely to be conservative—that is, to be against abortion—than are higher-income groups (of course, there are many exceptions).

Where a person works also affects her or his opinions. Co-workers who spend a great deal of time working together tend to influence one another. For example, labor union members working together for a company may have similar political opinions, at least on issues of government involvement in the economy. Individuals working for a nonprofit agency that depends on government funds will tend to support government spending in that area. Business managers are more likely to favor tax laws helpful to businesses than are factory workers.

FOR CRITICAL THINKING

Thinking about your own life, what sources of political socialization were most important to you? How did they influence your beliefs?

8–3 Why People Vote as They Do

What prompts some citizens to vote Republican and others to vote Democratic? What persuades voters to choose certain kinds of candidates? Researchers have collected more information on voting than on any other form of political participation in the United States. These data shed some light on why people decide to vote for particular candidates.

Learning Outcome 8–3

Discuss the different factors that affect voter choices.

8–3a Party Identification

Many voters have a standing allegiance to a political party, or a *party identification*, although the proportion of the population that does so has fallen in recent decades. For established voters, party identification is one of the most important and lasting predictors of how a person will vote. Party identification is an emotional attachment to a party that is influenced by family, age, peer groups, and other factors that play a role in the political socialization process discussed earlier.

A large number of voters call themselves independents. Despite this label, many independents actually support one or the other of the two major parties quite regularly.

8–3b Perception of the Candidates

Voters often base their decisions on the perceived character of the candidates rather than on their

peer group Associates, often close in age to one another; may include friends, classmates, co-workers, club members, or religious group members.

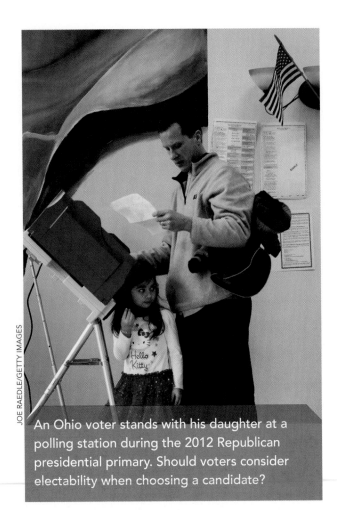

An Ohio voter stands with his daughter at a polling station during the 2012 Republican presidential primary. Should voters consider electability when choosing a candidate?

JOE RAEDLE/GETTY IMAGES

qualifications or policy positions. Such perceptions were important in 2010 and 2012. Following each of these elections, many political analysts concluded that the Republican Party had forfeited two to three U.S. Senate races by nominating Tea Party–supported candidates that were regarded by many voters as "too extreme." This perception was, to a large extent, based not on the political positions taken by the candidates, but on personal attitudes.

In 2010, for example, Christine O'Donnell, a Tea Party favorite, beat a popular former governor in the Republican Senate primary in Delaware. Before the primary, experts thought that the Republicans would easily win the seat. O'Donnell, however, was accused by members of her own party of lying and misusing campaign funds. The final straw was the revelation that she had dabbled in witchcraft as a young woman. The Democratic candidate scored a 17-point victory in November.

In 2012, Tea Party–backed Republicans in Missouri and Indiana looked like sure bets to gain Senate seats. Missouri's Todd Akin, however, made the mistake of claiming that women cannot become pregnant as a result

of "legitimate rape." In Indiana, Richard Mourdock stated that pregnancies resulting from rape were "intended by God." The perception that these two men were hostile toward women's rights sank both of their candidacies.

8-3c Policy Choices

When people vote for candidates who share their positions on particular issues, they are engaging in policy voting. If a candidate for senator in your state opposes gun control laws, for example, and you decide to vote for him or her for that reason, you have engaged in policy voting.

Historically, economic issues have had the strongest influence on voters' choices. When the economy is doing well, it is very difficult for a challenger, particularly at the presidential level, to defeat the incumbent. In contrast, when the country is experiencing inflation, rising unemployment, or high interest rates, the incumbent may be at a disadvantage. The main issue in the elections of 2008, 2010, and 2012 was the financial crisis facing Americans.

Some of the most heated debates in American political campaigns have involved social issues, such as abortion, gay and lesbian rights, the death penalty, and religion in the schools. Often, presidential candidates prefer to avoid emphasizing their stand on these types of issues, because voters who have strong opinions about such issues are likely to be offended if a candidate does not share their views.

8-3d Socioeconomic Factors

Some factors that influence how people vote can be described as socioeconomic. These factors include educational attainment, occupation and income, age, gender, religion and ethnicity, and geographic location. Some of these factors have to do with the circumstances into which individuals are born. Others have to do with personal choices. Figure 8–2 on the following page shows how various groups voted in the 2012 presidential elections.

Educational Attainment As a general rule, people with more education are more likely to vote Republican, although, in recent years, voters with postgraduate degrees have tended to vote Democratic. Educational attainment, of course, can be linked to income level. Recent studies show that among students from families with income in the bottom fifth of the population, only 12 percent earn a bachelor's degree by the

FIGURE 8-2

Voting by Groups
in the 2012 Presidential Elections

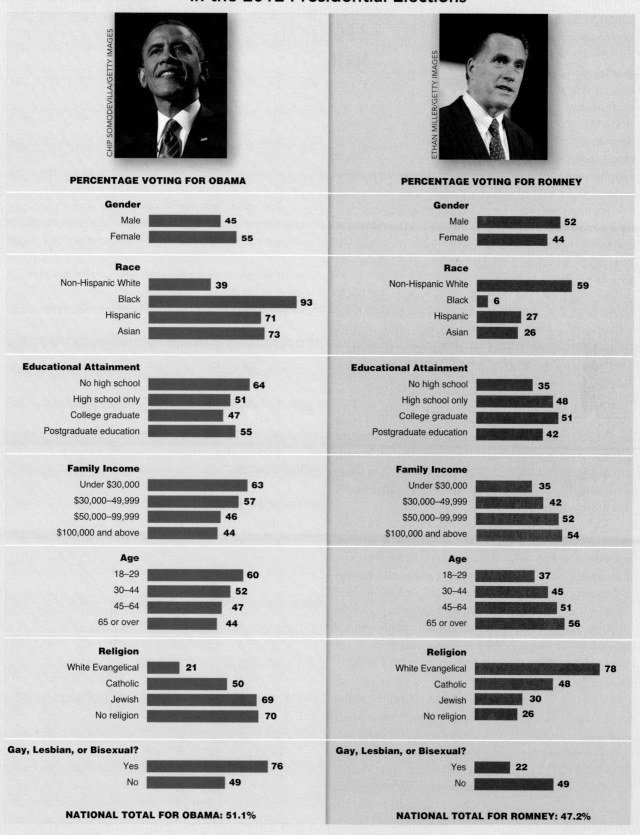

PERCENTAGE VOTING FOR OBAMA

PERCENTAGE VOTING FOR ROMNEY

CHIP SOMODEVILLA/GETTY IMAGES

ETHAN MILLER/GETTY IMAGES

Gender
	Obama	Romney
Male	45	52
Female	55	44

Race
	Obama	Romney
Non-Hispanic White	39	59
Black	93	6
Hispanic	71	27
Asian	73	26

Educational Attainment
	Obama	Romney
No high school	64	35
High school only	51	48
College graduate	47	51
Postgraduate education	55	42

Family Income
	Obama	Romney
Under $30,000	63	35
$30,000–49,999	57	42
$50,000–99,999	46	52
$100,000 and above	44	54

Age
	Obama	Romney
18–29	60	37
30–44	52	45
45–64	47	51
65 or over	44	56

Religion
	Obama	Romney
White Evangelical	21	78
Catholic	50	48
Jewish	69	30
No religion	70	26

Gay, Lesbian, or Bisexual?
	Obama	Romney
Yes	76	22
No	49	49

NATIONAL TOTAL FOR OBAMA: 51.1%

NATIONAL TOTAL FOR ROMNEY: 47.2%

age of twenty-four. In the top fifth, the figure is 73 percent.

Occupation and Income

Businesspersons tend to vote Republican and have done so for many years. This is understandable, given the pro-business stand traditionally adopted by that party. Recently, professionals (such as attorneys, professors, and physicians) have been more likely to vote Democratic than in earlier years. It appears that institutional and social changes have made it less likely that professionals will see themselves as small businesspersons or identify with business interests. Manual laborers, factory workers, and especially union members are more likely to vote for the Democrats, who have a history of pro-labor positions.

In the past, the higher the income, the more likely it was that a person would vote Republican. Conversely, a much larger percentage of low-income individuals voted Democratic. But this pattern is also breaking down. (For more on this topic, see the *Perception versus Reality* feature in Chapter 7.)

Age

The conventional wisdom is that the young are liberal and the old are conservative. Certainly, younger voters were unusually supportive of Barack Obama in the 2008 and 2012 elections. Yet in years past, age differences in support for the parties have often been quite small.

One age-related effect is that people's attitudes are shaped by the events that unfolded as they grew up. Many voters who came of age during Franklin Roosevelt's New Deal held on to a preference for the Democrats. Voters who were young when Ronald Reagan was president have had a tendency to prefer the Republicans. Younger voters are noticeably more liberal on one set of issues, however—those dealing with the rights of minorities, women, and gay males and lesbians.

Gender

Until about thirty years ago, there seemed to be no fixed pattern of voter preferences by gender in presidential elections. Women and men tended to vote for the various candidates in roughly equal numbers.

gender gap The difference between the percentage of votes cast for a particular candidate by women and the percentage of votes cast for the same candidate by men.

"In politics, an organized minority is

A POLITICAL MAJORITY."

~ REV. JESSE JACKSON ~
CIVIL RIGHTS ACTIVIST
1941–PRESENT

Some political analysts believe that a **gender gap** became a major determinant of voter decision making in the 1980 presidential elections, however. In that year, Ronald Reagan outdrew Jimmy Carter by 16 percentage points among male voters, whereas women gave about an equal number of votes to each candidate. In the years since, the gender gap has been a continuing phenomenon. For example, in 2012 Barack Obama carried the female vote by 55 to 44 percentage points, while losing the male vote by a 45 to 52 point margin.

The modern feminist movement and the recognition that women have suffered from various types of discrimination doubtless have something to do with the gender gap. It also appears, however, that compared with men, women on average have a stronger commitment to the liberal value of the common welfare and a weaker belief in the conservative value of self-reliance.

Religion and Ethnic Background

A century ago, at least in the northern states, white Catholic voters were likely to be Democrats, and white Protestant voters were probably Republicans. There are a few places around the country where this pattern continues to hold, but for the most part, white Catholics are now almost as likely as their Protestant neighbors to support the Republicans.

REGULAR CHURCH ATTENDANCE. In recent years, a different religious variable has become important in determining voting behavior. Regardless of their denomination, white Christian voters who attend church regularly have favored the Republicans by substantial margins. White Christian voters who attend church rarely or who find religion less important in their lives are more likely to vote Democratic.

Although some churches do promote liberal ways of thinking, the number of churches that promote conservative values is much larger. Note, too, that Jewish voters are strongly Democratic, regardless of whether they attend services.

MINORITY GROUP MEMBERS. Most African Americans are Protestants, but African Americans are one of the most solidly Democratic constituencies in the United States. This is a complete reversal of the circumstances that existed a century ago. As noted in Chapter 7, for many years after the Civil War, those African Americans who could vote were overwhelmingly Republican. Not until President Franklin Roosevelt's New Deal did black voters begin to turn to the Democrats. While we would predict that today's African American voters would trend Democratic based on their low average income, black support for the Democrats far exceeds the levels that could be deduced from economics alone.

Latino voters have supported the Democrats by margins of about two to one, with some exceptions: Cuban Americans are strongly Republican. In contrast to support from African Americans, Hispanic support for the Democrats is only modestly greater than what we would predict based on low average income. This fact might encourage those Republicans who, in the wake of the 2012 elections, sought to win Latino votes by such measures as immigration reform.

Most Asian Americans favor the Democrats. Vietnamese Americans, however, are strongly Republican.

MUSLIM AMERICANS. Muslim Americans are an interesting example of changing preferences. In 2000, a majority of Muslims of Middle Eastern background voted for Republican presidential candidate George W. Bush because of Islamic cultural conservatism. Today, Muslims are the most Democratic religious group in the nation. Anti-Muslim campaigns by certain conservative groups appear to be a major cause of this transformation.

Geographic Region

In today's presidential contests, states in the South, the Great Plains, and parts of the Rocky Mountains are strongly Republican. The Northeast, the West Coast, and Illinois are firmly Democratic. Many of the swing states that decide elections are located in the Midwest, although several Rocky Mountain states swing between the parties as well.

THE SOLID SOUTH. A very different pattern existed a century ago. In those years, most white southerners were Democrats, and people spoke of the **Solid South**—solidly Democratic, that is. The Solid South lasted for a century after the Civil War. In large part, it resulted from southern resentment of the Republicans for their role in the "War between the States" and their support of African Americans in the postwar era. At the end of the nineteenth century, the Republicans were strong in the Northeast and much of the Midwest, while the Democrats were able to find support outside the South in the Great Plains and the Far West.

The ideologies of the two parties have likewise undergone something of a reversal. One hundred years ago, the Democrats were seen as *less* likely than the Republicans to support government intervention in the economy. The Democrats were also the party that opposed civil rights. Today, the Democrats are often regarded as the party that supports "big government" and affirmative action programs.

SOUTHERN CONSERVATISM. One consequence of the distinctive conservatism of southern white voters is that the concept of a "white vote" is misleading. It is better to think of a southern white vote and a northern white vote. In the run-up to the 2012 elections, some pundits claimed that Obama had a "white working-class problem" because Republican Mitt Romney was winning this group. In fact, polls showed white working-class voters breaking evenly between the parties in the West and the Northeast. Obama was narrowly ahead in the Midwest. Only in the South were white working-class voters solidly for Romney—just like every other class of whites in the South.

Southern white support for the Republicans greatly exceeds what could be predicted from average incomes. In this, southern whites are a mirror image of African Americans. The contrast between these groups has deep historical roots. Southern white support has led some Republicans to reject the post-2012 strategy of attempting to appeal to Latinos and to "double-down" on the white vote instead. Liberal economist Paul Krugman describes this strategy as "an attempt to persuade Ohio whites to start voting like Alabama whites, which I guess could happen. But what if the effect is, instead, to persuade Hispanics to start voting like African Americans?"

8–3e Ideology

Ideology is another indicator of voting behavior. A significant percentage of Americans today identify themselves as conservatives. Recent polls indicate that 40 percent of Americans consider themselves to be conservatives, 21 percent consider themselves liberals, and 35 percent identify themselves as moderates.

For many Americans, where they fall in the political spectrum is a strong indicator of how they will vote: liberals and some moderates vote for Democrats, and conservatives vote for Republicans. The large numbers of Americans who fall in the political center do

Solid South A term used to describe the tendency of the southern states to vote Democratic after the Civil War.

not adhere strictly to an ideology. In most elections, the candidates compete aggressively for these voters because they know their "base"—on the political left or right—is secure.

Ideology and the 2010 Elections

In 2008, Barack Obama swept the liberal vote, won a majority among moderates, and even captured 20 percent of the vote of self-identified conservatives. In the 2010 midterm elections, Democrats continued to win the liberal vote, but their support among moderates and conservatives fell by several points.

What really contributed to Republican victories in that year, however, was turnout. The only ideological category to display a large increase in turnout compared with earlier midterm elections was "conservative Republican." Even moderate Republicans did not vote significantly more than in the past.

As noted earlier in this text, the result was a large number of new Republican members of Congress, many elected with Tea Party support, who were pledged to resist all compromise. Also, many moderate Democratic candidates were defeated in 2010. The subsequent severe polarization in Congress and in American politics generally made it hard for moderates to play a role.

Ideology and the 2012 Elections

Observers have remarked that Americans often voice conservative, small-government principles even as they defend the specific benefits that government provides. In 2011 and 2012, House Republicans endorsed long-term budget plans that would dramatically scale back federal support for Medicaid and privatize Medicare for future generations. These plans and other Republican steps alarmed independent voters. Fears about what the Republicans might do to entitlement programs now counterbalanced concerns about Democratic affection for "big government." It is possible that such attitudes may have helped turn what looked like an extremely close election into a modest success for the Democrats.

FOR CRITICAL THINKING

For what reasons might Cuban Americans and Vietnamese Americans be more conservative than members of other minority groups?

"WHENEVER A FELLOW TELLS ME HE IS BIPARTISAN, I know he is going to vote against me."

~ HARRY TRUMAN ~
THIRTY-THIRD PRESIDENT
OF THE UNITED STATES
1945–1953

8–4 Voting and Voter Turnout

Voting is arguably the most important way in which citizens participate in the political process. Because we do not live in a direct democracy, Americans use the vote to elect politicians to represent their interests, values, and opinions in government. In many states, public-policy decisions—for example, access to medical marijuana—are also decided by voters through referendums and initiatives. Our right to vote also helps keep elected officials accountable because they must face reelection.

> **Learning Outcome 8–4**
>
> Indicate some of the factors that affect voter turnout, and discuss what has been done to improve voter turnout and voting procedures.

8–4a Factors Affecting Voter Turnout

If voting is so important, then why do so many Americans fail to exercise their right to vote? Why is *voter turnout*—the percentage of those who actually turn out to vote from among those eligible to vote—relatively low? In many foreign countries, voter turnout is greater than in the United States. (Sometimes, this is due to laws that actually require citizens to cast a ballot, as we explain in *The Rest of the World* feature on page 182.)

As you will read shortly, in the past, legal restrictions based on income, gender, race, and other factors kept a number of people from voting. In the last decades of the twentieth century, these restrictions were almost completely eliminated, and yet voter turnout in presidential elections still hovered around 55 percent, as shown in Figure 8–3 on the following page. In the last three presidential elections, however, turnout showed a welcome, if modest, improvement.

According to a Pew Research Center survey, one of the reasons for low voter turnout is that many nonvoters (close to 40 percent) do not feel that they have a duty to vote. The survey also found that nearly 70 percent of nonvoters said that they did not vote because they lacked information about the candidates.[6] Finally, some people believe that their vote will not make any difference, so they do not bother to become informed about the candidates and issues or go to the polls.

8–4b The Legal Right to Vote

In the United States today, citizens who are at least eighteen years of age and who are not felons have the right to vote. This was not always true. Recall from Chapter 5 that restrictions on *suffrage*, the legal right to vote, have existed since the founding of our nation. Expanding the right to vote has been an important part of the gradual democratization of the American electoral process. Table 8–1 on page 181 summarizes the major amendments, Supreme Court decisions, and laws that extended the right to vote to various American groups.

Historical Restrictions on Voting Those who drafted the Constitution left the power to set suffrage qualifications to the individual states. Most states limited suffrage to adult white males who owned property, but these restrictions were challenged early on in the

ALEX WONG/GETTY IMAGES

This Maryland voter is participating in early voting in November 2012. Does early voting improve voter turnout?

history of the republic. By 1828, laws restricting the right to vote to Christians were abolished in all states, and property ownership and tax-payment requirements gradually began to disappear as well. By 1850, all white males were allowed to vote. Restrictions based on race and gender continued, however.

FIGURE 8–3 Voter Turnout since 1968

The figures in this chart show voter turnout as a percentage of the population that is eligible to vote.

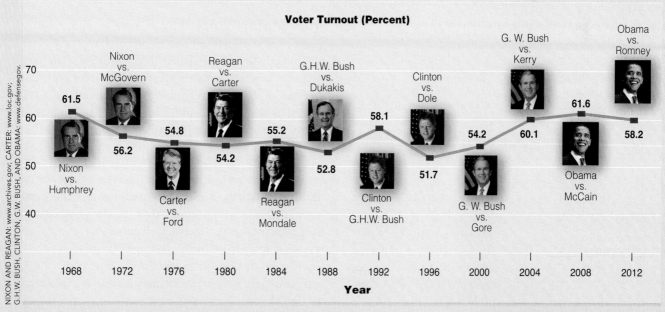

Sources: *Statistical Abstract of the United States*, various issues; the Committee for the Study of the American Electorate; and authors' updates.

The Fifteenth Amendment, ratified in 1870, guaranteed suffrage to African American males. Yet, for many decades, African Americans were effectively denied the ability to exercise their voting rights. Using methods ranging from mob violence to economic pressure, groups of white southerners kept black Americans from voting. We briefly listed some of these techniques in Chapter 5.

Some states required citizens to pass **literacy tests** and to answer complicated questions about government and history before they could register to vote. Registrars made sure that African Americans would always fail such tests. The **poll tax,** a fee of several dollars, was another device used to discourage African Americans from voting. At the time, this tax was a sizable burden, not only for most blacks but also for poor whites.

Another restriction was the **grandfather clause,** which had the effect of restricting voting rights to those whose ancestors had voted before the 1860s. This technique was prohibited by the United States Supreme Court in 1915.[7]

Still another voting barrier was the **white primary**—African Americans were prohibited from voting in Democratic primary elections. (In southern states at that time, winning the Democratic primary almost always guaranteed victory in the general election.) The Supreme Court initially upheld this practice on the grounds that the political parties were private entities, not public, and thus could do as they wished. Eventually, in 1944, the Court banned the use of white primaries.[8]

Voting Rights Today

Today, these devices for restricting voting rights are explicitly outlawed by constitutional amendments and by the Voting Rights Act of 1965, as discussed in Chapter 5. Furthermore, the Nine-teenth Amendment gave women the right to vote in 1920. In 1971, the Twenty-sixth Amendment reduced the minimum voting age to eighteen.

Some restrictions on voting rights still exist. Every state except North Dakota requires voters to register with the appropriate state or local officials before voting. Residency requirements are also usually imposed for voting. Since 1970, however, no state can impose a residency requirement of more than thirty days. Twenty-five states require that length of time, while the other twenty-five states require fewer or no days.

Another voting requirement is citizenship. Non-citizens may not vote in any public election held anywhere in the United States. (Until the early twentieth century, several states allowed noncitizens to cast ballots.) Most states also do not permit prison inmates, mentally ill people, felons, or election-law violators to vote. Should former prison inmates regain the right to vote? We discuss that issue in the *Join the Debate* feature on page 183.

8–4c Attempts to Improve Voter Turnout

Various attempts have been made to improve voter turnout. Typically, these attempts have a partisan dimension, because the kinds of people who find it difficult to register to vote tend to be disproportionately Democratic in their sympathies. Many, for example, are African Americans, a reliably Democratic voting bloc. As a result, Republicans are generally wary of efforts to make registration easier.

The Motor Voter Law The National Voter Registration Act (the "Motor Voter Law") of 1993 simplified the voter-registration process. The act requires states to provide all eligible citizens with the opportunity to register to vote when they apply for or renew a driver's license. The law also requires that states allow mail-in registration. Forms are available at public assistance agencies. The law, which took effect in 1995, has facilitated millions of registrations.

Mail-in Voting In 1998, Oregon voters approved a ballot initiative requiring that all elections in that state, including presidential elections, be conducted exclusively by mail. In the 2012 presidential elections, 65 percent of Oregonians eligible to vote cast ballots, a figure that is somewhat higher than the national average but not exceptionally so.

The state of Washington now also relies almost exclusively on mail-in ballots. Many states have

literacy test A test given to voters to ensure that they could read and write and thus evaluate political information. This technique was used in many southern states to restrict African American participation in elections.

poll tax A fee of several dollars that had to be paid before a person could vote. This device was used in some southern states to discourage African Americans and low-income whites from voting.

grandfather clause A clause in a state law that had the effect of restricting voting rights to those whose ancestors had voted before the 1860s. It was one of the techniques used in the South to prevent African Americans from exercising their right to vote.

white primary A primary election in which African Americans were prohibited from voting. The practice was banned by the Supreme Court in 1944.

TABLE 8-1

Extension of the Right to Vote

Year	Action	Impact
1870	Fifteenth Amendment	Discrimination based on race outlawed.
1915	*Guinn v. United States*	Grandfather clause ruled unconstitutional by the Supreme Court.
1920	Nineteenth Amendment	Discrimination based on gender outlawed.
1924	Congressional act	All Native Americans given citizenship.
1944	*Smith v. Allwright*	Supreme Court prohibits white primary.
1957	Civil Rights Act of 1957	Justice Department can sue to protect voting rights in various states.
1960	Civil Rights Act of 1960	Courts authorized to appoint referees to assist voter-registration procedures.
1961	Twenty-third Amendment	Residents of District of Columbia given right to vote for president and vice president.
1964	Twenty-fourth Amendment	Poll tax in national elections outlawed.
1965	Voting Rights Act of 1965	Literacy tests prohibited; federal voter registrars authorized in seven southern states.
1970	Voting Rights Act Amendments of 1970	Voting age for federal elections reduced to eighteen years; maximum thirty-day residency required for presidential elections; state literacy tests abolished.
1971	Twenty-sixth Amendment	Minimum voting age reduced to eighteen for all elections.
1975	Voting Rights Act Amendments of 1975	Federal voter registrars authorized in ten more states; bilingual ballots to be used in certain circumstances.
1982	Voting Rights Act Amendments of 1982	Extended provisions of Voting Rights Act Amendments of 1970 and 1975; private parties allowed to sue for violations.
2006	Voting Rights Act extension	Extended Voting Rights Act for another twenty-five years.

recently made such ballots an option for all voters. In the past, absentee ballots were often available only to those who clearly could not make it to a polling place on Election Day. Reasons for an *absentee ballot* might include military service, business travel, or ill health.

Laws That May Discourage Voting   In recent years, a number of states have passed laws that may have the effect of making it harder to vote, not easier. The most common such law requires that voters produce photographic identification before they are allowed to register or vote. Supporters of such laws contend that they reduce voter fraud. Opponents argue that the net effect is to deter voters—mostly lower income and often minority—who do not have easy access to ID cards. We discussed this issue in the chapter-opening *America at Odds* feature.

8-4d Attempts to Improve Voting Procedures

Because of serious problems in achieving accurate vote counts in recent elections, particularly in the 2000 presidential elections, steps have been taken to attempt to ensure more accuracy in the voting process. In 2002, Congress passed the Help America Vote Act, which, among other things, provided funds to the states to help them purchase new electronic voting equipment. Concerns about the possibility of fraudulent manipulation of electronic voting machines then replaced the worries over inaccurate vote counts caused by the previous equipment.

Problems in 2006   In the 2006 elections, about half of the states that were using new electronic voting systems reported problems. Some systems "flipped" votes from the selected candidate to the opposing

Compulsory Voting Improves Voter Turnout

No matter what the election is, no matter what the issues are, and no matter who is running, voter turnout in the United States is low compared with that in many other countries. Obviously, the United States would have higher voter participation if we had a compulsory voting law. Australia is a good example of how such a system works.

Compulsory Voting in Australia

In Australia, citizens over the age of eighteen must register to vote, and they must show up at the polls on Election Day. Otherwise, they are subject to fines. This law has been in effect since 1924.

Australia does make voting easier than it is in America, however. Elections are always held on Saturday, not Tuesday. Voters can vote from anywhere in the country.

The Effects of Australia's Law

Before 1924, in a typical year Australia saw a turnout of registered voters that was about on a par with that in the United States—an average of 47 percent. Currently, voter turnout is roughly 95 percent. Candidates in Australia therefore do not have to engage in "get out the vote" activities. In other words, campaigns can focus on issues rather than on encouraging voters to go to the polls. In the United States, much effort goes into getting citizens to register and then to vote.

One odd result of compulsory voting is known as the "donkey vote." Citizens who do not care about the elections may simply vote for the first name on a list of candidates. Before 1984, when lists were typically in alphabetical order, candidates could obtain a detectable advantage if their last name began with the letter A. Since that year, however, names have been listed in random order.

Compulsory Voting in Other Countries

Australia is not alone in enforcing compulsory voting. The following nations also do so:

Argentina	Nauru
Brazil	Peru
Congo (Kinshasa)	Singapore
Ecuador	Uruguay
Luxembourg	

Twelve other countries have compulsory voting laws but do not attempt to enforce them.

FOR CRITICAL ANALYSIS Some critics of compulsory voting claim that it is undemocratic. Why do you think they would make this argument?

candidate. In one Florida district, about eighteen thousand votes apparently were unrecorded by electronic equipment, and this may have changed the outcome of a congressional race. Many experts have demanded that electronic systems create a "paper trail," so that machine errors can be tracked and fixed.

Voting Systems in Recent Elections Because of problems with electronic systems, fewer polling places used them in 2008 and 2010. Indeed, more than half of all votes cast in these years used old-fashioned paper ballots. As a result, vote counting was slow.

In 2012, the development of voter-verified paper audit trail (VVPAT) printers led to the reintroduction of electronic machines in many states. Often, however, only a limited number of such machines were installed to serve voters with disabilities. Two-thirds of all votes nationwide were still cast using paper ballots.

In seventeen states, some or all of the votes were cast through electronic devices that lacked a paper audit trail. A full quarter of all votes were cast using these questionable systems.[9]

One feature of the elections was the large number of states that allowed early voting at polling places that opened weeks before Election Day. A benefit of early voting was that it allowed election workers time to ensure that all systems were working properly by Election Day. As we have noted in this chapter, however, since 2012 some states have attempted to cut back on early voting.

8–4e Who Actually Votes

Just because an individual is eligible to vote does not necessarily mean that the person will cast a ballot. Why do some eligible voters go to the polls while others do

Should Felons Be Allowed to Vote?

Suppose that you commit a crime that is punishable by a prison term. You serve your time and are released. You are now a felon—someone who has been convicted of a serious crime. You may believe that you have "repaid your debt to society" by going to prison, but that does not mean that all of your rights are restored after you have served your sentence. In quite a few states, felons—ex-convicts, or ex-cons—do not have the right to vote. A substantial number of people will agree that those who are actually serving time in prison should not be able to vote. But what about those who have rejoined society?

Because America puts a larger share of its people behind bars than any other nation, the number of ex-cons is staggering. At least 13 percent of the nation's African American male population is disenfranchised (can't vote). The United States takes a much harder line on this issue than most countries. A substantial number of our allies, in fact, allow people to vote while they are still in prison. Among our European allies, only Belgium permanently disenfranchises felons. Should such people have the right to vote?

No One Should Be Denied the Right to Vote

Felony disenfranchisement affects almost 6 million persons in the United States. That means that 6 million Americans cannot express their political beliefs by voting. One negative result of this exclusion is racial discrimination. The percentage of African Americans who are felons is much greater than their share of the total population. The result: compared with whites, a disproportionate number of blacks are excluded from the democratic process because of state laws that prevent felons from voting.

Regardless of race, those who are convicted of felonies are disproportionately poor. By excluding many poor persons and minority group members from the voting rolls, we bias the vote. Some question how we can call ourselves a fully democratic country if we disenfranchise so many people. Those who want felons to regain the right to vote contend that our current situation is patently unfair.

When You Break the Rules, You Lose Some Rights

No one questions the right of society to incarcerate those convicted of serious crimes. No one questions the need for punishment when individuals violate our accepted rules of behavior. Therefore, why should anyone question each state's right to prevent convicts and former convicts from exercising all of the rights enjoyed by law-abiding citizens? Felons are not the kind of people we want to choose our leaders.

Furthermore, proponents of felon enfranchisement may be making a mountain out of a molehill. When Florida passed a law allowing former convicts to register to vote, the results were not encouraging. Only about 10,000 out of a potential 120,000 former convicts actually registered. Those in favor of allowing felons to vote are misplacing their efforts. They should instead attempt to reduce incentives for Americans to commit crimes.

FOR CRITICAL ANALYSIS If the millions of former convicts in America could register to vote, would it make any difference? Why or why not?

not? Although nobody can answer this question with absolute conviction, certain factors appear to affect voter turnout.

Educational Attainment Among the factors affecting voter turnout, education appears to be the most important. The more education a person has, the more likely it is that she or he will be a regular voter. People who graduated from high school vote more regularly than those who dropped out, and college graduates vote more often than high school graduates.

Income Level and Age Differences in income also lead to differences in voter turnout. Wealthy people tend to be overrepresented among regular voters. Generally, older voters turn out to vote more regularly than younger voters do, although participation tends to decline among the very elderly. Participation

A Rock the Vote bus visits the campus of the University of North Carolina at Charlotte. Rock the Vote encourages young people to register to vote.

likely increases with age because older people tend to be more settled, are already registered, and have had more experience with voting.

Minority Status

Racial and ethnic minorities traditionally have been underrepresented among the ranks of voters. In several recent elections, however, participation by these groups, particularly African Americans and Hispanics, has increased. In part because the number of Latino citizens has grown rapidly, the increase in the Hispanic vote has been even larger than the increase in the black vote.

Immigration and Voter Turnout

The United States has experienced high rates of immigration in recent decades, and that has had an effect on voter-turnout figures. In the past, voter turnout was often expressed as a percentage of the **voting-age population,** the number of people residing in the United States who are at least eighteen years old. Due to legal and illegal immigration, however, many people of voting age are not eligible to vote because they are not citizens. Millions more cannot vote because they are felons. Additionally, the voting-age population excludes Americans abroad, who are eligible to cast absentee ballots.

Today, political scientists calculate the **vote-eligible population,** the number of people who are actually entitled to vote in American elections. They have found that there may be 20 million fewer eligible voters than the voting-age population suggests. Therefore, voter turnout is actually greater than the percentages sometimes cited.

Some experts have argued that the relatively low levels of voter turnout often reported for the years between 1972 and 2000 were largely due to immigration.[10] Beginning in 2004, voter turnout has improved by any calculation method.

voting-age population The number of people residing in the United States who are at least eighteen years old.

vote-eligible population The number of people who are actually eligible to vote in an American election.

AMERICA AT ODDS Public Opinion and Voting

Public opinion polls reveal that Americans are in broad agreement on many issues, such as the basic political structure of our nation. Nevertheless, polls also report that Americans are at odds with one another on many other issues. After all, the questions posed by poll takers are typically divisive ones. Issues surrounding who votes and why can also be contentious. Some examples include the following:

- Is the disenfranchisement of felons a form of racial discrimination—or a rational part of the punishment process?

- Given that historical events shape popular attitudes toward the parties, when all is said and done, will the impact of the Great Recession benefit one of the major parties—or will the effects of the recession prove trivial?

- Should legislators follow public opinion as faithfully as they can—or, as the Democrats did on health-care reform, should lawmakers do what they think is best for the country regardless of the polls?

- We discussed push polls earlier in this chapter. Should push polls be banned—or would that violate First Amendment guarantees of free speech?

- Should voters be more concerned with the policy positions of the presidential candidates—or are the presidential candidates' personalities and personal characteristics of equal or greater concern?

STUDY TOOLS

Fill-In

Learning Outcome 8–1

1. A random sample means that _____.

2. When a pollster's results appear to consistently favor a particular political party, polling experts refer to the phenomenon as a _____.

3. A _____ is a campaign tactic used to feed false or misleading information to potential voters, under the guise of conducting an opinion poll.

Learning Outcome 8–2

4. Agents of political socialization include _____.

Learning Outcome 8–3

5. For established voters, _____ is one of the most important and lasting predictors of how a person will vote.

6. When people vote for candidates who share their positions on particular issues, they are engaging in _____.

7. Socioeconomic factors that influence how people vote include _____.

Learning Outcome 8–4

8. Methods used to keep African Americans from voting even after the Fifteenth Amendment to the U.S. Constitution was ratified included _____.

Multiple Choice

Learning Outcome 8–1

9. A *Literary Digest* poll incorrectly predicted that Alfred Landon would win the presidential election in 1936 because the
   a. pollsters used an unrepresentative sample.
   b. pollsters used a random sample.
   c. sample size was too small.

Learning Outcome 8–2

10. Most political socialization is informal, and it usually begins
    a. in college.
    b. in high school.
    c. during early childhood.

11. The family is an important agent of political socialization because
    a. most families deliberately set out to form their children's political ideas and beliefs.
    b. a child first sees the political world through the eyes of his or her family.
    c. parents are responsible for registering their children to vote.

Learning Outcome 8–3

12. Historically, ____ issues have had the strongest influence on voters' choices.
    a. foreign policy   b. social   c. economic

13. The term *gender gap*
    a. refers to the difference between the percentage of votes cast for a particular candidate by women and the percentage of votes cast for the same candidate by men.
    b. describes the difference in voter turnout between men and women.
    c. describes the differences in the campaign styles of male and female candidates.

Learning Outcome 8–4

14. In 1971, the Twenty-sixth Amendment reduced the minimum voting age to
    a. sixteen.   b. eighteen.   c. twenty-one.

15. Among the factors affecting voter turnout, ____ appears to be the most important.
    a. educational attainment   c. income level
    b. race

Campaigns and Elections

TOM WILLIAMS/CQ ROLL CALL

The **Learning Outcomes** labeled 1 through 5 are designed to help improve your understanding of the chapter. After reading this chapter, you should be able to:

9–1 Explain how elections are held and how the electoral college functions in presidential elections.

9–2 Discuss how candidates are nominated.

9–3 Indicate what is involved in launching a political campaign today, and describe the structure and functions of a campaign organization.

9–4 Describe how the Internet has transformed political campaigns.

9–5 Summarize the current laws that regulate campaign financing and the role of money in modern political campaigns.

Remember to visit page 211 for additional Study Tools

Learning Outcomes

AMERICA AT
ODDS
Should We Elect the President by Popular Vote?

WWW.SHUTTERSTOCK.COM

When Americans go to the polls every four years to cast their ballots for president, many are unaware that they are not, in fact, voting directly for the candidates. Rather, they are voting for electors—individuals chosen in each state by political parties to cast the state's electoral votes for the candidate who wins that state's popular vote. The system by which electors cast their votes for president is known as the *electoral college.*

Each state is assigned electoral votes based on the number of its members in the U.S. Senate and House of Representatives. Each state has the same number of senators (two), and the number of representatives a state has is determined by the size of its population. There are currently 538 electoral votes.[1] To win in the electoral college, a presidential candidate must win 270 of these votes.

Most states have a "winner-take-all" system in which the candidate who receives more of the popular votes than any other candidate receives *all* of that state's electoral votes, even if the margin of victory is very slight. A candidate who wins the popular vote nationally may yet lose in the electoral college. Many Americans believe that we should let the popular vote, not the electoral college, decide who becomes president.[2] Others are not so sure.

Let the People Elect Our President

In 2000, Democratic candidate Al Gore won the popular vote yet narrowly lost to Republican George W. Bush in the electoral college. Many Americans questioned the legitimacy of Bush's election. If the 2012 presidential elections had been closer than they were, Democrat Barack Obama could easily have been elected with fewer popular votes than Republican Mitt Romney—or vice versa.

The electoral college was designed to ensure that the interests of smaller states are not overshadowed by those of their more populous neighbors. Yet the college gives the smaller states a disproportionate amount of clout. Consider, for example, that one electoral vote in California now corresponds to roughly 690,000 people, while an electoral vote in more sparsely settled Wyoming represents only about 190,000. Clearly, the votes of Americans are not weighted equally, and this voting inequality is contrary to the "one person, one vote" principle of our democracy.

The Electoral College Protects the Small States and Ensures Stability

Supporters of the electoral college argue that it helps to protect the small states from being overwhelmed by the large states. The electoral college also helps to maintain a relatively stable and coherent party system. If the president were elected by popular vote, we might have multiple parties vying for the nation's highest office—as occurs in such nations as France, Germany, and Italy.

The current system helps to discourage single-issue or regional candidates—candidates who are not focused on the interests of the nation as a whole. To prevail in the electoral college, a candidate must build a national coalition.

Finally, the electoral college vote has diverged from the popular vote in only three elections during our nation's history—in 1876, 1888, and 2000. These exceptions do not justify abolishing the system. There is a relevant saying, "If it ain't broke, don't fix it." Let's apply it to the electoral college debate.

Where do you stand?

1. Do you believe that a candidate elected by the popular vote would be more representative of the entire nation than a candidate elected by the electoral college? Why or why not?

2. Suppose that states awarded their electoral votes according to the share of the popular vote each candidate received. How would this affect presidential elections?

Explore this issue online

- To see proposals to elect the president by popular vote, enter "fair vote inequalities" into your favorite search engine.
- To find articles defending the electoral college, search on "case for electoral college."

Introduction

During elections, candidates vie to become representatives of the people in both national and state offices. Campaigning for election has become an arduous task for every politician. As you will see in this chapter, American campaigns are long and expensive undertakings. The rules that govern our elections can be complicated, as we discussed in the chapter-opening *America at Odds* feature. Yet America's campaigns are an important part of our political process, because it is through campaigns that citizens learn about the candidates and decide how they will cast their votes.

American democracy would be impossible without campaigns and elections. Otherwise, there would be no way for the people to control the government. For freedom to thrive, however, elections are not enough. Democracy also requires the kind of shared political culture that we described in Chapter 1. We explain what can happen in countries that do not enjoy such a political culture in *The Rest of the World* feature on the following page.

9–1 How We Elect Candidates

The ultimate goal of a political campaign and the associated fund-raising efforts is, of course, winning the election. The most familiar kind of election is the **general election,** which is a regularly scheduled election held in even-numbered years on the Tuesday after the first Monday in November. During general elections, the voters decide who will be the U.S. president, vice president, and senators and representatives in Congress. The president and vice president are elected every four years, senators every six years, and representatives every two years.

General elections are also held to choose state and local government officials, often at the same time as those for national offices. A **special election** is held at the state or local level when the voters must decide an issue before the next general election or when vacancies occur by reason of death or resignation.

9–1a Conducting Elections and Counting the Votes

Since 1888, all states in the United States have used the **Australian ballot**—a secret ballot that is prepared, distributed, and counted by government officials at public expense. As its name implies, this ballot was first developed in Australia.

Recall from Chapter 8 that local units of government, such as cities, are divided into smaller voting districts, or precincts. Within each precinct, voters cast their ballots at a designated polling place.

An election board supervises the polling place and the voting process in each precinct. The board sets hours for the polls to be open according to the laws of the state and sees that ballots or voting machines are available.

In most states, the board provides the list of registered voters and makes certain that only qualified voters cast ballots in each precinct. When the polls close, staff members count the votes and report the results, usually to the county clerk or the board of elections.

Representatives from each party, called **poll watchers,** are allowed at each polling place to make sure the election is run fairly and that fraud doesn't occur.

9–1b Presidential Elections and the Electoral College

When citizens vote for president and vice president, they are not voting directly for the candidates. Instead, they are voting for **electors** who will cast their ballots in the **electoral college.** The electors are selected during

Learning Outcome 9–1

Explain how elections are held and how the electoral college functions in presidential elections.

general election A regularly scheduled election to choose the U.S. president, vice president, and senators and representatives in Congress. General elections are held in even-numbered years on the Tuesday after the first Monday in November.

special election An election that is held at the state or local level when the voters must decide an issue before the next general election or when vacancies occur by reason of death or resignation.

Australian ballot A secret ballot that is prepared, distributed, and counted by government officials at public expense; used by all states in the United States since 1888.

poll watcher A representative from one of the political parties who is allowed to monitor a polling place to make sure that the election is run fairly and that fraud doesn't occur.

elector A member of the electoral college.

electoral college The group of electors who are selected by the voters in each state to elect officially the president and vice president. The number of electors in each state is equal to the number of that state's representatives in both chambers of Congress.

Elections Are Not Enough

In recent decades, more and more nations have sought to choose their leaders through elections. Often, however, elections have done little to address a nation's problems. Most conspicuously, elections in Afghanistan and Iraq that were relatively free and fair have not curbed the violence in those two countries. Russia's Vladimir Putin first came to power in a reasonably fair election, but he is fast turning into an absolute dictator. Apparently, elections are not enough. Why not?

Playing by the Rules

First, consider the obvious: Elections can only settle national questions when most of a country's citizens are willing to accept the election results. Political leaders must be willing to follow the "rules of the game." Voters must be willing to punish rule breakers, even when an offender is a member of their own party. In Iraq and Afghanistan, large groups of citizens are flatly unwilling to accept a loss at the polls. In Russia, Putin has been able to institutionalize lawlessness without effective reprisals from anyone.

On a deeper level, a free society relies on a shared political culture such as the one described in "American Democracy" in Chapter 1. The nation's people must recognize one another as fellow citizens. Furthermore, a free society cannot survive without a broad popular commitment to such values as freedom of expression, the right to personal property, and equality under the law.

Finally, freedom is dependent on the flourishing of *civil society*—that is, all the organizations, businesses, churches, unions, and social groups that bring people together outside of the control of government. When elections fail, one or more of these preconditions for freedom are invariably lacking.

The Example of Egypt

In 2013, Egypt's short experiment with representative democracy collapsed. After huge demonstrations against Mohamed Morsi, the nation's first freely elected president, the military seized power. Elected in 2012, Morsi was a member of the Muslim Brotherhood, Egypt's main Islamist organization. Days after the military coup, security forces broke up pro-Morsi demonstrations, killing hundreds.

Earlier, in 2011, massive demonstrations had forced out the former Egyptian dictator, Hosni Mubarak. Egypt at that time contained three important political forces.

- The weakest group was made up of the often-youthful liberals who led the demonstrations.
- The second group was the Islamists, especially the well-organized Muslim Brotherhood. This group won the 2012 election campaign.
- The third group was the "deep state," the military and government officials who owned or controlled Egypt's most important institutions. This centralized control of social institutions crippled civil society.

Of these forces, only the liberals were committed to democratic values. Yet after a year of disastrously incompetent rule by Morsi, even the liberals had given up on accepting election results. When liberals allied with the deep state against the Brotherhood, Egyptian democracy no longer had any defenders at all.

FOR CRITICAL ANALYSIS Do you think there are people in the United States who would refuse to abide by election results if they thought they could get away with it?

---

winner-take-all system
A system in which the candidate who receives the most votes wins. In contrast, proportional systems allocate votes to multiple winners.

each presidential election year by the states' political parties, subject to the laws of the state. Each state has as many electoral votes as it has U.S. senators and representatives (see Figure 9–1 on the following page). In addition, there are three electors from the District of Columbia, even though it is not a state.

The Winner-Take-All System The electoral college system is primarily a **winner-take-all system**, in which the candidate who receives the largest popular vote in a state is credited with all that state's electoral votes. The only exceptions are Maine and Nebraska.[3]

FIGURE 9-1

State Electoral Votes in 2012

The size of each state reflects the number of electoral votes that state has, following the changes required by the 2010 census. The colors show which party the state voted for in the 2012 presidential elections: red for Republican, blue for Democratic. A candidate must win 270 electoral votes to be elected president.

In December, after the general election, electors (either Republicans or Democrats, depending on which candidate has won the state's popular vote) meet in their state capitals to cast their votes for president and vice president. When the Constitution was drafted, the framers intended that the electors would use their own discretion in deciding who would make the best president. Beginning as early as 1796, however, electors have usually voted for the candidates to whom they are pledged. The electoral college ballots are then sent to the U.S. Senate, which counts and certifies them before a joint session of Congress held early in January. The candidates who receive a majority of the electoral votes are officially declared president and vice president.

What It Takes to Win   To be elected, a candidate must receive more than half of the 538 electoral votes available. Thus, a candidate needs 270 votes to win. If no presidential candidate gets an electoral college majority (which has happened twice—in 1800 and 1824), the House of Representatives votes on the candidates, with each state delegation casting only a single vote. If no candidate for vice president gets a majority of electoral votes, the vice president is chosen by the Senate, with each senator casting one vote.

Even when a presidential candidate wins by a large margin in the electoral college and in the popular vote—a *landslide election*—it does not follow that the candidate has won the support of the majority of those eligible to vote. We explore this paradox in this chapter's *Perception versus Reality* feature on the following page.

FOR CRITICAL THINKING

Should the District of Columbia be admitted as a state—and therefore elect members to the U.S. House and Senate in addition to participating in the electoral college?

9-2 How We Nominate Candidates

The first step on the long road to winning an election is the nomination process. Nominations narrow the field of possible candidates and limit each political party's choice to one person.

Perception versus Reality

Presidents and the "Popular Vote"

Some presidential contests are very close, such as the 2000 race between Al Gore and George W. Bush. Others are less so, such as the one between Lyndon B. Johnson and Barry Goldwater in 1964. When a presidential candidate wins the race by a wide margin, as Johnson did, the result is called a *landslide victory* for the winning candidate.

THE PERCEPTION

The traditional perception has been that, in general, our presidents are elected by a majority of eligible American voters. A president who has been swept into office by a landslide victory may thus claim to have received a "mandate from the people" to govern the nation. Moreover, a president may assert that his or her landslide victory proves that a policy or program endorsed in campaign speeches is backed by popular support.

THE REALITY

In reality, the "popular vote" is not all that popular, in the sense of representing the wishes of a majority of American citizens who are eligible to vote. In fact, the president of the United States has never received the votes of a majority of all eligible adults. Lyndon Johnson, in 1964, came the closest of any president in history, and even he won the votes of fewer than 40 percent of those who were eligible to cast a ballot.

The hotly contested presidential elections of 2000 and 2004 were divisive, leaving the millions of Americans who had voted for the losing candidates unhappy with the results. Nonetheless, George W. Bush assumed that his reelection in 2004—in which he received the votes of 30.5 percent of eligible citizens—was a signal from the American people to push his controversial foreign policy and the war on terrorism. Barack Obama likewise claimed a personal mandate based on his strong performance in 2008, and he parlayed it into a sweeping program of domestic initiatives. Yet Obama had won the support of only 32.6 percent of eligible voters. In the 2012 elections, he won just 29.7 percent.

It is useful to keep these figures in mind whenever a president claims to have received a mandate from the people. The truth is, no president has ever been elected with sufficient popular backing to make this a serious claim.

BLOG ON   Dave Leip's Atlas of U.S. Presidential Elections provides detailed figures on presidential election results. Find the Atlas by searching on "leip."

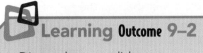

Learning Outcome 9–2

Discuss how candidates are nominated.

For many local government posts, which are often nonpartisan, self-nomination is the most common way to become a candidate. A self-proclaimed candidate usually files a petition to be listed on the ballot. Each state has laws that specify how many signatures a candidate must obtain to show that he or she has some public support. An alternative is to be a *write-in candidate*—voters write the candidate's name on the ballot on Election Day.

Candidates for major offices are rarely nominated in these ways, however. As you read in Chapter 7, most candidates for high office are nominated by a political party and receive considerable support from party activists throughout their campaigns.

9–2a Party Control over Nominations

The methods used by political parties to nominate candidates have changed during the course of American history. Broadly speaking, the process has grown more open over the years, with the involvement of ever-greater numbers of local leaders and ordinary citizens. Today, any voter can participate in choosing party candidates. This was not true as recently as 1968, however, and was certainly not possible during the first years of the republic.

The Caucus System

George Washington was essentially unopposed in the first U.S. presidential elections in 1789—no other candidate was seriously considered in any state. By the end of Washington's eight years in office, however, political divisions among the nation's leaders had solidified into political parties, the Federalists and the Jeffersonian Republicans (see Chapter 7). These early parties were organized by gatherings of important persons, who often met in secret. The meetings came to be called **caucuses.**[4]

Beginning in 1800, members of Congress who belonged to the two parties held caucuses to nominate candidates for president and vice president. The Republican caucus chose Thomas Jefferson in 1800, as expected, and the Federalist caucus nominated the incumbent president, John Adams. By 1816, the Federalist Party had ceased to exist, and the Jeffersonian Republican congressional caucus was in complete control of selecting the president of the United States.

The Death of "King Caucus"

The congressional caucus system collapsed in 1824.[5] It was widely seen as undemocratic—opponents derided it as "King Caucus." A much-diminished caucus nominated a presidential candidate who then came in third in the electoral vote. The other three major candidates were essentially self-nominated.[6] The four candidates split the electoral vote so completely that the House of Representatives had to decide the contest. It picked John Quincy Adams, even though Andrew Jackson had won more popular and electoral votes.

In the run-up to the 1828 elections, two new parties grew up around the major candidates. Adams's supporters called themselves the National Republicans (later known as the Whigs). Jackson's supporters organized as the Democratic Party, which won the election.

9–2b A New Method: The Nominating Convention

In 1832, both parties settled on a new method of choosing candidates for president and vice president—the national nominating convention. A number of state parties had already adopted the convention system for choosing state-level candidates. New Jersey held conventions as early as 1800.

Nominating Conventions

A **nominating convention** is an official meeting of a political party to choose its candidates. Those who attend the convention are called **delegates,** and they are chosen to represent the people of a particular geographic area. Conventions can take place at multiple levels. A county convention might choose delegates to attend a state convention. The state convention, in turn, might select delegates to the national convention. By 1840, the convention system was the most common method of nominating political party candidates at the state and national levels.

Limits of the Convention System

While the convention system drew in a much broader range of leaders than had the caucus, it was not a particularly democratic institution. Convention delegates were rarely chosen by a vote of the party's local members. Typically, they were appointed by local party officials, who were usually, with good reason, called bosses. These local leaders often gained their positions in ways that were far from democratic. Not until 1972 did ordinary voters in all states gain the right to select delegates to the national presidential nominating conventions.

9–2c Primary Elections and the Loss of Party Control

The corruption that so often accompanied the convention system led reformers to call for a new way to choose candidates—the **primary election,** in which voters go to the polls to decide among candidates who seek the nomination of their party. Candidates who win a primary election then go on to compete against the candidates from other parties in the general election.

The first primary election may have been held in 1842 by Democrats in Crawford County, Pennsylvania. The technique was not widely used, however, until the end of the nineteenth

caucus A meeting held to choose political candidates or delegates.

nominating convention An official meeting of a political party to choose its candidates. Nominating conventions at the state and local levels also select delegates to represent the citizens of their geographic areas at a higher-level party convention.

delegate A person selected to represent the people of one geographic area at a party convention.

primary election An election in which voters choose the candidates of their party, who will then run in the general election.

century and the beginning of the twentieth. These were years in which reform was a popular cause.

Direct and Indirect Primaries

The rules for conducting primary elections are highly variable, and a number of different types of primaries exist. One major distinction is between a direct primary and an indirect primary.

In a **direct primary,** voters cast their ballots directly for candidates. The elections that nominate candidates for Congress and for state or local offices are almost always direct primaries.

In an *indirect primary,* voters choose delegates, who in turn choose the candidates. The delegates may be pledged to a particular candidate but sometimes run as *unpledged delegates.* The major parties use indirect primaries to elect delegates to the national nominating conventions that choose candidates for president and vice president.

The Role of the States

Primary elections are normally conducted by state governments. States set the dates and conduct the elections. They provide polling places, election officials, and registration lists, and they then count the votes. By sponsoring the primaries, state governments have obtained considerable influence over the rules by which the primaries are conducted. The power of the states is limited, however, by the parties' First Amendment right to freedom of association, a right that has been repeatedly confirmed by the United States Supreme Court.[7]

On occasion, parties that object to the rules imposed by state governments have opted out of the state-sponsored primary system altogether.[8] Note that third parties typically do not participate in state-sponsored primaries, but hold nominating conventions instead. The major parties rarely opt out of state elections, however, because the financial—and political—costs of going it alone are high. (When primary elections are used to choose candidates for local *nonpartisan* positions, state control is uncontested.)

Primary Voters

Voter turnout for primaries is lower than it is in general elections. The voters who do go to the polls are often strong supporters of their party. Indeed, as you will learn shortly, independents cannot participate in primary elections in some states, even if they lean toward one or the other of the two major parties. As a result, the Republican primary electorate is very conservative, and Democratic primary voters are quite liberal. Candidates often find that they must run to the political right or left during the primaries. They may then move to the center during the general election campaign.

Insurgent Candidates

Primary elections were designed to take nominations out of the hands of the party bosses. Indeed, the most important result of the primary system has been to reduce dramatically the power of elected and party officials over the nominating process.

Ever since primary elections were established, the insurgent candidate who runs against the party

When Senator John Kerry became secretary of state, Massachusetts had to call a special election to replace him. The candidates were Republican Gabriel Gomez, a former Navy Seal (left), and Democratic representative Edward Markey (right). In the end, Markey won.

---

direct primary

An election held within each of the two major parties—Democratic and Republican—to choose the party's candidates for the general election. Voters choose the candidate directly, rather than through delegates.

"establishment" has been a common phenomenon. Running against the "powers that be" is often a very effective campaign strategy, and many insurgents have won victories at the local, state, and national levels.

Occasionally, an insurgent's platform is strikingly different from that of the party as a whole. Yet even when an insurgent's politics are abhorrent to the rest of the party—for example, an insurgent might make an outright appeal to racism—the party has no way of denying the insurgent the right to the party label in the general election.

Closed and Open Primaries

Primaries can be classified as closed or open.

CLOSED PRIMARIES. In a **closed primary,** only party members can vote to choose that party's candidates, and they may vote only in the primary of their own party. Thus, only registered Democrats can vote in the Democratic primary, and only registered Republicans can vote for the Republican candidates. A person usually establishes party membership when she or he registers to vote. Some states have a *semiclosed* primary, which allows voters to register with a party or change their party affiliations on Election Day.

Regular party workers favor the closed primary because it promotes party loyalty. Independent voters usually oppose it because it forces them to select a party if they wish to participate in the nominating process.

OPEN PRIMARIES. In an **open primary,** voters can vote for a party's candidates regardless of whether they belong to the party. In most open primaries, all voters receive both a Republican ballot and a Democratic ballot. Voters then choose either the Democratic or the Republican ballot in the privacy of the voting booth. In a *semiopen* primary, voters request the ballot for the party of their choice.

MIXED FORMS. The fifty states have developed dozens of variations on the open and closed primary plans. In some states, primaries are closed only to persons registered to another party, and independents can vote in either primary. In several states, an independent who votes in a party primary is automatically enrolled in that party. In other states, the voter remains an independent. The two major parties often have different rules. For example, the Democrats allow independents to vote in the primaries in two states, but the Republicans do not.

Blanket and "Top Two" Primaries Until 2000, California and a few other states employed a *blanket primary,* in which voters could choose the candidates of more than one party. A voter might participate in choosing the Republican candidate for governor, for example, and at the same time vote to pick the Democratic candidate for the U.S. Senate. In that year, however, the Supreme Court ruled that the blanket primary violated the parties' right to freedom of association.[9] Similar primary systems in Washington and Alaska were struck down in later cases.

THE LOUISIANA MODEL. Louisiana for many years had a unique system in which all candidates participated in the same primary, regardless of party. The two candidates receiving the most votes then proceeded on to the general election. In 2008, Louisiana abandoned this system for the U.S. House and Senate, but kept it for state and local offices.

THE "TOP TWO" PRIMARY. Even as Louisiana was backing away from its system, other states began picking it up. Washington adopted the Louisiana system in 2004, and in 2008 the Supreme Court ruled that it was constitutional.[10] In June 2010, California voters adopted a system known as the *"top two" primary* that was patterned on the one in Washington. The California system went into effect in 2011, and in the 2012 general elections, eight U.S. House contests featured two members of the same party facing off against each other.

In such systems, political parties continue to have the right to designate preferred candidates, using conventions or other means, but their endorsements do not appear on the ballot. An insurgent Republican and a "regular" Republican, for example, would both be labeled simply "Republican."

9–2d Nominating Presidential Candidates

In some respects, being nominated for president is more difficult than being elected. The nominating process narrows a very large number of hopefuls down to a single candidate from each party. Choosing a presidential candidate is unlike nominating candidates for any other office.

closed primary
A primary in which only party members can vote to choose that party's candidates.

open primary A primary in which voters can vote for a party's candidates regardless of whether they belong to the party.

Republican presidential candidates: former Pennsylvania senator Rick Santorum, former Massachusetts governor Mitt Romney, former House Speaker Newt Gingrich, and Representative Ron Paul (R., Tex.) take the stage before one of the numerous Republican presidential candidate debates during 2011 and 2012.

AP PHOTO/MATT ROURKE

One reason for this is that the nomination process combines several different methods.

Presidential Primaries

Most of the states hold presidential primaries, beginning early in the election year. For a candidate, a good showing in the early primaries results in plenty of media attention as television networks and newspaper reporters play up the results. Subsequent primaries tend to eliminate candidates unlikely to be successful.

The presidential primaries do not necessarily follow the same rules the states use for nominating candidates for the U.S. Congress or for state and local offices. Often, the presidential primaries are not held on the same date as the other primaries. States frequently hold the presidential primaries early in hope of exercising greater influence on the outcome.

Caucuses

The caucus system is an alternative to primary elections. Strictly speaking, the caucus system is a convention system. The caucuses are party conventions held at the local level that elect delegates to conventions at the county or congressional district level. These midlevel conventions then choose the delegates to the state convention, which finally elects the delegates to the national party convention.

Unlike the caucuses of two centuries ago, modern caucuses are open to all party members. It is not hard to join a party. At the famous Iowa caucuses, you become a party member simply by attending a local caucus.

While some states, such as Iowa and Minnesota, rely on the caucus/convention system to nominate candidates for state and local positions, the system is more frequently used only to choose delegates to the Democratic and Republican national conventions. Most states with presidential caucuses use primaries to nominate state and local candidates. Twelve states choose national convention delegates through caucuses. Four states use caucuses to allocate some of the national convention delegates and use primaries to allocate the others.

Primaries—The Rush to Be First

Traditionally, states have held their presidential primaries at various times over the first six months of a presidential election year. In an effort to make their primaries prominent in the media and influential in the political process, however, many states have moved the date of their primary to earlier in the year—a practice known as *front-loading*. In 1988, a group of southern states created a "Super Tuesday" by hold-

196   PART 3: THE POLITICS OF DEMOCRACY

ing their primaries on the same day in early March. Then, other states moved their primaries to an earlier date, too.

The practice of front-loading primaries has gained momentum over the last decade. The states with later primary dates found that most nominations were decided early in the season, leaving their voters "out of the action." As more states moved up their primary dates, the early primaries became even more important, and other states, to compete, also moved up their primaries. This rush to be first was particularly notable in the year or so preceding the 2008 presidential primaries.

> ## "THERE IS NO EXCITEMENT
> anywhere in the world . . .
> to match the excitement of
> an American presidential
> campaign."
> ~ THEODORE H. WHITE ~
> AMERICAN JOURNALIST AND HISTORIAN
> 1915–1986

The Impact of Front-Loading

Many Americans worried that with a shortened primary season, long-shot candidates would no longer be able to propel themselves into serious contention by doing well in small early-voting states, such as New Hampshire and Iowa. Traditionally, a candidate who had a successful showing in the New Hampshire primary had time to obtain enough financial backing to continue in the race. The fear was that an accelerated schedule of presidential primaries would favor the richest candidates.

FRONT-LOADING IN 2008. In practice, front-loading did not have this effect in 2008. True, on the Republican side, Arizona senator John McCain had developed a clear lead by February 5. (A number of states that had moved their primaries to an earlier date held primaries on February 5.) The Republican primaries were mostly conducted on a winner-take-all basis, a rule that allowed McCain to wrap up the nomination on March 4.

The Democrats, however, allocated delegates on a proportional basis, so that each candidate received delegates based on his or her share of the vote. That rule made an early decision impossible, and Barack Obama did not obtain a majority of the Democratic delegates until June 3. As a result, many of the most important Democratic primaries took place late in the season. States that had moved their primaries to February 5 discovered that they were lost in the crowd of early contests. Front-loading, in other words, had become counterproductive.

FRONT-LOADING IN 2012. In 2012, the Democrats were expected to renominate President Obama without opposition, and so the Republican primaries were the only ones that mattered. In an attempt to reduce front-loading, the Republican National Committee ruled that only four traditionally early states, including Iowa and New Hampshire, could choose delegates before March 6. States choosing delegates through the rest of March would have to allocate them proportionally. From April 1 on, delegates could be selected on a winner-take-all basis. Several states violated these rules and had their delegations to the national convention cut in half.

The 2012 Republican Primaries

Two characteristics of the 2011–2012 Republican primary cycle stood out. One was the importance of a series of debates among the presidential candidates, held from May 2011 through February 2012. The second was the long-running attempt by Republican conservatives to find an alternative to former Massachusetts governor Mitt Romney, the eventual winner.

THE REPUBLICAN PRESIDENTIAL DEBATES. In previous years, the parties had often scheduled debates among the presidential candidates. During 2011, however, the Republican debates assumed an importance never before seen. During 2011, millions of Republicans and others tuned in to view them. As a result, campaign finance was temporarily of little importance, a striking development.

ANYBODY BUT ROMNEY. Throughout 2011 and early 2012, ultraconservative Republicans backed a series of candidates in an attempt to challenge Romney, the presumed front-runner. During the 2011–2012 campaigns, Romney's position on the issues was as conservative as that of any other candidate. Romney, however, had a history that was not particularly conservative. The state-level health-care insurance reforms he sponsored as governor of Massachusetts were particularly notable. This legislation bore a striking resemblance to Obamacare.

Michele Bachmann was the first candidate backed by conservatives who distrusted Romney, but her campaign faded early. In August, Texas governor Rick Perry entered the race. Perry proved to be a

disaster as a debater, however, and his support soon collapsed. Conservatives then pinned their hopes on Georgia businessman Herman Cain, an African American and an excellent speaker. In November, Cain's campaign was destroyed when several women alleged that he had harassed them sexually.

ROMNEY STRIKES BACK. By the time the primaries actually took place in 2012, the two conservative champions were former House Speaker Newt Gingrich of Georgia and former Pennsylvania senator Rick Santorum. Romney, however, was finally able to take advantage of his immense financial war chest. Romney defeated Gingrich in the Florida primary with the help of a barrage of negative advertisements. For his part, Santorum was unable to assemble the campaign necessary to compete with Romney on a level basis. Romney effectively secured the nomination in April.

National Party Conventions Created in the 1830s, the American national political convention is unique in Western democracies. Elsewhere, candidates for prime minister or chancellor are chosen within the confines of party councils. That is actually closer to the way the framers of the Constitution wanted it done.

GIANT PEP RALLIES. At one time, national conventions were often giant free-for-alls. It wasn't always clear who the winning presidential and vice-presidential candidates would be until the delegates voted.

As more states opted to hold presidential primaries, however, the drama of national conventions diminished. Today, the conventions have been described as massive pep rallies. Nonetheless, each convention's task remains a serious one. In late summer, two thousand to three thousand delegates gather at each convention to represent the wishes of the voters and political leaders of their home states.

THE CONVENTION SCHEDULE. On the first day of the convention, delegates hear the reports of the **Credentials Committee,** which inspects each prospective delegate's claim to be seated as a legitimate representative of her or his state. When the eligibility of delegates is in question, the committee decides who will be seated. Then, a carefully chosen keynote speaker whips up enthusiasm among the delegates. Later, the convention deals with committee reports and debates on the party platform. Finally, it turns to nominations and voting.

Balloting takes place with an alphabetical roll call in which states and territories announce their votes. The vice-presidential nomination takes place later. Acceptance speeches by the presidential and vice-presidential candidates are timed to take place during prime-time television hours. We provided more details on the national party conventions in Chapter 7.

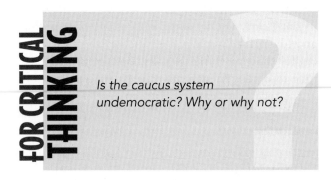

FOR CRITICAL THINKING

Is the caucus system undemocratic? Why or why not?

9–3 The Modern Political Campaign

Once nominated, candidates focus on their campaigns. The term *campaign* originated in the military context. Generals mounted campaigns, using their scarce resources (soldiers and materials) to achieve military objectives. Using the term in a political context is apt. In a political campaign, candidates also use scarce resources (time and funds) in an attempt to defeat their adversaries in the battle for votes.

9–3a Responsibilities of the Campaign Staff

To run a successful campaign, a candidate's campaign staff must be able to raise funds, get media coverage, produce and pay for political ads, schedule the candidate's time effectively with constituent groups

Credentials Committee
A committee of each national political party that evaluates the claims of national party convention delegates to be the legitimate representatives of their states.

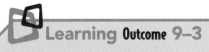

Learning Outcome 9-3

Indicate what is involved in launching a political campaign today, and describe the structure and functions of a campaign organization.

and potential supporters, convey the candidate's position on the issues, conduct research on the opposing candidate, and persuade the voters to go to the polls.

When party identification was firmer and TV campaigning was still in its infancy, a strong party organization on the local, state, or national level could furnish most of the services and expertise that the candidate needed. Today, party organizations are no longer as important as they once were in providing campaign services. Instead of relying so extensively on political parties, candidates now turn to professionals to manage their campaigns.

The fact that party organizations no longer provide large quantities of campaign services, however, should not lead anyone to believe that the parties are unimportant in campaigns. Because of the intense political polarization that has taken place in recent years, the parties are in some ways more important than ever. Political experts know that today, the party label allows them to predict how a senator or representative will vote on almost all issues. Many voters are also aware of this reality.

9-3b The Professional Campaign Organization

As mentioned, the role of the political party in managing campaigns has declined, although the party continues to play an important role in recruiting volunteers and getting out the vote. Professional **political consultants** now manage nearly all aspects of a presidential candidate's campaign. Most candidates for governor, the House, and the Senate also rely on consultants. Political consultants generally specialize in a particular area of the campaign, such as researching the opposition, conducting polls, developing the candidate's advertising, or organizing "get-out-the-vote" efforts. Nonetheless, most candidates have a campaign manager who coordinates and plans the **campaign strategy.** Figure 9–2 on the following page shows a typical presidential campaign organization.

A major development in contemporary American politics is the focus on reaching voters through effective use of the media, particularly television. At least half of the budget for a major political campaign is consumed by television advertising. Media consultants are therefore pivotal members of the campaign staff. The nature of political advertising is discussed in more detail in Chapter 10.

9-3c Opposition Research

Major campaigns, such as those for governor, senator, and U.S. president, typically make use of **opposition research.** A staff member—or even an entire team—spends time discovering as much negative information about opposing candidates as possible. Journalists often rely on opposition researchers for their stories.

One campaign adviser described the 2011–2012 political season as a "golden age of opposition research." In many ways, it was. A notable characteristic of opposition research in this period, though, was that candidate campaigns played a relatively modest role. Much of the research was undertaken by political activists operating independently of the campaigns.

Republican versus Republican Republican candidates for president in 2012 had little reason to fund opposition research on President Obama. This research had already been done in the 2008 elections, and there was little prospect of finding anything new. It was necessary only to repeat themes that had been developed earlier, such as Obama's alleged radicalism.

Republican candidates for president were much more vulnerable to opposition research because these politicians were not as well known to voters as Obama was. Because the Republican presidential primary campaigns were long and hard-fought, some of the damage done to various anti-Romney candidates was done by other Republicans, possibly including the Romney campaign organization.

Attempts to Define Mitt Romney Opposition research aimed at Mitt Romney himself, in contrast, was clearly tied to the Obama campaign. Obama supporters focused on Romney's time as CEO of Bain Capital, a financial

political consultant
A professional political adviser who, for a fee, works on an area of a candidate's campaign. Political consultants include campaign managers, pollsters, media advisers, and "get out the vote" organizers.

campaign strategy
The comprehensive plan developed by a candidate and his or her advisers for winning an election.

opposition research
The attempt to learn damaging information about an opponent in a political campaign.

FIGURE 9-2

A Typical Presidential
Campaign Organization

Most aspects of a candidate's campaign are managed by professional political consultants, as this figure illustrates.

CANDIDATE

Campaign Manager
Develops overall campaign strategy, manages finances, oversees staff

Campaign Staff
Undertakes the various tasks associated with campaigning

MEDIA CONSULTANTS	**FUND-RAISERS**	**SPEECHWRITERS**	**PRESS SECRETARY**	**POLICY EXPERTS**
Help to shape candidate's image, manage campaign advertising	Raise money to subsidize campaign	Prepare speeches for candidate's public appearances	Maintains press contacts, is responsible for disseminating campaign news	Provide input on foreign and domestic policy issues
LAWYERS AND ACCOUNTANTS	**PRIVATE POLLSTER**	**RESEARCHERS**	**TRAVEL PLANNER**	**WEB CONSULTANT**
Monitor legal and financial aspects of campaign	Gathers up-to-the-minute data on public opinion	Investigate opponents' records and personal history	Arranges for candidate's transportation and accommodations	Oversees candidate's Internet presence

State Campaign Chairpersons
Monitor state and local campaigns

Local Committees
Direct efforts of local volunteers

Volunteers
Publicize candidate at local level through personal visits, phone calls, direct mailings, and online activities

firm. Democrats accused Romney of sabotaging profitable companies and of shipping jobs overseas. They also publicized Romney's failure to release any income tax returns for years before 2010, and the relatively low 14 percent average tax rate on his income that he paid on the returns he did release. Clearly, the intent of these allegations was to define Romney as a cold-hearted businessman with little concern for the problems of ordinary Americans.

FOR CRITICAL THINKING

Some people have accused political consultants of "managing the candidate" too well, making the candidate appear stilted and unnatural. *How could a candidate prevent that from happening?*

9-4 The Internet Campaign

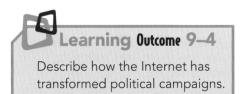

Learning Outcome 9-4

Describe how the Internet has transformed political campaigns.

Over the years, political leaders have benefited from understanding and using new communications technologies. In the 1930s, command of a new medium—radio—gave President Franklin D. Roosevelt an edge. In 1960, Democratic presidential candidate John F. Kennedy gained an advantage over Republican Richard Nixon because Kennedy had a better understanding of the visual requirements of television.

Today, the ability to make effective use of social media and the Internet is essential to a candidate. In the 2008 presidential elections, Barack Obama gained an edge on his rivals in part because of his superior use of the new technologies. His team relied on the Internet for fund-raising, targeting potential supporters, and creating local political organizations. His 2012 campaign was even more sophisticated.

9-4a Fund-Raising on the Internet

Internet fund-raising grew out of an earlier technique: the direct-mail campaign. In direct mailings, campaigns send solicitations to large numbers of likely prospects, typically seeking contributions. Developing good lists of prospects is central to an effective direct-mail operation, because postage, printing, and the rental of address lists make the costs of each mailing high. In many direct-mail campaigns, most of the funds raised are used up by the costs of the campaign itself. In contrast to the costs, response rates are low—a 1 percent response rate is a tremendous success. From the 1970s on, conservative organizations became especially adept at managing direct-mail campaigns. For a time, this expertise gave conservative causes and candidates an advantage over liberals.

To understand the old system is to recognize the superiority of the new one. The cost of e-mailing is very low. Lists of prospects need not be prepared as carefully, because e-mail sent to unlikely prospects does not waste resources. E-mail fund-raising did face one problem when it was new—many people were not yet online. Today, that issue is no longer so important.

The new technology brought with it a change in the groups that benefited the most. Conservatives were no longer the most effective fund-raisers. Instead, liberal and libertarian organizations enjoyed some of the greatest successes.

Obama Online Barack Obama took Internet fund-raising to a new level. One of the defining characteristics of his fund-raising has been its decentralization. The Obama campaign has attempted to recruit as many supporters as possible to act as fund-raisers who will solicit contributions from their friends and neighbors. As a result, Obama has been spared much of the personal fund-raising effort that consumes the time of most national politicians.

Obama's online operation in 2011–2012 made a major contribution to his $1.25 billion fund-raising total. Even more than in his first race, the sums came largely from smaller donors. Many of the wealthy individuals who had contributed to Obama earlier

AP PHOTO/CHARLES DHARAPAK

President Obama sends a tweet during a "Twitter Town Hall" at the White House. How important was the Internet to Obama's reelection?

had been alienated by the president's policies and his rhetorical attacks on the rich.

Republicans Online Already in 2008, one Republican candidate was able to use the Internet with great success—Texas representative Ron Paul, who espoused a libertarian philosophy that was highly appealing to many high-tech enthusiasts. Paul pioneered the online *moneybomb* technique, described by the San José *Mercury News* as "a one-day fund-raising frenzy." A moneybomb organized by Paul supporters in December 2007 raised $6.3 million, a new record for one-day fund-raising. (Obama's moneybombs soon bested Paul's totals, however.) Despite Paul's fund-raising prowess, his libertarian politics were sufficiently far from the conservative Republican mainstream that he was able to win only a handful of national convention delegates.

In 2012, Mitt Romney was less reliant on the Internet than many other recent candidates. In part, this was because much of his campaign finance came in large chunks from wealthy individuals—the reverse of Obama's experience. Romney's campaign fund-raising roughly matched Obama's—about $1.25 billion in total.

9–4b Targeting Supporters

In 2004, President George W. Bush's chief political adviser, Karl Rove, pioneered a new campaign technique known as *microtargeting*. The process involves collecting as much information as possible about voters in a gigantic database and then filtering out various groups for special attention.

Through microtargeting, for example, the Bush campaign could identify Republican prospects living in heavily Democratic neighborhoods—potential supporters whom the campaign might otherwise have neglected because the neighborhood as a whole seemed so unpromising. In 2004, the Democrats had nothing to match Republican efforts. In 2012, however, Obama's microtargeting operation vastly outperformed Romney's.

9–4c Support for Local Organizing

Perhaps the most effective use of the Internet has been as an organizing tool. One of the earliest Internet techniques was to use the site **Meetup.com** to organize real-world meetings. In this way, campaigns were able to gather supporters without relying on the existing party and activist infrastructure.

Obama's Campaign As with fund-raising, Barack Obama took Web-based organizing to a new level. In 2012, Obama had seven times as many Facebook supporters as Romney (28 million versus 4 million). Although this was a substantial advantage, it was not necessarily as significant as you might think. The problem is that the Facebook demographic is heavily weighted toward young people who either cannot or do not vote. Indeed, surveys in 2012 showed that those least likely to vote supported Obama by a two-to-one margin. The question for the Obama campaign, therefore, was whether it could turn politically disengaged social media participants into actual voters.

> **"IN CONSTANT PURSUIT OF MONEY** to finance campaigns, the political system is simply unable to function. Its deliberative powers are paralyzed."
>
> ~ JOHN RAWLS ~
> AMERICAN EDUCATOR
> 1921–2000

The Ground Game A modern campaign collects as much data as it can—in part, through use of Internet resources—to identify the people whose votes it wants. The data are used to make human contact more efficient by directing volunteers toward the voters they most need to reach. Such get-out-the-vote drives have been called the *ground game* (as opposed to advertising, called the *air game*).

By 2012, Obama had had years to perfect his ground game, and it showed. The Obama campaign was able to create active local support groups in towns and counties across the country—many in areas that had traditionally supported Republicans. By comparison, Romney's ground game sometimes looked like a comedy of errors. His volunteers often called the wrong voters. The team developed a major Web program called Orca to allocate resources on Election Day. It crashed. A staffer reported, "Orca is lying on the beach with a harpoon in it." Even if Orca had worked perfectly, Election Day would have been far too late for it to be effective.

Some candidates are more successful than others in using the Internet. *Do such candidates have any traits in common? If so, what might these be?*

9–5 What It Costs to Win

Learning Outcome 9–5

Summarize the current laws that regulate campaign financing and the role of money in modern political campaigns.

The modern political campaign is an expensive undertaking. Candidates must spend huge sums for professional campaign managers and consultants, television and radio ads, the printing of campaign literature, travel, office rent, equipment, and other necessities.

To get an idea of the cost of waging a campaign for Congress today, consider that the average House candidate appearing on the 2012 general election ballot spent about $1.1 million on his or her own campaign. Outside organizations nominally unaffiliated with the campaign spent another $0.4 million. In Senate races, the comparable amounts were $6.4 million and $4 million.

Of course, some contests were much more expensive than the average. In the Massachusetts Senate race, Republican Scott Brown spent $35 million, while Democrat Elizabeth Warren, the winner, laid out $42 million. Each candidate benefited from an additional $4 million in outside spending. In a highly contested House race in Florida, Tea Party favorite Allen West spent more than $18 million and enjoyed another $4 million in outside funds. His Democratic opponent, Patrick Murphy, spent only $4.5 million, plus $2.5 million in outside money. Murphy, however, won the race. West's loss is a reminder that money doesn't necessarily win elections. For one thing, when political advertising exceeds a certain saturation level, voters tune out. Additional commercials are simply wasted.

9–5a Presidential Spending

Presidential campaigns are even more costly than congressional campaigns. As noted, in the 2011–2012 presidential election cycle, spending by the two major candidates approached $2.5 billion. Despite restrictions on how the major political parties could raise funds, each had accumulated about $600 million by September 2012.

Furthermore, in today's campaign-finance environment, the sums spent by the candidates themselves and by the parties are only part of the story. Independent expenditures by outside groups nominally unconnected with the campaigns have become as important as spending by the candidates themselves. (We discuss independent expenditures in more detail later in this chapter.) Total presidential campaign spending, including spending by candidates who lost in the primaries and by outside groups, reached $4.5 billion in the 2011–2012 cycle.

The groups responsible for much of this spending, known as *super PACs,* are a new development. They became prominent only in the 2011–2012 campaign cycle. Super PACs resulted from recent court decisions, especially the Supreme Court's ruling in *Citizens United v. Federal Election Commission.* We discuss that decision later in this section. First, however, we examine the development of our campaign-finance system.

9–5b The Federal Election Campaign Act

The high cost of campaigns gives rise to the fear that campaign contributors and special interest groups will try to buy favored treatment from those who are elected to office. In an attempt to prevent these abuses, the government has tried to regulate campaign financing.

Legislation to regulate campaign finance was passed in 1925 and 1939, but these early efforts were almost completely ineffective. The first reform that actually had teeth was the Federal Election Campaign Act (FECA) of 1971.[11] The act was amended in 1974. As amended, the new law did the following:

- Restricted the amount that could be spent on mass media advertising, including television.

- Limited how much individuals and groups could contribute to candidates.

- Limited the amount that candidates and their families could contribute to their own campaigns.

- Prevented corporations and labor unions from participating directly in political campaigns, but allowed them to set up political action committees (discussed shortly).

Ben Cohen, co-founder of Ben & Jerry's Ice Cream, holds up a one-dollar bill he stamped with the words "Not to be used for bribing politicians." Cohen advocates getting money out of politics.

SAUL LOEB/AFP/GETTY IMAGES

- Required disclosure of all contributions and expenditures of more than $100.

- Created the Federal Election Commission (FEC) to administer and enforce the act's provisions.

In addition, the act provided public financing for presidential primaries and general elections, funded by a checkoff on federal income tax returns. From 1976 through 2000, presidential campaigns were largely funded by the public purse. Beginning in 2004, however, leading Democratic and Republican presidential candidates were refusing public funding for the primaries. By 2012, the public financing of presidential campaigns was effectively over.

soft money Campaign contributions not regulated by federal law, such as some contributions that are made to political parties instead of to particular candidates.

independent expenditure An expenditure for activities that are independent from (not coordinated with) those of a political candidate or a political party.

Freeing Up Self-Financing In 1976, the United States Supreme Court declared unconstitutional the provision in the 1971 act that limited the

amount each individual could spend on his or her own campaign. The Court held that a "candidate, no less than any other person, has a First Amendment right to engage in the discussion of public issues and vigorously and tirelessly to advocate his own election."[12]

The Rise of PACs The FECA allowed corporations, labor unions, and special interest groups to set up national *political action committees (PACs)* to raise money for candidates. PACs can contribute up to $5,000 per candidate in each election, but there is no limit on the total amount of PAC contributions during an election cycle.

As discussed in Chapter 6, the number of PACs grew significantly from the 1970s, as did their campaign contributions. In the 2004 election cycle, about 36 percent of campaign funds spent on House races came from PACs.[13] Since 2004, however, other methods of raising campaign funds have reduced the relative importance of traditional PACs.

9–5c Skirting the Campaign-Financing Rules

The FECA was designed to regulate funds given to the campaign organizations of candidates for office. There are ways, however, to influence the political process without giving money directly to a candidate's campaign. Individuals and corporations soon developed such practices. One way to skirt the rules was to contribute to the political parties instead of the candidates. A second was to make independent expenditures not coordinated with a candidate's campaign or a political party.

Soft Money The FECA and its amendments did not prohibit individuals or corporations from contributing to political parties. Contributors could make donations to the parties to cover the costs of registering voters, printing flyers, advertising, developing campaigns to get out the vote, and holding fundraising events. Contributions to political parties were called **soft money.**

By 2000, the parties were raising nearly $463 million per election season through soft money contributions. Soft dollars became the main source of campaign money in the presidential race until after the 2002 elections, when soft money was banned, as you will read shortly.

Independent Expenditures The campaign-financing laws did not prohibit corporations, labor unions, and special interest groups from making **independent expenditures** in an election campaign.

Independent expenditures, as the term implies, are expenditures for activities that are independent of (not coordinated with) those of a candidate or a political party.

Decisions by the courts have distinguished two types of independent expenditures. In the first type, an interest group or other contributor wages an "issue campaign" without going so far as to say "Vote for Candidate X." An issue campaign might, however, go so far as to publish voter guides informing voters of candidates' positions. The courts have repeatedly upheld the right of groups to advocate their positions in this way.

Alternatively, a group might explicitly campaign for particular candidates. The Supreme Court has held that an issue-oriented group has a First Amendment right to advocate the election of its preferred candidates as long as it acts independently of the candidates' campaigns. In 1996, the Court held that these guidelines apply to expenditures by political parties as well.[14]

9–5d The Bipartisan Campaign Reform Act of 2002

The increasing use of soft money and independent expenditures led to a demand for further campaign-finance reform. In 2002, Congress passed, and the president signed, the Bipartisan Campaign Reform Act. The measure is also known as the McCain-Feingold Act after its chief sponsors, Senators John McCain (R., Ariz.) and Russell Feingold (D., Wisc.).

The new law banned soft money at the national level. It also regulated campaign ads paid for by interest groups and prohibited any such issue-advocacy commercials within thirty days of a primary election or sixty days of a general election.

The 2002 act set the amount that an individual could contribute to a federal candidate at $2,000 and the amount that an individual could give to all federal candidates at $95,000 over a two-year election cycle. (Under the law, some individual contribution limits are indexed for inflation and thus may change slightly with every election cycle.) Individuals could still contribute to state and local parties, so long as the contributions did not exceed $10,000 per year per individual. The new law went into effect the day after the 2002 general elections.

The Supreme Court Upholds McCain-Feingold Several groups immediately filed lawsuits challenging the constitutionality of the new law. Supporters of the restrictions on campaign ads by special interest groups argued that the large amounts of funds spent on these ads create an appearance of corruption in the political process. In contrast, an attorney for the National Rifle Association (NRA) argued that because the NRA represents "millions of Americans speaking in unison ... [it] is not a *corruption* of the democratic political process; it *is* the democratic political process."[15] In December 2003, the Supreme Court upheld nearly all of the clauses of the act in *McConnell v. Federal Election Commission.*[16]

> "A PROMISING YOUNG MAN
>
> should go into politics so that he can go on promising for the rest of his life."
>
> ~ ROBERT BYRNE ~
> AMERICAN AUTHOR
> B. 1930

The Supreme Court Changes Its Mind

Beginning in 2007, however, the Supreme Court began to chip away at the limits on independent expenditures contained in McCain-Feingold. In that year, in *Federal Election Commission v. Wisconsin Right to Life, Inc.,* the Court invalidated a major part of the 2002 law and overruled a portion of its own 2003 decision upholding the act. In the four years since the earlier ruling, Chief Justice John Roberts, Jr., and Associate Justice Samuel Alito, Jr., had been appointed, and both were conservatives.

In a five-to-four decision, the Court held that issue ads could not be prohibited in the time period preceding elections (thirty days before primary elections and sixty days before general elections) *unless* they were "susceptible of no reasonable interpretation other than as an appeal to vote for or against a specific candidate."[17] The Court concluded that restricting *all* television ads paid for by corporate or labor union treasuries in the weeks before an election amounted to censorship of political speech.

Citizens United v. Federal Election Commission (FEC)

A January 2010 Supreme Court ruling helped establish our current wide-open campaign-finance system. This decision, *Citizens United v. FEC,* was initially seen as fostering a vast new wave of corporate spending on elections. The actual results were somewhat different, as you will read shortly.

In this artist's rendering, U.S. Solicitor General Elena Kagan, right, argues her first case before the Supreme Court, *Citizens United v. Federal Election Commission*, in Washington, D.C.

In the *Wisconsin Right to Life* case described earlier, the Court ruled out bans on issue ads placed by corporations and other organizations in the run-up to an election. In *Citizens United v. FEC*, the Court extended this protection to ads that attack or praise specific candidates, including ads that suggest voting for particular candidates.[18] Two months later, in *Speechnow v. FEC*, a federal court of appeals held that it was not possible to limit contributions to independent-expenditure groups based on the size or source of the contribution.[19]

As a result of these two decisions, *Citizens United* and *Speechnow*, there is now no limit on the ability of corporations, unions, nonprofit groups, or individuals to fund advertising, provided that they do not contribute directly to a candidate's campaign. While Republican leaders applauded the *Citizens United* ruling as a victory for free speech, most Democratic leaders were appalled. They feared that the ruling would result in a massive tilting of the political landscape toward corporate wealth.

9–5e The Current Campaign-Finance Environment

Because the *Citizens United* decision was issued less than a year before the 2010 elections, its impact in that year was modest. By 2012, however, the new rules had changed the shape of the campaign-finance environment. Individuals and PACs still faced limits on what they could contribute directly to candidates' campaigns and to the parties. Despite these limits, the campaigns and parties were still able to raise huge sums. Meanwhile, independent organizations stood out as the wildcard in American politics. We list the largest independent expenditures in the 2012 election cycle in Table 9–1 on the following page.

Super PACs A new type of organization came into existence to take advantage of the new rules. Known officially as "independent-expenditure only committees," the new bodies were soon dubbed super PACs.

THE MYTH OF INDEPENDENCE. The super PACs' supposed independence from campaigns turned out to be a convenient fiction. By 2011, every major presidential candidate had one or more affiliated super PACs, usually run by former members of the candidate's own campaign. Newt Gingrich, Ron Paul, Rick Perry, Mitt Romney, Rick Santorum—and Barack Obama—each had an associated super PAC. A division of labor soon developed. Super PACs would run

TABLE 9-1

The Twenty Top Groups Making Independent Expenditures during the 2011-2012 Cycle

This table lists independent expenditures only. Some groups, such as the party committees, have designated only a small part of their total fund-raising as independent expenditures.

Committee	Affiliation	Raised 2011–2012	Type	Disclosure of Contributors
American Crossroads & Crossroads GPS	Republican	$176,429,025	Super PAC, 501c	partial
Restore Our Future	Mitt Romney	$142,097,336	Super PAC	full
Priorities USA & Priorities USA Action	Barack Obama	$65,166,859	Super PAC	partial
National Republican Congressional Committee	Republican	$64,653,078	party committee	full
Democratic Congressional Campaign Committee	Democratic	$60,545,352	party committee	full
Democratic Senatorial Campaign Committee	Democratic	$52,834,293	party committee	full
Republican National Committee	Republican	$43,629,275	party committee	full
Majority PAC	Senate Democrats	$37,498,257	Super PAC	full
Americans for Prosperity	Koch brothers (conservative)	$36,352,928	501c	none
U.S. Chamber of Commerce	business	$35,657,029	501c	none
National Republican Senatorial Committee	Republican	$32,114,674	party committee	full
House Majority PAC	Democratic	$30,470,122	Super PAC	full
American Future Fund	conservative	$25,415,969	501c	none
Service Employees International Union	labor	$23,011,004	Super PAC, 501c	full
National Rifle Association	special interest	$19,767,043	501c	partial
Freedom Works	Dick Armey (conservative)	$19,638,968	Super PAC	partial
American Federation of State, County & Municipal Employees	labor	$18,012,198	501c	full
Club for Growth	antitax	$17,960,737	Super PAC, 501c	partial
Winning Our Future	Newt Gingrich	$17,007,762	Super PAC	full
Americans for Job Security	conservative	$15,872,864	501c	none

Source: Center for Responsive Politics.

negative ads to damage a candidate's opponents, while candidate committees accentuated the positive about the candidate.

THE ROLE OF THE INDIVIDUAL DONOR. When the *Citizens United* decision was handed down, a flood of corporate cash was expected to enter the political system. The ruling did result in more corporate (and union) spending but far less than anticipated. Apparently, many companies were reluctant to take stands that might alienate a large number of customers. What caught everyone by surprise was the huge volume of finance poured into super PACs by individuals, notably individuals of great wealth.

For example, Charles and David Koch, two brothers with a long-standing commitment to conservative politics, set up their own independent committee, which soon became one of the largest. In January 2012, Sheldon Adelson, a casino billionaire, contributed $5 million to Newt Gingrich's super PAC, and shortly thereafter Adelson's wife kicked in another $5 million. The Adelsons are credited with keeping Gingrich's campaign alive for an extra month. In June, Adelson donated $10 million to Mitt Romney's super

Casino billionaire Sheldon Adelson and his wife each donated $5 million to Newt Gingrich's super PAC. Adelson's total donations to all candidates may have exceeded $100 million.

tax code that covers it. Spending by 527s rose rapidly after 2002, and in the 2004 election cycle, the committees spent about $612 million to "advocate positions," as they were not allowed to "expressly advocate" voting for specific candidates. By 2008, 527 committees began to decline in importance, and by 2012 they had been replaced almost completely by super PACS, which were allowed to campaign for and against candidates.

One reason for the decline of the 527 in 2008 was the creation of a new kind of body, the *501(c)4 organization,* known as the *501c.* Like the 527, this type of committee was named after a provision in the tax code. According to some lawyers, a 501c could make limited contributions directly to campaigns and—perhaps more importantly—could conceal the identities of its donors. So far, the FEC has refused to rule on the legality of this technique. Table 9–1 indicates which major independent committees are super PACs and which are 501c organizations. Some groups have organized both types.

The 501c's ability to hide its contributors created a new campaign-finance issue. Republicans argued that donors needed the right to remain anonymous so that they would not have to fear retribution. Democrats contended that anonymous contributions were simply a further corruption of the political process. Attempts to end donor anonymity through legislation failed. We discuss the issue of anonymous donations in the *Join the Debate* feature on the following page.

PAC. While conservative donors gained much attention, some billionaires also backed Democrats. As far back as 2004, for example, financier George Soros gave almost $24 million to independent groups dedicated to defeating Republican president George W. Bush. The largest Democratic donor in 2012 was Chicago businessman Fred Eychaner, who gave more than $8 million to Democratic super PACs and committees.

527 and 501c Committees
In addition to super PACs, another type of independent committee is the *527 committee,* named after the provision of the

FOR CRITICAL THINKING

Under what circumstances would you consider political contributions to be free speech— and under what circumstances would you see them as thinly veiled bribes to public officials?

Should We Let Political Contributors Conceal Their Identities?

In the run-up to every November general election, television watchers can be certain that they will be bombarded with negative political ads. Such ads must identify their sponsors. If you see an ad by the Committee for the Advancement of Everything Good, though, how can you tell who actually funded it?

Many of these ads are put together by super PACs or 501c organizations, which we described in this chapter. If you go to the Web sites of these organizations, you are not likely to learn who provided the funds. In some cases, you might be able to find the answer at the Web site of the Federal Election Commission or a watchdog organization such as OpenSecrets. As you can see from Table 9–1 on page 207, however, four of the twenty largest independent expenditure organizations hide the identities of all their donors. Another five offer donors the option of hiding their identities.

Full Disclosure, Please

Polls show that a strong majority of voters are concerned about the role of money in politics. No one believes that special interest money is going to disappear, but most voters from both parties say that we should know who is making the contributions.

Opponents of anonymous contributions point to a number of reasons why they should have no place in our democracy. When voters evaluate a candidate, they have the right to know who stands behind that person. Which unions, corporations, trade associations, or individual billionaires are supporting him or her? How can we battle undue influence on the part of special interests if we don't know which interests are supporting which candidates? Also, those who fund misleading advertisements or even flat-out lies should take responsibility for their messages. Furthermore, small campaign contributors lose out when they are up against well-funded super PACs with anonymous donors. Candidates can compete fairly for public office only when we eliminate secret funding of political campaigns.

Political Privacy Should Be a Civil Right

Not everyone is in favor of forcing secret donors to political campaigns out into the open. Consider that in 1958, the United States Supreme Court ruled that Alabama could not require the NAACP to disclose its membership rolls. Why not? Because if segregationists in Alabama were able to identify NAACP members, they could retaliate against the most vulnerable ones. Some members might lose their jobs or be threatened with violence. Publicizing the membership list of an organization such as the NAACP would make a mockery of the constitutional rights to free association and free speech. According to the Court, the privacy of group membership is critical to "effective advocacy of both public and private points of view, particularly controversial ones."

If all political contributions were exposed, what could happen to a supporter of a liberal cause such as gay rights if he or she worked for a conservative employer? In California, supporters of same-sex marriage picketed and boycotted various groups that funded opposition to gay marriage. Banning anonymous donations harms free speech—not the other way around.

FOR CRITICAL ANALYSIS Who would benefit from full disclosure of all financial supporters of super PACs?

AMERICA AT
ODDS Campaigns and Elections

Some observers believe that if the founders could see how presidential campaigns are conducted today, they would be shocked at how candidates "pander to the masses." Whether they would be shocked at the costliness of modern campaigns is not as clear. After all, the founders themselves were an elitist, wealthy group, as are many of today's successful candidates for high political office. In any event, Americans today are certainly stunned by how much it takes to win an election. Some of the specific controversies that divide Americans concerning campaigns are the following:

- Is the electoral college a dangerous anachronism—or a force for stability within our political system?

- Should all voters be free to participate in any party primary—or does such a step make it too difficult for the parties to present a coherent group of candidates and policies?

- Should states retain their treasured right to set the dates of their presidential primaries—or should the national parties assume responsibility for establishing a rational primary schedule?

- Are campaign contributions a constitutionally protected form of free speech—or are they too often a source of corruption within the political system?

- Should all politically active groups be required to furnish the identities of their major contributors—or should we allow contributors to remain anonymous because they might suffer reprisals due to their contributions?

STUDY TOOLS

Ready to study?

- **Review** what you've read with the quiz below.
- Check your answers on the **Chapter in Review** card at the back of the book.
- For any questions you miss, read the corresponding **Learning Outcome** section again to prepare for class and your exam.
- Rip out and study the **Chapter in Review** card (at the back of the book).

Fill-In

Learning Outcome 9–1

1. The electoral college system is primarily a winner-take-all system, in which the candidate _____.

2. A candidate must win at least _____ electoral votes, cast by the electors, to become president through the electoral college system.

Learning Outcome 9–2

3. In a _____ primary, voters cast their ballots directly for candidates.

4. In the context of presidential primaries, the practice known as front-loading refers to _____.

Learning Outcome 9–3

5. The attempt to learn damaging information about an opponent in a political campaign is called _____ research.

Learning Outcome 9–4

6. A campaign technique known as microtargeting involves _____.

Learning Outcome 9–5

7. The Federal Election Campaign Act of 1971 and its amendments provided public financing for presidential primaries and general elections, funded by a checkoff on _____

8. As a result of the Supreme Court's decision in *Citizens United v. Federal Election Commission* (2010), a new type of organization came into existence. Known officially as "independent-expenditure only committees," the new bodies were soon dubbed _____.

Multiple Choice

Learning Outcome 9–1

9. The total number of electoral votes available is
   a. 538.   b. 535.   c. 435.

10. If no presidential candidate receives the required number of electoral votes,
    a. a runoff election is held in January.
    b. the House of Representatives votes on the candidates, with each state delegation casting only a single vote.
    c. the Senate votes on the candidates, with each senator casting one vote.

Learning Outcome 9–2

11. In a(n) ____ primary, only party members can vote to choose that party's candidates, and they may vote only in the primary of their own party.
    a. closed   b. open   c. indirect

12. In late summer of a presidential election year, ____ gather at their party's national convention to adopt the party platform and to nominate the party's presidential and vice-presidential candidates.
    a. poll watchers   b. delegates   c. electors

Learning Outcome 9–3

13. With the rise of candidate-centered campaigns in the past several decades, the role of the political party in managing campaigns has
    a. increased.   c. declined.
    b. stayed about the same.

Learning Outcome 9–4

14. Barack Obama gained an edge on his rivals in part because of his superior use of
    a. radio.   c. social media and the Internet.
    b. television.

Learning Outcome 9–5

15. The Federal Election Campaign Act allows corporations, labor unions, and interest groups to set up PACs to raise money for candidates. PACs can contribute up to ____ per candidate in each election, but there is no limit on the total amount of PAC contributions during an election cycle.
    a. $2,000   b. $5,000   c. $95,000

GOVT

10

Politics and the Media

The **Learning Outcomes** labeled 1 through 5 are designed to help improve your understanding of the chapter. After reading this chapter, you should be able to:

10–1 Explain the role of the media in a democracy.

10–2 Summarize how television influences the conduct of political campaigns.

10–3 Explain why talk radio has been described as the Wild West of the media.

10–4 Describe types of media bias and explain how such bias affects the political process.

10–5 Indicate the extent to which the Internet is reshaping news and political campaigns.

Remember to visit page 232 for additional Study Tools

ALEX WONG/GETTY IMAGES FOR MEET THE PRESS

AMERICA AT
ODDS Do We Still Need Newspapers?

The *New York Times.* The *Washington Post.* The *Wall Street Journal.* The *Christian Science Monitor.* These and hundreds of other major and minor newspapers have generated and disseminated the nation's news for more than one hundred years. But recent times have brought great changes to the newspaper industry.

The Great Recession was hard on newspaper revenues. Some famous newspapers have filed for bankruptcy protection. The following newspapers no longer exist: the *Tucson Citizen,* the *Rocky Mountain News,* the *Baltimore Examiner,* the *Cincinnati Post,* and the *Albuquerque Tribune.* Other newspapers have reduced their printing schedules or have gone completely online.

The online revolution has changed the newspaper business—and may destroy it. The key blow was financial. Classified advertising has always been a major revenue source for newspapers, but various Internet sites such as Craigslist have taken over this function in recent years.

True, newspapers have gone online, but most have been unable to sell enough advertisements to pay for their online editions. The dean of the U.S. investing community, Warren Buffett, has said that the newspaper business faces "unending losses."

We Don't Need Newspapers— Free Content Is Everywhere

Those who do not mourn the loss of newspapers—particularly the younger generation—point out the obvious. Americans have more access to more news than ever before. Online news is available and updated day and night. An enormous number of citizen bloggers will help you find out what is happening anywhere in the world, at any time you want. So who needs newspapers?

In the past, local newspapers were monopolies. Today, journalists have to put up with competition just like everyone else, and that is for the best. Even if your hometown newspaper shuts down, "hyperlocal" Web sites are increasingly available to deliver local news. Many of these sites are organized by companies such as EveryBlock, Outside.In, Placeblogger, and Patch.

In the past, most Americans had to put up with whatever point of view their local newspaper provided. That is no longer the case. You can find the news—presented in whatever way you like—on thousands of Internet news sites and millions of blogs. Variety is the spice of life, and we certainly have more variety in news gathering and presentation than ever before. Newspapers are dead. Long live the news.

We Need Real Reporters, and Newspapers Offer Them

The reality of this world is that people have to be paid to do a good job, no matter what that job is. Journalists have families to feed. Rarely are they independently wealthy amateurs. Where does all that free content on the Web come from? Most of it can ultimately be traced back to journalists working for the print media. This is true of hyperlocal sites as well. Even today, newspapers employ the overwhelming majority of all journalists. How many bloggers bother to attend city council meetings and report what happens? Precious few do.

A British reporter sums up the entire argument: "The real value that newspapers provide, whether in print or online, is organization, editing, and reputation." The issue is not the survival of the newspaper industry, but the survival of an informed citizenry. If citizens believe that all information, no matter where it comes from—blogs, tweets, Web sites that promote conspiracy theories—is of the same value, then these citizens are in trouble.

We need to change the way newspapers work. We need to figure out ways in which online versions of publications can earn enough revenue to be self-supporting. If we do this, we can ensure that newspapers remain the mainstay of American news gathering and distribution.

Where do you stand?

1. Most young people rarely, if ever, read a newspaper. Does that mean they are not getting any news? Why or why not?
2. How much do you think the reputation of a news source really matters?

Explore this issue online

Newspapers have been harder hit in Michigan than in any other state. Ann Arbor, home of the University of Michigan, is the largest urban area in the country to lose its only daily newspaper. Papers in Flint, Saginaw, and Bay City now publish only three times a week, and the Detroit papers have drastically cut back their distribution. Statewide coverage is now provided by the online service www.mlive.com. For details of how the *Ann Arbor News* came to close its doors, search on "Ann Arbor News wiki."

Introduction

The debate over whether we need newspapers, described in the chapter-opening *America at Odds* feature, is just one aspect of an important topic: the role of the media in American politics. Strictly defined, the term *media* means communication channels. It is the plural form of *medium,* as in a medium, or means, of communication. In this strict sense, any method used by people to communicate—including the telephone—is a communication medium.

In this chapter, though, we look at the **mass media**—channels through which people can communicate to large audiences. These channels include the **print media** (newspapers and magazines) and the **electronic media** (radio, television, and the Internet).

10–1 The Role of the Media in a Democracy

What the media say and do has an impact on what Americans think about political issues. But just as clearly, the media also *reflect* what Americans think about politics. Some scholars argue that the media are the fourth "check" in our political system—checking and balancing the power of the president, the Congress, and the courts. The power of the media today is enormous, but how the media use their power is an issue about which Americans are often at odds.

10–1a Media Characteristics

The media are a dominant presence in our lives largely because they provide entertainment. Americans today enjoy more leisure than at any time in history, and we fill it up with e-books, movies, Web surfing, texting, and television—a huge amount of television. But the media play a vital role in our political lives as well, particularly during campaigns and elections. Politicians and political candidates have learned—often the hard way—that positive media exposure and news coverage are essential to winning votes.

As you read in Chapter 4, one of the most important civil liberties protected in the Bill of Rights is freedom of the press. Like free speech, a free press is considered a vital tool of the democratic process. If people are to cast informed votes, they must have access to a forum in which they can discuss public affairs fully and assess the conduct and competency of their officials. The media provide this forum.

In contrast, government censorship of the press is common in many nations around the globe. One example is China, where the Web is heavily censored, even though China now has more Internet users than any other country on earth.

10–1b The New Media and the Old

From the founding of the nation through the early years of the twentieth century, all media were print media—newspapers, magazines, and books. Beginning in the twentieth century, however, new media forms were introduced. Radio and motion pictures were the first new media, and they became important in the first half of the twentieth century.

Following World War II (1939–1945), broadcast television became the dominant form of communication. Cable television networks arrived in the 1970s. The Internet, including e-mail and the World Wide Web, came into widespread use by the general public in the 1990s.

The Decline of the Old Media   Film and radio did not displace print media in the early twentieth century. Television, though, had a much greater effect. Beginning about 1950, the number of adults reading a daily paper began to decline, although circulation remained steady due to population growth.

Later, the Internet proved to be even more devastating to newspapers. Newspaper circulation fell modestly in the 1990s. In 2006, however, circulation began to collapse, declining more than 5 percent each

mass media
Communication channels, such as newspapers and radio and television broadcasts, through which people can communicate to large audiences.

print media
Communication channels that consist of printed materials, such as newspapers and magazines.

electronic media
Communication channels that involve electronic transmissions, such as radio, television, and the Internet.

A surprisingly large number of young people get much of their news from comedians Jon Stewart (left) and Stephen Colbert (right). Both have shows on the Comedy Central network.

FRANK MICELOTTA/INVISION/AP

politics and government. Older Americans largely rely on these more traditional media outlets, and older voters outnumber the young. As of the 2010 census, approximately 100 million Americans were age fifty or older. The number of U.S. residents age eighteen through twenty-nine was about half that figure. Older voters are also much more likely to turn out to vote than younger ones. Finally, some of the most enthusiastic adopters of new media are not yet eighteen and cannot vote even if they want to.

To give an example, many young people may find radio host Rush Limbaugh—with his audience largely composed of middle-aged white men—to be irrelevant to their lives. Limbaugh is not irrelevant to American politics, however. His millions of listeners vote, and they can influence the outcome of Republican presidential primaries.

Considering the electorate as a whole, television remains the dominant medium in terms of political influence. Much of this chapter, therefore, deals with the impact of television.

10–1c The Media and the First Amendment

As noted earlier, freedom of the press is essential if the media are to play their role in supporting the democratic process. The concept of freedom of the press has been applied to print media since the adoption of the Bill of Rights. Such freedoms were not, however, immediately extended to other types of media as they came into existence.

Film was one of the first types of new media to be considered under the First Amendment, and in 1915 the United States Supreme Court ruled that "as a matter of common sense," freedom of the press did not apply to the movies.[1] Radio received no protection upon its development, and neither did television. The Court did not extend First Amendment protections to the cinema until 1952.[2] Although the Court has stated that the First Amendment is relevant to broadcast media such as radio and television, to this day it has not granted these media complete protection.

In contrast, the Court extended First Amendment protections to the Internet in 1997, in its first opportunity to rule on the issue.[3] Cable TV received substantial protections in 2000.[4]

Although First Amendment protections now clearly prohibit the U.S. government from restricting speech on the Internet, other threats exist. We examine some of them in *The Rest of the World* feature on the following page.

year. The *America at Odds* feature discussed some of the problems of the newspaper industry, and we will return to these problems later in the chapter.

Youth and the New Media Today, millions of Americans have developed unprecedented habits of media consumption. Leaders of the revolution include the wealthy and "early adopters" of new technology. Above all, the new consumers include the young. As one might expect, the upcoming generation of media users rarely read newspapers. But even television is now of lesser importance.

True, young people still watch a variety of television programs. Many of them, however, primarily view such shows online, as streaming video. Even e-mail has been abandoned by many of today's youth. Instead, messages are transmitted via Facebook, Twitter, Tumblr, Google+, and the smartphone. For such persons, old-media personalities such as television news anchors and radio talk-show hosts are completely obsolete.

New Media versus Old Voters Yet radio, television, and print media remain important to American

Worldwide Threats to the World Wide Web

The Internet was created by the U.S. military through the Defense Advanced Research Projects Agency—DARPA (formerly ARPA). Soon it was opened to university researchers and later to the public at large. Censoring it was almost impossible. "The Internet interprets censorship as damage," one early administrator exalted. "We will route around you!"

In time, the Internet, now mostly the World Wide Web, became an international—not just an American—institution. Every nation with a modern economy has embraced the Internet. Poorer countries that want to develop must do so as well. A worldwide Internet, however, means participation by unfree nations. Leaders of these nations have no interest in free speech. Given this, how can the Internet remain both free and worldwide?

Threats from Abroad

No other nation can prevent a country such as China from censoring the Internet within its own borders. Is it possible, however, for unfree nations to export their controls to the rest of the world? Fear of such a development was fueled by an international treaty proposed in 2012 at a meeting of the World Conference on International Telecommunications, a United Nations body. The treaty was backed by eighty-nine nations—including China, Cuba, Iran, and Russia. Fifty-five nations, including the United States, Japan, and most Western European countries, voted "no."

Under the proposed treaty, international bodies made up of governments would run the Internet. Censorship could have international support. New financial rules could be crippling. Russia has proposed, for example, that Facebook, Google, and other sites pay cable companies a fee every time someone accesses them. No international body has the power to impose such a regime on the United States or any other nation. What the proposed treaty could do, however, is fragment the Internet—divide it between an open system and a variety of other systems under the control of repressive governments.

Threats from Ourselves

In 2013, the world learned that the U.S. National Security Agency (NSA), through its PRISM program, has been downloading massive amounts of data from Google, Microsoft, Yahoo, AOL, and other firms. While the exposure of PRISM touched off a debate over privacy in America, NSA snooping may have other consequences that the government never anticipated. President Obama has claimed that the NSA's actions do not violate the rights of U.S. citizens. But what about the rights of foreigners? Michael Hayden, a former NSA director, was blunt: the Fourth Amendment to the Constitution, which prohibits unreasonable searches, "is not an international treaty."

With the growth in *cloud computing*, more and more individuals and businesses now store important data on remote servers owned by such companies as Google and Microsoft. Europeans as well as Americans use cloud computing. But Europeans have just been informed that they have no privacy rights in data stored on American servers. The U.S. government can look at any data, at any time, for any reason, and U.S. high-tech firms will cooperate.

If you were a European concerned about your privacy, you might consider moving your data to your own country, where you would be protected by your own government. You might also support laws to restrict access to your country by firms that cooperate with foreign intelligence agencies such as the NSA.

 **FOR CRITICAL ANALYSIS** How might high-tech companies' cooperation with U.S. security agencies affect America's dominance of the high-tech sector?

10–1d The Agenda-Setting Function of the Media

One of the criticisms often levied against the media is that they play too large a role in determining the issues, events, and personalities that are in the public eye. When people take in the day's top news stories, they usually assume that these stories concern the most important issues facing the nation. In actuality, the media decide the relative importance of issues by publicizing some issues and ignoring others, and by giving some stories high priority and others low priority.

By helping to determine what people will talk and think about, the media set the *political agenda*—the issues that politicians will address. In other words, the media are engaged in **agenda setting.** To borrow from Bernard Cohen's classic statement on the media and public opinion, the press (media) may not be successful in telling people what to think, but it is "stunningly successful in telling its readers what to think about."[5]

For example, television played a significant role in shaping public opinion about the Vietnam War (1965–1975), which has been called the first "television war." Part of the public opposition to the war in the late 1960s came about as a result of the daily portrayal of the war's horrors on TV news programs. Film footage and narrative accounts of the destruction, death, and suffering in Vietnam brought the war into living rooms across the United States.

Priming and Framing
Two additional concepts related to agenda setting are *priming* and *framing*. In **priming,** a television show or an Internet blogger publicizes facts or ideas that may influence how the public thinks about a particular issue. As an example of priming, if the public is informed that the general rate of taxation in the United States is lower than it has been at any time since the 1950s, people are likely to be more receptive to the idea of raising tax rates on upper-income individuals.

In contrast, if the media point out that compared with other wealthy nations, the United States collects a much larger share of its tax revenue from the upper classes, then popular responses to proposals to tax our richer citizens may be quite different.

Framing an issue involves establishing the context in which it is understood. Frames are stories about how the world works. As an example, consider the different stories that can be told about someone who is experiencing poverty. A TV news show might cover a man whose condition was, to all appearances, due primarily to bad luck. Perhaps he suffered from a life-threatening disease, could not work, lost his job, and then became homeless. This description would set up a particular frame, encouraging viewers to take a positive attitude toward social spending that would provide aid to such an individual.

Another TV report might show a woman who became addicted to alcohol or drugs at an early age, dropped out of high school, and became pregnant without a partner to help support her. Such an account could lead to an entirely different frame, which could lead to a much more skeptical attitude toward spending that benefits the poor.

Limits of Agenda Setting
The degree to which the media influence public opinion is not always that clear, however. As you read in Chapter 8, some studies show that people filter the information they receive from the media through their own preconceived ideas about issues. People bring their own frames to political stories, in other words, and these frames can be very powerful.

Scholars who try to analyze the relationship between American politics and the media inevitably confront the chicken-and-egg conundrum: Do the media cause the public to hold certain views, or do the media merely reflect the public's views?

10–1e The Medium Does Affect the Message

Of all the media, television still has the greatest impact on most Americans, especially older ones. Television reaches almost every home in the United States. Even outside their homes, Americans can watch television—in airports, shopping malls, golf clubhouses, and medical offices. People can view television shows on their computers, and they can download TV programs to their smartphones and tablet devices and view the programs whenever and wherever they want.

Today, Americans watch more television than ever, and it is the primary news source for more than 65 percent of the citizenry. As you will read shortly, politicians take maximum advantage of the power and influence of television. But does the television medium alter the presentation of political information in any way? Compare the coverage given to an important political issue by the print media—including the online sites of major newspapers and magazines—with the coverage provided by broadcast and cable TV networks. You will note some striking differences.

For one thing, the print media (particularly leading newspapers such as the *Washington Post,* the *New York Times,* and the *Wall Street Journal*) treat an important issue in much more detail than television does. In addition

agenda setting The media's ability to determine which issues are considered important by the public and by politicians.

priming An agenda-setting technique in which a media outlet promotes specific facts or ideas that may affect the public's thinking on related topics.

framing An agenda-setting technique that establishes the context of a media report. Framing can mean fitting events into a familiar story or filtering information through preconceived ideas.

> "The press may not be successful much of the time in telling people what to think, but it is stunningly successful in telling its readers **what to think about.**"
>
> ~ BERNARD C. COHEN ~
> AMERICAN POLITICAL SCIENTIST
> B. 1926

to news stories based on reporters' research, you will find editorials taking positions on the issue and arguments supporting those positions. Television news, in contrast, is often criticized as being too brief and too superficial.

Time Constraints   The medium of television necessarily imposes constraints on how political issues are presented. Time is limited. News stories must be reported quickly, in only a few minutes or occasionally in only a **sound bite,** a televised comment lasting for just a few seconds that captures a thought or a perspective and has an immediate impact on the viewers.

A Visual Medium   Television reporting also relies extensively on visual elements, rather than words, to capture the viewers' attention. Inevitably, the photos or videos selected to depict a particular political event have exaggerated importance to viewers. The visual aspect of television contributes to its power, but it also creates a potential bias. Those watching the news presentation do not know what portions of a video being shown have been deleted, what other photos may have been taken, or whether other records of the event exist. This kind of "selection bias" will be discussed in more detail later in this chapter.

Television Is Big Business   Today's TV networks compete aggressively with one another to air "breaking news" and to produce interesting news programs. Competition in the television industry understandably has had an effect on how the news is presented. To make profits, or even stay in business, TV stations need viewers. And to attract viewers, the news industry has turned to "infotainment"—programs that inform and entertain at the same time. Slick sets, attractive reporters, and animated graphics that dance across the television screen are commonplace on most news programs, particularly on the cable news channels.

> **sound bite** A televised comment, lasting for only a few seconds, that captures a thought or a perspective and has an immediate impact on viewers.

TV networks also compete with one another for advertising income. Although the media in the United States are among the freest in the world, their programming nonetheless remains vulnerable to the influence of their advertising sponsors.

10–1f Ownership of the Media

Concentrated ownership of media is another issue. Many mainstream media outlets are owned by giant corporations, such as Time Warner, Rupert Murdoch's News Corporation, and Disney. An often expressed concern is that these giant corporations will influence news coverage to benefit their interests.

There is little evidence, however, that these corporations significantly influence reporting. Their media outlets do show a generalized support of the capitalist economic system, but capitalism is so widely accepted in this country that the press would probably endorse it under any form of media ownership.

In some circumstances, it may benefit a media outlet to have owners with deep pockets. Consider the *Washington Post,* one of the nation's most important publications. Like many other newspapers, the *Post* has faced serious financial difficulties. Its previous owners, aware that they did not have the means to ensure the paper's quality, sold it to Jeff Bezos, founder and chief executive officer of Amazon.com. Bezos has a record of innovation and a deep understanding of the Internet. He bought the *Post* as an individual—Amazon does not own it. Still, his wealth may allow the paper the time and resources it needs to establish a new, viable business model.

Local Monopolies   Concentrated ownership may be a more serious problem at the local level than at the national level. If only one or two companies own a city's newspaper and its TV stations, these outlets may not present a diversity of opinion. Further, the owners are unlikely to air information that could be damaging either to their advertisers or to themselves, or even to publicize views that they disagree with politically. For example, TV networks have refused to run antiwar commercials created by religious groups. Still, some media observers are not particularly concerned about

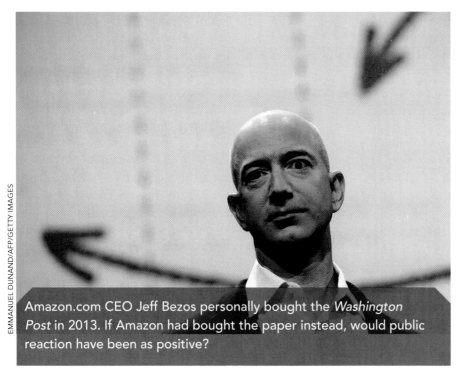

Amazon.com CEO Jeff Bezos personally bought the *Washington Post* in 2013. If Amazon had bought the paper instead, would public reaction have been as positive?

EMMANUEL DUNAND/AFP/GETTY IMAGES

10–2 The Candidates and Television

Given the TV-saturated environment in which we live, it should come as no surprise that candidates spend a great deal of time—and money—obtaining a TV presence through political ads, debates, and general news coverage. Candidates and their campaign managers realize that the time and money are well spent because television has an important impact on the way people see the candidates, understand the issues, and cast their votes.

10–2a Political Advertising

Today, televised **political advertising** consumes at least half of the total budget for a major political campaign. According to the research firm PQ Media, spending on all forms of political advertising reached $4.5 billion in the 2007–2008 election cycle, including $2.3 billion for broadcast TV in 2008 alone. For the 2012 election cycle, the Sunlight Foundation has estimated that total spending on political advertisements may have reached $9.8 billion.

Spending on the Swing States One characteristic of campaign advertising that was more noticeable in 2012 than ever before was its uneven distribution. As of September 2012, residents of the Pacific states had seen almost no presidential campaign ads. The only visible ads were those run nationwide. Voters in many other parts of the country could report the same.

In highly contested states such as Florida and Ohio, however, the main limitation on television spending appeared to be a shortage of advertising slots available for purchase. By early October, the presidential campaigns had spent more than $100 million in Florida and more than $90 million in Ohio. In contrast, the campaigns had purchased

concentrated ownership of traditional outlets, because the Internet has generated a massive diversification of media.

The Murdoch Empire A possible exception to the claim that major corporations do not influence reporting is the Murdoch media conglomerate. Murdoch's holdings in the United States, which include the Fox television networks, the *Wall Street Journal,* and the *New York Post,* are famous for promoting conservative politics. Still, Fox News is only one voice among many in America.

The role of Murdoch's holdings have been more troubling in Britain, where they make up a much larger share of the national media than they do in the United States. In 2011, however, a major scandal curbed Murdoch's influence in Britain. (Murdoch newspaper personnel were caught hacking into the cell phones of hundreds of persons.)

FOR CRITICAL THINKING

How do you typically obtain information about political events? Does it differ from how your parents obtain information? Your grandparents?

political advertising
Advertising undertaken by or on behalf of a political candidate to familiarize voters with the candidate and his or her views on campaign issues; advertising for or against policy issues.

almost no ads in California and Texas. These states have huge populations, but no amount of advertising would make California vote Republican or Texas Democratic.

Negative Advertising

Political advertising first appeared on television during the 1952 presidential campaign. At that time, there were only about 15 million television sets. Today, there are as many TV sets as people. Initially, political TV commercials were more or less like any other type of advertising. Instead of focusing on the positive qualities of a product, thirty-second or sixty-second ads focused on the positive qualities of a political candidate. Within the decade, however, **negative political advertising** began to appear on TV.

PERSONAL ATTACKS GO WAY BACK. Despite the barrage of criticism levied against the candidates' use of negative political ads during recent election cycles, such ads are not new. Indeed, **personal attack ads**—advertising that attacks the character of an opposing candidate—have a long tradition. In 1800, an article in the *Federalist Gazette of the United States* described Thomas Jefferson as having a "weakness of nerves, want of fortitude, and total imbecility of character."

negative political advertising Political advertising undertaken for the purpose of discrediting an opposing candidate in voters' eyes. Attack ads are one form of negative political advertising.

personal attack ad A negative political advertisement that attacks the character of an opposing candidate.

issue ad A political advertisement that focuses on a particular issue. Issue ads can be used to support or attack a candidate's position or credibility.

PERSONAL ATTACKS IN 2012. In the 2012 general election, the Obama campaign had much more to gain by "going personal" than the Romney campaign did. Romney's problem was that the voters now had four years of experience with President Obama, and almost all of them had already made up their minds as to what kind of person he was.

Many conservatives regarded the president with outright loathing, and so personal attacks on Obama were useful in mobilizing the faithful. Independents, however, often thought well of Obama as a person, even when they disagreed with his policies. Romney's task was to persuade these independents that the Republican team could do better, and attacking Obama personally would not help reach that goal.

For his part, Obama confronted a candidate who was not as well known to the public as he himself was. The Democrats, therefore, had an opportunity to define Romney in highly negative ways. The Obama campaign and its allies sought to portray Romney as a ruthless, wealthy financier who was out of touch with ordinary people and who was indifferent to the suffering his policies would cause. Romney's response was to "go positive" about himself and seek ways to show his genuine concern for other people.

Issue Ads

Candidates use negative **issue ads** to focus on flaws in their opponents' positions on various issues, such as health care and the bank-bailout legislation. Candidates also try to undermine their opponents' credibility by pointing to discrepancies between what the opponents say in their campaign speeches, on the one hand, and their political records, such as their voting records, on the other hand. Their records are available to the public and thus can be easily verified.

Issue ads can be even more devastating than personal attacks—as Barry Goldwater learned in 1964 when his opponent in the presidential race, President Lyndon Johnson, aired the "daisy girl" ad. This ad, a new departure in negative advertising, showed a little girl standing quietly in a field of daisies. She held a daisy and pulled off the petals, counting to herself. Suddenly, a deep voice was heard counting: "10, 9, 8, 7, 6, ..." When the countdown hit zero, the unmistak-

CHARLES BARSOTTI/THE NEW YORKER COLLECTION/ WWW.CARTOONBANK.COM

"It's Lamar, Senator, he's going to take our attack ads door to door."

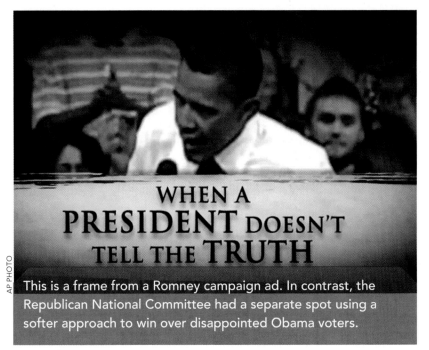

This is a frame from a Romney campaign ad. In contrast, the Republican National Committee had a separate spot using a softer approach to win over disappointed Obama voters.

lic debate, thereby enriching the democratic process. This is the position taken by Vanderbilt University political science professor John Geer. He contends that negative ads are likely to focus on substantive political issues instead of candidates' personal characteristics. Thus, negative ads do a better job of informing the voters about important campaign issues than positive ads do.[8]

10–2b Television Debates

Televised debates have been a feature of presidential campaigns since 1960, when presidential candidates Republican Richard M. Nixon and Democrat John F. Kennedy squared off in four great TV debates. Television debates provide an opportunity for voters to find out how candidates differ on issues. They also allow candidates to capitalize on the power of television to improve their images or point out the failings of their opponents.

It is widely believed that Kennedy won the first of the 1960 debates in large part because of Nixon's haggard appearance and poor makeup—many people who heard the debate on the radio thought that Nixon had done well. No presidential debates were held during the general election campaigns of 1964, 1968, or 1972, but the debates have been a part of every election since 1976.

The 1992 debates, which starred Republican George H. W. Bush and Democrat Bill Clinton, also included a third-party candidate, H. Ross Perot. Since 1996, however, the Commission on Presidential Debates, which now organizes the events, has limited the participants to candidates of the two major parties.[9] The commission also organizes debates between the vice-presidential candidates.

able mushroom cloud of an atomic explosion filled the screen. Then President Johnson's voice was heard saying, "These are the stakes: to make a world in which all of God's children can live, or to go into the dark. We must either love each other or we must die." A message on the screen then read: "Vote for President Johnson on November 3." The implication, of course, was that Goldwater would lead the country into a nuclear war.[6]

Negative Advertising—Is It Good or Bad for Our Democracy? The debate over the effect of negative advertising on our political system is ongoing. Some observers argue that negative ads can backfire. Extreme ads may create sympathy for the candidate being attacked rather than support for the attacker, particularly when the charges against the candidate being attacked are not credible. Many people fear that attack ads and "dirty tricks" used by both parties during a campaign may alienate citizens from the political process itself and thus lower voter turnout in elections.

Yet candidates and their campaign managers typically assert that they use negative advertising simply because it works. Negative TV ads are more likely than positive ads to grab the viewers' attention and make an impression. Also, according to media expert Shanto Iyengar, "the more negative the ad, the more likely it is to get free media coverage. So there's a big incentive to go to extremes."[7] Others believe that negative advertising is a force for good because it sharpens pub-

TV Debates and Election Outcomes Many contend that the presidential debates help shape the outcome of the elections. Others doubt that the debates—or the postdebate "spin" applied by campaign operatives and political commentators—have changed many votes. Evidence on this question is mixed.

Gallup polling figures suggest that in 1960 the debates helped Kennedy to victory. In 1980, Republican Ronald Reagan did well in a final debate with Democratic incumbent Jimmy Carter. Reagan im-pressed many voters with his sunny temperament, which helped dispel fears that he was a right-wing radical. In Gallup's opinion, however, Reagan would have won the election even without the debate.

The 2012 Presidential Elections

The 2012 presidential debates, held in October, gave Mitt Romney's campaign a substantial boost. In the months leading up to the debate, the Obama campaign enjoyed some success in defining Romney as a rich man who only cared about the interests of other upper-class Americans. This impression was reinforced by the release of a video in which Romney appeared contemptuous of citizens who were not wealthy enough to pay income taxes.

During the first debate, however, Romney was able to present himself as a caring and moderate candidate. Obama, in contrast, seemed lethargic and unprepared. Obama turned in much better performances in the second and third debates, but the damage to his campaign had been done. Nevertheless, in the end, Romney's debate performance was not enough to propel him to victory.

10-2c News Coverage

Whereas political ads are expensive, coverage by the news media is free. Accordingly, the candidates try to take advantage of the media's interest in campaigns to increase the quantity and quality of news coverage. This is not always easy. Often, the media devote the lion's share of their coverage to polls and other indicators of which candidate is ahead in the race.

In recent years, candidates' campaigns have shown increasing sophistication in creating newsworthy events for journalists and TV camera crews to cover. This effort is commonly referred to as **managed news coverage**. For example, typically one of the jobs of the campaign manager is to create newsworthy events that demonstrate the candidate's strong points so that the media can capture this image of the candidate.[10]

Many aspects of the campaign focus on potential news coverage.

managed news coverage News coverage that is manipulated (managed) by a campaign manager or political consultant to gain media exposure for a political candidate.

spin doctor A political candidate's press adviser who tries to convince reporters to give a story or event concerning the candidate a particular "spin" (interpretation, or slant).

spin A reporter's slant on, or interpretation of, a particular event or action.

Political consultants plan political events to accommodate the press. The campaign staff attempts to make what the candidate is doing appear interesting. The staff also knows that journalists and political reporters compete for stories and that these individuals can be manipulated. Hence, they frequently are granted favors, such as exclusive personal interviews with the candidate. Each candidate also has press advisers, often called **spin doctors,** who try to convince reporters to give the story or event a **spin,** or interpretation, that is favorable to the candidate.[11]

10-2d "Popular" Television

Although not normally regarded as a forum for political debate, television programs such as dramas, sitcoms, and late-night comedy shows often use political themes. For example, the popular courtroom drama *Law & Order* regularly broached controversial topics such as the death penalty, the USA Patriot Act, and the rights of the accused. For years, the sitcom *Will and Grace* consistently brought to light issues regarding gay and lesbian rights. The dramatic *West Wing* series gave viewers a glimpse into national politics as it told the story of a fictional presidential administration. Late-night shows and programs such as *The Daily Show with Jon Stewart* and *The Colbert Report* provide a forum for politicians to demonstrate their lighter sides.

FOR CRITICAL THINKING

Media experts believe that negative political advertisements often include statements that are flatly untrue. *What, if anything, should the media do when that happens?*

10-3 Talk Radio— The Wild West of the Media

Ever since Franklin D. Roosevelt held his first "fireside chats" on radio, politicians have realized the power of that medium. From the beginning, radio has been a favorite outlet for the political right.

During the 1930s, for example, the nation's most successful radio commentator was Father Charles Edward Coughlin, a Roman Catholic priest based at the National Shrine of the Little Flower church in Royal

Learning Outcome 10–3

Explain why talk radio has been described as the Wild West of the media.

Oak, Michigan. Coughlin's audience numbered more than 40 million listeners—in a nation that had only 123 million inhabitants in 1930. Coughlin started out as a Roosevelt supporter, but he soon moved to the far right, advocating anti-Semitism and expressing sympathy for Adolf Hitler. Coughlin's fascist connections eventually destroyed his popularity.

Modern talk radio took off in the United States during the 1990s. In 1988, there were 200 talk-show radio stations. Today, there are more than 1,200. The growth of talk radio was made possible by the Federal Communications Commission's repeal of the fairness doctrine in 1987.

Introduced in 1949, the *fairness doctrine* required the holders of broadcast licenses to present controversial issues of public importance in a manner that was

"For a politician to complain about the press is like **a ship's captain complaining about the sea.**"

~ ENOCH POWELL ~
BRITISH POLITICIAN
1912–1998

(in the commission's view) honest, equitable, and balanced. That doctrine would have made it difficult for radio stations to broadcast conservative talk shows exclusively, as many now do.

Today, eight of the top ten talk-radio shows, as measured by Arbitron ratings, are politically conservative. No liberal commentator ranks higher than twentieth place in the ratings. (Several of the shows ranked higher than twentieth are not political but deal with subjects such as personal finance and paranormal activities.)

10–3a Audiences and Hosts

The Pew Research Center for the People and the Press reports that 17 percent of the public regularly listen to talk radio. This audience is predominantly male, middle-aged, and conservative. Among those who regularly listen to talk radio, 41 percent consider themselves Republicans and 28 percent, Democrats.

Talk radio is sometimes characterized as the Wild West of the media. Talk-show hosts do not attempt to hide their political biases. If anything, they exaggerate them for effect. No journalistic conventions are observed. Leading shows, such as those of Rush Limbaugh, Sean Hannity, Andrew Wilkow, and Michael Savage, espouse a brand of conservatism that is robust, even radical. Opponents are regularly characterized as Nazis, Communists, or both at the same time. Limbaugh, for example, consistently refers to feminists as "feminazis."

Talk-show hosts sometimes appear to care more about the entertainment value of their statements than whether they are, strictly speaking, true. Hosts have often publicized fringe beliefs, such as the contention that President Barack Obama was not really born in the United States. The government of Britain actually banned Michael Savage from entry into that country based on his remarks about Muslims.

Conservative radio talk-show host Rush Limbaugh.

ALEXIS C. GLENN/UPI/LANDOV

10–3b The Wild West Migrates to Television

Commentators at Fox News have always been predominantly conservative, just as liberals are the rule at the smaller MSNBC network. Still, until recently it was widely seen as inappropriate for television personalities to employ the radical style characteristic of such talk-show hosts as Rush Limbaugh. That understanding began to crumble after October 2008, when Fox News hired radio talk-show host Glenn Beck.

In contrast to his large radio audience, Beck's TV audience was smaller than those of his Fox colleagues Bill O'Reilly and Sean Hannity. In short order, however, Beck transformed himself into one of the nation's most politically polarizing figures. Beck's emotional style—he frequently broke into tears—his over-the-top statements, and his apocalyptic views were a new development on television.

VOA/UIG VIA GETTY IMAGES

Press photographers at a 2012 campaign event held by First Lady Michelle Obama in Las Vegas.

Beck gained further attention by using his on-air pulpit as a political organizing tool. Throughout 2009, Beck promoted the Tea Party movement, and in August 2010 he sponsored the Restoring Honor rally at the Lincoln Memorial in Washington, D.C., which was attended by nearly 200,000 people. Beck's activism appears to be the primary reason that Fox News canceled his show in 2011. The head of Fox News, Roger Ailes, said that Beck's "goals were different from our goals. . . . I need people focused on a daily television show."

"A nation that is afraid to let its people judge truth and falsehood in an **OPEN MARKET** is a nation that is afraid of its people."

~ JOHN FITZGERALD KENNEDY ~
THIRTY-FIFTH PRESIDENT
OF THE UNITED STATES
1961–1963

Those who claim that talk-show hosts go too far ultimately have to deal with the constitutional issue of free speech. While the courts have always given broad support to freedom of expression, broadcast media have been something of an exception, as was explained in Chapter 4. The United States Supreme Court, for example, upheld the fairness doctrine in a 1969 ruling.[12]

Presumably, the doctrine could be reinstated. In 2009, after the Democratic victories in the 2008 elections, a few liberals advocated doing just that. President Obama and the Democratic leadership in Congress, however, quickly put an end to this notion. Americans have come to accept talk radio as part of the political environment, and any attempt to curtail it would be extremely unpopular.

10–3c The Impact of Talk Radio

The overwhelming dominance of strong conservative voices on talk radio is justified by supporters as a good way to counter what they perceive as the liberal bias in the mainstream print and TV media. (We discuss the question of bias in the media in the following section.) Supporters say that such shows are simply a response to consumer demand. Those who think that talk radio is good for the country argue that talk shows, taken together, provide a great populist forum. Others are uneasy because they fear that talk shows empower fringe groups, perhaps magnifying their rage.

FOR CRITICAL THINKING

Why, in your opinion, have liberal commentators found it so difficult to develop successful talk-radio shows?

10-4 The Question of Media Bias

Learning Outcome 10-4

Describe types of media bias and explain how such bias affects the political process.

The question of media bias is important in any democracy. After all, for our political system to work, citizens must be well informed. And they can be well informed only if the news media, the source of much of their information, do not slant the news. Today, however, relatively few Americans believe that the news media are unbiased in their reporting. Accompanying this perception is a notable decline in the public's confidence in the news media in recent years.

In a 2013 Gallup poll measuring the public's confidence in various institutions, only 23 percent of the respondents stated that they had "a great deal" or "quite a lot" of confidence in newspapers, and 23 percent had the same degree of confidence in television news. Because of these low percentages, some analysts believe that the media are facing a crisis of confidence.

Despite these low figures, however, the public does believe that the press is successful in fulfilling its role as a watchdog. In a 2013 poll by the Pew Research Center, 68 percent of respondents agreed that "press criticism of political leaders keeps them from doing things that should not be done." Republicans, Democrats, and independents were equally likely to agree with this statement.

10-4a Partisan Bias

For years, conservatives have argued that there is a liberal bias in the media, and liberals have complained that the media reflect a conservative bias. The majority of Americans think that the media reflect a bias in one direction or another. According to a recent poll, 46 percent of the respondents believed that the news media leaned left, whereas only 26 percent thought that the news media had a conservative bias.

The Attitudes of Journalists Surveys and analyses of the attitudes and voting habits of reporters have suggested that journalists do indeed hold liberal views. The Web site CampaignMoney.com has calculated that from 1999 to 2013, campaign contributors who list their occupation as journalist or reporter gave 74 percent of their donations to Democrats. Only 13 percent of the donations went to Republicans. Among journalists working for national outlets, 22 percent described themselves as liberal and only 5 percent as conservative. In contrast, 14 percent of local reporters called themselves liberals, and 18 percent adopted the conservative label.

There is substantial evidence that top journalists working for the nation's most famous newspapers and networks do tend to be liberal. Many journalists themselves perceive the *New York Times* as liberal (although an even larger number view Fox News as conservative).

Still, members of the press are likely to view themselves as moderates. In a recent study, the Pew Research Center for the People and the Press found that 64 percent of reporters in both national and local media applied the term *moderate* to themselves.

The Impact on Reporting A number of media scholars, including Kathleen Hall Jamieson, suggest that even if many reporters hold liberal views, these views are not reflected in their reporting.[13] Media analysts Debra Reddin van Tuyll and Hubert P. van Tuyll have similarly concluded that left-leaning reporters do not automatically equate to left-leaning news coverage. They point out that reporters are only the starting point for news stories. Before any story goes to print or is aired on television, it has to go through a progression of editors and perhaps even the publisher. Because employees at the top of the corporate ladder in news organizations are more right leaning than left leaning, the end result of the editorial and oversight process is more balanced coverage.[14]

Perhaps the most important protection against bias in reporting is a commitment to professionalism on the part of most journalists. Professional ethics dictate a commitment to "objectivity" and truthfulness. Reporters may sometimes violate this code, but it does have an impact.

In addition, a recent, helpful development is the growing number of fact-checking operations such as PolitiFact and FactCheck. FactCheck, for example, is a project of the Annenberg Public Policy Center of the University of Pennsylvania. Services such as these enable journalists to be more objective in identifying and cracking down on political lies and misrepresentations.

10-4b The Bias against Losers

Kathleen Hall Jamieson believes that media bias does play a significant role in shaping presidential campaigns and elections, but she argues that it is not a partisan bias. Rather, it is a bias against losers. A candidate who falls behind in the race is immediately labeled a "loser," making it even more difficult for the candidate to regain favor in the voters' eyes.[15]

Jamieson says that the media use the winner-loser paradigm to describe events throughout the campaigns. Even a presidential debate is regarded as a "sporting match" that results in a winner and a loser. In the days leading up to the 2012 debates, reporters focused on what each candidate had to do to "win" the debate. When the debate was over, reporters immediately speculated about who had "won" as they waited for post-debate polls to answer that question. According to Jamieson, this approach "squanders the opportunity to reinforce learning." The debates are an important source of political information for the voters, and this fact is eclipsed by the media's win-lose focus.

10–4c Selection Bias

As mentioned earlier, television is big business, and maximizing profits from advertising is a major consideration in what television stations choose to air. After all, a station or network that incurs losses will eventually go bankrupt. The expansion of the media universe to include cable channels and the Internet has also increased the competition among news sources. As a result, news directors *select* programming they believe will attract the largest audiences and garner the highest advertising revenues.

Competition for viewers and readers has become even more challenging in the wake of a declining news audience. A recent Pew survey and analysis of reporters' attitudes found that all media sectors except two are losing popularity. The two exceptions are the ethnic press, such as Latino newspapers and TV programs, and online sources—but even the online sector has stopped growing.[16]

Selection Bias and the Bottom Line The Pew study also indicated that news organizations' struggles to stay afloat are having a notable effect on news coverage. The survey showed that a larger number of reporters than ever before (about 66 percent) agreed that "increased bottom-line pressure is seriously hurting the quality of news coverage." About one-third of the journalists—again, more than in previous surveys—stated that they have felt pressure from either advertisers or corporate owners concerning what to write or broadcast. In other words, these journalists believe that economic pressure—the need for revenues—is making significant inroads on independent editorial decision making.

A Changing News Culture Today's news culture is in the midst of change. News organizations are redefining their purpose and increasingly looking for special niches in which to build their audiences. For some markets the niche is *hyperlocalism*—that is, narrowing the focus of news to the local area.

For others, it is personal commentary, revolving around highly politicized TV figures such as Bill O'Reilly (conservative) and Rachel Maddow (liberal). In a sense, news organizations have begun to base their appeal more on *how* they cover the news and less on *what* they cover. Traditional journalism—fact-based reporting instead of opinion and punditry—is becoming a smaller part of this mix.

Another development is the move toward highly specific subject matter that appeals strongly to a limited number of viewers. Magazines have always done this—consider the many magazine titles on topics such as model railroading or home decorating. With the large number of cable channels, *narrowcasting* has become important on television as well. Networks now appeal to members of particular ethnic groups (BET—Black Entertainment Television), hobbyists (Cooking Channel), or history buffs (Military Channel).

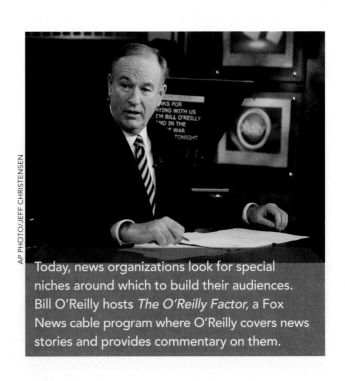

AP PHOTO/JEFF CHRISTENSEN

Today, news organizations look for special niches around which to build their audiences. Bill O'Reilly hosts *The O'Reilly Factor,* a Fox News cable program where O'Reilly covers news stories and provides commentary on them.

WILLIAM B. PLOWMAN/NBC/NBC NEWSWIRE/GETTY IMAGES

Political commentator and journalist Rachel Maddow appears on MSNBC, where she has had a daily show since 2008.

FOR CRITICAL THINKING

Often, media consumers prefer outlets that confirm their own personal biases. *What problems might this create for American democracy?*

10–5 Political News and Campaigns on the Web

Learning Outcome 10–5

Indicate the extent to which the Internet is reshaping news and political campaigns.

Cyberspace is getting bigger every day. Almost 40 percent of the world's inhabitants currently use the Internet, a total of about 2.75 billion people. According to Technorati, a blog search site, bloggers around the world update their blogs with new posts in eighty-one languages at a rate of almost 4 million posts every day. Among U.S. Internet users, 77 percent read blogs, and one blog tracker has identified more than 180 million blogs.

In addition, popular networking sites have enormous numbers of personalized pages—Twitter has 550 million accounts, and Facebook has more than one billion.

Not surprisingly, the Internet is a major source of information. All major newspapers are online, as are transcripts of major television news programs. About two-thirds of Internet users consider the Internet to be an important source of news. In addition, having an Internet strategy has become an integral part of political campaigning. The Internet is also important in countries that do not have free elections, as you will see in the *Perception versus Reality* feature on the following page.

10–5a News Organizations Online

Almost every major news organization, both print and broadcast, delivers news via the Web. Indeed, an online presence is required to compete effectively with other traditional news companies for revenues. The online share of newspaper company revenues has increased over the years. Still, only 12 percent of U.S. newspaper revenues come from online sources.

Characteristics of Newspaper Sites Some newspaper sites simply copy articles from their printed versions. The Web sites for major newspapers, however, including those for the *Washington Post* and the *New York Times,* offer a different array of coverage and options than their printed editions, Web sites have a notable advantage over their printed counterparts. They can add breaking news, informing readers of events that occurred just minutes ago. They can also link readers to more extensive reports on particular topics. (Many papers shy away from in-text linking, though, perhaps fearing that if readers leave the news organization's site, they might not return.)

Inadequate Revenues A major problem facing news organizations is that readers or viewers of online newspapers and news programs are typically the same people who read the printed news editions and view the news programs on TV. Web-only readers of a particular newspaper make up a relatively small percentage of those going online for their news. Therefore, investing heavily in online news delivery may not be a solution for news companies seeking to increase readership and revenues.

In fact, the additional revenues that newspapers have gained from their online editions do not come close to making up for the massive losses in advertising revenue suffered by their print editions. In many

Perception versus Reality

Social Media Give Rebels an Advantage over the Authorities

It happened in Iran. It happened in Egypt. It happened in Tunisia. It has happened in China and in other countries with authoritarian regimes. Facebook, Twitter, and other social media have provided the communications necessary to organize demonstrations and other acts of rebellion. In Egypt and elsewhere, such demonstrations have helped bring down the government.

THE PERCEPTION

Those who rebel against any type of authority can now use social media and cell phones to do more than just "get out the vote." They can generate massive demonstrations against dictatorial governments. Hooligans have also used such media to organize violent "flash mobs" that overwhelm any police presence. Rioters used smartphones to coordinate the vandalism, arson, and massive looting that took place in Britain in the summer of 2011.

THE REALITY

Authoritarian governments might seem anachronistic, slow moving, and even foolish. But dictatorships are not blind to the uses of advanced technology. Consider Iran. It was widely believed that incumbent

president Mahmoud Ahmadinejad rigged the 2009 elections, guaranteeing his reelection. Rebels, including many young people, took to the streets. Many thought that the corrupt and repressive regime was finished. Far from it. The Green Revolution, as it was called, used Twitter, Facebook, and YouTube to its advantage—at first. But the Iranian government soon began using the same social media to identify activists, determine their connections with each other, and track down support from outside Iran. The government even used what it learned from social media when it put the rebels on trial.

Today, in countries such as Russia and China, government-paid bloggers support the regime. Many citizens who read such blogs do not realize that the government pays these bloggers. Other government supporters are paid to participate in Facebook and Twitter communities. Their "sincere" posts and tweets never fail to support government policies. Facial recognition software is another tool employed by oppressive regimes. Governments can compare the faces of protesters with photos that activists themselves have uploaded on social networks.

In short, social media can help organize a rebellion, but unless the rebellion wins, the advantage in using such media may quickly swing to the authorities.

BLOG ON You can find more information on how rebels have used social media by searching on "social media rebellion" and "flash mobs." Evgeny Morozov is a major analyst of how authoritarian regimes have used social media. Search on his name to locate his blog and videos of interviews he has given.

---

instances, publications have not sold enough advertising in their online editions even to make up for the additional expense of publishing on the Web.

"All Your Online Ad Revenue Are Belong to Google"
The problem is not that there is an absolute shortage of online advertising revenue. In fact, by 2012, the advertising industry was spending more on Internet advertising than it spent on all print newspapers and magazines put together—$39.5 billion online versus $33.8 billion. The site eMarketer predicted that by 2016, print ad spending would be

down slightly to $32.3 billion while online advertising would be up to $62.0 billion.

The real problem is that *content providers*—such as newspaper sites that hire journalists and create new material—receive a very small share of the online advertising revenue. Most of the revenue goes to *aggregators*, including search engine sites that develop little new content but mostly direct users elsewhere. Google, by far the largest of these aggregators, collects one-third of all online ad revenues.

By 2010, the ad revenues of this single company exceeded the revenues of the entire newspaper industry, as shown in Figure 10–1 below. (Hence, the title of this section—a blogger's reference to a popular online gaming joke).[17] Of course, if the business of journalism were to collapse, Google would have little to aggregate. As of now, the cybersphere is nowhere close to resolving this issue.

10–5b Blogs and the Emergence of Citizen Journalism

As mentioned earlier, the news culture is changing, and at the heart of this change—and of most innovation in news delivery today—is the blogosphere. There has been a veritable explosion of blogs in recent years. To make their Web sites more competitive and appealing, and to counter the influence of blogs run by private citizens and those not in the news business, the mainstream news organizations have themselves been adding blogs to their Web sites.

Blogs are offered by independent journalists, various scholars, political activists, and the citizenry at large. Anyone who wants to can create a blog and post news or information, including videos, to share with others. Many blogs are political in nature, both reporting political developments and discussing politics. Taken as a whole, the collection, analysis, and dissemination of information online by the citizenry is referred to as **citizen journalism.** Other terms that have been used to describe the news blogosphere include *people journalism* and *participatory journalism.* When blogs focus on news and developments in a spe-

cific community, the term *community journalism* is often applied.

The increase in news blogs and do-it-yourself journalism on the Web clearly poses a threat to mainstream news sources. Compared with the operational costs faced by a major news organization, the cost of creating and maintaining blogs is trivial. Moreover, the most successful blogs are able to sell advertising. Because of their low costs, it does not take much advertising to keep such sites in business. How can major news sources adhere to their traditional standards and still compete with this new world of news generated by citizens?

10–5c Podcasting the News

Another nontraditional form of news distribution is **podcasting**—the distribution of audio or video files to personal computers or mobile devices such as smartphones.[18] Though still a relatively small portion of the overall news-delivery system, podcasts are becoming increasingly popular. Almost anyone can create a podcast and make it available for downloading onto computers or mobile devices, and like blogging, podcasting is inexpensive. As you will read next, political candidates are using both blogging

citizen journalism The collection, analysis, and dissemination of information online by independent journalists, scholars, politicians, and the general citizenry.

podcasting The distribution of audio or video files to personal computers or mobile devices such as smartphones.

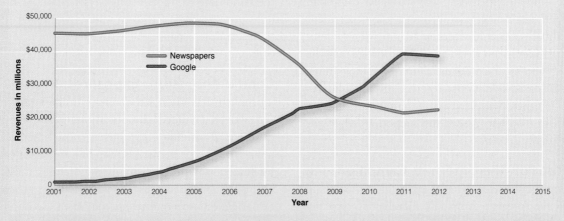

FIGURE 10-1

Advertising Revenues:
Google versus the Newspaper Industry, 2001–2012

Source: Dan McCarthy, The Media Transformation (blog).

and podcasting as part of their Internet campaign strategies.

10–5d Cyberspace and Political Campaigns

Today's political parties and candidates realize the benefits of using the Internet to conduct online campaigns and raise funds. Voters also are increasingly using the Web to access information about parties and candidates, promote political goals, and obtain political news. Generally, the use of the Internet is an inexpensive way for candidates to contact, recruit, and mobilize supporters, as well as to disseminate information about their positions on issues. In effect, the Internet can replace brochures, letters, and position papers. Individual voters or political party supporters can use the Internet to avoid having to go to special meetings or to a campaign site to do volunteer work or obtain information on a candidate's positions.

That the Internet is now a viable medium for communicating political information and interacting with voters was made clear in the campaigns preceding the 2008 and 2012 elections. According to a Pew Research Center survey following the 2012 presidential elections, 47 percent of Americans said that they had gone online for election news—up from 36 percent who had done so in the 2008 campaign. Among Internet users, 18 percent had posted political comments in a blog or on a social networking site. Fully 45 percent of users had watched online videos related to the campaigns. One in three had forwarded political content to someone else.

Online Fund-Raising

The Internet can be an effective—and inexpensive—way to raise campaign funds. Fund-raising on the Internet by presidential candidates became widespread after the Federal Election Commission decided, in June 1999, that the federal government could distribute matching funds for credit-card donations received by candidates via the Internet. We discussed Internet fund-raising in depth in Chapter 9—see the section titled *Fund-Raising on the Internet.*

The Rise of the Internet Campaign

An increasingly important part of political campaigning today is the Internet campaign. Candidates typically hire Web managers to manage their Internet campaigns.

AP PHOTO/BARACKOBAMA.COM

This 2012 image is from the Spanish-language version of the Obama Web site. Obama's Spanish-language ads were relatively upbeat. Why might that have been so?

The job of the Web manager, or Web strategist, is to create a well-designed, informative, and user-friendly campaign Web site to attract viewers, hold their attention, manage their e-mails, and track their credit-card contributions. The Web manager also hires bloggers to promote the candidate's views, arranges for podcasting of campaign information and updates to supporters, and hires staff to monitor the Web for news about the candidates and to track the online publications of *netroots groups*—online activists who support the candidate but are not controlled by the candidate's organization.

Controlling the Netroots   One of the challenges facing candidates today is delivering a consistent campaign message to voters. Netroots groups may make this task more difficult. Such a group may publish online promotional ads or other materials that do not represent a candidate's position, for example, or attack the candidate's opponent in ways that the candidate does not approve. Yet no candidate wants to alienate these groups, because they can raise significant sums of money and garner votes for the candidate.

Candidates' 24/7 Exposure   Just as citizen journalism has altered the news culture, so have citizen videos changed the traditional campaign. For example, a candidate can never know when a comment that she or he makes may be caught on camera by someone with a cell phone or digital camera and published on the Internet for all to see.

A candidate's opponents may post a compilation of video clips showing the candidate's inconsistent comments over time on a specific topic, such as abortion or the health-care reform legislation. The effect can be very damaging, because it makes the candidate's "flip-flopping" on the issue apparent.

Gaffes during the 2012 Campaigns

Both major-party presidential candidates experienced the dangers of 24/7 exposure during the 2012 campaigns. Republican Mitt Romney became rather well known for *gaffes*—poorly chosen words. The most damaging of these was a video of Romney speaking to wealthy donors: "There are 47 percent of the people who will vote for the president no matter what . . . who believe that they are victims, who believe the government has a responsibility to care for them, who believe that they are entitled to health care, to food, to housing. . . . These are people who pay no income tax. . . . My job is not to worry about those people. I'll never convince them they should take personal responsibility and care for their lives." This comment powerfully reinforced the Democratic theme of Romney as a rich man out of touch with ordinary citizens. In fact, about half of the 47 percent who pay no income tax vote Republican.

Barack Obama occasionally put his foot in his mouth as well. Speaking to supporters, Obama tried to explain why the wealthy should pay more taxes: "If you were successful . . . somebody helped to create this unbelievable American system that we have that allowed you to thrive. Somebody invested in roads and bridges. If you've got a business—you didn't build that. Somebody else made that happen." In saying "you didn't build that," Obama was referring to infrastructure. A clumsy choice of words, however, made it sound as if he were referring to private businesses themselves. Republicans repeated the shorter version of the quote endlessly.

FOR CRITICAL THINKING *To what extent do the media— in particular, the new media— encourage political participation? To what extent might they discourage participation by providing apolitical entertainment?*

AMERICA AT ODDS Politics and the Media

Americans love to hate the media, possibly because we spend so much time watching and reading them. Without a doubt, the media are undergoing a revolution today. With the loss of classified ads to the Internet, newspapers are in serious financial jeopardy. Online news sources, meanwhile, have yet to hit upon a reliable method of generating adequate income. In this changing environment, Americans are at odds over a number of media topics:

- Do the difficulties faced by newspapers threaten the existence of competent journalism—or is this not an important problem?

- Is the media's agenda-setting function a vital contribution to the democratic process—or an improper attempt to manipulate viewers?

- Should protection of the First Amendment be extended to broadcast media without exception—or would such a move threaten the morals of the country and make it impossible for viewers to avoid sexual content?

- Are negative advertisements an inevitable and unremarkable aspect of political campaigns—or should the voters punish politicians who employ them?

- Does talk radio add to the vigor of our political discourse—or is it a corrupting influence that divides the nation?

- Do the mainstream media have a liberal bias—or do they merely publicize facts that do not square with conservative beliefs?

STUDY TOOLS

Ready to study?

- **Review** what you've read with the quiz below.
- Check your answers on the **Chapter in Review** card at the back of the book.
- For any questions you miss, read the corresponding **Learning Outcome** section again to prepare for class and your exam.
- Rip out and study the **Chapter in Review** card (at the back of the book).

Fill-In

Learning Outcome 10–1

1. _____ is an agenda-setting technique in which a media outlet promotes specific facts or ideas that may affect the public's thinking on related topics.

2. Of all the media, _____ still has the greatest impact on most Americans.

3. A sound bite is _____.

4. Newspapers today are in financial difficulty because _____.

Learning Outcome 10–2

5. The first televised presidential debate, between _____, took place in 1960.

6. Spin doctors are _____.

Learning Outcome 10–3

7. The talk-radio audience is predominantly _____.

8. Talk radio is sometimes characterized as the Wild West of the media because _____.

Learning Outcome 10–4

9. It has been suggested that the media use the winner-loser framework to describe events throughout the campaigns, contributing to a bias against _____.

Learning Outcome 10–5

10. Citizen journalism refers to _____.

Multiple Choice

Learning Outcome 10–1

11. In the news business, framing refers to
    a. fitting events into a familiar story or filtering information through preconceived ideas.
    b. news coverage that is managed by a political consultant to gain media exposure for a political candidate.
    c. narrowing the focus of news to the local area.

Learning Outcome 10–2

12. The 1964 "daisy girl" ad is an example of
    a. a personal attack ad.
    b. citizen journalism.
    c. a negative issue ad.

Learning Outcome 10–3

13. Modern talk radio took off in the United States during the
    a. 1930s, after Franklin Roosevelt's first "fireside chat."
    b. 1950s, after political advertising first appeared on television.
    c. 1990s, after the repeal of the fairness doctrine.

Learning Outcome 10–4

14. In a 2013 Gallup poll measuring the public's confidence in various institutions, ____ percent of the respondents stated that they had a "great deal" or "quite a lot" of confidence in television news.
    a. 67
    b. 42
    c. 23

Learning Outcome 10–5

15. ____ refers to the distribution of audio or video files to personal computers or mobile devices such as smartphones.
    a. Blogging
    b. Podcasting
    c. Narrowcasting

The Congress

The **Learning Outcomes** labeled 1 through 6 are designed to help improve your understanding of the chapter. After reading this chapter, you should be able to:

11–1 Explain how seats in the House of Representatives are apportioned among the states.

11–2 Describe the power of incumbency.

11–3 Identify the key leadership positions in Congress, describe the committee system, and indicate some important differences between the House of Representatives and the Senate.

11–4 Summarize the specific steps in the lawmaking process.

11–5 Identify Congress's oversight functions and explain how Congress fulfills them.

11–6 Indicate what is involved in the congressional budgeting process.

Remember to visit page 256 for additional Study Tools

Learning Outcomes

AMERICA AT ODDS

WWW.SHUTTERSTOCK.COM

Should It Take Sixty Senators to Pass Important Legislation?

The number of Senate votes required to force an end to a *filibuster* is sixty. A filibuster takes place when senators use the chamber's tradition of unlimited debate to block legislation. In years past, filibustering senators would speak for hours—even reading names from the telephone book—to prevent a vote on a proposed bill. In recent decades, however, Senate rules have permitted filibusters in which actual continuous floor speeches are not required. Senators merely announce that they are filibustering.

The threat of a filibuster has created an *ad hoc* rule that important legislation needs the support of sixty senators. (There are exceptions. Budget bills can be handled using a special *reconciliation* rule that does not permit filibusters.) If one party can elect sixty or more U.S. senators, and if they all follow the party line, they can force through any legislation they want. The Democrats, in fact, enjoyed a supermajority in the Senate for seven months, from July 7, 2009, until February 4, 2010, when they lost a seat in a special election.

Are sixty votes an appropriate requirement for passing important legislation in the Senate? Should the number be reduced to fifty-five or even to fifty-one—a simple majority of all sitting senators?

Don't Let the Majority Trample on the Minority

In the course of our history, the filibuster in the U.S. Senate has served us well. Filibusters provide the minority with an effective means of preventing the majority from ramming legislation down the throats of American voters. Rule by a simple majority can be scary. Support for a measure can shift between forty-nine votes and fifty-one votes very quickly. Should such small changes be the basis for passing major legislation?

A simple majority does not signify an adequate degree of consensus. It takes two-thirds of both chambers of Congress to override a veto by the president. That's another supermajority. Changing the Constitution requires a very substantial supermajority—three-quarters of the state legislatures. If these supermajority rules were good enough for the founders, then the principle still is good enough for the Senate.

In the past, the American public has supported the filibuster in public opinion polls—for good reason. One of the most important characteristics of our political system is that it is not easy to create new laws. The existence of two chambers of Congress—and the president's veto power—ensures this. In particular, the Senate was always meant to be a body that could delay legislation. As President George Washington allegedly said, "We pour legislation into the senatorial saucer to 'cool' it."

Don't Let Obstructionists Determine Legislation

Supermajority rules allow a minority to block the preference of the majority. Even James Madison, who worried about the tyranny of the majority over the minority, recognized the opposite possibility. He said that "the fundamental principle of free government" might be reversed by requiring supermajorities. "It would be no longer majority that would rule: the power would be transferred to the minority."

Madison's warning has been amply justified. At one time, the filibuster was reserved for the defense of major principles. Not all of these principles were laudable—the filibuster was used to defend Jim Crow laws and to prevent African Americans from voting in much of the South. Still, the procedure was rare. Today, it is used for most legislation.

A second development makes the filibuster even more of a problem. In recent years, the major parties have become politically unified and monolithic. Members of the minority are prepared to cast party-line votes to frustrate the will of the majority on most legislation. Such votes make governance almost impossible. Congress has never passed so few bills in each session as it does under current circumstances.

The Senate should reduce the votes required to end a filibuster to fifty-five or even fifty-one. The public now supports such a measure. Let's get on with government by the majority, not the minority.

Where do you stand?

1. Why might it be appropriate to require supermajority voting for important legislation?
2. Under what circumstances do supermajority voting rules prevent democracy from being fully realized?

Explore this issue online

You can find out more about the filibuster by entering "filibuster" into a search engine. For debates on the merits of the tradition, search on "filibuster pro con."

Introduction

Congress is the lawmaking branch of government. When someone says, "There ought to be a law," at the federal level it is Congress that will make that law. The framers had a strong mistrust of powerful executive authority. Consequently, they made Congress—not the executive branch (the presidency)—the central institution of American government. Yet, as noted in Chapter 2, the founders created a system of checks and balances to ensure that no branch of the federal government, including Congress, could exercise too much power.

Many Americans view Congress as a largely faceless, anonymous legislative body that is quite distant and removed from their everyday lives. Yet the people you elect to Congress represent and advocate for your interests at the very highest level of power.

Furthermore, the laws created by the men and women in the U.S. Congress affect the daily lives of every American in one way or another. Getting to know about your congressional representatives and how they are voting in Congress on issues that concern you is an important step toward becoming an informed voter. Even the details of how Congress makes law—such as the Senate rules described in the chapter-opening *America at Odds* feature—should be of interest to the savvy voter.

11–1 The Structure and Makeup of Congress

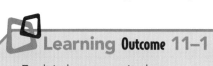

Learning Outcome 11–1

Explain how seats in the House of Representatives are apportioned among the states.

The framers agreed that the Congress should be the "first branch of the government," as James Madison said, but they did not immediately agree on its organization. Ultimately, they decided on a *bicameral legislature*—a Congress consisting of two chambers. This was part of the Great Compromise, which you read about in Chapter 2.

The framers favored a bicameral legislature so that the two chambers, the House and the Senate, might serve as checks on each other's power and activity. The House was to represent the people. The Senate was to represent the states and would protect the interests of small states by giving them the same number of senators (two per state) as the larger states.

11–1a Apportionment of House Seats

The Constitution provides for the **apportionment** (distribution) of House seats among the states on the basis of their respective populations. States with larger populations, such as California, have many more representatives than states with smaller populations, such as Wyoming. California, for example, currently has fifty-three representatives in the House. Wyoming has only one.

Every ten years, House seats are reapportioned based on the outcome of the decennial (ten-year) census conducted by the U.S. Census Bureau. Figure 11–1 on the following page indicates the states that gained and lost seats based on population changes reported by the 2010 census. This redistribution of seats took effect with the 113th Congress, elected in 2012.

> **SOCIAL MEDIA In Politics**
>
> If you are interested in Congress, two sources are worth investigating. Politico is a political news blog, and *Roll Call* is a newspaper covering Congress. Both have Facebook pages, and you can also follow either of them on Twitter.

Each state is guaranteed at least one House seat, no matter what its population. Today, seven states have only one representative.[1] The District of Columbia, American Samoa, Guam, the Northern Mariana Islands, and the U.S. Virgin Islands all send nonvoting delegates to the House. Puerto Rico, a self-governing possession of the United States, is represented by a nonvoting resident commissioner.

11–1b Congressional Districts

Whereas senators are elected to represent all of the people in a state, representatives are elected by the voters of a particular area known as a **congressional district.** The Constitution makes no provisions for congressional districts. In

apportionment The distribution of House seats among the states on the basis of their respective populations.

congressional district The geographic area that is served by one member in the House of Representatives.

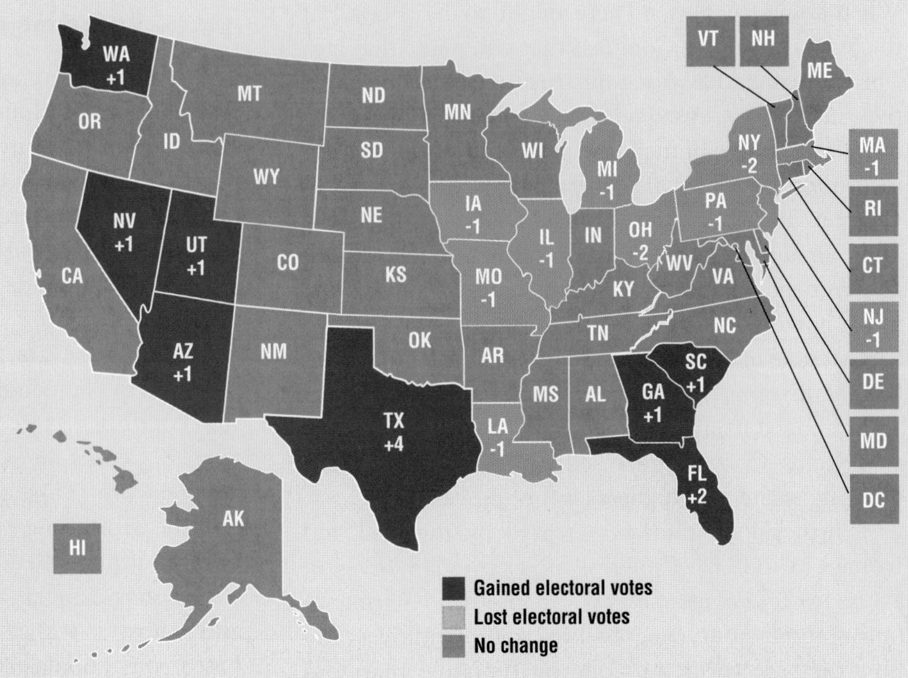

the early 1800s, each state was given the right to decide whether to have districts at all.

Most states set up single-member districts, in which voters in each district elected one of the state's representatives. In states that chose not to have districts, representatives were chosen at large, from the state as a whole. In 1842, however, Congress passed an act that required all states to send representatives to Congress from single-member districts.

The Size of the House

For many years, the number of House members increased as the population expanded. In 1929, however, a federal law fixed House membership at 435 members. Thus, today the 435 members of the House are chosen by the voters in 435 separate congressional districts across the country. If a state's population allows it to have only one representative, the entire state is one congressional district. In contrast, states with large populations have many districts. California, for example, because its population entitles it to send fifty-three representatives to the House, has fifty-three congressional districts.

As a result of the rule limiting the size of the House to 435 members, U.S. congressional districts on average now have very substantial populations—about 730,000 people. We compare the size of the U.S. House with the size of parliamentary bodies of other nations in this chapter's *The Rest of the World* feature on the following page.

The Requirement of Equal Representation

malapportionment
A condition in which the voting power of citizens in one district is greater than the voting power of citizens in another district.

By default, the lines of the congressional districts are drawn by the state legislatures. Alternatively, the task may be handed off to a designated body such as an independent commission. States must meet certain requirements in drawing district boundaries. To ensure equal representation in the House, districts in a given state must contain, as nearly as possible, equal numbers of people. Additionally, each district must have contiguous boundaries and must be "geographically compact," although this last requirement is not enforced very strictly.

If congressional districts are not made up of equal populations, people's votes are not equally valuable. In the past, state legislators often used this fact to their advantage. For example, traditionally, many state legislatures were controlled by rural areas. By drawing districts that were not equal in population, rural leaders attempted to curb the number of representatives from growing urban centers. At one point in the 1960s, in many states the largest district had twice the population of the smallest district. In effect, this meant that a person's vote in the largest district had only half the value of a person's vote in the smallest district.

For some time, the United States Supreme Court refused to address this problem. In 1962, however, in *Baker v. Carr*,[2] the Court ruled that the Tennessee state legislature's **malapportionment** was an issue that could be heard in the federal courts because it affected the constitutional requirement of equal pro-

FIGURE 11–1

Electoral Votes Gained
and Lost after the 2010 Census

Gained electoral votes
Lost electoral votes
No change

The Size of Congress—How the United States Stacks Up

The U.S. House of Representatives is the "lower" chamber of our Congress. (In international terminology, it is the *lower house*.) The U.S. House consists of 435 members, a number established in 1929. That means, today, the average member of the House represents about 730,000 Americans. In other democracies, members of the lower house represent a far smaller number of people.

Almost all large nations—and even many of the smaller ones—have lower houses that are larger than the U.S. House. Britain's House of Commons has 650 members, each of whom represents almost 100,000

inhabitants. The French National Assembly has 577 members, each representing about 114,000 people.

Only one nation in the entire world has a lower house with members who represent more people than House representatives do in America. That nation is India. Each of the 552 members of the House of the People represents more than 2.2 million citizens. This makes a certain amount of sense—India has a total population in excess of 1.2 billion.

Build a Bigger House?
New York University professor of sociology Dalton Connelly argues that as

the third most populous nation on earth, the United States should have a larger House of Representatives. The average House member spoke for only 200,000 citizens in 1913. If that ratio were kept today, we would have almost 1,600 representatives. Because districts would be smaller, campaigns would be cheaper. We might have more citizen-legislators and fewer lifetime politicians. We would certainly see our representatives more often. Members of the House would do more of the work of the House, and there would be less reliance on staff members.

FOR CRITICAL ANALYSIS To create a larger House of Representatives, Congress itself would have to pass the necessary legislation. Why might current members of Congress be reluctant to do this?

---

tection under the law. Two years later, in *Wesberry v. Sanders*,[3] the Supreme Court held that congressional districts must have equal populations. This principle has come to be known as the **"one person, one vote" rule.** In other words, one person's vote has to count as much as another's vote.

Gerrymandering Although in the 1960s the Supreme Court ruled that congressional districts must be equal in population, it continued to be silent on the issue of gerrymandered districts. **Gerrymandering** occurs when a district's boundaries are drawn to maximize the influence of a certain group or political party.

Where a party's voters are scarce, the boundaries of a district can be drawn to include as many of the party's voters as possible. Where the party is strong, the lines are drawn so that the opponent's supporters are spread across two or more districts, thus diluting the opponent's strength. (The term *gerrymandering* was originally used to describe the district lines drawn to favor the party of Governor Elbridge Gerry of Massachusetts prior to the 1812 elections—see Figure 11–2 on the following page.)

Although there have been constitutional challenges to political gerrymandering,[4] the practice continues. It was certainly evident following the 2010 census. Sophisticated computer programs were now able to analyze the partisan leanings of individual neighborhoods and city blocks. District lines were drawn to "pack" the opposing party's voters into the smallest number of districts or "crack" the opposing party's voters into several different districts. Packing and cracking make congressional races less competitive.

HOW GERRYMANDERING WORKS. For a better understanding of how gerrymandering works, look at the examples in Figure 11–3 on page 239. In the examples, sixty-four voters must be distributed among four districts, each of which will have a population of

"one person, one vote" rule A rule, or principle, requiring that congressional districts have equal populations so that one person's vote counts as much as another's vote.

gerrymandering The drawing of a legislative district's boundaries in such a way as to maximize the influence of a certain group or political party.

FIGURE 11-2

The First "Gerrymander"

Prior to the 1812 elections, the Massachusetts legislature divided up Essex County in a way that favored Governor Elbridge Gerry's party. The result was a district that looked something like a salamander. A newspaper editor of the time referred to it as a "gerrymander," and the name stuck.

Source: *Congressional Quarterly's Guide to Congress*, 3d ed. (Washington, D.C.: Congressional Quarterly Press, 1982), p. 695.

the X Party. The district in the lower right is an example of packing—the maximum possible number of O voters is packed into the district. In the other three districts, O Party supporters are cracked apart so that they do not have a majority in any of the districts. In these districts, the X Party has majorities of eleven to five, ten to six, and eleven to five.

GERRYMANDERING AFTER THE 2010 CENSUS. The 2010 elections were a Republican triumph, and the party won control of state legislatures across the country. These victories occurred just before the states were required to redraw the boundaries of congressional districts following the 2010 census. The result was a large number of Republican gerrymanders, which had a substantial effect on the 2012 elections. In the elections, Democratic candidates for the U.S. House actually collected more votes than Republican candidates. The Democrats picked up only eight seats, however. In the end, the partisan breakdown was 200 Democrats and 235 Republicans.

Consider Pennsylvania, which went for Barack Obama by 5.4 percentage points in 2012. Pennsylvania voters cast 2.72 million votes for Democratic House candidates and 2.65 million votes for Republicans. These votes elected five Democratic representatives and thirteen Republicans—even though more votes were cast for Democrats. Fortunately for the Democrats, the effects of a gerrymander wear off in time. Still, the Republicans looked set to enjoy the fruits of their 2010 redistricting for years to come.

RACIAL GERRYMANDERING. Although political gerrymandering has a long history, gerrymandering to empower minority groups is a relatively new phenomenon. In the early 1990s, the U.S. Department of Justice instructed state legislatures to draw district lines to maximize the voting power of minority groups. As a result, several **minority-majority districts** were created. Many of these districts took on bizarre shapes. For example, North Carolina's newly drawn Twelfth Congressional District was 165 miles long—a narrow strip that, for the most part, followed Interstate 85.

LIMITS ON RACIAL GERRYMANDERING. The practice of racial gerrymandering has generated heated arguments on both sides of the issue. Some groups contend that minority-majority districts are necessary to ensure equal representation of minority groups, as mandated by the Voting Rights Act of 1965. They further contend that these districts have been instrumental in

sixteen. The two political parties are the O Party and the X Party.

In Example 1, each district contains only one kind of voter. This type of gerrymander is sometimes created when a state legislature is more interested in preserving the seats of incumbents than in benefiting a particular party. In this case, it would be almost impossible for a sitting member to lose in a general election.

In Example 2, every district is divided evenly between the parties. The slightest swing toward one of the parties could give that party all four seats. A legislature would almost never come up with these boundaries, but an independent redistricting board might do so.

Example 3 is a partisan gerrymander favoring

minority-majority district A district in which minority groups make up a majority of the population.

FIGURE 11-3

Examples of Voter Distribution

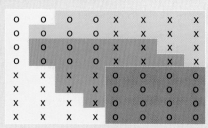

Example 1: A bipartisan gerrymander that protects incumbents of both parties.

Example 2: An unstable system. All districts have the same number of voters from each party.

Example 3: A classic partisan gerrymander. The X Party should carry three districts.

increasing the number of African Americans holding political office. Before 1990, redistricting plans in the South often created only white-majority districts.[5]

Opponents of racial gerrymandering argue that such race-based districting is unconstitutional because it violates the equal protection clause. In a series of cases in the 1990s, the Supreme Court agreed and held that when race is the dominant factor in the drawing of congressional district lines, the districts are unconstitutional and must be redrawn.[6]

In 2001, however, the Supreme Court issued a ruling that seemed to suggest that it would not police racial gerrymandering very closely. North Carolina's Twelfth District, which had been redrawn in 1997, was again challenged in court as unconstitutional, and a lower court agreed. Yet when the case reached the Supreme Court, the justices concluded that there was insufficient evidence that race had been the dominant factor in redrawing the district's boundaries.[7]

11-1c The Representation Function of Congress

Of the three branches of government, Congress has the closest ties to the American people. Members of Congress represent the interests and wishes of the constituents in their home states. At the same time, they must also consider larger national issues, such as the economy and the environment. Often, legislators find that the interests of their constituents are at odds with the demands of national policy.

For example, limits on emissions of carbon dioxide may help reduce climate change, to the benefit of all Americans and the people of the world generally. Yet members of Congress who come from states where most electricity comes from coal-burning power plants may fear that new laws would hurt the local economy and cause companies to lay off workers.

All members of Congress face difficult votes that set representational interests against lawmaking realities. There are several views on how legislators should decide such issues.

The Trustee View of Representation Some believe that representatives should act as **trustees** of the broad interests of the entire society, rather than serving only the narrow interests of their constituents. Under the trustee view, a legislator should act according to her or his conscience and perception of national needs. For example, a senator from North Carolina might support laws regulating the tobacco industry, even though the state's economy could be negatively affected.

The Instructed-Delegate View of Representation In contrast, others believe that members of Congress should behave as **instructed delegates.** The instructed-delegate view requires representatives to mirror the views of their constituents, regardless of their opinions. Under this view, a senator from Nebraska would strive to obtain subsidies for corn growers, and a representative from the Detroit area would seek to protect the automobile industry.

The Partisan View of Representation Because the political parties often take different positions on legislative issues, there are times when members of Congress are very attentive to the wishes of the party leadership. Especially on matters that are controversial, the Democratic members of Congress will

trustee A representative who tries to serve the broad interests of the entire society and not just the narrow interests of his or her constituents.

instructed delegate A representative who deliberately mirrors the views of the majority of his or her constituents.

be more likely to vote in favor of policies endorsed by a Democratic president, while Republicans will be more likely to oppose them.

Typically, members of Congress combine these three approaches. Legislators may take a trustee approach on some issues, adhere to the instructed-delegate view on other matters, and follow the party line on still others.

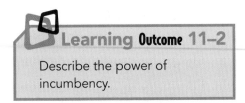

Some states have tried to prevent gerrymandering by establishing independent redistricting commissions. *What kinds of individuals should serve on such commissions? Why?*

11–2 Congressional Elections

Learning Outcome 11–2

Describe the power of incumbency.

The U.S. Constitution requires that representatives to Congress be elected every second year by popular vote. Senators are elected every six years, also by popular vote (since the ratification of the Seventeenth Amendment). Under Article I, Section 4, of the Constitution, state legislatures control the "Times, Places and Manner of holding Elections for Senators and Representatives." Congress, however, "may at any time by Law make or alter such Regulations." You can see the results of the 2012 House elections in Figure 11–4 on the following page.

11–2a Who Can Be a Member of Congress?

The Constitution sets forth only a few qualifications that those running for Congress must meet. To be a member of the House, a person must have been a citizen of the United States for at least seven years before his or her election, must be a legal resident of the state from which he or she is to be elected, and must be at least twenty-five years of age.

To be elected to the Senate, a person must have been a citizen for at least nine years, must be a legal resident of the state from which she or he is to be elected, and must be at least thirty years of age. The Supreme Court has ruled that neither the Congress nor the states can add to these three qualifications.[8]

Once elected to Congress, a senator or representative receives an annual salary from the government—$174,000 for rank-and-file members as of 2012. He or she also enjoys certain perks and privileges. Additionally, if a member of Congress wants to run for reelection in the next congressional elections, that person's chances are greatly enhanced by the power that incumbency brings to a reelection campaign.

11–2b The Power of Incumbency

The power of incumbency has long been noted in American politics. Typically, incumbents win so often and by such large margins that some observers have claimed that our electoral system involves something similar to a hereditary entitlement. As you can see in Figure 11–5 on page 242, most incumbents in Congress are reelected if they run.

Incumbent politicians enjoy several advantages over their opponents. A key advantage is their fundraising ability. Most incumbent members of Congress have a much larger network of contacts, donors, and lobbyists than their opponents have. Incumbents raise, on average, twice as much in campaign funds as their challengers. Other advantages that incumbents can put to work to aid their reelection include:

- *Congressional franking privileges*—members of Congress can mail newsletters and other correspondence to their constituents at the taxpayers' expense. (In an era of e-mail and social networking, however, the franking privilege is much less valuable than it used to be.)

- *Professional staffs*—members have large administrative staffs both in Washington, D.C., and in their home districts.

- *Lawmaking power*—members can back legislation that will benefit their states or districts and then campaign on that legislative record in the next election.

- *Access to the media*—because they are elected officials, members have many opportunities to stage events for the press and thereby obtain free publicity.

- *Name recognition*—incumbent members are usually far better known to the voters than challengers are.

Critics argue that the advantages enjoyed by incumbents reduce the competition necessary for a healthy democracy. These incumbency advantages also serve to suppress voter turnout. Voters are less likely to turn out when an incumbent candidate is practically guaranteed reelection.

11–2c Congressional Terms

As noted earlier, members of the House of Representatives serve two-year terms, and senators serve six-year terms. This means that every two years we hold congressional elections: the entire House of Representatives and a third of the Senate are up for election. In January of every odd-numbered year, a "new" Congress con-venes (of course, two-thirds of the senators are not new, and most House incumbents are reelected, so they are not new to Congress either). Each Congress has been numbered consecutively, dating back to 1789. The Congress that convened in 2013 was the 113th.

Congressional Sessions Each congressional term is divided into two regular sessions, one for each year. Until about 1940, Congress remained in session for only four or five months, but the complicated rush of legislation and the public's increased demand for services in recent years have forced Congress to remain in session through most of each year.[9] Both chambers, however, schedule short recesses, or breaks, for holidays and vacations. The president may call a

---

FIGURE 11–4

Members of the U.S. House
Following the 2012 Elections

Each dot represents one congressional district. Red dots show a Republican representative, and blue dots show a Democrat. In three metropolitan areas—Chicago, Los Angeles, and New York—the dots on the main map overlap so much that many of them are hidden. That is the reason for the three metro area close-ups.

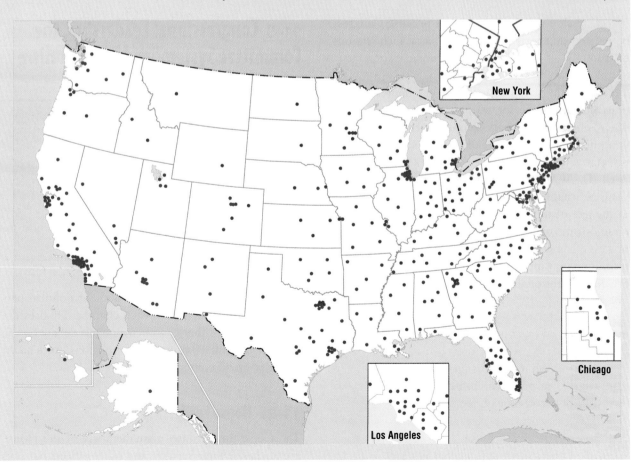

FIGURE 11-5   The Power of Incumbency

While incumbents who run are usually reelected, this chart reveals occasional periods of some turbulence when fewer incumbents than usual won reelection. One was in the years 1992 and 1994, and another was in 2010 and 2012.

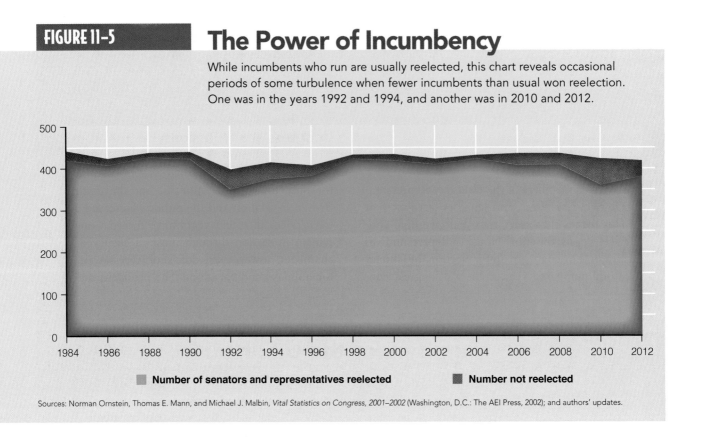

■ **Number of senators and representatives reelected**   ■ **Number not reelected**

Sources: Norman Ornstein, Thomas E. Mann, and Michael J. Malbin, *Vital Statistics on Congress, 2001–2002* (Washington, D.C.: The AEI Press, 2002); and authors' updates.

special session during a recess, but because Congress now meets on nearly a year-round basis, such sessions are rare.

Term Limits   As you will read in Chapter 12, the president can serve for no more than two terms in office, due to the Twenty-second Amendment. There is no limit on the number of terms a senator or representative can serve, however. For example, Robert Byrd (D., W.V.) served more than fifty-two years in the U.S. Senate, from 1959 until he died in June 2010, at the age of ninety-two. Some observers favor term limits for members of Congress. The Supreme Court, however, has ruled that state-level attempts to impose term limits on members of the U.S. House or Senate are unconstitutional.[10]

FOR CRITICAL THINKING

What benefits could a state hope to gain from representation by a long-serving legislator?

11–3 Congressional Leadership, the Committee System, and Bicameralism

The Constitution provides for the presiding officers of both the House and the Senate, and each chamber has added other leadership positions as it has seen fit. Leadership and organization in both chambers are

Learning Outcome 11–3

Identify the key leadership positions in Congress, describe the committee system, and indicate some important differences between the House of Representatives and the Senate.

based on membership in the two major political parties. The majority party in each chamber chooses the major officers of that chamber, controls debate on the floor, selects all committee chairpersons, and has a majority on all committees.

11–3a House Leadership

The Constitution states that members of the House are to choose their Speaker and other officers but says

AP PHOTO/EVAN VUCCI

COURTESY OF WWW.WIKIPEDIA.ORG

MICHAEL REYNOLDS/EPA/LANDOV

When the Republicans took control of the House after the 2010 elections, former minority leader John Boehner (R., Ohio), left, was elected Speaker of the House, and Eric Cantor (R., Va.), center, was elected House majority leader. Former Speaker Nancy Pelosi (D., Calif.), right, became the new House minority leader. These leaders remained in their posts after the 2012 elections.

nothing more about these positions. Today, important "other officers" include the majority and minority leaders and whips.

Speaker of the House

Chief among the leaders in the House of Representatives is the **Speaker of the House.** This office is filled by a vote taken at the beginning of each congressional term. The Speaker has traditionally been a longtime member of the majority party who has risen in rank and influence through years of service in the House. The candidate for Speaker is selected by the majority-party caucus. The House as a whole then approves the selection.

As the presiding officer of the House and the leader of the majority party, the Speaker has a great deal of power. In the nineteenth century, the Speaker had even more authority. Speakers known by such names as "Uncle Joe Cannon" and "Czar Reed" ruled the House with a firm hand. A revolt in 1910 reduced the Speaker's powers and gave some of them to various committees. Nevertheless, the Speaker still has many important powers, including the following:

- The Speaker has substantial control over what bills are assigned to which committees.

- The Speaker may preside over the sessions of the House, recognizing or ignoring members who wish to speak.

- The Speaker votes in the event of a tie, interprets and applies House rules, rules on points of order

(questions about procedures asked by members), puts questions to a vote, and interprets the outcome of most of the votes taken.

- The Speaker plays a major role in making important committee assignments

- The Speaker schedules bills for action.

The Speaker may choose whether to vote on any measure. If the Speaker chooses to vote, he or she appoints a temporary presiding officer (called a Speaker pro tempore), who then occupies the Speaker's chair. Under the House rules, the only time the Speaker *must* vote is to break a tie. Otherwise, a tie automatically defeats a bill. The Speaker does not often vote, but by choosing to vote in some cases, the Speaker can actually cause a tie and defeat a proposal.

Majority Leader

The **majority leader** of the House is elected by the majority-party caucus to act as spokesperson for the party and to keep the party together. The majority leader's job is to help plan the party's legislative program, organize other party members to support legislation favored by the party, and make

Speaker of the House
The presiding officer in the House of Representatives. The Speaker is a member of the majority party and is the most powerful member of the House.

majority leader
The party leader elected by the majority party in the House or in the Senate.

sure the chairpersons on the many committees finish work on bills that are important to the party. The majority leader makes speeches on important bills, stating the majority party's position.

Minority Leader

The House **minority leader** is the leader of the minority party. Although not as powerful as the majority leader, the minority leader has similar responsibilities. The primary duty of the minority leader is to maintain solidarity within the minority party. The minority leader persuades influential members of the party to follow the party's position and organizes fellow party members in criticism of the majority party's policies and programs.

Whips

The leadership of each party includes assistants to the majority and minority leaders known as **whips.** Whips originated in the British House of Commons, where they were named after the "whipper in," the rider who keeps the hounds together in a fox hunt. The term is applied to assistant party leaders because of the pressure that they place on party members to uphold the party's positions.

Whips try to determine how each member is going to vote on an issue and then advise the party leaders on the strength of party support. Whips also try to see that members are present when important votes are to be taken and that they vote with the party leadership. For example, if the Republican Party strongly supports a tax-cut bill, the Republican Party whip might meet with other Republican Party members in the House to try to ensure that they will show up and vote with the party.

11–3b Senate Leadership

The Constitution makes the vice president of the United States the president of the Senate. As presiding officer, the vice president may call on members to speak and put questions to a vote. The vice president is not an elected member of the Senate, however, and may not take part in Senate debates. The vice president may cast a vote in the Senate only in the event of a tie.

President Pro Tempore

Because vice presidents are rarely available—and do not often desire—to preside over the Senate, senators elect another presiding officer, the president pro tempore ("pro tem"), who serves in the absence of the vice president. The president pro tem is elected by the whole Senate and is ordinarily the member of the majority party with the longest continuous term of service in the Senate. In the absence of both the president pro tem and the vice president, a temporary presiding officer is selected from the ranks of the Senate, usually a junior member of the majority party.

Party Leaders

The real power in the Senate is held by the majority leader, the minority leader, and their whips. The majority leader is the most powerful individual and chief spokesperson of the majority party. The majority leader directs the legislative program and party strategy. The minority leader commands the minority party's opposition to the policies of the majority party and directs the legislative strategy of the minority party.

In 2006, Democratic senator Harry Reid of Nevada, left, became the Senate majority leader, and Republican senator Mitch McConnell of Kentucky became the Senate minority leader. Both retained their offices following the 2012 elections.

AP PHOTO/CAROLYN KASTER

MCCONNELL.SENATE.GOV/OFFICIAL_PHOTOS.CFM

minority leader
The party leader elected by the minority party in the House or in the Senate.

whip A member of Congress who assists the majority or minority leader in the House or in the Senate in managing the party's legislative program.

11-3c Congressional Committees

Thousands of bills are introduced during every session of Congress, and no single member can possibly be adequately informed on all the issues that arise. The committee system is a way to provide for specialization, or a division of the legislative labor. Members of a committee concentrate on just one area or topic—such as agriculture or transportation—and develop sufficient expertise to draft appropriate legislation when needed. The flow of legislation through both the House and the Senate is determined largely by the speed with which these committees act on bills and resolutions.

Standing Committees The permanent and most powerful committees of Congress are called **standing committees.** Their names are listed in Table 11–1 below. Normally, before any bill can be considered by the entire House or Senate, it must be approved by a majority vote in the standing committee to which it was assigned.

As mentioned, standing committees are controlled by the majority party in each chamber. Committee membership is generally divided between the parties according to the number of members in each chamber. In both the House and the Senate, committee *seniority*—the length of continuous service on a particular committee—typically plays a role in determining the committee chairpersons.

standing committee A permanent committee in Congress that deals with legislation concerning a particular area, such as agriculture or foreign relations.

subcommittee A division of a larger committee that deals with a particular part of the committee's policy area. Most standing committees have several subcommittees.

Subcommittees and Other Committees

Most House and Senate committees also have **subcommittees** with limited areas of jurisdiction. Today, there are more than two hundred subcommittees.

There are also other types of committees in Congress. Special, or select, committees are formed to study specific problems or issues. These committees may be either permanent or temporary.

Joint committees are created by the concurrent action of both chambers of Congress and consist of members from each chamber. Joint committees have dealt with the economy, taxation, and the Library of Congress.

Conference committees, which also include members from both chambers, are formed for the purpose of achieving agreement between the House and the Senate on the exact wording of legislative acts when the two

TABLE 11–1

Standing Committees in the 113th Congress, 2013–2015

House Committees	Senate Committees
Agriculture	Agriculture, Nutrition, and Forestry
Appropriations	Appropriations
Armed Services	Armed Services
Budget	Banking, Housing, and Urban Affairs
Education and the Workforce	Budget
Energy and Commerce	Commerce, Science, and Transportation
Financial Services	Energy and Natural Resources
Foreign Affairs	Environment and Public Works
Homeland Security	Finance
House Administration	Foreign Relations
Judiciary	Health, Education, Labor, and Pensions
Natural Resources	Homeland Security and Governmental Affairs
Oversight and Government Reform	Judiciary
Rules	Rules and Administration
Science and Technology	Small Business and Entrepreneurship
Small Business	Veterans' Affairs
Standards of Official Conduct	
Transportation and Infrastructure	
Veterans' Affairs	
Ways and Means	

chambers pass legislative proposals in different forms. No bill can be sent to the White House to be signed into law unless it first passes both chambers in identical form.

If the leadership in either chamber believes that an acceptable compromise with the other chamber is impossible, it can block legislation simply by refusing to appoint members to a conference committee. In 2013, the Republicans employed this technique on several bills, beginning with the 2014 federal budget resolution.

Most of the actual work of legislating is performed by the committees and subcommittees (the "little legislatures"[11]) within Congress. In creating or amending laws, committee members work closely with relevant interest groups and administrative agency personnel. For more details on the interaction among these groups, see the discussion of "issue networks" and "iron triangles" in Chapter 13.

11–3d The Differences between the House and the Senate

To understand what goes on in the chambers of Congress, we need to look at the effects of bicameralism. Each chamber has developed certain distinct features. The major differences between the House and the Senate are listed in Table 11–2 below.

Size Matters Obviously, with 435 voting members, the House cannot operate the same way as the Senate, which has only 100 members. With its larger size, the House needs both more rules and more formality—otherwise, no work would ever get done. The

Rules Committee A standing committee in the House of Representatives that provides special rules governing how particular bills will be considered and debated by the House. The Rules Committee normally proposes time limits on debate for any bill.

most obvious formal rules have to do with debate on the floor.

The Senate normally permits extended debate on all issues that arise before it. In contrast, the House uses an elaborate system: The House **Rules Committee** normally proposes time limits on debate for any bill. The rules are then accepted or modified by the House. Despite its greater size, as a consequence of its stricter time limits on debate, the House is often able to act on legislation more quickly than the Senate.

The "Hastert Rule" in the House One informal rule affecting only House Republicans can prevent consideration of legislation even if it has passed in the Senate. That is the *Hastert Rule,* named after a former Republican Speaker. Under the rule, when the Republicans have a majority in the House, the Speaker will not allow any measure to reach the floor unless it has the support of a majority of the Republican members of the House. Democratic Speakers, of course, also have the power to block legislation in this way, and they often do. They have not turned this procedure into an informal rule, however.

The Hastert Rule came under considerable pressure in late 2012 and 2013, when Republican Speaker John Boehner felt compelled to violate it repeatedly. Legislation in December 2012 prevented large-scale tax increases at the cost of allowing taxes to rise for the wealthiest citizens. It passed without the support

TABLE 11–2

Major Differences between the House and the Senate

House*	Senate*
Members chosen from local districts	Members chosen from entire state
Two-year term	Six-year term
Always elected by voters	Originally (until 1913) elected by state legislatures
May impeach (accuse, indict) federal officials	May convict federal officials of impeachable offenses
Larger (435 voting members)	Smaller (100 members)
More formal rules	Fewer rules and restrictions
Debate limited	Debate extended
Floor action controlled	Unanimous consent rules
Less prestige and less individual notice	More prestige and media attention
Originates bills for raising revenues	Has power of "advice and consent" on presidential appointments and treaties
Local or narrow leadership	National leadership

*Some of these differences, such as term of office, are provided for in the Constitution, while others, such as debate rules, are not.

of most Republicans. Boehner also lifted the rule so that he could win aid for states suffering the effects of Superstorm Sandy (October 2012) and for several other bills.

In the Senate, Debate Can Just Keep Going and Going

At one time, both the House and the Senate allowed unlimited debate, but the House ended this practice in 1811. The use of unlimited debate in the Senate to obstruct legislation is called **filibustering** (as discussed in the chapter-opening *America at Odds* feature).

Today, under Senate Rule 22, filibusters may be ended by invoking **cloture**—a procedure for closing debate and bringing the matter under consideration to a vote in the Senate. Sixteen senators must sign a petition requesting cloture. Then, after two days have elapsed, three-fifths of the entire membership must vote for cloture. Normally, that means sixty senators. Once cloture is invoked, each senator may speak on a bill for no more than one hour before a vote is taken. Additionally, a final vote must take place within one hundred hours after cloture has been invoked.

The Senatorial Hold

Senators have an additional tool they can use to delay legislation. Individual senators may place a *hold* on a particular bill. A senator simply informs the leader of his or her party of the hold. Party leaders do not announce who has placed a hold, so holds are often anonymous. Recent rule changes designed to curb anonymous holds have been ineffective. Cloture can be used to lift a hold.

Senators often place holds on nominees for executive or judicial positions in an attempt to win concessions from the executive branch. For example, in 2010, Senator Richard Shelby (R., Ala.) placed holds on at least seventy of President Obama's nominations in an attempt to force the administration to support two military spending programs in Alabama.

The Senate Wins the Prestige Race, Hands Down

Because of the large number of representatives, few can garner the prestige that a senator enjoys. Senators have relatively little difficulty in gaining access to the media. Members of the House, who run for reelection every two years, have to survive many reelection campaigns before they can obtain such recognition. Usually, a representative must become an important committee leader to enjoy the consistent attention of the national news media.

One consequence of the prestige difference is that it has been very difficult for a member of the House to win a presidential nomination. In contrast, the parties have often nominated senators, and a number of senators have gone on to become president.

FOR CRITICAL THINKING Vice presidents typically avoid presiding over the Senate, even though that is their chief constitutional responsibility. *Why might they be so reluctant?*

11–4 The Legislative Process

Look at Figure 11–6 on the following page, which shows the basic process through which a bill becomes law at the national level. Not all of the complexities of the process are shown, to be sure. For example, the figure does not indicate the extensive lobbying and media politics that are often involved in the legislative process, nor does it mention the informal negotiations and "horse trading" that occur to get a bill passed.

Learning Outcome 11–4

Summarize the specific steps in the lawmaking process.

The basic steps in the process are as follows:

1. ***Introduction of legislation.*** Although individual members of Congress or their staffs—as well as private citizens and lobbying groups—may come up with ideas for new legislation, most bills are proposed by the executive branch. Only a member of Congress can formally introduce legislation, however. In reality, many bills are proposed, developed, and even written by the White House or an executive agency. Then a "friendly" senator or representative introduces the bill in Congress. Such bills are rarely ignored entirely, although they are often amended or defeated.

filibustering The Senate tradition of unlimited debate undertaken for the purpose of preventing action on a bill.

cloture A procedure for ending filibusters in the Senate and bringing the matter under consideration to a vote.

FIGURE 11-6 How a Bill Becomes a Law

This illustration shows the most typical way in which proposed legislation is enacted into law. It follows two hypothetical bills, House bill No. 100 (HR 100) and Senate bill No. 200 (S 200). The path of HR 100 is traced by an orange line, and that of S 200 by a purple line. In practice, most bills begin as similar proposals in both chambers. Bills must be passed by both chambers in identical form before they can be sent to the president.

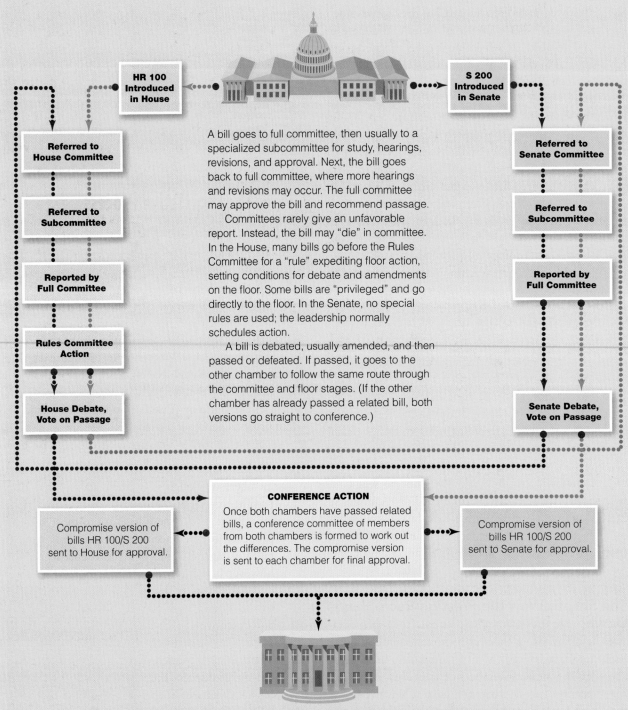

HR 100 Introduced in House

S 200 Introduced in Senate

Referred to House Committee

Referred to Subcommittee

Reported by Full Committee

Rules Committee Action

House Debate, Vote on Passage

Referred to Senate Committee

Referred to Subcommittee

Reported by Full Committee

Senate Debate, Vote on Passage

A bill goes to full committee, then usually to a specialized subcommittee for study, hearings, revisions, and approval. Next, the bill goes back to full committee, where more hearings and revisions may occur. The full committee may approve the bill and recommend passage.

Committees rarely give an unfavorable report. Instead, the bill may "die" in committee. In the House, many bills go before the Rules Committee for a "rule" expediting floor action, setting conditions for debate and amendments on the floor. Some bills are "privileged" and go directly to the floor. In the Senate, no special rules are used; the leadership normally schedules action.

A bill is debated, usually amended, and then passed or defeated. If passed, it goes to the other chamber to follow the same route through the committee and floor stages. (If the other chamber has already passed a related bill, both versions go straight to conference.)

CONFERENCE ACTION
Once both chambers have passed related bills, a conference committee of members from both chambers is formed to work out the differences. The compromise version is sent to each chamber for final approval.

Compromise version of bills HR 100/S 200 sent to House for approval.

Compromise version of bills HR 100/S 200 sent to Senate for approval.

A compromise bill approved by both chambers is sent to the president, who can sign it, veto it, or let it become law without a signature. Congress may override a veto by a two-thirds majority vote in each chamber.

To a degree not seen for some decades, the Obama administration during his first term let Congress take the lead on writing important new legislation dealing with issues such as health-care reform and financial regulation. Even under Obama, however, a majority of the legislation considered by Congress has come from the executive branch.

2. *Referral to committees.* As soon as a bill is introduced and assigned a number, it is sent to the appropriate standing committee. In the House, the Speaker assigns the bill to the committee. In the Senate, the presiding officer does so. For example, a farm bill in the House would be sent to the Agriculture Committee, and a gun control bill would be sent to the Judiciary Committee.

A committee chairperson will typically send the bill on to a subcommittee. For example, a Senate bill concerning NATO (the North Atlantic Treaty Organization) in Europe would be sent to the Senate Foreign Relations Subcommittee on European Affairs. Alternatively, the chairperson may decide to put the bill aside and ignore it. Most bills that are pigeonholed in this manner receive no further action.

If a bill is not pigeonholed, committee staff members go to work researching it. The committee may hold public hearings during which people who support or oppose the bill can express their views. Committees also have the power to order witnesses to testify at public hearings. Witnesses may be executive agency officials, experts on the subject, or representatives of interest groups concerned about the bill.

The subcommittee must meet to approve the bill as it is, add new amendments, or draft a new bill. This meeting is known as the **markup session.** If members cannot reach a consensus on changes, a vote on the changes is taken.

When a subcommittee completes its work, the bill goes to the full standing committee, which then meets for its own markup session. The committee may hold its own hearings, amend the subcommittee's version, or simply approve the subcommittee's recommendations.

3. *Reports on a bill.* Finally, the committee will report the bill back to the full chamber. It can report the bill favorably, report the bill with amendments, or report a newly written bill. It can also report a bill unfavorably, but usually such a bill will have been pigeonholed earlier instead. Along with the bill, the committee will send to the House or Senate a written report that explains the committee's actions, describes the bill, lists the major changes made by the committee, and gives opinions on the bill.

4. *The Rules Committee and scheduling.* Scheduling is an extremely important part of getting a bill enacted into law. A bill must be put on a calendar. Typically, in the House the Rules Committee plays a major role in the scheduling process. This committee, along with the House leaders, regulates the flow of the bills through the House. The Rules Committee will also specify how much time can be spent on debate and whether amendments can be made by a floor vote.

In the Senate, a few leading members control the flow of bills. The Senate brings a bill to the floor by "unanimous consent," a motion by which all members present on the floor set aside the formal

BILL CLARK/CQ ROLL CALL

Senator Elizabeth Warren (D., Mass.) and Senator Joe Manchin (D., W. Va.) at a Banking, Housing and Urban Affairs Committee hearing.

markup session A meeting held by a congressional committee or subcommittee to approve, amend, or redraft a bill.

Senate rules and consider a bill. In contrast to the procedure in the House, individual senators have the power to disrupt work on legislation—refusing to agree to unanimous consent is the way in which a senatorial hold is enforced.

5. *Floor debate.* Because of its large size, the House imposes severe limits on floor debate. The Speaker recognizes those who may speak and can force any member who does not "stick to the subject" to give up the floor. Normally, the chairperson of the standing committee reporting the bill will take charge of the session during which it is debated. You can often watch such debates on C-SPAN.

Only on rare occasions does a floor debate change anybody's mind. The written record of the floor debate completes the legislative history of the proposed bill in the event that the courts have to interpret it later on. Floor debates also give the full House or Senate the opportunity to consider amendments to the original version of the bill.

6. *Vote.* In both the House and the Senate, the members present generally vote for or against the bill. There are several methods of voting, including voice votes, standing votes, and recorded votes (also called roll-call votes). Since 1973, the House has had electronic voting. The Senate does not have such a system, however.

7. *Conference committee.* To become a law, a bill must be passed in identical form by both chambers. When the two chambers pass differing versions of the same bill, the measure is turned over

CHIP SOMODEVILLA/GETTY IM-

John Mica (R., Fla.) of the House Oversight and Government Reform Committee. The committee investigated allegations that the Internal Revenue Service targeted conservative organizations for extra scrutiny.

to a **conference committee**—a temporary committee with members from the two chambers, as mentioned earlier.

Most members of the committee are drawn from the standing committees that handled the bill in both chambers. In theory, the conference committee can consider only those points in a bill on which the two chambers disagree. No proposals are supposed to be added. In reality, however, the conference committee sometimes makes important changes in the bill or adds new provisions.

Once the conference committee members agree on the final compromise bill, a **conference report** is submitted to each chamber. The bill must be accepted or rejected by both chambers as it was written by the committee, with no further amendments made. If the bill is approved by both chambers, it is ready for action by the president.

8. *Presidential action.* All bills passed by Congress must be submitted to the president for approval. The president has ten days to decide whether to sign the bill or veto it. If the president does nothing, the bill goes into effect unless Congress has adjourned before the ten-day period expires. In that case, the bill dies in what is called a **pocket veto.**

9. *Overriding a veto.* If the president decides to veto a bill, Congress can still get the bill enacted into law. With a two-thirds majority vote in both chambers, Congress can override the president's veto.

conference committee
A temporary committee that is formed when the two chambers of Congress pass differing versions of the same bill. The conference committee consists of members from the House and the Senate who work out a compromise bill.

conference report
A report submitted by a conference committee after it has drafted a single version of a bill.

pocket veto A special type of veto power used by the chief executive after the legislature has adjourned. Bills that are not signed die after a specified period of time.

Why do debates on the floor of the House or the Senate almost never change anyone's mind?

11–5 Investigation and Oversight

Learning Outcome 11–5

Identify Congress's oversight functions and explain how Congress fulfills them.

Steps 8 and 9 of the legislative process described illustrate the interlocking roles that the executive and the legislative branches play in making laws. The relationship between Congress and the president is at the core of our system of government, although, to be sure, the judicial branch plays a vital role as well (see Chapter 14).

One of the most important functions of Congress is its oversight (supervision) of the executive branch and its many federal departments and agencies. The executive bureaucracy, which includes the president's cabinet departments, wields tremendous power, as you will read in Chapters 12 and 13. Congress can rein in that power by choosing not to provide the money nec-

essary for the bureaucracy to function. (The budgeting process will be discussed later in this chapter.)

11–5a The Investigative Function

Congress also has the authority to investigate the actions of the executive branch, the need for certain legislation, and even the actions of its own members. The numerous congressional committees and subcommittees regularly hold hearings to investigate the actions of the executive branch. Congressional committees receive opinions, reports, and assessments on a broad range of issues.

A widely held belief is that between 2001 and 2007, when Republicans controlled both chambers of Congress and the presidency, Congress neglected its oversight function out of deference to President Bush. Many also believe that Congress neglected its oversight function from 2009 to 2011, when the Democrats controlled both chambers of Congress and the presidency.

One way in which Congress has "kept itself honest" is by establishing oversight bodies separate from—but responsible to—Congress. One such body is the Congressional Budget Office (CBO), which evaluates the impact of proposed legislation on the federal budget and the budget deficit. The CBO has frequently been in the news in recent years due to its "scoring" of various proposals considered by the House and the Senate. Members of Congress have found themselves tailoring measures to earn a better score from the CBO.

11–5b Impeachment Power

Congress has the power to impeach and remove from office the president, vice president, and other "civil officers," such as federal judges. To *impeach* means to accuse a public official of—or charge him or her with—improper conduct in office. The House of Representatives is vested with this power and has exercised it twice against a president.

Impeaching Presidents The House voted to impeach Andrew Johnson in 1868 and Bill Clinton in 1998. After a vote to impeach in the full House, the accused official is then tried in the Senate. If convicted by a two-thirds vote, the official

General Keith Alexander, director of the National Security Agency (NSA), testifies before the Senate Appropriations Committee in response to charges that the agency's data collection methods violate privacy rights.

SAUL LOEB/AFP/GETTY IMAGES

"LAWS ARE LIKE SAUSAGES.

It is better if the public does not see how they are made."

~ JOHN GODFREY SAXE ~
AMERICAN POET 1816–1887
(MISATTRIBUTED TO OTTO VON BISMARCK,
CHANCELLOR OF GERMANY
1871–1890)

is removed from office. Both Johnson and Clinton were acquitted by the Senate. A vote to impeach President Richard Nixon was pending before the full House of Representatives in 1974 when Nixon chose to resign. Nixon is the only president ever to resign from office.

Impeaching Other Officers Congress has taken action to remove officials other than the president. For example, the House of Representatives voted to impeach Judge Thomas Porteous in March 2010 on charges of bribery and perjury. In December of that year, the Senate convicted Porteous and disqualified him from ever holding any "office of honor or profit under the United States," as the formal language puts it. Only one United States Supreme Court justice has ever been impeached. The House impeached Samuel Chase in 1804, but he was later acquitted by the Senate.

11–5c Senate Confirmation

Article II, Section 2, of the Constitution states that the president may appoint ambassadors, justices of the Supreme Court, and other officers of the United States "with the Advice and Consent of the Senate." The Constitution leaves the precise nature of how the Senate will give this "advice and consent" up to the lawmakers.

In practice, the Senate either confirms or fails to confirm the president's nominees for the Supreme Court, other federal judgeships, members of the president's cabinet, and other top executive branch officers. Nominees appear first before the appropriate Senate committee—the Judiciary Committee for federal judges or the Foreign Relations Committee for the secretary of state, for example. If the individual committee approves the nominee, the full Senate will vote on the nomination.

As you will read further in Chapters 12 and 14, Senate confirmation hearings have been very politicized at times. Judicial appointments often receive the most intense scrutiny by the Senate, because federal judges serve for life.

The president has a somewhat freer hand with cabinet appointments, because the heads of executive departments (unlike federal judges) are expected to be loyal to the president. Nonetheless, Senate confirmation remains an important check on the president's power. We will discuss the relationship between Congress and the president in more detail in Chapter 12.

FOR CRITICAL THINKING

More and more often in recent years, senators have blocked a president's appointments to make an unrelated point. *Should such an act be considered a legitimate political tactic? Why or why not?*

11–6 The Budgeting Process

The Constitution makes it very clear that Congress has the power of the purse, and this power is significant. Only Congress can impose

Learning Outcome 11–6

Indicate what is involved in the congressional budgeting process.

taxes, and only Congress can authorize expenditures. To be sure, the president submits a budget, but all final decisions are up to Congress.

The congressional budget is, of course, one of the most important determinants of what policies will or will not be implemented. For example, the president might order executive agencies under presidential control to undertake specific programs, but these orders are meaningless if there is no money to pay for their execution. For any program that receives an annual appropriation, Congress can nullify a president's ambitious plans simply by refusing to allocate the necessary money to executive agencies to implement the program.

11–6a Authorization and Appropriation

The budgeting process is a two-part procedure. **Authorization** is the first part. It involves the creation of the legal basis for government programs. In this phase, Congress passes authorization bills outlining the rules governing the expenditure of funds. Limits may be placed on how much money can be spent and for what period of time.

Appropriation is the second part of the budgeting process. In this phase, Congress determines how many dollars will actually be spent in a given year on a particular government activity. Appropriations must never exceed the authorized amounts, but they can be less.

An exception to this process involves **entitlement programs,** which require the government to provide benefits, such as Social Security benefits, veterans' benefits, and the like, to persons who qualify under entitlement laws. Many such programs operate under open-ended authorizations that, in effect, place no limits on how much can be spent (although it is usually possible to estimate the cost of a particular entitlement program fairly accurately). The Affordable Care Act, also known as Obamacare, is, for the most part, an entitlement program. For this reason, repeated votes by the Republican-led house to "defund" Obamacare have had no practical effect.

The remaining federal programs fall into the category of discretionary spending, and so they can be altered at will by Congress. National defense is the most important item in the discretionary-spending part of the budget. Discretionary spending also includes earmarks, or "pork," as described in this chapter's *Perception versus Reality* feature on the following page.

11–6b The Actual Budgeting Process

Figure 11–7 on page 255 outlines the lengthy budgeting process. The process runs from January, when the president submits a proposed federal budget for the next **fiscal year,** to the start of that fiscal year on October 1. In actuality, about eighteen months prior to October 1, the executive agencies submit their requests to the Office of Management and Budget (OMB), and the OMB outlines a proposed budget. If the president approves it, the budget is officially submitted to Congress.

The legislative budgeting process begins eight to nine months before the start of the fiscal year. The **first budget resolution** is supposed to be passed in May. It sets overall revenue goals and spending targets and, by definition, the size of the federal budget deficit or surplus.

The **second budget resolution,** which sets "binding" limits on taxes and spending, is supposed to be passed in September, before the beginning of the fiscal year on October 1. When Congress is unable to pass a complete budget by October 1, it usually passes **continuing resolutions,** which enable the executive agencies to keep on doing whatever they were doing the previous year with the same amount of funding. But even continuing resolutions have not always been passed on time.

The budget process involves making predictions about the state of the U.S. economy for years to come. This process is necessarily very imprecise. Since 1996, both Congress and the president have attempted to make ten-year projections for income (from taxes) and spending, but no one can really know what the financial picture of the United States will look like in ten years. The workforce could grow or shrink, which would drastically alter government revenue from taxes. Any number of emergencies could arise that would require increased government spending—from going to war against terrorists to inoculating federal employees against smallpox.

---

authorization A part of the congressional budgeting process—the creation of the legal basis for government programs.

appropriation A part of the congressional budgeting process—the determination of how many dollars will be spent in a given year on a particular government activity.

entitlement program A government program (such as Social Security) that allows, or entitles, a certain class of people (such as elderly persons) to receive benefits. Entitlement programs operate under open-ended budget authorizations that, in effect, place no limits on how much can be spent.

fiscal year A twelve-month period that is established for bookkeeping or accounting purposes. The government's fiscal year runs from October 1 through September 30.

first budget resolution A budget resolution, which is supposed to be passed in May, that sets overall revenue goals and spending targets for the next fiscal year, beginning on October 1.

second budget resolution A budget resolution, which is supposed to be passed in September, that sets "binding" limits on taxes and spending for the next fiscal year.

continuing resolution A temporary resolution passed by Congress that enables executive agencies to continue work with the same funding that they had in the previous fiscal year.

Perception versus Reality

Congress Has Banned Pork-Barrel Spending

In recent years, Congress voted to fund a "bridge to nowhere" in Alaska, a program to combat wild hogs in Missouri, and payment of storage fees for Georgia peanut farmers. Such special interest spending is called *pork-barrel* spending—members of Congress "bring home the bacon" this way to benefit local businesses and workers.

Formally, an item of pork is called an *earmark*. The Congressional Research Service defines earmarks as spending provisions that apply to a very limited number of individuals or entities. The Office of Management and Budget defines earmarks as direct allocations of funds that bypass merit-based or competitive allocation processes of the executive branch. Those who defend earmarks often contend that Congress has a right to determine who benefits from government spending. After all, directing money to particular purposes is a core constitutional function of Congress.

THE PERCEPTION

In 2010, immediately after the elections that would give them control of the U.S. House, Republicans announced that they would ban earmarks. It follows that pork must be history.

THE REALITY

The House Republican ban on earmarks certainly made it more difficult for members of Congress to do favors for the folks back home. Still, many members devoted considerable ingenuity to creating end-runs around the rules. A simple method was simply to deny that a particular funding request was an earmark. One senator identified more than one hundred such mislabeled provisions in a single House defense bill.

A common technique was to lobby executive agencies to place specific projects on their approved lists. If the appropriate agency endorsed a project ostensibly on merit-based grounds, then, as if by magic, the project was no longer an earmark. For example, Republicans from Texas and Virginia who opposed a (non-earmarked) high-speed rail project in California were happy to submit letters from the Department of Transportation that endorsed high-speed rail projects—in Texas and Virginia.

One technique for benefiting specific corporations is to lower the tariff (import tax) on goods imported by that firm—and often imported by no one else. You might think that this kind of help would be an unusual procedure. You would be wrong. Congress regularly passes a Miscellaneous Tariff Bill that contains hundreds of such requests.

A final point: presidents are fond of inserting special funding requests into their budget proposals at the last minute, regardless of whether executive agencies signed off on these expenditures. The president, in short, is often the biggest "porkmeister" of all.

BLOG ON You can visit the Web sites of two groups that oppose pork-barrel spending: Citizens against Government Waste and Taxpayers for Common Sense. Do the recommendations of these groups suggest that they have particular ideological leanings? If so, what are they?

In any event, when you read about what the administration predicts the budget deficit (or surplus) will be in five or ten years, take such predictions with a grain of salt. While one- or two-year predictions are often fairly realistic, long-term predictions have never come close to being accurate. Moreover, most times, the longest-term predictions made by administrations will depend on decisions made when *another* administration is in office later on.

FOR CRITICAL THINKING

Why do you think Congress created entitlement programs that operate under open-ended authorizations instead of reauthorizing each of them every year?

FIGURE 11-7

The Budgeting Process

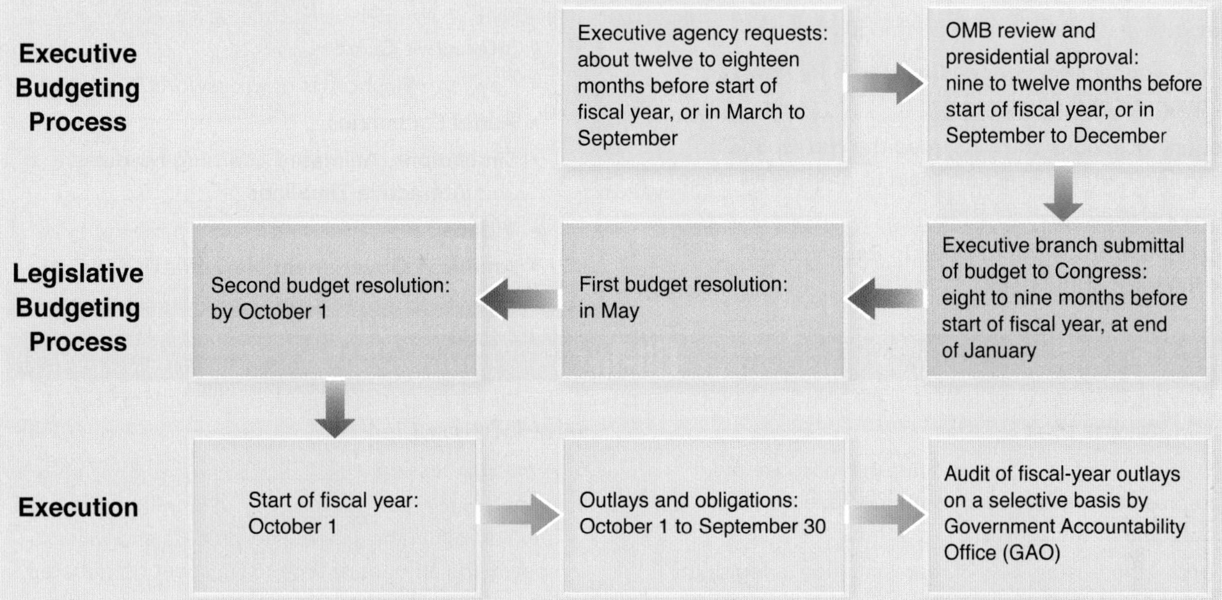

Executive Budgeting Process		Executive agency requests: about twelve to eighteen months before start of fiscal year, or in March to September	OMB review and presidential approval: nine to twelve months before start of fiscal year, or in September to December
Legislative Budgeting Process	Second budget resolution: by October 1	First budget resolution: in May	Executive branch submittal of budget to Congress: eight to nine months before start of fiscal year, at end of January
Execution	Start of fiscal year: October 1	Outlays and obligations: October 1 to September 30	Audit of fiscal-year outlays on a selective basis by Government Accountability Office (GAO)

AMERICA AT
ODDS The Congress

The founders thought that Congress would be the branch of government that was closest to the people. Yet Congress is one of the least popular institutions in America. It seems that anything that Congress does annoys a substantial share of the electorate. Needless to say, Americans are at odds over Congress on a variety of issues:

- Is the Senate's filibuster rule a legitimate safeguard of minority rights—or a disastrous handicap on Congress's ability to address the nation's problems?

- Is political gerrymandering just a normal part of the political game—or does it deprive voters of their rights?

- Does racial gerrymandering allow the voices of minority groups to be heard—or is it an unconstitutional violation of the equal protection clause?

- When voting on legislation, should members of Congress faithfully represent the views of their constituents—or should they stay true to their own beliefs about what is good for the nation?

- Should legislative earmarks, or "pork," be banned as a waste of taxpayers' resources—or is it appropriate for members of Congress to support specific projects in their own districts?

STUDY TOOLS

Ready to study?

- **Review** what you've read with the quiz below.
- Check your answers on the **Chapter in Review** card at the back of the book.
- For any questions you miss, read the corresponding **Learning Outcome** section again to prepare for class and your exam.
- Rip out and study the **Chapter in Review** card (at the back of the book).

Fill-In

Learning Outcome 11–1

1. Every _____ years, seats in the House of Representatives are reapportioned based on the outcome of the census.

2. Under the trustee view of representation, a legislator should try to _____.

Learning Outcome 11–2

3. Incumbent members of Congress enjoy several advantages over their challengers in elections, including _____.

Learning Outcome 11–3

4. The Speaker of the House has the power to _____.

5. Filibusters may be ended by invoking _____.

Learning Outcome 11–4

6. A markup session is _____.

7. In the House, the _____ Committee plays a major role in the scheduling process and will also specify the amount of time to be spent on debate.

Learning Outcome 11–5

8. In practice, the Senate's power of "advice and consent" means that the Senate confirms or fails to confirm the president's nominees to _____.

Learning Outcome 11–6

9. The budgeting process is a two-part procedure that includes _____.

Multiple Choice

Learning Outcome 11–1

10. To ensure equal representation in the House, congressional districts in a given state must contain, as nearly as possible, equal numbers of
    a. men and women.
    b. Republicans and Democrats.
    c. people.

Learning Outcome 11–2

11. The U.S. Constitution requires that members of the House of Representatives be elected every
    a. second year by popular vote.
    b. six years by popular vote.
    c. second year by state legislatures.

Learning Outcome 11–3

12. In the Senate, the ____ is typically the most powerful individual and directs the legislative program and strategy of his or her party.
    a. vice president
    b. majority leader
    c. president pro tempore

Learning Outcome 11–4

13. As soon as a bill is introduced in either the House or the Senate, it is sent to
    a. the floor of the chamber.
    b. the appropriate standing committee.
    c. a conference committee.

Learning Outcome 11–5

14. The Senate
    a. voted to impeach Richard Nixon.
    b. convicted Bill Clinton of impeachable offenses by a two-thirds vote.
    c. tries officials who have been impeached in the House of Representatives.

Learning Outcome 11–6

15. When Congress is unable to pass a complete budget by the beginning of the fiscal year, it usually passes ____, which enable the executive agencies to keep on doing whatever they were doing the previous year with the same amount of funding.
    a. continuing resolutions   c earmarks
    b. entitlement programs

The Presidency

MANDEL NGAN/AFP/GETTY IMAGES

The **Learning Outcomes** labeled 1 through 5 are designed to help improve your understanding of the chapter. After reading this chapter, you should be able to:

12–1 List the constitutional requirements for becoming president.

12–2 Explain the roles that a president adopts while in office.

12–3 Indicate the scope of presidential powers.

12–4 Describe advantages enjoyed by Congress and by the president in their institutional relationship.

12–5 Discuss the organization of the executive branch and the role of cabinet members in presidential administrations.

Remember to visit page 282 for additional Study Tools

AMERICA AT
ODDS
Should Obama Have Asked Congress for Permission to Bomb Syria?

Under the U.S. Constitution, only Congress has the right to declare war. Yet as commander in chief of the armed forces, the president has the power to send our soldiers into harm's way, whether Congress has acted or not. In the early twentieth century, presidents ordered troops into Cuba, the Dominican Republic, Haiti, Honduras, Mexico, and Nicaragua. Before the United States entered World War II in 1941, Franklin D. Roosevelt ordered the Navy to "shoot on sight" any German submarine that appeared off our shores.

In 2011, a civil war broke out in Syria. A variety of insurgent groups sought to overthrow the dictator Bashar al-Assad. By mid-2013, the death toll had passed 100,000, and almost 5 million people had been displaced from their homes. The Syrian government has a large stock of chemical weapons, which are considered weapons of mass destruction. In 2012, President Obama warned that the use of such weapons would "cross a red line." In August 2013, the Syrian government released poison gas in a Damascus suburb controlled by the insurgents. The attack killed about 1,300 men, women, and children.

In September, President Obama announced plans for an air strike on Syrian government facilities as punishment for the use of chemical weapons. Rather than immediately moving forward with an attack, however, Obama asked Congress to approve the mission. Was Obama on the right track?

Consulting Congress Was the Right Thing to Do

As soon as U.S. military action against Syria became likely, dozens of senators and representatives demanded that Obama consult with Congress before taking action. They were right to do so. To be sure, as we have just noted, many presidents have initiated military action without asking Congress's permission. The circumstances in Syria, however, were novel. Neither America nor any of its allies were under attack. The United States planned to act almost alone, without the support of the United Nations Security Council or of our European allies in the North Atlantic Treaty Organization (NATO). A unilateral attack launched by the American president might lack legitimacy, and gaining the support of Congress would provide the necessary backing. Indeed, the mere threat of a U.S. strike backed by Congress appears to have been enough to persuade Syria to yield its chemical weapons to international authorities. As a result, a strike was not even necessary.

Obama's Request to Congress Made No Sense

The most vehement advocates of an attack on Syria believed that asking Congress for a vote was an error. What would happen if the administration lost the vote? In fact, such a result seemed probable. Charles Krauthammer, a leading hawk, claimed that the request showed that Obama was "deeply unserious." As it turned out, Russian president Vladimir Putin persuaded Syria to put its weapons under international control. This step may have resolved the issue for now, but it added greatly to the prestige of a leader—Putin—who did not deserve such respect. Further, Obama himself wound up looking foolish.

Many opponents of the request, however, thought that an attack on Syria would have been the real mistake. Hawks claimed that without it, foreign nations would doubt American resolve, but doves found such reasoning unacceptable. Also, an attack on Syria might doom any chance of a deal with the new president of Iran to stop that country from acquiring nuclear weapons.

Where do you stand?

1. How important is it that America have a reputation for carrying out any threats it might make?
2. Under what circumstances should the United States act only with the support of other nations, and when should we be prepared to go it alone?

Explore this issue online

- Historian Joyce Appleby believes that institutional conflict between the president and Congress is one of the virtues of the American system. Blogger Matt Yglesias disagrees. You can read their opinions if you search on, respectively, "warring ambitions" and "founding falter."

Introduction

President Lyndon B. Johnson (1963–1969) stated in his autobiography[1] that "of all the 1,886 nights I was President, there were not many when I got to sleep before 1 or 2 A.M., and there were few mornings when I didn't wake up by 6 or 6:30." President Harry Truman (1945–1953) once observed that no one can really understand what it is like to be president: there is no end to "the chain of responsibility that binds him," and he is "never allowed to forget that he is president." These responsibilities are, for the most part, unremitting. Unlike Congress, the president never adjourns.

At the apex of the political ladder, the presidency is the most powerful and influential political office that any one individual can hold. Presidents can help to shape not only domestic policy but also global developments.

Since the demise of the Soviet Union and the Communist-controlled governments in eastern Europe in the early 1990s, the president of the United States has been the leader of the most powerful nation on earth. The president heads the greatest military force anywhere. Presidents have more power to reach their political objectives than any other players in the American political system. (We discussed the president's ability to initiate military action with or without congressional consent in this chapter's opening *America at Odds* feature.) It is not surprising, therefore, that many Americans aspire to attain this office.

12–1 Who Can Become President?

The notion that anybody can become president of this country has always been a part of the American mythology. Certainly, the requirements for becoming president set forth in Article II, Section 1, of the Constitution are not difficult to meet:

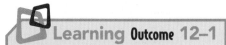

Learning Outcome 12–1

List the constitutional requirements for becoming president.

> No Person except a natural born Citizen, or a Citizen of the United States, at the time of the Adoption of this Constitution, shall be eligible to the Office of President; neither shall any Person be eligible to that Office who shall not have attained to the Age of thirty-five Years, and been fourteen Years a Resident within the United States.

This language does make it impossible for a foreign-born naturalized citizen to become president, even if that person came to this country as an infant. For more on that issue, see this chapter's *Join the Debate* feature on the following page.

12–1a Perks of the President

Given the demands of the presidency, why would anyone seek the office? There are some very special perks associated with the presidency. The president enjoys, among other things, the use of the White House. The White House has 132 rooms located on 18.3 acres of land in the heart of the nation's capital. At the White House, the president in residence has a staff of more than eighty persons, including chefs, gardeners, maids, butlers, and a personal tailor.

Amenities also include a tennis court, a swimming pool, bowling lanes, and a private movie theater. Additionally, the president has at his or her disposal a fleet of automobiles, helicopters, and jets (including *Air Force One*, which costs about $180,000 an hour to run). For relaxation, the presidential family can go to Camp David, a resort hideaway in the Catoctin

Promotional poster for the feature film *Hellcats of the Navy,* starring future president Ronald Reagan.

A Foreign-Born President?

As you just read, Article II of the Constitution states that "[n]o Person except a natural born Citizen . . . shall be eligible to the Office of President." This restriction has long been controversial, for it has kept many otherwise qualified Americans from running for president. These persons have included former California governor Arnold Schwarzenegger, who was born in Austria, and former Michigan governor Jennifer M. Granholm, who was born in Canada, both of whom have been U.S. citizens for decades. In all, some 13 million Americans born outside the United States are excluded by this provision. The requirement of native birth has come up most recently because of claims by conspiracy theorists that President Obama was not born in the United States. These individuals claim that Obama's Hawaiian birth certificate was forged, and they are undeterred by the fact that Obama's birth was also announced in Honolulu newspapers.

An Obsolete Provision

America is a nation of immigrants, so it strikes some as odd that a foreign-born person would be barred from aspiring to the presidency. Naturalized U.S. citizens are allowed to vote, to serve on juries, and to serve in the military. They are also allowed to serve as secretary of state and represent the nation in foreign affairs. Why can't they run for president? Critics of the Constitution's citizenship requirement think that the requirement should be abolished by a constitutional amendment. They point out that the clause was initially included in the Constitution to prevent European princes from attempting to force the young republic back under monarchical rule in the late 1700s. Clearly, the clause is now obsolete and should no longer apply.

A Requirement Still Valid Today

Other Americans believe that the constitutional ban should remain. They argue that national security could be compromised by a foreign-born president. With the immense power that the president wields, especially in foreign policy, loyalty is of the utmost concern.

In addition, the Constitution is difficult to amend, requiring support from two-thirds of both chambers of Congress and ratification by three-fourths of the states. The need for an amendment that would allow immigrants to run for president is hardly as pressing as the prior need for antidiscrimination amendments, such as the ones that abolished slavery and gave women the right to vote, opponents argue.

FOR CRITICAL ANALYSIS Do you see a problem with someone born in a foreign country serving as president? Why or why not?

Mountains of Maryland. Other perks include free dental and medical care.

12–1b Presidential Age and Occupation

Modern presidents have included a haberdasher (Harry Truman), a peanut farmer (Jimmy Carter), and an actor (Ronald Reagan), although all of these men also had significant political experience before assuming the presidency. The most common previous occupation of U.S. presidents, however, has been the legal profession. Out of forty-four presidents, twenty-seven have been lawyers. Many presidents have also been wealthy.

Although the Constitution states that anyone who is thirty-five years of age or older can become president, the average age at inauguration has been fifty-five. The youngest person elected president was John F. Kennedy (1961–1963), who assumed the presidency at the age of forty-three (the youngest person to hold the office was Theodore Roosevelt, who was forty-two when he became president after the assassination of William McKinley). The oldest was Ronald Reagan (1981–1989), who was sixty-nine years old when he became president.

12–1c Race, Gender, and Religion

For most of American history, all presidential candidates, even those of minor parties, were white, male, and of the Protestant religious tradition. In recent years, however, the pool of talent has expanded. In 1928, Democrat Al Smith became the first Roman

Catholic to run for president on a major-party ticket, and in 1960 Democrat John F. Kennedy was elected as the first Catholic president. Among recent unsuccessful Democratic presidential candidates, Michael Dukakis was Greek Orthodox and John Kerry was Roman Catholic.

In 2008, the doors swung wide in the presidential primaries as the Democrats chose between a white woman, Hillary Clinton, and an African American man, Barack Obama. By that time, about 90 percent of Americans told pollsters that they would be willing to support an African American for president, and the same number would support a woman.

In 2012, none of the top three finishers in the Republican primaries was Protestant. Newt Gingrich and Rick Santorum were Catholic. Mitt Romney was a member of the Latter-Day Saints, commonly called the Mormons.

NATIONAL PHOTO COMPANY COLLECTION/LIBRARY OF CONGRESS

President Woodrow Wilson throwing out the first pitch on the opening day of the Major League Baseball season in 1916. This action is part of the president's role as head of state.

FOR CRITICAL THINKING

Why do some people believe so strongly that Barack Obama must have been born in a foreign country?

12–2 The President's Many Roles

Learning Outcome 12–2

Explain the roles that a president adopts while in office.

The president has the authority to exercise a variety of powers. Some of these are explicitly outlined in the Constitution, and some are simply required by the office—such as the power to persuade. In the course of exercising these powers, the president performs a variety of roles. For example, as commander in chief of the armed services, the president can exercise significant military powers.

Which roles a president executes successfully usually depends on what is happening domestically and internationally, as well as on the president's personality. Some presidents, including Bill Clinton (1993–2001) during his first term, have shown much more interest in domestic policy than in foreign policy. Others, such as George H. W. Bush (1989–1993), were more interested in foreign affairs than in domestic ones.

Table 12–1 on the following page summarizes the major roles of the president. An important role is, of course, that of chief executive. Other roles include those of commander in chief, head of state, chief diplomat, chief legislator, and political party leader.

12–2a Chief Executive

According to Article II of the Constitution,

> The executive Power shall be vested in a President of the United States of America. . . . [H]e may require the Opinion, in writing, of the principal Officer in each of the executive Departments, upon any Subject relating to the Duties of their respective Offices . . . and he shall nominate, and by and with the Advice and Consent of the Senate, shall appoint . . . Officers of the United States . . . . [H]e shall take Care that the Laws be faithfully executed.

This constitutional provision makes the president of the United States the nation's **chief executive,** or the head of the executive branch of the federal government.

chief executive The head of the executive branch of government; in the United States, the president.

TABLE 12–1

Roles of the President

	ROLE/DESCRIPTION	EXAMPLES
	**Chief executive** Enforces laws and federal court decisions, along with treaties approved by the United States	• Can appoint, with Senate approval, and remove high-ranking officers of the federal government • Can grant reprieves, pardons, and amnesties • Can handle national emergencies during peacetime, such as riots or natural disasters
	**Commander in chief** Leads the nation's armed forces	• Can commit troops for up to ninety days in response to a military threat (War Powers Resolution) • Can make secret agreements with other countries • Can set up military governments in conquered lands • Can end fighting by calling a cease-fire (armistice)
	**Head of state** Performs ceremonial activities as a personal symbol of the nation	• Decorates war heroes • Dedicates parks and post offices • Throws out first pitch of baseball season • Lights national Christmas tree • Receives foreign heads of state
	**Chief diplomat** Directs U.S. foreign policy and is the nation's most important representative in dealing with foreign countries	• Can negotiate and sign treaties with other nations, which go into effect with Senate approval • Can make pacts (executive agreements) with other heads of state, without Senate approval • Can accept the legitimacy of another country's government (power of recognition)
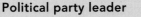	**Chief legislator** Informs Congress about the condition of the country and recommends legislative measures	• Proposes legislative program to Congress in traditional State of the Union address • Suggests budget to Congress and submits annual economic report • Can veto a bill passed by Congress • Can call special sessions of Congress
	**Political party leader** Heads political party	• Chooses a vice president • Makes several thousand top government appointments, often to party faithful (patronage) • Tries to execute the party's platform • Attends party fund-raisers • May help reelect party members running for office as mayors, governors, or members of Congress

VACCLAV/SHUTTERSTOCK · RAFAL OIKIS/SHUTTERSTOCK · R CARNER/SHUTTERSTOCK · PEER GRIMM/DPA/LANDOV · BRANDON BOURDAGES/SHUTTERSTOCK · GARY HATHAWAY/SHUTTERSTOCK

When the framers created the office of the president, they created a uniquely American institution. Nowhere else in the world at that time was there a democratically elected chief executive. The executive branch is also unique among the branches of government because it is headed by a single individual—the president.

12–2b Commander in Chief

The Constitution states that the president "shall be Commander in Chief of the Army and Navy of the United States, and of the Militia of the several States, when called into the actual Service of the United

States." As **commander in chief** of the nation's armed forces, the president exercises tremendous power.

Under the Constitution, war powers are divided between Congress and the president. Congress was given the power to declare war and the power to raise and maintain the country's armed forces. The president, as commander in chief, was given the power to deploy the armed forces. The president's role as commander in chief has evolved over the last century. We mentioned this shared power of the president and Congress in the chapter-opening *America at Odds* feature and will examine it in more detail later in this chapter.

WIN MCNAMEE/GETTY IMAGES

As chief diplomat, the president regularly meets foreign leaders. Here, Obama greets India's prime minister Manmohan Singh.

12–2c Head of State

Traditionally, a country's monarch has performed the function of **head of state**—the country's representative to the rest of the world. The United States, of course, has no king or queen to act as head of state. Thus, the president of the United States fulfills this role.

The president engages in many symbolic or ceremonial activities, such as throwing out the first pitch to open the baseball season and turning on the lights of the national Christmas tree. The president also decorates war heroes, dedicates parks and post offices, receives visiting heads of state at the White House, and goes on official state visits to other countries.

Some argue that presidents should not perform such ceremonial duties because they take time that the president should be spending on "real work." Most presidents, however, have found the role of head of state to be politically useful. (See this chapter's *The Rest of the World* feature on the following page for more information on how one other country handles this issue.)

12–2d Chief Diplomat

A **diplomat** is a person who represents one country in dealing with representatives of another country. In the United States, the president is the nation's **chief diplomat**. The Constitution did not explicitly reserve this role to the president, but since the beginning of this nation, presidents have assumed the role based on their explicit constitutional powers to "receive [foreign] Ambassadors" and, with the advice and consent of the Senate, to appoint U.S. ambassadors and make treaties. As chief diplomat, the president directs the foreign policy of the United States and is our nation's most important representative.

12–2e Chief Legislator

Nowhere in the Constitution do the words *chief legislator* appear. The Constitution, however, does require that the president "from time to time give to the Congress Information of the State of the Union, and recommend to their Consideration such Measures as he shall judge necessary and expedient." The president has, in fact, become a major player in shaping the congressional agenda—the set of measures that actually get discussed and acted on.

This was not always the case. In the nineteenth century, some presidents preferred to let Congress lead the way in proposing and implementing

commander in chief The supreme commander of a nation's military force.

head of state The person who serves as the ceremonial head of a country's government and represents that country to the rest of the world.

diplomat A person who represents one country in dealing with representatives of another country.

chief diplomat The role of the president of the United States in recognizing and interacting with foreign governments.

The Unusual Role of the French President

Earlier in this text, you read about the parliamentary system used by many countries. In that system, the chief executive is chosen by the legislature, not the people. A few countries, however, have a hybrid system that is part parliamentary and part presidential. The best-known example of such a system is in France.

The Presidential-Parliamentary System

France has both a president, currently François Hollande, and a prime minister. Both represent the left-of-center party in France, the Socialists. In France, the president names the prime minister and the members of the cabinet. The prime minister and the cabinet, though, are responsible to the legislature, not the president.

The National Assembly, which is the lower house of Parliament, can force the entire cabinet to resign by passing a motion of no confidence.

In other words, "the government"—the prime minister and the other cabinet members—cannot survive politically unless a majority in the National Assembly supports them, regardless of the president's preferences.

The Unique French Practice of Cohabitation

For much of the history of the modern French Republic, the legislature's ability to throw out the government was not important, because the president's party had a majority in the National Assembly. French legislators were willing to let the president—the head of the majority party—choose the government. In 1981, the French elected a Socialist president for the first time, and they also gave the Socialists a majority in the National Assembly. In the 1986 elections, however, France voted for a center-right

Assembly majority. The Socialist president, François Mitterrand, still had two years left in his term of office. The French have a quaint term for the resulting situation: "cohabitation." During cohabitation, the prime minister and the rest of the cabinet are from one party and the president is from another.

Who Does What?

Nowhere in the French constitution is there an explicit statement of the division of powers between the president and the prime minister. The division of duties that exists today has evolved over time. Typically, the president is responsible for foreign policy and the prime minister for domestic policy. This distinction is most carefully observed during periods of cohabitation. When one party is in full control of the government, however, the president tends to take over completely.

FOR CRITICAL ANALYSIS Would our government work better if a prime minister served under the president?

policy. Since the administration of Theodore Roosevelt (1901–1909), however, presidents have taken an activist approach. Presidents are now expected to develop a legislative program and propose a budget to Congress every year.

In the past, this shared power has often put Congress and the president at odds. President Bill Clinton's administration, for example, drew up a health-care reform package in 1993 and presented it to Congress almost on a take-it-or-leave-it basis. Congress left it. To avoid such confrontations, President Obama frequently let Congress determine much of the content of important new legislation, such as the health-care reform bills.

In the example of health-care reform, President Obama's deference to Congress had several negative

consequences. These included an unusually large number of earmarks, a protracted and unpopular legislative process, and opportunities for conservatives to mobilize against the reforms. Still, in the end, Obama succeeded where Clinton had failed.

12-2f Political Party Leader

The president of the United States is also the *de facto* leader of his or her political party. The Constitution, of course, does not mention this role because, in the eyes of the founders, parties should have no place in the American political system.

As party leader, the president exercises substantial powers. For example, the president chooses the chairperson of the party's national committee. The president can also exert political power within the party by using presidential appointment and removal powers.

Naturally, presidents are beholden to the party members who put them in office. Thus, usually they indulge in the practice of **patronage**—appointing individuals to government or public jobs to reward those who helped them win the presidential contest.

The president may also reward party members with fund-raising assistance. (Campaign financing was discussed in Chapter 9.) The president is, in a sense, "fund-raiser in chief" for his or her party, and recent presidents, including Bill Clinton, George W. Bush, and Barack Obama, have proved themselves to be prodigious fund-raisers.

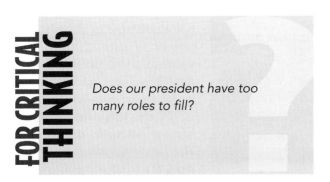

Does our president have too many roles to fill?

12–3 Presidential Powers

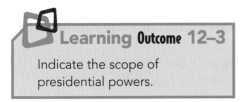

Learning Outcome 12–3

Indicate the scope of presidential powers.

The president exercises numerous powers. Some of these powers are set forth in the Constitution. Others, known as *inherent powers,* are those that are necessary to carry out the president's constitutional duties. We look next at these powers, as well as at the expansion of presidential powers over time.

12–3a The President's Constitutional Powers

As you have read, the constitutional source for the president's authority is found in Article II of the Constitution, which states, "The executive Power shall be vested in a President of the United States of America." The Constitution then sets forth the president's relatively limited constitutional responsibilities.

The Specified Powers Article II grants the president broad but vaguely described powers. From the very beginning, there were different views as to

what exactly the "executive Power" clause enabled the president to do. Nonetheless, Sections 2 and 3 of Article II list the following specific presidential powers. These powers parallel the roles of the president discussed in the previous section:

- To serve as commander in chief of the armed forces and the state militias.
- To appoint, with the Senate's consent, the heads of the executive departments, ambassadors, justices of the Supreme Court, and other top officials.
- To make treaties, with the advice and consent of the Senate.
- To grant reprieves and pardons, except in cases of impeachment.
- To deliver the annual State of the Union address to Congress and to send other messages to Congress from time to time.
- To call either house or both houses of Congress into special sessions.
- To receive ambassadors and other representatives from foreign countries.
- To commission all officers of the United States.
- To ensure that the laws passed by Congress "be faithfully executed."

In addition, Article I, Section 7, gives the president the power to veto legislation. We will now discuss some of these powers in more detail. As you will see, many of the president's powers are balanced by the powers of Congress. We return to the complex relationship between the president and Congress later in this chapter.

Proposal and Ratification of Treaties A **treaty** is a formal agreement between two or more countries. The president has the sole power to negotiate and sign treaties with other countries. The Senate, however, must approve a treaty by a two-thirds vote of the members present before it becomes effective. If the treaty is approved by the Senate and signed by the president, it becomes law.

Presidents have not always succeeded in winning the Senate's approval for treaties. In 1999, Bill Clinton was unable to persuade the Senate to

patronage The practice by which elected officials give government jobs to individuals who helped them gain office.

treaty A formal agreement between the governments of two or more countries.

approve the Comprehensive Test Ban Treaty, which would have prohibited all signers from testing nuclear weapons. Clinton argued that the United States no longer needed to test its nuclear weapons and that the treaty's restrictions on other countries would enhance our national security. The treaty was defeated largely on a party-line vote, with the Republicans opposed.

In contrast, Barack Obama convinced the Senate to approve the New Strategic Arms Reduction Treaty (New START) with Russia in December 2010. The treaty reduced by half the number of nuclear missiles in both countries and provided for inspections. New START was supported by all of the Democrats and by many Republicans.

AP PHOTO

Lyndon B. Johnson came the closest of any presidential candidate ever to winning a majority of the votes of all citizens eligible to cast a ballot.

The Power to Grant Reprieves and Pardons

The president's power to grant a pardon serves as a check on judicial power. A *pardon* is a release from punishment or the legal consequences of a crime. It restores a person to the full rights and privileges of citizenship.

In 1925, the United States Supreme Court upheld an expansive interpretation of the president's pardon power in a case involving an individual convicted for contempt of court. The Court held that the power covers all offenses "either before trial, during trial, or after trial, by individuals, or by classes, conditionally or absolutely, and this without modification or regulation by Congress."[2] The president can grant a pardon for any federal offense, except in cases of impeachment.

One of the most controversial pardons was that granted by President Gerald Ford (1974–1977) to former president Richard Nixon (1969–1974) after the Watergate affair (to be discussed later in the chapter) before any formal charges were brought in court.

veto A Latin word meaning "I forbid"; the refusal by an official, such as the president of the United States or a state governor, to sign a bill into law.

Sometimes pardons are granted to a class of individuals as a general amnesty. For example, President Jimmy Carter granted amnesty to tens of thousands of people who had resisted the draft during the Vietnam War by failing to register for the draft or by moving abroad.

The President's Veto Power

As noted in Chapter 11, the president can **veto** a bill passed by Congress. Congress can override the veto with a two-thirds vote by the members present in each chamber. The result of a veto override is that the bill becomes law against the wishes of the president.

If the president does not send a bill back to Congress after ten congressional working days, the bill becomes law without the president's signature. If the president refuses to sign the bill and Congress adjourns within ten working days after the bill has been submitted to the president, however, the bill is killed for that session of Congress. As mentioned in Chapter 11, this is called a *pocket veto*.

Presidents used the veto power sparingly until the administration of Andrew Johnson (1865–1869). Johnson vetoed twenty-one bills. Franklin D. Roosevelt (1933–1945) vetoed more bills by far than any of his predecessors or successors in the presidency. During his administration, there were 372 regular vetoes, 9 of which were overridden by Congress, and 263 pocket vetoes.

The Veto in Recent Administrations

President George W. Bush (2001–2009) used his veto power very sparingly. Indeed, during the first six years of his presidency, Bush vetoed only one bill—a proposal to expand the scope of stem-cell research. Bush vetoed so few bills largely because the Republican-led Congress during those years strongly supported his agenda. After the Democrats took control of Congress in 2007, Bush vetoed eleven bills. Congress overrode four of the vetoes.

With a Congress led by his own party during the first two years of his presidency, President Obama

President Jimmy Carter (center) met with Egyptian president Anwar Sadat (left) and Israeli prime minister Menachem Begin (right) at the White House for the signing of the Camp David Accords on September 18, 1978. Since then, Egypt and Israel have remained at peace with each other.

DAVID HUME KENNERLY/GETTY IMAGES

faced circumstances similar to those enjoyed by George W. Bush. Consequently, in his first two years in office, Obama exercised the veto power only twice. Surprisingly, Obama issued no vetoes during his second two years even though the Republicans were in control of the House. Apparently, no measure that Obama would have opposed was able to make its way through the Democratic-controlled Senate.

The Line-Item Veto Many presidents have complained that they cannot control "pork-barrel" legislation—federal expenditures tacked onto bills to "bring home the bacon" to a particular congressional member's district. For example, expenditures on a specific sports stadium might be added to a bill involving crime. The reason is simple: the president would have to veto the entire bill to eliminate the pork—and that might not be feasible politically. Presidents have often argued in favor of a *line-item veto* that would enable them to veto just one (or several) items in a bill. In 1996, Congress passed and President Clinton signed a line-item veto bill. In 1998, though, the Supreme Court concluded that the bill was unconstitutional.[3]

12–3b The President's Inherent Powers

In addition to the powers explicitly granted by the Constitution, the president also has *inherent powers*—powers that are necessary to carry out the specific responsibilities of the president as set forth in the Constitution. The presidency is, of course, an institution of government, but it is also an institution that consists, at any one moment in time, of one individual. That means the lines between the presidential office and the person who holds that office often become blurred.

Certain presidential powers that are generally recognized today were simply assumed by strong presidents to be inherent powers of the presidency, and their successors then continued to exercise these powers.

President Woodrow Wilson clearly indicated this interplay between presidential personality and presidential powers in the following observation:

The President is at liberty, both in law and conscience, to be as big a man as he can. His capacity will set the limit; and if Congress be overborne by him, it will be no fault of the makers of the Constitution—it will be from no lack of constitutional powers on his part, but only because the President has the nation behind him, and Congress has not.[4]

In other words, because the Constitution is vague as to the actual carrying out of presidential powers, presidents are left to define the limits of their authority—subject, of course, to obstacles raised by the other branches of government.

12–3c The Expansion of Presidential Powers

The Constitution defines presidential powers in very general language, and even the founders were uncertain just how the president would perform the various functions. George Washington (1789–1797) set many of the precedents that have defined presidential power. For example, he removed officials from office, interpreting the constitutional power to appoint officials as implying power to remove them as well.[5]

President Clinton signs a bill promoting trade with China. He is surrounded by cabinet members and, to the right, House Speaker Dennis Hastert (R., Ill.).

closely with members of Congress to persuade them to support particular programs. The president writes, telephones, and meets with various congressional leaders to discuss pending bills. The president also sends aides to lobby on Capitol Hill.

One study of the legislative process found that "no other single actor in the political system has quite the capability of the president to set agendas in given policy areas." As one lobbyist told a researcher, "Obviously, when a president sends up a bill [to Congress], it takes first place in the queue. All other bills take second place." As noted earlier, however, compared with some recent presidents, Barack Obama has showed a surprising willingness to let Congress determine the details of important legislation.

THE POWER TO PERSUADE. The president's political skills and ability to persuade others play a large role in determining the administration's success. According to Richard Neustadt in his classic work *Presidential Power,* "Presidential power is the power to persuade."[7] For all of the resources at the president's disposal, the president still must rely on the cooperation of others if the administration's goals are to be accomplished. After three years in office, President Harry Truman made this remark about the powers of the president:

> The president may have a great many powers given to him in the Constitution and may have certain powers under certain laws which are given to him by the

Washington established the practice of meeting regularly with the heads of the three departments that then existed (plus the attorney general) and of turning to them for political advice. He set a precedent for the president to act as chief legislator by submitting proposed legislation to Congress.

Expansion under Later Presidents

Abraham Lincoln (1861–1865), confronting the problems of the Civil War during the 1860s, took several important actions while Congress was not in session. He suspended certain constitutional liberties, spent funds that Congress had not appropriated, blockaded southern ports, and banned "treasonable correspondence" from the U.S. mail. Lincoln carried out all of these actions in the name of his power as commander in chief and his constitutional responsibility to "take Care that the Laws be faithfully executed."[6]

Other presidents, including Thomas Jefferson, Andrew Jackson, Woodrow Wilson, Franklin D. Roosevelt, and George W. Bush, also greatly expanded the powers of the president. The power of the president continues to evolve, depending on the person holding the office, the relative power of Congress, and events at home and abroad.

The President's Expanded Legislative Powers

Congress has come to expect the president to develop a legislative program. From time to time, the president submits special messages on certain subjects. These messages call on Congress to enact laws that the president thinks are necessary. The president also works

> "All the president is, is a glorified public relations man who spends his time flattering, kissing, and kicking people to get them to do what they are supposed to do anyway."
>
> ~ HARRY TRUMAN ~
> THIRTY-THIRD PRESIDENT
> OF THE UNITED STATES
> 1945–1953

As chief diplomat, George Washington made foreign policy decisions without consulting Congress. This action laid the groundwork for an active presidential role in foreign policy.

By the time Abraham Lincoln gave his Inauguration Day speech, seven southern states had already seceded from the Union. Some scholars believe that Lincoln's skillful and vigorous handling of the Civil War increased the power and prestige of the presidency.

In its attempts to counter the effects of the Great Depression, Franklin D. Roosevelt's administration not only extended the role of the national government in regulating the nation's economic life but also further increased the power of the president.

Congress of the United States; but the principal power that the president has is to bring people in and try to persuade them to do what they ought to do without persuasion. That's what the powers of the president amount to.[8]

Persuasive powers are particularly important when divided government exists. If a president from one political party faces a Congress dominated by the other party, the president must overcome more opposition than usual to get legislation passed.

GOING PUBLIC. The president may also use a strategy known as "going public"[9]—that is, using press conferences, public appearances, and televised events to arouse public opinion in favor of certain legislative programs. The public may then pressure legislators to support the administration's programs. A president who has the support of the public can wield significant persuasive power over Congress. Presidents who are voted into office through "landslide" elections have increased bargaining power because of their widespread popularity. Those with less popular support have less bargaining leverage.

The ability of the president to "go public" effectively is dependent on popular attitudes toward the president. It is also dependent on the political climate in Washington, D.C. In periods of severe political

polarization—such as the last several years—going public can actually be counterproductive. Simply by endorsing a proposal that might have had bipartisan support, the president can turn the question into a partisan issue. Without support from at least some members of both parties, the proposal then fails to pass.

THE POWER TO INFLUENCE THE ECONOMY. Some of the greatest expansions of presidential power occurred during Franklin Roosevelt's administration. Roosevelt claimed the presidential power to regulate the economy during the Great Depression in the 1930s. Since that time, Americans have expected the president to be actively involved in economic matters and social programs. That expectation becomes especially potent during a major economic downturn, such as the Great Recession that began in December 2007.

Each year, the president sends Congress a suggested budget and the *Economic Report of the President.* The budget message proposes what amounts of money the government will need for

SOCIAL MEDIA
In Politics

The Gallup poll has a major social media presence where you can follow news about the president's popularity and many other topics. On Facebook, look for "gallup." On Twitter, follow "gallupnews."

its programs. The *Economic Report of the President* presents the state of the nation's economy and recommends ways to improve it.

Voters may rate a president based on the state of the economy. Experts have observed that the president's ability to control the level of economic activity is subject to severe limits. From the public's point of view, however, evaluating its leaders based on results makes good sense. If a president is under constant political pressure to improve the economy, he or she is likely to do whatever is possible to reach that goal. How much can a president actually do to affect the economy? We examine that question in the *Perception versus Reality* feature on the following page.

THE LEGISLATIVE SUCCESS OF VARIOUS PRESIDENTS. Look at Figure 12–1 on page 272. It shows the success records of presidents in getting their legislation passed. Success is defined as how often the president got his way on roll-call votes on which he took a clear position. As you can see, typically a president's success record was very high when he first took office and then gradually declined. This is sometimes attributed to the president's "honeymoon period," when Congress may be most likely to work with the president to achieve the president's legislative agenda.

The media often put a great deal of emphasis on how successful a president is during the "first hundred days" in office. Ironically, this is also the period when the president is least experienced in the ways of the White House, particularly if the president was a Washington outsider, such as a state governor, before becoming president.

In 2009, President Obama had the most successful legislative year of any president in half a century. Large Democratic majorities in both chambers of Congress were surely important in explaining Obama's ability to obtain the legislation that he sought. Obama was also

> "If one morning I walked on top of the water across the Potomac River, the headline that afternoon would read: **'PRESIDENT CAN'T SWIM.'**"
>
> ~ LYNDON B. JOHNSON ~
> THIRTY-SIXTH PRESIDENT
> OF THE UNITED STATES
> 1963–1969

successful in 2010. After the Democrats lost control of the U.S. House in November 2010, however, Obama's success rate fell considerably.

The Increasing Use of Executive Orders As the nation's chief executive, the president is considered to have the inherent power to issue **executive orders,** which are presidential orders to carry out policies described in laws that have been passed by Congress. These orders have the force of law.

Presidents have issued executive orders for a variety of purposes, including to establish procedures for appointing noncareer administrators, to restructure the White House bureaucracy, and to ration consumer goods and administer wage and price controls under emergency conditions. Other goals have included classifying government information as secret, implementing affirmative action policies, and regulating the export of certain items. Presidents issue executive orders frequently, sometimes as many as one hundred a year.

An Unprecedented Use of Signing Statements A **signing statement** is a written statement issued by a president at the time he or she signs a bill into law. James Monroe (1817–1825) was the first president to issue such a statement. For many years, signing statements were rare—prior to the presidency of Ronald Reagan, only seventy-five were issued. Most were "rhetorical" in character. They might praise the legislation or the Congress that passed it, or criticize the opposition. On occasion, however, the statements noted constitutional problems with one or more clauses of a bill or provided details as to how the executive branch would interpret legislative language.

Reagan issued a grand total of 249 signing statements. For the first time, each statement was published in the *U.S. Code Congressional and Administrative News,* along with the text of the bill in question. A substantial share of the statements addressed constitutional issues. Reagan staff member Samuel Alito, Jr.—who now sits on the United States Supreme Court—issued a memo in favor of using signing statements to "increase the power of the Executive to shape the law."

executive order A presidential order to carry out a policy or policies described in a law passed by Congress.

signing statement A written statement, appended to a bill at the time the president signs it into law, indicating how the president interprets that legislation.

Perception versus Reality

Can the President Really Fix the Economy?

The economy has been in poor shape since the end of 2007. As political scientists know, a president running for reelection often won't be reelected if the state of the economy is not improving. There is clearly a public perception that the president can engage in numerous actions to "fix the economy." So, if the economy isn't growing, it's the president's fault.

THE PERCEPTION

What the president wants, the president gets. If the president has the right ideas about how to improve the economy, he or she just has to make sure that those ideas become public policy. Therefore, when the economy is not adding jobs and the rate of economic growth is slow or nonexistent, clearly the president is responsible.

THE REALITY

What presidents say and what happens are not necessarily related. When it comes to the economy, that statement is especially true. Consider *monetary policy*—changing the amount of money in circulation to warm up or cool down the economy. Presidents have almost no control over monetary policy because the independent Federal Reserve System (Fed) carries it out. Presidents can, to be

sure, "jawbone" the current head of the Fed—try to exert influence—but that is about the extent of presidential power over monetary policy.

Fiscal policy—tax rates, subsidies, decreases and increases in government spending levels—is another policy lever. People often believe that the president can control such variables. The reality is often quite the opposite.

Only Congress can pass laws that change our tax code and that change the amount of taxpayer dollars spent. This is not to say that a president is incapable of influencing tax rates and the level of government spending, but such influence does not usually go very far if one or both chambers of Congress are in the hands of the other party. This is especially true today, given high levels of political polarization. President Ronald Reagan could dramatically lower tax rates when Democrats controlled Congress, but that was another era.

President Obama was able to get a stimulus bill passed in 2009 because the Democrats controlled both chambers of Congress. Since 2011, in contrast, the Republicans have controlled the House. Attempts by the Obama administration to negotiate with the House Republican leadership have proved to be extraordinarily difficult. As a result, the president has had little influence on taxing and spending decisions.

BLOG ON To learn more about economic policy, try consulting two talented bloggers. A search on "mankiw" will lead you to the blog of Greg Mankiw, currently chair of the Harvard Economics Department and a moderate Republican. Matt Yglesias is a pro-market progressive, and you can find his Slate blog by searching on "yglesias."

Signing Statements under Bush President George W. Bush took the use of signing statements to an entirely new level. Bush's 161 statements challenged more than 1,100 clauses of federal law—more legal provisions than were challenged by all previous presidents put together. The powers that the statements claimed for the president alarmed some people. One statement rejected Congress's authority to ban torture. Another affirmed that the president could have anyone's mail opened without a warrant.

As a presidential candidate, Barack Obama criticized Bush's use of signing statements and promised to limit his use of them. As president, he has reduced the number of signing statements substantially.

Evolving Presidential Power in Foreign Affairs The precise extent of the president's power in foreign affairs is constantly evolving. The president is commander in chief and chief diplomat, but only Congress has the power to formally declare war, and

FIGURE 12-1

Presidential Success Records

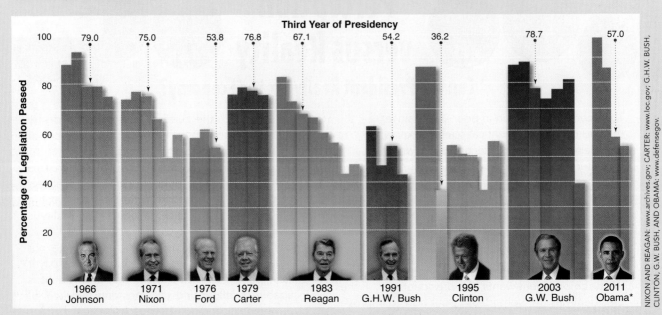

Third Year of Presidency

*Obama's first-year success rate (2009) was 96 percent, the highest since the opening days of Franklin Roosevelt's presidency.

Source: *Congressional Quarterly Almanac.*

the Senate must ratify any treaty that the president has negotiated with other nations. Nevertheless, from the beginning, our country has been led by the president in foreign affairs.

George Washington laid the groundwork for our long history of the president's active role in foreign policy. For example, when war broke out between Britain and France in 1793, Washington chose to disregard a treaty of alliance with France and to pursue a course of strict neutrality. Since that time, on many occasions presidents have taken military actions and made foreign policy without consulting Congress.

EXECUTIVE AGREEMENTS. In foreign affairs, presidential power is enhanced by the ability to make **executive agreements,** which are pacts between the president and other heads of state. Executive agreements do not require Senate approval (even though Congress may refuse to appropriate the necessary money to carry out the agreements), but they have the same legal status as treaties.

Presidents form executive agreements for a wide range of purposes.

executive agreement
A binding international agreement, or pact, that is made between the president and another head of state and that does not require Senate approval.

Some involve routine matters, such as promises of assistance to other countries. Others concern matters of great importance. In 1940, for example, President Franklin Roosevelt formed an important executive agreement with British prime minister Winston Churchill. The agreement provided that the United States would lend American destroyers to Britain to help protect that nation and its shipping during World War II. In return, the British allowed the United States to use military and naval bases on British territories in the Western Hemisphere.

To prevent presidential abuse of the power to make executive agreements, Congress passed a law in 1972 that requires the president to inform Congress within sixty days of making any executive agreement. The law did not limit the president's power to make executive agreements, however, and they continue to be used far more than treaties in making foreign policy.

MILITARY ACTIONS. As you read in the chapter-opening *America at Odds* feature, the U.S. Constitution gives Congress the power to declare war. Consider however, that although Congress has declared war in only five different conflicts during our nation's history,[10] the United States has engaged in more than two hundred activities involving the armed services.

President George W. Bush with Secretary of State Condoleezza Rice in 2008, shortly after Russia invaded the small nation of Georgia.

1970s. Criticism of the president's role in the Vietnam conflict led to the passage of the War Powers Resolution of 1973.

The law, which was passed over President Nixon's veto, requires the president to notify Congress within forty-eight hours of deploying troops. It also prevents the president from keeping troops abroad for more than sixty days (or ninety days, if more time is needed for a successful withdrawal). If Congress does not authorize a longer period, the troops must be removed.

THE WAR ON TERRORISM. President George W. Bush did not obtain a declaration of war from Congress for the war against terrorism that began on September 11, 2001. Instead, Congress passed a joint resolution authorizing the president to use "all necessary and appropriate force against those nations, organizations, or persons he determines planned, authorized, committed, or aided the terrorist attacks that occurred on September 11, 2001."

This resolution was the basis for America's subsequent involvement in Afghanistan. Also, in October 2002, Congress passed a joint resolution authorizing the use of U.S. armed forces against Iraq.

As a consequence of these resolutions, the president was able to invoke certain emergency wartime measures. For example, through executive order the president created military tribunals for trying terrorist suspects. The president also held some American citizens as "enemy combatants," denying them access to their attorneys.

Without a congressional declaration of war, President Truman sent U.S. armed forces to Korea in 1950, thus involving American troops in the conflict between North and South Korea. The United States also entered the Vietnam War (1965–1975) without a declaration of war. President Nixon did not consult Congress when he made the decision to invade Cambodia in 1970. Neither did President Reagan when he sent troops to Lebanon and Grenada in 1983.

No congressional vote was taken before President George H. W. Bush sent troops into Panama in 1989. Bush did, however, obtain congressional approval to use American troops to force Iraq to withdraw from Kuwait in 1991. Without Congress, President Clinton made the decision to send troops to Haiti in 1994 and to Bosnia in 1995, as well as to bomb Iraq in 1998. In 1999, he also decided on his own authority to send U.S. forces under the command of NATO (the North Atlantic Treaty Organization) to bomb Yugoslavia.

THE WAR POWERS RESOLUTION. As commander in chief, the president can respond quickly to a military threat without waiting for congressional action. This power to involve the nation in a war upset many members of Congress as the undeclared war in Vietnam dragged on for years into the

> "As to the presidency, the two happiest days of my life were those of my entrance upon the office and my surrender of it."
>
> ~ MARTIN VAN BUREN ~
> EIGHTH PRESIDENT
> OF THE UNITED STATES
> 1837–1841

NUCLEAR WEAPONS. Since 1945, the president, as commander in chief, has been responsible for the most difficult of all military decisions—if and when to use nuclear weapons. In 1945, Harry Truman made the awesome decision to drop atomic bombs on the Japanese cities of Hiroshima and Nagasaki. "The final decision," he said, "on where and when to use the atomic bomb

President George H. W. Bush often seemed at ease during White House press conferences.

was up to me. Let there be no mistake about it." Today, the president travels at all times with the "football"—the briefcase containing the codes used to launch a nuclear attack.

Some observers believe that it is almost impossible for the president to change the nation's policies simply by delivering a speech, no matter how important the topic. *Do you think this is true? Why or why not?*

12–4 Congressional and Presidential Relations

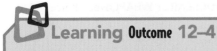

Learning **Outcome** 12–4

Describe advantages enjoyed by Congress and by the president in their institutional relationship.

Despite the seemingly immense powers at the president's disposal, the president is limited in what he or she can accomplish, or even attempt. In our system of checks and balances, the president must share some powers with the legislative and judicial branches of government. The president's power is checked not only by these institutions but also by the media, public opinion, and the voters. The founders hoped that this system

of shared power would lessen the chance of tyranny.

Some scholars believe the relationship between Congress and the president is the most important one in the American system of government. Congress traditionally has had the upper hand in some areas, primarily in passing legislation. In some other areas, though, particularly in foreign affairs, the president can exert tremendous power that Congress has almost no ability to check.

12–4a Advantage: Congress

Congress has the advantage over the president in the areas of legislative authorization, the regulation of foreign and interstate commerce, and some budgetary matters. Of course, as you have already read, the president today proposes a legislative agenda and a budget to Congress every year. Nonetheless, only Congress has the power to pass the legislation and appropriate the money. The most the president can do constitutionally is veto an entire bill if it contains something that she or he does not like. (As noted, however, recent presidents have frequently used signing statements in an attempt to nullify portions of bills that they did not approve.)

Presidential popularity is a source of power for the president in dealings with Congress. Presidents spend a great deal of time courting public opinion, eyeing the "presidential approval ratings," and meeting with the press. Much of this activity is for the purpose of gaining leverage with Congress. Yet even when the president puts all of his or her persuasive powers to work in achieving a legislative agenda, Congress still retains the ultimate lawmaking authority.

Divided Government When government is divided—with at least one house of Congress controlled by a different party than the White House—the president can have difficulty even getting a legislative agenda to the floor for a vote. President Barack Obama faced such a problem in 2011, when the Republicans gained a majority in the House of Representatives. During his first two years as president, Obama had worked with a very cooperative Democrat-led Congress. After the Republicans became the majority party in the House, however, divided government existed again. Indeed, few people in public life could remember a time when partisan hostilities had been so intense.

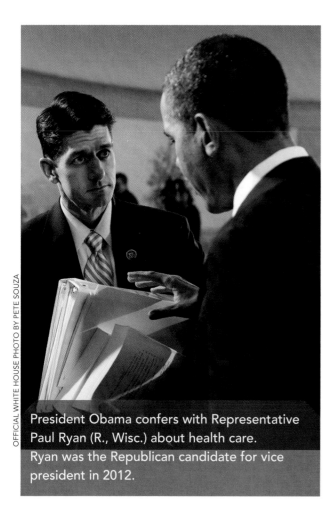

President Obama confers with Representative Paul Ryan (R., Wisc.) about health care. Ryan was the Republican candidate for vice president in 2012.

OFFICIAL WHITE HOUSE PHOTO BY PETE SOUZA

Different Constituencies Congress and the president have different constituencies, and this fact influences their relationship. Members of Congress represent a state or a local district, and this gives them a regional focus. As we discussed in Chapter 11, members of Congress like to have legislative successes of their own to bring home to their constituents—military bases that remain operative, public-works projects that create local jobs, or trade rules that benefit a big local employer. Ideally, the president's focus should be on the nation as a whole: national defense, homeland security, the national economy. At times, this can put the president at odds even with members of his or her own party in Congress.

Furthermore, members of Congress and the president face different election cycles (every two years in the House, every six years in the Senate, and every four years for the president), and the president is limited to two terms in office. Consequently, the president and Congress sometimes feel a different sense of urgency about implementing legislation. For example, the president often senses the need to demonstrate leg-

islative success during the first year in office, when the excitement over the elections is still fresh in the minds of politicians and the public.

12–4b Advantage: The President

The president has the advantage over Congress in dealing with a national crisis, in setting foreign policy, and in influencing public opinion. In times of crisis, the presidency is arguably the most crucial institution in government because, when necessary, the president can act quickly, speak with one voice, and represent the nation to the world.

Some scholars have argued that recent presidents have abused the powers of the presidency by taking advantage of crises. Others have argued that there is an unwritten "doctrine of necessity" under which presidential powers can and should be expanded during a crisis. When this has happened in the past, however, Congress has always retaken some control when the crisis was over, in a natural process of institutional give-and-take.

The War on Terrorism A problem faced during the George W. Bush administration was that the "war on terrorism" had no obvious end or conclusion. It was not clear when the crisis would be over and the nation could return to normal government relations and procedures. Many supporters of Barack Obama believed that upon election, he would restore civil liberties lost during Bush's war on terrorism. As it turned out, the Obama administration has kept most of Bush's policies in place. (You learned about this issue in greater detail in Chapter 4, in the section "Personal Privacy and National Security.")

Executive Privilege As you read in Chapter 11, Congress has the authority to investigate and oversee the activities of other branches of government. Nonetheless, both Congress and the public have accepted that a certain degree of secrecy by the executive branch is necessary to protect national security. Some presidents have claimed an inherent executive power to withhold information from, or to refuse to appear before, Congress or the courts. This is called **executive privilege,** and it has

> **executive privilege** An inherent executive power claimed by presidents to withhold information from, or to refuse to appear before, Congress or the courts. The president can also accord the privilege to other executive officials.

President Nixon delivering his resignation speech in August 1974. Why did Nixon leave office?

CBS PHOTO ARCHIVE/GETTY IMAGES

been invoked by presidents from the time of George Washington to the present.

Abuses of Executive Privilege

One of the problems with executive privilege is that it has been used for more purposes than simply to safeguard national security. President Nixon invoked executive privilege in an attempt to avoid handing over taped White House conversations to Congress during the **Watergate scandal.** President Clinton invoked the privilege in an attempt to keep details of his sexual relationship with White House intern Monica Lewinsky a secret.

After the Democrats took control of Congress in 2007 and began to investigate various actions undertaken by the Bush administration, they were frequently blocked in their attempts to obtain information by the claim of executive privilege. For example, during Congress's investigation of the Justice Department's firing of several U.S. attorneys for allegedly political reasons, the Bush administration raised the claim of executive privilege to prevent several people from testifying or submitting requested documents to Congress.

Watergate scandal A scandal involving an illegal break-in at the Democratic National Committee offices in 1972 by members of President Richard Nixon's reelection campaign staff.

cabinet An advisory group selected by the president to assist with decision making. Traditionally, the cabinet has consisted of the heads of the executive departments and other officers whom the president may choose to appoint.

Would we be better off if executive privilege didn't exist, or are there some matters a president must be able to keep private? Discuss.

12–5 The Organization of the Executive Branch

In the early days of this nation, presidents answered their own mail. Only in 1857 did Congress authorize a private secretary for the president, to be paid by the federal government. Even Woodrow Wilson typed most of his correspondence, although by that time several secretaries were assigned to the president. When Franklin Roosevelt became president in 1933, the entire staff consisted of thirty-seven employees. Not until Roosevelt's New Deal and World War II did the presidential staff become a sizable organization.

Learning Outcome 12–5

Discuss the organization of the executive branch and the role of cabinet members in presidential administrations.

12–5a The President's Cabinet

The Constitution does not specifically mention presidential assistants and advisers. The Constitution states only that the president "may require the Opinion, in writing, of the principal Officer in each of the executive Departments." Since the time of our first president, however, presidents have had an advisory group, or **cabinet,** to turn to for counsel. Originally, the cabinet consisted of only four officials—the secretaries of state, treasury, and war and the attorney general.

Today, the cabinet includes fourteen department secretaries, the attorney general, and a number of other officials. (See Table 12–2 on the following page for the names of the major executive departments represented in the cabinet.) Additional cabinet members vary from one presidency to the next. Typically, the vice president is a member. President Clinton added ten officials to the cabinet, and George W. Bush added five. Barack

Obama added the following members, in addition to the vice president:

- The administrator of the Environmental Protection Agency.
- The chair of the Council of Economic Advisers.
- The director of the Office of Management and Budget.
- The United States ambassador to the United Nations.
- The United States trade representative.
- The White House chief of staff.

Use of the Cabinet Because the Constitution does not require the president to consult with the cabinet, the use of this body is purely discretionary. Some presidents have relied on the counsel of their cabinets more than others. After a cabinet meeting in which a vote was seven nays against his one aye, President Lincoln supposedly said, "Seven nays and one aye, the ayes have it."[11]

Still other presidents have sought counsel from so-called **kitchen cabinets,** informal groups of unofficial advisers. The term *kitchen cabinet* originated during the presidency of Andrew Jackson, who relied on the counsel of close friends who allegedly met with him in the kitchen of the White House.

In general, presidents usually don't rely heavily on the advice of the formal cabinet. They are aware that department heads are often more responsive to the wishes of their own staffs, to their own political ambitions, or to obtaining resources for their departments than they are to the presidents they serve.

Obama's "Czars" President Obama's response to the need to seek advice was to centralize the advisory function within the White House Office (discussed below) by appointing a large number of in-house "czars." Each of these White House czars has responsibility for a certain policy area.

Critics of the Obama administration believe that the czar system tends to undercut the authority of cabinet members. Congress also loses leverage, because cabinet members must be confirmed by the Senate, whereas czars are responsible only to the president.

12–5b The Executive Office of the President

In 1939, President Franklin Roosevelt set up the **Executive Office of the President (EOP)** to cope with the increased responsibilities brought on by the Great Depression. Since then, the EOP has grown significantly to accommodate the increasingly expansive role played by the national government, including the executive branch, in the nation's economic and social life.

The EOP is made up of the top advisers and assistants who help the president carry out major duties. Over the years, the EOP has changed according to the needs and leadership style of each president. It has become an increasingly influential and important part of the executive branch.

TABLE 12–2

The Major Executive Departments

The heads of all of these departments are members of the president's cabinet.

Department	Year of First Establishment
Department of State	1789
Department of the Treasury	1789
Department of Defense*	1789
Department of Justice (headed by the attorney general)[†]	1789
Department of the Interior	1849
Department of Agriculture	1889
Department of Commerce[‡]	1903
Department of Labor[‡]	1903
Department of Health and Human Services[§]	1953
Department of Housing and Urban Development	1965
Department of Transportation	1967
Department of Energy	1977
Department of Education	1979
Department of Veterans Affairs	1989
Department of Homeland Security	2002

*Established in 1947 by merging the Department of War, created in 1789, and the Department of the Navy, created in 1798.
[†]Formerly the Office of the Attorney General; renamed and reorganized in 1870.
[‡]Formed in 1913 by splitting the Department of Commerce and Labor, which was created in 1903.
[§]Formerly the Department of Health, Education, and Welfare; renamed when the Department of Education was spun off in 1979.

kitchen cabinet The name given to a president's unofficial advisers. The term was coined during Andrew Jackson's presidency.

Executive Office of the President (EOP) A group of staff agencies that assist the president in carrying out major duties.

Table 12–3 alongside lists various offices within the EOP as of 2013. Note that the organization of the EOP is subject to change. Presidents have frequently added new bodies to its membership and subtracted others. President Obama has made a number of changes to the EOP's table of organization during his years in office.

The White House Office Of all of the executive staff agencies, the **White House Office** has the most direct contact with the president. The White House Office is headed by the **chief of staff,** who advises the president on important matters and directs the operations of the presidential staff. A number of other top officials, assistants, and special assistants to the president also provide aid in such areas as national security, the economy, and political affairs. The **press secretary** meets with reporters and makes public statements for the president. The counsel to the president serves as the White House lawyer and handles the president's legal matters.

The White House staff also includes speechwriters, researchers, the president's physician, and a correspondence secretary. Altogether, the White House Office has more than four hundred employees.

The White House staff has several duties. First, the staff investigates and analyzes problems that require the president's attention. Staff members who are specialists in certain areas, such as diplomatic relations or foreign trade, gather information for the president and suggest solutions. White House staff members also screen the questions, issues, and problems that people present to the president, so matters

TABLE 12–3
The Executive Office of the President as of 2013
Agency
Council of Economic Advisers
Council on Environmental Quality
Executive Residence
National Security Staff
Office of Administration
Office of Management and Budget
Office of National Drug Control Policy
Office of Science and Technology Policy
Office of the U.S. Trade Representative
Office of the Vice President
White House Office

Source: www.whitehouse.gov.

that can be handled by other officials do not reach the president's desk.

Additionally, the staff provides public relations support. For example, the press staff handles the president's relations with the White House press corps and schedules news conferences. Finally, the White House staff ensures that the president's initiatives are effectively transmitted to the relevant government personnel. Several staff members are usually assigned to work directly with members of Congress for this purpose.

PETE SOUZA/THE WHITE HOUSE/GETTY IMAGES

President Barack Obama, Vice President Joe Biden, Secretary of State Hillary Clinton, and members of the national security team receive an update on the mission against Osama bin Laden in the Situation Room of the White House on May 1, 2011.

The First Lady The White House Office also includes the staff of the president's spouse. First Ladies have at times taken important roles within the White House. For example, Franklin Roosevelt's wife, Eleanor, advocated the rights of women, labor, and African Americans. As First Lady, Hillary Clinton helped develop an unsuccessful plan for a national health-care system. In 2008, she was a leading contender for the Democratic presidential nomination. Had she won the presidency, Bill Clinton would have become the nation's First Gentleman.

The Office of Management and Budget The **Office of Management and Budget (OMB)** was originally the Bureau of the Budget. Under recent presidents, the OMB has become an important and influential unit of the Executive Office of the President. The main function of the OMB is to assist the president in preparing the proposed annual budget, which the president must submit to Congress in January of each year (see Chapter 11 for details).

The federal budget lists the revenues and expenditures expected for the coming year. It indicates which programs the federal government will pay for and how much they will cost. Thus, the budget is an annual statement of the public policies of the United States translated into dollars and cents. Making changes in the budget is a key way for presidents to influence the direction and policies of the federal government.

The president appoints the director of the OMB with the consent of the Senate. The director oversees the OMB's work and argues the administration's positions before Congress. The director also lobbies members of Congress to support the president's budget or to accept key features of it. Once the budget is approved by Congress, the OMB has the responsibility of putting it into practice. The OMB oversees the execution of the budget, checking on federal agencies to ensure that they use funds efficiently.

Beyond its budget duties, the OMB also reviews new bills prepared by the executive branch. It checks all legislative matters to be certain that they agree with the president's own positions.

The National Security Council The **National Security Council (NSC)** was established in 1947 to manage the defense and foreign policy of the United States. Its members are the president, the vice president, and the secretaries of state and defense. It also

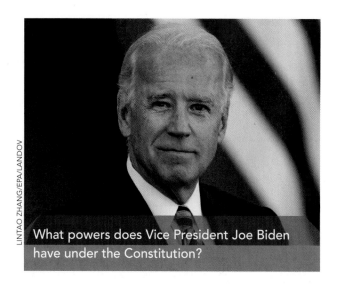

What powers does Vice President Joe Biden have under the Constitution?

LINTAO ZHANG/EPA/LANDOV

includes several informal advisers. The NSC is the president's link to his or her key foreign and military advisers. The president's special assistant for national security affairs heads the NSC staff.

12–5c The Vice Presidency and Presidential Succession

As a rule, presidential nominees choose running mates who balance the ticket or whose appointment rewards or appeases party factions. For example, to balance the ticket geographically, a presidential candidate from the South may solicit a running mate from the West.

In 2008, Republican candidate John McCain chose as his running mate Alaska governor Sarah Palin. Palin shored up McCain's support among cultural conservatives. President Barack Obama picked Senator Joe Biden, who had thirty-five years of experience in Congress. Obama wished to counter detractors who claimed that he was too inexperienced.

In 2012, Republican presidential candidate Mitt Romney chose Representative Paul Ryan of Wisconsin to join his ticket. Ryan helped Romney appeal to the party's conservative wing. Ryan had gained recognition as chair of the House Budget Committee when

Office of Management and Budget (OMB) An agency in the Executive Office of the President that has the primary duty of assisting the president in preparing and supervising the administration of the federal budget.

National Security Council (NSC) A council that advises the president on domestic and foreign matters concerning the safety and defense of the nation.

President Gerald Ford (right) confers with Vice President Nelson Rockefeller in 1974. For the first time in the history of the United States, neither leader had obtained office by winning a general election.

Presidential Succession

One of the questions left unanswered by the Constitution was what the vice president should do if the president becomes incapable of carrying out necessary duties while in office. The Twenty-fifth Amendment to the Constitution, ratified in 1967, filled this gap.

THE TWENTY-FIFTH AMENDMENT. The amendment states that when the president believes that he or she is incapable of performing the duties of the office, he or she must inform Congress in writing of this fact.

When the president is unable to communicate, a majority of the cabinet, including the vice president, can declare that fact to Congress. In either case, the vice president then serves as acting president until the president resumes normal duties. If a dispute arises over the return of the president's ability to discharge the normal functions of the presidential office, a two-thirds vote of both chambers of Congress is required if the vice president is to remain acting president. Otherwise, the president resumes these duties.

VICE-PRESIDENTIAL VACANCIES. The Twenty-fifth Amendment also addresses the question of how the president should fill a vacant vice presidency. Section 2 of the amendment states, "Whenever there is a vacancy in the office of the Vice President, the President shall nominate a Vice President who shall take office upon confirmation by a majority vote of both Houses of Congress."

In 1973, Gerald Ford became the first appointed vice president of the United States after Spiro Agnew was forced to resign. One year later, President Richard Nixon resigned, and Ford advanced to the office of president. President Ford named Nelson Rockefeller as his vice president. For the first time in U.S. history, neither the president nor the vice president had been elected to his position.

What if both the president and the vice president die, resign, or are disabled? According to the Succession Act

he authored a series of proposed budgets that won near-universal Republican support.

The Role of Vice Presidents For much of our history, the vice president has had almost no responsibilities. Still, the vice president is in a position to become the nation's chief executive should the president die, be impeached, or resign the presidential office. Nine vice presidents have become president because of the death or resignation of the president.

In recent years, the responsibilities of the vice president have grown immensely. The vice president has become one of the most—if not *the* most—important of the president's advisers. The first modern vice president to act as a major adviser was Walter Mondale, who served under Jimmy Carter. Later, Bill Clinton relied heavily on Vice President Al Gore, who shared many of Clinton's values and beliefs.

Without question, however, the most powerful vice president in American history was Dick Cheney, who served under George W. Bush. The unprecedented delegation of power that Cheney enjoyed would not have been possible without the president's agreement, and Bush clearly approved of it. Vice President Joe Biden has been one of President Barack Obama's most important advisers, but not at the level of Cheney.

of 1947, the Speaker of the House of Representatives will then act as president on her or his resignation as Speaker and as representative. If the Speaker is unavailable, next in line is the president pro tem of the Senate, followed by the permanent members of the president's cabinet in the order of the creation of their departments (see Table 12–2 earlier in this chapter).

FOR CRITICAL THINKING

Members of the Washington political community often harbor a degree of resentment toward those who work in the White House Office. *What might cause these feelings?*

AMERICA AT
ODDS The Presidency

The president is the most conspicuous figure in our political system. Everyone has opinions about what the president should do—and in a presidential election year, who the president should be. To an extent not seen in regard to other offices, the public also has a serious interest in the president's personality and character. The president, after all, represents all of us. Americans are at odds over a variety of questions relating to the presidency. These include the following:

- Should the president try, whenever possible, to compromise with other political players, such as the Congress—or should the president generally stand on principle?

- Should the president seek to expand his or her authority so as to deal more effectively with the nation's problems—or should the president try to adhere to a strict constitutional understanding of the powers of the office?

- Is it appropriate for the president to rely primarily on staff members within the White House Office when determining policy—or should the president offer the cabinet a substantial policymaking role?

- Should voters evaluate presidential candidates primarily on the positions they take on the issues—or are the president's character, personality, and decision-making style more important considerations?

- Should the president be the "moral leader" of the country in the sense of basing policies on religious values—or should the president avoid any intermingling of religion and policy?

STUDY TOOLS

Ready to study?

- **Review** what you've read with the quiz below.
- Check your answers on the **Chapter in Review** card at the back of the book.
- For any questions you miss, read the corresponding **Learning Outcome** section again to prepare for class and your exam.
- Rip out and study the **Chapter in Review** card (at the back of the book).

Fill-In

Learning Outcome 12–1

1. The most common previous occupation of U.S. presidents has been _____.

Learning Outcome 12–2

2. The president leads the nation's armed forces in his or her role as _____.

3. In his or her role as _____, the president delivers the traditional State of the Union address and has the power to veto bills passed by Congress.

Learning Outcome 12–3

4. The president has the power to issue executive orders, which are _____.

5. The _____ requires the president to notify Congress within forty-eight hours of deploying troops.

Learning Outcome 12–4

6. Executive privilege is _____.

Learning Outcome 12–5

7. Traditionally, the cabinet has consisted of _____.

8. The Executive Office of the President (EOP) is made up of a number of executive staff agencies, including the _____.

Multiple Choice

Learning Outcome 12–1

9. Which of the following is a constitutional requirement for becoming president of the United States?
   a. Must be at least thirty years old.
   b. Must be of sound moral character.
   c. Must be a natural born citizen of the United States.

Learning Outcome 12–2

10. When the president ____, he or she is performing the role of head of state.
    a. attends party fund-raisers
    b. makes executive agreements
    c. receives foreign dignitaries

11. When the president negotiates and signs treaties with other nations, he or she is performing the role of
    a. chief diplomat.
    b. chief executive.
    c. commander in chief.

Learning Outcome 12–3

12. The presidential strategy known as "going public" refers to
    a. using press conferences, public appearances, and televised events to arouse public opinion in favor of certain legislative programs.

    b. publicly acknowledging mistakes or misconduct.
    c. appearing on talk shows.

13. Legislative success for presidents is defined as how often they
    a. got their way on roll-call votes on which they took a clear position.
    b. were able to get presidential legislative proposals introduced in Congress.
    c. were able to veto legislation.

Learning Outcome 12–4

14. The term *divided government* refers to the
    a. cultural and political differences between the red states and the blue states.
    b. case when at least one chamber of Congress is held by a different party than the president.
    c. separation of powers.

Learning Outcome 12–5

15. If a vacancy occurs in the vice presidency,
    a. there is currently no provision for filling the office.
    b. the Speaker of the House acts as vice president.
    c. a vice president is nominated by the president and confirmed by a majority vote in both chambers of Congress.

The Bureaucracy

National Park Service
U.S. Department of the Interior

Because of the
Federal Government SHUTDOWN,
All National Parks
Are CLOSED.

JEWEL SAMAD/AFP/GETTY IMAGES

The **Learning Outcomes** labeled 1 through 5 are designed to help improve your understanding of the chapter. After reading this chapter, you should be able to:

13–1 Describe the size and functions of the U.S. bureaucracy and the major components of federal spending.

13–2 Discuss the structure and basic components of the federal bureaucracy.

13–3 Describe how the federal civil service was established and how bureaucrats get their jobs.

13–4 Explain how regulatory agencies make rules and how issue networks affect policymaking in government.

13–5 Identify some of the ways in which the government has attempted to curb waste and improve efficiency in the bureaucracy.

Learning Outcomes

Remember to visit page 305 for additional Study Tools

AMERICA AT
ODDS What Happened to Privacy?

WIN MCNAMEE/GETTY IMAGES

DISSENT = DEMOCRACY

In 2013, a disgruntled programmer working for a contractor to the National Security Agency (NSA) decided to act. Edward Snowden revealed to America and the world that the NSA was collecting data through U.S. companies such as Google and Verizon. What data? Well, data on every text message, phone call, and e-mail generated by every resident in the United States and in many other nations as well. It all started in 2005, during the war in Iraq. The NSA was seeking information on Iraqi bomb makers. The head of the NSA, General Keith B. Alexander, decided not to "look for a needle in a haystack." Rather, the agency would "collect the whole haystack"—*every* Iraqi text message, e-mail, and phone call—and then tag it and store it.

Soon, this strategy was implemented in the United States as well, with the aim of safeguarding Americans from terrorism and cyberattacks. Today, the NSA collects information on billions of phone calls and e-mails every single day. By 2013, the agency had accumulated 20 trillion transactions among U.S. citizens. It is no wonder that the NSA is constructing a massive new facility in Utah to hold all the communications it collects.

Is this massive data collection a violation of our privacy rights? Leading members of Congress and the president tell us not to worry. After all, the U.S. Foreign Intelligence Surveillance Court (FISC) has to approve the constitutionality of NSA actions. But should we accept these reassurances? Americans remain at odds over this issue.

Protect Us From Our Protectors

Many journalists and scholars argue that we should put a stop to the NSA's data seizures because they are unconstitutional. The Fourth Amendment to the Constitution says that we have the right to be secure from unreasonable searches of our "papers." That means the Fourth Amendment protects the privacy of our information. The NSA has no right to seize the records of private communications companies such as AT&T and Verizon. The "terms of service" agreements of these companies do not say that they can share our data with the government.

NSA data banks give government workers information about our electronic communications and our financial transactions not only without our consent, but also without our knowledge. Government officials may say that they are collecting the data only to protect us against terrorism, but they said that about the Patriot Act as well. Information collected as a result of that act forced a New York governor out of office because call records revealed that he had been visiting prostitutes. Is this kind of snooping what we want? The NSA is effectively destroying the privacy not only of residents of the United States, but also of residents in our ally nations in Europe and the Pacific.

So Much Ado About So Little

Despite the hyperventilation by NSA critics, there is no real reason to be worried. No evidence shows that the NSA is intentionally spying on Americans or abusing any of our civil liberties. The rare cases in which the agency has collected data improperly were the result of simple mistakes. The NSA is required to destroy inadvertently acquired communications concerning a "U.S. person" if such information does not contain foreign intelligence or evidence of a crime. The NSA at all times has an ongoing dialogue with the FISC. That court is regularly informed of NSA's activities and its compliance with the court's judgments.

Fourth Amendment zealots live in a dream world. The world in which we live today simply doesn't permit the kind of privacy envisioned by the framers of the Constitution. Obtaining that level of privacy would require that we never use a phone, e-mail, social media, credit cards, or bank accounts. It isn't just the government that collects information, after all. Private businesses have huge collections of data on their customers. As far as privacy is concerned, the barn door is already open, and the horse is long gone.

Where do you stand?

1. How much information can someone glean from knowledge about phone calls and e-mails without actually examining their contents?
2. Today, people—especially young people—voluntarily reveal their whereabouts, actions, and thoughts on a daily basis through Facebook posts and tweets. Have these people given up their privacy rights? Why or why not?

Explore this issue online

- For arguments by constitutional law professor Randy Barnett that the NSA's actions are unconstitutional, search on "nsa barnett unconstitutional."
- Edward Snowden released his materials to journalist Glenn Greenwald. For Greenwald's take on the NSA, search on "collect it all greenwald."
- For defenses of the NSA, check out Gene Lyons at "lyons hysteria" and Benjamin Wittes at "wittes nsa."

Introduction

Did you eat breakfast this morning? If you did, **bureaucrats**—individuals who work in the offices of government—had a lot to do with that breakfast.

If you had bacon, the meat was inspected by federal agents. If you drank milk, the price was affected by rules and regulations of the Department of Agriculture. If you looked at a cereal box, you saw fine print about fat and vitamins, which was the result of regulations made by several other federal agencies, including the Food and Drug Administration. If you ate leftover pizza for breakfast, state or local inspectors made sure that the kitchen of the pizza eatery was sanitary and safe. Other bureaucrats ensured that the employees who put together (and perhaps delivered) the pizza were protected against discrimination in the workplace.

SOCIAL MEDIA
In Politics

Several federal agencies have large presences on social media. The National Aeronautics and Space Administration, for example, has 2.2 million "likes" on Facebook and 3.8 million followers on Twitter.

Today, the word *bureaucracy* often evokes a negative reaction. For some, it conjures up visions of depersonalized automatons performing chores without any sensitivity toward the needs of those they serve. For others, it is synonymous with government "red tape." A **bureaucracy,** however, is simply a large, complex administrative organization that is structured hierarchically in a pyramid-like fashion.[1] Government bureaucrats carry out the policies of elected government officials.

Members of the bureaucracy—government employees—deliver our mail, clean our streets, teach in our public schools, run our national parks, and attempt to ensure the safety of our food and the prescription drugs that we take. Life as we know it would be quite different without the bureaucrats who keep our governments—federal, state, and local—in operation. Still, Americans differ about the positive and negative aspects of various federal bureaucracies, as discussed in the chapter-opening *America at Odds* feature.

GOVERNMENT BUREAUCRACY:

"A marvelous labor-saving device which enables ten men to do the work of one."

~ ATTRIBUTED TO JOHN MAYNARD KEYNES ~
BRITISH ECONOMIST
1883–1946

13–1 The Nature and Size of the Bureaucracy

The concept of a bureaucracy is not confined to the federal government. Any large organization must have a bureaucracy. In each bureaucracy, everybody (except the head of the bureaucracy) reports to at least one other person. In the federal government, the head of the bureaucracy is the president of the United States, and the bureaucracy is part of the executive branch.[2]

Learning Outcome 13–1

Describe the size and functions of the U.S. bureaucracy and the major components of federal spending.

13–1a The Uses of Bureaucracy

A bureaucratic form of organization allows each person to concentrate on her or his area of knowledge and expertise. In your college or university, for example, you do not expect the basketball coach to solve the problems of the finance office. The reason the federal government bureaucracy exists is that Congress, over time, has delegated certain tasks to specialists.

For example, in 1914 Congress passed the Federal Trade Commission Act, which established the Federal Trade Commission to regulate deceptive and unfair trade practices. Those appointed to the commission were specialists in that area. Similarly, Congress passed the Consumer Product Safety Act in 1972, which established the Consumer Product Safety Commission to investigate the safety of consumer products. The commission is one of many federal administrative agencies.

Another key aspect of any bureaucracy is that the power to act resides in the *position* rather than in the *person*. In your college or university, the person who is

bureaucrat An individual who works in a bureaucracy. As generally used, the term refers to a government employee.

bureaucracy A large, complex, hierarchically structured administrative organization that carries out specific functions.

president now has more or less the same authority as any previous president. Additionally, bureaucracies usually entail *standard operating procedures*—directives on what procedures should be followed in specific circumstances. Bureaucracies normally also have a merit system, meaning that people are hired and promoted on the basis of demonstrated skills and achievements.

13–1b The Growth of Bureaucracy

The federal government that existed in 1789 was small. It had three departments, each with only a few employees: (1) the Department of State (nine employees), (2) the Department of War (two employees), and (3) the Department of the Treasury (thirty-nine employees). By 1798, nine years later, the federal bureaucracy was still quite small. The secretary of state had seven clerks. His total expenditures on stationery and printing amounted to $500, or about $10,050 in 2014 dollars. The Department of War spent, on average, a grand total of $1.4 million each year, or about $28.2 million in 2014 dollars.

Growing Government Employment Times have changed. Figure 13–1 below shows the number of government employees at the local, state, and national levels from 1959 to 2013 as a percentage of the total U.S. population. Most growth has been at the state and local levels. All in all, the three levels of government employ about 16 percent of the civilian labor force. Today, more Americans are employed by government (at all three levels) than by the entire manufacturing sector of the U.S. economy.

As you examine Figure 13–1, you will notice a substantial increase in government employment relative to the population from 1959 up to about 1980. During those years, the absolute number of government workers nearly doubled. Government employment has been more stable since 1980, when Republican Ronald Reagan was elected president.

The Impact of President Reagan Indeed, during Reagan's first four years in office, government employment fell. Most of this decrease was at the local level. The drop was caused in part by the reces-

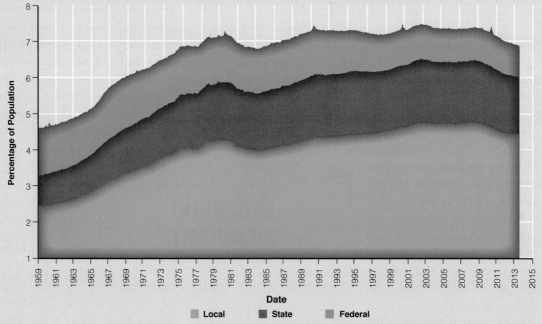

FIGURE 13–1

Government Employees:
Local, State, and Federal, as a Percentage of the Total U.S. Population (1959–2013)

The number of local government employees has the greatest effect on total government employment. The brief spikes in 1980, 1990, 2000, and 2010 represent temporary federal census workers.

Source: The Federal Reserve Economic Data (FRED) service of the St. Louis Federal Reserve.

sion of 1980–1982 and in part by the elimination of revenue sharing. This program had transferred large sums from the federal government to state and especially local governments. The loss of government jobs was made up in Reagan's second term, but the rapid rise in government employment relative to population seen before 1980 did not return.

Recently, government employment has once again dropped, in absolute as well as relative terms. President Obama's 2009 stimulus program, which transferred large sums to local governments, helped stabilize government employment through 2010. By August 2013, however, almost 750,000 fewer people worked for the various levels of government. Most of those who lost their jobs had worked at the local level.

13-1c The Costs of Maintaining the Government

The costs of maintaining the government are high and growing. In 1929, government at all levels accounted for about 11 percent of the nation's gross domestic product (GDP). Today, that figure is about 38 percent. Average citizens pay a significant portion of their income to federal, state, and local governments. They do this by paying income taxes, sales taxes, property taxes, and many other types of taxes and fees.

The government is costly, to be sure, but it also provides numerous services for Americans. Cutting back on the size of government inevitably means a reduction in those services. The trade-off between government spending and popular services has been central to American politics throughout our history.

13-1d Where Does All the Money Go?

It is worth examining where federal spending actually goes. If you ask people on the street, you will get varied responses—from too much spent on wars in Iraq and Afghanistan to too much spent on welfare or foreign aid. As it turns out, none of those categories makes up a very large percentage of federal government spending. Consider Figure 13–2 below.

Social Spending As you can see in Figure 13–2, over half of the federal budget consists of various social programs, shown in shades of blue and green. Some of these programs, such as Social Security, Medicare, and unemployment compensation, are funded by payroll taxes and paid out to all qualifying persons, regardless of income. Together, these three programs make up 38 percent of the federal budget.

FIGURE 13-2 Major Components of Federal Government Spending

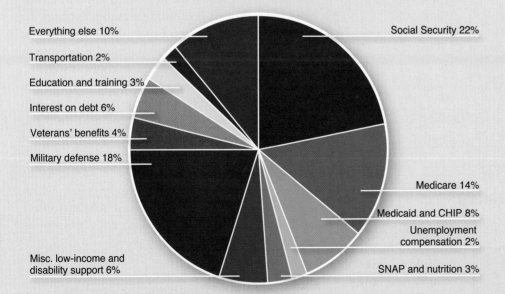

Everything else 10%
Transportation 2%
Education and training 3%
Interest on debt 6%
Veterans' benefits 4%
Military defense 18%
Misc. low-income and disability support 6%
Social Security 22%
Medicare 14%
Medicaid and CHIP 8%
Unemployment compensation 2%
SNAP and nutrition 3%

Note: Percentages do not sum to 100 due to rounding.
Source: Office of Management and Budget.

Other programs, including Medicaid and the Supplemental Nutrition Assistance Program (SNAP, formerly "food stamps"), are available only to low-income individuals. The three "low-income" pie slices make up 17 percent of spending, or almost $700 billion in Fiscal Year 2014. Temporary Assistance for Needy Families (TANF)—traditional cash welfare—is hiding in the "miscellaneous low-income" slice. It accounts for only 0.5 percent of the federal budget—$17 billion. It is completely overshadowed within its pie slice by disability payments, low-income housing programs, and tax refunds.

Defense Defense spending is a big number—with veterans' benefits, it amounts to almost a quarter of the whole. The wars in Iraq and Afghanistan were obviously expensive. One recent estimate of their cost was $170 billion a year, or 4.6 percent of the total. That is serious money, but it's not really "busting the bank." Furthermore, spending on wars is dropping quickly.

Everything Else At 10 percent of the total, "everything else" includes a vast range of programs. One example is military and economic foreign aid, at 1.5 percent of the total, or $57 billion. That's a substantial sum, but it is less than many people imagine it to be. One item that bears watching is the interest on the national debt, which currently exceeds $200 billion per year. Federal budget deficits will cause this figure to grow in future years.

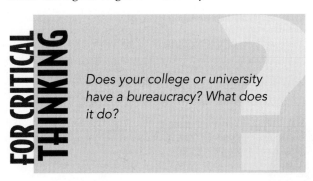

Does your college or university have a bureaucracy? What does it do?

13-2 How the Federal Bureaucracy Is Organized

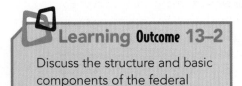

Learning Outcome 13-2

Discuss the structure and basic components of the federal bureaucracy.

A complete organization chart of the federal government would cover an entire wall. A simplified version is provided in Figure 13-3 on the following page. The executive branch consists of a number of bureaucracies that provide services to Congress, to the federal courts, and to the president directly.

The executive branch of the federal government includes four major types of structures:

- Executive departments.
- Independent executive agencies.
- Independent regulatory agencies.
- Government corporations.

Each type of structure has its own relationship to the president and its own internal workings.

13-2a The Executive Departments

You were introduced to the various executive departments in Chapter 12, when you read about how the president works with the cabinet and other close advisers. The fifteen executive departments, which are directly accountable to the president, are the major service organizations of the federal government. They are responsible for performing government functions such as training troops (Department of Defense), printing currency (Department of the Treasury), and enforcing federal laws setting minimum safety and health standards for workers (Department of Labor).

Table 13-1 on page 290–291 provides an overview of each of the departments within the executive branch. The table lists a few of the many activities undertaken by each department. Because the president appoints the department heads, they are expected to help carry out the president's policy objectives. Often, they attempt to maximize the president's political successes as well.

Each executive department was created by Congress as the perceived need for it arose, and each department manages a specific policy area. In 2002, for example, Congress created the Department of Homeland Security to deal with terrorism and other threats. The head of each department is known as the secretary, except for the Department of Justice, which is headed by the attorney general. Each department head is appointed by the president and confirmed by the Senate.

13-2b A Typical Departmental Structure

Each cabinet department consists of the department's top administrators (the secretary of the department,

FIGURE 13-3

The Organization
of the Federal Government

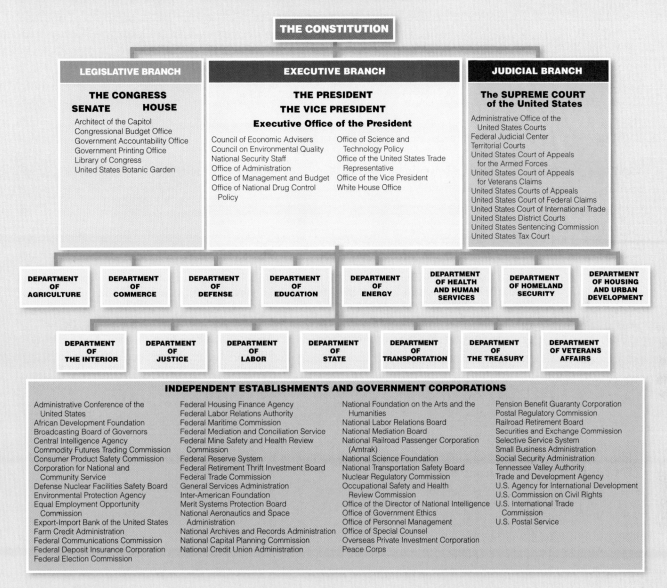

Sources: *United States Government Manual 2013* (National Archives and Records Administration, Office of the Federal Register) and whitehouse.gov.

deputy secretary, undersecretaries, and the like), plus a number of agencies. For example, the National Park Service is an agency within the Department of the Interior. The Drug Enforcement Administration is an agency within the Department of Justice.

Although there are organizational differences among the departments, each department generally follows a typical bureaucratic structure. The Department of Agriculture provides a model for how an executive department is organized (see Figure 13–4 on page 292).

One aspect of the secretary of agriculture's job is to carry out the president's agricultural policies. Another aspect is to promote and protect the department. The secretary spends time ensuring that Congress allocates enough money for the department to work effectively. The secretary also makes sure that constituents, or the people the department serves—farmers and major agricultural corporations—are happy. In general, the secretary tries to maintain or improve the status of the department with respect to all of the other departments and units of the federal bureaucracy.

TABLE 13-1

Executive Departments

Department (Year of Original Establishment)	Principal Duties	Selected Subagencies
State (1789)	Negotiates treaties; develops our foreign policy; protects citizens abroad.	Bureau of Diplomatic Security; Foreign Service; Bureau of Democracy, Human Rights, and Labor; Bureau of Consular Affairs (passports).
Treasury (1789)	Pays all federal bills; borrows money; collects federal taxes; mints coins and prints paper currency; supervises national banks.	Internal Revenue Service; U.S. Mint.
Defense (1789)*	Manages the armed forces (Army, Navy, Air Force, Marines); operates military bases.	National Security Agency; Joint Chiefs of Staff; Departments of the Air Force, Navy, Army; Defense Intelligence Agency; the service academies.
Justice (1789)†	Furnishes legal advice to the president; enforces federal criminal laws; supervises the federal corrections system (prisons).	Federal Bureau of Investigation; Drug Enforcement Administration; Bureau of Prisons; U.S. Marshals Service.
Interior (1849)	Supervises federally owned lands and parks; operates federal hydroelectric power facilities; supervises Native American affairs.	U.S. Fish and Wildlife Service; National Park Service; Bureau of Indian Affairs; Bureau of Land Management.
Agriculture (1889)	Provides assistance to farmers and ranchers; conducts research to improve agriculture; works to protect forests.	Natural Resources Conservation Service; Agricultural Research Service; Food Safety and Inspection Service; Federal Crop Insurance Corporation; Forest Service.
Commerce (1903)‡	Grants patents and trademarks; conducts national census; monitors the weather; protects the interests of businesses.	Bureau of the Census; Bureau of Economic Analysis; Minority Business Development Agency; Patent and Trademark Office; National Oceanic and Atmospheric Administration.
Labor (1903)‡	Administers federal labor laws; promotes the interests of workers.	Occupational Safety and Health Administration; Bureau of Labor Statistics; Labor-Management Standards Administration; Employment and Training Administration; Wage and Hour Division.

Continued

The secretary of agriculture is assisted by a deputy secretary and several assistant secretaries and undersecretaries, all of whom are nominated by the president and put into office with Senate approval. The secretary and assistant secretaries have staffs that help with all sorts of jobs, such as hiring new people and generating positive public relations for the Department of Agriculture.

13–2c Independent Executive Agencies

independent executive agency
A federal agency that is not located within a cabinet department.

Independent executive agencies are federal bureaucratic organizations that have a single function. They are independent in the sense that they are not located within a cabinet department. Rather, independent executive agency heads report directly to the president. A new federal independent executive agency can be created only through cooperation between the president and Congress.

The Creation of Independent Agencies

Prior to the twentieth century, the federal government did almost all of its work through the executive departments. In the twentieth century, in contrast, presidents began to ask for certain executive agencies to be kept separate, or independent, from existing departments. Today, there are more than two hundred independent executive agencies.

TABLE 13-1

Executive Departments—(Continued)

Department (Year of Original Establishment)	Principal Duties	Selected Subagencies
Health and Human Services (1953)§	Promotes public health; enforces pure food and drug laws; sponsors health-related research.	Food and Drug Administration; Centers for Disease Control and Prevention; National Institutes of Health; Administration for Children and Families; Centers for Medicare and Medicaid Services.
Housing and Urban Development (1965)	Deals with the nation's housing needs; develops and rehabilitates urban communities; oversees resale of mortgages.	Government National Mortgage Association; Office of Multifamily Housing Programs; Office of Single Family Housing; Office of Fair Housing and Equal Opportunity.
Transportation (1967)	Finances improvements in mass transit; develops and administers programs for highways, railroads, and aviation.	Federal Aviation Administration; Federal Highway Administration; National Highway Traffic Safety Administration; Federal Transit Administration.
Energy (1977)	Promotes the conservation of energy and resources; analyzes energy data; conducts research and development.	Office of Civilian Radioactive Waste Management; National Nuclear Security Administration; Energy Information Administration.
Education (1979)	Coordinates federal programs and policies for education; administers aid to education; promotes educational research.	Office of Special Education and Rehabilitation Services; Office of Elementary and Secondary Education; Office of Postsecondary Education; Office of Vocational and Adult Education.
Veterans Affairs (1989)	Promotes the welfare of veterans of the U.S. armed forces.	Veterans Health Administration; Veterans Benefits Administration; National Cemetery Administration.
Homeland Security (2002)	Works to prevent terrorist attacks within the United States, control America's borders, and minimize the damage from potential attacks and natural disasters.	U.S. Customs and Border Protection; U.S. Bureau of Citizenship and Immigration Services; U.S. Coast Guard; Secret Service; Federal Emergency Management Agency.

*Established in 1947 by merging the Department of War, created in 1789, and the Department of the Navy, created in 1798.
†Formerly the Office of the Attorney General; renamed and reorganized in 1870.
‡Formed in 1913 by splitting the Department of Commerce and Labor, which was created in 1903.
§Formerly the Department of Health, Education, and Welfare; renamed when the Department of Education was spun off in 1979.

The Danger of Partisan Politics Sometimes, agencies are kept independent because of the sensitive nature of their functions. But at other times, Congress creates independent agencies to protect them from **partisan politics**—politics in support of a particular party. The U.S. Commission on Civil Rights, which was created in 1957, is a case in point. Congress wanted to protect the work of the commission from the influences not only of Congress's own political interests but also of the president.

The Central Intelligence Agency (CIA), which was formed in 1947, is another good example. Both Congress and the president know that the intelligence activities of the CIA could be abused if it were not independent. Finally, the General Services Administration (GSA) was created as an independent executive agency in 1949 to provide services and office space for most federal agencies. To serve all parts of the government, the GSA has to be an independent agency.

Among the more than two hundred independent executive agencies, a few stand out in importance either because of the mission they were established to accomplish or because of their large size. We list selected independent executive agencies in Table 13–2 on the following page.

partisan politics Political actions or decisions that benefit a particular party.

FIGURE 13-4

The Organization
of the Department of Agriculture

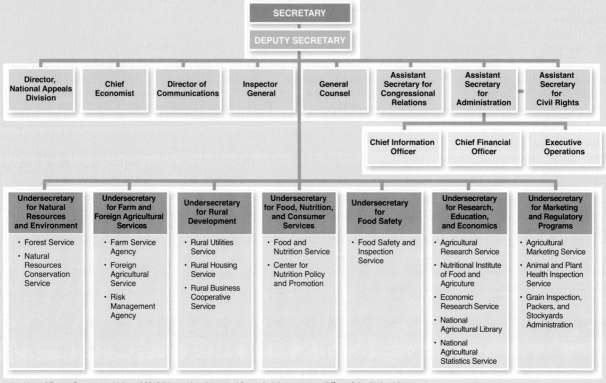

Source: *United States Government Manual 2013* (National Archives and Records Administration, Office of the Federal Register).

TABLE 13-2

Selected Independent Executive Agencies

Name	Date Formed	Principal Duties
Central Intelligence Agency (CIA)	1947	Gathers and analyzes political and military information about foreign countries so that the United States can improve its own political and military status; conducts covert operations outside the United States.
General Services Administration (GSA)	1949	Purchases and manages property of the federal government; acts as the business arm of the federal government, overseeing federal government spending projects; discovers overcharges in government programs.
Small Business Administration (SBA)	1953	Promotes the interests of small businesses; provides low-cost loans and management information to small businesses.
National Aeronautics and Space Administration (NASA)	1958	Is responsible for the U.S. space program, including building, testing, and operating space vehicles.
Environmental Protection Agency (EPA)	1970	Undertakes programs aimed at reducing air and water pollution; works with state and local agencies to fight environmental hazards.
Social Security Administration (SSA)*	1994	Manages the government's Social Security programs, including Retirement and Survivors Insurance, Disability Insurance, and Supplemental Security Income.

*Separated from the Department of Health and Human Services in 1994; originally established in 1946.

13–2d Independent Regulatory Agencies

An **independent regulatory agency** is responsible for a specific type of public policy. Its function is to create and implement rules that regulate private activity and protect the public interest in a particular sector of the economy. These agencies are sometimes called the "alphabet soup" of government because most of them are known in Washington by their initials.

One of the earliest independent regulatory agencies was the Interstate Commerce Commission (ICC), established in 1887. (This agency was abolished in 1995.) After the ICC was formed, other agencies were created to regulate aviation (the Civil Aeronautics Board, or CAB, which was abolished in 1985), communications (the Federal Communications Commission, or FCC), the stock market (the Securities and Exchange Commission, or SEC), and many other areas of business. Table 13–3 below lists some major independent regulatory agencies.

13–2e Government Corporations

Another form of federal bureaucratic organization is the **government corporation,** a business that is owned by the government. Government corporations are not exactly like corporations in which you buy stock and become a shareholder. The U.S. Postal Service (USPS) is a government corporation, for example, but it does not sell shares.

Government corporations are like private corporations in that they provide a service that could be handled by the private sector. They are also like private corporations in that they charge for their services, though sometimes they charge less than private-sector corporations do for similar services. Table 13–4 on the following page lists selected government corporations.

Facing Losses When a private business fails to make a profit, its shareholders have a problem. The value of the company may drop, in some instances to zero. If a small business loses money, its owners must either raise more capital or shut down the firm. If a government corporation runs at a loss, taxpayers may be forced to foot the bill.

The U.S. Postal Service is an example of this problem. In recent years, as Americans have increasingly relied on the Internet for communications, the volume of first-class mail had dropped considerably. As a result,

independent regulatory agency
A federal organization that is responsible for creating and implementing rules that regulate private activity and protect the public interest in a particular sector of the economy.

government corporation An agency of the government that is run as a business enterprise. Such agencies engage primarily in commercial activities, produce revenues, and require greater flexibility than most government agencies have.

TABLE 13–3

Selected Independent Regulatory Agencies

Name	Date Formed	Principal Duties
Federal Reserve System (Fed)	1913	Determines policy on interest rates, credit availability, and the money supply.
Federal Trade Commission (FTC)	1914	Works to prevent businesses from engaging in unfair trade practices and to stop the formation of business monopolies; protects consumers' rights.
Securities and Exchange Commission (SEC)	1934	Regulates the nation's stock exchanges, where shares of stock are bought and sold; requires full disclosure of the financial profiles of companies that wish to sell stocks and bonds to the public.
Federal Communications Commission (FCC)	1934	Regulates interstate and international communications by radio, television, wire, satellite, and cable.
National Labor Relations Board (NLRB)	1935	Protects employees' rights to join unions and to bargain collectively with employers; attempts to prevent unfair labor practices by both employers and unions.
Equal Employment Opportunity Commission (EEOC)	1964	Works to eliminate discrimination that is based on religion, gender, race, color, national origin, age, or disability; examines claims of discrimination.

TABLE 13-4

Selected Government Corporations

Name	Date Formed	Principal Duties
Tennessee Valley Authority (TVA)	1933	Operates a Tennessee River control system and generates power for a seven-state region; promotes the economic development of the Tennessee Valley; controls floods and promotes the navigability of the Tennessee River.
Federal Deposit Insurance Corporation (FDIC)	1933	Insures individuals' bank deposits up to $250,000 and oversees the business activities of banks.
National Railroad Passenger Corporation (Amtrak)	1970	Provides a national and intercity rail passenger service network; controls more than 23,000 miles of track with about 505 stations.
U.S. Postal Service (formed from the old U.S. Post Office department—the Post Office itself is older than the Constitution)	1971	Delivers mail throughout the United States and its territories. Is the largest government corporation.

the USPS has been losing money. (This in spite of the fact that parcel deliveries have gone up, also because of the Internet—specifically, as a result of online shopping.) Losses in 2012 amounted to $16 billion. In August 2012, the service defaulted on a monthly $5.5 billion payment due to the U.S. Treasury to finance retirees' health-care expenses. Since then, the USPS has cut costs dramatically, spending $4 billion less in 2013 than it did in 2012. Still, it lost $2.6 billion in the first half of 2013. Some observers claim that the service's real problem is that Congress has forced it to pre-fund retiree benefits in a way that no other business or government agency must do.

To solve the problem permanently, the USPS proposed to lay off additional employees, close rural post offices, reduce pension benefits, and even end Saturday delivery. Many of these steps require congressional approval, which was not forthcoming. The alternative would be direct federal subsidies to the service, which has been self-supporting since the early 1980s.

Intermediate Forms of Organization A number of intermediate forms of organization exist that fall between a government corporation and a private one. In some circumstances, the government can take control of a private corporation. When a company goes bankrupt, for example, it is subject to the supervision of a federal judge until it exits from bankruptcy or is liquidated. The government can also purchase stock in a private corporation. The government used this technique to funnel funds into major banks during the financial crisis that began in September 2008. In addition, the government can set up a corporation and sell stock to the public.

The Federal Home Loan Mortgage Corporation (Freddie Mac) and the Federal National Mortgage Association (Fannie Mae) are examples of stockholder-owned government-sponsored enterprises. Fannie Mae (founded in 1938) and Freddie Mac (created in 1970) buy, resell, and guarantee home mortgages. In September 2008, the government placed the two businesses into a conservatorship—effectively a bankruptcy overseen by the Federal Housing Finance Agency instead of a federal judge. The government also took an 80 percent share of the stock of each firm. Fannie Mae and Freddie Mac became examples of almost every possible way that the government can intervene in a private company.

FOR CRITICAL THINKING Some people have advocated selling off government corporations, such as the U.S. Postal Service, and turning them into truly private enterprises. *Would it be a good idea to "privatize" the U.S. Postal Service? Why or why not?*

13-3 How Bureaucrats Get Their Jobs

As already noted, federal bureaucrats holding top-level positions are appointed by the president and confirmed by the Senate. These bureaucrats include department and agency heads, their deputy and assistant secretaries, and the like. The list of positions that are

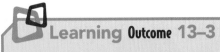

Learning Outcome 13–3

Describe how the federal civil service was established and how bureaucrats get their jobs.

filled by appointments is published after each presidential election in a document called *Policy and Supporting Positions.* The volume is more commonly known as the *Plum Book,* because the eight thousand jobs it summarizes are known as "political plums." Normally, these jobs go to those who supported the winning presidential candidate.

13–3a The Civil Service

The rank-and-file bureaucrats—the rest of the federal bureaucracy—are part of the **civil service** (nonmilitary employees of the government). They obtain their jobs through the Office of Personnel Management (OPM), an agency established by the Civil Service Reform Act of 1978. The OPM recruits, interviews, and tests potential government workers and determines who should be hired. The OPM makes recommendations to individual agencies as to which persons meet relevant standards (typically, the top three applicants for a position), and the agencies then generally decide which of the recommended individuals they will hire.

The 1978 act also created the Merit Systems Protection Board (MSPB) to oversee promotions, employees' rights, and other employment matters. The MSPB evaluates charges of wrongdoing, hears employee appeals from agency decisions, and can order corrective action against agencies and employees.

civil service Nonmilitary government employees.

13–3b Origins of the Merit System

The idea that the civil service should be based on a merit system dates back more than a century. The Civil Service Reform Act of 1883 established the principle of government employment on the basis of merit through open, competitive examinations.

Initially, only about 10 percent of federal employees were covered by the merit system. Today, more than 90 percent of the federal civil service is recruited on the basis of merit. Are public employees paid as well as workers in the private sector? For a discussion of this question, see this chapter's *Perception versus Reality* feature on the following page.

© LAWRENCE MIGDALE /SCIENCE SOURCE

FOR CRITICAL THINKING

When most private companies hire new employees, they don't use systems similar to those of the civil service. *Why is this so?*

13–4 Regulatory Agencies: Are They the Fourth Branch of Government?

In Chapter 2, we considered the system of checks and balances among the three branches of the U.S. government—executive, legislative, and judicial. Recent history, however, shows that it may be time to regard the regulatory agencies as a fourth

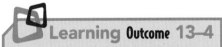

Learning Outcome 13–4

Explain how regulatory agencies make rules and how issue networks affect policymaking in government.

Perception versus Reality

Working for the Government at Low Pay

Not all parents jump for joy at the thought that their children might go to work for the government. In the United States, government work in general has never been considered the road to riches. Indeed, the common picture of government employment is quite negative.

THE PERCEPTION

It is often assumed that only individuals working in the private sector can hope to receive large paychecks. Top-level staff members in the executive branch of the federal government make much less than senior executives in the private sector. Although even rank-and-file workers in the public sector receive paid-for medical insurance and a generous retirement program, these benefits do not make up for the lower pay they earn.

THE REALITY

It can be difficult to determine just how the pay of government employees compares to pay in the private sector because this question is so politically loaded. Consider two studies that tried to compare state and local employees with private-sector workers doing similar jobs. A paper by a Boston College team concluded that state and local workers are paid 9.5 percent less than comparable workers in the private sector, although generous benefits reduce the gap to 4 percent. In contrast, an article by two U.S. Bureau of Labor Statistics (BLS) economists found that, on average, workers in state government have total compensation 3 to 10 percent greater than workers in the private sector, while in local government the gap is 10 to 19 percent.[3] Some experts believe that even the BLS study undercounts the value of government pensions.

Move now to the federal government. In 2012, many Republican candidates cited figures from the U.S. Bureau of Economic Analysis that showed federal government workers earning an average of $123,049 in wages and benefits, about twice the $61,051 in total compensation for the average private-sector worker. These figures came under criticism for flawed methodology, however.

For one thing, federal workers don't do the same kind of work as employees in the private sector. On average, federal workers are much better educated and more likely to be employed in jobs that are also well paid in the private sector.

The Congressional Budget Office, which has a reputation for impartiality, studied federal pay in 2012. It found that the federal government paid 16 percent more than the private sector for comparable jobs. Workers with only a high school education came out best, with 36 percent higher compensation than in the private sector. In contrast, employees with professional degrees actually received 18 percent less.[4] A final point: as of the beginning of 2014, the pay of federal workers had been frozen for four years.

BLOG ON You can find a variety of articles on the issue of government pay by searching on "state local government workers pay" and "federal workers overpaid."

branch of the government. Although the U.S. Constitution does not mention regulatory agencies, these agencies can and do make **legislative rules** that are as legally binding as laws passed by Congress. With such powers, regulatory agencies have an influence that rivals that of the president, Congress, and the courts. Indeed, most Americans do not realize how much of our "law" is created by regulatory agencies.

Regulatory agencies have been on the American political scene since the nineteenth century, but their golden age came during the regulatory explosion of the 1960s and 1970s. Congress itself could not have overseen the actual implementation of all of the laws that it was enacting at that time to control pollution and deal with other social problems. It therefore chose (and still chooses) to delegate to administrative agencies the tasks

legislative rule An administrative agency rule that carries the same weight as a statute enacted by a legislature.

involved in implementing its laws. By delegating some of its authority to an administrative agency, Congress can indirectly monitor a particular area in which it has passed legislation without becoming bogged down in the details relating to the enforcement of that legislation—details that are often best left to specialists.

13–4a Agency Creation

To create a federal administrative agency, Congress passes **enabling legislation,** which specifies the name, purpose, composition, and powers of the agency being created.

An Example: The FTC The Federal Trade Commission (FTC), for example, was created in 1914 by the Federal Trade Commission Act, as mentioned earlier. The act prohibits unfair and deceptive trade practices. The act also describes the procedures that the agency must follow to charge persons or organizations with violations of the act, and it provides for judicial review of agency orders.

Other portions of the act grant the agency powers to "make rules and regulations for the purpose of carrying out the Act," to conduct investigations of business practices, to obtain reports on business practices from interstate corporations, to investigate possible violations of federal antitrust statutes, to publish findings of its investigations, and to recommend new legislation.

Finally, the act empowers the FTC to hold trial-like hearings and to **adjudicate** (formally resolve) certain kinds of disputes that involve FTC regulations or federal antitrust laws. When adjudication takes place, within the FTC or any other regulatory agency, an administrative law judge (ALJ) conducts the hearing and, after weighing the evidence presented, issues an *order.* Unless it is overturned on appeal, the ALJ's order becomes final.

The Power of Regulatory Agencies Enabling legislation makes the regulatory agency a potent organization. For example, the Securities and Exchange Commission (SEC) imposes rules regarding the disclosures a company must make to those who purchase its new stock. Under its enforcement authority, the SEC also investigates and prosecutes alleged violations of these regulations. Finally, SEC judges decide whether its rules have been violated and, if so, what punishment should be imposed on the offender (although the judgment may be appealed to a federal court).

13–4b Rulemaking

A major function of a regulatory agency is **rulemaking**—the formulation of new regulations. The power that an agency has to make rules is conferred on it by Congress in the agency's enabling legislation.

For example, the Occupational Safety and Health Administration (OSHA) was authorized by the Occupational Safety and Health Act of 1970 to develop and issue rules governing safety in the workplace. Under this authority, OSHA has issued various safety standards, including rules to prevent the spread of certain diseases, such as acquired immune deficiency syndrome (AIDS). The rules specify various standards—on how contaminated instruments should be handled, for instance—with which health-care workers must comply.

> **enabling legislation** A law enacted by a legislature to establish an administrative agency. Enabling legislation normally specifies the name, purpose, composition, and powers of the agency being created.
>
> **adjudicate** To render a judicial decision. In administrative law, it is the process in which an administrative law judge hears and decides issues that arise when an agency charges a person or firm with violating a law or regulation enforced by the agency.
>
> **rulemaking** The process undertaken by an administrative agency when formally proposing, evaluating, and adopting a new regulation.

Requirements for Making Rules Agencies cannot just make a rule whenever they wish. Rather, they must follow certain procedural requirements, particularly those set forth in the Administrative Procedure Act of 1946. Agencies must also make sure that their rules are based on substantial evidence and are not "arbitrary and capricious." Therefore, before proposing a new rule, an agency may engage in extensive investigation to obtain data on the problem to be addressed by the rule. Based on this information, the agency may undertake a cost-benefit analysis of a new rule to determine whether its benefits outweigh its costs.

A Cost-Benefit Analysis As an example of cost-benefit analysis in rulemaking, consider the Clean Air Fine Particle Implementation Rule, issued by the Environmental Protection Agency (EPA) in 2007. The EPA estimated the costs of the regulation as $7.3 billion per year, with benefits ranging from $19 billion to $167 billion per year. The benefits largely consist of reductions in health-care costs and premature deaths—and, as these figures suggest, such calculations can be highly uncertain. Does the United States suffer from excessive regulation, as some have claimed? We examine that question in the *Join the Debate* feature on the following page.

13–4c Policymaking

Bureaucrats in federal agencies are expected to exhibit **neutral competency,** which means that they are supposed to apply their technical skills to their jobs without regard to political issues. In principle, they should not be swayed by the thought of personal or political gain. In reality, each independent agency and each executive department is interested in its own survival and expansion. All agencies and departments wish to retain or expand their functions and staffs. To do this, they must gain the goodwill of both the White House and Congress.

Support from Congress While the administrative agencies of the federal government are prohibited from directly lobbying Congress, departments and agencies have developed techniques to help them gain congressional support. Each organization maintains a congressional information office, which specializes in helping members of Congress by supplying any requested information and solving casework problems.

For example, if a member of the House of Representatives receives a complaint from a constituent that his Social Security payments are not arriving on time, that member of Congress may go to the Social Security Administration and ask that

something be done. Typically, requests from members of Congress receive immediate attention.

Iron Triangles Analysts have determined that one way to understand the bureaucracy's role in policymaking is to examine the **iron triangle,** which is a three-way alliance among legislators (members of Congress), bureaucrats, and interest groups. Presumably, the laws that are passed and the policies that are established benefit the interests of all three corners of the iron triangle, which is shown in Figure 13–5 on page 300. Iron triangles are well established in almost every part of the bureaucracy.

WHO BELONGS TO AN IRON TRIANGLE? As an example, consider agricultural policy. The Department of Agriculture consists of about 100,000 individuals working directly for the federal government and thousands of other individuals who work indirectly for the department as contractors, subcontractors, or consultants. Now think about the various interest groups and client groups that are concerned with what the bureaus and agencies in the Agriculture Department can do for them. These groups include the American Farm Bureau Federation, the National Milk Producers Federation, various regional citrus growers associations, and many others. Finally, in Congress two major committees are concerned with agriculture: the House Committee on Agriculture

neutral competency
The application of technical skills to jobs without regard to political issues.

iron triangle A three-way alliance among legislators, bureaucrats, and interest groups to make or preserve policies that benefit their respective interests.

LUKE SHARRETT/GETTY IMAGES

In Kentucky, workers from Mexico and Nicaragua hang tobacco to start the curing process. These farm workers are here legally under a federal program.

How Much Regulation Do We Need?

Many people believe that the financial crisis of 2008 and 2009 was caused by inadequate regulation of financial enterprises. As a result, these businesses took on far too much risk. It's not surprising, therefore, that Congress later imposed a large number of new regulations on the financial industry. Compliance will be costly.

In the distant past, there was very little government regulation of health care or other industries. One hundred years ago, drugs were not tested before they were put on the market. Physicians were licensed by the states, but that was about it.

Today, regulation is widespread. Estimates of its costs vary dramatically. According to the Office of Management and Budget (OMB), the annual cost of federal regulations lies between $62 billion and $73 billion, with total benefits of $153 billion to $806 billion. Others argue that the OMB's sums are not comprehensive. One study quoted by conservatives puts total costs at $1.75 trillion per year. Liberals do not find this figure credible—it puts the costs at 10 percent of the entire economy. Whatever the true costs are, the question remains: Are current levels of regulation appropriate?

Unbridled Capitalism Is Dead

The law of the capitalist jungle is what got us into the biggest financial crisis since the Great Depression. Investment banking firms created ever-riskier financial assets, which they sold to unsuspecting individuals and even to local governments as solid, gold-plated investments. In the mortgage industry, unscrupulous salespeople who earned big commissions tricked unsuspecting families into buying homes that were too expensive for their modest means. These problems were largely due to an absence of proper regulation.

Even with something as important as the prescription drugs that we take, the government is not giving us enough protection. Recently, despite its staff members' misgivings, the Food and Drug Administration allowed a drug named Avandia to hit the market. That drug turned out to have potential cardiac side effects, and no safety statement on the drug's label warned of them. We need more regulation to protect our lives and our pocketbooks.

Too Much of Anything Is Bad

While no one proposes that all regulation should be eliminated, many believe that the amount of regulation in effect today is too costly relative to the benefits received. We all want safer products, but the Consumer Product Safety Commission now requires that warning labels appear on even common products. A standard ladder has six hundred words of warning pasted on it, including a warning not to place it in front of a swinging door. What are we, idiots? Every toy has a warning that says, "Small parts may cause a choking risk." Parents don't know this?

Studies indicate that almost no one reads warning labels anymore because the warnings are either too obvious or too long. What happened to personal responsibility in America? The average American is no longer expected to use common sense about any of her or his purchases or activities. Regulation has its place, but it shouldn't control the entire life of a nation.

FOR CRITICAL ANALYSIS How much do you think you benefit from regulation in our economy? Give some examples.

and the Senate Committee on Agriculture, Nutrition, and Forestry.

The bureaucrats, interest groups, and legislators who make up this iron triangle cooperate to create mutually beneficial regulations and legislation. Because of the connections between agricultural interest groups and policymakers within the government, the agricultural industry has benefited greatly over the years from significant farm subsidies.

CONGRESS'S ROLE. The Department of Agriculture is headed by the secretary of agriculture, who is nominated by the president (and confirmed by the Senate). But that secretary cannot even buy a desk lamp if Congress does not approve the appropriations for the department's budget.

Within Congress, the responsibility for considering the Department of Agriculture's request for funding belongs first to the House and Senate appropriations

FIGURE 13-5

An Iron Triangle

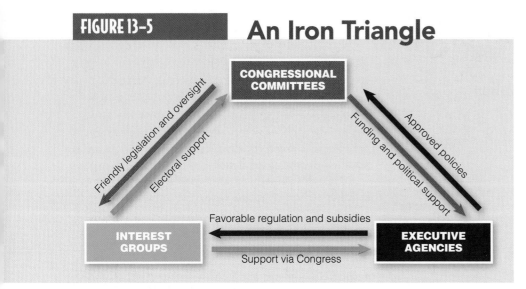

These experts have frequently served variously as interest group lobbyists and as public-sector staff members during their careers, creating a revolving-door effect. They often have strong opinions and interests regarding the direction of policy and are thus able to exert a great deal of influence on legislators and bureaucratic agencies.

The relationships among these experts, which are less structured than iron triangles, are often referred to as **issue networks.** Like iron triangles, issue networks are made up of people with similar policy concerns. Issue networks are less interdependent and unified than iron triangles, however, and often include more players, such as media outlets.[5] (See Figure 13-6 on the following page.)

A key characteristic of issue networks is that there can be more than one network in a given policy area. To take the example of the environment, one issue network tends to advocate greater environmental regulation, while another network opposes such regulations as undue burdens on businesses and landowners. In other words, competing interests often form rival issue networks that tend to limit each other's power.

committees and then to the agriculture subcommittees of the appropiations committees. The members of those committees, most of whom represent agricultural states, have been around a long time and have their own ideas about what is appropriate for the Agriculture Department's budget. They carefully scrutinize the ideas of the president and the secretary of agriculture.

THE INFLUENCE OF INTEREST GROUPS. The various interest groups—including producers of farm chemicals and farm machinery, agricultural cooperatives, grain dealers, and exporters—have vested interests in what the Department of Agriculture does and in what Congress lets the department do. Those interests are well represented by the lobbyists who crowd the halls of Congress. Many lobbyists have been working for agricultural interest groups for decades. They know the congressional committee members and Agriculture Department staff very well and meet with them routinely.

Issue Networks
The iron triangle relationship does not apply to all policy domains. When making

policy decisions on environmental and welfare issues, for example, many members of Congress and agency officials rely heavily on "experts." Legislators and agency heads tend to depend on their staff members for specialized knowledge of rules, regulations, and legislation.

issue networks Groups of individuals or organizations—which consist of legislators and legislative staff members, interest group leaders, bureaucrats, the media, scholars, and other experts—that support particular policy positions on a given issue.

FOR CRITICAL THINKING

Who—or what—can stop an iron triangle from absorbing ever-greater amounts of government resources?

13-5 Curbing Waste and Improving Efficiency

There is no doubt that our bureaucracy is costly. There is also little doubt that at times it can be wasteful and inefficient. The government has made many attempts to reduce waste, inefficiency, and wrongdoing. For example, federal and state governments have passed laws requiring more openness in government. Other laws encourage employees to report any waste and

FIGURE 13-6

Issue Network:
The Environment

Executive Departments and Agencies
- Environmental Protection Agency
- Agriculture Department
- Energy Department
- Department of the Interior
- National Oceanic and Atmospheric Admin.
- Bureau of Land Management
- Army Corps of Engineers

Key Congressional Committees
- **Senate**
  Appropriations, Energy and Natural Resources, Environment and Public Works, Finance, Commerce, Science, and Transportation
- **House of Representatives**
  Agriculture, Appropriations, Natural Resources, Transportation and Infrastructure

Selected Interest Groups
- **Environmental Groups**
  Environmental Defense, Friends of the Earth, National Audubon Society, Clean Water Action, National Wildlife Federation, The Ocean Conservancy, American Forests
- **Industry Groups**
  Citizens for a Sound Economy, Edison Electric Institute, U.S. Chamber of Commerce, National Food Processors Association, International Wood Products Association, National Mining Association, American Resort Development Association

Learning Outcome 13-5

Identify some of the ways in which the government has attempted to curb waste and improve efficiency in the bureaucracy.

wrongdoing that they observe.

13-5a Helping Out the Whistleblowers

The term **whistle-blower,** as applied to the federal bureaucracy, has a special meaning: it is someone who blows the whistle, or reports, on gross governmental inefficiency, illegal activities, or other wrongdoing. Whistleblowers often take their complaints to the press.

Laws Protecting Whistleblowers Federal employees may be reluctant to blow the whistle on their superiors for fear of reprisals. To encourage federal employees to report government wrongdoing, Congress has passed laws to protect whistleblowers. The Whistle-Blower Protection Act of 1989 authorized the Office of Special Counsel (OSC), an independent agency, to investigate complaints of reprisals against whistleblowers. Many federal agencies also have toll-free hotlines that employees can use to anonymously report bureaucratic waste and inappropriate behavior.

One set of laws encourages reports by making cash rewards to whistleblowers. Under four differ-

ent programs, if the government saves or retrieves a significant sum as a result of a tip-off, a percentage of the government's gain can be paid to the whistleblower. Under the False Claims Act, a private individual can even pursue a claim in court if the Justice Department fails to proceed.

Many such cases involve tax fraud by corporations and individuals, not government malfeasance. In September 2012, the government paid out the largest such reward ever—$104 million. The money went to a banker who blew the whistle on a Swiss bank that was helping U.S. citizens defraud the Internal Revenue Service. The whistleblower, however, also had to serve forty months in prison for his part in the fraud.

Whistleblowers Continue to Face Problems In spite of these laws, there is little evidence that whistleblowers are adequately protected against retaliation. According to a study conducted by the Government Accountability Office, 41 percent of the whistleblowers who turned to the OSC for protection during a recent three-year period reported that they were no longer employed by the agencies on which they blew the whistle. Indeed, given how difficult it is to fire a federal employee under normal circumstances, it is amazing how quickly most whistleblowers are "shown the door."

Many federal employees who have blown the whistle say that they would not do so again because it was so difficult to get help. Even when they did get help, they faced a stressful ordeal. Barack Obama's supporters expected that, as president, he would protect whistleblowers. Many of them were disappointed, however, when the new administration took an unusually harsh line regarding information disclosures.

> **whistleblower** In the context of government employment, someone who "blows the whistle" (reports to authorities or the press) on gross governmental inefficiency, illegal action, or other wrongdoing.

Indeed, some believe that Obama's record on whistle-blowers is the worst of any president's. By late 2013, the Obama administration had charged seven individuals with violations of the Espionage Act of 1917. Before Obama took office, only three persons had ever been charged under that act. Some of those charged may have endangered national security. In other cases, though, the true crime may simply have been embarrassing the government.

13–5b Improving Efficiency and Getting Results

The Government Performance and Results Act, which went into effect in 1997, has forced the federal government to change the way it does business. Since 1997, almost every agency (except the intelligence agencies) has had to describe its goals and identify methods for evaluating how well those goals are met. A goal can be as broad as lowering the number of highway traffic deaths or as narrow as reducing the number of times an agency's phone rings before it is answered.

As one example, consider the National Oceanic and Atmospheric Adminstration (NOAA). It has improved the effectiveness of its short-term forecasting services, particularly in issuing warnings of tornadoes. The warning time has increased from seven to fifteen minutes. This may not seem significant, but it provides additional critical time for those in the path of a tornado.

President Obama's contribution to the attempt to improve government effectiveness was to create a chief performance officer. This individual reports directly to the president and works with other economic officials in an attempt to increase efficiency and eliminate waste in government.

13–5c Another Approach— Pay-for-Performance Plans

privatization The transfer of the task of providing services traditionally provided by government to the private sector.

For some time, the private sector has used pay-for-performance plans as a means to increase employee productivity and efficiency. About one-third of the major firms in

> ## "The only thing that saves us from the bureaucracy
> is its inefficiency."
>
> ~ EUGENE J. MCCARTHY ~
> U.S. SENATOR FROM MINNESOTA
> 1959–1971

this country use some kind of alternative pay system, such as team-based pay, skill-based pay, profit-sharing plans, or individual bonuses. In contrast, workers for the federal government traditionally have received fixed salaries. Promotions and salary increases are given on the basis of seniority, not output.

The federal government has been experimenting with pay-for-performance systems. For example, the U.S. Postal Service has implemented the Economic Value Added Variable Pay Program, which ties bonuses to performance. As part of a five-year test of a new pay system, three thousand scientists working in Air Force laboratories received salaries based on results.

13–5d Privatization

Another idea for reforming government bureaucracies is **privatization,** which means turning over certain types of government work to the private sector. Privatization can take place by contracting out (outsourcing) work to the private sector or by *managed competition,* in which the task of providing public services is opened up to competition. In managed competition, both the relevant government agency and private firms can compete for the work.

State and local governments have been experimenting with privatization for some time. Almost all of the states have privatized at least a few of their services, and some states, including California, Colorado, and Florida, have privatized more than one hundred activities formerly undertaken by government. In Scottsdale, Arizona, the city contracts for fire protection. In Baltimore, Maryland, nine of the city's schools are outsourced to private entities.

13–5e Government in the Sunshine

The last four decades of the twentieth century saw a trend toward more openness in government. The theory was that because Americans pay for the government, they own it—and they have a right to know what the government is doing with the taxpayers' dollars.

In response to pressure for more government openness and disclosure, Congress passed the Freedom of Information Act in 1966. This act requires federal agencies to disclose any information in agency files, with some exceptions, to any persons requesting it.

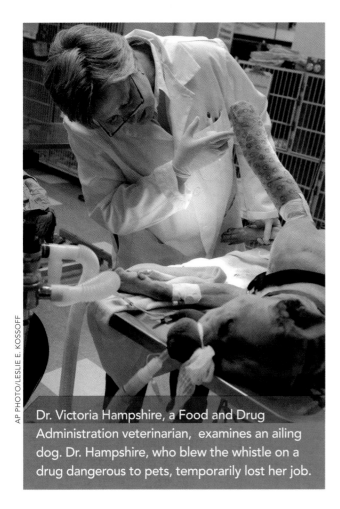

Dr. Victoria Hampshire, a Food and Drug Administration veterinarian, examines an ailing dog. Dr. Hampshire, who blew the whistle on a drug dangerous to pets, temporarily lost her job.

AP PHOTO/LESLIE E. KOSSOFF

Since the 1970s, *sunshine laws*, which require government meetings to be open to the public, have been enacted at all levels of American government.

The trend toward greater openness in government came to an abrupt halt on September 11, 2001. In the wake of the terrorist attacks on the World Trade Center and the Pentagon, the government began tightening its grip on information. In the months following the attacks, hundreds of thousands of documents were removed from government Web sites. No longer can the public access plans of nuclear power plants, descriptions of airline security violations, or maps of pipeline routes. Agencies were instructed to be more cautious about releasing information in their files and were given new guidelines on what should be considered public information.

13–5f Government Online

Increasingly, government agencies have attempted to improve their effectiveness and efficiency by making use of the Internet. One method has been to make information available to the public online. This may appear to run counter to the information restrictions imposed following 9/11, but much government information is not relevant to national security issues.

Under the Obama administration, for example, it is possible to get annual data on immigration, airline flight delays, and job-related deaths that name employers. The *Federal Register*, a record of government notices, can now be read online.

Local governments have posted such information as real estate records, restaurant health inspection scores, and the geographic locations of crimes. Some parts of the government have resisted the trend toward openness, however. Lawyers and other interested parties must often pay to obtain information held by the courts.

Filing Forms Online   Another way that government agencies are using the Internet to improve services is to let citizens file forms and apply for services online. For example, if you change your address, you may be able to request an update sticker for your driver's license by visiting a state Web site. Also, you may be able to apply for unemployment benefits without visiting an unemployment office, and receive payments through a government-issued debit card. The federal government distributes payments for Medicare, tax refunds, and a variety of other programs automatically and electronically.

E-Fraud   One danger of automatic payments is the possibility of fraud. This problem is not new. Criminals have long attempted to defraud the government—and the taxpayer—by filing false income tax forms or by making improper claims following natural disasters. The Internet, however, has made it possible for crooks to "game the system" more easily. Claims can be processed without examination by an actual person. Such faulty payment systems demonstrate that bureaucrats still have a role to play, even in the high-tech era.

FOR CRITICAL THINKING   In the name of security, some states have gone so far as to bar access to emergency evacuation plans. *Why might these states have done this? What problems could result if citizens lack access to this information?*

AMERICA AT
ODDS The Bureaucracy

Although the story is often told about red tape and wasteful spending generated by our bureaucracy, all in all, the U.S. bureaucracy compares favorably with bureaucracies in other countries. Citizens typically overestimate the amount of "government waste" by very large margins. Still, the U.S. government faces the same problems with its bureaucracy—sluggishness, inefficiency, and even incompetence—that large businesses and organizations throughout the country face. Americans are at odds over a number of issues relating to the bureaucracy, including the following:

- Can new financial regulations eliminate the danger of a catastrophe such as the one we experienced in September 2008—or will clever financiers find ways around any new regulations?

- Do the recent health-care reforms provide vital protection to the citizenry—or are they an example of excessive government meddling in the private sector?

- Are government employees overpaid—or is their pay appropriate, given their responsibilities?

- Is the outsourcing of government services a way to improve efficiency—or does it mostly serve to hide the true cost and scope of government?

- Should our leaders focus on openness and transparency in government—or are such measures dangerous during the war on terrorism?

STUDY TOOLS

Ready to study?

- **Review** what you've read with the quiz below.
- Check your answers on the **Chapter in Review** card at the back of the book.
- For any questions you miss, read the corresponding **Learning Outcome** section again to prepare for class and your exam.
- Rip out and study the **Chapter in Review** card (at the back of the book).

Fill-In

Learning Outcome 13–1

1. All in all, the three levels of government employ about _____ percent of the civilian labor force.

Learning Outcome 13–2

2. The head of each executive department is known as the _____, except for the Department of Justice, which is headed by the attorney general.

3. The _____ Department grants patents and trademarks, conducts the national census, and monitors the weather.

Learning Outcome 13–3

4. Federal bureaucrats holding top-level positions are appointed by the _____ and confirmed by the _____.

5. The Civil Service Reform Act of 1883 established the principle of government employment on the basis of _____.

Learning Outcome 13–4

6. To create a federal administrative agency, Congress passes _____, which specifies the name, purpose, composition, and powers of the agency being created.

7. An iron triangle is _____.

Learning Outcome 13–5

8. A whistleblower is someone who _____.

Multiple Choice

Learning Outcome 13–1

9. The amount spent on defense, together with veterans' benefits, accounts for about ____ percent of federal spending.
   a. 5   b. 22   c. 49

Learning Outcome 13–2

10. The principal duties of the ____ Department include negotiating treaties, developing foreign policy, and protecting citizens abroad.
    a. State
    b. Homeland Security
    c. Defense

11. The independent executive agencies
    a. are businesses owned by the government.
    b. create and implement rules that regulate private activity and protect the public interest in a particular sector of the economy.
    c. are federal bureaucratic organizations that have a single function.

12. The ____ is a government corporation.
    a. General Services Administration
    b. U.S. Postal Service
    c. Securities and Exchange Commission

Learning Outcome 13–3

13. The document called *Policy and Supporting Positions* (the *Plum Book*) summarizes about ____ jobs that are filled by appointments after each presidential election.
    a. six hundred
    b. one thousand
    c. eight thousand

Learning Outcome 13–4

14. The process undertaken by an administrative agency when formally proposing, evaluating, and adopting a new regulation is called
    a. adjudication.
    b. rulemaking.
    c. neutral competency.

Learning Outcome 13–5

15. "Sunshine laws" require government
    a. meetings to be open to the public.
    b. agencies to outsource work to the private sector.
    c. agencies to let citizens file forms and apply for services online.

14

The Judiciary

JEWEL SAMAD/AFP/GETTY IMAGES

Learning Outcomes

The **Learning Outcomes** labeled 1 through 6 are designed to help improve your understanding of the chapter. After reading this chapter, you should be able to:

14–1 Summarize the origins of the American legal system and the basic sources of American law.

14–2 Delineate the structure of the federal court system.

14–3 Say how federal judges are appointed.

14–4 Explain how the federal courts make policy.

14–5 Describe the role of ideology and judicial philosophies in judicial decision making.

14–6 Identify some of the criticisms of the federal courts and some of the checks on the power of the courts.

Remember to visit page 329 for additional Study Tools

AMERICA AT
ODDS
Are There Prisoners We Must Detain without Trial?

After the September 11, 2001, attacks in the United States, the George W. Bush administration interned hundreds of suspected terrorists at the Guantánamo Bay Naval Base in Cuba. Most of them were foreign fighters captured during the war in Afghanistan, a war initiated just after 9/11. All prisoners were labeled *unlawful enemy combatants* and therefore were afforded neither the legal protections guaranteed to prisoners of war (POWs) under the Geneva Conventions nor the protections required under the conventions for dealing with civilians who commit crimes. Indeed, the Bush administration established the prison at Guantánamo in the belief that the facility would lie outside the reach of American law.

President Barack Obama promised to close the Guantánamo prison, but he failed to do so. Obama furthermore stated that it may be necessary to hold some of the detainees more or less forever without bringing them to trial. It's true that, as of 2013, 84 Guantánamo prisoners had been cleared for release—yet the government freed only 2 of them in the first eight months of that year. A hundred of the prison's 166 detainees staged a hunger strike and were force-fed by authorities.

We Release Terrorists at the Civilized World's Peril

Look back over U.S. history. Federal judges never heard cases brought by Confederate prisoners of war held during the Civil War. During World War II, no civilian courts reviewed the cases of the thousands of German prisoners housed in the United States. At the end of that war, the Supreme Court agreed that enemy aliens held by the United States in Europe and Asia had no right to appear in front of an American judge.

Today, if the president deems that certain terrorist prisoners are too dangerous to be tried and perhaps freed, that is the president's prerogative. After all, under our Constitution, the president has wartime decision-making powers. We also have evidence that at least thirty detainees released from the Guantánamo prison rejoined terrorist organizations and have been responsible for the deaths of innocent people overseas.

Who will be responsible for the deaths caused by terrorists if they cannot be convicted and we then let them go? Terrorists do not deserve the civil liberties we offer to fellow Americans. If we cannot be sure that a trial will result in a conviction, we must not let these people stand trial at all.

Indefinite Detention Is Unconstitutional and Damages Our Image Abroad

It is wrong to hold persons deemed "dangerous" by the government indefinitely. How can we know that the government is correct in its allegations against these people? We have learned that some of the Afghans held at Guantánamo and elsewhere were arrested due to false accusations resulting from long-standing feuds between rival families. U.S. officials were reluctant to release these innocents because it meant admitting that the officials had made a mistake.

The way our government has handled prisoners of war in the past is irrelevant. Traditional POWs were captured during battle, on the field, in uniform. The potential for capturing a POW by mistake was minimal. In contrast, the danger of error when arresting an alleged unlawful enemy combatant is enormous. Most of the Guantánamo detainees were arrested nowhere near a battlefield. How can we know whether such detainees are truly dangerous if there is no trial? The world contains thousands of potential terrorists who might harm us. We cannot protect ourselves from them by keeping the few people we now have in custody locked up forever.

Where do you stand?

1. Could Congress fashion a law providing a procedure to determine when an alleged terrorist should never be let out of prison? Could such a law withstand Supreme Court review? Why or why not?
2. Why is it easier to falsely arrest a purported terrorist than a regular military soldier?

Explore this issue online

- One of the strongest voices in favor of indefinite detention has been John Yoo, who served in President Bush's Justice Department when the detention policies were crafted. You'll find some of Yoo's articles if you enter "john yoo wall street journal" into a search engine.
- One of the many bloggers who oppose indefinite detentions is Digby. You can find his work by searching on "digby terrorism."

Introduction

As you read in this chapter's opening *America at Odds* feature, the question of whether certain alleged terrorists should be imprisoned indefinitely without trial has elicited a great deal of controversy. Also controversial is the policymaking function of the United States Supreme Court. After all, when the Court renders an opinion on how the Constitution is to be interpreted, it is, necessarily, making policy on a national level.

To examine the nature of this controversy, we first need to explain how the **judiciary** (the courts) functions in this country. We begin by looking at the origins and sources of American law. We then describe the federal court system, at the apex of which is the United States Supreme Court, and consider various issues relating to the courts.

14–1 The Origins and Sources of American Law

Learning Outcome 14–1

Summarize the origins of the American legal system and the basic sources of American law.

The American colonists brought with them the legal system that had developed in England over hundreds of years. Thus, to understand how the American legal system operates, we need to go back in time to the early English courts and the traditions they established.

14–1a The Common Law Tradition

After the Normans conquered England in 1066, William the Conqueror and his successors began the process of unifying the country under their rule. One of the methods they used was the establishment of the "king's courts," or *curiae regis*. Before the Norman Conquest, disputes had been settled according to the local legal customs in various regions of the country. The law developed in the king's courts, however, applied to the country as a whole. What evolved in these courts was the beginning of the **common law**— the body of general rules that was applied throughout the entire English realm.

The Rule of Precedent The early English courts developed the common law rules from the principles underlying judges' decisions in actual legal controversies. Judges attempted to be consistent, and whenever possible, they based their decisions on the principles applied in earlier cases. They also considered new kinds of cases with the awareness that their decisions would make new law. Each interpretation became part of the law on the subject and served as a legal **precedent**—that is, a decision that furnished an example or authority for deciding subsequent cases involving identical or similar legal issues and facts.

Stare Decisis The practice of deciding new cases with reference to former decisions, or precedents, eventually became a cornerstone of the English and American judicial systems. The practice formed a doctrine called **stare decisis** ("to stand on decided cases").

Under this doctrine, judges are obligated to follow the precedents established in their jurisdictions. For example, if the Supreme Court of Georgia holds that a state law requiring candidates for state office to pass drug tests is unconstitutional, that decision will control the outcome of future cases on that issue brought before the state courts in Georgia.

Similarly, a decision made on a given issue by the United States Supreme Court (the nation's highest court) is binding on all inferior (lower) courts. For example, if the Georgia case on drug testing is appealed to the United States Supreme Court and the

> **"It is confidence** in the men and women who administer the judicial system, **that is the true backbone of the rule of law."**
>
> ~ JOHN PAUL STEVENS ~
> ASSOCIATE JUSTICE OF THE
> UNITED STATES SUPREME COURT
> 1975–2010

Court agrees that the Georgia law is unconstitutional, the high court's ruling will be binding on *all* courts in the United States. In other words, similar drug-testing laws in other states will be invalid and unenforceable.

Departures from Precedent Sometimes a court will depart from the rule of precedent if it decides that a precedent is simply incorrect or that technological or social changes have rendered the precedent inapplicable. Cases that overturn precedent often receive a great deal of publicity.

For example, in 1954, in *Brown v. Board of Education of Topeka*,[1] the United States Supreme Court expressly overturned precedent when it concluded that separate educational facilities for African Americans, which had been upheld as constitutional in many earlier cases under the "separate-but-equal" doctrine[2] (see Chapter 5), were inherently unequal and violated the equal protection clause. The Supreme Court's departure from precedent in *Brown* received a tremendous amount of publicity as people began to realize the political and social ramifications of this change in the law.

More recently, the Supreme Court departed from precedent in its 2010 ruling *Citizens United v. Federal Election Commission*.[3] In this decision, the Court determined that the government may not ban political spending by corporations in elections when the spending is undertaken independently of the campaigns of individual candidates. (The ruling implicitly covers unions and nonprofit groups as well.) The Court's verdict overturned two precedents that had upheld restrictions on corporate spending: *Austin v. Michigan Chamber of Commerce* (1990)[4] and *McConnell v. Federal Election Commission* (2003).[5]

> **"IT IS BETTER,**
> so the Fourth Amendment teaches, **THAT THE GUILTY SOMETIMES GO FREE**
> than that citizens be subject to easy arrest."
>
> ~ WILLIAM O. DOUGLAS ~
> ASSOCIATE JUSTICE OF THE
> UNITED STATES SUPREME COURT
> 1939–1975

14–1b Primary Sources of American Law

In any governmental system, the primary function of the courts is to interpret and apply the law. In the United States, the courts interpret and apply several sources of law when deciding cases. We look here only at the **primary sources of law**—that is, sources that *establish* the law—and the relative priority of these sources when particular laws come into conflict.

Constitutional Law The U.S. government and each of the fifty states have separate written constitutions that set forth the general organization, powers, and limits of their respective governments. **Constitutional law** consists of the rights and duties set forth in these constitutions.

The U.S. Constitution is the supreme law of the land. As such, it is the basis of all law in the United States. Any law that violates the Constitution is invalid and unenforceable. Because of the paramount importance of the U.S. Constitution in the American legal system, the complete text of the Constitution is found in Appendix B.

The Tenth Amendment to the U.S. Constitution reserves to the states and to the people all powers not granted to the federal government. Each state in the union has its own constitution. Unless they conflict with the U.S. Constitution or a federal law, state constitutions are supreme within the borders of their respective states.

Statutory Law Statutes enacted by legislative bodies at any level of government make up another source of law, which is generally referred to as **statutory law.** Federal statutes—laws enacted by the U.S. Congress—apply to all of the states. State statutes—laws enacted by state legislatures—apply

SOCIAL MEDIA In Politics

Unlike the other branches of government, the judiciary tends to take a dim view of social media because jurors in trials use social media to obtain information they are not supposed to have. Still, you can follow one of several services that regularly tweet new rulings by the United States Supreme Court. One of the most informative of these is Supreme Court USA (@iSupremeCourt.)

primary source of law A source of law that establishes the law. Primary sources of law include constitutions, statutes, administrative agency rules and regulations, and decisions rendered by the courts.

constitutional law Law based on the U.S. Constitution and the constitutions of the various states.

statutory law The body of law enacted by legislatures (as opposed to constitutional law, administrative law, or case law).

only within the state that enacted the laws. Any state statute that conflicts with the U.S. Constitution, with federal laws enacted by Congress, or with the state's constitution will be deemed invalid if challenged in court and will not be enforced.

Statutory law also includes the ordinances (such as local zoning or housing-construction laws) passed by cities and counties. None of these may violate the U.S. Constitution, the relevant state constitution, or any existing federal or state laws.

Administrative Law Another important source of American law consists of **administrative law**—the rules, regulations, orders, and decisions of administrative agencies. As you read in Chapter 13, at the federal level Congress creates executive agencies, such as the Food and Drug Administration and the Environmental Protection Agency, to perform specific functions. Typically, when Congress establishes an agency, it authorizes the agency to create rules that have the force of law and to enforce those rules by bringing legal actions against violators.

Rules issued by various government agencies now affect nearly every aspect of our lives. For example, almost all of a business's operations, including the firm's capital structure and financing, its hiring and firing procedures, its relations with employees and unions, and the way it manufactures and markets its products, are subject to government regulation.

Government agencies exist at the state and local levels as well. States commonly create agencies that parallel federal agencies. Just as federal statutes take precedence over conflicting state statutes, federal agency regulations take precedence over conflicting state regulations.

Case Law As is evident from the earlier discussion of the common law tradition, another basic source of American law consists of the rules of law announced in court decisions, or **case law.** These rules of law include interpretations of constitutional provisions, of statutes enacted by legislatures, and of regulations issued by administrative agencies.

Thus, even though a legislature passes a law to govern a certain area, how that law is interpreted and applied depends on the courts. The importance of case law, or *judge-made law,* is one of the distinguishing characteristics of the common law tradition.

14–1c Civil Law and Criminal Law

All of the sources of law just discussed can be classified in other ways as well. One of the most significant classification systems divides all law into two categories: civil law and criminal law.

Civil law spells out the duties that individuals in society owe to other persons or to their governments, excluding the duty not to commit crimes. Typically, in a civil case, a private party sues another private party (although the government can also sue a party for a civil law violation). The object of a civil lawsuit is to make the defendant—the person being sued—comply with a legal duty (such as a contractual promise) or pay money damages for failing to comply with that duty.

Criminal law, in contrast, has to do with wrongs committed against the public as a whole. Criminal acts are prohibited by local, state, or federal government statutes. Thus, criminal defendants are prosecuted by public officials, such as a district attorney (D.A.), on behalf of the government, not by their victims or other private parties.

In a criminal case, the government seeks to impose a penalty (usually a fine and/or imprisonment) on a person who has violated a criminal law. For example, when someone robs a convenience store, that person has committed a crime and, if caught and proved guilty, will usually spend time in prison.

> ## "Our Constitution is colorblind, and neither knows nor tolerates classes among citizens."
>
> ~ JOHN MARSHALL HARLAN ~
> ASSOCIATE JUSTICE OF THE
> UNITED STATES SUPREME COURT
> 1877–1911

administrative law The body of law created by administrative agencies (in the form of rules, regulations, orders, and decisions) in order to carry out their duties and responsibilities.

case law The rules of law announced in court decisions. Case law includes the aggregate of reported cases that interpret judicial precedents, statutes, regulations, and constitutional provisions.

civil law The branch of law that spells out the duties that individuals in society owe to other persons or to their governments, excluding the duty not to commit crimes.

criminal law The branch of law that defines and governs actions that constitute crimes. Generally, criminal law has to do with wrongful actions committed against society for which society demands redress.

14–1d Basic Judicial Requirements

A court cannot decide just any issue at any time. Before a court can hear and decide a case, specific requirements must be met. To a certain extent, these requirements act as restraints on the judiciary because they limit the types of cases that courts can hear and decide. Courts also have procedural requirements that judges must follow.

Jurisdiction In Latin, *juris* means "law," and *diction* means "to speak." Therefore, **jurisdiction** literally refers to the power "to speak the law." Jurisdiction applies either to the geographic area in which a court has the right and power to decide cases, or to the right and power of a court to decide matters concerning certain persons, types of property, or subjects. Before any court can hear a case, it must have jurisdiction over the person against whom the suit is brought, the property involved in the suit, and the subject matter.

THE JURISDICTION OF STATE COURTS. A state trial court usually has jurisdictional authority over the residents of a particular area of the state, such as a county or district. (A **trial court** is, as the term implies, a court in which trials are held and testimony is taken.) A state's highest court (often called the *state supreme court*)[6] has jurisdictional authority over all residents within the state. In some cases, if an individual has committed an offense such as injuring someone in an automobile accident or selling defective goods within the state, the court can exercise jurisdiction even if the individual is a resident of another state.

State courts can also exercise jurisdiction over those who do business within the state. A New York company that distributes its products in California, for example, can be sued by a California resident in a California state court.

FEDERAL COURT JURISDICTION. Because the federal government is a government of limited powers, the jurisdiction of the federal courts is limited. Article III, Section 2, of the Constitution states that the federal courts can exercise jurisdiction over all cases "arising under this Constitution, the Laws of the United States, and Treaties made, or which shall be made, under their Authority." Whenever a case involves a claim based, at least in part, on the U.S. Constitution, a treaty, or a federal law, a **federal question** arises. Any lawsuit involving a federal question can originate in a federal court.

Federal courts can also exercise jurisdiction over cases involving **diversity of citizenship.** Such cases may arise when the parties in a lawsuit live in

jurisdiction The authority of a court to hear and decide a particular case.

trial court A court in which trials are held and testimony is taken.

federal question A question that pertains to the U.S. Constitution, acts of Congress, or treaties. A federal question provides a basis for federal court jurisdiction.

diversity of citizenship A basis for federal court jurisdiction over a lawsuit that arises when (1) the parties in the lawsuit live in different states or when one of the parties is a foreign government or a foreign citizen, and (2) the amount in controversy is more than $75,000.

When a criminal case fails, sometimes a victim may file a civil lawsuit instead. Here, the attorney for a New York hotel maid is pursuing a civil suit against French diplomat Dominique Strauss-Kahn. It was alleged that Strauss-Kahn sexually assaulted the woman.

STAN HONDA/AFP/GETTY IMAGES

different states or when one of the parties is a foreign government or a foreign citizen. Before a federal court can take jurisdiction in a diversity case, the amount in controversy must be more than $75,000. (Congress raised the limit to $75,000 in 1996. In 1789, the sum was $500.)

One interesting question concerning jurisdiction is the extent to which U.S. courts have the authority to resolve issues that arise outside our borders. We examine that question in *The Rest of the World* feature on page 314.

Standing to Sue To bring a lawsuit before a court, a person must have **standing to sue,** or a sufficient "stake" in the matter to justify bringing a suit. Thus, the party bringing the suit must have suffered a harm or been threatened with a harm by the action at issue, and the issue must be justiciable. A **justiciable controversy** is one that is real and substantial, as opposed to hypothetical or academic.

The requirement of standing to sue clearly limits the issues that can be decided by the courts. Furthermore, both state and federal governments can specify by law when an individual or group has standing to sue. For example, the federal government will not allow a taxpayer to sue the Department of Defense for spending tax dollars wastefully.

standing to sue
The requirement that an individual must have a sufficient stake in a controversy before he or she can bring a lawsuit. The party bringing the suit must demonstrate that he or she has either been harmed or been threatened with a harm.

justiciable contro-versy A controversy that is not hypothetical or academic but real and substantial; a requirement that must be satisfied before a court will hear a case. *Justiciable* is pronounced jus-*tish*-a-bul.

contempt of court
A ruling that a person has disobeyed a court order or has shown disrespect to the court or to a judicial proceeding.

Court Procedures
Both the federal and the state courts have established procedural rules that apply in all cases. These procedures are designed to protect the rights and interests of the parties, ensure that the litigation proceeds in a fair and orderly manner, and identify the issues that must be decided by the court—thus saving court time and costs. Different procedural rules apply in criminal and civil cases. Generally, criminal procedural rules attempt to ensure that defendants are not deprived of their constitutional rights.

Parties involved in civil or criminal cases must comply with court procedural rules or risk being held in **contempt of court.** A party who is held in contempt of court can be fined, taken into custody, or both. A court must take care to ensure that the parties—and the court itself—comply with procedural requirements. Procedural errors often serve as grounds for a mistrial or for appealing the court's decision to a higher tribunal.

FOR CRITICAL THINKING

Why does national law—even administrative law established by a federal agency—overrule conflicting law that the people of a state have written into their state constitution?

14–2 The Federal Court System

The federal court system is a three-tiered model consisting of U.S. district courts (trial courts), U.S. courts of appeals, and the United States Supreme Court. Figure 14–1 on the following page shows the organization of the federal court system.

Learning Outcome 14–2

Delineate the structure of the federal court system.

Bear in mind that the federal courts constitute only one of the fifty-two court systems in the United States. Each of the fifty states has its own court system, as does the District of Columbia. No two state court systems are exactly the same. In general, though, the states have different levels, or tiers, of courts, just as the federal system does.

Normally, state courts deal with questions of state law, and the decisions of a state's highest court on matters of state law are normally final. If a federal question is involved, however, a decision of a state supreme court may be appealed within the federal court system. We will discuss the federal court system in the pages that follow.

14–2a U.S. District and Specialized Courts

On the lowest tier of the federal court system are the U.S. district courts, or federal trial courts—the courts in which cases involving federal laws begin. The cases in these courts are decided by a judge or a jury. There

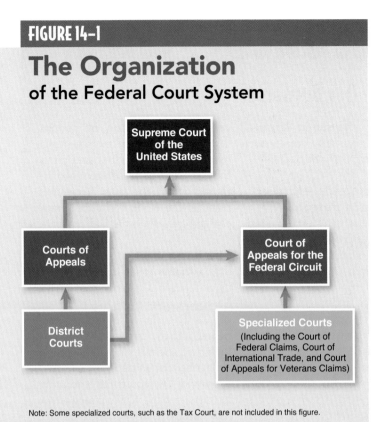

FIGURE 14-1

The Organization
of the Federal Court System

Supreme Court of the United States

Courts of Appeals

Court of Appeals for the Federal Circuit

District Courts

Specialized Courts
(Including the Court of Federal Claims, Court of International Trade, and Court of Appeals for Veterans Claims)

Note: Some specialized courts, such as the Tax Court, are not included in this figure.

is at least one federal district court in every state, and there is one in the District of Columbia. The number of judicial districts varies over time, primarily owing to population changes and corresponding caseloads. Currently, there are ninety-four judicial districts. Figure 14–2 on page 315 shows their geographic boundaries.

The federal system also includes other trial courts, such as the Court of International Trade and others shown in Figure 14–1. These courts have limited, or specialized, subject-matter jurisdiction—that is, they can exercise authority over only certain kinds of cases.

One specialized court has recently received exceptional scrutiny—the Foreign Intelligence Surveillance Court (FISC). This court was initially created to issue search warrants against suspected foreign spies inside the United States. The Patriot Act of 2001 greatly expanded its powers. The FISC almost never rejects a warrant request. It meets in secret and releases no information on individual cases.

More controversially, the court does not report the legal interpretations under which it issues its rulings. In 2013, revelations of large-scale surveillance by the National Security Agency (NSA) raised questions about the FISC's practices. (As mentioned in Chapter 13, NSA actions must be approved by the

FISC.) Some legal experts doubted that the FISC's decisions could be squared with the Fourth Amendment to the U.S. Constitution, which bars unreasonable searches.

14–2b U.S. Courts of Appeals

On the middle tier of the federal court system are the U.S. courts of appeals. Courts of appeals, or **appellate courts,** do not hear evidence or testimony. Rather, an appellate court reviews the transcript of the trial court's proceedings, other records relating to the case, and attorneys' arguments as to why the trial court's decision should or should not stand.

In contrast to a trial court, where normally a single judge presides, an appellate court consists of a panel of three or more judges. The task of the appellate court is to determine whether the trial court erred in applying the law to the facts and issues involved in a particular case.

There are thirteen federal courts of appeals in the United States. The courts of appeals for twelve of the circuits, including the Court of Appeals for the D.C. Circuit, hear appeals from the U.S. district courts located within their respective judicial circuits (see Figure 14–2).

Decisions made by federal administrative agencies may be reviewed either by a district court or the court of appeals, depending on the agency. The Court of Appeals for the Federal Circuit has national jurisdiction over certain types of cases, such as those concerning patent law and some claims against the national (federal) government.

The decisions of the federal appellate courts may be appealed to the United States Supreme Court. If a decision is not appealed, or if the high court declines to review the case, the appellate court's decision is final.

14–2c The United States Supreme Court

The highest level of the three-tiered model of the federal court system is the United States Supreme Court. According to Article III of the U.S. Constitution, there is only one national Supreme

appellate court A court having appellate jurisdiction. An appellate court normally does not hear evidence or testimony but reviews the transcript of the trial court's proceedings, other records relating to the case, and attorneys' arguments as to why the trial court's decision should or should not stand.

Can American Courts Reach outside Our Borders?

For almost two centuries, the Alien Tort Statute (ATS) of 1789 lay dormant. In 1979, however, a federal court of appeals decided that a Paraguayan citizen, then living in America, could use the statute to sue a Paraguayan policeman for torture committed in Paraguay. Fifteen years later, a federal court let a group of Burmese nationals sue a California oil company accused of participating in a scheme of forced labor, torture, and rape by the Burmese Army during the construction of a pipeline.

More than one hundred fifty lawsuits have been brought against American and foreign corporations under the ATS. These companies have been accused of violating international law—often through human rights abuses or environmental destruction. The question of whether foreign nationals should have the ability to sue in America for actions purportedly committed abroad, however, is controversial.

A Recent Example—*Kiobel v. Royal Dutch Petroleum*

In 2013, the Supreme Court provided the most recent precedent concerning overseas jurisdiction. The Royal Dutch Petroleum Company—which is not a U.S. firm—had engaged in oil exploration and production in Nigeria. Some local residents had conducted demonstrations alleging that these activities resulted in environmental disasters. The Nigerian government violently suppressed the demonstrations. Some of the protesters, now living in the United States, sued under the ATS.

The Court found for the oil company. It pointed out that U.S. law does not rule the world. The ATS "covers actions by aliens for violations of the law of nations, but does not imply extraterritorial reach." The Court further stated that the ATS was not passed to make the United States the most hospitable place in the world for enforcement of international norms.[7]

The Long Arm of the Law

Still, extraterritorial jurisdiction has its defenders. Consider that in the European Union, which is made up of twenty-eight countries, a European company can be sued at home for aiding and abetting human rights violations committed anywhere in the world. Our courts have no problem applying the ATS to piracy on the high seas. Why not also enforce such treaties as the Convention against Torture, the third Geneva Convention, and the International Convention for the Protection of All Persons from Forced Disappearance?

FOR CRITICAL ANALYSIS If the federal judiciary can exercise extraterritorial jurisdiction, can the judicial systems of other countries try American citizens living in the United States? Discuss.

Court, but Congress is empowered to create additional ("inferior") courts as it deems necessary. The inferior courts that Congress has created include the second tier in our model—the U.S. courts of appeals—as well as the district courts and any other courts of limited, or specialized, jurisdiction.

The United States Supreme Court consists of nine justices—a chief justice and eight associate justices—although that number is not mandated by the Constitution. The Supreme Court has original, or trial, jurisdiction only in unusual instances (set forth in Article III, Section 2). In other words, only rarely does a case originate at the Supreme Court level. Most of the Court's work is as an appellate court. The Supreme Court has appellate authority over cases decided by the U.S. courts of appeals, as well as over some cases decided in the state courts when federal questions are at issue.

writ of *certiorari* An order from a higher court asking a lower court for the record of a case. *Certiorari* is pronounced sur-shee-uh-*rah*-ree.

The Writ of *Certiorari* To bring a case before the Supreme Court, a party may request that the Court issue a **writ of *certiorari*,** often called "cert." The writ of *certiorari* is an order that the Supreme Court issues to a lower court requesting the latter to send it the record of the case in question.

Parties can petition the Supreme Court to issue a writ of *certiorari*, but whether the Court will do so is entirely within its discretion. The Court will not issue

FIGURE 14-2

U.S. Courts of Appeals
and U.S. District Courts

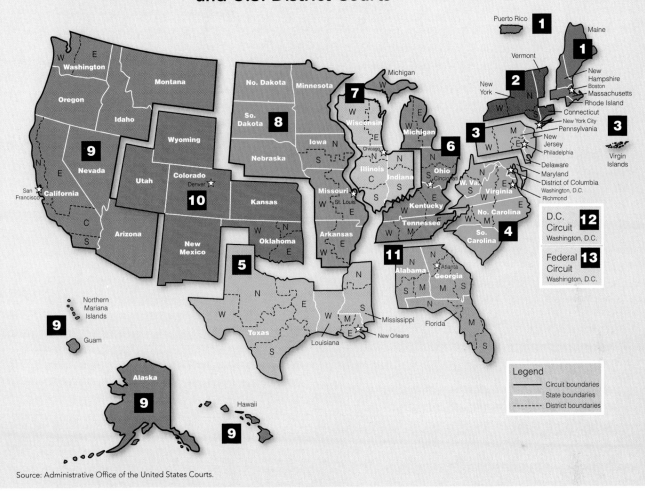

Source: Administrative Office of the United States Courts.

a writ unless at least four of the nine justices approve. In no instance is the Court required to issue a writ of *certiorari*.[8]

Most petitions for writs of *certiorari* are denied. A denial is not a decision on the merits of a case, nor does it indicate that the Court agrees with a lower court's opinion. The denial of a writ has no value as a precedent. A denial simply means that the decision of the lower court remains the law within that court's jurisdiction.

Which Cases Reach the Supreme Court?

There is no absolute right to appeal to the United States Supreme Court. Although thousands of cases are filed with the Supreme Court each year, on average the Court hears fewer than one hundred. As Figure 14–3 on the following page shows, the number of cases heard by the Court each year has declined significantly since the 1980s. In large part, this has occurred because the Court has raised its standards for accepting cases in recent years.

Typically, the Court grants petitions for cases that raise important policy issues that need to be addressed. In its 2012–2013 term, for example, the Court heard cases involving such issues as the following:

- Whether it is possible to patent a naturally occurring DNA sequence. (The Court ruled that it is not.)[9]

- Whether public college admissions programs can continue to use affirmative action policies to promote diversity. (The Court found that affirmative action is still acceptable if it is tightly controlled.)[10]

- Whether, under the Voting Rights Act of 1965, certain state and local governments are still required to "pre-clear" changes to voting procedures and districts with the federal government. (The Court held that the formulas determining which localities

FIGURE 14-3

The Number of
Supreme Court Opinions

The number of Supreme Court opinions peaked at 151 in the Court's 1982 term, declined more or less steadily through 1995, and then leveled off. During the 2012 term (ending in June 2013), the Court issued 75 opinions.

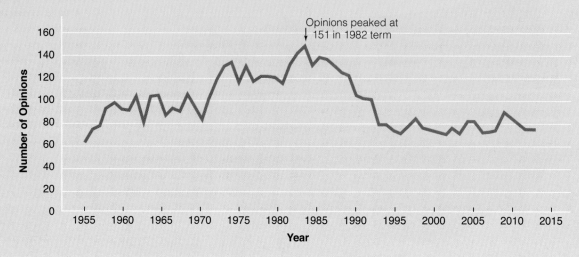

needed pre-clearance were obsolete. Congress can restore pre-clearance if it adopts new formulas.)[11]

- Whether the federal government can refuse to recognize same-sex marriages authorized by the states. (The Court ruled that it may not.)[12]

If the lower courts have rendered conflicting opinions on an important issue, the Supreme Court may review one or more cases involving that issue to define the law on the matter. For example, in 2010 and 2011, various federal appellate courts issued conflicting opinions as to whether it is constitutional to require citizens to purchase health-care insurance, as provided by the health-care reforms enacted in 2010. The conflicting rulings were eventually resolved by the Court in *National Federation of Independent Business v. Sebelius*.[13]

Supreme Court Opinions
Like other appellate courts, the United States Supreme Court normally does not hear any evidence. The Court's decision in a particular case is based on the written record of the case and the written arguments (legal briefs) that the attorneys submit. The attorneys also present **oral arguments**—spoken arguments presented in person rather than on paper—to the Court.

REACHING AN OPINION. After considering all this information, the justices discuss the case in **conference.** The conference is strictly private—only the justices are allowed in the room.

When the Court has reached a decision, the chief justice, if in the majority, assigns the task of writing the Court's **opinion** to one of the justices. When the chief justice is not in the majority, the most senior justice vot-

oral argument A spoken argument presented to a judge in person by an attorney on behalf of her or his client.

conference In regard to the Supreme Court, a private meeting of the justices in which they present their arguments concerning a case under consideration.

opinion A written statement by a court expressing the reasons for its decision in a case.

> **"AS NIGHTFALL DOESN'T COME AT ONCE, NEITHER DOES OPPRESSION.**
> In both instances, . . . we must be aware of change in the air, however slight, lest we become unwitting victims of the darkness."
> ~ WILLIAM O. DOUGLAS ~
> ASSOCIATE JUSTICE OF THE
> UNITED STATES SUPREME COURT
> 1939–1975

ing with the majority assigns the writing of the Court's opinion. The opinion outlines the reasons for the Court's decision, the rules of law that apply, and the judgment.

CONCURRING AND DISSENTING OPINIONS. Often, one or more justices who agree with the Court's decision do so for reasons different from those outlined in the majority opinion. These justices may write **concurring opinions,** setting forth their own legal reasoning on the issue. Frequently, one or more justices disagree with the Court's conclusion. These justices may write **dissenting opinions,** outlining the reasons they feel the majority erred in arriving at its decision.

Although a dissenting opinion does not affect the outcome of the case before the Court, it may be important later. In a subsequent case concerning the same issue, a jurist or attorney may use the legal reasoning in the dissenting opinion as the basis for an argument to reverse the previous decision and establish a new precedent.

Some people believe that the Supreme Court should accept more cases and thereby resolve more issues. Others contend that such a move would result in less well-thought-out opinions. *Who do you think has the better argument, and why?*

14–3 Federal Judicial Appointments

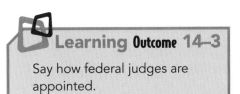

Learning Outcome 14–3

Say how federal judges are appointed.

Unlike state court judges, who are often elected, all federal judges are appointed. Article II, Section 2, of the Constitution authorizes the president to appoint the justices of the Supreme Court with the advice and consent of the Senate. Laws enacted by Congress provide that the same procedure is to be used for appointing judges to the lower federal courts as well. Does the practice of appointing judges yield better results than elections—or vice versa? We examine that question in this chapter's *Join the Debate* feature on page 319.

Federal judges receive lifetime appointments (because under Article III of the Constitution they "hold their Offices during good Behaviour"). Federal judges

may be removed from office through the impeachment process, but such proceedings are extremely rare and are usually undertaken only if a judge engages in blatantly illegal conduct, such as bribery. In the history of this nation, only fifteen federal judges have been impeached, and only eleven left office due to a conviction or resignation. Normally, federal judges serve until they resign, retire, or die.

Although the Constitution sets no specific qualifications for those who serve on the Supreme Court, those who have done so share one characteristic: all have been attorneys. The backgrounds of the Supreme Court justices have been far from typical of the characteristics of the American public as a whole. Table 14–1 on the following page summarizes the backgrounds of all of the 112 United States Supreme Court justices to 2014.

14–3a The Nomination Process

The president receives suggestions and recommendations as to potential nominees for judicial positions from various sources, including the Justice Department, senators, other judges, the candidates themselves, state political leaders, bar associations, and other interest groups. After selecting a nominee, the president submits her or his name to the Senate for approval. The Senate Judiciary Committee then holds hearings and makes its recommendation to the Senate, where it takes a majority vote to confirm the nomination.

Senatorial Courtesy When judges are nominated to the district courts (and, to a lesser extent, the U.S. courts of appeals), a senator of the president's political party from the state where there is a vacancy traditionally has been allowed to veto the president's choice. This practice is known as **senatorial courtesy.** At times, senatorial courtesy even permits senators from the opposing party to veto presidential choices. Because of senatorial courtesy, home-state senators of the president's party may be able to influence the choice of the nominee.

concurring opinion A statement written by a judge or justice who agrees (concurs) with the court's decision, but for reasons different from those in the majority opinion.

dissenting opinion A statement written by a judge or justice who disagrees with the majority opinion.

senatorial courtesy A practice that allows a senator of the president's party to veto the president's nominee to a federal court judgeship within the senator's state.

TABLE 14–1

Backgrounds of United States Supreme Court Justices to 2014

	Number of Justices (112 = Total)
Occupational Position before Appointment	
Private legal practice	25
State judgeship	21
Federal judgeship	31
U.S. attorney general	7
Deputy or assistant U.S. attorney general	2
U.S. solicitor general	3
U.S. senator	6
U.S. representative	2
State governor	3
Federal executive post	9
Other	3
Religious Affiliation	
Protestant	83
Roman Catholic	14
Jewish	7
Unitarian	7
No religious affiliation	1
Age on Appointment	
Under 40	5
41–50	33
51–60	60
61–70	14
Political Party Affiliation	
Federalist (to 1835)	13
Jeffersonian Republican (to 1828)	7
Whig (to 1861)	1
Democrat	46
Republican	44
Independent	1
Education	
College graduate	96
Not a college graduate	16
Gender	
Male	108
Female	4
Race	
White (non-Hispanic)	109
African American	2
Hispanic	1

Sources: *Congressional Quarterly's Guide to the U.S. Supreme Court* (Washington, D.C.: Congressional Quarterly Press, 1997); and authors' updates.

Partisanship It should come as no surprise that partisanship plays a significant role in the president's selection of nominees to the federal bench, particularly to the Supreme Court, the crown jewel of the federal judiciary. Traditionally, presidents have attempted to strengthen their legacies by appointing federal judges with political and philosophical views similar to their own. In the history of the Supreme Court, fewer than 13 percent of the justices nominated by a president have been from an opposing political party.

That said, presidents have often discovered that the justices they appointed took very different positions than expected. President Dwight D. Eisenhower (1953–1961), for example, had no idea when he appointed Chief Justice Earl Warren that Warren would seek to overturn the system of racial segregation. The Court accomplished this goal through rulings such as *Brown v. Board of Education* (see Chapter 5).[14]

Courts of Appeals Appointments to the U.S. courts of appeals can also have a lasting impact. Recall that these courts occupy the level just below the Supreme Court in the federal court system. Also recall that the decisions rendered by these courts—about 60,000 per year—are final unless overturned by the Supreme Court. Given that the Supreme Court renders opinions in fewer than one hundred cases a year, the decisions of the federal appellate courts have a wide-reaching effect on American society.

For example, a decision interpreting the federal Constitution by the U.S. Court of Appeals for the Ninth Circuit, if not overruled by the Supreme Court, establishes a precedent that will be followed in the states of Alaska, Arizona, California, Hawaii, Idaho, Montana, Nevada, Oregon, and Washington.

14–3b Confirmation or Rejection by the Senate

The president's nominations are not always confirmed. In fact, almost 20 percent of presidential nominations for the Supreme Court have been either rejected or not acted on by the Senate. The process of nominating and confirming federal judges, especially Supreme Court justices, often involves political debate and controversy. Many bitter battles over Supreme Court appointments have ensued when the Senate and the president have disagreed on political issues.

From 1893 until 1968, the Senate rejected only three Court nominees. From 1968 through 1986,

JOIN THE DEBATE

Should the People Elect Judges?

The founders of the American republic were concerned that too great a degree of popular control over the government could lead to "mob rule," and so they sought to insulate various institutions from direct popular elections. Federal judges, in particular, were to be appointed and serve for life. In contrast, in many states, all judges are popularly elected.

From time to time, judges are defeated at the polls. The most common way to defeat a judge is to accuse that official of being "soft on crime." Some people believe that despite the long prison sentences common in recent years, the judicial system is still too friendly to criminals. Others believe that elections tempt judges to cut corners on civil liberties. Should state judges be named through appointment? Or should the states rely on popular election?

The People Should Rule

Those who favor electing judges do not believe that judges can be insulated from politics. Governors, who often do the appointing when judges aren't elected, are highly political creatures. They tend to appoint supporters of their own party. If politics is going to play a role in judicial selection, then the people ought to have their say directly. Let the voters decide whether a judge is tough enough on crime or too tough on business. We admit ordinary people into the judicial process through juries, and

judges should respond to public opinion as well. Officials who do not have to win a popular election may become remote from the people. Living in upscale neighborhoods, they will never experience what it is like to walk home at night fearing for their safety. Instead, they can end up living in a legal never-never land where abstractions matter more than the real world. It takes elections to give us the kinds of judges that we really want.

The Courts Must Be Insulated from Popular Pressure

Many opponents of judicial elections believe that they allow too much opportunity for popular panics and prejudices to influence the process. Popular "lock 'em up" attitudes toward criminals do not lead to an optimum strategy for crime reduction. Rather, we need to study what works and what doesn't. In some states, "get tough" policies have led to absurd cases of individuals serving life sentences for trivial offenses. The last thing we need is to place additional pressure on judges by threatening them with removal.

Any move toward greater use of elections would bring with it a further problem—the corrupting influence of campaign contributions. Several states that use judicial elections are famous for their harsh sentences and enthusiasm for the death penalty. Judges in these states are also conspicuously friendly toward the moneyed interests that helped get them elected.

FOR CRITICAL ANALYSIS If judges must raise campaign contributions, what kinds of people would be most likely to contribute? Why?

however, two presidential nominees to the highest court were rejected, and two more nominations, both by President Ronald Reagan, failed in 1987. The most significant of these nominees was Robert Bork, who faced hostile questioning about his views on the Constitution during the confirmation hearings. The Bork hearings are often considered to be a turning point after which confirmation hearings became much more contentious.

One of President George H. W. Bush's nominees to the Supreme Court—Clarence Thomas—was also the subject of considerable controversy. The nation watched on television as Anita Hill, a former aide,

leveled charges of sexual harassment at Thomas, who nevertheless was confirmed.

George W. Bush's Appointments During George W. Bush's second term, Chief Justice William Rehnquist died, and Sandra Day O'Connor, the Court's first woman justice, retired. These events allowed Bush to nominate John G. Roberts, Jr., to replace Rehnquist and Samuel A. Alito, Jr., to replace O'Connor. Both nominations were confirmed by the Senate with relatively little difficulty. The appointment of Alito, in particular, changed the character of the Court, because he was distinctly more conservative than O'Connor.

Sonia Sotomayor became the first Latina on the Supreme Court when she was confirmed by the Senate in 2009.

JOSE CABEZAS/AFP/GETTY IMAGES

Obama's Nominees   In May 2009, as a result of a judicial retirement, President Barack Obama named Sonia Sotomayor to the Court. Sotomayor had served for more than a decade as a judge of the U.S. Court of Appeals for the Second Circuit and was the first Hispanic American ever nominated to the Supreme Court.

A second retirement gave Obama an additional chance to pick a nominee, in May 2010. He chose Elena Kagan, his solicitor general. At her confirmation hearings, several Republicans seized on an incident that had occurred when Kagan was dean of Harvard Law School. In line with Harvard policy, Kagan placed restrictions on military recruiters. The restrictions were in response to the military's "don't ask, don't tell" policy, which prevented lesbians and gay men from serving openly. Still, Kagan was confirmed. It was a sign of the increased political polarization in the Senate that neither Sotomayor nor Kagan received more than a handful of votes from Republican senators.

FOR CRITICAL THINKING

In recent years, senators have increasingly made use of the filibuster to delay or prevent the approval of judicial nominees. *Is this a legitimate tactic or an example of partisan excess? Explain.*

14-4 The Courts as Policymakers

In the United States, judges and justices play a major role in government. Unlike judges in some other countries, U.S. judges have the power to decide on the constitutionality of laws or actions undertaken by the other branches of government.

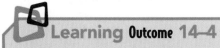

Learning Outcome 14-4

Explain how the federal courts make policy.

Clearly, the function of the courts is to interpret and apply the law, not to make law—that is the function of the legislative branch of government. Yet judges can and do "make law." Indeed, they cannot avoid making law in some cases, because the law does not always provide clear answers to questions that come before the courts.

14-4a The Issue of Broad Language

The text of the U.S. Constitution is set forth in broad terms. When a court interprets a constitutional provision and applies that interpretation to a specific set of circumstances, the court is essentially "making the law" on that issue. Examples of how the courts, and especially the United States Supreme Court, make law abound.

Consider privacy rights, which we discussed in Chapter 4. Nothing in the Constitution or its amendments specifically states that we have a right to privacy. Yet the Supreme Court, through various decisions, has established such a right by deciding that it is implied by several constitutional amendments. The Court has also held that this right to privacy includes a number of specific rights, such as the right to have an abortion.

Statutory provisions and other legal rules also tend to be expressed in general terms, and the courts must decide how those general provisions and rules apply to specific cases. The Americans with Disabilities Act of 1990 is an example. The act requires employers to reasonably accommodate the needs of employees with disabilities. But the act does not say exactly what employers must do to "reasonably accommodate" such persons. Thus, the courts must decide, on a case-by-case basis, what this phrase means.

Additionally, in some cases there is no relevant law or precedent to follow. In recent years, for example, courts have been struggling with new kinds of legal issues stemming from new communications technologies, including the Internet. Until legislative bod-

As Chief Justice John G. Roberts, Jr., looks on, Justice Elena Kagan signs the Oaths of Office.

STEVE PETTEWAY/COLLECTION OF THE SUPREME COURT OF JUSTICE VIA GETTY IMAGES

ies enact laws governing these issues, it is up to the courts to fashion the law that will apply—and thus make policy.

14–4b The Impact of Court Decisions

As already mentioned, how the courts interpret particular laws can have a widespread impact on society. For example, in May 2008, the California Supreme Court ruled that limiting marriage to opposite-sex couples violated the state constitution. California became the second state, after Massachusetts, to allow same-sex marriages. In November 2008, however, California voters passed Proposition 8, a state constitutional amendment to ban same-sex marriages. In May 2009, the California Supreme Court affirmed Proposition 8—although same-sex marriages contracted from June to November 2008 remained valid.

In August 2010, a U.S. district court found that Proposition 8, by revoking existing marriage rights, violated the Fourteenth Amendment to the U.S. Constitution.[15] Proponents of Proposition 8 appealed the verdict to the Ninth Circuit Court of Appeals. In February 2012, the appeals court sided with the district court against Proposition 8.[16] While the Ninth District's jurisdiction covers nine western states, the ruling in this case applied only to California, because a California law was in question.

Decisions rendered by the United States Supreme Court, of course, have a broader impact. For example, as mentioned earlier, the Supreme Court ruled in 2013 that the federal government must recognize same-sex marriages authorized by individual states. This decision affected couples in thirteen states, plus the District of Columbia.

At the same time, the Court heard California's Proposition 8 case, which had been appealed after the circuit court decision mentioned earlier. Some hoped that the result might be the legalization of same-sex marriages everywhere. The Court's decision, however, was limited to California. The Court found that those who had appealed had lacked standing to sue. Therefore, the Court issued no ruling, and the district court's original ruling was allowed to stand.[17] By declining to act, in other words, the Court allowed same-sex marriages in California.

When the Supreme Court interprets laws that have national effect, it establishes national policy. If the Court deems that a law passed by Congress or a state legislature violates the Constitution, for example, that law will be void and unenforceable in any court within the United States.

14–4c The Power of Judicial Review

Recall from Chapter 2 that the U.S. Constitution divides government powers among the executive, legislative, and judicial branches. This division of powers is part of our system of checks and balances. Essentially, the founders gave each branch of government the constitutional authority to check the other two branches. The federal judiciary can exercise a check on the actions of either of the other branches through its power of **judicial review.**

The Constitution does not actually mention judicial review. Rather, the Supreme Court claimed the power for itself in *Marbury v. Madison.*[18] In that case, which was decided by the Court in 1803, Chief Justice John Marshall held that a provision of a 1789 law affecting the Supreme

judicial review The power of the courts to decide on the constitutionality of legislative enactments and of actions taken by the executive branch.

Court's jurisdiction violated the Constitution and was thus void. Marshall declared, "It is emphatically the province and duty of the judicial department [the courts] to say what the law is. . . . If two laws conflict with each other, the courts must decide on the operation of each. . . . [I]f a law be in opposition to the constitution . . . the court must determine which of these conflicting rules governs the case. This is the very essence of judicial duty."

Most constitutional scholars believe that the framers intended that the federal courts should have the power of judicial review. In *Federalist Paper* No. 78, Alexander Hamilton clearly espoused the doctrine. Hamilton stressed the importance of the "complete independence" of federal judges and their special duty to "invalidate all acts contrary to the manifest tenor of the Constitution." Without judicial review by impartial courts, there would be nothing to ensure that the other branches of government stayed within constitutional limits when exercising their powers, and "all the reservations of particular rights or privileges would amount to nothing." Chief Justice Marshall shared Hamilton's views and adopted Hamilton's reasoning in *Marbury v. Madison*.

14–4d Judicial Activism versus Judicial Restraint

As already noted, making policy is not the primary function of the federal courts. Yet it is unavoidable that courts do, in fact, influence or even establish policy when they interpret and apply the law. Further, the power of judicial review gives the courts, and particularly the Supreme Court, an important policymaking tool. When the Supreme Court upholds or invalidates a state or federal statute, the consequences for the nation can be profound.

One issue that is often debated is how the federal courts should wield their policymaking power, particularly the power of judicial review. Often, this debate is couched in terms of judicial activism versus judicial restraint.

Activist versus Restraintist Justices The terms *judicial activism* and *judicial restraint* do not have precise meanings. Generally, however, an activist judge or justice believes that the courts should actively use their powers to check the legislative and executive branches to ensure that they do not exceed their authority. A restraintist judge or justice, in contrast, generally assumes that the courts should defer to the

decisions of the legislative and executive branches. After all, members of Congress and the president are elected by the people, whereas federal court judges are not. In other words, the courts should not thwart the implementation of legislative acts unless those acts are clearly unconstitutional.

Political Ideology and Judicial Activism/ Restraint One of the Supreme Court's most activist eras occurred during the period from 1953 to 1969 under the leadership of Chief Justice Earl Warren. The Warren Court propelled the civil rights movement forward by holding, among other things, that laws permitting racial segregation violated the equal protection clause (see Chapter 5).

Because of the activism of the Warren Court, the term *judicial activism* has often been linked with liberalism. Indeed, many liberals are in favor of an activist federal judiciary because they believe that the judiciary can "right" the "wrongs" that result from unfair laws or from "antiquated" legislation at the state and local levels. Neither judicial activism nor judicial restraint is necessarily linked to a particular political ideology, however. In fact, many observers claim that today's Supreme Court is often activist on behalf of a conservative agenda.

FOR CRITICAL THINKING

If a judge rules that it is unconstitutional for a state to ban same-sex marriage, is this judicial activism? Why or why not?

14–5 Ideology and the Courts

The policymaking role of the courts gives rise to an important question: To what extent do ideology and personal policy preferences affect judicial

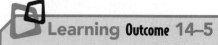

Learning Outcome 14–5

Describe the role of ideology and judicial philosophies in judicial decision making.

decision making? Numerous scholars have attempted to answer this question, especially with respect to Supreme Court justices.

14-5a Ideology and Supreme Court Decisions

Few doubt that ideology affects judicial decision making, although, of course, other factors play a role as well. Certainly, there are numerous examples of ideology affecting Supreme Court decisions. As new justices replace old ones and new ideological alignments are formed, the Court's decisions are affected. Yet many scholars argue that there is no real evidence that personal preferences influence Supreme Court decisions to an *unacceptable* extent.

Keep in mind that judicial decision making, particularly at the Supreme Court level, can be very complex. When deciding cases, the Supreme Court often must consider any number of sources of law, including constitutions, statutes, and administrative agency regulations—as well as cases interpreting relevant portions of those sources. At times, the Court may also take demographic data, public opinion, foreign laws, and other factors into account. How much weight is given to each of these sources or factors will vary from justice to justice. After all, reasoning of any kind, including judicial reasoning, does not take place in a vacuum.

It is only natural that a justice's life experiences, personal biases, and intellectual abilities and predispositions will touch on the reasoning process. Nevertheless, it is expected that when reviewing a case, a Supreme Court justice does not start out with a conclusion (such as "I don't like this particular law that Congress passed") and then look for legal sources to support that conclusion.

14-5b Ideology and the Supreme Court

In contrast to the liberal Supreme Court under Earl Warren, today's Court is generally conservative. The Court began its rightward shift after President Ronald Reagan (1981–1989) appointed conservative William Rehnquist as chief justice in 1986, and the Court moved further to the right as other conservative appointments to the bench were made by Reagan and George H. W. Bush (1989–1993).

The Roberts Court Many Supreme Court scholars believe that the appointments of John Roberts (as chief justice) and especially Samuel Alito (as associate justice) caused the Court to drift even further to the right.[19] Certainly, the five conservative justices on the bench during the Roberts Court's first five terms voted together and cast the deciding votes in numerous cases. The remaining justices held liberal to moderate views and often formed an opposing bloc.

A notable change in the Court occurred when Alito replaced retiring justice Sandra Day O'Connor. O'Connor had often been the "swing" vote on the Court, sometimes voting with the liberal bloc and at other times siding with the conservatives.

On the Roberts Court, the swing voter is usually Justice Anthony Kennedy, who is generally more conservative in his views than O'Connor was. Although Justice Kennedy dislikes being described as a swing voter, he often decides the outcome of a case. In the 2012–2013 term, for example, Kennedy was in the majority in 91 percent of all cases, substantially more than any other justice.

President Obama's naming of Justices Elena Kagan and Sonia Sotomayor to the Court did not change its ideological balance. Both women joined the liberal bloc, but the men they replaced had been liberal as well.

The Supreme Court Today In recent years, the nature of the Court's conservatism has come into sharper focus. It is a mistake to equate the ideology of the Court's majority with the conservatism, say, of the Republicans in Congress or with the ideology of the conservative movement. To be sure, there are members of the Court who are unmistakably *movement conservatives*. Justices Antonin Scalia and Clarence Thomas are in this camp.

Yet Justice Kennedy and Chief Justice Roberts—and even Justice Alito—often "march to their own drummer." A leading example was Chief Justice Roberts's ruling on Obamacare, in which he found that incentives to

Chief Justice John Roberts, Jr.

Justice Samuel Alito, Jr.

obtain health-care insurance could be written into the tax code. Any conservative hostility that Roberts may have felt toward the health-care reform legislation was clearly checked by his commitment to judicial restraint. In contrast to this position, the four other conservative justices contended that the Affordable Care Act was unconstitutional as a whole. The four liberal justices believed that the *individual mandate* to obtain insurance followed from the Constitution's commerce clause.

Another area in which Court conservatives have frequently parted from the conservative movement is that of gay rights. Justice Kennedy, in particular, has favored gay rights ever since *Lawrence v. Texas*, a 2003 ruling that abolished laws against homosexual acts.[20] Justice Kennedy joined the Court's liberals in this case, providing the fifth vote that decided the issue. Kennedy also wrote the opinion. (In contrast, Kennedy's views on the Affordable Care Act were more conventionally conservative. During oral arguments, Kennedy made his opposition to the health reform legislation very clear.)

14–5c Approaches to Legal Interpretation

It would be a mistake to look at the judicial philosophy of today's Supreme Court solely in terms of the political ideologies of liberalism and conservatism. In fact, some Supreme Court scholars have suggested that other factors are as important as, or more important

> ## "THE CONSTITUTION ITSELF SHOULD BE OUR GUIDE,
> not our own concept of what is fair, decent, and right."
>
> ~ HUGO L. BLACK ~
> ASSOCIATE JUSTICE OF THE
> UNITED STATES SUPREME COURT
> 1937–1971

than, the justices' political philosophies in determining why they decide as they do. These factors include the justices' attitudes toward legal interpretation and their perceptions of the Supreme Court's role in the federal judiciary. Two important judicial philosophies, both of which are often associated with conservative principles, are *strict construction* and *originalism*.

Strict Construction The term *strict construction* is widely used in the press and by politicians. Republican presidential candidates routinely promise to appoint justices who will interpret the Constitution strictly and not "legislate from the bench." The opposite of strict construction is *broad construction*. Advocates of strict construction often contend that the government should do nothing that is not specifically mentioned in the Constitution. In 1803, for example, some strict constructionists argued that the national government had no power to double the size of the country by purchasing the Louisiana Territory. Such radical strict constructionism had little support in 1803 and is accepted by few people today.

Despite the wide popularity of strict construction as a concept, members of the Supreme Court generally reject the description. Justice Scalia, for example, who is normally considered one of the purest examples of a strict constructionist on the Court, prefers to call himself a *textualist* instead. Scalia writes, "I am not a strict constructionist, and no one ought to be. . . . A text should not be construed strictly, and it should not be construed leniently; it should be construed reasonably, to contain all that it fairly means."[21]

What Scalia means by textualism is that when determining the meaning of legislation, he refuses to consider the legislative debates that took place when the measure was passed, the nature of the problem the legislation was meant to address, or anything other than the actual text of the law.

Original Intent A second conservative philosophy is called *originalism*. Justice Thomas is a well-known advocate of this approach. Originalists believe that to determine the meaning of a par-

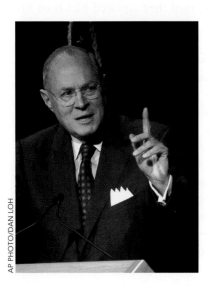

Although often considered a conservative when he served on the Rehnquist Court, Justice Anthony Kennedy has typically held the "swing" vote on the closely divided Roberts Court.

AP PHOTO/DAN LOH

Justice Stephen Breyer   Justice Ruth Bader Ginsburg   Justice Clarence Thomas   Justice Antonin Scalia

ticular constitutional phrase, the Court should look to the intentions of the founders. What did the framers of the Constitution themselves intend when they included the phrase in the document? To discern the intent of the founders, justices might look to sources that shed light on the founders' views. These sources could include writings by the founders, newspaper articles from that period, the *Federalist Papers,* and notes taken during the Constitutional Convention.

Originalism, Textualism, and Modernism

Such analysis is precisely what textualists wish to avoid when it comes to assessing modern-day statutory law. Nevertheless, Justice Scalia considers himself an originalist as well as a textualist. In the 2012–2013 term, Scalia was in agreement with Justice Thomas 86 percent of the time.

Originalism can be contrasted with what has been called *modernism.* Modernists seek to examine the Constitution in the context of today's society and to consider how modern life affects the words in the document. For an example of how originalism and modernism contrast, consider *Lawrence v. Texas,* a case mentioned earlier.

Justice Kennedy's majority opinion in the case held that laws that criminalize same-sex intimate relations are unconstitutional under the Fourteenth Amendment. An originalist could object to this judgment because the legislators who adopted the amendment never considered that it might apply to gay men and lesbians. In fact, both Scalia and Thomas opposed the ruling. In contrast, modernists might argue that discrimination against gays and lesbians is exactly the type of evil that

the amendment sought to prevent, even though such an application never occurred to those who wrote it.

FOR CRITICAL THINKING

If President Obama is able to replace one of the justices on the Supreme Court because of death or retirement, how might the new Court rule on abortion? On affirmative action?

14–6 Assessing the Role of the Federal Courts

The federal courts have often come under attack, particularly in the last decade or so, for many reasons. This should come as no surprise in view of the policymaking

Learning Outcome 14–6

Identify some of the criticisms of the federal courts and some of the checks on the power of the courts.

power of the courts. After all, a Supreme Court decision can establish national policy on such issues as abortion, racial segregation, and gay rights. Critics, especially on the political right, frequently accuse the judiciary of "legislating from the bench." We discuss these criticisms in this chapter's *Perception versus Reality* feature on the following page.

Perception versus Reality

The Supreme Court Legislates from the Bench

Our Constitution gives legislative powers to the Congress exclusively. All executive powers are granted to the president. And all judicial powers are given to the judiciary. The United States Supreme Court is the final arbiter and interpreter of what is and is not constitutional. Because of its power of judicial review, it has the ability to "make law," or so it seems.

THE PERCEPTION

Using the power of judicial review, the Supreme Court creates new laws. In 1954, the Court determined that racial segregation is illegal, a position that is universally accepted today but was hugely controversial back in the 1950s. The Court has also legalized sexual acts between same-sex adults and, of course, abortion. These decisions, especially the legalization of abortion, remain very divisive today.

Such decisions have had a major impact on the nature of American society. Because citizens elect members of Congress and the president only—and not members of the Supreme Court—it is undemocratic to allow these nine justices to determine laws for our nation.

THE REALITY

The Supreme Court cannot actually write new laws. It can only eliminate old ones. When the Court threw out laws that criminalized adult sexual activity by gay men and lesbians, it was abolishing laws, not creating them. The Court does not have the power to legislate—to create new laws.

Consider what would happen if the Court decided that some basic level of health care is a constitutional right—a highly unlikely event. Could the Court establish mechanisms by which such a right could be enforced? It could not. It takes members of Congress months of hard work to craft bills that affect our health-care system. Such legislation fills thousands of pages and can be developed only with the assistance of large numbers of experts and lobbyists. The federal courts could not undertake such projects even if they wanted to.

The courts must decide how they will handle the cases that are brought before them. To do so establishes judicial policy. It does not constitute lawmaking. In any event, we have no alternative to judicial review when it comes to determining what is or is not constitutional. Without the Supreme Court, Congress and the president could make all sorts of laws that violate our Constitution and infringe on our rights, and there would be nothing to stop them. As Chief Justice John Roberts said during his confirmation hearings, "Judges are like umpires. Umpires don't make the rules; they apply them."

BLOG ON Plenty of bloggers follow the activities of the Supreme Court. You can find some of these blogs by searching on "us supreme court blog." One of the best is SCOTUSblog, sponsored by the law firm Goldstein & Russell. Another is the U.S. Supreme Court Blog, written by Paul M. Rashkind, a Florida lawyer.

14–6a Criticisms of the Federal Courts

Certainly, policymaking by unelected judges and justices in the federal courts has serious implications in a democracy. Some Americans, including many conservatives, contend that making policy from the bench has upset the balance of powers envisioned by the framers of the Constitution. They cite Thomas Jefferson, who once said, "To consider the judges as the ultimate arbiters of all constitutional questions [is] a very dangerous doctrine indeed, and one which would place us under the despotism of an oligarchy."[22] This group believes that we should rein in the power of the federal courts, and particularly judicial activism.

14–6b The Case for the Courts

On the other side of the debate over the courts are those who argue in favor of leaving the courts alone. Several federal court judges have sharply criticized congressional efforts to interfere with their authority. They claim that such efforts violate the Constitution's separation of powers. James M. Jeffords, a former independent senator from Vermont, likened the federal court system to a referee: "The first lesson we teach children when they enter competitive sports is to respect the referee, even if we think he [or she] might have made the wrong call. If our children can understand this, why can't our political leaders?"[23]

Others argue that there are already sufficient checks on the courts. We look at some of those next.

Judicial Traditions and Doctrines

One check on the courts is judicial restraint. Supreme Court justices traditionally have exercised a great deal of self-restraint. Justices sometimes admit to making decisions that fly in the face of their personal values and policy preferences, simply because they feel obligated to do so in view of existing law.

Self-restraint is also mandated by various established judicial traditions and doctrines, including the doctrine of *stare decisis*, which theoretically obligates the Supreme Court to follow its own precedents. Furthermore, the Supreme Court will not hear a meritless appeal just so it can rule on the issue.

Finally, more often than not, the justices narrow their rulings to focus on just one aspect of an issue, even though there may be nothing to stop them from broadening their focus and thus widening the impact of their decisions.

Other Checks

The judiciary is subject to other checks as well. Courts may make rulings, but they cannot force federal and state legislatures to appropriate the funds necessary to carry out those rulings. For example, if a state supreme court decides that prison conditions must be improved, the state legislature has to find the funds to carry out the ruling or the improvements will not take place.

Additionally, legislatures can revise old laws or pass new ones in an attempt to negate a court's ruling. This may happen when a court interprets a statute in a way that Congress did not intend. Congress may also propose amendments to the Constitution to reverse Supreme Court rulings, and Congress has the authority to limit or otherwise alter the jurisdiction of the lower federal courts. Finally, although it is most unlikely, Congress could even change the number of justices on the Supreme Court, in an attempt to change the ideological balance on the Court. (President Franklin D. Roosevelt proposed such a plan in 1937—without success.)

The Public's Regard for the Supreme Court

Some have proposed that Congress, not the Supreme Court, be the final arbiter of the Constitution. In debates on this topic, one factor is often overlooked: the American public's high regard for the Supreme Court and the federal courts generally. The Court continues to be respected as a fair arbiter of conflicting interests and the protector of constitutional rights and liberties.

Even when the Court issued its decision to halt the manual recount of votes in Florida following the 2000 elections, which effectively handed the presidency to George W. Bush, Americans respected the Court's decision-making authority—although many disagreed with the Court's decision. Polls continue to show that Americans have much more trust and confidence in the Supreme Court than they do in Congress.

FOR CRITICAL THINKING

Why do you think that Americans trust the Supreme Court much more than they do Congress?

AMERICA AT
ODDS The Judiciary

A Supreme Court decision can affect the lives of millions of Americans. For example, in 1973 the Supreme Court, in *Roe v. Wade*, held that the constitutional right to privacy included the right to have an abortion. The influence wielded by the Court today is a far cry from the Court's relative obscurity at the founding of this nation. Initially, the Supreme Court was not even included in the plans for government buildings in the national capital. It did not have its own building until 1935. Over time, however, the Court has established a reputation with the public for dispensing justice in a fair and reasonable manner. Still, Americans are at odds over a number of judicial issues:

- Are there terrorist suspects who must be detained indefinitely without trial to protect our safety—or is such an act a violation of our Constitution that does us more damage in the world than a detainee could possibly accomplish if freed?

- Should the United States Supreme Court accept more cases to provide a greater number of definitive rulings—or should it take on relatively few cases so that it can treat each one thoroughly?

- Should senators accept a Supreme Court nomination by a president of the opposing party whenever the nominee appears to have sound judicial temperament—or should senators vote only for those nominees who share their political philosophies?

- Should judges defer to the decisions of legislatures and administrative agencies whenever possible—or should they strictly police the constitutionality of legislative and executive decisions?

- Is it crucial that the Constitution be interpreted in terms of the beliefs of the founders—or should justices take account of modern circumstances that the founders could not have envisioned?

STUDY TOOLS

Ready to study?

- **Review** what you've read with the quiz below.
- Check your answers on the **Chapter in Review** card at the back of the book.
- For any questions you miss, read the corresponding **Learning Outcome** section again to prepare for class and your exam.
- Rip out and study the **Chapter in Review** card (at the back of the book).

Fill-In

Learning Outcome 14–1

1. Primary sources of American law include _____.

Learning Outcome 14–2

2. To bring a case before the Supreme Court, a party may request a _____, which is an order that the Court issues to a lower court requesting that court to send it the record of the case in question.

3. The attorneys involved with a case will present _____ to the Supreme Court, after which the justices discuss the case in conference.

4. A _____ opinion is a statement written by a justice who agrees with the Court's decision, but for reasons different from those outlined by the majority.

Learning Outcome 14–3

5. Because of a practice known as _____, home-state senators of the president's political party may

be able to influence the choice of a nominee for the U.S. district court in that state.

Learning Outcome 14–4

6. A restraintist judge or justice generally assumes that the courts should _____.

Learning Outcome 14–5

7. Two important judicial philosophies that describe justices' attitudes toward legal interpretation, both of which are often associated with conservative principles, are _____.

Learning Outcome 14–6

8. Congress can check the power of the courts in several ways, including _____.

Multiple Choice

Learning Outcome 14–1

9. A precedent is best defined as a
   a. controversy that is real and substantial.
   b. court decision that furnishes an example or authority for deciding subsequent cases.
   c. ruling that a person has disobeyed a court order.

Learning Outcome 14–2

10. The U.S. courts of appeals
    a. are the courts in which cases involving federal law begin.
    b. hear appeals from the U.S. district courts located within their respective judicial circuits.
    c. hear testimony and evidence before they make decisions in cases.

Learning Outcome 14–3

11. A nominee for the Supreme Court must be confirmed by a
    a. majority vote in the Senate.
    b. two-thirds vote in the Senate.

c. majority vote in the House Judiciary Committee.

Learning Outcome 14–4

12. The power of the courts to decide on the constitutionality of legislative enactments and of actions taken by the executive branch is called
    a. judicial review.   b. *stare decisis.*   c. jurisdiction.

Learning Outcome 14–5

13. Justice _____ typically has held the "swing vote" on the closely divided Roberts Court.
    a. Antonin Scalia   c. Anthony Kennedy
    b. Clarence Thomas

Learning Outcome 14–6

14. Judicial self-restraint is mandated by various judicial traditions and doctrines, such as _____, which theoretically obligates the Supreme Court to follow its own precedents.
    a. *curiae regis*   c. justiciable controversy
    b. *stare decisis*

15

Domestic Policy

CHIP SOMODEVILLA/GETTY IMAGES

Learning **Outcomes**

The **Learning Outcomes** labeled 1 through 4 are designed to help improve your understanding of the chapter. After reading this chapter, you should be able to:

15–1 Explain what domestic policy is, and summarize the steps in the policymaking process.

15–2 Discuss the issue of health-care funding and recent legislation on universal health insurance.

15–3 Summarize the issues of energy independence, climate change, and alternative energy sources.

15–4 Describe the two major areas of economic policymaking, and discuss the issue of the public debt.

Remember to visit page 351 for additional **Study Tools**

AMERICA AT ODDS
Do We Send Too Many People to Prison?

Currently, there are about 2.2 million U.S. residents in prison or jail. That's roughly one in every one hundred adults. We are setting records—the share of our population in prison is thirteen times more than in Japan, nine times more than in Germany, and five times more than in Britain.

In 1970, the proportion of Americans behind bars—the *incarceration rate*—was only one-fourth of what it is today. Not surprisingly, the number of drug offenders in prison is responsible for much of this increase. Such lockups have multiplied thirteenfold since 1980.

Defense attorney Jim Felman of Tampa, Florida, said that America is conducting "an experiment in imprisoning first-time nonviolent offenders for periods of time previously reserved only for those who had killed someone." Holding that many prisoners is not cheap. It costs about $50,000 a year to house a convicted criminal in a state prison. Because of these costs, a number of conservative governors have begun to rethink their commitment to high rates of incarceration. Indeed, the massive growth in prison populations that marked the last few decades appears to have come to an end, and the incarceration rate is no longer growing. Given all this, do we still send too many Americans to prison?

Keep Criminals behind Bars—It Works

Supporters of aggressive incarceration policies argue that still more criminals should be behind bars. Putting more people in prison reduces crime rates. After all, incentives matter. If potential criminals know that they will be thrown in jail more readily and stay there longer, they will have less incentive to engage in illegal activities.

Also, the crime rate is strongly determined by the number of criminals at large. When we remove a criminal from the streets and put that person in prison, the prisoner can no longer commit crimes that harm the public. This effect of removal is called *incapacitation*. The evidence shows that during the 1960s, when incarceration rates fell, the crime rate more than doubled. As incarceration rates rose sharply in the 1990s, the crime rate went steadily down. As a comparison, the risk of criminal punishment in England has been falling. In consequence, crime rates have risen in England while they have fallen in the United States.

Tough sentencing is effective. We should not turn career criminals loose on the streets.

Too Many Laws and Too Many Prisoners

Those who argue against our high rates of incarceration point out that many individuals are convicted of nonviolent crimes. The government should not be spending $50,000 a year or more to keep such people in prison.

Too many acts have been criminalized, particularly at the federal level. Many crimes are so vaguely defined that most Americans would not know if they were breaking the law. Granted, hard-core criminals should be behind bars. But what about the casual pot smoker? (In 2013, about 700,000 people were arrested for possession of marijuana.) Or someone convicted under a federal statute designed to protect the environment? Lying to a federal official is a felony. Who can say how many people might be imprisoned based on such an act?

Many states have "habitual-offender" laws. In California, for example, more than 4,000 individuals are serving life sentences because they were convicted of a third offense—one that was neither violent nor serious. The cost to society of putting drug users behind bars is much greater than the benefits. Wouldn't that money be better spent on rehabilitation?

Where do you stand?

1. Could factors other than high incarceration rates be causing our current low crime rates? What might they be?
2. Why do you think federal, state, and local governments arrest so many drug-law violators?

Explore this issue online

- You can find several articles in the *Economist,* a British magazine, arguing that the United States imprisons too many people. Search on "economist us prison."
- The Criminal Justice Legal Foundation is among the few groups that advocate increased rates of incarceration. See its arguments by entering "cjlf" into a search engine.

Introduction

Whether we send too many people to prison is just one of the issues that confront our nation's policymakers today. How are questions of national importance, such as this one, decided? Who are the major participants in the decision-making process?

To learn the answers to these questions, we need to delve into the politics of policymaking. *Policy*, or *public policy*, can be defined as a plan or course of action taken by the government to respond to a political issue or to enhance the social or political well-being of society. Public policy is the end result of the policymaking process, which will be described shortly.

In this chapter, after discussing how policy is made through the policymaking process, we look at several aspects of **domestic policy**, which consists of public policy concerning issues *within* a national unit. Specifically, we examine health-care policy, energy policy, and economic policy. We focus on these policy areas because they have been among the Obama administration's top priorities.

Bear in mind that although the focus here is on policy and policymaking at the national level, state and local governments also engage in policymaking and establish policies to achieve goals relating to activities within their boundaries. This is certainly true in relation to the criminal justice issues discussed in this chapter's opening *America at Odds* feature.

domestic policy Public policy concerning issues within a national unit, such as national policy concerning health care or the economy.

policymaking process The procedures involved in getting an issue on the political agenda; formulating, adopting, and implementing a policy with regard to the issue; and then evaluating the results of the policy.

agenda setting Getting an issue on the political agenda to be addressed by Congress; part of the first stage of the policymaking process.

15–1 The Policymaking Process

A new law does not appear out of nowhere. First, the problem addressed by the new law has to become part of the political agenda—that is, the problem must be defined as a political issue to be resolved by government action. Furthermore, once the issue gets on the political agenda, proposed solutions to the problem have to be formulated and then adopted. Issue identification and agenda setting, policy formulation, and policy adoption are all parts of the **policymaking process**, which is illustrated in Figure 15–1 on the following page.

Learning Outcome 15–1

Explain what domestic policy is, and summarize the steps in the policymaking process.

The process does not end there, however. Once the law is passed, it has to be implemented and then evaluated.

Each phase of the policymaking process involves interactions among various individuals and groups. The president and members of Congress are obviously important participants in the process. Remember from Chapter 6 that interest groups also play a key role. Groups that may be affected adversely by a new policy will try to convince Congress not to adopt the policy. Groups that will benefit from the policy will exert whatever influence they can on Congress to do the opposite. Congressional committees and subcommittees may investigate the problem to be addressed by the policy and, in so doing, solicit input from members of various groups or industries.

The participants in policymaking and the nature of the debates involved depend on the particular policy being proposed, formed, or implemented. Whatever the policy, however, debate over its pros and cons occurs during each stage of the policymaking process. Additionally, making policy decisions inevitably involves *trade-offs*, in which policymakers must sacrifice one goal to achieve another because of budget constraints and other factors.

15–1a Issue Identification and Agenda Setting

If no one recognizes a problem, then no matter how important the problem may be, politically it does not yet really exist. Thus, *issue identification* is part of the first stage of the policymaking process. Some group—whether it be the media, the public, politicians, or even foreign commentators—must identify a problem that can be solved politically. The second part of this stage of the policymaking process involves getting the issue on the political agenda to be addressed by Congress. This is called **agenda setting**, or *agenda building*.

A problem in society may be identified as an issue and included on the political agenda when an event or series of events leads to a call for action. For example, the failure of a major bank may lead to the conclusion

FIGURE 15-1

The Policymaking Process

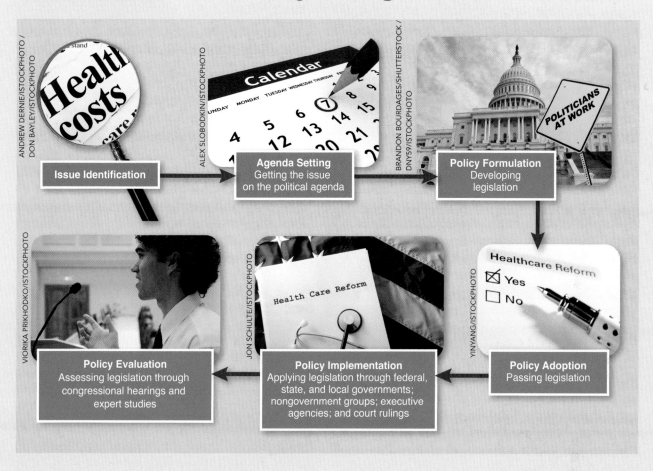

Issue Identification

Agenda Setting
Getting the issue
on the political agenda

Policy Formulation
Developing
legislation

Policy Adoption
Passing legislation

Policy Implementation
Applying legislation through federal,
state, and local governments;
nongovernment groups; executive
agencies; and court rulings

Policy Evaluation
Assessing legislation through
congressional hearings and
expert studies

that the financial industry is in trouble and that the government should take action to rectify the problem. Dramatic increases in health-care costs may cause the media or other groups to consider health care a priority that should be on the national political agenda. Sometimes, the social or economic effects of a national calamity, such as the Great Depression of the 1930s or the terrorist attacks of September 11, 2001, create a pressing need for government action.

15–1b Policy Formulation and Adoption

The second stage in the policymaking process involves the formulation and adoption of specific plans for achieving a particular goal, such as health-care reform. The president, members of Congress, administrative agencies, and interest group leaders typically are the key participants in developing proposed legislation. Remember from Chapter 13 that iron triangles and issue networks work together in forming mutually

beneficial policies. To a certain extent, the courts also establish policies when they interpret statutes passed by legislative bodies or make decisions concerning disputes not yet addressed by any law, such as disputes involving new technology.

Note that some issues may become a part of the political agenda but never proceed beyond that stage of the policymaking process. Usually, this happens when it is impossible to achieve a consensus on what policy should be adopted.

15–1c Policy Implementation

Because of our federal system, the implementation of national policies necessarily requires the cooperation of the federal government and the various state and local governments. A case in point is the Obama administration's Race to the Top program, which was included in the February 2009 stimulus package. Race to the Top was a competition among state governments to win up to $4.35 billion in federal education grants. The states competed by undertaking reforms to their kindergarten–through–high school educational systems. Reforms included performance-based standards for teachers and promotion of charter schools. All but four states entered the competition.

Successful implementation usually requires the support of groups outside the government. For example, the first-round Race to the Top winners—Delaware and Tennessee—were able to persuade their teachers' unions to support the reforms.

Policy implementation also involves agencies in the executive branch (see Chapter 13). Once Congress establishes a policy by enacting legislation, the executive branch, through its agencies, enforces the new policy. Furthermore, the courts are involved in policy implementation, because the legislation and administrative regulations enunciating the new policy must be interpreted and applied to specific situations by the courts.

15–1d Policy Evaluation

The final stage of policymaking involves evaluating the success of a policy during and following its implementation. Groups both inside and outside the government participate in the evaluation process.

Congress may hold hearings to obtain feedback from different groups on how a statute or regulation has affected them. Scholars and scientists may conduct studies to determine whether a particular law, such as an environmental law designed to reduce air pollution, has actually achieved the desired result—less air pollution. Sometimes, feedback obtained in these or other ways indicates that a policy has failed, and a new policymaking process may be undertaken to modify the policy or create a more effective one.

15–1e Policymaking and Special Interests

The policymaking steps just discussed may seem straightforward, but they are not. Every bill that passes through Congress is a compromise. Every bill that passes through Congress is also an opportunity for individual members of Congress to help constituents, particularly those who were kind enough to contribute financially to the members' reelection campaigns.

Consider the Emergency Economic Stabilization Act of 2008, known as the "bank bailout" bill. This was a $700 billion financial rescue plan that the U.S. Treasury Department urgently requested on September 19, 2008. After the House defeated the initial "clean" version of the bill, the Senate drafted a second version. This second version was inserted into landmark health-care legislation requiring that insurance companies provide coverage for mental health treatment equivalent to that provided for the treatment of physical illnesses.

The bill also contained almost $14 billion in tax-break extensions for businesses. Special provisions benefited rural schools, film and television producers, makers of toy wooden arrows, victims of the 1989 *Exxon Valdez* oil spill in Alaska, rum distillers in the Virgin Islands and Puerto Rico, auto racetracks, and wool researchers. The second bill passed the House on October 3. Clearly, policymaking, particularly on the economic front, remains a complicated process.

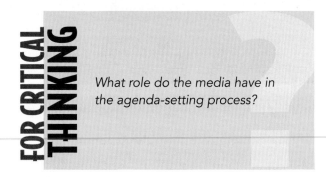

FOR CRITICAL THINKING

What role do the media have in the agenda-setting process?

15–2 Health-Care Policy

In March 2010, Congress passed the Patient Protection and Affordable Care Act and a companion bill. The two bills, which President Barack Obama immediately signed, contained health-care reforms that were among the most consequential government initiatives in many years.

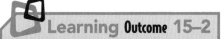

Learning Outcome 15–2

Discuss the issue of health-care funding and recent legislation on universal health insurance.

Even before the new legislation was adopted, the federal government was paying the health-care costs of more than 100 million Americans. When President Obama took office, the government was picking up the tab for about 50 percent of the nation's health-care costs. Private insurance was responsible for about a third of all health-care payments, and the rest was met either by patients themselves or by charity. Paying for health-care expenses, in other words, was already a

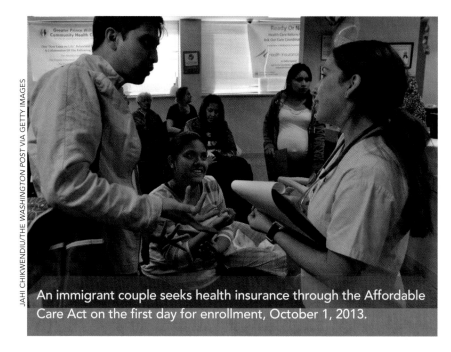

An immigrant couple seeks health insurance through the Affordable Care Act on the first day for enrollment, October 1, 2013.

to Americans aged sixty-five and over, and **Medicaid**, which funds health-care coverage for low-income persons.

15–2b Medicaid and Medicare

The federal government pays for health care in a variety of ways. Like many major employers, it buys health-care insurance for its employees. Members of the armed forces, veterans, and Native Americans receive medical services provided directly by the government. Most federal spending on health care, however, is accounted for by Medicare and Medicaid. Both are costly, and each in its own way poses a serious financial problem for the government.

major federal responsibility, and questions about how the government should carry out that function in the future were unavoidable.

15–2a Two Problems with U.S. Health Care

Our system for funding health care has suffered from two major problems. One is that health care is expensive. About 17.7 percent of national spending in the United States goes to health care, compared with 11.2 percent in Canada, 9.4 percent in Britain, and 7.7 percent in Israel. U.S. health-care costs have been rising for years, as you can see in Figure 15–2 on the following page.

Also, 50 million Americans—close to 16 percent of the population—still had no health-care insurance as of 2013. Lack of coverage means that people may put off seeing a physician until it is too late for effective treatment or may be forced into bankruptcy due to large medical bills. One study has estimated that 20,000 people each year die prematurely because they lack health insurance.[1] (Others dispute these findings.) All other economically advanced nations provide health insurance to everyone, typically through a government program similar to Social Security or Medicare in the United States.

Before discussing the recently passed health-care reforms, let's first look at the programs that are already in place. The most important of these is **Medicare**, which provides health-care insurance

Medicaid   A joint federal-state program, Medicaid provides health-care subsidies to low-income persons. The federal government provides about 60 percent of the Medicaid budget, and the states provide the rest. More than 60 million people are in the program. Many Medicaid recipients are elderly residents of nursing homes—the Medicare program does not pay for nursing home expenses.

Although recent cost-containment measures have slowed the growth of Medicaid spending, the cost of Medicaid has doubled in the last decade. This has put a considerable strain on the budgets of many states. About 17 percent of the average state general fund budget now goes to Medicaid. Another program, the **Children's Health Insurance Program (CHIP)**, covers children in families with incomes that are modest but too high to qualify for Medicaid. By fiscal year 2013, the total cost of Medicaid and CHIP for all levels of government was about $325 billion.

The Great Recession put a considerable strain on the states' ability to pick up their share of Medicaid payments. The Obama administration's

Medicare A federal government program that pays for health-care insurance for Americans aged sixty-five years and over.

Medicaid A joint federal-state program that pays for health-care services for low-income persons.

Children's Health Insurance Program (CHIP) A joint federal-state program that provides health-care insurance for low-income children.

FIGURE 15-2

Percentage of Total National
Income Spent on Health Care in the United States

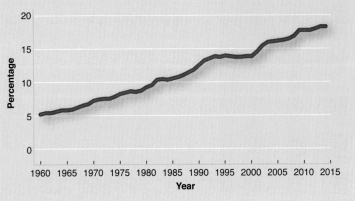

Source: National Health Expenditure Accounts, Centers for Medicare & Medicaid Services.

February 2009 stimulus package, therefore, included $87 billion to reduce temporarily the Medicaid burden on the states. Congressional Democrats also substantially increased the size of CHIP within weeks of Obama's inauguration.

Medicare Medicare is the federal government's health-care program for persons sixty-five years of age and older. Medicare is now the government's second-largest domestic spending program, after Social Security. In 1970, Medicare accounted for only 0.7 percent of total annual U.S. national income (gross domestic product, or GDP). It currently accounts for about 3.1 percent of GDP, and costs are expected to soar as millions of "baby boomers" retire over the next two decades.

By 2030, the sixty-five-and-older population is expected to double. Further, technological developments in health care and the advancement of medical science are driving medical costs up every year. There are simply more actions that medical science can take to keep people alive—and Americans naturally want to take advantage of these services.

entitlement program
A government program that provides benefits to all persons who meet specified requirements.

Entitlement Programs
Medicare and Medicaid are examples of federal **entitlement programs.** Social Security and unemployment compensation are two other examples. Entitlement programs pay out benefits to persons who meet specified requirements. In the case of Social Security, for example, the government issues payments based on a recipient's age at retirement and past wage or salary income.

A special characteristic of entitlement programs is that they continue from year to year, regardless of whether Congress passes an annual funding measure. An entitlement continues until the government explicitly adopts a new law to change the benefits or otherwise alter the program. Further, Congress has no direct control over how much an entitlement program will cost in any particular year. It is usually possible to estimate the costs, but the actual amount of spending depends on how many eligible persons sign up for the benefits.

In this way, entitlements are different from *discretionary spending*. In a discretionary program, Congress establishes a binding annual budget for a government agency that the agency cannot exceed. Note that "discretionary" does not mean "unimportant." As an example, the nation's armed forces are funded through discretionary spending.

Entitlements lie at the heart of the political differences between liberals and conservatives. For liberals, entitlements are an essential part of the social compact that binds us together. For conservatives, entitlements breed a dangerous dependency on the government. In understanding the 2010 Affordable Care Act—commonly called Obamacare—it is important to realize that the program was primarily designed as an entitlement.

15-2c The Democrats Propose Universal Coverage

As noted earlier, the United States has been the only economically advanced nation that did not provide universal health-insurance coverage to its citizens. Democratic president Bill Clinton (1993–2001) and then-First Lady Hillary Clinton made a serious push for a universal plan during President Clinton's first term, but the project failed to pass Congress.

Many universal health-insurance plans—for example, the systems in Canada and France—involve government monopolies. In these nations, the government is responsible for providing basic health-care insurance to everyone through **national health insurance.** Some wealthy nations, such as the Netherlands and Switzerland, provide universal coverage through private insurance companies instead. The plan that the United States has adopted also provides a large role for the private sector.

Congress Addresses the Issue   As Congress began to address the health-care issue in 2009, all of the various proposals had common features. All assumed that employer-provided health insurance would continue to be a major part of the system. Large employers that did not offer a plan would be required to pay a penalty. Medicaid would be available to individuals with incomes up to about 1.5 times the federal poverty level. (In 2013, the poverty level for a family of four was $23,550.) A new health-insurance marketplace, the Health Insurance Exchange, would allow individuals and small employers to shop for plans. Insurance companies would not be allowed to deny anyone coverage.

Most individuals would be required to obtain coverage or pay an income tax penalty. This requirement is known as the **individual mandate** or the *personal mandate.* Those with low-to-middle incomes would receive help in paying their premiums. Subsidies would be phased out for those earning more than four times the federal poverty level.

The individual mandate was controversial, because it would require all Americans to have health insurance, whether they wanted it or not. Supporters of reform, however, pointed out that without an individual mandate, reform would not work. Any system that let healthy people avoid buying insurance would face financial collapse.

To fund the program, Congress adopted various new taxes and fees, such as a new tax on investments for high-income persons, an increased Medicare tax rate, and a new tax on high-end ("Cadillac") health policies that cost more than a specified amount.

Support and Opposition   The Obama administration won considerable support for reform from interest groups that had opposed universal health-care systems in the past. For the first time, the American Medical Association was on board. The greater part of

> "It helps to think of the government as **an insurance company with an army."**
>
> ~ MIKE HOLLAND ~
> OFFICE OF SCIENCE AND
> TECHNOLOGY POLICY UNDER
> PRESIDENT GEORGE W. BUSH

the opposition came not from interest groups but from conservatives.

Opponents were not just hostile to health-care reform. They were upset over what they saw as the growing power of government in general. They believed that health-care reform was only one of several steps toward a mammoth federal government that would crush individual freedoms.

Expected Results   The bills passed by Congress and signed by President Obama were to become effective over a period of several years. One immediate change was that young people could remain covered by their parents' insurance until they turned twenty-six. Another immediate result was subsidies to small employers that obtained insurance plans for their employees.

The most important provisions, however, would not take effect until January 1, 2014. From that day on, subsidies would help citizens purchase health-care insurance if they were not covered by Medicare, Medicaid, or an employer's plan. Individuals and families with incomes up to four times the federal poverty level would be eligible for at least some subsidies. (Currently, the income cutoff would be $94,200 for a family of four, but the exact value will surely change.) About 32 million Americans who did not have health-care insurance would gain coverage.

The Conservative Reaction   Conservatives argued that the Democrats had ignored the will of the people, who were against the reform legislation. In a typical poll in March 2010, immediately after the legislation was adopted, 56 percent of respondents opposed Obamacare. That figure was slightly misleading, however. Only 43 percent opposed the reforms because they were "too liberal." Another 13 percent opposed them because they were "not liberal enough."

> **national health insurance** A program, found in many of the world's economically advanced nations, under which the central government provides basic health-care insurance coverage to everyone in the country.
>
> **individual mandate** In the context of health-care reform, a requirement that all persons obtain health-care insurance from one source or another. Those failing to do so must pay a penalty.

A CONSTITUTIONAL CHALLENGE. One last-ditch method of opposing the reforms was to challenge their constitutionality. Attorney generals in twenty states challenged the measure on the basis that the individual mandate violated the Constitution. In the end, the Supreme Court did not accept this argument.

The Court did rule, however, that states could not be required to participate in the Medicaid expansion portion of the reforms. Obamacare addressed the health-insurance needs of the nation's lowest-income families through a substantial expansion in Medicaid eligibility. States that refused to participate would lose all of their Medicaid funding. A majority on the Court found this penalty to be too harsh.[2]

ATTEMPTS TO REPEAL THE LEGISLATION. A second method of attack would be to repeal the legislation, and the Republicans made repeal part of their platform for the 2010 and 2012 elections. Because Obamacare was primarily an entitlement program, however, repeal would require specific legislation passed by Congress and signed by the president. To prevent a veto, a Republican president would be necessary. The Republicans would also need to keep control of the House, and they would need sixty votes in the Senate to override a Democratic filibuster.[3] In the 2012 elections, the Republicans failed to win control of either the presidency or the Senate.

Despite their failure to win control of the Senate or the presidency, Republicans kept trying to repeal Obamacare. The Republican-controlled House voted to overturn the legislation more than forty times, without effect.

In September 2013, weeks away from the October 1 initial signup for the insurance exchanges, House Republicans threatened to force a so-called government shutdown unless Democrats agreed to delay Obamacare for one year. (In principle, a "government shutdown" would halt all discretionary spending. In practice, it would suspend all "nonessential services.") Abolition of Obamacare was also a demand in the October 2013 debate over raising the federal government's debt ceiling. We discuss these developments later in this chapter.

15–3 Energy Policy

Energy policy was a second major priority for the Obama administration, but its accomplishments in this area have been relatively modest. The Democrats did move a major energy bill through the House in 2009, but it died in the Senate. Energy policy is important because of two problems: (1) our reliance on imported oil, and (2) the possibility of global climate change.

Learning Outcome 15–3

Summarize the issues of energy independence, climate change, and alternative energy sources.

15–3a The Problem of Imported Oil

Our nation currently imports 40 percent of its petroleum supply. This figure has fallen substantially in recent years. In 2005, imports were more than 60 percent of consumption. Still, oil imports are a potential problem largely because many of the nations that export oil are not particularly friendly to the United States. Some, such as Iran, are outright adversaries. Other oil exporters that could pose difficulties include Iraq, Libya, Nigeria, Russia, and Venezuela.

Fortunately for the United States, the sources of our imported oil are highly diversified, and we are not excessively dependent on any one nation. Canada and Mexico, friendly neighbors, supply 40 percent of our imports. Many of our European and Asian allies, however, are dependent on imports from questionable regimes.

> ## "NATURE PROVIDES A FREE LUNCH,
> but only if we control our appetites."
> ~ WILLIAM DOYLE RUCKELSHAUS ~
> FIRST HEAD OF THE ENVIRONMENTAL PROTECTION AGENCY
> 1970–1973

The Price of Oil Until fairly recently, the price of oil was low, and the U.S. government was under little pressure to address our dependence on imports. In 1998, the price per barrel fell below $12. In July 2008, however, the price of oil spiked to more than $125 a barrel, forcing U.S. gasoline prices above $4 per gallon. Thereafter, oil prices fell dramatically when demand collapsed due to the global economic panic of that period. Oil prices then rose again along with the economic recovery—the price of gasoline reached $4 per gallon in some states in 2011 and 2012.

Fuel Efficiency Standards In the 1970s, the federal government responded to an earlier spurt in oil prices by imposing fuel-mileage standards on cars and trucks sold in this country. Under the **Corporate Average Fuel Economy (CAFE) standards**, each vehicle manufacturer had to meet a miles-per-gallon benchmark, which was averaged across all cars and trucks that it sold.

With the steep rise in oil prices in 2007 and 2008, measures to restrain U.S. fuel consumption were on the agenda again. In 2009, President Obama issued higher fuel efficiency standards for cars and trucks. In August 2012, the Obama administration raised fuel efficiency standards even higher. By 2025, the nation's combined fleet of new cars and trucks must have an average fuel efficiency of 54.5 miles per gallon.[4]

15–3b Climate Change

Observations collected by agencies such as the National Aeronautics and Space Administration (NASA) suggest that during the last half century, average global temperatures increased by about 0.74 degrees Celsius (1.33 degrees Fahrenheit). Figure 15–3 below illustrates this phenomenon. Most climatologists believe that this **global warming** is the result of human activities, especially the release of **greenhouse gases** such as CO_2 into the atmosphere.

A United Nations body, the Intergovernmental Panel on Climate Change (IPCC), estimated in 2013 that during the twenty-first century, global temperatures could rise an additional 1.0 to 4.8 degrees

Corporate Average Fuel Economy (CAFE) standards A set of federal standards under which each vehicle manufacturer (or the industry as a whole) must meet a miles-per-gallon benchmark averaged across all new cars or trucks.

global warming An increase in the average temperature of the Earth's surface over the last half century and its projected continuation; referred to more generally as *climate change*.

greenhouse gas A gas that, when released into the atmosphere, traps the sun's heat and slows its release into outer space. Carbon dioxide (CO_2) is a major example.

FIGURE 15–3

Global Warming

This map shows the changes in average temperature around the world between two periods of time. The first period is the years from 1951 to 1980. The second is 2000 to 2010. Temperatures are in degrees Celsius (°C). The orange area in the north of the earth indicates that average temperatures there increased by between 1 and 2 degrees Celsius.

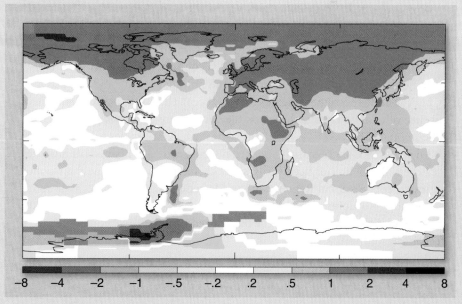

Source: NASA/GISS (Goddard Institute for Space Studies).

Celsius (1.8 to 8.6 degrees Fahrenheit). Warming may continue in subsequent centuries.

The predicted outcomes of climate change vary, depending on the climate models on which they are based. If the oceans grow warmer, seawater will expand, and polar ice will melt. (This last event is already underway.) These two developments will cause sea levels to rise, possibly negatively affecting some coastal areas. Rainfall patterns are expected to change, turning some areas into deserts but allowing agriculture to expand elsewhere. Other likely effects could include increases in extreme weather.

The Climate Change Debate   Some scientists dispute the consensus view of climate change. They argue that any observed warming is due largely to natural causes and may not continue into the future. Although this position is rare among scientists, it has been common in the broader community of Americans. Some public opinion polls taken in 2010, for example, revealed that only a third of Americans believed that climate change is the result of human activities.

Furthermore, attitudes toward climate change have become highly politicized. Some commentators on the political right contend that global warming is a giant liberal hoax designed to clear the way for increased government control of the economy and society. At the same time, many on the political left believe that the right-wing refusal to accept the existence of climate change threatens the very future of the human race.

Members of Congress are influenced by these attitudes even if they do not necessarily share them, and as a result, congressional Republicans and Democrats have almost no common ground on questions of how potential climate change might be reduced or its effects mitigated.

By 2013, however, belief that human activities were responsible for global warming had risen from one-third to about half of all respondents in some polls. Hot summers, widespread drought, and severe storms may have contributed to these results.

SOCIAL MEDIA In Politics

To learn what the natural gas industry has to say about fracking, search on "natural gas" on Facebook to bring up the page of America's Natural Gas Alliance. Artists against Fracking, a major antifracking group, has a presence on Facebook and Twitter.

15–3c New Energy Sources

The issues of U.S. energy security and climate change raise the question of whether we can develop new energy sources. Energy security means finding energy sources that are produced either in this country or by friendly neighbors such as Canada. A reduction in global warming means deploying energy sources that do not release CO_2 and other greenhouse gases into the atmosphere. As explained next, however, new energy sources may be accompanied by problems.

Expanded Supplies of Oil and Natural Gas

By 2012, many Americans had begun to realize that they were entering a new era of energy production. U.S. oil production, which declined rapidly after 1985, began to grow again in 2009. As noted earlier, crude oil imports are at 40 percent of consumption, down from more than 60 percent. In 2011, U.S. exports of petroleum *products*—refined goods such as gasoline—exceeded imports for the first time since 1949.

These developments are based in part on technological improvements and in part on higher prices. For example, production from oil sands in Alberta, Canada, was not profitable when prices for petroleum were low. With gasoline prices approaching $4 per gallon, however, extraction is quite feasible. In the United States itself, novel extraction techniques have allowed oil companies to open new oilfields.

THE NATURAL GAS BOOM.   An even more dramatic development is the increase in supplies of natural gas. Only a few years ago, experts believed that the United States would soon need to import natural gas. Because gas cannot be transported by ship efficiently unless it is converted to *liquefied natural gas (LNG)*, imports would be costly.

By 2012, however, gas producers were planning to *export* LNG. The nation was running out of facilities to store all the new gas, some of which was simply flamed off into the atmosphere. Low natural gas prices plus new air-pollution regulations made coal uncompetitive as a source of electricity. As a result, about one hundred coal-based power plants were closed or scheduled for retirement, and construction of new coal-based plants was at a standstill. Coal-producing regions such as eastern Kentucky and West Virginia faced serious economic difficulties.

An unexpected consequence of the boom in natural gas production was its environmental impact. Burning natural gas does release some CO_2 into the atmosphere, but less than half as much as coal. By 2011, U.S. emissions of CO_2 were actually down from 2008. The main cause was electricity generation using natural gas instead of coal. More fuel-efficient vehicles on the road added to the reduction.

THE FRACKING REVOLUTION. Why has it been possible for the United States to ramp up oil and natural gas production so greatly during the last several years? The answer is an extraction technique known as hydraulic fracturing, or **fracking.** This method involves pumping a high-pressure mixture of water, sand, and chemicals into oil- or gas-bearing underground rock, usually shale, to release the oil or gas. Fracking is not actually a new technique. High prices of oil and gas combined with improvements in the process, however, have made fracking cost-effective.

New oilfields in Texas and North Dakota are based on fracking. Twenty states now produce natural gas through fracking. A growing concern, though, is that the technology could lead to the contamination of underground water sources. Accordingly, various state governments are developing regulations aimed at preventing such contamination.

Offshore Drilling

Another method of reducing our reliance on foreign oil is additional exploration and drilling for oil and natural gas in waters off the American coastline. For twenty years, however, the federal government prohibited offshore drilling in much of the ocean. The concern was that oil spills could severely damage the environment.

During the 2008 elections, Republicans demanded that vast new areas be made available for drilling. Barack Obama also endorsed additional drilling, but in fewer areas. In March 2010, Obama proposed opening up a number of new areas for drilling.

In April 2010, three weeks after Obama's announcement, an offshore drilling platform in the Gulf of Mexico exploded and sank. The drilling platform was leased to BP, formerly known as British Petroleum. By the time the well was permanently plugged, 4.9 million barrels of oil had spilled into the Gulf—the largest oil spill in American history. In reaction to the disaster, President Obama placed a temporary moratorium on new deepwater-drilling projects.

Nuclear Energy

One energy source that cannot contribute to global warming is nuclear power—nuclear reactors do not release greenhouse gases. Still, due to concern over possible dangers and the difficulty of storing spent nuclear fuel, no new nuclear power plants have been built in the United States in more than thirty years. Because nuclear power appears to solve the problems of both energy security and greenhouse gas emissions, it recently attracted renewed interest. Only one new nuclear power plant is currently under construction, however.

The key obstacle to the construction of new nuclear plants is cost. Uranium, which is used to power these plants, must compete on price with natural gas as a fuel for new power plants. Currently, nuclear energy simply cannot compete on price.

Nuclear power also suffered a severe blow in 2011 as a result of a series of disasters in Japan. In March, a giant tsunami devastated the northeast coast of the country, and

Commercial windmills tower above a farm in upstate New York. What negative consequences might result from installing banks of very large windmills?

RON ANTONELLI/BLOOMBERG VIA GETTY IMAGES

fracking Technique for extracting oil or natural gas from underground rock by the high-power injection of a mixture of water, sand, and chemicals.

renewable energy
Energy from technologies that do not rely on extracted resources, such as oil and coal, that can run out.

economic policy
All actions taken by the national government to address ups and downs in the nation's level of business activity.

recession A period in which the level of economic activity falls; usually defined as two or more quarters of economic decline.

unemployment The state of not having a job even when actively seeking one.

more than 25,000 people died. Four reactors located on the coast were flooded, and radioactive material was released. Following the disaster, support for new nuclear plants in the United States fell from 57 percent to 43 percent in opinion polls.

Renewable Energy

Not all methods of supplying energy come with potentially hazardous by-products, such as greenhouse gases or nuclear waste. For example, hydroelectric energy, generated by water flowing through dams, is a widely used technology that employs no coal, natural gas, oil, or other fossil fuels.

Energy from such technologies is referred to as **renewable energy,** because it does not rely on extracting resources that can run out, such as oil, coal, or uranium ore. Obviously, renewable energy can reduce our dependence on imported oil, and as noted, it produces no greenhouse gases that may contribute to climate change. The problem has been that most existing renewable technologies, such as solar power cells, were expensive. Hydropower is an exception, but the number of feasible locations for new dams in the United States is small, and dams create their own environmental problems.

In recent years, however, the cost of solar power and wind energy has been falling fast. In response, the number of solar- and wind-power installations has grown rapidly. Of course, the wind does not always blow, and the sun does not always shine, so there are practical limits to how much of our electricity can be provided by these technologies.

FOR CRITICAL THINKING

One possible way to reduce greenhouse gas emissions would be to tax them by imposing a "carbon tax" on fuels that contain carbon. *Why hasn't Congress considered such a solution?*

15–4 Economic Policy

Under our current troubled economic conditions, policies that affect the economy are more important than any other set of activities the government undertakes.

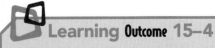

Learning Outcome 15–4

Describe the two major areas of economic policymaking, and discuss the issue of the public debt.

Economic policy consists of all actions taken by the government to address the ups and downs in the nation's level of business activity. National economic policy is solely the responsibility of the national government.

15–4a The Goals of Economic Policy

Everyone understands that the nation's economy passes through periods of "boom and bust" and that we recently experienced a major bust. Even in times when the economy has been less turbulent, however, the nation has alternated between periods of strong economic growth and periods of weak or no growth. This rhythm seems to be inherent in the capitalist system, and it is called the *business cycle*. A period in which the economy stops growing altogether and undergoes a contraction is called a **recession.** The most recent recession began in December 2007 and officially ended in June 2009. We say "officially," because even though economic growth resumed in 2009, the nation's economy is still operating well below its potential.

Unemployment The most important sign that the economy was still troubled was the high rate of **unemployment.** The rate of unemployment is measured by a government survey. People are defined as unemployed if they are without a job and are actively looking for one. An unemployment rate of 7 percent means that there are seven people looking for work for every ninety-three people who have a job. If "discouraged workers," who have given up looking for work, are also counted, the unemployment rate is substantially higher.

Even in the best of times, there is always a degree of unemployment, because some people are between jobs. Unemployment rates of 8 or 9 percent, however, are clear signs of economic and social distress. Few experiences are more psychologically damaging than extended unemployment. Reducing unemployment is a major policy objective.

Inflation Unemployment and recession go hand in hand. A second economic problem that the government must occasionally address is associated with economic booms. That problem is **inflation,** a sustained rise in average prices. A rise in prices is equivalent to a decline in the value of the dollar. High rates of inflation were a serious problem in the 1970s, but rates have fallen since. Even though the rate of inflation is now relatively low, many people are fearful that high rates could return at some point in the future.

The national government has two main tools to smooth the business cycle and to reduce unemployment and inflation. These tools are monetary policy and fiscal policy, and we describe them in the following sections.

15–4b Monetary Policy

One of the tools used in managing the economy is **monetary policy,** which involves changing the amount of money in circulation to affect interest rates, credit markets, the rate of inflation, the rate of economic growth, and the rate of unemployment. Monetary policy is under the control of the Federal Reserve System, an independent regulatory agency that is one of the government's most important sources of economic power.

The Federal Reserve System (the Fed) was established by Congress as the nation's central banking system in 1913. The Fed is governed by a board of seven governors, including the very influential chairperson. The president appoints the members of the board of governors, and the Senate must approve the nominations. Members of the board serve for fourteen-year terms. In addition to controlling the money supply, the Fed has a number of responsibilities in supervising and regulating the nation's banking system.

Easy Money, Tight Money The Fed and its **Federal Open Market Committee (FOMC)** make decisions about monetary policy several times each year. In theory, monetary policy is relatively straightforward. In periods of recession and high unemployment, the Fed pursues an **easy-money policy** to stimulate the economy by expanding the rate of growth of the money supply. An easy-money policy supposedly will lead to lower interest rates and induce consumers to spend more and producers to invest more.

In periods of rising inflation, the Fed does the reverse: it reduces the rate of growth in the amount of money in circulation—this is called a *tight-money policy.* This policy should cause interest rates to rise,

President Obama picked Janet Yellen, vice chair of the U.S. Federal Reserve, to replace Ben Bernanke as chair of the Fed. Bernanke retired in January 2014. Yellen is the first woman to lead the Fed.

thus inducing consumers to spend less and businesses to invest less.

"Pushing on a String" Although an easy-money policy may sound simple, the reality is not simple at all. To give one example, if times are hard enough, people and businesses may not want to borrow even if interest rates go down to zero. The government cannot force anyone to borrow, after all.

This state of affairs is not hypothetical—it has characterized the economy since 2008. The Fed has managed to keep the interest rate for short-term federal debt almost at zero, but rates of borrowing remain depressed. Instead of percolating into the actual economy, much of the extra money created by the Fed has piled up in excess bank reserves. With some reason, the failure of easy-money policy to spur the economy has been described as "pushing on a string."

inflation A sustained rise in average prices; equivalent to a decline in the value of the dollar.

monetary policy Actions taken by the Federal Reserve Board to change the amount of money in circulation to affect interest rates, credit markets, the rate of inflation, the rate of economic growth, and the rate of unemployment.

Federal Open Market Committee (FOMC) The most important body within the Federal Reserve System; decides how monetary policy should be carried out.

easy-money policy A monetary policy that involves stimulating the economy by expanding the rate of growth of the money supply.

The Fed has responded to the failure of its easy-money policy by adopting some unorthodox tactics. Ordinarily, the Fed expands the money supply by using the newly created money to purchase short-term federal government debt. Since 2010, however, it has undertaken programs of buying long-term federal debt in the hope that long-term purchases will be more effective than short-term ones. In addition, the Fed has begun purchasing private-sector debt obligations, such as securities based on residential mortgages.

Conservative Criticisms   The Fed's recent policies have alarmed some conservatives. A number of economists fear that at some point in the future the extra money created by the Fed—which is currently just sitting there—could pass into the real economy with explosive speed. The result would be increased inflation. In 2011, the Republican leadership in Congress sent a joint letter to the Fed demanding that it halt its activist policies. Texas governor Rick Perry, a candidate for president, went so far as to call the Fed's actions "treasonous."

A second response to the Fed's actions has been the growth in the philosophy of "hard money" among radical conservatives. Led by Representative Ron Paul of Texas, hard-money advocates believe that the government should not be in the business of creating money at all, but should tie the value of the dollar to commodities such as gold. Mainstream economists, both liberal and conservative, believe that such a policy would lead to a dramatic contraction in the money supply and a recession of unprecedented severity.

15–4c Fiscal Policy

Prior to the onset of the Great Recession, mainstream economists agreed on one point: under ordinary circumstances, monetary policy would be sufficient to steer the economy. If monetary policy proved to be inadequate, however, many economists also recommended use of a second tool—fiscal policy.

The principle underlying **fiscal policy,** like the one that underlies monetary policy, is relatively simple: when unemployment is rising and the economy is going into a recession, fiscal policy should stimulate economic activity by increasing government spending, decreasing taxes, or both. When unemployment is decreasing and prices are rising (that is, when we have inflation), fiscal policy should curb economic activity by reducing government spending, increasing taxes, or both.

In the past, fiscal policy meant raising or lowering rates of taxation. Such changes could be accomplished quickly and would not trigger disputes about government spending. The severity of the Great Recession, however, led some economists to recommend increases in government spending as well.

U.S. fiscal policy is associated with the economic theories of the British economist John Maynard Keynes (1883–1946). Keynes's theories, which we address next, were the result of his study of the Great Depression of the 1930s.

Keynes and the Great Depression   According to **Keynesian economics,** the nation cannot automatically recover from a disaster such as the Great Depression—or for that matter, the Great Recession. In both cases, the shock that initiates the crisis frightens consumers and businesses so much that they, in great numbers, begin to reduce their borrowing and spending.

Unfortunately, if everyone in the economy tries to cut spending at the same time, demand for goods and services drops sharply. That, in turn, reduces the income of everyone selling these goods and services. People become even more reluctant to borrow and spend. The cycle feeds on itself.

fiscal policy The use of changes in government expenditures and taxes to alter national economic variables.

Keynesian economics An economic theory proposed by British economist John Maynard Keynes that is typically associated with the use of fiscal policy to alter national economic variables.

British economist John Maynard Keynes developed theories of how to pull the world out of the Great Depression in the 1930s.

WALTER STONEMAN/SAMUEL BOURNE/GETTY IMAGES

The Keynesian solution to this type of impasse is for the government to provide the demand by a huge, if temporary, spending program. The spending has to be financed by borrowing. The government, in other words, begins borrowing when the private sector stops. Some economists believe that just such a spending program broke the back of the Great Depression—that is, the "spending program" known as World War II (1939–1945).

Keynes and the Great Recession Until recently, support for Keynesianism was relatively bipartisan. Republican president Richard Nixon once said, "I am now a Keynesian." Even President George W. Bush justified his tax cuts with Keynesian rhetoric. From the years after World War II until the first years of the twenty-first century, it was relatively easy to be a Keynesian. After all, Keynesian solutions could be implemented through relatively small changes to rates of taxation. The Bush administration sponsored just such a tax-based stimulus in early 2008, when the Great Recession had already begun but was not yet a major disaster.

OBAMA VERSUS THE REPUBLICANS. In February 2009, with the full scope of the recession evident, Obama proposed and Congress passed a stimulus package of roughly $800 billion, made up mostly of spending, not tax cuts. This was a classical Keynesian response to the recession, but it turned out to be a one-time measure. From 2009 on, Republicans in Congress strongly rejected Keynesianism. An important group of economists had long opposed Keynesian theories. They argued that it is not possible to stimulate the economy through federal borrowing. The borrowing just drains funds from some other part of the economy. A few members of Congress turned to these thinkers. Most of the Republicans, however, simply objected to the use of budget deficits as a recession-fighting tool.

THE ECLIPSE OF KEYNESIANISM. If it took World War II to eliminate unemployment in the 1940s, Keynesian economics faced a problem in 2009. The increase in the federal budget deficit necessary to end the economic crisis could be very large. Some Keynesians outside the Obama administration calculated that, to have a

real impact, stimulus spending would have to be three times the $800 billion already committed.[5] That type of program was politically impossible. Few Americans would accept new government spending programs amounting to trillions of dollars. By the time of his State of the Union address in 2010, Obama himself was employing rhetoric that was substantially anti-Keynesian.

State and local government spending dropped sharply after the expiration of the 2009 stimulus, and more than half a million state and local workers lost their jobs. At the federal level, even though explicitly Keynesian fiscal policies were off the table, the government continued to run trillion-dollar budget deficits through 2012. The size of these deficits became a major political issue. By 2013, however, the deficit had begun to decline noticeably. Is the federal deficit still a problem today? We address that question in the *Join the Debate* feature on the following page.

15–4d The Federal Tax System

The government raises money to pay its expenses in two ways: through taxes levied on business and personal income and through borrowing. The American income tax system is progressive—meaning that as you earn more income, you pay a higher tax rate on the additional income earned.

The 2013 tax rates are shown in Table 15–1 below. More than 40 percent of American families earn so little that they have no income tax liability at all, and this figure temporarily hit 47 percent at the height of the

TABLE 15–1

Tax Rates for Single Persons and Married Couples: Tax Year 2013, Filed in April 2014

Single Persons		Married Filing Jointly	
Marginal Tax Bracket	Marginal Tax Rate	Marginal Tax Bracket	Marginal Tax Rate
$0–$8,925	10%	$0–$17,850	10%
$8,926–$36,250	15%	$17,851–$72,500	15%
$36,251–$87,850	25%	$72,501–$146,400	25%
$87,851–$183,250	28%	$146,401–$223,050	28%
$183,251–$398,350	33%	$223,051–$398,350	33%
$398,351–$400,000	35%	$398,351–$450,000	35%
$400,001 and higher	39.6%	$450,001 and higher	39.6%

Source: Internal Revenue Service.

Does the Size of the Federal Budget Deficit Still Matter?

If a family lets its spending exceed its income, it is running a "deficit." It can only do this if it dips into savings or goes into debt to make up the difference. If a family goes into debt, sooner or later it will have to pay back that obligation. For the last half century, in contrast, the federal government has run a budget deficit in all but four years. Whenever there is a deficit, the government borrows from domestic and foreign residents, firms, and governments. Each deficit adds to the national debt, and so each year the national debt grows.

Do we have to worry about the federal deficit and the growing national debt? Some argue that we do, whereas others believe the problem is exaggerated.

We Should Always Worry about Federal Deficits

Many people believe that the federal deficit is a major problem. Today, we are still borrowing hundreds of billions of dollars per year. Of course, that's better than the trillions of dollars that we borrowed from 2009 through 2012, but it's still too much. We should try to reduce the federal debt, not raise it. Someday, we are sure to have another recession. If by that time we haven't paid down some of what we borrowed during the last recession, the debt could become truly unsustainable. Even now, we face a potential danger from the interest on the national debt. For the moment, the federal government can borrow at abnormally low rates. What happens when those rates go back to normal?

Lurking behind the deficit is federal government spending. The deficit—and the public debt—has allowed the size of government to increase relative to the rest of the economy. For a healthy economy, we need to grow the private sector, not the government.

The Deficit Is Falling, So What's the Worry?

Those who believe that the deficit is not an important problem now point to the fact that it is falling. Spending cuts and tax increases enacted from 2010 through 2013 have had their effect, and the slow-but-sure recovery has added to federal tax receipts.

The last thing our economy needs is to cut the deficit further when unemployment is still high. Consider what happened in the Great Recession. Everyone tried to pay off debts—in effect, to be a lender, not a borrower. But *for every lender there has to be a borrower*. If everyone tries to get out of debt at the same time, the economy crashes, and some people are forced to go deeper in debt instead. Better that the *government* should go into debt—it can afford to do so. That was Keynes's insight. For decades, our economy has grown even with substantial deficits. We should worry less about the federal deficit and more about creating jobs for young people and controlling health-care costs.

FOR CRITICAL **ANALYSIS** Unlike a family, the federal government has the power to create money out of thin air. What could happen if the government abused this power?

recession. (For a discussion of the amount of taxes paid by the rich versus other groups in American society, see this chapter's *Perception versus Reality* feature on the following page.)

The Action-Reaction Syndrome
The Internal Revenue Code consists of thousands of pages, thousands of sections, and thousands of subsections. In other words, our tax system is not simple. Part of the reason for this complexity is that tax policy has always been plagued by the **action-reaction syndrome,** a term describing the following phenomenon: *for every government action, there will be a reaction by the public.*

Often, the government will react with another action, and the public will follow with further reaction. The ongoing action-reaction cycle is clearly operative in policymaking on taxes.

action-reaction syndrome The principle that for every government action, there will be a reaction by the public.

Perception versus Reality

Tax-Rate Cuts Allow the Rich to Pay Lower Taxes

As the saying goes, only two things are certain— death and taxes. In recent years, though, different presidents have instituted a number of tax-rate cuts. A major reduction occurred in 2003 under the administration of George W. Bush.

THE PERCEPTION

You often hear or read that the Bush tax-rate cuts favored the rich. After all, it's the rich who received the lion's share of the benefits from these tax-rate cuts.

THE REALITY

First, we must distinguish between tax rates and taxes paid. It is true that the Bush tax cuts lowered the top marginal income tax rate from 39.6 percent to 35 percent and that the long-term capital gains tax rate dropped from 20 percent to 15 percent. Also, the rate applied to dividends fell. Therefore, the tax rates on the highest-income individuals did indeed fall after the tax cuts of 2003 were enacted.

At the same time, though, the percentage of taxes paid by the rich went up, not down. Indeed, the share of individual income taxes paid by the top 1 percent of income earners rose steadily from about 1981 to 2000, dropped off a bit from 2000 to 2003, and has risen ever since.

According to the nonpartisan Congressional Budget Office, the top 40 percent of income earners in the United States pay 99.1 percent of all income taxes. The top 10 percent pay more than 70 percent of all income taxes. At the bottom end of the scale, more than 40 percent of this nation's households pay no income taxes at all (though they do pay Social Security and Medicare contributions). Finally, it is true that the rich have been getting richer in the United States. Nevertheless, their individual tax liabilities have gone up more quickly than their share of income.

These data give us some indication of what may happen now that Congress has failed to extend the Bush tax cuts on the upper tax brackets. As a result of the changes made in December 2012, the top long-term capital gains tax rate rose to 23.8 percent. The marginal income tax rate for a couple making more than $450,000 per year went up from 35 percent to 39.6 percent. Wealthy individuals are likely to respond to these higher tax rates by adjusting their behavior. The higher rates could actually result in the rich paying less in taxes, not more.

BLOG ON Scott Adams, creator of the *Dilbert* comic strip, makes hilarious and fresh observations about all sorts of things on his blog. Taxing the rich is just one of his topics—try searching on "dilbert blog tax 2007."

Tax Loopholes Generally, the action-reaction syndrome means that the higher the tax rate—the action on the part of the government—the greater the public's reaction to that tax rate. Individuals and corporations facing high tax rates will react by making concerted attempts to get Congress to add various loopholes to the tax law that will allow them to reduce their taxable incomes.

Years ago, when Congress imposed very high tax rates on high incomes, it also provided for more loopholes. These loopholes enabled many wealthy individuals to decrease their tax bills significantly. For example, special tax provisions allowed investors in oil and gas wells to reduce their taxable income. Additional loopholes permitted individuals to shift income from one year to the next—which meant that they could postpone the payment of their taxes for one year. Still more loopholes let U.S. citizens form corporations outside the United States in order to avoid some taxes completely. We discussed tax loopholes in the *Join the Debate* feature in Chapter 6.

Will We Ever Have a Truly Simple Tax System? The Tax Reform Act of 1986 was intended to lower taxes and simplify the tax code—and it did just that for most taxpayers. A few years later, however, large federal deficits forced Congress to choose between cutting spending and raising taxes, and Congress opted to do the latter. Tax increases occurred under the administrations of both George H. W. Bush (1989–1993) and Bill Clinton (1993–2001). In fact, the tax rate for the highest income bracket rose from 28 percent in 1986 to 39.6 percent in 1993. Thus, the effective highest marginal tax rate increased significantly.

In response to this sharp increase in taxes, those who were affected lobbied Congress to legislate special exceptions and loopholes so that the full impact of the rate increase would not be felt by the wealthiest Americans. As a result, the tax code is more complicated than it was before the 1986 Tax Reform Act.

While in principle everyone is for a simpler tax code, in practice Congress rarely is able to pass tax-reform legislation. Why? The reason is that those who now benefit from our complicated tax code will not give up their tax breaks without a fight.

These groups include homeowners who deduct interest on their mortgages (and therefore the home-building industry as well), charities that receive tax-deductible contributions, and businesses that get tax breaks for research and development. Two other groups also benefit greatly from the current complicated tax code: tax accountants and tax lawyers.

15–4e The Public Debt

When the government spends more than it receives, it has to finance this shortfall. Typically, it borrows. The U.S. Treasury sells IOUs on behalf of the U.S. government. They are

public debt The total amount of money that the national government owes as a result of borrowing; also called the *national debt*.

called U.S. Treasury bills, notes, or bonds, depending on how long the funds are borrowed. All are commonly called *treasuries*.

The sale of these obligations to corporations, private individuals, pension plans, foreign governments, foreign companies, and foreign individuals is big business. After all, except for a few years in the late 1990s and early 2000s, federal government expenditures have always exceeded federal government revenues.

Every time there is a federal government deficit, there is an increase in the total accumulated **public debt** (also called the *national debt*), which is defined as the total value of all outstanding federal government borrowing. If the existing public debt is $5 trillion and the government runs a deficit of $100 billion, then at the end of the year the public debt is $5.1 trillion. Figure 15–4 below shows what has happened to the *net* public debt over time, in comparison with the overall size of the economy. (The net public debt doesn't count sums that the government owes to itself, although it does include funds held by the Fed.)

The Burden of the Public Debt We often hear about the burden of the public debt. Some even maintain that the government will eventually go bankrupt. As long as the government can collect taxes to pay interest on its public debt, however, that will never happen. What happens instead is that when treasuries come due, they are simply "rolled over," or refinanced.

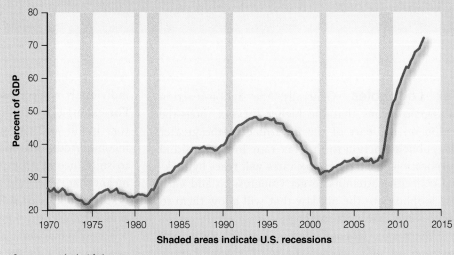

FIGURE 15–4

The Net Public Debt
as a Percentage of the Gross Domestic Product (GDP)

Shaded areas indicate U.S. recessions

Source: research.stlouisfed.org.

Every time Congress must raise the national debt ceiling, there are protesters who want the federal government to "Hold the Line."

JONATHAN ERNST/REUTERS

That is, if a $1 million Treasury bond comes due today and is cashed in, the U.S. Treasury pays it off with the money it gets from selling another $1 million bond.

The interest on treasuries is paid by federal taxes. Even though much of the interest is being paid to American citizens, the more the federal government borrows to meet these payments, the greater the percentage of its budget that is committed to making interest payments. This reduces the government's ability to supply funds for anything else, including transportation, education, housing programs, and the military.

Public Debt Explosion, 2009–2012 As discussed earlier, the initial response of the federal government to the Great Recession was to increase spending. At the same time, the economy was shrinking, so tax revenues were shrinking, too. Between increased spending and lower revenues, the federal budget deficit shot up. The deficit for 2011 was $1.3 trillion. That was about 8.6 percent of the entire economy. (The estimated deficit for 2013 was down to about $760 billion.) If we look at all levels of government together, for every five dollars of spending, three were backed up by tax receipts. The other two were borrowed.

Debt Held by Foreigners An additional problem with a growing federal debt involves how much non-Americans own. Today, about half of the U.S. net public debt is owned by foreign individuals,

foreign businesses, and foreign central banks.

The largest debt holder is the People's Republic of China. The federal government owes China about $1.28 trillion. Japan is in second place, with $1.14 trillion in federal obligations. As long as China sells us more in exports than it imports from the United States, it accumulates dollars. China (and Japan) have chosen to use those dollars to buy U.S. government treasuries rather than to import more American-made goods.

Some worry that these foreigners might not want to keep all of the U.S. debt they now hold. In such a situation, efforts to sell U.S. government treasuries might lead to a collapse in the markets for government obligations in this country. The result could be much higher interest rates. If the value of U.S. treasuries fell sharply, however, countries such as China and Japan would lose tremendous sums on their investments.[6]

So far, there have been no signs that foreign investors are losing their appetite for treasuries. Indeed, during the recent economic crises, frightened investors bought more treasuries in the belief that they were the safest possible investment. As a result, the government has been able to borrow at very low interest rates. For example, the September 2013 rate for four-week bills, the shortest-term obligations, was 0.015 percent. (The rate for five-year notes was 1.375 percent, and the rate for thirty-year bonds was 3.625 percent.) With the rate of inflation below just 2 percent in 2013, those buying four-week and five-year treasuries were actually losing money on their loans to the federal government.

The Debt Ceiling One threat to U.S. obligations does not come from foreign nations, but is entirely domestic. That is the danger that at some point the U.S. Congress will fail to raise the *debt ceiling*. Possible results of such a failure include federal default on payments to vendors, employees, recipients of entitlement spending, and even investors holding U.S. treasuries.

Almost uniquely among nations, the U.S. government cannot automatically borrow to fund spending over and above what is paid for by taxes or other government income. Congress has long set a cap, or ceiling, on the total amount of borrowing. Due to the growth of the national debt, it is necessary from time to time to raise the cap. Raising the debt ceiling does not authorize future government spending. It simply determines how much the government may borrow to fund already-existing obligations.

THE DEBT-CEILING CRISIS OF 2011.   In the past, raising the debt ceiling gave various members of Congress a chance to show off politically by voting against a measure that was guaranteed to pass. In 2011, however, House Republicans demanded real cuts to the federal budget in return for raising the ceiling. In the resulting negotiations, the Obama administration and the Republicans agreed to $917 billion in budget cuts over the following ten years.

A congressional committee was established to negotiate additional reductions. If the committee failed to report, a series of automatic cuts would apply to discretionary programs, both domestic and military. In fact, the committee deadlocked, and the cuts, known as the "sequester," finally took effect in March 2013.

THE CRISIS OF OCTOBER 2013.   In October 2013, the government again approached a debt-ceiling crisis. This time, the debt-ceiling crisis was entwined with the issue of a federal government shutdown. On October 1, a continuing resolution to fund the activities of the federal government expired. (We discussed continuing resolutions in Chapter 11.) A majority of the Republicans in the House refused to accept a renewal unless it defunded or delayed the Affordable Care Act. As a result, about 800,000 federal employees were furloughed. Another 1.3 million, who were considered "essential," were required to work (temporarily) without pay.

House Republicans also stated that they would not raise the debt ceiling without concessions on Obamacare. The Treasury announced that it would exhaust its borrowing ability on October 17. Obama and congressional Democrats refused to engage in budget negotiations until the crisis was over.

Reaction by the public and the business community to these developments was highly negative. On October 16, the Republicans gave in. Speaker John Boehner submitted a "clean" continuing resolution and debt-ceiling increase. The bill, which contained only trivial concessions by the Democrats, was supported by all Democrats and a minority of Republicans. (It therefore violated the *Hastert rule*—see Chapter 11.) Ironically, the standoff drew attention away from the very rocky start-up of the Obamacare insurance exchanges. The national Web site for the exchanges was almost non-functional for weeks after the October 1 start date.

FOR CRITICAL THINKING

Why would anyone make an almost no-interest loan to the U.S. federal government?

AMERICA AT
ODDS Domestic Policy

The Preamble to the U.S. Constitution states that one of the goals of the new government was to "promote the general Welfare." Domestic policy is certainly the main way in which our government seeks to promote the general welfare. But how should this be done? Americans are at odds over many domestic issues. A few of them are listed here:

- Do we send too many people to prison—or do our current incarceration policies protect the public?

- Should health-care insurance be a right of all citizens—or does such a program sap individual initiative and lead to an over-mighty government?

- Is climate change a serious problem that must be addressed now—or are the risks overblown and the proposed solutions a danger to our economy?

- Is new offshore drilling essential to our energy independence—or is it an unacceptable threat to the environment?

- Is a budgetary stimulus a necessary tool to fight recessions—or does it simply worsen the long-term budget deficit?

STUDY TOOLS

Ready to study?

- **Review** what you've read with the quiz below.
- Check your answers on the **Chapter in Review** card at the back of the book.
- For any questions you miss, read the corresponding **Learning Outcome** section again to prepare for class and your exam.
- Rip out and study the **Chapter in Review** card (at the back of the book).

Fill-In

Learning Outcome 15–1

1. The stages of the policymaking process are _____.

Learning Outcome 15–2

2. _____ is now the federal government's second-largest domestic spending program, after Social Security.

3. The individual mandate in the 2010 health-care reform legislation is a requirement that _____.

Learning Outcome 15–3

4. The nations of _____ supply 40 percent of our oil imports.

5. The predicted outcomes of climate change include _____.

6. Renewable energy technologies include _____.

Learning Outcome 15–4

7. A period in which the economy stops growing altogether and undergoes a contraction is called a _____.

8. Monetary policy is under the control of the _____, an independent regulatory agency.

9. Today, about half of the U.S. net public debt is owned by foreign individuals, foreign businesses, and foreign central banks. The largest debt holder is _____.

Multiple Choice

Learning Outcome 15–1

10. A discussion in the media about a problem that might have a political solution is an example of
    a. policy adoption.
    b. policy implementation.
    c. issue identification.

Learning Outcome 15–2

11. About ____ percent of national spending in the United States goes to health care.
    a. 4
    b. 17.7
    c. 29.5

12. One immediate change brought about by the health-care reform bills that passed in 2010 was that young people can remain covered by their parents' insurance until they turn
    a. 26.
    b. 21.
    c. 18.

Learning Outcome 15–3

13. The CAFE standards
    a. regulate offshore drilling.
    b. measure the effect of greenhouse gases.
    c. are designed to force auto and truck manufacturers to increase the fuel efficiency of their vehicles.

Learning Outcome 15–4

14. ____ policy uses changes in government expenditures and taxes to alter national economic variables.
    a. Monetary
    b. Fiscal
    c. Domestic

15. According to the nonpartisan Congressional Budget Office, more than ____ percent of this nation's households pay no income taxes at all.
    a. 10
    b. 23
    c. 40

Foreign Policy

Remember to visit page 373 for additional **Study Tools**

WIN MCNAMEE/GETTY IMAGES

AMERICA AT ODDS
Do Russia's Ambitions Mean Trouble?

ASTAPKOVICH VLADIMIR/ITAR-TASS/LANDOV

In August 2008, the Russian army invaded the small neighboring country of Georgia. The invasion was Russia's first use of troops outside its own borders since the dissolution of the Soviet Union in 1991. Many people around the world drew the obvious conclusion: the "Russian bear" was back—and it posed a threat to world peace.

During the years of the Cold War, from the late 1940s until the end of the 1980s, the Russian-dominated Soviet Union clearly was a threat to peace. The Soviets had occupied Eastern Europe. By the 1960s, even the Chinese were worried that the Soviets might attack them. Soviet nuclear weapons were at least equal to those of the United States. In 1985, the Soviet Union also had a population of 278 million, compared with 238 million in the United States.

The impact of the Soviet breakup on Russian power was almost beyond belief. With the loss of the fourteen other Soviet republics, Russia's population fell to 149 million. Its economy was in a state of collapse. Its inventory of main battle tanks had fallen from 51,000 to 19,500.[1] Russia was unable to prevent its former "satellite states" in Eastern Europe from joining NATO, the American-led alliance originally established to defend the West against the Soviets.

Russia today is not nearly as formidable as the Soviet Union was—but how much of a threat is it, really? Americans who take an interest in foreign affairs are at odds over this issue.

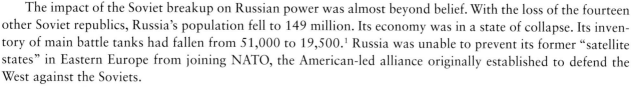

A Stronger Russia Is Bad News

Those who believe that Russia poses a threat to world peace point to its attack on Georgia, threats made against Ukraine, and the cyberwar it launched against the tiny nation of Estonia. Russia is regaining the economic power needed to support a large military. Its economy experienced a substantial recovery during the first two terms of President Vladimir Putin (2000–2008). Putin was popular, and he has retained much of his popularity despite his undermining of Russia's democratic institutions. Putin reclaimed the presidency in 2012.

Russia is the world's largest exporter of natural gas and the second-largest oil exporter. It currently provides 34 percent of Europe's oil imports and 32 percent of its natural gas. Russia has repeatedly used its energy exports for political purposes. It has temporarily cut off gas supplies to Belarus, the Czech Republic, Georgia, Lithuania, and Ukraine.

Russia's Future Looks Grim

Those who are less worried about the return of the Russian bear point out several factors that may undermine its future as a world power. In many countries, oil wealth has led to gross corruption and inefficiency, and this has happened in Russia. The greatest threat to Russia's future, however, is its collapsing population. Russia's population is now down to 143 million, and the United Nations estimates that it may fall to 132 million by 2050.

Several developed nations expect to lose people in forthcoming years. No nation, however, is experiencing losses that come close to what is predicted for Russia. If Russia is no longer one of the world's most populous countries, it will not be able to maintain its position as a great power. Russia has not only a low birth rate, but a very high death rate. The life expectancy of a Russian male is only about sixty-three years. Experts attribute this in part to extremely high rates of alcoholism among men.

Where do you stand?

1. What factors might cause Russia to take a belligerent stand toward neighboring countries?
2. In 2009, President Barack Obama and Secretary of State Hillary Clinton stated that they would "push the reset button" in relations with Russia in an attempt to move beyond the negative feelings that had developed during the Bush administration. Was this attempt successful? Why or why not?

Explore this issue online

- Entering "russia" into a search engine will provide background information from a variety of sources, including Wikipedia, the Central Intelligence Agency, and the *New York Times*. Searching on "russia demographic" yields stories on Russia's decreasing population—and some arguments that the decline is overestimated.

Introduction

What we call **foreign policy** is a systematic and general plan that guides a country's attitudes and actions toward the rest of the world. Foreign policy includes all of the economic, military, commercial, and diplomatic positions and actions that a nation takes in its relationships with other countries. Although foreign policy may seem quite removed from the concerns of everyday life, it can and does have a significant impact on the day-to-day lives of Americans.

American foreign policy has been shaped by two principles that are often seen as contradicting each other. One is **moral idealism,** the belief that the most important goal in foreign policy is to do what is right. Moral idealists think that it is possible for nations to relate to each other as part of a rule-based community. Moral idealism appeals to the often-held American belief that our nation is special and should provide an example to the rest of the world.

A contrasting view is **political realism,** the belief that nations are inevitably selfish. Foreign countries, therefore, are by definition dangerous. Foreign policy must be based on protecting our national security, regardless of moral arguments. Although there have been times when one or the other of these two principles has dominated, U.S. foreign policy has usually been a mixture of both.

16–1 Who Makes U.S. Foreign Policy?

The framers of the Constitution envisioned that the president and Congress would cooperate in developing American foreign policy. The Constitution did not spell out exactly how this was to be done, though. As commander in chief, the president has assumed much of the decision-making power in the area of foreign policy. Nonetheless, members of Congress, a number of officials, and a vast national security bureaucracy help to shape the president's decisions and to limit the president's powers.

foreign policy A systematic and general plan that guides a country's attitudes and actions toward the rest of the world. Foreign policy includes all of the economic, military, commercial, and diplomatic positions and actions that a nation takes in its relationships with other countries.

moral idealism In foreign policy, the belief that the most important goal is to do what is right. Moral idealists think that it is possible for nations to cooperate as part of a rule-based community.

political realism In foreign policy, the belief that nations are inevitably selfish and that we should seek to protect our national security, regardless of moral arguments.

Learning Outcome 16–1
Discuss how foreign policy is made, and identify the key players in this process.

16–1a The President's Role

Article II, Section 2, of the Constitution names the president commander in chief of the armed forces. As commander in chief, the president oversees the military and guides defense policies. Presidents have interpreted this role broadly, sending American troops, ships, and weapons to trouble spots at home and around the world.

The Constitution authorizes the president to make treaties, which must be approved by two-thirds of the Senate. In addition, the president is empowered to form executive agreements—pacts between the president and the heads of other nations. These executive agreements do not require Senate approval.

The president's foreign policy responsibilities have special significance in that the president has ultimate control over the use of nuclear weapons. The president also influences foreign policymaking in the role of head of state. As the symbolic head of our government, the president represents the United States to the rest of the world. When a serious foreign policy issue or international question arises, the nation expects the president to make a formal statement on the matter.

16–1b The Cabinet

Many members of the president's cabinet concern themselves with international problems and recommend policies to deal with them. As U.S. power in the world has grown and as economic factors have become increasingly important, the departments of Commerce, Agriculture, Treasury, and Energy have become more involved in foreign policy decisions. The secretary of state and the secretary of defense, however, are the only cabinet members who concern themselves with foreign policy matters on a full-time basis.

The Department of State The Department of State is, in principle, the government agency most directly involved in foreign policy. The department is responsible for diplomatic relations with nearly two hundred independent nations around the globe, as well as with the United Nations and other multilateral organizations, such as the Organization of American

States. Most U.S. relations with other countries are maintained through embassies, consulates, and other U.S. offices around the world.

As the head of the State Department, the secretary of state has traditionally played a key role in foreign policymaking, and many presidents have relied heavily on the advice of their secretaries of state. Since the end of World War II, though, the preeminence of the State Department in foreign policy has declined dramatically.

The Department of Defense   The Department of Defense is the principal executive department that establishes and carries out defense policy and protects our national security. The secretary of defense advises the president on all aspects of U.S. military and defense policy, supervises all of the military activities of the U.S. government, and works to see that the decisions of the president as commander in chief are carried out. The secretary advises and informs the president on the nation's military forces, weapons, and bases and works closely with the U.S. military, especially the Joint Chiefs of Staff, in gathering and studying defense information.

> ## "TO BE PREPARED FOR WAR
> is one of the most effectual means of preserving peace."
>
> ~ GEORGE WASHINGTON ~
> COMMANDER OF THE CONTINENTAL ARMY
> AND FIRST PRESIDENT OF THE
> UNITED STATES
> 1789–1797

The Joint Chiefs of Staff include the chief of staff of the Army, the chief of staff of the Air Force, the chief of naval operations, and the commandant of the Marine Corps. The chairperson of the Joint Chiefs of Staff is appointed by the president for a four-year term.

The joint chiefs regularly serve as the key military advisers to the president, the secretary of defense, and the National Security Council. They are responsible for handing down the president's orders to the nation's military units, preparing strategic plans, and recommending military actions. They also propose military budgets, new weapons systems, and military regulations.

16-1c Other Agencies

Several other government agencies are also involved in the foreign relations of the United States. Two key agencies in the area of foreign policy are the National Security Council and the Central Intelligence Agency.

The National Security Council   The National Security Council (NSC) was established by the National Security Act of 1947. The formal members of the NSC include the president, the vice president, the secretary of state, and the secretary of defense. Meetings are often attended by the chairperson of the Joint Chiefs of Staff, the director of the Central Intelligence Agency, and representatives from other departments.

The national security adviser, who is a member of the president's White House staff, is the director of the NSC. The adviser informs the president, coordinates advice and information on foreign policy, and serves as a liaison with other officials.

The NSC and its members can be as important and powerful as the president wants them to be. Some presidents have made frequent use of the NSC, whereas others have

JACQUELYN MARTIN-POOL/GETTY IMAGES

U.S. Secretary of Defense Chuck Hagel visits a U.S. naval base in Japan in 2013. Why does the United States continue to station troops in Japan and South Korea?

convened it infrequently. Similarly, the importance of the role played by the national security adviser in shaping foreign policy can vary significantly, depending on the administration and the adviser's identity.

The Central Intelligence Agency The Central Intelligence Agency (CIA) was created after World War II to coordinate American intelligence activities abroad. The CIA provides the president and his or her advisers with up-to-date information about the political, military, and economic activities of foreign governments.

The CIA gathers much of its intelligence from overt sources, such as foreign radio broadcasts and newspapers, people who travel abroad, the Internet, and satellite photographs. Other information is gathered from covert activities, such as the CIA's own secret investigations into the economic or political affairs of other nations. Covert operations may involve secretly supplying weapons to a force rebelling against an unfriendly government or seizing suspected terrorists in a clandestine operation and holding them for questioning.

The CIA has tended to operate autonomously, and the details of its work, methods, and operating funds have been kept secret. Intelligence reform passed by Congress in 2004, however, makes the CIA accountable to a national intelligence director. The CIA is now required to cooperate more with other U.S. intelligence agencies and has lost a degree of the autonomy it once enjoyed.

16–1d Powers of Congress

Although the executive branch takes the lead in foreign policy matters, Congress also has some power over foreign policy. Remember that Congress alone has the power to declare war. It also has the power to appropriate funds to build new weapons systems, equip the U.S. armed forces, and provide for foreign aid. The Senate has the power to approve or reject the implementation of treaties and the appointment of ambassadors.

In 1973, Congress passed the War Powers Resolution, which limits the president's use of troops in military action without congressional approval. Presidents since then, however, have not interpreted the resolution to mean that Congress must be consulted before military action is taken. On several occasions, presidents have

isolationism A political policy of noninvolvement in world affairs.

ordered military action and then informed Congress after the fact.

A few congressional committees are directly concerned with foreign affairs. The most important are the Armed Services Committee and the Committee on Foreign Affairs in the House, and the Armed Services Committee and the Foreign Relations Committee in the Senate. Other congressional committees deal with matters that indirectly influence foreign policy, such as oil, agriculture, and imports.

FOR CRITICAL THINKING

Should American citizens know more about what the CIA does, or would such knowledge merely benefit our opponents? In either case, why?

16–2 A Short History of American Foreign Policy

Many U.S. foreign policy initiatives have been rooted in moral idealism. A primary consideration in U.S. foreign policy, though, has always been

Learning Outcome 16–2

Summarize the history of American foreign policy through the years.

national security—the protection of the independence and political integrity of the nation.

Over the years, the United States has attempted to preserve its national security in many ways. These ways have changed over time and are not always internally consistent. This inconsistency results from the fact that foreign policymaking, like domestic policymaking, reflects the influence of various political groups in the United States. These groups—including the voting public, interest groups, Congress, and the president and relevant agencies of the executive branch—are often at odds over what the U.S. position should be on particular foreign policy issues.

16–2a Isolationism

The nation's founders and the early presidents believed that **isolationism**—avoiding political involvement

STOCK MONTAGE/GETTY IMAGES

President James Monroe (1817–1825) said that the United States would not accept foreign intervention in the Western Hemisphere.

lost and subsequently ceded control of several of its possessions, including Guam, Puerto Rico, and the Philippines, to the United States. The United States thus acquired a **colonial empire** and was acknowledged as a world power.

The growth of the United States as an industrial economy also confirmed the nation's position as a world power. For example, in the early 1900s, President Theodore Roosevelt proposed that the United States could invade Latin American countries when it was necessary to guarantee political or economic stability.

16–2c The World Wars

When World War I broke out in 1914, President Woodrow Wilson initially proclaimed a policy of **neutrality**—the United States would not take sides in the conflict. The United States did not enter the war until 1917, after U.S. ships in international waters were attacked by German submarines that were blockading Britain.

Wilson called the war a way to "make the world safe for democracy." In his eyes, Germany was not merely dangerous but evil. Wilson, in short, was our most famous presidential advocate of *moral idealism.*

After World War I ended in 1918, the United States returned to a policy of isolationism. Consequently, we refused to join the League of Nations, an international body intended to resolve peacefully any future conflicts between nations.

But the U.S. policy of isolationism ended when the Japanese attacked Pearl Harbor in 1941. We joined the Allies— Australia, Britain, Canada, China, France, and the Soviet Union—to fight the Axis nations of Germany, Italy, and Japan. One of the most significant foreign policy actions during World War II was the dropping of atomic bombs on the Japanese cities of Hiroshima and Nagasaki

with other nations—was the best way to protect American interests. The United States was certainly not yet strong enough to directly influence European developments. As president of the new nation, George Washington did little in terms of foreign policy. Indeed, in his Farewell Address in 1797, he urged Americans to "steer clear of permanent alliances with any portion of the foreign world." During the 1700s and 1800s, the United States generally attempted to avoid conflicts and political engagements elsewhere.

In accordance with this isolationist philosophy, President James Monroe in 1823 proclaimed what became known as the **Monroe Doctrine.** In his message to Congress in December 1823, Monroe stated that the United States would not tolerate foreign intervention in the Western Hemisphere. In return, promised Monroe, the United States would stay out of European affairs. The Monroe Doctrine buttressed the policy of isolationism toward Europe.

16–2b The Beginning of Interventionism

Isolationism gradually gave way to **interventionism** (direct involvement in foreign affairs). The first true step toward interventionism occurred with the Spanish-American War of 1898. The United States fought this war to free Cuba from Spanish rule. Spain

Monroe Doctrine A U.S. policy, announced in 1823 by President James Monroe, that the United States would not tolerate foreign intervention in the Western Hemisphere, and in return, the United States would stay out of European affairs.

interventionism Direct involvement by one country in another country's affairs.

colonial empire A group of dependent nations that are under the rule of a single imperial power.

neutrality The position of not being aligned with either side in a dispute or conflict, such as a war.

CHAPTER 16: FOREIGN POLICY **357**

The United States entered World War II after the surprise Japanese attack on Pearl Harbor, Hawaii, on December 7, 1941.

minister, Winston Churchill, established the tone for a new relationship between the Soviet Union and the Western allies in a famous speech in 1946:

> An iron curtain has descended across the Continent. Behind that line all are subject in one form or another, not only to Soviet influence but to a very high . . . measure of control from Moscow.

The reference to an **iron curtain** described the political boundaries between the democratic countries in Western Europe and the Soviet-controlled Communist countries in Eastern Europe.

The Marshall Plan and the Policy of Containment

In 1947, when it appeared that local Communists, backed by the Soviets, would take over Greece and Turkey, President Harry Truman took action. He convinced Congress to appropriate $400 million ($4.25 billion in 2014 dollars) in aid for those countries to prevent the spread of communism.

THE TRUMAN DOCTRINE AND THE MARSHALL PLAN. The president also proclaimed what became known as the *Truman Doctrine*. It would be "the policy of the United States to support free peoples who are resisting attempted subjugation by armed minorities or by outside pressures."[2]

The Truman administration also instituted a policy of economic assistance to war-torn Europe, called the **Marshall Plan** after George Marshall, who was then the U.S. secretary of state. During the next five years, Congress appropriated $17 billion (about $168 billion in 2014 dollars) for aid to sixteen European countries. By 1952, the nations of Western Europe, with U.S. help, had recovered and were again prospering.

THE CONTAINMENT POLICY AND NATO. These actions marked the beginning of a policy of **containment** designed to contain (prevent) the spread of communism by offering threatened nations U.S. military and economic aid.[3] To make the policy of containment effective, the United States initiated a program of collective security involving the formation of mutual defense alliances with other nations.

In 1949, through the North Atlantic Treaty, the United States, Canada, and ten European nations

Soviet bloc The group of Eastern European nations that fell under the control of the Soviet Union following World War II.

iron curtain A phrase coined by Winston Churchill to describe the political boundaries between the democratic countries in Western Europe and the Soviet-controlled Communist countries in Eastern Europe.

Marshall Plan A plan providing for U.S. economic assistance to European nations following World War II to help those nations recover from the war. The plan was named after George C. Marshall, secretary of state from 1947 to 1949.

containment A U.S. policy designed to contain the spread of communism by offering military and economic aid to threatened nations.

in August 1945 in a successful attempt to force Japan to surrender.

16–2d The Cold War

After World War II ended in 1945, the wartime alliance between the United States and the Soviet Union began to deteriorate quickly. The Soviet Union opposed America's political and economic systems. Many Americans considered Soviet attempts to spread Communist systems to other countries a major threat to democracy. After the war ended, countries in Eastern Europe—Bulgaria, Czechoslovakia, East Germany, Hungary, Poland, and Romania—fell under Soviet domination, forming what became known as the **Soviet bloc**.

The Iron Curtain

Britain's wartime prime

Britain's Winston Churchill was a valuable ally of the United States during World War II.

formed a military alliance—the North Atlantic Treaty Organization (NATO). The treaty declared that an attack on any member of the alliance would be considered an attack against all members.

The Cold War Begins

Thus, by 1949, almost all illusions of friendship between the Soviet Union and the Western allies had disappeared. The United States became the leader of a bloc of democratic nations in Western Europe, the Pacific, and elsewhere.

The tensions between the Soviet Union and the United States became known as the **Cold War**—a war of words, warnings, and ideologies that lasted from the late 1940s through the late 1980s. Although the Cold War was mainly a war of words and belief systems, "hot" wars in Korea (1950–1953) and Vietnam (1965–1975) grew out of the efforts to contain communism.

The Arms Race and Deterrence

The tensions induced by the Cold War led both the Soviet Union and the United States to try to surpass each other militarily. They began competing for more and better weapons, particularly nuclear weapons, with greater destructive power.

This phenomenon, known as the *arms race,* was supported by a policy of **deterrence**—of rendering ourselves and our allies so strong militarily that our very strength would deter (stop or discourage) any attack on us. Out of deterrence came the theory of **mutually assured destruction (MAD)**, which held that if the forces of two nations were capable of destroying each other, neither nation would take a chance on war.

The Cuban Missile Crisis

In 1962, the United States and the Soviet Union came close to a nuclear confrontation in what became known as the **Cuban missile crisis.** The United States learned that the Soviet Union had placed nuclear weapons on the island of Cuba, ninety miles from the coast of Florida.

The crisis was defused diplomatically. A U.S. naval blockade of Cuba convinced the Soviet Union to agree to remove the missiles. The United States also agreed to remove some of its missiles near the Soviet border in Turkey. Both sides recognized that a nuclear war between the two superpowers was unthinkable.

Détente and Arms Control

In 1969, the United States and the Soviet Union began negotiations on a treaty to limit the number of antiballistic missiles (ABMs) and offensive missiles that each country could develop and deploy. In 1972, both sides signed the Strategic Arms Limitation Treaty (SALT I). This event marked the beginning of a period of **détente**, a French word that means a "relaxation of tensions."

In 1983, President Ronald Reagan (1981–1989) nearly reignited the arms race by proposing a missile defense system known as the strategic defense initiative (SDI, or "Star Wars"). Nonetheless, Reagan pursued arms control agreements with Soviet leaders, as did Reagan's successor, President George H. W. Bush (1989–1993).

Cold War The war of words, warnings, and ideologies between the Soviet Union and the United States that lasted from the late 1940s through the late 1980s.

deterrence A policy of building up military strength for the purpose of discouraging (deterring) military attacks by other nations; the policy that supported the arms race between the United States and the Soviet Union during the Cold War.

mutually assured destruction (MAD) A phrase referring to the assumption that if the forces of two nations are capable of destroying each other, neither nation will take a chance on war.

Cuban missile crisis A nuclear standoff that occurred in 1962 when the United States learned that the Soviet Union had placed nuclear warheads in Cuba.

détente A French word meaning a "relaxation of tensions." Détente characterized the relationship between the United States and the Soviet Union in the 1970s as they attempted to pursue cooperative dealings and arms control.

The Dissolution of the Soviet Union In the late 1980s, the political situation inside the Soviet Union began to change rapidly. Mikhail Gorbachev, the new leader, had initiated an effort to democratize the Soviet political system and decentralize the economy. The reforms quickly spread to other countries in the Soviet bloc. In 1989, the Berlin Wall, constructed nearly thirty years earlier to separate Soviet-dominated East Berlin from West Berlin, was torn down. East Germany and West Germany were reunited in 1990.

In August 1991, a number of disgruntled Communist Party leaders who wanted to reverse the reforms briefly seized control of the Soviet central government. Russian citizens rose up in revolt and defied those leaders. The democratically elected president of the Russian republic (the largest republic in the Soviet Union), Boris Yeltsin, confronted troops in Moscow that were under the control of the conspirators. The attempted coup collapsed after three days. The Communist Party in the Soviet Union lost almost all of its power.

The fifteen republics constituting the Soviet Union—including the Russian republic—declared their independence. By the end of the year, the Union of Soviet Socialist Republics (USSR) no longer existed.

16–2e Post–Cold War Foreign Policy

The demise of the Soviet Union altered the framework and goals of U.S. foreign policy. During the Cold War, the moral underpinnings of American foreign policy were clear to all—the United States was the defender of the "free world" against the Soviet aggressor.

When the Cold War ended, U.S. foreign policymakers were forced, for the first time in decades, to rethink the nation's foreign policy goals and adapt them to a world arena in which, at least for a while, the United States was the only superpower.

U.S. foreign policymakers have struggled since the end of the Cold War to determine the degree of intervention that is appropriate and prudent for the U.S. military. Should we intervene in a humanitarian crisis, such as a famine? Should the U.S. military participate in peacekeeping missions, such as those instituted after civil or ethnic strife in other countries?

"Soviet Union foreign policy is a puzzle, inside **a riddle wrapped in an enigma."**

~ WINSTON CHURCHILL ~
BRITISH PRIME MINISTER
DURING WORLD WAR II
1874–1965

Americans have faced these questions in Bosnia, Kosovo, Rwanda, Somalia, and Sudan.

Yet no overriding framework emerged in U.S. foreign policy until September 11, 2001. Since that date, our goal has been to capture and punish the terrorists who planned and perpetrated the events of that day and to prevent future terrorist attacks against Americans. Sometimes, that goal has involved "regime change," one of the objectives of the war against Iraq in 2003.

FOR CRITICAL THINKING

The Cold War between the United States and the Soviet Union never turned into a shooting war. *Why not?*

16–3 The War on Terrorism

One of the most difficult challenges faced by governments around the world is how to control terrorism. *Terrorism* is defined as the use of staged violence, often against civilians, to achieve political goals. Terrorism has occurred in almost every region of the world.

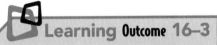

Learning Outcome 16–3

Identify the foreign policy challenges presented by terrorism.

The most devastating terrorist attack in U.S. history occurred on September 11, 2001, when radical Islamist terrorists used hijacked airliners as missiles to bring down the World Trade Center towers in New York City and to destroy part of the Pentagon building in Washington, D.C. A fourth airplane crashed in a Pennsylvania field after passengers fought back against the hijackers. In all, almost three thousand innocent civilians were killed as a result of these terrorist acts.

Other examples of terrorist acts include the Palestinian attacks on Israeli Olympic athletes in

Munich, Germany in 1972; the Libyan suitcase bombing of an American airliner over Lockerbie, Scotland, in 1988; the bombing of two U.S. embassies in Africa in 1998; the bombing of the Navy ship USS *Cole* in a Yemeni port in 2000; and coordinated bomb attacks on London's transportation system in 2005.

16–3a Varieties of Terrorism

Terrorists are willing to destroy others' lives and property, and often sacrifice their own lives, for a variety of reasons. Terrorist acts generally fall into one of the three broad categories discussed next.

Local or Regional Terrorism Some terrorist acts have been committed by extremists motivated by the desire to obtain freedom from a nation or government that they regard as an oppressor. Another motivation for terrorism is to disrupt peace talks. In Israel, for example, numerous suicide bombings by Palestinians against Israeli civilians have served to stall efforts to negotiate a peace between Israel and the Palestinians.

SEPARATIST GROUPS. The Irish Republican Army, which sought to unite British-governed Northern Ireland with the independent Republic of Ireland, conducted bombings and other terrorist acts in Northern Ireland and England over a period of many years. The attacks came to an end in 1997 as part of a peace process that lasted from 1995 until 2005.

Basque separatists in Spain have engaged in terrorism for decades. The separatists were initially—and

incorrectly—blamed for bombing a commuter train in Madrid, Spain, on March 11, 2004. That terrorist attack, actually perpetrated by Islamic radicals, killed 191 people and injured hundreds of others.

DOMESTIC TERRORISM IN THE UNITED STATES. The United States has also been the victim of homegrown terrorists. The bombing of the Oklahoma City federal building in 1995 was the act of vengeful extremists in the United States who claimed to fear an oppressive federal government. Although Timothy McVeigh and Terry Nichols, who were convicted of the crime, were not directly connected to a particular political group, they expressed views characteristic of the extreme right-wing militia movement in the United States.

A more recent problem in the United States has been attacks by domestic Islamists who have been "self-radicalized" through the Internet. While these individuals may communicate with foreign terrorist organizations, they are not under foreign control. An example is the two self-radicalized Muslim brothers who set bombs at the Boston Marathon in 2013. Three people died in this incident, and many more lost the use of one or both of their legs.

State-Sponsored Terrorism Some terrorist attacks have been planned and sponsored by governments. For example, the bombing of Pan Am Flight 103—which exploded over Lockerbie, Scotland, in 1988, killing all 259 people on board and 11 on the

Smoke pours from the twin towers of the World Trade Center after they were hit by two hijacked airliners in a terrorist attack on September 11, 2001, in New York City.

ROBERT GIROUX/GETTY IMAGES

ground—was later proved to be the work of an intelligence officer working for Libya.

The United Nations imposed economic sanctions against Libya in an effort to force Libyan dictator Moammer Gadhafi to extradite those who were suspected of being responsible for the bombing. More than a decade after the bombing, Libya agreed to hand the men over for trial.

The case of Pan Am Flight 103 illustrates the difficulty in punishing the perpetrators of state-sponsored terrorism. The victim country must first prove who the terrorists are and for whom they were working. Then it must decide what type of retribution is warranted.

Foreign Terrorist Networks

A relatively new phenomenon in the late 1990s and early 2000s was the emergence of nonstate terrorist networks, such as al Qaeda. Al Qaeda is the nongovernmental terrorist organization that planned and carried out the terrorist attacks of September 11, 2001. Its leader until his death in 2011 was the Saudi dissident Osama bin Laden.

Throughout the 1990s, al Qaeda conducted training camps in the mountains of Afghanistan, which was ruled by an ultraconservative Islamic faction known as the Taliban. The U.S. government determined that al Qaeda was responsible for terrorist attacks on two U.S. embassies in Africa in 1998 and the bombing of the USS *Cole* in 2000. In 1998, President Bill Clinton (1993–2001) ordered the bombing of terrorist camps in Afghanistan in retaliation for the embassy bombings, but with little effect. Al Qaeda cells continued to operate largely unimpeded until the terrorist attacks of September 11.

16–3b The U.S. Response to 9/11— The War in Afghanistan

Immediately after the 9/11 terrorist attacks, Congress passed a joint resolution authorizing President George W. Bush (2001–2009) to use "all necessary and appropriate force" against nations, organizations, or individuals that the president determined had "planned, authorized, committed, or aided the terrorist attacks."

In late 2001, supported by a **coalition** of allies, the U.S. military attacked al Qaeda camps in Afghanistan and the ruling Taliban regime that harbored those terrorists. Once the Taliban had been ousted, the United States helped to establish a government in Afghanistan that did not support terrorism. Instead of continuing the hunt for al Qaeda members in Afghanistan, however, the Bush administration increasingly looked to Iraq as a threat to U.S. security.

16–3c The Focus on Iraq

On March 20, 2003, U.S. and British forces attacked the nation of Iraq. Iraqi military units crumbled quickly. Saddam Hussein, Iraq's dictator, was captured in December 2003 and executed in 2006.

The First Gulf War

The Iraq War was in fact the second U.S. conflict with that country. In 1990, Hussein had attacked and occupied Kuwait, a small neighboring country. This unprovoked aggression was perhaps the most flagrant violation of international law since World War II. U.S. President George H. W. Bush (George W. Bush's father) organized an international coalition to free Kuwait. The coalition forces did not advance into Iraq to unseat Hussein, however.

Reasons for the Second War

The cease-fire that ended the first Gulf War required Iraq to submit to inspections for chemical, biological, and nuclear weapons—**weapons of mass destruction**. In 1998, however, Hussein ceased to cooperate with the inspections. The George W. Bush administration believed that Hussein was developing an atomic bomb and that the Iraqi regime was in some way responsible for the 9/11 terrorist attacks. (Both beliefs later proved to be incorrect.) Bush sought United Nations support

> ## "FIGHTING TERRORISM IS LIKE BEING A GOALKEEPER.
>
> You can make a hundred brilliant saves but the only shot that people remember is the one that gets past you."
>
> ~ PAUL WILKINSON ~
> BRITISH TERRORISM EXPERT
> B. 1937

coalition An alliance of nations formed to undertake a foreign policy action, particularly a military action. A coalition is often a temporary alliance that dissolves after the action is concluded.

weapons of mass destruction Chemical, biological, or nuclear weapons that can inflict massive casualties.

for the use of military force, but China, France, and Russia blocked the move. In March 2003, Bush told Hussein to leave Iraq or face war. Hussein was defiant, and war followed.

Rise and Fall of the Insurgency
Iraq is divided into three main ethnic or religious groups: Kurds, Arabs of the Sunni branch of Islam, and Arabs of the Shiite branch of Islam. The Kurdish-speaking people live in the north. The Sunni Muslims live mostly in central Iraq and had been the group in power under Hussein's rule. The Shiite Muslims, who live mostly in the south, make up the majority of the population, but they had been persecuted by the Sunni under Hussein.

After the overthrow of Hussein's government, Sunni rebels soon launched an insurrection against the occupation forces. The insurgents, including the newly organized al Qaeda in Iraq, attacked not only U.S. and Iraqi government forces but also Shiite civilians. Shiite radicals responded with attacks on Sunnis, and Iraq appeared to be drifting toward interethnic civil war. American voters began to turn against the war, and in the 2006 elections they handed Congress to the Democrats.

Instead of withdrawing U.S. troops, however, the Bush administration increased troop levels in 2007. The "surge," as it was called, was surprisingly successful. Many Sunnis, who also had been terrorized by al Qaeda, turned against the insurgency and allied with the Americans.

With the insurgency fatally undermined, the United States planned its withdrawal. President Barack Obama announced that U.S. combat forces would leave Iraq by the end of August 2010, and the rest of the troops would be out by the end of 2011. In fact, U.S. forces departed slightly ahead of schedule.

16–3d Again, Afghanistan
The war in Iraq tended to draw the Bush administration's attention away from Afghanistan, which was never completely at peace even after the Taliban had been ousted from Kabul, the capital. By 2006, the Taliban had regrouped and were waging a war of insurgency against the new government. The United States and its NATO allies were now the new government's principal military defenders.

The Afghan-Pakistani Border
A problem for the coalition forces was that the Taliban were able to take shelter on the far side of the Afghan-Pakistani bor-

der, in Pakistan's Federally Administered Tribal Areas. These districts are largely free from central government control.

In 2009, Taliban forces began to take complete control of districts in the Tribal Areas and adjacent districts in the Northwest Frontier Province. Facing a direct challenge to Pakistan's sovereignty, the Pakistani military began to engage the Taliban forces in what soon became a major struggle.

U.S. Attacks in Pakistan
Under the George W. Bush administration, the CIA began operating remote-controlled aircraft (drones) known as Predators over Pakistan. Predators are equipped with small missiles, which were used to kill a number of Taliban and al Qaeda leaders. President Obama ramped up the Predator program significantly.

One result was increasing tensions with Pakistan, which could not openly support the Predator campaign. Pakistan's role in Afghanistan, in fact, has been quite complicated. The nation has been nominally allied with the United States. At the same time, Pakistan's intelligence agency, Inter-Services

TAYLOR HILL/GETTY IMAGES

Malala Yousafzai of Pakistan. In 2008, when Malala was eleven, she began writing a blog about Taliban attempts to ban girls' schools. In 2012, she barely survived a Taliban assassination attempt.

Intelligence has funded a variety of Islamist militant groups, including units that have engaged in terrorist attacks on the government of Afghanistan and U.S. forces in that country.

The Death of Bin Laden During the winter of 2010–2011, U.S. intelligence agencies learned that al Qaeda leader Osama bin Laden might be hiding in the Pakistani city of Abbottabad. On May 1, 2011, U.S. Navy Seals entered bin Laden's residential compound and killed him.

The reaction in America was one of relief and satisfaction. The reaction in Pakistan was quite different. Many Pakistanis considered the incident a violation of their country's sovereignty. American commentators speculated that bin Laden could not have hidden in Abbottabad without support from elements of the military, as that city is home to the Pakistan Military Academy.

A common perception following the death of Bin Ladens, is that al Qaeda is now effectively out of business and no longer a threat to the United States or other Western nations. Such a conclusion may be premature, however, as we explain in the *Perception versus Reality* feature on the following page.

Obama and Afghanistan In 2009, President Obama increased the number of U.S. troops in Afghanistan by 47,000. At the same time, he indicated that he hoped to withdraw some U.S. forces as early as 2011. In fact, only 10,000 U.S. soldiers left Afghanistan that year. Withdrawals picked up speed in 2012, however, and current plans are that almost all U.S. troops are to be out of Afghanistan by the end of 2014.

FOR CRITICAL THINKING

Sometimes, it is possible to negotiate with certain terrorist groups, such as the Irish Republican Army, and "bring them in from the cold." *Why might such a strategy be impossible with al Qaeda?*

16–4 The Israeli-Palestinian Conflict

The long-running conflict between Israel and its Arab neighbors has poisoned the atmosphere in the Middle East for more than half a century. Some experts have argued that resolving this conflict is key to solving additional problems, such as terrorism. Others doubt that a resolution would really have that effect. Regardless, the conflict has caused enough bloodshed and heartbreak over the years to deserve attention on its own merits. American presidents dating back at least to Richard Nixon (1969–1974) have attempted to persuade the parties to reach a settlement. Barack Obama is only the latest American leader to address the problem.

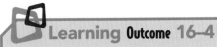

Learning Outcome 16–4

Explain the principal issues dividing the Israelis and the Palestinians and the solutions proposed by the international community.

16–4a The Arab-Israeli Wars

For many years after Israel was founded in 1948, the neighboring Arab states did not accept its legitimacy as a nation. The result was a series of wars between Israel and neighboring states, including Egypt, Jordan, and Syria, waged in 1948, 1956, 1967, and 1973. Following the 1948 Arab-Israeli War, a large number of Palestinians—Arab residents of the area, known as Palestine until 1948—were forced into exile, adding to Arab grievances.

The failure of the Arab states in the 1967 war led to additional Palestinian refugees and the rise of the **Palestine Liberation Organization (PLO)**, a nonstate body committed to armed struggle against Israel. In the late 1960s and early 1970s, Palestinian groups launched a wave of terrorist attacks against Israeli targets around the world.

Following the 1973 Yom Kippur War, Egyptian president Anwar el-Sadat launched a major peace initiative. He traveled to Israel in 1977 and addressed the Israeli parliament, a major turning point. U.S. president Jimmy Carter (1977–1981) then sponsored intensive negotiations.

Egypt and Israel signed a peace treaty in 1979 that marked the end to an era of major wars between Israel and other states. Lower-level conflicts continued, however. On several occasions, Israel launched attacks against nonstate militias in Lebanon in response to

Perception versus Reality

Al Qaeda Has Been Defeated

Some twenty-five years ago, a Saudi Arabian named Osama bin Laden founded the al Qaeda terrorist organization. In time, branches of al Qaeda spread across the globe. Al Qaeda was responsible for the September 11, 2001, attacks that killed almost three thousand people in the United States.

THE PERCEPTION

U.S. forces killed bin Laden in May 2011. Two months later, Leon Panetta, U.S. secretary of defense at that time, told reporters that America was "within reach of strategically defeating" the al Qaeda network. According to Panetta, intelligence materials gathered during the raid on bin Laden's headquarters in Pakistan had revealed that al Qaeda was broke and crippled by American drone strikes.

THE REALITY

The founder of al Qaeda may be dead, but al Qaeda affiliates and "fellow travelers" are alive and expanding. Consider the Westgate Shopping Mall incident in Nairobi, Kenya. In September 2013, a group from Somalia called Shabab killed almost seventy people in the mall and injured hundreds of others. Shabab is al Qaeda's Somali affiliate. Shabab had recently been forced out of much of southern Somalia, in part by Kenyan troops. Many thought that it could not regroup, but it did. Many other al Qaeda branches are also returning to serious terrorist activities.

In 2013, the U.S. State Department closed nineteen diplomatic missions in North Africa and the Middle East. Why? Because it had intercepted communications between bin Laden's successor in Pakistan and the head of al Qaeda's Yemen-based affiliate. Al Qaeda central in Pakistan was demanding that the Yemeni branch initiate terrorist operations against American interests.

The former al Qaeda in Iraq, renamed the Islamic State of Iraq and al Sham (ISIS), has recently pushed into Syria. (*Al Sham* is Arabic for "the eastern Mediterranean.") Another al Qaeda–linked group, Jabhat al Nusrah (JAN), is also active in Syria. Radical Islamists may now make up 80 percent of the active fighters attempting to overthrow the government of the Syrian president, Bashar al-Assad. Additionally, the North African branch of al Qaeda is now entrenched in Mali, Nigeria, Libya, and elsewhere. This group has vowed to carry out attacks against France and Spain.

Bin Laden may be dead, but his legacy lives on.

BLOG ON For current details on al Qaeda's activities, search on "al qaeda" using an Internet search engine. Be aware that the "alqaeda" account on Twitter, if it has not yet been taken down, is a satire.

---

incursions across the Israeli-Lebanon border. Israel and Jordan eventually signed a peace treaty in 1994, but no peace treaty between Israel and Syria has yet been negotiated, and the conflict between Israel and the Palestinians has remained.

16–4b The Israeli-Palestinian Dispute

Resolving the Israeli-Palestinian dispute has always presented more difficulties than achieving peace between Israel and neighbors such as Egypt. One problem is that the hostilities between the two parties run deeper. On the Palestinian side, many families lost their homes after the 1948 war. Then, after the 1967 war, the West Bank of the Jordan River and the Gaza Strip fell under Israeli control, and the Palestinians living in these areas became an occupied people.

On the Israeli side, the sheer viciousness of the Palestinian terrorist attacks—which frequently resulted in the deaths of civilians, including children—made negotiations with those responsible hard to imagine. A further complication was the Israeli settlements on the West Bank and the Gaza Strip, which the Palestinians considered their own. Israeli settlers living on the West Bank had an obvious interest in opposing any peace deal that required them to move.

Despite the difficulties, the international community, including the United States, was in agreement on several principles for settling the conflict. Lands seized by Israel in the 1967 war should be restored to the Palestinians, who could organize their own independent nation-state there. In turn, the Palestinians would have to recognize Israel's right to exist and take concrete steps to guarantee Israel's security.

The international consensus did not address some important issues. These include what compensation, if any, should go to Palestinians who lost homes in what is now Israel. A second issue is whether Israel could adjust its borders to incorporate some of the Israeli settlement areas, plus part or all of eastern Jerusalem, which had been under Arab control before 1967.

16–4c Negotiations

In 1993, Israel and the PLO met officially for the first time in Oslo, Norway. The resulting **Oslo Accords** were signed in Washington under the watchful eye of President Bill Clinton. A major result was the establishment of a Palestinian Authority, under Israeli control, on the West Bank and the Gaza Strip.

Negotiations Collapse In 2000, attempts to reach a settlement collapsed in acrimony. After the failure of these talks, an uprising by Palestinian militants led to Israeli military incursions into the West Bank and the almost complete collapse of the Palestinian Authority. In 2005, Israeli prime minister Ariel Sharon, concluding that he had no credible peace partner, carried out a plan to unilaterally withdraw from the Gaza Strip and to build an enormous security fence between Israel and the West Bank. The fence came under strong international criticism because it incorporated parts of the West Bank into Israel.

Oslo Accords The first agreement signed between Israel and the PLO; led to the establishment of the Palestinian Authority in the occupied territories.

> ## "THE PURPOSE OF FOREIGN POLICY
> is not to provide an outlet for our own sentiments of hope or indignation; **IT IS TO SHAPE REAL EVENTS IN A REAL WORLD."**
>
> ~ JOHN F. KENNEDY ~
> THIRTY-FIFTH PRESIDENT
> OF THE UNITED STATES
> 1961–1963

A Divided Palestine

Gaza was taken over in 2007 by Hamas, a radical Islamist party that refuses to recognize Israel. After the imposition of an Israeli blockade, Hamas launched missile attacks on Israel, which in turn briefly occupied the strip in December 2008. The West Bank remained under the control of the PLO-led Palestinian Authority, and so the Palestinians, now politically divided, were in an even worse bargaining position than before.

Turkish activists attempted in 2010 to "run" the Israeli blockade of Gaza with a flotilla of six ships, which led to the death of nine activists. The incident drew international attention to the blockade, and Israel subsequently eased its terms.

On the West Bank, the Palestinian Authority succeeded in reestablishing itself as an effective government, and the territory entered a period of relative stability and economic growth.

Obama and the Negotiations In 2009, Israel chose Benjamin Netanyahu, a staunch conservative, as its new prime minister. Attempts by the Obama administration to restart Israeli-Palestinian talks were frustrated by disagreements about Israeli settlements on the West Bank—Netanyahu strongly supported the settlers. The resulting chill in U.S.-Israeli relations thawed in 2011 when the Palestinians appealed to the United Nations to recognize the West Bank and Gaza as an independent state. To Israel's relief, Obama vehemently opposed this step. In 2013, Netanyahu and Palestinian leader Mahmoud Abbas formally reopened negotiations with U.S. assistance, but any agreement seemed to be very far off.

FOR CRITICAL THINKING

Why do you think that Americans support Israel so strongly?

WIN MCNAMEE/GETTY IMAGES

U.S. Secretary of State John Kerry (center) with Palestinian and Israeli negotiators. Justice Minister Tzipi Livni (right) represents Israel, and Saeb Erekat (left) speaks for the Palestinians.

16–5 Weapons Proliferation in an Unstable World

Learning Outcome 16–5

Outline some of the actions taken by the United States to curb the threat of nuclear weapons.

The Cold War may be over, but the threat of nuclear warfare—which formed the backdrop of foreign policy during the Cold War—has by no means disappeared. The existence of nuclear weapons in Russia and in other countries around the world continues to challenge U.S. foreign policymakers.

Concerns about nuclear proliferation mounted in 1998 when India and Pakistan detonated nuclear devices within a few weeks of each other—events that took U.S. intelligence agencies by surprise. Increasingly, American officials have focused on the threat of an attack by a rogue nation or a terrorist group that possesses weapons of mass destruction. Of most concern today are attempts by North Korea and Iran to develop nuclear capabilities and the recent use of chemical weapons by the Assad regime in Syria.

16–5a North Korea's Nuclear Program

North Korea signed the Treaty on the Non-Proliferation of Nuclear Weapons in 1985 and sub-mitted to weapons inspections by the International Atomic Energy Agency (IAEA) in 1992. Throughout the 1990s, however, there were discrepancies between North Korean declarations and IAEA inspection findings. In 2002, North Korea expelled the IAEA inspectors.

Opening Negotiations The administration of George W. Bush had been reluctant to engage in diplomatic relations with North Korea. Bush insisted that any talks with North Korea must also include all of North Korea's neighbors—China, Japan, Russia, and South Korea. In 2003, North Korea finally agreed to such talks.

Since that time, it has proved quite difficult to keep North Korea at the bargaining table—its representatives have stormed out of the talks repeatedly, for the most trivial reasons. China is the one power with substantial economic leverage over North Korea, and typically, Chinese leaders have been the ones to lead the North Koreans back to the table.

Tensions heightened in October 2006, when North Korea conducted its first nuclear test. Nevertheless, the Bush administration continued to participate with North Korea's neighbors in multilateral negotiations. In the spring of 2007, North Korea agreed that it would begin to dismantle its nuclear facilities and would allow inspectors from the United Nations (UN) into the country.

In return, the other nations agreed to provide various kinds of aid, and the United States would begin to discuss normalization of relations with North Korea. By mid-2007, North Korea had shut down one of its nuclear reactors and had admitted a permanent UN inspection team into the country.

The Collapse of Negotiations In April 2009, North Korea tested a long-range missile under the guise of attempting to launch a satellite. The UN Security Council voted unanimously to condemn the test. This vote demonstrated that the Chinese, who have a permanent Security Council seat, were annoyed as well. North Korea then pulled out of the six-party talks and expelled all nuclear inspectors from the country. In May 2009, North Korea tested another nuclear device, to universal disapproval.

Protesters against the proposed U.S. air strike on Syria in 2013. A majority of Americans opposed the action, but most of the U.S. foreign policy establishment favored it. Why might that be so?

GREG WOOD/AFP/GETTY IMAGES

In spite of numerous UN resolutions, Iran is still producing uranium, and at a faster rate. The existence of a second uranium enrichment plant was made public in the fall of 2009. Simultaneously, Iran has been developing missiles that eventually could be capable of carrying a nuclear payload.

Iranian leaders have publicly stated that they have no intention of using their nuclear program for destructive purposes. They claim that they are seeking only to develop nuclear energy plants.

Iran as a Security Threat Like North Korea, Iran has been openly hostile to the United States. Iran has implemented an extensive terrorism campaign in hopes of undermining U.S. influence in the Middle East. Many analysts have also tied Iran to Iraqi insurgency efforts against American occupation forces.

Mahmoud Ahmadinejad, president of Iran from 2005 to 2013, repeatedly called for the complete destruction of Israel. It is no surprise, therefore, that Israel considers Iranian nuclear weapons to be a threat to its existence. Perhaps more surprising is that Iran's Arab neighbors consider these weapons a threat as well. Leaked U.S. diplomatic cables reveal that Arab leaders have urged the United States to take out the Iranian nuclear program by force.

Diplomatic Efforts The George W. Bush administration refused to negotiate directly with the Iranians. Therefore, Britain, France, and Germany took the lead in diplomatic efforts to encourage Iran to abandon its nuclear program. The United Nations has imposed sanctions on Iran, as has the United States. Past attempts to strengthen UN sanctions, however, have been frustrated by the opposition of China and Russia.

The Obama administration was open to negotiations with Iran, and so when talks resumed in 2009, the United States was also at the table, as was Russia. Up to 2014, however, no agreement was reached.

War or Peace? Because negotiations with Iran appeared to be going nowhere, the United States and its allies increasingly turned to coercive measures. The

After a third test in 2013, China for the first time imposed significant economic restrictions—or *sanctions*—on North Korea. The UN Security Council imposed its own sanctions, which led to an explosion of violent rhetoric from the northern regime directed at South Korea and the United States.

North Korea's aggressive behavior may have been linked to a succession crisis. In 2011, the dictator Kim Jong Il died and was succeeded by his youngest son, Kim Jong Un. Kim Jong Il himself was the son of North Korea's first Communist dictator. North Korea, therefore, is unique in that it is effectively a Communist monarchy.

16–5b Iran: An Emerging Nuclear Threat?

In November 1979, militant students in Tehran, Iran, seized the U.S. embassy and took fifty-two American citizens hostage. The crisis lasted 444 days. Ever since, Iran and the United States have been at odds with each other.

In the years that followed, the rest of the world discovered that Iran was engaged in a covert nuclear program. Investigators for the International Atomic Energy Agency reported that Iran was enriching uranium that could be used in the fabrication of a nuclear bomb.

Hassan Rouhani during his campaign to be elected Iran's new president in 2013.

United States was able to persuade or pressure a majority of the world's nations not to buy Iran's oil. The United States was also able to cut Iran off from the international banking system. This step made it extremely difficult for Iran to finance imports and exports. By 2013, the Iranian economy was in serious trouble.

Another coercive measure would be to bomb Iran's nuclear sites. In 2008, Israel began preparations that would allow it to launch such a strike if necessary. After Benjamin Netanyahu became prime minister of Israel in 2009, he called for air strikes with increasing urgency. One type of attack, in fact, was launched immediately. In 2010, a sophisticated U.S. computer "worm" took down about a thousand of the five thousand centrifuges used in Iran's uranium enrichment program. Many were completely destroyed.

Again, Negotiations In 2013, Iran elected a new president, Hassan Rouhani. In short order, Rouhani initiated a charm offensive aimed at re-establishing diplomatic negotiations. The new leader repudiated the anti-Israel rhetoric of previous Iranian president Ahmadinejad. After making a speech at the United Nations calling for a diplomatic resolution of the nuclear issue, Rouhani spoke briefly by phone with President Obama. For the moment, at least, military measures were off the table, and diplomacy had resumed.

16–5c Use of Chemical Weapons by Syria

Most nations have signed treaties banning the use of chemical weapons—they were, in fact, one of the few instruments of horror that were never used on the battlefield in World War II. Only a handful of nations have refused to sign, including North Korea, Iraq (under Saddam Hussein), and Syria. In August 2013, the government of Syria used the nerve gas sarin against suburbs of Damascus that were under the control of antiregime rebels. The attack killed more than a thousand civilians. Syrian dictator Bashar al-Assad may have used chemical weapons earlier, but this incident was so conspicuous that it could not be ignored.

As described in the *America at Odds* feature in Chapter 12, President Obama proposed to punish the Assad regime for its use of poison gas by launching air strikes. Obama took the unusual step of asking Congress for its approval of the strikes. It seemed quite possible that Congress would vote such a resolution down. In September, however, the government of Russia announced that Syria was willing to sign the Chemical Weapons Convention, a treaty governing chemical weapons, and place its weapons under international control. This initiative was a diplomatic triumph for Russian president Vladimir Putin. The U.S. Senate postponed the vote on the bombing resolution indefinitely. By October, to the surprise of many, the Assad regime was cooperating with international inspectors.

FOR CRITICAL THINKING

If the United States were to bomb Iran's uranium enrichment sites, what might be the consequences?

16–6 China—The Next Superpower?

Some of the foreign policy challenges faced by the United States do not necessarily involve issues of

Learning Outcome 16–6

Describe China's emerging role as a world power.

war and peace. Economic matters, including international trade and currency problems, can be very important. One example is the recent European economic crisis, which at times has affected the U.S. economy as well. We discuss that problem in the *Join the Debate* feature below.

An even greater challenge may be the growing importance of China. Following President

JOIN THE DEBATE

Is the Euro Doomed?

Decades ago, European leaders had a dream of forging a European union of nations so that world war could never happen again. They created the Common Market and then the European Union (EU). In 2000, sixteen EU countries adopted a common currency called the *euro*. Today, out of the twenty-eight European Union countries, eighteen use the euro. This group of nations is often referred to as the *euro zone*. Since the Great Recession, the euro zone has suffered serious debt crises. As a result, some people wonder whether the euro can survive.

Adopting the euro allowed poorer nations on the periphery of Europe to borrow as cheaply as the richer core nations, such as France and Germany. Investors from the core nations—including large European banks—lent huge sums of money to the periphery countries. When the Great Recession struck, it became clear that people in Greece, Ireland, Portugal, and Spain had borrowed too many euros and would have trouble paying them back. The problem was especially bad in Greece, where the government had shown exceptional irresponsibility. A system of bailouts from richer euro-zone countries to poorer ones began. The process is still ongoing.

The question remains: Can the euro survive? The United States has a stake in what happens in Europe, because trouble there can drag down our economy as well.

The Euro Is Here to Stay

The euro's defenders say that reports of the euro's demise are premature and, indeed, misguided. Germany, in particular, will not let the euro zone break apart. Germany has benefited greatly from the euro zone and especially from the way that the euro has kept Germany's exports cheap and competitive. True, a monetary union without a political union can lead to problems. It will take time to establish agreements that allow the eighteen different economies in the euro zone to be guided by a set of binding rules that cover government spending and financing. Also, the European Central Bank (ECB) established by the EU can, if necessary, buy the debt of countries that are in trouble. It has done so already.

As long as the ECB helps poorer countries to avoid defaulting on their debts, you can bet that the euro will be around for a long time.

The Euro Cannot Last

Pessimists contend that, although the euro may not be doomed immediately, it cannot last much longer. The euro is forcing the nations of the periphery into endless economic depression, with staggering unemployment levels. Eventually, these countries will rebel. True, these nations tend to have excessive regulation and rules making it hard to fire and hire workers. Germany and other northern nations claim that if the nations in the periphery would only reform, everything would be fine. Yet such reforms wouldn't change the fact that the Mediterranean nations are stuck with a currency that is priced too high, making their exports too expensive. Because these countries do not have their own currencies, they cannot devalue their currency and become competitive. If Germany and other countries were to pursue expansionary policies, countries in the periphery might have someplace to which they could export. But Germany is too afraid of inflation to follow such a strategy. So don't bet that the euro will last.

FOR CRITICAL ANALYSIS What might happen to the value of the dollar in international trade if the euro disappeared?

Workers at a Chinese refrigerator factory. Haier, the manufacturer, is the world's largest producer of refrigerators and washing machines.

16–6b A Future Challenger to American Dominance?

Many U.S. observers have warned that China is destined to challenge American global supremacy. China has one of the fastest-growing economies in the world, along with a population of 1.3 billion, and its gross domestic product (GDP) is expected to surpass that of the United States by 2020. China's GDP is nearly *one hundred times* what it was in 1978, when China implemented reforms to make the economy more market oriented. Never in the history of the world have so many people been lifted out of poverty so quickly.

Richard Nixon's historic visit to China in 1972, American diplomatic and economic relations with the Chinese gradually improved. Diplomacy with China focused on cultivating a more pro-Western disposition in the formerly isolationist nation. Relations with China are important in part because that nation has enjoyed economic growth averaging almost 10 percent a year for more than thirty years in a row. Such growth has turned China into a great power.

U.S. Relations with China   Diplomatic relations between China and the United States have been uneven. China offered its full support of the U.S. war on terrorism following the September 11 attacks, even providing intelligence about terrorist activities. But the Chinese did not support the American invasion of Iraq in 2003. Also, recent attempts by Chinese hackers to steal U.S. intellectual property have raised questions about China's attitudes toward the West.

16–6a Chinese-American Trade Relations

The rapid growth of the Chinese economy and increasingly close trade ties between the United States and China have helped bring about a policy of diplomatic outreach. Many Americans protested, however, when the U.S. government extended **normal trade relations (NTR) status** to China on a year-to-year basis. Labor groups objected because they feared that American workers would lose jobs that could be performed at lower wages in Chinese factories. Human rights organizations denounced the Chinese government's well-documented mistreatment of its people.

Despite this heavy opposition, Congress granted China permanent NTR status in 2000 and endorsed China's application to join the World Trade Organization in 2001.

The Issues of Taiwan and Tibet   Although China has not demonstrated any ambition to acquire more territory in general or to become militarily aggressive, it has expressed a desire to take control of the island of Taiwan. China considers Taiwan, a former Chinese province, to be a legal part of China. In practice, however, since 1949 the island has functioned as an independent nation. The United States has historically supported a free and separate Taiwan and has reiterated that any

> **normal trade relations (NTR) status** A trade status granted through an international treaty by which each member nation must treat other members at least as well as it treats the country that receives its most favorable treatment. This status was formerly known as *most-favored-nation status.*

reunion of China and Taiwan must come about by peaceful means.

Relations between China and several Western nations have become strained in recent years due to criticisms by these nations of Chinese behavior in Tibet. While supposedly autonomous, Tibet is under tight Chinese control.

FOR CRITICAL THINKING

If we have strong trade relations with a country, does that make it less likely that we would ever go to war with that country? Why or why not?

AMERICA AT ODDS Foreign Policy

In 1947, Republican senator Arthur Vandenberg of Michigan announced, "Politics stops at the water's edge." By this, Vandenberg, formerly a fierce isolationist, meant that Republicans and Democrats should cooperate in dealing with such foreign policy issues as the Cold War with the Soviet Union.

Bipartisanship was never complete even in Vandenberg's day, however, and it is much less common today. True, the two major parties are more likely to cooperate over a foreign policy issue than over domestic policy. Nevertheless, Americans are at odds over many foreign policy issues, as reflected in Congress. The following are a few of these issues:

- In foreign policy, is it best to ally with other nations whenever possible—or should America carefully guard its ability to act alone?

- Should the president take complete charge of the foreign policy process, including the use of armed force—or should the president collaborate closely with Congress?

- Should the war on terrorism be the central focus of U.S. foreign policy—or should we devote equal energy to managing our relations with rising powers such as China?

- Was President Obama's plan to withdraw forces from Afghanistan in 2011 and 2012 a wise method of putting pressure on the Afghan government—or a recipe for failure in that country?

- In attempting to promote peace between Israelis and Palestinians, should the United States put most of its pressure on the Palestinians—or should it also pressure the Israelis to, for example, suspend the construction of new Jewish settlements on the West Bank?

STUDY TOOLS

Ready to study?

- **Review** what you've read with the quiz below.
- Check your answers on the **Chapter in Review** card at the back of the book.
- For any questions you miss, read the corresponding **Learning Outcome** section again to prepare for class and your exam.
- Rip out and study the **Chapter in Review** card (at the back of the book).

Fill-In

Learning Outcome 16–1

1. The executive departments and other government agencies that are most directly involved in foreign policy include the _____.

Learning Outcome 16–2

2. The nation's founders and the early presidents believed that a policy of _____ was the best way to protect American interests.

3. The _____ was a war of words, warnings, and ideologies between the Soviet Union and the United States that lasted from the late 1940s through the late 1980s.

Learning Outcome 16–3

4. In 2001, supported by a coalition of allies, the U.S. military attacked al Qaeda camps in _____ and the ruling Taliban regime that harbored those terrorists.

5. In 2011, U.S. Navy Seals killed Osama bin Laden in Abbottabad, a city in _____.

Learning Outcome 16–4

6. The 1993 Oslo Accords led to the establishment of the _____ in the occupied territories.

Learning Outcome 16–5

7. With respect to the prospects of nuclear proliferation, American officials are most concerned about recent developments in the countries of _____.

Learning Outcome 16–6

8. The danger exists of a possible future crisis in U.S.-Chinese relations over the status of _____.

Multiple Choice

Learning Outcome 16–1

9. The power to declare war belongs to
   a. the president.
   b. Congress.
   c. the Joint Chiefs of Staff.

Learning Outcome 16–2

10. Direct involvement by one country in another country's affairs best describes
    a. political realism.
    b. collective security.
    c. interventionism.

11. Actions taken under the Truman Doctrine and the Marshall Plan marked the beginning of a policy of
    a. containment.   c. mutually assured destruction.
    b. deterrence.

Learning Outcome 16–3

12. The phrase *weapons of mass destruction* refers to
    a. landmines and cluster munitions.
    b. Improvised Explosive Devices (IEDs).
    c. chemical, biological, or nuclear weapons.

Learning Outcome 16–4

13. For many years after Israel was founded in 1948,
    a. the neighboring Arab states did not accept its legitimacy as a nation.
    b. the only peace treaty that it was able to negotiate was one with Syria.
    c. it lived in peace with its neighbors in the Middle East.

Learning Outcome 16–5

14. During 2010, a sophisticated computer "worm" attacked centrifuges used in _____ uranium enrichment program.
    a. North Korea's   b. Iran's   c. Israel's

Learning Outcome 16–6

15. The U.S. government granted China permanent ____ (NTR) status in 2000.
    a. normal trade relations
    b. national trade reservation
    c. no tariff records

USE THE TOOLS.

- Rip out the Review Cards in the back of your book to study.

Or Visit CourseMate to:

- Read, search, highlight, and take notes in the Interactive eBook
- Review Flashcards (Print or Online) to master key terms
- Test yourself with Auto-Graded Quizzes
- Bring concepts to life with Games, Videos, and Animations!

Go to CourseMate for **GOVT** to begin using these tools.
Access at **www.cengagebrain.com**

Complete the Speak Up
survey in CourseMate at
www.cengagebrain.com

f Follow us at
www.facebook.com/4ltrpress

NOTES

Chapter 1

1. Harold Lasswell, *Politics: Who Gets What, When, and How* (New York: McGraw-Hill, 1936).
2. Charles Lewis, *The Buying of Congress* (New York: Avon Books, 1998), p. 346.
3. As quoted in Paul M. Angle and Earl Schenck Miers, *The Living Lincoln* (New York: Barnes & Noble, 1992), p. 155.
4. Martin J. Wade and William F. Russell, *The Short Constitution* (Iowa City: American Citizen Publishing, 1920), p. 38.

Chapter 2

1. The first *European* settlement in today's United States was St. Augustine, Florida (a city that still exists), which was founded on September 8, 1565, by the Spaniard Pedro Menéndez de Ávilés.
2. Archaeologists recently discovered the remains of a colony at Popham Beach, on the southern coast of what is now Maine, that was established at the same time as the colony at Jamestown. The Popham colony disbanded after thirteen months, however, when the leader, after learning that he had inherited property back home, returned—with the other colonists—to England.
3. John Camp, *Out of the Wilderness: The Emergence of an American Identity in Colonial New England* (Middleton, Conn.: Wesleyan University Press, 1990).
4. Ironically, the colonists were in fact protesting a tax reduction. The British government believed that if tea were cheaper, Americans would be more willing to drink it, even though it was still taxed. The Americans viewed the tax reduction as an attempt to trick them into accepting the principle of taxation. If the tea had been expensive, it would have been easy to organize a boycott. Because the tea was so cheap, the protesters destroyed it so that no one would be tempted to buy it. (Also, many of the protesters were in the business of smuggling tea, and they would have been put out of business by the cheap competition.)
5. Much of the colonists' fury over British policies was directed personally at King George III, who had ascended the British throne in 1760 at the age of twenty-two, rather than at Britain or British rule *per se*. If you look at the Declaration of Independence in Appendix A, you will note that much of that document focuses on what "He" (George III) has or has not done. George III's lack of political experience, his personality, and his temperament all combined to lend instability to the British government at this crucial point in history.
6. *The Political Writings of Thomas Paine,* Vol. 1 (Boston: J. P. Mendum Investigator Office, 1870), p. 46.
7. The equivalent in today's publishing world would be a book that sells between 9 million and 11 million copies in its first year of publication.
8. As quoted in Winthrop D. Jordan *et al., The United States,* 6th ed. (Englewood Cliffs, N.J.: Prentice Hall, 1987).
9. Some scholars feel that Locke's influence on the colonists, including Thomas Jefferson, has been exaggerated. For example, Jay Fliegelman states that Jefferson's fascination with the ideas of Homer, Ossian, and Patrick Henry "is of greater significance than his indebtedness to Locke." Jay Fliegelman, *Declaring Independence: Jefferson, Natural Language, and the Culture of Performance* (Stanford, Calif.: Stanford University Press, 1993).
10. Well before the Articles were ratified, many of them had, in fact, already been implemented. The Second Continental Congress and the thirteen states conducted American military, economic, and political affairs according to the standards and form specified later in the Articles of Confederation. See Robert W. Hoffert, *A Politics of Tensions: The Articles of Confederation and American Political Ideas* (Niwot, Colo.: University Press of Colorado, 1992).
11. Shays' Rebellion was not merely a small group of poor farmers. The participants and their supporters represented whole communities, including some of the wealthiest and most influential families of Massachusetts. Leonard L. Richards, *Shays' Rebellion: The American Revolution's Final Battle* (Philadelphia: University of Pennsylvania Press, 2003).
12. Madison, however, was much more "republican" in his views—that is, less of a centralist—than Hamilton. See Lance Banning, *The Sacred Fire of Liberty: James Madison and the Founding of the Federal Republic* (Ithaca, N.Y.: Cornell University Press, 1995).
13. The State House was later named Independence Hall. The East Room was the same room in which the Declaration of Independence had been signed eleven years earlier.
14. Charles A. Beard, *An Economic Interpretation of the Constitution of the United States* (New York: Macmillan, 1913; New York: Free Press, 1986).
15. Morris was partly of French descent, which is why his first name may seem unusual. Note, however, that naming one's child *Gouverneur* was not common at the time in any language, including French.
16. Quoted in J. J. Spengler, "Malthusianism in Late Eighteenth-Century America," *American Economic Review* 25 (1935), p. 705.

17. For further detail on Wood's depiction of the founders' views, see Gordon S. Wood, *Revolutionary Characters: What Made the Founders Different* (New York: Penguin Press, 2006).
18. Some scholarship suggests that the *Federalist Papers* did not play a significant role in bringing about the ratification of the Constitution. Nonetheless, the papers have lasting value as an authoritative explanation of the Constitution.
19. The papers written by the Anti-Federalists are online. (Locate them by entering "wepin anti-federalist papers" into a search engine.) For essays on the positions, arranged in topical order, of both the Federalists and the Anti-Federalists in the ratification debate, see John P. Kaminski and Richard Leffler, *Federalists and Antifederalists: The Debate over the Ratification of the Constitution,* 2d ed. (Madison, Wis.: Madison House, 1998).
20. The concept of the separation of powers generally is credited to the French political philosopher Montesquieu (1689–1755), who included it in his monumental two-volume work entitled *The Spirit of the Laws,* published in 1748.
21. The Constitution does not explicitly mention the power of judicial review, but the delegates at the Constitutional Convention probably assumed that the courts would have this power. Indeed, Alexander Hamilton, in *Federalist Paper* No. 78, explicitly outlined the concept of judicial review. In any event, whether the founders intended for the courts to exercise this power is a moot point, because in an 1803 decision, *Marbury v. Madison,* the Supreme Court successfully claimed this power for the courts—see Chapter 14.
22. Eventually, Supreme Court decisions led to legislative reforms relating to apportionment. The amendment concerning compensation of members of Congress became the Twenty-seventh Amendment to the Constitution when it was ratified 203 years later, in 1992.
23. The Twenty-first Amendment repealed the Eighteenth Amendment, which had prohibited the manufacture or sale of alcoholic beverages nationwide (Prohibition). Special conventions were necessary because prohibitionist forces controlled too many state legislatures for the standard ratification method to work.

Chapter 3

1. The federal models used by the German and Canadian governments provide interesting comparisons with the U.S. system. See Arthur B. Gunlicks, *Laender and German Federalism* (Manchester, England: Manchester University Press, 2003); and Jennifer Smith, *Federalism* (Vancouver: University of British Columbia Press, 2004).
2. Text of an address by the president to the National Conference of State Legislatures, Atlanta, Georgia (Washington, D.C.: The White House, Office of the Press Secretary, July 30, 1981).
3. An excellent illustration of this principle was President Dwight Eisenhower's disciplining of Arkansas governor Orval Faubus when Faubus refused to allow a Little Rock high school to be desegregated in 1957. Eisenhower federalized the National Guard to enforce the court-ordered desegregation of the school.
4. 5 U.S. 137 (1803).
5. 17 U.S. 316 (1819).
6. 22 U.S. 1 (1824).
7. *Hammer v. Dagenhart,* 247 U.S. 251 (1918). This decision was overruled in *United States v. Darby,* 312 U.S. 100 (1941).
8. *Wickard v. Filburn,* 317 U.S. 111 (1942).
9. *McLain v. Real Estate Board of New Orleans, Inc.,* 444 U.S. 232 (1980).
10. 514 U.S. 549 (1995).
11. *Printz v. United States,* 521 U.S. 898 (1997).
12. *United States v. Morrison,* 529 U.S. 598 (2000).
13. 549 U.S. 497 (2007).
14. *Arizona v. United States,* 567 U.S. ___ (2012).
15. *National Federation of Independent Business v. Sebelius,* 567 U.S. ___ (2012).

Chapter 4

1. 32 U.S. 243 (1833).
2. 330 U.S. 1 (1947).
3. 370 U.S. 421 (1962).
4. 449 U.S. 39 (1980).
5. *Wallace v. Jaffree,* 472 U.S. 38 (1985).
6. See, for example, *Brown v. Gwinnett County School District,* 112 F.3d 1464 (1997).
7. *Santa Fe Independent School District v. Doe,* 530 U.S. 290 (2000).
8. 393 U.S. 97 (1968).
9. *Edwards v. Aguillard,* 482 U.S. 578 (1987).
10. *Kitzmiller v. Dover Area School District,* 400 F.Supp.2d 707 (M.D.Pa. 2005).

11. 403 U.S. 602 (1971).
12. *Zelman v. Simmons-Harris*, 536 U.S. 639 (2002).
13. *Holmes v. Bush* (Fla.Cir.Ct. 2002). For details about this case, see David Royse, "Judge Rules School Voucher Law Violates Florida Constitution," *USA Today*, August 6, 2002, p. 7D.
14. 98 U.S. 145 (1878).
15. *Police v. City of Newark*, 170 F.3d 359 (3d Cir. 1999).
16. *Schenck v. United States*, 249 U.S. 47 (1919).
17. Ibid.
18. *Gitlow v. New York*, 268 U.S. 652 (1925).
19. 341 U.S. 494 (1951).
20. *Brandenburg v. Ohio*, 395 U.S. 444 (1969).
21. *Liquormart v. Rhode Island*, 517 U.S. 484 (1996).
22. 413 U.S. 15 (1973).
23. *Reno v. American Civil Liberties Union*, 521 U.S. 844 (1997); and *Ashcroft v. American Civil Liberties Union*, 542 U.S. 656 (2004). In *United States v. American Library Association*, 539 U.S. 194 (2003), the Court finally found that the government could require libraries that received certain federal subsidies to install filtering software to prevent minors from viewing pornographic material. The filters could be turned off at adult request. The subsidies were small, however, and about one-third of libraries nationwide rejected them and did not install the software.
24. *Morse v. Frederick*, 551 U.S. 393 (2007).
25. See, for example, *Doe v. University of Michigan*, 721 F.Supp. 852 (1989).
26. 484 U.S. 260 (1988).
27. Brandeis made this statement in a dissenting opinion in *Olmstead v. United States*, 277 U.S. 438 (1928).
28. 381 U.S. 479 (1965).
29. The state of South Carolina challenged the constitutionality of this act, claiming that the law violated states' rights under the Tenth Amendment. The Supreme Court, however, held that Congress had the authority, under its commerce power, to pass the act because drivers' personal information had become an article of interstate commerce. *Reno v. Condon*, 528 U.S. 141 (2000).
30. *Sorrell v. IMS Health*, 131 S.Ct. 857 (2011).
31. 410 U.S. 113 (1973). Jane Roe was not the real name of the woman in this case. It is a common legal pseudonym used to protect a party's privacy.
32. See, for example, the Supreme Court's decision in *Lambert v. Wicklund*, 520 U.S. 1169 (1997). The Court held that a Montana law requiring a minor to notify one of her parents before getting an abortion was constitutional.
33. *Schenck v. ProChoice Network*, 519 U.S. 357 (1997); and *Hill v. Colorado*, 530 U.S. 703 (2000).
34. *Stenberg v. Carhart*, 530 U.S. 914 (2000).
35. *Gonzales v. Carhart*, 550 U.S. 124 (2007).
36. *Washington v. Glucksberg*, 521 U.S. 702 (1997).
37. *Gonzales v. Oregon*, 546 U.S. 243 (2006).
38. Initially, the data collection appeared to be limited to a single telephone service provider, but Internet experts soon concluded the program was almost certainly universal.
39. 372 U.S. 335 (1963).
40. *Mapp v. Ohio*, 367 U.S. 643 (1961).
41. 384 U.S. 436 (1966). In 1968, Congress passed legislation including a provision that reinstated the previous rule that statements made by defendants can be used against them as long as the statements were made voluntarily. This provision was never enforced, however, and only in 1999 did a court try to enforce it. The case ultimately came before the Supreme Court, which held that the *Miranda* rights were based on the Constitution and thus could not be overruled by legislative act. See *Dickerson v. United States*, 530 U.S. 428 (2000).
42. *Moran v. Burbine*, 475 U.S. 412 (1986).
43. *Arizona v. Fulminante*, 499 U.S. 279 (1991).
44. *Davis v. United States*, 512 U.S. 452 (1994).
45. *Berghuis v. Thompkins*, 130 S.Ct. 2250 (2010).
46. *J.D.B. v. North Carolina*, 564 U.S. ___ (2011).
47. Thomas P. Sullivan, *Police Experiences with Recording Custodial Interrogations* (Chicago: Northwestern University School of Law Center on Wrongful Convictions, Summer 2004), p. 4.

Chapter 5

1. *Michael M. v. Superior Court*, 450 U.S. 464 (1981).
2. See, for example, *Craig v. Boren*, 429 U.S. 190 (1976).
3. *Orr v. Orr*, 440 U.S. 268 (1979).
4. *Mississippi University for Women v. Hogan*, 458 U.S. 718 (1982).
5. 518 U.S. 515 (1996).
6. 163 U.S. 537 (1896).
7. 347 U.S. 483 (1954).
8. 349 U.S. 294 (1955).
9. *Swann v. Charlotte-Mecklenburg Board of Education*, 402 U.S. 1 (1971).
10. *Keyes v. School District No. 1*, 413 U.S. 189 (1973).
11. *Milliken v. Bradley*, 418 U.S. 717 (1974).
12. *Riddick v. School Board of City of Norfolk*, 627 F.Supp. 814 (E.D.Va. 1984).
13. 570 U.S. ___ (2013).
14. Emily Bazelon, "The Next Kind of Integration," *The New York Times Magazine*, July 20, 2008.
15. *Oncale v. Sundowner Offshore Services*, 523 U.S. 75 (1998).
16. *Faragher v. City of Boca Raton*, 524 U.S. 775 (1998).

17. The Supreme Court upheld these actions in *Hirabayashi v. United States*, 320 U.S. 81 (1943); and *Korematsu v. United States*, 323 U.S. 214 (1944).
18. Historians in the early and mid-twentieth century gave much smaller figures for the pre-Columbian population—as low as 14 million people for the entire New World. Today, 40 million is considered a conservative estimate, and an estimate of 100 million has much support among demographers. If 100 million is correct, the epidemics that followed the arrival of the Europeans killed one out of every five people alive in the world at that time. See Charles C. Mann, *1491* (New York: Vintage, 2006).
19. The 1890 siege was the subject of Dee Brown's best-selling book *Bury My Heart at Wounded Knee* (New York: Holt, Rinehart & Winston, 1971).
20. *County of Oneida, New York v. Oneida Indian Nation*, 470 U.S. 226 (1985).
21. *Sutton v. United Airlines*, 527 U.S. 471 (1999); and *Toyota v. Williams*, 534 U.S. 184 (2002).
22. *Board of Trustees of the University of Alabama v. Garrett*, 531 U.S. 356 (2001).
23. 539 U.S. 558 (2003).
24. 517 U.S. 620 (1996).
25. *Goodridge v. Department of Public Health*, 798 N.E.2d 941 (Mass. 2003).
26. *Hollingsworth v. Perry*, 570 U.S. ___ (2013).
27. 570 U.S. ___ (2013).
28. *Log Cabin Republicans v. United States*, 716 F.Supp.2d 884 (C.D.Cal. 2010).
29. 438 U.S. 265 (1978).
30. 515 U.S. 200 (1995).
31. 84 F.3d 720 (5th Cir. 1996).
32. 539 U.S. 244 (2003).
33. 539 U.S. 306 (2003).
34. 551 U.S. 701 (2007).
35. 570 U.S. ___ (2013).
36. *Coalition to Defend Affirmative Action v. University of Michigan*, ___ F.3d ___ (2012).

Chapter 6

1. David Bicknell Truman, *The Governmental Process: Political Interests and Public Opinion*, 2d rev. ed. (New York: Alfred A. Knopf, 1971). This work is a political science classic.
2. Robert H. Salisbury, *Interests and Institutions: Substance and Structure in American Politics* (Pittsburgh: University of Pittsburgh Press, 1992).
3. *Democracy in America*, Vol. 1, ed. Phillip Bradley (New York: Knopf, 1980), p. 191.
4. Mancur Olson, *The Logic of Collective Action: Public Goods and the Theory of Groups*, rev. ed. (Cambridge, Mass.: Harvard University Press, 1971).
5. Pronounced ah-*mee*-kus *kure*-ee-*eye*.
6. Fred McChesney, *Money for Nothing: Politicians, Rent Extraction and Political Extortion* (Cambridge, Mass.: Harvard University Press, 1997).
7. The Agricultural Adjustment Act of 1933 (declared unconstitutional) was replaced by the 1937 Agricultural Adjustment Act, which later was changed and amended several times.
8. 558 U.S. 50 (2010).
9. 567 U.S. ___ (2012).
10. *Caperton v. A. T. Massey Coal Co.*, 556 U.S. 868 (2009).
11. *United States v. Harriss*, 347 U.S. 612 (1954).

Chapter 7

1. Letter to Francis Hopkinson written from Paris while Jefferson was ambassador to France, as cited in John P. Foley, ed., *The Jeffersonian Cyclopedia* (New York: Russell & Russell, 1967), p. 677.
2. The U.S. Senate presents the text of the address at **www.access.gpo.gov/congress/senate/farewell/sd106-21.pdf**.
3. The association of red with the Republicans and blue with the Democrats is barely a decade old. The terms *red* and *blue* are derived from the colors used by the major television networks to show the states carried by the Republican and Democratic presidential candidates. This use of colors deliberately reverses a traditional pattern. In most European countries, the right-of-center party uses blue, while the left-of-center party employs red. The use of red originated in the socialist movement, from which most European left-of-center parties descend. From time to time, Republicans have accused Democrats of socialism. U.S. television networks thus assigned red to the Republicans precisely so that the networks would not appear to be endorsing that accusation.
4. For an interesting discussion of the pros and cons of patronage from a constitutional perspective, see the majority opinion versus the dissent in the Supreme Court case *Board of County Commissioners v. Umbehr*, 518 U.S. 668 (1996).
5. The term *third party*, although not literally accurate (because sometimes there has been a fourth party, a fifth party, and even more), is commonly used to refer to a minor party.
6. Thomas Nast, the cartoonist who drew these images, was a Republican. "Copperhead" was a derisive term for northern Democrats who sympathized with the South during the Civil War, and in the first cartoon Nast condemned Democratic newspapers for abusing Edwin Stanton, Lincoln's secretary of war, following Stanton's death. The elephant in the second cartoon referred to the large size of the Republican vote in the North. Nast

depicted the elephant as stampeded into a pit by a jackass dressed in a lion skin. This referred to the *New York Herald,* a Democratic newspaper, which made accusations against Republican president Ulysses S. Grant that caused Republicans to panic.
7. Today, twelve states have multimember districts for their state houses, and a handful also have multimember districts for their state senates.

Chapter 8

1. The elections that Gallup predicted incorrectly were usually close ones. In 2004, Gallup reported a statistical tie—49 percent each—between Republican George W. Bush and Democrat John Kerry. In 1976, Gallup falsely predicted that Republican incumbent Gerald Ford would prevail over Democrat Jimmy Carter. In 1948, Gallup wrongly predicted that Republican Thomas Dewey would defeat Democratic incumbent Harry Truman. The 2012 elections, however, may have been Gallup's biggest embarrassment to date. Assuming very low Democratic voter turnout, Gallup had Romney well in the lead throughout October. It corrected its last poll to reflect greater turnout, but it still predicted a Romney victory.
2. John M. Benson, "When Is an Opinion Really an Opinion?" *Public Perspective,* September/October 2001, pp. 40–41.
3. As quoted in Karl G. Feld, "When Push Comes to Shove: A Polling Industry Call to Arms," *Public Perspective,* September/October 2001, p. 38.
4. Doris A. Graber, *Mass Media and American Politics,* 8th ed. (Washington, D.C.: CQ Press, 2009).
5. Jimmy Carter, *Palestine: Peace Not Apartheid* (New York: Simon & Schuster, 2007).
6. Pew Research Center for the People and the Press, survey conducted September 21–October 4, 2006, and reported in "Who Votes, Who Doesn't, and Why," released October 28, 2006.
7. *Guinn v. United States,* 238 U.S. 347 (1915).
8. *Smith v. Allwright,* 321 U.S. 649 (1944).
9. For more information on voting systems, see the Web site of **verifiedvoting.org**.
10. The argument about the vote-eligible population was first made by Michael P. McDonald and Samuel L. Popkin, "The Myth of the Vanishing Voter," *American Political Science Review,* Vol. 95, No. 4 (December 2001), p. 963.

Chapter 9

1. Today, there are 100 senators in the Senate and 435 members of the House of Representatives. In addition, the District of Columbia has three electoral votes, as provided for by the Twenty-third Amendment to the Constitution.
2. This group includes those who support the National Popular Vote movement, a proposed interstate compact that would cast the electoral votes of each participating state for the candidate who won the national popular vote. The compact would go into effect if participating states controlled a majority of the votes in the electoral college.
3. These states award one electoral vote to the candidate who wins the popular vote in a congressional district and an additional two electoral votes to the winner of the statewide popular vote. Other states have considered similar plans.
4. The word *caucus* apparently was first used in the name of a men's club, the Caucus Club of colonial Boston, sometime between 1755 and 1765. (Many early political and government meetings took place in pubs.) We have no certain knowledge of the origin of the word, but it may be from an Algonquin term meaning "elder" or from the Latin name of a drinking vessel.
5. Today, the Democratic and Republican caucuses in the House and Senate (the Republicans now use the term *conference* instead of *caucus*) choose each party's congressional leadership and sometimes discuss legislation and legislative strategy.
6. Due to the customs of the time, none of the candidates could admit that he had made a personal decision to run. All claimed to have entered the race in response to popular demand.
7. Parties cannot use their freedom-of-association rights to practice racial discrimination in state-sponsored elections: *Smith v. Allwright,* 321 U.S. 649 (1944). When racial discrimination is not involved, the parties have regularly won freedom-of-association suits against state governments. Examples are *Tashjian v. Republican Party of Connecticut,* 479 U.S. 208 (1986), and *California Democratic Party v. Jones,* 530 U.S. 567 (2000).
8. In Washington, the state government holds presidential primaries for both parties. The Democratic Party, however, ignores the Democratic primary and chooses its national convention delegates through a caucus/convention system. In 1984, following a dispute with the state of Michigan over primary rules, the state Democratic Party organized a presidential primary election that was run completely by party volunteers. In 2008, after a similar dispute with its state, the Virginia Republican Party chose its candidate for the U.S. Senate at its state party convention instead of through the Virginia primary elections.
9. The case was *California Democratic Party v. Jones,* cited in footnote 7.
10. *Washington State Grange v. Washington State Republican Party et al.,* 552 U.S. 442 (2008).
11. This act is sometimes referred to as the Federal Election Campaign Act of 1972 because it became effective in that year. The official date of the act, however, is 1971.

12. *Buckley v. Valeo,* 424 U.S. 1 (1976).
13. This figure is from the Center for Responsive Politics.
14. *Colorado Republican Federal Campaign Committee v. Federal Election Commission,* 518 U.S. 604 (1996).
15. Quoted in George Will, "The First Amendment on Trial," *The Washington Post,* December 1, 2002, p. B7.
16. 540 U.S. 93 (2003).
17. 551 U.S. 449 (2007).
18. 558 U.S. 50 (2010).
19. 599 F.3d 686 (D.C.Cir. 2010).

Chapter 10

1. *Mutual Film Corporation v. Industrial Commission of Ohio,* 236 U.S. 230 (1915).
2. *Joseph Burstyn, Inc. v. Wilson,* 343 U.S. 495 (1952).
3. *Reno v. American Civil Liberties Union,* 521 U.S. 844 (1997).
4. *United States v. Playboy Entertainment Group,* 529 U.S. 803 (2000).
5. Bernard Cohen, *The Press and Foreign Policy* (Princeton, N.J.: Princeton University Press, 1963), p. 81.
6. Interestingly, in the 2000 campaigns, a Texas group supporting George W. Bush's candidacy paid for a remake of the "daisy" commercial, but the target in the new ad was Al Gore.
7. As quoted in Michael Grunwald, "The Year of Playing Dirtier," *The Washington Post,* October 27, 2006, p. A1.
8. John G. Geer, *In Defense of Negativity: Attack Ads in Presidential Campaigns* (Chicago: University of Chicago Press, 2006).
9. The commission's action was upheld by a federal court. See *Perot v. Federal Election Commission,* 97 F.3d 553 (D.C.Cir. 1996).
10. For more details on how political candidates manage news coverage, see Doris A. Graber, *Mass Media and American Politics,* 7th ed. (Washington, D.C.: CQ Press, 2005).
11. For suggestions on how to dissect spin and detect when language is steering one toward a conclusion, see Brooks Jackson and Kathleen Hall Jamieson, *unSpun: Finding Facts in a World of Disinformation* (New York: Random House, 2007).
12. *Red Lion Broadcasting Co. v. FCC,* 395 U.S. 367 (1969).
13. Kathleen Hall Jamieson, *Everything You Think You Know about Politics . . . and Why You're Wrong* (New York: Basic Books, 2000), pp. 187–195.
14. Debra Reddin van Tuyll and Hubert P. van Tuyll, "Political Partisanship," in William David Sloan and Jenn Burleson Mackay, eds., *Media Bias: Finding It, Fixing It* (Jefferson, N.C.: McFarland, 2007), pp. 35–49.
15. Jamieson, *Everything You Think You Know about Politics,* pp. xiii–xiv.
16. Pew Research Center for the People and the Press and the Project for Excellence in Journalism, *The State of the News Media 2007: An Annual Report on American Journalism.*
17. For details, search on "all your base wiki" and "revenue are belong to."
18. The term *podcasting* is used for this type of information delivery because initially podcasts were downloaded onto Apple's iPods.

Chapter 11

1. These states are Alaska, Delaware, Montana, North Dakota, South Dakota, Vermont, and Wyoming.
2. 369 U.S. 186 (1962).
3. 376 U.S. 1 (1964).
4. See, for example, *Davis v. Bandemer,* 478 U.S. 109 (1986).
5. *Amicus curiae* brief filed by the American Civil Liberties Union (ACLU) in support of the appellants in *Easley v. Cromartie,* 532 U.S. 234 (2001).
6. See, for example, *Shaw v. Reno,* 509 U.S. 630 (1993); *Miller v. Johnson,* 515 U.S. 900 (1995); *Shaw v. Hunt,* 517 U.S. 899 (1996); and *Bush v. Vera,* 517 U.S. 952 (1996).
7. *Easley v. Cromartie,* 532 U.S. 234 (2001).
8. *Powell v. McCormack,* 395 U.S. 486 (1969).
9. Some observers maintain that another reason Congress stays in session longer is the invention of air-conditioning. Until the advent of air-conditioning, no member of Congress wanted to stay in session during the hot and sticky late spring, summer, and early fall months in Washington, D.C.
10. *U.S. Term Limits, Inc. v. Thornton,* 514 U.S. 779 (1995).
11. A term used by Woodrow Wilson in *Congressional Government* (New York: Meridian Books, 1956 [first published in 1885]).

Chapter 12

1. Lyndon B. Johnson, *The Vantage Point: Perspectives of the Presidency, 1963–1969* (New York: Henry Holt & Co., 1971).
2. *Ex parte Grossman,* 267 U.S. 87 (1925).
3. *Clinton v. City of New York,* 524 U.S. 417 (1998).
4. As cited in Lewis D. Eigen and Jonathan P. Siegel, *The Macmillan Dictionary of Political Quotations* (New York: Macmillan, 1993), p. 565.
5. The Constitution does not grant the president explicit power to remove from office officials who are not performing satisfactorily or who do not agree

with the president. In 1926, however, the Supreme Court prevented Congress from interfering with the president's ability to fire those executive-branch officials whom he had appointed with Senate approval. See *Myers v. United States,* 272 U.S. 52 (1926).

6. Ironically, Lincoln believed that the actions of the president ought to be strictly limited when war powers were not concerned. He therefore left most domestic issues that did not involve the war entirely to Congress. In doing so, Lincoln was true to the ideas of his former party, the Whigs. That party advocated a limited role for the presidency in reaction to the sweeping assumption of authority by President Andrew Jackson, their great opponent. See David Donald's classic essay "Abraham Lincoln: Whig in the White House," in *Lincoln Reconsidered: Essays on the Civil War Era,* 3d ed. (New York: Vintage, 2001), pp. 133–147.

7. Richard E. Neustadt, *Presidential Power: The Politics of Leadership* (New York: John Wiley, 1960), p. 10.

8. As quoted in Richard M. Pious, *The American Presidency* (New York: Basic Books, 1979), pp. 51–52.

9. A phrase coined by Samuel Kernell in *Going Public: New Strategies of Presidential Leadership,* 2d ed. (Washington, D.C.: Congressional Quarterly Press, 1992).

10. Congress used its power to declare war in the War of 1812, the Mexican War (1846–1848), the Spanish-American War (1898), and World War I (U.S. involvement lasted from 1916 until 1918) and on six different occasions during World War II (U.S. involvement lasted from 1941 until 1945).

11. As quoted in Thomas E. Cronin, *The State of the Presidency,* 2d ed. (Boston: Little, Brown, 1980), p. 11.

Chapter 13

1. This definition follows the classic model of bureaucracy put forth by German sociologist Max Weber. See Max Weber, *Theory of Social and Economic Organization,* ed. Talcott Parsons (New York: Oxford University Press, 1974).

2. It should be noted that although the president is technically the head of the bureaucracy, the president cannot always control the bureaucracy—as you will read later in this chapter.

3. Alicia Munnell, Jean-Pierre Aubry, Josh Hurwitz, and Laura Quinby, *Comparing Compensation: State-Local Versus Private Sector Workers,* Center for Retirement Research at Boston College, September 2011 (slge .org/publications/comparing-compensation-state-local-versus-private-sector -workers). Also, Maury Gittleman and Brooks Pierce, "Compensation for State and Local Government Workers," *Journal of Economic Perspectives,* Vol. 26, No. 1, Winter 2012, pp. 217–242 (www.aeaweb.org/articles .php?doi=10.1257/jep.26.1.217).

4. Dennis Cauchon, "Federal Workers Earning Double Their Private Counterparts," *USA Today,* August 13, 2010. According to FactCheck.org, however, the total wage figure from which the $123,049 estimate was derived includes approximately $10,000 per current employee that was actually paid to other employees who retired earlier. Thus, the true average is closer to $113,000. Also, Congressional Budget Office, "Comparing the Compensation of Federal and Private-Sector Employees," January 30, 2012 (www.cbo.gov/publication/42921).

5. For an insightful analysis of the policymaking process in Washington, D.C., and the role played by various groups in the process, see Morton H. Halperin and Priscilla A. Clapp, with Arnold Kanter, *Bureaucratic Politics and Foreign Policy,* 2d ed. (Washington, D.C.: The Brookings Institution, 2006). Although the focus of the book is on foreign policy, the analysis applies in many ways to the general policymaking process.

Chapter 14

1. 347 U.S. 483 (1954).
2. See *Plessy v. Ferguson,* 163 U.S. 537 (1896).
3. 130 S.Ct. 876 (2010).
4. 494 U.S. 652 (1990).
5. 540 U.S. 93 (2003).
6. Although a state's highest court is often referred to as the state supreme court, there are exceptions. In the New York court system, for example, the supreme court is a trial court, and the highest court is called the New York Court of Appeals.
7. 569 U.S. ___ (2013).
8. Between 1790 and 1891, Congress allowed the Supreme Court almost no discretion over which cases to decide. After 1925, in almost 95 percent of appealed cases the Court could choose whether to hear arguments and issue an opinion. Beginning in October 1988, mandatory review was nearly eliminated.
9. *Association for Molecular Pathology v. Myriad Genetics,* 569 U.S. ___ (2013).

10. *Fisher v. University of Texas,* 570 U.S. ___ (2013).
11. *Shelby County v. Holder,* 570 U.S. ___ (2013).
12. *United States v. Windsor,* 570 U.S. ___ (2013).
13. 132 S.Ct. 2566 (2012).
14. 347 U.S. 483 (1954).
15. *Perry v. Brown,* 704 F.Supp.2d 921 (N.D.Cal. 2010).
16. *Perry v. Brown,* 671 F.3d 1052 (9th Cir. 2012).
17. *Hollingsworth v. Perry,* 570 U.S. ___ (2013).
18. 5 U.S. 137 (1803). The Supreme Court had considered the constitutionality of an act of Congress in *Hylton v. United States,* 3 U.S. 171 (1796), in which Congress's power to levy certain taxes was challenged. That particular act was ruled constitutional, rather than unconstitutional, however, so this first federal exercise of judicial review was not clearly recognized as such. Also, during the decade before the adoption of the federal Constitution, courts in at least eight states had exercised the power of judicial review.
19. For an analysis of the Roberts Court's first term by a Georgetown University law professor, see Jonathan Turley, "The Roberts Court: Seeing Is Believing," *USA Today,* July 6, 2006, p. 11A.
20. 539 U.S. 558 (2003).
21. Antonin Scalia, *A Matter of Interpretation: Federal Courts and the Law* (Princeton, N.J.: Princeton University Press, 1997).
22. Letter by Thomas Jefferson to William C. Jarvis, 1820, in Andrew A. Lipscomb and Albert Ellery Bergh, *The Writings of Thomas Jefferson,* Memorial Edition (Washington, D.C.: Thomas Jefferson Memorial Association of the United States, 1904).
23. As quoted in Carl Hulse and David D. Kirkpatrick, "DeLay Says Federal Judiciary Has 'Run Amok,' Adding Congress Is Partly to Blame," *The New York Times,* April 8, 2005, p. 5.

Chapter 15

1. Stan Dorn, *Uninsured and Dying because of It: Updating the Institute of Medicine Analysis on the Impact of Uninsurance on Mortality* (Washington, D.C.: Urban Institute, 2008).
2. *National Federation of Independent Business v. Sebelius,* 567 U.S. ___ (2012).
3. An alternative possibility would be to change the Senate rules so that sixty votes would no longer be necessary to pass legislation. Changing the rules, however, could easily prove more difficult than assembling sixty votes.
4. The CAFE standards that go into effect fully in 2025 are different from the ones first imposed in the 1970s. At first, the benchmarks were imposed on a manufacturer-by-manufacturer basis. The new standards will be based on vehicle type. A company that manufactures only luxury vehicles, such as Mercedes Benz, will therefore face lower mile-per-gallon standards than a company that specializes in small cars. The figure of 54.5 miles per gallon is an estimate based on the predicted mix of vehicles sold in 2025. Examples of standards follow:

Small car	61.1	Small SUV	47.5	Minivan	39.2
Midsize car	54.9	Midsize SUV	43.4	Large pickup	33.0
Large car	48.0				

5. Paul Krugman, "Romer and Bernstein on Stimulus," in the blog Conscience of a Liberal, The *New York Times,* January 10, 2009.
6. Recent Keynesian analyses, however, suggest that under current conditions, a crisis of confidence in the dollar would result in a fall in its value relative to other currencies, with no direct impact on interest rates. This outcome would benefit U.S. exporters by making exports cheaper and more competitive. Note that it is widely accepted that China buys treasuries to keep the value of its currency down and the value of the dollar up, benefiting its exporters. It can be argued that if China *sold* treasuries, it would unwind this process. See Paul Krugman, "Currency Regimes, Capital Flows, and Crises" (keynote lecture, IMF Annual Research Conference, Washington, D.C., November 7, 2013).

Chapter 16

1. David L. Rousseau, *Identifying Threats and Threatening Identities: The Social Construction of Realism and Liberalism* (Palo Alto, Calif.: Stanford University Press, 2006), p. 154.
2. *Public Papers of the Presidents of the United States: Harry S. Truman, 1947* (Washington, D.C.: U.S. Government Printing Office, 1963), pp. 176–180.
3. The containment policy was outlined by George F. Kennan, the chief of the policy-planning staff for the Department of State at that time, in an article that appeared in *Foreign Affairs,* July 1947, p. 575. The author's name was given as "X."

THE DECLARATION OF INDEPENDENCE

IN CONGRESS, JULY 4, 1776

A Declaration by the Representatives of the United States of America, in General Congress assembled. When in the Course of human Events, it becomes necessary for one People to dissolve the Political Bands which have connected them with another, and to assume among the Powers of the Earth, the separate and equal Station to which the Laws of Nature and of Nature's God entitle them, a decent Respect to the Opinions of Mankind requires that they should declare the causes which impel them to the Separation.

We hold these Truths to be self-evident, that all Men are created equal, that they are endowed by their Creator with certain unalienable Rights, that among these are Life, Liberty, and the Pursuit of Happiness— That to secure these Rights, Governments are instituted among Men, deriving their just Powers from the Consent of the Governed, that whenever any Form of Government becomes destructive of these Ends, it is the Right of the People to alter or to abolish it, and to institute new Government, laying its Foundation on such Principles, and organizing its Powers in such Forms, as to them shall seem most likely to effect their Safety and Happiness. Prudence, indeed, will dictate that Governments long established should not be changed for light and transient Causes; and accordingly all Experience hath shewn, that Mankind are more disposed to suffer, while Evils are sufferable, than to right themselves by abolishing the Forms to which they are accustomed. But when a long Train of Abuses and Usurpations, pursuing invariably the same Object, evinces a Design to reduce them under absolute Despotism, it is their Right, it is their Duty, to throw off such Government, and to provide new Guards for their future Security. Such has been the patient Sufferance of these Colonies; and such is now the Necessity which constrains them to alter their former Systems of Government. The History of the present King of Great-Britain is a History of repeated Injuries and Usurpations, all having in direct Object the Establishment of an absolute Tyranny over these States. To prove this, let Facts be submitted to a candid World.

He has refused his Assent to Laws, the most wholesome and necessary for the public Good.

He has forbidden his Governors to pass Laws of immediate and pressing Importance, unless suspended in their Operation till his Assent should be obtained; and when so suspended, he has utterly neglected to attend to them.

He has refused to pass other Laws for the Accommodation of large Districts of People, unless those People would relinquish the Right of Representation in the Legislature, a Right inestimable to them, and formidable to Tyrants only.

He has called together Legislative Bodies at Places unusual, uncomfortable, and distant from the Depository of their Public Records, for the sole Purpose of fatiguing them into Compliance with his Measures.

He has dissolved Representative Houses repeatedly, for opposing with manly Firmness his Invasions on the Rights of the People.

He has refused for a long Time, after such Dissolutions, to cause others to be elected; whereby the Legislative Powers, incapable of Annihilation, have returned to the People at large for their exercise; the State remaining in the mean time exposed to all the Dangers of Invasion from without, and Convulsions within.

He has endeavoured to prevent the Population of these States; for that Purpose obstructing the Laws for Naturalization of Foreigners; refusing to pass others to encourage their Migrations hither, and raising the Conditions of new Appropriations of Lands.

He has obstructed the Administration of Justice, by refusing his Assent to Laws for establishing Judiciary Powers.

He has made Judges dependent on his Will alone, for the Tenure of their offices, and the Amount and payment of their Salaries.

He has erected a Multitude of new Offices, and sent hither Swarms of Officers to harrass our People, and eat out their Substance.

He has kept among us, in Times of Peace, Standing Armies, without the consent of our Legislatures.

He has affected to render the Military independent of, and superior to the Civil Power.

He has combined with others to subject us to a Jurisdiction foreign to our Constitution, and unacknowledged by our Laws; giving his Assent to their Acts of pretended Legislation:

For quartering large Bodies of Armed Troops among us:

For protecting them, by a mock Trial, from Punishment for any Murders which they should commit on the Inhabitants of these States:

For cutting off our Trade with all Parts of the World:

For imposing Taxes on us without our Consent:

For depriving us, in many cases, of the Benefits of Trial by Jury:

For transporting us beyond Seas to be tried for pretended Offences:

For abolishing the free System of English Laws in a neighbouring Province, establishing therein an arbitrary Government, and enlarging its Boundaries, so as to render it at once an Example and fit Instrument for introducing the same absolute Rule into these Colonies:

For taking away our Charters, abolishing our most valuable Laws, and altering fundamentally the Forms of our Governments:

For suspending our own Legislatures, and declaring themselves invested with Power to legislate for us in all Cases whatsoever.

He has abdicated Government here, by declaring us out of his Protection and waging War against us.

He has plundered our Seas, ravaged our Coasts, burnt our towns, and destroyed the Lives of our People.

He is, at this Time, transporting large Armies of foreign Mercenaries to compleat the works of Death, Desolation, and Tyranny, already begun with circumstances of Cruelty and Perfidy, scarcely paralleled in the most barbarous Ages, and totally unworthy the Head of a civilized Nation.

He has constrained our fellow Citizens taken Captive on the high Seas to bear Arms against their Country, to become the Executioners of their Friends and Brethren, or to fall themselves by their Hands.

He has excited domestic Insurrections amongst us, and has endeavoured to bring on the Inhabitants of our Frontiers, the merciless Indian Savages, whose known Rule of Warfare, is an undistinguished Destruction, of all Ages, Sexes and Conditions.

In every state of these Oppressions we have Petitioned for Redress in the most humble Terms: Our repeated Petitions have been answered only by repeated Injury. A Prince, whose Character is thus marked by every act which may define a Tyrant, is unfit to be the Ruler of a free People.

Nor have we been wanting in Attentions to our British Brethren. We have warned them from Time to Time of Attempts by their Legislature to extend an unwarrantable Jurisdiction over us. We have reminded them of the Circumstances of our Emigration and Settlement here. We have appealed to their native Justice and Magnanimity, and we have conjured them by the Ties of our common Kindred to disavow these Usurpations, which, would inevitably interrupt our Connections and Correspondence. They too have been deaf to the Voice of Justice and of Consanguinity. We must, therefore, acquiesce in the Necessity, which denounces our Separation, and hold them, as we hold the rest of Mankind, Enemies in War, in Peace, Friends.

We, therefore, the Representatives of the UNITED STATES OF AMERICA, in General Congress Assembled, appealing to the Supreme Judge of the World for the Rectitude of our Intentions, do, in the Name, and by the Authority of the good People of these Colonies, solemnly Publish and Declare, That these United Colonies are, and of Right ought to be, Free and Independent States; that they are absolved from all Allegiance to the British Crown, and that all political Connection between them and the State of Great-Britain, is and ought to be totally dissolved; and that as Free and Independent States, they have full Power to levy War, conclude Peace, contract Alliances, establish Commerce, and to do all other Acts and Things which Independent States may of right do. And for the support of this declaration, with a firm Reliance on the Protection of divine Providence, we mutually pledge to each other our lives, our Fortunes, and our sacred Honor.

THE CONSTITUTION OF THE UNITED STATES

PREAMBLE

We the People of the United States, in Order to form a more perfect Union, establish Justice, insure domestic Tranquility, provide for the common defence, promote the general Welfare, and secure the Blessings of Liberty to ourselves and our Posterity, do ordain and establish this Constitution for the United States of America.

ARTICLE I

Section 1.   All legislative Powers herein granted shall be vested in a Congress of the United States, which shall consist of a Senate and House of Representatives.

Section 2.   The House of Representatives shall be composed of Members chosen every second Year by the People of the several States, and the Electors in each State shall have the Qualifications requisite for Electors of the most numerous Branch of the State Legislature.

No Person shall be a Representative who shall not have attained to the Age of twenty five Years, and been seven Years a Citizen of the United States, and who shall not, when elected, be an Inhabitant of that State in which he shall be chosen.

Representatives and direct Taxes shall be apportioned among the several States which may be included within this Union, according to their respective Numbers, which shall be determined by adding to the whole Number of free Persons, including those bound to Service for a Term of Years, and excluding Indians not taxed, three fifths of all other Persons. The actual Enumeration shall be made within three Years after the first Meeting of the Congress of the United States, and within every subsequent Term of ten Years, in such Manner as they shall by Law direct. The Number of Representatives shall not exceed one for every thirty Thousand, but each State shall have at Least one Representative; and until such enumeration shall be made, the State of New Hampshire shall be entitled to chuse three, Massachusetts eight, Rhode Island and Providence Plantations one, Connecticut five, New York six, New Jersey four, Pennsylvania eight, Delaware one, Maryland six, Virginia ten, North Carolina five, South Carolina five, and Georgia three.

When vacancies happen in the Representation from any State, the Executive Authority thereof shall issue Writs of Election to fill such Vacancies.

The House of Representatives shall chuse their Speaker and other Officers; and shall have the sole Power of Impeachment.

Section 3.   The Senate of the United States shall be composed of two Senators from each State, chosen by the Legislature thereof, for six Years; and each Senator shall have one Vote.

Immediately after they shall be assembled in Consequence of the first Election, they shall be divided as equally as may be into three Classes. The Seats of the Senators of the first Class shall be vacated at the Expiration of the second Year, of the second Class at the Expiration of the fourth Year, and of the third Class at the Expiration of the sixth Year, so that one third may be chosen every second Year; and if Vacancies happen by Resignation, or otherwise, during the Recess of the Legislature of any State, the Executive thereof may make temporary Appointments until the next Meeting of the Legislature, which shall then fill such Vacancies.

No Person shall be a Senator who shall not have attained to the Age of thirty Years, and been nine Years a Citizen of the United States, and who shall not, when elected, be an Inhabitant of that State for which he shall be chosen.

The Vice President of the United States shall be President of the Senate, but shall have no Vote, unless they be equally divided.

The Senate shall chuse their other Officers, and also a President pro tempore, in the Absence of the Vice President, or when he shall exercise the Office of President of the United States.

The Senate shall have the sole Power to try all Impeachments. When sitting for that Purpose, they shall be on Oath or Affirmation. When the President of the United States is tried, the Chief Justice shall preside: And no Person shall be convicted without the Concurrence of two thirds of the Members present.

Judgment in Cases of Impeachment shall not extend further than to removal from Office, and disqualification to hold and enjoy any Office of honor, Trust, or Profit under the United States: but the Party convicted shall nevertheless be liable and subject to Indictment, Trial, Judgment, and Punishment, according to Law.

Section 4. The Times, Places and Manner of holding Elections for Senators and Representatives, shall be prescribed in each State by the Legislature thereof; but the Congress may at any time by Law make or alter such Regulations, except as to the Places of chusing Senators.

The Congress shall assemble at least once in every Year, and such Meeting shall be on the first Monday in December, unless they shall by Law appoint a different Day.

Section 5. Each House shall be the Judge of the Elections, Returns, and Qualifications of its own Members, and a Majority of each shall constitute a Quorum to do Business; but a smaller Number may adjourn from day to day, and may be authorized to compel the Attendance of absent Members, in such Manner, and under such Penalties as each House may provide.

Each House may determine the Rules of its Proceedings, punish its Members for disorderly Behavior, and, with the Concurrence of two thirds, expel a Member.

Each House shall keep a Journal of its Proceedings, and from time to time publish the same, excepting such Parts as may in their Judgment require Secrecy; and the Yeas and Nays of the Members of either House on any question shall, at the Desire of one fifth of those Present, be entered on the Journal.

Neither House, during the Session of Congress, shall, without the Consent of the other, adjourn for more than three days, nor to any other Place than that in which the two Houses shall be sitting.

Section 6. The Senators and Representatives shall receive a Compensation for their Services, to be ascertained by Law, and paid out of the Treasury of the United States. They shall in all Cases, except Treason, Felony and Breach of the Peace, be privileged from Arrest during their Attendance at the Session of their respective Houses, and in going to and returning from the same; and for any Speech or Debate in either House, they shall not be questioned in any other Place.

No Senator or Representative shall, during the Time for which he was elected, be appointed to any civil Office under the Authority of the United States, which shall have been created, or the Emoluments whereof shall have been increased during such time; and no Person holding any Office under the United States, shall be a Member of either House during his Continuance in Office.

Section 7. All Bills for raising Revenue shall originate in the House of Representatives; but the Senate may propose or concur with Amendments as on other Bills.

Every Bill which shall have passed the House of Representatives and the Senate, shall, before it become a Law, be presented to the President of the United States; If he approve he shall sign it, but if not he shall return it, with his Objections to the House in which it shall have originated, who shall enter the Objections at large on their Journal, and proceed to reconsider it. If after such Reconsideration two thirds of that House shall agree to pass the Bill, it shall be sent together with the Objections, to the other House, by which it shall likewise be reconsidered, and if approved by two thirds of that House, it shall become a Law. But in all such Cases the Votes of both Houses shall be determined by Yeas and Nays, and the Names of the Persons voting for and against the Bill shall be entered on the Journal of each House respectively. If any Bill shall not be returned by the President within ten Days (Sundays excepted) after it shall have been presented to him, the Same shall be a Law, in like Manner as if he had signed it, unless the Congress by their Adjournment prevent its Return in which Case it shall not be a Law.

Every Order, Resolution, or Vote, to which the Concurrence of the Senate and House of Representatives may be necessary (except on a question of Adjournment) shall be presented to the President of the United States; and before the Same shall take Effect, shall be approved by him, or being disapproved by him, shall be repassed by two thirds of the Senate and House of Representatives, according to the Rules and Limitations prescribed in the Case of a Bill.

Section 8. The Congress shall have Power To lay and collect Taxes, Duties, Imposts and Excises, to pay the Debts and provide for the common Defence and general Welfare of the United States; but all Duties, Imposts and Excises shall be uniform throughout the United States;

To borrow Money on the credit of the United States;

To regulate Commerce with foreign Nations, and among the several States, and with the Indian Tribes;

To establish an uniform Rule of Naturalization, and uniform Laws on the subject of Bankruptcies throughout the United States;

To coin Money, regulate the Value thereof, and of foreign Coin, and fix the Standard of Weights and Measures;

To provide for the Punishment of counterfeiting the Securities and current Coin of the United States;

To establish Post Offices and post Roads;

To promote the Progress of Science and useful Arts, by securing for limited Times to Authors and Inventors the exclusive Right to their respective Writings and Discoveries;

To constitute Tribunals inferior to the supreme Court;

To define and punish Piracies and Felonies committed on the high Seas, and Offenses against the Law of Nations;

To declare War, grant Letters of Marque and Reprisal, and make Rules concerning Captures on Land and Water;

To raise and support Armies, but no Appropriation of Money to that Use shall be for a longer Term than two Years;

To provide and maintain a Navy;

To make Rules for the Government and Regulation of the land and naval Forces;

To provide for calling forth the Militia to execute the Laws of the Union, suppress Insurrections and repel Invasions;

To provide for organizing, arming, and disciplining, the Militia, and for governing such Part of them as may be employed in the Service of the United States, reserving to the States respectively, the Appointment of the Officers, and the Authority of training the Militia according to the discipline prescribed by Congress;

To exercise exclusive Legislation in all Cases whatsoever, over such District (not exceeding ten Miles square) as may, by Cession of particular States, and the Acceptance of Congress, become the Seat of the Government of the United States, and to exercise like Authority over all Places purchased by the Consent of the Legislature of the State in which the Same shall be, for the Erection of Forts, Magazines, Arsenals, dock-Yards, and other needful Buildings;—And

To make all Laws which shall be necessary and proper for carrying into Execution the foregoing Powers, and all other Powers vested by this Constitution in the Government of the United States, or in any Department or Officer thereof.

Section 9. The Migration or Importation of such Persons as any of the States now existing shall think proper to admit, shall not be prohibited by the Congress prior to the Year one thousand eight hundred and eight, but a Tax or duty may be imposed on such Importation, not exceeding ten dollars for each Person.

The privilege of the Writ of Habeas Corpus shall not be suspended, unless when in Cases of Rebellion or Invasion the public Safety may require it.

No Bill of Attainder or ex post facto Law shall be passed.

No Capitation, or other direct, Tax shall be laid, unless in Proportion to the Census or Enumeration herein before directed to be taken.

No Tax or Duty shall be laid on Articles exported from any State.

No Preference shall be given by any Regulation of Commerce or Revenue to the Ports of one State over those of another: nor shall Vessels bound to, or from, one State be obliged to enter, clear, or pay Duties in another.

No Money shall be drawn from the Treasury, but in Consequence of Appropriations made by Law; and a regular Statement and Account of the Receipts and Expenditures of all public Money shall be published from time to time.

No Title of Nobility shall be granted by the United States: And no Person holding any Office of Profit or Trust under them, shall, without the Consent of the Congress, accept of any present, Emolument, Office, or Title, of any kind whatever, from any King, Prince, or foreign State.

Section 10. No State shall enter into any Treaty, Alliance, or Confederation; grant Letters of Marque and Reprisal; coin Money; emit Bills of Credit; make any Thing but gold and silver Coin a Tender in Payment of Debts; pass any Bill of Attainder, ex post facto Law, or Law impairing the Obligation of Contracts, or grant any Title of Nobility.

No State shall, without the Consent of Congress, lay any Imposts or Duties on Imports or Exports, except what may be absolutely necessary for executing its inspection Laws: and the net Produce of all Duties and Imposts, laid by any State on Imports or Exports, shall be for the Use of the Treasury of the United States; and all such Laws shall be subject to the Revision and Controul of the Congress.

No State shall, without the Consent of Congress, lay any Duty of Tonnage, keep Troops, or Ships of War in time of Peace, enter into any Agreement or Compact with another State, or with a foreign Power, or engage in War, unless actually invaded, or in such imminent Danger as will not admit of delay.

ARTICLE II

Section 1. The executive Power shall be vested in a President of the United States of America. He shall hold his Office during the Term of four Years, and, together with the Vice President, chosen for the same Term, be elected, as follows:

Each State shall appoint, in such Manner as the Legislature thereof may direct, a Number of Electors, equal to the whole Number of Senators and Representatives to which the State may be entitled in the Congress; but no Senator or Representative, or Person holding an Office of Trust or Profit under the United States, shall be appointed an Elector.

The Electors shall meet in their respective States, and vote by Ballot for two Persons, of whom one at least shall not be an Inhabitant of the same State with themselves. And they shall make a List of all the Persons voted for, and of the Number of Votes for each; which List they shall sign and certify, and transmit sealed to the Seat of the Government of the United States, directed to the President of the Senate. The President of the Senate shall, in the Presence of the Senate and House of Representatives, open all the Certificates, and the Votes shall then be counted. The Person having the greatest Number of Votes shall be the President, if such Number be a Majority of the whole Number of Electors appointed; and if there be more than one who have such Majority, and have an equal Number of Votes, then the House of Representatives shall immediately chuse by Ballot one of them for President; and if no Person have a Majority, then from the five highest on the List the said House shall in like Manner chuse the President. But in chusing the President, the Votes shall be taken by States, the Representation from each State having one Vote; A quorum for this Purpose shall consist of a Member or Members from two thirds of the States, and a Majority of all the States shall be necessary to a Choice. In every Case, after the Choice of the President, the Person having the greater Number of Votes of the Electors shall be the Vice President. But if there should remain two or more who have equal Votes, the Senate shall chuse from them by Ballot the Vice President.

The Congress may determine the Time of chusing the Electors, and the Day on which they shall give their Votes; which Day shall be the same throughout the United States.

No person except a natural born Citizen, or a Citizen of the United States, at the time of the Adoption of this Constitution, shall be eligible to the Office of President; neither shall any Person be eligible to that Office who shall not have attained to the Age of thirty five Years, and been fourteen Years a Resident within the United States.

In Case of the Removal of the President from Office, or of his Death, Resignation or Inability to discharge the Powers and Duties of the said Office, the same shall devolve on the Vice President, and the Congress may by Law provide for the Case of Removal, Death, Resignation or Inability, both of the President and Vice President, declaring what Officer shall then act as President, and such Officer shall act accordingly, until the Disability be removed, or a President shall be elected.

The President shall, at stated Times, receive for his Services, a Compensation, which shall neither be increased nor diminished during the Period for which he shall have been elected, and he shall not receive within that Period any other Emolument from the United States, or any of them.

Before he enter on the Execution of his Office, he shall take the following Oath or Affirmation: "I do solemnly swear (or affirm) that I will faithfully execute the Office of President of the United States, and will to the best of my Ability, preserve, protect and defend the Constitution of the United States."

Section 2. The President shall be Commander in Chief of the Army and Navy of the United States, and of the Militia of the several States, when called into the actual Service of the United States; he may require the Opinion, in writing, of the principal Officer in each of the executive Departments, upon any Subject relating to the Duties of their respective Offices, and he shall have Power to grant Reprieves and Pardons for Offenses against the United States, except in Cases of Impeachment.

He shall have Power, by and with the Advice and Consent of the Senate to make Treaties, provided two thirds of the Senators present concur; and he shall nominate, and by and with the Advice and Consent of the Senate, shall appoint Ambassadors, other public Ministers and Consuls, Judges of the supreme Court, and all other Officers of the United States, whose Appointments are not herein otherwise provided for, and which shall be established by Law; but the Congress may by Law vest the Appointment

of such inferior Officers, as they think proper, in the President alone, in the Courts of Law, or in the Heads of Departments.

The President shall have Power to fill up all Vacancies that may happen during the Recess of the Senate, by granting Commissions which shall expire at the End of their next Session.

Section 3. He shall from time to time give to the Congress Information of the State of the Union, and recommend to their Consideration such Measures as he shall judge necessary and expedient; he may, on extraordinary Occasions, convene both Houses, or either of them, and in Case of Disagreement between them, with Respect to the Time of Adjournment, he may adjourn them to such Time as he shall think proper; he shall receive Ambassadors and other public Ministers; he shall take Care that the Laws be faithfully executed, and shall Commission all the Officers of the United States.

Section 4. The President, Vice President and all civil Officers of the United States, shall be removed from Office on Impeachment for, and Conviction of, Treason, Bribery, or other high Crimes and Misdemeanors.

ARTICLE III

Section 1. The judicial Power of the United States, shall be vested in one supreme Court, and in such inferior Courts as the Congress may from time to time ordain and establish. The Judges, both of the supreme and inferior Courts, shall hold their Offices during good Behaviour, and shall, at stated Times, receive for their Services a Compensation, which shall not be diminished during their Continuance in Office.

Section 2. The judicial Power shall extend to all Cases, in Law and Equity, arising under this Constitution, the Laws of the United States, and Treaties made, or which shall be made, under their Authority;—to all Cases affecting Ambassadors, other public Ministers and Consuls;—to all Cases of admiralty and maritime Jurisdiction;—to Controversies to which the United States shall be a Party;—to Controversies between two or more States;—between a State and Citizens of another State;—between Citizens of different States;—between Citizens of the same State claiming Lands under Grants of different States, and between a State, or the Citizens thereof, and foreign States, Citizens or Subjects.

In all Cases affecting Ambassadors, other public Ministers and Consuls, and those in which a State shall be a Party, the supreme Court shall have original Jurisdiction. In all the other Cases before mentioned, the supreme Court shall have appellate Jurisdiction, both as to Law and Fact, with such Exceptions, and under such Regulations as the Congress shall make.

The Trial of all Crimes, except in Cases of Impeachment, shall be by Jury; and such Trial shall be held in the State where the said Crimes shall have been committed; but when not committed within any State, the Trial shall be at such Place or Places as the Congress may by Law have directed.

Section 3. Treason against the United States, shall consist only in levying War against them, or, in adhering to their Enemies, giving them Aid and Comfort. No Person shall be convicted of Treason unless on the Testimony of two Witnesses to the same overt Act, or on Confession in open Court.

The Congress shall have Power to declare the Punishment of Treason, but no Attainder of Treason shall work Corruption of Blood, or Forfeiture except during the Life of the Person attainted.

ARTICLE IV

Section 1. Full Faith and Credit shall be given in each State to the public Acts, Records, and judicial Proceedings of every other State. And the Congress may by general Laws prescribe the Manner in which such Acts, Records and Proceedings shall be proved, and the Effect thereof.

Section 2. The Citizens of each State shall be entitled to all Privileges and Immunities of Citizens in the several States.

A Person charged in any State with Treason, Felony, or other Crime, who shall flee from Justice, and be found in another State, shall on Demand of the executive Authority of the State from which he fled, be delivered up, to be removed to the State having Jurisdiction of the Crime.

No Person held to Service or Labour in one State, under the Laws thereof, escaping into another, shall, in Consequence of any Law or Regulation therein, be discharged from such Service or Labour, but shall be delivered up on Claim of the Party to whom such Service or Labour may be due.

Section 3. New States may be admitted by the Congress into this Union; but no new State shall be formed or erected within the Jurisdiction of any other

State; nor any State be formed by the Junction of two or more States, or Parts of States, without the Consent of the Legislatures of the States concerned as well as of the Congress.

The Congress shall have Power to dispose of and make all needful Rules and Regulations respecting the Territory or other Property belonging to the United States; and nothing in this Constitution shall be so construed as to Prejudice any Claims of the United States, or of any particular State.

Section 4. The United States shall guarantee to every State in this Union a Republican Form of Government, and shall protect each of them against Invasion; and on Application of the Legislature, or of the Executive (when the Legislature cannot be convened) against domestic Violence.

ARTICLE V

The Congress, whenever two thirds of both Houses shall deem it necessary, shall propose Amendments to this Constitution, or, on the Application of the Legislatures of two thirds of the several States, shall call a Convention for proposing Amendments, which, in either Case, shall be valid to all Intents and Purposes, as part of this Constitution, when ratified by the Legislatures of three fourths of the several States, or by Conventions in three fourths thereof, as the one or the other Mode of Ratification may be proposed by the Congress; Provided that no Amendment which may be made prior to the Year One thousand eight hundred and eight shall in any Manner affect the first and fourth Clauses in the Ninth Section of the first Article; and that no State, without its Consent, shall be deprived of its equal Suffrage in the Senate.

ARTICLE VI

All Debts contracted and Engagements entered into, before the Adoption of this Constitution shall be as valid against the United States under this Constitution, as under the Confederation.

This Constitution, and the Laws of the United States which shall be made in Pursuance thereof; and all Treaties made, or which shall be made, under the Authority of the United States, shall be the supreme Law of the Land; and the Judges in every State shall be bound thereby, any Thing in the Constitution or Laws of any State to the Contrary notwithstanding.

The Senators and Representatives before mentioned, and the Members of the several State Legislatures, and all executive and judicial Officers, both of the United States and of the several States, shall be bound by Oath or Affirmation, to support this Constitution; but no religious Test shall ever be required as a Qualification to any Office or public Trust under the United States.

ARTICLE VII

The Ratification of the Conventions of nine States shall be sufficient for the Establishment of this Constitution between the States so ratifying the Same.

AMENDMENT I [1791]

Congress shall make no law respecting an establishment of religion, or prohibiting the free exercise thereof; or abridging the freedom of speech, or of the press; or the right of the people peaceably to assemble, and to petition the Government for a redress of grievances.

AMENDMENT II [1791]

A well regulated Militia, being necessary to the security of a free State, the right of the people to keep and bear Arms, shall not be infringed.

AMENDMENT III [1791]

No Soldier shall, in time of peace be quartered in any house, without the consent of the Owner, nor in time of war, but in a manner to be prescribed by law.

AMENDMENT IV [1791]

The right of the people to be secure in their persons, houses, papers, and effects, against unreasonable searches and seizures, shall not be violated, and no Warrants shall issue, but upon probable cause, supported by Oath or affirmation, and particularly describing the place to be searched, and the persons or things to be seized.

AMENDMENT V [1791]

No person shall be held to answer for a capital, or otherwise infamous crime, unless on a presentment or indictment of a Grand Jury, except in cases arising in the land or naval forces, or in the Militia, when in actual service in time of War or public danger; nor shall any person be subject for the same offense to be twice put in jeopardy of life or limb; nor shall be compelled in any criminal case to be a witness against himself, nor be deprived of life, liberty, or property, without due process of law; nor shall private property be taken for public use, without just compensation.

AMENDMENT VI [1791]

In all criminal prosecutions, the accused shall enjoy the right to a speedy and public trial, by an impartial jury of the State and district wherein the crime shall have been committed, which district shall have been previously ascertained by law, and to be informed of the nature and cause of the accusation; to be confronted with the witnesses against him; to have compulsory process for obtaining witnesses in his favor, and to have the Assistance of Counsel for his defence.

AMENDMENT VII [1791]

In Suits at common law, where the value in controversy shall exceed twenty dollars, the right of trial by jury shall be preserved, and no fact tried by a jury, shall be otherwise re-examined in any Court of the United States, than according to the rules of the common law.

AMENDMENT VIII [1791]

Excessive bail shall not be required, nor excessive fines imposed, nor cruel and unusual punishments inflicted.

AMENDMENT IX [1791]

The enumeration in the Constitution, of certain rights, shall not be construed to deny or disparage others retained by the people.

AMENDMENT X [1791]

The powers not delegated to the United States by the Constitution, nor prohibited by it to the States, are reserved to the States respectively, or to the people.

AMENDMENT XI [1798]

The Judicial power of the United States shall not be construed to extend to any suit in law or equity, commenced or prosecuted against one of the United States by Citizens of another State, or by Citizens or Subjects of any Foreign State.

AMENDMENT XII [1804]

The Electors shall meet in their respective states, and vote by ballot for President and Vice-President, one of whom, at least, shall not be an inhabitant of the same state with themselves; they shall name in their ballots the person voted for as President, and in distinct ballots the person voted for as Vice-President, and they shall make distinct lists of all persons voted for as President, and of all persons voted for as Vice-President, and of the number of votes for each, which lists they shall sign and certify, and transmit sealed to the seat of the government of the United States, directed to the President of the Senate;—The President of the Senate shall, in the presence of the Senate and House of Representatives, open all the certificates and the votes shall then be counted;—The person having the greatest number of votes for President, shall be the President, if such number be a majority of the whole number of Electors appointed; and if no person have such majority, then from the persons having the highest numbers not exceeding three on the list of those voted for as President, the House of Representatives shall choose immediately, by ballot, the President. But in choosing the President, the votes shall be taken by states, the representation from each state having one vote; a quorum for this purpose shall consist of a member or members from two-thirds of the states, and a majority of all states shall be necessary to a choice. And if the House of Representatives shall not choose a President whenever the right of choice shall devolve upon them, before the fourth day of March next following, then the Vice-President shall act as President, as in the case of the death or other constitutional disability of the President.—The person having the greatest number of votes as Vice-President, shall be the Vice-President, if such number be a majority of the whole number of Electors appointed, and if no person have a majority, then from the two highest numbers on the list, the Senate shall choose the Vice-President; a quorum for the purpose shall consist of two-thirds of the whole number of Senators, and a majority of the whole number shall be necessary to a choice. But no person constitutionally ineligible to the office of President shall be eligible to that of Vice-President of the United States.

AMENDMENT XIII [1865]

Section 1. Neither slavery nor involuntary servitude, except as a punishment for crime whereof the party shall have been duly convicted, shall exist within the United States, or any place subject to their jurisdiction.

Section 2. Congress shall have power to enforce this article by appropriate legislation.

AMENDMENT XIV [1868]

Section 1. All persons born or naturalized in the United States, and subject to the jurisdiction thereof, are citizens of the United States and of the State wherein they reside. No State shall make or enforce any law which shall abridge the privileges or immunities of citizens of the United States; nor shall any State deprive any person of life, liberty, or property, without due process of law; nor deny to any person within its jurisdiction the equal protection of the laws.

Section 2. Representatives shall be apportioned among the several States according to their respective numbers, counting the whole number of persons in each State, excluding Indians not taxed. But when the right to vote at any election for the choice of electors for President and Vice President of the United States, Representatives in Congress, the Executive and Judicial officers of a State, or the members of the Legislature thereof, is denied to any of the male inhabitants of such State, being twenty-one years of age, and citizens of the United States, or in any way abridged, except for participation in rebellion, or other crime, the basis of representation therein shall be reduced in the proportion which the number of such male citizens shall bear to the whole number of male citizens twenty-one years of age in such State.

Section 3. No person shall be a Senator or Representative in Congress, or elector of President and Vice President, or hold any office, civil or military, under the United States, or under any State, who having previously taken an oath, as a member of Congress, or as an officer of the United States, or as a member of any State legislature, or as an executive or judicial officer of any State, to support the Constitution of the United States, shall have engaged in insurrection or rebellion against the same, or given aid or comfort to the enemies thereof. But Congress may by a vote of two-thirds of each House, remove such disability.

Section 4. The validity of the public debt of the United States, authorized by law, including debts incurred for payment of pensions and bounties for services in suppressing insurrection or rebellion, shall not be questioned. But neither the United States nor any State shall assume or pay any debt or obligation incurred in aid of insurrection or rebellion against the United States, or any claim for the loss or emancipation of any slave; but all such debts, obligations and claims shall be held illegal and void.

Section 5. The Congress shall have power to enforce, by appropriate legislation, the provisions of this article.

AMENDMENT XV [1870]

Section 1. The right of citizens of the United States to vote shall not be denied or abridged by the United States or by any State on account of race, color, or previous condition of servitude.

Section 2. The Congress shall have power to enforce this article by appropriate legislation.

AMENDMENT XVI [1913]

The Congress shall have power to lay and collect taxes on incomes, from whatever source derived, without apportionment among the several States, and without regard to any census or enumeration.

AMENDMENT XVII [1913]

Section 1. The Senate of the United States shall be composed of two Senators from each State, elected by the people thereof, for six years; and each Senator shall have one vote. The electors in each State shall have the qualifications requisite for electors of the most numerous branch of the State legislatures.

Section 2. When vacancies happen in the representation of any State in the Senate, the executive authority of such State shall issue writs of election to fill such vacancies: Provided, That the legislature of any State may empower the executive thereof to make temporary appointments until the people fill the vacancies by election as the legislature may direct.

Section 3. This amendment shall not be so construed as to affect the election or term of any Senator chosen before it becomes valid as part of the Constitution.

AMENDMENT XVIII [1919]

Section 1. After one year from the ratification of this article the manufacture, sale, or transportation of intoxicating liquors within, the importation thereof into, or the exportation thereof from the United States and all territory subject to the jurisdiction thereof for beverage purposes is hereby prohibited.

Section 2. The Congress and the several States shall have concurrent power to enforce this article by appropriate legislation.

Section 3. This article shall be inoperative unless it shall have been ratified as an amendment to the Constitution by the legislatures of the several States, as provided in the Constitution, within seven years from the date of the submission hereof to the States by the Congress.

AMENDMENT XIX [1920]

Section 1. The right of citizens of the United States to vote shall not be denied or abridged by the United States or by any State on account of sex.

Section 2. Congress shall have power to enforce this article by appropriate legislation.

AMENDMENT XX [1933]

Section 1. The terms of the President and Vice President shall end at noon on the 20th day of January, and the terms of Senators and Representatives at noon on the 3d day of January, of the years in which such terms would have ended if this article had not been ratified; and the terms of their successors shall then begin.

Section 2. The Congress shall assemble at least once in every year, and such meeting shall begin at noon on the 3d day of January, unless they shall by law appoint a different day.

Section 3. If, at the time fixed for the beginning of the term of the President, the President elect shall have died, the Vice President elect shall become President. If the President shall not have been chosen before the time fixed for the beginning of his term, or if the President elect shall have failed to qualify, then the Vice President elect shall act as President until a President shall have qualified; and the Congress may by law provide for the case wherein neither a President elect nor a Vice President elect shall have qualified, declaring who shall then act as President, or the manner in which one who is to act shall be selected, and such person shall act accordingly until a President or Vice President shall have qualified.

Section 4. The Congress may by law provide for the case of the death of any of the persons from whom the House of Representatives may choose a President whenever the right of choice shall have devolved upon them, and for the case of the death of any of the persons from whom the Senate may choose a Vice President whenever the right of choice shall have devolved upon them.

Section 5. Sections 1 and 2 shall take effect on the 15th day of October following the ratification of this article.

Section 6. This article shall be inoperative unless it shall have been ratified as an amendment to the Constitution by the legislatures of three-fourths of the several States within seven years from the date of its submission.

AMENDMENT XXI [1933]

Section 1. The eighteenth article of amendment to the Constitution of the United States is hereby repealed.

Section 2. The transportation or importation into any State, Territory, or possession of the United States for delivery or use therein of intoxicating liquors, in violation of the laws thereof, is hereby prohibited.

Section 3. This article shall be inoperative unless it shall have been ratified as an amendment to the Constitution by conventions in the several States, as provided in the Constitution, within seven years from the date of the submission hereof to the States by the Congress.

AMENDMENT XXII [1951]

Section 1. No person shall be elected to the office of the President more than twice, and no person who has held the office of President, or acted as President, for more than two years of a term to which some other person was elected President shall be elected to the office of President more than once. But this Article shall not apply to any person holding the office of President when this Article was proposed by the Congress, and shall not prevent any person who may be holding the office of President, or acting as President, during the term within which this Article becomes operative from holding the office of President or acting as President during the remainder of such term.

Section 2. This article shall be inoperative unless it shall have been ratified as an amendment to the Constitution by the legislatures of three-fourths of the several States within seven years from the date of its submission to the States by the Congress.

AMENDMENT XXIII [1961]

Section 1. The District constituting the seat of Government of the United States shall appoint in such manner as the Congress may direct:

A number of electors of President and Vice President equal to the whole number of Senators and Representatives in Congress to which the District would be entitled if it were a State, but in no event more than the least populous state; they shall be in addition to those appointed by the states, but they shall be considered, for the purposes of the election of President and Vice President, to be electors appointed by a state; and they shall meet in the District and perform such duties as provided by the twelfth article of amendment.

Section 2. The Congress shall have power to enforce this article by appropriate legislation.

AMENDMENT XXIV [1964]

Section 1. The right of citizens of the United States to vote in any primary or other election for President or Vice President, for electors for President or Vice President, or for Senator or Representative in Congress, shall not be denied or abridged by the United States, or any State by reason of failure to pay any poll tax or other tax.

Section 2. The Congress shall have power to enforce this article by appropriate legislation.

AMENDMENT XXV [1967]

Section 1. In case of the removal of the President from office or of his death or resignation, the Vice President shall become President.

Section 2. Whenever there is a vacancy in the office of the Vice President, the President shall nominate a Vice President who shall take office upon confirmation by a majority vote of both Houses of Congress.

Section 3. Whenever the President transmits to the President pro tempore of the Senate and the Speaker of the House of Representatives his written declaration

that he is unable to discharge the powers and duties of his office, and until he transmits to them a written declaration to the contrary, such powers and duties shall be discharged by the Vice President as Acting President.

Section 4. Whenever the Vice President and a majority of either the principal officers of the executive departments or of such other body as Congress may by law provide, transmit to the President pro tempore of the Senate and the Speaker of the House of Representatives their written declaration that the President is unable to discharge the powers and duties of his office, the Vice President shall immediately assume the powers and duties of the office as Acting President.

Thereafter, when the President transmits to the President pro tempore of the Senate and the Speaker of the House of Representatives his written declaration that no inability exists, he shall resume the powers and duties of his office unless the Vice President and a majority of either the principal officers of the executive department or of such other body as Congress may by law provide, transmit within four days to the President pro tempore of the Senate and the Speaker of the House of Representatives their written declaration that the President is unable to discharge the powers and duties of his office. Thereupon Congress shall decide the issue, assembling within forty-eight hours for that purpose if not in session. If the Congress, within twenty-one days after receipt of the latter written declaration, or, if Congress is not in session, within twenty-one days after Congress is required to assemble, determines by two-thirds vote of both Houses that the President is unable to discharge the powers and duties of his office, the Vice President shall continue to discharge the same as Acting President; otherwise, the President shall resume the powers and duties of his office.

AMENDMENT XXVI [1971]

Section 1. The right of citizens of the United States, who are eighteen years of age or older, to vote shall not be denied or abridged by the United States or by any State on account of age.

Section 2. The Congress shall have power to enforce this article by appropriate legislation.

AMENDMENT XXVII [1992]

No law, varying the compensation for the services of the Senators and Representatives, shall take effect, until an election of Representatives shall have intervened.

FEDERALIST PAPERS NO. 10 AND NO. 51

The founders completed drafting the U.S. Constitution in 1787. It was then submitted to the thirteen states for ratification, and a major debate ensued. As you read in Chapter 2, on the one side of this debate were the Federalists, who urged that the new Constitution be adopted. On the other side of the debate were the Anti-Federalists, who argued against ratification.

During the course of this debate, three men well known for their Federalist views—Alexander Hamilton, James Madison, and John Jay—wrote a series of essays in which they argued for immediate ratifcation of the Constitution. The essays appeared in the New York City Independent Journal in October 1787, just a little over a month after the Constitutional Convention adjourned. Later, Hamilton arranged to have the essays collected and published in book form. The articles filled two volumes, both of which were published by May 1788. The essays are often referred to collectively as the Federalist Papers.

Scholars disagree as to whether the Federalist Papers *had a significant impact on the decision of the states to ratify the Constitution. Nonetheless, many of the essays are masterpieces of political reasoning and have left a lasting imprint on American politics and government. Above all, the Federalist Papers shed an important light on what the founders intended when they drafted various constitutional provisions.*

Here we present just two of these essays, Federalist Paper No. 10 *and* Federalist Paper No. 51. *Each essay was written by James Madison, who referred to himself as "Publius." We have annotated each document to clarify the meaning of particular passages. The annotations are set in italics to distinguish them from the original text of the documents.*

#10

Federalist Paper No. 10 is a classic document that is often referred to by teachers of American government. Authored by James Madison, it sets forth Madison's views on factions in politics. The essay was written, in large part, to counter the arguments put forth by the Anti-Federalists that small factions might take control of the government, thus destroying the representative nature of the republican form of government established by the Constitution. The essay opens with a discussion of the "dangerous vice" of factions and the importance of devising a form of government in which this vice will be controlled.

Among the numerous advantages promised by a well-constructed Union, none deserves to be more accurately developed than its tendency to break and control the violence of faction. The friend of popular governments never finds himself so much alarmed for their character and fate as when he contemplates their propensity to this dangerous vice. He will not fail, therefore, to set a due value on any plan which, without violating the principles to which he is attached, provides a proper cure for it. The instability, injustice, and confusion introduced into the public councils have, in truth, been the mortal diseases under which popular governments have everywhere perished, as they continue to be the favorite and fruitful topics from which the adversaries to liberty derive their most specious declamations. The valuable improvements made by the American constitutions on the popular models, both ancient and modern, cannot certainly be too much admired; but it would be an unwarrantable partiality to contend that they have as effectually obviated the danger on this side, as was wished and expected. Complaints are everywhere heard from our most considerate and virtuous citizens, equally the friends of public and private faith and of public and personal liberty, that our governments are too unstable, that the public good is disregarded in the conflicts of rival parties, and that measures are too often decided, not according to the rules of justice and the rights of the minor party, but by the superior force of an interested and overbearing majority. However anxiously we may wish that these complaints had no foundation, the evidence of known facts will not permit us to deny that they are in some degree true. It will be found, indeed, on a candid review of our situation, that some of the distresses under which we labor have been erroneously charged on the operation of our governments; but it will be found, at the same time, that other causes will not alone account for many of our heaviest misfortunes; and, particularly, for that prevailing and increasing distrust of public engagements and alarm for private rights which are echoed from one end of the continent to the other. These must be chiefly, if not wholly, effects of the unsteadiness and injustice with which a factious spirit has tainted our public administration.

In the following paragraph, Madison clarifies for his readers his understanding of what the term faction means.

By a faction I understand a number of citizens, whether amounting to a majority or minority of the whole, who are united and actuated by some common impulse of passion, or of interest, adverse to the rights of other citizens, or the permanent and aggregate interests of the community.

In the following passages, Madison looks at the two methods of curing the "mischiefs of factions." One of these methods is removing the causes of faction. The other is to control the effects of factions.

There are two methods of curing the mischiefs of faction: the one, by removing its causes; the other, by controlling its effects.

There are again two methods of removing the causes of faction: the one, by destroying the liberty which is essential to its existence; the other, by giving to every citizen the same opinions, the same passions, and the same interests.

It could never be more truly said than of the first remedy that it was worse than the disease. Liberty is to faction what air is to fire, an aliment without which it instantly expires. But it could not be a less folly to abolish liberty, which is essential to political life, because it nourishes faction than it would be to wish the annihilation of air, which is essential to animal life, because it imparts to fire its destructive agency.

The second expedient is as impracticable as the first would be unwise. As long as the reason of man continues fallible, and his is at liberty to exercise it, different opinions will be formed. As long as the connection subsists between his reason and his self-love, his opinions and his passions will have a reciprocal influence on each other; and the former will be objects to which the latter will attach themselves. The diversity in the faculties of men, from which the rights of property originate, is not less an insuperable obstacle to a uniformity of interests. The protection of these faculties is the first object of government. From the protection of different and unequal faculties of acquiring property, the possession of different degrees and kinds of property immediately results; and from the influence of these on the sentiments and views of the respective proprietors ensues a division of the society into different interests and parties.

The latent causes of faction are thus sown in the nature of man; and we see them everywhere brought into different degrees of activity, according to the different circumstances of civil society. A zeal for different opinions concerning religion, concerning government, and many other points, as well of speculation as of practice; an attachment to different leaders ambitiously contending for pre-eminence and power; or to persons of other descriptions whose fortunes have been interesting to the human passions, have, in turn, divided mankind into parties, inflamed them with mutual animosity, and rendered them much more disposed to vex and oppress each other than to co-operate for their common good. So strong is this propensity of mankind to fall into mutual animosities that where no substantial occasion presents itself the most frivolous and fanciful distinctions have been sufficient to kindle their unfriendly passions and excite their most violent conflicts. But the most common and durable source of factions has been the various and unequal distribution of property. Those who hold and those who are without property have ever formed distinct interests in society. Those who are creditors, and those who are debtors, fall under a like discrimination. A landed interest, a manufacturing interest, a mercantile interest, a moneyed interest, with many lesser interests, grow up of necessity in civilized nations, and divide them into different classes, actuated by different sentiments and views. The regulation of these various and interfering interests forms the principal task of modern legislation and involves the spirit of party and faction in the necessary and ordinary operations of government.

No man is allowed to be a judge in his own cause, because his interest would certainly bias his judgment, and, not improbably, corrupt his integrity. With equal, nay with greater reason, a body of men are unfit to be both judges and parties at the same time; yet what are many of the most important acts of legislation but so many judicial determinations, not indeed concerning the rights of single persons, but concerning the rights of large bodies of citizens? And what are the different classes of legislators but advocates and parties to the causes which they determine? Is a law proposed concerning private debts? It is a question to which the creditors are parties on one side and the debtors on the other. Justice ought to hold the balance between them. Yet the parties are, and must be, themselves the judges; and the most numerous party, or in other words, the most powerful faction must be expected to prevail. Shall domestic manufacturers be encouraged, and in what degree, by restrictions on foreign manufacturers? Are questions which would be differently decided by the landed and the manufacturing classes, and probably by neither with a sole regard to justice and the public good. The apportionment of taxes on the various descriptions of property is an act which seems to require the most exact impartiality; yet there is, perhaps, no legislative act in which greater opportunity and temptation are given to a predominant party to trample on the rules of justice. Every shilling with which they overburden the inferior number is a shilling saved to their own pockets.

It is in vain to say that enlightened statesmen will be able to adjust these clashing interests and render them all subservient to the public good. Enlightened statesmen will not always be at the helm. Nor, in many cases, can such an adjustment be made at all without taking into view indirect and remote considerations, which will rarely prevail over the immediate interest which one party may find in disregarding the rights of another or the good of the whole.

The inference to which we are brought is that the causes of faction cannot be removed and that relief is only to be sought in the means of controlling its effects.

In the preceding passages, Madison has explored the causes of factions and has concluded that they cannot "be removed" without removing liberty itself, which is one of the causes, or altering human nature. He now turns to a discussion of how the effects of factions might be controlled.

If a faction consists of less than a majority, relief is supplied by the republican principle, which enables the majority to defeat its sinister views by regular vote. It may clog the administration, it may convulse the society; but it will be unable to execute and mask its violence under the forms of the Constitution. When a majority is included in a faction, the form of popular government, on the other hand, enables it to sacrifice to its ruling passion or interest both the public good and the rights of other citizens. To secure the public good and private rights against the danger of such a faction, and at the same time to preserve the spirit and the form of popular government, is then the great object to which our inquiries are directed. Let me add that it is the great desideratum by which alone this form of government can be rescued from the opprobrium under which it has so long labored and be recommended to the esteem and adoption of mankind.

According to Madison, one way of controlling the effects of factions is to make sure that the majority is not able to act in "concert," or jointly, to "carry into effect schemes of oppression."

By what means is this object attainable? Evidently by one of two only. Either the existence of the same passion or interest in a majority at the same time must be prevented, or the majority, having such coexistent passion or interest, must be rendered, by their number and local situation, unable to concert and carry into effect schemes of oppression. If the impulse and the opportunity be suffered to coincide, we well know that neither moral nor religious motives can be relied on as an adequate control. They are not found to be such on the injustice and violence of individuals, and lose their efficacy in proportion to the number combined together, that is, in proportion as their efficacy becomes needful.

From this view of the subject it may be concluded that a pure democracy, by which I mean a society consisting of a small number of citizens, who assemble and administer the government in person, can admit of no cure for the mischiefs of faction. A common passion or interest will, in almost every case, be felt by a majority of the whole; a communication and concert results from the form of government itself; and there is nothing to check the inducements to sacrifice the weaker party or an obnoxious individual. Hence it is that such democracies have ever been spectacles of turbulence and contention; have ever been found incompatible with personal security or the rights of property; and have in general been as short in their lives as they have been violent in their deaths. Theoretic politicians, who have patronized this species of government, have erroneously supposed that by reducing mankind to a perfect equality in their political rights, they would at the same time be perfectly equalized and assimilated in their possessions, their opinions, and their passions.

In the following six paragraphs, Madison sets forth some of the reasons why a republican form of government promises a "cure" for the mischiefs of factions. He begins by clarifying the difference between a republic and a democracy. He then describes how in a large republic, the elected representatives of the people will be large enough in number to guard against factions—the "cabals," or concerted actions, of "a few." On the one hand, representatives will not be so removed from their local districts as to be unacquainted with their constituents' needs. On the other hand, they will not be "unduly attached" to local interests and unfit to understand "great and national objects." Madison concludes that the Constitution "forms a happy combination in this respect."

A republic, by which I mean a government in which the scheme of representation takes place, opens a different prospect and promises the cure for which we are seeking. Let us examine the points in which it varies from pure democracy, and we shall comprehend both the nature of the cure and the efficacy which it must derive from the Union.

The two great points of difference between a democracy and a republic are: first, the delegation of the government, in the latter, to a small number of citizens elected by the rest; secondly, the greater number of citizens and greater sphere of country over which the latter may be extended.

The effect of the first difference is, on the one hand, to refine and enlarge the public views by passing them through the medium of a chosen body of citizens, whose wisdom may best discern the true interest of their country and whose patriotism and love of justice will be least likely to sacrifice it to temporary or partial considerations. Under such a regulation it may well happen that the public voice, pronounced by the representatives of the people, will be more consonant to the public good than if pronounced by the people themselves, convened for the purpose. On the other hand, the effect may be inverted. Men of factious tempers, of local prejudices, or of sinister designs, may, by intrigue, by corruption, or by other means, first obtain the suffrages, and then betray the interests of the people. The question resulting is, whether small or extensive republics are most favorable to the election of proper guardians of the public weal; and it is clearly decided in favor of the latter by two obvious considerations.

In the first place it is to be remarked that however small the republic may be the representatives must be raised to a certain number in order to guard against the cabals of a few; and that however large it may be they must be limited to a certain number in order to guard against the confusion of a multitude. Hence, the number of representatives in the two cases not being in proportion to that of the constituents, and being proportionally greatest in the small republic, it follows that if the proportion of fit characters be not less in the large than in the small republic, the former will present a greater option, and consequently a greater probability of a fit choice.

In the next place, as each representative will be chosen by a greater number of citizens in the large than in the small republic, it will be more difficult for unworthy candidates to practice with success the vicious arts by which elections are too often carried; and the suffrages of the people being more free, will be more likely to center on men who possess the most attractive merit and the most diffusive and established characters.

It must be confessed that in this, as in most other cases, there is a mean, on both sides of which inconveniencies will be found to lie. By enlarging too much the number of electors, you render the representative too little acquainted with all their local circumstances and lesser interests; as by reducing it too much, you render him unduly attached to these, and too little fit to comprehend and pursue great and national objects. The federal Constitution forms a happy combination in this respect; the great and aggregate interests being referred to the national, the local and particular to the State legislatures.

In the remaining passages of this essay, Madison looks at another "point of difference" between a republic and a democracy. Specifically, a republic can encompass a larger territory and a greater number of citizens than a democracy can. This fact, too, argues Madison, will help to control the influence of factions because the interests that draw people together to act in concert are typically at the local level and would be unlikely to affect or dominate the national government. As Madison states, "The influence of factious leaders may kindle a flame within their particular States but will be unable to spread a general conflagration through the other States." Generally, in a large republic, there will be numerous factions, and no particular faction will be able to "pervade the whole body of the Union."

The other point of difference is the greater number of citizens and extent of territory which may be brought within the compass of republican than of democratic government; and it is this circumstance principally which renders factious combinations less to be dreaded in the former than in the latter. The smaller the society, the fewer probably will be the distinct parties and interests composing it; the fewer the distinct parties and interests, the more frequently will a majority be found of the same party; and the smaller the number of individuals composing a majority, and the smaller the compass within which they are placed, the more easily will they concert and execute their plans of oppression. Extend the sphere and you take in a greater variety of parties and interests; you make it less probable that a majority of the whole will have a common motive to invade the rights of other citizens; or if such a common motive exists, it will be more difficult for all who feel it to discover their own strength and to act in unison with each other. Besides other impediments, it may be remarked that, where there is a consciousness of unjust or dishonorable purposes, communication is always checked by distrust in proportion to the number whose concurrence is necessary.

Hence, it clearly appears that the same advantage which a republic has over a democracy in controlling the effects of faction is enjoyed by a large over a small republic—is enjoyed by the Union over the States composing it. Does this advantage consist in the substitution of representatives whose enlightened views and virtuous sentiments render them superior to local prejudices and to schemes of injustice? It will not be denied that the representation of the Union will be most likely to possess these requisite endowments. Does it consist in the greater security afforded by a greater variety of parties, against the event of any one party being able to outnumber and oppress the rest? In an equal degree does the increased variety of parties comprised within the Union increase this security. Does it, in fine, consist in the greater obstacles opposed to the concert and accomplishment of the secret wishes of an unjust and interested majority? Here again the extent of the Union gives it the most palpable advantage.

The influence of factious leaders may kindle a flame within their particular States but will be unable to spread a general conflagration through the other States. A religious sect may degenerate into a political faction in a part of the Confederacy; but the variety of sects dispersed over the entire face of it must secure the national councils against any danger from that source. A rage for paper money, for an abolition of debts, for an equal division of property, or for any other improper or wicked project, will be less apt to pervade the whole body of the Union than a particular member of it, in the same proportion as such a malady is more likely to taint a particular county or district than an entire State.

In the extent and proper structure of the Union, therefore, we behold a republican remedy for the diseases most incident to republican government. And according to the degree of pleasure and pride we feel in being republicans ought to be our zeal in cherishing the spirit and supporting the character of federalists.

Publius
(James Madison)

#51

Federalist Paper *No. 51, which was also authored by James Madison, is one of the classics in American political theory. Recall from Chapter 2 that a major concern of the founders was to create a relatively strong national government but one that would not be capable of tyrannizing over the populace. In the following essay, Madison sets forth the theory of "checks and balances." He explains that the new Constitution, by dividing the national government into three branches (executive, legislative, and judicial), offers protection against tyranny.*

To what expedient, then, shall we finally resort, for maintaining in practice the necessary partition of power among the several departments as laid down in the Constitution? The only answer that can be given is that as all these exterior provisions are found to be inadequate the defect must be supplied, by so contriving the interior structure of the government as that its several constituent parts may, by their mutual relations, be the means of keeping each other in their proper places. Without presuming to undertake a full development of this important idea I will hazard a few general observations which may perhaps place it in a clearer light, and enable us to form a more correct judgment of the principles and structure of the government planned by the convention.

In the following two paragraphs, Madison explains that to ensure that the powers of government are genuinely separated, it is important that each of the three branches of government (executive, legislative, and judicial) should have a "will of its own." Among other things, this means that persons in one branch should not depend on persons in another branch for the "emoluments annexed to their offices" (pay, perks, and privileges). If they did, then the branches would not be truly independent of one another.

In order to lay a due foundation for that separate and distinct exercise of the different powers of government, which to a certain extent is admitted on all hands to be essential to the preservation of liberty, it is evident that each department should have a will of its own; and consequently should be so constituted that the members of each should have as little agency as possible in the appointment of the members of the others. Were this principle rigorously adhered to, it would require that all the appointments for the supreme executive, legislative, and judiciary magistracies should be drawn from the same fountain of authority, the people, through channels having no communication whatever with one another. Perhaps such a plan of constructing the several departments would be less difficult in practice than it may in contemplation appear. Some difficulties, however, and some additional expense would attend the execution of it. Some deviations, therefore, from the principle must be admitted. In the constitution of the judiciary department in particular, it might be inexpedient to insist rigorously on the principle: first, because peculiar qualifications being essential in the members, the primary consideration ought to be to select that mode of choice which best secures these qualifications; second, because the permanent tenure by which the appointments are held in that department must soon destroy all sense of dependence on the authority conferring them.

It is equally evident that the members of each department should be as little dependent as possible on those of the others for the emoluments annexed to their offices. Were the executive magistrate, or the judges, not independent of the legislature in this particular, their independence in every other would be merely nominal.

One of the striking qualities of the theory of checks and balances as posited by Madison is that it assumes that persons are not angels but driven by personal interests and motives. In the following two paragraphs, which are among the most widely quoted of Madison's writings, he stresses that the division of the government into three branches helps to check personal ambitions. Personal ambitions will naturally arise, but they will be linked to the constitutional powers of each branch. In effect, they will help to keep the three branches separate and thus serve the public interest.

But the great security against a gradual concentration of the several powers in the same department consists in giving to those who administer each department the necessary constitutional means and personal motives to resist encroachments of the others. The provision for defense must in this, as in all other cases, be made commensurate to the danger of attack. Ambition must be made to counteract ambition. The interest of the man must be connected with the constitutional rights of the place. It may be a reflection on human nature that such devices should be necessary to control the abuses of government. But what is government itself but the greatest of all reflections on human nature? If men were angels, no government would be necessary. If angels were to govern men, neither external nor internal controls on government would be necessary. In framing a government which is to be administered by men over men, the great difficulty lies in this: you must first enable the government to control the governed; and in the next place oblige it to control itself. A dependence on the people is, no doubt, the primary control on the government; but experience has taught mankind the necessity of auxiliary precautions.

This policy of supplying, by opposite and rival interests, the defect of better motives, might be traced through the whole system of human affairs, private as well as public. We see it particularly displayed in all the subordinate distributions of power, where the constant aim is to divide and arrange the several offices in such a manner as that each may be a check on the other—that the private interest of every individual may be a sentinel over the public rights. These inventions of prudence cannot be less requisite in the distribution of the supreme powers of the State.

In the next two paragraphs, Madison first points out that the "legislative authority necessarily predominates" in a republican form of government. The "remedy" for this lack of balance with the other branches of government is to divide the legislative branch into two chambers with "different modes of election and different principles of action."

But it is not possible to give to each department an equal power of self-defense. In republican government, the legislative authority necessarily predominates. The remedy for this inconveniency is to divide the legislature into different branches; and to render them, by different modes of election and different principles of action, as little connected with each other as the nature of their common functions and their common dependence on the society will admit. It may even be necessary to guard against dangerous encroachments by still further precautions. As the weight of the legislative authority requires that it should be thus divided, the weakness of the executive may require, on the other hand, that it should be fortified. An absolute negative on the legislature appears, at first view, to be the natural defense with which the executive magistrate should be armed. But perhaps it would be neither altogether safe nor alone sufficient. On ordinary occasions it might not be exerted with the requisite firmness, and on extraordinary occasions it might be perfidiously abused. May not this defect of an absolute negative be supplied by some qualified connection between this weaker department and the weaker branch of the stronger department, by which the latter may be led to support the constitutional rights of the former, without being too much detached from the rights of its own department?

If the principles on which these observations are founded be just, as I persuade myself they are, and they be applied as a criterion to the several State constitutions, and to the federal Constitution, it will be found that if the latter does not perfectly correspond with them, the former are infinitely less able to bear such a test.

In the remaining passages of this essay, Madison discusses the importance of the division of government powers between the states and the national government. This division of powers, by providing additional checks and balances, offers a "double security" against tyranny.

There are, moreover, two considerations particularly applicable to the federal system of America, which place that system in a very interesting point of view.

First. In a single republic, all the power surrendered by the people is submitted to the administration of a single government; and the usurpations are guarded against by a division of the government into distinct and separate departments. In the compound republic of America, the power surrendered by the people is first divided between two distinct governments, and then the portion allotted to each subdivided among distinct and separate departments. Hence a double security arises to the rights of the people. The different governments will control each other, at the same time that each will be controlled by itself.

Second. It is of great importance in a republic not only to guard the society against the oppression of its rulers, but to guard one part of the society against the injustice of the other part. Different interests necessarily exist in different classes of citizens. If a majority be united by a common interest, the rights of the minority will be insecure. There are but two methods of providing against this evil: the one by creating a will in the community independent of the majority—that is, of the society itself; the other, by comprehending in the society so many separate descriptions of citizens as will render an unjust combination of a majority of the whole very improbable, if not impracticable. The first method prevails in all governments possessing an hereditary or self-appointed authority. This, at best, is but a precarious security; because a power independent of the society may as well espouse the unjust views of the major as the rightful interests of the minor party, and may possibly be turned against both parties. The second method will be exemplified in the federal republic of the United States. Whilst all authority in it will be derived from and dependent on the society, the society itself will be broken into so many parts, interests and classes of citizens, that the rights of individuals, or of the minority, will be in little danger from interested combinations of the majority. In a free government the security for civil rights must be the same as that for religious rights. It consists in the one case in the multiplicity of interests, and in the other in the multiplicity of sects. The degree of security in both cases will depend on the number of interests and sects; and this may be presumed to depend on the extent of country and number of people comprehended under the same government. This view of the subject must particularly recommend a proper federal system to all the sincere and considerate friends of republican government, since it shows that in exact proportion as the territory of the Union may be formed into more circumscribed Confederacies, or States, oppressive combinations of a majority will be facilitated; the best security, under the republican forms, for the rights of every class of citizen, will be diminished; and consequently the stability and independence of some member of the government, the only other security, must be proportionally increased. Justice is the end of government. It is the end of civil society. It ever has been and ever will be pursued until it be obtained, or until liberty be lost in the pursuit. In a society under the forms of which the stronger faction can readily unite and oppress the weaker, anarchy may as truly be said to reign as in a state of nature, where the weaker individual is not secured against the violence of the stronger; and as, in the latter state, even the stronger individuals are prompted, by the uncertainty of their condition, to submit to a government which may protect the weak as well as themselves; so, in the former state, will the more powerful factions or parties be gradually induced, by a like motive, to wish for a government which will protect all parties, the weaker as well as the more powerful. It can be little doubted that if the State of Rhode Island was separated from the Confederacy and left to itself, the insecurity of rights under the popular form of government within such narrow limits would be displayed by such reiterated oppressions of factious majorities that some power altogether independent of the people would soon be called for by the voice of the very factions whose misrule had proved the necessity of it. In the extended republic of the United States, and among the great variety of interests, parties, and sects which it embraces, a coalition of a majority of the whole society could seldom take place on any other principles than those of justice and the general good; whilst there being thus less danger to a minor from the will of a major party, there must be less pretext, also, to provide for the security of the former, by introducing into the government a will not dependent on the latter, or, in other words, a will independent of the society itself. It is no less certain than it is important, notwithstanding the contrary opinions which have been entertained, that the larger the society, provided it lie within a practicable sphere, the more duly capable it will be of self-government. And happily for the *republican cause*, the practicable sphere may be carried to a very great extent by a judicious modification and mixture of the *federal principle*.

Publius
(James Madison)

INFORMATION ON U.S. PRESIDENTS

	Term of Service	Age at Inauguration	Party Affiliation	College or University	Occupation or Profession
1. George Washington	1789–1797	57	None		Planter
2. John Adams	1797–1801	61	Federalist	Harvard	Lawyer
3. Thomas Jefferson	1801–1809	57	Democratic-Republican	William and Mary	Planter, Lawyer
4. James Madison	1809–1817	57	Democratic-Republican	Princeton	Lawyer
5. James Monroe	1817–1825	58	Democratic-Republican	William and Mary	Lawyer
6. John Quincy Adams	1825–1829	57	Democratic-Republican	Harvard	Lawyer
7. Andrew Jackson	1829–1837	61	Democrat		Lawyer
8. Martin Van Buren	1837–1841	54	Democrat		Lawyer
9. William H. Harrison	1841	68	Whig	Hampden-Sydney	Soldier
10. John Tyler	1841–1845	51	Whig	William and Mary	Lawyer
11. James K. Polk	1845–1849	49	Democrat	U. of N. Carolina	Lawyer
12. Zachary Taylor	1849–1850	64	Whig		Soldier
13. Millard Fillmore	1850–1853	50	Whig		Lawyer
14. Franklin Pierce	1853–1857	48	Democrat	Bowdoin	Lawyer
15. James Buchanan	1857–1861	65	Democrat	Dickinson	Lawyer
16. Abraham Lincoln	1861–1865	52	Republican		Lawyer
17. Andrew Johnson	1865–1869	56	National Union[†]		Tailor
18. Ulysses S. Grant	1869–1877	46	Republican	U.S. Mil. Academy	Soldier
19. Rutherford B. Hayes	1877–1881	54	Republican	Kenyon	Lawyer
20. James A. Garfield	1881	49	Republican	Williams	Lawyer
21. Chester A. Arthur	1881–1885	51	Republican	Union	Lawyer
22. Grover Cleveland	1885–1889	47	Democrat		Lawyer
23. Benjamin Harrison	1889–1893	55	Republican	Miami	Lawyer
24. Grover Cleveland	1893–1897	55	Democrat		Lawyer
25. William McKinley	1897–1901	54	Republican	Allegheny College	Lawyer
26. Theodore Roosevelt	1901–1909	42	Republican	Harvard	Author
27. William H. Taft	1909–1913	51	Republican	Yale	Lawyer
28. Woodrow Wilson	1913–1921	56	Democrat	Princeton	Educator
29. Warren G. Harding	1921–1923	55	Republican		Editor
30. Calvin Coolidge	1923–1929	51	Republican	Amherst	Lawyer
31. Herbert C. Hoover	1929–1933	54	Republican	Stanford	Engineer
32. Franklin D. Roosevelt	1933–1945	51	Democrat	Harvard	Lawyer
33. Harry S Truman	1945–1953	60	Democrat		Businessman
34. Dwight D. Eisenhower	1953–1961	62	Republican	U.S. Mil. Academy	Soldier
35. John F. Kennedy	1961–1963	43	Democrat	Harvard	Author
36. Lyndon B. Johnson	1963–1969	55	Democrat	Southwest Texas State	Teacher
37. Richard M. Nixon	1969–1974	56	Republican	Whittier	Lawyer
38. Gerald R. Ford[‡]	1974–1977	61	Republican	Michigan	Lawyer
39. James E. Carter, Jr.	1977–1981	52	Democrat	U.S. Naval Academy	Businessman
40. Ronald W. Reagan	1981–1989	69	Republican	Eureka College	Actor
41. George H. W. Bush	1989–1993	64	Republican	Yale	Businessman
42. William J. Clinton	1993–2001	46	Democrat	Georgetown	Lawyer
43. George W. Bush	2001–2009	54	Republican	Yale	Businessman
44. Barack Obama	2009–	47	Democrat	Columbia	Lawyer

*Church preference; never joined any church.
†The National Union Party consisted of Republicans and War Democrats. Johnson was a Democrat.
**Inaugurated Dec. 6, 1973, to replace Agnew, who resigned Oct. 10, 1973.
‡Inaugurated Aug. 9, 1974, to replace Nixon, who resigned that same day.
§Inaugurated Dec. 19, 1974, to replace Ford, who became president Aug. 9, 1974.

Religion	Born	Died	Age at Death	Vice President	
1. Episcopalian	Feb. 22, 1732	Dec. 14, 1799	67	John Adams	(1789–1797)
2. Unitarian	Oct. 30, 1735	July 4, 1826	90	Thomas Jefferson	(1797–1801)
3. Unitarian*	Apr. 13, 1743	July 4, 1826	83	Aaron Burr	(1801–1805)
				George Clinton	(1805–1809)
4. Episcopalian	Mar. 16, 1751	June 28, 1836	85	George Clinton	(1809–1812)
				Elbridge Gerry	(1813–1814)
5. Episcopalian	Apr. 28, 1758	July 4, 1831	73	Daniel D. Tompkins	(1817–1825)
6. Unitarian	July 11, 1767	Feb. 23, 1848	80	John C. Calhoun	(1825–1829)
7. Presbyterian	Mar. 15, 1767	June 8, 1845	78	John C. Calhoun	(1829–1832)
				Martin Van Buren	(1833–1837)
8. Dutch Reformed	Dec. 5, 1782	July 24, 1862	79	Richard M. Johnson	(1837–1841)
9. Episcopalian	Feb. 9, 1773	Apr. 4, 1841	68	John Tyler	(1841)
10. Episcopalian	Mar. 29, 1790	Jan. 18, 1862	71		
11. Methodist	Nov. 2, 1795	June 15, 1849	53	George M. Dallas	(1845–1849)
12. Episcopalian	Nov. 24, 1784	July 9, 1850	65	Millard Fillmore	(1849–1850)
13. Unitarian	Jan. 7, 1800	Mar. 8, 1874	74		
14. Episcopalian	Nov. 23, 1804	Oct. 8, 1869	64	William R. King	(1853)
15. Presbyterian	Apr. 23, 1791	June 1, 1868	77	John C. Breckinridge	(1857–1861)
16. Presbyterian*	Feb. 12, 1809	Apr. 15, 1865	56	Hannibal Hamlin	(1861–1865)
				Andrew Johnson	(1865)
17. Methodist*	Dec. 29, 1808	July 31, 1875	66		
18. Methodist	Apr. 27, 1822	July 23, 1885	63	Schuyler Colfax	(1869–1873)
				Henry Wilson	(1873–1875)
19. Methodist*	Oct. 4, 1822	Jan. 17, 1893	70	William A. Wheeler	(1877–1881)
20. Disciples of Christ	Nov. 19, 1831	Sept. 19, 1881	49	Chester A. Arthur	(1881)
21. Episcopalian	Oct. 5, 1829	Nov. 18, 1886	57		
22. Presbyterian	Mar. 18, 1837	June 24, 1908	71	Thomas A. Hendricks	(1885)
23. Presbyterian	Aug. 20, 1833	Mar. 13, 1901	67	Levi P. Morton	(1889–1893)
24. Presbyterian	Mar. 18, 1837	June 24, 1908	71	Adlai E. Stevenson	(1893–1897)
25. Methodist	Jan. 29, 1843	Sept. 14, 1901	58	Garret A. Hobart	(1897–1899)
				Theodore Roosevelt	(1901)
26. Dutch Reformed	Oct. 27, 1858	Jan. 6, 1919	60	Charles W. Fairbanks	(1905–1909)
27. Unitarian	Sept. 15, 1857	Mar. 8, 1930	72	James S. Sherman	(1909–1912)
28. Presbyterian	Dec. 29, 1856	Feb. 3, 1924	67	Thomas R. Marshall	(1913–1921)
29. Baptist	Nov. 2, 1865	Aug. 2, 1923	57	Calvin Coolidge	(1921–1923)
30. Congregationalist	July 4, 1872	Jan. 5, 1933	60	Charles G. Dawes	(1925–1929)
31. Friend (Quaker)	Aug. 10, 1874	Oct. 20, 1964	90	Charles Curtis	(1929–1933)
32. Episcopalian	Jan. 30, 1882	Apr. 12, 1945	63	John N. Garner	(1933–1941)
				Henry A. Wallace	(1941–1945)
				Harry S Truman	(1945)
33. Baptist	May 8, 1884	Dec. 26, 1972	88	Alben W. Barkley	(1949–1953)
34. Presbyterian	Oct. 14, 1890	Mar. 28, 1969	78	Richard M. Nixon	(1953–1961)
35. Roman Catholic	May 29, 1917	Nov. 22, 1963	46	Lyndon B. Johnson	(1961–1963)
36. Disciples of Christ	Aug. 27, 1908	Jan. 22, 1973	64	Hubert H. Humphrey	(1965–1969)
37. Friend (Quaker)	Jan. 9, 1913	Apr. 22, 1994	81	Spiro T. Agnew	(1969–1973)
				Gerald R. Ford**	(1973–1974)
38. Episcopalian	July 14, 1913	Dec. 26, 2006	93	Nelson A. Rockefeller§	(1974–1977)
39. Baptist	Oct. 1, 1924			Walter F. Mondale	(1977–1981)
40. Disciples of Christ	Feb. 6, 1911	June 5, 2004	93	George H. W. Bush	(1981–1989)
41. Episcopalian	June 12, 1924			J. Danforth Quayle	(1989–1993)
42. Baptist	Aug. 19, 1946			Albert A. Gore	(1993–2001)
43. Methodist	July 6, 1946			Dick Cheney	(2001–2009)
44. United Church of Christ	August 4, 1961			Joe Biden	(2009–)

PARTY CONTROL OF CONGRESS SINCE 1900

Congress	Years	President	Majority Party in House	Majority Party in Senate
57th	1901–1903	T. Roosevelt	Republican	Republican
58th	1903–1905	T. Roosevelt	Republican	Republican
59th	1905–1907	T. Roosevelt	Republican	Republican
60th	1907–1909	T. Roosevelt	Republican	Republican
61st	1909–1911	Taft	Republican	Republican
62d	1911–1913	Taft	Democratic	Republican
63d	1913–1915	Wilson	Democratic	Democratic
64th	1915–1917	Wilson	Democratic	Democratic
65th	1917–1919	Wilson	Democratic	Democratic
66th	1919–1921	Wilson	Republican	Republican
67th	1921–1923	Harding	Republican	Republican
68th	1923–1925	Coolidge	Republican	Republican
69th	1925–1927	Coolidge	Republican	Republican
70th	1927–1929	Coolidge	Republican	Republican
71st	1929–1931	Hoover	Republican	Republican
72d	1931–1933	Hoover	Democratic	Republican
73d	1933–1935	F. Roosevelt	Democratic	Democratic
74th	1935–1937	F. Roosevelt	Democratic	Democratic
75th	1937–1939	F. Roosevelt	Democratic	Democratic
76th	1939–1941	F. Roosevelt	Democratic	Democratic
77th	1941–1943	F. Roosevelt	Democratic	Democratic
78th	1943–1945	F. Roosevelt	Democratic	Democratic
79th	1945–1947	Truman	Democratic	Democratic
80th	1947–1949	Truman	Republican	Democratic
81st	1949–1951	Truman	Democratic	Democratic
82d	1951–1953	Truman	Democratic	Democratic
83d	1953–1955	Eisenhower	Republican	Republican
84th	1955–1957	Eisenhower	Democratic	Democratic
85th	1957–1959	Eisenhower	Democratic	Democratic
86th	1959–1961	Eisenhower	Democratic	Democratic
87th	1961–1963	Kennedy	Democratic	Democratic
88th	1963–1965	Kennedy/Johnson	Democratic	Democratic
89th	1965–1967	Johnson	Democratic	Democratic
90th	1967–1969	Johnson	Democratic	Democratic
91st	1969–1971	Nixon	Democratic	Democratic
92d	1971–1973	Nixon	Democratic	Democratic
93d	1973–1975	Nixon/Ford	Democratic	Democratic
94th	1975–1977	Ford	Democratic	Democratic
95th	1977–1979	Carter	Democratic	Democratic
96th	1979–1981	Carter	Democratic	Democratic
97th	1981–1983	Reagan	Democratic	Republican
98th	1983–1985	Reagan	Democratic	Republican
99th	1985–1987	Reagan	Democratic	Republican
100th	1987–1989	Reagan	Democratic	Democratic
101st	1989–1991	G. H. W. Bush	Democratic	Democratic
102d	1991–1993	G. H. W. Bush	Democratic	Democratic
103d	1993–1995	Clinton	Democratic	Democratic
104th	1995–1997	Clinton	Republican	Republican
105th	1997–1999	Clinton	Republican	Republican
106th	1999–2001	Clinton	Republican	Republican
107th	2001–2003	G. W. Bush	Republican	Democratic
108th	2003–2005	G. W. Bush	Republican	Republican
109th	2005–2007	G. W. Bush	Republican	Republican
110th	2007–2009	G. W. Bush	Democratic	Democratic
111th	2009–2011	Obama	Democratic	Democratic
112th	2011–2013	Obama	Republican	Democratic
113th	2013–2015	Obama	Republican	Democratic

GLOSSARY

A

action-reaction syndrome The principle that for every government action, there will be a reaction by the public.

adjudicate To render a judicial decision. In administrative law, it is the process in which an administrative law judge hears and decides issues that arise when an agency charges a person or firm with violating a law or regulation enforced by the agency.

administrative law The body of law created by administrative agencies (in the form of rules, regulations, orders, and decisions) in order to carry out their duties and responsibilities.

affirmative action A policy that gives special consideration, in jobs and college admissions, to members of groups that have been discriminated against in the past.

agenda setting The media's ability to determine which issues are considered important by the public and by politicians.

agents of political socialization People and institutions that influence the political views of others.

Anti-Federalists A political group that opposed the adoption of the Constitution.

appellate court A court having appellate jurisdiction. An appellate court normally does not hear evidence or testimony but reviews the transcript of the trial court's proceedings, other records relating to the case, and attorneys' arguments as to why the trial court's decision should or should not stand.

apportionment The distribution of House seats among the states on the basis of their respective populations.

appropriation A part of the congressional budgeting process—the determination of how many dollars will be spent in a given year on a particular government activity.

Articles of Confederation The nation's first national constitution, which established a national form of government following the American Revolution. The Articles provided for a confederal form of government in which the central government had few powers.

Australian ballot A secret ballot that is prepared, distributed, and counted by government officials at public expense; used by all states in the United States since 1888.

authority The ability to legitimately exercise power, such as the power to make and enforce laws.

authorization A part of the congressional budgeting process—the creation of the legal basis for government programs.

autocracy A form of government in which the power and authority of the government are in the hands of a single person.

B

biased sample A poll sample that does not accurately represent the population.

bicameral legislature A legislature made up of two chambers, or parts.

bill of attainder A legislative act that inflicts punishment on particular persons or groups without granting them the right to a trial.

Bill of Rights The first ten amendments to the U.S. Constitution. They list the freedoms—such as the freedoms of speech, press, and religion—that a citizen enjoys and that cannot be infringed on by the government.

block grant A federal grant given to a state for a broad area, such as criminal justice or mental-health programs.

bureaucracy A large, complex, hierarchically structured administrative organization that carries out specific functions.

bureaucrat An individual who works in a bureaucracy. As generally used, the term refers to a government employee.

busing The transportation of public school students by bus to schools physically outside their neighborhoods to eliminate school segregation based on residential patterns.

C

cabinet An advisory group selected by the president to assist with decision making. Traditionally, the cabinet has consisted of the heads of the executive departments and other officers whom the president may choose to appoint.

campaign strategy The comprehensive plan developed by a candidate and his or her advisers for winning an election.

capitalism An economic system based on the private ownership of wealth-producing property, free markets, and freedom of contract. The privately owned corporation is the preeminent capitalist institution.

case law The rules of law announced in court decisions. Case law includes the aggregate of reported cases that interpret judicial precedents, statutes, regulations, and constitutional provisions.

categorical grant A federal grant targeted for a specific purpose as defined by federal law.

caucus A meeting held to choose political candidates or delegates.

checks and balances A major principle of American government in which each of the three branches is given the means to check (to restrain or balance) the actions of the others.

chief diplomat The role of the president of the United States in recognizing and interacting with foreign governments.

chief executive The head of the executive branch of government; in the United States, the president.

chief of staff The person who directs the operations of the White House Office and advises the president on important matters.

Children's Health Insurance Program (CHIP) A joint federal-state program that provides health-care insurance for low-income children.

citizen journalism The collection, analysis, and dissemination of information online by independent journalists, scholars, politicians, and the general citizenry.

civil disobedience The deliberate and public act of refusing to obey laws thought to be unjust.

civil law The branch of law that spells out the duties that individuals in society owe to other persons or to their governments, excluding the duty not to commit crimes.

civil liberties Individual rights protected by the Constitution against the powers of the government.

civil rights The rights of all Americans to equal treatment under the law, as provided by the Fourteenth Amendment to the Constitution.

civil rights movement The movement in the 1950s and 1960s, by minorities and concerned whites, to end racial segregation.

civil service Nonmilitary government employees.

closed primary A primary in which only party members can vote to choose that party's candidates.

cloture A procedure for ending filibusters in the Senate and bringing the matter under consideration to a vote.

coalition An alliance of individuals or groups with a variety of interests and opinions who join together to support all or part of a political party's platform.

Cold War The war of words, warnings, and ideologies between the Soviet Union and the United States that lasted from the late 1940s through the late 1980s.

colonial empire A group of dependent nations that are under the rule of a single imperial power.

commander in chief The supreme commander of a nation's military force.

commerce clause The clause in Article I, Section 8, of the Constitution that gives Congress the power to regulate interstate commerce (commerce involving more than one state).

commercial speech Advertising statements that describe products. Commercial speech receives less protection under the First Amendment than ordinary speech.

common law The body of law developed from judicial decisions in English and U.S. courts, not attributable to a legislature.

competitive federalism A model of federalism in which state and local governments compete for businesses and citizens, who in effect "vote with their feet" by moving to jurisdictions that offer a competitive advantage.

concurrent powers Powers held by both the federal and the state governments in a federal system.

concurring opinion A statement written by a judge or justice who agrees (concurs) with the court's decision, but for reasons different from those in the majority opinion.

confederal system A league of independent sovereign states, joined together by a central government that has only limited powers over them.

confederation A league of independent states that are united only for the purpose of achieving common goals.

conference In regard to the Supreme Court, a private meeting of the justices in which they present their arguments concerning a case under consideration.

conference committee A temporary committee that is formed when the two chambers of Congress pass differing versions of the same bill. The conference committee consists of members from the House and the Senate who work out a compromise bill.

conference report A report submitted by a conference committee after it has drafted a single version of a bill.

congressional district The geographic area that is served by one member in the House of Representatives.

conservatism A set of political beliefs that include a limited role for the national government in helping individuals and in the economic affairs of the nation, as well as support for traditional values and lifestyles.

conservative movement An ideological movement that arose in the 1950s and 1960s and continues to shape conservative beliefs.

Constitutional Convention The convention of delegates from the states that was held in Philadelphia in 1787 for the purpose of amending the Articles of Confederation. In fact, the delegates wrote a new constitution (the U.S. Constitution) that established a federal form of government.

constitutional law Law based on the U.S. Constitution and the constitutions of the various states.

containment A U.S. policy designed to contain the spread of communism by offering military and economic aid to threatened nations.

contempt of court A ruling that a person has disobeyed a court order or has shown disrespect to the court or to a judicial proceeding.

continuing resolution A temporary resolution passed by Congress that enables executive agencies to continue work with the same funding that they had in the previous fiscal year.

cooperative federalism A model of federalism in which the states and the federal government cooperate in solving problems.

Corporate Average Fuel Economy (CAFE) standards A set of federal standards under which each vehicle manufacturer (or the industry as a whole) must meet a miles-per-gallon benchmark averaged across all new cars or trucks.

Credentials Committee A committee of each national political party that evaluates the claims of national party convention delegates to be the legitimate representatives of their states.

criminal law The branch of law that defines and governs actions that constitute crimes. Generally, criminal law has to do with wrongful actions committed against society for which society demands redress.

Cuban missile crisis A nuclear standoff that occurred in 1962 when the United States learned that the Soviet Union had placed nuclear warheads in Cuba.

D

dealignment Among voters, a growing detachment from both major political parties.

de facto segregation Racial segregation that occurs not as a result of deliberate intentions but because of social and economic conditions and residential patterns.

de jure segregation Racial segregation that occurs because of laws or decisions by government agencies.

delegate A person selected to represent the people of one geographic area at a party convention.

democracy A system of government in which the people have ultimate political authority. The word is derived from the Greek *demos* ("the people") and *kratia* ("rule").

détente A French word meaning a "relaxation of tensions." Détente characterized the relationship between the United States and the Soviet Union in the 1970s as they attempted to pursue cooperative dealings and arms control.

deterrence A policy of building up military strength for the purpose of discouraging (deterring) military attacks by other nations; the policy that supported the arms race between the United States and the Soviet Union during the Cold War.

devolution The surrender or transfer of powers to local authorities by a central government.

dictatorship A form of government in which absolute power is exercised by an individual or group whose power is not supported by tradition.

diplomat A person who represents one country in dealing with representatives of another country.

direct democracy A system of government in which political decisions are made by the people themselves rather than by elected representatives. This form of government was practiced in some parts of ancient Greece.

direct primary An election held within each of the two major parties—Democratic and Republican—to choose the party's candidates for the general election. Voters choose the candidate directly, rather than through delegates.

direct technique Any method used by an interest group to interact with government officials directly to further the group's goals.

dissenting opinion A statement written by a judge or justice who disagrees with the majority opinion.

diversity of citizenship A basis for federal court jurisdiction over a lawsuit that arises when (1) the parties in the lawsuit live in different states or when one of the parties is a foreign government or a foreign citizen, and (2) the amount in controversy is more than $75,000.

divine right theory The theory that a monarch's right to rule was derived directly from God rather than from the consent of the people.

division of powers A basic principle of federalism established by the U.S. Constitution, by which powers are divided between the national and state governments.

domestic policy Public policy concerning issues within a national unit, such as national policy concerning health care or the economy.

double jeopardy The prosecution of a person twice for the same criminal offense; prohibited by the Fifth Amendment in all but a few circumstances.

dual federalism A system of government in which the federal and the state governments maintain diverse but sovereign powers.

due process clause The constitutional guarantee, set out in the Fifth and Fourteenth Amendments, that the government will not illegally or arbitrarily deprive a person of life, liberty, or property.

due process of law The requirement that the government use fair, reasonable, and standard procedures whenever it takes any legal action against an individual; required by the Fifth and Fourteenth Amendments.

E

easy-money policy A monetary policy that involves stimulating the economy by expanding the rate of growth of the money supply.

economic policy All actions taken by the national government to address ups and downs in the nation's level of business activity.

electoral college The group of electors who are selected by the voters in each state to elect officially the president and vice president. The number of electors in each state is equal to the number of that state's representatives in both chambers of Congress.

elector A member of the electoral college.

electorate All of the citizens eligible to vote in a given election.

electronic media Communication channels that involve electronic transmissions, such as radio, television, and the Internet.

enabling legislation A law enacted by a legislature to establish an administrative agency. Enabling legislation normally specifies the name, purpose, composition, and powers of the agency being created.

entitlement program A government program (such as Social Security) that allows, or entitles, a certain class of people (such as elderly persons) to receive benefits. Entitlement programs operate under open-ended budget authorizations that, in effect, place no limits on how much can be spent.

equality A concept that holds, at a minimum, that all people are entitled to equal protection under the law.

equal protection clause Section 1 of the Fourteenth Amendment, which states that no state shall "deny to any person within its jurisdiction the equal protection of the laws."

establishment clause The section of the First Amendment that prohibits Congress from passing laws "respecting an establishment of religion."

exclusionary rule A criminal procedural rule stating that illegally obtained evidence is not admissible in court.

executive agreement A binding international agreement, or pact, that is made between the president and another head of state and that does not require Senate approval.

Executive Office of the President (EOP) A group of staff agencies that assist the president in carrying out major duties.

executive order A presidential order to carry out a policy or policies described in a law passed by Congress.

executive privilege An inherent executive power claimed by presidents to withhold information from, or to refuse to appear before, Congress or the courts. The president can also accord the privilege to other executive officials.

ex post facto law A criminal law that punishes individuals for committing an act that was legal when the act was committed.

expressed powers Constitutional or statutory powers that are expressly provided for by the U.S. Constitution; also called *enumerated powers.*

F

faction A group of persons forming a cohesive minority.

federalism A system of shared sovereignty between two levels of government—one national and one subnational—occupying the same geographic region.

Federalists A political group, led by Alexander Hamilton and John Adams, that supported the adoption of the Constitution and the creation of a federal form of government.

federal mandate A requirement in federal legislation that forces states and municipalities to comply with certain rules.

Federal Open Market Committee (FOMC) The most important body within the Federal Reserve System; decides how monetary policy should be carried out.

federal question A question that pertains to the U.S. Constitution, acts of Congress, or treaties. A federal question provides a basis for federal court jurisdiction.

federal system A form of government that provides for a division of powers between a central government and several regional governments.

feminism A doctrine advocating full political, economic, and social equality for women.

filibustering The Senate tradition of unlimited debate undertaken for the purpose of preventing action on a bill.

first budget resolution A budget resolution, which is supposed to be passed in May, that sets overall revenue goals and spending targets for the next fiscal year, beginning on October 1.

First Continental Congress A gathering of delegates from twelve of the thirteen colonies, held in 1774 to protest the Coercive Acts.

fiscal federalism The allocation of taxes collected by one level of government (typically the national government) to another level (typically state or local governments).

fiscal policy The use of changes in government expenditures and taxes to alter national economic variables.

fiscal year A twelve-month period that is established for bookkeeping or accounting purposes. The government's fiscal year runs from October 1 through September 30.

foreign policy A systematic and general plan that guides a country's attitudes and actions toward the rest of the world. Foreign policy includes all of the economic, military, commercial, and diplomatic positions and actions that a nation takes in its relationships with other countries.

fracking Technique for extracting oil or natural gas from underground rock by the high-power injection of a mixture of water, sand, and chemicals.

framing An agenda-setting technique that establishes the context of a media report. Framing can mean fitting events into a familiar story or filtering information through pre-conceived ideas.

free exercise clause The provision of the First Amendment stating that the government cannot pass laws "prohibiting the free exercise" of religion.

free rider problem The difficulty that exists when individuals can enjoy the outcome of an interest group's efforts without having to contribute, such as by becoming members of the group.

fundamental right A basic right of all Americans, such as First Amendment rights. Any law or action that prevents some group of persons from exercising a fundamental right is subject to the *strict scrutiny standard*.

G

gender gap The difference between the percentage of votes cast for a particular candidate by women and the percentage of votes cast for the same candidate by men.

general election A regularly scheduled election to choose the U.S. president, vice president, and senators and representatives in Congress. General elections are held in even-numbered years on the Tuesday after the first Monday in November.

gerrymandering The drawing of a legislative district's boundaries in such a way as to maximize the influence of a certain group or political party.

glass ceiling An invisible but real discriminatory barrier that prevents women and minorities from rising to top positions of power or responsibility.

global warming An increase in the average temperature of the Earth's surface over the last half century and its projected continuation; referred to more generally as *climate change*.

government The individuals and institutions that make society's rules and possess the power and authority to enforce those rules.

government corporation An agency of the government that is run as a business enterprise. Such agencies engage primarily in commercial activities, produce revenues, and require greater flexibility than most government agencies have.

grandfather clause A clause in a state law that had the effect of restricting voting rights to those whose ancestors had voted before the 1860s. It was one of the techniques used in the South to prevent African Americans from exercising their right to vote.

Great Compromise A plan for a bicameral legislature in which one chamber would be based on population and the other chamber would represent each state equally. The plan was also known as the Connecticut Compromise.

greenhouse gas A gas that, when released into the atmosphere, traps the sun's heat and slows its release into outer space. Carbon dioxide (CO_2) is a major example.

H

head of state The person who serves as the ceremonial head of a country's government and represents that country to the rest of the world.

I

ideology Generally, a system of political ideas that are rooted in religious or philosophical beliefs concerning human nature, society, and government.

imminent lawless action test The current Supreme Court doctrine for assessing the constitutionality of subversive speech. To be illegal, speech must be "directed to inciting . . . imminent lawless action."

implied powers The powers of the federal government that are implied by the expressed powers in the Constitution, particularly in Article I, Section 8.

independent executive agency A federal agency that is not located within a cabinet department.

independent expenditure An expenditure for activities that are independent from (not coordinated with) those of a political candidate or a political party.

independent regulatory agency A federal organization that is responsible for creating and implementing rules that regulate private activity and protect the public interest in a particular sector of the economy.

indirect technique Any method used by interest groups to influence government officials through third parties, such as voters.

individual mandate In the context of health-care reform, a requirement that all persons obtain health-care insurance from one source or another. Those failing to do so must pay a penalty.

inflation A sustained rise in average prices; equivalent to a decline in the value of the dollar.

inherent powers The powers of the national government that, although not always expressly granted by the Constitution, are necessary to ensure the nation's integrity and survival as a political unit.

institution An ongoing organization that performs certain functions for society.

instructed delegate A representative who deliberately mirrors the views of the majority of his or her constituents.

interest group An organized group of individuals sharing common objectives who actively attempt to influence policymakers.

interstate commerce Trade that involves more than one state.

interventionism Direct involvement by one country in another country's affairs.

iron curtain A phrase coined by Winston Churchill to describe the political boundaries between the democratic countries in Western Europe and the Soviet-controlled Communist countries in Eastern Europe.

iron triangle A three-way alliance among legislators, bureaucrats, and interest groups to make or preserve policies that benefit their respective interests.

isolationism A political policy of noninvolvement in world affairs.

issue ad A political advertisement that focuses on a particular issue. Issue ads can be used to support or attack a candidate's position or credibility.

issue networks Groups of individuals or organizations—which consist of legislators and legislative staff members, interest group leaders, bureaucrats, the media, scholars, and other experts—that support particular policy positions on a given issue.

J

judicial review The power of the courts to decide on the constitutionality of legislative enactments and of actions taken by the executive branch.

judiciary The courts; one of the three branches of government in the United States.

jurisdiction The authority of a court to hear and decide a particular case.

justiciable controversy A controversy that is not hypothetical or academic but real and substantial; a requirement that must be satisfied before a court will hear a case. *Justiciable* is pronounced jus-*tish*-a-bul.

K

Keynesian economics An economic theory proposed by British economist John Maynard Keynes that is typically associated with the use of fiscal policy to alter national economic variables.

kitchen cabinet The name given to a president's unofficial advisers. The term was coined during Andrew Jackson's presidency.

L

labor force All of the people over the age of sixteen who are working or actively looking for jobs.

legislative rule An administrative agency rule that carries the same weight as a statute enacted by a legislature.

***Lemon* test** A three-part test enunciated by the Supreme Court in the 1971 case of *Lemon v. Kurtzman* to determine whether government aid to parochial schools is constitutional.

libel A published report of a falsehood that tends to injure a person's reputation or character.

liberalism A set of political beliefs that include the advocacy of active government, including government intervention to improve the welfare of individuals and to protect civil rights.

libertarianism The belief that government should do as little as possible, not only in the economic sphere, but also in regulating morality and personal behavior.

liberty The freedom of individuals to believe, act, and express themselves as they choose so long as doing so does not infringe on the rights of other individuals in the society.

limited government A form of government based on the principle that the powers of government should be clearly limited either through a written document or through wide public understanding. It is characterized by institutional checks to ensure that government serves public rather than private interests.

literacy test A test given to voters to ensure that they could read and write and thus evaluate political information. This technique was used in many southern states to restrict African American participation in elections.

lobbying All of the attempts by organizations or by individuals to influence the passage, defeat, or contents of legislation or to influence the administrative decisions of government.

lobbyist An individual who handles a particular interest group's lobbying efforts.

M

Madisonian Model The model of government devised by James Madison, in which the powers of the government are separated into three branches: legislative, executive, and judicial.

majority leader The party leader elected by the majority party in the House or in the Senate.

majority party The political party that has more members in the legislature than the opposing party.

malapportionment A condition in which the voting power of citizens in one district is greater than the voting power of citizens in another district.

managed news coverage News coverage that is manipulated (managed) by a campaign manager or political consultant to gain media exposure for a political candidate.

markup session A meeting held by a congressional committee or subcommittee to approve, amend, or redraft a bill.

Marshall Plan A plan providing for U.S. economic assistance to European nations following World War II to help those nations recover from the war. The plan was named after George C. Marshall, secretary of state from 1947 to 1949.

mass media Communication channels, such as newspapers and radio and television broadcasts, through which people can communicate to large audiences.

material incentive A reason to join an interest group—practical benefits such as discounts, subscriptions, or group insurance.

Mayflower Compact A document drawn up by Pilgrim leaders in 1620 on the ship *Mayflower*. The document stated that laws were to be made for the general good of the people.

media Newspapers, magazines, television, radio, the Internet, and any other printed or electronic means of communication.

Medicaid A joint federal-state program that pays for health-care services for low-income persons.

Medicare A federal government program that pays for health-care insurance for Americans aged sixty-five years and over.

minority leader The party leader elected by the minority party in the House or in the Senate.

minority-majority district A district in which minority groups make up a majority of the population.

minority party The political party that has fewer members in the legislature than the opposing party.

***Miranda* warnings** A series of statements informing criminal suspects, on their arrest, of their constitutional rights, such as the right to remain silent and the right to counsel; required by the Supreme Court's 1966 decision in *Miranda v. Arizona.*

moderates Persons whose views fall in the middle of the political spectrum.

monarchy A form of autocracy in which a king, queen, emperor, empress, tsar, or tsarina is the highest authority in the government. Monarchs usually obtain their power through inheritance.

monetary policy Actions taken by the Federal Reserve Board to change the amount of money in circulation to affect interest rates, credit markets, the rate of inflation, the rate of economic growth, and the rate of unemployment.

Monroe Doctrine A U.S. policy, announced in 1823 by President James Monroe, that the United States would not tolerate foreign intervention in the Western Hemisphere, and in return, the United States would stay out of European affairs.

moral idealism In foreign policy, the belief that the most important goal is to do what is right. Moral idealists think that it is possible for nations to cooperate as part of a rule-based community.

mutually assured destruction (MAD) A phrase referring to the assumption that if the forces of two nations are capable of destroying each other, neither nation will take a chance on war.

N

national convention The meeting held by each major party every four years to nominate presidential and vice-presidential candidates, write a party platform, and conduct other party business.

national health insurance A program, found in many of the world's economically advanced nations, under which the central government provides basic health-care insurance coverage to everyone in the country.

national party chairperson An individual who serves as a political party's administrative head at the national level and directs the work of the party's national committee.

national party committee The political party leaders who direct party business during the four years between the national party conventions, organize the next national convention, and plan how to obtain a party victory in the next presidential election.

National Security Council (NSC) A council that advises the president on domestic and foreign matters concerning the safety and defense of the nation.

natural rights Rights that are not bestowed by governments but are inherent within every man, woman, and child by virtue of the fact that he or she is a human being.

necessary and proper clause Article I, Section 8, Clause 18, of the Constitution, which gives Congress the power to make all laws "necessary and proper" for the federal government to carry out its responsibilities; also called the *elastic clause.*

negative political advertising Political advertising undertaken for the purpose of discrediting an opposing candidate in voters' eyes. Attack ads are one form of negative political advertising.

neutral competency The application of technical skills to jobs without regard to political issues.

neutrality The position of not being aligned with either side in a dispute or conflict, such as a war.

New Deal The policies ushered in by the Roosevelt administration in 1933 in an attempt to bring the United States out of the Great Depression.

new federalism A plan to limit the federal government's role in regulating state governments and to give the states increased power in deciding how they should spend government revenues.

nominating convention An official meeting of a political party to choose its candidates. Nominating conventions at the state and local levels also select delegates to represent the citizens of their geographic areas at a higher-level party convention.

normal trade relations (NTR) status A trade status granted through an international treaty by which each member nation must treat other members at least as well as it treats the country that receives its most favorable treatment. This status was formerly known as *most-favored-nation status.*

O

obscenity Indecency or offensiveness in speech, expression, behavior, or appearance.

Office of Management and Budget (OMB) An agency in the Executive Office of the President that has the primary duty of assisting the president in preparing and supervising the administration of the federal budget.

"one person, one vote" rule A rule, or principle, requiring that congressional districts have equal populations so that one person's vote counts as much as another's vote.

open primary A primary in which voters can vote for a party's candidates regardless of whether they belong to the party.

opinion A written statement by a court expressing the reasons for its decision in a case.

opposition research The attempt to learn damaging information about an opponent in a political campaign.

oral argument A spoken argument presented to a judge in person by an attorney on behalf of her or his client.

Oslo Accords The first agreement signed between Israel and the PLO; led to the establishment of the Palestinian Authority in the occupied territories.

P

Palestine Liberation Organization (PLO) An organization formed in 1964 to represent the Palestinian people. The PLO has a long history of terrorism but for some years has functioned primarily as a political party.

parliament The name of the national legislative body in countries governed by a parliamentary system, such as Britain and Canada.

partisan politics Political actions or decisions that benefit a particular party.

party activist A party member who helps to organize and oversee party functions and planning during and between campaigns, and may even become a candidate for office.

party identifier A person who identifies himself or herself as being a supporter of a particular political party.

party platform The document drawn up by each party at its national convention that outlines the policies and positions of the party.

party ticket A list of a political party's candidates for various offices. In national elections, the party ticket consists of the presidential and vice-presidential candidates.

patronage The practice by which elected officials give government jobs to individuals who helped them gain office.

peer group Associates, often close in age to one another; may include friends, classmates, co-workers, club members, or religious group members.

personal attack ad A negative political advertisement that attacks the character of an opposing candidate.

picket-fence federalism A model of federalism in which specific policies and programs are administered by all levels of government —national, state, and local.

pluralist theory A theory that views politics as a contest among various interest groups—at all levels of government—to gain benefits for their members.

pocket veto A special type of veto power used by the chief executive after the legislature has adjourned. Bills that are not signed die after a specified period of time.

podcasting The distribution of audio or video files to personal computers or mobile devices such as smartphones.

police powers The powers of a government body that enable it to create laws for the protection of the health, safety, welfare, and morals of the people. In the United States, most police powers are reserved to the states.

policymaking process The procedures involved in getting an issue on the political agenda; formulating, adopting, and implementing a policy with regard to the issue; and then evaluating the results of the policy.

political action committee (PAC) A committee that is established by a corporation, labor union, or special interest group to raise funds and make campaign contributions on the establishing organization's behalf.

political advertising Advertising undertaken by or on behalf of a political candidate to familiarize voters with the candidate and his or her views on campaign issues; advertising for or against policy issues.

political consultant A professional political adviser who, for a fee, works on an area of a candidate's campaign. Political consultants include campaign managers, pollsters, media advisers, and "get out the vote" organizers.

political culture The set of ideas, values, and attitudes about government and the political process held by a community or a nation.

political party A group of individuals who organize to win elections, operate the government, and determine policy.

political realism In foreign policy, the belief that nations are inevitably selfish and that we should seek to protect our national security, regardless of moral arguments.

political socialization The learning process through which most people acquire their political attitudes, opinions, beliefs, and knowledge.

politics The process of resolving conflicts over how society should use its scarce resources and who should receive various benefits, such as public health care and public higher education.

poll tax A fee of several dollars that had to be paid before a person could vote. This device was used in some southern states to discourage African Americans and low-income whites from voting.

poll watcher A representative from one of the political parties who is allowed to monitor a polling place to make sure that the election is run fairly and that fraud doesn't occur.

power The ability to influence the behavior of others, usually through the use of force, persuasion, or rewards.

precedent A court decision that furnishes an example or authority for deciding subsequent cases involving identical or similar facts and legal issues.

precinct A political district within a city, such as a block or a neighborhood, or a rural portion of a county; the smallest voting district at the local level.

preemption A doctrine rooted in the supremacy clause of the Constitution that provides that national laws or regulations governing a certain area take precedence over conflicting state laws or regulations governing that same area.

press secretary A member of the White House staff who holds news conferences for reporters and makes public statements for the president.

primary A preliminary election held for the purpose of choosing a party's final candidate.

primary election An election in which voters choose the candidates of their party, who will then run in the general election.

primary source of law A source of law that establishes the law. Primary sources of law include constitutions, statutes, administrative agency rules and regulations, and decisions rendered by the courts.

priming An agenda-setting technique in which a media outlet promotes specific facts or ideas that may affect the public's thinking on related topics.

print media Communication channels that consist of printed materials, such as newspapers and magazines.

privatization The transfer of the task of providing services traditionally provided by government to the private sector.

probable cause Cause for believing that there is a substantial likelihood that a person has committed or is about to commit a crime.

progressivism An alternative, more popular term for the set of political beliefs also known as liberalism.

public debt The total amount of money that the national government owes as a result of borrowing; also called the *national debt*.

public-interest group An interest group formed for the purpose of working for the "public good." Examples are the American Civil Liberties Union and Common Cause.

public opinion The views of the citizenry about politics, public issues, and public policies; a complex collection of opinions held by many people on issues in the public arena.

public opinion poll A survey of the public's opinion on a particular topic at a particular moment.

public services Essential services that individuals cannot provide for themselves, such as building and maintaining roads, establishing welfare programs, operating public schools, and preserving national parks.

purposive incentive A reason to join an interest group—satisfaction resulting from working for a cause in which one believes.

push poll A campaign tactic used to feed false or misleading information to potential voters, under the guise of taking an opinion poll, with the intent to "push" voters away from one candidate and toward another.

Q

quota system A policy under which a specific number of jobs, promotions, or other types of placements, such as university admissions, are given to members of selected groups.

R

random sample In the context of opinion polling, a sample in which each person within the entire population being polled has an equal chance of being chosen.

rating system A system by which a particular interest group evaluates (rates) the performance of legislators based on how often the legislators have voted with the group's position on particular issues.

rational basis test A test (also known as the *ordinary scrutiny standard*) used by the Supreme Court to decide whether a discriminatory law violates the equal protection clause of the Constitution. It is used only when there is no classification—such as race or gender—that would require a higher level of scrutiny.

realignment A process in which the popular support for and relative strength of the parties shift and the parties are reestablished with different coalitions of supporters.

recession A period in which the level of economic activity falls; usually defined as two or more quarters of economic decline.

renewable energy Energy from technologies that do not rely on extracted resources, such as oil and coal, that can run out.

representative democracy A form of democracy in which the will of the majority is expressed through groups of individuals elected by the people to act as their representatives.

republic Essentially, a representative democracy in which there is no king or queen and the people are sovereign.

reverse discrimination Discrimination against those who have no minority status.

right-to-work laws Laws that ban unions from collecting dues or other fees from workers whom they represent but who have not actually joined the union.

rulemaking The process undertaken by an administrative agency when formally proposing, evaluating, and adopting a new regulation.

rule of law A basic principle of government that requires those who govern to act in accordance with established law.

Rules Committee A standing committee in the House of Representatives that provides special rules governing how particular bills will be considered and debated by the House. The Rules Committee normally proposes time limits on debate for any bill.

S

sample In the context of opinion polling, a group of people selected to represent the population being studied.

sampling error In the context of opinion polling, the difference between what the sample results show and what the true results would have been had everybody in the relevant population been interviewed.

school voucher An educational certificate, provided by a government, that allows a student to use public funds to pay for a private or a public school chosen by the student or his or her parents.

secession The act of formally withdrawing from membership in an alliance; the withdrawal of a state from the federal Union.

second budget resolution A budget resolution, which is supposed to be passed in September, that sets "binding" limits on taxes and spending for the next fiscal year.

Second Continental Congress The congress of the colonies that met in 1775 to assume the powers of a central government and to establish an army.

seditious speech Speech that urges resistance to lawful authority or that advocates the overthrow of a government.

self-incrimination Providing damaging information or testimony against oneself in court.

senatorial courtesy A practice that allows a senator of the president's party to veto the president's nominee to a federal court judgeship within the senator's state.

separate-but-equal doctrine A Supreme Court doctrine holding that the equal protection clause of the Fourteenth Amendment did not forbid racial segregation as long as the facilities for blacks were equal to those for whites.

separation of powers The principle of dividing governmental powers among the legislative, the executive, and the judicial branches of government.

sexual harassment Unwanted physical contact, verbal conduct, or abuse of a sexual nature that interferes with a recipient's job performance, creates a hostile environment, or carries with it an implicit or explicit threat of adverse employment consequences.

Shays' Rebellion A rebellion of angry farmers in western Massachusetts in 1786, led by former Revolutionary War captain Daniel Shays.

signing statement A written statement, appended to a bill at the time the president signs it into law, indicating how the president interprets that legislation.

sit-in A tactic of nonviolent civil disobedience. Demonstrators enter a business, college building, or other public place and remain seated until they are forcibly removed or until their demands are met.

slander The public utterance (speaking) of a statement that holds a person up for contempt, ridicule, or hatred.

social conflict Disagreements among people in a society over what the society's priorities should be.

social contract A voluntary agreement among individuals to create a government and to give that government adequate power to secure the mutual protection and welfare of all individuals.

socialism A political ideology that lies to the left of liberalism on the traditional political spectrum. Socialists are scarce in the United States but common in many other countries.

soft money Campaign contributions not regulated by federal law, such as some contributions that are made to political parties instead of to particular candidates.

solidarity Mutual agreement among the members of a particular group.

solidary incentive A reason to join an interest group—pleasure in associating with like-minded individuals.

Solid South A term used to describe the tendency of the southern states to vote Democratic after the Civil War.

sound bite A televised comment, lasting for only a few seconds, that captures a thought or a perspective and has an immediate impact on viewers.

Soviet bloc The group of Eastern European nations that fell under the control of the Soviet Union following World War II.

Speaker of the House The presiding officer in the House of Representatives. The Speaker is a member of the majority party and is the most powerful member of the House.

special election An election that is held at the state or local level when the voters must decide an issue before the next general election or when vacancies occur by reason of death or resignation.

spin A reporter's slant on, or interpretation of, a particular event or action.

spin doctor A political candidate's press adviser who tries to convince reporters to give a story or event concerning the candidate a particular "spin" (interpretation, or slant).

standing committee A permanent committee in Congress that deals with legislation concerning a particular area, such as agriculture or foreign relations.

standing to sue The requirement that an individual must have a sufficient stake in a controversy before he or she can bring a lawsuit. The party bringing the suit must demonstrate that he or she has either been harmed or been threatened with a harm.

stare decisis A common law doctrine under which judges normally are obligated to follow the precedents established by prior court decisions. Pronounced *ster*-ay dih-*si*-sis.

statutory law The body of law enacted by legislatures (as opposed to constitutional law, administrative law, or case law).

straw poll A nonscientific poll in which there is no way to ensure that the opinions expressed are representative of the larger population.

strict scrutiny standard A standard under which a law or action must be necessary to promote a compelling state interest and must be narrowly tailored to meet that interest.

subcommittee A division of a larger committee that deals with a particular part of the committee's policy area. Most standing committees have several subcommittees.

suffrage The right to vote; the franchise.

supremacy clause Article VI, Clause 2, of the Constitution, which makes the Constitution and federal laws superior to all conflicting state and local laws.

suspect classification A classification, such as race, that provides the basis for a discriminatory law. Any law based on a suspect classification is subject to strict scrutiny by the courts, meaning that the law must be justified by a compelling state interest.

symbolic speech The expression of beliefs, opinions, or ideas through forms other than verbal speech or print; speech involving actions and other nonverbal expressions.

T

Tea Party movement A grassroots conservative movement that arose in 2009 after Barack Obama became president. The movement opposes big government and current levels of taxation, and also rejects political compromise.

third party In the United States, any party other than one of the two major parties (Republican and Democratic).

three-fifths compromise A compromise reached during the Constitutional Convention by which three-fifths of all slaves were to be counted for purposes of representation in the House of Representatives.

trade organization An association formed by members of a particular industry, such as the oil industry or the trucking industry, to develop common standards and goals for the industry. Trade organizations, as interest groups, lobby government for legislation or regulations that specifically benefit their members.

treaty A formal agreement between the governments of two or more countries.

trial court A court in which trials are held and testimony is taken.

trustee A representative who tries to serve the broad interests of the entire society and not just the narrow interests of his or her constituents.

two-party system A political system in which two strong and established parties compete for political offices.

tyranny The arbitrary or unrestrained exercise of power by an oppressive individual or government.

U

unemployment The state of not having a job even when actively seeking one.

unicameral legislature A legislature with only one chamber.

unitary system A centralized governmental system in which local or subdivisional governments exercise only those powers given to them by the central government.

V

veto A Latin word meaning "I forbid"; the refusal by an official, such as the president of the United States or a state governor, to sign a bill into law.

veto power A constitutional power that enables the chief executive (president or governor) to reject legislation and return it to the legislature with reasons for the rejection. This either prevents or delays the bill from becoming law.

vote-eligible population The number of people who are actually eligible to vote in an American election.

voting-age population The number of people residing in the United States who are at least eighteen years old.

W

ward A local unit of a political party's organization, consisting of a division or district within a city.

Watergate scandal A scandal involving an illegal break-in at the Democratic National Committee offices in 1972 by members of President Richard Nixon's reelection campaign staff.

weapons of mass destruction Chemical, biological, or nuclear weapons that can inflict massive casualties.

whip A member of Congress who assists the majority or minority leader in the House or in the Senate in managing the party's legislative program.

whistleblower In the context of government employment, someone who "blows the whistle" (reports to authorities or the press) on gross governmental inefficiency, illegal action, or other wrongdoing.

White House Office The personal office of the president. White House Office personnel handle the president's political needs and manage the media, among other duties.

white primary A primary election in which African Americans were prohibited from voting. The practice was banned by the Supreme Court in 1944.

winner-take-all system A system in which the candidate who receives the most votes wins. In contrast, proportional systems allocate votes to multiple winners.

writ of *certiorari* An order from a higher court asking a lower court for the record of a case. *Certiorari* is pronounced sur-shee-uh-*rah*-ree.

writ of *habeas corpus* An order that requires an official to bring a specified prisoner into court and explain to the judge why the person is being held in jail.

INDEX

legislative success of, 272
lobbying reform, 138–139
No Child Left Behind Act, 61
North Korea and talks with, 367
as opinion leader, 172
oversight of, by Congress, 251
Partial Birth Abortion Ban Act, 85
response to 9/11, 362
September 11, 2001 terrorist attacks and, 275
signing statements and, 271
Supreme Court appointments, 319
tax cuts for rich, 347
veto power exercised by, 266
war on terrorism, 86, 273, 362–363
Business cycle, 342
Business interest groups, 125–126
Busing, 98
Byrd, Robert, 242

C

Cabinet, 276–277
defined, 276
executive departments, 276–277, 288–289
foreign policymaking and, 354–355
kitchen, 277
Obama's czars, 277
use of, 277
Cain, Herman, 198
Campaign(s)
campaign strategy, 199
cost of, 203–209
direct-mail campaigns, 201
financing, 203–209
ground and air games, 202
Internet and, 230–231
candidates' 24/7 exposure, 230–231
controlling netroots, 230
fund-raising on, 201–202
online fund-raising, 230
rise of Internet campaign, 230
support for local organizing, 202
targeting supporters, 202
nominating candidates, 191–198
opposition research, 199
political parties role in running, 152
professional campaign organization, 199
responsibilities of campaign staff, 198–199
typical organization for presidential, 200
Campaign financing, 203–209
Bipartisan Campaign Reform Act, 205–206
bundled campaign contributions, 138
by business interest groups, 126
Citizens United decision, 133, 203, 205–206, 207
corporate funding, 205–206, 207, 309
direct-mail campaigns, 201
favoring two-party system, 157
Federal Election Campaign Act, 203–204
501(c)4 and 527s, 134, 208
incumbent and, 240
independent expenditures, 204–206
Internet fund-raising, 201–202
issue campaigns, 205
lobbying regulation and reform, 138–139
political action committees (PACs) and, 204
skirting campaign-financing rules, 204–205
soft money, 134, 204
super PAC's, 132–133, 203, 206–208
Campaign strategy, 199
Camp David, 259–260
Canada, 48
Canadian vs. American federalism, 50
health-care spending, 335
North Atlantic Treaty Organization (NATO), 359
as oil exporter, 338, 340
powers of provinces, 50
two languages and, 50
World War II and, 357
Candidates
incumbent, power of, 240–241, 242
insurgent candidates, 194–195
nomination process, 191–198
perception of, and voting behavior, 173–174
policy choice and voting behavior, 174
presidential, 195–198
selecting, 151
television and
debates, 221–222
news coverage, 222
political advertising, 219–221
popular television, 222
use of Internet, 230–231
write-in, 192
Cantor, Eric, 243
Cantwell v. Connecticut, 73
Capitalism, 12–13
Carpenters & Joiners Union, 127
Carter, Jimmy, 260, 267
amnesty for draft resisters, 266
election of 1980
presidential debate and, 221–222
public opinion polls, 168
legislative success of, 272
Middle East peace efforts and, 364
Mondale as vice president, 280
as opinion leader, 172
Case law, 310
Castro, Fidel, 106
Categorical grants, 63
Catholics
insurance for birth control, 78, 168
voting behavior, 176
Catt, Carrie Chapman, 102
Caucuses
defined, 193
historical perspective on, 193
presidential, 196
Cell phones, public opinion polls and, 166
Censorship, 83
of Internet, 214, 216
Central America–Dominican Republic–United States Free Trade Agreement, 137
Central Intelligence Agency (CIA)
creation of, 356
foreign policymaking and, 356
formation of, 291
function of, 356
principal duties of, 292
Chamber of Commerce, 125
Change to Win federation, 126
Charitable contribution tax break, 124
Chase, Samuel, 252
Checks and balances
Congress and, 235, 274
defined, 39
judicial review, 321–322
media and, 214
of president, 39, 40
as principle of Constitution, 39–40
Chemical Weapons Convention, 369
Cheney, Dick, power of, as vice president, 280
Chief diplomat, 263
Chief executive role of president, 261–262
Chief of staff, 278
Child labor, 57
Children, media and opinion formation, 172
Children's Health Insurance Program (CHIP), 335, 336
China
American trade relations with, 371
Communist Party of, and dictatorial power, 7
as debt holder of U.S. public debt, 349
government-paid bloggers, 228
gross domestic product, 371
Internet censorship and, 214
negotiations with North Korea nuclear cooperation treaty, 367
normal trade relations status, 371
political party affiliation in, 153
religious intolerance in, 74
Taiwan and Tibet, 371–372
Tibet and, 5
World War II, 357
WTO membership, 371
Chinese Americans, 107
Chinese Exclusion Act, 107
Christian nation, 22
Christian Science Monitor, 213
Chrysler, 148
Churchill, Winston, 358, 359
executive agreement with Roosevelt, 272
Cincinnati Post, 213
Citigroup, Inc., 126
Citizen journalism, 229
Citizens Against Government Waste, 501(c)4 group, 134
Citizens United v. Federal Elections Commission, 133, 203, 205–206, 207, 309
Civil Aeronautics Board, 293
Civil disobedience, 98–99
Civil law, 310
Civil liberties, 70–90. *See also* Bill of Rights; Constitution of United States; *individual amendments*
Bill of Rights and, 70–72
vs. civil rights, 70
defined, 70
First Amendment protections, 73–83
freedom of expression, 78–83
freedom of press, 83
freedom of religion, 74–78
freedom of speech, 78–83
importance of, 70
rights of the accused, 87–90
right to die, 86
right to privacy, 84–85
safeguards in original constitution, 70
Civil rights, 93–116. *See also* Civil rights movement
affirmative action, 112–115
of African Americans, 96–101
of Asian Americans, 107
vs. civil liberties, 70
Civil Rights Movement and, 98–99
civil rights plank of Democratic Party platform of 1948, 146
defined, 94

Gender discrimination, 103
Gender gap, 176
General election, 189
General fund budget, 64
General Motors, 148
General Services Administration
    formation of, 291
    principal duties of, 292
Geographic region, voting behavior and, 177
George III, King (England), 25, 26, 27
Georgia, Russian attack on, 353
Germany, 48
    Berlin Wall, 360
    end of Cold War, 360
    Greece bailout, 370
    World War II, 357
Gerry, Elbridge, 237
Gerrymandering
    after 2010 census, 238
    racial, 238–239
Gibbons, Thomas, 56
Gibbons v. Ogden, 56, 59
Gideon v. Wainwright, 73, 88
Gingrich, Newt, 196, 198, 206, 207, 261
Ginsburg, Ruth Bader, 85, 103, 325
Gitlow v. New York, 73
Glass ceiling, 104
Global warming, 339–340
    debate on, 340
    renewable energy and, 342
Going public strategy, 269
Goldman Sachs, 126
Goldwater, Barry, 16, 192, 220–221
Gomez, Gabriel, 194
Google, 87, 216, 228–229
Google+, 215
Gorbachev, Mikhail, 360
Gore, Al
    election of 2000, 160
        exit polls, 168
        popular vote, 147, 188
    as vice president, 280
Government
    access to, and interest groups, 123
    aristocracy, 9
    authority of, 4, 5
    autocracy, 7
    coalition, 41
    cost of maintaining, 287–288
    defending nation and culture, 5
    defined, 4
    dictatorship, 7
    direct democracy, 7–8
    limited, 10, 38
        vs. effective, 40
    managing economy, 5
    minority, 41
    monarchy, 7
    need for, 2, 3
    online, 303
    plutocracy, 9
    power of, 4
    principles of, in Constitution
        checks and balances, 39–40
        federalism, 38–39
        limited government, 38
        popular sovereignty, 38
        separation of powers, 39
    privatization, 302
    providing public service, 5
    representative, 10
    representative democracy, 8–9
    resolving conflicts, 4–5
    salary for workers, 296

size of, 2
    in sunshine, 302–303
    theocracy, 9
    types of, 6–9
Government Accountability Office (GAO), 301
Government corporations
    defined, 293
    list of selected, 294
Government Performance and Results Act, 302
Government regulation. *See* Regulation/regulatory agencies
Graber, Doris A., 172
Grandfather clause, 97, 180
Grand jury, 71, 73
Granholm, Jennifer M., 260
Grassroots organizing, 134–135
Gratz v. Bollinger, 114
Great Britain. *See also* England; United Kingdom
    American independence from, 26–28
    coalition government, 41
    Cold War and, 358–360
    fusion of powers, 41
    health-care spending, 335
    House of Commons, 237
    Murdoch's News Corporation scandal, 219
    Parliament, 10
    parliamentary system, 41
    Seven Years' War, 24–25
    as unitary system, 48
    World War II, 357
Great Charter, 10
Great Compromise, 33–34, 235
Great Depression
    cooperative federalism and, 58–59
    Farm Bureau and fair prices during, 128
    federalism in Canada vs. U.S. during, 50
    formation of public opinion, 172
    Keynes on, 344–345
    Republican and Democratic Parties, 146
Great Recession
    deficit spending to fight, 349
    Emergency Economic Stabilization Act, 334
    Europe and Greek bailout, 370
    Fannie Mae and Freddie Mac, 294
    federalism and, 61–62
    food stamps, 131
    formation of public opinion, 173
    Keynesian economics and, 345
    number of jobs created and, 6
    public debt and, 349
    regulation and financial crisis, 299
    spending on Medicaid by states, 335–336
    state and federal spending during, 61–62
    unemployment during, 5, 6
Great Society, 58, 63
Greece
    communist threat to, 358
    direct democracy and, 8
    financial bailout and austerity measures, 370
Greenhouse gas emissions, 60, 339
Green Party, 158, 160
Greenpeace USA, 130
Green Revolution, 228
Griswold v. Connecticut, 73, 83

Ground game, 202
Grutter v. Bollinger, 114
Guam, 235, 357
Guantánamo prisoners, 307
Gun control
    Brady Handgun Violence Prevention Act, 60
    Gun-Free School Zones Act, 60
    military-style rifles/magazines, 69
    right to bear arms, 5
Gun-Free School Zones Act, 60

H

Habeas corpus, writ of, 70
Hagel, Chuck, 355
Hamas, 366
Hamilton, Alexander, 28
    at Constitutional Convention, 31, 32
    judicial review, 322
    leader of Federalist Party, 144
    ratification of Constitution and, 36, 37
Hannity, Sean, 223, 224
Happiness, pursuit of, 12
Harassment
    hostile-environment, 104–105
    sexual, 104–105
Hard money, 344
Harlan, John Marshall, 96
Harris Poll, 166
Haskins, Ron, 131
Hastert Rule, 246–247
Hate speech, 79
Hayden, Michael, 216
Hazelwood School District v. Kuhlmeier, 83
Head of state, 263
Head Start, 58, 59
Health and Human Services, Department of, 277, 291
Health care/health-care reform, 334–338.
    See also Obamacare
    attempts to repeal, 338
    Clinton and, 264, 336
    conservative reaction, 337–338
    constitutionality of, 46, 323–324, 338
    current system of funding, 334–335
    Democrats' proposal, 336–337
    employer-provided health-insurance tax break, 124
    entitlement programs and, 336
    Health Insurance Exchange, 337
    individual mandate, 62, 324, 337
    information privacy, 84
    lack of coverage, 335
    Medicaid expansion, 62
    Medicare and Medicaid overview, 335–336
    national health insurance, 337
    Obama and content of legislation, 264
    Patient Protection and Affordable Care Act, 334–338
    as percent of national spending, 335, 336
    popularity of Democrats and, 148
    public option, 337
    regulation of, 299
    states' rights and, 62
    support and opposition to, 337
Health Insurance Exchange, 337
Help America Vote Act, 181
Henry, Patrick, 32
    as Anti-Federalist, 37
    on slavery, 36

Lebanon, 364
Lee, Richard Henry, 27
Legislation
    enabling, 297
    supermajority to pass important
        legislation, 234
    by Supreme Court, 325–327
Legislative branch
    checks and balances and, 39–40
    separation of powers, 39
Legislative process, 247–250
Legislative rules, 296
Legislature
    bicameral, 33
    success of various presidents, 272
    unicameral, 28
Lemon test, 77
Lemon v. Kurtzman, 77
Lesbians
    changing attitude toward, 111
    changing legal landscape, 110–111
    civil rights of, 110–112, 324, 325
    "Don't ask, don't tell" policy, 112
    in military, 112
    same-sex marriage, 53, 54, 61,
        111–112, 321
Lewinsky, Monica, 276
Lexington, Battle of, 26
Libel, 81
Liberalism/liberals
    bias in media, 225
    big government and, 16
    civil rights movement, 16–17
    defined, 14
    entitlement programs and, 336
    progressives and, 17
    roots of, 16
    Supreme Court and, 324
    in traditional political spectrum, 17–19
    Vietnam War and, 17
    voting behavior, 177–178
Libertarianism, 18
Libertarian Party, 159
Liberty
    civil liberties, 11
    defined, 11–12
    as political value, 11–12
Libya, 338, 365
    Pan Am Flight 103 bombing, 361–362
Life events, major, formation of political
    opinion and, 172–173
Limbaugh, Rush, 215, 223, 224
Limited government
    American democracy and, 10
    defined, 10
    vs. effective, 40
    Magna Carta and, 10
    popular sovereignty, 38
    principle of Constitution, 38
Lincoln, Abraham, 269, 277
    election of 1860, 146
    powers of president under, 268
    role of government, 5, 9
Line-item veto, 267
Liquefied natural gas (LNG), 340
Literacy test, 97, 180
Literary Digest, 165
Little legislatures, 246
Livingston, Robert, 56
Livni, Tzipi, 367
Lobbying Disclosure Act, 138
Lobbying/lobbyists. *See also* Interest
    groups
    astroturf lobbying, 135
    defined, 132

    direct techniques of, 131–133
    professional, 136
    reform efforts, 138–139
    regulation of, 136–138
    revolving door syndrome, 136
Local government
    number of, in U.S., 49
    privatization, 302
    size of bureaucracy, 286
    state government and powers of, 48
Local party organization, 154–155
Locke, John, 10, 23
    Declaration of Independence and, 28
    natural rights, 10–11
Lockerbie, Scotland Pan Am Flight 103
    bombing, 361–362
Logic of Collective Action, The (Olson),
    122
Louisiana Science Education Act, 76
Luxembourg, 197
Lynching, 97

M

Maddow, Rachel, 226, 227
Madison, James, 3, 22, 144, 234, 235
    Bill of Rights, 40
    at Constitutional Convention, 31, 32
    as Federalist, 36, 37
    Madisonian Model, 39
    ratification of Constitution and, 36, 37
Madisonian Model, 39
Magna Carta, 10
Majority leader
    of the House, 243–244
    in Senate, 244
Majority party, 152
Majority rule and minority rights, 11
Major League Baseball Players Association,
    126
Malapportionment, 236–237
Malaysia, 48
Malcolm X, 99, 100
Malloy v. Hogan, 73
Managed competition, 302
Manchin, Joe, 249
Mapp v. Ohio, 73
Marbury v. Madison, 55, 321–322
March on Washington for Jobs and
    Freedom, 99
Marijuana, medical, 130
Marine Corps., 355
Markey, Edward, 194
Markup session, 249
Marriage
    same-sex, 43, 53, 54, 61, 111–112, 3
        21
    state power and, 53, 54
Marshall, George, 358
Marshall, John, 55, 56, 57, 59, 321–322
Marshall Plan, 358
Martin, Trayvon, 102
Mason, George, 32
Massachusetts Bay Colony, 23
Massachusetts Body of Liberties, 23
*Massachusetts v. Environmental Protection
    Agency,* 60
Mass media, 214
Material incentive, 122
Mayflower Compact, 23
McCain, John
    Bipartisan Campaign Reform Act, 205
    election of 2000, push poll and,
        169–170

    election of 2008
        choice of Palin as running mate, 279
        primaries, 197
McCain-Feingold Act, 205
McChesney, Fred, 126
McConnell, Mitch, 244
*McConnell v. Federal Election
    Commission,* 205, 309
McCulloch, James, 56
McCulloch v. Maryland, 55–56, 59
McDonald v. Chicago, 73
McKinley, William, 260
McVeigh, Timothy, 361
Media
    bias in, 225–227
        attitudes of journalists, 225
        against losers, 225–226
        partisan bias, 225
        selection bias, 226
    changing news culture, 226
    checks and balances, 214
    decline of old media, 214–215
    defined, 172, 214
    electronic, 214
    First Amendment and, 215
    formation of political opinion and, 172
    framing, 217
    freedom of press and, 214, 215
    increased bottom-line pressure, 226
    Internet
        blogs, 229
        censorship of, in China, 214
        citizen journalism, 229
        news organizations online, 227–229
        podcasting news, 229–230
        political campaigns, 230–231
    issue advertising, 205
    managed news coverage, 222
    mass, 214
    medium's affect on message, 217–218
    misuse of polls, 169
    Murdoch empire, 219
    older voters and, 215
    ownership of, 218–219
    presidential elections and effective use
        of, 199
    priming, 217
    print, 214
    role of
        agenda-setting function, 216–217
        new media and old, 214–215
    social, limits on free speech, 79
    sound bites, 218
    talk radio, 222–224
    television
        debates, 221–222
        impact of, 217–218
        news coverage, 222
        political advertising, 219–221
        popular television, 222
    usage of, by consumers, 214–215
Medicaid
    cost of, 335
    creation of, 58
    establishment of, 16
    expansion under Obamacare, 46
    federal budget spent on, 287, 288
    federal funding to states for, 64
    Great Recession and spending on,
        335–336
    health-care reform and, 338
    Obama care and, 62, 64
    overview, 335–336
    presidential elections of 2012, 178
    Republican proposed cuts to, 14

size of government and, 2
spending on, 335
Medical-marijuana initiative, 61
Medicare
    cost of, 336
    creation of, 58
    establishment of, 16
    federal budget spent on, 287
    health-care reform and, 338
    overview of, 336
    presidential elections of 2012, 178
    Republican proposed cuts to, 14
    size of government and, 2
    spending on, 336
Meetup.com, 202
Members of Parliament (MPs), 41
Men, voting behavior and, 176
Merit Systems Protection Board (MSPB), 295
Mexican Americans, 106
Mexico, 48
    as oil exporter, 338
Meyerson, Harold, 164
Mica, John, 250
Microsoft, 126, 216
Microtargeting, 202
Mid-term elections, of 2010
    economy as number one issue, 174
    ideology and voter behavior, 178
    perception of candidates and, 173–174
Military
    congressional power to declare war, 272–273, 273–274
    "Don't ask, don't tell" policy, 112
    dropping atomic bomb, 273–274
    federal budget spent on, 287, 288
    gays and lesbians in, 112
    presidential powers in military action, 258, 273–274
    president as commander in chief, 262–263
    War Powers Resolution, 273
Military-style rifles/magazines, 69
Miller v. California, 81
Minimum-wage laws, 49
Minority government, 41
Minority groups. *See also specific groups*
    distribution of U.S. population by, 13, 14
    voter turnout, 184
Minority leader
    of the House, 103, 244
    of Senate, 244
Minority-majority district, 238
Minority party, 152
Minority rights, majority rule and, 11
Minor parties, 156
Minutemen, 26
Miranda v. Arizona, 88
Miranda warning, 88–90
Mitterrand, François, 264
Moderates, 18
    voting behavior and, 177–178
Modernism, original intent vs., 325
Monarchy, 7, 9
Mondale, Walter, 280
Monetary policy, 343–345
    conservative reaction, 344
    hard-money, 344
    president's control over, 271
    pushing on a string, 343–344
Money
    coining of, 51
    monetary policy, 343–344
Moneybomb, 202
Monroe, James, 22, 270, 357

Monroe Doctrine, 357
Moral idealism, 354, 357
Mormons, 78
Morris, Gouverneur, 35
Morris, Robert, 32
Morsi, Mohamed, 190
Mothers Against Drunk Driving (MADD), 46, 130
Motor Voter Law, 180
Mott, Lucretia, 101
Mourdock, Richard, 174
MoveOn, 129
MSNBC, 223
Mubarak, Hosni, 190
Multiculturalism, 13
Municipalities, number of, in U.S., 49
Murdoch, Rupert, 219
Murphy, Patrick, 203
Muslim Americans, 78
    voting behavior, 177
Muslim Brotherhood, 190
Mutually assured destruction (MAD), 359

N

Nader, Ralph, 160
Nagasaki, 273, 357–358
NARAL Pro-Choice America, 130
Narrowcasting, 226
National Aeronautics and Space Administration (NASA), 292, 339
National American Woman Suffrage Association, 101–102
National Assembly, 264
National Association for the Advancement of Colored People (NAACP), 97, 129
National Association of Manufacturers (NAM), 125
National Association of Realtors, 126
National Association of Social Workers, 128
National Automobile Dealers Association, 126
National conventions
    Credentials Committee, 198
    defined, 155
    function of, 155
    historical perspective of, 198
National Council on Public Polls, 169
National debt, 348. *See also* Public debt
    federal budget spent on, 287, 288
National defense
    as discretionary spending, 253
    government's role in, 5
    as public good, 122
National Education Association (NEA), 126–127
National Farmers Union, 128
National Federation of Independent Business v. Sebelius, 62
National government. *See also* Federalism
    authority of, and shifting boundary with state authority, 60–62
    commerce clause, 38
    devolution, 60
    division of powers, 51–52
    federalism, 38–39
    federal lands, 52
    interstate relations, 52–53
    Native American tribal governments and, 51
    necessary and proper clause, 51
    new federalism, 60
    organization of, 288–294

powers of, 38, 48
    concurrent powers, 53
    expressed, 51
    implied, 51
    inherent, 51–52
    prohibited, 52
    separation of powers, 39
    size of, 286
    supremacy clause, 53–54
    supremacy of
        Civil War, 57
        cooperative federalism, 58–59
        dual federalism, 57–58
        early Supreme Court decisions, 55–56
        struggle for, 55–59
    term of, 47–48
National Grange, 128
National Guard, federalized to quell violence from school integration, 97
National health insurance, 337
Nationalist, during Revolutionary Era, 28
National Labor Relations Board (NLRB), 293
National Milk Producers Federation, 298
National Oceanic and Atmospheric Administration, 302
National Organization for Women (NOW), 103
National Park Service, 289
National party chairperson, 156
National party committees, 156
National party organization, 155–156
National Railroad Passenger Corporation (AMTRAK), 294
National Republicans, 145, 193
National Rifle Association (NRA), 69
    Bipartisan Campaign Reform Act challenged by, 205
    contributions to, 130
    defending group's interest, 121
    historical perspective of, 121
    mobilizing constituents, 134
    as single-issue interest group, 130
    from social to interest group, 121
National Right to Life Committee, 121
National security, 356
    personal privacy and, 84, 86–87
National Security Act, 355
National Security Agency (NSA)
    Foreign Intelligence Surveillance Court (FISC) and, 313
    information collected by and privacy concerns, 284
    phone surveillance, 86
    PRISM data collection, 87, 216
National Security Council (NSC), 279
    foreign policymaking and, 355–356
    functions of, 355
National Security Letter, 86
National Transportation Safety Board, 46
National Urban League, 129
National Voter Registration Act, 180
National Wildlife Federation, 130
National Woman Suffrage Association, 101
Nation-centered federalism, 60
Nation of Islam, 99
Native American Languages Act, 109
Native Americans
    assimilation of, 109
    casinos and, 109
    civil rights of, 107–109
    compensation for past injustices, 109
    decline in population of, 107–108
    early policies toward, 108–109
    poverty and, 105

Guantánamo prisoners and rights of, 307
openness of government afterwards, 303
personal privacy and national security since, 84, 86–87
planned and carried out by al Qaeda, 362
U.S. response to, 362
war on terrorism afterwards, 273, 275
Service Employees International Union (SEIU), 127
Seventeenth Amendment, 240
Seventh Amendment, text of, 71
Seven Years' War, 24–25
Sexual harassment, 104–105
Sharon, Ariel, 366
Shays, Daniel, 30
Shays' Rebellion, 30–31
Shelby, Richard, 247
Shelby County v. Holder, 100
Sherman, Roger, 33
Shiite Muslims, 363
Sierra Club
501(c)4 group, 134
litigation used by, 135
Signing statements, 270–271
defined, 270–271
by George W. Bush, 271
Silver, Nate, 166, 169, 170
Singapore, 182
Singh, Manmohan, 263
Single-member district, 158
Sit-ins, 99
Sixteenth Amendment, 51
Sixth Amendment, 71, 87–88
Skype, 87, 166
Slander, 81
Slaves/slavery
Civil War and, 57
Constitutional Convention and, 34, 35, 36
Constitution of United States and, 34, 35, 36
Declaration of Independence, 35, 36
importation of, 34
as presidential election issue, 146
Republican Party and, 146
three-fifths compromise, 34
Small Business Administration, 292
Smith, Al, 260–261
Smith Act, 80
Smith v. Allwright, 181
SNAP, 131
Snowden, Edward, 284
Social conflict, 3–4
Social contract, 10
Socialism, 18
Socialist Labor Party, 158–159
Socialist Party, 158
Social media
limits on free speech, 79
rebels and government's use of, 228
Social Security
AARP preserving benefits for, 121
as entitlement program, 336
federal budget spent on, 287
size of government and, 2
Social Security Administration (SSA), 292
Socioeconomic factors, voting behavior and, 174–177
Sodomy laws, 110–111
Soft money, 134, 204
Solidarity, 153
Solidary incentive, 122
Solid South, 177

Somalia, 360
Soros, George, 208
Sotomayor, Sonia, 103, 320, 323
Sound bite, 218
Southern Christian Leadership Conference (SCLC), 98, 129
Sovereignty
Articles of Confederation, 29
popular, 38
Soviet bloc, 358
Soviet Union. *See also* Russia
arms race and deterrence, 359
breakup of, 353
Cold War and, 358–360
Cuban missile crisis, 359
détente and arms control, 359
dissolution of, 360
Soviet bloc, 358
Strategic Arms Limitation Treaty (SALT I), 359
World War II, 357
Spain
Basque separatists terrorism in, 361
constitutional monarchy in, 7
financial bailout and, 370
Madrid commuter train bombing, 361
Spanish-American War and, 357
Spanish-American War, 357
Speaker of the House, 103, 243
presidential succession and, 281
Speaker pro tempore of the House, 243
Special districts, number of, in U.S., 49
Special election, 189
Special interest groups. *See* Interest groups
Speech
commercial, 80
libel and slander, 81
obscene, 81
seditious, 79–80
symbolic, 78
unprotected, 80–81
Speech, freedom of, 11, 71, 73, 78–83
early restrictions on expression, 80
libel and slander, 81
limited protection for commercial speech, 80
obscenity, 81
social media and, 79
for students, 82–83
symbolic speech, 78
unprotected speech, 80–81
Speechnow v. FEC, 206
Spin, 222
Spin doctors, 222
Splinter party, 159
Stalin, Joseph, 7
Stamp Act, 25
Standard operating procedures, 286
Standing committees, 245
Standing to sue, 312
Stanton, Elizabeth Cady, 101
Stare decisis, 308–309, 327
State, Department of, 277
foreign policymaking and, 354–355
original size of, 286
principal duties of, 290
State-centered federalism, 60
State court system
court procedures, 312
jurisdiction, 311
supreme court, 311
State government. *See also* States
affirmative action, 114–115
authority of, and shifting boundary with federal authority, 60–62

cooperative federalism, 58–59
devolution, 60
division of powers, 52
dual federalism, 57–58
federal grants to control, 64
federal revenue for state spending, 64
Hispanics holding office in, 106
interstate relations, 52–53
Native American tribal governments and, 51
new federalism, 60
number of, in U.S., 49
powers of, 48
concurrent powers, 53
police power, 52
prohibited, 52
privatization, 302
size of bureaucracy, 286
state spending as procyclical, 61–62
supremacy clause, 53–54
women holding office in, 103–104
State party organization, 154
States. *See also* State government
competitive federalism, 64–65
confederation of, 29–31
constitutions of, 28
electoral college, 190, 191
federalism, 39
general fund budget, 64
Medicaid spending by, 335
primaries and role in, 194
rights of, and Civil War, 57
transformed from colonies, 28
States' Rights Party, 159
Statistical modeling, public opinion polls and, 167–168
Statutory law, 309–310
Stein, Jill, 160
Stewart, Jon, 215
Stimulus package
federal grants to states, 62
government employment and, 287
Medicaid payments and, 336
Obama's ability to get passed, 271
popularity of Democrats and, 148
Race to the Top, 333–334
size of, to have real impact, 345
Stone, Lucy, 101
Stone v. Graham, 75
Stonewall Inn incident, 110
Strategic Arms Limitation Treaty (SALT I), 359
Straw polls, 165
Strict construction, 324
Strict scrutiny standard, 94–95, 113
Student Nonviolent Coordinating Committee (SNCC), 98, 129
Subcommittees, 245–246
Subsidies, agricultural, 119, 129
Substantive due process, 72–73
Succession Act, 280–281
Sudan, 360
Suffrage, 101, 179
Sugar Act, 25
Suicide, assisted, 86
Sullivan, Thomas P., 89–90
Sunlight Foundation, 219
Sunni Muslims, 363
Sunshine laws, 302–303
Super PACs, 132–133, 203, 206–208
Super Tuesday, 196
Supplemental Nutrition Assistance Program (SNAP), 131
Supremacy clause, 53–54, 55–56, 59
Supreme court, state, 311

Treaty on the Non-Proliferation of Nuclear Weapons, 367
Trial courts, 311
    federal, 312–313, 315
Trials
    jury
        common law tradition, 308–309
        right to, 71
    right to, 73
    Sixth Amendment and, 87
Truman, David B., 121
Truman, Harry, 259, 260
    armed forces ordered, to Korea, 273
    bombs dropped on Hiroshima and Nagasaki, 273–274
    Marshall Plan, 358
    on presidential power, 268–269
Truman Doctrine, 358
Trustee, 239
Tucson Citizen, 213
Tumblr, 215
Turkey
    communist threat to, 358
    Cuban missile crisis, 359
Twenty-fifth Amendment, 280
Twenty-fourth Amendment, 181
Twenty-second Amendment, 242
Twenty-sixth Amendment, 180, 181
Twenty-third Amendment, 181
Twitter, 215, 227, 228
    India and, 79
Two-party system
    defined, 156
    election laws favoring, 157
    institutional barriers to multiparty system, 157–158
    political socialization and, 157
Two Treatises (Locke), 23
Tyranny, 37

U

Unemployment
    economic policy and, 342
    federal budget spent on unemployment compensation, 287
    during Great Recession, 5, 6
    number of jobs created and, 6
    political impact of, 6
    rate of, 342
    young people and, 6
Unemployment compensation, as entitlement program, 336
Unicameral legislature, 28
Unions
    decline of membership, 127–128
    goals of, 126–127
    public-sector unions, 128
    right-to-work laws and, 127–128
Unitary system
    compared to federal system, 48
    defined, 48
United Auto Workers, 127
United Electrical Workers (UE), 126
United Kingdom. *See also* Great Britain
    constitutional monarchy in, 7
United Nations, 354
    North Korea nuclear missile test and, 367–368
    Palestine, 366
    sanctions by, 368
United Parcel Service, 126
United States
    Canadian vs. American federalism, 50

federal system of, 47–51
    governmental units in, 49
    racial and ethnic distribution of, 13, 14
United States v. Lopez, 60
United States v. Virginia, 95
United States v. Windsor, 112
Unlawful enemy combatants, 307
Unpledged delegates, 194
Unprotected speech, 80–81
Unreasonable search and seizure, 87
Uruguay, 182
USA Patriot Act, 86
U.S. Code Congressional and Administrative News, 270
U.S. district courts, 312–313, 315
U.S. Postal Service (USPS)
    Economic Value Added program, 302
    facing losses, 293–294
    as government corporation, 293–294
USS *Cole,* terrorist attack on, 361, 362

V

Vandenberg, Arthur, 372
van Tuyll, Debra, 225
van Tuyll, Hubert, 225
Vargas, José Antonio, 134
Venezuela, 338
Ventura, Jesse, 161
Veterans Affairs, Department of, 277, 291
Veterans benefits, federal budget spent on, 287
Veto
    defined, 266
    line-item veto, 267
    overriding, 250
    pocket, 250, 266
    president's power of, 39, 266–267
Veto power, 39
Vice president
    presidential succession, 280–281
    as president of Senate, 244
    role of, 280–281
Vietnamese Americans, 107
    voting behavior of, 177
Vietnam War, 147, 266, 273, 359
    formation of public opinion, 173
    liberals and, 17
    media and public opinion, 217
    protests against, 135
Violence Against Women Act, 60
Virginia Company, 23
Virginia House of Burgesses, 24
Virginia Military Institute, 95
Virginia Plan, 33
Virgin Islands, 235
Voluntary consent to be governed, 11
Vote-eligible population, 184
Voter fraud, 164
Voter News Service (VNS), 168
Voter turnout
    age and, 183–184
    attempts to improve, 180–181
    compulsory voting, 182, 189
    educational attainment and, 183
    factors affecting, 178–179
    Hispanics, 106
    immigration and, 184
    impact of voting restrictions and, 100
    income and, 183–184
    mail-in voting, 180–181
    minority status and, 184
    primaries, 194
    since 1968, 179

Voter-verified paper audit trail (VVPAT), 182
Votes/voting, 178–184
    affected by third party, 160
    African Americans, 97, 100
    age and, 176
    attempts to improve voter turnout, 180–181
    attempt to improve procedures for, 181–182
    compulsory voting, 182
    education and income, 174
    electronic voting systems, 181–182
    equality in, 11
    factors affecting voter turnout, 178–179
    felons, 180, 183
    gender and, 176
    geographic region and, 177
    historical restrictions on, 179–180
    income and, 150
    legal right to vote, 179–180
    photo ID requirement, 164, 181
    policy voting, 174
    popular vote and presidents, 192
    preclearance for changes in rules for, 164, 315–316
    registration for, 180
    religion and ethnic background, 176–177
    types of elections, 189
    voting behavior
        candidate policy choices, 174
        ideology, 177–178
        party identification, 173
        perception of candidate, 173–174
        socioeconomic factors, 174–177
Voting-age population, 184
Voting rights
    for African Americans, 97, 100
    African Americans and, 180
    for women, 101–103, 180, 181
Voting Rights Act, 99, 164, 180, 181, 239, 315
    weakening of, 100
Vouchers, school, 77, 168

W

Wage discrimination, 104
Wallace, Henry, 159
Wall Street Journal, 213, 217, 219
War, congressional power to declare, 258, 263, 272–273, 273–273, 356
War, Department of, original size of, 286
Ward, 154–155
War on terrorism, 360–364. *See also* September 11, 2001 terrorist attacks
    Afghanistan and, 363–364
    al Qaeda, 362–365
    Bush and, 362–363
    death of Bin Laden, 364
    First Gulf War background to, 362
    focus on Iraq, 362–363
    foreign terrorist networks, 362
    invasion of Iraq in 2003, 363
    local or regional, 361
    openness of government afterwards, 303
    Pakistan and, 363–364
    presidential power and, 275
    Second Gulf War, 362–363
    state-sponsored, 361–362
    types of terrorism, 361–362

U.S. response to 9/11, 362
War Powers Resolution, 273, 356
Warrants, 87
    NSA and, 86
Warren, Earl, 97, 318, 322
Warren, Elizabeth, 203, 249
Warren Court, 322, 323
Washington, George, 22, 26, 28, 30, 32,
    193, 269
    farewell address, 143, 357
    on political parties, 143
    powers of president under, 267–268
    president's role in foreign affairs and,
        272
    on slavery, 36
Washington Post, 213, 217, 218, 227
Wasserman Schultz, Debbie, 155
Watergate scandal, 266, 276
Wealthy people, perception of, as
    Republicans, 150
Weapons of mass destruction
    defined, 362
    Iran as emerging threat, 368–369
    Iraq and, 362–363
    North Korea's nuclear program,
        367–368
Web. *See* Internet
Web sites, selling ads on government sites,
    303
Webster, Daniel, 145
Welfare
    cooperative federalism and, 58
    picket-fence federalism, 59
    reform, as devolution, 60, 61
Wesberry v. Sanders, 237
West, Allen, 203
Westgate Shopping Mall incident, 365
West Germany, Berlin Wall, 360

West Wing, 222
Whig Party, 145–146, 193
Whips, 244
Whistle-Blower Protection act, 301
Whistleblowers, 301–302
White House, 259
White House chief of staff, 278
White House Office, 278
White primary, 97, 180
Wilkow, Andrew, 223
Will and Grace, 222
William the Conqueror, 308
Wilson, Woodrow, 102, 146, 261, 268, 276
    election of 1912, 160
    moral idealism and, 357
    neutrality policy, 357
    on presidential powers, 267
Wind power, 342
Winner-take-all system, 157, 190–191
Wolf v. Colorado, 73
Women
    civil rights of, 101–105
        feminist movement, 103
        World War I and, 102
    in federal office, 103
    feminist movement, 103
    glass ceiling, 104
    in politics today, 103–104
    sexual harassment, 104–105
    voting behavior and, 176
    voting rights, 101–103, 180, 181
    wage discrimination, 104
    World War I and women's rights, 102
Wood, Gordon S., 36
Workplace
    religious practices in, 78
    sexual harassment, 104–105
    women in, 104

World Conference on International
    Telecommunications, 216
World Trade Center. *See also* September
    11, 2001 terrorist attacks
        terrorist attack on, in 2001, 360, 361
World Trade Organization (WTO), China's
    membership in, 371
World War I
    clear and present danger, 80
    neutrality policy, 357
    women's rights and, 102
World War II
    attack on Pearl Harbor, 357, 358
    dropping atomic bomb, 273–274,
        357–358
    formation of public opinion, 173
Wounded Knee, South Dakota, 109
Write-in candidate, 192
Writ of *certiorari*, 314–315
Writ of *habeas corpus*, 70

Y

Yahoo, 216
Yellen, Janet, 343
Yeltsin, Boris, 360
Yglesias, Matt, 124
Yom Kippur War, 364
Yousafzai, Malala, 363
YouTube, 228

Z

Zimmerman, George, 102
Zuckerberg, Mark, 150

KEY TERMS

authority The ability to legitimately exercise power, such as the power to make and enforce laws. **5**

autocracy A form of government in which the power and authority of the government are in the hands of a single person. **7**

capitalism An economic system based on the private ownership of wealth-producing property, free markets, and freedom of contract. The privately owned corporation is the preeminent capitalist institution. **12**

conservatism A set of political beliefs that include a limited role for the national government in helping individuals and in the economic affairs of the nation, as well as support for traditional values and lifestyles. **14**

conservative movement An ideological movement that arose in the 1950s and 1960s and continues to shape conservative beliefs. **15**

democracy A system of government in which the people have ultimate political authority. The word is derived from the Greek *demos* ("the people") and *kratia* ("rule"). **7**

dictatorship A form of government in which absolute power is exercised by an individual or group whose power is not supported by tradition. **7**

direct democracy A system of government in which political decisions are made by the people themselves rather than by elected representatives. This form of government was practiced in some parts of ancient Greece. **7**

divine right theory The theory that a monarch's right to rule was derived directly from God rather than from the consent of the people. **7**

equality A concept that holds, at a minimum, that all people are entitled to equal protection under the law. **12**

government The individuals and institutions that make society's rules and possess the power and authority to enforce those rules. **4**

ideology Generally, a system of political ideas that are rooted in religious or philosophical beliefs concerning human nature, society, and government. **14**

institution An ongoing organization that performs certain functions for society. **3**

liberalism A set of political beliefs that

SUMMARY

LearningOutcome 1–1 Explain what is meant by the terms politics and government. **1** Resolving conflicts over how the society should use its scarce resources and who should receive various benefits is the essence of **politics**. **2** Government—the individuals and institutions that make society's rules and possess the **power** and **authority** to enforce those rules—resolves **social conflicts**, provides **public services**, and defends the nation and its culture against attacks by other nations.

LearningOutcome 1–2 Identify the various types of government systems. **3** Authoritarian rule by an individual is called **autocracy**. **Monarchs** are hereditary autocrats. A **dictatorship** is authoritarian rule by an individual or group unsupported by tradition. **4 Democracy** is a system of government in which the people have ultimate political authority. In a **representative democracy**, the will of the people is expressed through groups of individuals elected by the people to act as their representatives. **5** Other forms of government include aristocracy and plutocracy. In a theocracy, the government rules according to religious precepts.

LearningOutcome 1–3 Summarize some of the basic principles of American democracy and the basic American political values. **6** In writing the U.S. Constitution, the framers incorporated two basic principles of government that had evolved in England: **limited government** and representative government. Our democracy resulted from a type of **social contract** among early Americans to create and abide by a set of governing rules. **7** American democracy is based on the principles of equality in voting, individual freedom, equal protection of the law, majority rule and minority rights, and collective voluntary consent to be governed. **8** The rights to **liberty, equality,** and property are fundamental political values shared by most Americans. Differences among Americans in interpreting these values underlie the division between the Democratic and Republican parties.

LearningOutcome 1–4 Define common American ideological positions, such as "conservatism" and "liberalism." **9** The emergence of the **conservative movement** in the 1950s and 1960s was essential to the development of modern American **conservatism**. Conservatives believe that individuals and families should take responsibility for their own economic circumstances, and they place a high value on the principle of order, on family values, and on patriotism. Religious conservatives believe that government should reflect traditional religious values. While tracing its roots to the New Deal programs of Franklin D. Roosevelt, American **liberalism** took its modern form in the 1960s. Support for minority rights of all kinds became an important part of liberal ideology. Liberals, or **progressives,** argue that big government is a necessary tool for promoting the common welfare, and strongly favor the separation of church and state. Liberals identify with the Democratic Party, and conservatives identify themselves as Republicans. People whose views fall in the middle are generally called **moderates. 10** Many Americans have opinions that do not fit neatly under the liberal or conservative label. Some Americans, for example, are both economic progressives and social conservatives. To the left of liberalism on the ideological spectrum lies **socialism. Libertarians,** on the right, oppose almost all forms of government regulation, not just the economic activities opposed by the conservative **Tea Party movement.**

include the advocacy of active government, including government intervention to improve the welfare of individuals and to protect civil rights. **16**

libertarianism The belief that government should do as little as possible, not only in the economic sphere, but also in regulating morality and personal behavior. **18**

liberty The freedom of individuals to believe, act, and express themselves as they choose so long as doing so does not infringe on the rights of other individuals in the society. **11**

limited government A form of government based on the principle that the powers of government should be clearly limited either through a written document or through wide public understanding. It is characterized by institutional checks to ensure that government serves public rather than private interests. **10**

moderates Persons whose views fall in the middle of the political spectrum. **18**

monarchy A form of autocracy in which a king, queen, emperor, empress, tsar, or tsarina is the highest authority in the government. Monarchs usually obtain their power through inheritance. **7**

natural rights Rights that are not bestowed by governments but are inherent within every man, woman, and child by virtue of the fact that he or she is a human being. **10**

parliament The name of the national legislative body in countries governed by a parliamentary system, such as Britain and Canada. **10**

political culture The set of ideas, values, and attitudes about government and the political process held by a community or a nation. **11**

politics The process of resolving conflicts over how society should use its scarce resources and who should receive various benefits, such as public health care and public higher education. **4**

power The ability to influence the behavior of others, usually through the use of force, persuasion, or rewards. **4**

progressivism An alternative, more popular term for the set of political beliefs also known as liberalism. **17**

public services Essential services that individuals cannot provide for themselves, such as building and maintaining roads, establishing welfare programs, operating public schools, and preserving national parks. **5**

representative democracy A form of democracy in which the will of the majority is expressed through groups of individuals elected by the people to act as their representatives. **8**

republic Essentially, a representative democracy in which there is no king or queen and the people are sovereign. **8**

social conflict Disagreements among people in a society over what the society's priorities should be. **3**

social contract A voluntary agreement among individuals to create a government and to give that government adequate power to secure the mutual protection and welfare of all individuals. **10**

socialism A political ideology that lies to the left of liberalism on the traditional political spectrum. Socialists are scarce in the United States but common in many other countries. **18**

Tea Party movement A grassroots conservative movement that arose in 2009 after Barack Obama became president. The movement opposes big government and current levels of taxation, and also rejects political compromise. **18**

ANSWERS TO STUDY TOOLS QUIZ

Fill-In

1. Government (LearningOutcome 1–1)
2. it resolves conflicts, provides public services, and defends the nation and its culture against attacks by other nations (LearningOutcome 1–1)
3. autocracy (LearningOutcome 1–2)
4. representative democracy (LearningOutcome 1–2)
5. life, liberty, and property (LearningOutcome 1–3)
6. equality in voting, individual freedom, equal protection of the law, majority rule and minority rights, and voluntary consent to be governed (LearningOutcome 1–3)
7. conservatives and liberals (LearningOutcome 1–4)
8. moderates (LearningOutcome 1–4)
9. Libertarians (LearningOutcome 1–4)

Multiple Choice

10. c. (LearningOutcome 1–1)
11. b. (LearningOutcome 1–2)
12. c. (LearningOutcome 1–2)
13. b. (LearningOutcome 1–3)
14. a. (LearningOutcome 1–3)
15. a. (LearningOutcome 1–4)

2 The Constitution

KEY TERMS

Anti-Federalists A political group that opposed the adoption of the Constitution. **36**

Articles of Confederation The nation's first national constitution, which established a national form of government following the American Revolution. The Articles provided for a confederal form of government in which the central government had few powers. **29**

bicameral legislature A legislature made up of two chambers, or parts. **33**

Bill of Rights The first ten amendments to the U.S. Constitution. They list the freedoms—such as the freedoms of speech, press, and religion—that a citizen enjoys and that cannot be infringed on by the government. **24**

checks and balances A major principle of American government in which each of the three branches is given the means to check (to restrain or balance) the actions of the others. **39**

commerce clause The clause in Article I, Section 8, of the Constitution that gives Congress the power to regulate interstate commerce (commerce involving more than one state). **38**

confederation A league of independent states that are united only for the purpose of achieving common goals. **29**

Constitutional Convention The convention of delegates from the states that was held in Philadelphia in 1787 for the purpose of amending the Articles of Confederation. In fact, the delegates wrote a new constitution (the U.S. Constitution) that established a federal form of government to replace the government. **31**

faction A group of persons forming a cohesive minority. **37**

Federalists A political group, led by Alexander Hamilton and John Adams, that supported the adoption of the Constitution and the creation of a federal form of government. **35**

federal system A form of government that provides for a division of powers between a central government and several regional governments. **38**

First Continental Congress A gathering of delegates from twelve of the thirteen colonies, held in 1774 to protest the Coercive Acts. **26**

SUMMARY

Learning Outcome 2–1 Point out some of the influences on the American political tradition in the colonial years. 1 American politics owes much to the English political tradition, but the colonists derived most of their understanding about limited government and representative government from their own experiences. In 1620, the Pilgrims drew up the **Mayflower Compact,** in which they set up a government and promised to obey its laws. Other colonies, in turn, established fundamental governing rules and principles that were later expressed in the U.S. Constitution and **Bill of Rights. 2** Colonial leaders became familiar with the practical problems of governing. They learned how to build coalitions among groups with diverse interests and how to make compromises.

Learning Outcome 2–2 Explain why the American colonies rebelled against Britain. 3 After the Seven Years' War (1756–1763), the British government decided to pay its war debts and to finance the defense of its North American empire by imposing taxes on the colonists. **4** The colonists protested, and Britain responded with even more repressive measures. The colonists established the **First Continental Congress** and sent a petition to King George III to explain their grievances. The congress also called for a continued boycott of British goods and required each colony to establish an army. **5** Soon after British soldiers fought colonial citizen soldiers in the first battles of the American Revolution in 1775, delegates gathered for the **Second Continental Congress,** which assumed the powers of a central government. The congress adopted the Declaration of Independence on July 4, 1776.

Learning Outcome 2–3 Describe the structure of government established by the Articles of Confederation and some of the strengths and weaknesses of the Articles. 6 The **Articles of Confederation** established the Congress of the Confederation as the central governing body. It was a unicameral assembly in which each state had one vote. Congress had several powers, including the power to declare war, to enter into treaties, and to settle disputes among the states under certain circumstances. Nevertheless, the central government created by the Articles was weak. Congress could not force the states to meet military quotas. It could not regulate commerce between the states or with other nations. There was no national judicial system and no executive branch. **7** Disruptions such as **Shays' Rebellion** persuaded American leaders that a true national government had to be created. Congress called on the states to send delegates to a meeting in Philadelphia in 1787 that became the **Constitutional Convention.**

Learning Outcome 2–4 List some of the major compromises made by the delegates at the Constitutional Convention, and discuss the Federalist and Anti-Federalist positions on ratifying the Constitution. 8 Delegates resolved the small-state/large-state controversy over representation in Congress with the **Great Compromise,** which established a **bicameral legislature.** The **three-fifths compromise** settled a deadlock on how slaves would be counted to determine representation in the House of Representatives. The delegates also agreed that Congress could prohibit the importation of slaves beginning in 1808. The South agreed to let Congress have the power to regulate both **interstate commerce** and commerce with other nations in exchange for a ban on export taxes. **9 Federalists** favored a strong central government and the new Constitution. **Anti-Federalists** argued that the Constitution would lead to aristocratic **tyranny** or an overly powerful central government that would limit personal freedom. To gain support for ratification, the Federalists promised to add a bill of rights to the Constitution.

Learning Outcome 2–5 Summarize the Constitution's major principles of government, and describe how the Constitution can be amended. 10 The Constitution incorporated the principles of limited government, popular sovereignty, and the **rule of law.** A **federal system,** in which the national government shares powers with the state governments, was established. **Separation of powers** and a system of **checks and balances** ensure that no one branch—legislative, executive, or judicial—can exercise exclusive control. **11** An amendment to the Constitution can be proposed either by a two-thirds vote in each chamber of Congress or by a national convention called at the request of two-thirds of the state legislatures. Ratification of an amendment requires either approval by three-fourths of the state legislatures or by three-fourths of the states in special conventions.

ANSWERS TO STUDY TOOLS QUIZ

Fill-In

1. Mayflower Compact
   (LearningOutcome 2–1)
2. imposing taxes on the American colonists and exercising more direct control over colonial trade
   (LearningOutcome 2–2)
3. Sugar Act, the Stamp Act, and taxes on glass, paint, and lead
   (LearningOutcome 2–2)
4. Congress of the Confederation
   (LearningOutcome 2–3)
5. Shays' Rebellion
   (LearningOutcome 2–3)
6. House of Representatives and the Senate
   (LearningOutcome 2–4)
7. "Treason, Bribery, or other high Crimes and Misdemeanors"
   (LearningOutcome 2–4)
8. bill of rights
   (LearningOutcome 2–4)
9. separation of powers
   (LearningOutcome 2–5)
10. president's veto power, the power of judicial review, and staggered terms of office
    (LearningOutcome 2–5)

Multiple Choice

11. c. (LearningOutcome 2–1)
12. b. (LearningOutcome 2–2)
13. b. (LearningOutcome 2–3)
14. a. (LearningOutcome 2–4)
15. a. (LearningOutcome 2–5)

Great Compromise A plan for a bicameral legislature in which one chamber would be based on population and the other chamber would represent each state equally. The plan was also known as the Connecticut Compromise. **33**

interstate commerce Trade that involves more than one state. **34**

Madisonian Model The model of government devised by James Madison, in which the powers of the government are separated into three branches: legislative, executive, and judicial. **39**

Mayflower Compact A document drawn up by Pilgrim leaders in 1620 on the ship *Mayflower*. The document stated that laws were to be made for the general good of the people. **23**

rule of law A basic principle of government that requires those who govern to act in accordance with established law. **38**

Second Continental Congress The congress of the colonies that met in 1775 to assume the powers of a central government and to establish an army. **26**

separation of powers The principle of dividing governmental powers among the legislative, the executive, and the judicial branches of government. **39**

Shays' Rebellion A rebellion of angry farmers in western Massachusetts in 1786, led by former Revolutionary War captain Daniel Shays. **30**

three-fifths compromise A compromise reached during the Constitutional Convention by which three-fifths of all slaves were to be counted for purposes of representation in the House of Representatives. **34**

tyranny The arbitrary or unrestrained exercise of power by an oppressive individual or government. **37**

unicameral legislature A legislature with only one chamber. **28**

veto power A constitutional power that enables the chief executive (president or governor) to reject legislation and return it to the legislature with reasons for the rejection. This either prevents or delays the bill from becoming law. **39**

3 Federalism

KEY TERMS

block grant A federal grant given to a state for a broad area, such as criminal justice or mental-health programs. **63**

categorical grant A federal grant targeted for a specific purpose as defined by federal law. **63**

competitive federalism A model of federalism, in which state and local governments compete for businesses and citizens, who in effect "vote with their feet" by moving to jurisdictions that offer a competitive advantage. **65**

concurrent powers Powers held by both the federal and the state governments in a federal system. **53**

confederal system A league of independent sovereign states, joined together by a central government that has only limited powers over them. **48**

cooperative federalism A model of federalism in which the states and the federal government cooperate in solving problems. **58**

devolution The surrender or transfer of powers to local authorities by a central government. **60**

division of powers A basic principle of federalism established by the U.S. Constitution, by which powers are divided between the national and state governments. **51**

dual federalism A system of government in which the federal and the state governments maintain diverse but sovereign powers. **57**

expressed powers Constitutional or statutory powers that are expressly provided for by the U.S. Constitution; also called *enumerated powers*. **51**

federalism A system of shared sovereignty between two levels of government—one national and one subnational—occupying the same geographic region. **47**

federal mandate A requirement in federal legislation that forces states and municipalities to comply with certain rules. **60**

fiscal federalism The allocation of taxes collected by one level of government (typically the national government) to another level (typically state or local governments). **63**

implied powers The powers of the federal government that are implied by the expressed powers in the Constitution, particularly in Article I, Section 8. **51**

SUMMARY

LearningOutcome 3–1 Explain what federalism means, how federalism differs from other systems of government, and why it exists in the United States. 1 Government powers in a federal system are divided between a national government and subnational governments. The powers of both levels of government are specified and limited. Alternatives to **federalism** include a **unitary system,** in which subnational governments exercise only those powers given to them by the national government, and a **confederal system,** in which the national government exists and operates only at the direction of the subnational governments. 2 The Articles of Confederation failed because they did not allow for a sufficiently strong central government, but the framers of the Constitution were fearful of a too-powerful central government. The appeal of federalism was that it retained state powers and local traditions while establishing a strong national government capable of handling common problems.

LearningOutcome 3–2 Indicate how the Constitution divides governing powers in our federal system. 3 The national government possesses three types of powers: **expressed, implied,** and **inherent.** The Constitution expressly enumerates twenty-seven powers that Congress may exercise, while the **"necessary and proper" clause** is the basis for implied powers. The national government also enjoys certain inherent powers—powers that governments must have simply to ensure the nation's integrity and survival. In addition, the Constitution expressly prohibits the national government from undertaking certain actions. 4 The Tenth Amendment states that powers that are not delegated to the national government by the Constitution, or prohibited to the states, are "reserved" to the states or to the people. In principle, each state has **police powers**—the ability to regulate its internal affairs and to enact whatever laws are necessary to protect the health, safety, welfare, and morals of its people. 5 The Constitution also contains provisions, such as the full faith and credit clause, relating to interstate relations. **Concurrent powers** can be exercised by both the state governments and the federal government. The **supremacy clause** asserts that national government power takes precedence over any conflicting state action.

LearningOutcome 3–3 Summarize the evolution of federal–state relationships in the United States over time. 6 The Supreme Court, in *McCulloch v. Maryland* (1819) and *Gibbons v. Ogden* (1824), played a key role in establishing the constitutional foundations for the supremacy of the national government. An increase in the political power of the national government was also a result of the Civil War. 7 The relationship between the states and the national government has evolved through several stages since the Civil War. The model of **dual federalism,** which prevailed until the 1930s, assumes that the states and the national government are more or less equals, with each level of government having separate and distinct functions and responsibilities. The model of **cooperative federalism,** which views the national and state governments as complementary parts of a single governmental mechanism, grew out of the need to solve the pressing national problems caused by the Great Depression. The 1960s and 1970s saw an even greater expansion of the national government's role in domestic policy, but the massive social programs undertaken during this period also resulted in greater involvement by state and local governments. The model in which every level of government is involved in implementing a policy is sometimes referred to as **picket-fence federalism.**

LearningOutcome 3–4 Describe developments in federalism in recent years. 8 Starting in the 1970s, several administrations favored a shift from nation-centered federalism to state-centered federalism. One of the goals of the **"new federalism"** was to return to the states certain powers that had been exercised by the national government since the 1930s. 9 The federal government and the states seem to be in a constant tug-of-war over federal regulations, federal programs, and federal demands on the states. Decisions made about welfare reform, educational funding, and same-sex marriages have involved the politics of federalism, as have recent rulings by the Supreme Court in cases involving a state immigration law and national health-care reform.

LearningOutcome 3–5 **Explain what is meant by the term** *fiscal federalism.* **10** To help the states pay for the costs associated with implementing national policies, the national government gives back some of the tax dollars it collects to the states—in the form of **categorical** and **block grants.** The states have come to depend on grants as an important source of revenue. By giving or withholding federal grant dollars, the federal government has been able to exercise control over matters that traditionally have been under the control of state governments. **11** Sometimes state and local governments engage in **competitive federalism** by offering lower taxes or more services to attract businesses and citizens.

ANSWERS TO STUDY TOOLS QUIZ

Fill-In

1. the ability to experiment with innovative polices at the state or local level, and the opportunity for the political and cultural interests of regional groups to be reflected in the laws governing those groups (LearningOutcome 3–1)
2. necessary and proper (LearningOutcome 3–2)
3. full faith and credit (LearningOutcome 3–2)
4. implied powers and national supremacy (LearningOutcome 3–3)
5. the Great Depression (LearningOutcome 3–3)
6. picket-fence (LearningOutcome 3–3)
7. federal mandate (LearningOutcome 3–4)
8. threatening to withhold federal highway funds from states that did not comply (LearningOutcome 3–5)

Multiple Choice

9. a. (LearningOutcome 3–1)
10. c. (LearningOutcome 3–1)
11. b. (LearningOutcome 3–2)
12. c. (LearningOutcome 3–2)
13. a. (LearningOutcome 3–3)
14. c. (LearningOutcome 3–4)
15. b. (LearningOutcome 3–5)

inherent powers The powers of the national government that, although not always expressly granted by the Constitution, are necessary to ensure the nation's integrity and survival as a political unit. **51**

necessary and proper clause Article I, Section 8, Clause 18, of the Constitution, which gives Congress the power to make all laws "necessary and proper" for the federal government to carry out its responsibilities; also called the *elastic clause.* **51**

New Deal The policies ushered in by the Roosevelt administration in 1933 in an attempt to bring the United States out of the Great Depression. **58**

new federalism A plan to limit the federal government's role in regulating state governments and to give the states increased power in deciding how they should spend government revenues. **60**

picket-fence federalism A model of federalism in which specific policies and programs are administered by all levels of government —national, state, and local. **59**

police powers The powers of a government body that enable it to create laws for the protection of the health, safety, welfare, and morals of the people. In the United States, most police powers are reserved to the states. **52**

preemption A doctrine rooted in the supremacy clause of the Constitution that provides that national laws or regulations governing a certain area take precedence over conflicting state laws or regulations governing that same area. **59**

secession The act of formally withdrawing from membership in an alliance; the withdrawal of a state from the federal Union. **57**

supremacy clause Article VI, Clause 2, of the Constitution, which makes the Constitution and federal laws superior to all conflicting state and local laws. **53**

unitary system A centralized governmental system in which local or subdivisional governments exercise only those powers given to them by the central government. **48**

4 Civil Liberties

KEY TERMS

bill of attainder A legislative act that inflicts punishment on particular persons or groups without granting them the right to a trial. **70**

civil liberties Individual rights protected by the Constitution against the powers of the government. **70**

commercial speech Advertising statements that describe products. Commercial speech receives less protection under the First Amendment than ordinary speech. **80**

double jeopardy The prosecution of a person twice for the same criminal offense; prohibited by the Fifth Amendment in all but a few circumstances. **87**

due process clause The constitutional guarantee, set out in the Fifth and Fourteenth Amendments, that the government will not illegally or arbitrarily deprive a person of life, liberty, or property. **72**

due process of law The requirement that the government use fair, reasonable, and standard procedures whenever it takes any legal action against an individual; required by the Fifth and Fourteenth Amendments. **72**

establishment clause The section of the First Amendment that prohibits Congress from passing laws "respecting an establishment of religion." Issues concerning the establishment clause often center on prayer in public schools, the teaching of fundamentalist theories of creation, and government aid to parochial schools. **74**

exclusionary rule A criminal procedural rule requiring that any illegally obtained evidence not be admissible in court. **88**

ex post facto law A criminal law that punishes individuals for committing an act that was legal when the act was committed. **70**

free exercise clause The provision of the First Amendment stating that the government cannot pass laws "prohibiting the free exercise" of religion. Free exercise issues often concern religious practices that conflict with established laws. **74**

imminent lawless action test The current Supreme Court doctrine for assessing the constitutionality of subversive speech. To be illegal, speech must be "directed to inciting . . . imminent lawless action." **80**

SUMMARY

LearningOutcome 4–1 Define the term *civil liberties*, explain how civil liberties differ from civil rights, and state the constitutional basis for our civil liberties. 1 Civil liberties are legal and constitutional rights that protect citizens from government actions. Civil rights specify what the government *must* do. Civil liberties set forth what the government *cannot* do. 2 Many of our liberties were added by the Bill of Rights. The United States Supreme Court has used the **due process clause** to incorporate most of the protections guaranteed by the Bill of Rights into the liberties protected from state government actions under the Fourteenth Amendment.

LearningOutcome 4–2 List and describe the freedoms guaranteed by the First Amendment and explain how the courts have interpreted and applied these freedoms. 3 The First Amendment prohibits government from passing laws "respecting an establishment of religion, or prohibiting the free exercise thereof." Issues involving the **establishment clause** include prayer in the public schools, the teaching of evolution versus creationism or intelligent design, and government aid to parochial schools. The Supreme Court has ruled that public schools cannot sponsor religious activities and has held unconstitutional state laws forbidding the teaching of evolution in the schools. Some aid to parochial schools has been held to violate the establishment clause, while other forms of aid have been held permissible. 4 The Court has ruled consistently that the right to hold any religious belief is absolute, but the right to practice one's beliefs may have some limits. 5 Although the Supreme Court has zealously safeguarded the right to free speech under the First Amendment, at times it has imposed limits on speech in the interests of protecting other rights. These rights include security against harm to one's person or reputation, the need for public order, and the need to preserve the government. 6 The First Amendment freedom of the press generally protects the right to publish a wide range of opinions and information. Over the years, the Court has developed various guidelines and doctrines to use in deciding whether freedom of expression can be restrained.

LearningOutcome 4–3 Discuss why Americans are increasingly concerned about privacy rights. 7 The Supreme Court has held that a right to privacy is implied by other constitutional rights guaranteed in the Bill of Rights, and during recent decades, Congress has passed laws ensuring the privacy rights of individuals. The nature and scope of this right, however, are not always clear. 8 In 1973, the Court held that the right to privacy is broad enough to encompass a woman's decision to terminate a pregnancy, though the right is not absolute throughout pregnancy. Since that decision, the Court has upheld restrictive state laws requiring certain actions prior to abortions. 9 Privacy issues have also been raised in the context of physician-assisted suicide. 10 Since the terrorist attacks of 9/11, the news media and Congress have debated how the United States can strengthen national security while still protecting civil liberties, particularly the right to privacy. Some Americans argue that when we abandon any of our civil liberties, we weaken our country rather than defend it. Others believe that those who have nothing to hide should not be concerned about government surveillance and other privacy intrusions undertaken with the intention of making our nation more secure against terrorist attacks.

LearningOutcome 4–4 Summarize how the Constitution and the Bill of Rights protect the rights of accused persons. 11 Constitutional safeguards include the Fourth Amendment protection from unreasonable searches and seizures and the requirement that no warrant for a search or an arrest be issued without **probable cause;** the Fifth Amendment prohibition against **double jeopardy** and the protection against **self-incrimination;** the Sixth Amendment guarantees of a speedy trial, a trial by jury, a public trial, the right to confront witnesses, and the right to counsel at various stages in some criminal proceedings; and the Eighth Amendment prohibitions against excessive bail and fines and against cruel and unusual punishments. The Constitution also provides for the **writ of *habeas corpus***—an order requiring that an official bring a specified prisoner into court and show the judge why the prisoner is being held in jail.

ANSWERS TO STUDY TOOLS QUIZ

Fill-In

1. due process (LearningOutcome 4–1)
2. (1) be for a clearly secular purpose; (2) neither advance nor inhibit religion in its primary effect; and (3) avoid an "excessive government entanglement with religion" (LearningOutcome 4–2)
3. subversive speech (LearningOutcome 4–2)
4. Libel (LearningOutcome 4–2)
5. preferred-position (LearningOutcome 4–2)
6. "National Security Letters" (LearningOutcome 4–3)
7. *Roe v. Wade* (1973) (LearningOutcome 4–3)
8. Fourth (LearningOutcome 4–4)
9. excessive bail and fines, as well as cruel and unusual punishments (LearningOutcome 4–4)

Multiple Choice

10. b. (Learning Outcome 4–1)
11. c. (Learning Outcome 4–2)
12. a. (Learning Outcome 4–2)
13. b. (Learning Outcome 4–3)
14. a. (Learning Outcome 4–4)
15. b. (Learning Outcome 4–4)

Lemon **test** A three-part test enunciated by the Supreme Court in the 1971 case of *Lemon v. Kurtzman* to determine whether government aid to parochial schools is constitutional. To be constitutional, the aid must (1) be for a clearly secular purpose, (2) neither advance nor inhibit religion in its primary effect, and (3) avoid an "excessive government entanglement with religion." The *Lemon* test has also been used in other types of cases involving the establishment clause. **77**

libel A published report of a falsehood that tends to injure a person's reputation or character. **81**

Miranda **warnings** A series of statements informing criminal suspects, on their arrest, of their constitutional rights, such as the right to remain silent and the right to counsel; required by the Supreme Court's 1966 decision in *Miranda v. Arizona*. **88**

obscenity Indecency or offensiveness in speech, expression, behavior, or appearance. Whether specific expressions or acts constitute obscenity is normally determined by community standards. **81**

probable cause Cause for believing that there is a substantial likelihood that a person has committed or is about to commit a crime. **87**

school voucher An educational certificate, provided by the government, that allows a student to use public funds to pay for a private or a public school chosen by the student or his or her parents. **77**

seditious speech Speech that urges resistance to lawful authority or that advocates the overthrowing of a government. **79**

self-incrimination Providing damaging information or testimony against oneself in court. **87**

slander The public utterance (speaking) of a statement that holds a person up for contempt, ridicule, or hatred. **81**

symbolic speech The expression of beliefs, opinions, or ideas through forms other than verbal speech or print; speech involving actions and other nonverbal expressions. **78**

writ of *habeas corpus* An order that requires an official to bring a specified prisoner into court and explain to the judge why the person is being held in jail. **70**

5 Civil Rights

KEY TERMS

affirmative action A policy that gives special consideration, in jobs and college admissions, to members of groups that have been discriminated against in the past. **112**

busing The transportation of public school students by bus to schools physically outside their neighborhoods to eliminate school segregation based on residential patterns. **98**

civil disobedience The deliberate and public act of refusing to obey laws thought to be unjust. **98**

civil rights The rights of all Americans to equal treatment under the law, as provided by the Fourteenth Amendment to the Constitution. **94**

civil rights movement The movement in the 1950s and 1960s, by minorities and concerned whites, to end racial segregation. **98**

de facto **segregation** Racial segregation that occurs not as a result of deliberate intentions but because of social and economic conditions and residential patterns. **98**

de jure **segregation** Racial segregation that occurs because of laws or decisions by government agencies. **97**

equal protection clause Section 1 of the Fourteenth Amendment, which states that no state shall "deny to any person within its jurisdiction the equal protection of the laws." **94**

feminism A doctrine advocating full political, economic, and social equality for women. **103**

fundamental right A basic right of all Americans, such as First Amendment rights. Any law or action that prevents some group of persons from exercising a fundamental right is subject to the *strict scrutiny standard.* **94**

glass ceiling An invisible but real discriminatory barrier that prevents women and minorities from rising to top positions of power or responsibility. **104**

quota system A policy under which a specific number of jobs, promotions, or other types of placements, such as university admissions, are given to members of selected groups. **113**

rational basis test A test (also known as the *ordinary scrutiny standard*) used by the Supreme Court to decide whether a discriminatory law violates the equal

SUMMARY

LearningOutcome 5–1 Explain the constitutional basis for our civil rights and for laws prohibiting discrimination. 1 Civil rights are the rights of all Americans to equal treatment under the law. The **equal protection clause** of the Fourteenth Amendment has been interpreted by the courts to mean that states may not discriminate unreasonably against a particular group or class of individuals. The amendment also provides a legal basis for federal civil rights legislation. The U.S. Supreme Court has developed various standards for determining whether the equal protection clause has been violated.

LearningOutcome 5–2 Discuss the reasons for the civil rights movement and the changes it caused in American politics and government. 2 The equal protection clause was originally intended to protect the newly freed slaves from discrimination after the Civil War. By the late 1880s, however, southern states had begun to pass a series of segregation laws. In 1896, the Supreme Court established the **separate-but-equal doctrine,** which was used to justify segregation for nearly sixty years. **3** In 1954, the Court held that segregation by race in public education was unconstitutional. One year later, the arrest of Rosa Parks for violating local segregation laws spurred a boycott of the bus system in Montgomery, Alabama. The protest was led by the Reverend Dr. Martin Luther King, Jr. In 1956, a federal court prohibited the segregation of buses in Montgomery, marking the beginning of the **civil rights movement. 4** Civil rights protesters in the 1960s applied the tactic of nonviolent **civil disobedience** in actions throughout the South. As the civil rights movement demonstrated its strength, Congress passed a series of civil rights laws, including the Civil Rights Act of 1964, the Voting Rights Act of 1965, and the Civil Rights Act of 1968. **5** Today, the percentages of voting-age blacks and whites registered to vote are nearly equal. Political participation by African Americans has increased, as has the number of African American elected officials. African Americans continue to struggle for income and educational parity with whites.

LearningOutcome 5–3 Describe the political and economic achievements of women in this country over time and identify some obstacles to equality that women continue to face. 6 The struggle of women for equal treatment initially focused on **suffrage.** In 1920, the Nineteenth Amendment was ratified, granting voting rights to women. **Feminism** shaped a new movement that began in the 1960s. Congress and several state legislatures enacted measures to provide equal rights for women, and the courts accepted the argument that gender discrimination violates the equal protection clause. Although women remain underrepresented in politics, increasingly women have gained power as public officials. **7** In spite of federal legislation to promote equal treatment of women in the workplace, women continue to face various forms of discrimination, including a lingering bias that has been described as the **glass ceiling. 8** The prohibition of gender discrimination has been extended to prohibit **sexual harassment.**

LearningOutcome 5–4 Summarize the struggles for equality that other groups in America have experienced. 9 Latinos constitute the largest ethnic minority in the United States. Economically, Latino households are often members of this country's working poor. Immigration reform has been an important issue for many Latinos. **10** Asian Americans suffered from discriminatory treatment in the late 1800s and early 1900s, and again during World War II. Today, Asian Americans lead other minority groups in median income and median education. **11** Native Americans had no civil rights under U.S. laws until 1924. Beginning in the 1960s, some Native Americans formed organizations to strike back at the U.S. government and to reclaim their heritage, including their lands. **12** Persons with disabilities first became a political force in the 1970s. The Americans with Disabilities Act

(ADA) of 1990 is the most significant legislation protecting the rights of this group of Americans. **13** In the decades following the 1969 Stonewall Inn incident, laws and court decisions protecting the rights of gay men and lesbians have reflected changing social attitudes. Same-sex marriage is legal in several states, and recent decisions by the Supreme Court have been supportive of same-sex couples.

LearningOutcome 5–5 Explain what affirmative action is and why it has been so controversial. **14 Affirmative action** policies give special consideration, in jobs and college admissions, to members of groups that have been discriminated against in the past. Such policies have been tested in court cases involving claims of **reverse discrimination.** Some states have banned affirmative action or replaced it with alternative policies.

ANSWERS TO STUDY TOOLS QUIZ

Fill-In

1. suspect classification (LearningOutcome 5–1)
2. separate-but-equal (LearningOutcome 5–2)
3. race, color, religion, gender, and national origin (LearningOutcome 5–2)
4. full political, economic, and social equality (LearningOutcome 5–3)
5. 80 cents (LearningOutcome 5–3)
6. Latinos (LearningOutcome 5–4)
7. Japanese (LearningOutcome 5–4)
8. that gives special consideration, in jobs and college admissions, to members of groups that have been discriminated against in the past (LearningOutcome 5–5)
9. strict (LearningOutcome 5–5)

Multiple Choice

10. b. (LearningOutcome 5–1)
11. a. (LearningOutcome 5–2)
12. c. (LearningOutcome 5–2)
13. a. (LearningOutcome 5–3)
14. c. (LearningOutcome 5–4)
15. a. (LearningOutcome 5–5)

protection clause of the Constitution. It is used only when there is no classification—such as race or gender—that would require a higher level of scrutiny. **95**

reverse discrimination Discrimination against those who have no minority status. **113**

separate-but-equal doctrine A Supreme Court doctrine holding that the equal protection clause of the Fourteenth Amendment did not forbid racial segregation as long as the facilities for blacks were equal to those for whites. **96**

sexual harassment Unwanted physical contact, verbal conduct, or abuse of a sexual nature that interferes with a recipient's job performance, creates a hostile environment, or carries with it an implicit or explicit threat of adverse employment consequences. **104**

sit-in A tactic of nonviolent civil disobedience. Demonstrators enter a business, college building, or other public place and remain seated until they are forcibly removed or until their demands are met. **99**

strict scrutiny standard A standard under which a law or action must be necessary to promote a compelling state interest and must be narrowly tailored to meet that interest. **94**

suffrage The right to vote; the franchise. **101**

suspect classification A classification, such as race, that provides the basis for a discriminatory law. Any law based on a suspect classification is subject to strict scrutiny by the courts, meaning that the law must be justified by a compelling state interest. **95**

6 Interest Groups

KEY TERMS

direct technique Any method used by an interest group to interact with government officials directly to further the group's goals. **132**

free rider problem The difficulty that exists when individuals can enjoy the outcome of an interest group's efforts without having to contribute, such as by becoming members of the group. **122**

independent expenditure An expenditure for activities that are independent from (not coordinated with) those of a political candidate or a political party. **133**

indirect technique Any method used by interest groups to influence government officials through third parties, such as voters. **133**

interest group An organized group of individuals sharing common objectives who actively attempt to influence policymakers. **120**

labor force All of the people over the age of sixteen who are working or actively looking for jobs. **127**

lobbying All of the attempts by organizations or by individuals to influence the passage, defeat, or contents of legislation or to influence the administrative decisions of government. **132**

lobbyist An individual who handles a particular interest group's lobbying efforts. **132**

material incentive A reason to join an interest group—practical benefits such as discounts, subscriptions, or group insurance. **122**

pluralist theory A theory that views politics as a contest among various interest groups—at all levels of government—to gain benefits for their members. **123**

political action committee (PAC) A committee that is established by a corporation, labor union, or special interest group to raise funds and make campaign contributions on the establishing organization's behalf. **132**

public-interest group An interest group formed for the purpose of working for the "public good." Examples are the American Civil Liberties Union and Common Cause. **125**

purposive incentive A reason to join an interest group—satisfaction resulting from working for a cause in which one believes. **122**

SUMMARY

LearningOutcome 6–1 Explain what an interest group is, why interest groups form, and how interest groups function in American politics. 1 An **interest group** is an organized group of people sharing common objectives who actively attempt to influence government policymakers through direct and indirect methods. The right to form interest groups and to lobby the government is protected by the First Amendment. Interest groups may form—and existing groups may become more politically active—when the government expands its scope of activities. Interest groups also come into existence in response to a perceived threat to a group's interests, or they can form in reaction to the creation of other groups. **Purposive incentives, solidary incentives,** and **material incentives** are among the reasons people join interest groups. **2** Interest groups (a) help bridge the gap between citizens and government; (b) help raise public awareness and inspire action on various issues; (c) provide public officials with specialized information that may be useful in making policy choices; and (d) serve as another check on public officials. The **pluralist theory** of American democracy views politics as a contest among various interest groups to gain benefits for their members. **3** Although interest groups and political parties are both groups of people joined together for political purposes, they differ in several ways.

LearningOutcome 6–2 Identify the various types of interest groups. 4 The most common interest groups are those that promote private interests. **Public-interest groups** are formed with the broader goal of working for the "public good," though in reality, all lobbying groups represent special interests. **5** Business has long been well organized for effective action. Hundreds of business groups operate at all levels of government, and there are also umbrella organizations, including the U.S. Chamber of Commerce, that represent business interests. **Trade organizations** support policies that benefit specific industries. Interest groups representing labor have been some of the most influential groups in the nation's history. While the strength and political power of labor unions have waned in the last several decades, more than one-third of all public-sector workers are union members. **6** Most professions that require advanced education or specialized training have organizations to protect and promote their interests. There are many groups working for general agricultural interests at all levels of government, and producers of various specific farm commodities have formed their own organizations. Groups organized for the protection of consumer rights were very active in the 1960s and 1970s, and some are still active today. **7** Americans who share the same race, ethnicity, gender, or other characteristic often have important common interests and form identity interest groups. Some interest groups, including environmental and religious groups, are organized to promote a shared political perspective or ideology. **8** Numerous interest groups focus on a single issue. Efforts by state and local governments to lobby the federal government have escalated in recent years.

LearningOutcome 6–3 Discuss how the activities of interest groups help to shape government policymaking. 9 Interest groups operate at all levels of government and use a variety of strategies to steer policies in ways beneficial to their interests. Sometimes, they attempt to influence policymakers directly, but at other times they try to exert indirect influence on policymakers by shaping public opinion. **10 Lobbying** and providing election support are two important **direct techniques** used by interest groups. Groups also try to influence public policy through third parties or the general public. Indirect techniques include advertising, **rating systems,** issue advocacy through **independent expenditures,** mobilizing constituents, going to court, and organizing demonstrations.

LearningOutcome 6–4 Describe how interest groups are regulated by government. **11** In spite of legislation designed to reduce the "revolving door" syndrome, it remains common for those who leave positions with the federal government to become lobbyists or consultants for the interest groups they helped to regulate. **12** The Lobbying Disclosure Act of 1995 reformed a 1946 law in several ways, particularly by creating stricter definitions of who is a lobbyist. In the wake of lobbying scandals in the early 2000s, additional lobbying reform efforts were undertaken. The Honest Leadership and Open Government Act of 2007 increased lobbying disclosure and placed further restrictions on the receipt of gifts and travel by members of Congress paid for by lobbyists and the organizations they represent.

ANSWERS TO STUDY TOOLS QUIZ

Fill-In

LearningOutcome 6–1

1. First (LearningOutcome 6–1)
2. Disturbance (LearningOutcome 6–1)
3. 11.3 (LearningOutcome 6–2)
4. Right-to-work (LearningOutcome 6–2)
5. all of the attempts by organizations or by individuals to influence the passage, defeat, or contents of legislation or to influence the administrative decisions of government (LearningOutcome 6–3)
6. *amicus curiae* briefs (LearningOutcome 6–3)
7. revolving door (LearningOutcome 6–4)

Multiple Choice

8. b. (LearningOutcome 6–1)
9. c. (LearningOutcome 6–1)
10. a. (LearningOutcome 6–2)
11. c. (LearningOutcome 6–2)
12. b. (LearningOutcome 6–3)
13. a. (LearningOutcome 6–3)
14. c. (LearningOutcome 6–3)
15. c. (LearningOutcome 6–4)

rating system A system by which a particular interest group evaluates (rates) the performance of legislators based on how often the legislators have voted with the group's position on particular issues. **134**

right-to-work laws Laws that ban unions from collecting dues or other fees from workers whom they represent but who have not actually joined the union. **127**

solidary incentive A reason to join an interest group—pleasure in associating with like-minded individuals. **122**

trade organization An association formed by members of a particular industry, such as the oil industry or the trucking industry, to develop common standards and goals for the industry. Trade organizations, as interest groups, lobby government for legislation or regulations that specifically benefit their members. **126**

7 Political Parties

KEY TERMS

coalition An alliance of individuals and groups with a variety of interests and opinions who join together to support all or part of a political party's platform. **152**

dealignment Among voters, a growing detachment from both major political parties. **149**

electorate All of the citizens eligible to vote in a given election. **152**

majority party The political party that has more members in the legislature than the opposing party. **152**

minority party The political party that has fewer members in the legislature than the opposing party. **152**

national convention The meeting held by each major party every four years to nominate presidential and vice-presidential candidates, write a party platform, and conduct other party business. **155**

national party chairperson An individual who serves as a political party's administrative head at the national level and directs the work of the party's national committee. **156**

national party committee The political party leaders who direct party business during the four years between the national party conventions, organize the next national convention, and plan how to obtain a party victory in the next presidential election. **156**

party activist A party member who helps to organize and oversee party functions and planning during and between campaigns, and may even become a candidate for office. **153**

party identifier A person who identifies himself or herself as being a supporter of a particular political party. **153**

party platform The document drawn up by each party at its national convention that outlines the policies and positions of the party. **155**

party ticket A list of a political party's candidates for various offices. In national elections, the party ticket consists of the presidential and vice-presidential candidates. **155**

patronage A system of rewarding the party faithful and workers with government jobs or contracts. **153**

political party A group of individuals who organize to win elections, operate the government, and determine policy. **143**

SUMMARY

LearningOutcome 7–1 Summarize the origins and development of the two-party system in the United States. 1 After the Constitution was ratified, the Federalist Party supported a strong central government that would encourage the development of commerce and manufacturing. Their opponents, the Jeffersonian Republicans, favored a more limited role for government. After suffering electoral defeats in the early 1800s, the Federalists went out of existence, resulting in a **realignment** of the party system. In the mid-1820s, the Republicans split into two groups—the Democrats and the National Republicans (later the Whig Party). As the Democrats and Whigs competed for the presidency during the 1840s and 1850s, the **two-party system** as we know it today emerged. **2** By the mid-1850s, most northern Whigs were absorbed into the new Republican Party, which opposed the extension of slavery. After the Civil War, the Republicans and Democrats were roughly even in strength, although the Republicans were more successful in presidential contests. After the realigning election of 1896, many Americans viewed the Republicans as the party that knew how to manage the nation's economy, and they remained dominant in national politics until the Great Depression. **3** The election of 1932 brought Franklin D. Roosevelt to the presidency and the Democrats back to power at the national level. In the 1960s, however, conservative Democrats did not like the direction in which their party seemed to be taking them, and over time most of them became Republican voters. The result of this "rolling realignment" was that by 2000, the two major parties were fairly evenly matched.

LearningOutcome 7–2 Describe the current status of the two major parties. 4 A key characteristic of recent politics has been the extreme partisanship of party activists and members of Congress. The rolling realignment after the elections of 1968 resulted in parties that were much more homogeneous. By 2009, the most conservative Democrat in the House was to the left of the most moderate Republican. **5** Ideological uniformity has made it easier for the parties to maintain discipline in Congress. Political polarization grew even more severe after the 2010 elections. Many of the new Republican members of Congress were pledged to the Tea Party philosophy of no-compromise conservatism. Also significant is the number of independent voters, contributing to a potential **dealignment** in the party system.

LearningOutcome 7–3 Explain how political parties function in our democratic system. 6 Political parties link the people's policy preferences to actual government policies. They select candidates for political office, and help educate the public about important political issues. Parties coordinate policy among the various branches and levels of government and balance the competing interests of those who support the party. Parties coordinate campaigns and take care of a large number of tasks that are essential to the smooth functioning of the electoral process. In government, the minority party checks the actions of the party in power.

LearningOutcome 7–4 Discuss the structure of American political parties. 7 The party in the **electorate** consists of **party identifiers** and **party activists.** Each party is decentralized, with national, state, and local organizations. Delegates to the **national convention** nominate the party's presidential and vice-presidential candidates, and they adopt the **party platform.** The national party organization includes a **national party committee,** a **national party chairperson,** and congressional campaign committees. The party in government consists of all of the party's candidates who have won elections and now hold public office. The party in government helps to organize the government's agenda by convincing its own party members in office to vote for its policies.

LearningOutcome 7–5 Describe the different types of third parties and how they function in the American political system. 8 The United States has a two-party system in which the Democrats and the Republicans dominate national politics. American election laws and the rules governing campaign financing tend to favor the major parties. There are also institutional barriers that prevent third parties from enjoying electoral success. Because third parties normally do not win elections, Americans tend not to vote for them. **9** There are different kinds of third parties. An issue-oriented party is formed to promote a particular cause or timely issue. An ideological party supports a particular political doctrine or a set of beliefs. A splinter party develops out of a split within a major party, which may be part of an attempt to elect a specific person. **10** Third parties have brought many issues to the public's attention and can influence election outcomes. Third parties also provide a voice for voters who are frustrated with the Republican and Democratic parties.

ANSWERS TO STUDY TOOLS QUIZ

Fill-In

1. Federalists and the Jeffersonian Republicans (LearningOutcome 7–1)
2. Republican (LearningOutcome 7–1)
3. a growing detachment from both major political parties (LearningOutcome 7–2)
4. selecting candidates, informing the public, coordinating policymaking, checking the power of the governing party, balancing competing interests, and running campaigns, linking the people's policy preferences to actual government policies (LearningOutcome 7–3)
5. primary (LearningOutcome 7–3)
6. national convention (LearningOutcome 7–4)
7. the document drawn up by each party at its national convention that outlines the policies and positions of the party (LearningOutcome 7–4)
8. bringing issues to the public's attention, affecting the vote, and providing a voice for voters who are frustrated with the Republican and Democratic parties (LearningOutcome 7–5)

Multiple Choice

9. a. (LearningOutcome 7–1)
10. b. (LearningOutcome 7–1)
11. b. (LearningOutcome 7–2)
12. c. (LearningOutcome 7–2)
13. b. (LearningOutcome 7–3)
14. c. (LearningOutcome 7–4)
15. b. (LearningOutcome 7–5)

precinct A political district within a city, such as a block or a neighborhood, or a rural portion of a county; the smallest voting district at the local level. **154**

primary A preliminary election held for the purpose of choosing a party's final candidate. **151**

realignment A process in which the popular support for and relative strength of the parties shift and the parties are reestablished with different coalitions of supporters. **144**

solidarity Mutual agreement among the members of a particular group. **153**

third party In the United States, any party other than one of the two major parties (Republican and Democratic). **156**

two-party system A political system in which two strong and established parties compete for political offices. **156**

ward A local unit of a political party's organization, consisting of a division or district within a city. **154**

8 Public Opinion and Voting

KEY TERMS

agents of political socialization People and institutions that influence the political views of others. **171**

biased sample A poll sample that does not accurately represent the population. **165**

gender gap The difference between the percentage of votes cast for a particular candidate by women and the percentage of votes cast for the same candidate by men. **176**

grandfather clause A clause in a state law that had the effect of restricting voting rights to those whose ancestors had voted before the 1860s. It was one of the techniques used in the South to prevent African Americans from exercising their right to vote. **180**

literacy test A test given to voters to ensure that they could read and write and thus evaluate political information. This technique was used in many southern states to restrict African American participation in elections. **180**

media Newspapers, magazines, television, radio, the Internet, and any other printed or electronic means of communication. **172**

peer group Associates, often close in age to one another; may include friends, classmates, co-workers, club members, or religious group members. **173**

political socialization The learning process through which most people acquire their political attitudes, opinions, beliefs, and knowledge. **171**

poll tax A fee of several dollars that had to be paid before a person could vote. This device was used in some southern states to discourage African Americans and low-income whites from voting. **180**

public opinion The views of the citizenry about politics, public issues, and public policies; a complex collection of opinions held by many people on issues in the public arena. **165**

public opinion poll A survey of the public's opinion on a particular topic at a particular moment. **165**

push poll A campaign tactic used to feed false or misleading information to potential voters, under the guise of taking an opinion poll, with the intent to "push" voters away from one candidate and toward another. **169**

SUMMARY

Learning Outcome 8–1 Explain how public opinion polls are conducted, problems with polls, and how they are used in the political process. 1 A **public opinion poll** is a survey of the public's opinion on a particular topic at a particular moment, as measured through the use of **samples. 2** Early polling efforts often relied on **straw polls.** The opinions expressed in straw polls, however, usually represent an atypical subgroup of the population, or a **biased sample.** Over time, more scientific polling techniques were developed. Today, polling is used extensively by political candidates and policymakers. Polls can be quite accurate when conducted properly. In-person surveys have been replaced by telephone interviews, often with prerecorded messages that solicit responses. Some pollsters specialize in Internet surveys. **3** To achieve the most accurate results possible, pollsters use **random samples,** in which each person within the entire population being polled has an equal chance of being chosen. If the sample is properly selected, the opinions of those in the sample will be representative of the opinions held by the population as a whole, though responses of various groups are sometimes weighted in an effort to achieve representativeness. Public opinion polls are fundamentally statistical. The true result of a poll is not a single figure, but a range of probabilities. Any poll contains a sampling error. **4** Problems with polls can stem from the way questions are worded, and polls often reduce complex issues to questions that simply call for "yes" or "no" answers. Moreover, polls of voter preferences cannot reflect rapid shifts in public opinion unless they are taken frequently. **5** Many journalists base their political coverage during campaigns almost exclusively on poll findings, and media companies often report only the polls conducted by their affiliated pollsters. Exit polls are used by news organizations to give an early indication of the outcome of elections. A tactic used in some political campaigns is a **push poll,** which asks "fake" polling questions that are designed to "push" voters toward one candidate or another.

Learning Outcome 8–2 Describe the political socialization process. 6 Most people acquire their political attitudes, opinions, beliefs, and knowledge through a complex learning process called **political socialization.** Most political socialization is informal. The strong early influence of the family later gives way to the multiple influences of schools, churches, the **media,** opinion leaders, major life events, **peer groups,** and economic status and occupation. People and institutions that influence the political views of others are called **agents of political socialization.**

Learning Outcome 8–3 Discuss the different factors that affect voter choices. 7 For established voters, party identification is one of the most important and lasting predictors of how a person will vote. Voters' choices often depend on the perceived character of the candidates rather than on their qualifications or policy positions. When people vote for candidates who share their positions on particular issues, they are engaging in policy voting. Historically, economic issues have had the strongest influence on voters' choices. **8** Socioeconomic factors, including educational attainment, occupation and income, age, gender, religion, ethnic background, and geographic region, also influence how people vote. Ideology is another indicator of voting behavior.

Learning Outcome 8–4 Indicate some of the factors that affect voter turnout, and discuss what has been done to improve voter turnout and voting procedures. 9 The Fifteenth Amendment to the Constitution (1870) guaranteed suffrage to African American males. Yet, for many decades, African Americans were effectively denied the ability to exercise their voting rights. Today, devices used to restrict voting rights, such as the **poll tax, literacy tests,** the **grandfather clause,** and **white primaries,** are explicitly prohibited by constitutional amendments, by the Voting

Rights Act of 1965, or by court decisions. The Nineteenth Amendment (1920) gave women the right to vote, and the Twenty-sixth Amendment (1971) reduced the minimum voting age to eighteen. **10** Some restrictions on voting rights, such as registration, residency, and citizenship requirements, still exist. Most states also do not permit prison inmates or felons to vote. Attempts to improve voter turnout and voting procedures include simplifying the voter-registration process, conducting voting by mail, updating voting equipment, and allowing early voting. In recent years, a number of states have passed laws that may have the effect of making it harder to vote, not easier. Voter turnout is affected by several factors, including educational attainment, income level, age, and minority status.

ANSWERS TO STUDY TOOLS QUIZ

Fill-In

1. each person within the entire population being polled has an equal chance of being chosen (LearningOutcome 8–1)
2. house effect (LearningOutcome 8–1)
3. push poll (LearningOutcome 8–1)
4. family, schools, churches, the media, opinion leaders, and peer groups (LearningOutcome 8–2)
5. party identification (LearningOutcome 8–3)
6. policy voting (LearningOutcome 8–3)
7. educational attainment, occupation and income, age, gender, religion and ethnic background, and geographic region (LearningOutcome 8–3)
8. literacy tests, poll taxes, the grandfather clause, and white primaries (LearningOutcome 8–4)

Multiple Choice

9. a. (LearningOutcome 8–1)
10. c. (LearningOutcome 8–2)
11. b. (LearningOutcome 8–2)
12. c. (LearningOutcome 8–3)
13. a. (LearningOutcome 8–3)
14. b. (LearningOutcome 8–4)
15. a. (LearningOutcome 8–4)

random sample In the context of opinion polling, a sample in which each person within the entire population being polled has an equal chance of being chosen. **166**

sample In the context of opinion polling, a group of people selected to represent the population being studied. **165**

sampling error In the context of opinion polling, the difference between what the sample results show and what the true results would have been had everybody in the relevant population been interviewed. **167**

Solid South A term used to describe the tendency of the southern states to vote Democratic after the Civil War. **177**

straw poll A nonscientific poll in which there is no way to ensure that the opinions expressed are representative of the larger population. **165**

vote-eligible population The number of people who are actually eligible to vote in an American election. **184**

voting-age population The number of people residing in the United States who are at least eighteen years old. **184**

white primary A primary election in which African Americans were prohibited from voting. The practice was banned by the Supreme Court in 1944. **180**

9 Campaigns and Elections

KEY TERMS

Australian ballot A secret ballot that is prepared, distributed, and counted by government officials at public expense; used by all states in the United States since 1888. **189**

campaign strategy The comprehensive plan developed by a candidate and his or her advisers for winning an election. **199**

caucus A meeting held to choose political candidates or delegates. **193**

closed primary A primary in which only party members can vote to choose that party's candidates. **195**

Credentials Committee A committee of each national political party that evaluates the claims of national party convention delegates to be the legitimate representatives of their states. **198**

delegate A person selected to represent the people of one geographic area at a party convention. **198**

direct primary An election held within each of the two major parties—Democratic and Republican—to choose the party's candidates for the general election. Voters choose the candidate directly, rather than through delegates. **194**

elector A member of the electoral college. **189**

electoral college The group of electors who are selected by the voters in each state to elect officially the president and vice president. The number of electors in each state is equal to the number of that state's representatives in both chambers of Congress. **189**

general election A regularly scheduled election to choose the U.S. president, vice president, and senators and representatives in Congress. General elections are held in even-numbered years on the Tuesday after the first Monday in November. **189**

independent expenditure An expenditure for activities that are independent from (not coordinated with) those of a political candidate or a political party. **214**

nominating convention An official meeting of a political party to choose its candidates. Nominating conventions at the state and local levels also select delegates to represent the citizens of their geographic areas at a higher-level party convention. **193**

SUMMARY

LearningOutcome 9–1 Explain how elections are held and how the electoral college functions in presidential elections. 1 During **general elections**, regularly scheduled elections held in even-numbered years in November, voters decide who will be the U.S. president, vice president, and members of Congress. 2 An election board supervises the voting process in each precinct. **Poll watchers** from each of the two major parties typically monitor the polling place as well. 3 Citizens do not vote directly for the president and vice president. Instead, they vote for **electors** who will cast their ballots in the **electoral college**. Each state has as many electoral votes as it has U.S. senators and representatives. There are also three electors from the District of Columbia. 4 The electoral college system is primarily a **winner-take-all system** because, in nearly all states, the candidate who receives the most popular votes in the state is credited with all that state's electoral votes. To be elected through this system, a candidate must receive at least 270 electoral votes, a majority of the 538 electoral votes available.

LearningOutcome 9–2 Discuss how candidates are nominated. 5 The methods used by political parties to nominate candidates have changed over time, and have included **caucuses** and **nominating conventions**. Today, candidates who win **primary elections** go on to compete against the candidates from other parties in the general election. In a **direct primary**, which can be either **closed** or **open**, voters cast their ballots directly for candidates. The elections that nominate candidates for Congress and for state or local offices are almost always direct primaries. 6 Most of the states hold presidential primaries, which are indirect primaries used to choose **delegates** to the national nominating conventions. In some states, delegates are chosen through a caucus/convention system. Each political party holds a national convention where delegates adopt the party platform and nominate the party's presidential and vice-presidential candidates.

LearningOutcome 9–3 Indicate what is involved in launching a political campaign today, and describe the structure and functions of a campaign organization. 7 To run a successful campaign, a candidate's campaign staff must be able to raise funds, get media coverage, produce and pay for political ads, schedule the candidate's time effectively with constituent groups and potential supporters, convey the candidate's position on the issues, conduct **opposition research**, and persuade the voters to go to the polls. Political party organizations are no longer as important as they once were in providing campaign services. Candidates now turn to political consultants who specialize in a particular area of the campaign such as conducting polls or developing the candidate's advertising. Most candidates have a campaign manager who coordinates and plans the **campaign strategy**.

LearningOutcome 9–4 Describe how the Internet has transformed political campaigns. 8 Today, the ability to make effective use of social media and the Internet is essential to a candidate. In 2008, Barack Obama gained an edge on his rivals in part because of his superior use of new technologies, and his 2012 campaign was even more sophisticated. Obama took Internet fund-raising to a new level. 9 Microtargeting, a technique that involves collecting as much information as possible about voters in a database and then filtering out various groups for special attention, was pioneered by the George W. Bush campaign in 2004. In 2012, Obama's microtargeting operation vastly outperformed Mitt Romney's. 10 Obama also took Web-based organizing to a new level. By 2012, the Obama campaign was able to create active local support groups in towns and counties across the country.

LearningOutcome 9–5 Summarize the current laws that regulate campaign financing and the role of money in modern political campaigns. **11** The modern campaign is an expensive undertaking. Campaign-financing laws enacted in the 1970s provided public funding for presidential primaries and general elections, required candidates to file periodic reports with the Federal Election Commission, and limited individual and group contributions to candidates. Beginning in 2004, leading Democratic and Republican presidential candidates were refusing public funding for the primaries. By 2012, the public financing of presidential campaigns was effectively over. **12** The Bipartisan Campaign Reform Act of 2002 addressed the issues of **soft money** and **independent expenditures** to a certain extent. Several court decisions, however, have altered the rules of campaign financing, especially with respect to independent expenditures. The most notable consequence of these rulings has been the rise of super PACs and the huge amounts of money poured into them by wealthy individuals. **13** Total presidential campaign spending, including spending by candidates who lost in the primaries, as well as spending by outside groups, reached $4.5 billion in the 2011–2012 election cycle.

ANSWERS TO STUDY TOOLS QUIZ

Fill-In

1. who receives the largest popular vote in a state is credited with all that state's electoral votes (LearningOutcome 9–1)
2. 270 (LearningOutcome 9–1)
3. direct (LearningOutcome 9–2)
4. the states moving their primaries to earlier in the year in an effort to make their primaries more prominent in the media and influential in the political process (LearningOutcome 9–2)
5. opposition (LearningOutcome 9–3)
6. collecting as much information as possible about voters in a database and then filtering out various groups for special attention (LearningOutcome 9–4)
7. federal income tax returns (LearningOutcome 9–5)
8. super PACs (LearningOutcome 9–5)

Multiple Choice

9. a. (LearningOutcome 9–1)
10. b. (LearningOutcome 9–1)
11. a. (LearningOutcome 9–2)
12. b. (LearningOutcome 9–2)
13. c. (LearningOutcome 9–3)
14. c. (LearningOutcome 9–4)
15. b. (LearningOutcome 9–5)

10 Politics and the Media

KEY TERMS

agenda setting The media's ability to determine which issues are considered to be important by the public and by politicians. **217**

citizen journalism The collection, analysis, and dissemination of information online by independent journalists, scholars, politicians, and the general citizenry. **229**

electronic media Communication channels that involve electronic transmissions, such as radio, television, and the Internet. **214**

framing An agenda-setting technique that establishes the context of a media report. Framing can mean fitting events into a familiar story or filtering information through preconceived ideas. **217**

issue ad A political advertisement that focuses on a particular issue. Issue ads can be used to support or attack a candidate's position or credibility. **220**

managed news coverage News coverage that is manipulated (managed) by a campaign manager or political consultant to gain media exposure for a political candidate. **222**

mass media Communication channels, such as newspapers and radio and television broadcasts, through which people can communicate to large audiences. **214**

negative political advertising Political advertising undertaken for the purpose of discrediting an opposing candidate in voters' eyes. Attack ads are one form of negative political advertising. **220**

personal attack ad A negative political advertisement that attacks the character of an opposing candidate. **220**

podcasting The distribution of audio or video files to personal computers or mobile devices such as smartphones. **229**

political advertising Advertising undertaken by or on behalf of a political candidate to familiarize voters with the candidate and his or her views on campaign issues; advertising for or against policy issues. **219**

priming An agenda-setting technique in which a media outlet promotes specific facts or ideas that may affect the public's thinking on related topics. **217**

print media Communication channels that consist of printed materials, such as newspapers and magazines. **214**

SUMMARY

LearningOutcome 10–1 Explain the role of the media in a democracy. **1** What the media say and do has an impact on what Americans think about political issues, but the media also reflect what Americans think about politics. While the new media based on the Internet are becoming increasingly important, the traditional media—radio, television, and print—remain important to American politics and government. **2** By helping to determine what people will talk and think about, the media play a role in setting the political agenda. Of all the media, television still has the greatest impact on most Americans, but the medium of television imposes constraints on how political issues are presented.

LearningOutcome 10–2 Summarize how television influences the conduct of political campaigns. **3** Candidates for political office spend a great deal of time and money obtaining a TV presence through political ads, debates, and general news coverage. Televised **political advertising** consumes at least half of the total budget for a major political campaign. **Personal attack ads** and **issue ads** frequently appear on TV. Televised debates are a routine feature of presidential campaigns. They provide an opportunity for voters to find out how candidates differ on issues and allow candidates to capitalize on the power of television to improve their images or point out the failings of their opponents. **4** Candidates' campaigns have become increasingly sophisticated in **managing news coverage,** while press advisers try to convince reporters to give a story or event a **spin** that is favorable to the candidate.

LearningOutcome 10–3 Explain why talk radio has been described as the Wild West of the media. **5** Talk-show hosts do not attempt to hide their political biases; if anything, they exaggerate them for effect. Sometimes, hosts appear to care more about the entertainment value of their statements than whether they are, strictly speaking, true. No journalistic conventions are observed. **6** Those who think that talk radio is good for the country argue that talk shows, taken together, provide a great populist forum. Others fear that talk shows empower fringe groups, perhaps magnifying their rage.

LearningOutcome 10–4 Describe types of media bias and explain how such bias affects the political process. **7** Relatively few Americans believe that the news media are unbiased in their reporting, and there has been a notable decline in the public's confidence in news media in recent years. Nevertheless, the public does believe that the press is successful in fulfilling its role as a watchdog. While the majority of Americans think that the media reflect a bias in either a liberal or conservative direction, it is a media bias against losers that may play a significant role in shaping presidential campaigns and elections. The media use the winner-loser framework to describe events throughout the campaigns. **8** The expansion of the media universe to include cable channels and the Internet has increased the competition among news sources. News directors select programming they believe will attract the largest audiences and garner the highest advertising revenues. Many journalists believe that economic pressure is making significant inroads on independent editorial decision making. News organizations are redefining their purpose and looking for special niches in which to build their audiences.

LearningOutcome 10–5 Indicate the extent to which the Internet is reshaping news and political campaigns. **9** The Internet is a major source of information. Almost every major news organization, both print and broadcast, delivers news online. In addition, there has been a veritable explosion of **citizen journalism** in recent years. Blogs are offered by independent journalists, scholars, political activists, and the citizenry at large. **Podcasting** is another nontraditional form of news distribution. **10** The Internet is an inexpensive way for candidates to contact, recruit, and mobilize supporters, as well as disseminate information about their positions on issues. Candidates hire Web managers to create well-designed Web sites to attract viewers, manage their e-mails, and track their credit-card contributions. The Web manager also hires bloggers to promote the candidate's views, arranges for podcasting of campaign information, and hires staff to monitor the Web for news about the candidates and to track the online publications of netroots groups. **11** Citizen videos have also changed the traditional campaign. A candidate can never know when a comment that he or she makes may be caught on camera by someone with a cell phone or digital camera and published on the Internet for all to see.

sound bite A televised comment, lasting for only a few seconds, that captures a thought or a perspective and has an immediate impact on viewers. **218**

spin A reporter's slant on, or interpretation of, a particular event or action. **222**

spin doctor A political candidate's press adviser who tries to convince reporters to give a story or event concerning the candidate a particular "spin" (interpretation, or slant). **222**

ANSWERS TO STUDY TOOLS QUIZ

Fill-In

1. Priming (LearningOutcome 10–1)
2. television (LearningOutcome 10–1)
3. televised comment, lasting for only a few seconds, that captures a thought or a perspective and has an immediate impact on the viewers (LearningOutcome 10–1)
4. they have lost a major share of their advertising revenue to online sites. (LearningOutcome 10–1)
5. John F. Kennedy and Richard Nixon (LearningOutcome 10–2)
6. political candidates' press advisers, who try to convince reporters to give a story or event concerning a candidate a particular interpretation or slant (LearningOutcome 10–2)
7. male, middle-aged, and conservative (LearningOutcome 10–3)
8. talk-show hosts often exaggerate their political biases for effect. Hosts sometimes appear to care more about the entertainment value of their statements than whether they are, strictly speaking, true. No journalistic conventions are observed (LearningOutcome 10–3)
9. losers (LearningOutcome 10–4)
10. the collection, analysis, and dissemination of information online by independent journalists, scholars, political activists, and the general citizenry (LearningOutcome 10–5)

Multiple Choice

11. a. (LearningOutcome 10–1)
12. c. (LearningOutcome 10–2)
13. c. (LearningOutcome 10–3)
14. c. (LearningOutcome 10–4)
15. b. (LearningOutcome 10–5)

11 The Congress

KEY TERMS

apportionment The distribution of House seats among the states on the basis of their respective populations. **235**

appropriation A part of the congressional budgeting process—the determination of how many dollars will be spent in a given year on a particular government activity. **253**

authorization A part of the congressional budgeting process—the creation of the legal basis for government programs. **253**

cloture A procedure for ending filibusters in the Senate and bringing the matter under consideration to a vote. **247**

conference committee A temporary committee that is formed when the two chambers of Congress pass differing versions of the same bill. The conference committee consists of members from the House and the Senate who work out a compromise bill. **250**

conference report A report submitted by a conference committee after it has drafted a single version of a bill. **250**

congressional district The geographic area that is served by one member in the House of Representatives. **235**

continuing resolution A temporary resolution passed by Congress that enables executive agencies to continue work with the same funding that they had in the previous fiscal year. **253**

entitlement program A government program (such as Social Security) that allows, or entitles, a certain class of people (such as elderly persons) to receive special benefits. Entitlement programs operate under open-ended budget authorizations that, in effect, place no limits on how much can be spent. **253**

filibustering The Senate tradition of unlimited debate undertaken for the purpose of preventing action on a bill. **247**

first budget resolution A budget resolution, which is supposed to be passed in May, that sets overall revenue goals and spending targets for the next fiscal year, beginning on October 1. **253**

fiscal year A twelve-month period that is established for bookkeeping or accounting purposes. The government's fiscal year runs from October 1 through September 30. **253**

gerrymandering The drawing of a legislative district's boundaries in such a way as to maximize the influence of a certain group or political party. **237**

SUMMARY

LearningOutcome 11–1 Explain how seats in the House of Representatives are apportioned among the states. **1** The Constitution provides for the **apportionment** of House seats among the states on the basis of their respective populations, though each state is guaranteed at least one seat. Every ten years, the 435 House seats are reapportioned based on the outcome of the census. **2** Each representative to the House is elected by voters in a **congressional district.** Within each state, districts must contain, as nearly as possible, equal numbers of people. This principle is known as the **"one person, one vote"** rule. Gerrymandering occurs when a district's boundaries are drawn to maximize the influence of a certain group or political party.

LearningOutcome 11–2 Describe the power of incumbency. **3** If legislators choose to run for reelection, they enjoy several advantages over their opponents, including name recognition, access to the media, congressional franking privileges, and lawmaking power. Members of Congress also have administrative staffs in Washington, D.C., and in their home districts. A key advantage is their fund-raising ability. Most incumbent members of Congress have a much larger network of contacts, donors, and lobbyists than their challengers have. While incumbents who run are usually reelected, there are occasional periods of some turbulence when fewer incumbents than usual win.

LearningOutcome 11–3 Identify the key leadership positions in Congress, describe the committee system, and indicate some important differences between the House of Representatives and the Senate. **4** The Constitution provides for the presiding officers of both the House and the Senate, and each chamber has added other leadership positions. The majority party in each chamber chooses the major officers of that chamber, selects committee chairpersons, and has a majority on all committees. **5** Chief among the leaders in the House of Representatives is the **Speaker of the House,** who has a great deal of power. Other leaders include the **majority and minority leaders,** and the **whips.** The vice president of the United States is the president of the Senate, and senators elect the president pro tempore ("pro tem"). The real power in the Senate is held by the majority and minority leaders, and their whips. **6** The committee system is a way to provide for specialization, or a division of legislative labor. Most of the work of legislating is performed by the **standing committees** and their **subcommittees** in the House and the Senate. Conference committees are formed for the purpose of achieving agreement between the House and Senate on the wording of legislative acts. **7** With its larger size, the House needs more rules and more formality than the Senate. The House **Rules Committee** proposes time limits on debate for most bills. The Senate normally permits extended debate. The use of unlimited debate to obstruct legislation is called **filibustering,** which may be ended by invoking **cloture.** There are other important differences between the House and the Senate as well.

LearningOutcome 11–4 Summarize the specific steps in the lawmaking process. **8** After a bill is introduced, it is sent to a standing committee. A committee chairperson will typically send the bill on to a subcommittee, where public hearings may be held. After a **markup session,** the bill goes to the full committee for further action. **9** After a bill is reported to the chamber, it is scheduled for floor debate. If, after votes are taken on the legislation, the House and Senate have passed differing versions of the same bill, a **conference committee** is formed to produce a compromise bill. A **conference report** is submitted to each chamber. If the bill is approved by both chambers, it is ready for action by the president.

LearningOutcome 11–5 Identify Congress's oversight functions and explain how Congress fulfills them. 10 Congress oversees the departments and agencies of the executive branch, and can rein in the power of the bureaucracy by refusing to fund government programs. Congress has the authority to investigate the actions of the executive branch, the need for certain legislation, and even the actions of its own members. It has the power to impeach federal officials and remove them from office. The Senate either confirms or fails to confirm the president's nominees for federal judgeships and top executive branch officers.

LearningOutcome 11–6 Indicate what is involved in the congressional budgeting process. 11 The budgeting process, which involves **authorization** and **appropriation,** begins when the president submits a proposed federal budget for the next **fiscal year.** In the **first budget resolution,** Congress sets overall revenue goals and spending targets. The **second budget resolution** sets "binding" limits on taxes and spending. When Congress is unable to pass a complete budget by October 1, it usually passes **continuing resolutions,** which enable executive agencies to keep on doing whatever they were doing the previous year with the same amount of funding.

ANSWERS TO STUDY TOOLS QUIZ

Fill-In

1. ten (LearningOutcome 11–1)
2. serve the broad interests of the entire society and act according to his or her perception of national needs (LearningOutcome 11–1)
3. fund-raising ability, franking privileges, professional staffs, lawmaking power, access to the media, and name recognition (LearningOutcome 11–2)
4. preside over sessions of the House, vote in the event of a tie, put questions to a vote, participate in making important committee assignments, and schedule bills for action (LearningOutcome 11–3)
5. cloture (LearningOutcome 11–3)
6. a meeting held by a congressional committee or subcommittee to approve, amend, or redraft a bill (LearningOutcome 11–4)
7. Rules (LearningOutcome 11–4)
8. the federal judiciary and to the cabinet (LearningOutcome 11–5)
9. authorization and appropriation (LearningOutcome 11–6)

Multiple Choice

10. c. (LearningOutcome 11–1)
11. a. (LearningOutcome 11–2)
12. b. (LearningOutcome 11–3)
13. b. (LearningOutcome 11–4)
14. c. (LearningOutcome 11–5)
15. a. (LearningOutcome 11–6)

instructed delegate A representative who deliberately mirrors the views of the majority of his or her constituents. **239**

majority leader The party leader elected by the majority party in the House or in the Senate. **243**

malapportionment A condition in which the voting power of citizens in one district is greater than the voting power of citizens in another district. **236**

markup session A meeting held by a congressional committee or subcommittee to approve, amend, or redraft a bill. **249**

minority leader The party leader elected by the minority party in the House or in the Senate. **244**

minority-majority district A district in which minority groups make up a majority of the population. **238**

"one person, one vote" rule A rule, or principle, requiring that congressional districts have equal populations so that one person's vote counts as much as another's vote. **237**

pocket veto A special type of veto power used by the chief executive after the legislature has adjourned. Bills that are not signed die after a specified period of time. **250**

Rules Committee A standing committee in the House of Representatives that provides special rules governing how particular bills will be considered and debated by the House. The Rules Committee normally proposes time limits on debate for any bill. **246**

second budget resolution A budget resolution, which is supposed to be passed in September, that sets "binding" limits on taxes and spending for the next fiscal year. **253**

Speaker of the House The presiding officer in the House of Representatives. The Speaker is a member of the majority party and is the most powerful member of the House. **243**

standing committee A permanent committee in Congress that deals with legislation concerning a particular area, such as agriculture or foreign relations. **245**

subcommittee A division of a larger committee that deals with a particular part of the committee's policy area. Most standing committees have several subcommittees. **245**

trustee A representative who tries to serve the broad interests of the entire society and not just the narrow interests of his or her constituents. **239**

whip A member of Congress who assists the majority or minority leader in the House or in the Senate in managing the party's legislative program. **244**

KEY TERMS

cabinet An advisory group selected by the president to assist with decision making. Traditionally, the cabinet has consisted of the heads of the executive departments and other officers whom the president may choose to appoint. **276**

chief diplomat The role of the president of the United States in recognizing and interacting with foreign governments. **263**

chief executive The head of the executive branch of government; in the United States, the president. **261**

chief of staff The person who directs the operations of the White House Office and advises the president on important matters. **278**

commander in chief The supreme commander of a nation's military force. **263**

diplomat A person who represents one country in dealing with representatives of another country. **263**

executive agreement A binding international agreement, or pact, that is made between the president and another head of state and that does not require Senate approval. **272**

Executive Office of the President (EOP) A group of staff agencies that assist the president in carrying out major duties. **277**

executive order A presidential order to carry out a policy or policies described in a law passed by Congress. **270**

executive privilege An inherent executive power claimed by presidents to withhold information from, or to refuse to appear before, Congress or the courts. The president can also accord the privilege to other executive officials. **275**

head of state The person who serves as the ceremonial head of a country's government and represents that country to the rest of the world. **263**

kitchen cabinet The name given to a president's unofficial advisers. The term was coined during Andrew Jackson's presidency. **277**

National Security Council (NSC) A council that advises the president on domestic and foreign matters concerning the safety and defense of the nation. **279**

Office of Management and Budget (OMB) An agency in the Executive Office of the President that has the primary duty of assisting the president in preparing and supervising the administration of the federal budget. **279**

SUMMARY

LearningOutcome 12–1 List the constitutional requirements for becoming president. **1** Article II of the Constitution sets forth relatively few requirements for becoming president. A person must be a natural born citizen, at least thirty-five years of age, and a resident within the United States for at least fourteen years.

LearningOutcome 12–2 Explain the roles that a president adopts while in office. **2** In the course of exercising his or her powers, the president performs a variety of roles. The president is the nation's **chief executive**—the head of the executive branch—and enforces laws and federal court decisions. The president leads the nation's armed forces as **commander in chief**. As **head of state**, the president performs ceremonial activities as a personal symbol of the nation. As **chief diplomat**, the president directs U.S. foreign policy and is the nation's most important representative in dealing with foreign governments. The president has become the chief legislator, informing Congress about the condition of the country and recommending legislative measures. As political party leader, the president chooses the chairperson of his or her party's national committee, attends party fund-raisers, and exerts influence within the party by using presidential appointment powers.

LearningOutcome 12–3 Indicate the scope of presidential powers. **3** The Constitution gives the president specific powers, such as the power to negotiate **treaties**, to grant reprieves and pardons, and to **veto** bills passed by Congress. The president also has inherent powers—powers that are necessary to carry out the specific constitutional duties of the presidency. **4** Several presidents have greatly expanded presidential powers. The president, for example, is now expected to develop a legislative program. The president's political skills, the ability to persuade others, and the strategy of "going public" all play a role in determining legislative success. **5** The president's executive authority has been expanded by the use of **executive orders** and **signing statements,** and the ability to make **executive agreements** has enhanced presidential power in foreign affairs. As commander in chief, the president can respond quickly to a military threat without waiting for congressional action, and since 1945, the president has been responsible for deciding if and when to use nuclear weapons.

LearningOutcome 12–4 Describe advantages enjoyed by Congress and by the president in their institutional relationship. **6** Congress has the advantage over the president in the areas of legislative authorization, the regulation of foreign and interstate commerce, and some budgetary matters. The president has the advantage over Congress in dealing with a national crisis, in setting foreign policy, and in influencing public opinion. **7** The relationship between Congress and the president is affected by their different constituencies and election cycles, and the fact that the president is limited to two terms in office. Their relationship is also affected when government is divided, with at least one house of Congress controlled by a different party than the White House.

LearningOutcome 12–5 Discuss the organization of the executive branch and the role of cabinet members in presidential administrations. **8** The heads of the fifteen executive departments are members of the president's **cabinet.** The president may add other officials to the cabinet as well. In general, presidents don't rely heavily on the advice of the formal cabinet. Department heads are often more responsive to the wishes of their own staffs, to their own political ambitions, or to obtaining resources for their departments than they are to the presidents they serve. **9** Since 1939, top advisers and assistants in the **Executive Office of the**

President (EOP) have helped the president carry out major duties. Some of the most important staff agencies in the EOP are the **White House Office,** headed by the **chief of staff,** the **Office of Management and Budget,** and the **National Security Council.** In recent years, the responsibilities of the vice president have grown immensely, and the vice president has become one of the most important of the president's advisers.

ANSWERS TO STUDY TOOLS QUIZ

Fill-In

1. the legal profession (LearningOutcome 12–1)
2. commander in chief (LearningOutcome 12–2)
3. chief legislator (LearningOutcome 12–2)
4. presidential orders to carry out policies described in laws passed by Congress (LearningOutcome 12–3)
5. War Powers Resolution (LearningOutcome 12–3)
6. an inherent executive power claimed by presidents to withhold information from, or to refuse to appear before, Congress or the courts (LearningOutcome 12–4)
7. the heads of the executive departments and other officials whom the president may choose to appoint (LearningOutcome 12–5)
8. White House Office, the Office of Management and Budget, and the National Security Council (LearningOutcome 12–5)

Multiple Choice

9. c. (LearningOutcome 12–1)
10. c. (LearningOutcome 12–2)
11. a. (LearningOutcome 12–2)
12. a. (LearningOutcome 12–3)
13. a. (LearningOutcome 12–3)
14. b. (LearningOutcome 12–4)
15. c. (LearningOutcome 12–5)

patronage The practice by which elected officials give government jobs to individuals who helped them gain office. **265**

press secretary A member of the White House staff who holds news conferences for reporters and makes public statements for the president. **278**

signing statement A written statement, appended to a bill at the time the president signs it into law, indicating how the president interprets that legislation. **270**

treaty A formal agreement between the governments of two or more countries. **265**

veto A Latin word meaning "I forbid"; the refusal by an official, such as the president of the United States or a state governor, to sign a bill into law. **266**

Watergate scandal A scandal involving an illegal break-in at the Democratic National Committee offices in 1972 by members of President Richard Nixon's reelection campaign staff. **276**

White House Office The personal office of the president. White House Office personnel handle the president's political needs and manage the media, among other duties. **278**

13 The Bureaucracy

KEY TERMS

adjudicate To render a judicial decision. In administrative law it is the process in which an administrative law judge hears and decides issues that arise when an agency charges a person or firm with violating a law or regulation enforced by the agency. **297**

bureaucracy A large, complex, hierarchically structured administrative organization that carries out specific functions. **285**

bureaucrat An individual who works in a bureaucracy. As generally used, the term refers to a government employee. **285**

civil service Nonmilitary government employees. **295**

enabling legislation A law enacted by a legislature to establish an administrative agency. Enabling legislation normally specifies the name, purpose, composition, and powers of the agency being created. **297**

government corporation An agency of the government that is run as a business enterprise. Such agencies engage primarily in commercial activities, produce revenues, and require greater flexibility than most government agencies have. **293**

independent executive agency A federal agency that is not located within a cabinet department. **290**

independent regulatory agency A federal organization that is responsible for creating and implementing rules that regulate private activity and protect the public interest in a particular sector of the economy. **293**

iron triangle A three-way alliance among legislators, bureaucrats, and interest groups to make or preserve policies that benefit their respective interests. **298**

issue networks Groups of individuals or organizations—which consist of legislators and legislative staff members, interest group leaders, bureaucrats, the media, scholars, and other experts—that support particular policy positions on a given issue. **300**

legislative rule An administrative agency rule that carries the same weight as a statute enacted by a legislature. **296**

neutral competency The application of technical skills to jobs without regard to political issues. **298**

SUMMARY

LearningOutcome 13–1 Describe the size and functions of the U.S. bureaucracy and the major components of federal spending. **1** In the federal government, the head of the bureaucracy is the president of the United States, and the **bureaucracy** is part of the executive branch. The federal bureaucracy exists because Congress, over time, has delegated certain tasks to specialists. The three levels of government employ about 16 percent of the civilian labor force. **2** Over half of the federal budget consists of various social programs, such as Social Security, Medicare, and Medicaid. With veterans' benefits, defense spending is almost 25 percent of total federal spending. Other categories of spending include military and economic foreign aid, as well as interest on the national debt.

LearningOutcome 13–2 Discuss the structure and basic components of the federal bureaucracy. **3** The fifteen executive departments are the major service organizations of the federal government. Each department was created by Congress as the perceived need for it arose, and each manages a specific policy area. Department heads are appointed by the president and confirmed by the Senate. Each department includes several subagencies. **4 Independent executive agencies** have a single function. Sometimes agencies are kept independent because of the sensitive nature of their functions, but at other times, Congress creates independent agencies to protect them from **partisan politics.** An **independent regulatory agency** is responsible for a specific type of policy. Its function is to create and implement rules that regulate private activity and protect the public interest in a particular sector of the economy. **5 Government corporations** are businesses owned by the government. They provide a service that could be handled by the private sector, and they charge for their services. A number of intermediate forms of organization exist that fall between a government corporation and a private one.

LearningOutcome 13–3 Describe how the federal civil service was established and how bureaucrats get their jobs. **6** Federal bureaucrats holding top-level positions are appointed by the president and confirmed by the Senate. The list of positions that are filled by appointments is published after each presidential election in a book that summarizes about eight thousand jobs. The rank-and-file bureaucrats—the rest of the federal bureaucracy—are part of the **civil service.** They obtain their jobs through the Office of Personnel Management (OPM). The OPM recruits, interviews, and tests potential government workers and makes recommendations to individual agencies as to which persons meet relevant standards. The Civil Service Reform Act of 1883 established the principle of government employment on the basis of merit through open, competitive examinations.

LearningOutcome 13–4 Explain how regulatory agencies make rules and how issue networks affect policymaking in government. **7** Regulatory agencies are sometimes regarded as the fourth branch of government. They make **legislative rules** that are as legally binding as laws passed by Congress. When they are engaging in **rulemaking,** agencies must follow certain procedural requirements and must also make sure that their rules are based on substantial evidence. Bureaucrats in federal agencies are expected to exhibit **neutral competency,** which means that they are supposed to apply their technical skills to their jobs without regard to political issues. In reality, however, each independent agency and each executive department is interested in its own survival and expansion. **8 Iron triangles** (alliances among legislators, bureaucrats, and interest groups to make or preserve policies that benefit their respective interests) are well established in almost every part of the bureaucracy. In some policy areas, there are less structured relationships among experts who have strong opinions and interests regarding the direction of policy. These **issue networks** are able to exert a great deal of influence on legislators and bureaucratic agencies.

LearningOutcome 13–5 Identify some of the ways in which the government has attempted to curb waste and improve efficiency in the bureaucracy. 9 To encourage government employees to report gross governmental inefficiency and wrongdoing, Congress has passed laws to protect **whistleblowers** and to make cash rewards to them. To improve efficiency, almost every federal agency has had to describe its goals and identify methods for evaluating how well those goals are met. President Obama created the position of a chief performance officer who works with other economic officials in an attempt to increase efficiency and eliminate waste in government. Other ideas for reforming government bureaucracies include **privatization** and allowing citizens to file forms and apply for services online.

ANSWERS TO STUDY TOOLS QUIZ

Fill-In

1. 16 (LearningOutcome 13–1)
2. secretary (LearningOutcome 13–2)
3. Commerce (LearningOutcome 13–2)
4. president; Senate (LearningOutcome 13–3)
5. merit through open, competitive examinations (LearningOutcome 13–3)
6. enabling legislation (LearningOutcome 13–4)
7. a three-way alliance among legislators, bureaucrats, and interest groups to make or preserve policies that benefit their respective interests (LearningOutcome 13–4)
8. reports on gross governmental inefficiency, illegal action, or other wrongdoing (LearningOutcome 13–5)

Multiple Choice

9. b. (LearningOutcome 13–1)
10. a. (LearningOutcome 13–2)
11. c. (LearningOutcome 13–2)
12. b. (LearningOutcome 13–2)
13. c. (LearningOutcome 13–3)
14. b. (LearningOutcome 13–4)
15. a. (LearningOutcome 13–5)

14 The Judiciary

KEY TERMS

administrative law The body of law created by administrative agencies (in the form of rules, regulations, orders, and decisions) in order to carry out their duties and responsibilities. **310**

appellate court A court having appellate jurisdiction. An appellate court normally does not hear evidence or testimony but reviews the transcript of the trial court's proceedings, other records relating to the case, and attorneys' arguments as to why the trial court's decision should or should not stand. **313**

case law The rules of law announced in court decisions. Case law includes the aggregate of reported cases that interpret judicial precedents, statutes, regulations, and constitutional provisions. **310**

civil law The branch of law that spells out the duties that individuals in society owe to other persons or to their governments, excluding the duty not to commit crimes. **310**

common law The body of law developed from judicial decisions in English and U.S. courts, not attributable to a legislature. **308**

concurring opinion A statement written by a judge or justice who agrees (concurs) with the court's decision, but for reasons different from those in the majority opinion. **317**

conference In regard to the Supreme Court, a private meeting of the justices in which they present their arguments concerning a case under consideration. **316**

constitutional law Law based on the U.S. Constitution and the constitutions of the various states. **309**

contempt of court A ruling that a person has disobeyed a court order or has shown disrespect to the court or to a judicial proceeding. **312**

criminal law The branch of law that defines and governs actions that constitute crimes. Generally, criminal law has to do with wrongful actions committed against society for which society demands redress. **310**

dissenting opinion A statement written by a judge or justice who disagrees with the majority opinion. **317**

SUMMARY

LearningOutcome 14–1 Summarize the origins of the American legal system and the basic sources of American law. **1** The American legal system evolved from the common law tradition that developed in England. The practice of deciding new cases with reference to **precedents (stare decisis)** became a cornerstone of the American judicial system. **2** Various **primary sources of law** provide the basis for **constitutional law, statutory law, administrative law,** and **case law. 3** Civil law spells out the duties that individuals in society owe to other persons or to their governments. **Criminal law** has to do with wrongs committed against the public as a whole. **4** A court must have **jurisdiction** to hear and decide a particular case. Any lawsuit involving a **federal question** can originate in federal court. Federal courts can also hear **diversity-of-citizenship** cases. To bring a lawsuit before a court, a person must have **standing to sue,** and the issue must be a **justiciable controversy.** The courts have also established procedural rules that apply in all cases.

LearningOutcome 14–2 Delineate the structure of the federal court system. **5** The U.S. district courts are trial courts—the courts in which cases involving federal laws begin. There is at least one federal district court in every state, and there is one in the District of Columbia. The U.S. courts of appeals are **appellate courts** that hear cases on review from the U.S. district courts located within their respective judicial circuits. Decisions made by federal agencies may be reviewed by a district court or a court of appeals, depending on the agency. The Court of Appeals for the Federal Circuit has national jurisdiction over certain types of cases. The United States Supreme Court has some original jurisdiction, but most of the Court's work is as an appellate court. The Supreme Court may take appeals of decisions made by the U.S. courts of appeals as well as appeals of cases decided in the state courts when federal questions are at issue. **6** To bring a case before the Supreme Court, a party may request that the Court issue a **writ of certiorari.** If the Court grants cert., it will typically hear **oral arguments.** The justices will then discuss the case in **conference.** When the Court has reached a decision, the justices explain their reasoning in written **opinions.**

LearningOutcome 14–3 Say how federal judges are appointed. **7** Federal judges are appointed by the president with the advice and consent of the Senate. They receive lifetime appointments. The Senate Judiciary Committee holds hearings on judicial nominees and makes its recommendation to the Senate, where it takes a majority vote to confirm a nomination. **Senatorial courtesy** gives home-state senators of the president's party influence over the president's choice of nominees for district courts (and, to a lesser extent, the U.S. courts of appeals). The process of nominating and confirming federal judges often involves political debate and controversy.

LearningOutcome 14–4 Explain how the federal courts make policy. **8** Federal judges can decide on the constitutionality of laws or actions undertaken by the other branches of government through the power of **judicial review.** And it is unavoidable that courts influence or even establish policy when they interpret and apply the law, because the law does not always provide clear answers to questions that come before the courts. **9** Generally, activist judges believe that the courts should actively use their powers to check the other two branches of government to ensure that they do not exceed their authority. Restraintist judges generally assume that the courts should defer to the decisions of the other branches.

LearningOutcome 14–5 Describe the role of ideology and judicial philosophies in judicial decision making. **10** There are numerous examples of ideology or policy preferences affecting Supreme Court decisions. Judicial decision making, however, can be complex. How much weight is given to the factors that may be taken into account depends, in part, on the approaches justices take toward the interpretation of laws and the Constitution. Important judicial philosophies include originalism, textualism, and modernism.

LearningOutcome 14–6 Identify some of the criticisms of the federal courts and some of the checks on the power of the courts. **11** Policymaking by unelected judges has important implications in a democracy. Critics, especially on the political right, frequently accuse the judiciary of "legislating from the bench." There are several checks on the courts, however, including judicial traditions and doctrines, the judiciary's lack of enforcement powers, and potential congressional actions in response to court decisions. The American public continues to have a fairly high regard for the federal judiciary.

ANSWERS TO STUDY TOOLS QUIZ

Fill-In

1. constitutions, statutes, administrative agency rules and regulations, and decisions by courts (LearningOutcome 14–1)
2. writ of *certiorari* (LearningOutcome 14–2)
3. oral arguments (LearningOutcome 14–2)
4. concurring (LearningOutcome 14–2)
5. senatorial courtesy (LearningOutcome 14–3)
6. defer to the decisions of the legislative and executive branches (LearningOutcome 14–4)
7. strict construction and originalism (LearningOutcome 14–5)
8. rewriting a statute to negate a court's ruling, proposing constitutional amendments to reverse Supreme Court decisions, or limiting the jurisdiction of the federal courts (LearningOutcome 14–6)

Multiple Choice

9. b. (LearningOutcome 14–1)
10. c. (LearningOutcome 14–2)
11. b. (LearningOutcome 14–2)
12. a. (LearningOutcome 14–3)
13. a. (LearningOutcome 14–4)
14. c. (LearningOutcome 14–5)
15. b. (LearningOutcome 14–6)

diversity of citizenship A basis for federal court jurisdiction over a lawsuit that arises when (1) the parties in the lawsuit live in different states or when one of the parties is a foreign government or a foreign citizen, and (2) the amount in controversy is more than $75,000. **311**

federal question A question that pertains to the U.S. Constitution, acts of Congress, or treaties. A federal question provides a basis for federal court jurisdiction. **311**

judicial review The power of the courts to decide on the constitutionality of legislative enactments and of actions taken by the executive branch. **321**

judiciary The courts; one of the three branches of government in the United States. **308**

jurisdiction The authority of a court to hear and decide a particular case. **311**

justiciable controversy A controversy that is not hypothetical or academic but real and substantial; a requirement that must be satisfied before a court will hear a case. *Justiciable* is pronounced jus-*tish*-a-bul. **312**

opinion A written statement by a court expressing the reasons for its decision in a case. **316**

oral argument A spoken argument presented to a judge in person by an attorney on behalf of her or his client. **316**

precedent A court decision that furnishes an example or authority for deciding subsequent cases involving identical or similar facts and legal issues. **308**

primary source of law A source of law that establishes the law. Primary sources of law include constitutions, statutes, administrative agency rules and regulations, and decisions rendered by the courts. **309**

senatorial courtesy A practice that allows a senator of the president's party to veto the president's nominee to a federal court judgeship within the senator's state. **317**

standing to sue The requirement that an individual must have a sufficient stake in a controversy before he or she can bring a lawsuit. The party bringing the suit must demonstrate that he or she has either been harmed or been threatened with a harm. **312**

stare decisis A common law doctrine under which judges normally are obligated to follow the precedents established by prior court decisions. Pronounced *ster*-ay dih-*si*-sis. **308**

statutory law The body of law enacted by legislatures (as opposed to constitutional law, administrative law, or case law). **309**

trial court A court in which trials are held and testimony is taken. **311**

writ of certiorari An order from a higher court asking a lower court for the record of a case. *Certiorari* is pronounced sur-shee-uh-*rah*-ree. **314**

15 Domestic Policy

KEY TERMS

action-reaction syndrome The principle that for every government action, there will be a reaction by the public. **346**

agenda setting Getting an issue on the political agenda to be addressed by Congress; part of the first stage of the policymaking process. **332**

Children's Health Insurance Program (CHIP) A joint federal-state program that provides health-care insurance for low-income children. **335**

Corporate Average Fuel Economy (CAFE) standards A set of federal standards under which each vehicle manufacturer (or the industry as a whole) must meet a miles-per-gallon benchmark averaged across all new cars or trucks. **339**

domestic policy Public policy concerning issues within a national unit, such as national policy concerning health care or the economy. **332**

easy-money policy A monetary policy that involves stimulating the economy by expanding the rate of growth of the money supply. **343**

economic policy All actions taken by the national government to address ups and downs in the nation's level of business activity. **342**

entitlement program A government program that provides benefits to all persons who meet specified requirements. **336**

Federal Open Market Committee (FOMC) The most important body within the Federal Reserve System; decides how monetary policy should be carried out. **343**

fiscal policy The use of changes in government expenditures and taxes to alter national economic variables. **344**

fracking Technique for extracting oil or natural gas from underground rock by the high-power injection of a mixture of water, sand, and chemicals. **341**

global warming An increase in the average temperature of the Earth's surface over the last half century and its projected continuation; referred to more generally as *climate change*. **339**

greenhouse gas A gas that, when released into the atmosphere, traps the sun's heat and slows its release into outer space. Carbon dioxide (CO_2) is a major example. **339**

SUMMARY

LearningOutcome 15–1 **Explain what domestic policy is, and summarize the steps in the policymaking process. 1** Domestic policy consists of public policy concerning issues within a national unit. **2** The **policymaking process** involves several phases. Identifying a problem that can be solved politically (issue identification) and getting the issue on the political agenda (**agenda-setting**) begin the process. The second stage involves the formulation and adoption of specific plans for achieving a particular goal. The final stages of the process focus on the implementation of the policy and evaluating its success. Each phase of the policymaking process involves interactions among various individuals and groups.

LearningOutcome 15–2 **Discuss the issue of health-care funding and recent legislation on universal health insurance. 3** Most federal spending on health care is accounted for by two **entitlement programs, Medicaid** and **Medicare,** which is the government's second largest domestic spending program. **4** In some countries, the government is responsible for providing basic health-care insurance to everyone through **national health insurance.** Major reform legislation adopted in the United States in 2010 provides a large role for the private sector. Employer-provided health insurance will continue, and a new health-insurance marketplace will allow small businesses and individuals to shop for plans. The legislation also includes an **individual mandate**—most individuals are required to obtain coverage or pay an income-tax penalty. **5** One immediate change brought about by the health-care bills is that young people could remain covered by their parents' insurance until they turn 26, but the most important provisions would not take effect until 2014, when subsidies would help eligible citizens purchase health-care insurance if they are not covered by Medicaid or an employer's plan. **6** Conservatives were opposed to the Affordable Care Act, and Republicans made repeal of it part of their platform for the 2010 and 2012 elections. The Republican-controlled House of Representatives voted to repeal Obamacare more than forty times, without effect.

LearningOutcome 15–3 **Summarize the issues of energy independence and alternative energy sources. 7** Our nation currently imports 40 percent of its petroleum supply. Many of the nations that export oil are not particularly friendly to the United States. Fortunately, Canada and Mexico supply 40 percent of our imports. In response to rising oil prices, the Obama administration has issued higher fuel efficiency standards for cars and trucks. By 2025, the nation's combined fleet of new cars and trucks must have an average fuel efficiency of 54.5 miles per gallon. **8** Most climatologists believe that **global warming** is the result of human activities, especially the release of **greenhouse gases** into the atmosphere. The predicted outcomes of climate change vary, and attitudes toward it have become highly politicized. **9** The issues of U.S. energy security and climate change raise the question of whether we can develop new energy sources. Due, in part, to technological improvements, there has recently been an increase in supplies of natural gas, and U.S. exports of petroleum products have exceeded imports. A key obstacle to the construction of new nuclear power plants is cost. While some **renewable energy** technologies were expensive, the cost of solar power and wind energy has been falling. As a result, the number of solar and wind-power installations has grown rapidly.

LearningOutcome 15–4 **Describe the two major areas of economic policymaking, and discuss the issue of the public debt. 10** The national government has two main tools to smooth the business cycle and to reduce **unemployment** and **inflation.** **11 Monetary policy** is under the control of the Federal Reserve System (the Fed), an independent regulatory agency. The Fed and its **Federal Open Market**

Committee make decisions about monetary policy several times each year. In periods of recession and high unemployment, the Fed pursues an **easy-money policy.** In periods of rising inflation, the Fed adopts a tight-money policy. **12** A second tool is **fiscal policy,** which usually involves raising or lowering taxes. The severity of the Great Recession led some economists to recommend increases in government spending as well. However, there is now strong political opposition to this aspect of **Keynesian economics. 13** The government raises money to pay its expenses through taxes levied on business and personal income and through borrowing. Tax policy is plagued by the **action-reaction syndrome,** resulting in a complicated tax system that is politically difficult to reform. When the government spends more than it receives, it borrows to finance the shortfall. Every time there is a federal government deficit, there is an increase in the total accumulated **public debt.** Today, about half of the U.S. net public debt is held by foreign individuals, foreign businesses, and foreign central banks. One threat to U.S. obligations does not come from foreign nations, but stems from the danger that the U.S. Congress will fail to raise the debt ceiling.

ANSWERS TO STUDY TOOLS QUIZ

Fill-In

1. issue identification and agenda setting, policy formulation and adoption, and policy implementation and evaluation (Learning Outcome 15–1)
2. Medicare (Learning Outcome 15–2)
3. all persons obtain health-care insurance from one source or another, or pay a penalty (LearningOutcome 15–2)
4. Canada and Mexico (LearningOutcome 15–3)
5. a rise in sea levels, changes in rainfall patterns, and increases in extreme weather (LearningOutcome 15–3)
6. solar power, hydropower, and wind power (LearningOutcome 15–3)
7. recession (LearningOutcome 15–4)
8. Federal Reserve System (LearningOutcome 15–4)
9. the People's Republic of China (LearningOutcome 15–4)

Multiple Choice

10. c. (LearningOutcome 15–1)
11. b. (LearningOutcome 15–2)
12. a. (LearningOutcome 15–2)
13. c. (LearningOutcome 15–3)
14. b. (LearningOutcome 15–4)
15. c. (LearningOutcome 15–4)

individual mandate In the context of health-care reform, a requirement that all persons obtain health-care insurance from one source or another. Those failing to do so must pay a penalty. **337**

inflation A sustained rise in average prices; equivalent to a decline in the value of the dollar. **343**

Keynesian economics An economic theory proposed by British economist John Maynard Keynes that is typically associated with the use of fiscal policy to alter national economic variables. **344**

Medicaid A joint federal-state program that provides health-care services to low-income persons. **335**

Medicare A federal government program that pays for health-care insurance for Americans aged sixty-five years and over. **335**

monetary policy Actions taken by the Federal Reserve Board to change the amount of money in circulation so as to affect interest rates, credit markets, the rate of inflation, the rate of economic growth, and the rate of unemployment. **343**

national health insurance A program, found in many of the world's economically advanced nations, under which the central government provides basic health-care insurance coverage to everyone in the country. **337**

policymaking process The procedures involved in getting an issue on the political agenda; formulating, adopting, and implementing a policy with regard to the issue; and then evaluating the results of the policy. **332**

public debt The total amount of money that the national government owes as a result of borrowing; also called the *national debt.* **348**

recession A period in which the level of economic activity falls; usually defined as two or more quarters of economic decline. **342**

renewable energy Energy from technologies that do not rely on extracted resources, such as oil and coal, that can run out. **342**

unemployment The state of not having a job even when actively seeking one. **342**

16 Foreign Policy

KEY TERMS

coalition An alliance of nations formed to undertake a foreign policy action, particularly a military action. A coalition is often a temporary alliance that dissolves after the action is concluded. **362**

Cold War The war of words, warnings, and ideologies between the Soviet Union and the United States that lasted from the late 1940s through the late 1980s. **359**

colonial empire A group of dependent nations that are under the rule of a single imperial power. **357**

containment A U.S. policy designed to contain the spread of communism by offering military and economic aid to threatened nations. **358**

Cuban missile crisis A nuclear standoff that occurred in 1962 when the United States learned that the Soviet Union had placed nuclear warheads in Cuba. **359**

détente A French word meaning a "relaxation of tensions." Détente characterized the relationship between the United States and the Soviet Union in the 1970s as they attempted to pursue cooperative dealings and arms control. **359**

deterrence A policy of building up military strength for the purpose of discouraging (deterring) military attacks by other nations; the policy that supported the arms race between the United States and the Soviet Union during the Cold War. **359**

foreign policy A systematic and general plan that guides a country's attitudes and actions toward the rest of the world. Foreign policy includes all of the economic, military, commercial, and diplomatic positions and actions that a nation takes in its relationships with other countries. **354**

interventionism Direct involvement by one country in another country's affairs. **357**

iron curtain A phrase coined by Winston Churchill to describe the political boundaries between the democratic countries in Western Europe and the Soviet-controlled Communist countries in Eastern Europe. **358**

isolationism A political policy of non-involvement in world affairs. **356**

SUMMARY

LearningOutcome 16–1 Discuss how foreign policy is made, and identify the key players in this process. 1 The president oversees the military, guides defense policies, and represents the United States to the rest of the world. The Department of State is responsible for diplomatic relations with other nations and with multilateral organizations. The Department of Defense establishes and carries out defense policy and protects our national security. Two key agencies in the area of **foreign policy** are the National Security Council and the Central Intelligence Agency. Congress has the power to declare war and the power to appropriate funds to equip the armed forces and provide for foreign aid. The Senate has the power to ratify treaties. A few congressional committees are directly concerned with foreign affairs.

LearningOutcome 16–2 Summarize the history of American foreign policy through the years. 2 Early leaders sought to protect American interests through **isolationism**. The Spanish-American War of 1898 marked the first step toward **interventionism**. **3** In World War I, the United States initially adopted a policy of **neutrality**, and after the war, returned to a policy of isolationism. That policy ended with the attack on Pearl Harbor in 1941. After World War II, the alliance between the United States and the Soviet Union deteriorated. The Truman Doctrine and the **Marshall Plan** marked the beginning of a policy of **containment** of communism. **4** During the **Cold War**, the United States and the Soviet Union engaged in an arms race supported by a policy of **deterrence**, which led to the theory of **mutually assured destruction (MAD)**. In 1962, the two countries came close to a nuclear confrontation during the **Cuban missile crisis.** The fall of the Berlin Wall in 1989 and the demise of the Soviet Union in 1991 altered the framework and goals of U.S. foreign policy.

LearningOutcome 16–3 Identify the foreign policy challenges presented by terrorism. 5 Terrorism is defined as the use of staged violence, often against civilians, to achieve political goals. Governments around the world face the challenges of dealing with local or regional terrorism, state-sponsored terrorism, and foreign terrorist networks. After the terrorist attacks on September 11, 2001, the U.S. military, supported by a **coalition** of allies, attacked al Qaeda camps in Afghanistan and the ruling Taliban regime that harbored those terrorists. **6** In 2003, U.S. and British forces attacked the nation of Iraq, believing (though incorrectly) that Iraq's dictator, Saddam Hussein, was developing **weapons of mass destruction** and that the Iraqi regime was in some way responsible for the 9/11 terrorist attacks. After overthrowing Hussein and undermining an insurgency that included the newly organized al Qaeda in Iraq, U.S. combat forces left Iraq in 2011. **7** By 2006, the Taliban had regrouped and were waging a war of insurgency against the new government in Afghanistan. During the winter of 2010–2011, U.S. intelligence agencies learned that al Qaeda leader Osama bin Laden might be hiding in a Pakistani city. In 2011, U.S. Navy Seals killed him in his residential compound. Al Qaeda affiliates, however, are alive and expanding.

LearningOutcome 16–4 Explain the principal issues dividing the Israelis and the Palestinians and the solutions proposed by the international community. 8 Following the 1967 war, the West Bank of the Jordan River and the Gaza Strip fell under Israeli control, and Palestinians living in these areas became an occupied people. Israeli settlements on the West Bank are controversial, and Palestinian terrorist attacks on Israel have impeded efforts toward peace. **9** The international community agrees that lands seized in the 1967 war should be restored to the Palestinians, who could organize their own independent nation-state there. In turn, the Palestinians would have to recognize Israel's right to exist and take

31

concrete steps to guarantee Israel's security. In 1993, Israel and the **Palestine Liberation Organization (PLO)** met officially for the first time. A major result of the **Oslo Accords** was the establishment of a Palestinian Authority, under Israeli control, on the West Bank and Gaza Strip. Any agreement between Israel and the Palestinians, however, seems far off.

LearningOutcome 16–5 Outline some of the actions taken by the United States to curb the threat of nuclear weapons. **10** Neither weapons inspections nor negotiations have resolved the issue of North Korea's nuclear ambitions. It conducted nuclear tests in 2006, 2009, and 2013. **11** Iran has been engaged in a covert nuclear program, and, like North Korea, has been openly hostile to the United States. Efforts to address Iran's pursuit of nuclear weapons include talks involving Britain, France, Germany, Iran, Russia, and the United States, as well as sanctions imposed by the United Nations and the United States. A majority of the world's nations have been persuaded not to buy Iran's oil, and Iran has been cut off from the international banking system. Iran's new president, Hassan Rouhani, has repudiated the anti-Israel rhetoric of his predecessor. For the moment, military measures, such as bombing Iran's nuclear sites, are off the table.

LearningOutcome 16–6 Describe China's emerging role as a world power. **12** China has one of the fastest-growing economies in the world and a population of 1.3 billion. Congress has granted China **normal trade relations status,** but diplomatic relations between China and the United States have been uneven. Recent attempts by Chinese hackers to steal U.S. intellectual property have raised questions about China's attitude toward the West, and relations between China and several Western nations have become strained in recent years due to criticisms of Chinese behavior in Tibet.

ANSWERS TO STUDY TOOLS QUIZ

Fill-In

1. departments of state and defense, and the National Security Council and the Central Intelligence Agency (LearningOutcome 16–1)
2. isolationism (LearningOutcome 16–2)
3. Cold War (LearningOutcome 16–2)
4. Afghanistan (LearningOutcome 16–3)
5. Pakistan (LearningOutcome 16–3)
6. Palestinian Authority (LearningOutcome 16–4)
7. North Korea and Iran (LearningOutcome 16–5)
8. Taiwan (LearningOutcome 16–6)

Multiple Choice

9. b. (LearningOutcome 16–1)
10. c. (LearningOutcome 16–2)
11. a. (LearningOutcome 16–2)
12. c. (LearningOutcome 16–3)
13. a. (LearningOutcome 16–4)
14. b. (LearningOutcome 16–5)
15. a. (LearningOutcome 16–6)

Marshall Plan A plan providing for U.S. economic assistance to European nations following World War II to help those nations recover from the war. The plan was named after George C. Marshall, secretary of state from 1947 to 1949. **358**

Monroe Doctrine A U.S. policy, announced in 1823 by President James Monroe, that the United States would not tolerate foreign intervention in the Western Hemisphere, and in return, the United States would stay out of European affairs. **357**

moral idealism In foreign policy, the belief that the most important goal is to do what is right. Moral idealists think that it is possible for nations to cooperate as part of a rule-based community. **354**

mutually assured destruction (MAD) A phrase referring to the assumption that if the forces of two nations are capable of destroying each other, neither nation will take a chance on war. **359**

neutrality The position of not being aligned with either side in a dispute or conflict, such as a war. **357**

normal trade relations (NTR) status A trade status granted through an international treaty by which each member nation must treat other members at least as well as it treats the country that receives its most favorable treatment. This status was formerly known as *most-favored-nation status.* **371**

Oslo Accords The first agreement signed between Israel and the PLO; led to the establishment of the Palestinian Authority in the occupied territories. **366**

Palestine Liberation Organization (PLO) An organization formed in 1964 to represent the Palestinian people. The PLO has a long history of terrorism but for some years has functioned primarily as a political party. **364**

political realism In foreign policy, the belief that nations are inevitably selfish and that we should seek to protect our national security, regardless of moral arguments. **354**

Soviet bloc The group of Eastern European nations that fell under the control of the Soviet Union following World War II. **358**

weapons of mass destruction Chemical, biological, or nuclear weapons that can inflict massive casualties. **362**